I believe there is hope in design.
Design evokes surprise and joy in people.

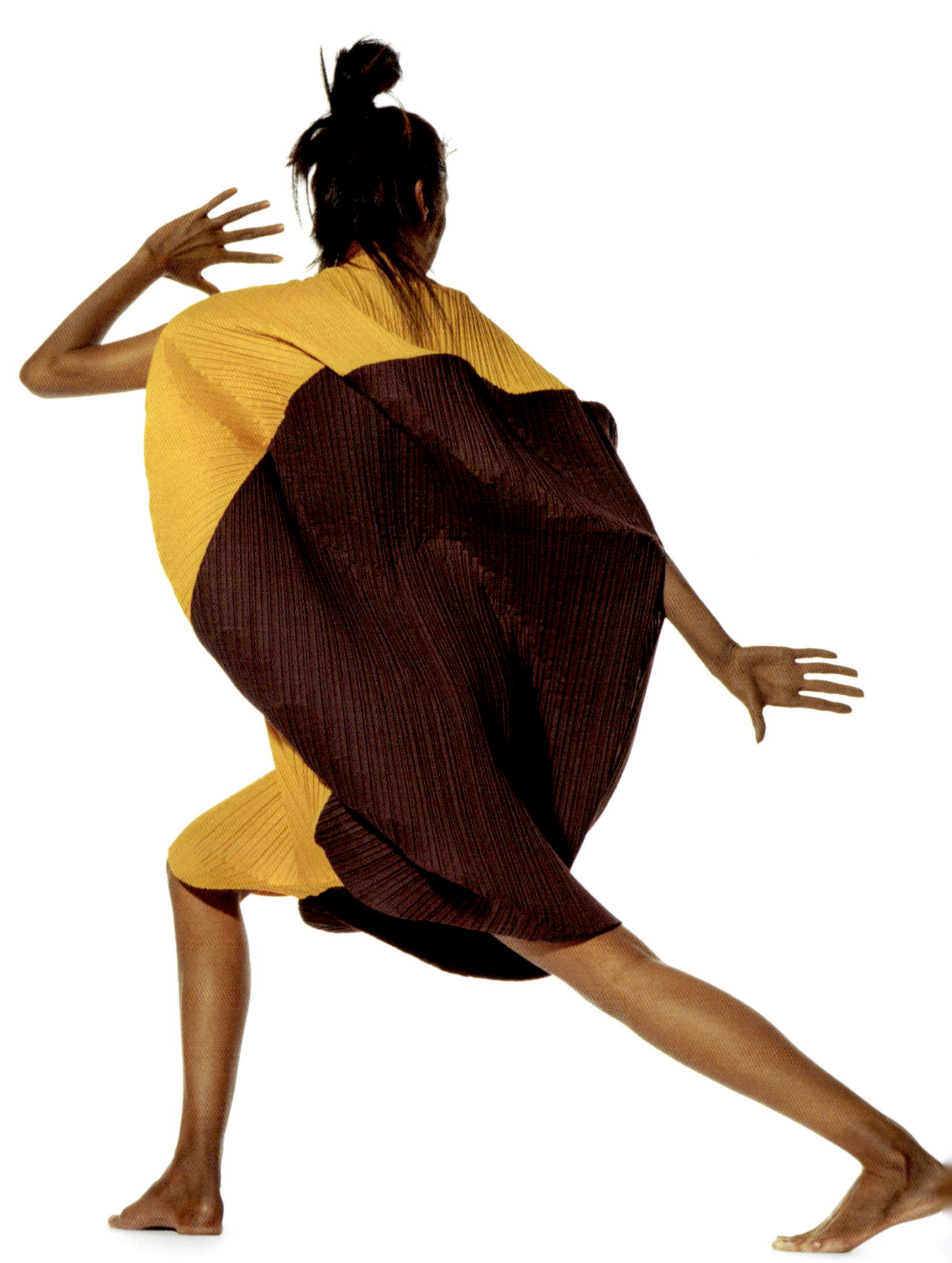

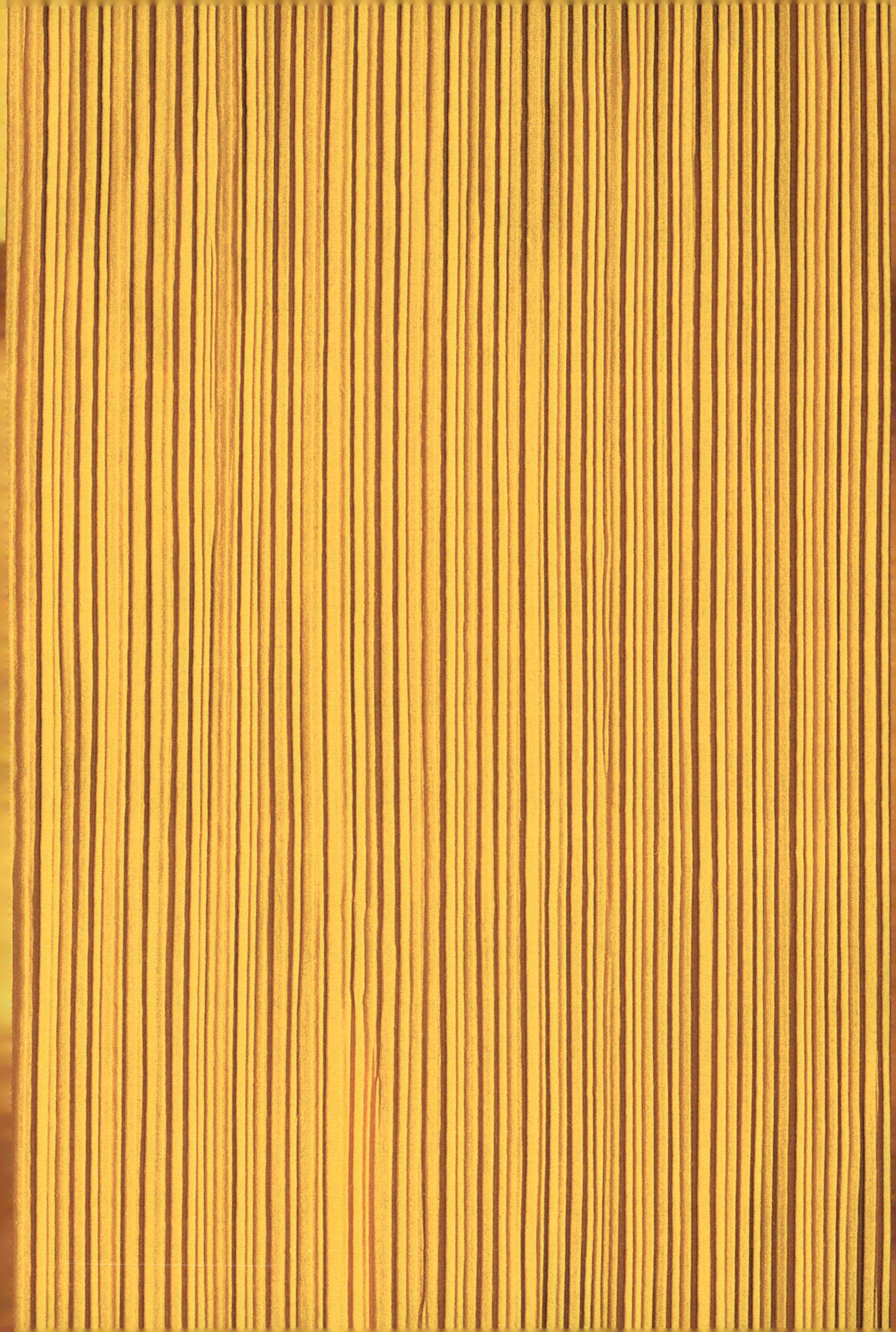

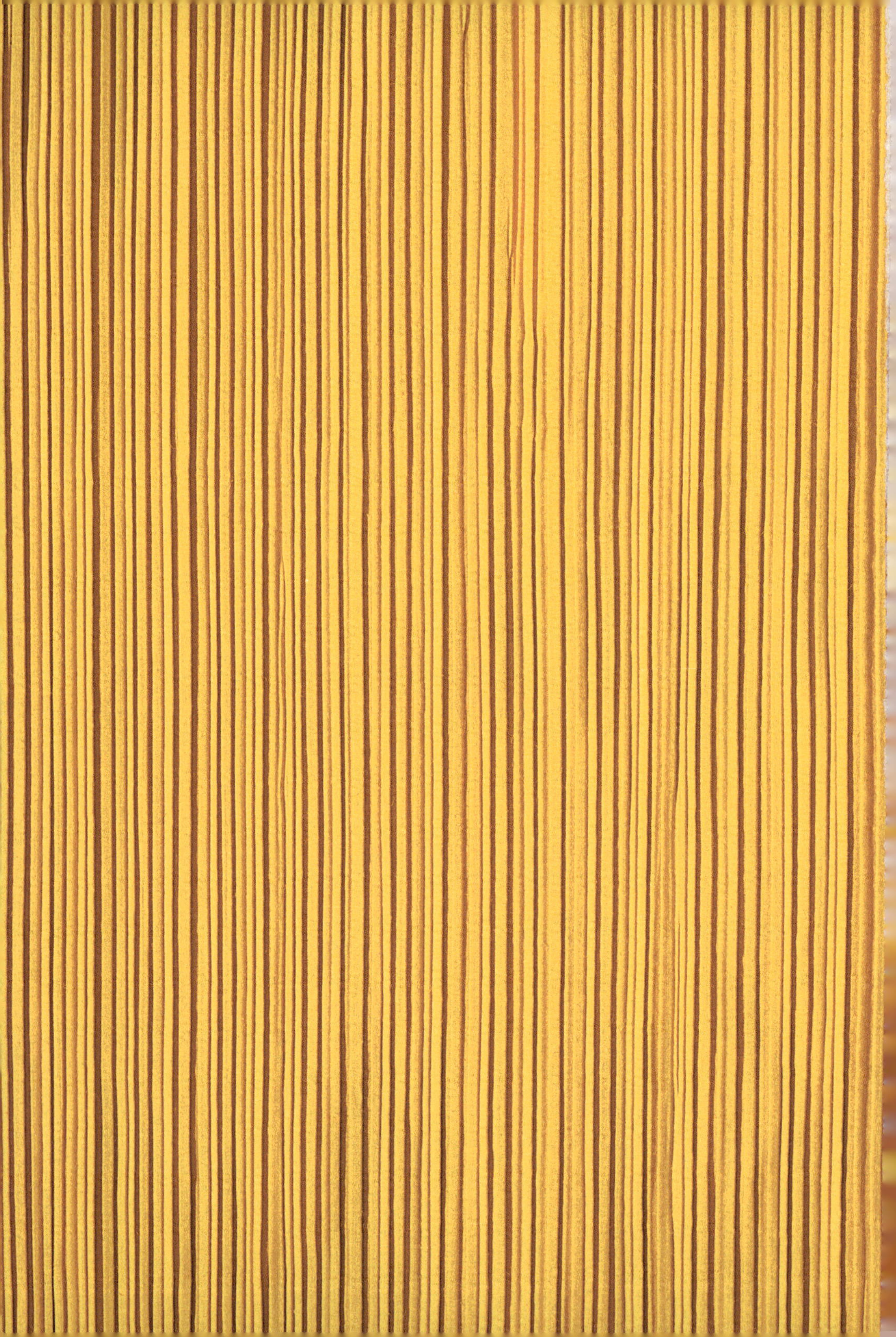

ISSEY MIYAKE
三宅一生

Concept and Editorial Direction
MIDORI KITAMURA

TASCHEN

FOREWORD
by Midori Kitamura
7

WHERE DID ISSEY COME FROM?
by Kazuko Koike
8

THE WORK OF ISSEY MIYAKE

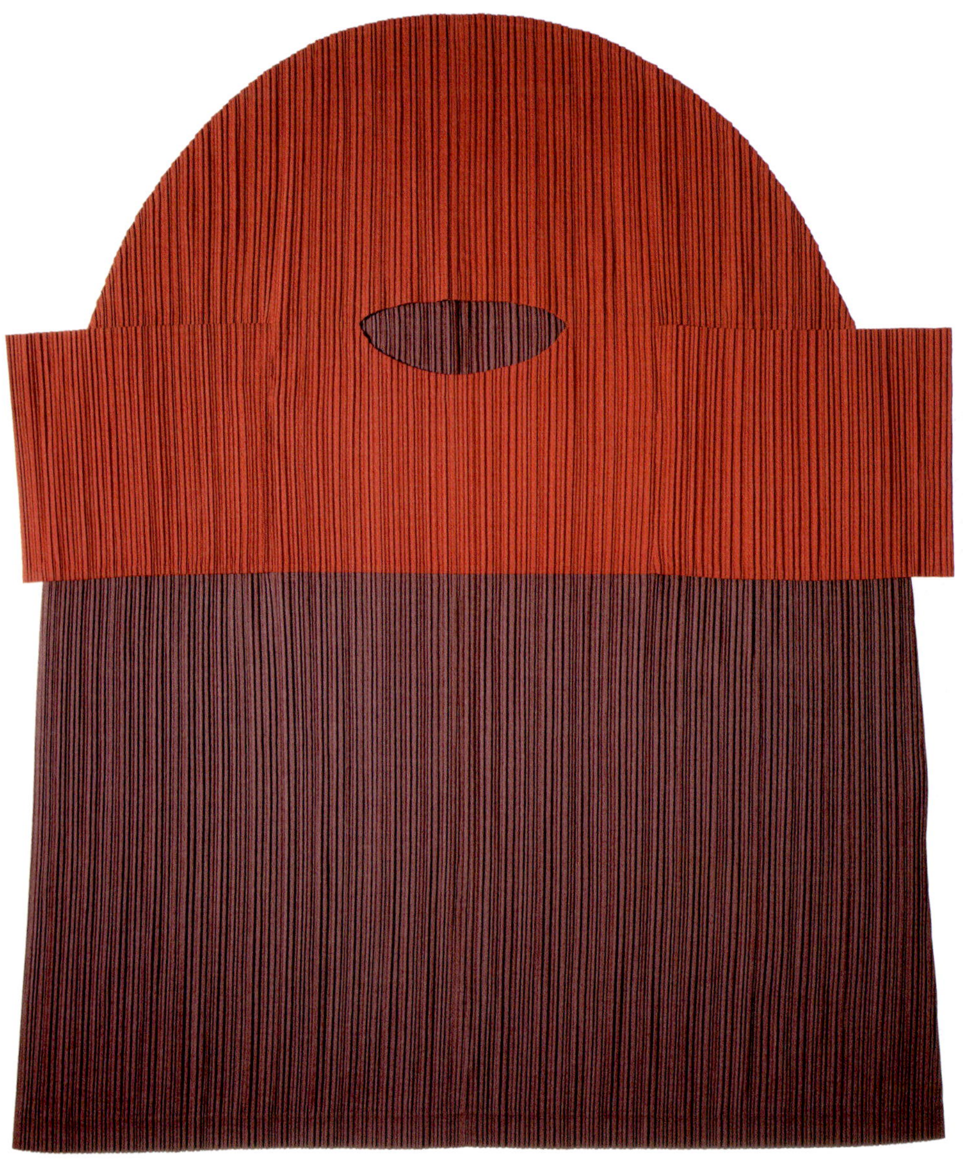

It has been nine years since the original publication of *Issey Miyake* by TASCHEN.
After returning home from New York, Miyake established Miyake Design Studio in Tokyo as
the atelier for his design work. I worked with him for nearly 50 years, and compiling all of his
activities into a single book required that I confront the question of who Issey Miyake was.

Miyake continued to work with the same enthusiasm after the publication of the book,
planning exhibitions and developing new brands. This revised and updated edition completes
the document by adding in the activities from 2015 until just prior to Miyake's passing. As
before, Kazuko Koike was asked to write the text as objectively as possible, which was added
as a new final chapter.

I believe there is hope in design.
Design evokes surprise and joy in people.

Issey Miyake often said this to the people around him.
Throughout his life, his gaze was firmly fixed on the future as both a designer
and a human being.

He continues to inspire us with new resolve to maintain that spirit of curiosity
and wonder, and to continue to design in ways that create hope and surprise.

Last but not least, I would like to express my heartfelt gratitude to all of the
many people who worked so generously to bring about this book.

Midori Kitamura
Chairman of Miyake Design Studio, 2025

WHERE DID ISSEY COME FROM?

Essay by
KAZUKO KOIKE

1—DAWN

A SUPERNOVA IN THE EASTERN SKY

Nippori. The name of the station where passengers traveling between Narita International Airport and Tokyo board the Skyliner railway link; it also happens to be next to Akihabara, a mecca for all things electronic and digital. I, however, would like to travel back in time and take you to Nippori as it used to be, a typical and traditional *shitamachi*, a working-class neighborhood, as it was in 1971.

Issey Miyake has been showing his work since his days as a student; he has begun to be noticed for his distinctive sensibility. On this particular day, he has been at the station since early morning for a photo shoot he has organized.

Nippori was a major train station with people transferring from a privately operated line to the Japan National Railway line (now called JR, following privatization). They came from Tokyo's eastern neighbor, Chiba prefecture, and the train carriages of early-morning commuters also carried throngs of farm women known as "Chiba Aunties" (*Chiba no obasan*), or "The Load-bearing Ladies" (*Katsugiya-san*). Arriving from northern Chiba, they fanned out all over Tokyo, going door-to-door selling their fresh vegetables. The sight of them streaming onto the station platforms shouldering their large bamboo baskets further wrapped and tied in huge indigo-dyed *furoshiki* was extraordinarily impressive. Bearing loads almost equal to their own heights and weighing upward of 70 kilograms, they trod silently and stoically, with so much dignity and presence that the "corporate warriors" who passed them would bow their heads in respect.

"I want to see these Japanese Amazons in their traditional farm clothing combined with the Issey Miyake international debut collection," the designer thought.

Before all of this could transpire, the Japan Society had invited Issey Miyake as one of Japan's rising designers to hold a fashion show in May at their headquarters, Japan House, on East 47th Street in New York. More than 60 pieces were shown, many of them bodywear[1] made of synthetics that represented the latest innovations from Japan's textile industry. They were worn under pants and jackets quilted with *sashiko*[2] stitches and

Portrait of Issey Miyake
So-en, August 1969, Bunka Publishing Bureau
Photography: Tatsuo Masubuchi

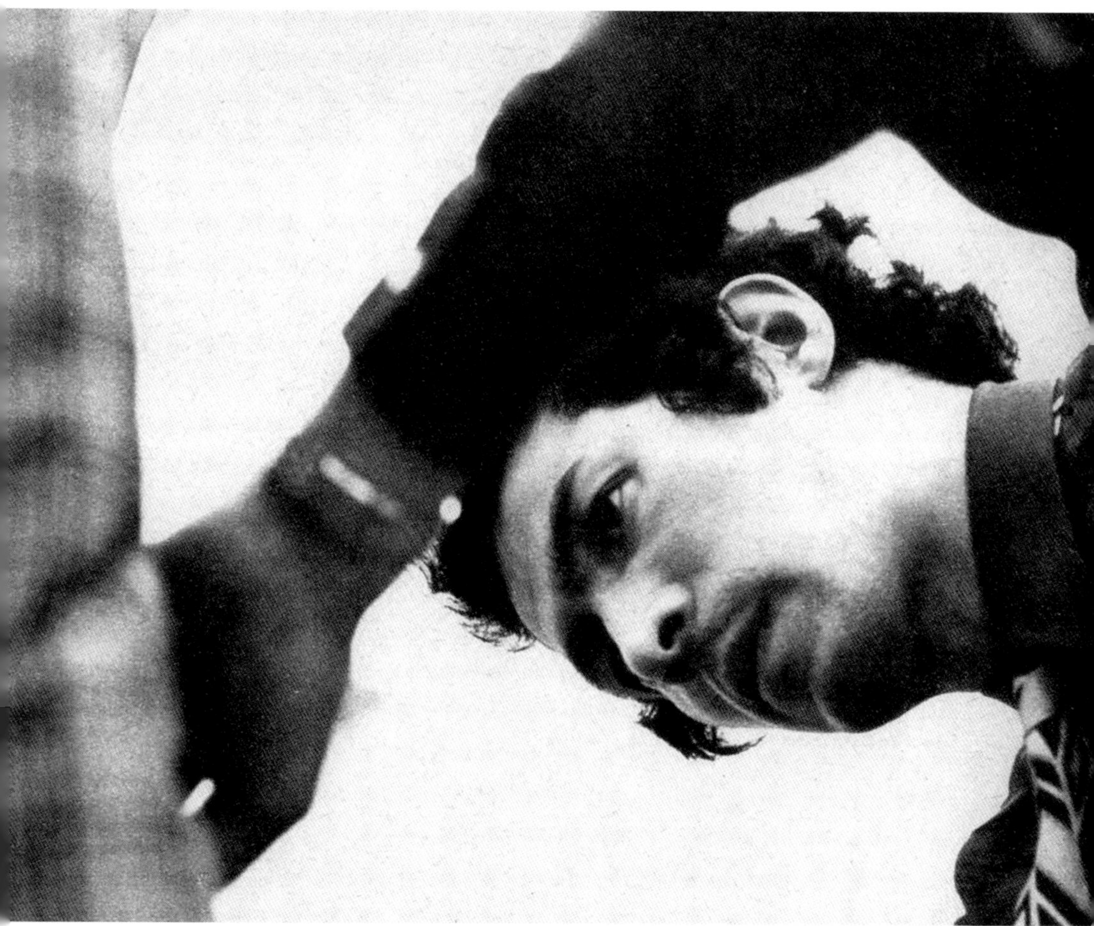

dyed with indigo, combinations that were both carefree and captured one's attention. The skintight cotton jersey was printed with what resembled tattoos of Jimi Hendrix and Janis Joplin, as a kind of personal statement honoring those rock icons who had died so young.

The models who strode down the runway[3] and on to the Japan House garden wearing the young Issey's collection included Donna Jordan,[4] who had worked with Andy Warhol, Loulou de la Falaise,[5] Elsa Peretti,[6] and Naomi Sims,[7] all women whose personal brilliance and presence went far beyond the level of "mere" fashion model. Issey's friendship with producer Joe Eula[8] had made this event possible; Eula had organized the staff and all of the other necessary elements for the show. The artist Tadanori Yokoo[9] happened to be in New York at the time, and was there to offer moral support. I was helping out at the reception desk, and recall how he was so caught up in the swirl of everyone's excitement. This was also an event which marked one of the early encounters between Tokyo's and New York's Pop generations.

The show itself may have been both experimental and modest in the context of today's fashion business, but it clearly indicated the further direction of Issey's work from the 1970s onward, as well as exhibiting design elements that would form currents that can be followed through to his work today.

When he was an art student, there was a shop in the Ginza district of Tokyo that Issey visited frequently – it was called *Kogei*, meaning handicraft, and had been founded by Masako Shirasu,[10] a woman known for her writings and for her profound knowledge of Japan's traditional arts and handicrafts. *Kogei* exhibited and sold outstanding examples of textiles and everyday utensils, including pottery, which had been made in various parts of Japan. The young, slender Issey Miyake would look intensely at the wide range of different types of woven cotton textiles and ask question after question, to which Ms. Shirasu would respond. This was the starting point of the encounter between two people who would over time come to express and communicate the essence of Japanese culture and arts in their respective fields.

The key to comprehending how Issey Miyake, a leading artist and designer in a variety of fields, was shaped as an individual and how the elements of his practice came into being lies in understanding his student-day interests and activities.

Issey Miyake was a student of graphic design at an art university, but his growing interest in clothing as a medium of expression led him to begin to design clothes. The brilliantly innovative art director Jo Murakoshi[11] noticed Issey, and this led to his becoming responsible for the visual direction of the corporate calendar of Toyo Rayon Co., Ltd. (now Toray Industries, Inc./TORAY). Design professionals such as architects and graphic designers were very impressed by the women draped in gauzy robes and refreshingly new pants, the work of this "new face" designer with his definitively "new era" aura.

Miyake then turned his attention to collaborating with contemporary musicians and composers. John Cage[12] had strongly influenced the composer Toshi Ichiyanagi[13] during his time in New York, and Ichiyanagi, who was by then back in Japan, collaborated with the composer/pianist Yuji Takahashi[14] on the music for *Nuno to Ishi no Uta* (*Poems of Cloth and Stone*),[15] resulting in a fashion presentation of a completely unprecedented kind. Organized by friends and well-wishers, and featuring the leading models of the time, this was not only Miyake's first collection show, but also a farewell event, as it marked both Issey's graduation from art school and his departure from Japan to study at l'École de la Chambre Syndicale de la Couture Parisienne.

But to jump further back in time for a moment, here is an episode which traces Miyake's central professional attitude back to his early days. In 1960, while he was still a student, Tokyo hosted the World Design Conference.[16] Realizing that clothing design was not included in the conference program, he wrote about this issue to the chairman of the organizing committee, architect Junzo Sakakura,[17] and to the editor Isao Imaida.[18] The organizers ultimately responded by formally including the field of clothing design and inviting designers to participate in the conference. The forthrightness shown by Miyake in taking action so that his chosen field of design would be properly acknowledged is still an integral part of who he is, and demonstrates the steadfastness of his principles.

ISSEYMAN FLIES

Sometimes I feel that even his contemporary fellow Japanese do not really understand much about the extraordinary person called Issey Miyake. What I am trying to say is that even a long-standing friend and collaborator such as myself cannot really claim to truly know the full scope of who he really is. One often talks of leaping or flying through time and space, and in Issey Miyake's case, it might not be inappropriate to think of him as being equipped with constantly whirring rotors of inspiration that allow him to make sudden takeoffs and landings.

He is the kind of person who makes one wonder not so much "where was he born?" as "what kind of place could he possibly come from?" This idea came to mind when I was mulling over the idea of writing *The Story of Issey Miyake* for children. The "place" does not necessarily mean somewhere on Earth; and the question arises precisely because he has such a special energy – indeed, an energy that makes one's own imagination begin to soar – that it seems only fitting to think of him as coming from somewhere else in the universe. This is the energy that made it possible to ensure that creative design be taken as a serious discipline in Japan, an island in the Far East where self-imposed restraint is an unspoken commandment of the psyche. His is the kind of energy that seizes uniquely inspired ideas and brings them to full fruition. When we mere mortals attempt to understand his sort of creative energy, we are tempted to entertain notions derived from science fiction, from the extraterrestrial.

In trying to understand the world that Issey was born into, I discover that Superman was one of his contemporaries. Both appeared on this planet in 1938. Superman was, of course, a fictional character who appeared in a comic book. He was born on Krypton, a planet with a highly developed civilization that was facing annihilation. In order to save his son, Superman's father, Jor-El, launched a capsule to send him to a relatively undeveloped planet, our Earth. Immediately after his escape, Krypton exploded, leaving the child an orphan and the sole survivor of Krypton. Traveling in a capsule, Superman lands in Kansas, in the United States, where he is discovered and brought up by a kindly couple.

Issey Miyake was born in Hiroshima. There is a photograph of him at about one and a half years old, handsomely dressed in a special festival costume which, he sometimes confided to friends, "had been handmade by my mother, and was the first piece of clothing that I distinctly recognized as being a favorite of mine." Behind the photograph we can infer the passage of time, days with his family, comings and goings about town, and the festivals and events that marked the passing seasons – the tranquility of everyday life in Japan.

This flow of ordinary Japanese life was interrupted and changed when the country entered World War II. And at the end, the atomic bomb was used for the first time in human history, and Japan was defeated.

ISAMU NOGUCHI'S BRIDGES

Kenzo Tange,[19] who had dedicated himself to the rebuilding of Hiroshima, asked Isamu Noguchi[20] to design two new bridges. They were completed around the time that Miyake was in junior high school. The bridges were initially named *Ikiru* (to live) and *Shinu* (to die), and then renamed *Tsukuru* (to build) and Yuku (to depart). What went through Noguchi's mind as he worked on this project for Hiroshima, only a few years after the end of World War II, was probably based on his understanding of life and death which he had had to confront during the war. In terms of Noguchi's work, the bridges are grounded in an orthodox structural form that also emanates an organic awakening, and since those teenage years they continued to exist deep in Issey Miyake's awareness.

Superman had to bear the collapse of his own planet and civilization. The Earth has nuclear weapons, mechanisms for self-destruction created by our own civilization. Their power to destroy has been tested twice. The children of Earth have no hope of possessing capsules that would allow them to fly to other planets and so escape annihilation.

Fly with Issey Miyake was the title of a show that was held in 1977.[21] The word "fly" was chosen as it suggested (among other things) euphoria, adventure, and the unleashing of the mind and body – sensations of which young people at the time were becoming aware. The show itself took free-wheeling flight.

"It succeeded in visualizing life itself," was the impression of the writer Aromu Mushiake.[22] Issey flies. Flying is the highest accolade. When artistry soars, the drama of life is encapsulated within.

1   Bodywear: Clothing that combines the functionality of underwear with the fashion attributes of outer layers. First observed from around 1960. Tops + panties are referred to as bodyshirts, bra + girdle combinations are bodysuits, stockings + shirts and bodytights are other examples of this category.

2   *Sashiko*: A Japanese sewing technique which can also refer to the cloth itself. Multiple layers of fabric, often previously used, are covered with tiny handsewn stitches to strengthen worn cloth and to add warmth. This technique of reinforcement led to the development of a particularly sturdy material that was adopted by firemen and judo athletes.

3   Runway: The term referring to the narrow stage where models walk to show clothes entered widespread use following the 1990s, but is used throughout this text.

4   Donna Jordan (1950–): Fashion model. Known for her bleached blonde hair and eyebrows, she was referred to as Disco Marilyn. An icon of the 1970s, she was one of Andy Warhol's muses, and appeared in his 1973 film *L'Amour*.

5   Loulou de la Falaise (1948–2011): Designer. Was a fashion journalist and model, but after meeting Yves Saint Laurent became his muse and joined the brand. Following his retirement in 2002, established her own brand, and created clothes and jewelry.

6   Elsa Peretti (1940–2021): Jewelry designer. Began working as a model and jewelry designer in New York from 1968, and from 1974 designed for Tiffany & Co., resulting in many creations that are noted for their long-lasting popularity.

7   Naomi Sims (1948–2009): Fashion model. Began modeling in the 1960s, and was the first black model to appear on the covers of *British Vogue* and *Harper's Bazaar*.

8   Joe Eula (1925–2004): Illustrator, and fashion show producer. Halston's right-hand man during the 1970s.

9   Tadanori Yokoo (1936–): Artist. Tokyo-based, he continues to create art in diverse styles and media. Has been featured in many exhibitions, including a solo exhibition at the Museum of Modern Art in New York in 1972, and has published many books.

10 Masako Shirasu (1910–1998): Essayist. The first woman to perform on the *Noh* theater stage, and, known for her deep understanding of *Noh*, and her love of antiques, she wrote extensively on Japanese aesthetics. Ran a handicraft shop of dyed and woven objects named *Kogei* between 1955 and 1970.

11 Jo Murakoshi (1925–1996): Art director. One of the founding members of the advertising agency Light Publicity Co., Ltd. He also worked with Yusaku Kamekura on the posters for the 1964 Tokyo Olympic Games.

12 John Milton Cage Jr. (1912–1992): Composer. His experimental work had a major influence on avant-garde art. Known for works such as "silent" piece *4'33"*, where the performer is instructed not to play his instrument.

13 Toshi Ichiyanagi (1933–2022): Composer and pianist. Went to the US at the age of 19 and returned to Japan in 1961. There his compositions explored ideas that focused on the spatial nature of music, while also merging elements of minimalism and Japanese traditional music.

14 Yuji Takahashi (1938–): Composer and pianist. Studied under Minao Shibata and Iannis Xenakis. Active as a pianist for contemporary music in France and Germany 1963–66; 1966–71 was based in the US, where he performed and also researched electronic music. Returned to Japan in 1972, where he continues to be active as a composer, performer, and writer.

15 *Poems of Cloth and Stone*: See p. 18.

16 World Design Conference: See pp. 14–15.

17 Junzo Sakakura (1901–1969): Architect. Studied under Le Corbusier, and was known as a practitioner of the modern style. His key projects include the Museum of Modern Art, Kamakura.

18 Isao Imaida (1915–1989): Editor. Became head of Bunka Publishing Bureau in 1952, founded many fashion magazines.

19 Kenzo Tange (1913–2005): Architect. Worked on many projects of nationwide importance such as the Hiroshima Peace Memorial Park and the Yoyogi National Gymnasium.

20 Isamu Noguchi (1904–1988): Sculptor. Born in the United States, he was brought up in Japan. Studied under Constantin Brâncuși in Paris. Known for a broad range of work, including monuments, environmental, furniture, lighting, and stage design. His lamps, *AKARI*, use a traditional craft method from Gifu prefecture, and are sold around the world. The Isamu Noguchi Museum is located in Long Island City, NY, where he had his studio. In Japan there is the Isamu Noguchi Garden Museum in Kagawa prefecture, and the Moerenuma Park in Sapporo, Hokkaido.

21 *Fly with Issey Miyake*: See pp. 79–81.

22 Aromu Mushiake (1923–1991): Writer and translator. Wrote widely on topics ranging from the arts to sports and racing.

1960

> February: Sent a letter to the World
  Design Conference while still a student
  at Tama Art University
> May: Began to frequent Light Publicity Co.,
  Ltd., an advertising agency in Ginza, after
  having been referred by a friend. First encounters with Jo Murakoshi, Kishin Shinoyama,
  and Katsumi Asaba. Began also to frequent
  Masako Shirasu's *Kogei*

**Letter to the secretariat of the
World Design Conference**
The World Design Conference was held in Tokyo
from May 11 to 16. It was its first conference in
Japan. It attracted more than 200 designers from
27 countries, and provided the impetus for the
word "design" to enter the Japanese vocabulary. At
the time, Issey Miyake was a student in the Graphic
Design Department at Tama Art University, and he
sent a letter to the secretariat asking why clothing
design had not been included in the Conference.
The letter and response created a sensation when
they appeared in the Conference newsletter.

Miyake's letter to the World Design Conference and the
secretariat's response, printed in the *WoDeCo Bulletin*,
No. 4 (February 25, 1960)

Why isn't clothing design included?
Issey Miyake, student
I am studying costume design. I think the WoDeCo
is a wonderful event. I wanted to attend myself (as
a student), but for some reason, the WoDeCo does
not include clothing design, even though it purports
to cover all areas of design! I find this difficult to
understand. There is no need to belabor how much of
a connection there is between clothing and ordinary
life. I would very much like to hear the opinion of the
Chair on this point.

[From the secretariat] We have received similar let-
ters from a number of different people. This response
was written by the secretariat at the direction of the
Standing Committee.

Broad interpretation of subcommittee names:
Article 7 of the Draft Organizing Committee Bylaws
contains the names and descriptions of the professional subcommittees, but Subcommittees 1 to 5 are
described in very abstract terms. In addition, people
attending the Conference are asked to select the
subcommittee most appropriate for themselves. Note
that, for example, Subcommittee No. 1 is for graphic
design "etc." And Subcommittee No. 3 is for industrial
design "etc." The subcommittees are meant to cover
a fairly broad range of disciplines.

One could come up with any number of special-
ties similar to clothing, for example, ship design, civil
engineering, photography, stage devices, or scientific
research. For some of these, it is relatively simple to

＝＝＝ひろば＝＝＝

服飾デザインは含まないか
学生　三宅一生

……私はコスチューム・デザインの勉強をしています。WoDeCo の行事は素晴らしいと思っています。私も参加したいと思っていました（学生として）しかしながら、この WoDeCo には、デザインの全分野と記されているにもかかわらず、何故服飾デザインが含まれていないのでしょうか！ 私には理解できません。衣服というものが生活とどれほど大きな連がりをもっているかなどということは、今さら言うまでもないことです。この点に関して委員長の御意見をお聞きしたいのです。

【事務局より】 同じような趣旨の御質問を他にもいろいろな方からいただきました。常任委員会できめられて考え方に従って、事務局からお答えします。

部会名称を広義に解釈して

実行委員会規約草案のなかで、第7条に各専門部会の名称と内容を記してありますが、第1部会……第5部会の分け方は非常に抽象的なものであります。そして、入会を希望される方々御自身で適当な部会を選んでいただくようになっています。第1部会はグラフィックデザイン《等》、第3部会はインダストリアル・デザイン《等》と、各部会ともそれぞれに相当ひろい分野をカバーできるように考えられております。

服飾と同じように、船舶デザイン、土木設計、写真、舞台装置、関連諸科学の研究など、個々に数えあげれば無数の専門分家があげられるのですが、その中で比較的簡単に特定の部会を選べるものもあり、また同一ジャンルでも、デザイン対象やデザイナーの立場によって異った部会に分れるものもあります。たとえば、テクスタイルデザインは、仕事の内容によって第1から第5まで、どの部会にも含まれる可能性があります。

もっとも、実行委員会の組織化がきわめて短かい期間に進められたため、規約（草案）の条文や、その解釈、運用などにいろいろの不備や片寄りがないとはいえませんし、また初期の組織活動に参加された方々の専門別分布の片寄りなどのために、入会の御案内も洩れている分野が多いと思います。WoDeCo の本来の趣旨として、「デザインという仕事に関するすべての分野を含んで綜合的に行なわれる。」（規約前文）と記されていますが、それを実現するためにも、ぜひ色々な立場の方の積極的な参加と交流をお願いしたいと思います。（組織係）

デザイン学生連合（仮称）結成へ

建築 造園　両学生会議との連絡組織も

世界デザイン会議の呼びかけを機会にデザイン専攻学生有志の集会が再三にわたってひらかれ、デザイン学生連合（仮称）の結成をめざして準備委員会がつくられた。2月6日までの会合に参加したのは芸大、多摩美、女子美、武蔵美、千葉大、教育大、日大、日女大、早大の8校から約100名である。学生連合は各校単位の組織を基盤に、代表者による委員会をもつ形になるものと思われる。なお日本建築学生会議、日本造園学生会議にも呼びかけて「デザイン学生団体連絡協議会」のような話し合いの機関をつくろうという提案がなされている。

デザイン学生連合の結成呼びかけに至るまでの経過は次の通り——
第1回集会：1月25日夜
決議事項——この会を世界デザイン会議第一期準備委員会とし、今人参加のたてまえから、個人参加とするが、学生として次の要望書を委員長に提出する。
1. 登録期限の延期
2. 登録会費の二期分納員は、この事に努力し、デザイン学生連合の準備委員を兼ねる。2. 第一期準備委員会は今迄通り WoDeCo に対して、学生のインフォメーション及び、企画のアイディア、デザインを学ぶ学生と交□りたい。2. パーティ、□開きたい。3. ゼミナー□会、討論会、座談会を開□ 4. 展示会、作品展を催□

第3回集会　2月3日夜
決議事項——1. 準備会□け：この準備委員会は、□イヤーを通じ、学生相互□のために有意義に活動し□を目的とする。2. デ□連合（仮称）はデザイン学□の利益をはかり、有意義□ていく学生団体である。□ザイン学生連合は WoD□二期学生準備委員会の仕□

3. WoDeCo の企画□ィアについて、第五部□本のデザイン教育につ□議してもらいたいとい□加する。4. 準備委員□は、総務、企画（Wo□ついて、デザインイヤ□て、その他）広報（組□の三つに分ける。デ□連合の規約委員会は□する事とする。総務□報の委員会設立

第1回企画委員会　2月□先の準備会で承認され□Co に対する学生の企画□ィアを具体的に検討、□にもっていこうとして□ 1. 世界のデザインを□交流をはかりたい——□イン学生の組織が出来□

---

select a specific subcommittee, but for others, different subcommittees may be appropriate even within the same genre, depending on what is being designed and the position of the designer. Textile design is a case in point. It could potentially be included in any one of the five subcommittees, depending upon the nature of the job.

We should also note that the Organizing Committee was brought together in a very short period of time and it is possible that there are mistakes or biases in the wording and interpretation of its bylaws (draft), or in how it is administered. Certainly, there were many areas that were left out of the initial information package due to biases in the professional distribution of the people involved in the initial organizing activities. The fundamental intent of the WoDeCo is to "comprehensively address all areas of the profession called 'design'" (preamble to the Bylaws), and we look forward to the active participation and interaction of people in many different positions and disciplines so that this goal is achieved. (Organizer)

1962

> **Produced clothing for Toyo Rayon (now Toray Industries, Inc.) 1963 calendar**

Toyo Rayon calendar

This was Issey Miyake's first job producing clothing; it came at the request of art director Jo Murakoshi.

"I was approached about working on the Toyo Rayon calendar, and was up all night on the job so that I could bring a design drawing to them the next morning. I was still studying graphic design at Tama Art University and had not decided on what I wanted to do in the future, though I was vaguely interested in fashion."

Issey Miyake, Geijutsu Shincho, *August 2000 edition*

Toyo Rayon (now Toray Industries, Inc.) 1963 calendar January on the left. October on the right shows a combination of Tanba cotton stripes, a checked vest, and knee-length pants. This calendar was awarded the Minister of International Trade and Industry's Prize.
Art direction: Jo Murakoshi; photography:
Osamu Hayasaki; layout: Kazunobu Shimura;
calendar photography: Hiroshi Iwasaki

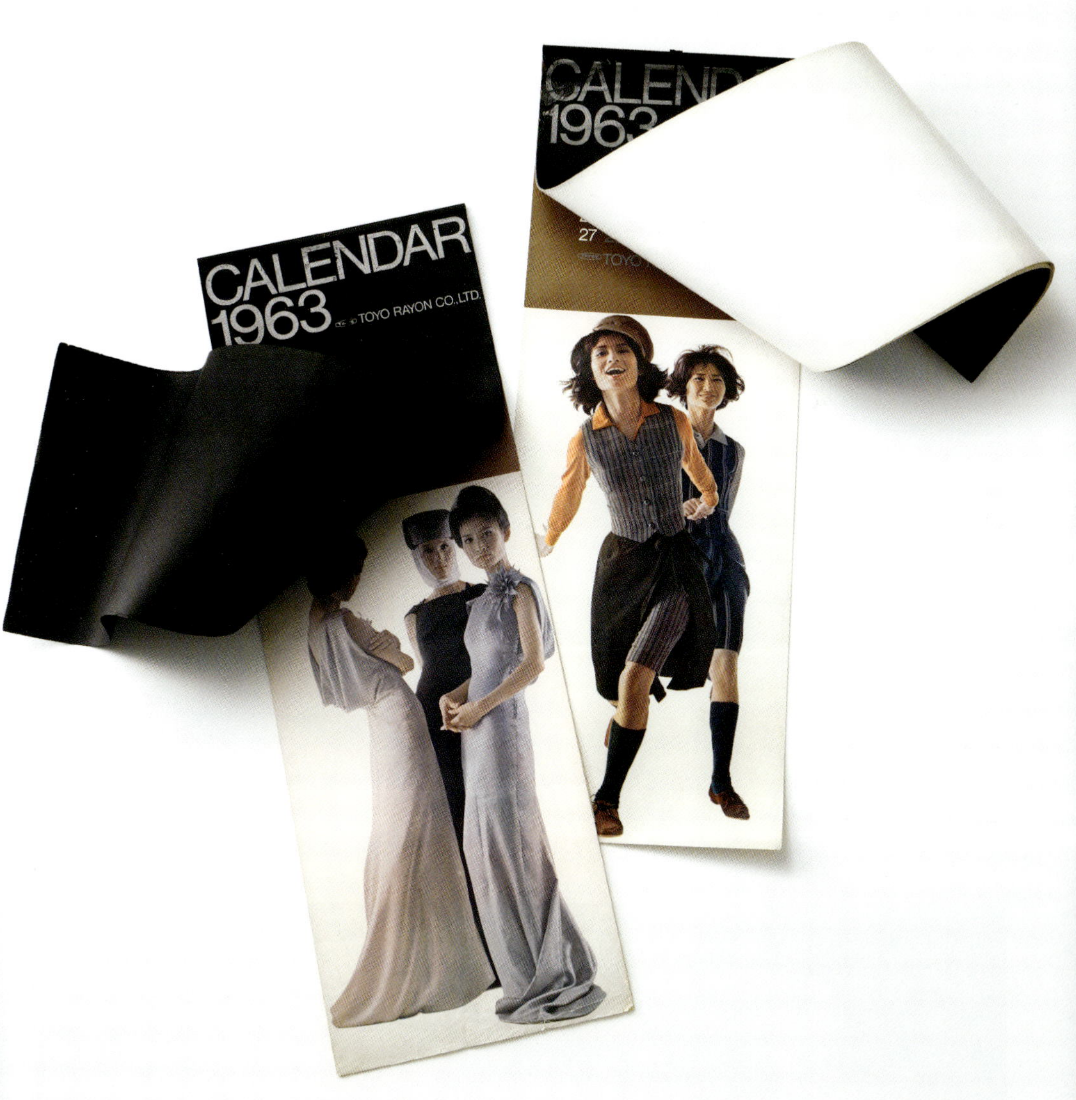

CALENDAR
1963 TORAY TOYO RAYON CO.,LTD.
CALENDAR
1963
27
TORAY TOYO

1963

> Produced clothing for the Shiseido Co., Ltd., spring campaign
> Produced clothing for the covers of *Hanatsubaki, Chainstore,* and other Shiseido publications (through 1965)
> March: Graduated from the Graphic Design Department at Tama Art University
> May: Showed first collection, *Poems of Cloth and Stone*, in Tokyo
> Produced clothing for the Canon Inc. 1964 calendar

Poems of Cloth and Stone

After graduation, Issey Miyake had his first show in the form of a joint collection with Kinya Hisamoto (hats) and Takashi Wada (accessories). The staging was experimental, with direction by Jo Murakoshi, strobe lighting, and an improvised piano performance by Yuji Takahashi and Toshi Ichiyanagi.

May 30: International Hall, Tokyo Chamber of Commerce and Industry
Direction: Jo Murakoshi; lighting: Toshiaki Ogawa; advertising: Hideaki Murase and Sho Akiyama; music: Yuji Takahashi and Toshi Ichiyanagi; narration: Kyoko Enami; makeup and hair: Shiseido Institute of Beauty Sciences; models: Mieko Imai, Hideko Kawahara, Kuniko Mitomi, Michiru Shono, Chieko Hirano, and Kyoko Enami (cameo)

Opposite left: 1964 Canon Inc. calendar
Art direction: Hideo Mukai; photography: Osamu Hayasaki; layout: Makoto Wada
This calendar won the Minister of International Trade and Industry's Prize.

Opposite right:
Shiseido Co., Ltd., spring campaign poster
Executive direction: Makoto Nakamura; photography: Noriaki Yokosuka

Poems of Cloth and Stone, May 30
International Hall, Tokyo Chamber of Commerce and Industry

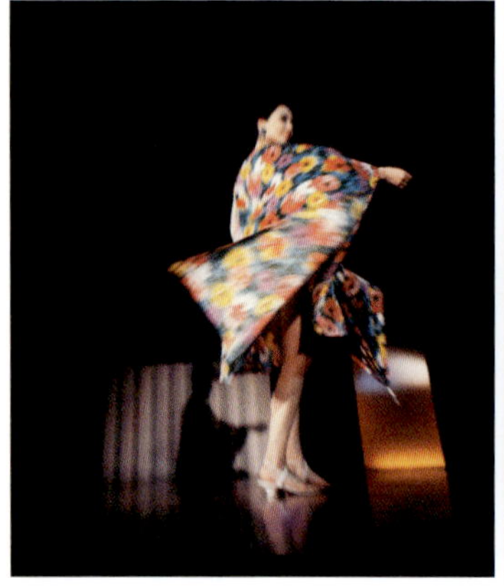

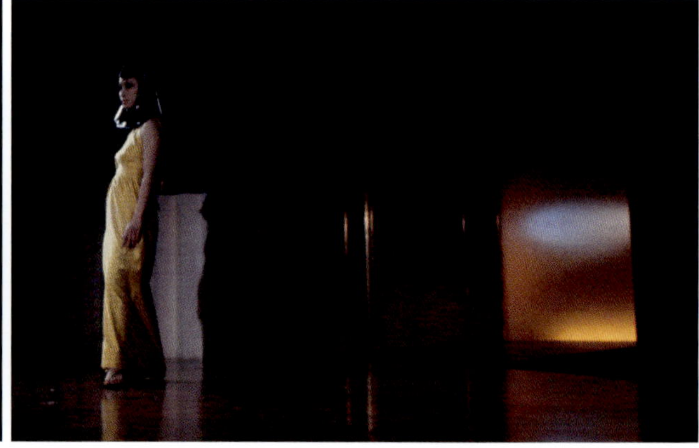

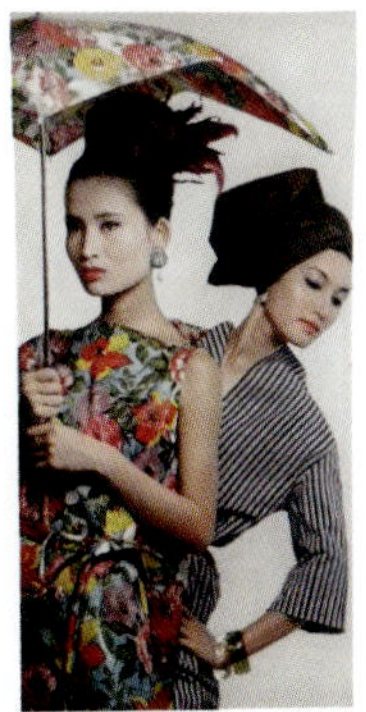

June

sun	mon	tue	wed	thur	fri	sat
	1	2	3	4	5	6
7	8	9	10	11	12	13
14	15	16	17	18	19	20
21	22	23	24	25	26	27
28	29	30				

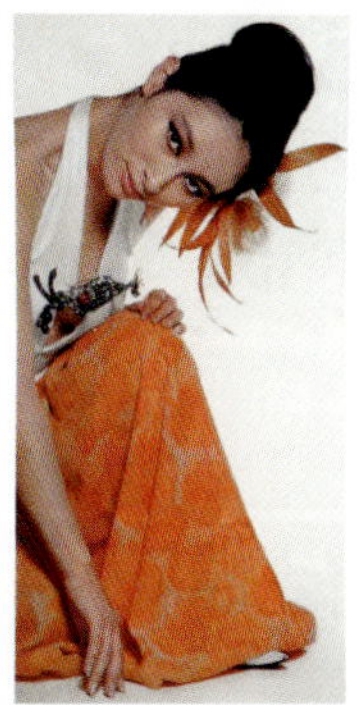

April

sun	mon	tue	wed	thur	fri	sat
			1	2	3	4
5	6	7	8	9	10	11
12	13	14	15	16	17	18
19	20	21	22	23	24	25
26	27	28	29	30		

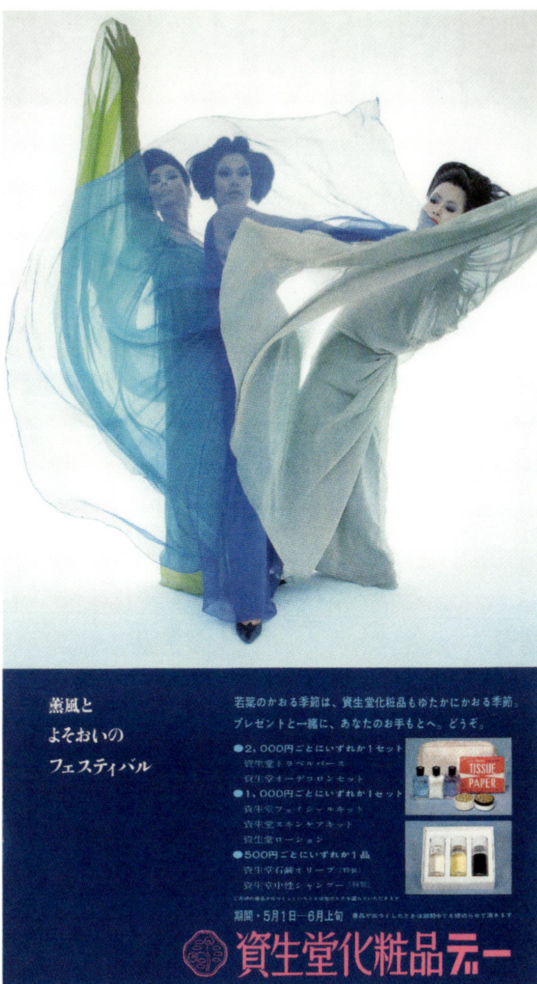

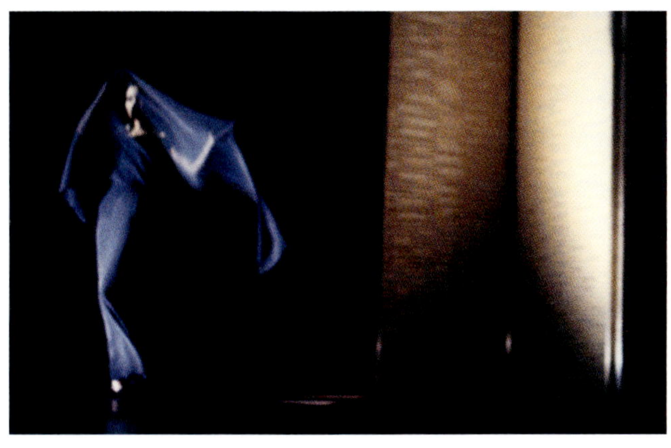

2—PARIS, WHAT HE SAW, AND THEN...

Essay by
KAZUKO KOIKE

WITNESS TO CHANGING TIMES

Issey Miyake's life in Paris was far from the culture and climate of Japan. Beginning in 1965, his studies at L'École de la Chambre Syndicale[1] were so vastly different from what he had experienced in Japan, it must have been equivalent to an encounter with advanced mathematics when one has known only elementary arithmetic. While he honed his skills at the school, Issey's attention was increasingly drawn to the diversity of nationalities and cultures he observed around him. The Musée de l'Homme and its displays of the clothing of ordinary people around the world seemed to indicate a universal state of humanity that went beyond the simple category of ethnic costume.

He could have explored the city to find hints of new fashion trends, but Miyake's interest in ethnography must have stemmed from the process of analysis that related to his own identity. This unceasing pursuit of knowledge, the way he would always spend his days, may perhaps be traced back to this period in Paris. He was like a warrior, balancing action with rest.

May 1968, Paris. Issey Miyake was there. The cobblestones of Boulevard Saint-Germain were ripped up by demonstrators in an outpouring of emotion. It was a revolt that was forged from an alliance between students and workers who questioned the state of things. Figures from the worlds of the various arts stood up in protest against a social system that had become sclerotic in the decades following World War II. The events of May 1968 and its momentum rippled throughout the world. Issey said, from time to time, "I seem to be present at occasions of great social change. Paris in May '68, Beijing at Tiananmen, New York on 9/11. Like a witness to history."

Having stared into the roiling development of current affairs, Miyake always returned to his creative process, but he never spoke about nor demonstrated through direct action what was going on in his mind. It seems that the new work developed when the time was ripe, and it was a crystallization of all that he felt about the events he experienced.

FOUNDING THE MIYAKE DESIGN STUDIO

In 1970, the *Toray Knit Exhibition*[2] was held in Tokyo. Miyake had already worked in ready-to-wear in New York, and so was asked to take part with other rising designers. Maïmé Arnodin,[3] a director who was achieving great work in the Parisian design industry, supervised the event. Starting in Paris, the tide of fashion had begun to show a worldwide shift away from couture toward ready-to-wear. Issey Miyake crystallized the atmosphere of the hall through a show that felt like the uncorking of a precious elixir that he had nurtured and whose intoxicating bouquet he now released. The models appeared without any accompanying music. What occurred instead was the sound of buttons being snapped open, and on the runway (bathed in the light and sound of cameras), pieces of the outfits danced in the air. The audience instantly grasped the fact that "Miyake's look" was built on a jumpsuit, but comprised of units, or elements, that structured the whole. This "combination" of parts became known as "unit fashion," and indicated Miyake's intention to discard the traditional Western concept of clothing, to create something completely different.

When he returned to Japan, Issey Miyake spoke of the hopes and expectations that he had for *mono zukuri* (making things) in Japan. The foundation for that was the Miyake Design Studio, which was established in 1970. It was also the year that he began to work on his collections. The New York collection described at the beginning of the previous chapter was born here.

Since the beginning of his collection creations, Miyake placed importance on the development of materials for the clothing. He had a clear vision that there are two possible directions: recreating traditional natural materials such as cotton, linen, wool, and silk, or developing new materials derived from even more advanced technology.

In Miyake's case, *mono zukuri* in Japan refers first and foremost to the making of materials. But the situation was vastly different in Paris, where fabric suppliers would bring quantities of materials to designers.

In the case of Japan, there's hardly anybody who is making fabric that we would like to have.
Issey Miyake East Meets West,
Heibonsha Limited, 1978

In addition to proposing new ideas for developing synthetics, Miyake and his team pursued their demands and desires in the workshops where traditional textiles were being woven. Makiko Minagawa[4] was one of the early members to join the Miyake Design Studio as a textile designer. Her entry established a strong foundation for the organization, as well as setting its creative aims ever higher in terms of the rarity and quality of its materials.

Makiko Minagawa was born into a family of skilled dyers and designers, and had an intimate knowledge of craft skills associated with textiles, particularly weaving and dyeing. She had studied design at art school, and was exceptionally prominent both as a cutting-edge creative artist and as the embodiment of modernity in lifestyle in Kyoto, a city that had felt the impact of the counterculture and the avant-garde art scenes at the time. Her finely honed sensibility responded to Issey Miyake's; their vast experience and great expertise were all-important foundations for the studio from the very beginning.

Issey Miyake focused on the study of Japanese clothing during his many years of apprenticeship. His basic premise was not to look at every single aspect of the transmission of Japanese traditions, but always to look for what possibilities could be found for their adoption and adaptation in contemporary everyday wear. He explored a world completely separate from traditional kimonos, which were becoming increasingly irrelevant, worn only on occasions such as weddings and funerals. In his case, he chose "grassroots Japanese beauty" and declared his intention to pursue a "populism of attire." Occupational clothing that was associated with farmers or construction workers, and the traditional costumes worn by firefighters, for example, became important sources of inspiration. Popular quilted *sashiko*, for instance, happened to be extremely diverse in terms of thickness and how stitches were applied, with different regions having different traditions. Visiting the places where these products and processes originated meant traveling across Japan. During these travels, his eyes were opened to the Tohoku (northeast) region, which became the source of the exhibition[5] that he proposed approximately a half-century later, in 2011, the year of the Great East Japan Earthquake.

The young and uncompromising Miyake also fixed his sights on Japan's recent history, when modern clothes came from the West and Western styles were imitated; these were called *Yofuku* (Western clothing). To create the unprecedented, to absorb regardless of Japanese (East) or Occidental (West) origins, and to transform it all into attire – Issey Miyake's willful intentions pulsated from the myriad of clothes that he presented in rapid succession.

JAPANESE SENSATIONS: CONTINUUM FROM ANCIENT HISTORY TO THE MEDIEVAL ERA

Issey and I once visited the philosopher Takeshi Umehara[6] in an attempt to understand the roots of the sensations that motivated the designer.

Many Europeans hold high esteem for the Japanese regarding their economic and technological achievements, but do not think much of their cultural creativity. ... It is hard to get Europe to acknowledge your academic findings, or art, purely on merit. In the past, there were, for example, D. T. Suzuki and Akira Kurosawa as figures in the arts, and today it is difficult to deny the presence of Issey Miyake at the forefront, and their continuum... If Europeans identify something Japanese within Issey Miyake, what would that be? If Japanese tradition is admitted, it would probably be medieval Basara.[7] *Issey Miyake's sensibilities are not Japanese in the way that we have typically regarded ourselves. ... For Japanese culture to resurrect itself robustly, we must look toward the tradition of* Jomon *culture... Mr. Issey Miyake may be aware of this or not, but his aesthetic is a resurrection of the tradition of* Basara, *of the tradition of* Jomon, *and is probably the international launch of this sense of beauty.*

Takeshi Umehara, *Issey Miyake Bodyworks*, Shogakukan, Inc., Tokyo, 1983

"His work is extremely intriguing as an analysis of civilization," said Professor Umehara after our visit; he later wrote the above article called *Issey Miyake: An Artist of Basara*.

IN SEARCH OF THE SOURCES OF CONTEMPORARY CLOTHING

Miyake sought the sources of clothing in the climate and culture of Japan, and his creations formed a series that could be described as "contemporary-universal" city wear. There were many international fashion critics, editors, and artists who were fans, and, reciprocally, there was a continuous stream of information about their activities that was sent to him. The announcement of Diana Vreeland's[8] costume exhibition at the

Metropolitan Museum of Art was one such example. Makiko Minagawa and I were enjoying our winter vacation in California, but Issey had rushed on to New York. Then, one day, he telephoned, asking us to join him right away, and so we did.

Diana Vreeland was famous as an editor of influential fashion magazines such as *Harper's Bazaar* and *Vogue*; she was a fashion leader, and had been invited to join the Costume Institute at the Metropolitan Museum of Art. The exhibition that she supervised was an overview of the most outstanding examples of Parisian couture from the first half of the 20th century, *Inventive Clothes: 1909–1939.*

What is noteworthy is the fact that the word "clothes" was chosen – not "fashion" or "mode." Also significant was the specific time frame indicated in the subtitle. Add to this the fact that the exhibition was about clothes, not costume. We felt this captured the meaning of "people's clothing" as a field of design. 1909 was the year that Serge Diaghilev and his Ballets Russes created a fervor for the arts of Russia in Paris; 1939 was marked by the events that led to World War II. These were the clothes made by Parisian couturiers in these three decades in the early 20th century, pieces which were both beautiful and useful. For the exhibition, the colors, space, lighting, and exhibition design were all carefully planned and seemed to breathe life back into clothes that had long slumbered in storage and were now exposed to the air of the 1970s. This was outstanding and went far beyond the level of an archive that simply keeps artifacts locked up in a museum basement. A glance was enough to understand, for example, the changes in clothing from the turn of the last century, or how the Art Deco style of 1925 was expressed in printed patterns.

The show matched the then prevailing concern here: at the time that it was mounted, the Japanese were discussing the need for a rule that was known as TPO, or Time, Place, Occasion.[9] TPO acknowledged the power of design and, hence, that certain types of dress were appropriate to different situations.

Issey Miyake came to a spontaneous decision at the exhibition. He would achieve what he could learn from it, and then express his own zeitgeist through his designs. Koichi Tsukamoto,[10] who was then a vice-chairman of the Kyoto Chamber of Commerce and Industry, responded to a proposal from Miyake. Kyoto had reason to wish for a resurgence in the culture of clothing. The decision to bring the exhibition *Inventive Clothes: 1909–1939* to The National Museum of Modern Art, Kyoto, as *Gendai Ifuku no Genryu Ten*[11] was made unusually quickly. Director Michiaki Kawakita,[12] like Miyake, was considering the future of crafts and design.

1   L'École de la Chambre Syndicale de la Couture Parisi-
     enne. Founded in 1927. Graduates include Yves Saint
     Laurent, Issey Miyake, Jean-Louis Scherrer, and Jean
     Colonna.
2   *Toray Knit Exhibition*: See p. 26.
3   Maïmé Arnodin (1916–2003): Fashion and advertising
     consultant. In 1968, after working as editor-in-chief
     at *Le Jardin des Modes*, she established MAFIA with
     her close friend Denise Fayolle. Both had been huge
     supporters of the prêt-à-porter since it began and had
     contributed enormously to raising public awareness
     about fashion and the use of public relations as a tool
     for promoting fashion as brands.
4   Makiko Minagawa: Textile designer. Has worked on
     developing original materials as textile director of the
     Miyake Design Studio immediately after it was estab-
     lished in 1970. Became total director of HaaT, an Issey
     Miyake Inc. brand, in 2000.
5   *The Spirit of Tohoku: "Clothing" by Issey Miyake*
     exhibition at 21_21 DESIGN SIGHT, July 2011:
     See pp. 308–309.
6   Takeshi Umehara (1925–2019): Philosopher. Reassessed
     the history of the Japanese psyche while advancing bold
     hypotheses relating to literature, history, and religion.
     Best known for his analysis of Japanese culture, specif-
     ically the cultures of the *Ainu* people and the region of
     Okinawa. Found them to have retained the strongest
     traces of *Jomon* influences. *Jomon* is a unique culture
     native to the Japanese archipelago which flourished
     between the latter half of the Later Stone Age and the
     Neolithic Era.
7   *Basara*: A trend that was at its height during the period
     known as *Nanbokucho* (latter part of 14th century), not-
     ed for admiration of bold deeds, flamboyance in dress,
     indulgence in luxury, and hedonism.
8   Diana Vreeland (1903–1989): Editor. Joined *Harper's
     Bazaar* in New York in 1937, fashion editor from 1937. In
     1963, appointed editor-in-chief of its rival, *Vogue*. After
     leaving this post, organized many exhibitions as special
     consultant to the Costume Institute of the Metropolitan
     Museum of Art in the 1970s.
9   TPO: Japanese acronym from Time, Place, Occasion.
     Refers to the need to dress appropriately as these
     conditions require.
10   Koichi Tsukamoto (1920–1998): Industrialist. Founder
     of Wacoal Corp. Achieved Wacoal's IPO in 1964, and
     became a key person in Kyoto's business circles.
     Established The Kyoto Costume Institute, KCI, in 1978.
11   *Gendai Ifuku no Genryu Ten – Inventive Clothes: 1909–
     1939*: See pp. 56–57.
12   Michiaki Kawakita (1914–1995): Art critic. Known for his
     work on modern and contemporary Japanese painting,
     and as a director of several art museums.

ISSEY MIYAKE Autumn-Winter 1971 Collection
at the Japan House in New York

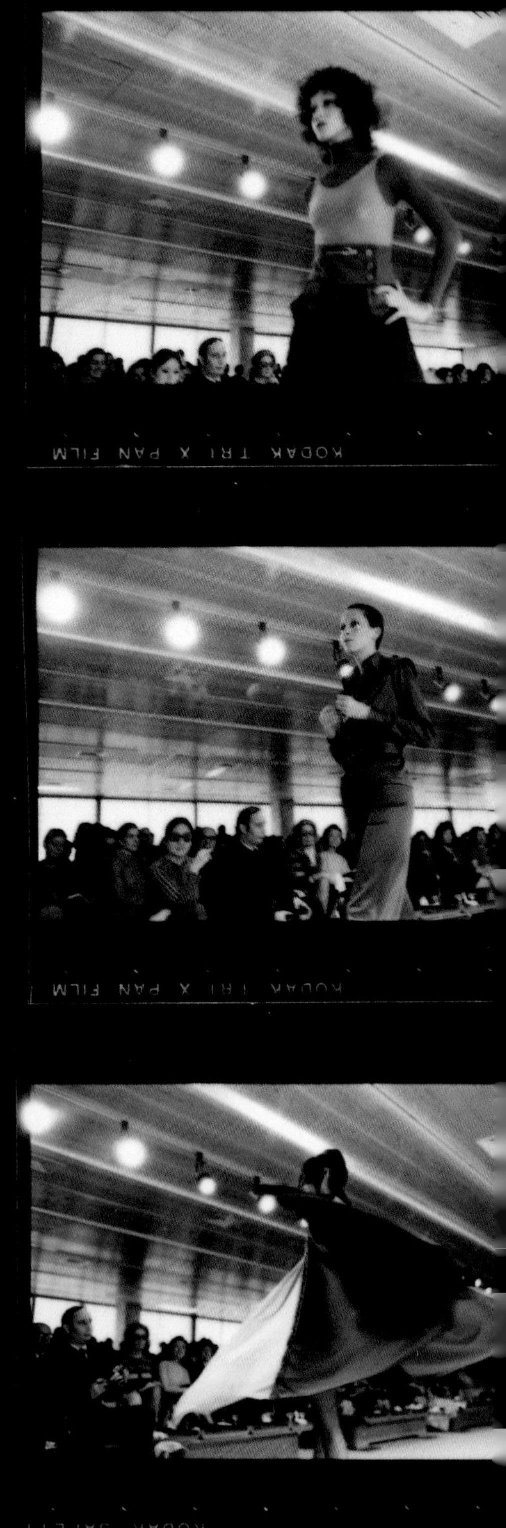

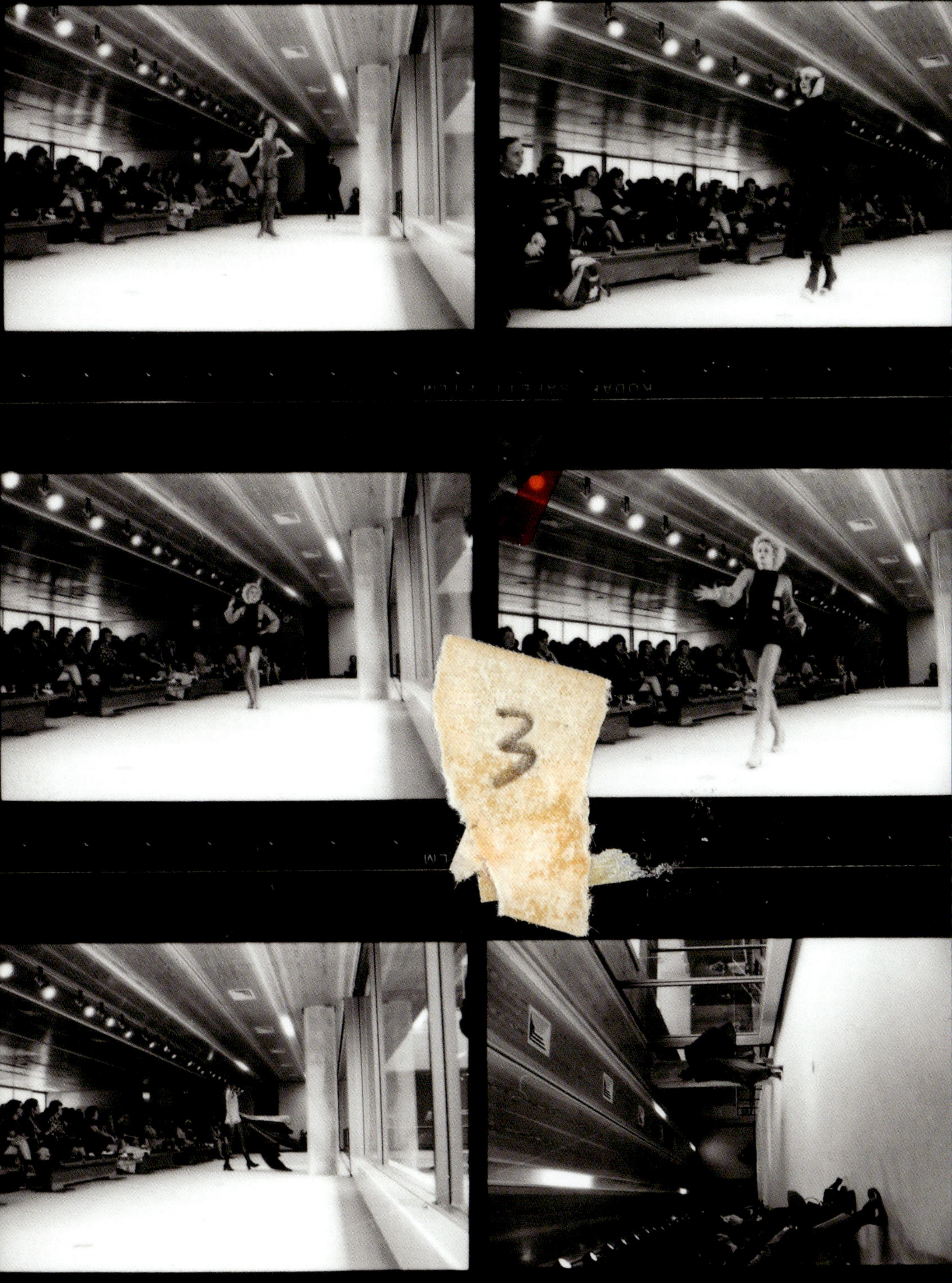

3

1970

> Designed the hostess uniforms for Shiseido Co., Ltd., Olivetti Press Center and International Wool Secretariat at Osaka World Exposition, held from March to September
> March: Participated in the *Toray Knit Exhibition*. Unveiled a unit fashion approach called *Constructible Clothes*
> April: Established Miyake Design Studio (MDS) with Tomoko Komuro

Toray Knit Exhibition and Constructible Clothes
Returning home from New York, Issey Miyake participated in a Toray Industries, Inc. event to highlight trends in knits. Miyake presented *Constructible Clothes* at an event featuring a speech by Maïmé Arnodin, the Paris fashion coordinator who coined the phrase "Knit Age," and a show of knit fabrics by three designers, including Miyake. The models took off pieces of clothing one by one on stage to demonstrate that the clothing has many separate units composed of individual parts. For Miyake's part of the program, there was no music in the hall, only the sound of the clothing as it was being put on and taken off.

March 26, Magnolia Hall, Tokyo Prince Hotel
Planning and composition: Akira Mishima

Opposite: *Constructible Clothes*
A jumpsuit made from a stretchy jersey fabric and a round cape divided into four parts and held in place with dot buttons. Designed and presented in 1970
Photography: Kishin Shinoyama; model: Yuri Hodaka

Toray Knit Exhibition, March 26, Magnolia Hall, Tokyo Prince Hotel

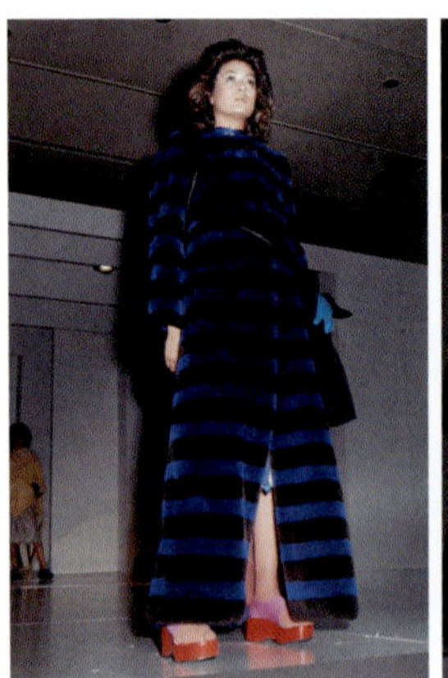
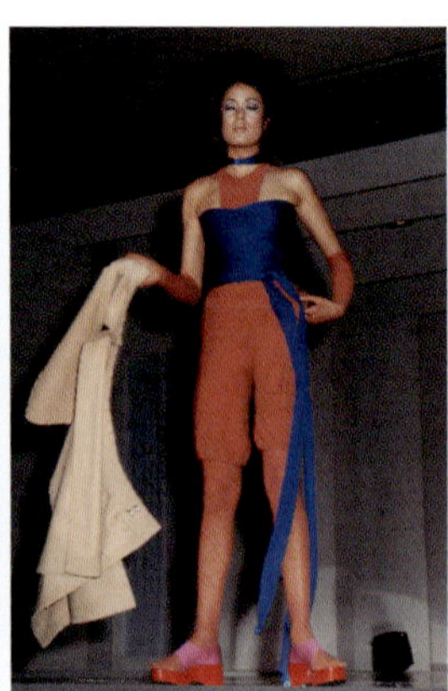
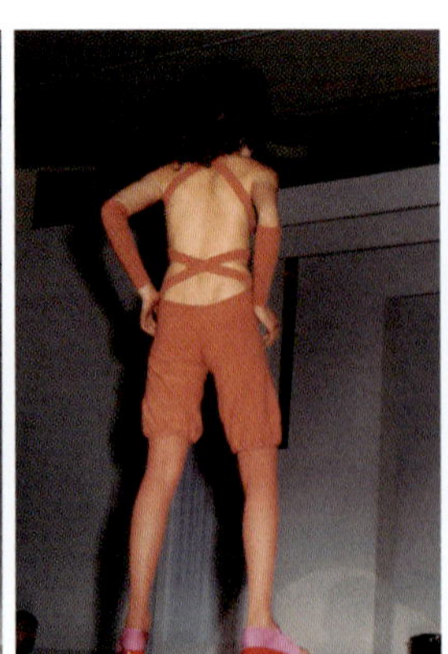
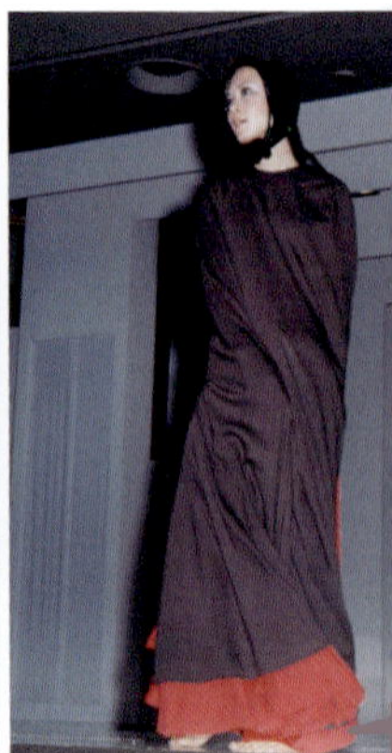

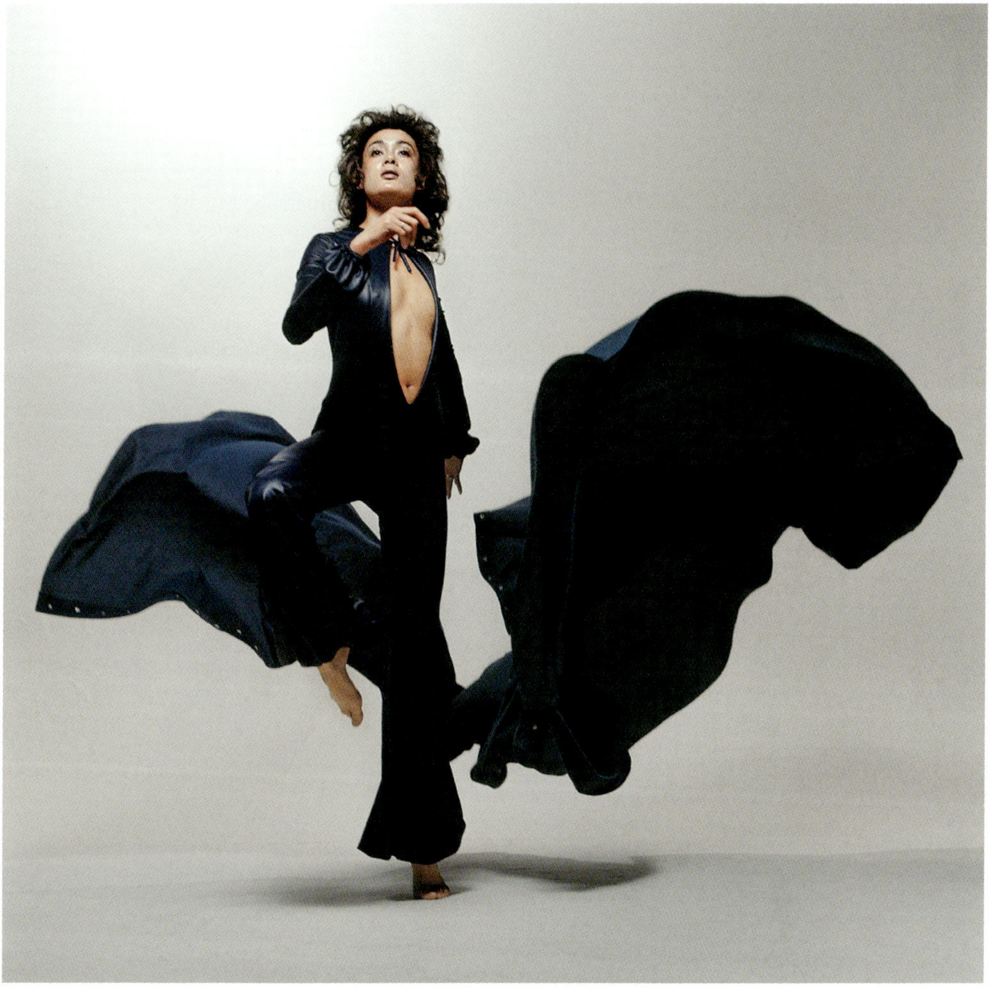

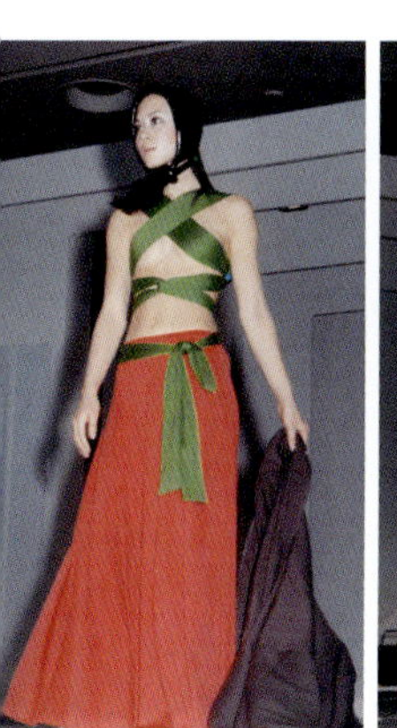
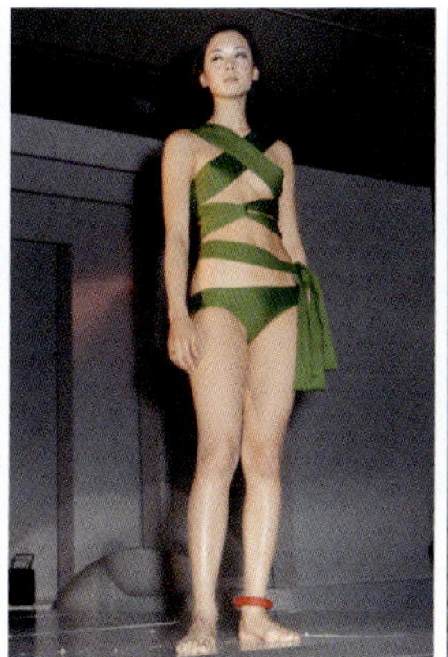
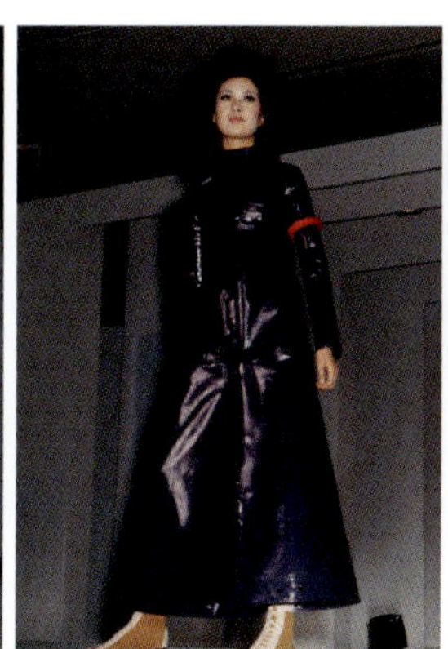
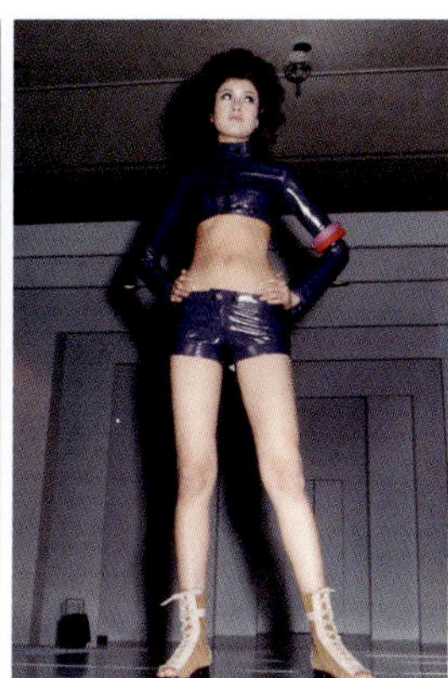

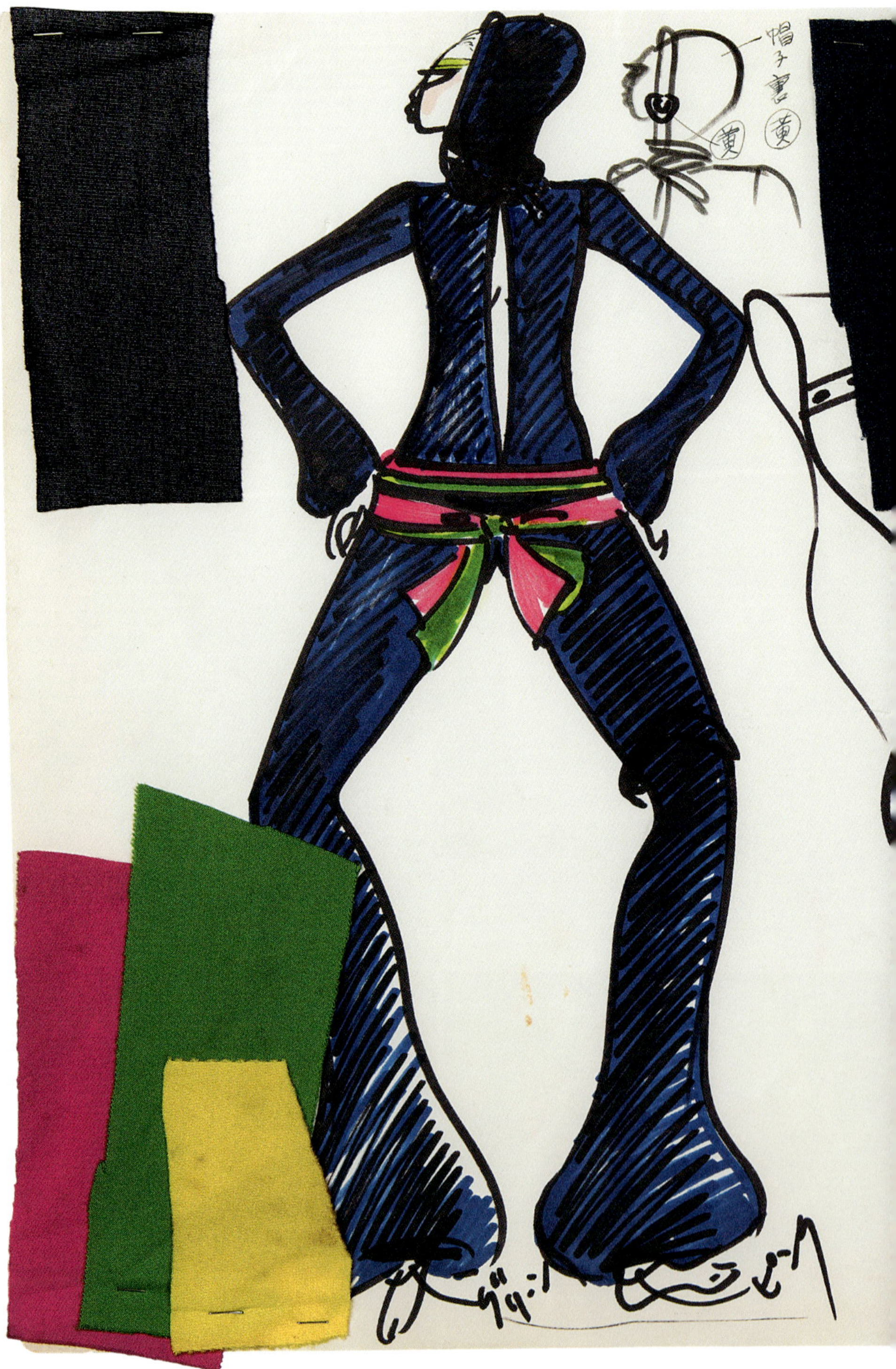
帽子裏
黄
黄

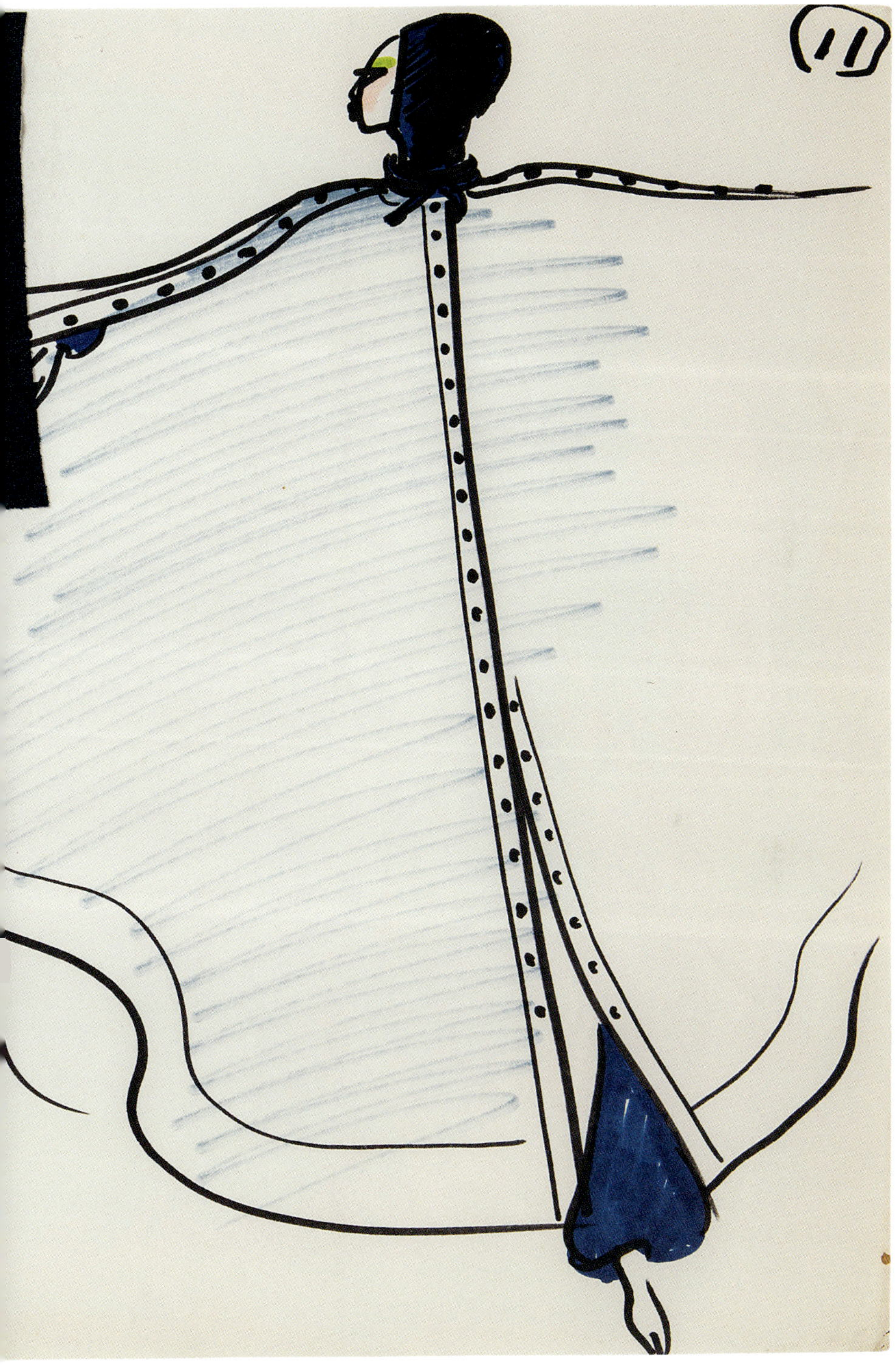

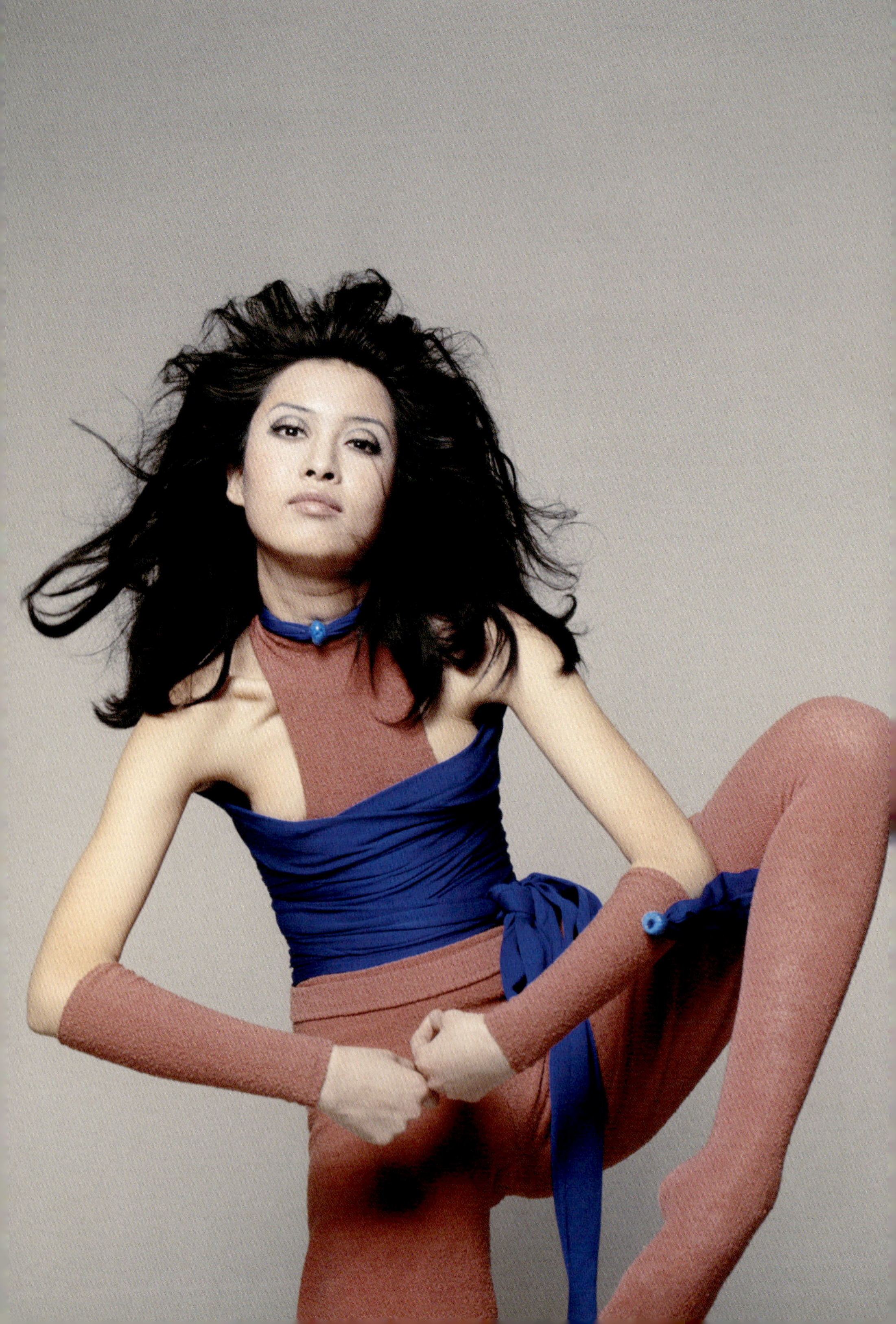

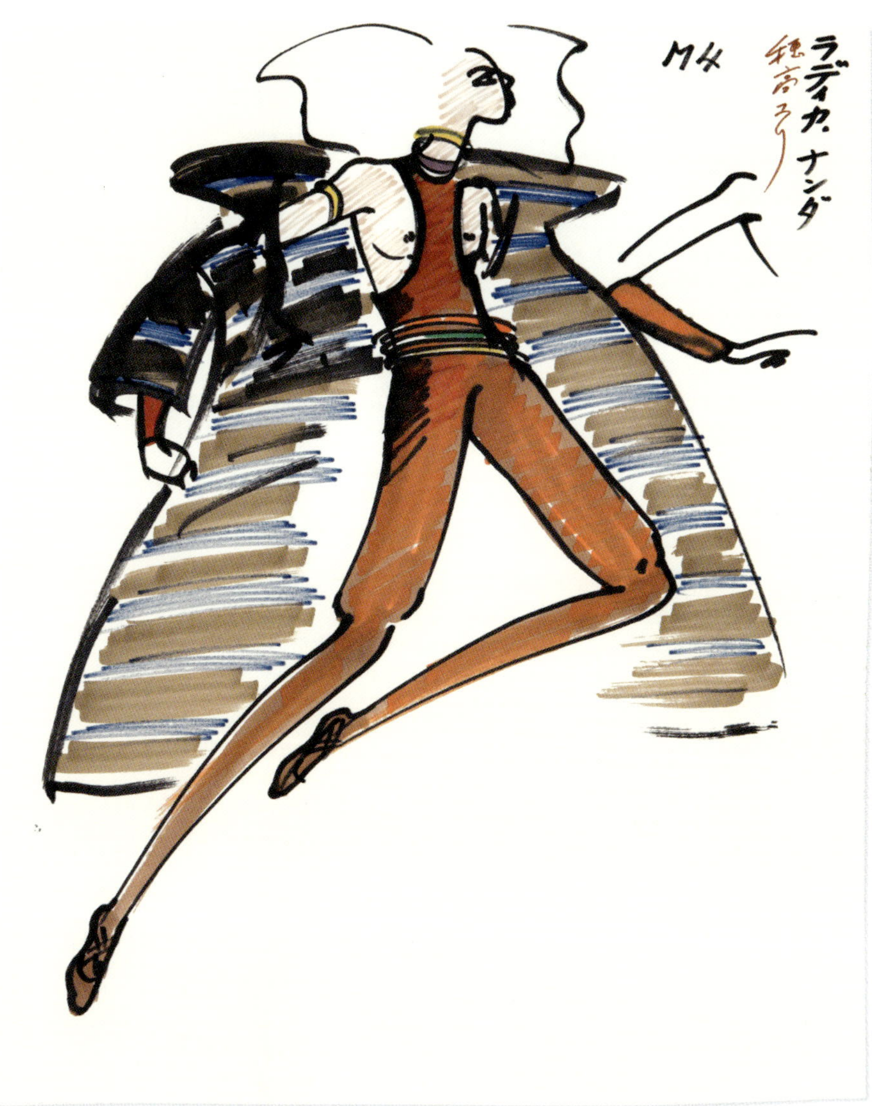

Opposite: *Constructible Clothes*
Knit overall with knee-high pants, socks, and arm covers. The overalls have long strings crossed in the back. At the *Toray Knit Exhibition*, a model appeared wearing the coat with the horizontal border, depicted in the design drawing on the right. Designed and presented in 1970
Photography: Kishin Shinoyama;
model: Sachiko Takeuchi

Constructible Clothes design drawing
1970: Design drawing: Issey Miyake
© Miyake Design Studio

Previous spread: Design drawing with fabric samples for ***Constructible Clothes***
1970: Design drawing: Issey Miyake
© Miyake Design Studio

1971

> January: *Toray/Ichiju ISSEY MIYAKE Ban-Lon Collection* released in Tokyo
> February: Showed first ISSEY MIYAKE collection (Spring-Summer 1971) at the Gotham Hotel in New York
> February: Began to develop bodywear, socks, and stockings in collaboration with Wacoal Corp.
> May: Held first solo fashion show, Autumn-Winter 1971 Collection at the Japan House in New York
> June: Showed the Autumn-Winter 1971 Collection, titled *ISSEY NOW: Something Will Happen in the Parking Garage Tonight*, at the C parking garage attached to the Shibuya Seibu department store in Tokyo
> November: Established Issey Miyake International, Inc. (now Issey Miyake Inc.)
> December: Opened press offices in New York and Paris

Show at the Japan House in New York
Designed by Junzo Yoshimura, the Japan House, which served as the headquarters of the Japan Society, was still under construction when Miyake held his first solo fashion show there. The show was directed by Joe Eula in collaboration with Japan House Gallery director Rand Castile, and made use of the open space in the construction site. That same month, an ISSEY MIYAKE corner opened in Bloomingdale's in New York.

Opposite: *Handkerchief Dress*
A one-size dress made using three square pieces of jersey cloth, with the bias used to cross the shoulder straps in back.
1970 design/Spring-Summer 1971 Collection
Photography: Tenmei Kanoh; models: Yasuko Yamayoshi and Marie Helvin

Autumn-Winter 1971 Collection
May 20, Japan House

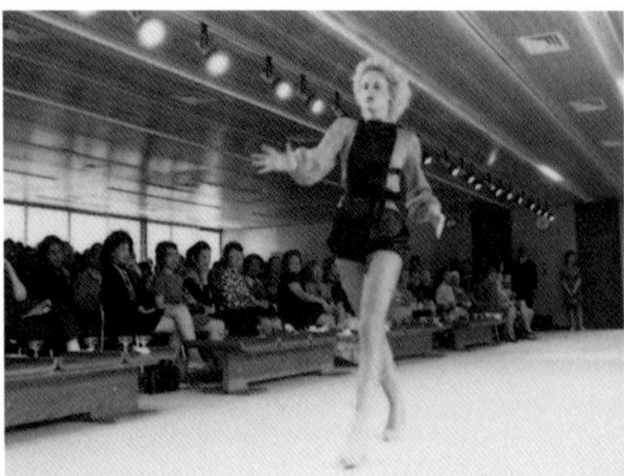
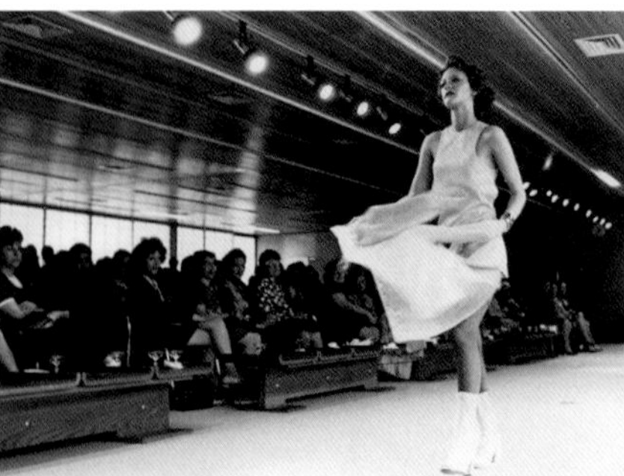
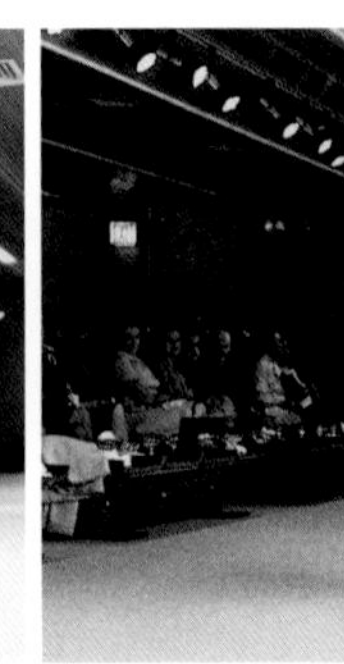

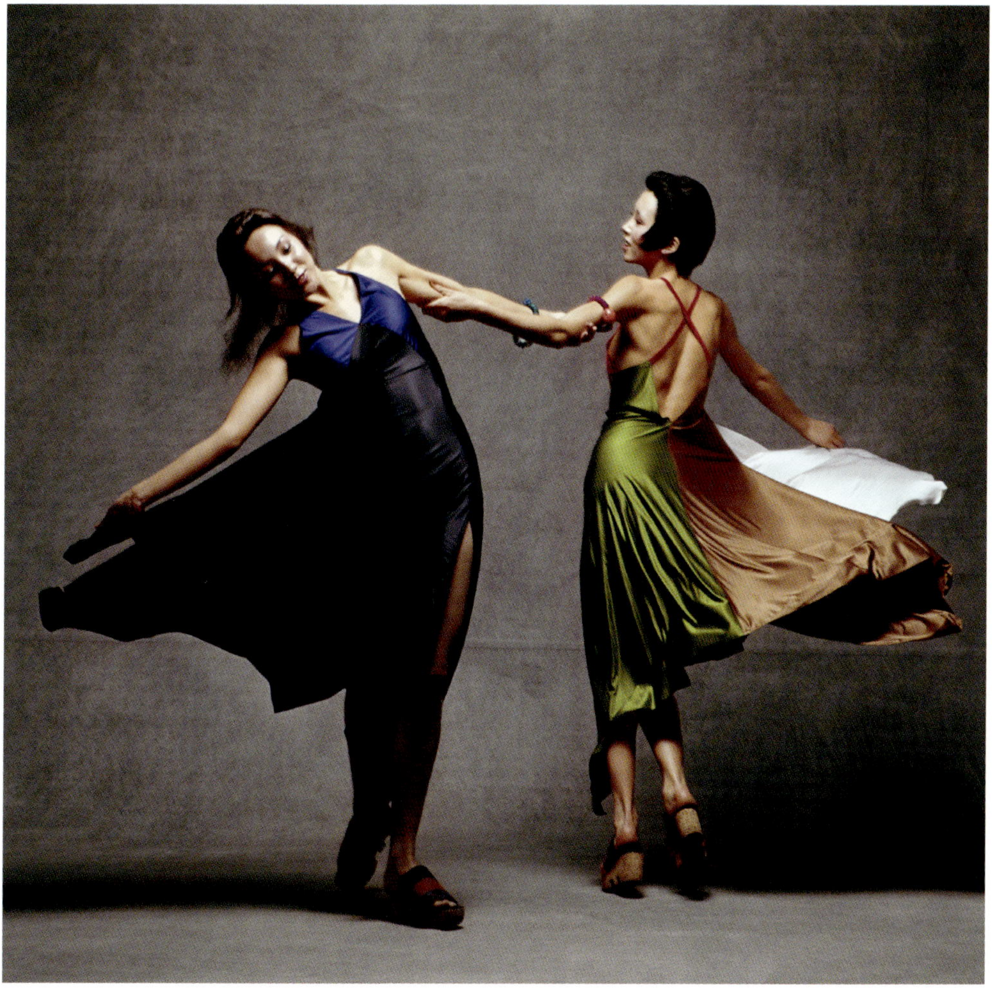

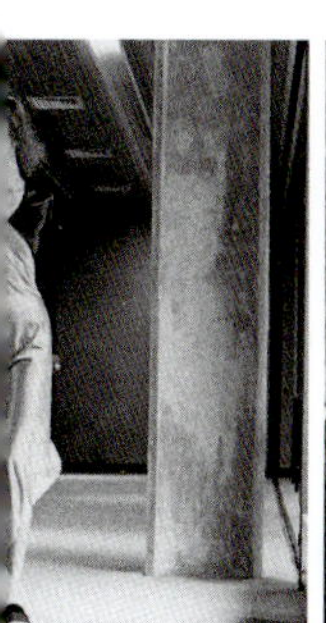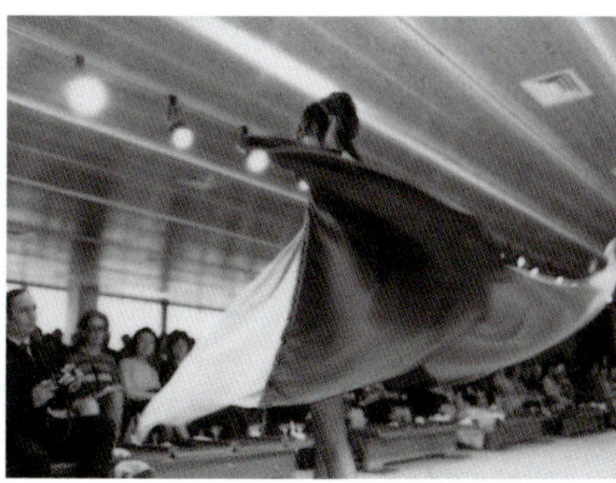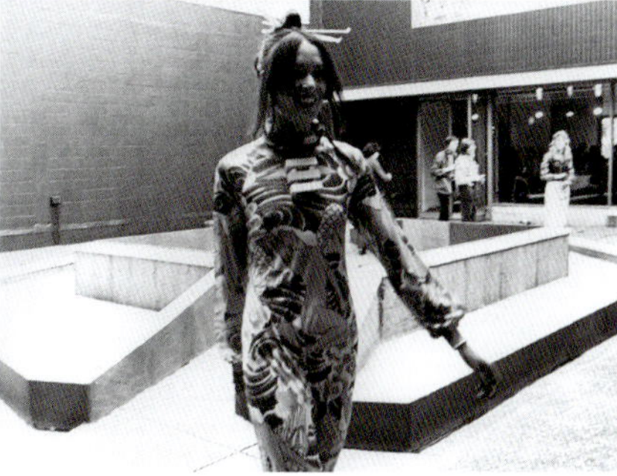

Below: ***Handkerchief Dress***
1970 design/Spring-Summer 1971 Collection
Photography: Kishin Shinoyama;
model: Yasuko Yamayoshi

Opposite: ***Handkerchief Dress*** design drawing
1970: Design drawing: Issey Miyake
© Miyake Design Studio

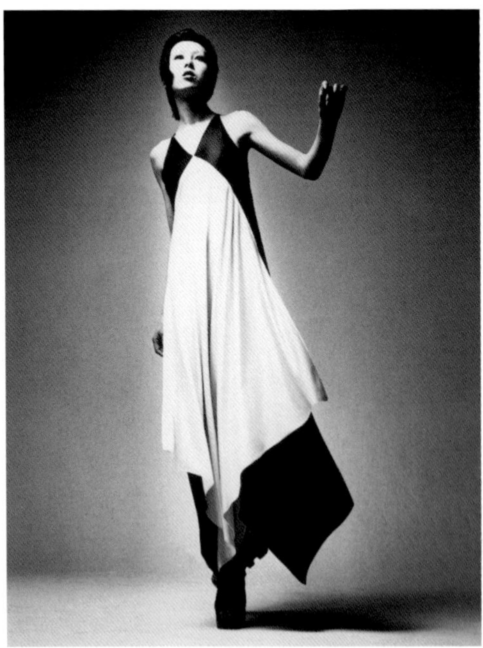

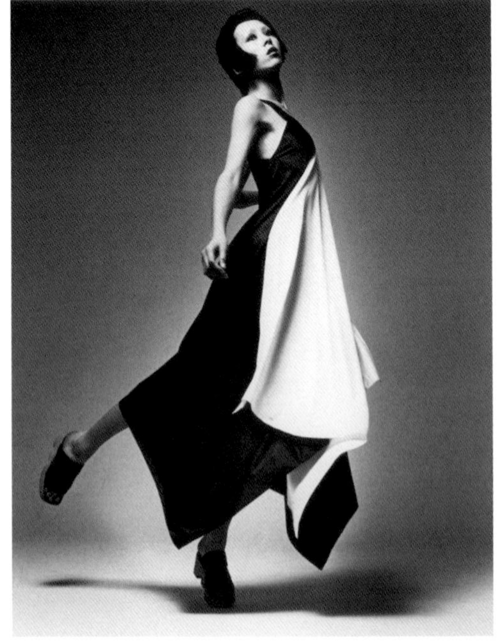

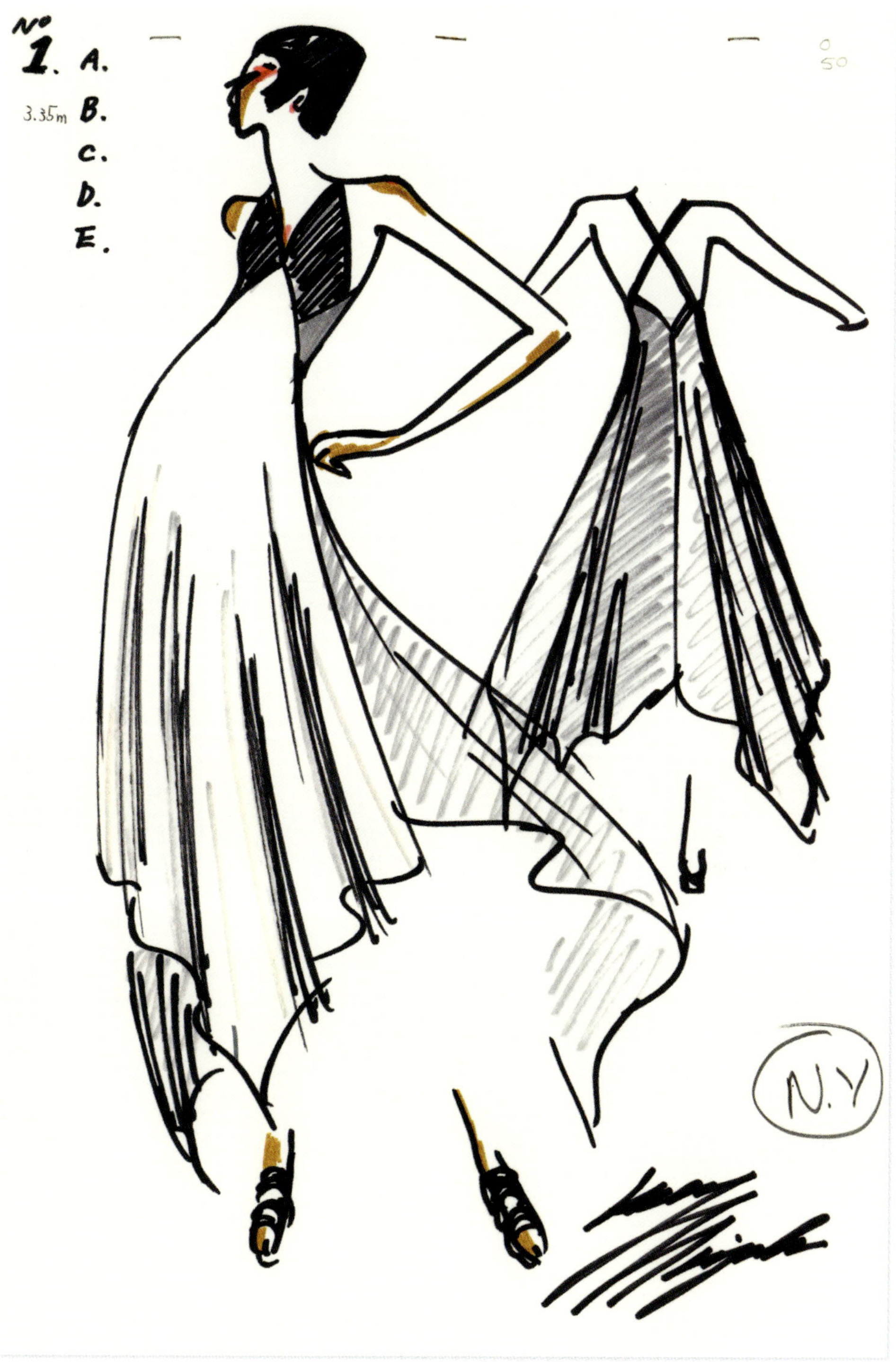
N° 1.
A.
B.
C.
D.
E.
3.35m
O
50
N.Y

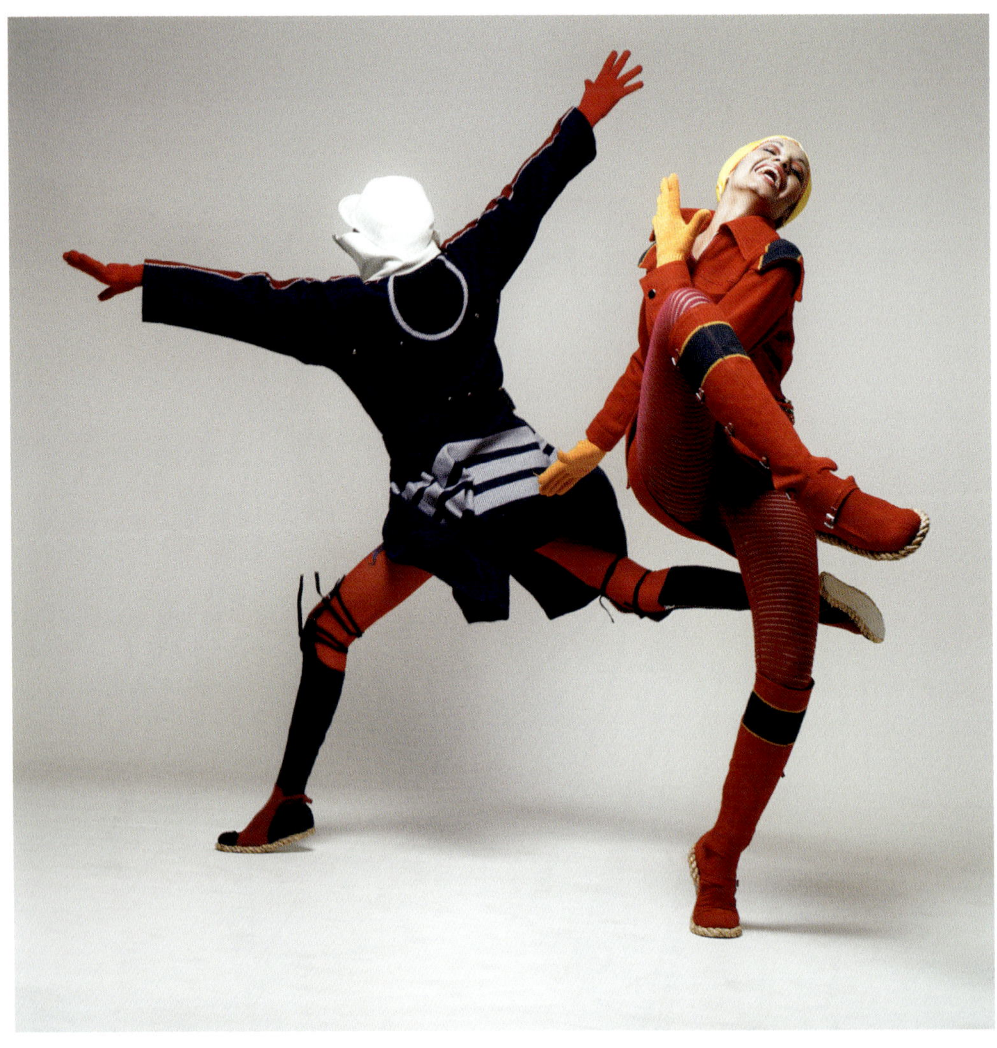

Sashiko coat and jacket
Coat and jacket made from thick *sashiko* cloth and
inspired by traditional "fireman's livery." Long *sashiko*
boots with straw along the bottom, combined with
"V-1" synthetic leather. *Sashiko* was the first fabric
that Issey Miyake explored as a commonplace, down-
to-earth fabric. It is a very robust cloth, similar to
denim in its use. The fabric was originally handmade
and is commonly used in judo wear and farm clothing.
1970 design/Autumn-Winter 1971 Collection
Photography: Kishin Shinoyama;
models: Radhika Nanda and Yasuko Yamayoshi

Opposite: ***Mainichi Graph***, August 1, 1971 edition
Early-morning photo session on the platform at
Nippori station. The models are wearing a *sashiko*
coat. In his search for comfortable clothing, Miyake
developed his own form of *sashiko* fabric by changing
the foreground and background colors of the *futsu*
weave (a style of Japanese double weave). Later, he
continued to change the coloring and weaving styles,
and to create *sashiko*-like designs in knits and prints.
1970 design/Autumn-Winter 1971 Collection
Photography: Hideko Yoshikawa (*Mainichi Shimbun*);
models: Yasuko Yamayoshi and Kayo Hasegawa

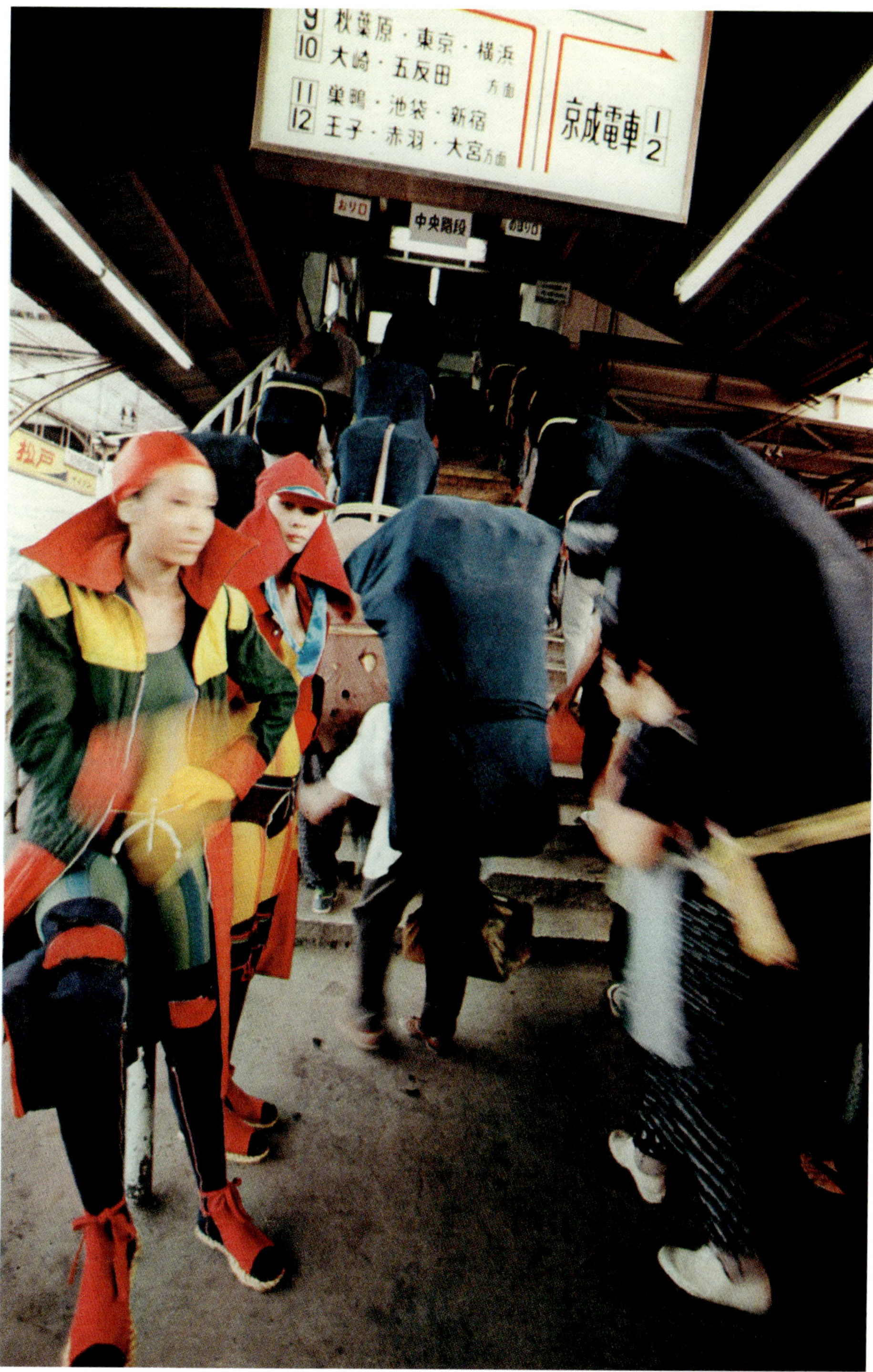
9 秋葉原・東京・横浜
10 大崎・五反田 方面
11 巣鴨・池袋・新宿
12 王子・赤羽・大宮 方面
京成電車 1 2
おり口 中央階段 のぼり口
松戸

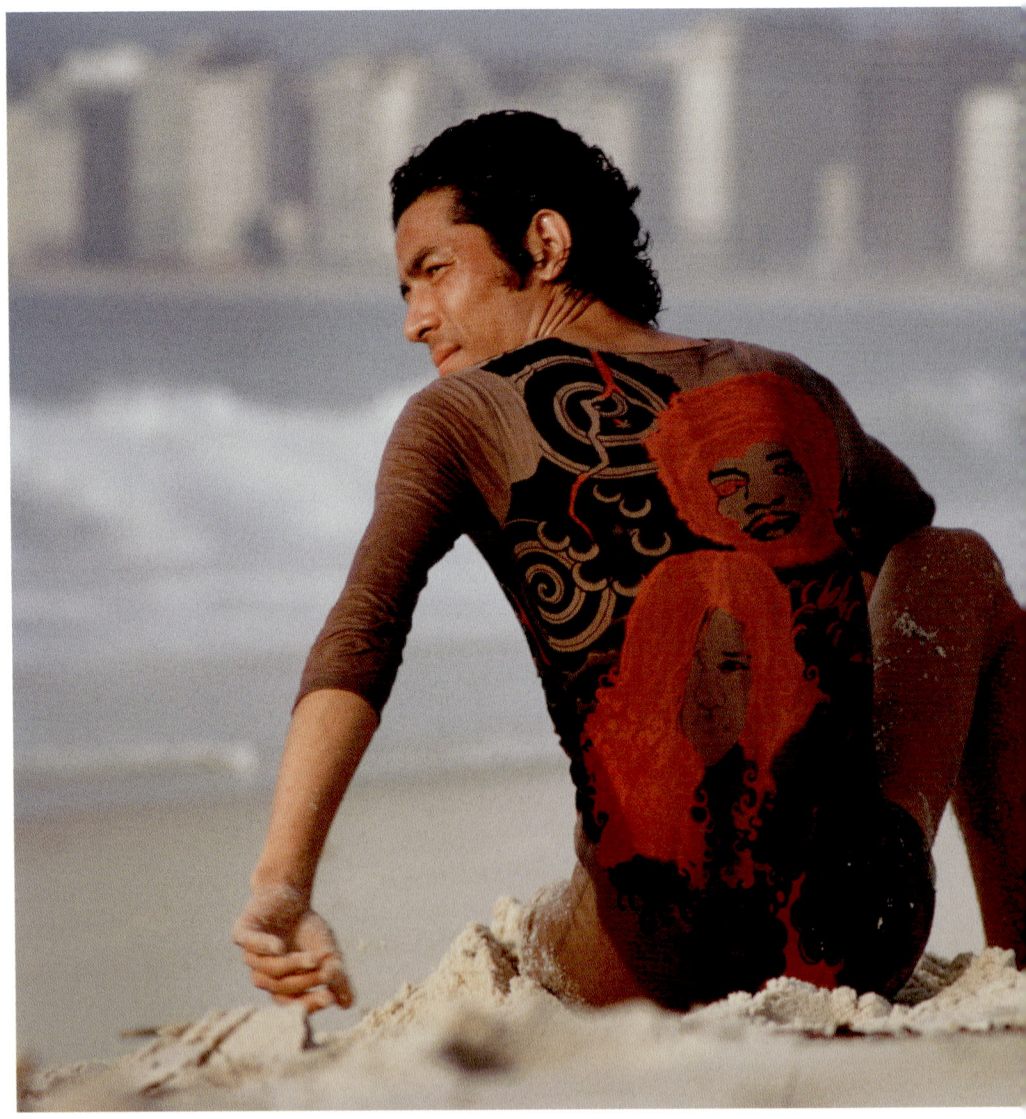

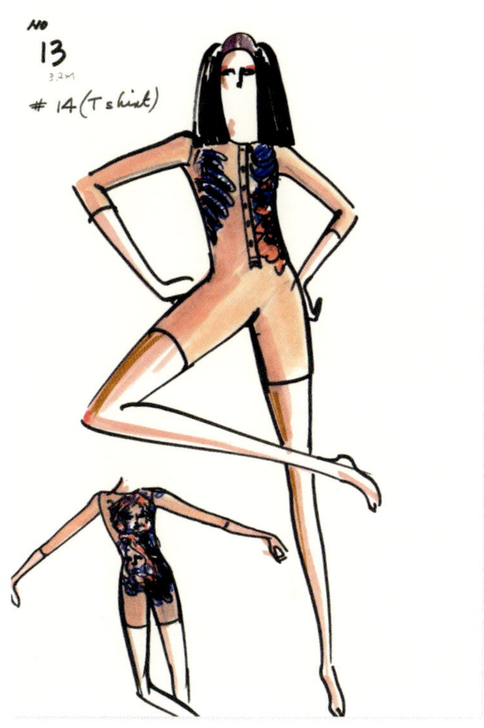

Tattoo

These prints were inspired by Japanese-style "tattoos," a unique art form in which the human body becomes a canvas and is used to express the person's unique psychological world. Miyake created it as an homage, using the likenesses of legendary rock musicians Jimi Hendrix and Janis Joplin, both of whom died in 1970. The original images were created by textile designer Makiko Minagawa.
1970 design/Spring-Summer 1971 Collection
Photography: Kishin Shinoyama; worn by: Issey Miyake
Design drawing: Issey Miyake © Miyake Design Studio

1972

> January: *What is Bodywear!?* show in Tokyo, sponsored by Wacoal Corp.
> February: Spring-Summer 1972 New York Collection at Paris Collections Inc.
> February: Opened corner in Escalade, London
> *Nova* (UK), April 1972 edition
> May: Autumn-Winter 1972 New York Collection at Paris Collections Inc.
> September: Autumn-Winter 1972 Tokyo Collection at Tokyo Prince Hotel
> November: Spring-Summer 1973 New York Collection at Paris Collections Inc.

What is Bodywear!?

In 1971, Issey Miyake became involved in the planning and design of *Bodywear*, the main line of clothing developed by Wacoal Corp. This led to the release of "*Bodywear Design* by Issey Miyake." While bodywear was the focus, it was a more general collection and also included socks, pants, skirts, and jackets. The *What is Bodywear!?* show was held in the same year to communicate the concept. *Bodywear* was also selected for the New York and Paris collections.

January 18: Imperial Hotel, Tokyo

Opposite: **Kappogi**
Inspired by the functional design of *kappogi*, a sort of apron to wear over a kimono while cooking and doing other housework. It has broad sleeves to accommodate the sleeves of the kimono, the cuffs are tightened with elastic and the front bodice is entirely covered and has two strings at the back to hold everything in place. Jurgen Lehl designed the *Rainbow Print* made by Kyoto's Marble Print workshop.
1971 design/Spring-Summer 1972 Collection
Photography: Irving Penn
Vogue (USA) © Condé Nast, May 1972

1 Spring-Summer 1972 New York Collection, Paris Collections Inc., February 9
2 Autumn-Winter 1972 New York Collection, Paris Collections Inc., May 22
3 Spring-Summer 1973 New York Collection, Paris Collections Inc., November 9

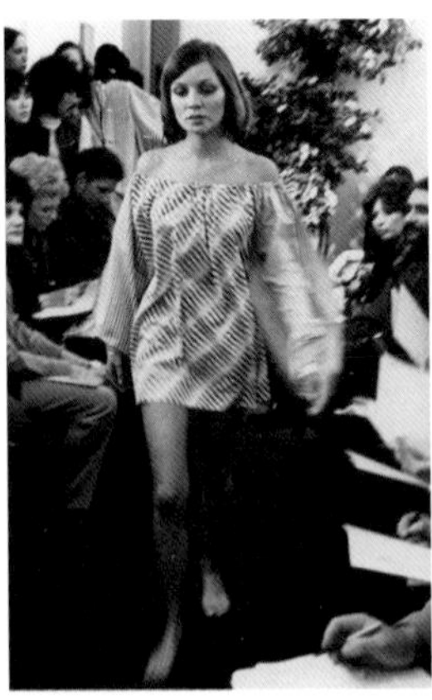
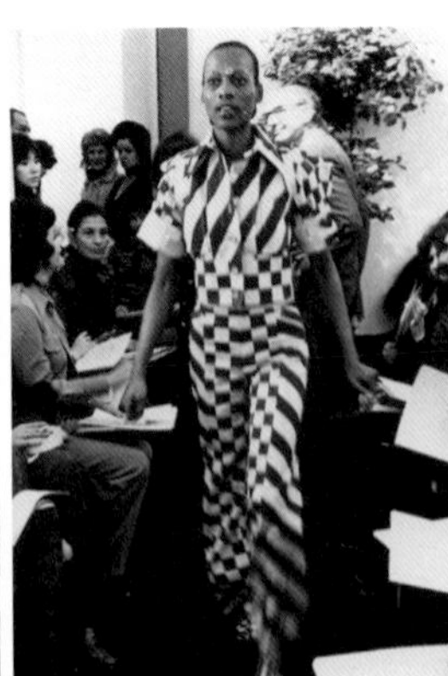
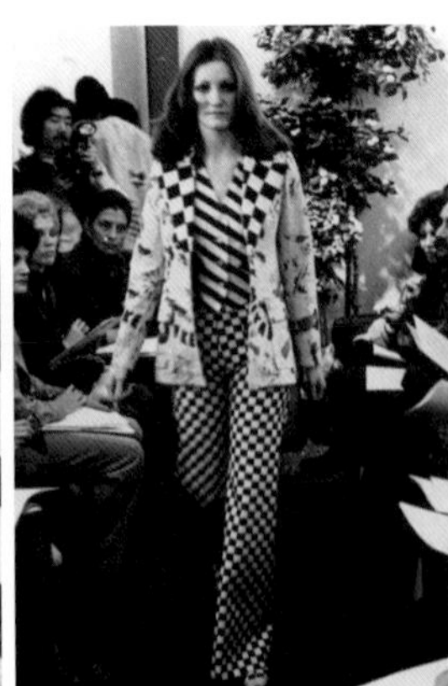
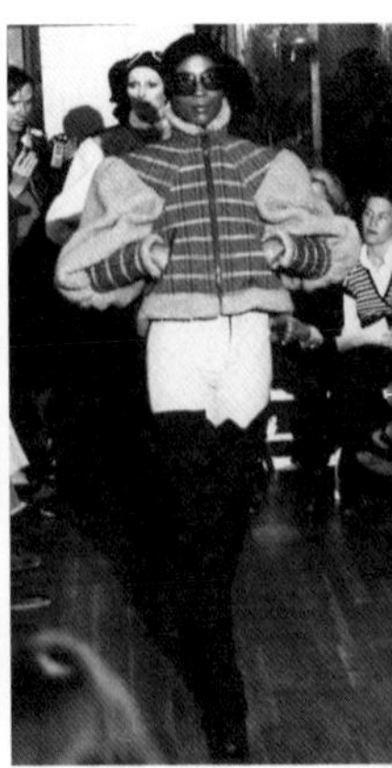

1

2

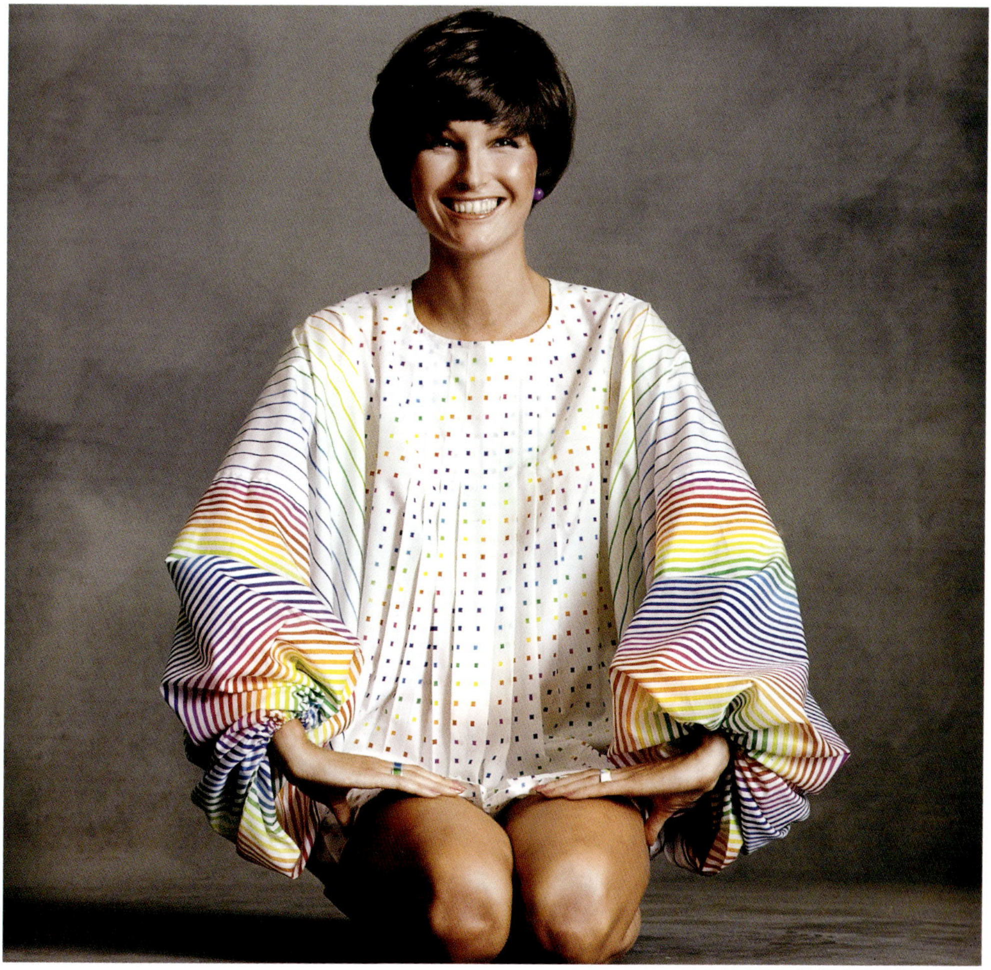

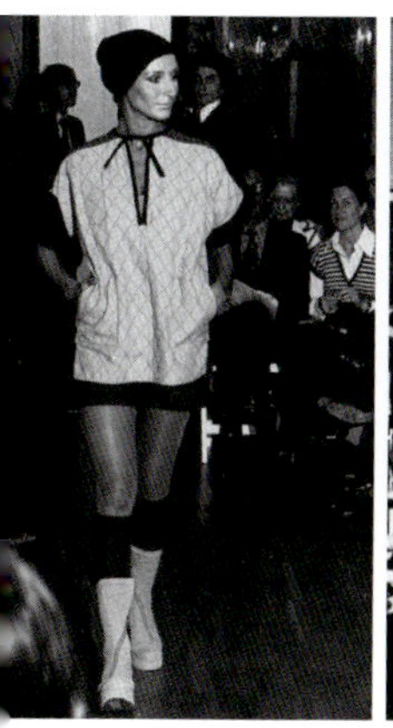
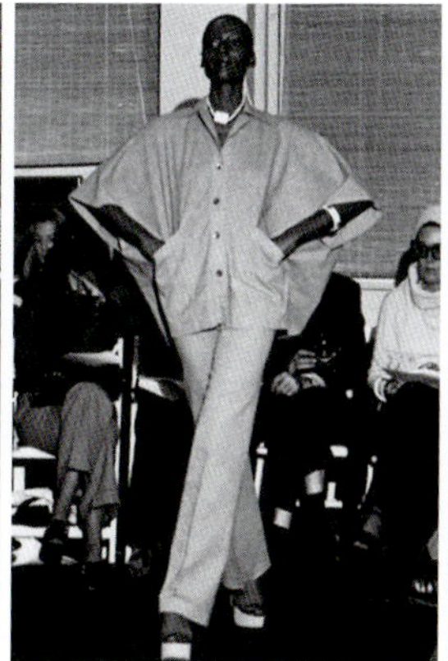
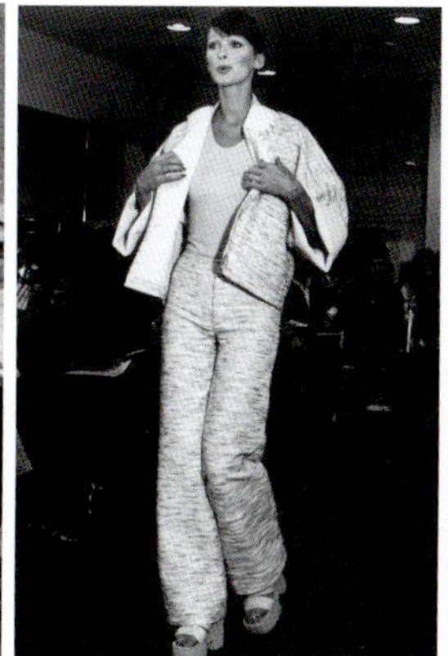
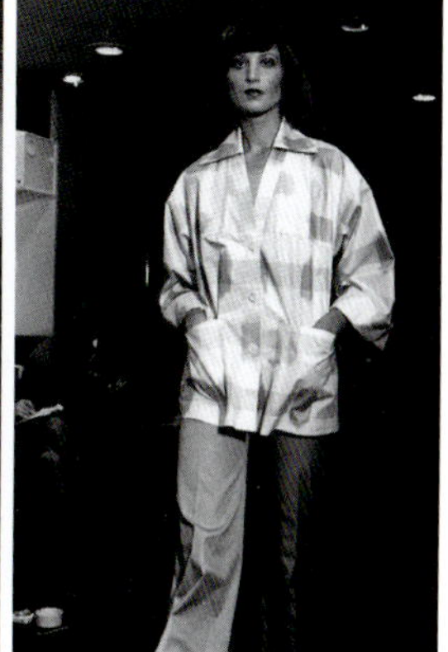

3

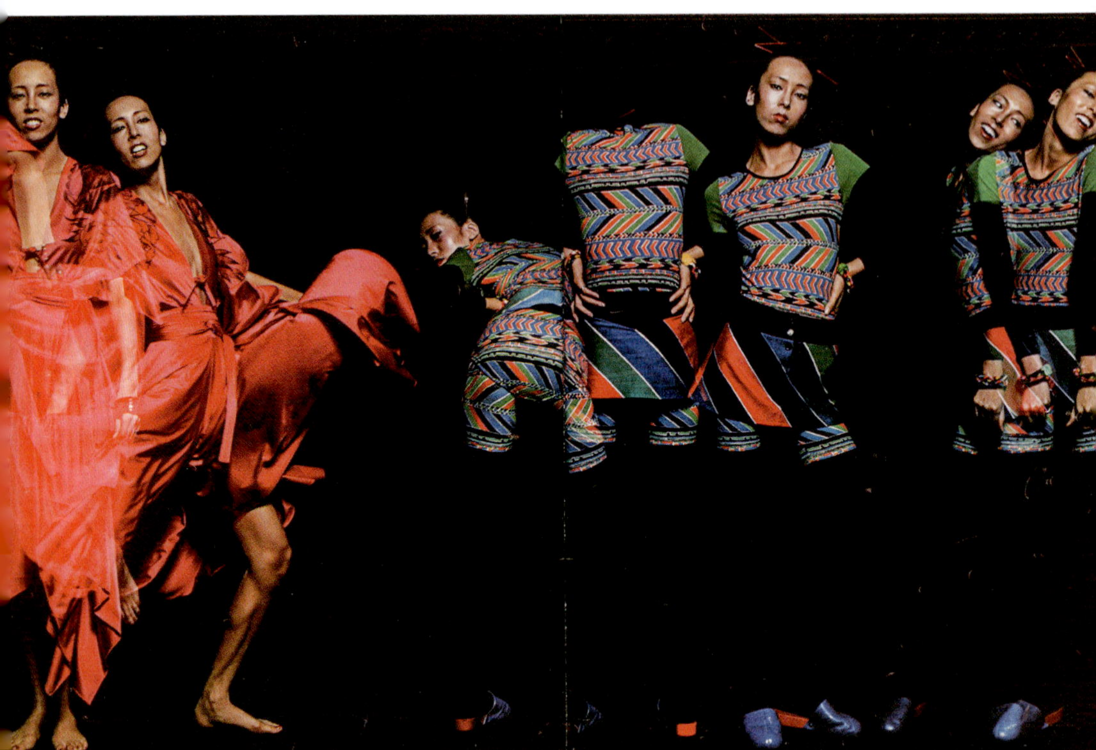
ASHIONS. HE THINKS FROM TOP TO BOTTOM, DESIGNING THE ACCESSORIES, CLOTHES AND UNDIES. SOME OF HIS CLOTHES ARE ON SALE HERE AT ESCALADE. FA

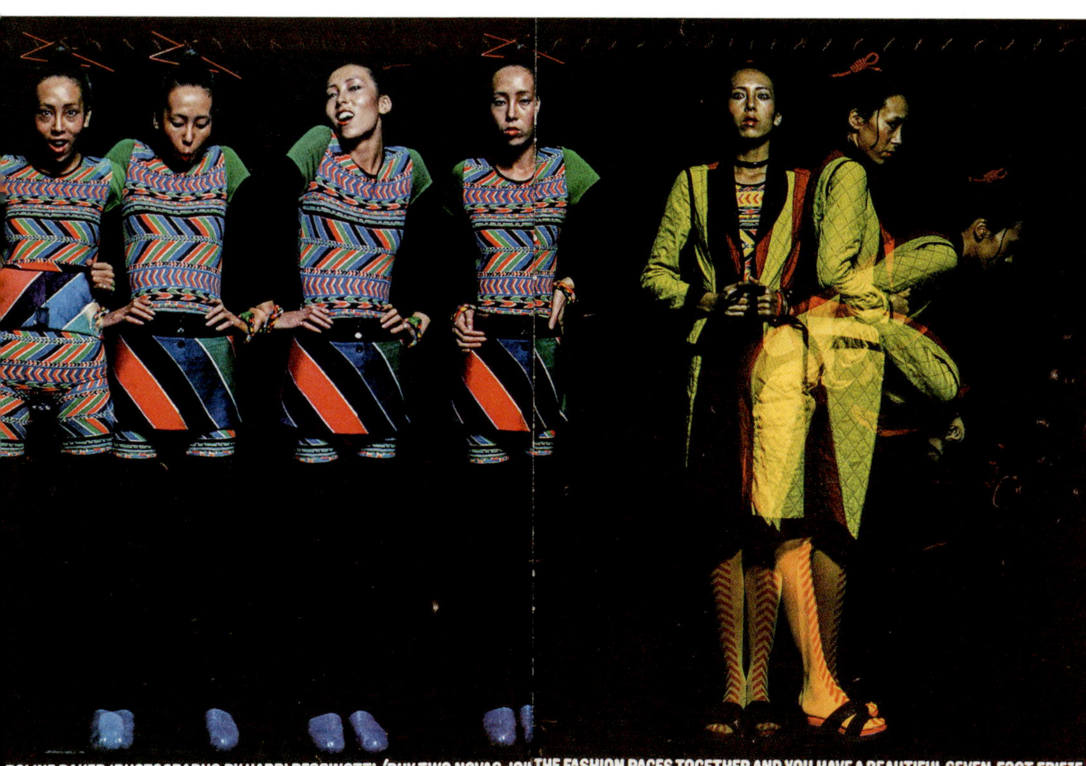

Nova (UK), April 1972 edition
The magazine served as the bible for the "Swinging London" that began in the mid-1960s and lasted to the mid-1970s. From the collection shown in New York in 1971.
Left: *Bat Print Dress*, a dress with a *hakama*-style skirt featuring a bat and peony pattern drawn with tattoo techniques. Print design: Makiko Minagawa
Center: *Bodywear*, combination of tights and skirt with the same pattern. Jointly developed with Wacoal Corp. Print design: Makiko Minagawa
Right: *Sashiko* jacket and skirt; bottom from *Bodywear* designed in 1970 and shown in 1971
Photography: Harri Peccinotti;
model: Yasuko Yamayoshi

3—DEVELOPING CONTEMPORANEITY

Essay by
KAZUKO KOIKE

MA AND SKIN

Issey Miyake pointed out that human beings breathe not only through their noses and mouths, but that the skin of our entire bodies also interacts with the air. Miyake was an early proponent of skin-hugging bodywear and explored the possibilities of this category before T-shirts became popular in Japan. In 1973, he used the intriguing phrase *hifu-zukuri* (skin-making) to describe his work.[1] It is a commonplace to describe clothing as a "second skin," but Miyake actually tried to achieve the equation skin=clothing, with his clothes being an organic substance that melds together with one's skin. To look at the human body in this manner – as one of the most exquisite forms in existence – is also a reinterpretation of nature, one that spurred Miyake on to further creativity.

At the same time, *matou* (to drape around the body) is a universal action that is seen in both the Orient and the Occident; there are both Greek and Buddhist statues that are draped in cloth. This simple relationship between the human body and the cloth that is draped about it captivated Miyake. This reassessment of the most fundamental issues is a position that coincided with his being a witness to the events of May 1968 in Paris.

Covering skin with cloth – the *ma* (the interval, the space in between) that is born when the human body is wrapped in cloth – is a sensation that can be experienced in wearing a Japanese kimono, but also exists in the context of European design. Madeleine Vionnet[2] was the greatest Western exponent of this idea, and was an important precursor and inspiration for Miyake. The philosophy of reducing clothing to *ichimai no nuno* (a piece of cloth) became a natural part of Miyake's fundamental beliefs.

While Miyake never made overt statements concerning for whom his clothes are intended, what is clear is that from early on he was convinced that independent women would lead Japan forward. When the image of a piece is born, the wearer of the clothes also becomes clear. When the new collection using *sashiko* stitches and knits was formed in an unprecedented way, Miyake requested the cooperation of a politician who was known for defending women's rights, and, in a stunning move, arranged for photographs of her wearing these clothes to be published as a cover story in one of Japan's photography magazines.[3] This was a designer who demonstrated his empathy with feminism even before the movement began to gain momentum in Japan. It was also an example of how Miyake demonstrated inspired direction, stemming from his belief in the power that graphic design and photographs could have upon society.

CONTEMPORARY COLLABORATIONS

The art director Eiko Ishioka[4] collaborated with Issey Miyake on an advertising campaign for the PARCO shopping complex. The poster designed by Ishioka featured Issey Miyake's latest creations, and was shot by the photographer Noriaki Yokosuka;[5] it was the essence of what felt contemporary at the time. Ishioka's friendship and collaboration with Miyake flourished and led to events that became the talk of "tout Tokyo," such as her staging an Issey Miyake show at the Seibu Theater.

Japan is extremely well attuned to foreign products and information, but historically has always taken its time in assimilating or adapting whatever it imports, and thus making that a part of its own distinctive culture. The changes that have occurred since the latter half of the 1960s, however, are marked differently due to that which is contemporary. While today's globalization might be said to be the result of computer technology, in those days other kinds of changes in people's actions and mindsets led to social phenomena. Underground, pop, counterculture, alternative culture – all were appearing in Japan, and around the world. Synchronously, they appeared in many cities in many countries. Japan, in particular, demonstrated such a flowering of young talent at this time that it is impossible to list the many names. Miyake's activities were regarded as the appearance of a megastar on the scene.

Tadanori Yokoo is noted for work that evokes the indigenous and uncanny elements inherent to Japanese visual art, and is an old comrade of Miyake's. Miyake entrusted Yokoo with the design of his Paris collection invitations from 1977 on, even though Miyake's position had changed and younger designers were now entrusted with the main collections. Shiro Kuramata[6] designed for the majority of Issey's shops, from the earliest days to the opening of his large overseas boutiques, creating an exquisite constellation of Kuramata's work. Issey Miyake's clothes became heavenly raiment flying in Shiro Kuramata's translucent universe.

In Japan, fashion design was unexplored territory in cultural terms for many years. Kimonos, which were predominant until World War II, had behind them a rich tradition of dyeing and weaving techniques, and were respected as an expression of craftsmanship. Women were expected to know how to sew kimonos for their families. This was the skill of *wasai* (Japanese sewing), while making Western clothes was referred to as *yosai* (Western sewing). Dressmaking was added to the curriculum for women's education. There were dressmakers, but no industrial development comparable to that in Europe or the United States. Japanese society needed the emergence of a leading figure such as Issey Miyake in order to develop an awareness of fashion design.

THE MAINICHI DESIGN AWARDS

The timing seemed symbolic – Miyake was chosen as the recipient of the most important award in Japanese design, the Mainichi Design Awards.[7]

The awards, which were presented for the 22nd time in 1976, had changed both their name and judges in accordance with the changing times. Until the previous year, there had been the *Mainichi Sangyo Dezain Sho* (The Mainichi Industrial Design Awards), but now the word "industrial" was no longer to be included. It is evident that the importance of design in diverse fields, as well as transformations and improvements in design quality, led to this new acknowledgment of a broad range of achievements in society and the arts. One of the judges was the architect Arata Isozaki,[8] and his comments on this decision let us feel the fresh breath of change that the year 1976 brought, and are an important record in Japanese design history.

... While "industry" and "design" are considered separately today, historically speaking, there was a relationship that was difficult to sever, when one looks back at their emergence ... Now, design is in a situation where the two must be separated. Products and advertisements are handled directly, but design has begun to stand independently, and transcends these categories. Design has started to orient itself toward culture, growing beyond its relationships with the fields of technology or business... The work of Issey Miyake in recent years in clothing design has not been limited to fashion, but has constituted an event in a field of culture that sends out forceful stimuli to other fields of design. To put it boldly, one may perhaps say that this demonstrates a decisive way of cutting through the tremendous stagnation that systems of modern design had brought about.

Arata Isozaki, *Mainichi Shimbun*,
January 26, 1977

The title of Isozaki's commentary was *Yasei no Shikou* (Thinking on the Wild Side), and besides being encouraging for Issey Miyake, it was especially heartening for those in the world of fashion design who were interested in such issues. The Japanese fashion industry was still following European thinking and methodologies, and despite the fact that Parisian couture had begun to search for ways to transform itself in response to the rise in ready-to-wear, the situation in Japan was still far from seeing any change, what with its business model so firmly based on department stores.

Fashion journalism was still undeveloped too, and while there were outliers such as the editor Isao Imaida, there was, in general, little interest or regard concerning editorial potential. Issey Miyake had great hopes for an awareness of fashion design, but was frustrated nonetheless. His experience abroad had made him realize that the then current journalism was not capable of understanding the meaning of what he was doing and he disliked the position taken by Japanese women's magazines, which were too caught up in trivialities.

When prior notification of Miyake's Mainichi Design Awards reached us, before the official announcement, I phoned Issey, who was in New York on a business trip. "Did they?!" was his joyous response.

"Clothes, I think, can even be considered in the context of skin, as a tool for a round-the-clock, human self-expression.... In fact, I'd had that prize in mind," Miyake said of that morning in New York.

I frankly confess that I've wanted this particular prize, and none other. Seven years have passed since I returned to Japan from Paris, days filled with continuous work, as I searched for the meaning of what clothes are ... whether designing clothing has really come into its own as a profession, and if it will contribute to the future of the fashion industry ... I cannot afford to consider such matters, and think of making clothes simply as proof of the fact that I am alive ...

Issey Miyake, *Mainichi Shimbun*,
January 26, 1977

EAST MEETS WEST

Miyake was a great admirer of the art director Ikko Tanaka,[9] who proposed that Miyake's work should be acknowledged in book form, leading to the world's first book created by a fashion designer who was also its subject. The photographers who took the specially commissioned photos provided material that went far beyond the level of work that could be seen in Japanese fashion magazines of the time; Noriaki Yokosuka's work, in particular, brimmed with "Miyake-ness."

Issey Miyake East Meets West[10] was the outcome. Tina Chow,[11] a model who was famous for her intelligence and erudition, argued strongly in favor of this name of the book out of a list of possible English titles. This was because of its message of contemporary beauty that, though launched in Japan, also looked ahead at what was to come in the future.

East Meets West. This large-format book, Miyake insisted, should be appropriately sized and priced, so that "students could simply roll it up and hold it in their hands." It quickly became wildly popular both across Japan and around the world. Although at that time there was no broad public interest in design even in Europe or the United States, the fact that it could be seen on the shelves of art and design offices all around the world gave to Miyake and all those who were connected to the project a sense of fulfillment.

1   *Detail*, No. 36, Spring issue, 1973, Shokokusha Publishing Co., Ltd., pp. 60–61.

2   Madeleine Vionnet (1876–1975): Fashion designer. Opened her couture house in Paris in 1912. Developed the bias cut, an innovative technique for garment construction. This placed cloth at a 45-degree angle to the body, rather than flat, allowing clothes to fit closely and flow sinuously and enhancing the figure of the wearer. Mme Vionnet's work looked deeply and seriously at the relationship of the body and clothing, and left a major impact on 20th-century dress.

3   "Fusae Ichikawa Wears Issey Miyake." *Asahi Graph*, October 11, 1974: See pp. 52–55.

4   Eiko Ishioka (1938–2012): Art director, designer. After working as a graphic designer and art director at Shiseido, went freelance and worked on numerous advertising campaigns in the 1970s. Based in New York from the 1980s, her work expanded internationally, with set and costume designs for films and theater. Winner of the Academy Award for Best Costume Design for her work on *Bram Stoker's Dracula*, 1992.

5   Noriaki Yokosuka (1937–2003): Photographer. Began working for Shiseido's in-house corporate newsletter while still a university student, later regarded as one of Japan's leading advertising photographers. In 1983, became the first Japanese photographer to join the freelance staff for Italian, German, and French *Vogue*.

6   Shiro Kuramata (1934–1991): Interior designer. Founded Kuramata Design Office in 1965, and designed retail spaces and furniture. A key characteristic of his work was the use of glass, acrylic, and mesh, creating spaces and objects that seemed to float. Designer of many Issey Miyake stores both in Japan and around the world.

7   Mainichi Design Awards: See pp. 74–79.

8   Arata Isozaki (1931–2022): Architect. Studied under Kenzo Tange. Established Arata Isozaki & Associates in 1963. He was active internationally, in philosophy, art, design, and criticism, in addition to architecture. Key projects include: Ōita Prefectural Library (1966); The Museum of Modern Art, Gunma (1974); Museum of Contemporary Art, Los Angeles (1986); Shenzhen Cultural Center (2008, China).

9   Ikko Tanaka (1934–2002): Graphic designer. Established the Ikko Tanaka Design Studio in 1963. Internationally renowned for his distinctive style that merged traditional Japanese aesthetics with modern design. A leader of Japanese graphic design, he also worked to promote art and culture in many different fields.

10   *Issey Miyake East Meets West*: See pp. 82–83.

11   Tina Chow (1951–1992): Fashion model. Featured in many Japanese advertising campaigns and magazines from the mid-1960s. Maiden name was Tina Lutz. Married Michael Chow, owner of Chinese restaurants in London, Los Angeles, and New York. Was known for her jewelry designs and her fashion collection. Died of AIDS at the age of 41.

1973

> April: Moved to Paris to show collections. The first was for the Autumn-Winter 1973 Collection at Bourse de Commerce, Paris
> June: Autumn-Winter 1973 Tokyo Collection at Issey Miyake International, Inc.
> The *sashiko* and knit combination made the cover of French *Elle*'s September 10 edition
> October: Spring-Summer 1974 Paris Collection at C&I Boutique

Participated in the Paris Collection

Didier Grumbach, president of Paris Collections and the ISSEY MIYAKE sales agent in New York, suggested moving the Miyake shows to Paris from New York. The Autumn-Winter 1973 Collection was shown on April 1, by participating in the collection program of C&I (Créateurs et Industriels) that was established by Grumbach. Bourse de Commerce, Paris was used as the venue, and in addition to Miyake, the show featured Christiane Bailly, Michèle Bruyère, Roland Chakkal, Jean-Jacques Martelli, Jean Muir, and Fernando Sánchez.

Opposite: *Elle* (France), No. 1447, September 10, 1973 cover
From the first collection in Paris, the combination of *sashiko* fabric and raw silk knits was chosen for the cover.
1973 design/Autumn-Winter 1973 Collection
Photography: Barry Lategan

1 Autumn-Winter 1973 Paris Collection, April 1, Bourse de Commerce, Paris
2 Spring-Summer 1974 Paris Collection, October 21, C&I Boutique

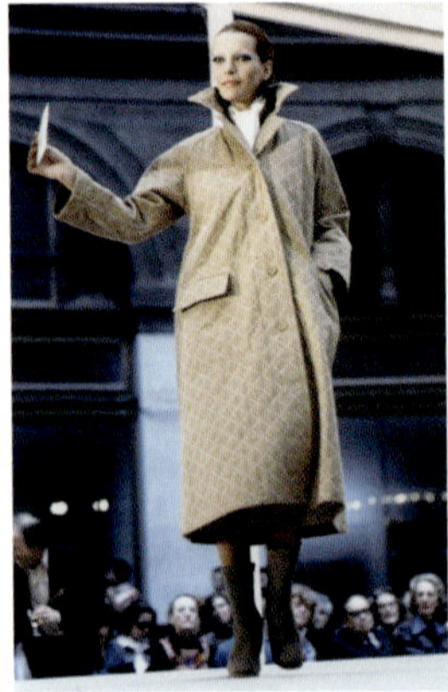
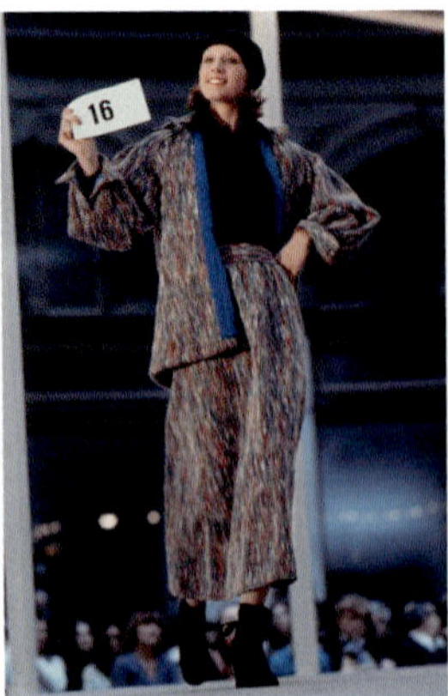
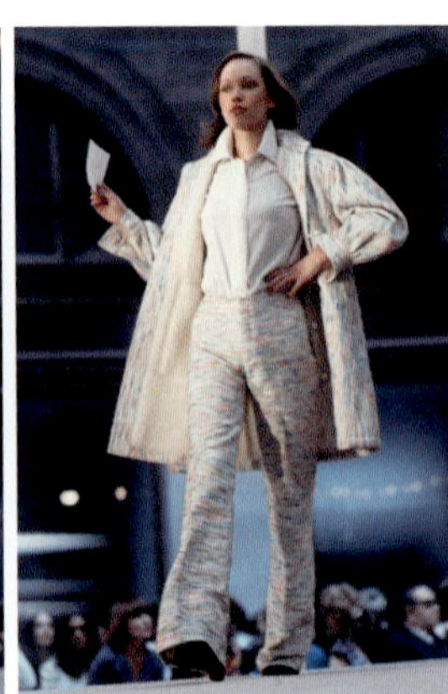
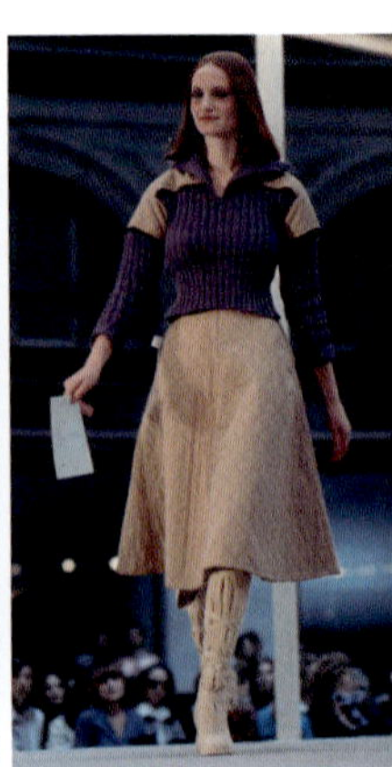

1

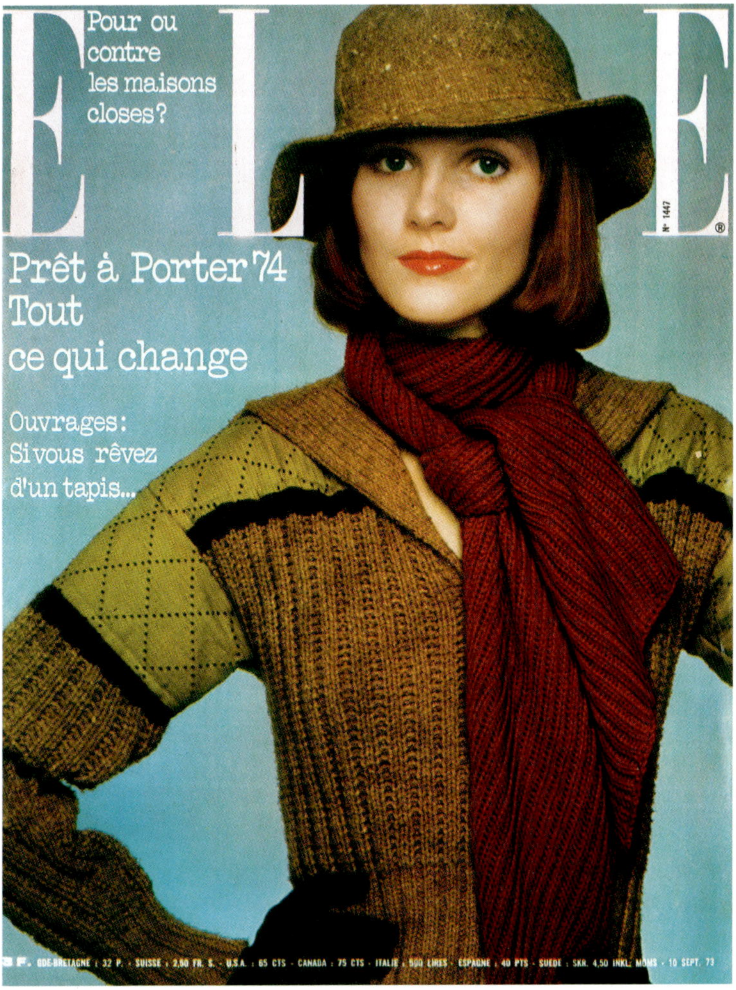

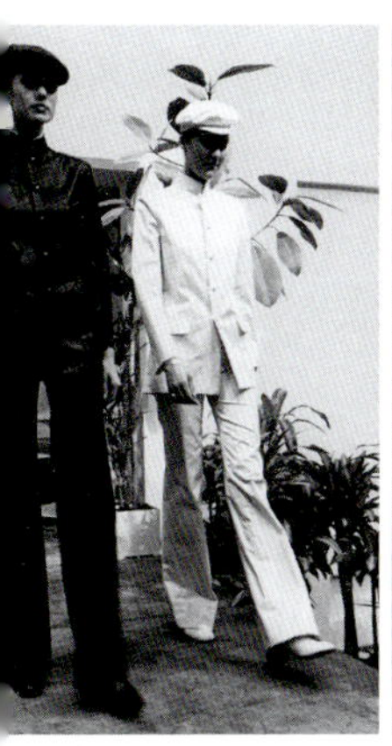
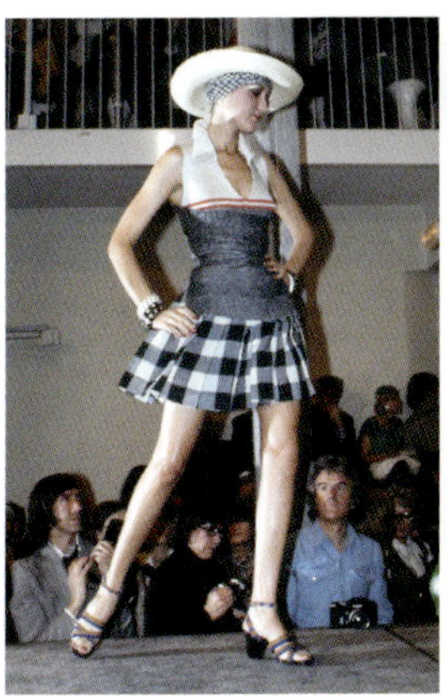
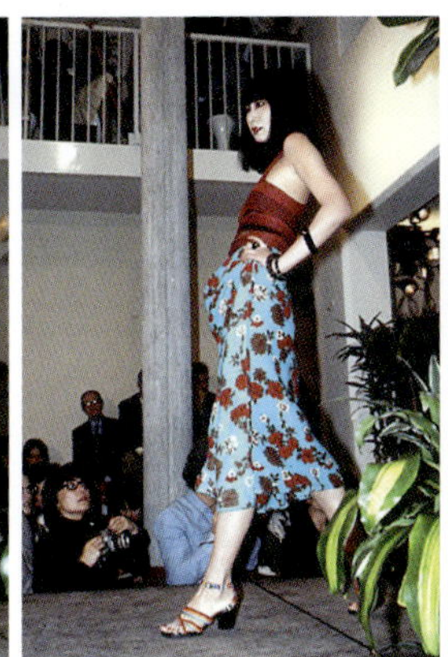
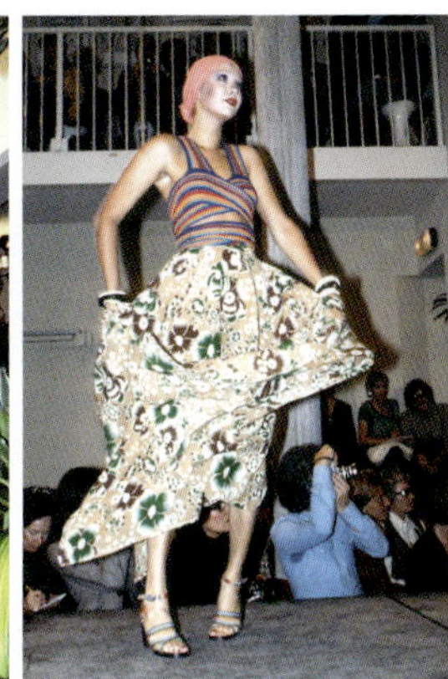

ELLE
Pour ou contre les maisons closes?
Prêt à Porter 74
Tout ce qui change
Ouvrages: Si vous rêvez d'un tapis...
N° 1447
2 F. BDE-BRETAGNE : 32 P. · SUISSE : 2,50 FR. S. · U.S.A. 65 CTS · CANADA : 75 CTS · ITALIE : 500 LIRES · ESPAGNE : 40 PTS · SUEDE : SKR. 4,50 INKL. MOMS · 10 SEPT. 73

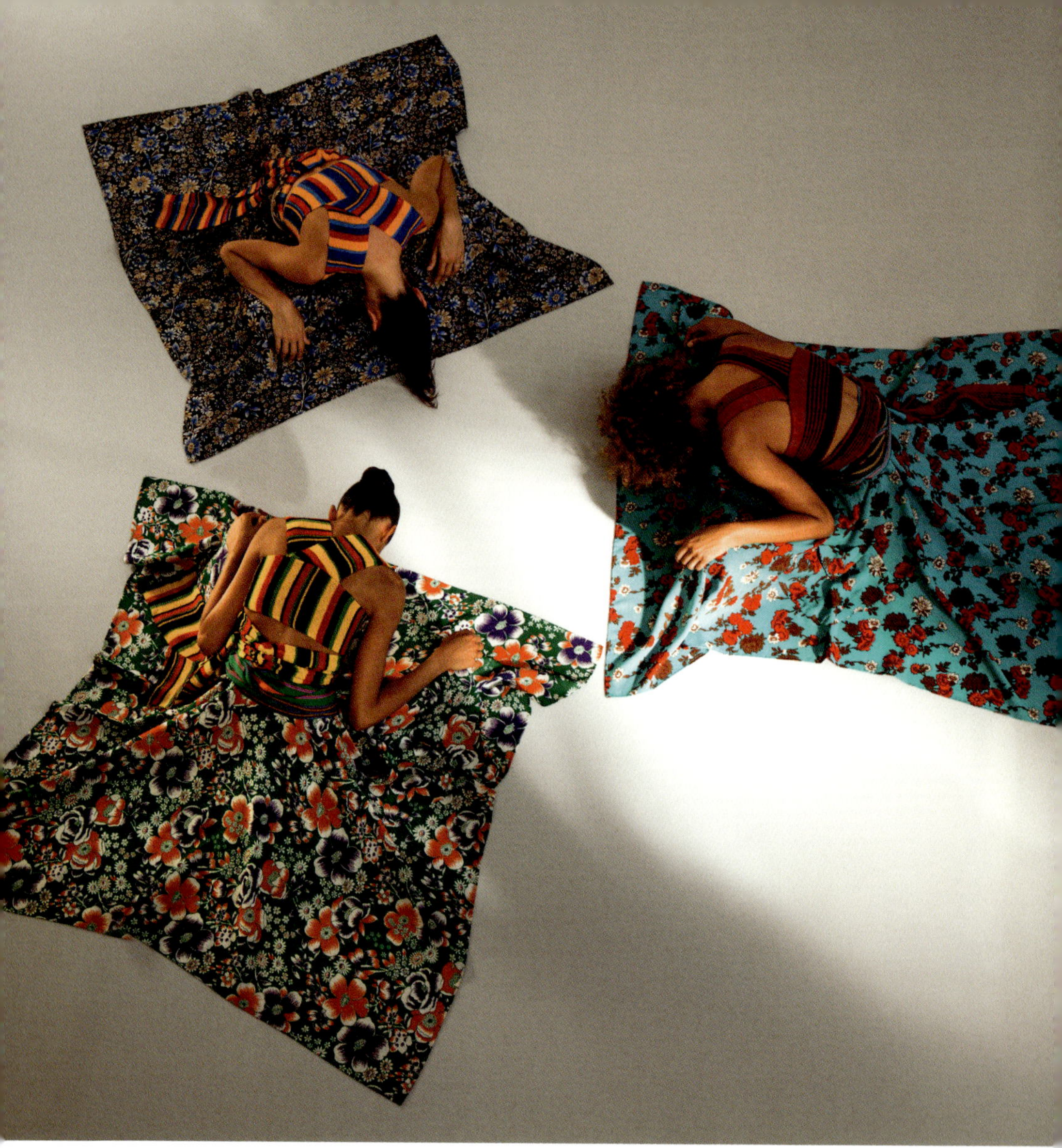

Bali Flowers
Square skirt with a Balinese floral print.
Top is made of knitted taping material.
1973 design/Spring-Summer 1974 Collection
Obi belt. 1975 design/Spring-Summer 1976 Collection
Photography: Yuriko Takagi

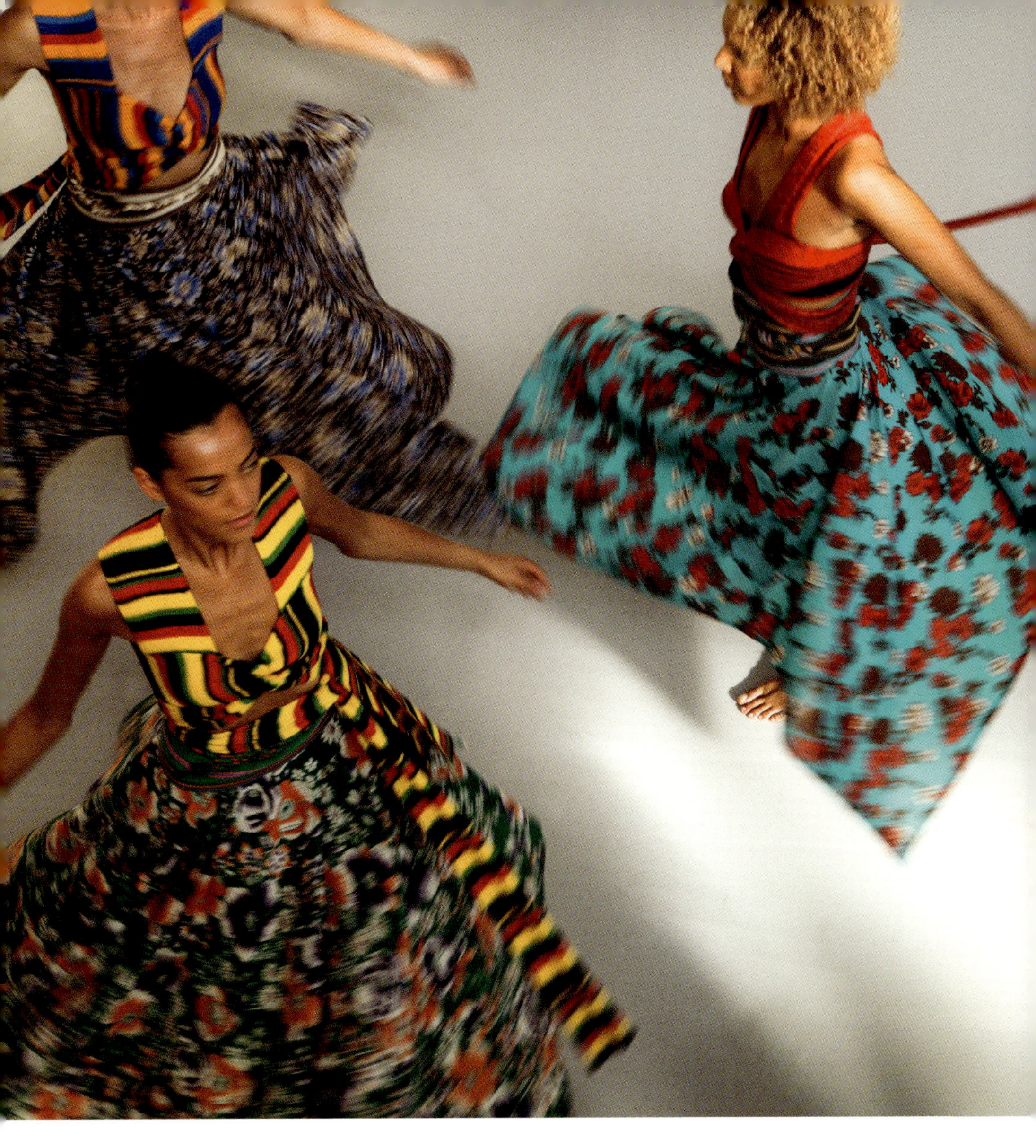

1974

> January: *Issey with Kansai* show at the National Olympics Memorial Youth Center in Tokyo
> March: Autumn-Winter 1974 Paris Collection at C&I Boutique
> March: Opened the first ISSEY MIYAKE store, in the Puzzle Aoyama Building in Tokyo
> June: Autumn-Winter 1974 Tokyo Collection at Van 99 Hall
> October: Photograph on the cover of *Asahi Graph* of Fusae Ichikawa wearing clothing designed by Miyake
> October: Spring-Summer 1975 Paris Collection at La Coupole

Asahi Graph cover: Fusae Ichikawa wears ISSEY MIYAKE

"Fusae Ichikawa, I am pleased to make your acquaintance. I am a professional clothing designer. Most people think that fashion is for young women, but clothing is one of the daily necessities of life, on par with food and shelter, and I believe that it is meaningless for clothing to depart from the lives and personalities of the people who wear it. What I try to do is to use materials that were developed and refined in the course of ordinary life in Japan to create clothing that people are comfortable moving around in, clothing that expresses the natural beauty of the body. Some of my clothing might be considered 'work clothes,' but the idea has been very well received in Paris and in New York. As I designed this clothing (ready-to-wear clothes), I asked myself who I would most like to see wearing it, and I decided it was you."

Issey Miyake, Asahi Graph, *October 11, 1974 edition*

1 Autumn-Winter 1974 Paris Collection, March 31, C&I Boutique
2 Spring-Summer 1975 Paris Collection, October 19, La Coupole

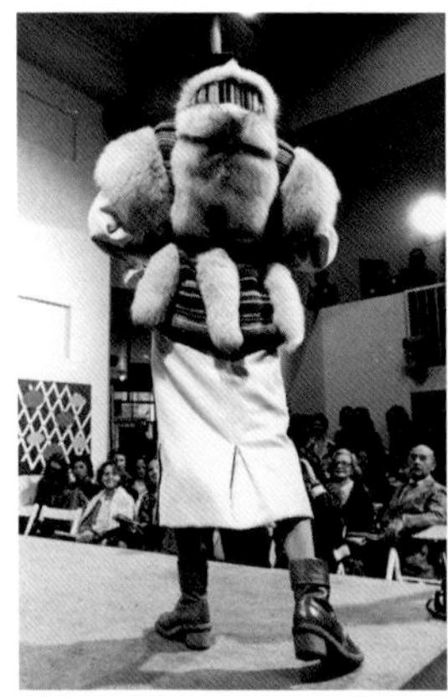 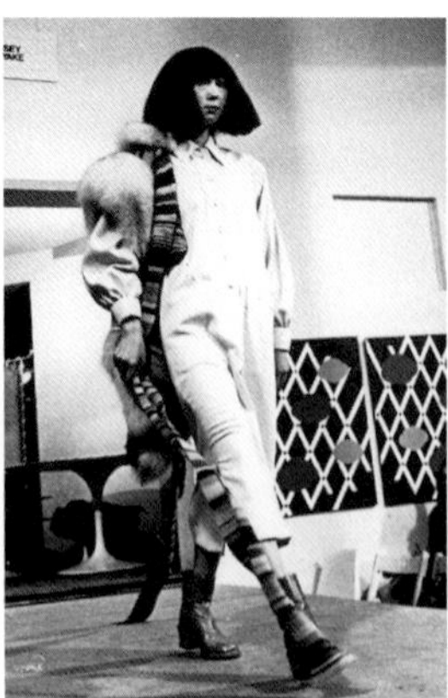 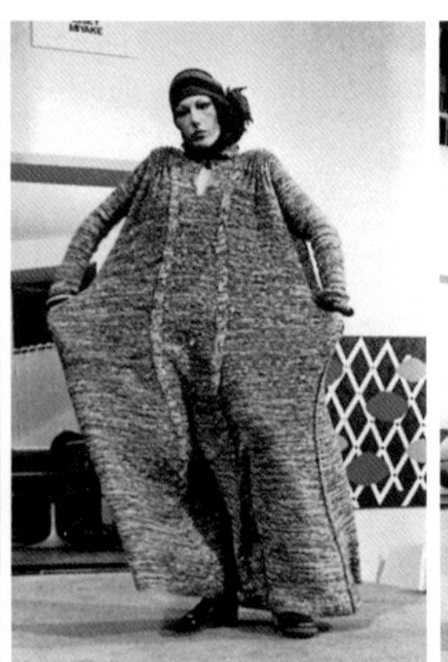 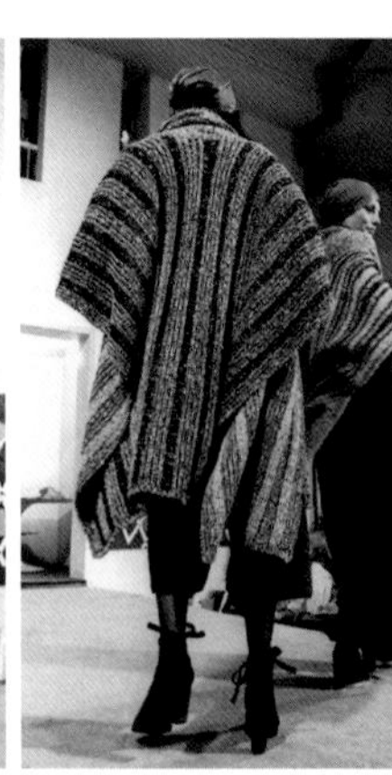

1

Asahi Graph, October 11, 1974 cover
The magazine is one of Japan's premier glossy photograph magazines, and it featured clothing by Issey Miyake in a photography series by photographer Kishin Shinoyama. Fusae Ichikawa was a Japanese women's rights activist and politician who endeavored to improve the status of women in society.
Photography: Kishin Shinoyama

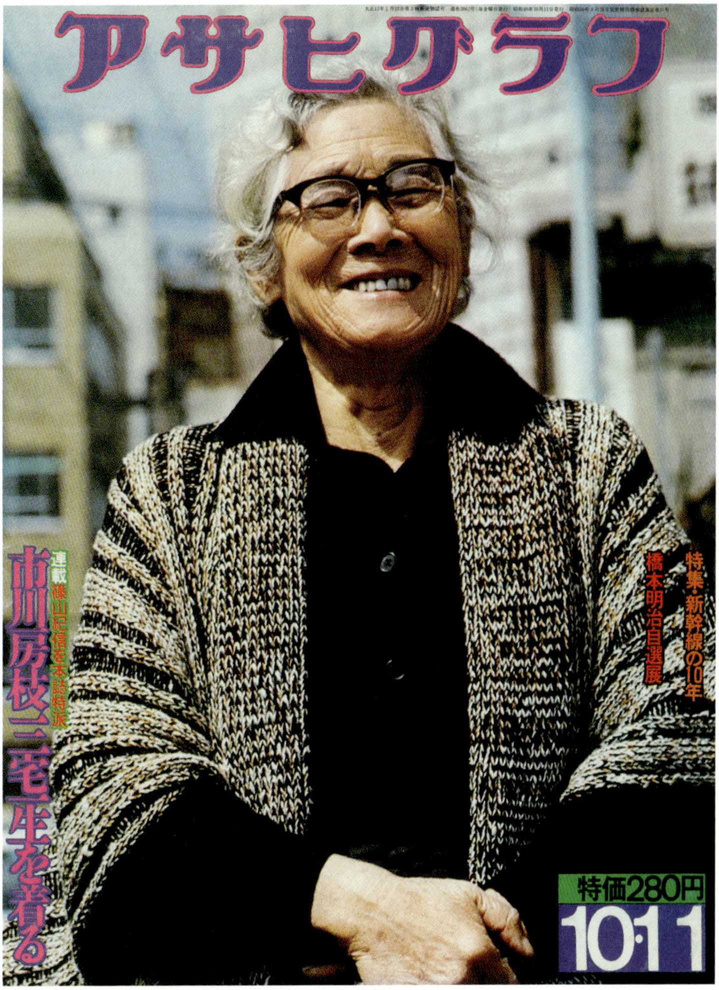

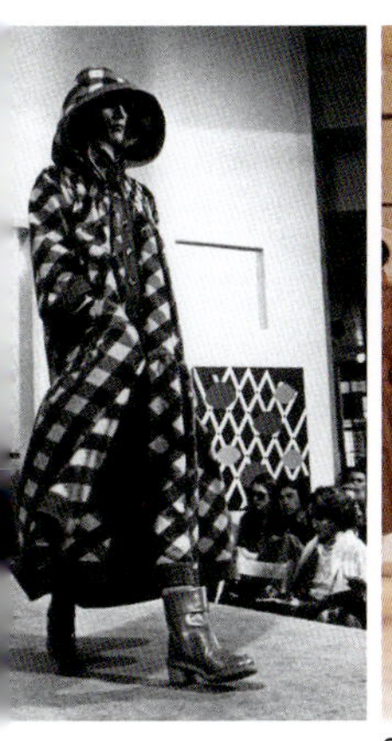
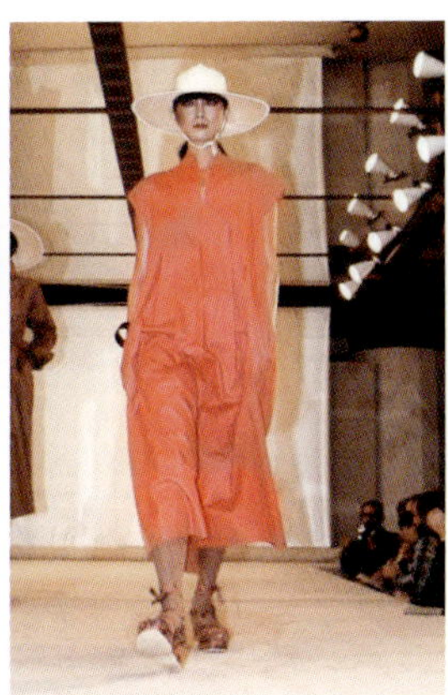
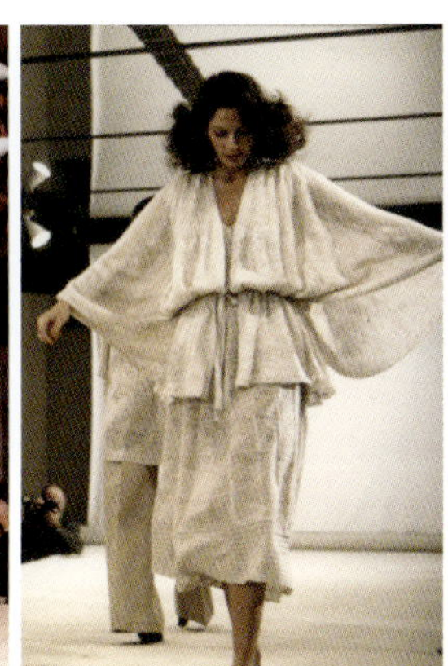
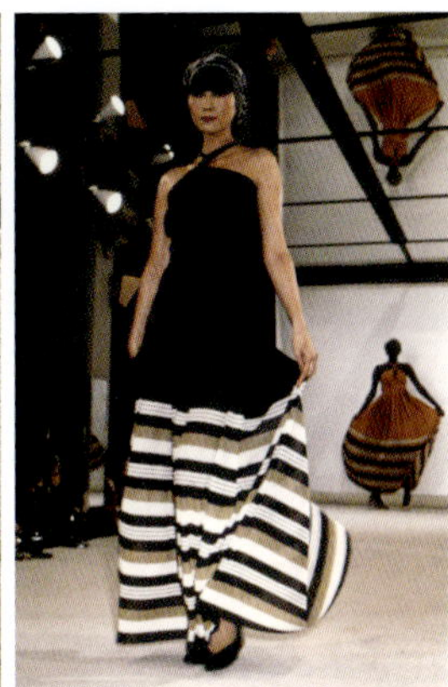

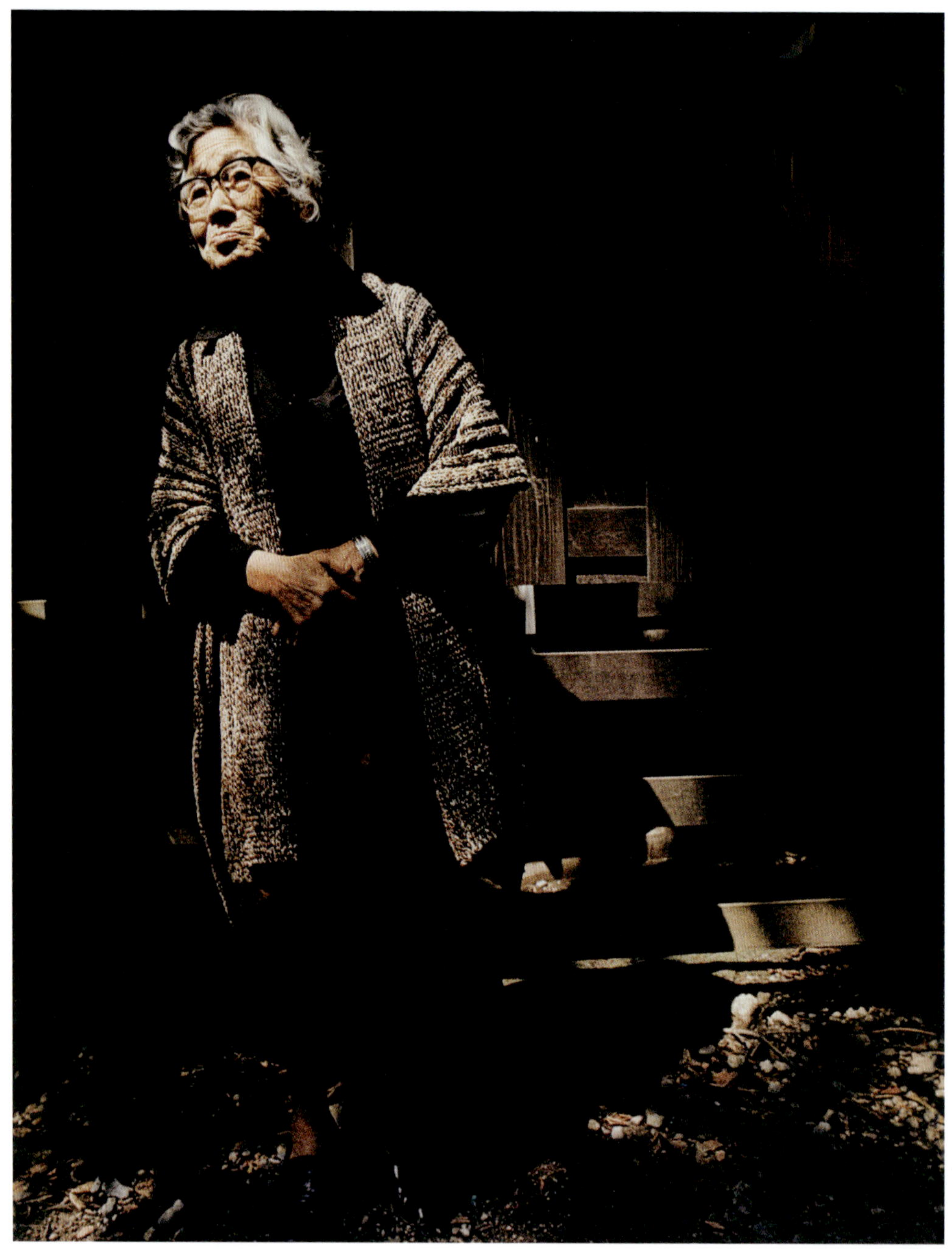

A raw silk knit jacket over a raw silk shirt (see p. 53)
1974 design/Autumn-Winter 1974 Collection
Photography: Kishin Shinoyama;
worn by: Fusae Ichikawa

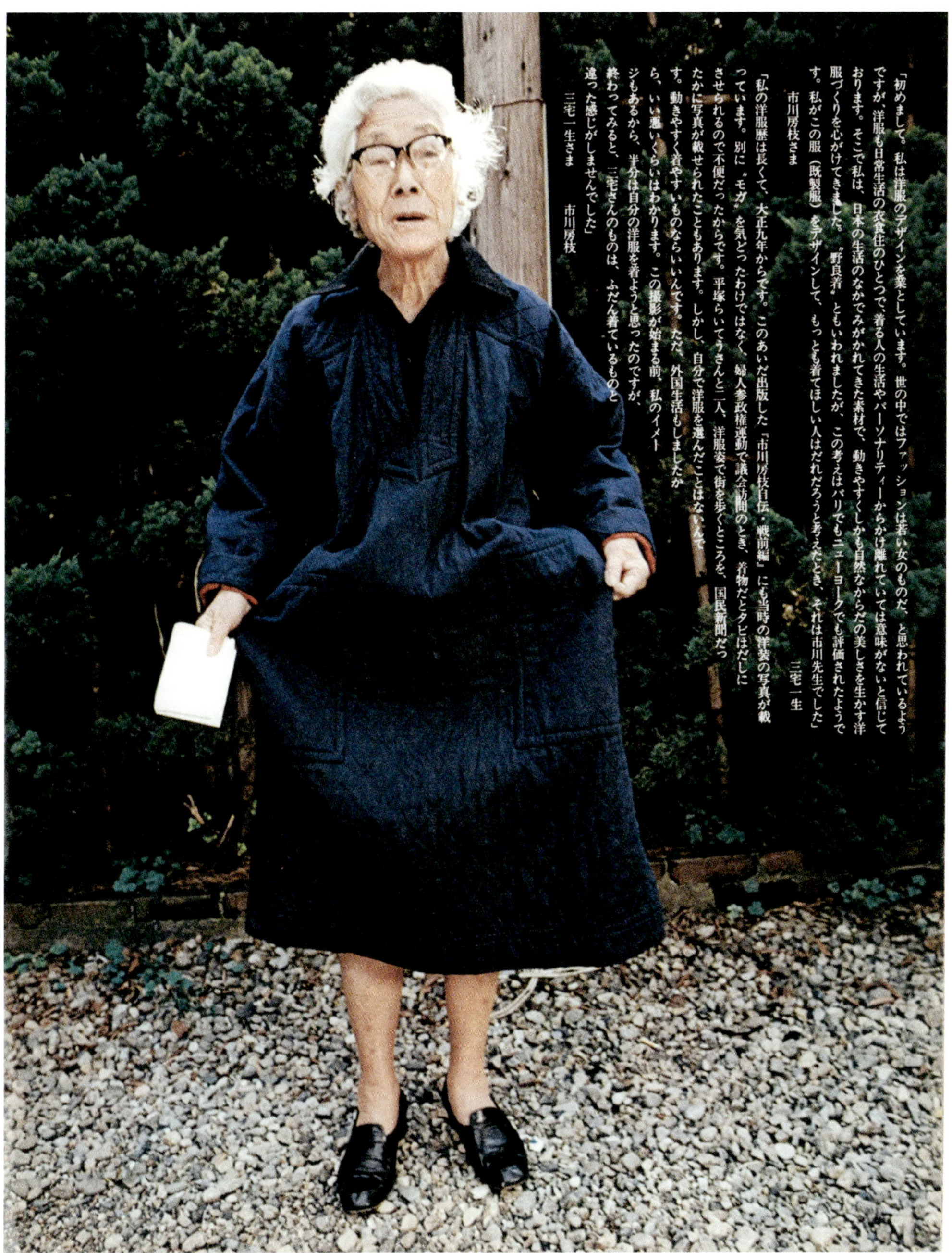

A double weave *sashiko* dress with red backing
1974 design/Autumn-Winter 1974 Collection
Photography: Kishin Shinoyama;
worn by: Fusae Ichikawa

1975

> January: First ISSEY MIYAKE store opened in the Place du Marché Saint-Honoré, Paris
> February: *Issey Miyake Show* at Seibu Theater in Tokyo (Spring-Summer 1975)
> February: Participated in the Milan Collection at the invitation of SNIA Viscosa in Milan, Italy
> Planned the exhibition *Gendai Ifuku no Genryu Ten – Inventive Clothes: 1909–1939* for March–May in Kyoto
> April: Autumn-Winter 1975 Paris Collection at Palais Galliera, Musée de la Mode de la Ville de Paris
> October: Spring-Summer 1976 Paris Collection at Place du Marché Saint-Honoré

Exhibition *Gendai Ifuku no Genryu Ten– Inventive Clothes: 1909–1939*

Inspired by an exhibition entitled *The Tens, The Twenties and The Thirties: Inventive Clothes: 1909–1939* on display at the Metropolitan Museum of Art in New York during 1973 and 1974, Issey Miyake obtained the approval of exhibition director Diana Vreeland to put together an exhibition in Japan featuring clothing designed by the likes of Paul Poiret, Madeleine Vionnet, and Jeanne Lanvin; he also negotiated with museums in France and the United States for use of the clothing in their collections. He also enlisted the cooperation of Koichi Tsukamoto, the president of Wacoal Corp. and vice-chair of the Kyoto Chamber of Commerce and Industry, to put together the exhibition *Gendai Ifuku no Genryu Ten – Inventive Clothes: 1909–1939*. It was at the time revolutionary for a Japanese museum to show Western clothing of historical value. The exhibition resulted in the establishment in 1978 of the Kyoto Costume Institute.

March 25 to May 25: The National Museum of Modern Art, Kyoto

1 Autumn-Winter 1975 Paris Collection, April 5, Palais Galliera, Musée de la Mode de la Ville de Paris
2 Spring-Summer 1976 Paris Collection, October 18, Place du Marché Saint-Honoré

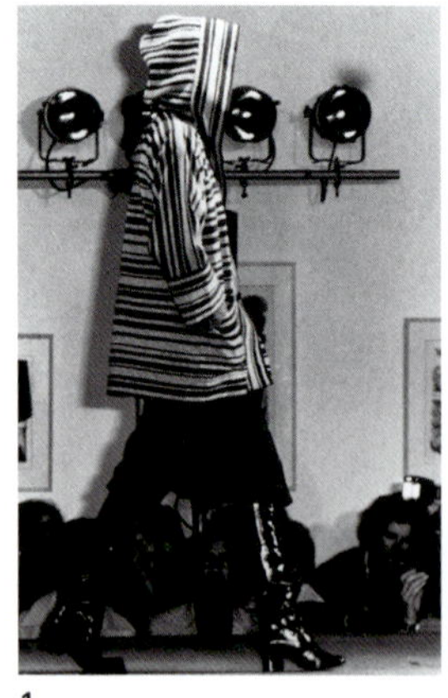
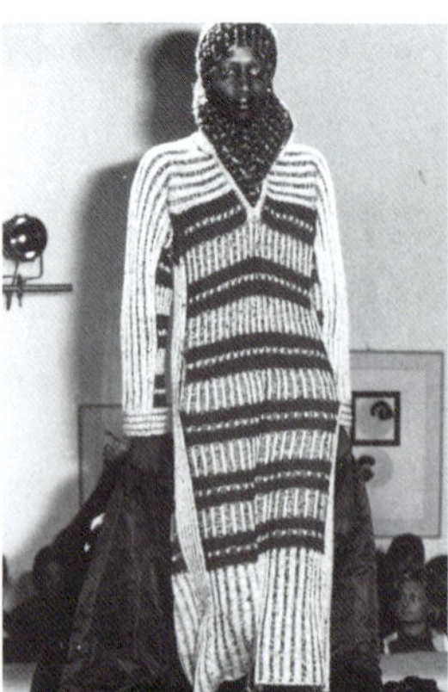
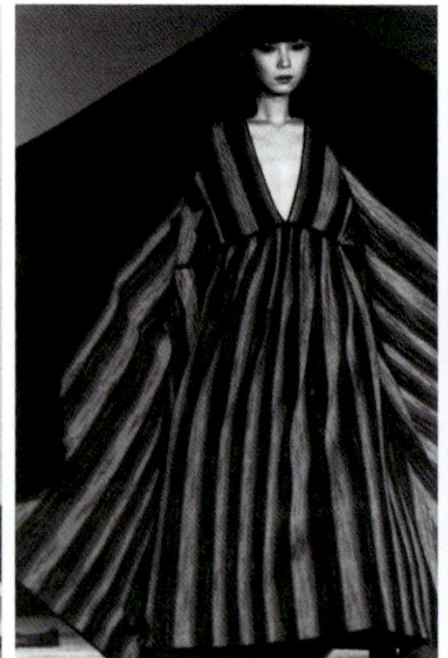
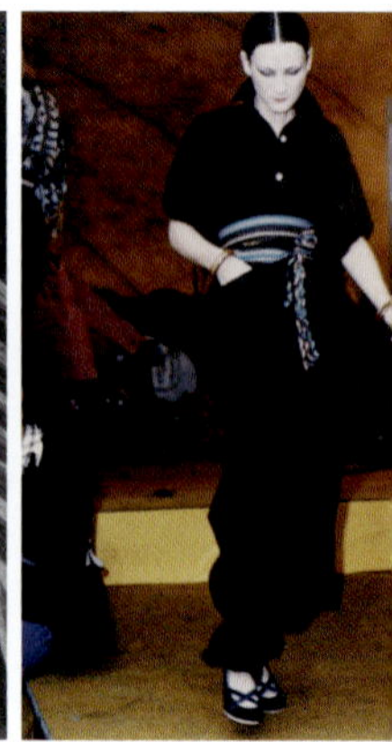

1

2

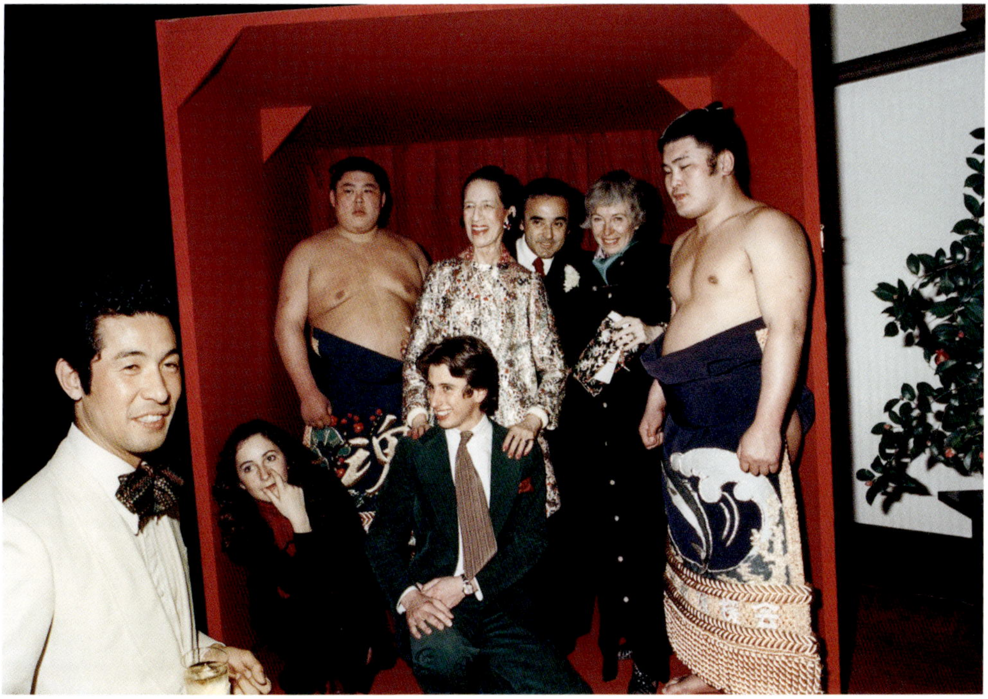

Opening of the exhibition *Gendai Ifuku no Genryu Ten – Inventive Clothes: 1909–1939*
Sumo wrestlers were on hand for the opening reception, a surprise that Miyake put together for Diana Vreeland, who was visiting Japan for the first time

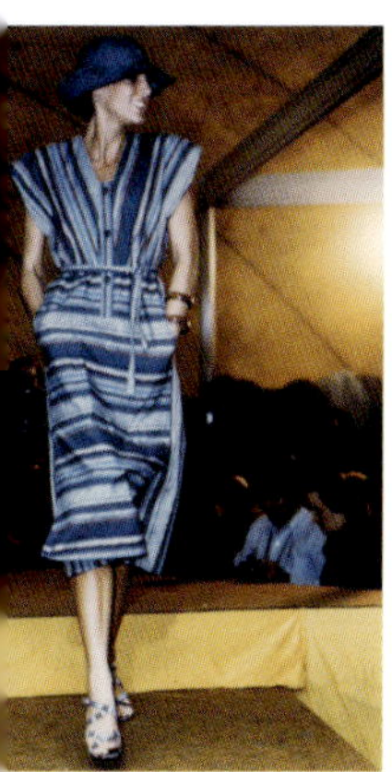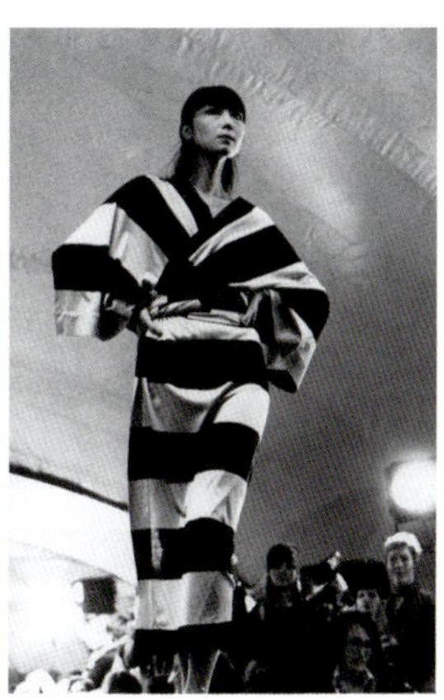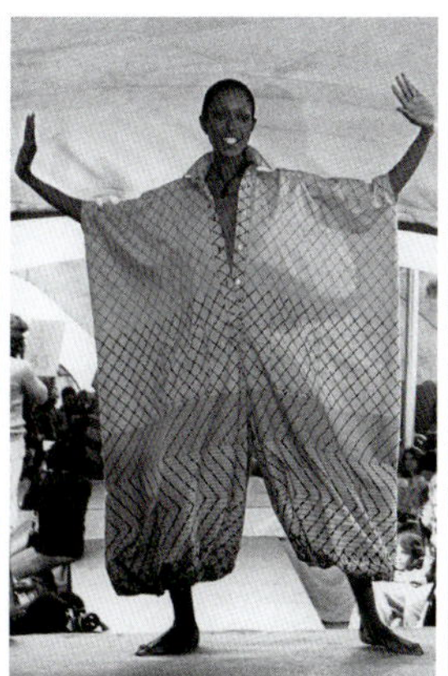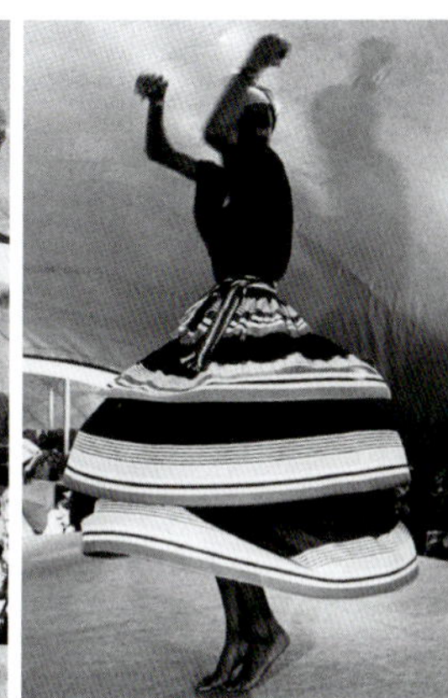

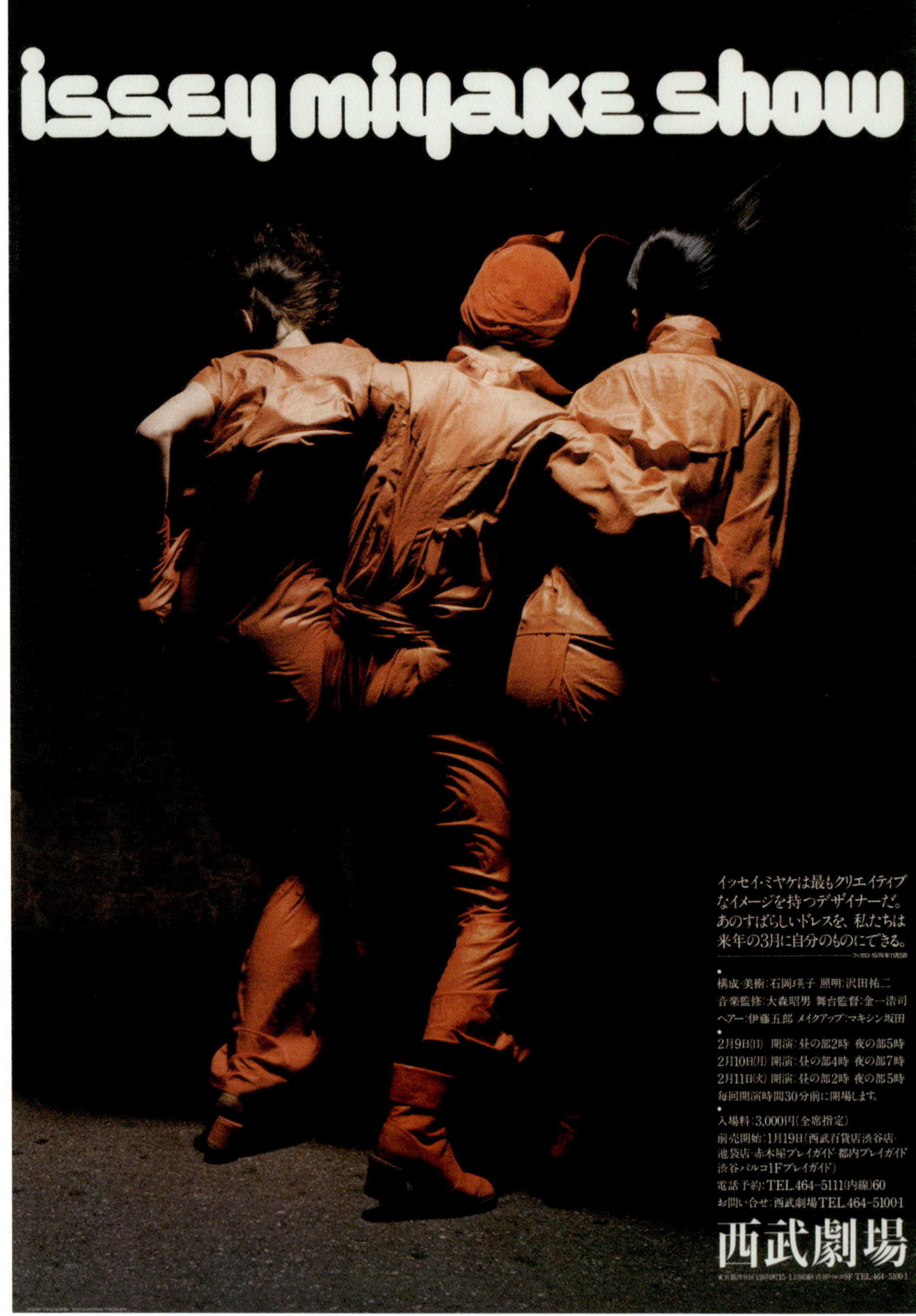

issey miyake show
イッセイ・ミヤケは最もクリエイティブなイメージを持つデザイナーだ。あのすばらしいドレスを、私たちは来年の3月に自分のものにできる。
——フィガロ・1974年11月5日
構成・美術:石岡瑛子　照明:沢田祐二
音楽監修:大森昭男　舞台監督:金一浩司
ヘアー:伊藤五郎　メイクアップ:マキシン坂田
2月9日(日) 開演:昼の部2時　夜の部5時
2月10日(月) 開演:昼の部4時　夜の部7時
2月11日(火) 開演:昼の部2時　夜の部5時
毎回開演時間30分前に開場します。
入場料:3,000円(全席指定)
前売開始:1月19日(西武百貨店渋谷店・池袋店・赤木屋プレイガイド・都内プレイガイド 渋谷パルコ1Fプレイガイド)
電話予約:TEL.464-5111(内線)60
お問い合せ:西武劇場 TEL.464-5100-1
西武劇場

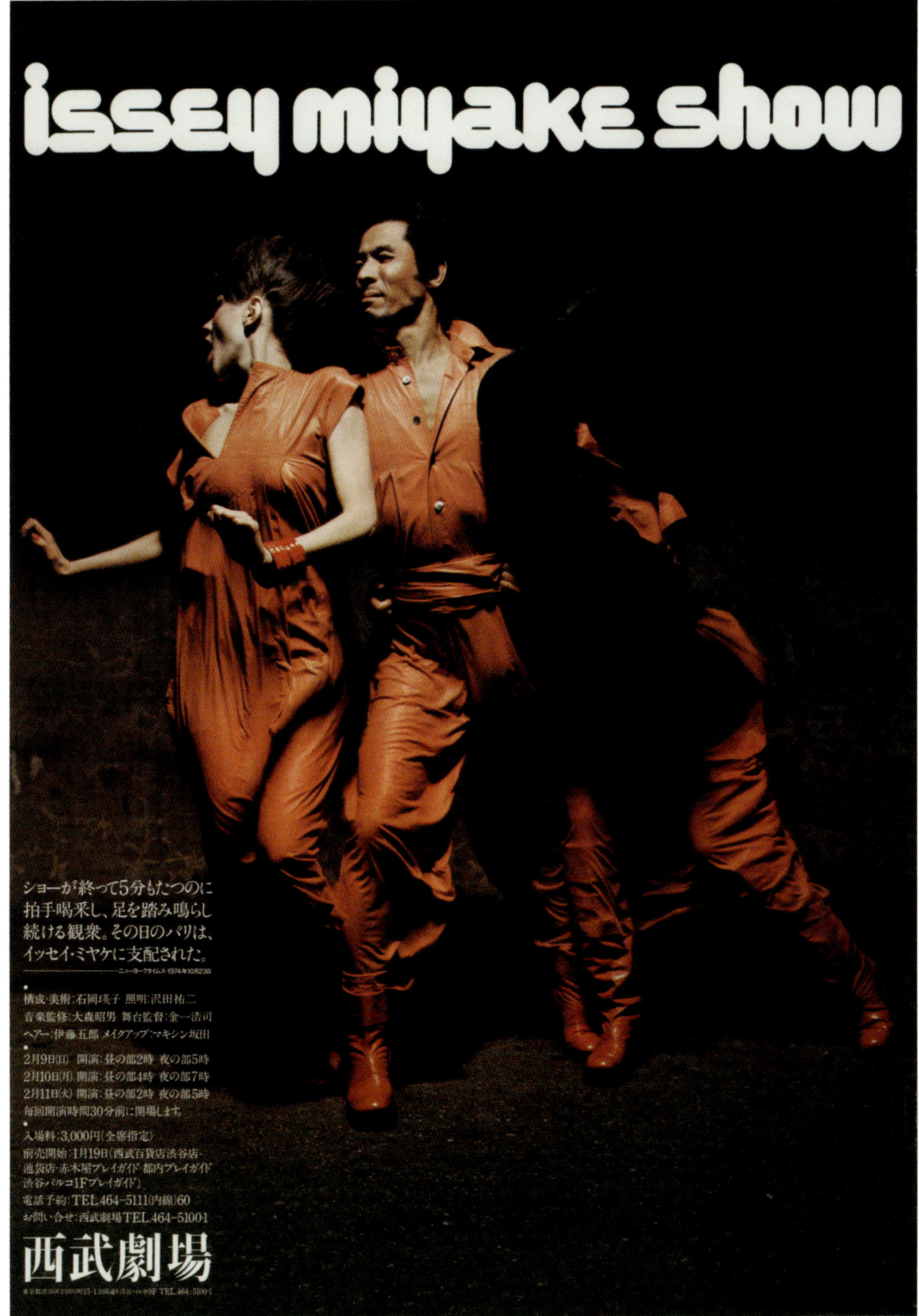
issey miyake show

ショーが終って5分もたつのに
拍手喝采し、足を踏み鳴らし
続ける観衆。その日のパリは、
イッセイ・ミヤケに支配された。
——————ニューヨークタイムズ・1974年10月23日

構成・美術：石岡瑛子　照明：沢田祐二
音楽監修：大森昭男　舞台監督：金一浩司
ヘアー：伊藤五郎　メイクアップ：マキシン坂田

2月9日(日)　開演：昼の部2時　夜の部5時
2月10日(月)　開演：昼の部4時　夜の部7時
2月11日(火)　開演：昼の部2時　夜の部5時
毎回開演時間30分前に開場します。

入場料：3,000円(全席指定)
前売開始：1月19日(西武百貨店渋谷店・
池袋店・赤木屋プレイガイド・都内プレイガイド
渋谷パルコ1Fプレイガイド)
電話予約：TEL.464-5111(内線)60
お問い合せ：西武劇場 TEL.464-51001

西武劇場

Previous spread: *Issey Miyake Show* poster
Miyake himself appeared as a model in the poster for
the *Issey Miyake Show*, which was held from February 9
to 11 at the Seibu Theater in the Shibuya Parco fashion
building. Six performances over three days attracted
approximately 4,000 people. During the mid-1970s,
Miyake often used new or unorthodox ways to show
his clothing that defied conventional assumptions
about fashion shows.
Art direction: Eiko Ishioka; photography:
Noriaki Yokosuka

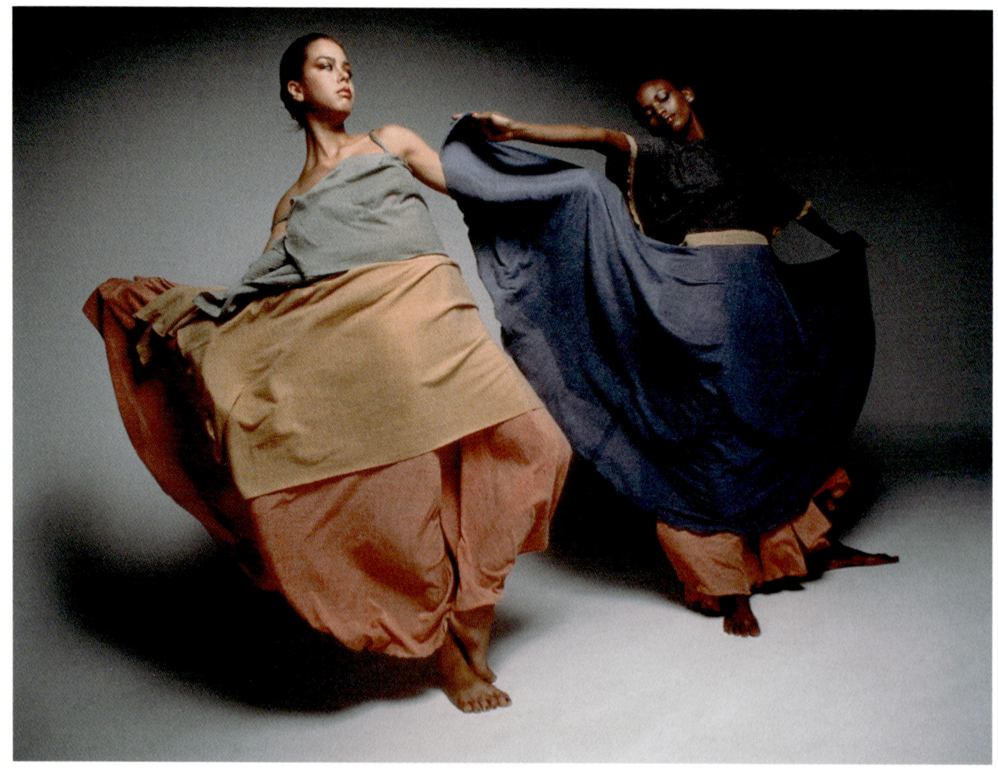

Opposite: **Thin yoryu crepe**
Redeveloped from the material commonly used
for men's underwear. Cotton and polyester *yoryu*
crepe with soft texture, made on the Rachel knitting
machine. All items use flat square, rectangular,
or circular shapes in the design.
1975 design/Spring-Summer 1976 Collection
Photography: Noriaki Yokosuka; models:
Debbie Dickinson and Toukie Smith

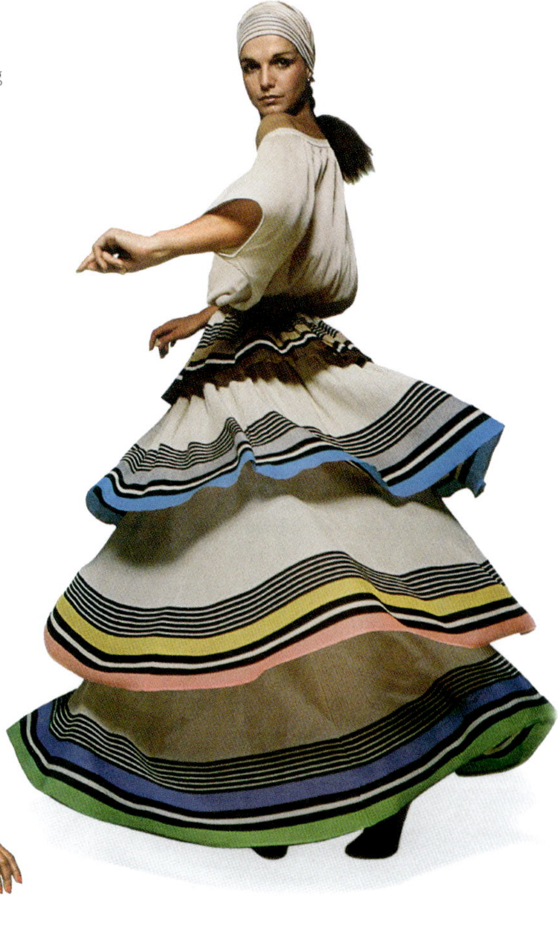

Top Dress
Miyake had bought a spinning top at a shop and got an
idea for a dress from the lines it made as it spun. The
dress came in two pieces, in a jersey made of "Pewlon,"
an acrylic filament that took and held strong colors;
developed by Asahi Kasei Corporation.
1975 design/Spring-Summer 1976 Collection
Photography: Noriaki Yokosuka; model:
Susie Dyson (above)

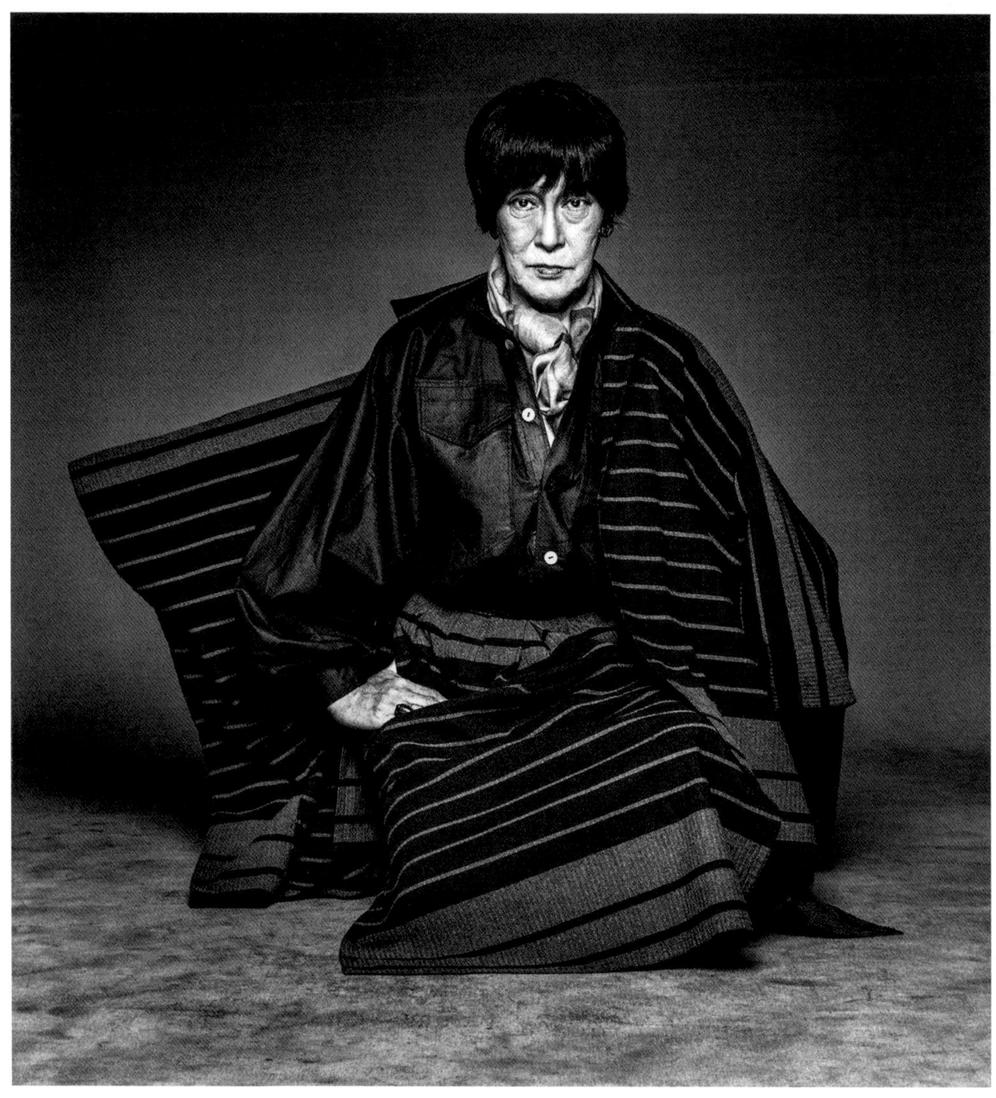

Shijira-ori
Redeveloped from the traditional *shijira-ori* weaving
technique that was once created by women in the Awa
area using cotton waste, in a wider-width fabric. Indigo
blue-dyed skirt and a jacket made with a piece of cloth.
1975 design/Spring-Summer 1976 Collection
Photography: Kazumi Kurigami; worn by:
Masako Shirasu

Opposite: **Oni-yoryu**
Oni-yoryu is a thick crepe woven in Niigata and given
deep wrinkles by being hand-wrung in cold water.
1975 design/Spring-Summer 1976 Collection
Photography: Noriaki Yokosuka; models: Sayoko
Yamaguchi and Atsuko Oka

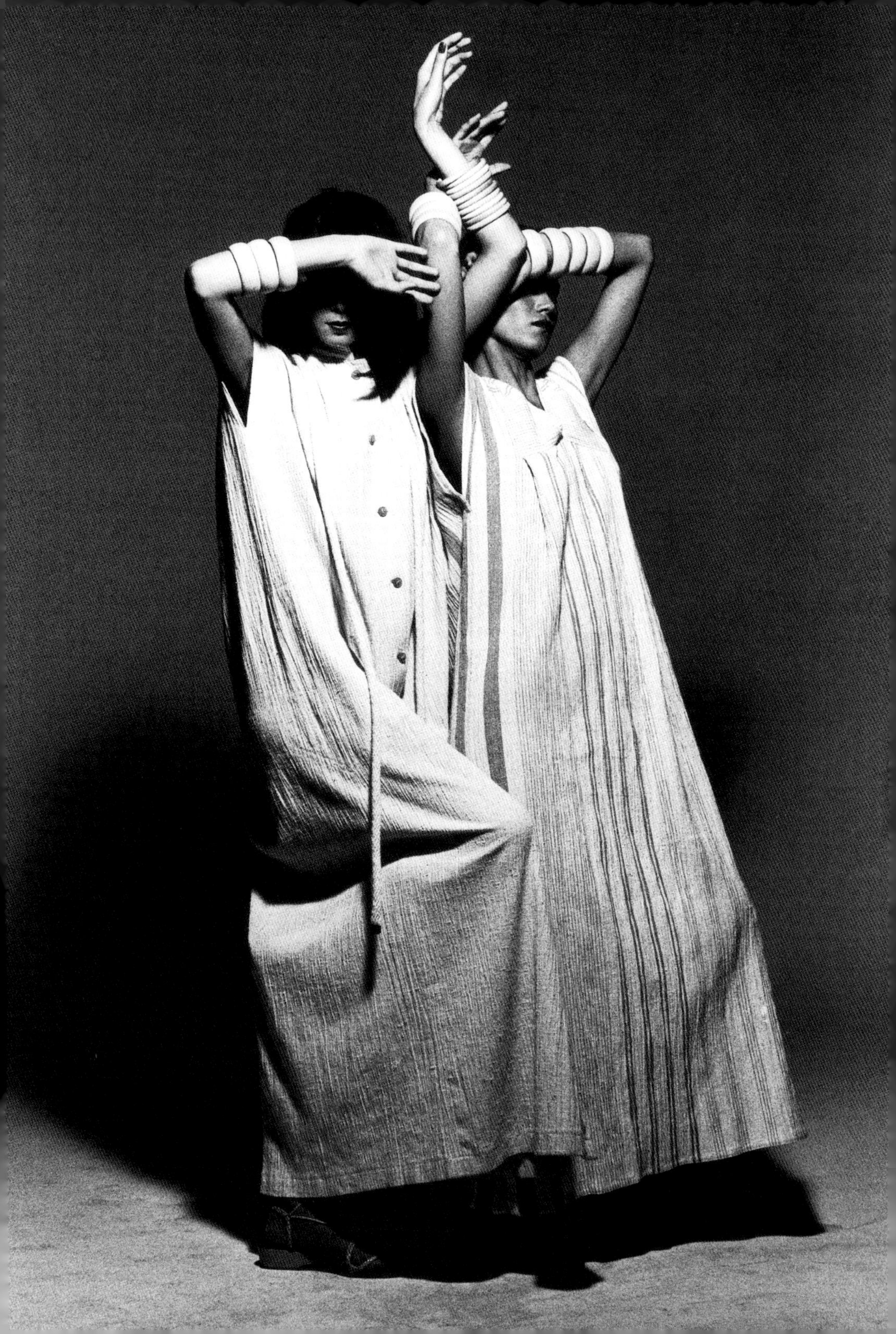

1976

> January–February: *Issey Miyake and Twelve Black Girls* show (Spring-Summer 1976) in Tokyo and Osaka
> April: Autumn-Winter 1976 Paris Collection at Hotel Intercontinental
> April: Autumn-Winter 1976 New York Collection at The Fashion Institute of Technology
> June: ISSEY MIYAKE flagship store opened in the From 1st Building in Minami Aoyama, Tokyo
> October: Spring-Summer 1977 Paris Collection at Salle Wagram
> December: Spring-Summer 1977 Tokyo Collection at Shiba Park Studio

1 Autumn-Winter 1976 Paris Collection, April 3, Hotel Intercontinental
2 Spring-Summer 1977 Paris Collection, October 23, Salle Wagram

Issey Miyake and Twelve Black Girls

Back at the Seibu Theater, he presented a new type of fashion show that featured 12 black models in a variety of theatrical settings, including plays, dances, and performance art.

January 29–February 2: Seibu Theater, Shibuya Parco fashion building; February 5: Osaka Prefectural Gymnasium. Seen by approximately 20,000 people in total. Concept, supervision: Eiko Ishioka, Issey Miyake; art: Eiko Ishioka; direction and music: Minoru Terada; models: Grace Jones, Barbara Summers, Carol Standifer, Doris Smith, Ramona Sanders, Jan Maiden, Dennis Pascal, June Murphy, Jessica Brown, Esther Kamatari, Barbara Jackson, and Karen Wilson; staff: Yuji Sawada, Kuma Harada, Morihisa Shibuya, Goro Ito, and Sachiko Kawabe; planning and production: Parco

ISSEY MIYAKE flagship store

The From 1st Building in Minami Aoyama was designed as a new form of urban living space, and quickly became a catalyst for a change to what until then had been a quiet residential neighborhood. The ISSEY MIYAKE store was on the first floor, and the space, which featured a large table jutting out from the wall, was designed by Shiro Kuramata. Kuramata went on to design many ISSEY MIYAKE stores in Japan and other countries.

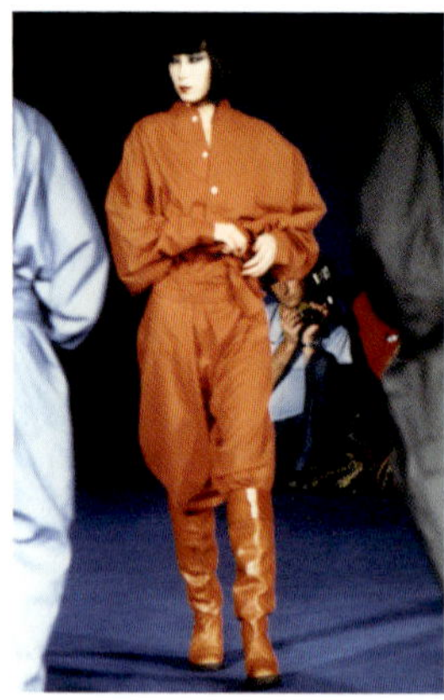
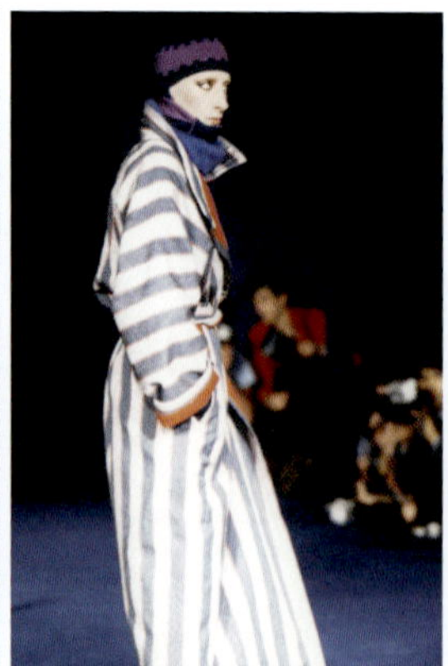
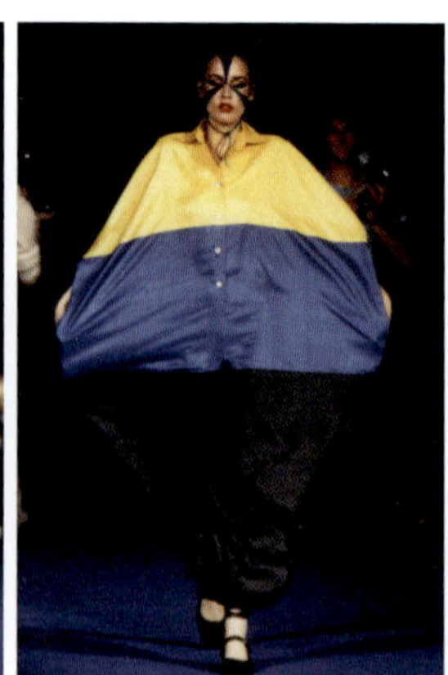
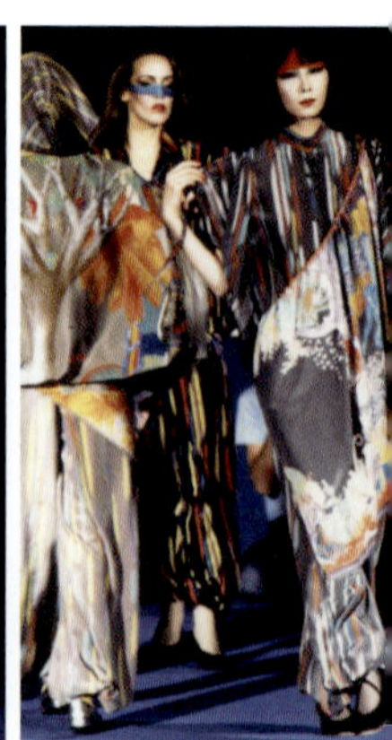

1

*Issey Miyake and
Twelve Black Girls* poster
Art direction: Eiko Ishioka;
photography: Hajime Sawatari;
models: Grace Jones and
Issey Miyake

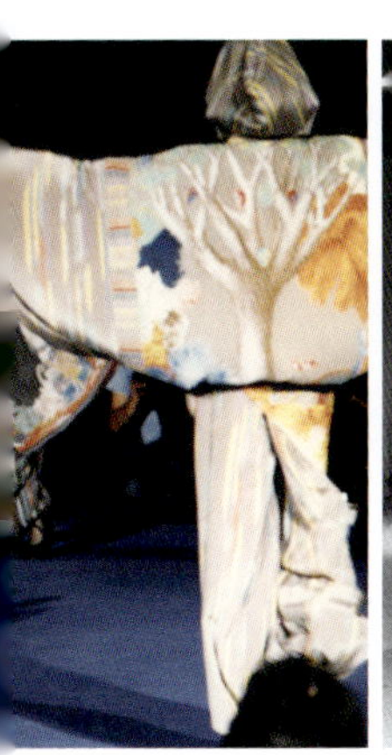
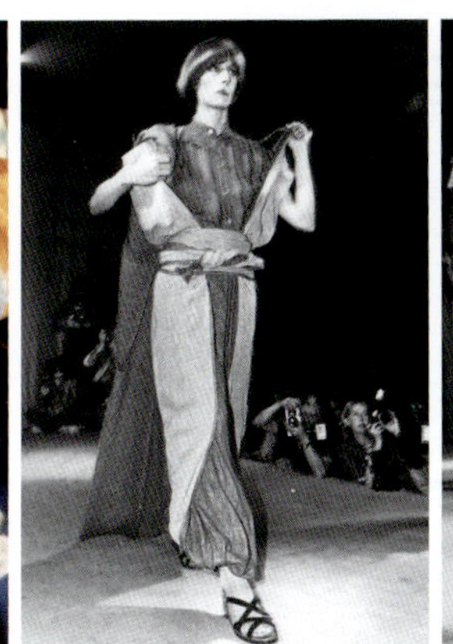
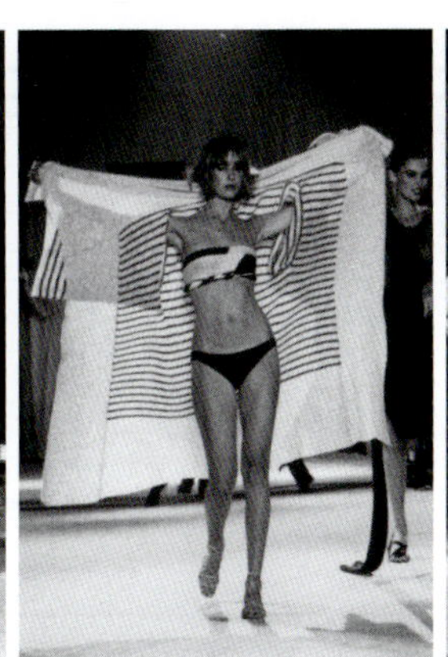
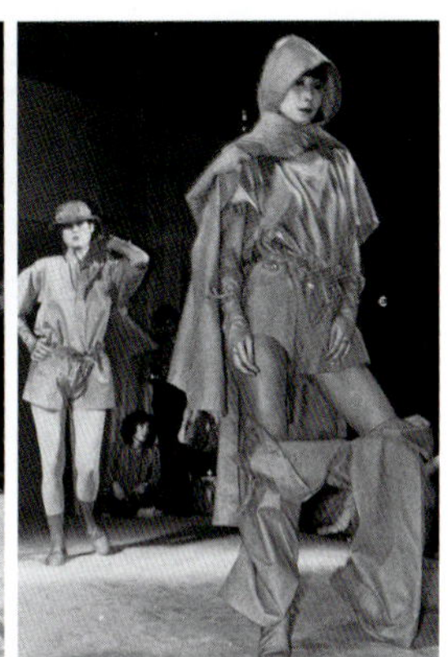

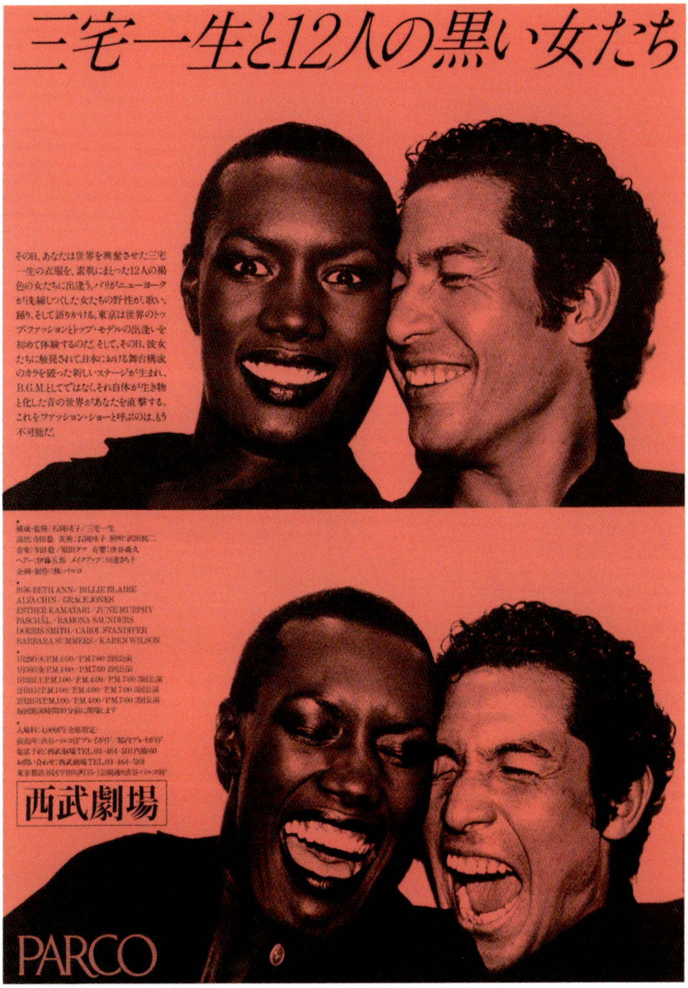

2

Below: PARCO poster
Hemp crepe dress. Made from a single piece of rectangular cloth that extends from the waist and is worn like a stole. 1975 design/Spring-Summer 1976 Collection
Art direction: Eiko Ishioka; photography:
Noriaki Yokosuka; model: Grace Jones

Opposite: **_Linen Jumpsuit_**
All of the models performing in _Issey Miyake and Twelve Black Girls_ wore soft linen jumpsuits that made use of the width of the cloth, with rubber to close the sleeves. 1975 design/Spring-Summer 1976 Collection
Photography: Hajime Sawatari; models:
full cast of _Issey Miyake and Twelve Black Girls_

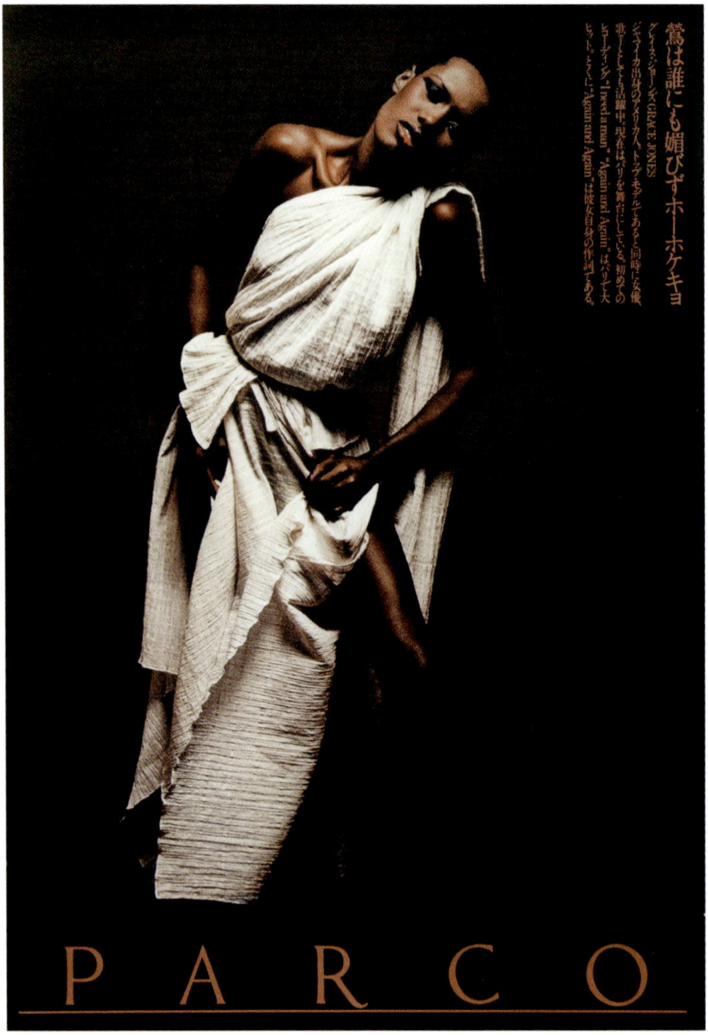

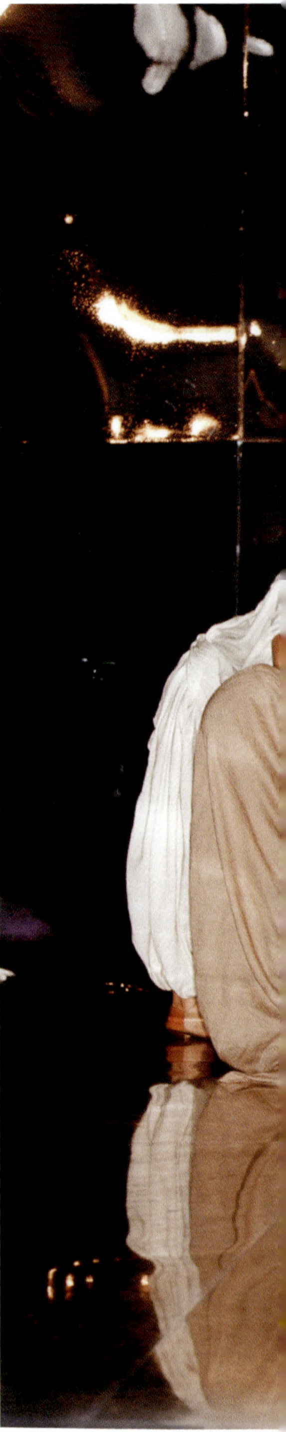

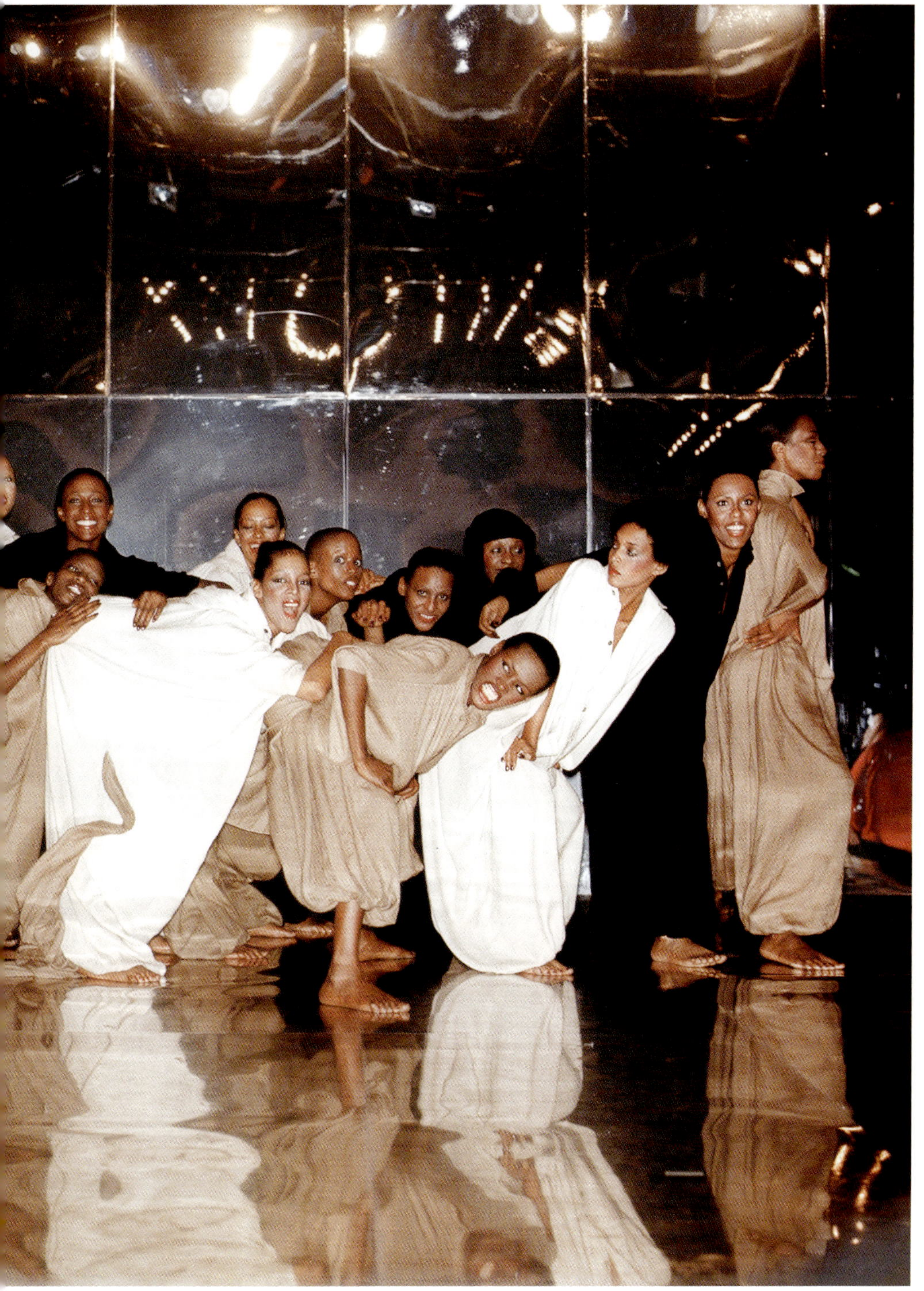

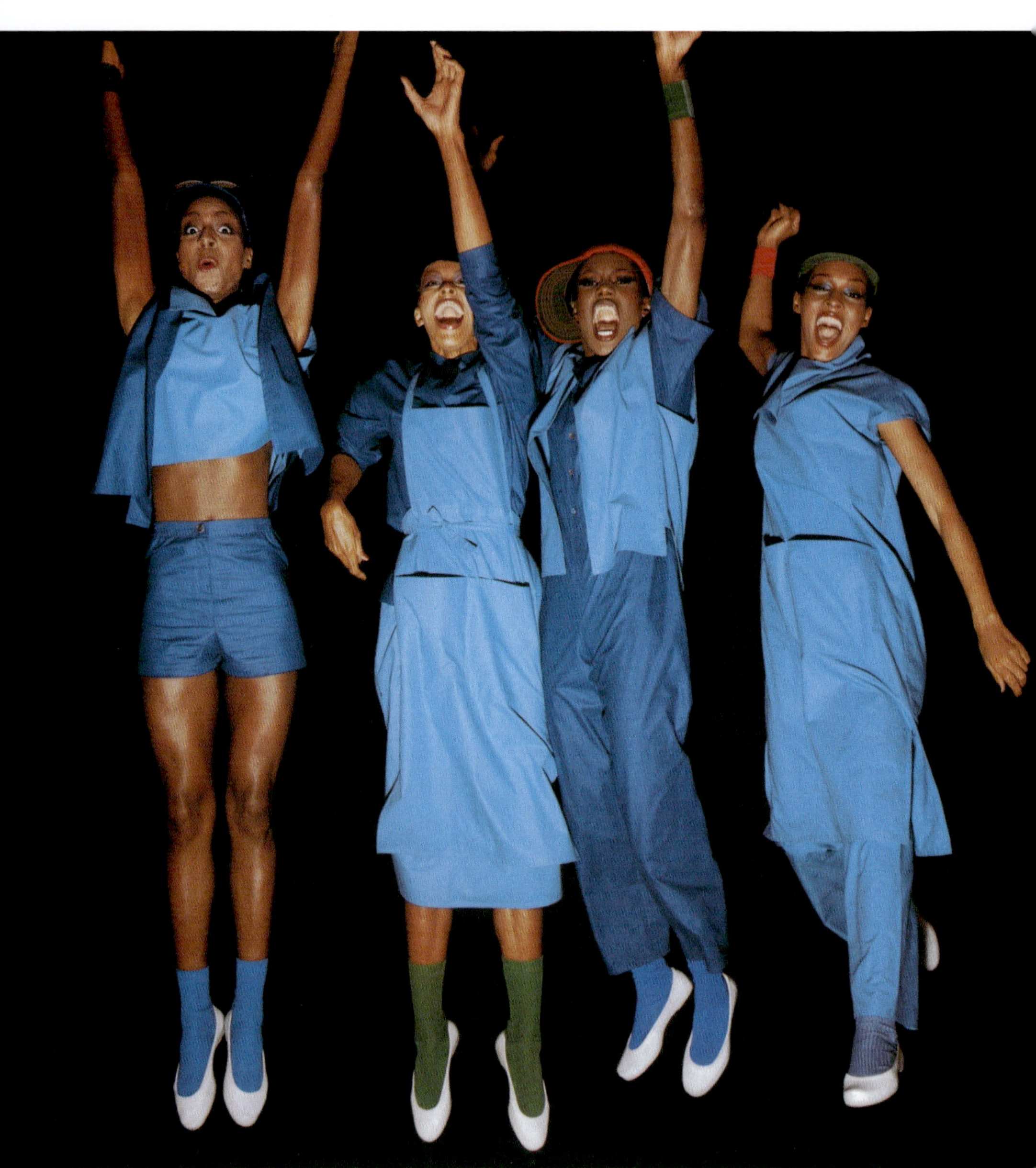

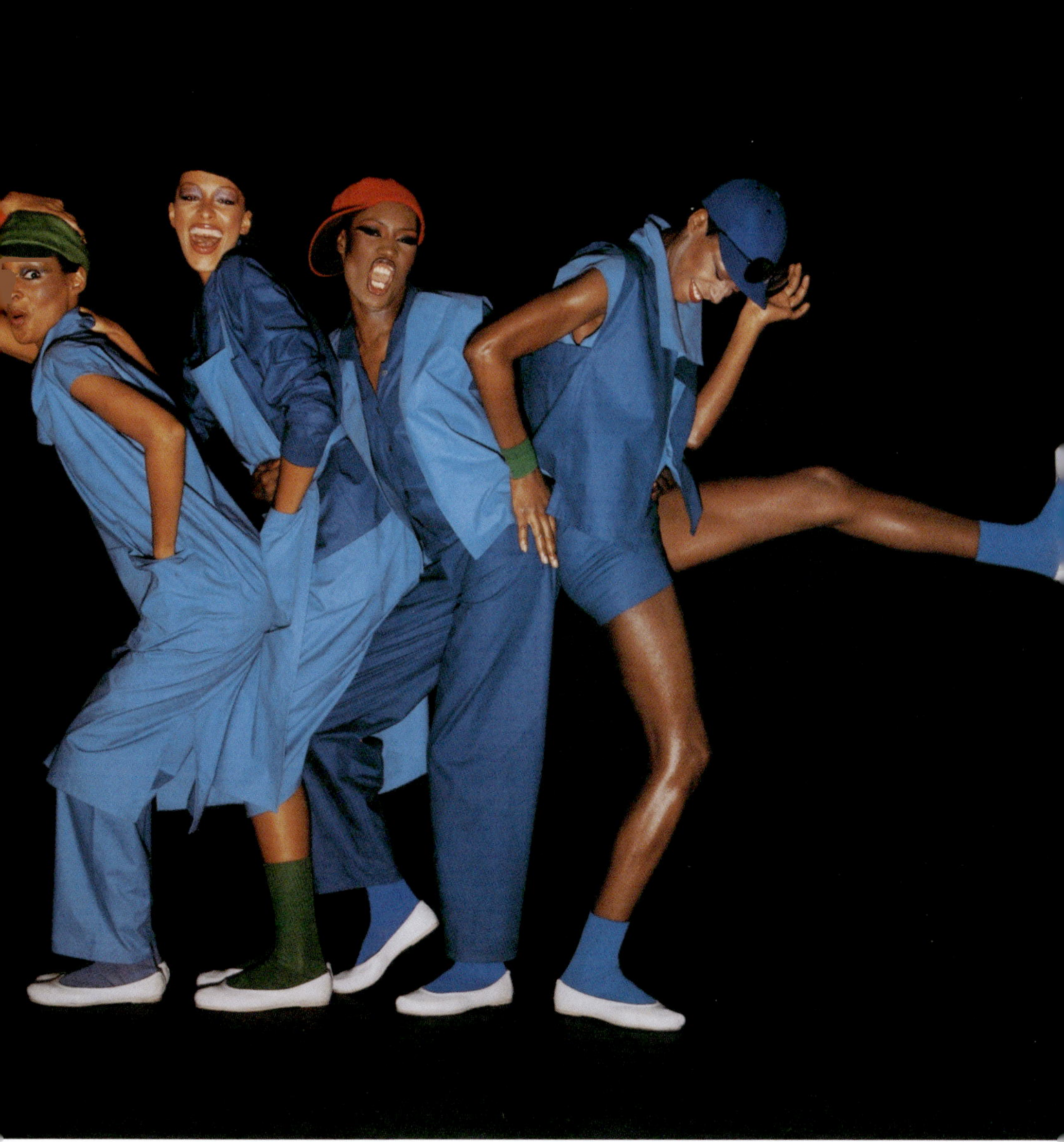

Hocho Cut

This takes its inspiration from the knife work of sushi chefs, and is cut in straight lines. Miyake created units in three shades of indigo, which could be put together in a variety of combinations. The material is an improved version of the fabric used to line men's kimonos and is made from slightly thicker *shohana-momen* cotton.
1975 design/Spring-Summer 1976 Collection
Photography: Tatsuo Masubuchi; models: Grace Jones, June Murphy, Barbara Summers, and Karen Wilson

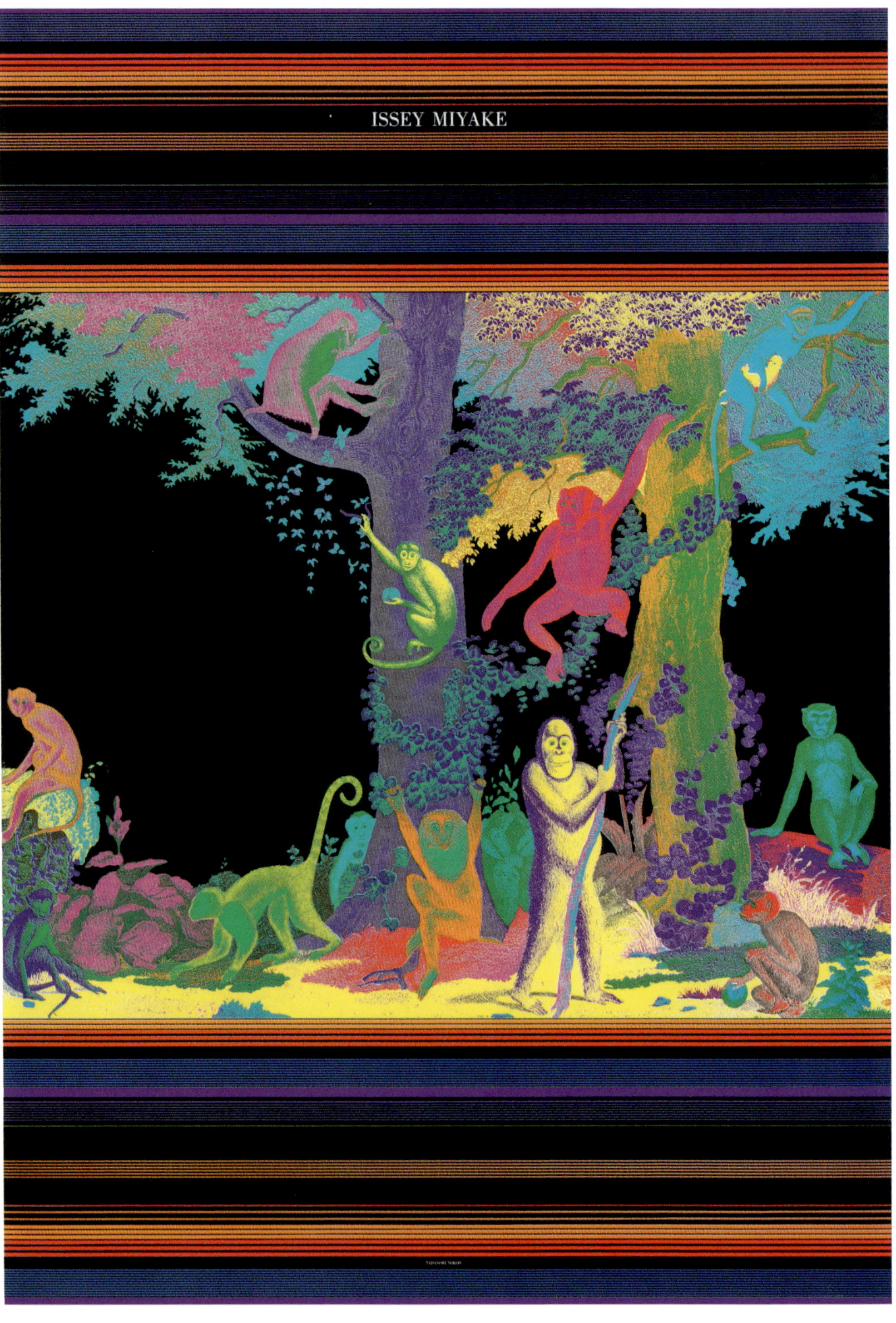

ISSEY MIYAKE

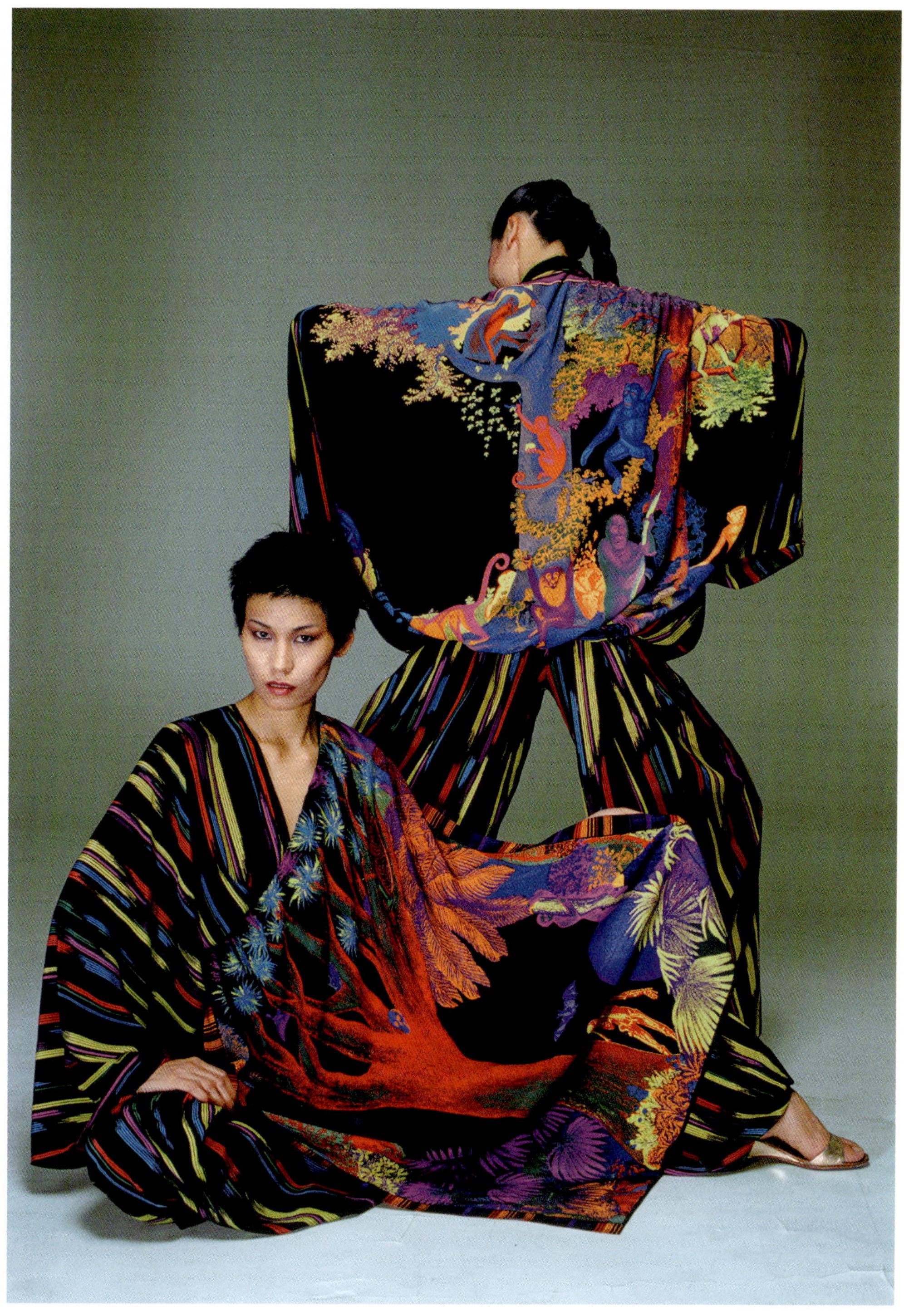

Page 70: *Paradise* poster
Poster created for Autumn-Winter 1976 Collection
Design: Tadanori Yokoo
Offset print

Page 71: *Paradise*
Print design by Tadanori Yokoo. Starting from this
season, the clothes created in collaboration with
Tadanori Yokoo continued to be presented until the
Spring-Summer 1978 Collection. All items made in silk.
The print is by Rainbow of Italy.
1976 design/Autumn-Winter 1976 Collection
Photography: Noriaki Yokosuka; model: Atsuko Oka

Below: *Paradise Lost* design drawings
1976: Design drawings: Issey Miyake
© Miyake Design Studio

Opposite: *Paradise Lost*
The original drawing used for the print
was created by Tadanori Yokoo.
1976 design/Spring-Summer 1977 Collection
Photography: Noriaki Yokosuka; model: Iman

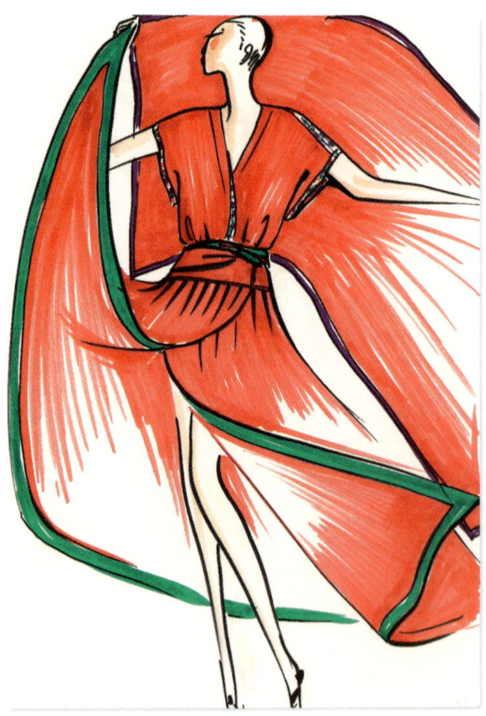
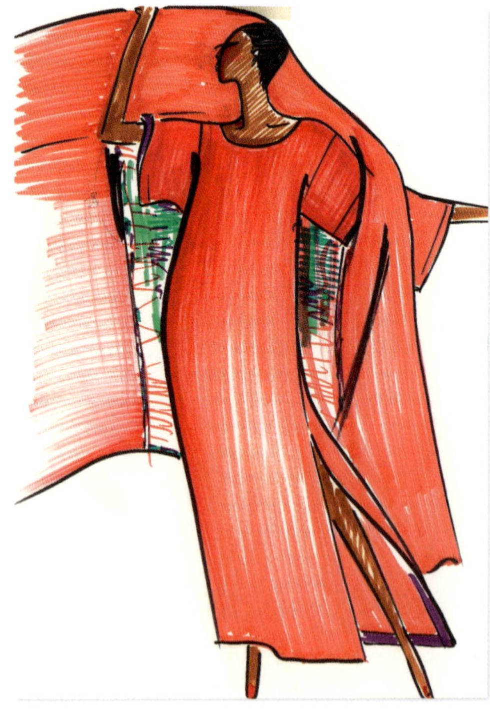

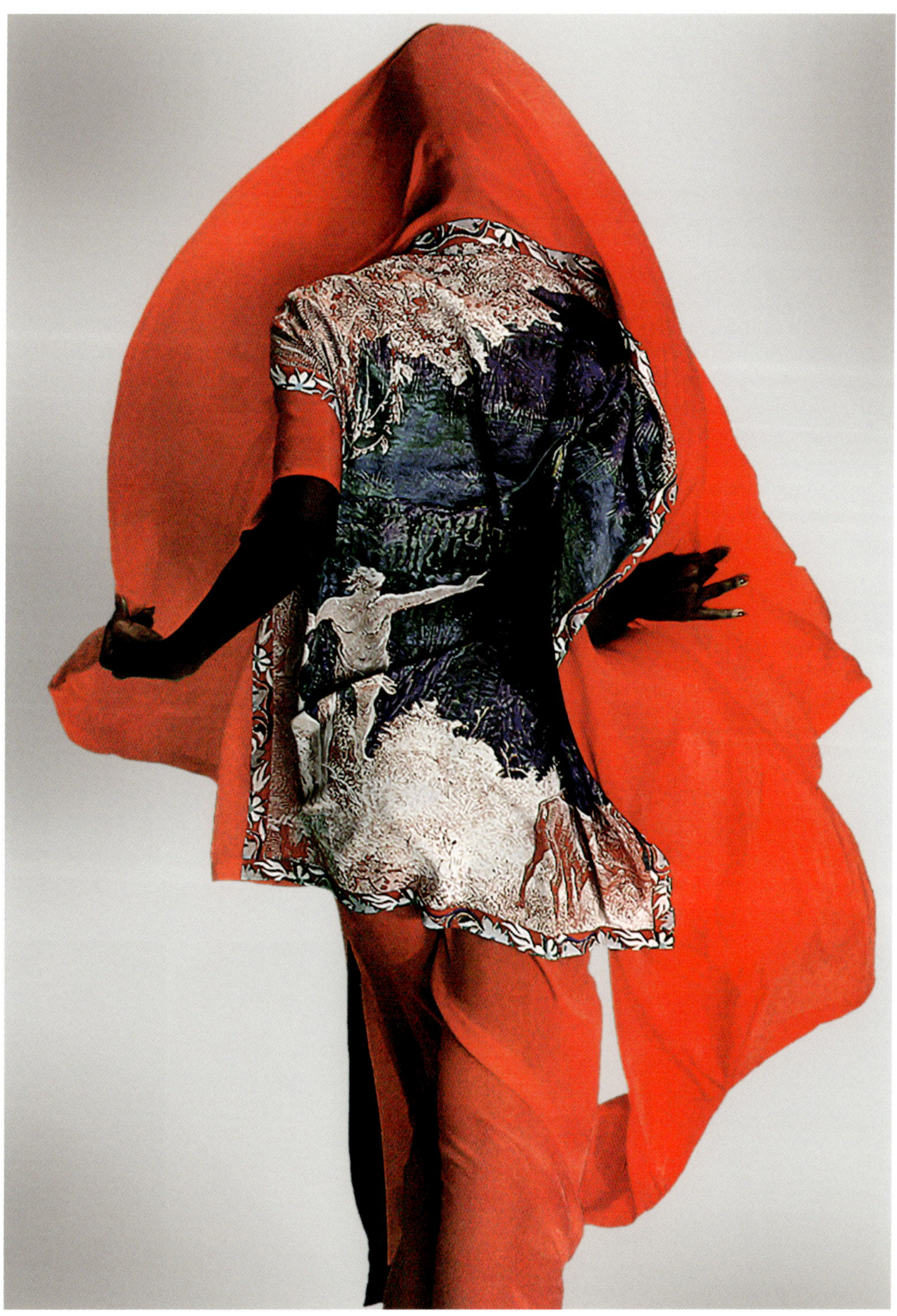

1977

> February: Mainichi Design Awards commemorative show, *A Piece of Cloth – Issey Miyake in Museum* in Tokyo
> March: Autumn-Winter 1977 Paris Collection at Salle Wagram. Tadanori Yokoo started to design the invitations from this collection
> July: *Fly with Issey Miyake* show (Autumn-Winter 1977) in Tokyo and Kyoto
> October: Spring-Summer 1978 Paris Collection at Salle Wagram
> Announced ISSEY MIYAKE MEN brand
> Designed uniforms for the ground staff of All Nippon Airways

A Piece of Cloth – Issey Miyake in Museum

Awarded the Mainichi Design Award in 1976, the first year after the name was changed from the Mainichi Industrial Design Awards. Arata Isozaki, a member of the selection committee, wrote an essay titled "Thinking on the Wild Side" under the headline "Issey Miyake's Work Is a Cultural Incident" (*Mainichi Shimbun*, January 26 edition). The commemorative show was put together by Kazuko Koike, Shiro Kuramata, and Ikko Tanaka. This was the first time that a fashion show had been held in a museum.

*February 19–20: Seibu Museum of Art, Tokyo
Production: Kazuko Koike; stage device: Shiro Kuramata; music: Shigeaki Saegusa; lighting: Harumi Fujimoto; advertising art: Ikko Tanaka and Noriaki Yokosuka; hair and makeup: Sachiko Kawabe; direction: Tomio Mohri; stylists: Rikako Nakamura and Akira Onozuka; production management: Tomoko Komuro and Sumako Kawayama; kimono fitting: Sun Design Group; models: Haruka Asami, Mari Azuma, Midori Ishizu, Atsuko Oka, Naomi Kawata, Masae Kawami, Christina Hyoi, Joanne Galecki, Mariko Takata, Lisa Tachiki, Seiko Ban, Yuri Hodaka, Manu Sekine, Mary Sano, Sayoko Yamaguchi, and Yasuko Yamayoshi*

1 Autumn-Winter 1977 Paris Collection, March 26, Salle Wagram
2 Spring-Summer 1978 Paris Collection, October 22, Salle Wagram

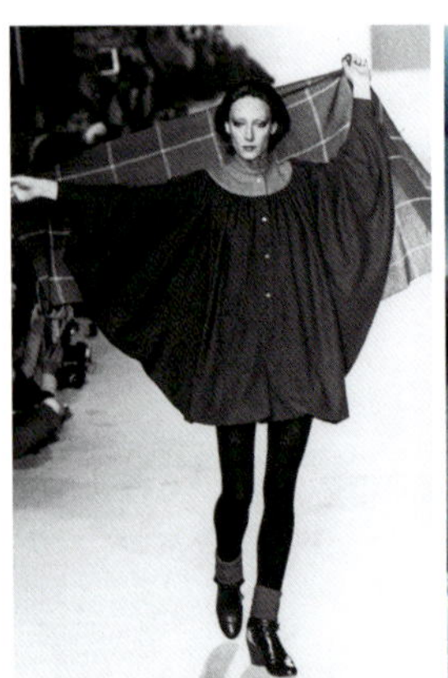
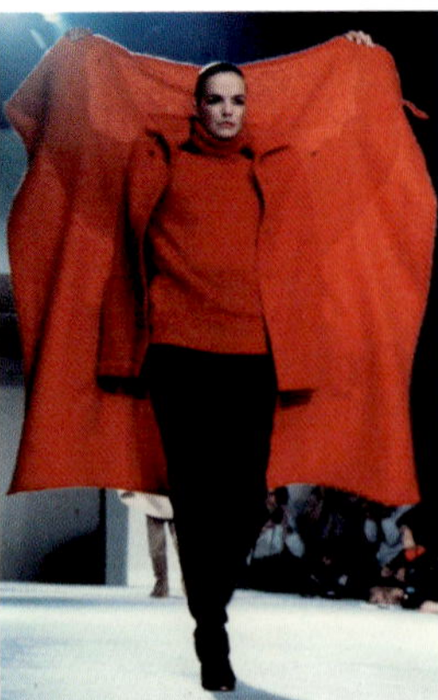
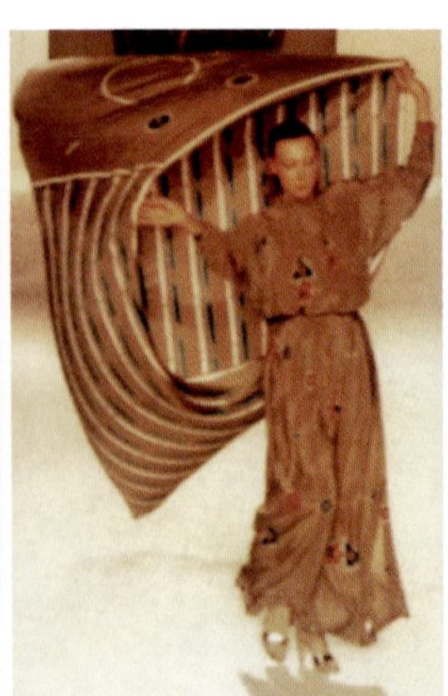
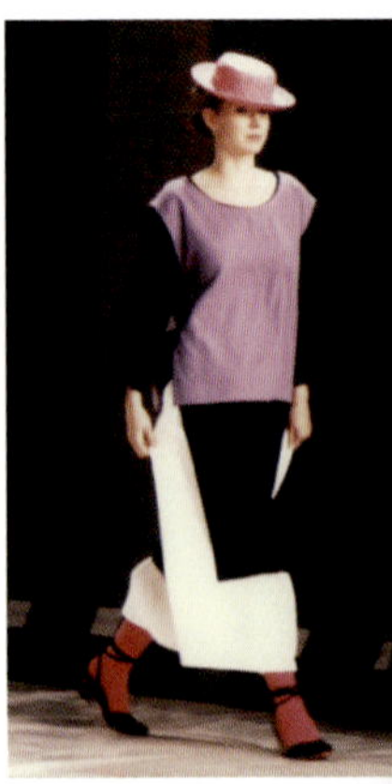

1

2

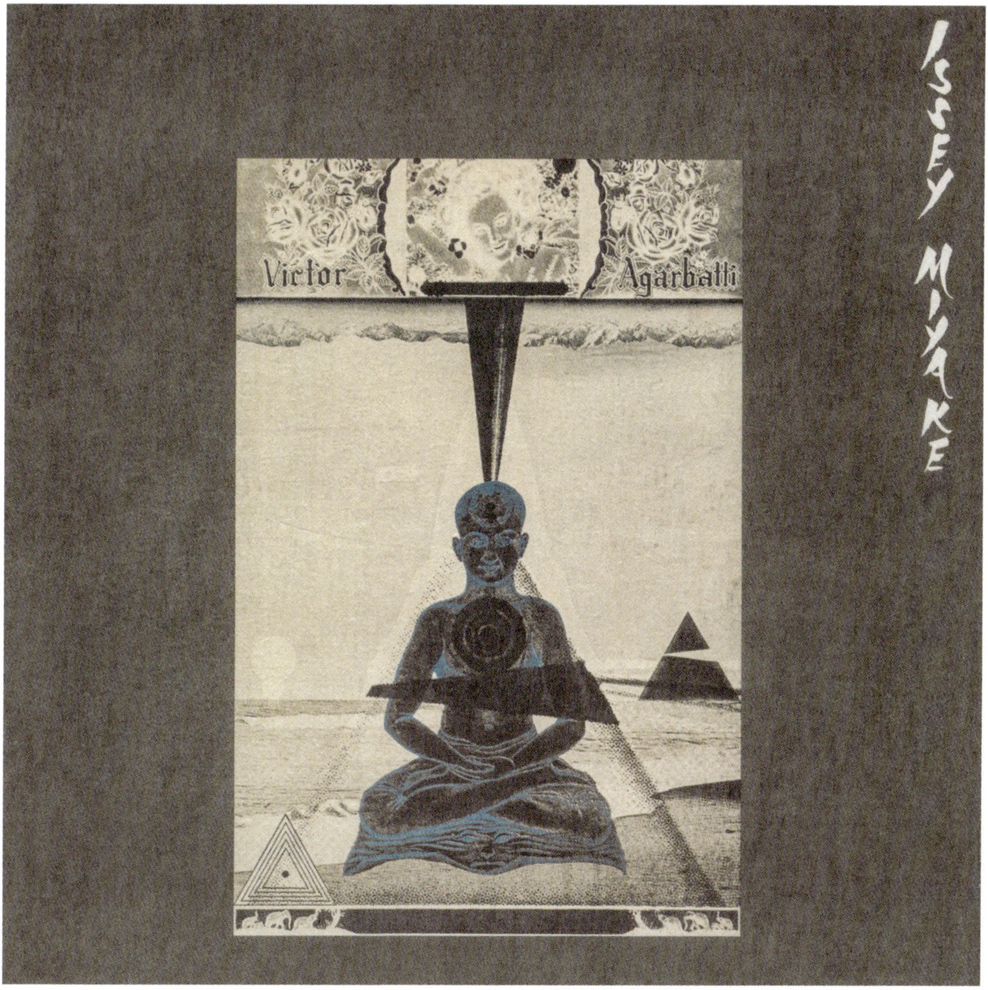

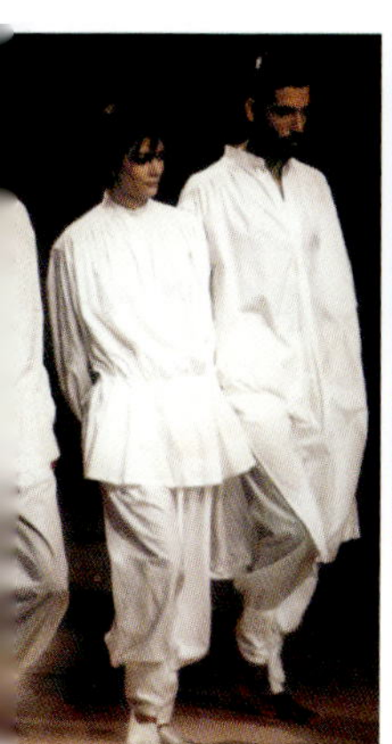

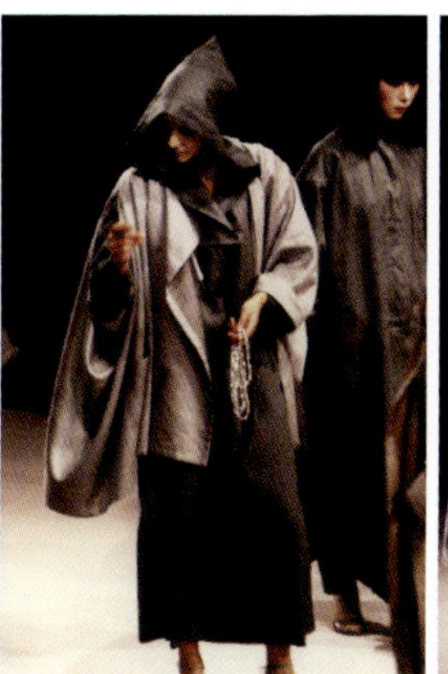

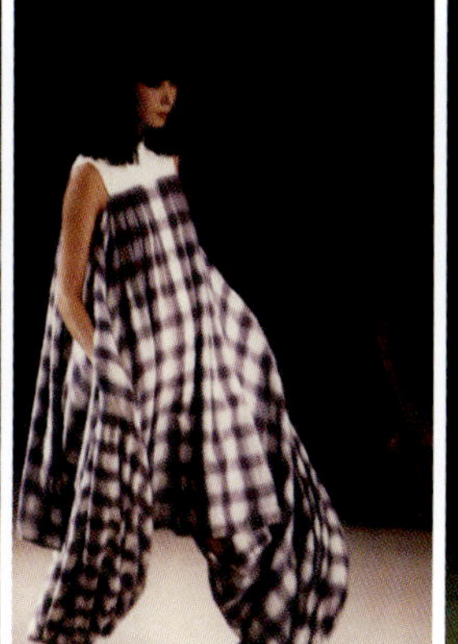

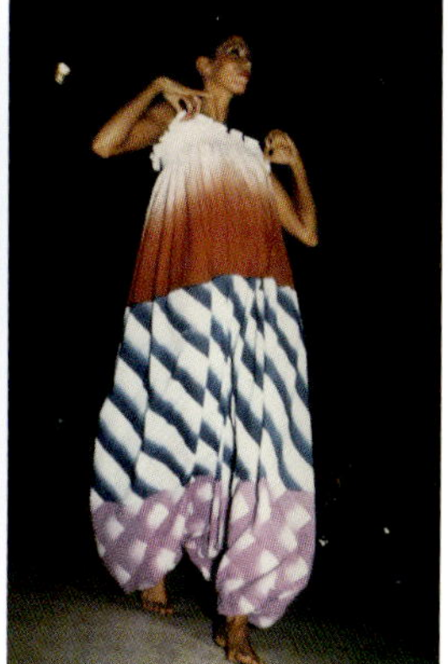

（15）　12版　特集　昭和52年（1977年）　1月26日　（水曜日）　朝日新聞

'76毎日デ

京・丸の内の東京会館で行われる。また受賞作品は三十一日から二月五日まで、東京・日本橋、大日本インキビル17階で開かれる「毎日デザイン展」に展示される。

【選考委員】磯崎新、栄久庵憲司、田中一光、中原佑介、森正洋

【調査委員】氷井一正、福田繁雄、梶祐輔、堀文彦、豊口克平、鶴岡善平、会田雄亮、森政弘、平尾収、粟辻博、石井幹子、倉俣史郎、毎日デザイン賞コーディネーター・斎藤豊人

――選考委員　磯崎　新――

野生の思考

三宅一生の活動は
文化領域の事件で
あったということ

選考委員の顔ぶれが一新したと同時に、まえまえから懸案になっていた賞の名前が問題にもなるように、昨年度の勝見勝氏の週評にもあるように、「産業デザイン賞」の「産業」を消すことに、関係者一同もはや異議はなかったのだが、永年のいきがかり上、改名はむずかしいことになっていた。それが選考委員が入れ替わるという機会に実現しただけで、必ずしも新しい委員の創意によるものではない。

しかし「産業デザイン」から「産業」を取り去ることは、かなり決定的な転換である。いまこそ「産業」と「デザイン」は別個に考えられるのだが、その発生を歴史的にみると、分かちがたい関係にあった。デザインは、近代の産業社会にあった。生産、流通の両過程にまたがってあらわれる商品をあつかうような広がりに向かって離脱であった。だから、単にデザインといわずに、産業をかぶせることは同義反復になるぐらいに正確（せいこう）を得たいいまわしであったといえるだろう。

それを分離せねばならないところに、まえまえから懸案がおかれている状況がある。デザインが置かれている状況がある今日、デザインという言葉に親しみ、これを大衆化する役割をしてきたにもかかわらず、プロダクト、グラフィック、建築、都市までが一貫したデザインの理念によってとらえられるようになったときには、いつもその対象からはずされていた。これは、自らの目標をファッションという閉ざされた世界に限定してきたことが大きい原因といえるだろう。

これは、かつてクラフトからいわゆる美術工芸が生まれ、ついには美的鑑賞の対象になったのと類似の現象ともいえるが、デザインはもっと多方面にわたり、いまや、現代文明の視覚領域のすべてをおおうような広がりに向かって離脱しつつある。

過去数年間の三宅一生の仕事は衣服デザインをファッションとしてだけではなく、ひとつの文化領域内での事件のおもむきがあった。おおげさにいうと、近代デザインがつくりあげてきた、ハイファッションの世界に出現する子やはんてんのような野良着が、突如として洋服と和服といった区別さえ失わせる。割しうる新しいデザインの方法であり、思案である、ということもできる。それゆえに、三宅一生のデザインは、洋服でなく、彼を選び出すことで「'76毎日デザイン賞」の性格を明確にできると、いった価値観の転換も用意している。デザイン賞を文化領域にまで広がった視界のなかにおいてみるためにも。

三宅一生の衣服デザイン活動が今年度の賞に選ばれたのには、以上のような背景がある。衣服は他領域よりも早くから新しいショーにつくりあげた点も見逃すことができない。

それは、衣服を着ることの原点にたちもどってとらえなおすという、一貫した姿勢が一体化していくという彼の思想を伝達する新しいスタイルが生まれたといっていいだろう。衣服とは、動く肉体にまとわりつく一枚の布であったという、もっとも基本的な事実を、三宅一生は改めて知らせてくれる。人類が初めて衣服を身にまとったときの感触が復活している。世界の諸民族の衣装を思わせるようなデザインが生まれるのは当然である。つまり、各民族が独自に一枚の布から衣装をつくりあげていった歴史が自らのなかにとり込まれている。

彼の活動を貫いているのは"野生の思考"とでもいうべき、近代化した制度が生み出した通念にとらわれない、いきいきとした発想である。それが単に閉ざされた個人のデザインだけでなく、新素材の開発といった、開いた行動に進むだけの柔軟さもあわせもっている。何よりも"作品のユニークさは決定的で、ファッション界における全世界的な活動がつづけられ評価されつつある。と同時に、広範なレベルにまで彼のデザインは浸透しつつあり、今後のデザイン界へ与える影響の大きいことも予想される。

今回、新しい委員によって、タイトルも変更して選考したとき、三宅一生につけでなく全員一致であった。だが、それだけではなく、彼を選び出すことで「'76毎日デザイン賞」の性格を明確にできると、デザイン賞を文化領域にまで広がった視界のなかにおいてみるためにも。

（建築家）

「この賞」だけは
欲しいと思った・
―受賞の言葉―

あれは随分前、日本で世界デザイン会議が開かれたことがあった。当時、多摩美大図案科の学生だった僕は、その内容を知りもしない幸運が知らされたのは、ニューヨークでの夢を彼る。ガク然とした記憶が、いまなおあざやかましい。高校時代から衣服のデザインが、最も日常身近で、デザインとしては認められていないのにも驚き、早速、個人の嗜好（このみ）にも左右されているから、そこに大きな可能性も感じるがゆえに、危険な落とし穴があるのも確かだが、衣服は、二十四時間の人間の自己表現の道具としては皮膚にさえ帰するものだと思ってきた。

一枚の布という、デザイン意欲の原初の形にたびたび立ち返ることで、私はこの答えを欲した。しかし、それは、どこまで行っても終わりのない影のような存在としてイスをもらったばかだった。

道念となったファッション・ショーでは、なく、動きの激しい、まさに衣服と肉体の動作が一体化していくという彼の思想を伝達する新しいスタイルが生まれたといっていいだろう。

彼の活動を貫いているのは"野生の思考"とでもいうべき、近代化した制度が生み出した通念にとらわれない、いきいきとした発想である。

将来を語（か）けようとした分野が、デザインとしては認められていないのにも驚き、早速、個人の嗜好（このみ）にも左右されているから、そこに大きな可能性も感じるがゆえに、危険な落とし穴があるのも確かだが、衣服は、二十四時間の人間の自己表現の道具としては皮膚にさえ帰するものだと思ってきた。

今、僕の頭を去来するのは、励ましつづけてくれた友人達と、みごとなチームワークを作りつづけてきたと考えている。いま、生きている証に服を作りつづけようとも考えている。スタッフ達のほほえみだ。

実は、私は、この賞を意識していた。ただ、この賞のみは欲しいと思っていた。正直にいってしまう。日本に帰って七年、その七年は、僕に正直にいってしまってきたことを、衣服とは何なのか、その意味を求め、いら立つ日々の連続だった。

事務局および文化出版局の今井田氏にこの点を疑うる結果、よ、うやくファッションは、特異な存在としてイスをもらったばか。果たして、それが衣服デザ帰するものだと思ってきた。

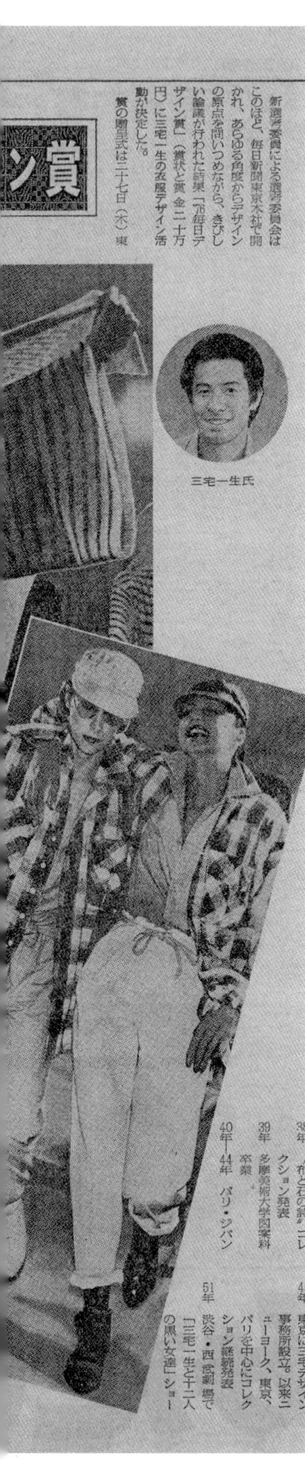

新選考委員会による選考委員会は
このほど、毎日新聞東京本社で開
かれ、あらゆる角度からデザイン
の原点を問いつめながら、きびし
い論議が行われた結果「76毎日デ
ザイン賞」（賞状と賞金二十万
円）に三宅一生の衣服デザイン活
動が決定した。
賞の贈呈式は二十七日（木）東

三宅一生氏

38年 "布と石の祭" コレ
クション発表
39年 多摩美術大学図案科
卒業
40年—44年 パリ・ジバン
38年 現在に三宅デザイン
事務所設立。以来ニ
ューヨーク、東京、
パリを中心にコレク
ション継続発表
51年 渋谷・西武劇場で
「三宅一生と十二人
の黒い女達」ショー

Page 75: *Invitation to the Autumn-Winter 1977 Paris Collection*

This was the first Paris Collection invitation designed by Tadanori Yokoo for ISSEY MIYAKE. The work *Chakra* (1974) was printed to nonwoven fabric. Yokoo continues to provide art direction for the Paris Collection invitations twice each year, and the format and size remain the same.
Design: Tadanori Yokoo; 375 x 340 mm

Essay titled **"Thinking on the Wild Side"** by architect Arata Isozaki, published in the January 26, 1977 edition of the *Mainichi Shimbun*

The removal of the word "industrial" from the "Industrial Design Award" marks a decisive transformation. Design today is expanding in all directions and covering every visual aspect of contemporary civilization. That is why Issey Miyake's work in clothing design was selected for this year's prize.

For the past several years, Issey Miyake's work has resembled more of a cultural incident. His clothing design has rocked not only the world of fashion, but many other areas of design as well. At the risk of overstatement, he has shown us how to blast through the stagnation that has become entrenched in the structures of modern design.

Miyake has consistently displayed an attitude of returning to the basics and re-examining what it means to wear clothes. He has caused us to think once again about the fact that clothing is one piece of cloth that wraps around moving bodies.

We should also note the completely new show that he has developed to present this work. This is not your ordinary fashion show, but a completely new style in which he communicates his ideas in sharp, energetic movements and the merger of the clothing and the body into a single whole.

Throughout Miyake's work there has been a consistent "wild thinking" that is not fettered by the systems and institutions of modernity. This is more than simply an individual closed off in his own world of design. Miyake has shown the flexibility to be able to move in the open, as can be seen in his development of new materials. More than anything else, however, it was the uniqueness of his work and his global prominence in the world of fashion that led to the prize. At the same time, his designs are making their way into a broad range of activities and areas, and we think that they will continue to exert significant influence on the world of design. (Paraphrased translation)

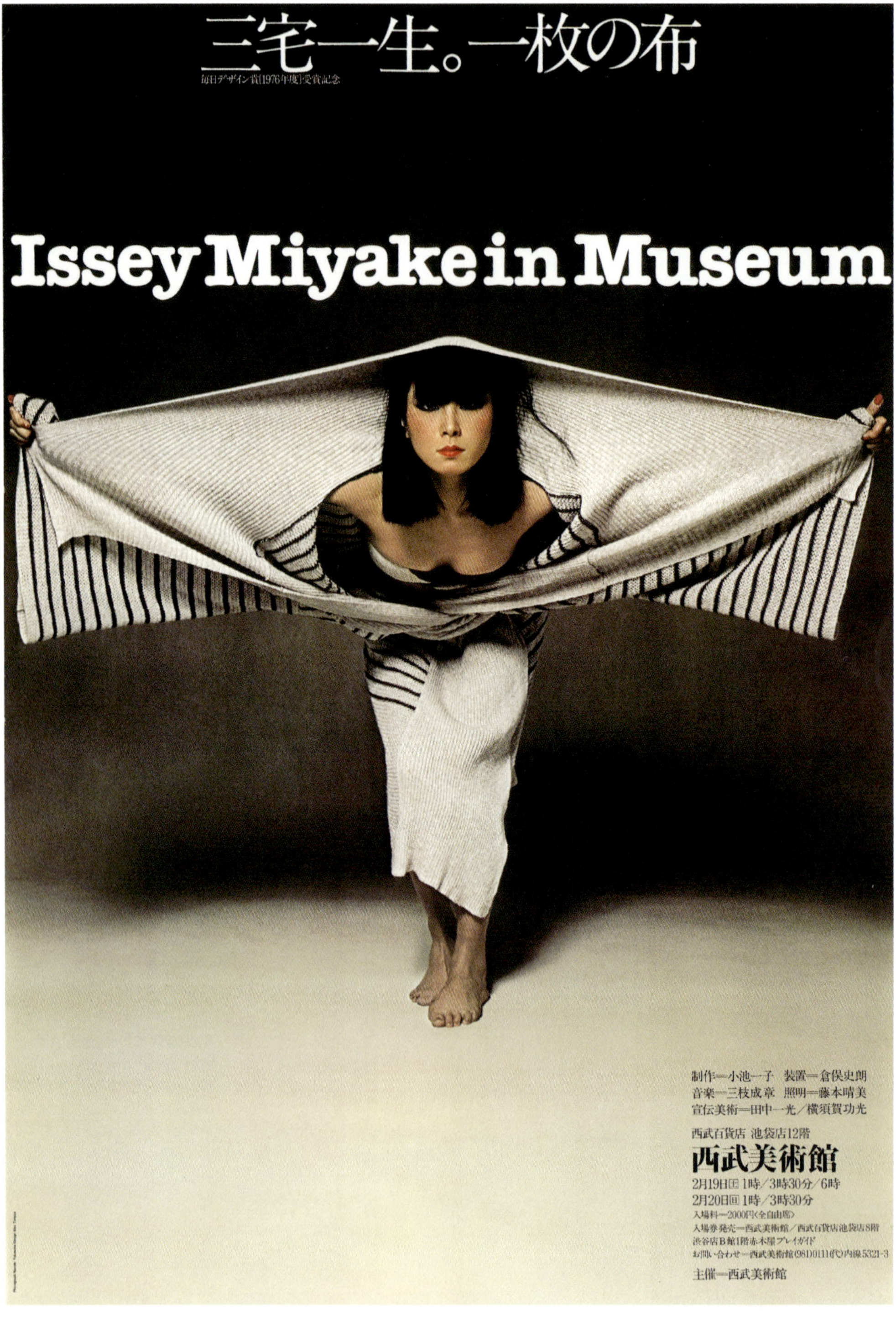

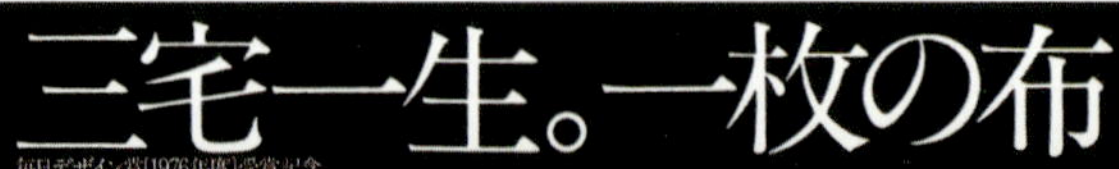
三宅一生。一枚の布
毎日デザイン賞[1976年度]受賞記念
Issey Miyake in Museum
制作＝小池一子　装置＝倉俣史朗
音楽＝三枝成章　照明＝藤本晴美
宣伝美術＝田中一光／横須賀功光
西武百貨店 池袋店12階
西武美術館
2月19日田 1時／3時30分／6時
2月20日回 1時／3時30分
入場料＝2000円〈全自由席〉
入場券 発売＝西武美術館／西武百貨店池袋店8階
渋谷店B館1階赤木屋プレイガイド
お問い合わせ＝西武美術館(980)0111(代)内線5321-3
主催＝西武美術館

Opposite: Poster for **A Piece of Cloth – Issey Miyake in Museum**, a show to commemorate the Mainichi Design Awards
The show featured the Spring-Summer 1977 Collection, including *A Piece of Cloth* cotton-linen knit coat used in the poster; and the *Paradise Lost* print design by Tadanori Yokoo.
Art direction: Ikko Tanaka; photography: Noriaki Yokosuka; model: Sayoko Yamaguchi

Fly with Issey Miyake

This was the third year of shows sponsored by Parco and open to the general public. It was held with production cooperation from Asahi Kasei Corporation and featured its "Pewlon" material, which made its appearance in the Miyake collections in 1974. The Autumn-Winter 1977 Collection was shown on a 45-meter-long cross-shaped stage. "In a word, it left me with the same excitement as seeing a very good performance of a very good musical." (Aromu Mushiake, *Sports Nippon*, July 13, 1977 edition)

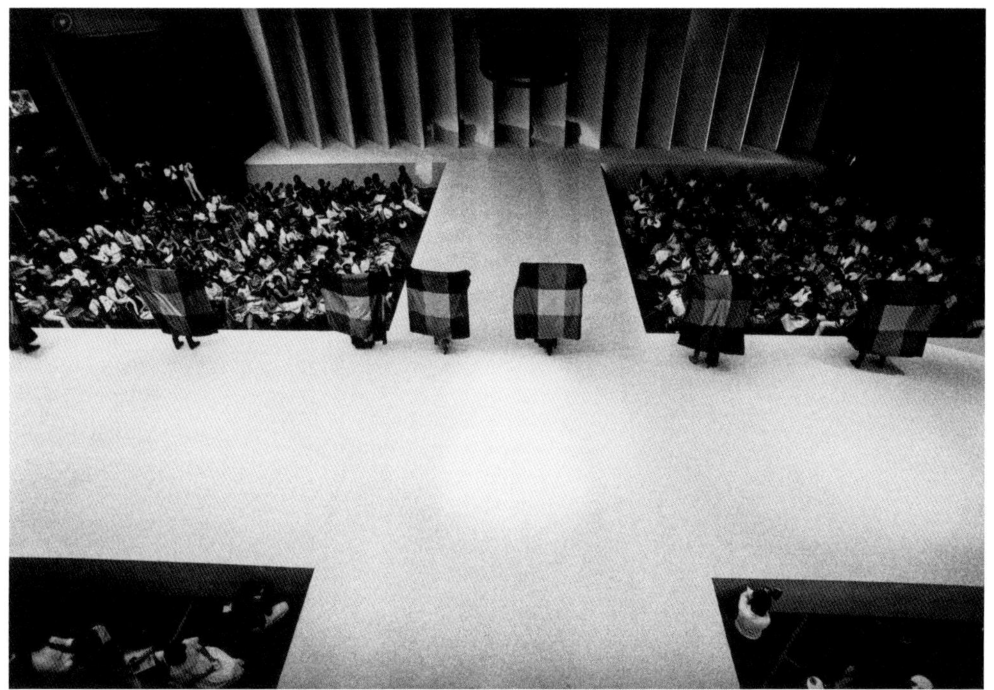

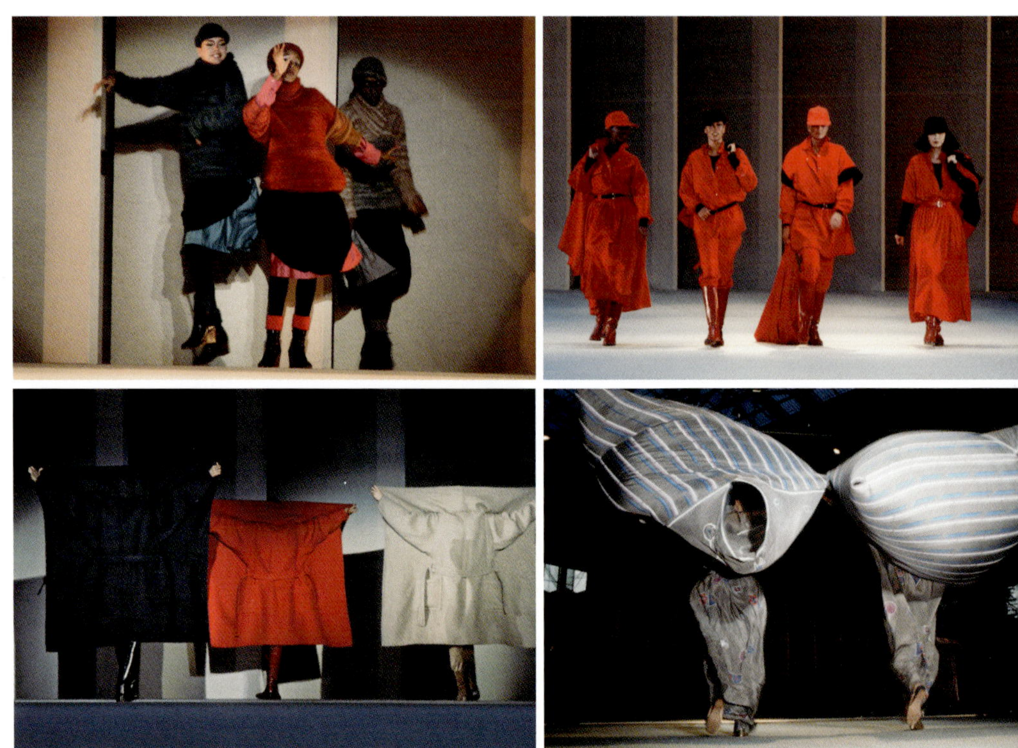

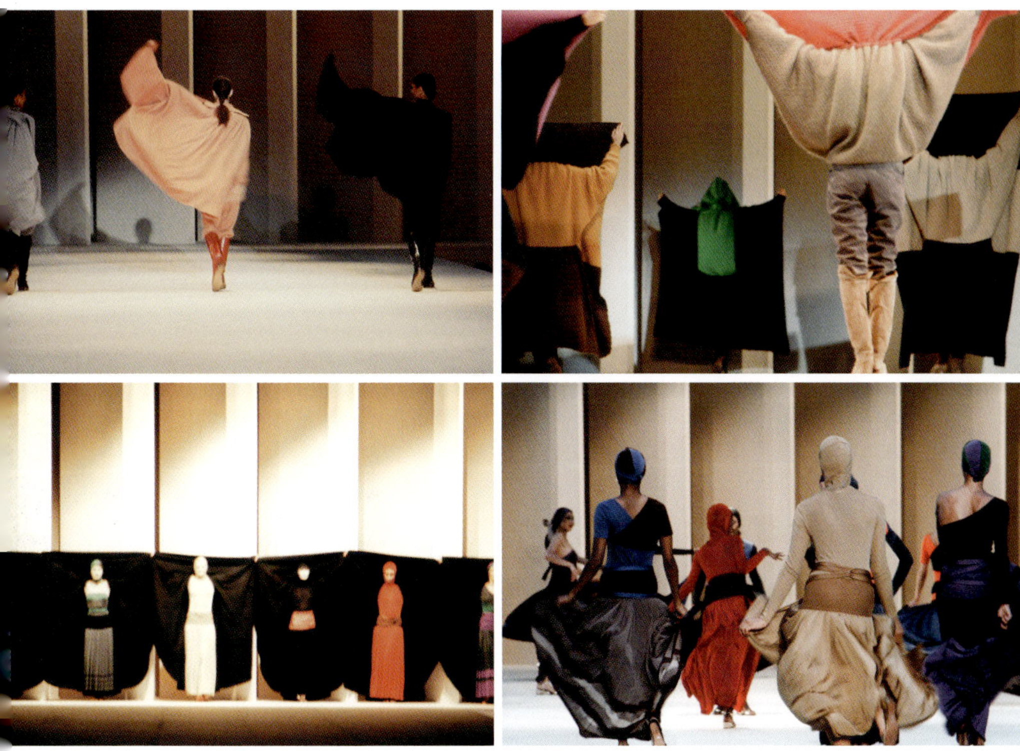

Page 79: From the **Fly with Issey Miyake** show
The show was held a total of five times, at the
Meiji Jingu Indoor Field on July 5–6, and at the Kyoto
Prefectural Gymnasium on July 9. Approximately
22,000 people attended.
Production: Tsuji Masuda; concept and direction:
Eiko Ishioka and Tomio Mohri; music: Yasohachi Ito
and Kiyoshi Ito; lighting: Harumi Fujimoto; audio:
Yoichi Yamanaka; stage director: Hisashi Akasaka;
hair and makeup: Sachiko Kawabe and Masayoshi
Otake; models: Bethann Hardison, Johna Johnson,
Susie Dyson, Sara Kapp, Toukie Smith, Ela Gerard,
Sayoko Yamaguchi, Atsuko Oka, Haruka Asami,
Rima Vetter, Iman, Masae Kawami, Peggy Dillard,
Seiko Ban, and Debbie Dickinson

From the **Fly with Issey Miyake** show
Top row from left: knit and cotton shirt with
two-colored skirt, thick twill wool series in red,
double-face cotton coat and jumpsuit, and *A Piece
of Cloth Knit* in wool
Bottom row from left: *Square-cut coat* in reversible
wool, *Spinnaker* with print design by Tadanori Yokoo,
"Pewlon" knit top and skirt with round wool coat,
"Pewlon" knit top and skirt
All designed in 1977 and included in the
Autumn-Winter 1977 Collection
Photography: Sachiko Kuru

1978

Issey Miyake East Meets West

Planned, organized, and edited by Ikko Tanaka and Kazuko Koike in honor of the Mainichi Design Awards. Contains an overview of Issey Miyake's work during the 1970s, including *A Piece of Cloth* and his exploration of new materials. The title was inspired by the Kipling poem and reflects Miyake's philosophy that clothing is universal.

Opposite: The book **Issey Miyake East Meets West**, Heibonsha Limited
Clothing on the front cover and right: "Pewlon" knit hooded shirt and skirt. 1977 design/Autumn-Winter 1977 Collection
Back cover clothing: *Paradise Lost* silk dress and coat. Print design by Tadanori Yokoo. 1976 design/Spring-Summer 1977 Collection
Art direction: Ikko Tanaka; book design: Ikko Tanaka and Kenichi Samura; cover photography: Noriaki Yokosuka; model: Iman; book photography: Yasuaki Yoshinaga

1 Autumn-Winter 1978 Paris Collection, April 8, Salle Wagram
2 Spring-Summer 1979 Paris Collection, October 21, Salle Wagram

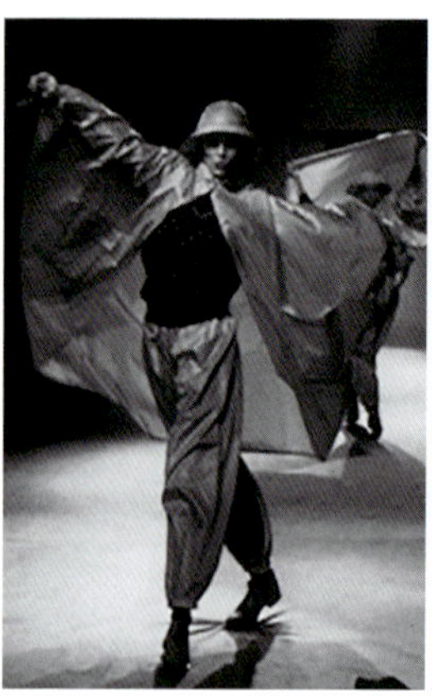
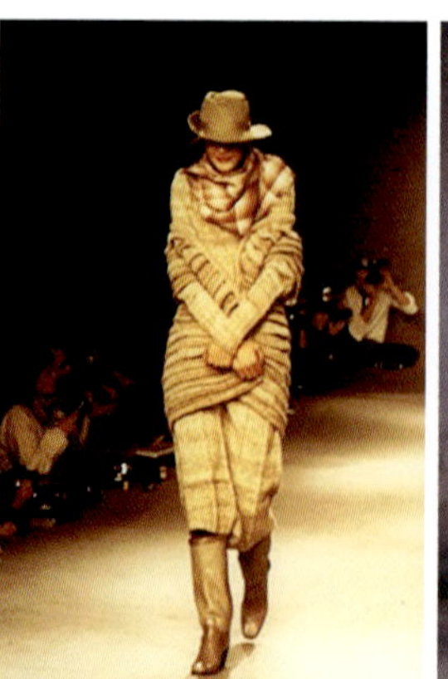
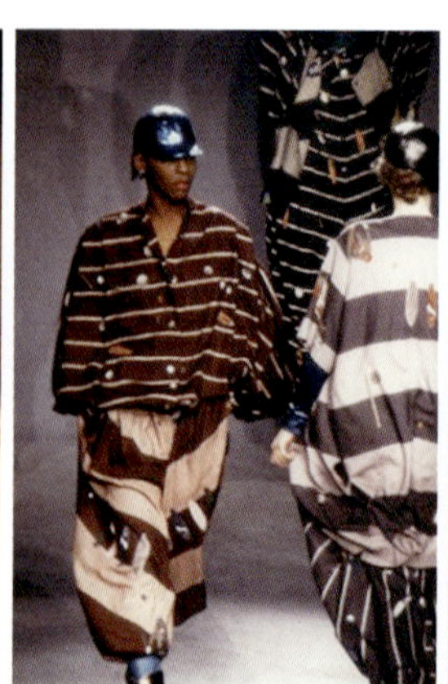
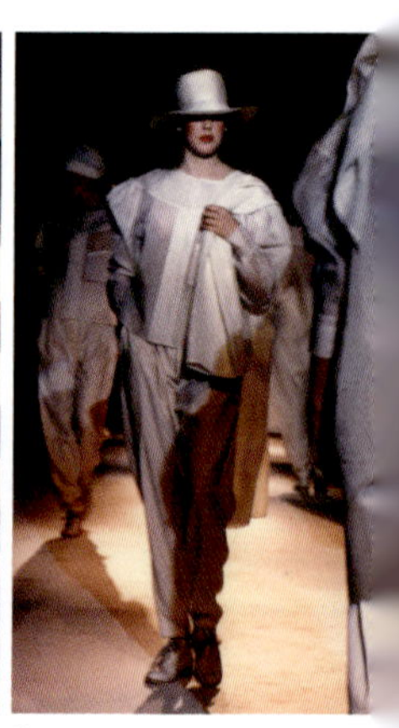

1

2

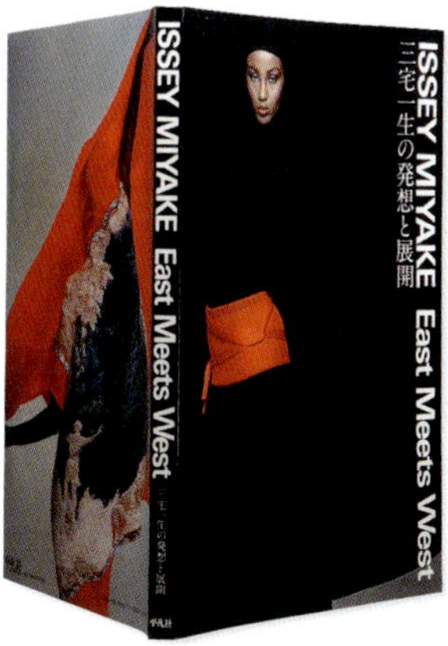

ISSEY MIYAKE East Meets West
三宅一生の発想と展開

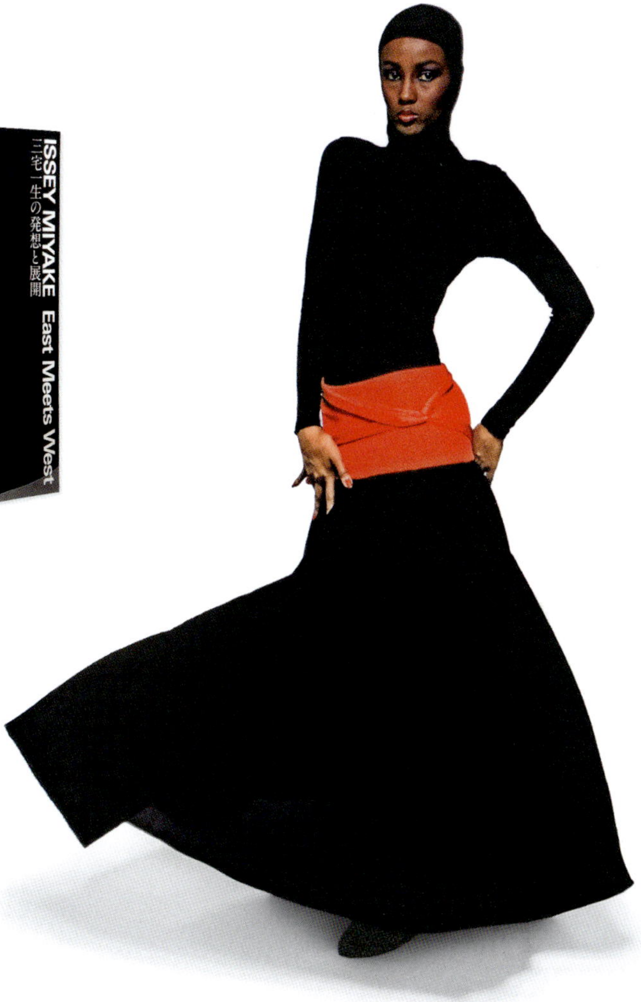

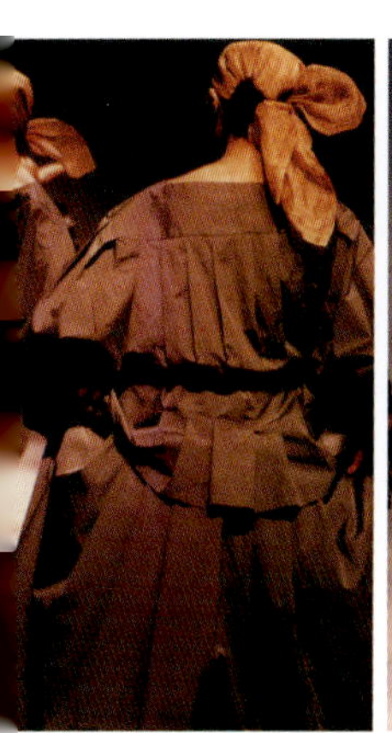
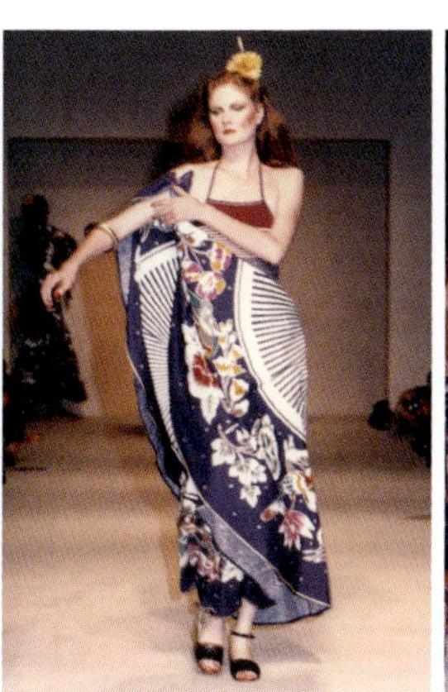
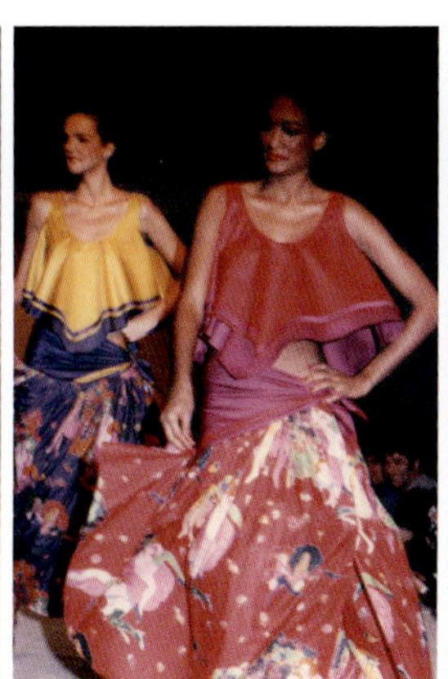
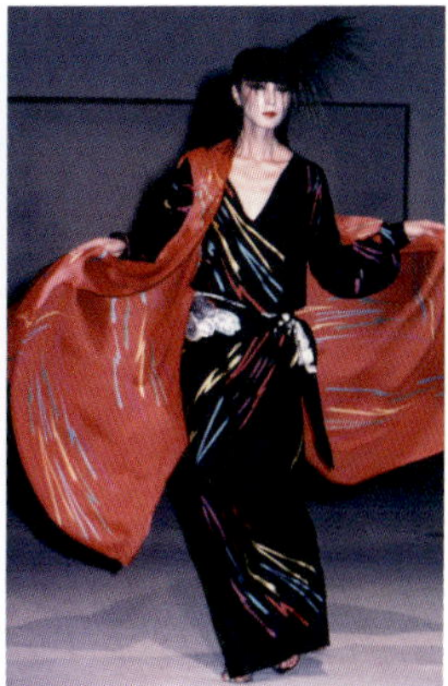

1979

> March: Autumn-Winter 1979 Milan Collection at Palazzo della Permanente
> April: Autumn-Winter 1979 Paris Collection at Salle Molière, Forum des Halles
> April: ISSEY MIYAKE flagship store opened on Boulevard Saint-Germain, Paris
> June: Invited as guest speaker to the International Design Conference in Aspen
> October: Spring-Summer 1980 Milan Collection at Palazzo della Permanente
> October: Spring-Summer 1980 Paris Collection at Salle Saint-Eustache, Forum des Halles
> October: Designed the logo for im ISSEY MIYAKE, a project for collaborating with multiple companies on product design and development
> November–February 1980: *Les Tissus Imprimés d'Issey Miyake* exhibition at Musée de l'Impression sur Étoffes de Mulhouse

International Design Conference in Aspen

Invited to the International Design Conference in Aspen for its theme of "Japan in Aspen: The Synthesis of Contradictions." Held a lecture-style show called *Issey Miyake East Meets West* as a workshop for the final day. Chairman Lou Dorfsman and other designers, scholars, and conference participants were enlisted as models.

June 17–22: Aspen, USA

Les Tissus Imprimés d'Issey Miyake exhibition

This exhibition was put together after Jacqueline Jacqué, the Director of the Musée de l'Impression sur Étoffes de Mulhouse, and assistant curator Miss De Bruignac saw ISSEY MIYAKE print clothing in a magazine. Print textiles and clothes designed by Issey Miyake from 1970 to 1979 were exhibited in a cathedral-ceilinged space.

November 29–February 24, 1980: Musée de l'Impression sur Étoffes de Mulhouse, France

1 Autumn-Winter 1979 Paris Collection, April 7, Salle Molière, Forum des Halles
2 Spring-Summer 1980 Paris Collection, October 13, Salle Saint-Eustache, Forum des Halles

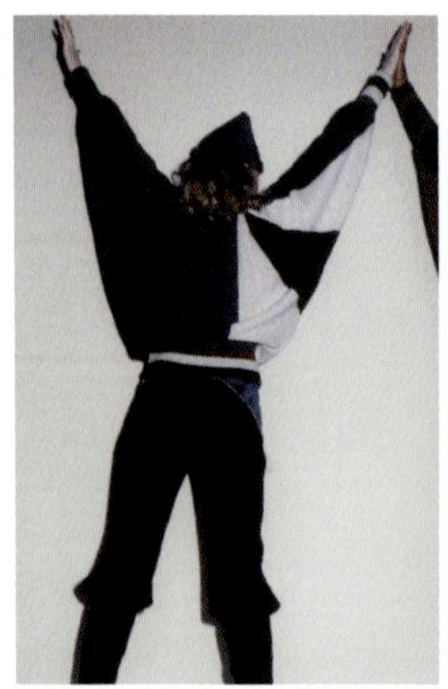
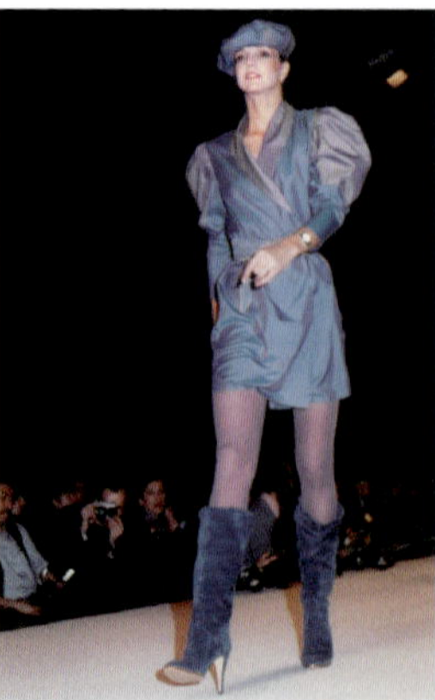
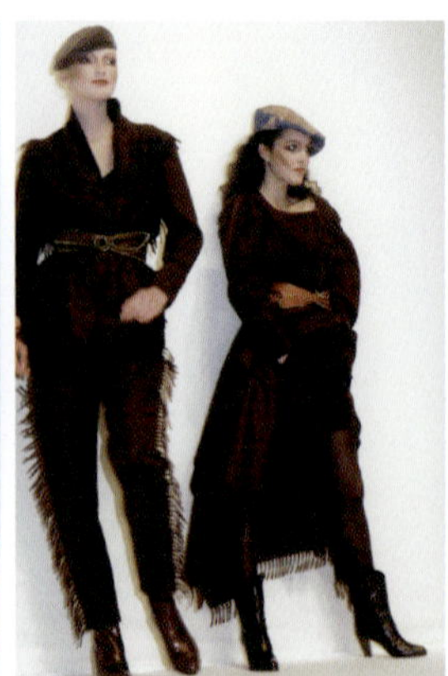
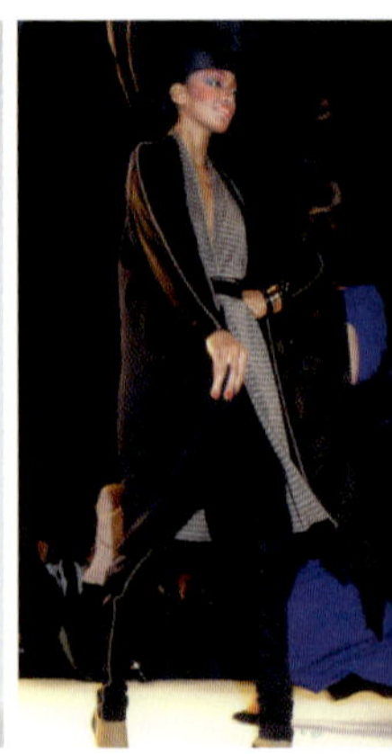

1

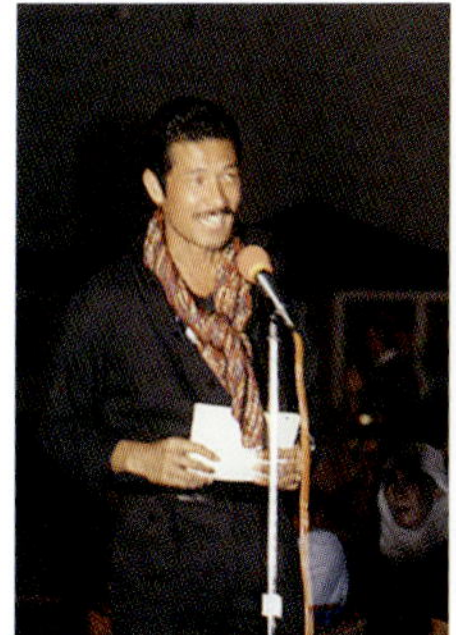
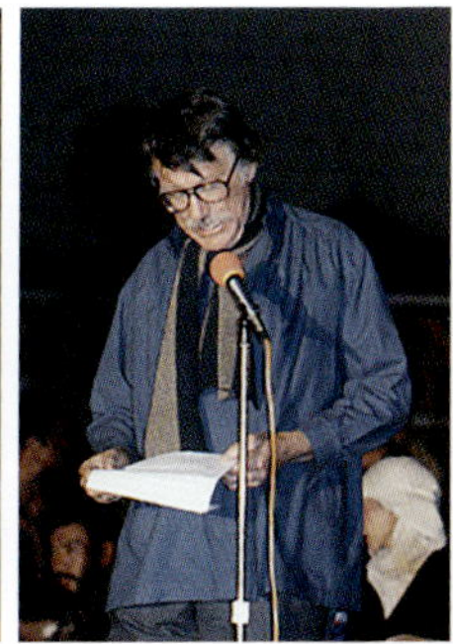
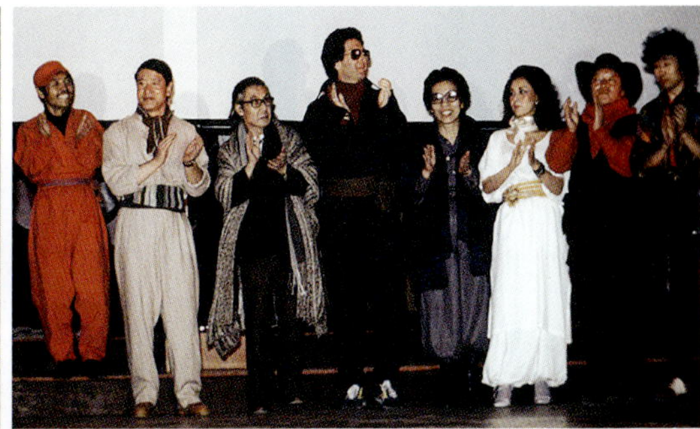
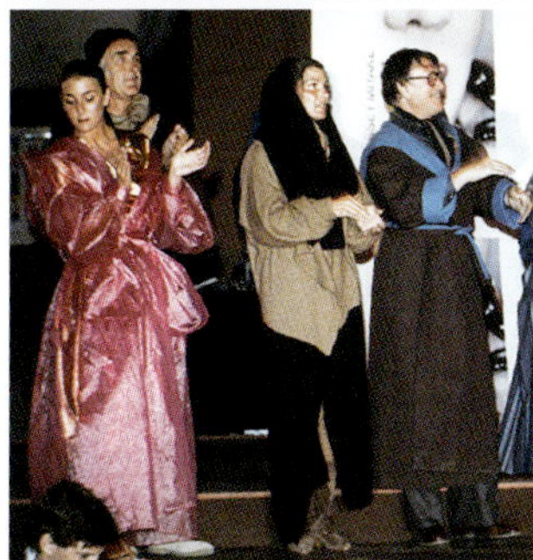
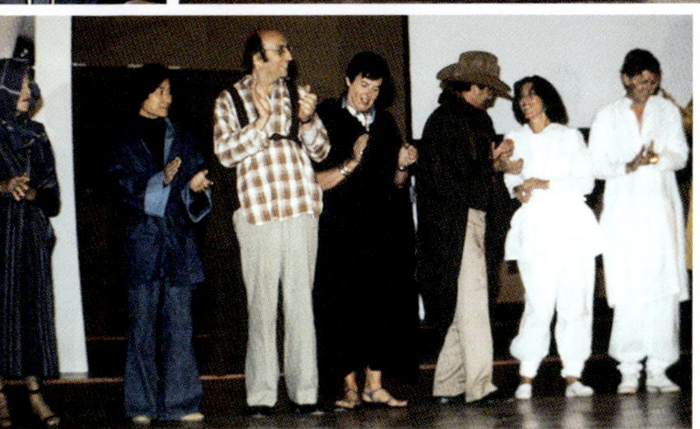

The finale from the show at the International Design Conference in Aspen. **Top left to right:** Issey Miyake, Lou Dorfsman, Toshihiro Katayama, Kazumasa Nagai, Masaru Katsumi, Michael Ross, Tsune Sesoko, Miyoko Urushibara, Ikko Tanaka, Tadanori Yokoo; **center left to right:** Lisa Farson, Richard and Dawn Farson, Lou Dorfsman, Madame Pepque, Kisho Kurokawa, Milton Glaser, Jane Thompson, Henry Wolff, Myrna Davis, Paul Davis; **bottom left to right:** Brian Bingham, Kiyoshi Awazu, Eiko Ishioka, Karen L. Otter, Shinya Izumi, anonymous person, Chieko Izumi, Jun Kanai, Kiyoshi Kanai. Photography: Grafton M. Smith

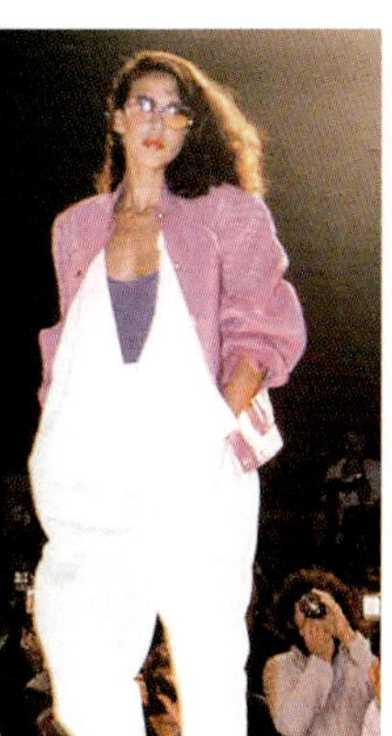
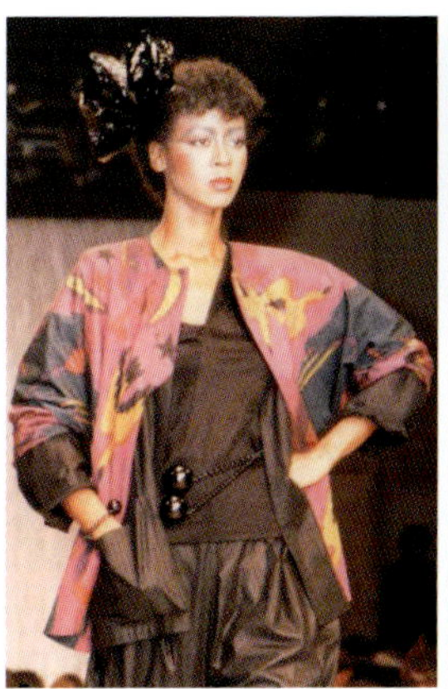
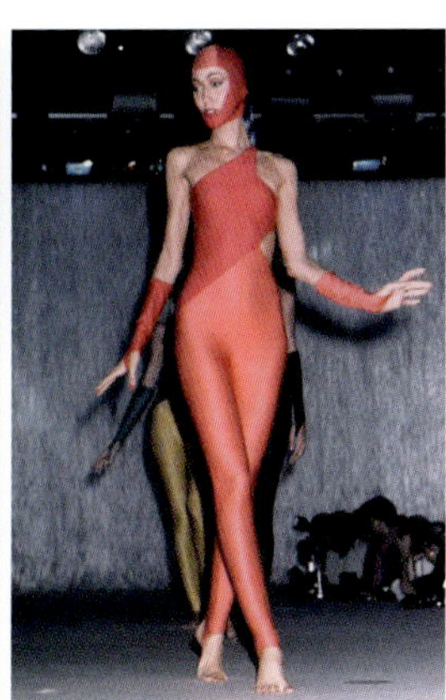
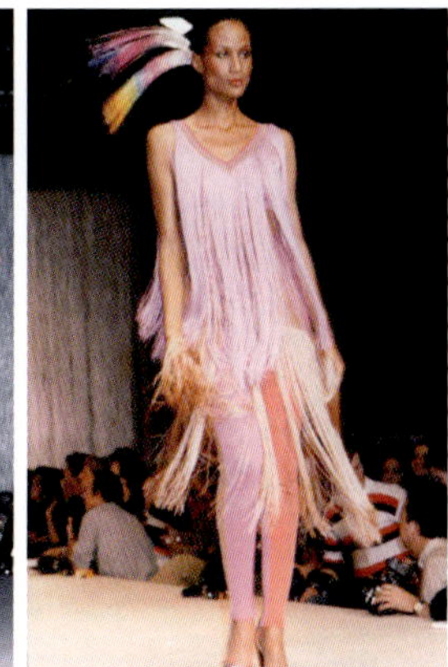

4—IN THE MAINSTREAM OF ART

Essay by
KAZUKO KOIKE

FROM EXPERIMENT TO APPLICATION

"There are no boundaries for what can be fabric, for what clothes can be made from. Anything can be clothing," said Miyake.[1]

In the 1980s, his interest in exploring new ideas increased dramatically and what have been referred to as Miyake's experiments in clothing went from the runway to the streets. This movement reflected that Japan was experiencing the emergence of mature consumers after the economic boom years.

There was a particular piece that was dubbed the *Plastic Body* by European and American journalists and which grabbed the world's attention.[2] The design office of Nanasai Co., Ltd., a company that made the mannequins that are indispensable to selling clothes, had found a way of molding plastic for the body, making it possible to fit the mold directly onto a woman's upper torso, providing coverage from her breasts to her hips. Miyake oversaw the final form and color design. The piece also has an aspect of functioning as a jewelry-like adornment of the body. But this piece – an *objet d'art* – was epoch-making in its subversion of the concept of clothing up to the 20th century.

But I would also like to draw attention to the fact that this was clothing that did not go through the usual process of cutting and sewing fabric, and that this methodology has been developed in subsequent collections, including the latest. Traditional materials such as *washi* (Japanese paper) are still being used and made into products, but this body-piece can be understood as a precursor to the innovative directions that have tapped the capabilities of new materials and technologies.

I would also point to the fact that *Plastic Body* reveals a nude body that fits the figures of models of differing contours, and gives them the appearance of nudity. While it may not be clear how far the models themselves found pleasure in the double structure of wearing a plastic nude body upon their own flesh, this was a prop that enabled the wearer to become another person. This sensation brings to mind the artifice/reality conundrum of the masks that are used in the *Noh* theater. The actors' masks transform their appearance, making an audience believe that they are seeing a young woman or an aged one (actually being played by a male actor). Viewers are captivated by the magic of the staged illusion.

The Paris collections at that time were also interested in bustiers, as corsets had resurfaced as a fashion item from within the context of ideas regarding the shape of the body in Western fashion history. But the piece created by Issey Miyake was inspired from wholly different origins. Whether he intended it or not, *Plastic Body* brims with an irony born in the Orient.

IN THE CITY OF ARTISTS

People who were connected to the arts in Paris understood Miyake's intentions in designing *Plastic Body*. "Paris is a place where outstanding artistic expression occurs," was Miyake's simple explanation for showing his creations there. A natural development of this "Paris connection" was a request to design stage costumes from the director of the Ballet of the 20th Century, ballet master Maurice Béjart.[3] Miyake had long been a great admirer of Béjart. Working with Tomio Mohri,[4] he studied the requirements of stage and body movements meticulously, and the result was a wondrous spectacle.[5]

"Big" was a word that was often used in connection with fashion directions in the 1980s; it referred to the many voluminous dresses and coats that blurred the body's silhouette. Miyake is often spoken of as a trendsetter, but as in the case of the Japanese designers who followed him and began to participate in the Paris collections, such as Rei Kawakubo[6] and Yohji Yamamoto,[7] he too was a part of the favorable currents that seemed at the time to all have their source in Japan. Around that time, the press reported how "Miyake had prepared the way, and then appeared Yamamoto and Kawakubo." In terms of styling, "Big" was typified by a reverse pyramid shape, with strong shoulders, but Miyake's *Rattan Body*[8] (fabricated by Emi Fukuzawa[9] and Shochikudo Kosuge[10]), which was reminiscent of armor, had such creative force that the trend-watchers had no choice but to fall silent.

Rattan Body was chosen for the cover of *Artforum*, one of the leading art magazines of the time.[11] This particular issue looked at contemporary art's ability to influence the public, and the editors, Germano Celant[12] and Ingrid Sischy,[13] analyzed the meaning of Miyake's work:

Equivalences are created between carving and modeling, between rigidity and softness, between the natural and the painted-over, between representation and showing. The outfit is a charged mnemonic device representing event and cumulative information.
Artforum, February 1982

These two incisive critics of the isolation of art, and its tendency to conservatism, pursued fashion from the perspective that work from other art-related fields could open up the traditional arts; indeed, in 1996, they organized a major international fashion biennale in Florence.[14]

ORIGINS AND THE CONTEMPORARY

Miyake continued to seek out new starting points. Making contemporary clothes for Japan out of materials that were unique to the country was the mission which was entrusted to the Plantation brand.[15] Some of these were textiles that Miyake had seen long ago in Masako Shirasu's shop, *Kogei,* while some were contemporary fabrics from other regions around Japan, but the main theme was working clothes, farming clothes, everyday clothes. These garments had enriched the day-to-day lives of people, and it was this aesthetic that he wanted to express. The breadth and diversity of Miyake's activities in the 1980s made it possible for him to work simultaneously on the two polar opposites of Plantation and *Plastic Body*.

Plantation was presented in a renovated space in the former Shokuryo Building, on the banks of the Sumida River in Tokyo. Nearby, I had opened the Sagacho Exhibit Space, an alternative space for contemporary art, and Issey introduced us to Momix,[16] the American dance company that he had invited to Japan. Their performance showcased many kinds of everyday clothes – all familiar, yet all refreshingly new. What was cast into sharp relief was the diversity of Miyake's ideas, and the creative direction that he was exploring, combining familiar clothing with forward-looking values.

Miyake had asked Shiro Kuramata to create his boutique interiors from his earliest years, but the unique wall that Kuramata created for the 1984 renovation of the Saint-Germain shop in Paris astonished Miyake. The concrete-walled space was draped all over in fabric. As if in response, in his next collection, Miyake revealed a piece which fixed draping on bodies.[17] This sort of "call-and-response" interaction between these two astounding artists was a wonderful sight to observe. Likewise, Kuramata wrapped a chair in metal, and then burned it, leaving only the metal to indicate the chair;[18] Miyake responded with a wire-metal torso.[19] Looking at pieces like these, we can trace the trajectory of creative inspiration between these two close friends.

TRAVEL AND PEOPLE

Issey Miyake traveled not only for relaxation, but also for what he finds interesting, or what attracts his attention, and then returns to Japan with something completely unexpected. India is an example of a trip that yielded exquisite results. His encounter with the Sarabhai family[20] of Ahmedabad revealed the rich variety and potential of Indian textiles and led to a collaboration. A proposal by Mrs. Sarabhai resulted in the Asha[21] brand, which utilized the magnificent fabrics and crafts of India. These materials in themselves seemed to contain the essence of Indian lifestyle and aesthetics, as well as revealing the origins of *ikat* and tie-dyeing techniques. The latter were known in Japan as *kasuri* and *shibori*. That they could also be found in India was something that the Japanese had not been aware of. Makiko Minagawa's work demonstrated the elegance that could be achieved when contemporary Japanese design was applied to traditional Indian textiles and clothing. This and other projects laid the foundations for Miyake to be invited by the Indian government to take part in the 1985 exhibition *L'Or, la Laine et le Soie, Cotons et Plumes de Paon. Les Textiles de l'Inde et les Modèles Créés par Issey Miyake*[22] at the Musée des Arts Décoratifs in Paris.

There were also cases of exhibitions for which Miyake did not travel, but had an impact nonetheless. Under Seiji Tsutsumi,[23] the Seibu Museum of Art in Tokyo had been involved in cultural exchanges with the Soviet Union and organized an exhibition called *Japanese Design: Traditional and Modern*, to which Miyake contributed his contemporary clothing.

There are no more dramatic moments than when eyes that are uncertain confront things that they have never seen, and are then transformed by the beauty and vibrancy of these objects from Japan. I was asked to curate the show, and gazed at the faces of the women who were astonished by the freedom that they were seeing for the first time and that was expressed by the ways Miyake's clothes could be worn, and the innovativeness of the materials. It seemed possible, I felt, that clothing could trigger changes in perceptions of value, and I wished that I could inform Miyake himself about the response on the other side of the Iron Curtain.

1 From *Issey Miyake, Photographs by Irving Penn*, New York Graphic Society Books + Little, Brown and Company + Callaway Editions, USA; Edipresse-Livres SA, France and Switzerland; Edition Stemmle, Germany; and Libro Port Publishing Co., Ltd., Japan, 1988.

2 *Plastic Body*: See pp. 90–93.

3 Maurice Béjart (1927–2007): Choreographer. Formed the Ballet of the 20th Century in 1960. Relocated to Lausanne, Switzerland, in 1987. Renowned for his many philosophical, sensuous, and joyous works.

4 Tomio Mohri: Artist, designer of spaces. Former staff member at the Miyake Design Studio, set up his own office, and worked on sets and costume design for opera, ballet, Super *Kabuki*, *Noh*, and contemporary drama.

5 *Casta Diva* created by Maurice Béjart: See pp. 90, 93.

6 Rei Kawakubo (1942–): Fashion designer. Founded COMME des GARÇONS in 1969. Has shown at the Paris collections since 1981. Known for provocative clothes that allow freedom from conventional concepts.

7 Yohji Yamamoto (1943–): Fashion designer. Founded his brand, Y's, in 1969. Has shown at the Paris collections since 1981.

8 *Rattan Body*: See pp. 94–95, 100–101.

9 Emi Fukuzawa (1946–2013): Artist. Worked in painting, sculpture, jewelry design, shop design.

10 Shochikudo Kosuge (1921–2003): Bamboo craft artist.

11 *Artforum* cover: See pp. 100–101.

12 Germano Celant (1940–2020): Art critic and curator. Known for coining the Arte Povera movement. Has been active in writing and exhibition curation.

13 Ingrid Sischy (1952–2015): Editor. Started her career at *Artforum* in 1979, editor-in-chief of *Interview* magazine from 1990 to 2008. Worked as both writer and editor for numerous publications, including *The New York Times Magazine*.

14 The Florence Fashion Biennale. The inaugural biennale in 1996 featured the Fashion/Art exhibition, curated by Celant and Sischy. Issey Miyake works that were featured included pieces from his pleats series, and *PLEATS PLEASE ISSEY MIYAKE Guest Artist Series No. 1 Yasumasa Morimura:* See pp. 204–205.

15 Plantation: See pp. 94, 96–99, 104–105.

16 *Momix*: The choreographer and dancer Moses Pendleton's dance performance called *Momix* for the 1980 Lake Placid Winter Olympic Games was followed the next year by the establishment of a dance company that adopted this name. Continues to be active in performance, film, and television: See pp. 97–99.

17 *Waterfall Body*: See pp. 115–118.

18 *Homage to Josef Hoffmann, Begin the Beguine,* 1985, Shiro Kuramata.

19 *Wire Body*: See pp. 106–109.

20 Sarabhai: A family of industrialists based in Ahmedabad, India. Owners of companies such as Sarabhai Textiles, Calico Mills, Sarabhai Chemicals, and also noted for their contributions to the arts and charity, such as the operation of the Calico Museum of Textiles.

21 Asha by MDS: See p. 114.

22 *L'Or, la Laine et le Soie, Cotons et Plumes de Paon. Les Textiles de l'Inde et les Modèles Créés par Issey Miyake* exhibition: See pp. 120, 126–127.

23 Seiji Tsutsumi (1927–2013): Businessman and head of organizations such as the Saison Group. Also had a notable career as a writer and poet under the pen name Takashi Tsujii.

1980

Produced costumes for *Casta Diva*, a spectacle based upon a script by Maurice Béjart
- March–July: Participated in *The Japan Style* exhibition at the Victoria and Albert Museum, London
- March: Autumn-Winter 1980 Paris Collection at Salle Wagram
- April–June: Participated in organizing the *Evolution of Fashion 1835–1895* exhibition at The National Museum of Modern Art, Kyoto
- June: *Paris–Tokyo Issey Miyake Collection en Route 1980* show (Autumn-Winter 1980) at Shinagawa Prince Hotel
- October: Spring-Summer 1981 Paris Collection at Salle Vaugirard, Parc des Expositions

Casta Diva

The spectacle *Casta Diva*, with a script by Maurice Béjart, was performed at the IRCAM at the Centre Pompidou, Paris, from March 18 to April 5. Issey Miyake collaborated with Tomio Mohri on the costumes. Béjart acceded to Miyake's request and appeared on stage in costume.

"Miyake's mode dances. It's similar to the sixth sense that I find within myself. It is the swells of life, a deep harmony. ... People who wear Miyake's work change their appearance, but even still, it is not unusual for them to become exactly themselves the moment they put the clothing on. We experience a Dionysian joy when we are freed from conventions. It doesn't matter what that is, it is dance."

Maurice Béjart, Spazio *(Japan), No. 23, 1980*

Opposite: *Plastic Body*
The first work in the Body Series. Formed from glass fibers infused with polyester resin.
1980 design/Autumn-Winter 1980 Collection
Photography: Daniel Jouanneau

1 Autumn-Winter 1980 Paris Collection, March 29, Salle Wagram
2 Spring-Summer 1981 Paris Collection, October 18, Salle Vaugirard, Parc des Expositions

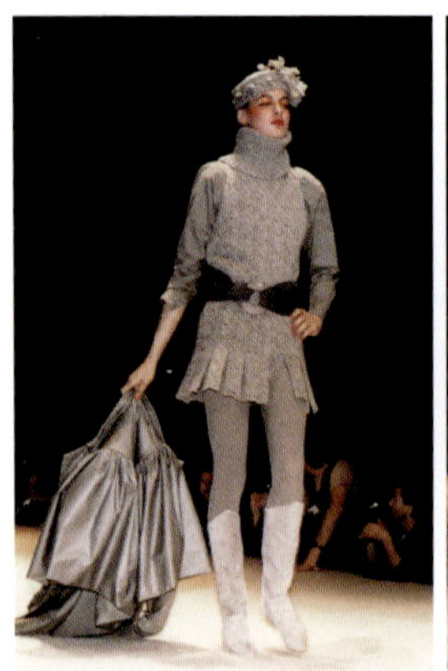
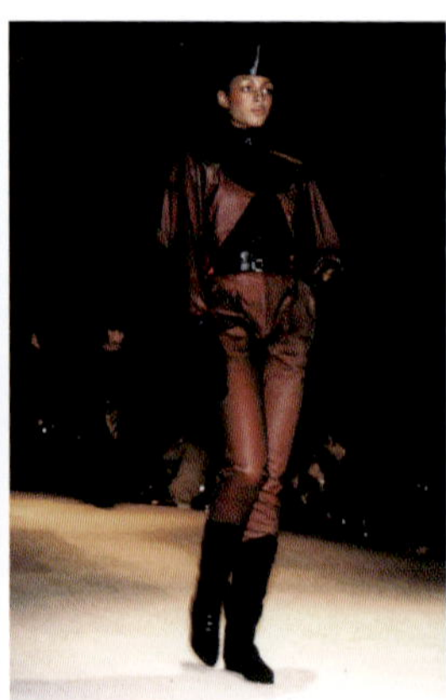
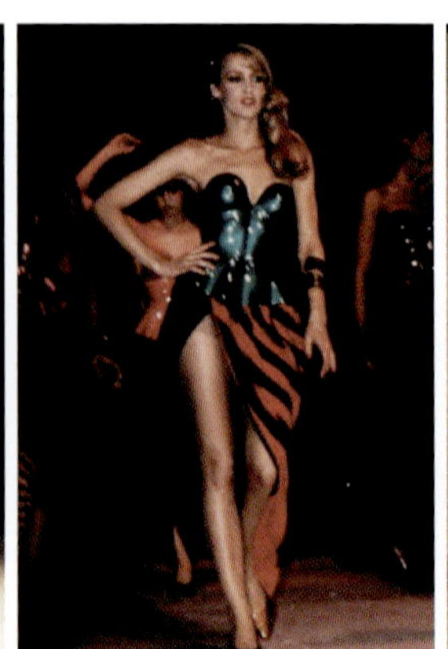
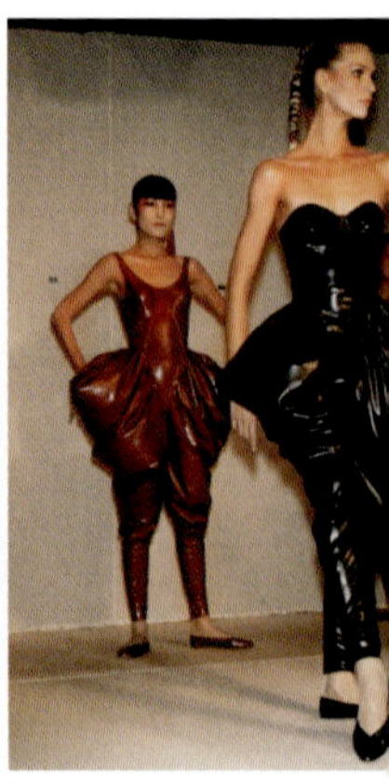

1

2

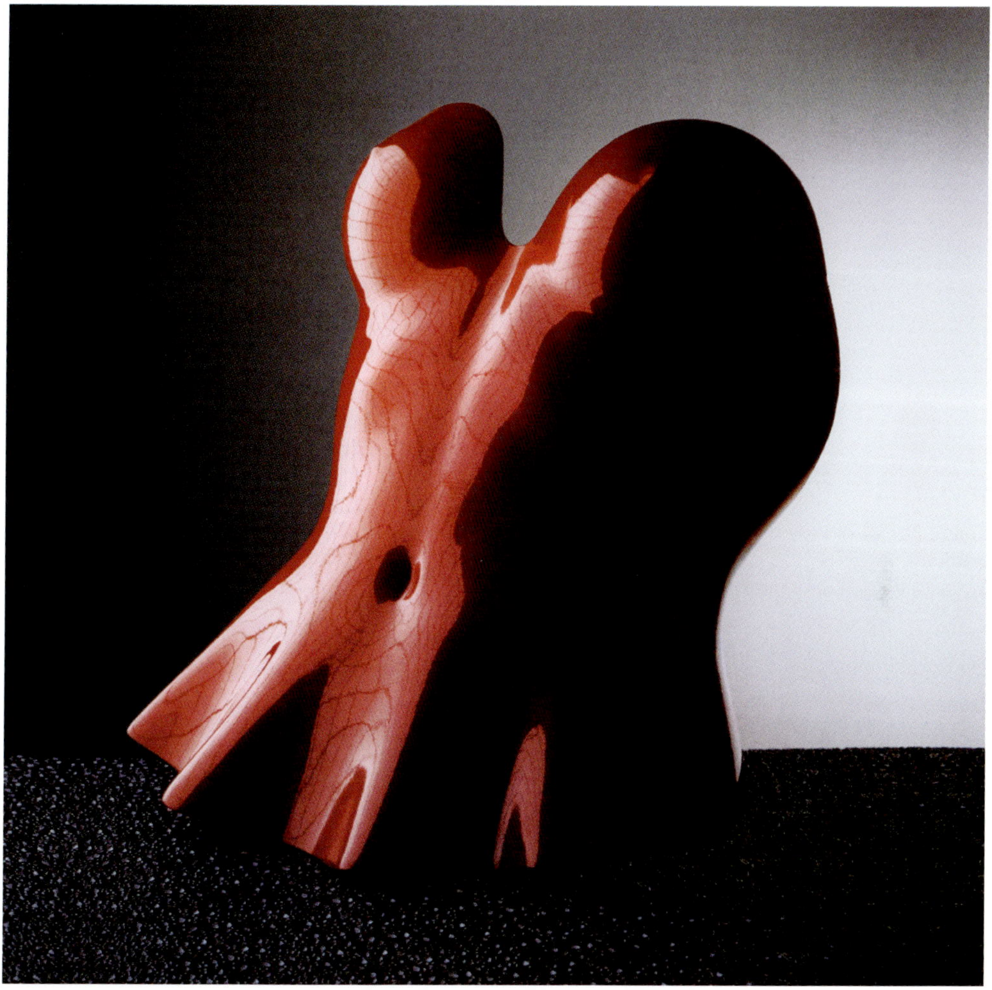

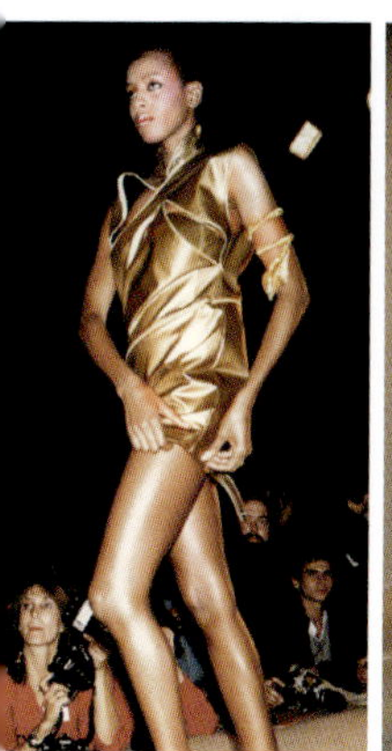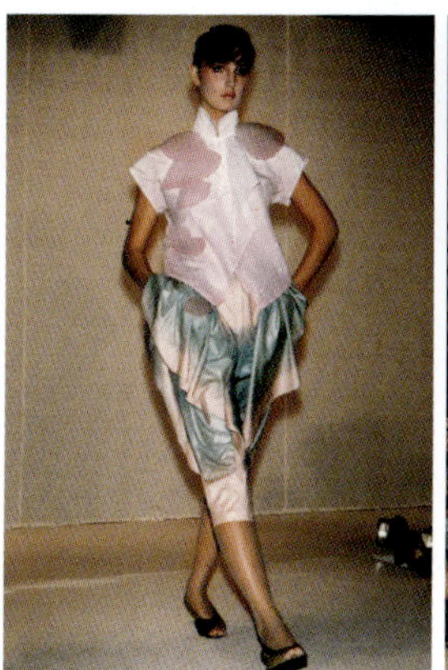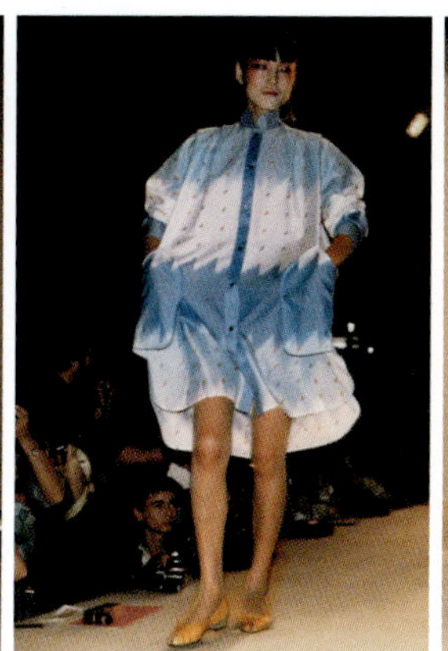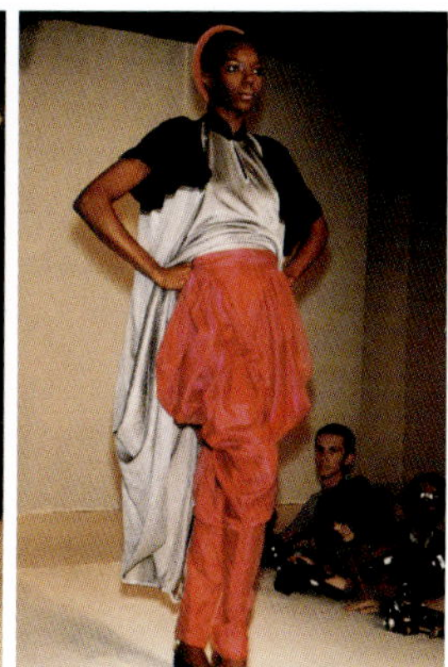

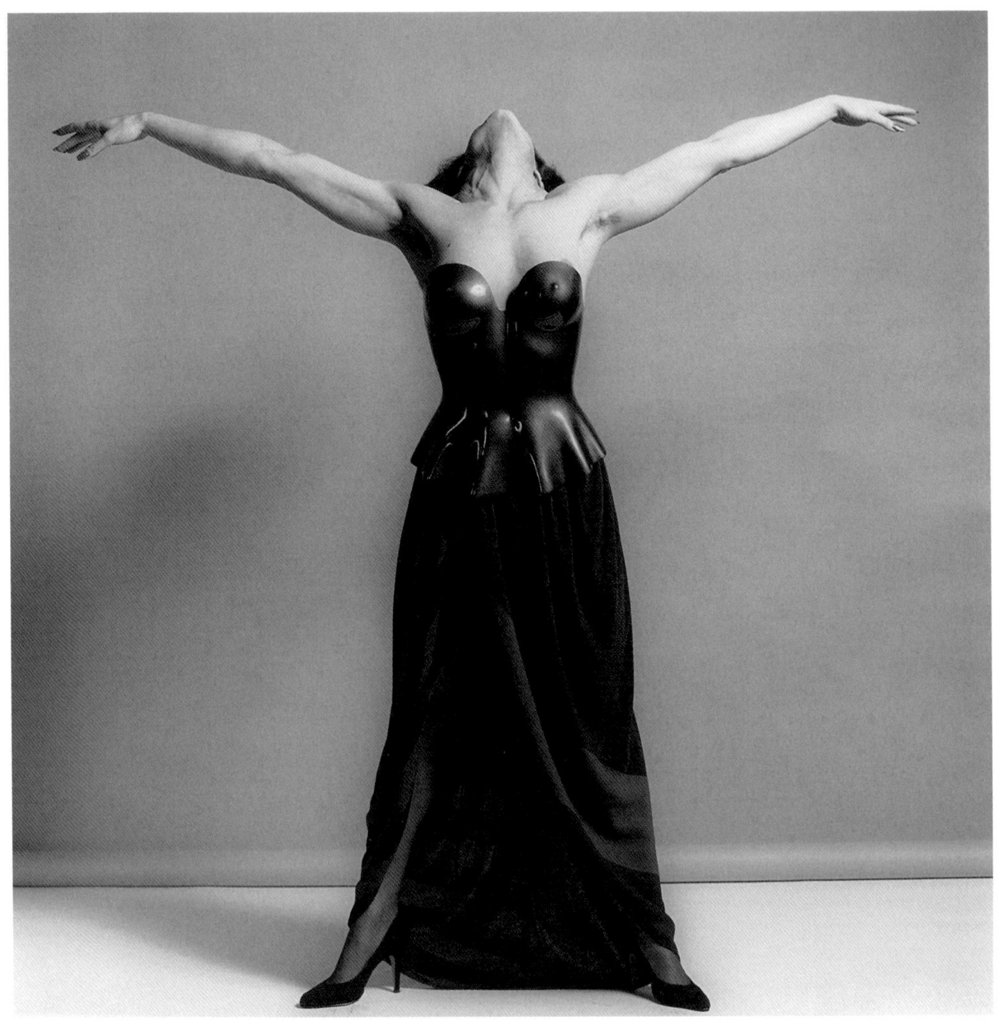

Lisa Lyon, 1982 © The Robert Mapplethorpe Foundation. Used by permission.

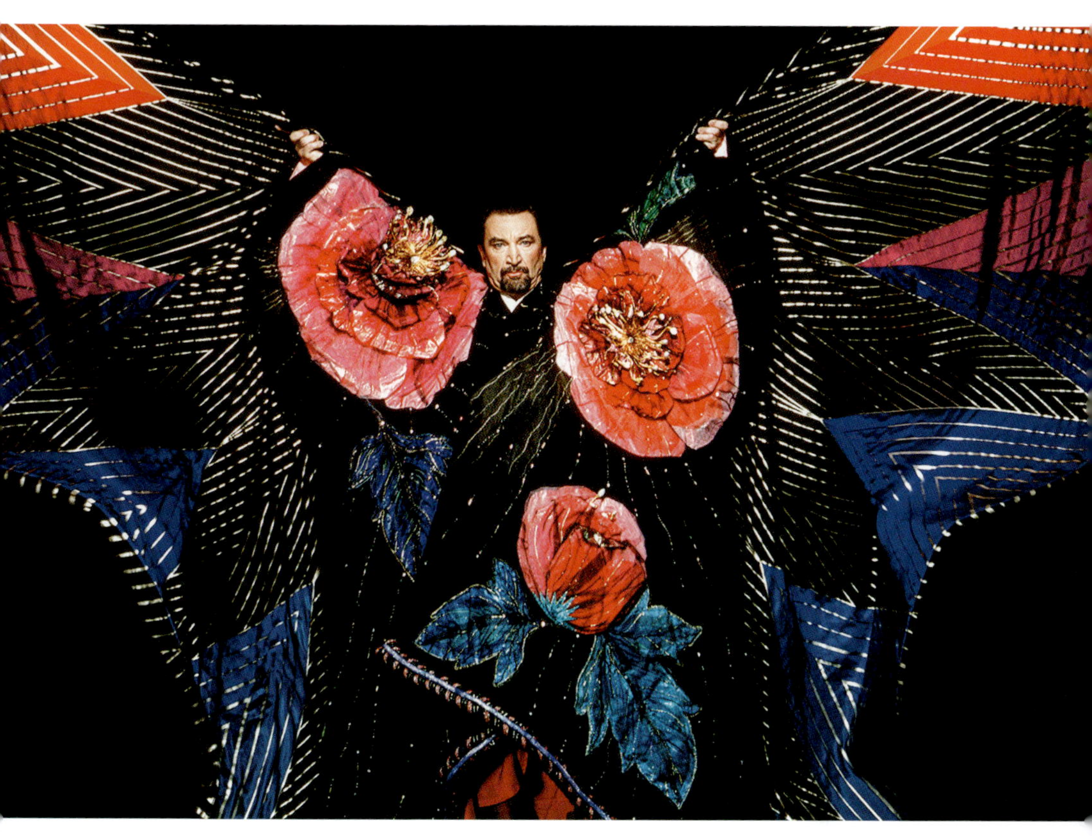

Opposite: ***Plastic Body*** worn by bodybuilder Lisa Lyon
Plastic Body and "Pewlon" wraparound skirt.
1980 design/Autumn-Winter 1980 Collection
This photograph was taken for an exhibition catalogue
called *Intimate Architecture: Contemporary Clothing
Design* that accompanied a 1982 exhibition at the
Hayden Gallery, at the Massachusetts Institute of
Technology. The exhibition used an innovative concept
to introduce the work of eight designers, each exploring
constructive form in contemporary clothes.
Photography: Robert Mapplethorpe; worn by: Lisa Lyon

Casta Diva costumes paid tribute to *Kabuki* costume
design techniques, which allow the hem to spread eight
meters long.
Photography: Kazumi Kurigami;
worn by: Maurice Béjart

1981

- January: *Issey Miyake It's so Neat* show at Meiji Jingu Indoor Field, Tokyo and Osaka Prefectural Gymnasium, Osaka (Spring-Summer 1981)
- April: Autumn-Winter 1981 Paris Collection at Salle Molière
- June: Autumn-Winter 1981 Tokyo Collection at Miyake Design Studio
- October: Spring-Summer 1982 Paris Collection at Salle Maillot
- October: Participated in *Japan Day Amsterdam 1981* at the invitation of the Art Directors Club Netherlands
- November: Participated in *The Best Six* at The Space in Tokyo
- November: Announced the Plantation brand
- Designed a uniform for Sony

Plantation

During the 1980s, the semiannual collections gradually became vehicles for showing more experimental ideas. Meanwhile, Miyake also introduced Plantation, a brand of natural, simple, ordinary clothes. The concepts were: "It's machine washable. Easy to care for. The idea is to use natural materials, mostly cotton. It develops more personality the more you wear it. Everything is done with flat-felled seams to make it stronger. Sizes are large enough to be worn by both men and women. It's multipurpose. Non-seasonal." From the start of his career, Miyake sought to create clothing that was comfortable and deferred to the person wearing it. Plantation provided him with a visual and tactile example of his view that clothes should be implements to be used in ordinary life.

Opposite: *Rattan Body*
This "body" was made from rattan and bamboo by bamboo craftsman Shochikudo Kosuge, with help from artist Emi Fukuzawa. 1981 design/Spring-Summer 1982 Collection
Photography: Daniel Jouanneau

Autumn-Winter 1981 Paris Collection, April 4, Salle Molière

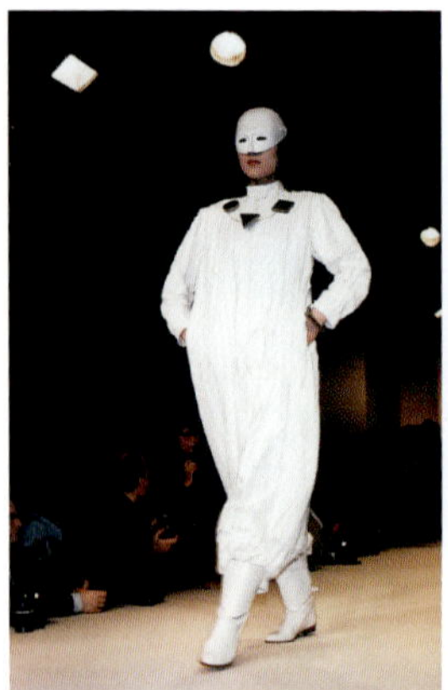
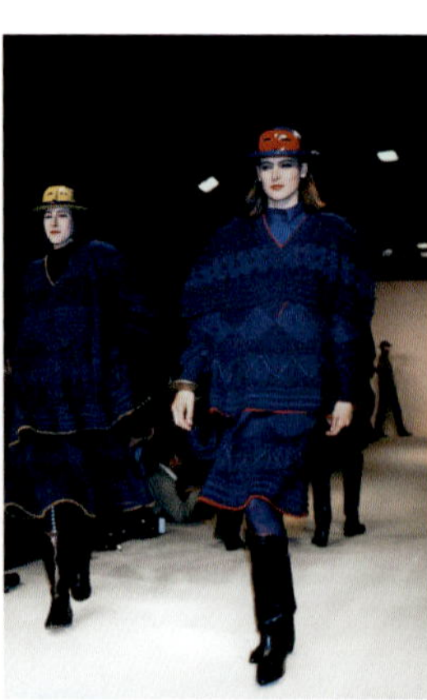
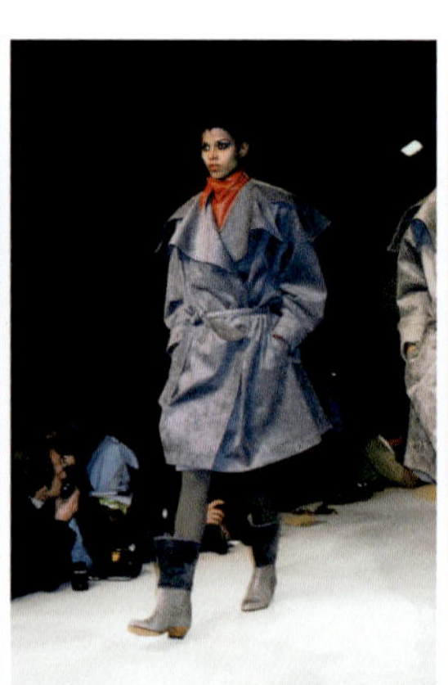
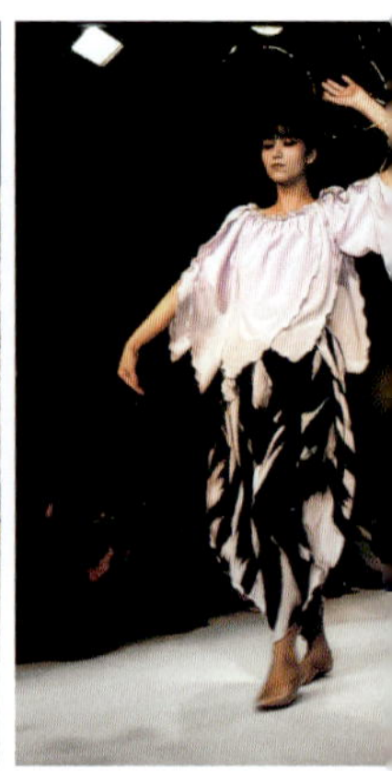

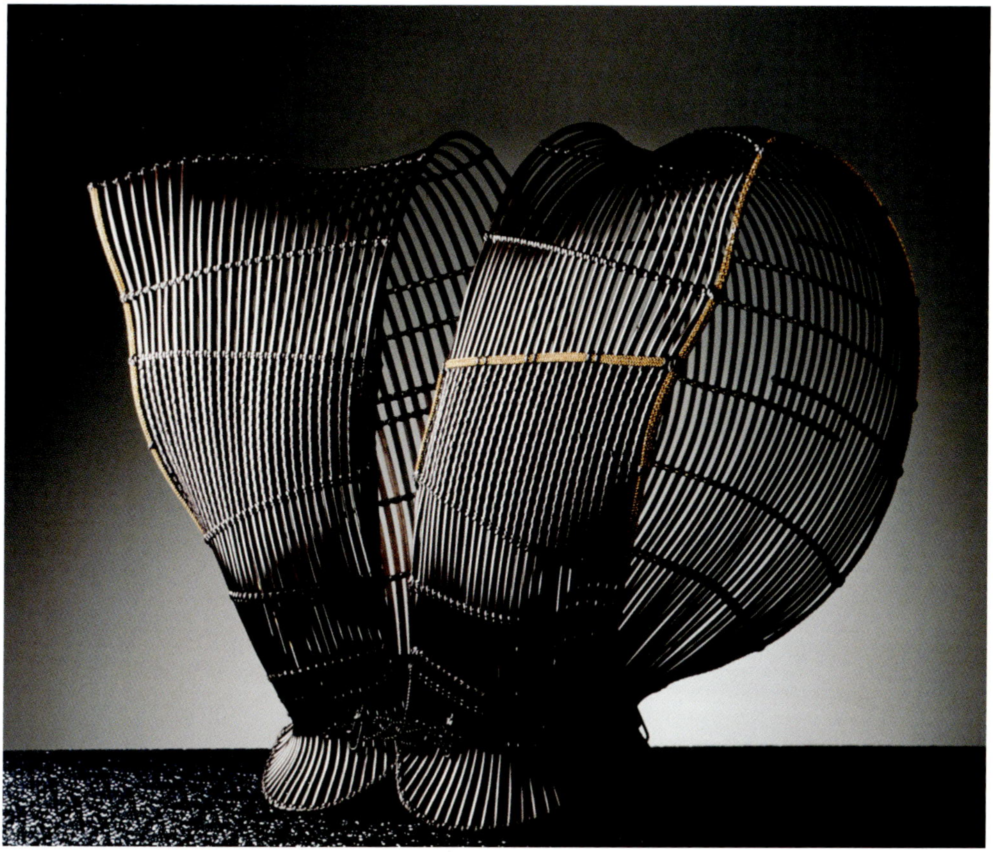

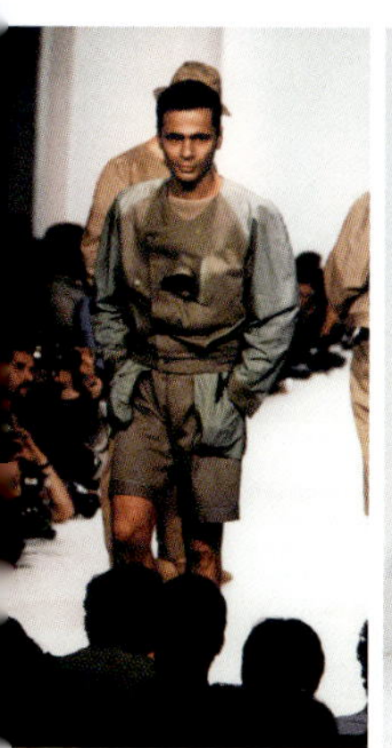

Spring-Summer 1982 Paris Collection,
October 17, Salle Maillot

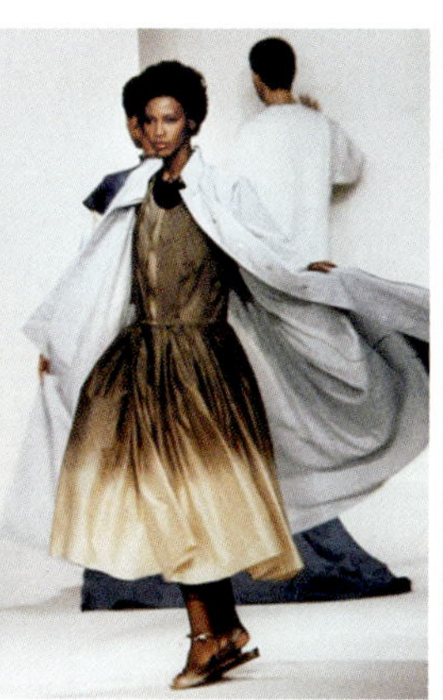
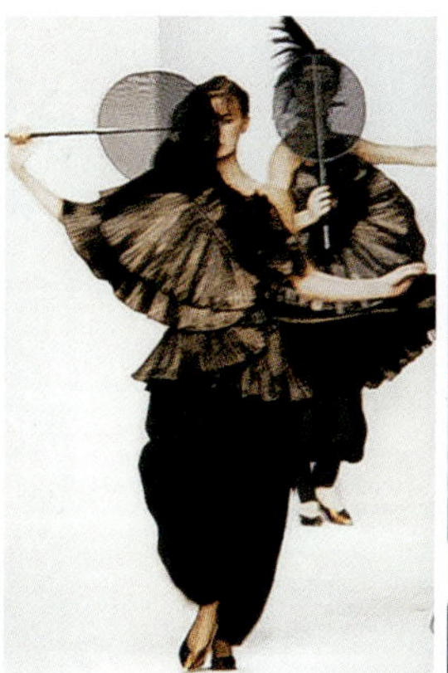
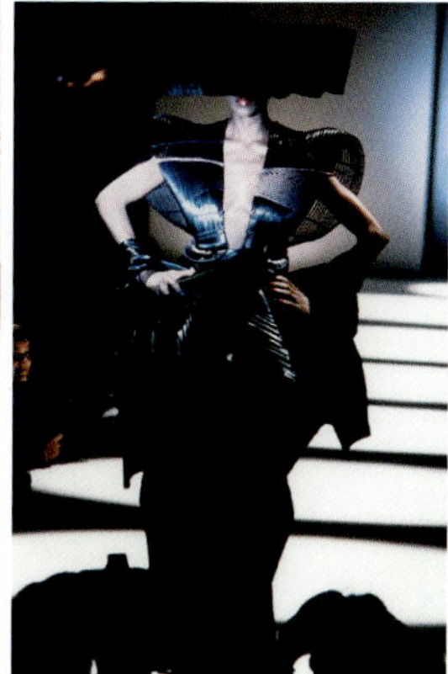

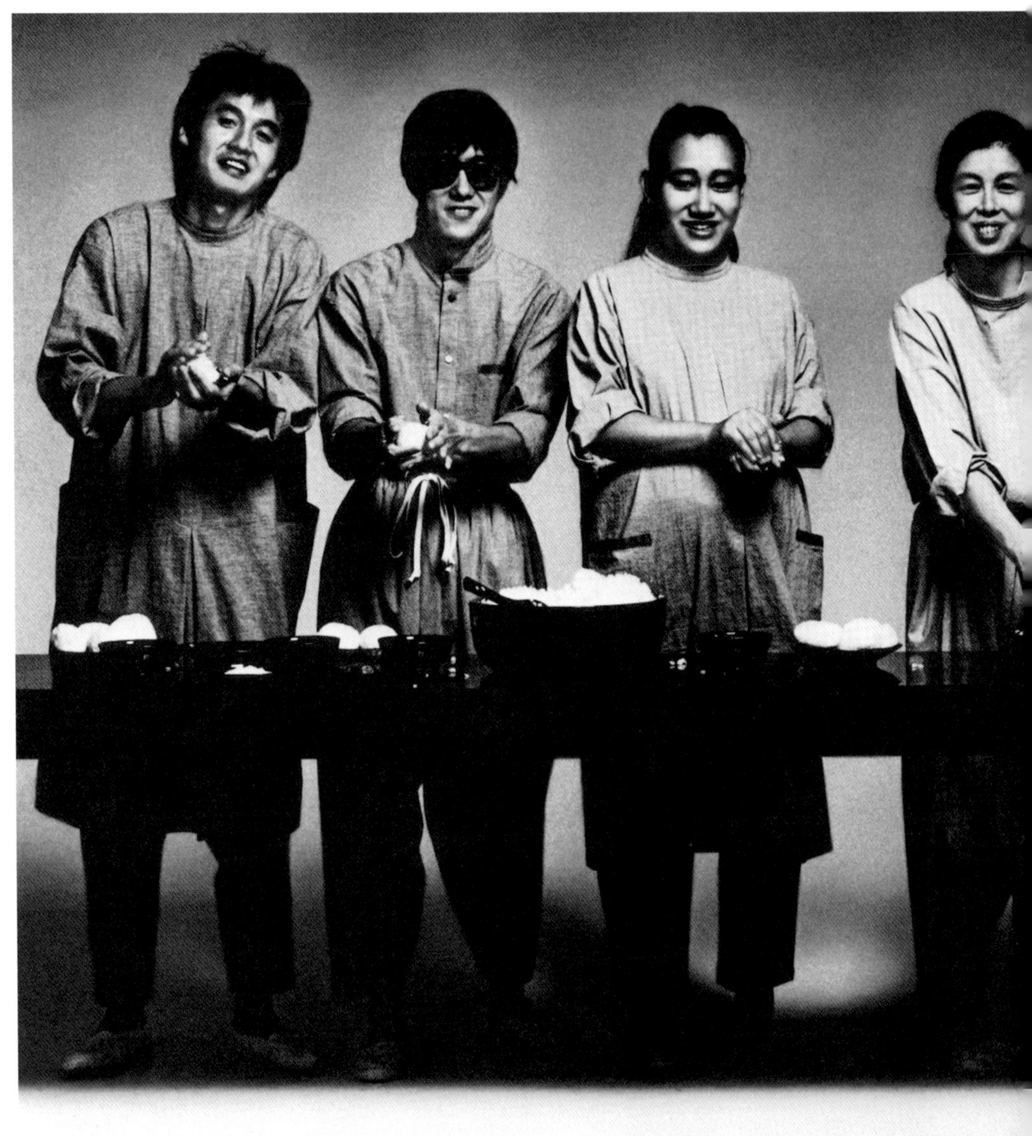

A pamphlet was produced about the brand concept. The first edition defined Plantation as being akin to an *onigiri* rice ball, and included photographs of men and women of all ages, body types, and professions making *onigiri*.
1981 design/Spring-Summer 1982 Collection
Photography: Eiichiro Sakata; worn by (from left): Yasuhiro Nakahara (guitarist), Itohiro (illustrator),

Kei Nakazawa (author), Yasue Kunieda (table coordinator), Masashi Ozaki (printer), Motoko Kitagawa (owner of "Borsalino" restaurant), and Yasunori Nakazawa (president of Sahata Moda, leather consultant); titles are from 1981
Logo mark art direction: Motoko Naruse; illustration: Katsu Yoshida

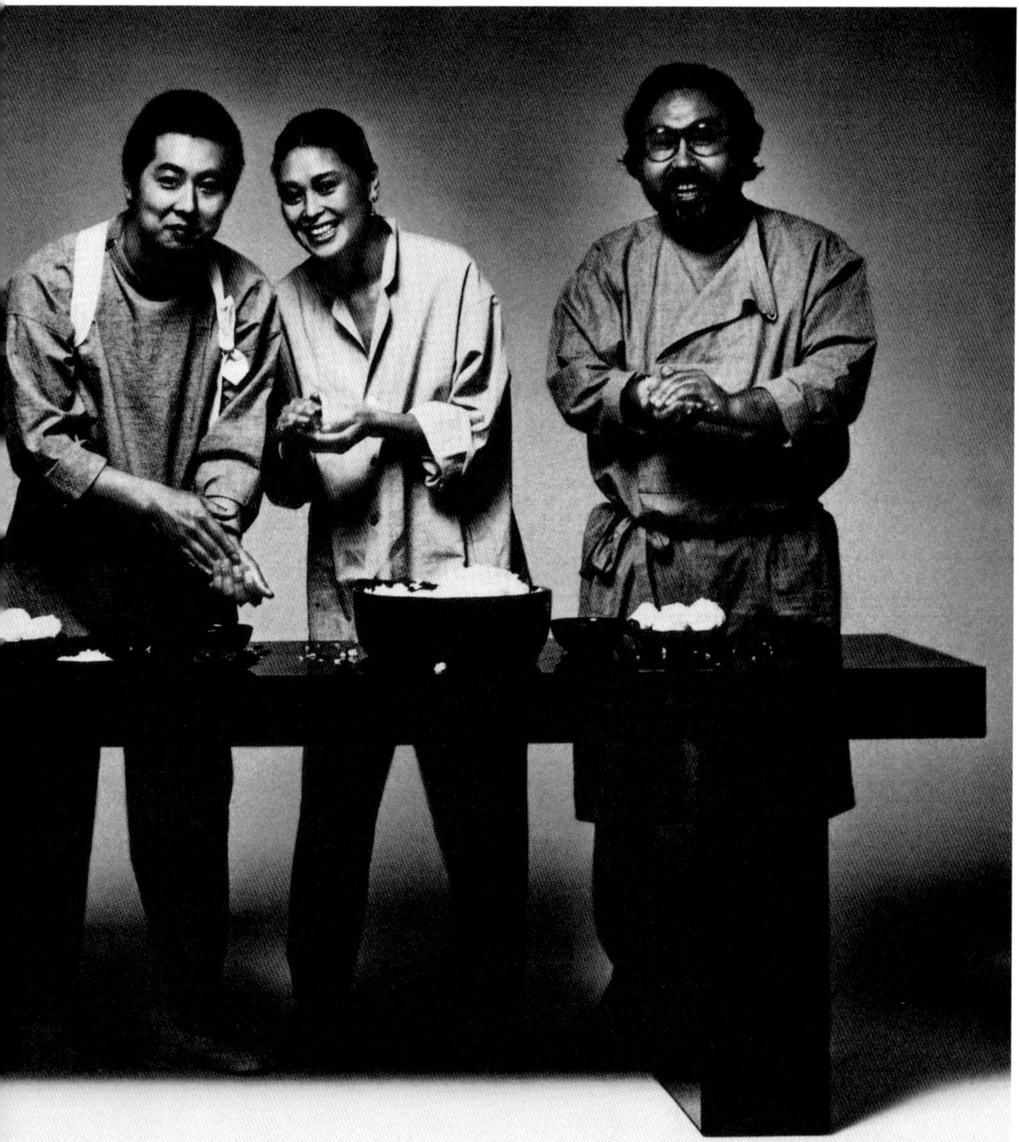

Plantation

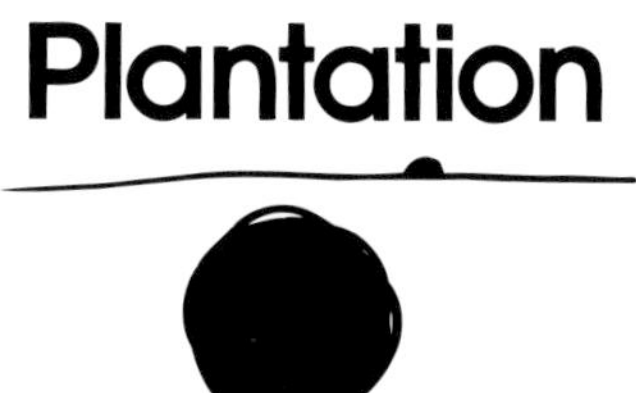

Following spread: Plantation worn by the American dance performance company Momix. Daniel Ezralow, Morleigh Steinberg, Ashley Roland, Jamey Hampton Combination of cotton speck-chambray, *katsuragi* and *dotera* stripes. The reversible vest has different materials on each side.
1984 design/Autumn-Winter 1984 Collection
Photography: Toru Kogure

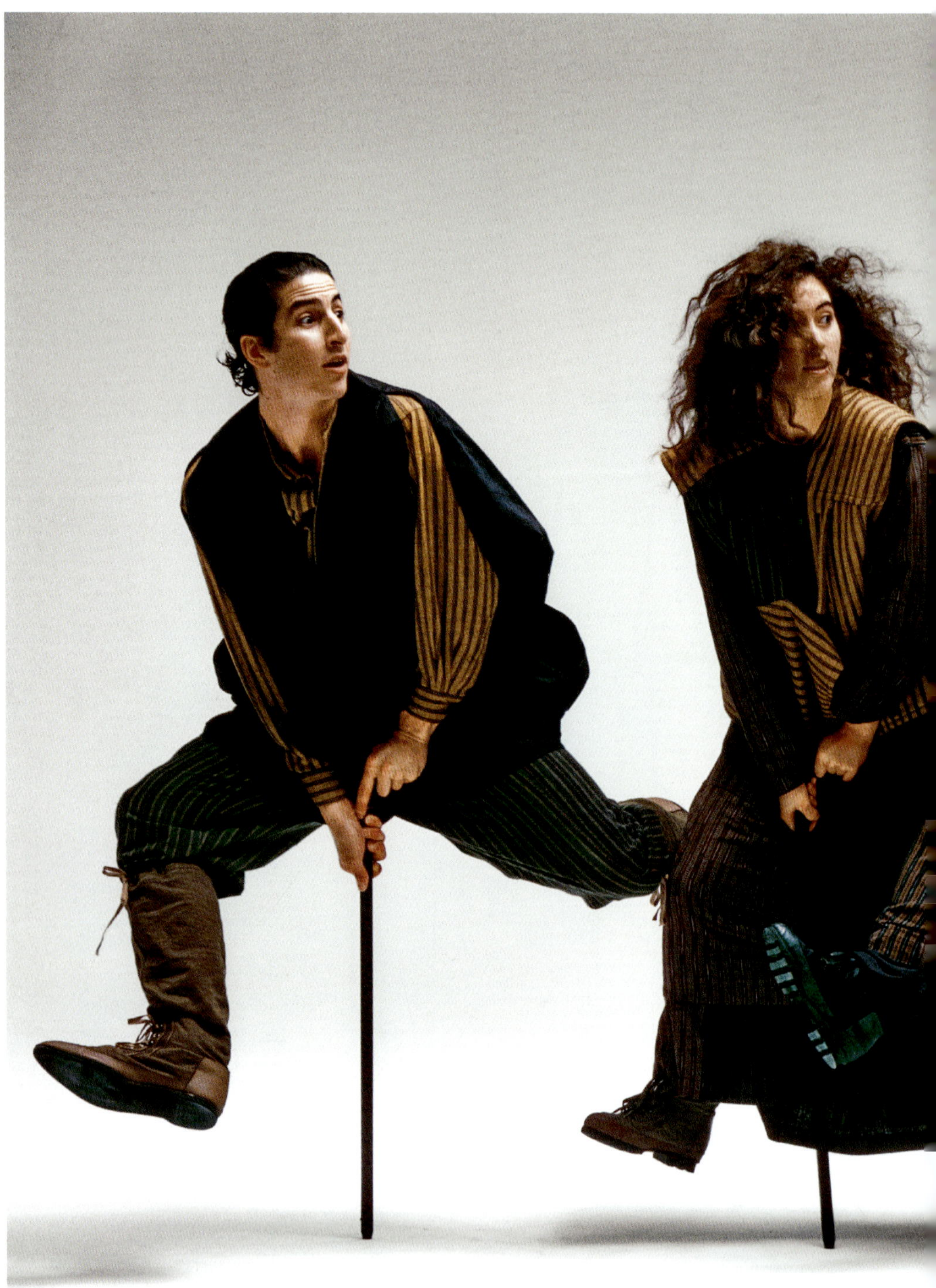

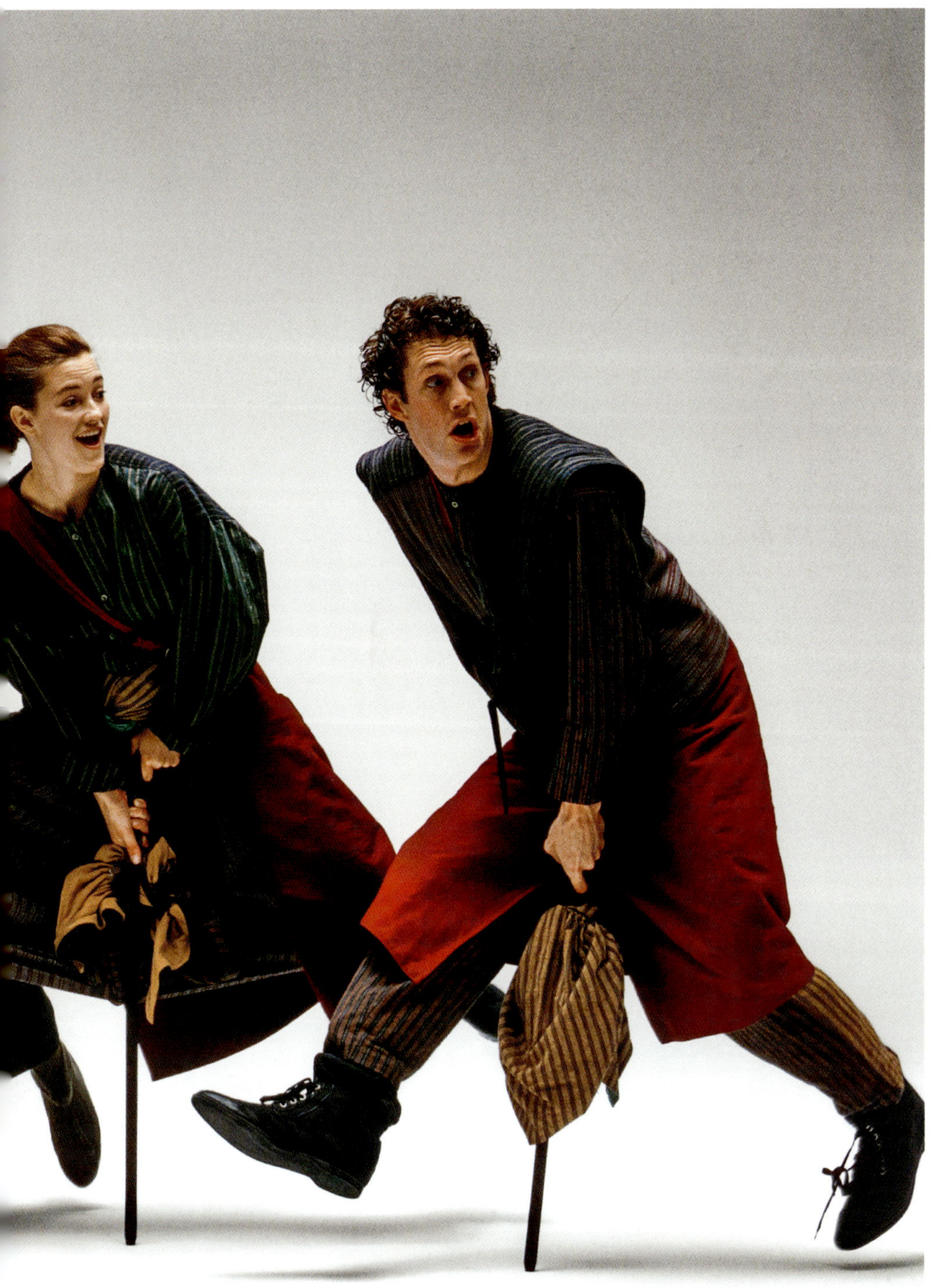

1982

> February: *Rattan Body* used as the cover of *Artforum* (USA), with accompanying article
> March: Autumn-Winter 1982 Paris Collection at Salle Médicis, Cour Carrée du Louvre
> May–June: Participated in the *Intimate Architecture: Contemporary Clothing Design* exhibition (see pp. 92–93)
> June: *Issey & Kenzo* show (Autumn-Winter 1982) at Shinagawa Prince Hotel in Tokyo, and at Osaka Prefectural Gymnasium in Osaka to commemorate the 110th anniversary of *The Mainichi Shimbun*
> October: Spring-Summer 1983 Paris Collection at Salle Médicis, Cour Carrée du Louvre
> November: *ISSEY MIYAKE* (Spring-Summer 1983) show in New York, with the announcement of Plantation at the beginning
> December: *Video Performance*, Tokyo (Spring-Summer 1983)

Cover story in *Artforum*

Artforum, a monthly arts magazine in the United States, featured *Rattan Body* on the cover. In the opening editorial, chief editors Ingrid Sischy and Germano Celant described Issey Miyake's *Rattan Body* as an icon of modernism, an intersection between past and future, East and West, rigidity and flexibility, nature and artifice. This was the first time that an arts magazine had dealt with clothes on its cover.

Opposite left: ***Artforum***, February 1982 cover
Photography: Eiichiro Sakata
Opposite right: ***Rattan Body* and pleated skirt made from synthetic leather**
1981 design/Spring-Summer 1982 Collection
Photography: Eiichiro Sakata

1 Autumn-Winter 1982 Paris Collection, March 27, Salle Médicis, Cour Carrée du Louvre
2 Spring-Summer 1983 Paris Collection, October 16, Salle Médicis, Cour Carrée du Louvre

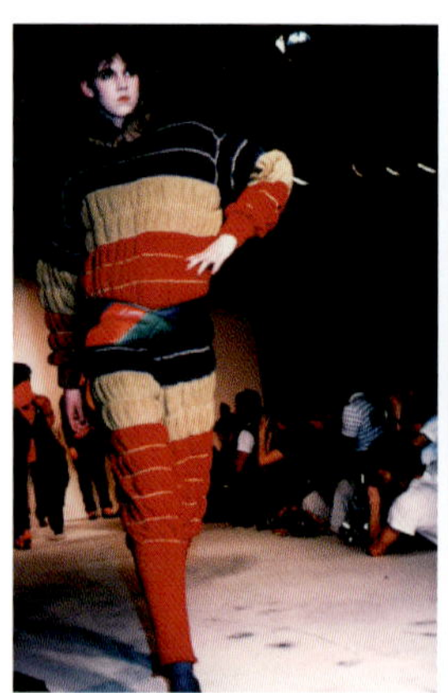
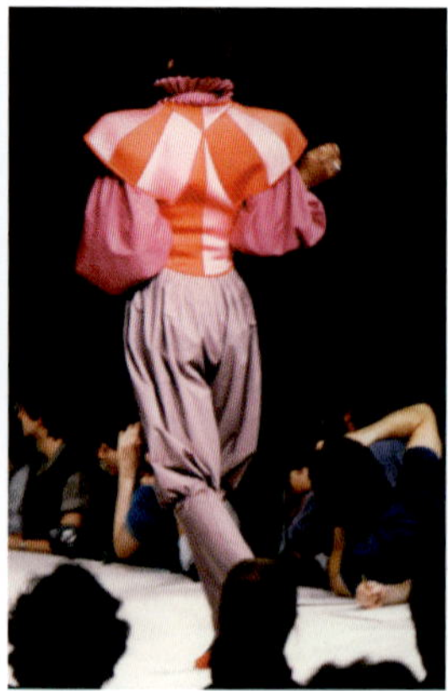
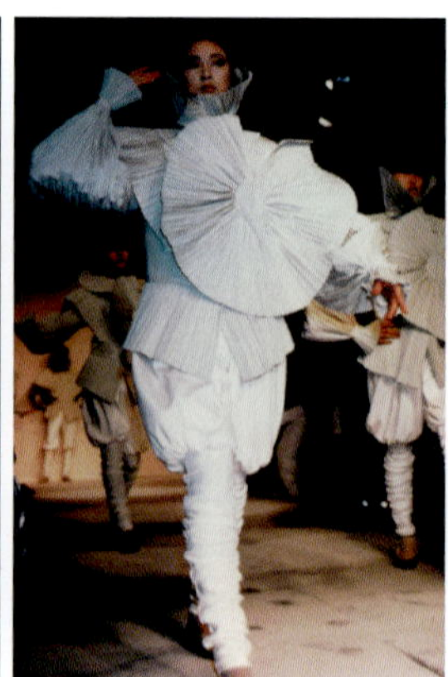
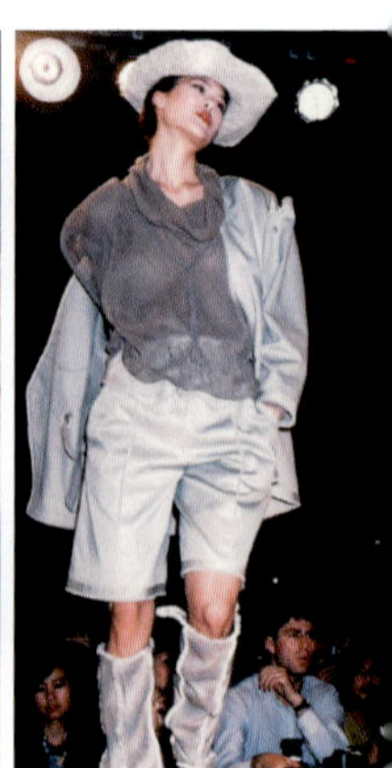

1

2

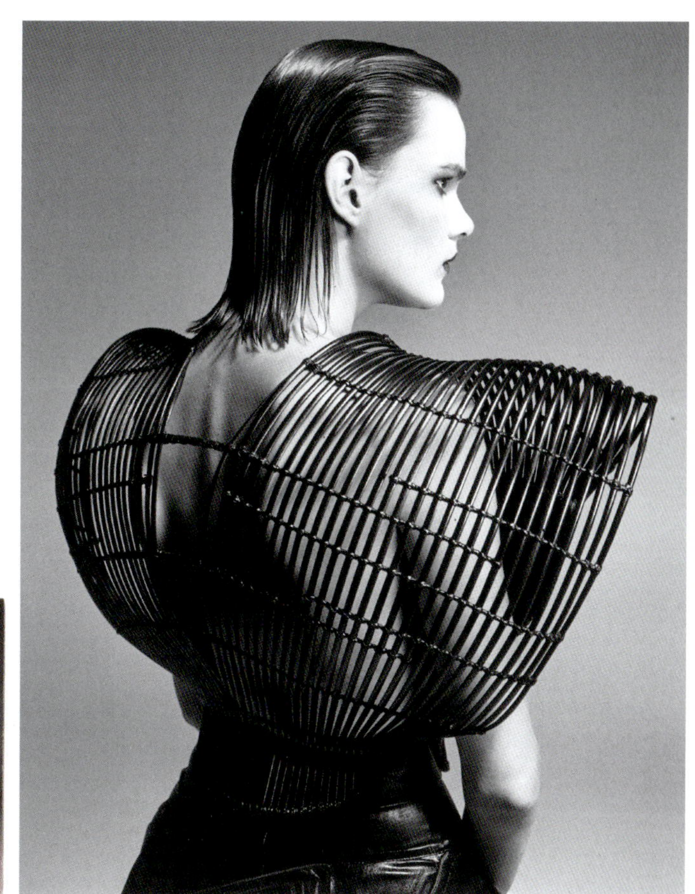

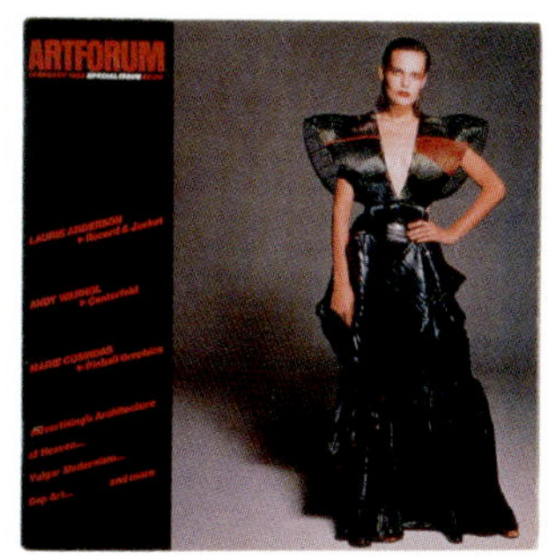

ARTFORUM
SPECIAL ISSUE
LAURIE ANDERSON
+ Record & Jacket
ANDY WARHOL
+ Centerfold
MARIE COSINDAS
+ Pinball Greatains
Advertising's Architecture
of Heaven...
Vulgar Modernism...
Pop Art... and more

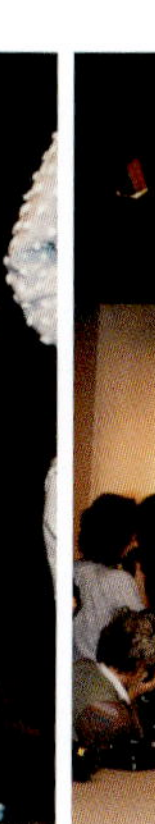

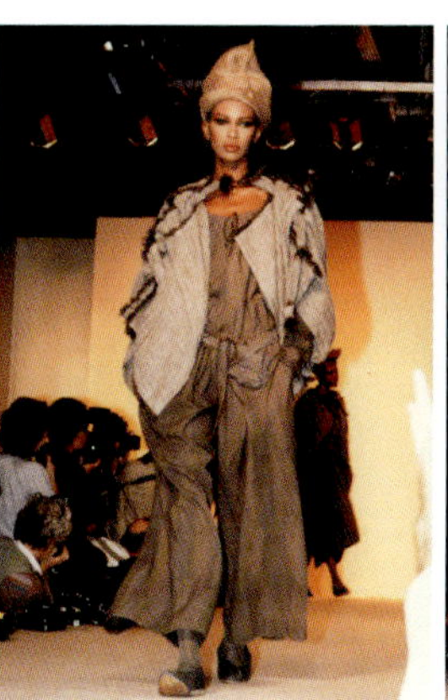

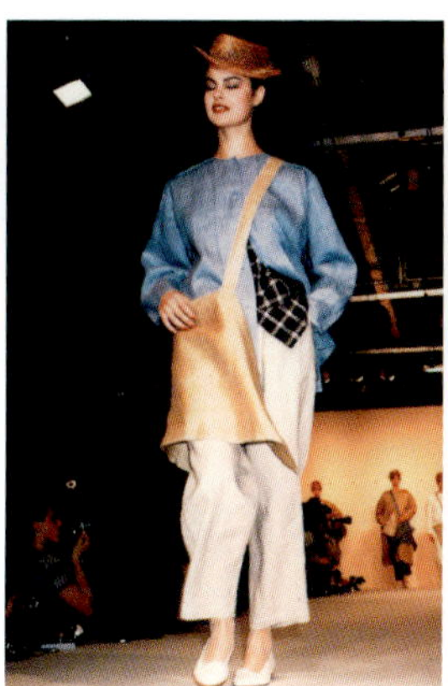

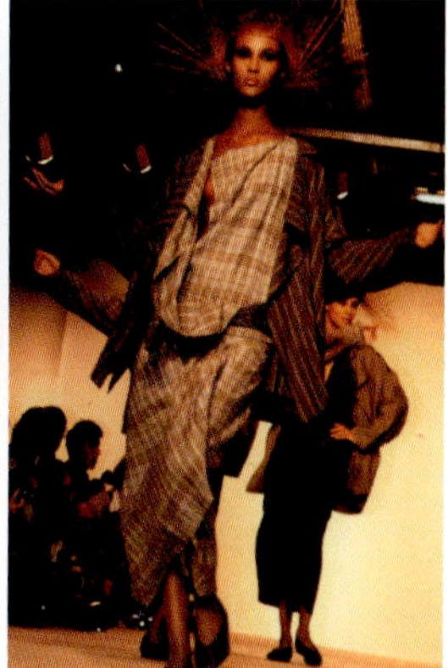

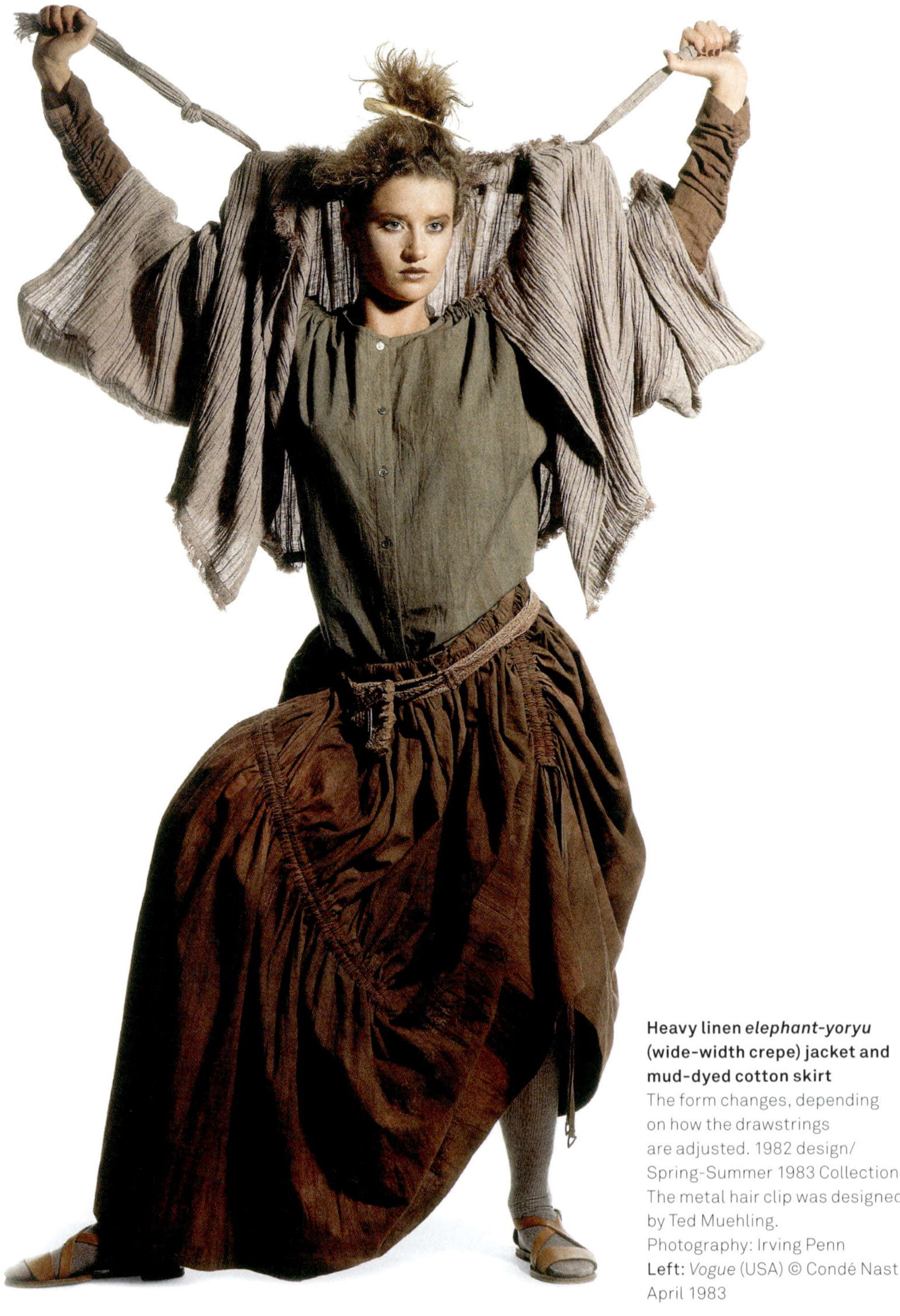

**Heavy linen *elephant-yoryu*
(wide-width crepe) jacket and
mud-dyed cotton skirt**
The form changes, depending
on how the drawstrings
are adjusted. 1982 design/
Spring-Summer 1983 Collection
The metal hair clip was designed
by Ted Muehling.
Photography: Irving Penn
Left: *Vogue* (USA) © Condé Nast,
April 1983

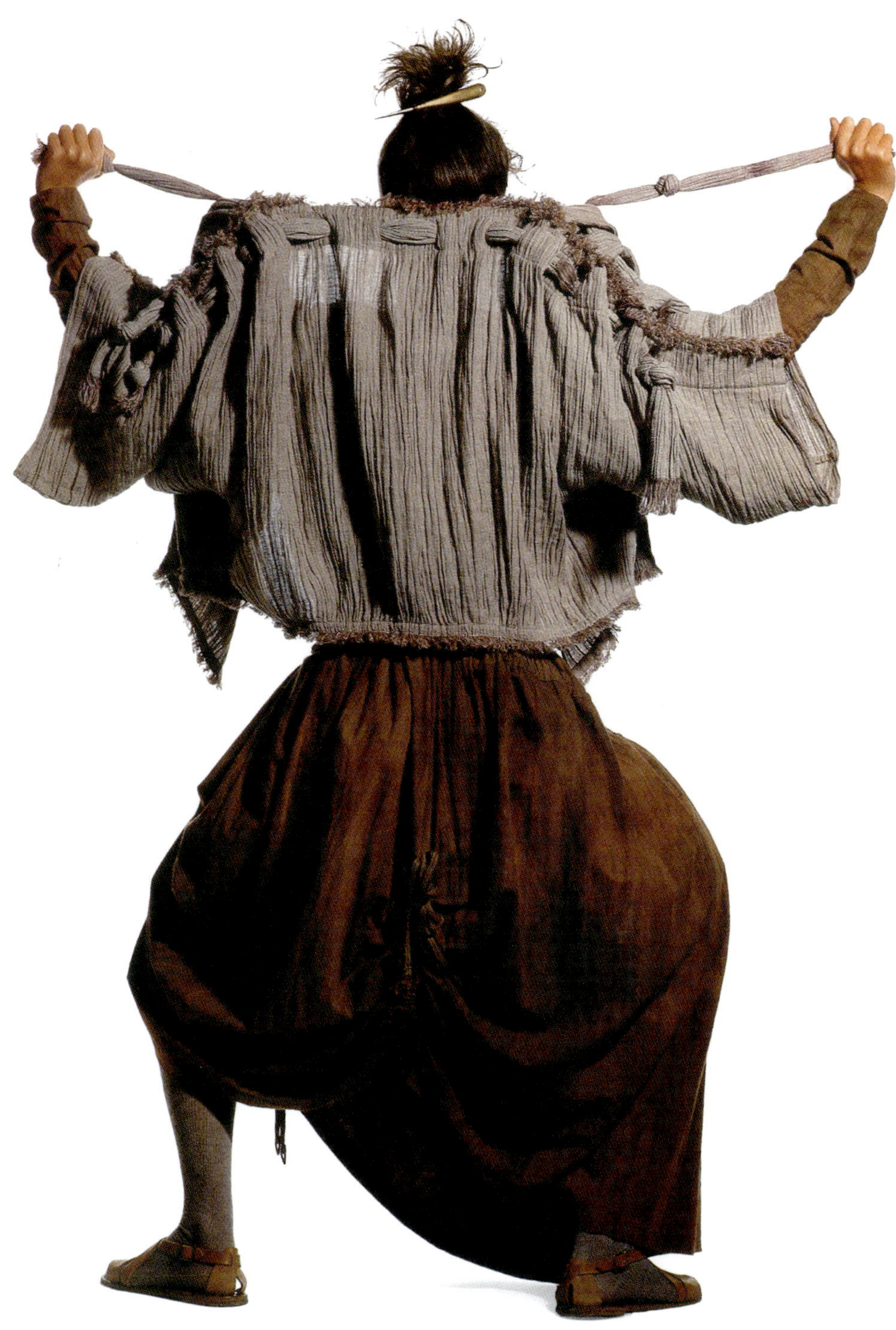

Miyake: Making Waves and Raves With His Simple Lines for Everyone

Washington Post, December 12, 1982

Text: Nina Hyde

When nearly 2,000 guests arrived on the deck hangar of the battleship *Intrepid** for the Issey Miyake show recently, they found 40 members of the New York Choral Society seated on stage and wearing the Japanese designer's easy-fit, washable cotton clothes from his new Plantation collection. Miyake's point was not only to open the show with a splendid "Gloriana" by Benjamin Britten, but also to show that absolutely anyone can wear these simple, neutral-colored clothes.

"I expect people who own these clothes to discover when and how to wear them and not just wear them one way," Miyake said. "My design is no design."

"Miyake restores my faith that there is something new under the sun in fashion," said Stella Blum, curator of costumes at the Metropolitan Museum of Art in New York.

The most important part of a Miyake collection is the fabric, and he will take as long as a year, if necessary, to get just the cloth he wants. He has made modern versions of traditional Japanese fabrics, including an *ikat-weave kasuri*, a farmer's check and *shijira-ori* weaving. Sometimes he'll change their scale or color and occasionally add synthetic fibers. He was the first to use Ultrasuede, later popularized by Halston… Everything inspires him. Fittingly, in 1977, Miyake won the coveted Mainichi Design Award, the first time that the Award was given to a fashion designer. It is usually given to architects and environmental designers. Now, Miyake wants to have a show for students in Paris and New York, as he'd done in Tokyo. …

"Paris is an old and traditional place; it needs new blood," he said. "The joining of the Japanese with the French should make a new movement. I think it should be good for Paris." It will be good for others, too. (Excerpt)

* A US aircraft carrier launched in 1943. Put on display at the Intrepid Sea, Air & Space Museum in New York City in 1982 after decommissioning.

Photography: Marcus Leatherdale (left), Joel Richardson (right)

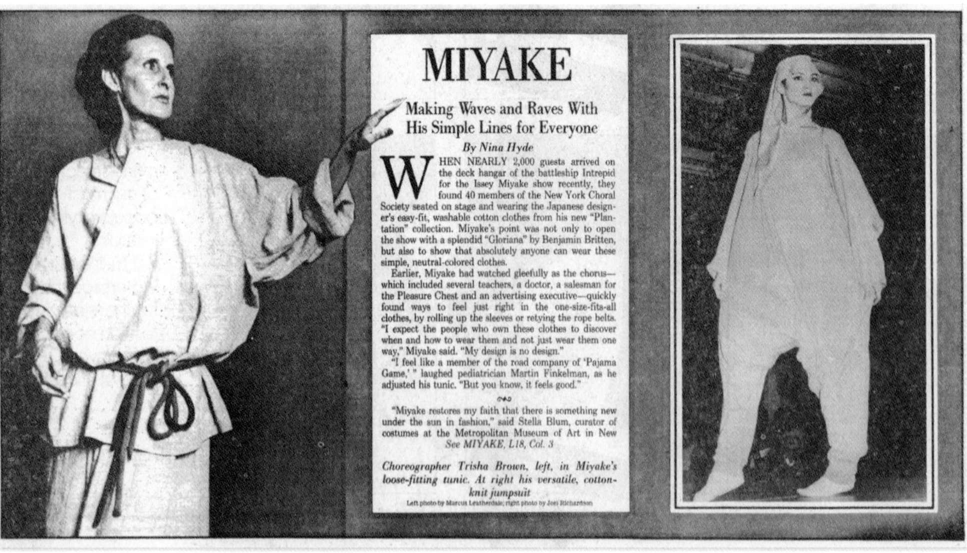

MIYAKE

Making Waves and Raves With His Simple Lines for Everyone

By Nina Hyde

WHEN NEARLY 2,000 guests arrived on the deck hangar of the battleship Intrepid for the Issey Miyake show recently, they found 40 members of the New York Choral Society seated on stage and wearing the Japanese designer's easy-fit, washable cotton clothes from his new "Plantation" collection. Miyake's point was not only to open the show with a splendid "Gloriana" by Benjamin Britten, but also to show that absolutely anyone can wear these simple, neutral-colored clothes.

Earlier, Miyake had watched gleefully as the chorus—which included several teachers, a doctor, a salesman for the Pleasure Chest and an advertising executive—quickly found ways to feel just right in the one-size-fits-all clothes, by rolling up the sleeves or retying the rope belts. "I expect the people who own these clothes to discover when and how to wear them and not just wear them one way," Miyake said. "My design is no design."

"I feel like a member of the road company of 'Pajama Game,'" laughed pediatrician Martin Finkelman, as he adjusted his tunic. "But you know, it feels good."

"Miyake restores my faith that there is something new under the sun in fashion," said Stella Blum, curator of costumes at the Metropolitan Museum of Art in New

See MIYAKE, L18, Col. 3

Choreographer Trisha Brown, left, in Miyake's loose-fitting tunic. At right his versatile, cotton-knit jumpsuit.

Left photo by Marcus Leatherdale; right photo by Joel Richardson

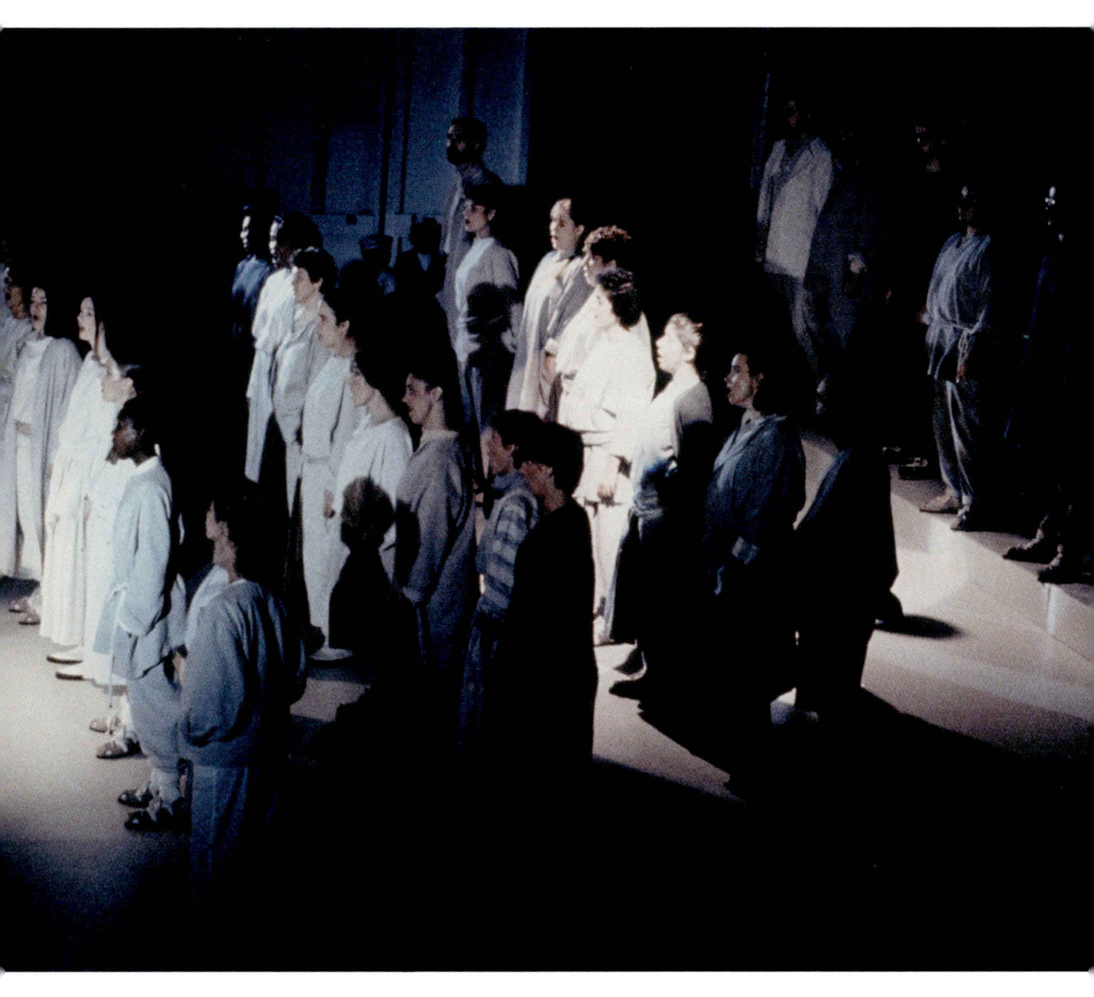

Members of the New York Choral Society singing and
wearing Plantation on stage on the *Intrepid*

1983

> March: Autumn-Winter 1983 Paris Collection at Salle Médicis, Cour Carrée du Louvre
> May: *Issey Miyake Spectacle: Bodyworks* exhibition in Tokyo. Also traveled to Los Angeles and San Francisco
> May: *Issey Miyake Bodyworks* published by Shogakukan, Inc.
> October: Spring-Summer 1984 Paris Collection at Salle Médicis, Cour Carrée du Louvre
> November: *Live Installation Part I* (Spring-Summer 1984), Tokyo

Opposite: **Wire Body**
1983 design/Autumn-Winter 1983 Collection
Photography: Daniel Jouanneau

1 Autumn-Winter 1983 Paris Collection, March 19, Salle Médicis, Cour Carrée du Louvre
2 Spring-Summer 1984 Paris Collection, October 15, Salle Médicis, Cour Carrée du Louvre

***Issey Miyake Spectacle: Bodyworks* exhibition**
This exhibition provided an overview of Miyake's work in the 1980s, focusing on the Body Series, which started with *Plastic Body*. The installation used models of the human body together with video and sound to create a spectacle on the theme of celebrating humanity and the body, the point of origin for all of Issey Miyake's clothes creations. It traveled to four locations, with changes to the space and environment at each venue.

May 1–22: Laforet Museum Iigura 800/500, Tokyo
Concept and art direction: Issey Miyake; concept, body model design: Tomio Mohri; concept: Kazuko Koike; body model fabrication: Masahiro Kano and Hiroyuki Onogi; installation design: Takashi Kato; kinetic art: Takuro Osaka; lighting design: Masao Nihei; computer software program: Hideo Dohmeki; video art: Vic Tannenberg and Taki Ono; music direction: Ryuichi Sakamoto; concept production: Shozo Tsurumoto
June 15–July 17: Otis Art Institute of Parsons School of Design, Los Angeles
September 20–November 20:
San Francisco Museum of Modern Art
February 27–April 9, 1985: Boilerhouse Project, Victoria and Albert Museum, London

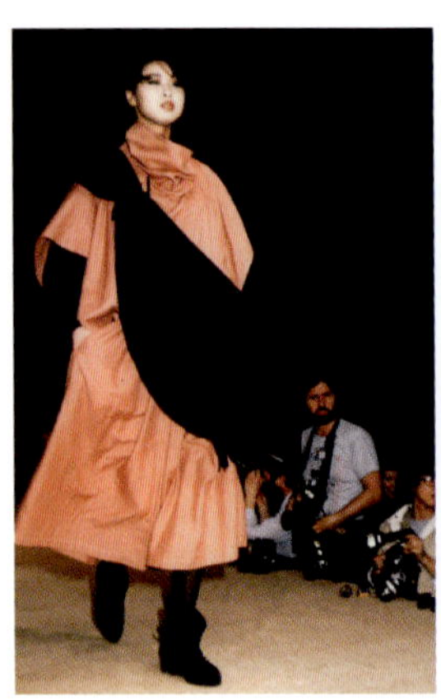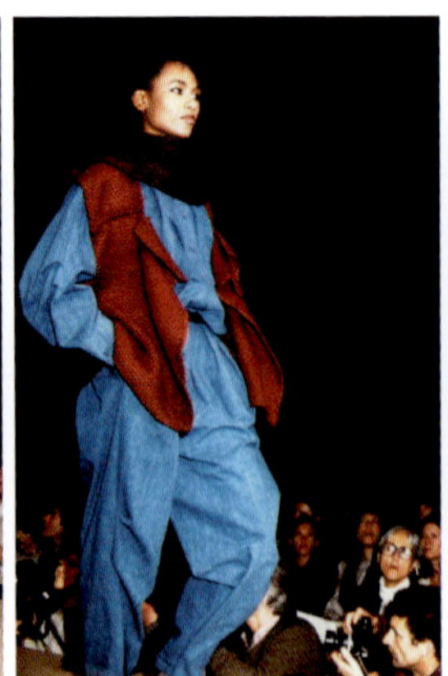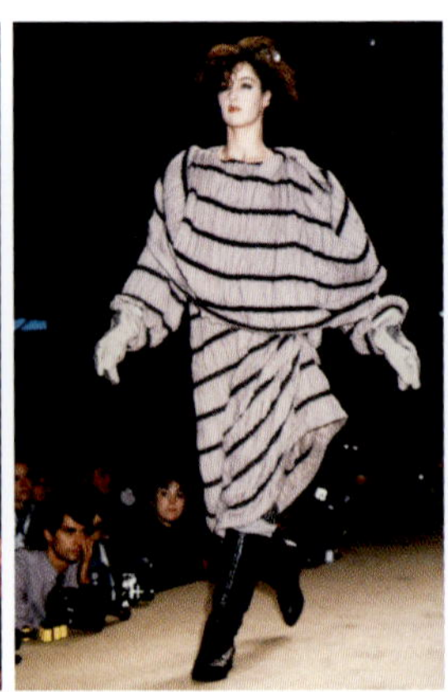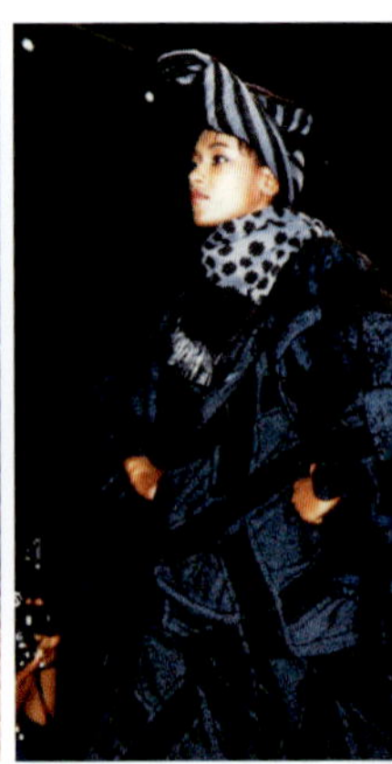

1

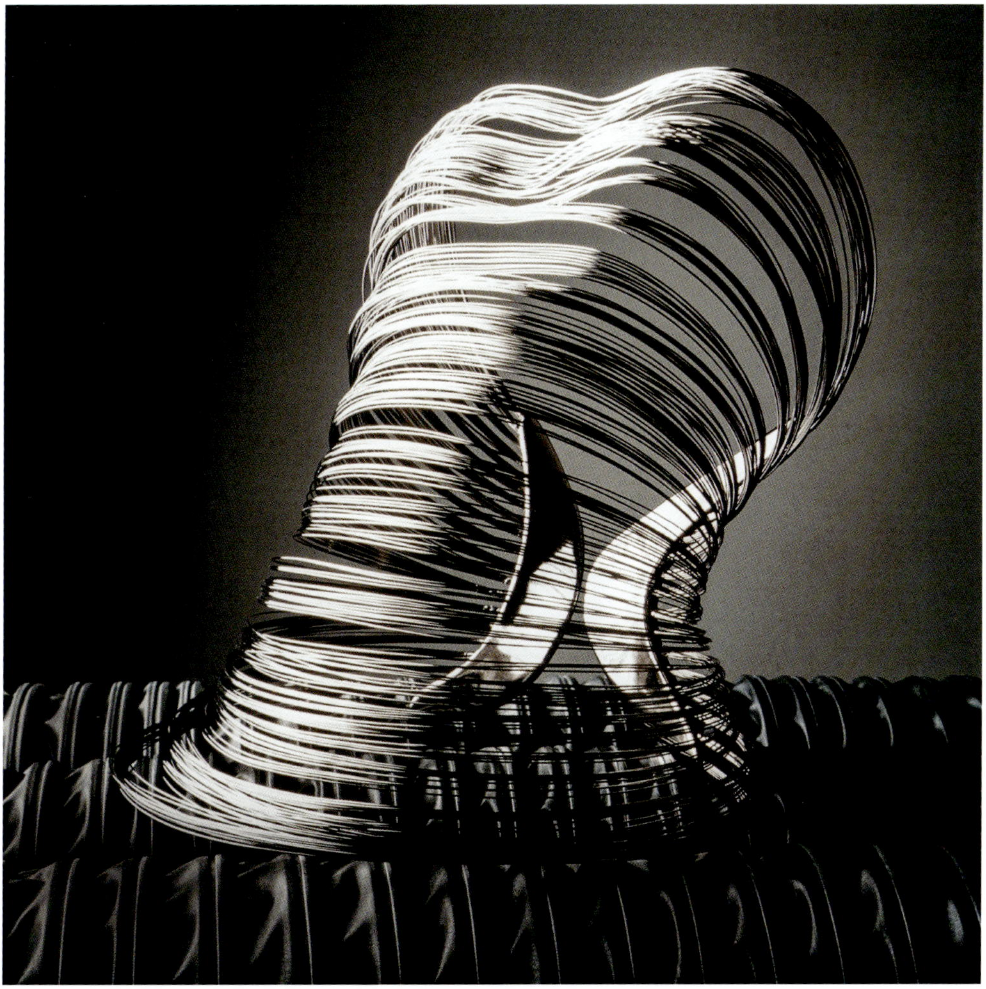

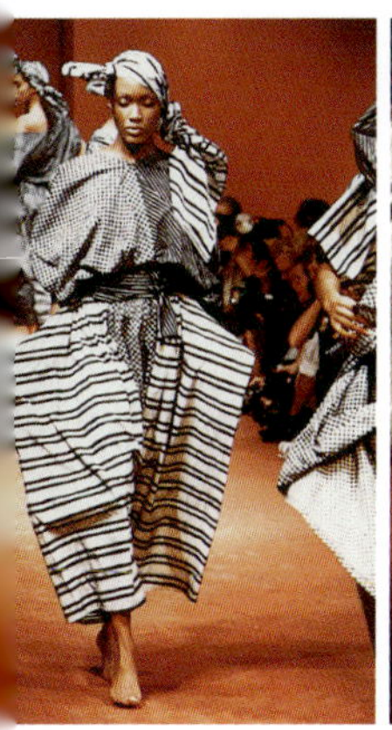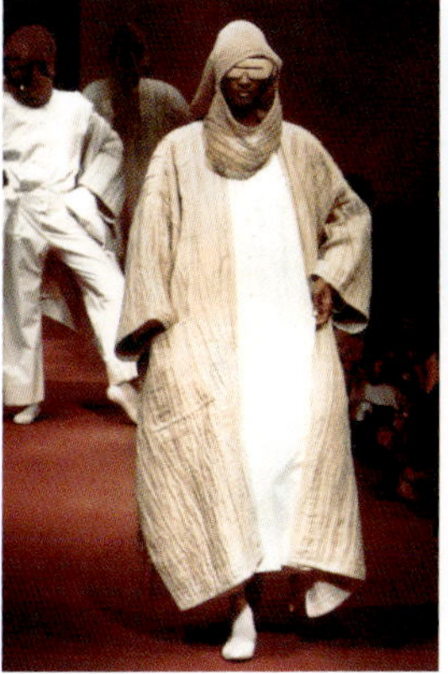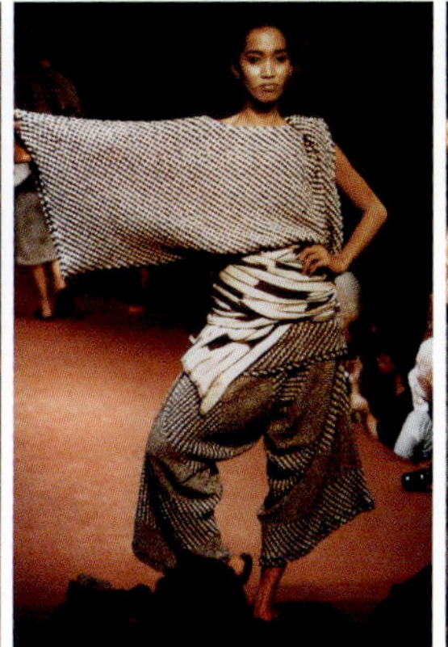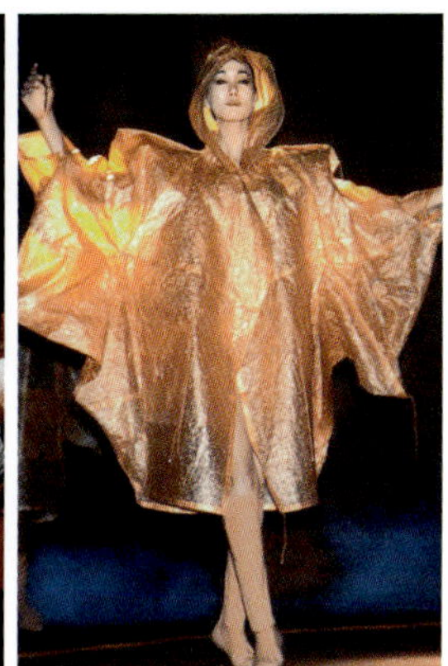

2

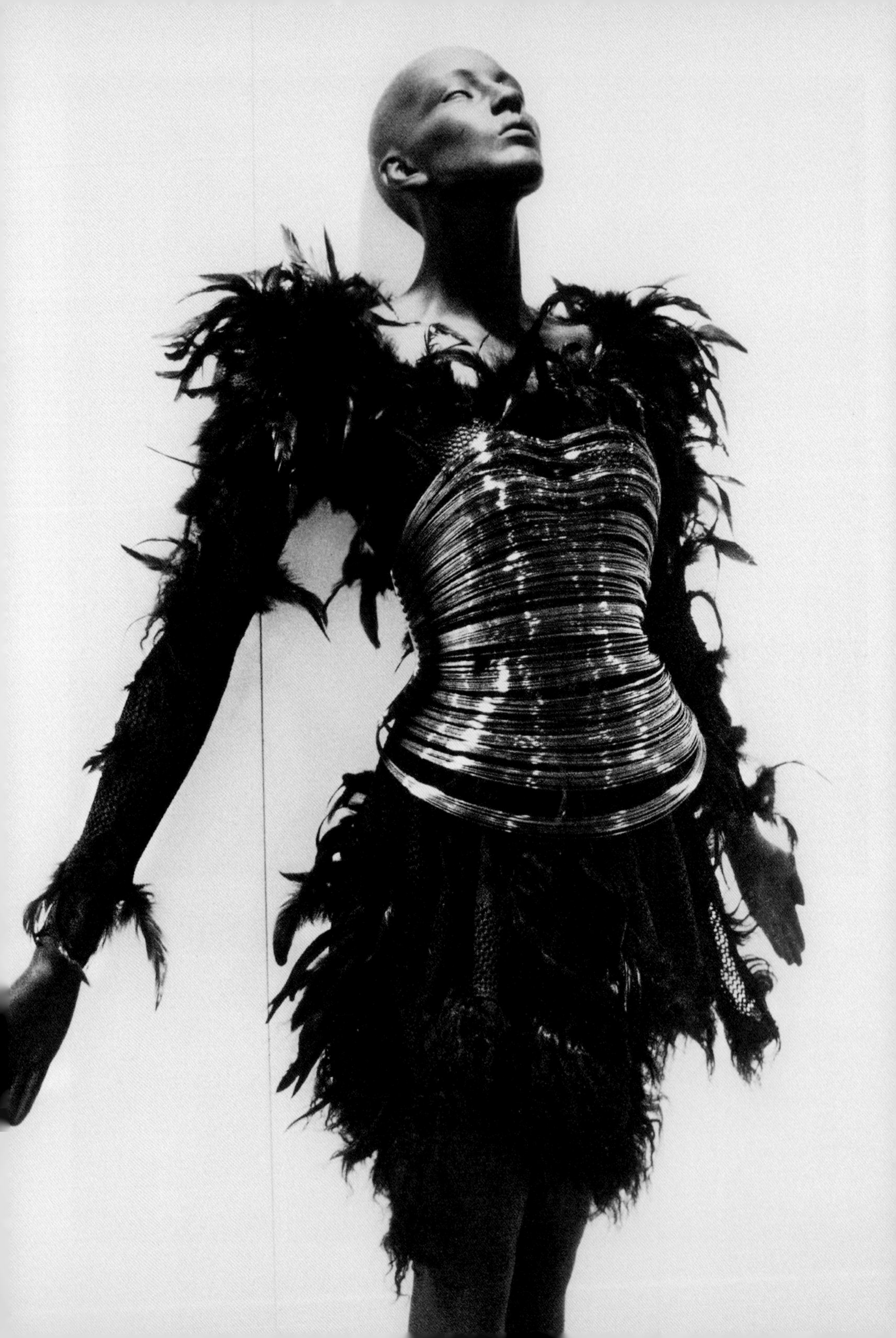

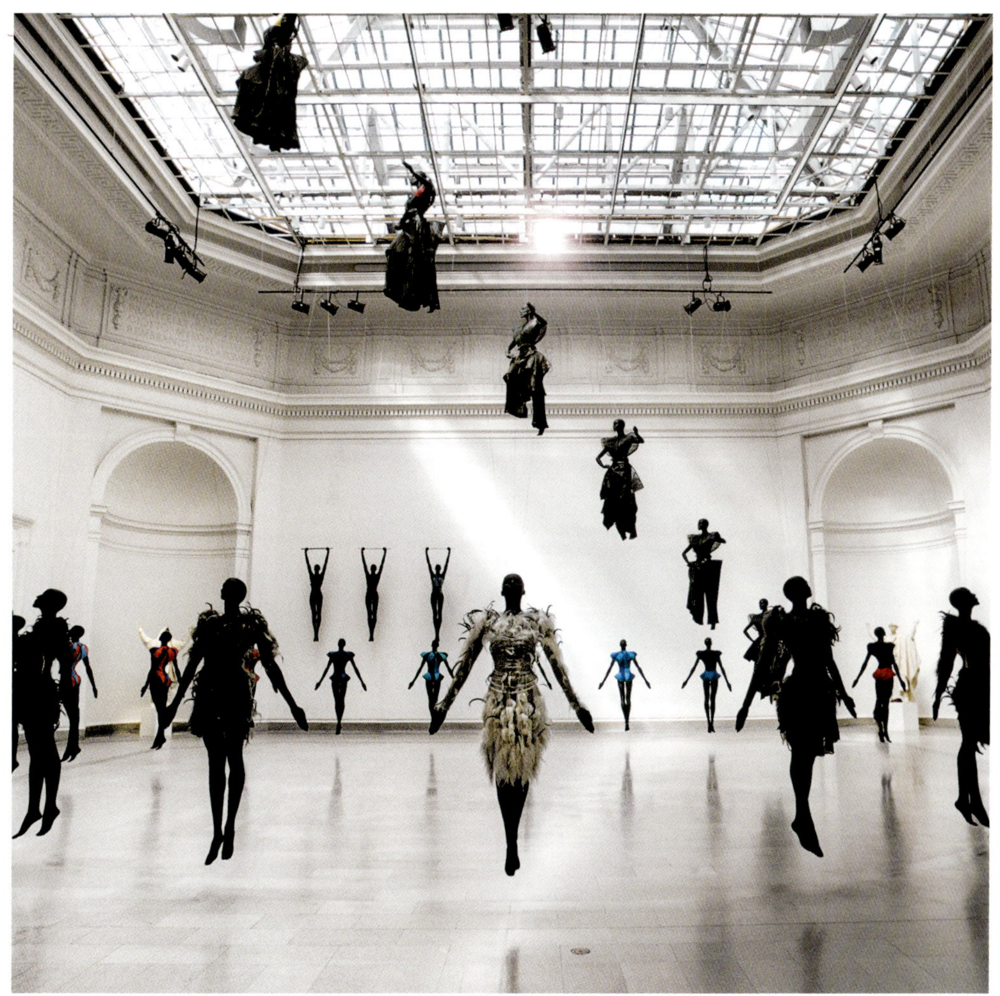

Opposite: *Wire Body*
As a symbol of the glow of health, mannequins with *Wire Body* were exhibited in the space. 1983 design/ Autumn-Winter 1983 Collection
Photography: Ben Blackwell
(San Francisco Museum of Modern Art)

Issey Miyake Spectacle: Bodyworks exhibition at the San Francisco Museum of Modern Art
Rattan Body 1981 design/Spring-Summer 1982 Collection; *Wire Body* 1983 design/Autumn-Winter 1983 Collection; *Urethane Body* 1982 design/ Autumn-Winter 1982 Collection; *Kamiko* 1982 design/ Autumn-Winter 1982 Collection
Photography: Mitsumasa Fujitsuka

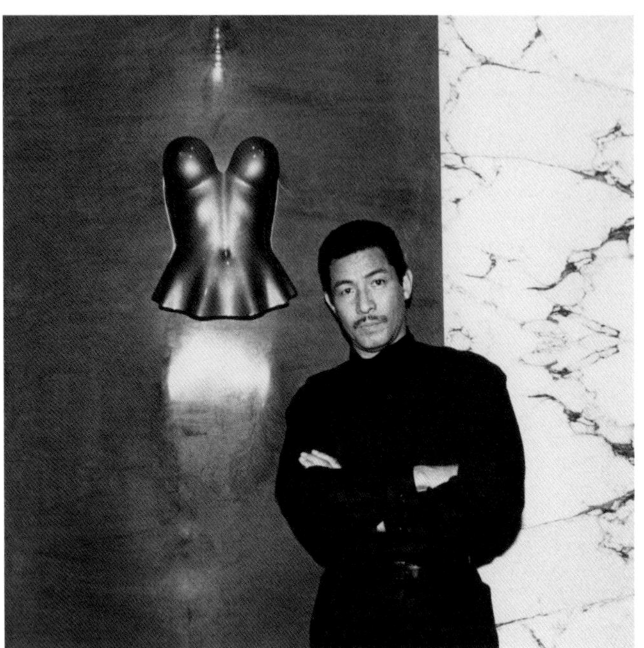

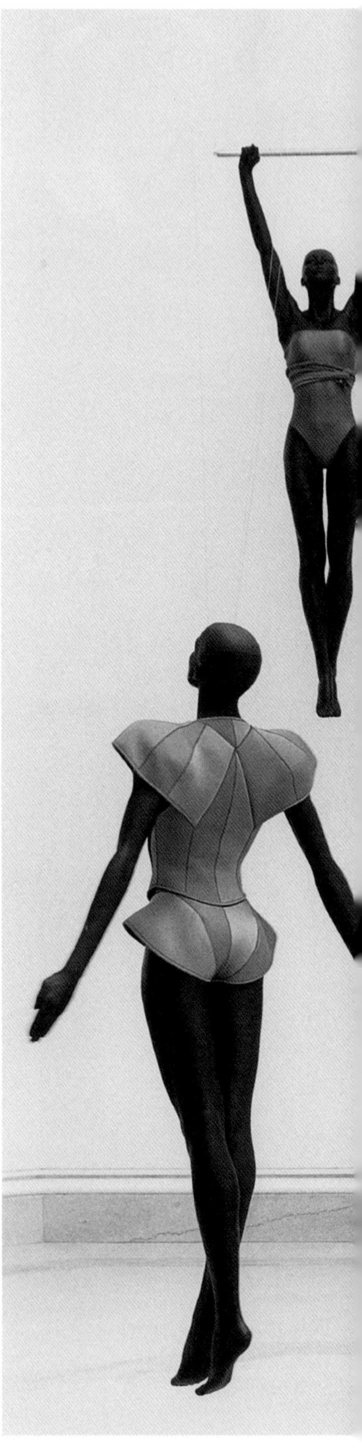

Above: **Plastic Body and Issey Miyake**
Issey Miyake Spectacle: Bodyworks exhibition at
Laforet Museum Iigura 800/500, Tokyo

Right: **Issey Miyake Spectacle: Bodyworks**
exhibition at the San Francisco Museum of Modern Art
Urethane Body 1982 design/Autumn-Winter
1982 Collection
Photography: Ben Blackwell
(San Francisco Museum of Modern Art)

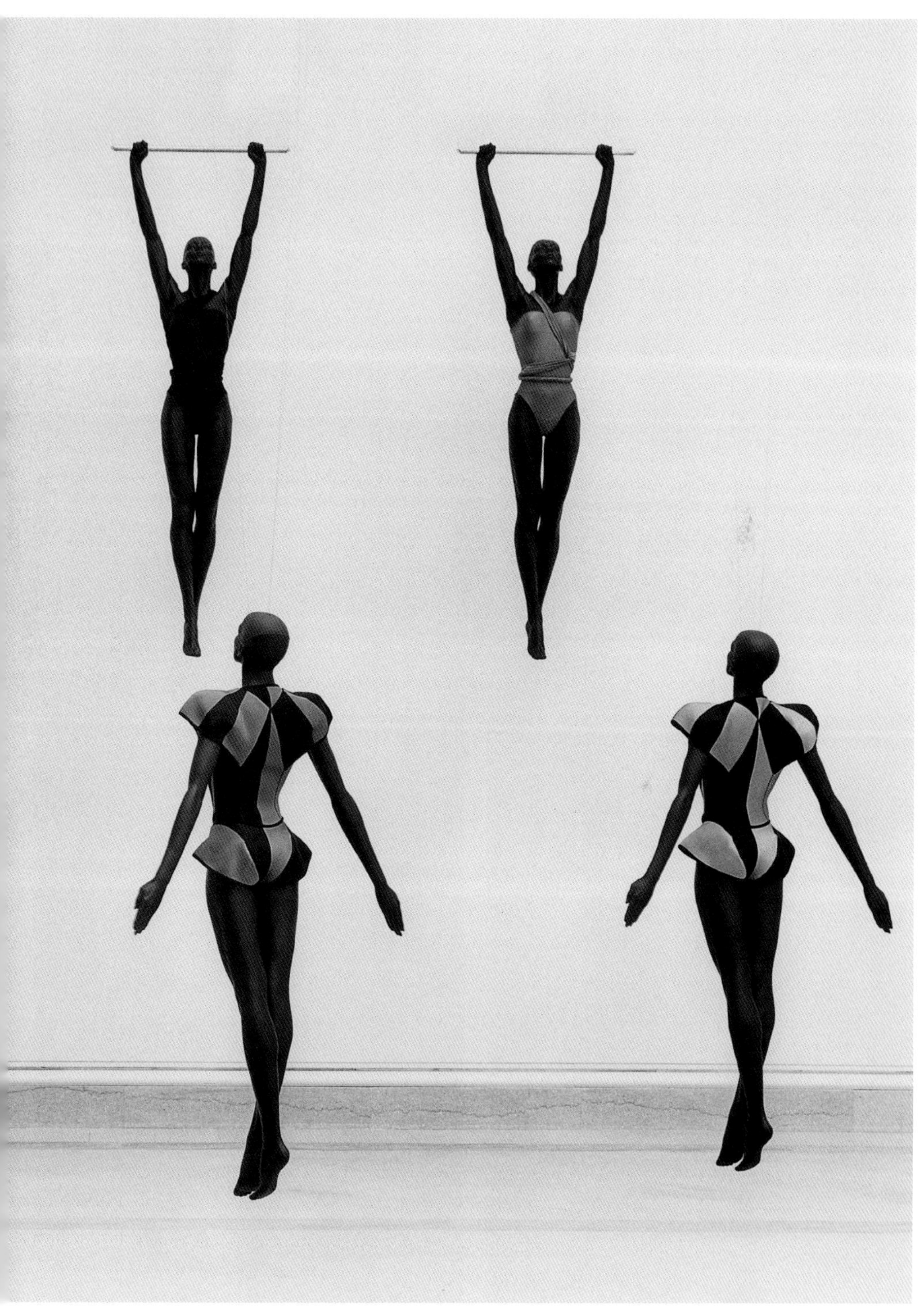

Live Installation Part I
Models wearing the same mask as the mannequins appear in the same space where the mannequins stand. The Spring-Summer 1984 Collection was introduced using a new approach at the intersection between the static and the active, in which the exhibit and the show become one. Tomio Mohri provided the direction.
November 29–30: Laforet Museum Iigura 800, Tokyo
Below left: Cotton batik with Indonesian hand-block processing worn by a sawdust mannequin.
Masked model: Junko Tajima
Photography: Mitsumasa Fujitsuka
Below right: The model appears at front; a mannequin with the same mask at back. Both are wearing a square-shaped knit top and striped bottom.
Masked model: Toshiko Shirai
Photography: Tsutomu Wakatsuki

Opposite: ***Abura-gami Coat***
Mino-washi Japanese paper is coated with persimmon juice to enhance strength, waterproofed with tung oil, and then rubbed to a shiny finish. Worn with the silicon shoulder from the same collection.
1983 design/Spring-Summer 1984 Collection
Photography: Kazumi Kurigami; models: Toshiko Shirai, Atsuko Oka

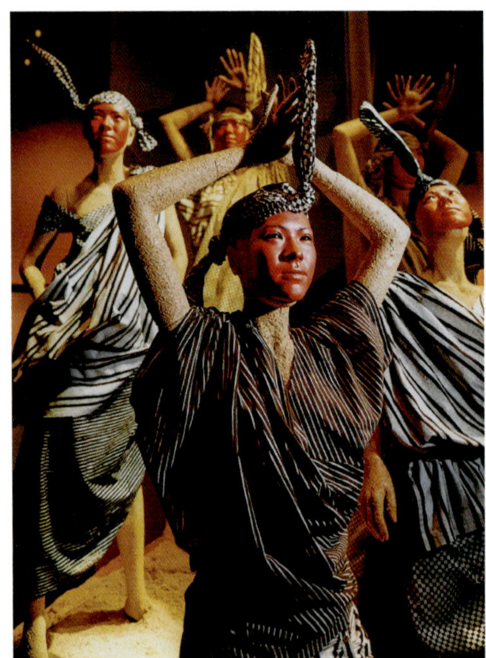

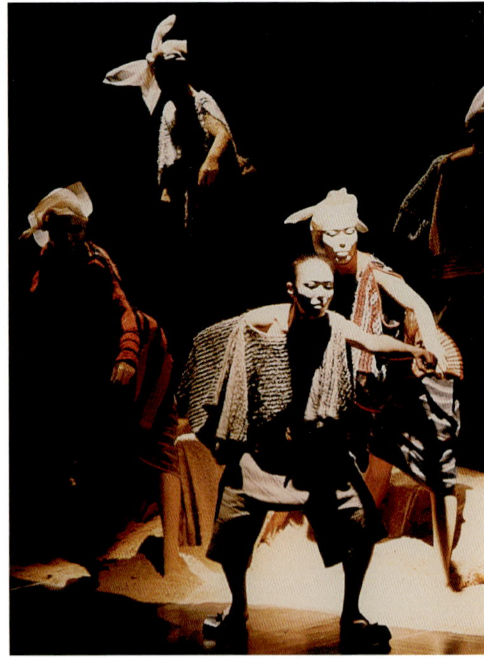

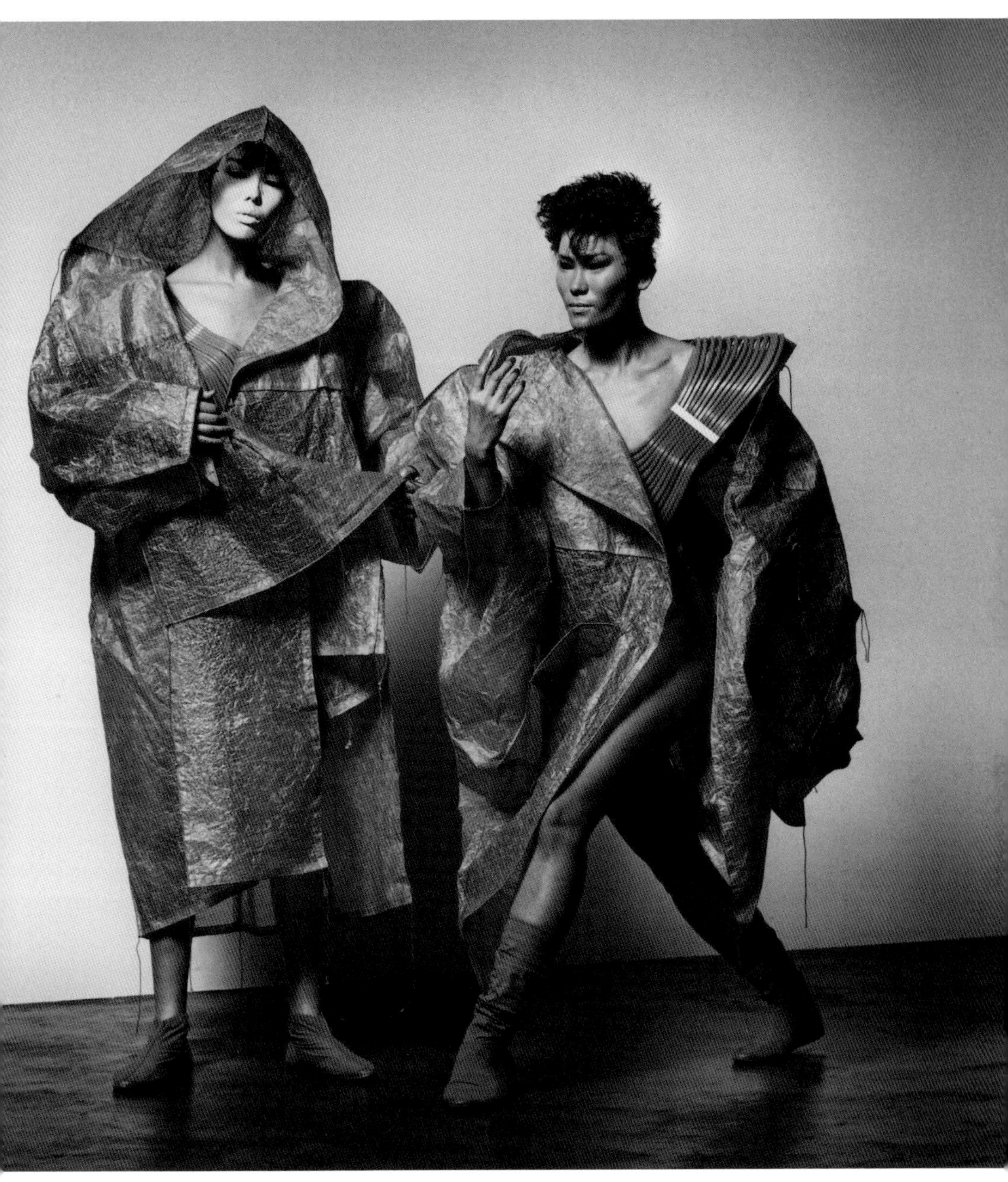

1984

> March: Autumn-Winter 1984 Paris Collection at Salle Médicis, Cour Carrée du Louvre
> May: *Live Installation Part II* (Autumn-Winter 1984), Tokyo
> May: Plantation Autumn-Winter 1984 show at Sagacho Exhibit Space, Tokyo; Momix dancers performed wearing the clothing
> September: Joint release of Asha by MDS in collaboration with Seibu Department Store
> October: Spring-Summer 1985 Paris Collection at Salle Médicis, Cour Carrée du Louvre
> November: Spring-Summer 1985 Tokyo Collection at Issey Miyake International, Inc. showroom
> Production of *Issey Miyake* program by a French national broadcasting station

Live Installation Part II

Multiscreen showing of footage from the Paris Collection; shown in alternation with real-time, live video of models on the stage. The 1984 Autumn-Winter Collection was shown in a spatial form that combined video monitors, mannequins, and models.

May 1: Laforet Museum Akasaka, Tokyo
Art direction: Tomio Mohri; lighting: Harumi Fujimoto (MGS); video production: Tokyo Eizo Kikaku; multi-vision system: Meiko Electronics multi-art; planning and production: Miyake Design Studio

Asha by MDS

At the end of 1981, Issey Miyake traveled to India with Makiko Minagawa and Kazuko Koike, where they were introduced to Asha Sarabhai. This led to a new clothing and lifestyle brand in collaboration with the Seibu Department Store. The use of traditional Indian fabrics and handwork with modern technology became the "haath" (hand) and the touchstone for the HaaT brand that Minagawa began directing in 2000. The Sarabhai family is based in Ahmedabad and has been involved in weaving for generations. They are also the owners of the Calico Museum, the best collection of textiles in India.

1 Autumn-Winter 1984 Paris Collection, March 24, Salle Médicis, Cour Carrée du Louvre
2 Spring-Summer 1985 Paris Collection, October 20, Salle Médicis, Cour Carrée du Louvre

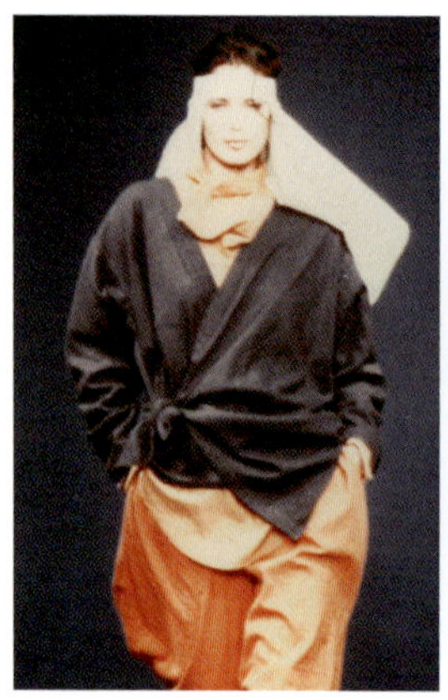
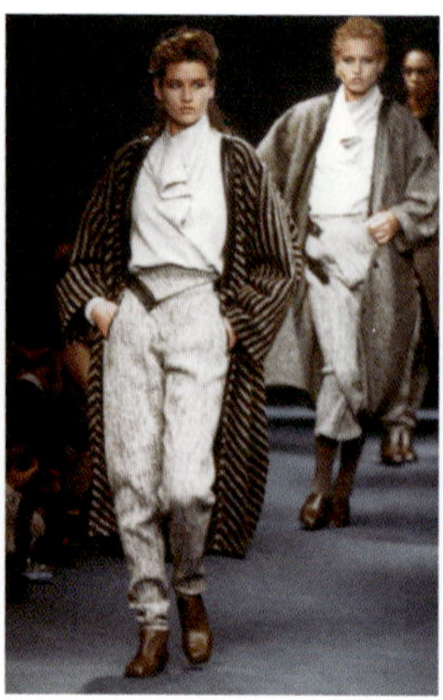
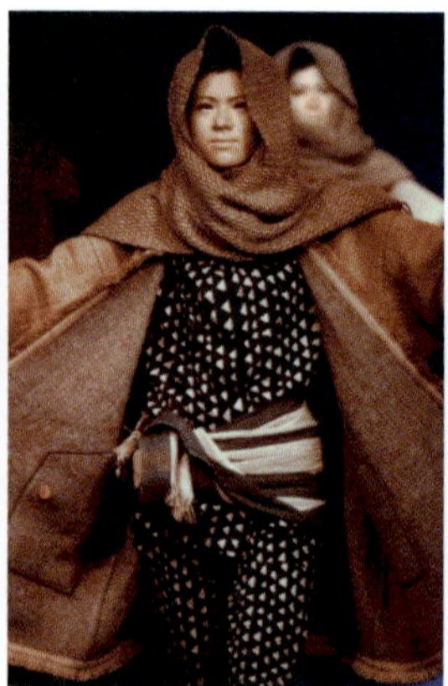
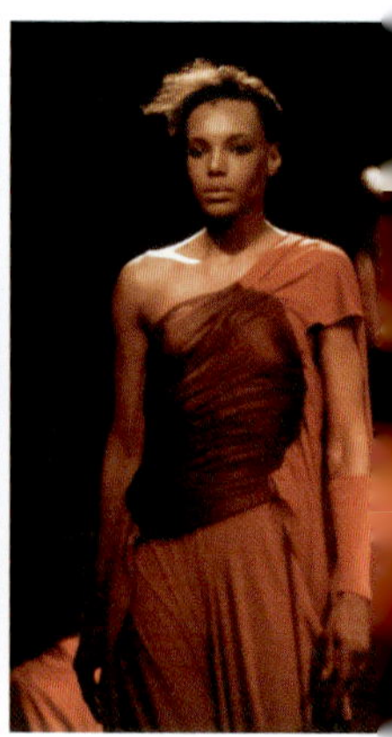

1

Waterfall Body
Formed and finished one
at a time by covering the
mannequin's body in cloth
partially infused with silicon.
1984 design/Autumn-Winter
1984 Collection
Photography: Art Kane;
model: Jun Kano; *Stern*
(Germany), October 4,
1984 edition

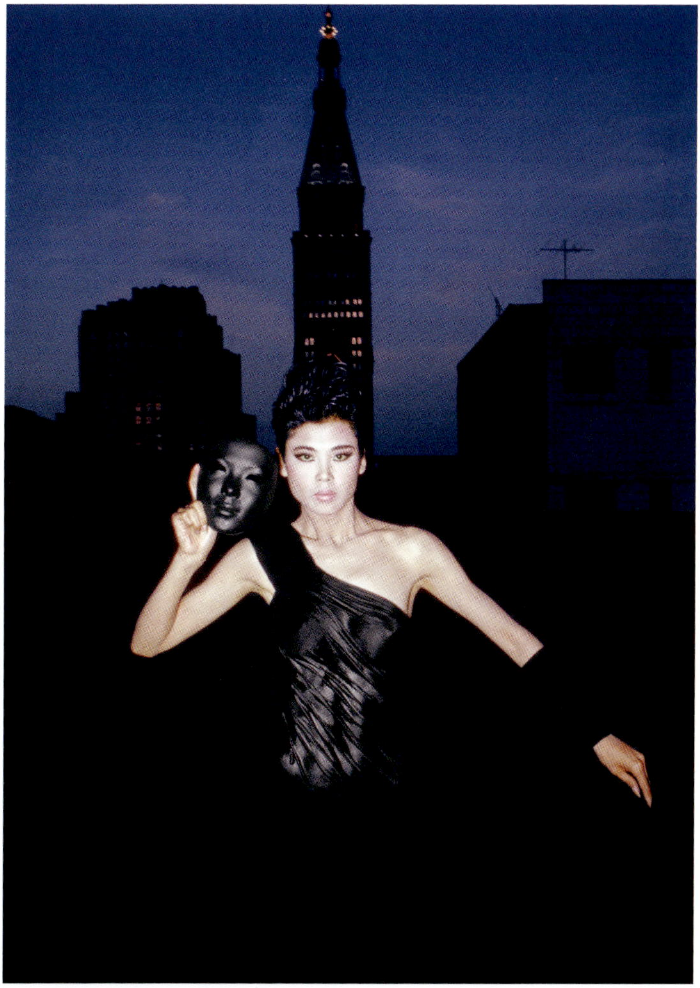

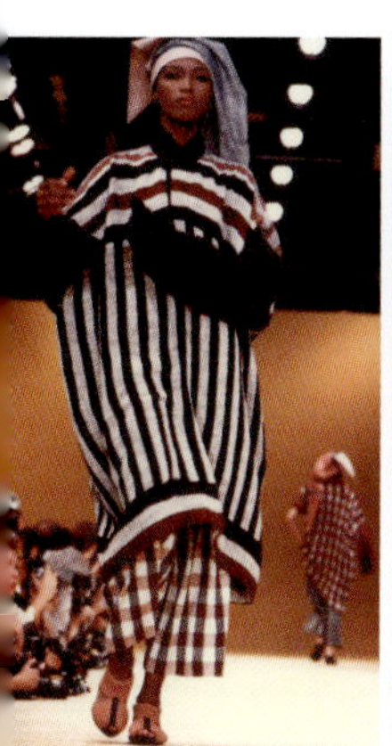

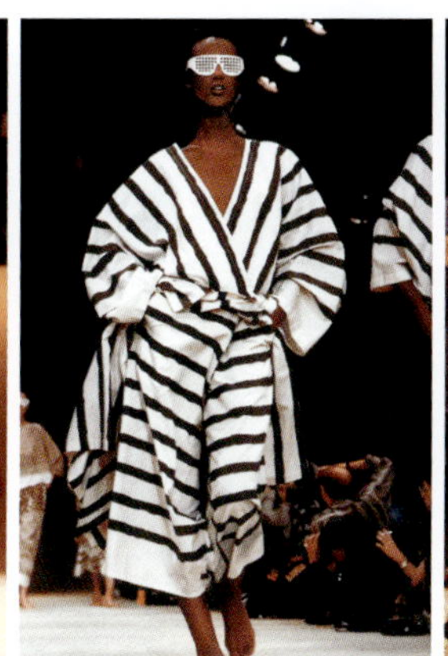

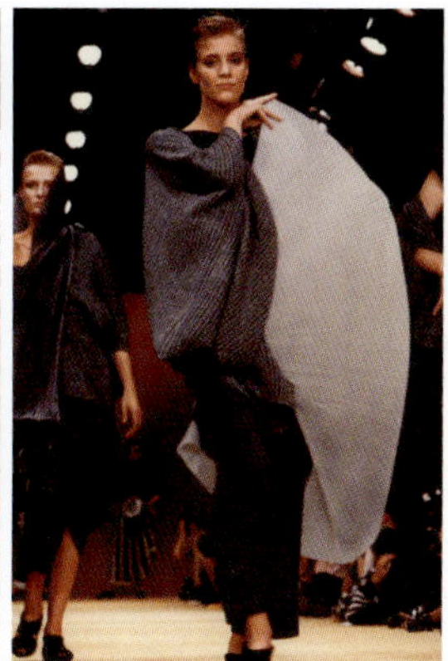

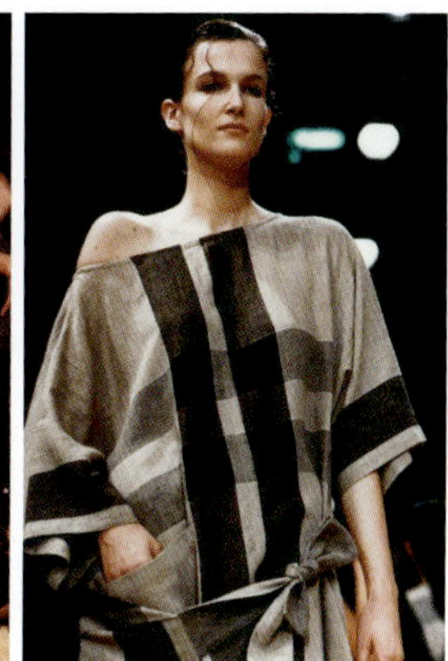

2

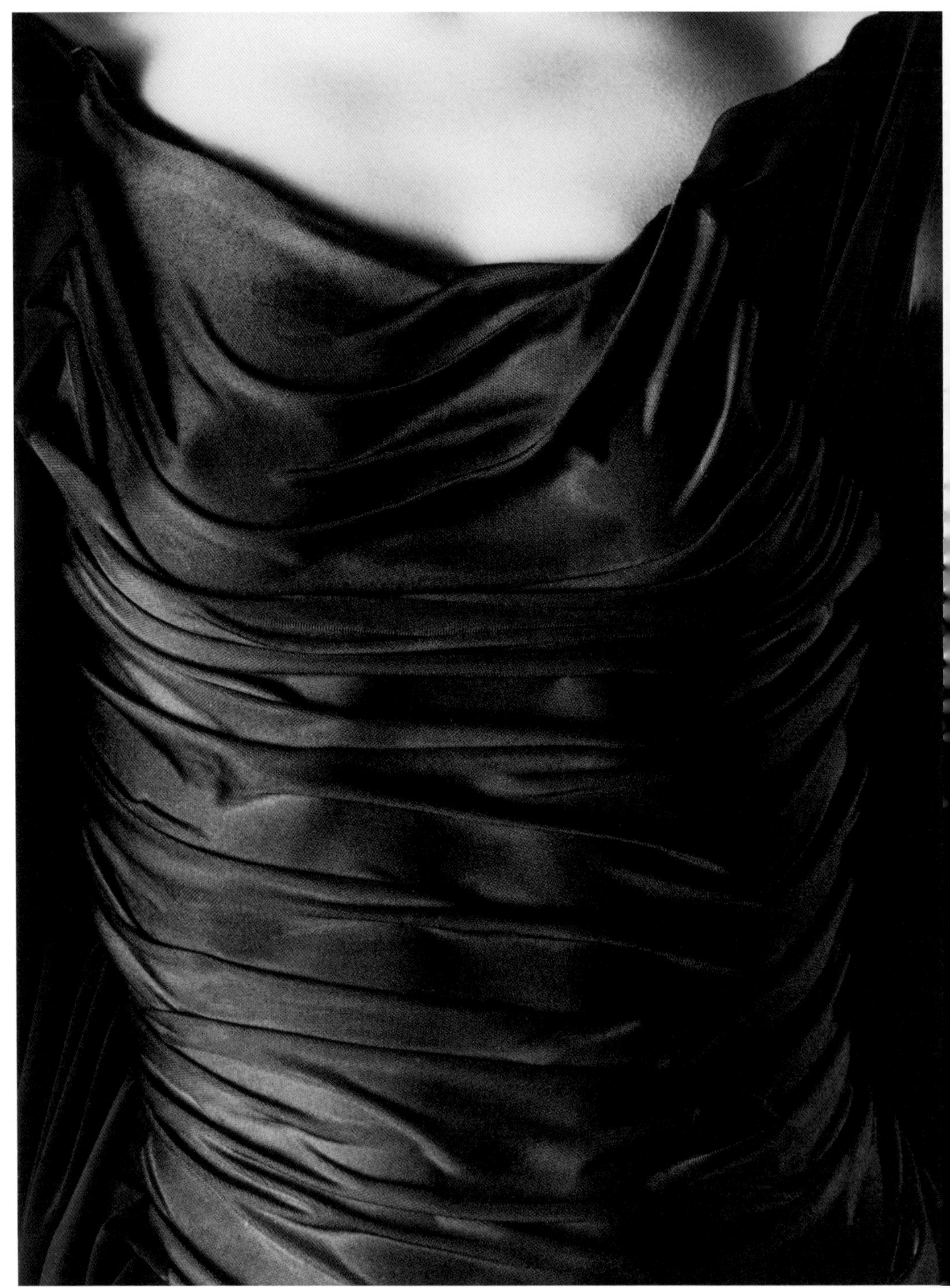

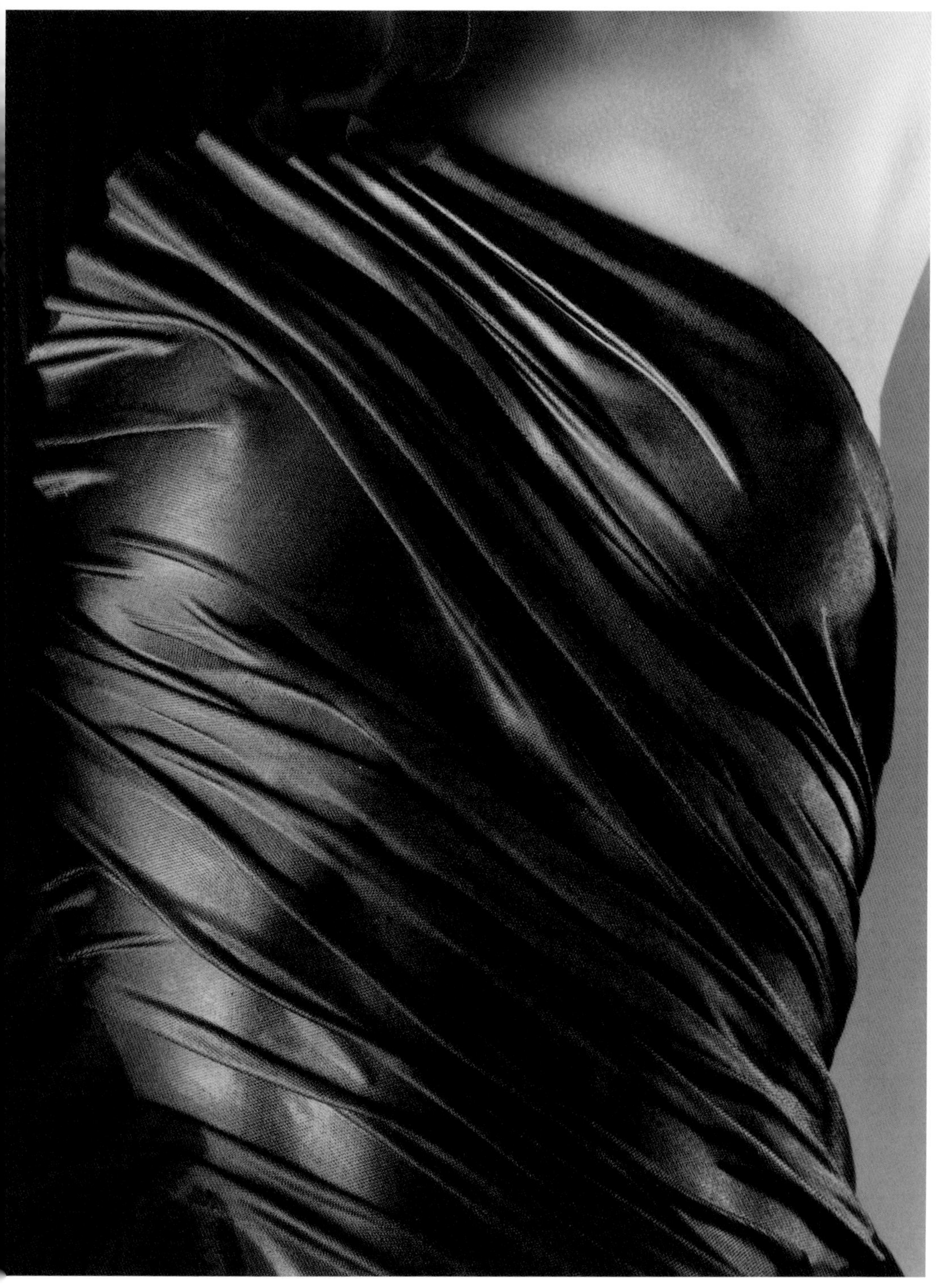

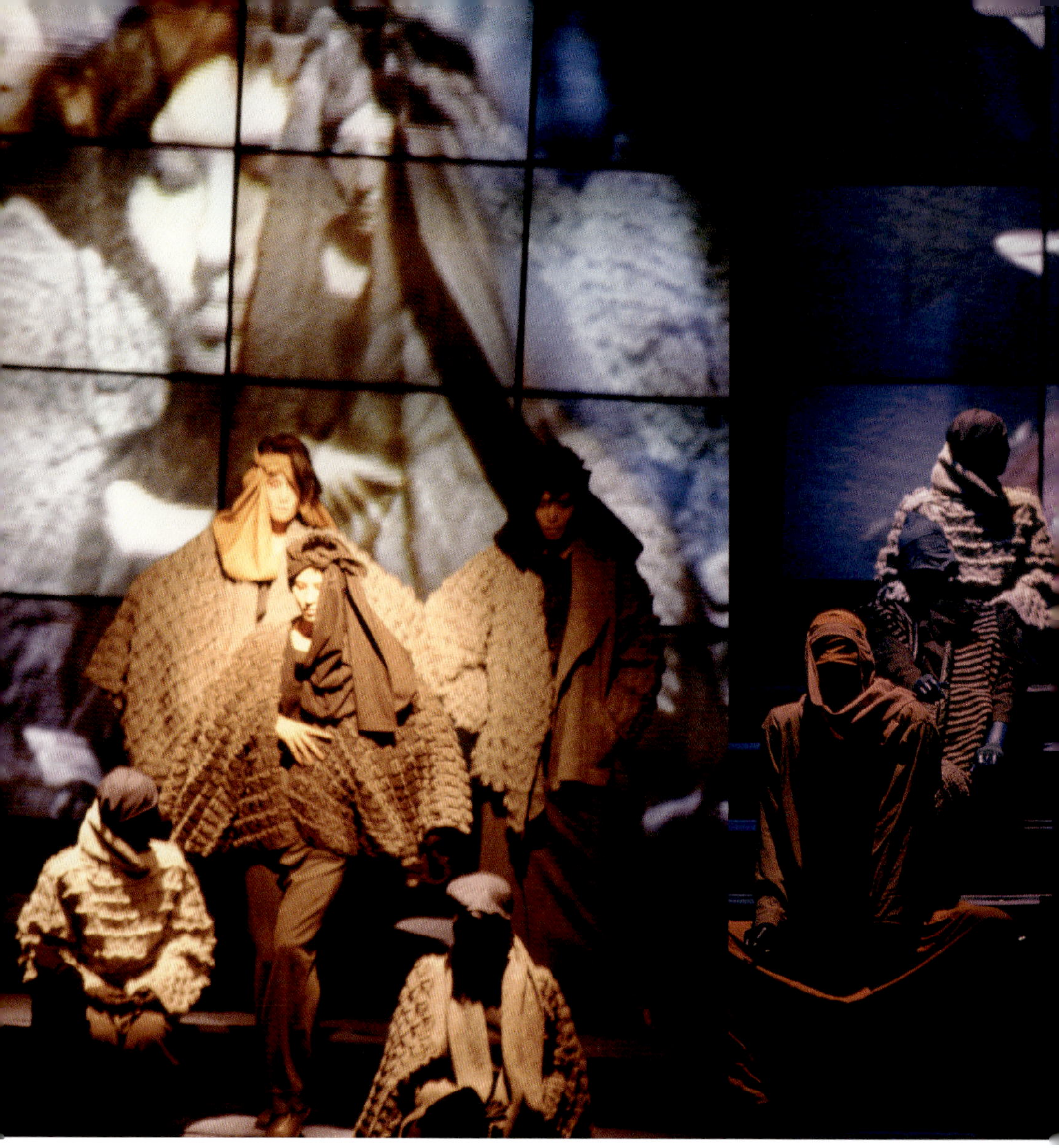

Pages 116–117: *Waterfall Body*
1984 design/Autumn-Winter 1984 Collection
Photography: Tsutomu Wakatsuki

Live Installation Part II
Left: *Bell Knit*
Center, from front left to back: Double-face cotton shirt and pants; tweed chambray vest; *Bell Knit*; **lower right:** tweed chambray coat and tweed stretch skirt; **upper right:** *Bell Knit*. All designed in 1984.
Autumn-Winter 1984 Collection
Right: *Waterfall Body* 1984 design/
Autumn-Winter 1984 Collection
Photography: Tsutomu Wakatsuki

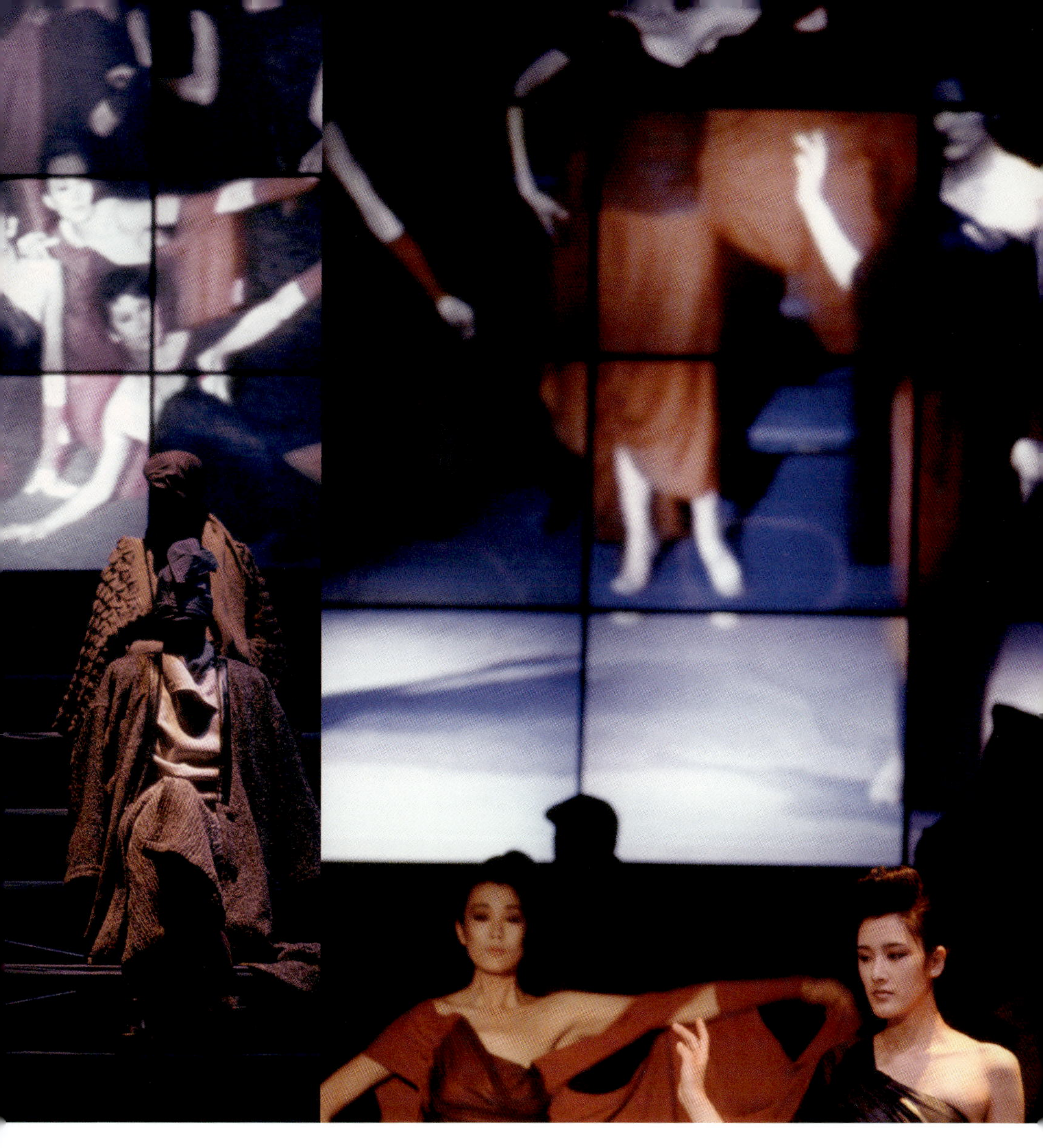

1985

> February: ISSEY MIYAKE MEN shown at Hotel Saint James Albany for the first time in Paris with the Autumn-Winter 1985 Collection (continued until 2020)

> February–April: *Issey Miyake Bodyworks: Fashion without Taboo* exhibition at the Boilerhouse Project, Victoria and Albert Museum in London

> March: Autumn-Winter 1985 Paris Collection at Salle Sully, Jardin des Tuileries

> April: Autumn-Winter 1985 Tokyo Collection at the Endo Commemoration Hall of Bunka Fukuso Gakuin

> October: Showed *Just A Moment* video installation filmed by Kazumi Kurigami at the opening of Aoyama Spiral, Tokyo

> October–December: Participated in *L'Or, la Laine et le Soie, Cotons et Plumes de Paon. Les Textiles de l'Inde et les Modèles Créés par Issey Miyake* exhibition at the Musée des Arts Décoratifs, Paris

L'Or, la Laine et le Soie, Cotons et Plumes de Paon. Les Textiles de l'Inde et les Modèles Créés par Issey Miyake exhibition

When Issey Miyake and Makiko Minagawa with some others traveled to India at the end of 1981, they met with the cultural advisers of the Indian government, which led to Miyake's participation in the exhibition that was held as part of the "Indian Year in France" events. Strongly urged by the Indian government, which was trying to maintain the country's textile techniques and to expand them internationally, Miyake created clothes using original Indian-inspired splashed patterns, 22-karat-gold thread *zari*, and hand-painting in collaboration with the Indian ateliers. They were not only shown in the exhibition, but also presented in the Spring-Summer 1986 Paris Collection that was held at the same time as the exhibition opening.

October 15–December 29:
Musée des Arts Décoratifs, Paris

Autumn-Winter 1985 Paris Collection,
March 23, Salle Sully, Jardin des Tuileries

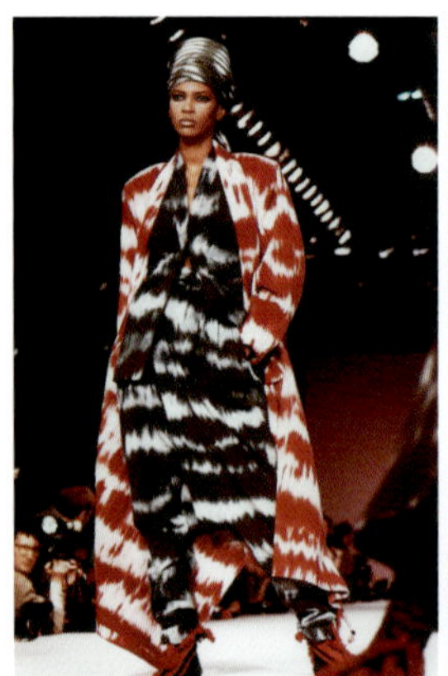
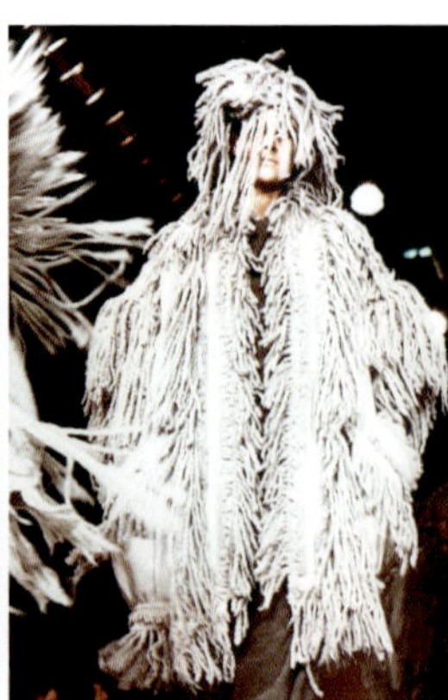
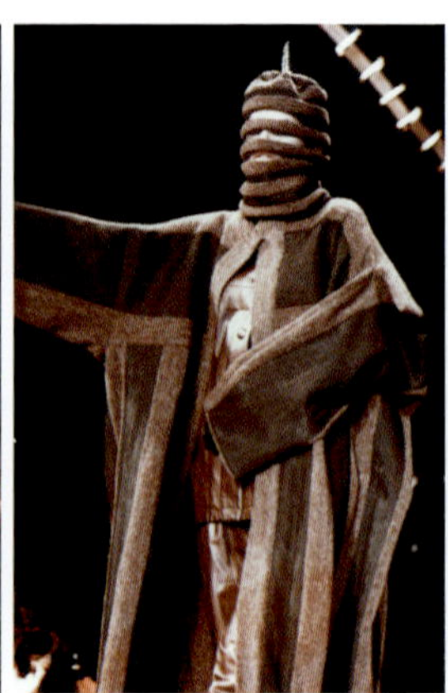
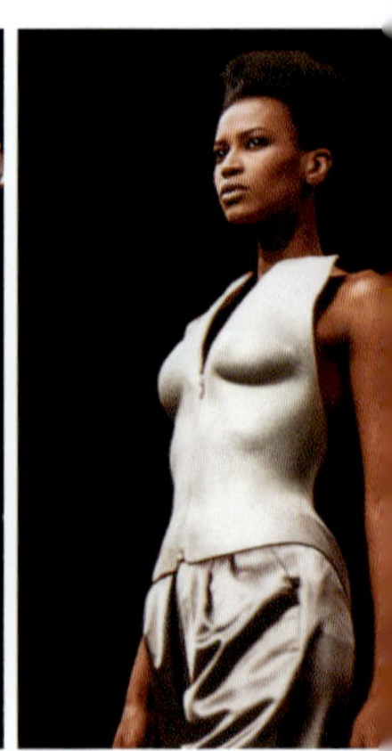

ISSEY MIYAKE PERMANENTE

There are such timeless clothes that people continue to wear for a long time among the variety of designs presented in each season's collections. While Issey Miyake always challenged in designing new clothes for the future, he also focused on the existence of such timeless clothes. This was the start of the Permanente brand into which Miyake tried to show new concepts with selections of special materials and forms based on his clothes-making experiences.

Spring-Summer 1986 Paris Collection,
October 19, Salle Sully, Jardin des Tuileries

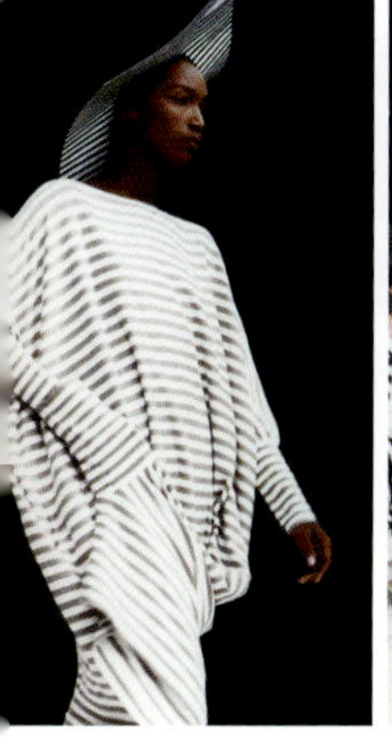
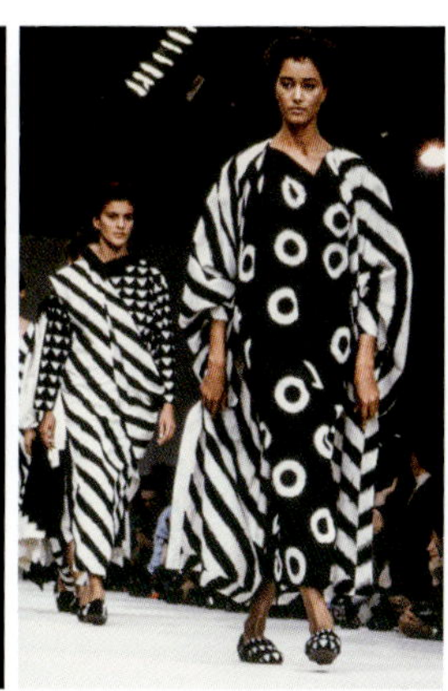
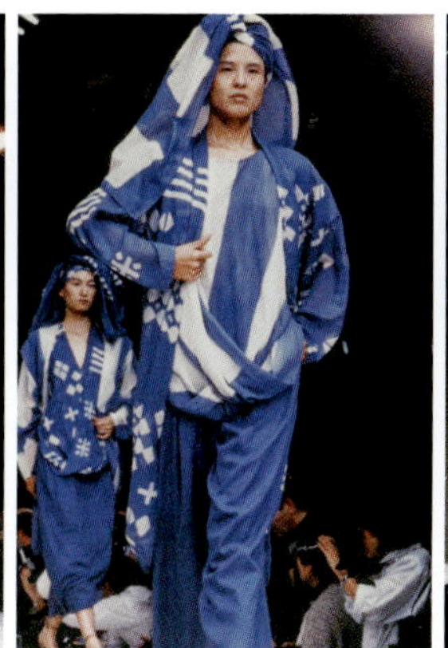
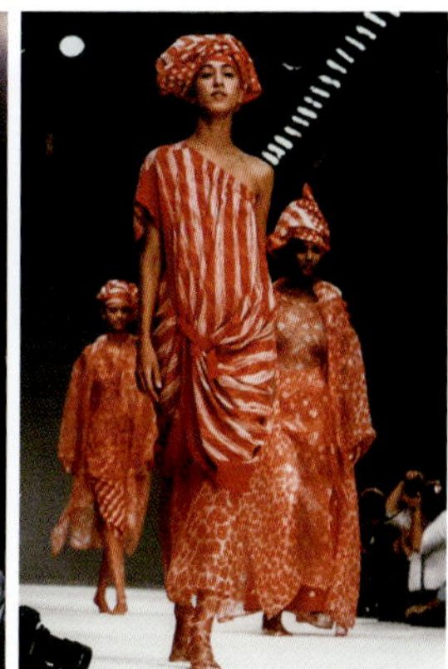

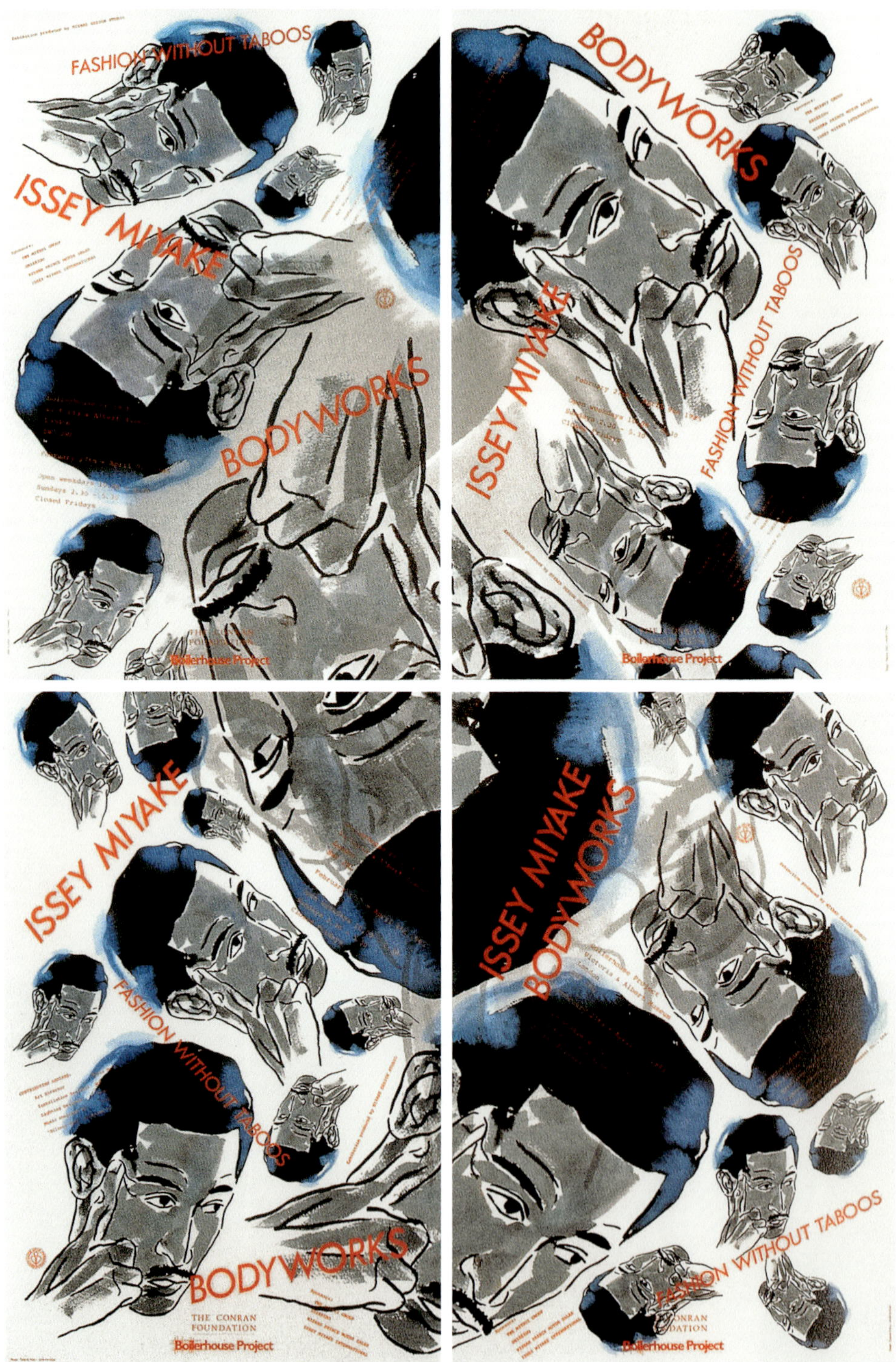

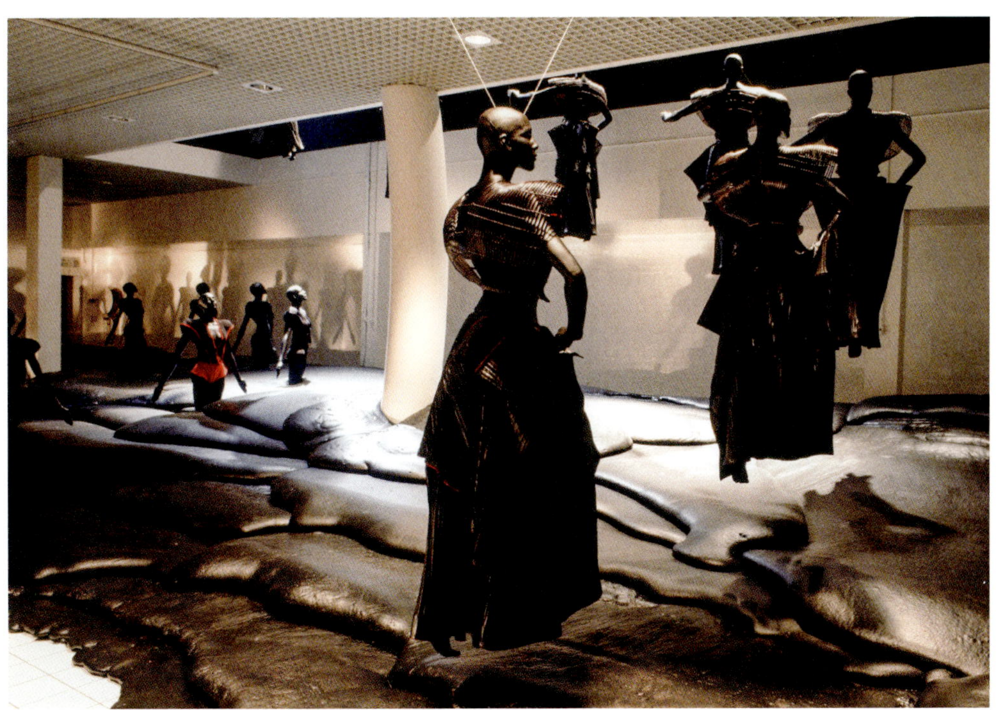

Opposite: Invitation for the *Issey Miyake Bodyworks: Fashion without Taboo* exhibition held at Victoria and Albert Museum in London. Illustrations and design by Tadanori Yokoo

Above and following spread: The *Issey Miyake Bodyworks: Fashion without Taboo* exhibition featured mannequins standing in black bubbles of what looked like a pool of coal tar. The space was designed by Shiro Kuramata and Tomio Mohri.

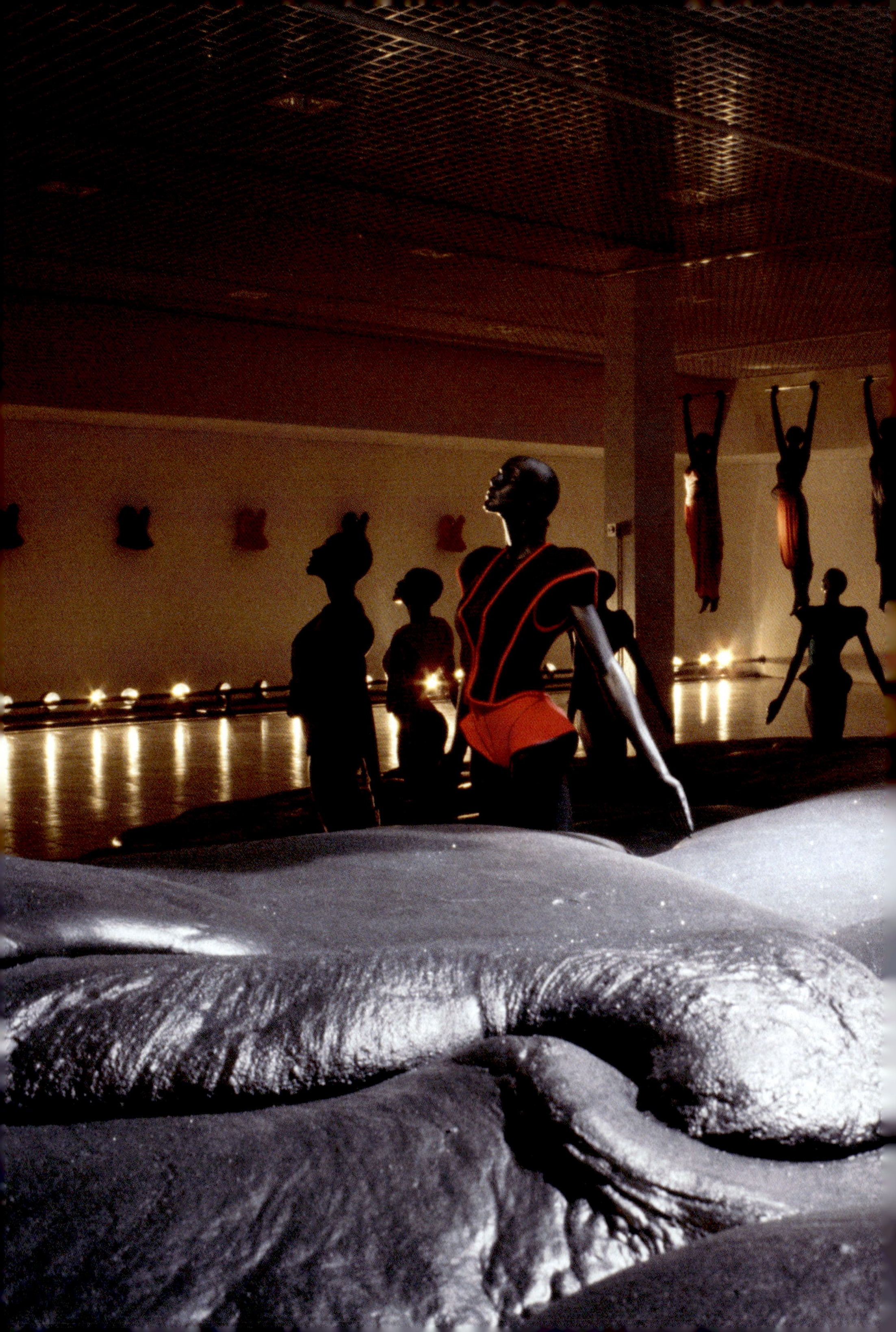

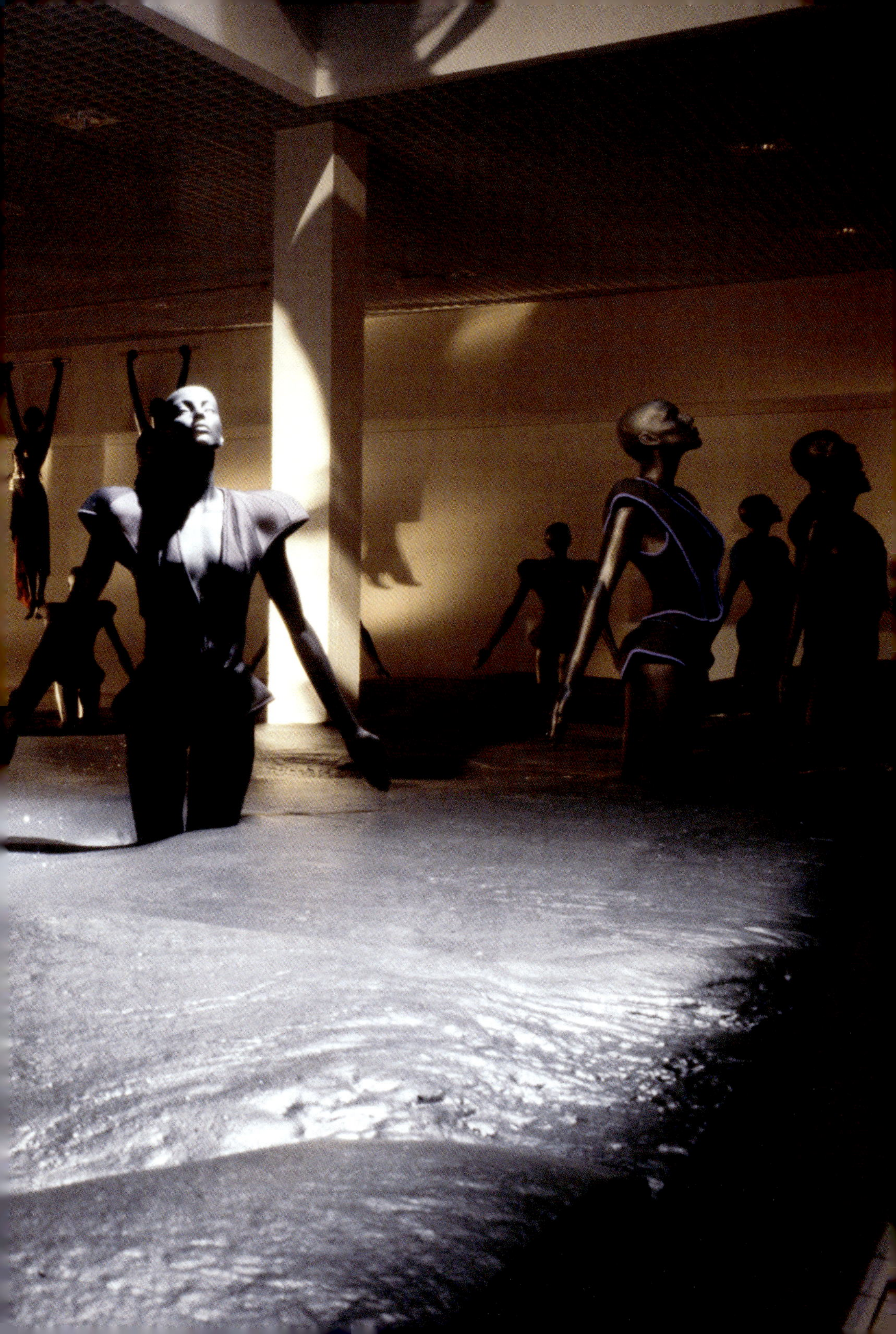

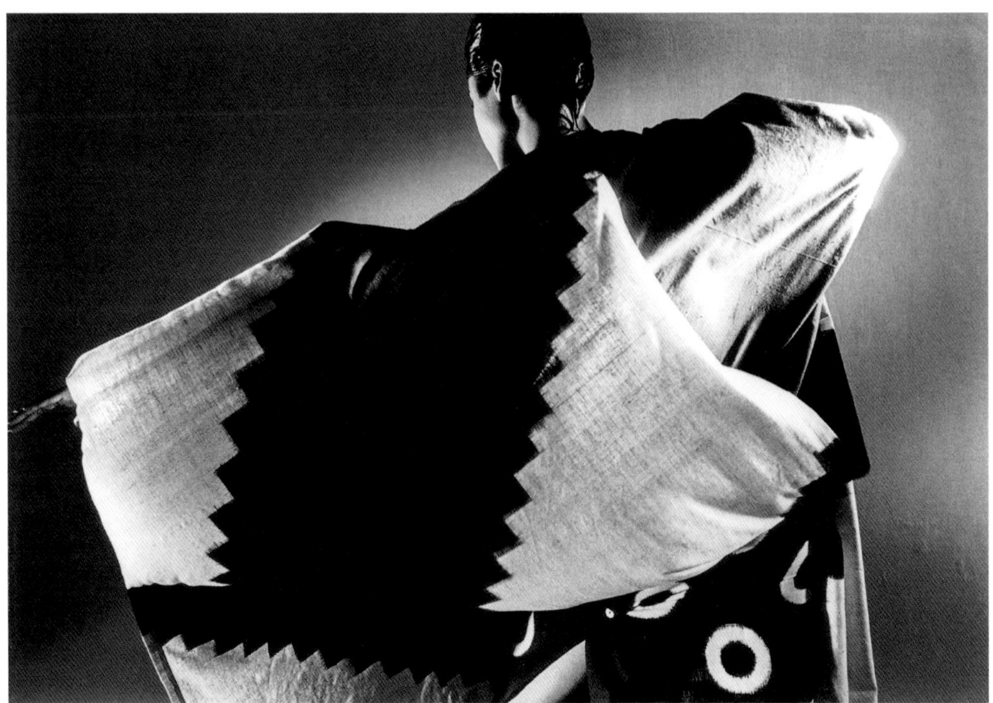

Indian *Ikat* dress and jacket
1985 design/Spring-Summer 1986 Collection
Photography: Keiichi Tahara

Opposite: ***L'Or, la Laine et le Soie, Cotons et Plumes de Paon. Les Textiles de l'Inde et les Modèles Créés par Issey Miyake*** exhibition
Hand-painted cotton circle skirt and patchwork T-shirt in the back. Large geometric patterns by Indian double *ikat* in the front.
1985 design/Spring-Summer 1986 Collection
Photography: Yasuhiko Ohgida

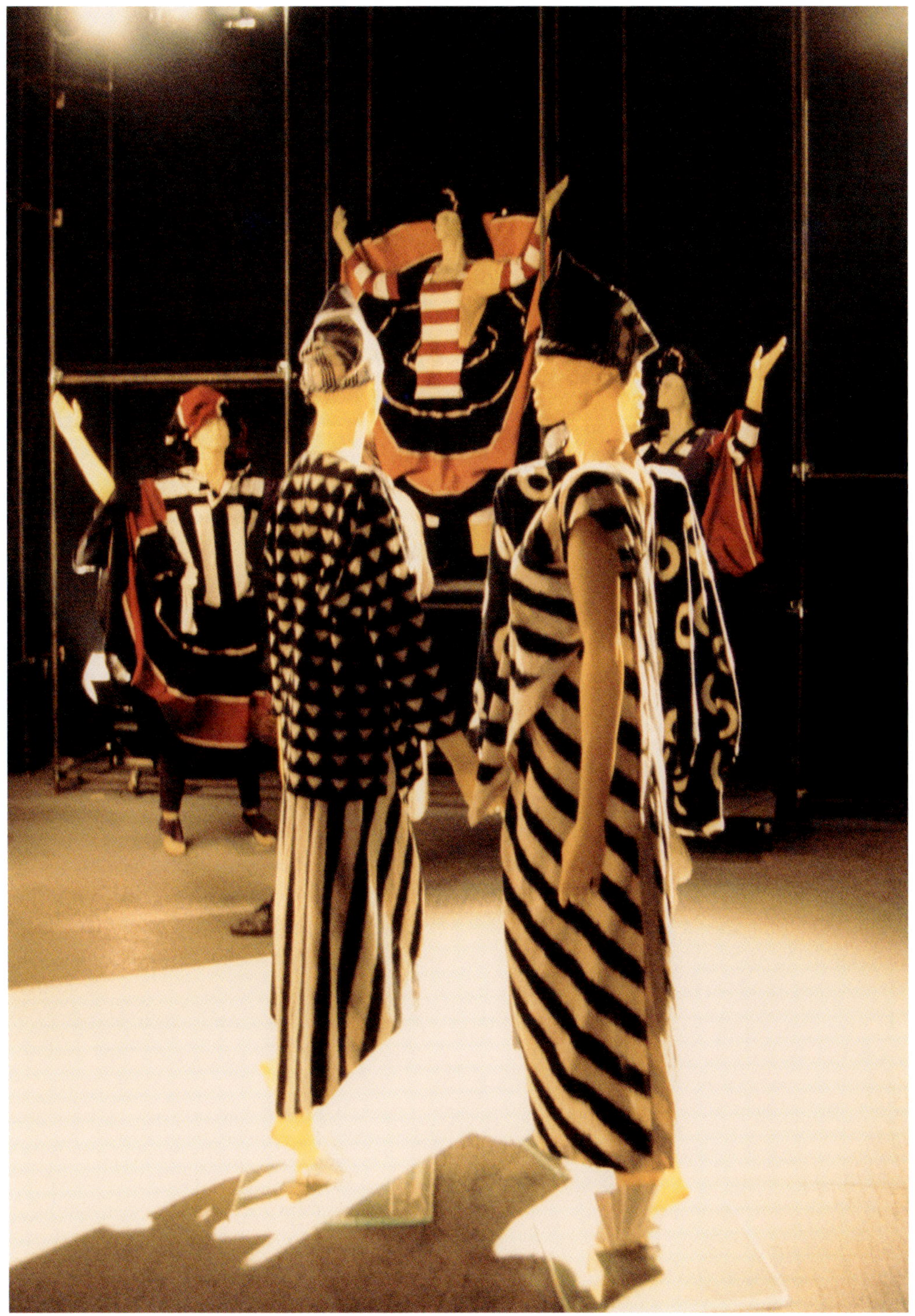

5—VISUAL DIALOGUE

Essay by
KAZUKO KOIKE

IP IM IT

Yet another adventure quickly began, another burst of Issey Miyake's inexhaustably creative mind, and, indeed, it was a challenge to be able to have the collections photographed continuously by the best photographer which one could possibly hope for, and to publish such photos.

Irving Penn.[1] Ever since his student days Issey would gaze, almost breathlessly, at Penn's photographs; this was his champion of fashion photography. Issey most probably discovered Penn in copies of American *Vogue*, which he had looked at regularly since his school days. Penn was his private hero. He always referred to him reverently as "Penn-san." An Irving Penn retrospective[2] toured major museums in the USA and around the world in 2009 and 2010. Visitors saw – many for the first time – the deep, rich variety of his subjects. Here, they encountered another aspect of this artist, aside from the historical achievement of his fashion photography. His portraits of the people of "marginal regions" of the world are testimony to his keen anthropological and ethnographical observation, and in them one finds the photographer's love for and curiosity about his subjects, and sometimes even a reflection of his humor. During his trips to remote places for pho-

tos commissioned by *Vogue* and other media, Penn had made these impressive series of portraits for his own private work. Among those places was Dahomey, now the Republic of Benin, where Penn depicted proud and pious people. These works were exhibited in 2004 at Tokyo's Japan Folk Crafts Museum.

Asking Irving Penn to take photographs was a major enterprise that went beyond a mere fashion photo assignment, and Issey Miyake was one such adventurer who had lived for years with this intense dream; this hope had become for him a *basso continuo*.

I had an expectation in mind when I made my request to Penn-san. There is in Japanese a word, A-ŪN. It describes a form of communication established when one person throws voiceless messages to another. I anticipated that our collaboration would have such sympathy. It would be our unspoken understanding.
Issey Miyake Photographs by Irving Penn,
Libro Port Publishing Co., Ltd., 1988

Miyake obliged himself not to be present with Penn at the photo sessions so as to allow the photographer full freedom of photographic interpretation and maneuvering. Miyake's *attaché de presse* at the time, Midori Kitamura,[3] took the responsibility to represent Miyake and realized their "*a-ūn* communication." The project continued over the course of 13 years at Penn's studio in New York, each time photographing a new Issey collection, and achieving overall a unique œuvre. One finds the silent power of teamwork behind every innovative project that Miyake Design Studio undertook. When Penn's photo sessions were over, the photographs were delivered to Tokyo, and then it was the graphic designer Ikko Tanaka's turn to work on the layout and typography for the posters.

IP: Irving Penn, IM: Issey Miyake, IT: Ikko Tanaka. Kitamura eventually punctuated the "crystallization" of their collaboration in the form of books and exhibitions promoting the idea of "visual dialogue."[4]

Dictionaries tell us that *a-ūn* means, in Sanskrit, a breathing out with the mouth open and breathing in with the mouth closed; the two together thus signifying the fundamental index of life. We are also told that these two sounds refer to the delicate mutual feelings of more than two people working or doing something together and the convergence of feeling between them. This reminds me of an occasion some time ago when Issey was enjoying an afternoon walk and saying aloud, "Mr. Guardian Dog," followed by "Mr. Guardian Dog, *a-ūn*." At Japanese Shinto shrines two stone statues of dogs stand guarding each side of the entrance — one with its mouth open and the other with its mouth closed, as if one were uttering the sound *a*, and the other the sound *ūn*. What Issey was saying on his walk was the very first phrases that Japanese children used to learn to read aloud as soon as they entered elementary school. In his case, the mountain village memory of a young boy had suddenly revisited him.

A-ŪN RAPPORT

Then came the *Issey Miyake A-ŪN* exhibition at the Musée des Arts Décoratifs, Paris, in 1988.[5] It would be easy to say that it showed what had been created through his "*a-ūn* rapport," but the actual display did not simply follow a chronological order, nor was it intended as a retrospective show. Yet the groundbreaking installation style of the show was fully appreciated by Parisian as well as international visitors. *A-ūn* rapport between and among specialized professionals at their studios, *a-ūn* rapport between designers and craftsmen, and among professionals of such divergent fields as graphic, lighting, and display design, and many others, most of whom usually have little to do with clothing design. And one could never overlook how important this was vis-à-vis "Penn-san." The scope of Issey Miyake's collaborators grew as broad and diverse as the credits of a feature film. Issey, as a creative director, screamed "a," and this was rapidly responded to with a wonderful "hum." Genuine fruition.

In the mid-1980s, while accepting the fashion industry custom of producing two collections per year (spring-summer and autumn-winter), Issey became increasingly skeptical about the prevailing attitude toward everyday life – that is, the consumption-oriented life cycle that allowed very little room for things to last for more than a short while and then to disappear. Prior to today's wide acceptance of the fact that the Earth's resources are limited, this was his intuition as well as his emotional resistance against ever-increasing consumption.

PERMANENT LIFE FOR CLOTHING

ISSEY MIYAKE PERMANENTE was conceived and presented as a new brand.[6] Though it may not be so well known to the general public, Lord Snowdon[7] photographed people wearing clothes from this group; the results were photos of a special quality and grace thanks to the intense presence and self-confidence of the models – people of accomplishment in their many respective fields. In fact, PERMANENTE was rooted in Issey's observing that his friends and customers cherished the clothes he had designed and wore them long after their debut season. This so moved him that he saw PERMANENTE at the base of his creativity, the embodiment of quality and style so fine and sophisticated as to make wearers convinced that "These are clothes for a lifetime." This belief was further augmented by his defiance of the status quo, as he confronted the idea of "New Design" with the best of his "Old Design." It was such a regal clothing series, and a testimony to his astute vision of "the life of a piece of clothing" in a period when it was still considered farfetched to uphold ecological consciousness or to discuss the virtues of "reuse." Further extensions of such consciousness came with the PLEATS PLEASE ISSEY MIYAKE, and the 132 5. ISSEY MIYAKE series.

These product series confirmed that there were numerous people around the world who were happy to see them made available, and happy to wear them as the creative masterpieces of materials and styles that they continue to be. Mightn't we call it then the fruition of the *a-ūn* rapport between clothes maker and clothes wearer?

AS EYES AND MIND DICTATE

Meanwhile, Miyake endeavored to have an exhibition in Japan of pottery by a longtime friend, Lucie Rie.[8] She had fled from her home in Vienna during the Nazi era, and now lived and worked in London. Her vases, bowls, and other works are imbued with a quietness of a traditional Oriental kind, but also appeal directly to our contemporary sensibilities, thus inviting the viewer into her rare and unique world.

Earlier on at a bookshop in London, Miyake had by chance come across a book featuring her work. This was a fortuitous encounter with work that might otherwise have remained the private knowledge of an experienced collector. After doing some research, it did not take long for Miyake to locate and visit Lucie Rie at her studio.

She was a petite woman with a lovable and expressive face. Her works remind us of the quiet atmosphere of white porcelain vases from Korea's Rhee Dynasty, while her very thinly baked pottery works show a sharp and even straightforward aggressiveness akin to the taste of our time. Despite the fact that they were meeting for the first time, the two were completely at ease with one another. Lucie welcomed Issey with great charm and they plunged into long conversations. She showed him a number of ceramic buttons she had baked under wartime austerities. Their encounter was inevitable: one was not simply a pottery maker, and the other not merely a creator of clothing. Now unrestricted by the hardships of war, they came together as phoenix-like immortal lovers both with eyes keen on the details of everyday life.

Issey Miyake's dedication culminated in Lucie Rie's exhibition at the Sogetsu Art Center in Tokyo thanks to the support of the *ikebana* (flower arrangement) grand master and filmmaker Hiroshi Teshigahara.[9] He was then the head of the Center, which in the 1960s was almost always Tokyo's first venue for the presentation of avant-garde and experimental events in contemporary music, cinema, performing arts, and so on. As such, Sogetsu made a major contribution to the enhancement of cultural exchange and merger on the non-governmental level.

Following the show in Tokyo, the Municipal Museum of Oriental Ceramics, Osaka, hosted the exhibition *Issey Miyake Meets Lucie Rie.*[10] The show was an opportunity for many people to see Rie's works for the first time, as well as for researchers and admirers of pottery to become fully cognizant of her achievement.

TEN SEN MEN
(POINT, LINE, AND PLANE)

The Hiroshima City Museum of Contemporary Art had decided to establish the Hiroshima Art Prize in order to recognize contemporary creative artists, and they announced that they would award the first prize (1990) to Issey Miyake. The selection committee consisted of museum directors, art critics, and other specialists from Japan, Korea, the USA, and Europe; the committee met many times in order to meet the Museum's founding mission to promote contemporary art from an international perspective. Michiaki Kawakita, the prize's organizing committee chairperson, announced in a speech, "Mr. Issey Miyake, a native of Hiroshima, was selected with overwhelming support out of a number of important recommended artists from around the world."

In his acceptance speech, Miyake said, "Without homage to human beings and Nature, one cannot make clothing, and at the basis of this act lies a wish for peace."[11]

Another of his exhibitions was named *Issey Miyake: Ten Sen Men*[12] and featured "only things that have been created in the recent two and a half years, centering around 'clothing' made of stretched and pleated fabrics."[13] The title (written in the Roman alphabet) adapted Japanese terms and contained conceptual and linguistic ingenuity. That is, as Miyake said, the three terms represented, in shortened form, TENSION, SENSIBILITY, and MENTALITY, with each Chinese character used in the Japanese-language notation respectively representing: POINT (Ten), indicating the design team's work; LINE (Sen), omnidirectional communication; and PLANE (Men), signifying a society consisting of networks of people. I could extend this message and say that this must be something like a motto or an ideal that keeps the connected unit of the Miyake Design Studio so intact. What, after all, is the secret of the fact that the Miyake Design Studio, this rare creative group, has been able to remain slim, flexible, and even robust? (Just compare it with other global organizations.) Their friends and fans are eager to know their secret!

It was in Paris one evening that a glowing full moon rose above the city. It brought light to the streets, bridges, and river. The moon came close to the Eiffel Tower, and when it crowned the Tower's top, I heard Issey say, "You see? It has become the fragrance bottle." Fantastic creative people, fantastic world! The perfume, L'Eau d'Issey, was launched in 1992.[14]

1   Irving Penn (1917–2009): Photographer. Studied design at the Philadelphia Museum School of Industrial Art under Alexey Brodovitch, *Harper's Bazaar* magazine's art director. Worked for numerous magazines and advertisers, but was especially noted for his long and fruitful collaboration with *Vogue* magazine, which lasted until his death. Published many books of his photographs throughout his career, and his photographs are in the collections of all the major museums in the world. The Museum of Modern Art in New York honored him with a retrospective exhibition in 1984. In 1997, he made a donation to the Art Institute of Chicago of prints and archival material, and the Art Institute mounted a retrospective that also toured to five museums around the world, beginning at the State Hermitage in St. Petersburg, Russia. In 1999, it was held as *Irving Penn: A Career in Photography* at the Tokyo Metropolitan Museum of Photography. In late 2015, a major retrospective exhibition opened at the Smithsonian American Art Museum in Washington, D.C.

2   *Irving Penn: Small Trades,* a collection of serial photographs of workers Penn took in 1950–51, which was exhibited at the J. Paul Getty Museum in Los Angeles in 2009. A collection of portraits of well-known writers and artists, *Portraits,* was presented at London's National Portrait Gallery in 2010.

3   Midori Kitamura: Chairman of Miyake Design Studio. Since 1976, as *attaché de presse* of ISSEY MIYAKE, has been involved in all activities, including collection creation, exhibitions, publications; has led fragrance and watch development projects as producer and creative director for products.

4   The books are: *Issey Miyake Photographs by Irving Penn*, 1988, New York Graphic Society Books + Little, Brown and Company + Callaway Editions, USA; Edipresse-Livres SA, France and Switzerland; Edition Stemmle, Germany; and Libro Port Publishing Co., Ltd., Japan.
Irving Penn Regards the Work of Issey Miyake, 1999, Jonathan Cape, UK; Bulfinch Press, USA; Editions Plum, France; Schirmer/Mosel, Germany; Kyuryudo, Japan. There are also privately published books.
The exhibition was titled *Irving Penn and Issey Miyake: Visual Dialogue (21_21 DESIGN SIGHT, 2011)*: See pp. 306–307.

5   *ISSEY MIYAKE A-ŪN*: See pp. 158, 160–163.

6   ISSEY MIYAKE PERMANENTE: See pp. 121, 148–151.

7   Lord Snowdon (1930–2017) Antony Armstrong-Jones, 1st Earl of Snowdon: Photographer. Did theater, fashion, and portrait photography. Established his own studio in 1952. After marrying Princess Margaret in 1960, he was granted the title Earl of Snowdon.

8   Lucie Rie (1902–1995): Pottery artist. Attended the Kunstgewerbeschule (University of Applied Arts), Vienna, to learn pottery. Studied closely under leading designers of the Wiener Werkstätte (Vienna Workshop), including Josef Hoffmann. After moving to London in 1938, learned a variety of ceramic and porcelain styles, while repeating high-precision experiments with glazes. Established a style of pottery that was uniquely her own, modern and elegant form combined with rich hue effects.

9   Hiroshi Teshigahara (1927–2001): *Ikebana* artist, filmmaker. Succeeded to the position of Sogetsu *ikebana* grand master, third generation, in 1980, created avant-garde *ikebana* works, and later came to be involved in a wide range of creative activities. Made a number of films based on scripts by his close friend, writer Kōbō Abe.

10 *Issey Miyake Meets Lucie Rie, Contemporary British Pottery Artist* exhibition: See p. 166.

11 Message by Issey Miyake from *Issey Miyake: Ten Sen Men* exhibition catalogue, 1990, p. 12.

12 Exhibition, *Issey Miyake: Ten Sen Men*: See pp. 176–177.

13 *Issey Miyake: Ten Sen Men* exhibition catalogue, p. 22.

14 L'Eau d'Issey: See pp. 186–187.

ISSEY MIYAKE Collection posters
Photography: Irving Penn; layout and typography: Ikko Tanaka

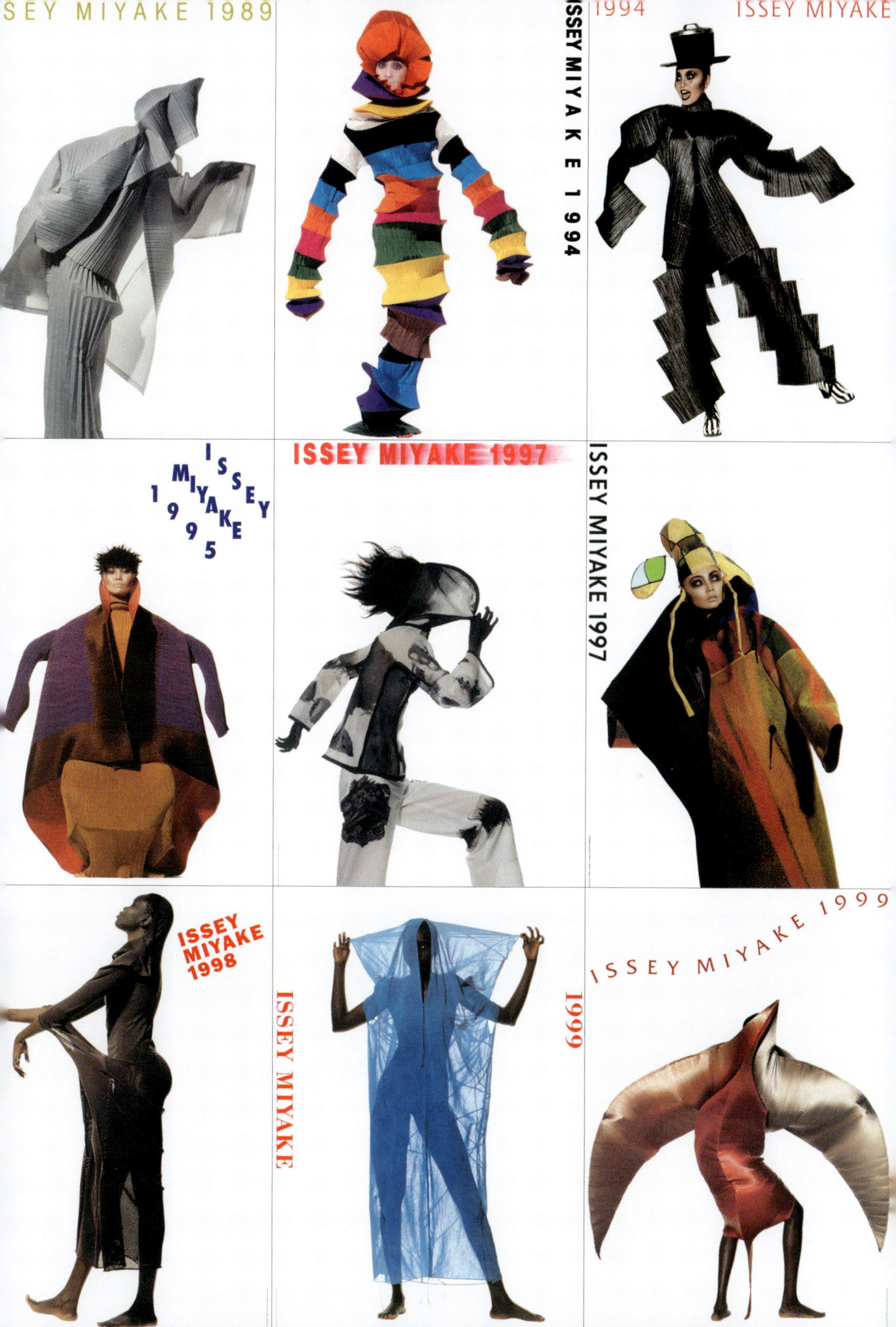

SEY MIYAKE 1989
ISSEY MIYAKE 1994
1994
ISSEY MIYAKE
ISSEY
MIYAKE
1995
ISSEY MIYAKE 1997
ISSEY MIYAKE 1997
ISSEY
MIYAKE
1998
ISSEY MIYAKE
ISSEY MIYAKE 1999
1999

1986

> January: The cover story of the Asian edition of *Time* magazine

> March: Autumn-Winter 1986 Paris Collection at Salle des Arts, Cour Carrée du Louvre

> April: Autumn-Winter 1986 Tokyo Collection at Yoyogi Tent South of the National Stadium

> May: Participated in the *HAATH: Hand Weaving of India and Issey Miyake* exhibition in Tokyo

> Participated in Nam June Paik's *Bye Bye Kipling: "From Ark Hills to the World / The Universe is Live"* East-West Television Competition

> October: Spring-Summer 1987 Paris Collection at Salle des Arts, Cour Carrée du Louvre

> November: Spring-Summer 1987 Tokyo Collection at Yoyogi Tent South of the National Stadium

> Irving Penn began to photograph the collections

> Publication began of Snowden's seasonal volumes of *ISSEY MIYAKE PERMANENTE* (private publication)

Collaboration with Irving Penn

Irving Penn, a master of still lifes, portraits, and fashion photography, began to photograph the ISSEY MIYAKE collections. The photo sessions were held twice a year, but Issey Miyake was never present. The sessions were led by a team in which Midori Kitamura was responsible for styling, Tyen did faces, and John Sahag handled hair. This unusual collaboration between Penn and Miyake was described as a "visual dialogue," which continued for 13 years, until 1999. Ikko Tanaka was in charge of poster layout and typography.

"Penn-san used his eyes to reinterpret clothing, breathing new life into it and providing completely different perspectives that I myself had not fully grasped. Without Penn-san mapping the way, I doubt I would have been able to find answers to any new challenges I might have taken on."

Issey Miyake, Irving Penn: A Career in Photography, *Tokyo Metropolitan Museum of Photography/The Asahi Shimbun Company, 1999*

1 Autumn-Winter 1986 Paris Collection, March 22, Salle des Arts, Cour Carrée du Louvre
2 Spring-Summer 1987 Paris Collection, October 18, Salle des Arts, Cour Carrée du Louvre

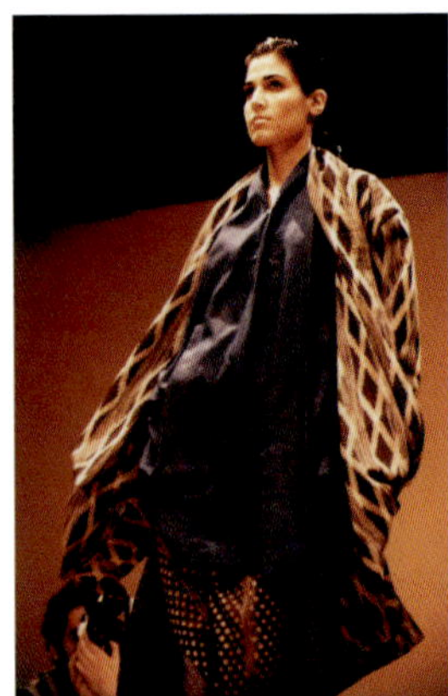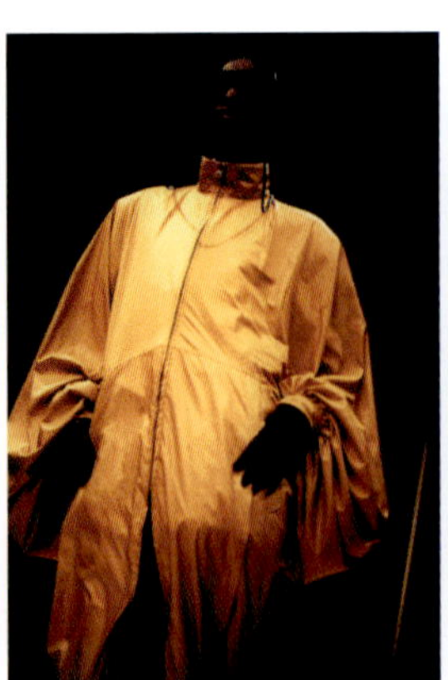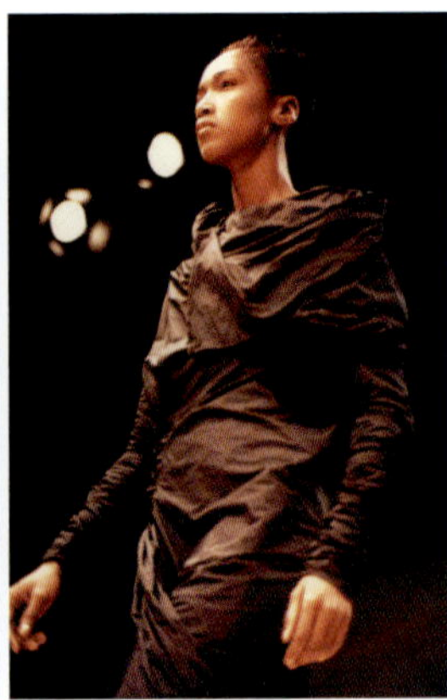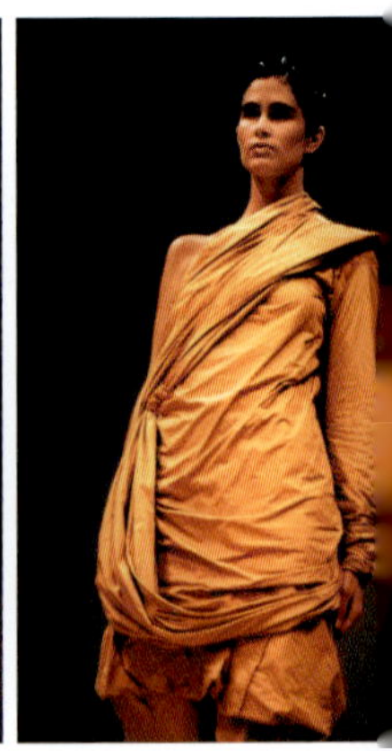

1

Spring-Summer 1987
Collection, poster
The *Balloon Raincoat* features
side tucks and drapes effort-
lessly across the back. The
Bird's Beak Cotton Cap was
designed alongside it in 1986
for the Spring-Summer 1987
Collection.
Photography: Irving Penn;
layout and typography:
Ikko Tanaka; model: Jun Kano

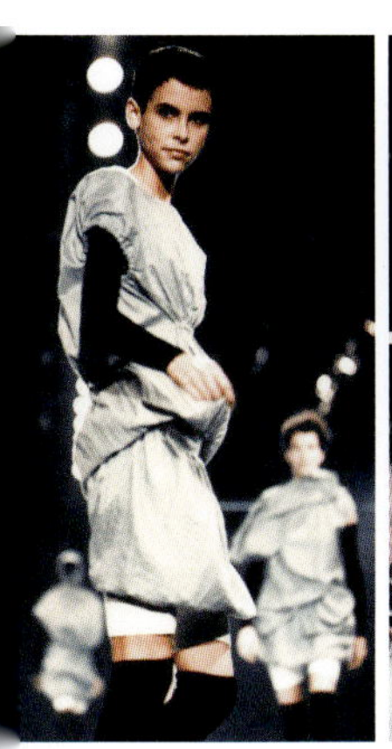
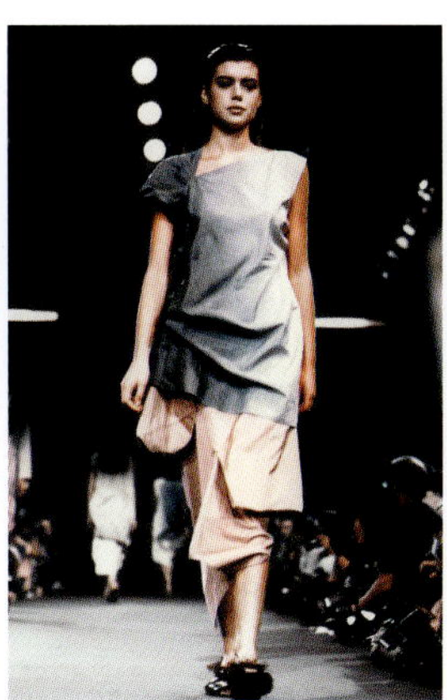
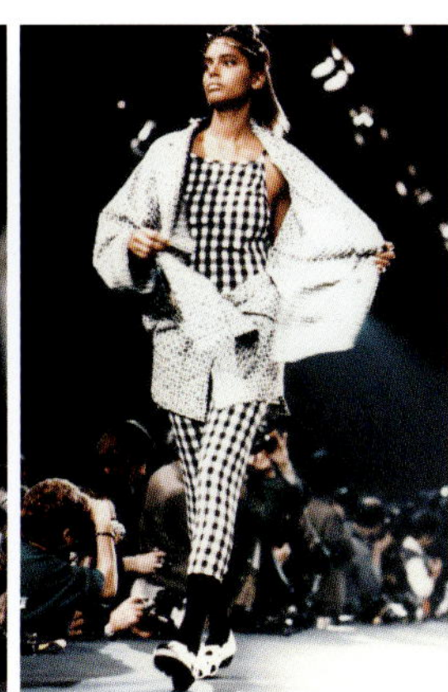
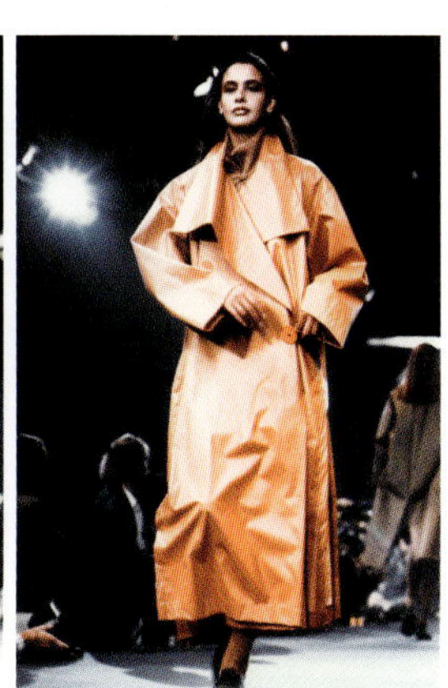

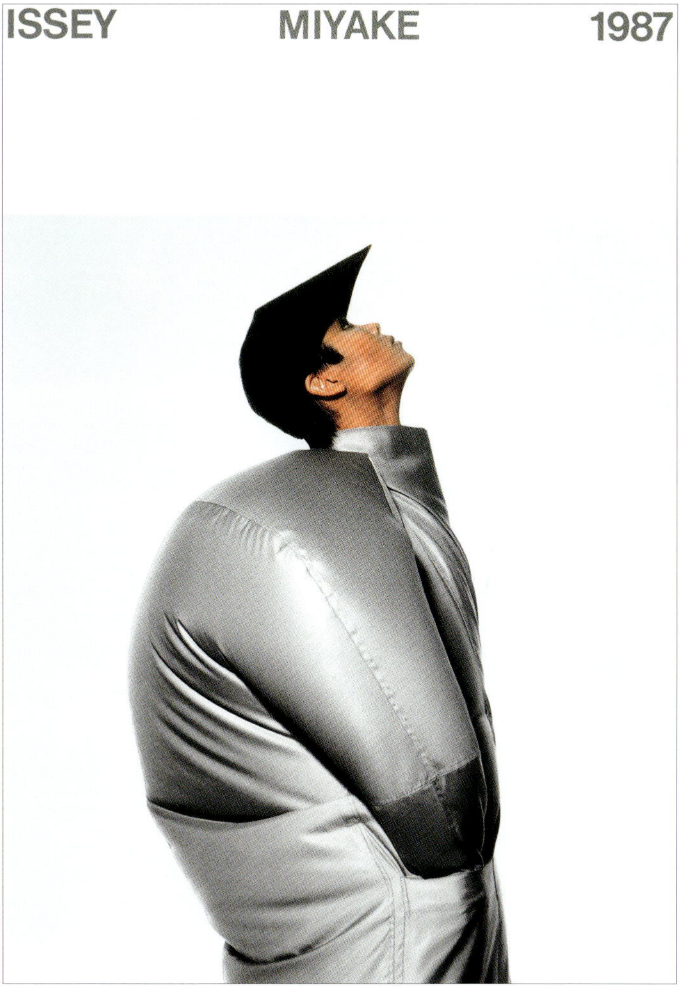

2

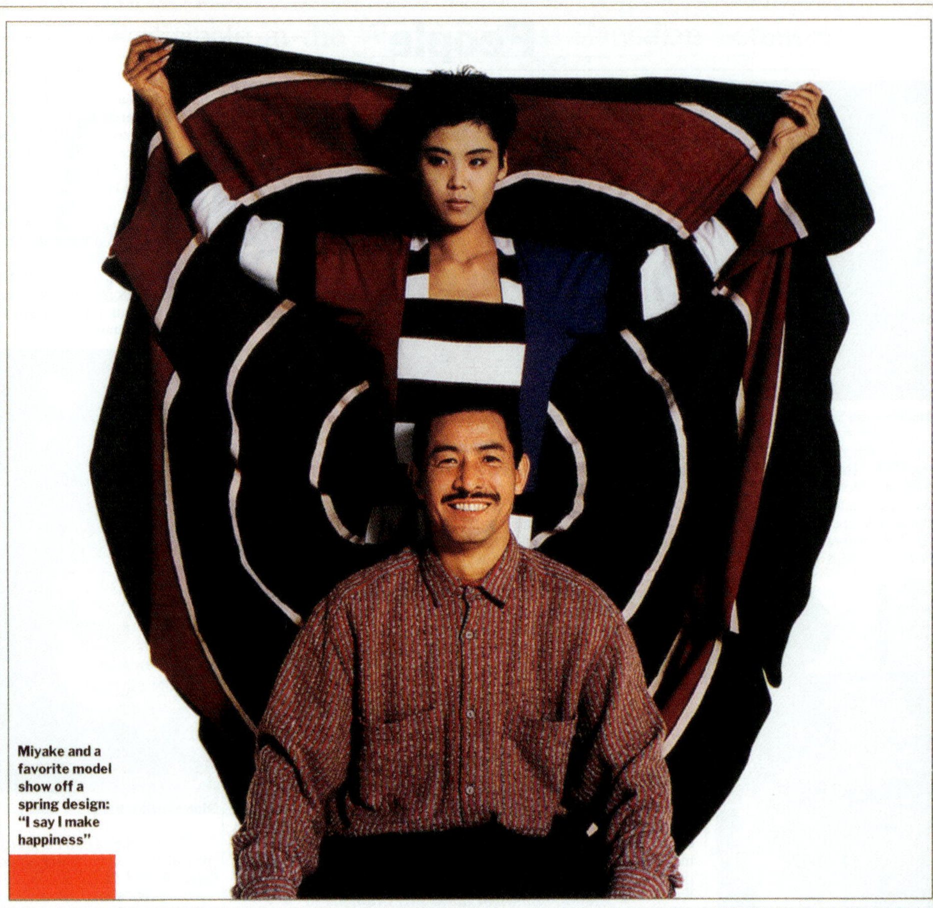

Living

COVER STORY

A Change of Clothes

Designer Issey Miyake shapes new forms into fashion for tomorrow

A general introduction, courtesy Issey Miyake: "I make clothes." A gentle caution: "We must not be too logical." And an all-purpose question: "How do you think it?"

"Issey," asks one of his friends, standing in the middle of a bustling hotel lobby, "how do I work this?" The friend is flapping about uncertainly in the enveloping intricacies of a new raincoat. "I made it like this," says the designer, improvising a fitting at the front desk. He unbuttons a half-cape that spans the sleeves, and puts the loose ends around his friend's neck. "Like a scarf, you see?"

"But what about this?" says a companion, trashing logic and pulling the cape over the friend's head, buttoning it under the neck to make a watertight hood. The designer looks; his head tilts slightly. "How do you think it?" his friend teases.

Miyake's face creases into the sort of smile that should come in a gift box. "Great!" he says, grabbing his companion in a tight hug as if some souvenir sphinx had suddenly surrendered a secret. To all the patrons in the hotel lobby, it looks as if old friends are reuniting at the end of a long trip; in fact, any voyage with Issey Miyake is ongoing. "Next time I make like that, and you do something different again," he laughs. "Always fresh, always

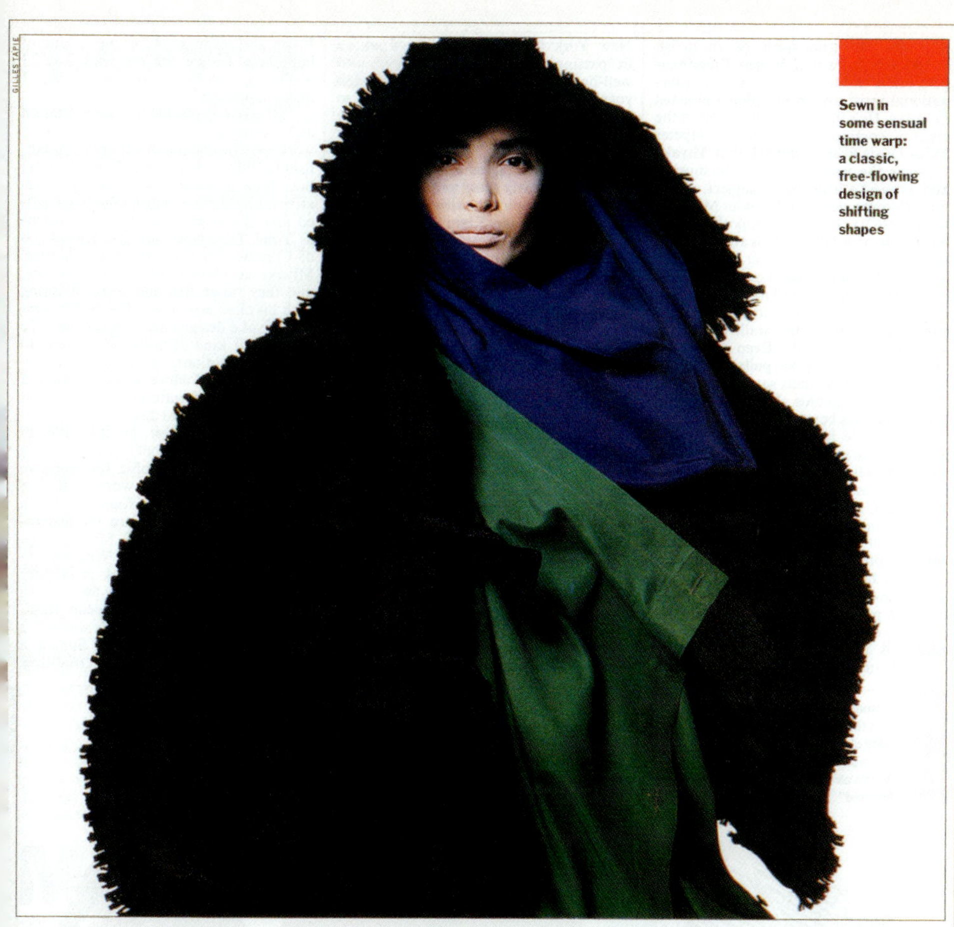

Sewn in some sensual time warp: a classic, free-flowing design of shifting shapes

different, always challenge. That way is best, I think. Want to eat?"

In a minute, maybe. Meanwhile, it is worth pointing out that some strenuous modification of that lobby styling session has produced, over the past 15 years, some of the best clothes there are, some of the most adventurous anyone has ever done. These are clothes that defy convention by flowing all around it, like so many pieces of whole cloth finding fresh form in the controlled accident of the fall, making the body under them feel as loose and free as the fabric. Miyake has even experimented with molding the body underneath. He designs *bustiers* for intrepid evening wear and mounts a museum project called "Bodyworks," which has appeared in Tokyo, Los Angeles, San Francisco, and at London's Victoria and Albert Museum.

Miyake's clothes, declarations of independence for the body, do not look at all out of place on exhibit in museums.

Yvonne Deslandres, a curator in charge of the costume collection at the Museum of Decorative Arts in Paris, casts traditional French fashion jingoism aside and calls Miyake "the greatest creator of clothing of our time." His designs challenge so many traditional expectations and break so many rules that they need different sets of standards to be understood or even worn. "I know many people resist or reject my clothing because it's not a package that's already formed, like European clothing," the designer will concede. "Without the wearer's ingenuity, my clothing isn't clothing. These are clothes where room is left for wearers to make things their own. That may need courage at first, but once you get the trick, it's not difficult."

The trick, most often, is simplicity. What may be difficult is the attitude that the clothes need and, indeed, can instill once they are on the body, making with every movement of the arm or arch of the

hip shapes full of gentle, sensual surprise. Miyake clothes, on women, are a revelation. On men, they are a relief. If most conventional clothing is, as the designer says, "a package," then wearing Miyake feels like being unwrapped at Christmas.

The lines of the garments, the tones of the fabrics, the unstructured and unstrictured social attitudes implicit in both the making and the wearing of Miyake clothes are, altogether, something rather more than an alternative form of dressing. They are Japanese in origin, Western in spirit and, finally, universal, not just in their impact but in the ravishing new images of the body they propose. These clothes taunt trend and defy style; they are not "fashion," except in its broadest generic definition. These are clothes that do not mean merely to decorate a body but to enhance it inside and out. They are objects made by a designer who has the true spirit of an artist. American Painter Robert Rauschenberg refers to Miyake easily as "an international artist, the most influential artist in Japan. He's supporting the whole of the artistic community." Jazz Trumpeter Miles Davis likes to remark that Miyake "designs the way I think about music," and, pressed a little on the subject, comes up with some elegant riffs about Miyake's work. "He has balance, composition; he's incredible with fabric. He is an artist, yes, more than a fashion designer. I hate to see anything he makes that I can't wear, like anything that's too small for me, or strictly ladies' things. I'd like to buy all of his stuff and put it on the wall, to look at when I get depressed." Even among his designer peers, Miyake pulls top points. Italy's Giorgio Armani says flat out that "Miyake is a genius. In image, in approach, he goes beyond fashion."

Commerce, however, does not go begging. Miyake's designs for his men's and women's collections and for a couple of spin-off lines like the lively, lower-priced Plantation, as well as royalties from assorted licensees supervised by him, pull in upward of $50 million yearly to the Miyake offices in Tokyo. Manageably pricey in Japan, where most of them are made, his clothes get expensive when sold in other parts of the world after freight charges, duties and store markups are added. A fall coat, for example, made of wool and nylon mesh costs $955 in New York City. Two pieces of advice in passing, then, to the intrepid and well-heeled consumer taking a maiden voyage into Miyake: the clothes, so unconstraining, can be addictive, and the name is pronounced Me-yah-kay. *Ee*-say Me-yah-kay.

Hefty retail prices and a more than $50 million yearly gross may be near beer to a fashion empire the size of Yves Saint Laurent's or Calvin Klein's, but that sum is quite robust for a designer who works in such free and unexpected forms. Miyake's collection for last fall, bursting with a natural landscape of shades and shifting silhouettes, moved briskly in the stores. His new spring collection, about to be shipped to shops worldwide, is a meteor shower of radiant colors, full of playful forms and unexpected but always amenable shapes.

The new collection is also a solid demonstration of the amplitude of Miyake's gifts, of all the discipline, restlessness and romance of his free-ranging creative spirit. *Challenge,* whether in his native Japanese, his fluent French or his serviceable English, is a favorite word: he uses it as a prod, a goal, a signpost and an explanation. *Fashion* fits into his vocabulary only as a practicality. "The semantics aren't important," he explains. "But in Japanese, we have three words: *yofuku,* which means Western clothing; *wafuku,* which means Japanese clothing; and *fuku,* which means clothing. It can also mean good fortune, a kind of happiness. People ask me what I do, I don't say *yofuku* or *wafuku.* I say I make happiness."

Miyake's implacable experimentation and perpetual reinvention of his own work were instrumental not only in establishing Tokyo as a world fashion center but, more important, in molding a creative atmosphere in which other such gifted and unconventional designing spirits as Yohji Yamamoto and Rei Kawakubo of Comme des Garçons could flourish. Miyake has his own influences, to be sure, and they range free and wide. Working with his close associate, Makiko Minagawa, Miyake designs his own textiles. "To know what kind of fabric he is going to want," she cautions, "is a matter of knowing what kind of dance and what kind of architecture he is interested in, or what color the sky was that day."

East Meets West is the title of Miyake's seminal book, published in 1978. It is a photographic retrospective and consolidation of his work, a kind of illustrated road map for round trips into the fashion ozone. "We are the generation who lived in limbo," Miyake says, "the first really raised with Western culture, the first who must look in another direction to search for a new identity. In fashion, I respect the European tradition. But they do it better." It was not a question, in the late '60s, of finding a radical alternative to that tradition;

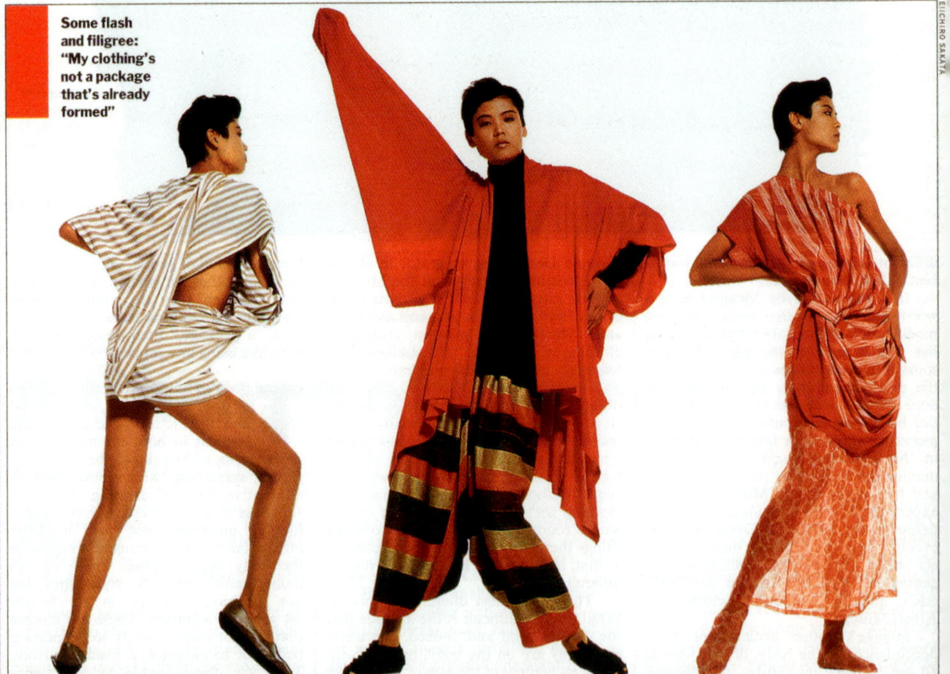

there was none. Miyake made his own.

Miyake, 47, grew up in Hiroshima during the war and emerged with his own brand of bedrock optimism, the sort of spirit that is perpetually renewed by being hard pressed, perhaps because all other challenges seem small after survival. "I say problem is opportunity," he explains. "When we have found a big problem, that is wonderful." In his work, he realized after a while that "my very disadvantage, my lack of Western heritage, would also be my advantage. I was free of Western tradition or convention. There was no other way for me to go but forward." The kimono may have been "a shape frozen in time," but Miyake not only took from it a way of cutting and wrapping clothes and a means for construction of a sleeve that did not constrict, he used its central concept of the space between body and cloth as a way to let wearer and garment interact, to make, from their respective shapes, a whole new form.

Says his friend Tomoko Komuro, who went into partnership with him to form the Miyake Design Studio (M.D.S.) in 1970: "He was attracted by some kind of excitement that goes beyond the limit of clothing." Miyake found the limit, then pushed past it. "Those '70s clothes were the work of a boy using all his energy," Miyake says now. "Those clothes seem to say, to shout, 'I've found it, I've found it!' " He used plastic, paper, rubber, insisting that "anything can be clothing." He often bypassed conventional fabric wholesalers and went right to the weavers. His clothes always seem to have been sewn together in some sensual time warp entirely of his own devising. They are ancestral and futuristic all at once. They do not go out of style because they have little relation to anything as evanescent as a trend.

Miyake approaches even the humblest bolt of cloth with the sophistication that comes from long practical experience, as well as from a grounding in the inward splendors of the classic Japanese tea ceremony. Two central concepts of tea culture are *sabi* and *wabi*. *Sabi* conveys the dull sheen of posterity, the finish, mystery and allure acquired by an object that has been well worn. *Wabi* suggests the use of a humble material for a higher purpose. Both qualities abound in Miyake's best clothes: his coats and dresses cut from one piece of cloth, a man's sweater that looks as if it could warm a wandering trapper but hangs on the shoulders no more heavily than a strand of loose hair.

Miyake has also used Irish wool, batik from Indonesia and silk from Italy. Whatever the material, and however it is worked, most people insist that it is "very Japanese" if they recognize Miyake's hand. Without a peek at the label, however, the garment's origin becomes more speculative. Miyake has the strongest kind of signature, emphatic but often elusive, in part because he gives his associates a lot of lead. Eiko Ishioka, a splendid art director and one of Miyake's oldest

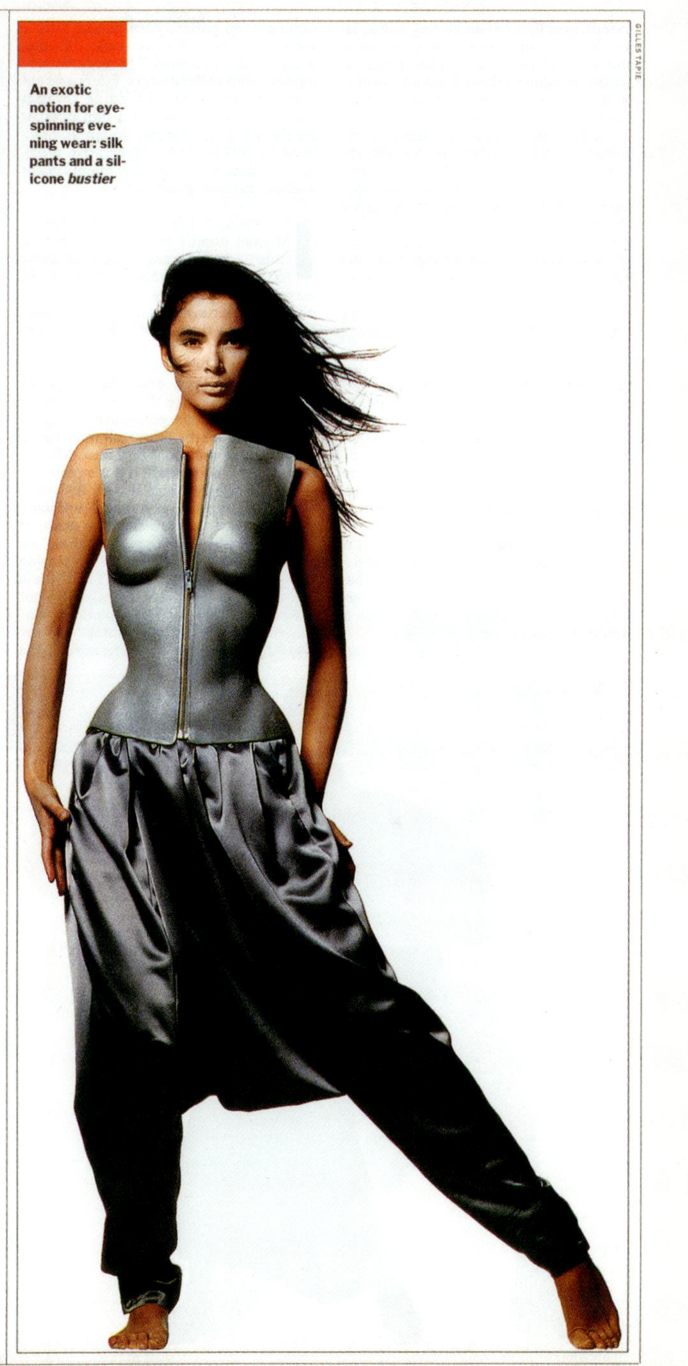

An exotic notion for eye-spinning evening wear: silk pants and a silicone *bustier*

friends, says that "when he was young, Issey lacked confidence and experience, and he could not control his emotional reactions or talent. His staff did not want to be slaves, they wanted to be equals, so he had to change his character."

Some substantial modification was required. Miyake's nickname around the workroom had been "Issey 3 mm." "I wouldn't compromise by even that much." Now he is proud to be called "Issey 1½ cm." "Once upon a time," he concedes, "I was not quite so happy to see all these eccentrics around the place. But now the sight of these people makes me happy." There are occasional heady references at M.D.S. to the Bauhaus and the 17th century Japanese school of painting called Rimpa. "I feel there are some possibilities that we might do something similar. That's why I'm not quitting yet," jokes Akira Onozuka, the studio's design director. "I was always worrying about what he would like and what he would want," confesses Tomio Mohri, who directs Miyake's fashion shows and special exhibits like "Bodyworks," all while supervising the spectacular range of knitwear for which Miyake is rightly renowned. "But then I told myself, 'I'm going to do what I want.'" "At M.D.S.," says Miyake, "everybody says what they think." But he also emphasizes, "If I see something at a fitting and I don't like it, whatever anyone else says, that's it."

This congenial and productive tension between group dynamics and artistic autocracy has a familiar echo. "Design work is not alone work," he says. Watching him with collaborators, fitters and apprentices, soliciting and sifting through ideas, one is reminded of a film director on the set. Like cinema, design as practiced by Miyake is a collaborative medium that deploys a myriad of talents under a single guiding sensibility.

In creating his fabric with Minagawa, Miyake usually works from what he calls "a broad image, not necessarily too specific. Something from daily life: leaves, trees, bark, sky, air. Anything. A noodle." After samples are redone ("usually a million times," Miyake says good-naturedly) and finally accepted, they are delivered to M.D.S., cut into 1½ meter pieces and draped over the designer's body. "Fabric is like the grain in wood," he says. "You can't go against it. I close my eyes and let the fabric tell me what to do." If the fabric could be a coat, Miyake wraps it around himself; if it is a potential shirt, the designer puts it over his chest. Then it is draped over a model, and only after that last step are sketches made of what the garment will be. "Clothes," he explains, "have to be seen on the outside as well as felt on the inside." Then, if it is something he can wear, Miyake will put the sample on himself and go into his single most characteristic fitting gesture: whirling an arm up, down and around in a quickly widening circle, making sure the garment has plenty of ease, he looks like a relief pitcher winding up to throw a high hard one that will retire the side.

The only thing that confounds him is the expected. He loves old wristwatches and wears them with zest, even though he says, "I don't like the correct time." He cannot drive and declines to learn, for the simple reason that "I don't like anything where, if you turn right, you go right." He seems perpetually beguiled by byways and the wisdom of the wrong direction. When he makes his yearly round of visits to fabricmakers, he will often tell them, "Show me your failures," because he can get fresh ideas, even inspiration, from them. It takes a very fleet eye to catch a surprise before it is forgotten as a mistake, and Miyake, ready for anything, can always see it almost as it starts. Onozuka remembers, several seasons ago, doing some larky variations on a woman's jacket. The garment was ultimately turned inside out and put back on the model. Miyake laughed, said, "This is how it should be," and left it like that. Says Onozuka: "That jacket sold immediately."

His personal life holds no such surprises. He is a major cultural celebrity on home turf, but he has not yet become so Westernized that his intimate life is common tender. He has kept company with the same woman for more than a decade, which is not nearly so interesting as the fact that many people who know him, and her, know nothing of the relationship. He is abstemious in matters of detailed autobiography, and it is easy enough to credit his reserve. It may be, as he says, that "the question creative people all ask—What can we do?—changes tomorrow." For Miyake, every tomorrow is a gift. "I just wanted to do something to feel good," he says, "to do something better. I grew up in Hiroshima. I thought that was life."

"I always say to people that I was far away in the mountains when the bomb was dropped, but in fact I was not," says Miyake, who was riding his bicycle to school. "I saw it all with my eyes. I can remember it; I can remember what I did. I remember. But I thought I'd better forget." That would not be possible. "In my memory, it was terrible because I lost my mother and most of my family. I saw my mother, and half her body was burned. There was no penicillin or anything else. We had no medicine, so we put eggs on her."

She lived for four more years, teaching flower arrangement, teaching cooking, teaching the samisen. "Even burned, she continued to teach," her son says. "My father was a professional soldier, so my mother had to learn how to live without him if he were to die. My mother was great. I am very much weaker than she." Certainly she had always known how to adapt. When Miyake, 2, had nothing to wear to an autumn harvest celebration, she cut up festival flags and made him a suit. She insisted that he always go to school, even if he was ailing. If he had a fever, she would take him on a bicycle.

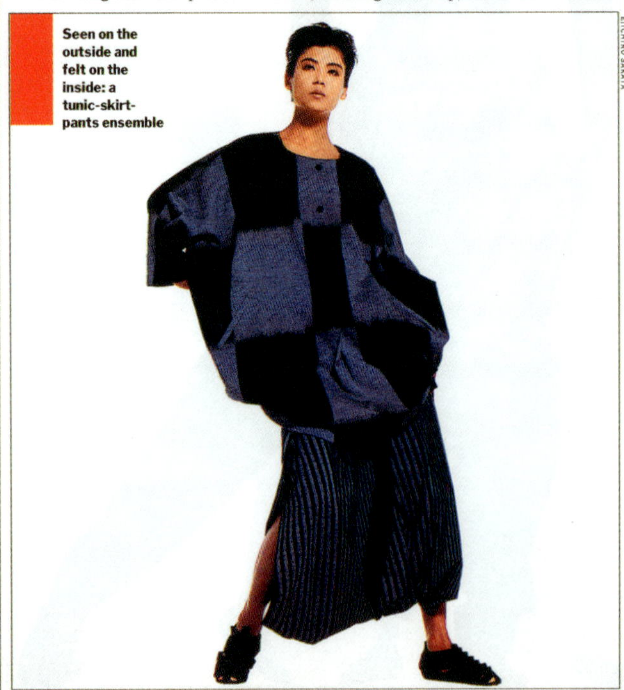

Seen on the outside and felt on the inside: a tunic-skirt-pants ensemble

140

"She never," he says, "gave me a chance to escape."

When he was ten years old, Miyake developed osteomyelitis, a bone-marrow disease. He makes light of it—"the 'osso buco' is disappearing," he will say—but he has been hospitalized twice for treatment, and he endured a seven-month siege of traction. At first, after the war, penicillin was the only available treatment for the condition. "My mother sold our land in the mountains to buy penicillin for me," he says. "After I had almost recovered, she died." The bone disease is not bomb related, he explains, but his left leg remains shorter than the right, and he often limps. An old friend says that when he limps, he is in pain. He limps a lot.

All that usually shows on his face is a smile or a look of dreamy, distracted concentration. "I don't know when it was I got my drive," he says, "but all the things that happened have been good for me." He thought he might become a painter, and he went to a special crafts school. At night, he remembers, "I went through drawings of naked *'femmes.'*" It was the clothed ones, however, that first seduced him. As a teenager, he recalls stopping his bike in front of a shop window, staring at the French-style mannequins inside, seeing his own reflection mirrored in the glass. He borrowed some books and started to copy French fashion sketches. His first drawing was a Balenciaga. "It was like a spiral," he says, still seeing it. "A woman with a long neck and bare arms and her back rounded."

Being a fashion designer in Japan was, he says, "frightening." It was not man's work, and it was not respected. Miyake attended the highly regarded Tama Art University, where he studied graphics and wrote a pointed and well-publicized letter to a major conference of international designers, inquiring why no one from fashion was represented on the program. It was inevitable that Miyake would wind up in France, and in 1965, after graduating from Tama, he arrived in Paris for further fashion studies. His sketches got him an apprenticeship with Guy Laroche in 1966, then in 1968 with Givenchy, who remembers his young assistant as "a charming young man, a gentleman. I think he has a lot of talent." He adds, with perhaps as much relief as regret, "I don't think I influenced him in any way."

Miyake mastered the intricacies of his craft from these apprenticeships, but he was also lastingly impressed, perhaps galvanized, by the idealistic force of the 1968 student rebellions in Paris. He pushed on to New York, where he worked with Geoffrey Beene, and then returned to Tokyo, where he founded the Miyake Design Studio in 1970. Friends contributed small amounts of money, like cronies chipping in at a rent party. An old pal, Kiyoshi Kanai, designed a logo for the new company. Kanai's wife Jun, who

"**In image, in approach, he goes beyond fashion**": a sumptuous print outfit

Living

worked as an editorial assistant at *Vogue,* carried four Miyake samples to the magazine office and to Bloomingdale's. She wore a fifth, a kind of nouveau Courrèges culotte suit made of heavy brown cotton traditionally used for judo uniforms. The response was uniformly enthusiastic.

Miyake himself reappeared soon after in New York with a small but complete collection, which included *sashiko* (the Japanese technique of cotton quilting) coats and fitted T shirts colored and cut to look like tattoos. Bloomingdale's promptly gave the debuting designer a small corner all his own. In Tokyo, he got himself space in two of the most prestigious department stores and staged a fashion show that had seismic reverberations not just within the design community but throughout the country. Models, in an indoor parking garage, swooped up and down car ramps in some good-humored approximation of handmaidens from the fourth dimension. "Suddenly," says Ishioka, "his name was famous." Japanese fashion seemed, all at once, to have found its focus and forward force.

This gave Miyake the confidence to initiate the design experiments that produced some of his greatest work: a graceful coat shaped like a cocoon, clothing made of a single piece of cloth or layered like segments of a child's spinning top, a man's raincoat that looks like a combination of an opera cape and an overturned circus tent. But it did not necessarily pay all the bills. A light drinker, he began to appear in a series of Suntory commercials, which featured him in various exotic climes, fortifying himself with drink to relieve the creative tensions of long days in the fitting room; one even showed him gamely leaning out the door of a helicopter as it hovered over a Hawaiian volcano.

Such remunerative celebrity may have stanched the red ink, but there were new burdens to contend with. By the time *East Meets West* appeared, Miyake was starting to get overworked, overextended and frightened. "I always tried to smile," he remembers, flashing a typical dazzler. "But after *East Meets West* I went to pieces." He was producing and showing a whole separate collection in Milan, which was punishing; seeing a decade's worth of work pressed between the covers of one book was daunting and brought him up against a dead end: Now what?

He bailed out of the Italian

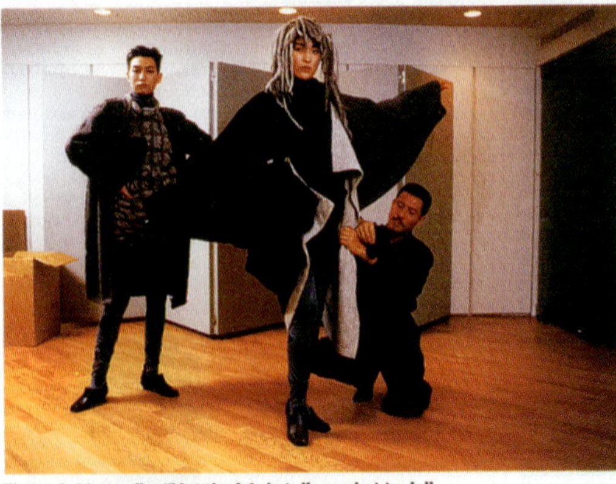

Fitting in his studio: "I let the fabric tell me what to do"

collection, retrenched and headed off for new territory. He began to bring his clothes into closer conformity with the body, changing the body's lines without constraining them, playing his frisky games with shape and size on a sharper silhouette. There are still occasional doubts. It has only been in the past few years that after a collection showing in Paris, "I haven't felt like calling Tokyo and saying, 'Is the company still there?'"

There, flourishing, and even expand-

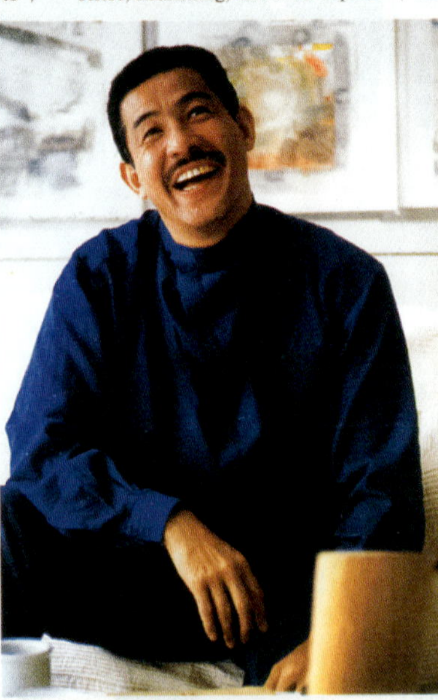

Miyake takes a break at his Tokyo apartment
Challenge as a prod, a goal, a signpost.

ing a little. Miyake is just about to pull off an exercise in the theoretical physics of fashion by moving ahead as he turns a little backward. In Japan, he has just launched a new line called Permanente, an excavation of his creative past that probably has no precedent in all of fashion. Most designers pack their old work off to some commercial attic; Miyake will turn his attic into a shop that trades evenly between past and present. Anyone who spots a vintage number on a Miyake fan and comes up with the familiar run-on question "God-that's-beautiful-where-can-I-get-one?" can now be directed to Permanente.

Repose is not a part of this picture, of course, and relaxation is mostly a rumor. Holidays usually have some sort of affiliated work benefits—"Sand," says his colleague Komuro, "can turn into an accessory"—and he likes challenges in his recreation as well as his vocation. On a trip in 1984 to the Kutch desert in the Indian state of Gujarat, his car broke down in the middle of a bridge spanning a salt sea. While friends fought off fantasies of sunstroke, dehydration and death in the wilderness, Miyake gazed at the weird water patterns below him, exclaiming, "This is really special." The travelers were eventually rescued and transported to a remote village, where they shared a room with a number of nimble rats. Recalls a friend, Museum Curator Kazuko Koike, "Issey snored through it all."

"I try sometimes to just go rest and not get ideas," Miyake says stoutly, but, Ishioka insists, "he cannot stay in one place for more than three days." Figuratively, at least, that is just as well. Last May he lived out a long-cherished goal and traveled the western U.S. by car; he spent Christmas in Tahiti. He dreams perpetually of further voyages: to South America, to Easter Island. "Make me a plan for my trip," he will ask of friends who have covered the same territory. "I'll go anywhere," he adds, although there is no mistaking that. "Where there are roads. Where there aren't any roads."

His body, animated with anticipation, seems already under way. "Where there aren't any roads . . . That's even better." And, just thinking of it, Issey is off. He moves a little, a short stride unbroken just at this moment, and takes a single, sure step in his accustomed direction. Forward. —*By Jay Cocks. Reported by Sandra Burton/Tokyo and Dorie Denbigh/Paris*

Time magazine cover, Asian edition, January 27, 1986
Photography: Eiichiro Sakata
Jay Cocks, the magazine's film and music critic, said
of Issey Miyake: "The roots of his clothes are Japan,
but the spirit is the West. It not only has strong impact,
but it brings a fresh, wonderful image to the body,
and in that is universal." Cocks went on to become
a screenwriter whose work includes two Academy
Award–nominated films.

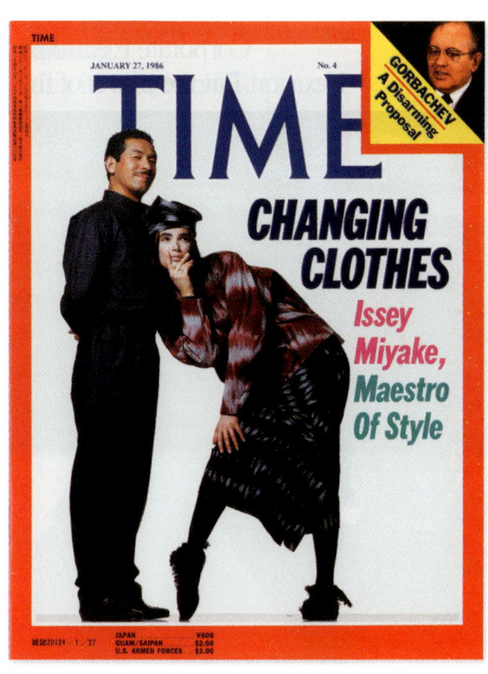

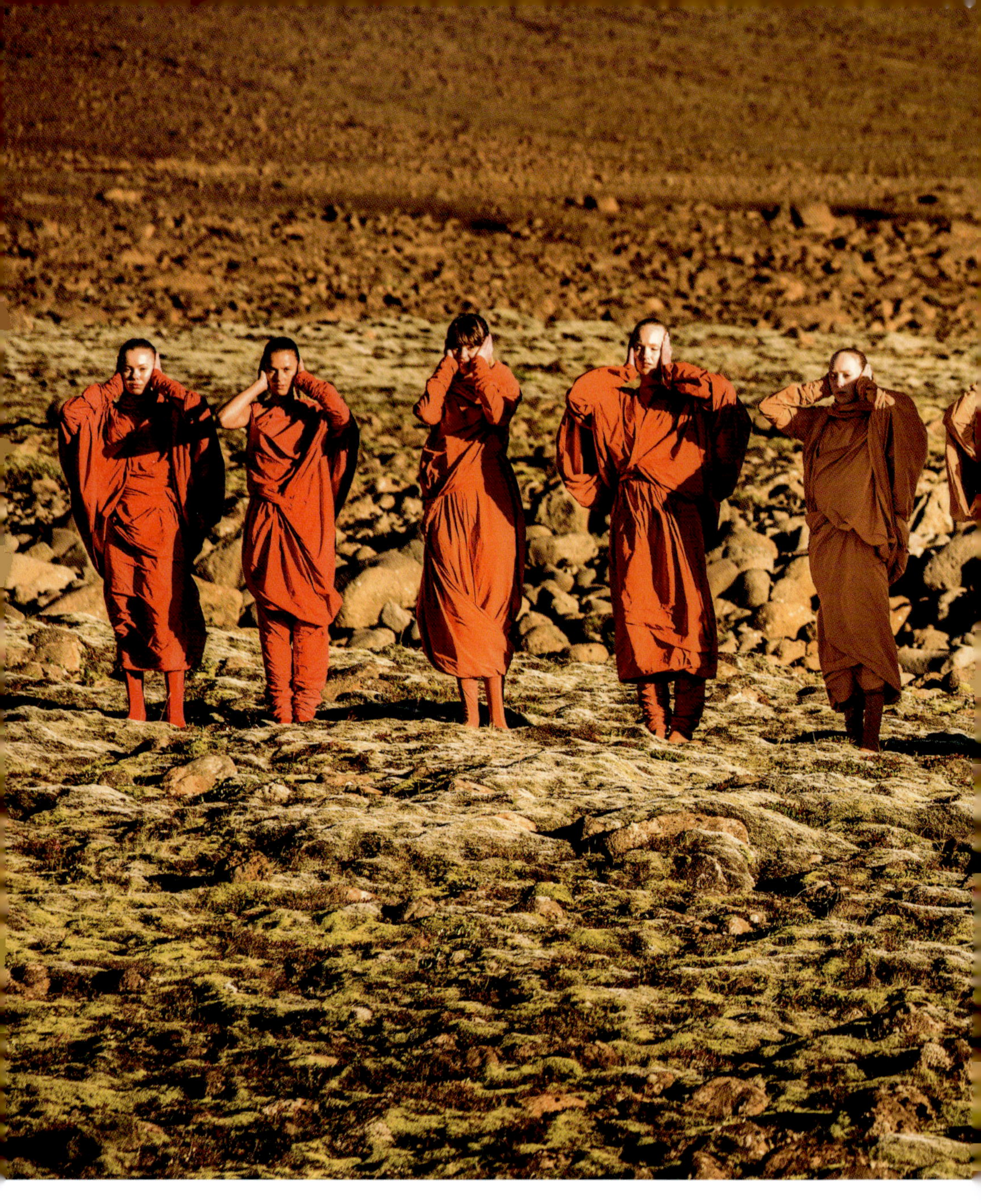

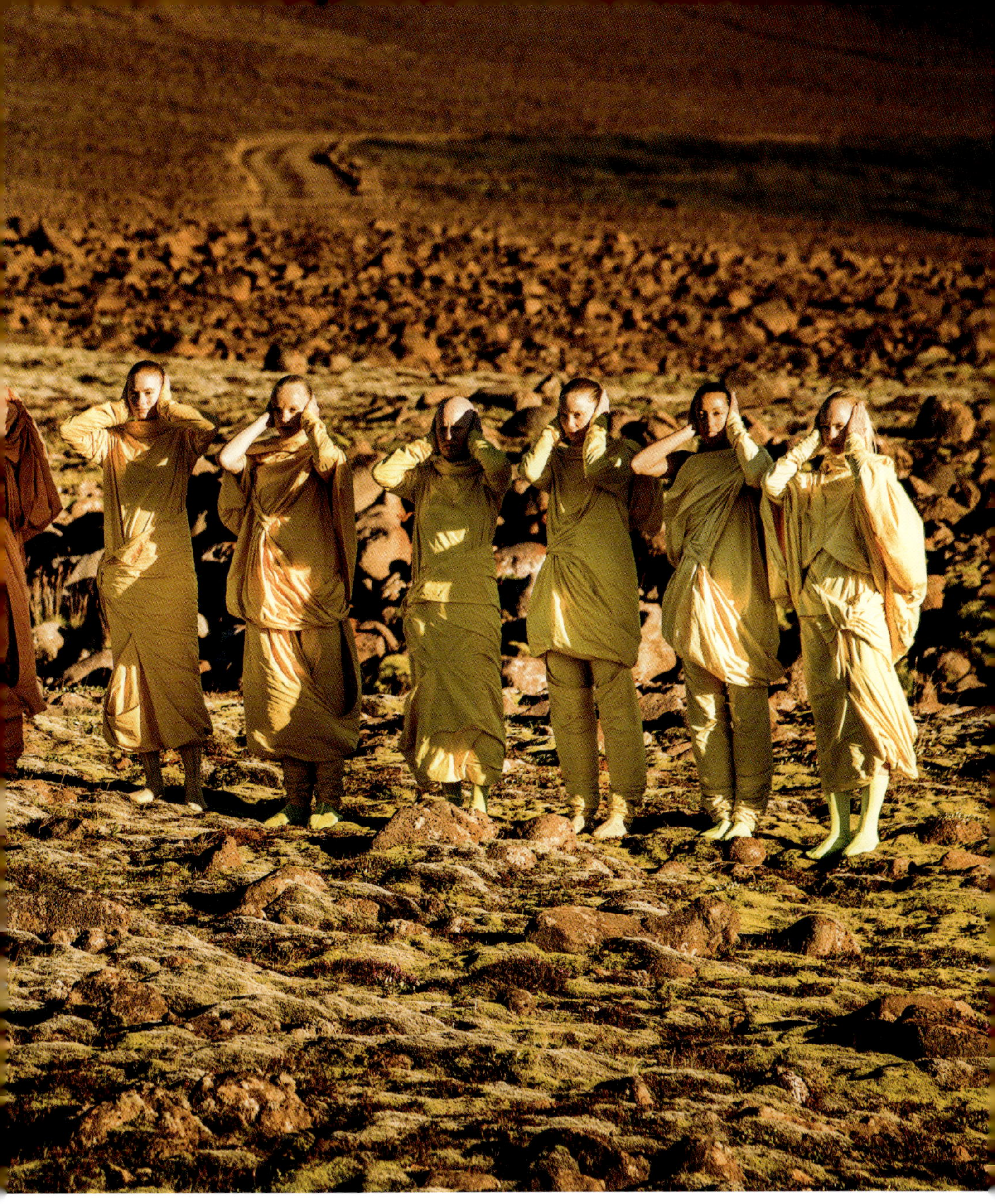

Above and following spread: Dress, shirt, poncho, vest, pants, and skirt made from a high-density, crease-free woven fabric using microfiber for the first time as a clothing material; thin and lightweight, with a texture like a piece of paper.
1986 design/Autumn-Winter 1986 Collection
Photography: Yuriko Takagi

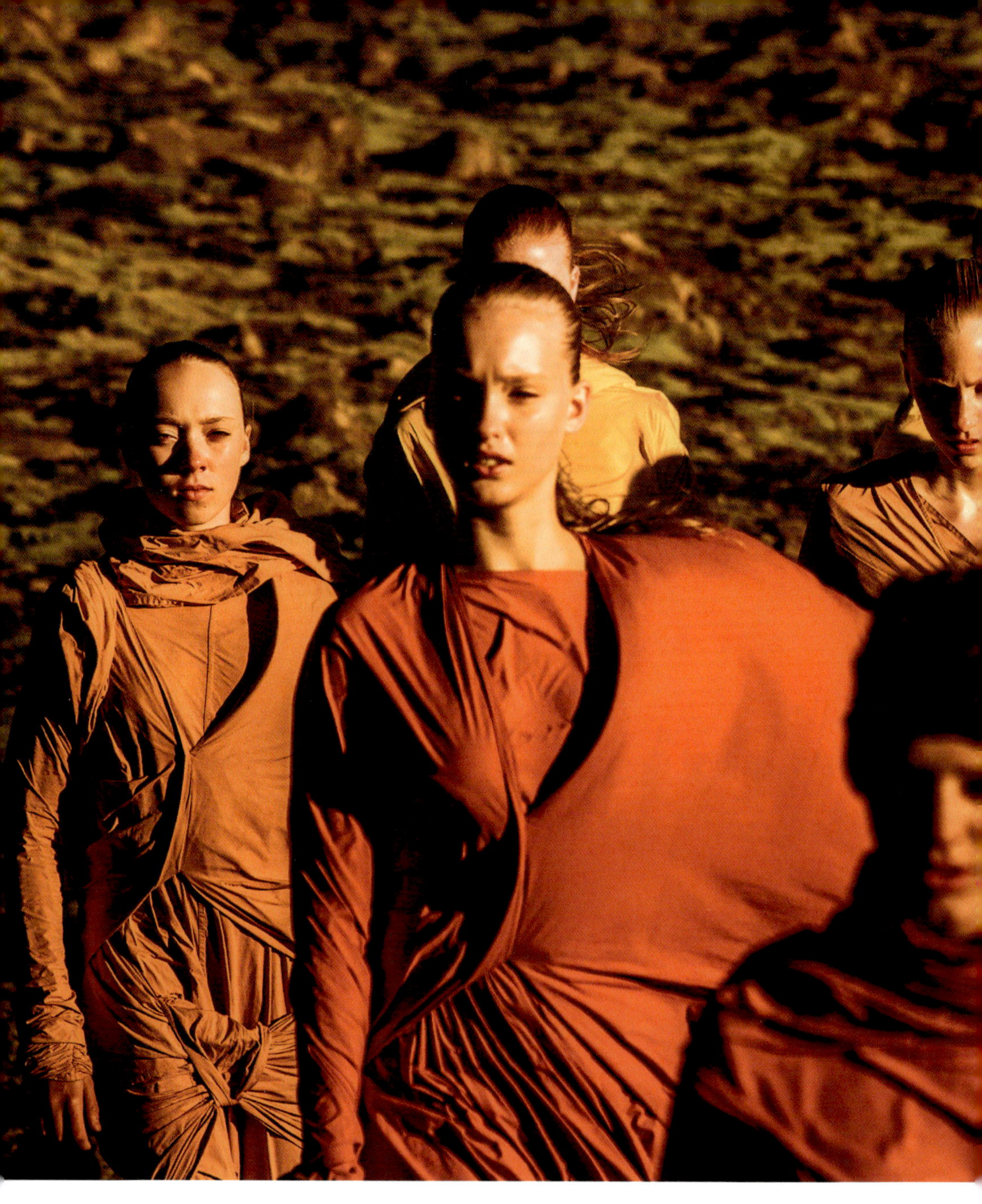

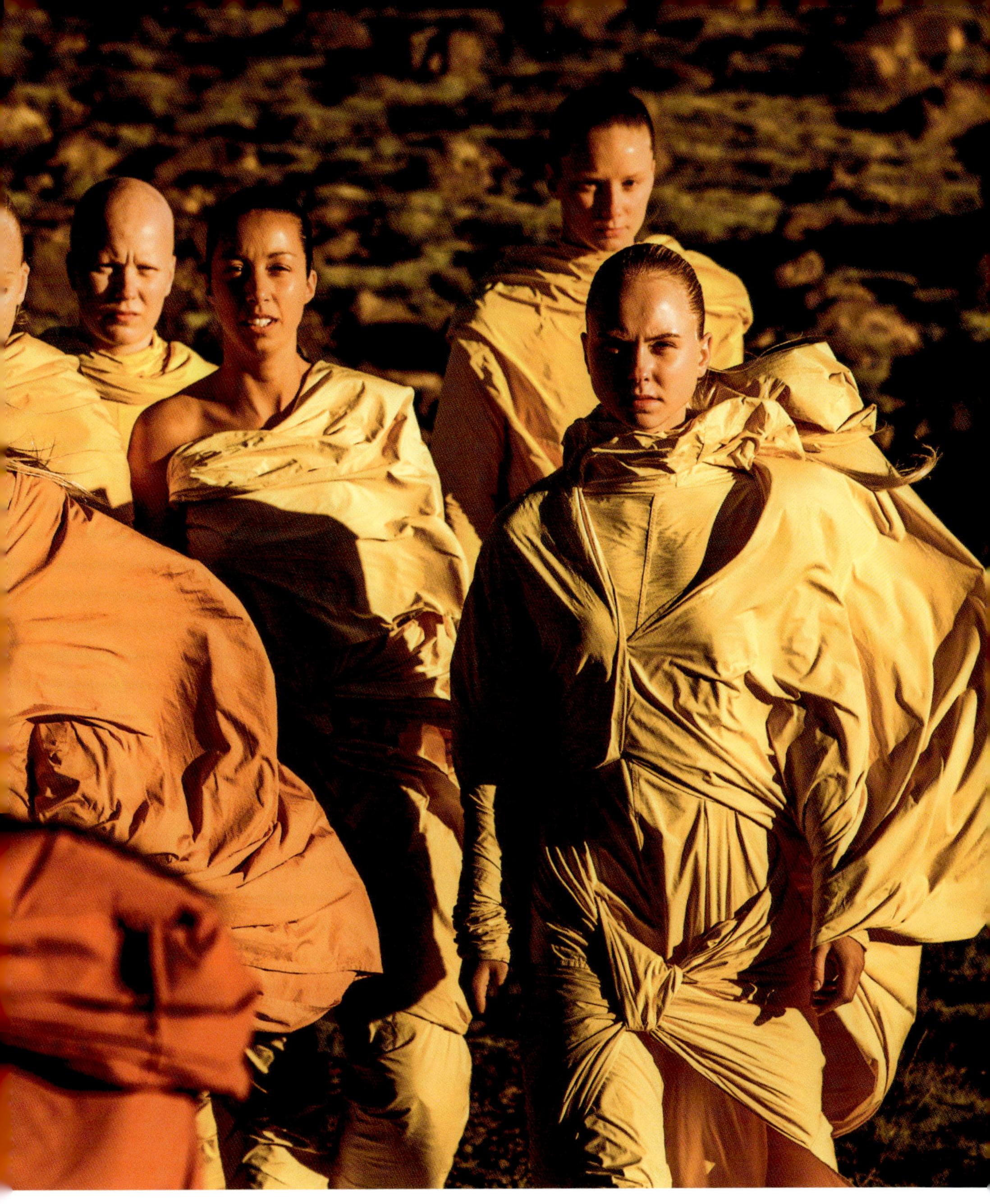

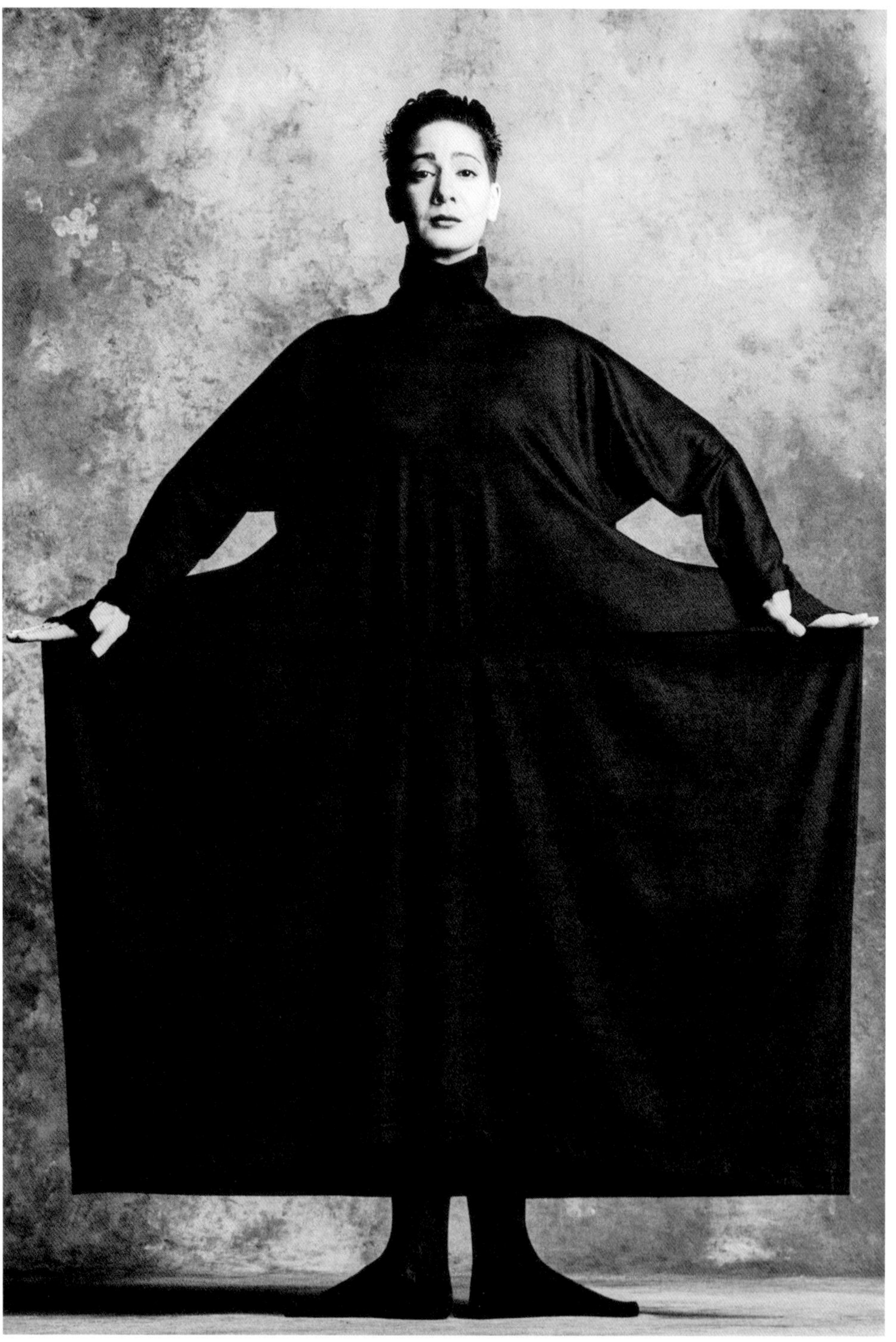

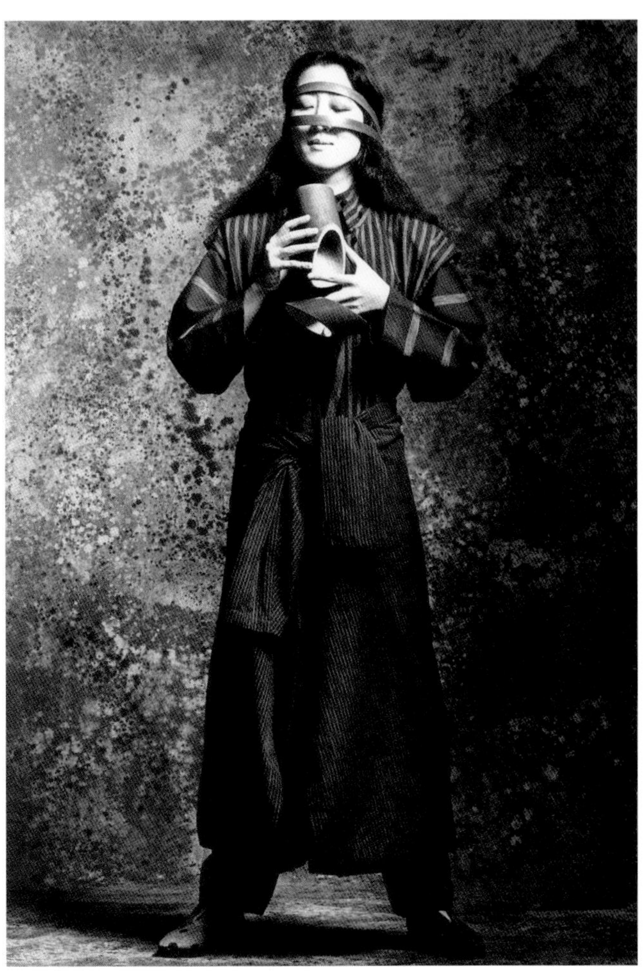

Opposite: ISSEY MIYAKE PERMANENTE
Simultaneously with the start of the brand, the
photography project by Lord Snowdon was initiated.
Nine photography books were produced between
1986 and 1990 with his portraits of people wearing
PERMANENTE clothes, who were active in various
fields. The texts were written by Susan Mann and art
direction was by Masatoshi Toda.
Photography: Snowdon; worn by:
Ellen Van Schuylenburch (dancer)
The angora jersey dress with a tape becomes a square
when unfolded. It can be worn in different ways,
depending on how the tape connection to both sides
of the square is arranged.
1986 design/Autumn-Winter 1986 Collection

ISSEY MIYAKE PERMANENTE
Photography: Snowdon; worn by:
Mitsuko Uchida (pianist)
Wide-striped shirt and a coatdress, which integrates
a dress and a coat at the hem, with combination of
different width of stripes. Sleeveless dress worn with
the coat whose sleeves are gathered around the waist.
The fabric is a cotton *kasurijima* variation.
1985 design/Spring-Summer 1986 Collection

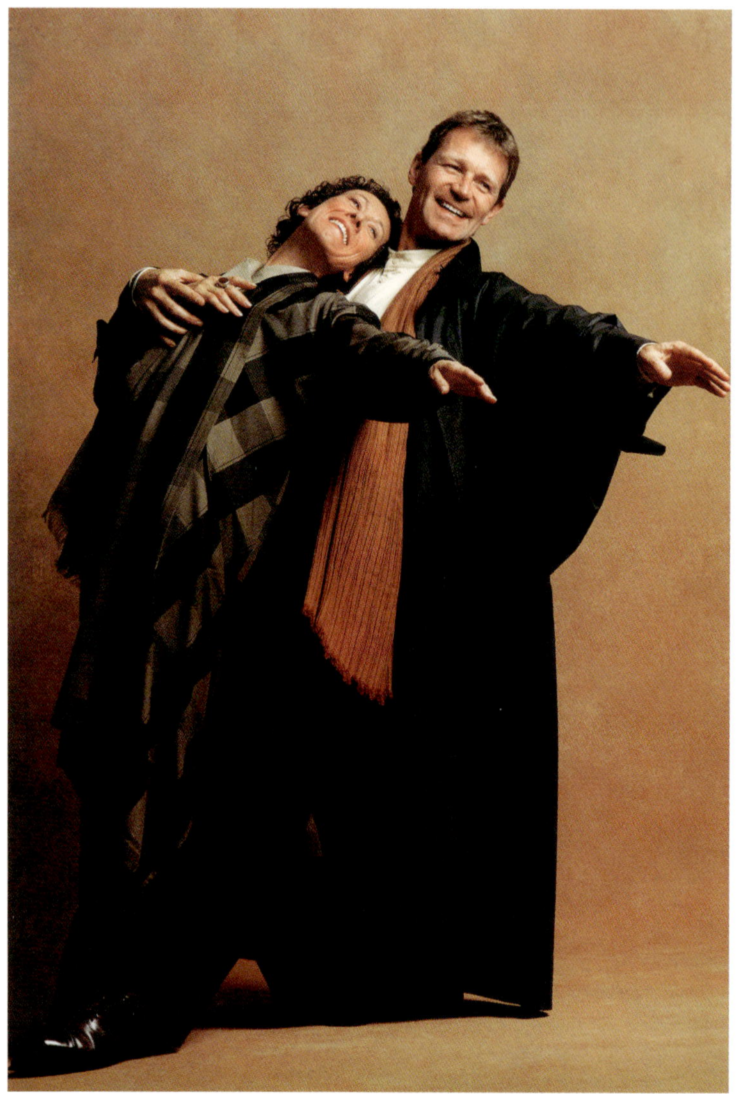

ISSEY MIYAKE PERMANENTE
Photography: Snowdon; worn by: Sir Nicholas Serota
(director of the Tate Gallery) and Lady Angela Serota
[at time of photo]
He wears an Oxford *Squid Coat* and silk pleated scarf.
She wears a cotton-silk check jacket.
1989 design/Autumn-Winter 1989 Collection

Opposite: **ISSEY MIYAKE PERMANENTE**
Photography: Snowdon;
worn by: Sir David Lean (movie director)
Double-face cotton shirt and pants. *Double-face cotton*
is a double weave material with gauze on one side.
Developed in the 1970s, it continues to be used by
ISSEY MIYAKE and other related brands. Stand-collar
and vertical slash chest pocket are a signature shirt
design of ISSEY MIYAKE MEN.
1988 design/Autumn-Winter 1988 Collection

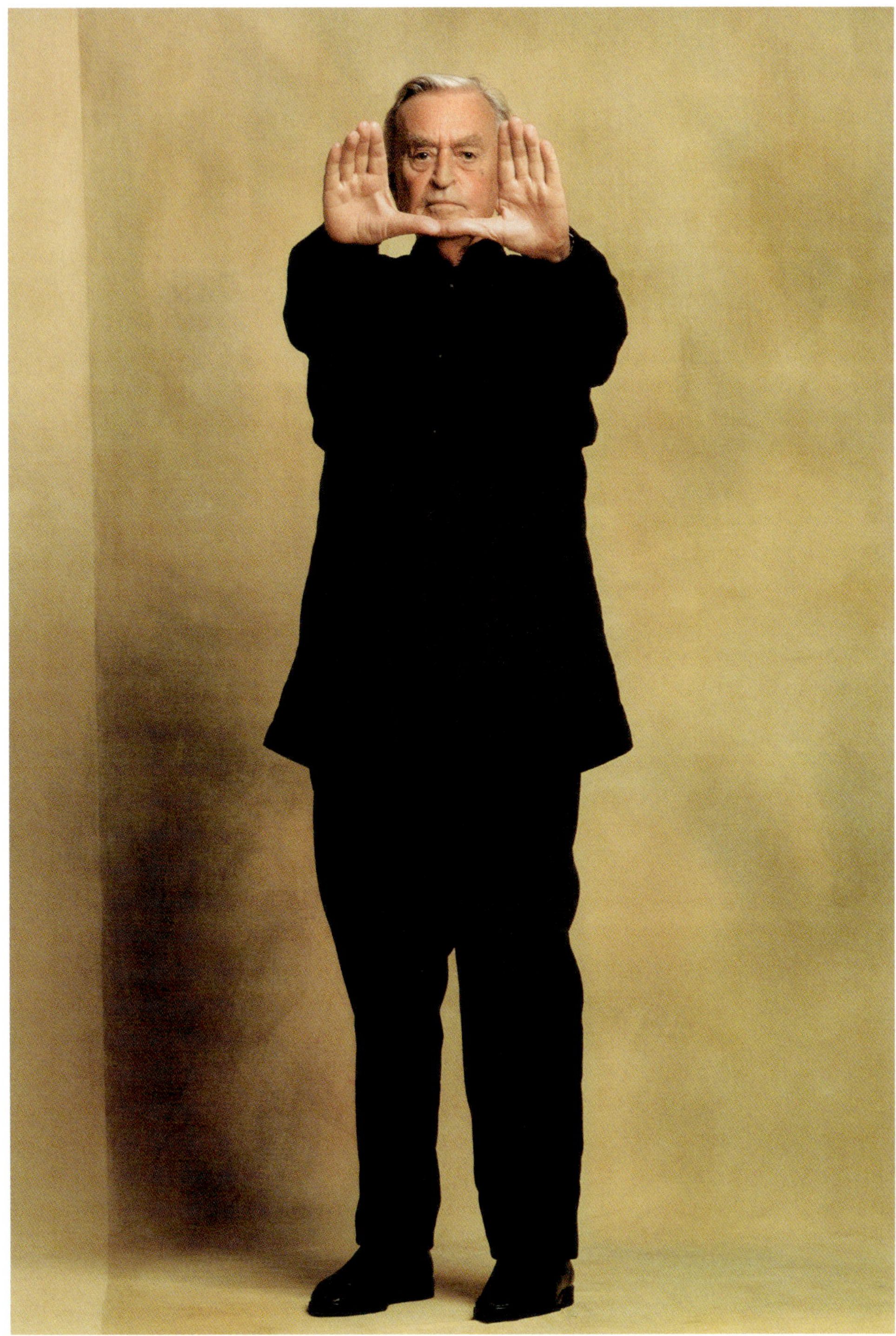

1987

> February–May: Participated in the
Fashion and Surrealism exhibition at The
Fashion Institute of Technology, New York
> March: Autumn-Winter 1987 Paris Collection
at Salle des Arts, Cour Carrée du Louvre
> April: Autumn-Winter 1987 Tokyo Collection at
Yoyogi Tent South of the National Stadium
> ISSEY MIYAKE store opened on Madison
Avenue, New York
> October: Spring-Summer 1988 Paris
Collection at Salle des Arts, Cour Carrée
du Louvre
> November: Spring-Summer 1988 Tokyo
Collection at Yoyogi Tent South of the
National Stadium

1 Autumn-Winter 1987 Paris Collection, March 21,
Salle des Arts, Cour Carrée du Louvre
2 Spring-Summer 1988 Paris Collection, October 17,
Salle des Arts, Cour Carrée du Louvre

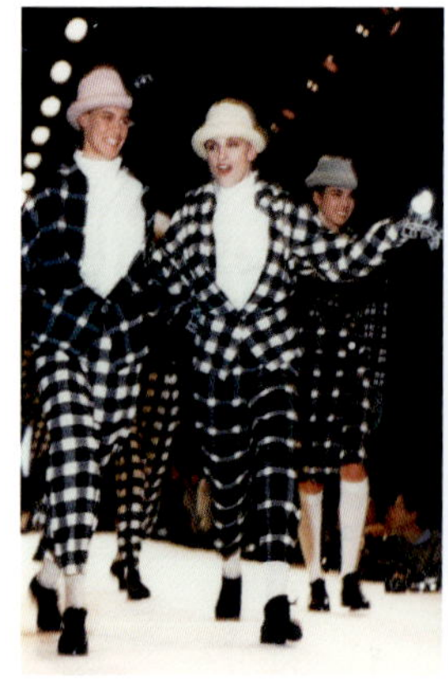
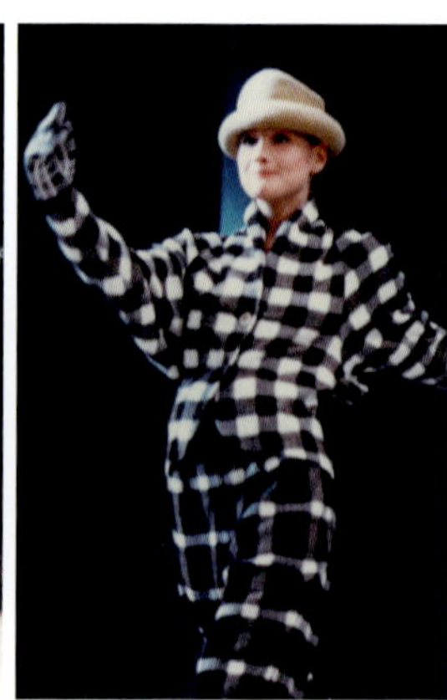
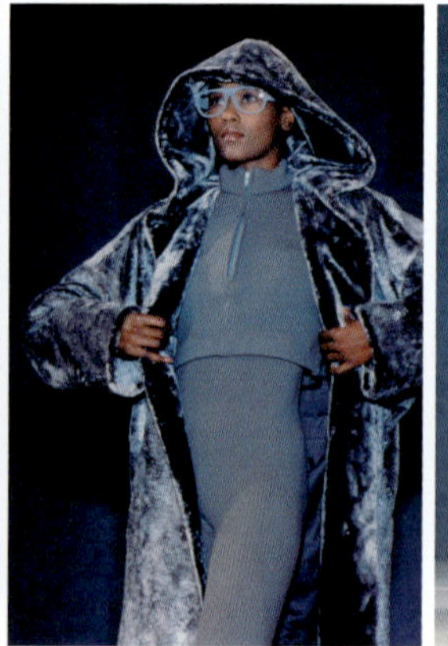
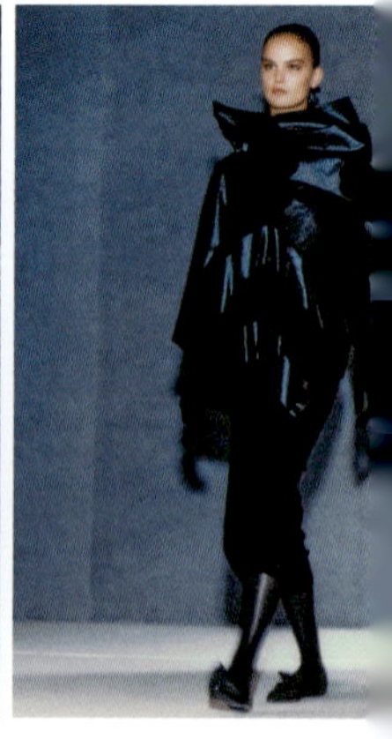

1

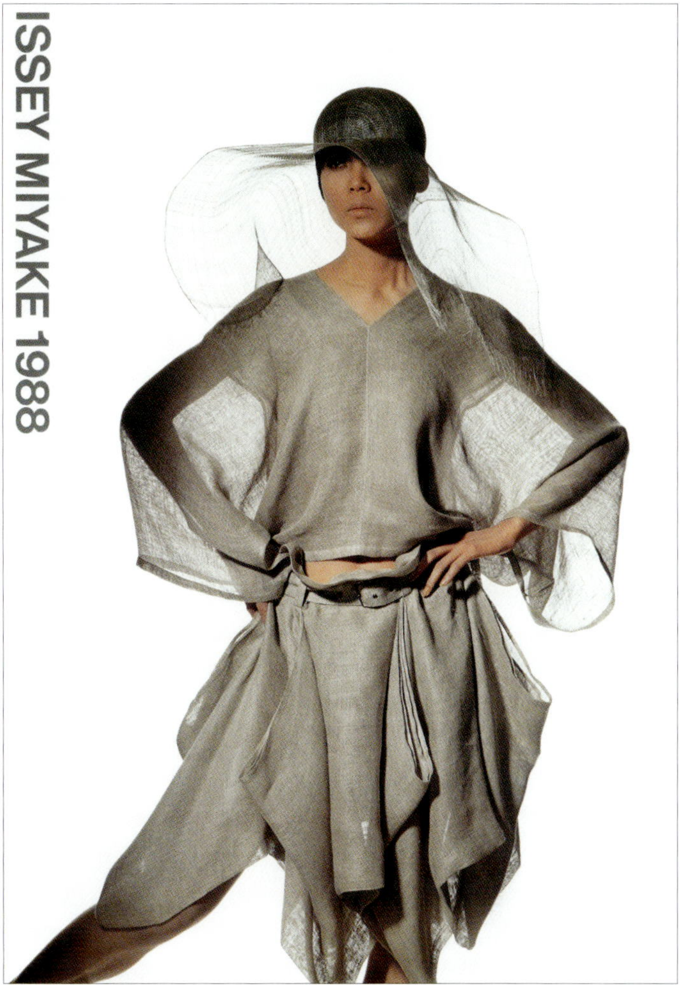

Spring-Summer 1988
Collection, poster
Kaya (mosquito net) linen gauze
skirt with large folds and shirt,
hat made from pineapple fibers
Photography: Irving Penn;
layout and typography:
Ikko Tanaka; model: Jun Kano

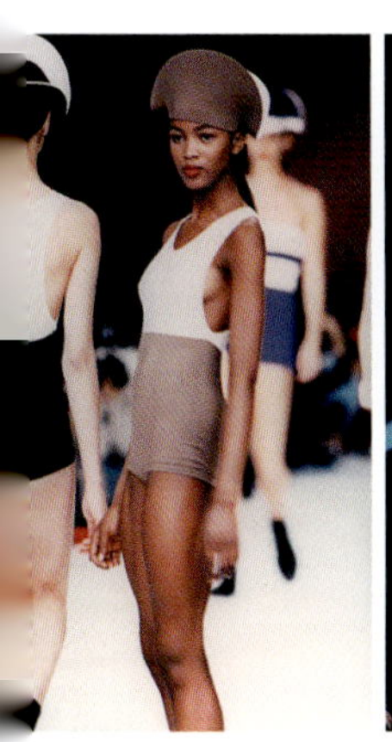
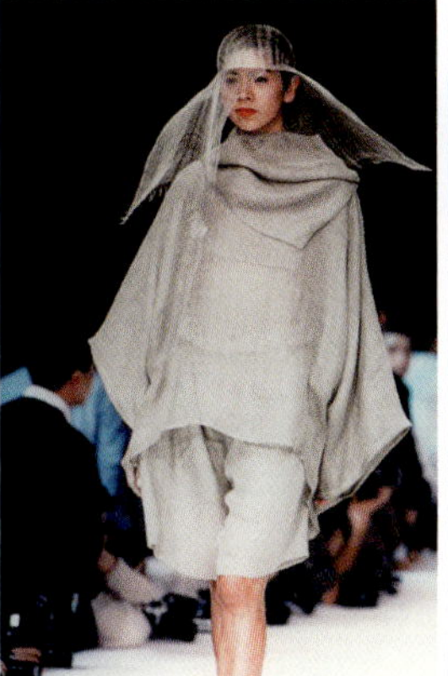
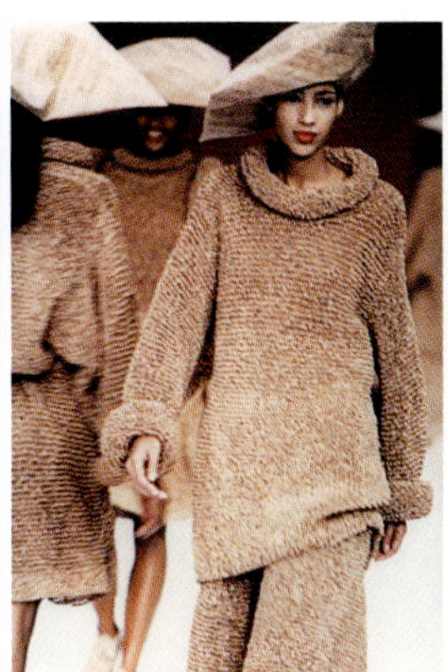
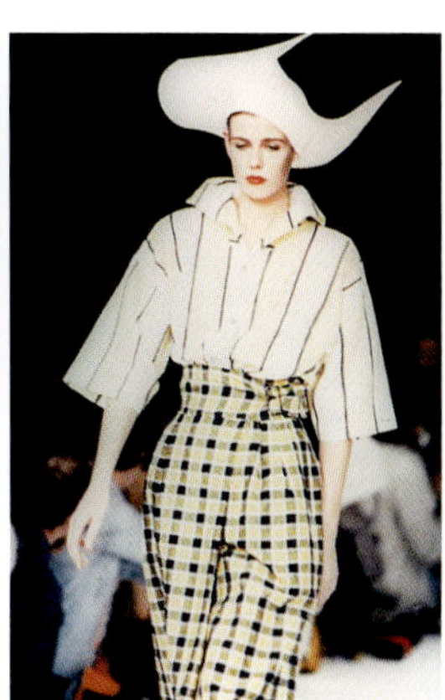

Essay by
KAZUKO KOIKE

PROFUNDITY OF FOLDS: PLEATS

It was a scarf that triggered it all.

Makiko Minagawa was looking for "a paper-light and quick-to-dry material," and she tentatively folded a piece of polyester and pleated it. By chance, Issey happened to notice.

Looking back, Miyake himself said, "By folding a square piece of fabric into quarters and then pleating these diagonally, a variety of clothing was born thanks to this new technique." Yet the bud, which would eventually become PLEATS PLEASE ISSEY MIYAKE (hereafter PLEATS PLEASE), itself was born as a result of Miyake's steadfast pursuit of materials development and imagination. I still remember a 1988 phone call clearly; he was busy preparing the 1989 Spring-Summer Collection. "You know a bread-baking oven? Just like that, a blouse is baked. Like a loaf of bread!" This was the announcement of a pleated shirt, a product with an intrinsic 3D shape. Miyake had long been eager to come up with "simple, ordinary clothes" for everyday life. And the new technique and polyester material were to fulfill just these conditions. Thus, Miyake Design Studio's research and trials leading up to production kicked off.

The prototypes of PLEATS PLEASE were first brought to people's attention in Amsterdam at the Stedelijk Museum. Conceived and organized around the theme of the power of creation, the exhibition *Energieën*[1] had invited artists, architects, designers, and others from around the world, including Anselm Kiefer,[2] Ettore Sottsass,[3] and many others. Issey covered the museum's white floor with a surface which had cut-out bumps of a few millimeters in depth. Large pleated clothes were displayed flat on the surface. While there were some clothed and standing mannequins, the scene was far from so-called "fashion." Many visitors wondered, "What is this?" – a reaction to his presentation that surely pleased Miyake. "Can I wear this?" "Do I dig it?" Questions of this type, which seem to infer a wearer's preconceptions concerning clothes, gradually disappeared from the minds of the museum visitors.

The aesthetic origins of pleats can be found in antiquity, for example in the statues of sibyls in Delphi, and at the beginning of the 20th century, in the work made by Mariano Fortuny[4] in Venice, including costumes featuring pleats. Both are considered important work in the history of clothing.

Miyake, however, was by then committed to creating pleated clothing for our contemporary times. He was also intrigued by the various features pleats embodied when using textiles devised not only in the West but in all parts of the world. At the time, he also enjoyed the lights and shadows that emanate throughout Nature in such elements as the desert and the ocean.

Paul Klee points out that the "movements" of lines make a plane. Thus, moving one line horizontally and another vertically, and following through their correlations, could be regarded as a series of endless pleats. Also, the force that brings together and compresses pleats incorporates within it an element of play. Issey Miyake applied the plastic principle that brings a thread to a line, and a line to a plane, to the polyester material, and gave this method the opportunity to prevail in today's clothing. What was epoch-making is that, predetermining the form of the clothes when worn on a body, the whole cloth is sewn and then put into a machine that gives the fabric its final feature, that is, its pleats. Conventionally, cutting and sewing fabric with its finished texture has been the standard approach, but PLEATS PLEASE clothes are made completely differently. PLEATS PLEASE was launched in 1993 and quickly became a hit product around the world. Further research into pleats is ongoing, including studying techniques of transforming tissues by heating, and exploring the possibility of making products mixed with cotton, wool, and other materials.

The success of PLEATS PLEASE in the global market, not as fashion items but as material products, had been preceded by a journey of 20 or so years by the Miyake Design Studio (including, of course, Makiko Minagawa) – an amazing journey of trial and research efforts. Moved by Miyake Design Studio's dedicated involvement, professionals of greatly varied specializations – people involved in the selection of the best polyester materials, in thread development, in the development of a technology to suppress static phenomena, in the study of knit materials – joined in the pursuit, and fully cooperated and contributed to the work of the Miyake Design Studio. The book *Pleats Please Issey Miyake* (2012, TASCHEN) revealed many of the details behind the work. Some people might sympathize with the decision to reveal what had happened "behind the scenes" of the textile industry, but now that there is a growing awareness regarding our coexistence with polyester materials, that Miyake Design Studio's attitude of sharing information has come to attract widespread interest.

CLOTHING AS AN ART MEDIUM

Lightweight, easy to wear, carry, and wash, PLEATS PLEASE clothing met the practical needs and desires of women who lead everyday lives as well as travel and perform other activities. But at the same time, it was Issey Miyake who showed us that clothing can also be a medium for art.

In the 1960s, T-shirts became not only a staple of everyday life for most people, but also a sort of manifesto for clothing as a "message medium." While PLEATS PLEASE clothing is strong enough as a versatile, stand-alone product, Issey Miyake also had a hunch that it could be used as a "canvas" on which to transmit distinctive visual messages. This idea became a series of clothes featuring works by contemporary artists. The first was Yasumasa Morimura,[5] who had portrayed his own identity in relation to famous paintings of Western Europe, in a solo exhibition called *Bijutushi no Musumetachi* (Daughters of Art History). For PLEATS PLEASE Morimura presented himself in the role of *La Source*, a famous work by Dominique Ingres. The work was commissioned by Issey himself, and thus it would be more appropriate to regard it as a commission rather than a collaboration. And the very piece of clothing was indeed a limited-edition artwork as well as a collector's item. This first-rate, imaginative artwork is also one that a person can wear, the image not merely a decoration stuck on the surface of a piece of cloth. It is an independent work of art that moves and transforms relative to the wearer's movements and gestures. Following Morimura, Nobuyoshi Araki,[6] Tim Hawkinson,[7] and Cai Guo-Qiang[8] participated in the project. The Artists Series culminated in being a playground of diverse and appealing artworks by a variety of artists.

At the opening of the *Issey Miyake Making Things* exhibition at the Fondation Cartier pour l'art contemporain in Paris, Cai Guo-Qiang created a strong impression with a performance in which he spread gunpowder over PLEATS PLEASE pieces, lit the powder, and then at a certain point put out the fire. He then displayed the remaining pieces of cloth with their scorch marks. Araki recalled how he thought that "I had assumed that Miyake would have picked an image of a flower or something of the sort, but was astonished that he proposed a much more risky one." Hawkinson incorporated images of various parts of his own body in an image that made a powerful graphic impression. All these were made possible thanks to Miyake's modus operandi of giving each artist maximum freedom. By combining the two pieces of work, the designer successfully confirmed that the clothing he had invented possessed the attribute of being an art medium.

MONO ZUKURI – MAKING THINGS: THE FIRST PRINCIPLE

Mono wo tsukuru toiu koto (On Making Things). This was the name Issey Miyake gave to an exhibition, and, as I think of it, I wonder if he might at the time have been haunted by a certain world in his mind that he wished to bid farewell to completely.

Like the calendar repeating itself year after year, so the fashion business continues to repeat past conventions, and both the industry and the media place their priority on marketing. Negative factors such as these, as well as established preconceptions and customs, surround the environment and together they discourage any serious *mono zukuri*.

Miyake even said laughingly at times, "My favorite word is *kusabi*, wedge."

I sometimes wonder what goes on in the deep reality of our time – and his time – in which he maintained a youthful sensibility – this tense, dense time. What converges upon and imbues Issey's idea of *mono zukuri* are nothing but confidence and pride regarding the past and the future:

"Making things" allows you to have the same state of mind as ordinary people. When I speak of "ordinary people," I mean our contemporaries, the people who are living in our era, at the same time. Making clothes that everyone can wear means making clothes for people who live with us, our contemporaries.
**Issey Miyake Making Things, AXIS,
Japanese edition, 1999**

The exhibition *Issey Miyake Making Things*[9] was presented in Paris and New York, and in both cities the sites were filled with joy. Pleats pieces were hung in vast spaces with high ceilings. The installation was entitled *Jumping*, and that's exactly what one felt the clothes were doing. It was realized by Tokujin Yoshioka,[10] a space designer who had inherited the best of genes from Shiro Kuramata and Issey Miyake.

Fundamentally, the show's organizers hoped and intended that the exhibition would make visitors feel good as they left the venue, and observing their reactions as they did so confirmed that the show had succeeded. I visited the Cartier Foundation venue one winter evening and witnessed how the hall had been turned into a joyful space and indeed the children were jumping. How many of them would recall, years later when they grew up, what they had seen on that day? If Issey Miyake entrusted anything to the exhibition as an art medium, I suspect that it might have been the expectation of this sort of recollection would prevail.

1   Exhibition *Energieën*: See pp. 170–171.
2   Anselm Kiefer (1945–): Artist. Has presented epic-like, large-scale works with historical, mythical, alchemical, and religious themes since his debut in 1969, in works that confront the Nazi past. Uses diverse materials and methods such as painting, installation, and others.
3   Ettore Sottsass (1917–2007): Designer and architect. He was involved in furniture and industrial design projects, as well as editing magazines and undertaking the "Memphis" project. As a thinker, too, he exerted a major influence over design work of the 20th century.
4   Mariano Fortuny (1871–1949): Fashion designer. Born in Spain and, after living in Paris, moved to Venice, where he spent most of the rest of his life. Designed dresses with pleated silk satin materials that were inspired by ancient Greek tube-shaped clothing. These were epoch-making in that the dress structure itself served as ornament.
5   Yasumasa Morimura (1951–): Artist. Since making his debut in 1985 with a photographic self-portrait as van Gogh, he has depicted himself in further works associated with not only important works in art history by artists such as Rembrandt, Ingres, and Goya, but also film stars and celebrities: See pp. 204–205 for the Guest Artist Series in which he participated.
6   Nobuyoshi Araki (1940–): Photographer. Has photographed nudes, portraits, flowers, bondage scenes, and street snapshots. Also known for having created over 400 photography books as well as holding solo exhibitions around the world: See pp. 206–207 for the Guest Artist Series in which he participated.
7   Tim Hawkinson (1960–): Artist. Active since the 1980s, making sculptural and installation works inspired by his own body; solo show at the Whitney Museum of American Art in 2005: See p. 228 for the Guest Artist Series in which he participated.
8   Cai Guo-Qiang (1957–): Artist. Studied stage design in Shanghai; lived in Japan from 1986 to 1995; now based in New York. Makes gigantic-scale installations and spectacles which reflect the Eastern view of the world, using Chinese gunpowder and herbal medicine: See p. 229 for the Guest Artist Series in which he participated.
9   Exhibition *Issey Miyake Making Things*: See pp. 218, 230–231, 234–239.
10 Tokujin Yoshioka (1967–): Designer. Worked under Shiro Kuramata and Issey Miyake. Established TOKUJIN YOSHIOKA INC. in 2000. Has undertaken diverse projects involving the design of products, architecture, interiors, packaging, etc. Known for his straightforward style, unusual ideas, and experimental creations. Has also designed many ISSEY MIYAKE shops.

1988

> March: Autumn-Winter 1988 Paris Collection at Salle des Arts, Cour Carrée du Louvre
> April: Autumn-Winter 1988 Tokyo Collection at Yoyogi Tent South of the National Stadium
> Publication of *Issey Miyake Photographs by Irving Penn* as international edition
> June: *i.i.i. at ggg Issey Miyake Posters* exhibition in Tokyo
> October–December: *Issey Miyake A-ŪN* exhibition at the Musée des Arts Décoratifs, Paris
> October: Spring-Summer 1989 Paris Collection at Salle des Arts, Cour Carrée du Louvre
> November: Spring-Summer 1989 Tokyo Collection at Yoyogi Tent South of the National Stadium
> Designed the rescue operations staff uniform for the Fire and Disaster Management Agency

Issey Miyake A-ŪN exhibition

The exhibition was an overview of Issey Miyake's work from 1978 to 1988. The title comes from the Japanese word "a-ūn," meaning "in synch." It was chosen to express both the relationship between the designer and the person receiving the design, and also the many different aspects of Miyake's work. The exhibition used wire "forms" (sculpted mannequins), with audio delivered from built-in speakers when visitors approached, to provide an interactive element. It was about this time that Miyake's focus shifted to exploring new materials.

October 5–December 31:
Musée des Arts Décoratifs, Paris
Exhibition direction: Issey Miyake; art direction and "form" design: Tomio Mohri; lighting: Masao Nihei; music: Yuji Kawashima; "form" production: Nanasai Co., Ltd.; graphic design: Ikko Tanaka; poster photography: Irving Penn

1 Autumn-Winter 1988 Paris Collection, March 19, Salle des Arts, Cour Carrée du Louvre
2 Spring-Summer 1989 Paris Collection, October 22, Salle des Arts, Cour Carrée du Louvre

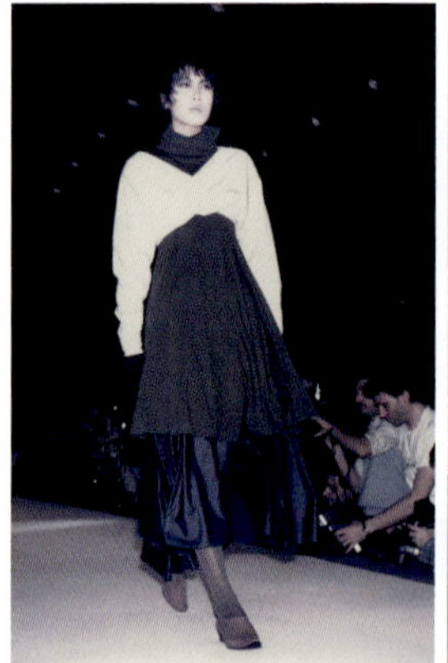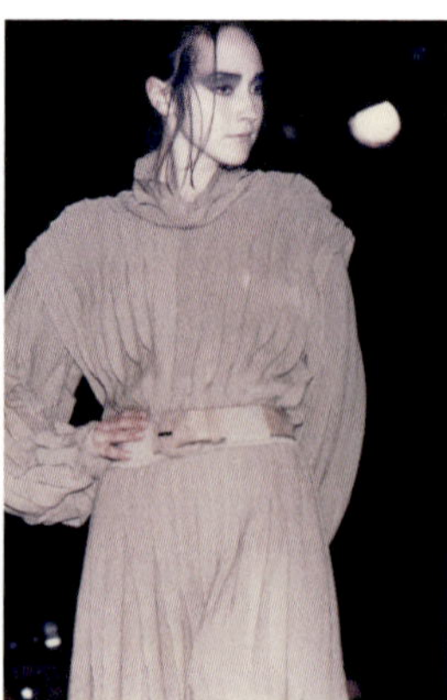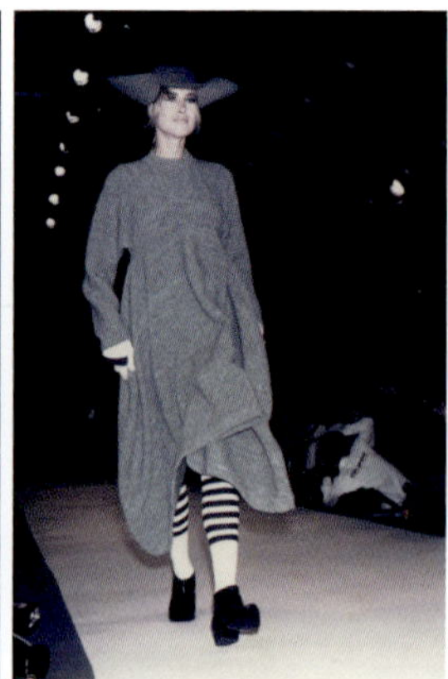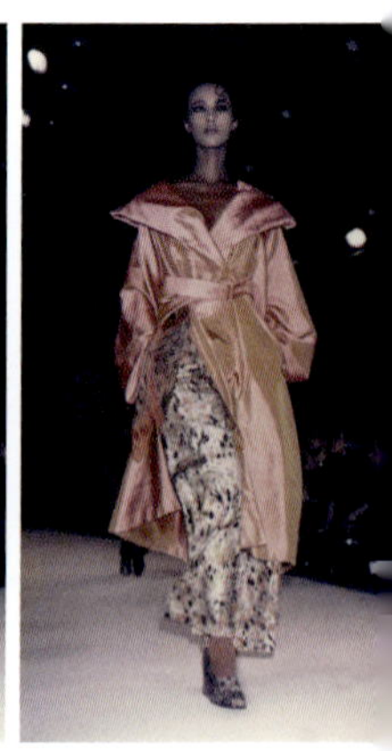

1

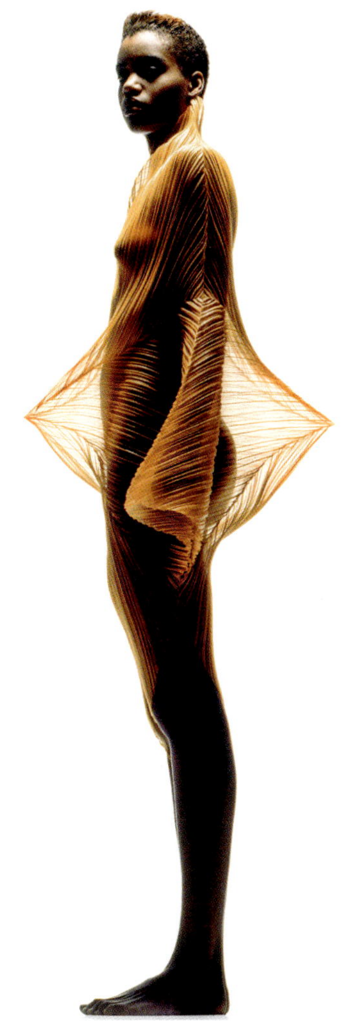

Cicada

A single scarf is folded up, given random pleats along the biased grain of the cloth, unfolded, and sewn in three locations to create a shirt. The starting point for this clothing was the idea of "garment pleating" that is applied after the clothing is sewn.
1988 design/Spring-Summer 1989 Collection
Photography: Albert Watson

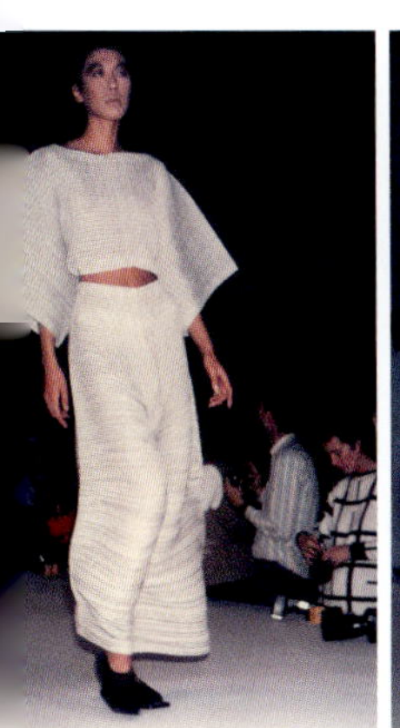
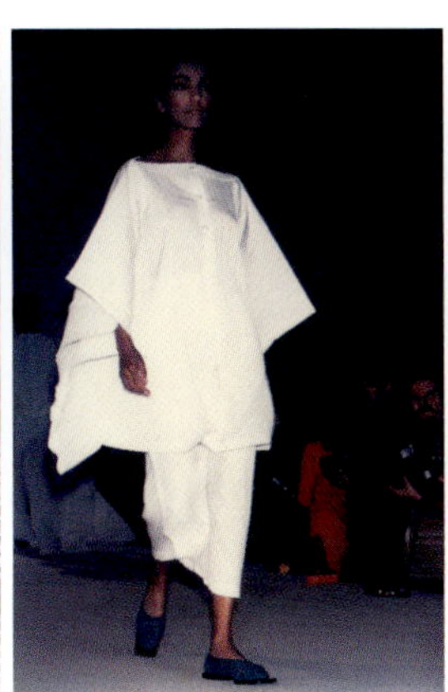
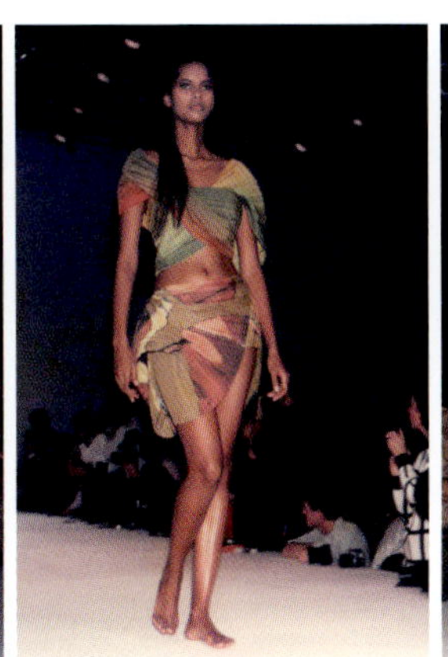
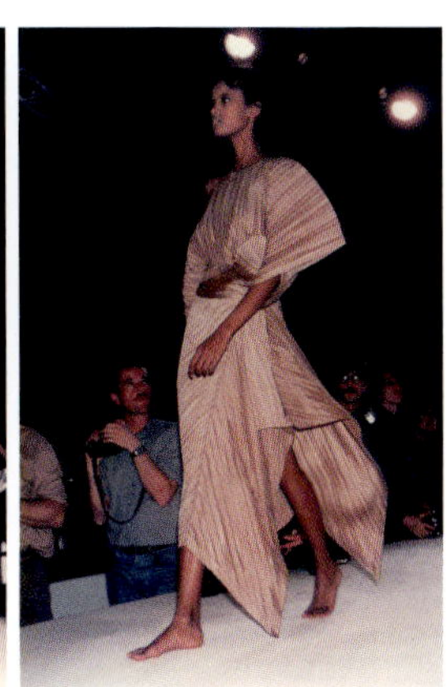

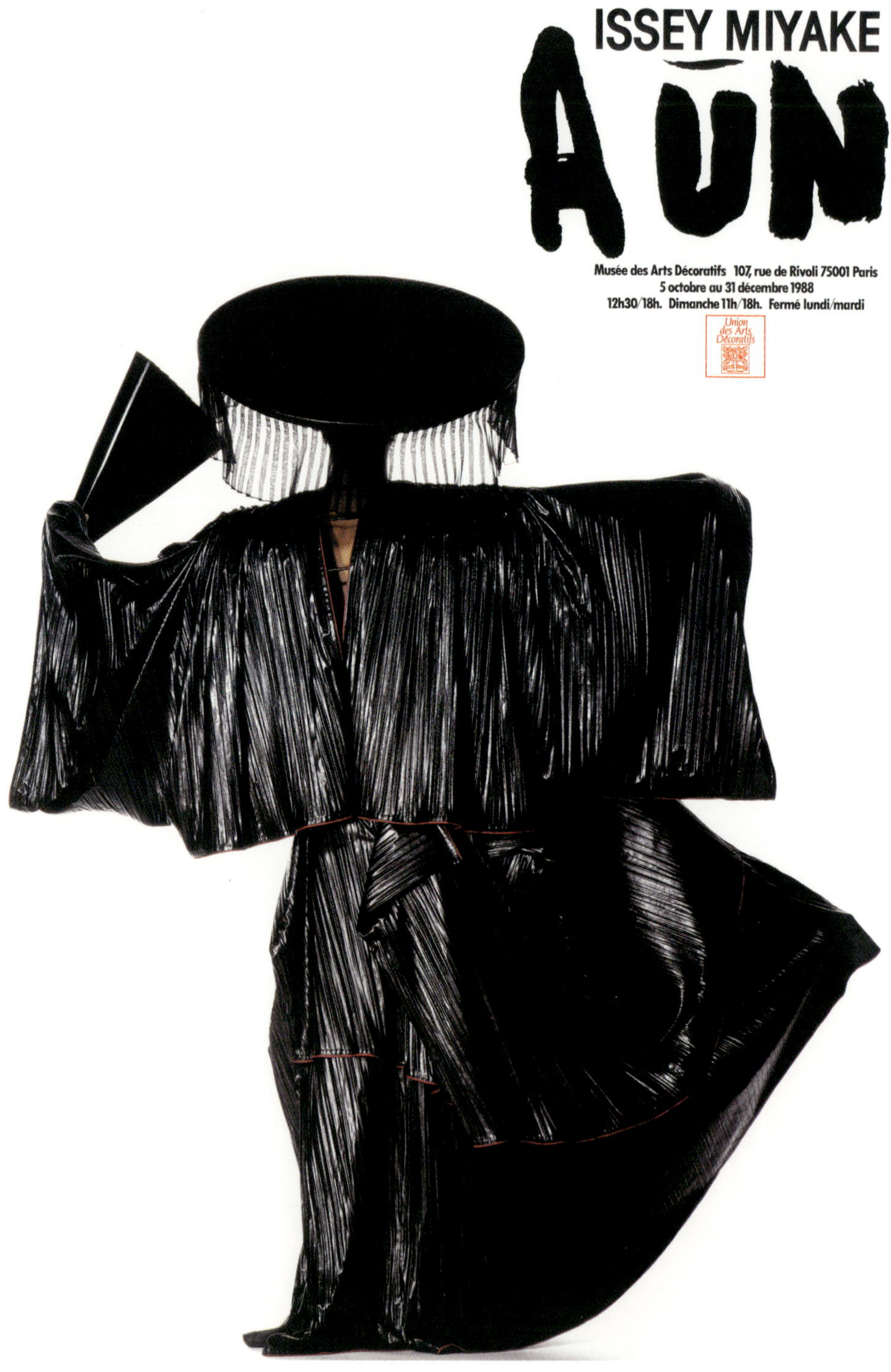
ISSEY MIYAKE
A ŪN
Musée des Arts Décoratifs 107, rue de Rivoli 75001 Paris
5 octobre au 31 décembre 1988
12h30/18h. Dimanche 11h/18h. Fermé lundi/mardi
Union
des Arts
Décoratifs

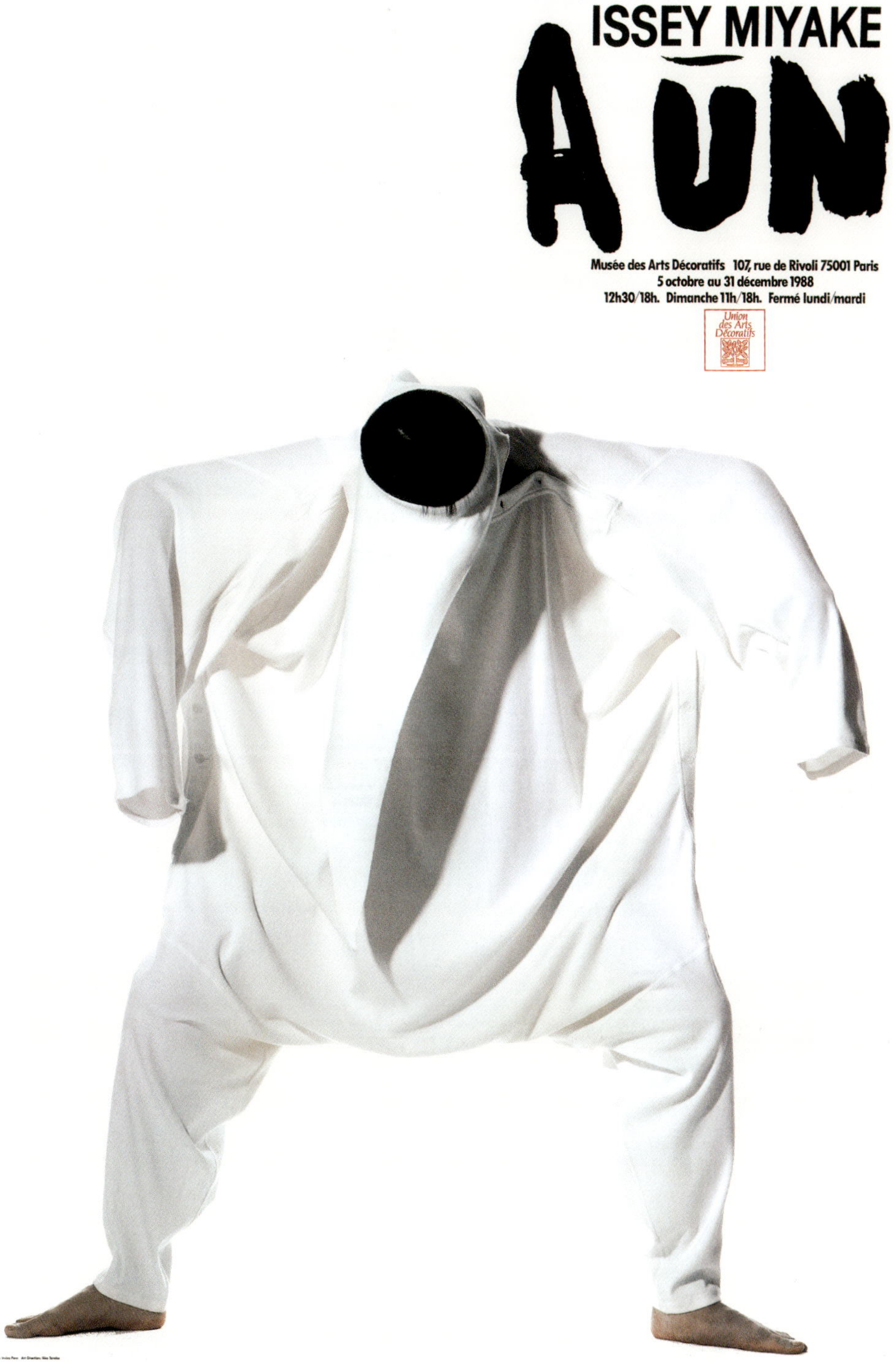

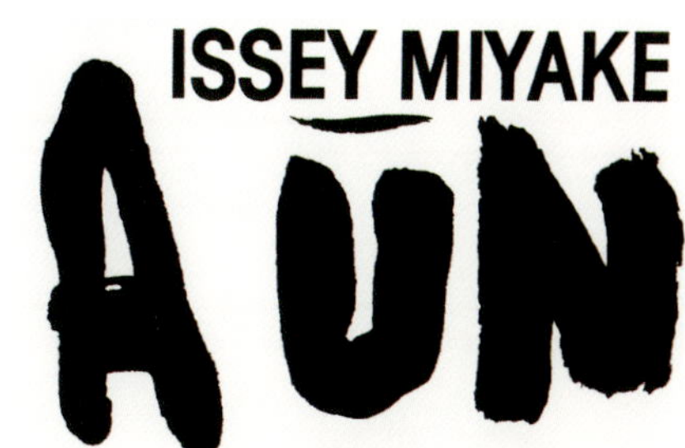
ISSEY MIYAKE
A UN
Musée des Arts Décoratifs 107, rue de Rivoli 75001 Paris
5 octobre au 31 décembre 1988
12h30/18h. Dimanche 11h/18h. Fermé lundi/mardi
Union
des Arts
Décoratifs

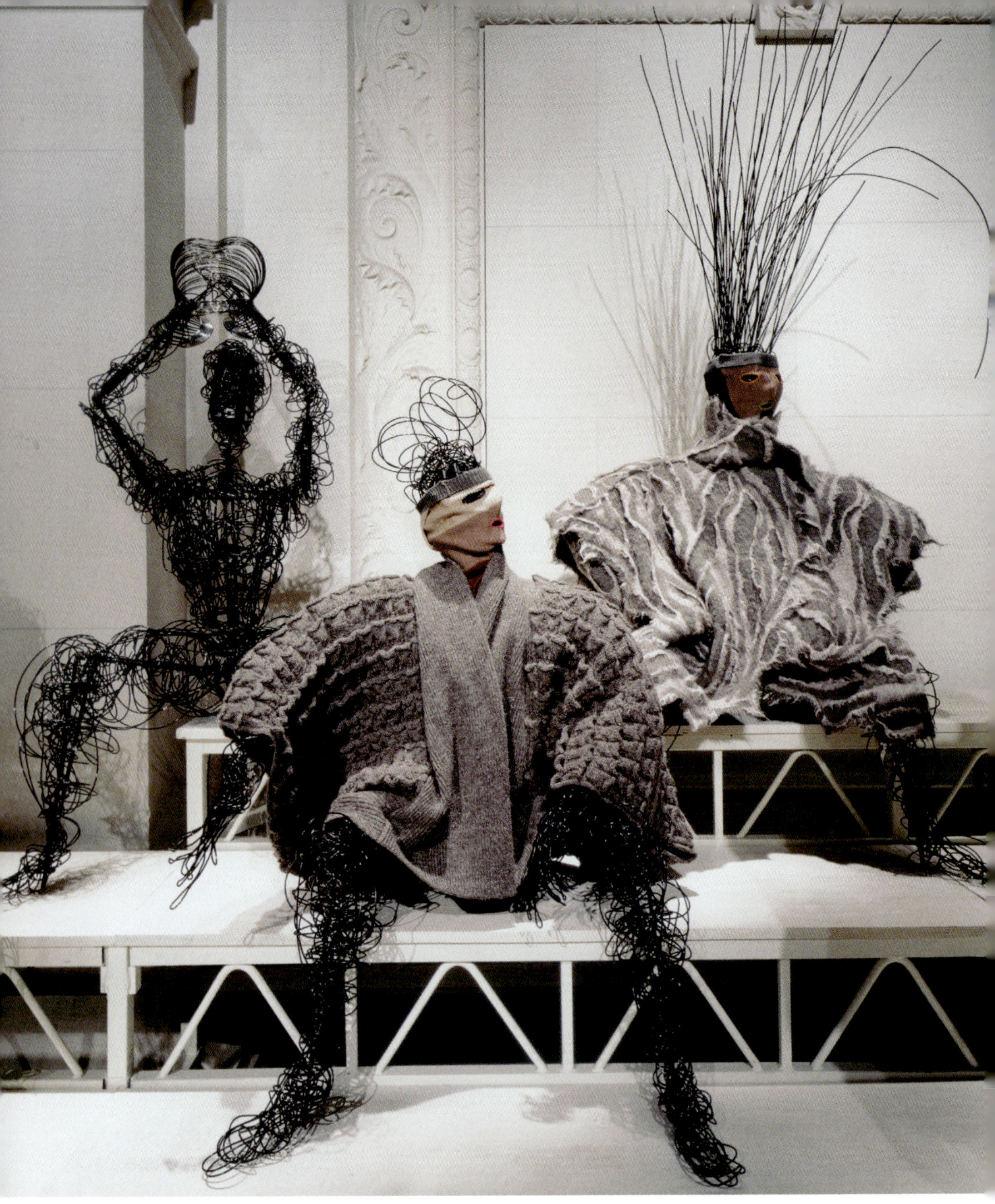

Previous spread: **Issey Miyake A-ŪN exhibition** poster
The poster was created from two sheets arranged side by side, the black representing "a," the white "ūn." The black clothing is a jacket and skirt made from pleated, synthetic leather. *Rattan Body* is underneath the jacket.
1981 design/Spring-Summer 1982 Collection

The white clothing is a *Turtle Jumpsuit*. With vertical and horizontal symmetry, any of the four buttoned openings may become the neckline. Asymmetrical headband.
1982 design/Spring-Summer 1983 Collection
Photography: Irving Penn; layout and typography: Ikko Tanaka; model: Jun Kano

Opposite: *Issey Miyake A-ŪN exhibition*
From left, *Wire Body* (1984 design/Autumn-Winter
1984 Collection), *Bell Knit* (1984 design/Autumn-
Winter 1984 Collection) and *Animal Knit* (1983 design/
Autumn-Winter 1983 Collection)
Photography: Shigeo Anzaï

Issey Miyake A-ŪN exhibition
Front: *Kanpan (hardtack) Coat.*
The material is a double weave of jute and cotton.
1983 design/Spring-Summer 1984 Collection
Back: Series made from high-density synthetic fibers.
Audio plays as guests approach.
1986 design/Autumn-Winter 1986 Collection
Photography: Shigeo Anzaï

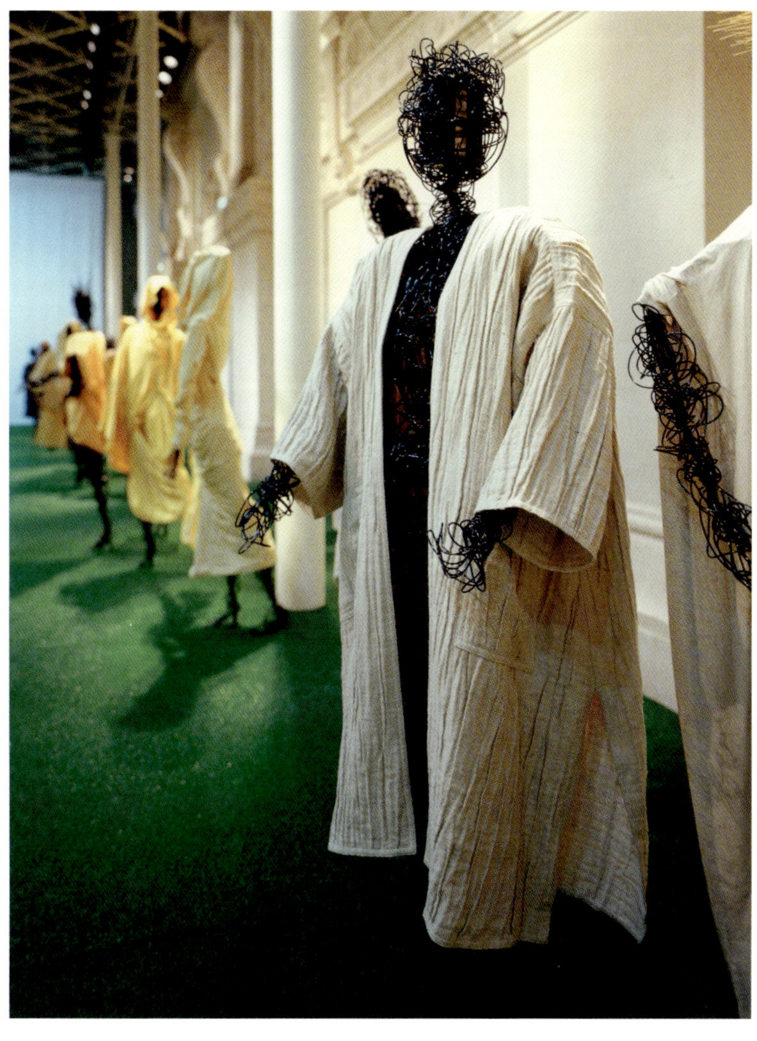

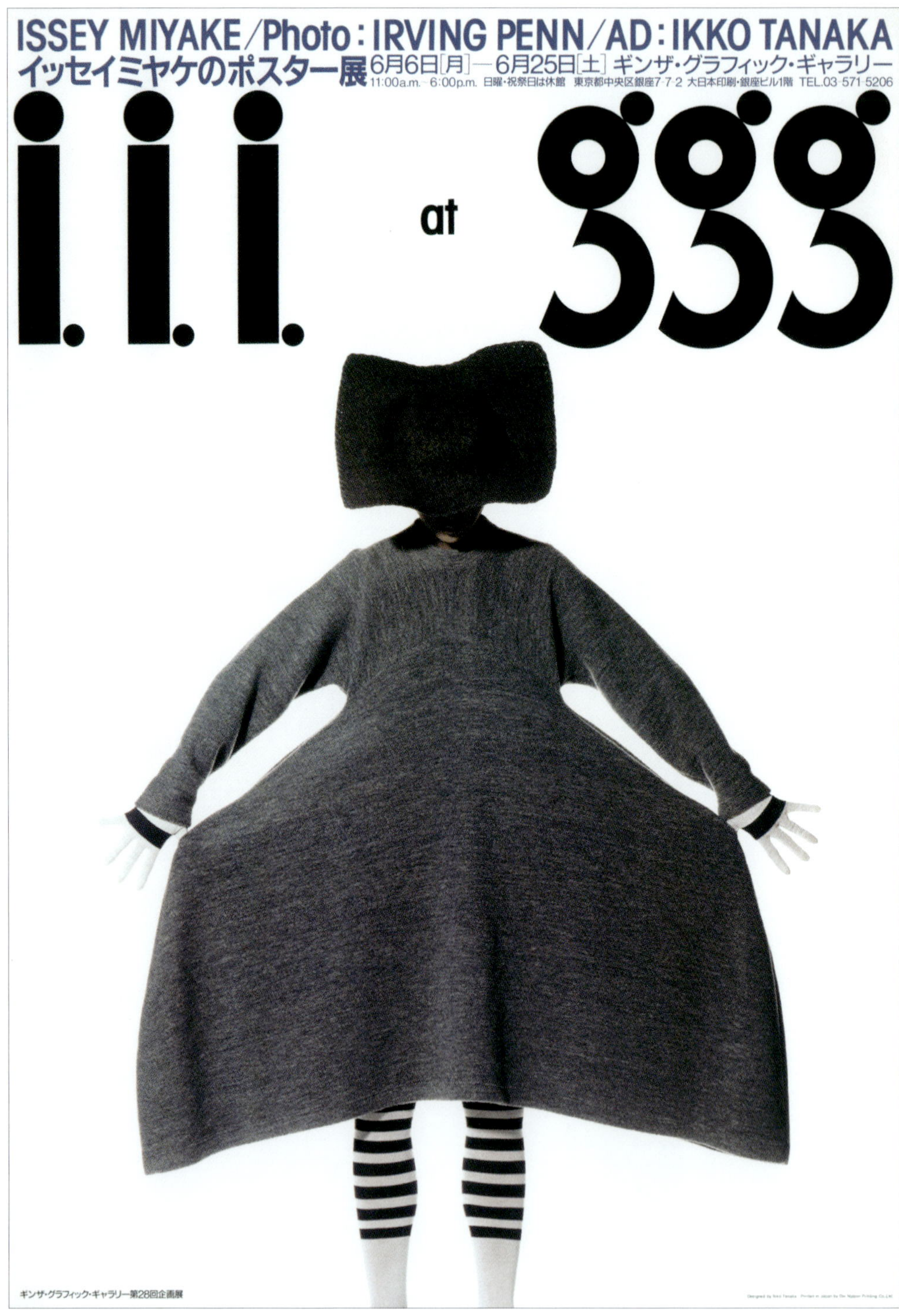
ISSEY MIYAKE／Photo：IRVING PENN／AD：IKKO TANAKA
イッセイミヤケのポスター展 6月6日［月］－6月25日［土］ ギンザ・グラフィック・ギャラリー
11:00a.m.－6:00p.m. 日曜・祝祭日は休館 東京都中央区銀座7-7-2 大日本印刷・銀座ビル1階 TEL.03-571-5206
i.i.i. at ggg
ギンザ・グラフィック・ギャラリー第28回企画展

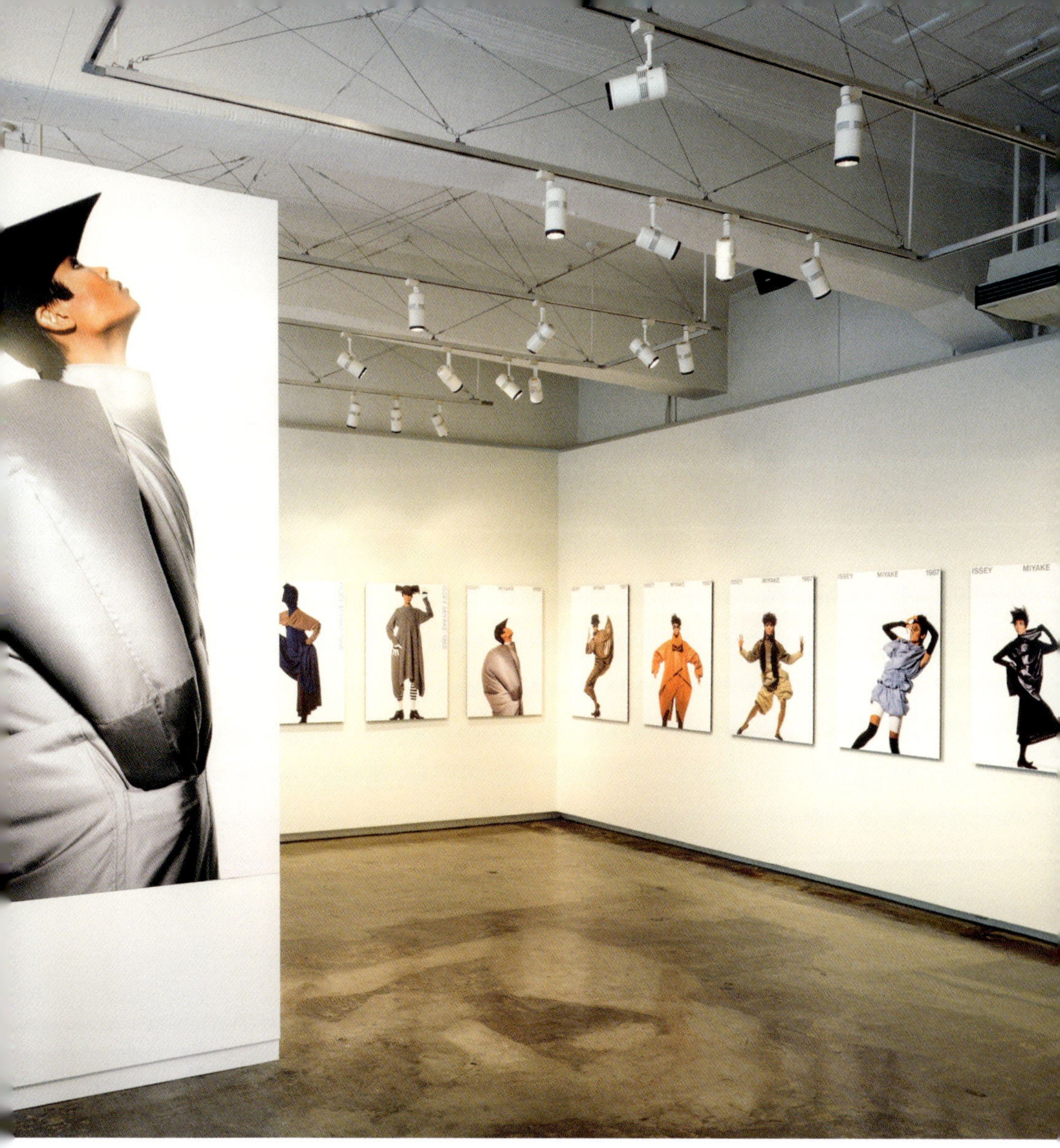

Opposite: *i.i.i. at ggg Issey Miyake Posters* exhibition poster
Crocheted raised mossa jersey dress. High-waist
transition with semicircular skirt. The body and skirt
use different warp and weft grains. Felt hat.
1988 design/Autumn-Winter 1988 Collection
Photography: Irving Penn; layout and typography:
Ikko Tanaka; model: Jun Kano

***i.i.i. at ggg Issey Miyake Posters* exhibition**
Installation view, Ginza Graphic Gallery
The poster exhibition's title was created by using the
first letter of the names of the three people who were
part of the collaboration: Issey Miyake, Irving Penn,
and Ikko Tanaka, plus the Ginza Graphic Gallery, the
exhibition's venue. Ikko Tanaka followed the directive
to use different typography in the layout of ISSEY
MIYAKE's collection posters.
Photography: Shigeyuki Morishita

1989

> March: Autumn-Winter 1989 Paris Collection at Salle des Arts, Cour Carrée du Louvre
> April: Autumn-Winter 1989 Tokyo Collection at Miyake Design Studio
> May–July: Organized *Issey Miyake Meets Lucie Rie* exhibition
> October: Spring-Summer 1990 Paris Collection at Salle des Arts, Cour Carrée du Louvre
> November: Spring-Summer 1990 Tokyo Collection at Yoyogi Tent South of the National Stadium
> Production began on *Issey Miyake by Irving Penn* (private publication) (1989, 1990, 1991–92, 1993–95, 1995–97)

***Issey Miyake Meets Lucie Rie* exhibition**

Miyake planned and organized the first Japanese exhibition for British pottery artist Lucie Rie. He happened upon Rie's catalogue by accident and was attracted by the work. He eventually visited her in London and they developed a friendship. Tadao Ando created the design for the space, which featured Rie's pottery arrayed in water. A catalogue was published with Yasuhiro Ishimoto providing the photography and Yusaku Kamekura the design.

May 10–June 7: Sogetsu Gallery, Tokyo
June 27–July 30: Museum of Oriental Ceramics, Osaka
Supervision: Issey Miyake; space design: Tadao Ando
Poster photograph: Yasuhiro Ishimoto; poster design: Yusaku Kamekura

1 Autumn-Winter 1989 Paris Collection, March 18, Salle des Arts, Cour Carrée du Louvre
2 Spring-Summer 1990 Paris Collection, October 21, Salle des Arts, Cour Carrée du Louvre

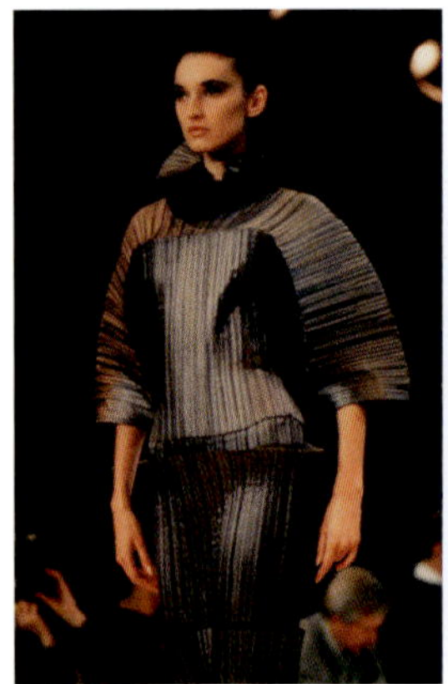
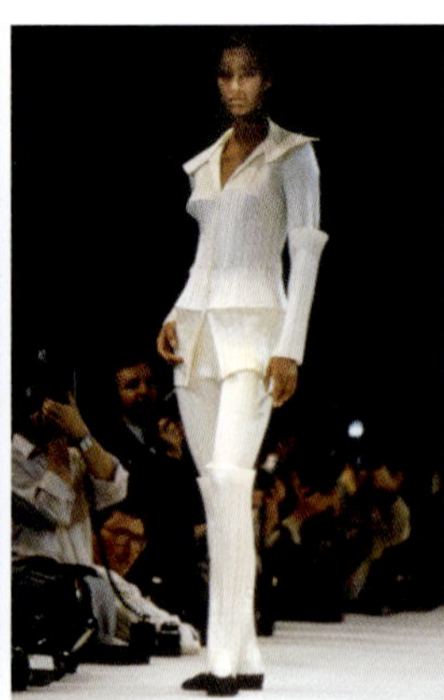
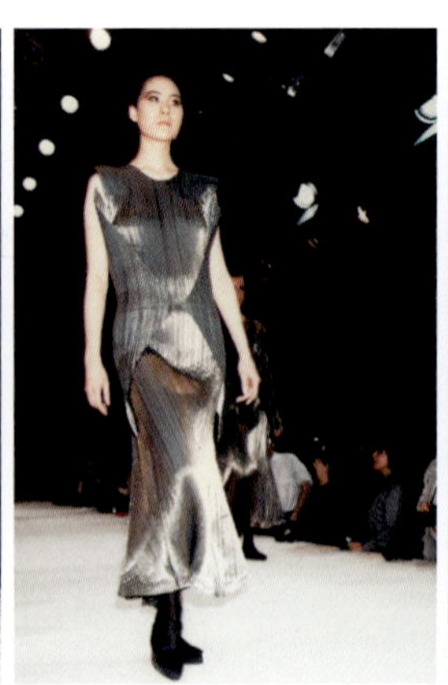
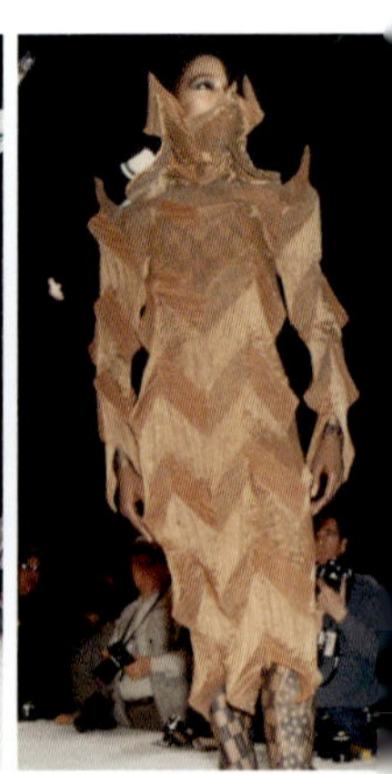

1

Advertisement in *Elle* (UK),
October 1989 edition
Mercury Pleats jacket.
1989 design/Autumn-Winter
1989 Collection
Photography: Irving Penn;
design: Kiyoshi Kanai
© Issey Miyake Inc.

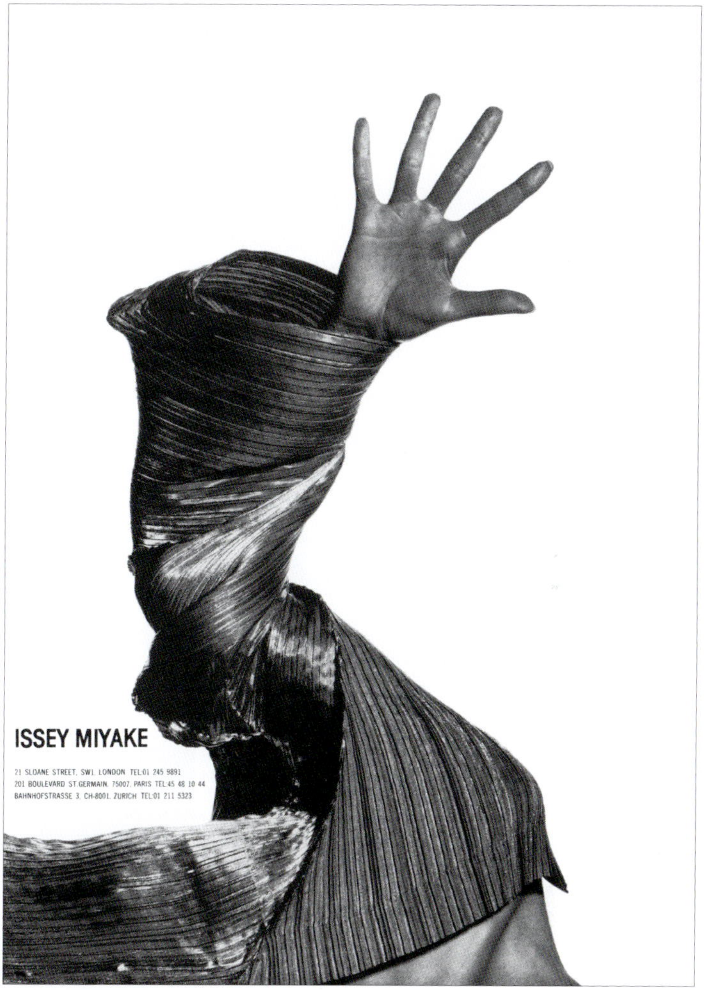

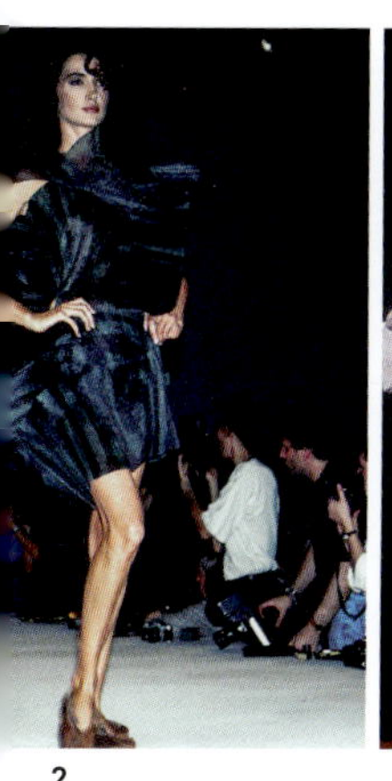
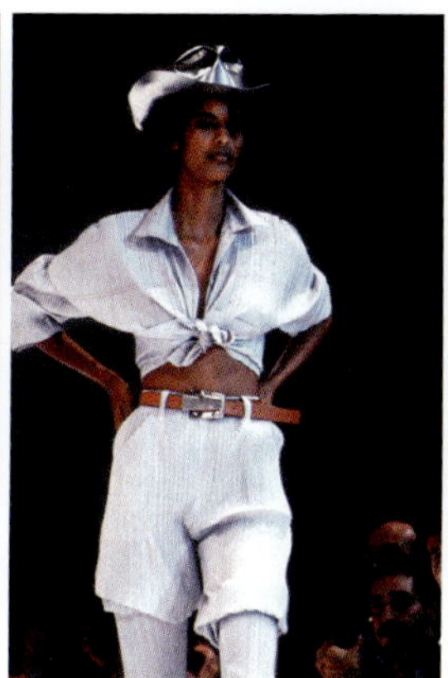
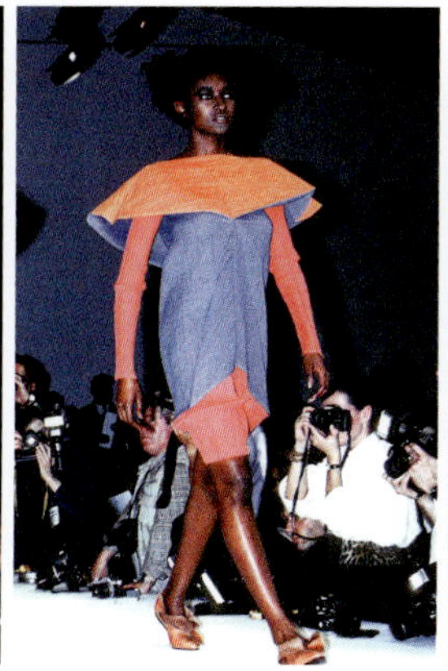
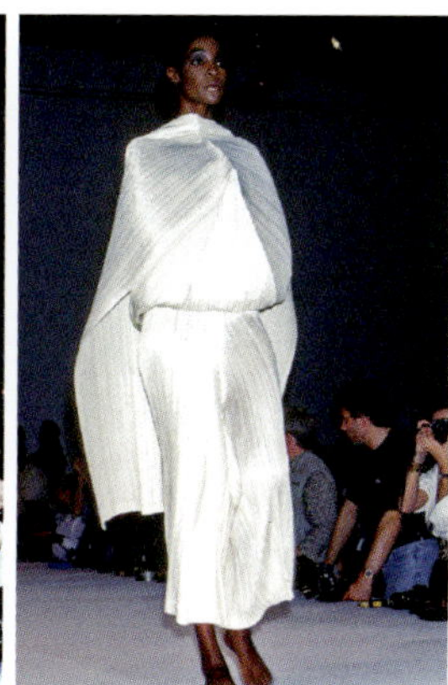

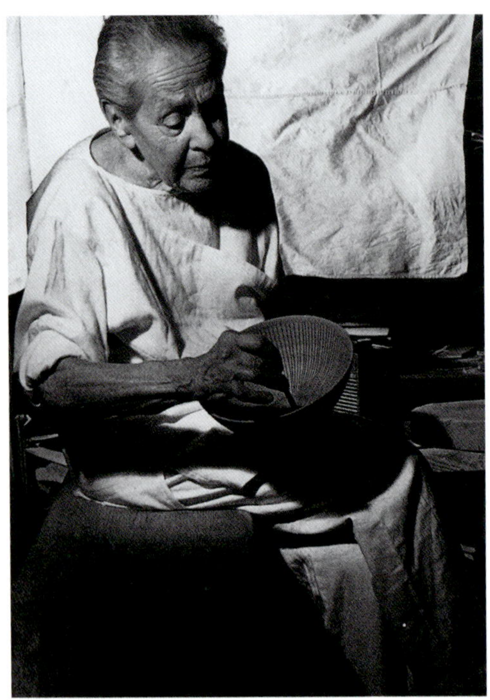

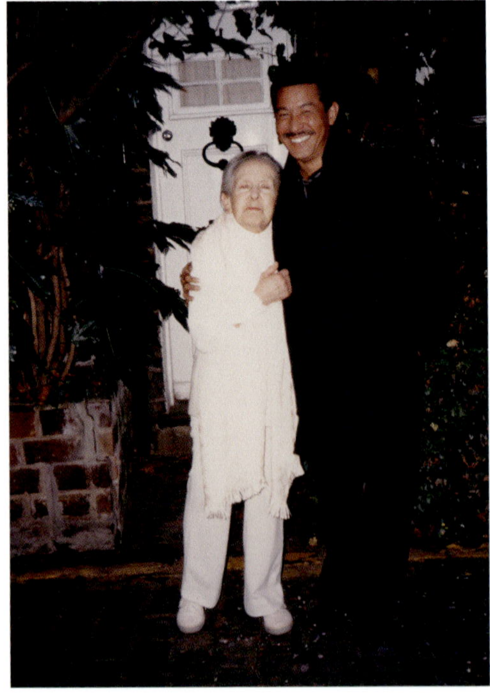

Above: Lucie Rie creates pottery wearing
a *double-face cotton shirt*
Photography: Sam Haskins

Right: Lucie Rie and Issey Miyake in front of Rie's
atelier in Albion Mews, London. Around 1990
Courtesy of Miyake Design Studio

Opposite: Jacket with buttons by Lucie Rie.
Silk wool mohair fabric woven to suit the buttons.
1989 design/Autumn-Winter 1989 Collection
Photography: Masaaki Miyazawa

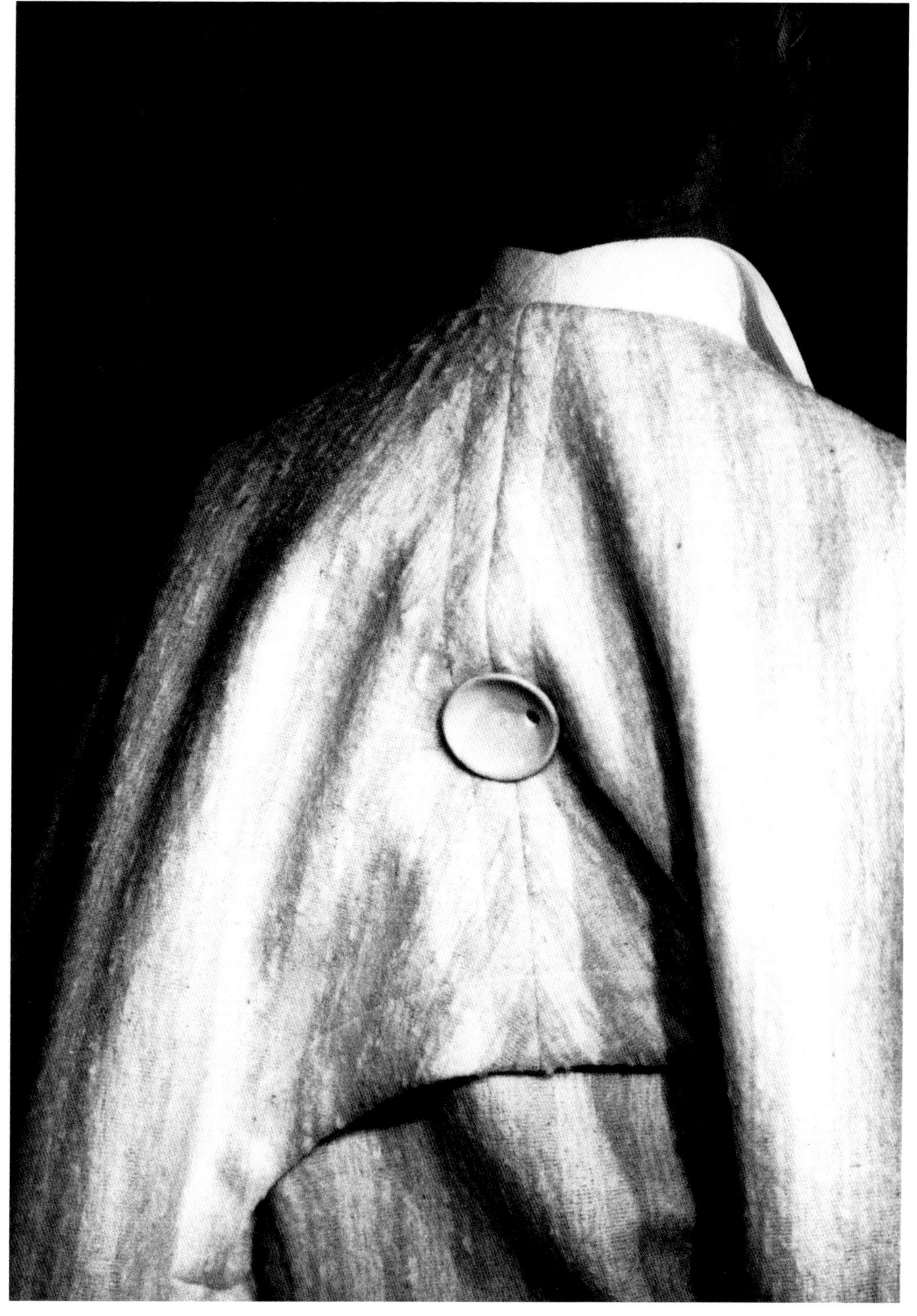

1990

- > March: Autumn-Winter 1990 Paris Collection at Salle des Arts, Cour Carrée du Louvre
- > April: Autumn-Winter 1990 Tokyo Collection at Ebisu Factory
- > April–July: Participated in the *Energieën* exhibition
- > September: *Issey Miyake Pleats Please* exhibition
- > October: Spring-Summer 1991 Paris Collection at Salle des Arts, Cour Carrée du Louvre
- > November: Spring-Summer 1991 Tokyo Collection at Hamilton Place
- > November–January 1991: *Issey Miyake: Ten Sen Men*, a commemorative exhibition in conjunction with the 1st Hiroshima Art Prize

Participated in the *Energieën* exhibition

Energieën was an innovative exhibition that focused upon the theme of "energy" in visual art and enlisted designers and artists from a wide range of multidisciplinary genres: painting, sculpture, architecture, performing arts, and film. Miyake was the only clothing designer selected and contributed an installation of *Rhythm Pleats*. The clothing was arranged on the floor as well as on mannequins, and visitors were invited to take off their shoes and walk around.

*April 8–July 29: Stedelijk Museum, Amsterdam
Planning, coordination, and organization: Wim Beeren; participating designers and artists: Luciano Fabro, Rem Koolhaas, Anselm Kiefer, Sigmar Polke, Cindy Sherman, Bruce Nauman, Frank Stella, Ettore Sottsass, Peter Struycken, Walter De Maria, Gary Hill, Jeff Koons, Robert Wilson, Bob Schulz, and Issey Miyake*

Autumn-Winter 1990 Paris Collection, March 17,
Salle des Arts, Cour Carrée du Louvre

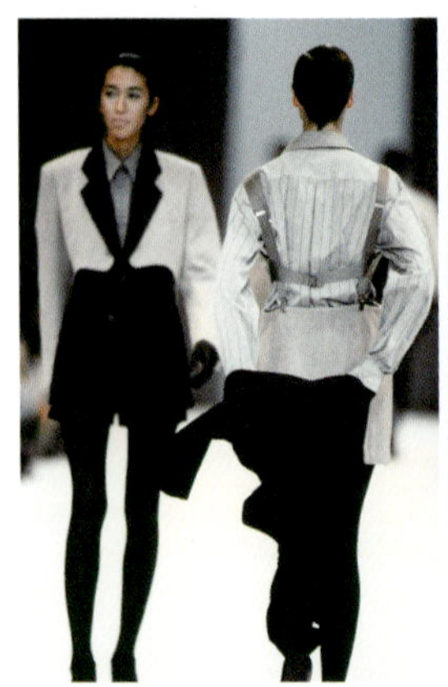
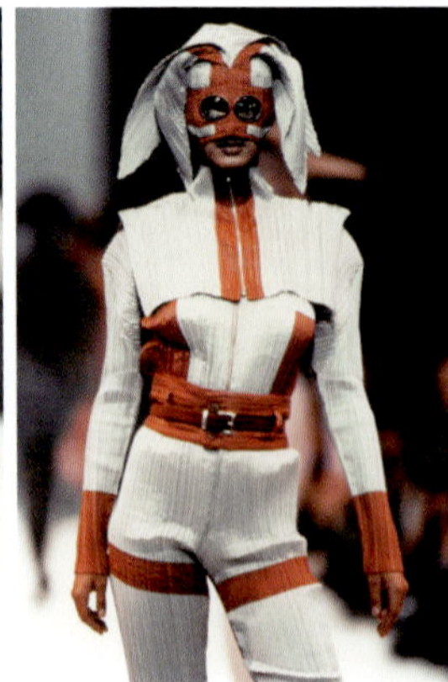
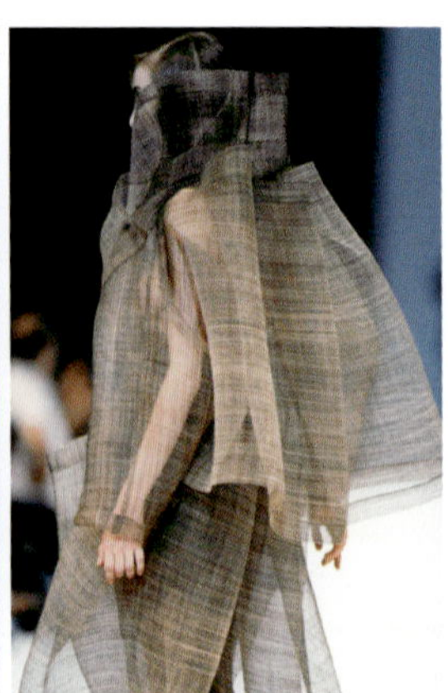
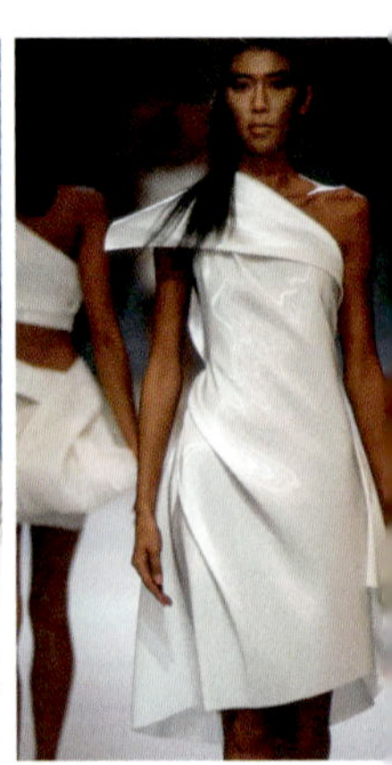

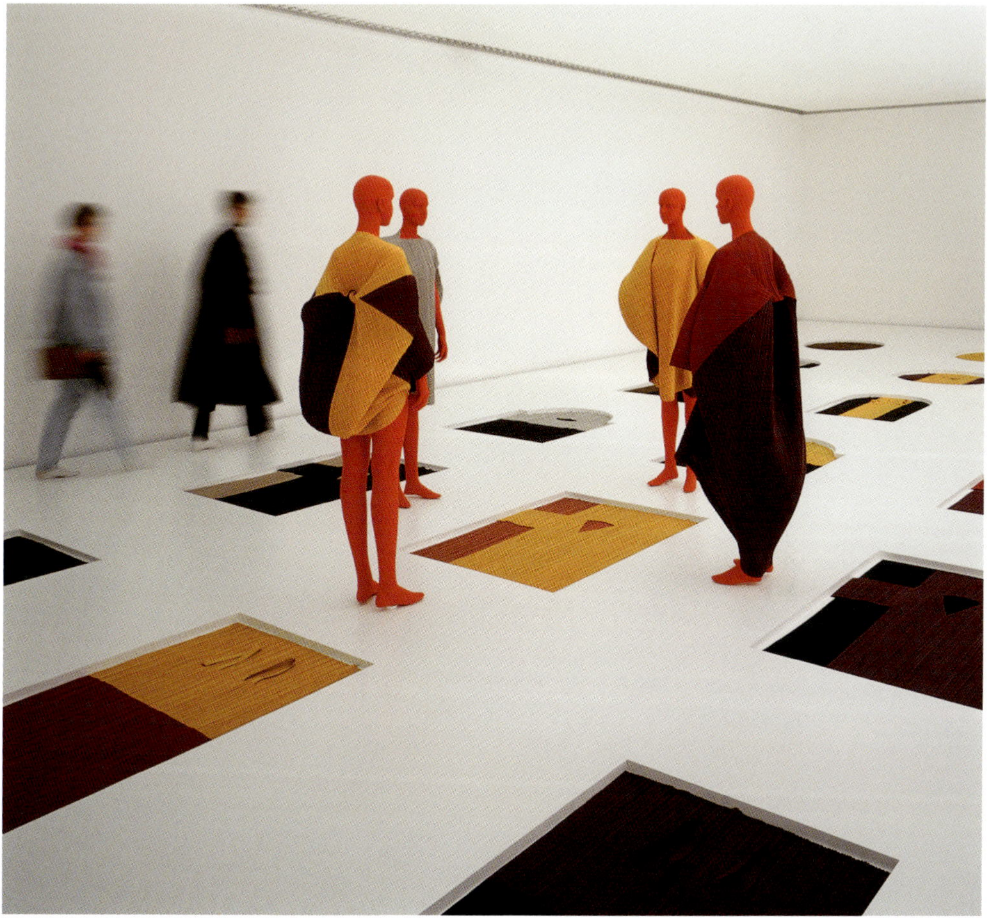

Spring-Summer 1991 Paris Collection, October 20,
Salle des Arts, Cour Carrée du Louvre

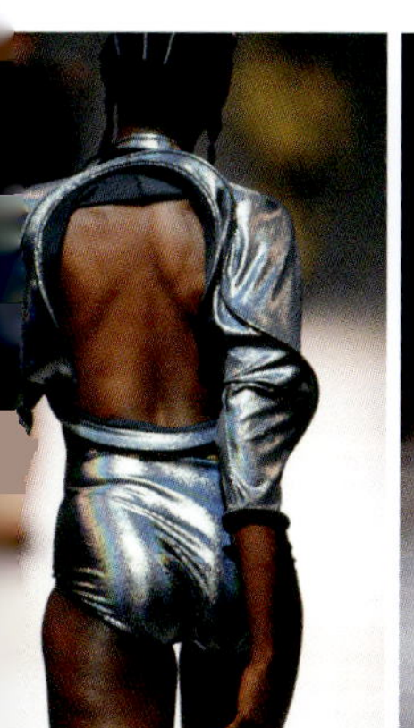
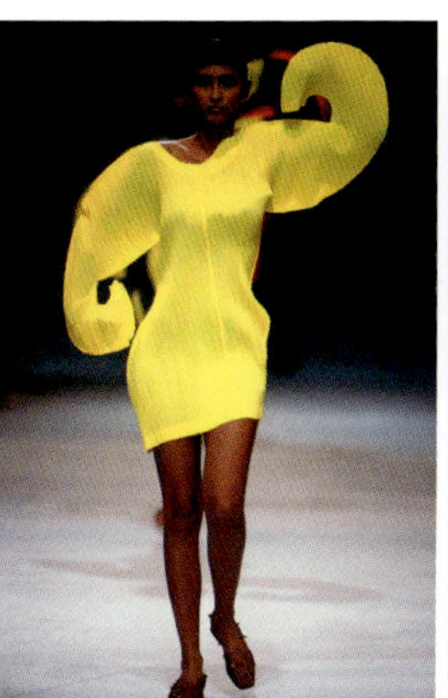
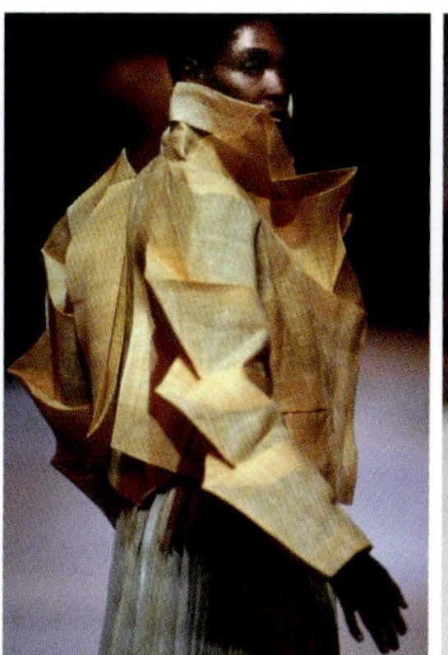
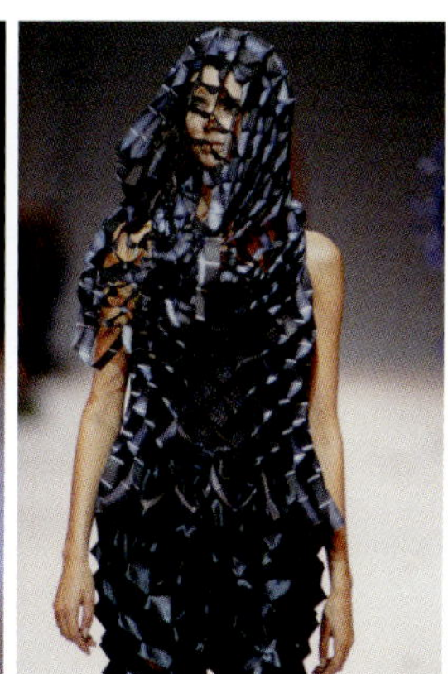

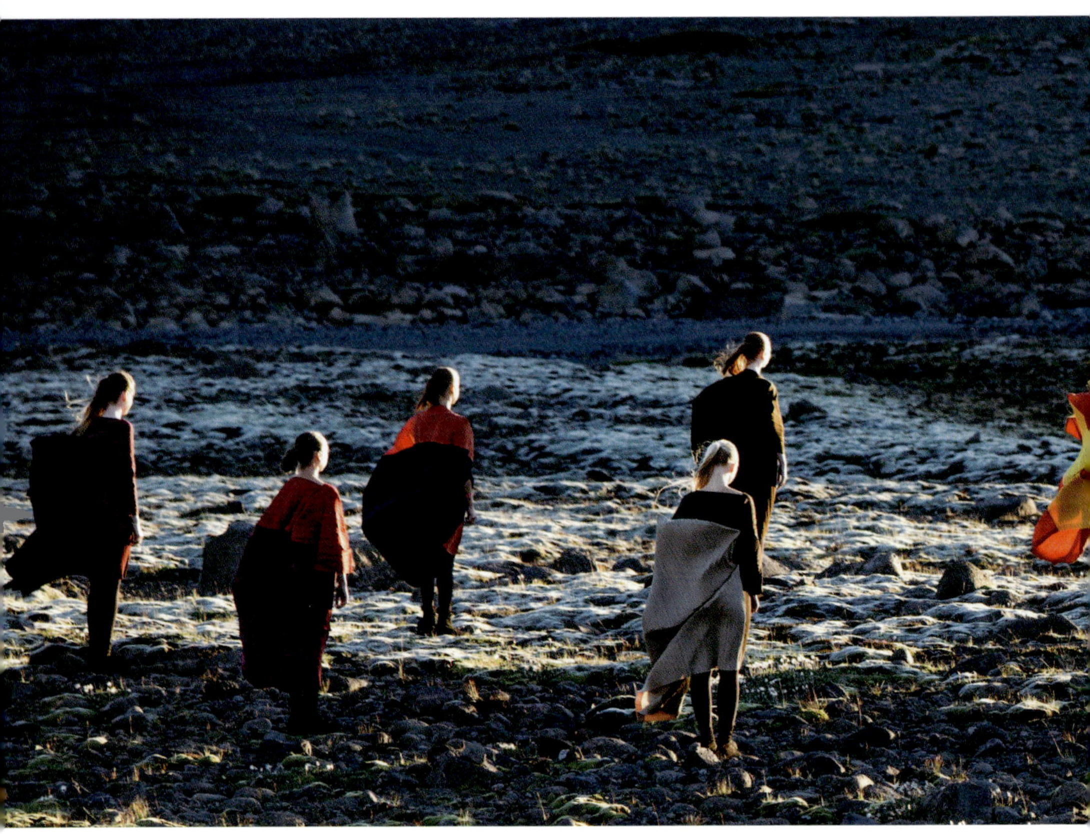

Page 171: *Energieën* exhibition at the Stedelijk Museum in Amsterdam
Rhythm Pleats (1989 design/Spring-Summer 1990 Collection) were exhibited. The clothes were inspired by Henri Rousseau's *Le Rêve*.
Space design: Tokujin Yoshioka
Photography: Shigeo Anzaï

Rhythm Pleats
Dresses in squares and ovals, with unusual placements of the collar and arm openings. Unexpected three-dimensional forms are created when worn.
1989 design/Spring-Summer 1990 Collection
Photography: Yuriko Takagi

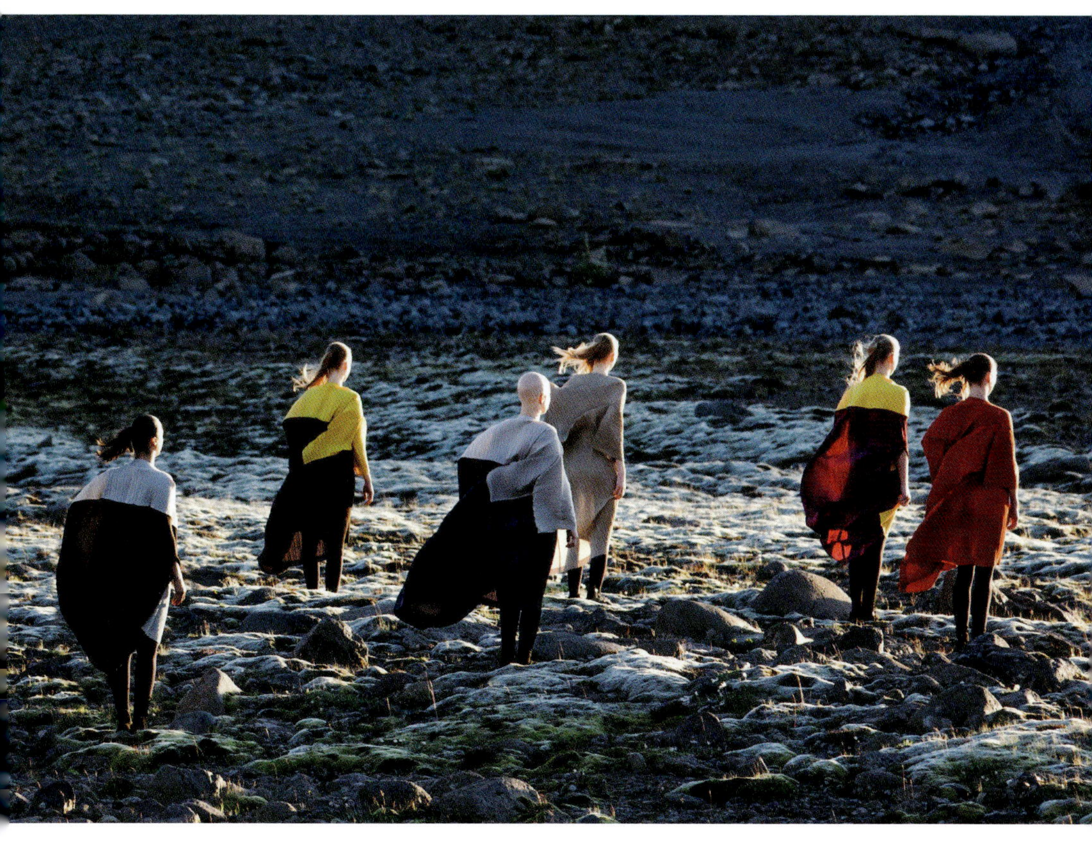

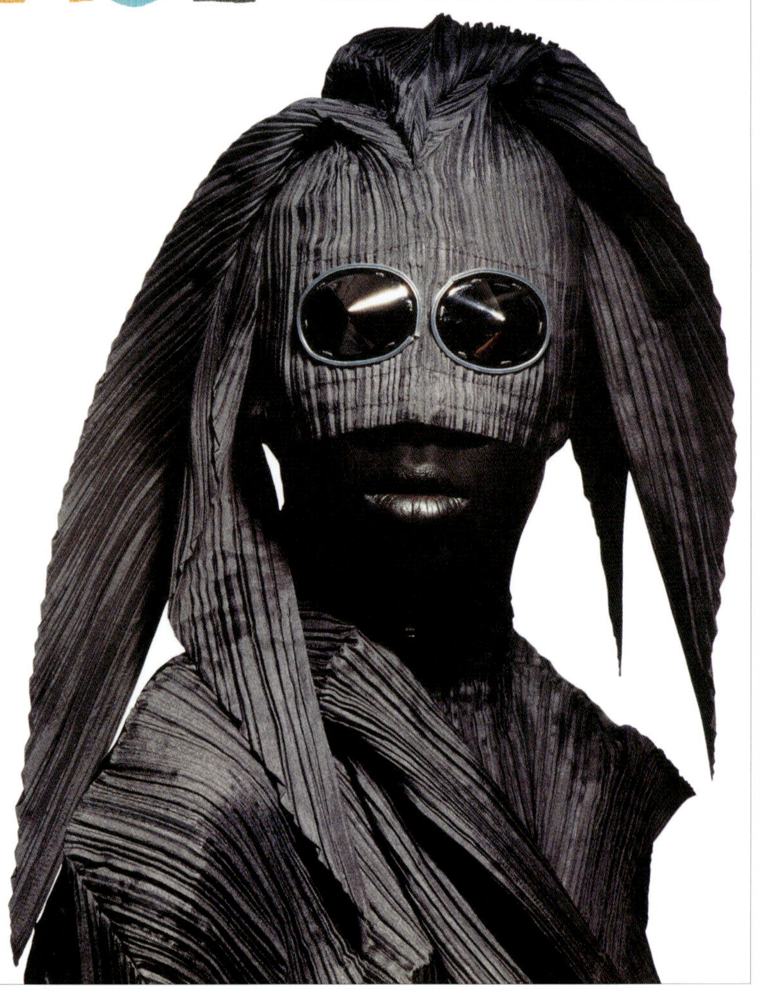

ISSEY MIYAKE
PLEATS
PLEASE

三宅一生展 プリーツ・プリーズ
1990年9月1日[土]—9月30日[日]
主催—東高現代美術館　入場料—一般1000円／大・高生500円　65歳以上・中学生以下無料
東高現代美術館　開館時間—11:00—20:00〔入館は19:30まで〕
月曜休館〔但し9月24日[月]は開館、25日[火]は休館〕
〒107 東京都港区北青山3-5-28 PHONE：03(404)1791 地下鉄［表参道駅］下車 A3出口
September 1–30, 1990 Touko Museum of Contemporary Art

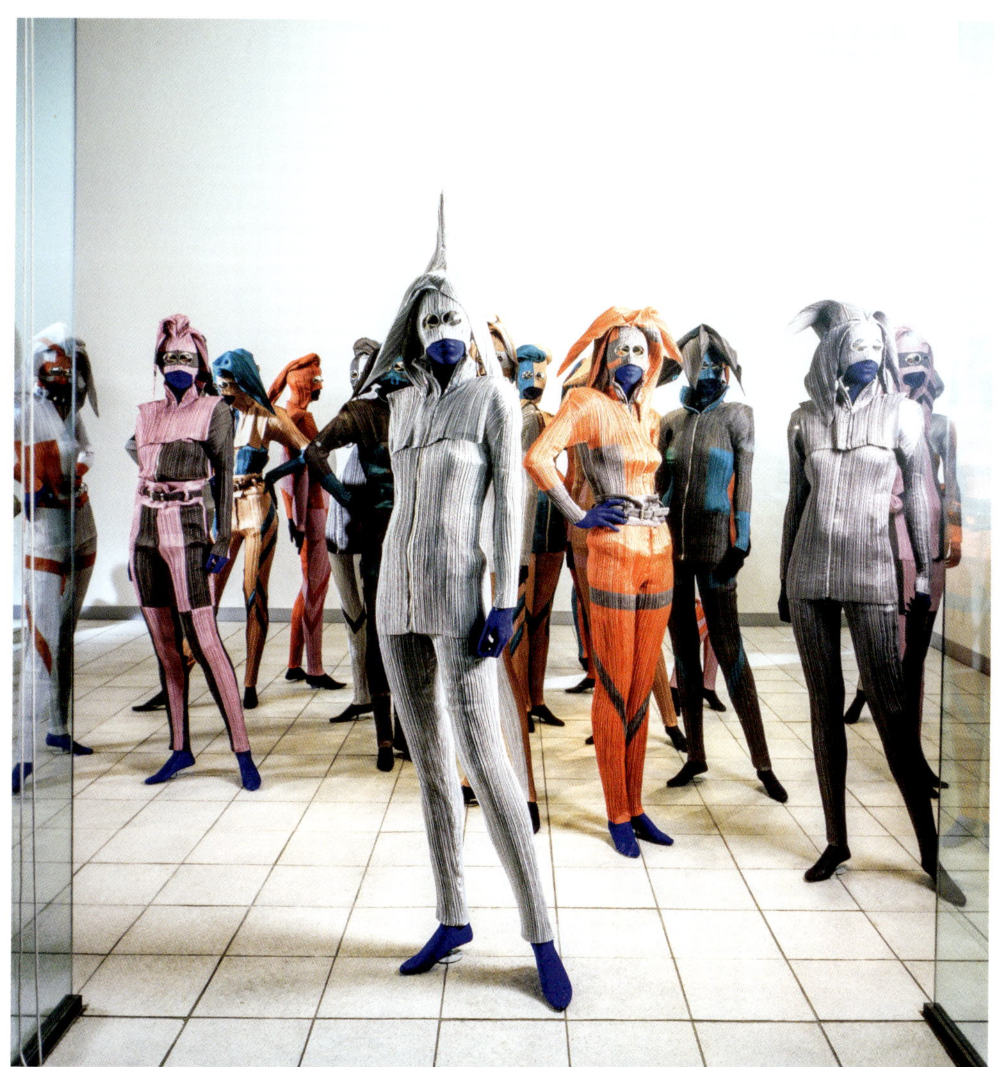

Issey Miyake Pleats Please
Research on pleated clothes began in 1988, and the results were shown as an exhibition for the first time in Japan. Part of the exhibition was taken from what had been done in *Energieën*, and *Body Pleats* were added to *Rhythm Pleats*. Tokujin Yoshioka designed the exhibition space. This was the first time that the name "Pleats Please" was used.
September 1–30: Touko Museum of Contemporary Art, Tokyo

Opposite: **Issey Miyake Pleats Please** poster
Body Pleats 1990 design/Autumn-Winter
1990 Collection
Photography: Irving Penn; layout and typography: Ikko Tanaka; model: Yuki Fujii

Above: **Issey Miyake Pleats Please** exhibition
Body Pleats 1990 design/Autumn-Winter
1990 Collection
Photography: Mitsumasa Fujitsuka

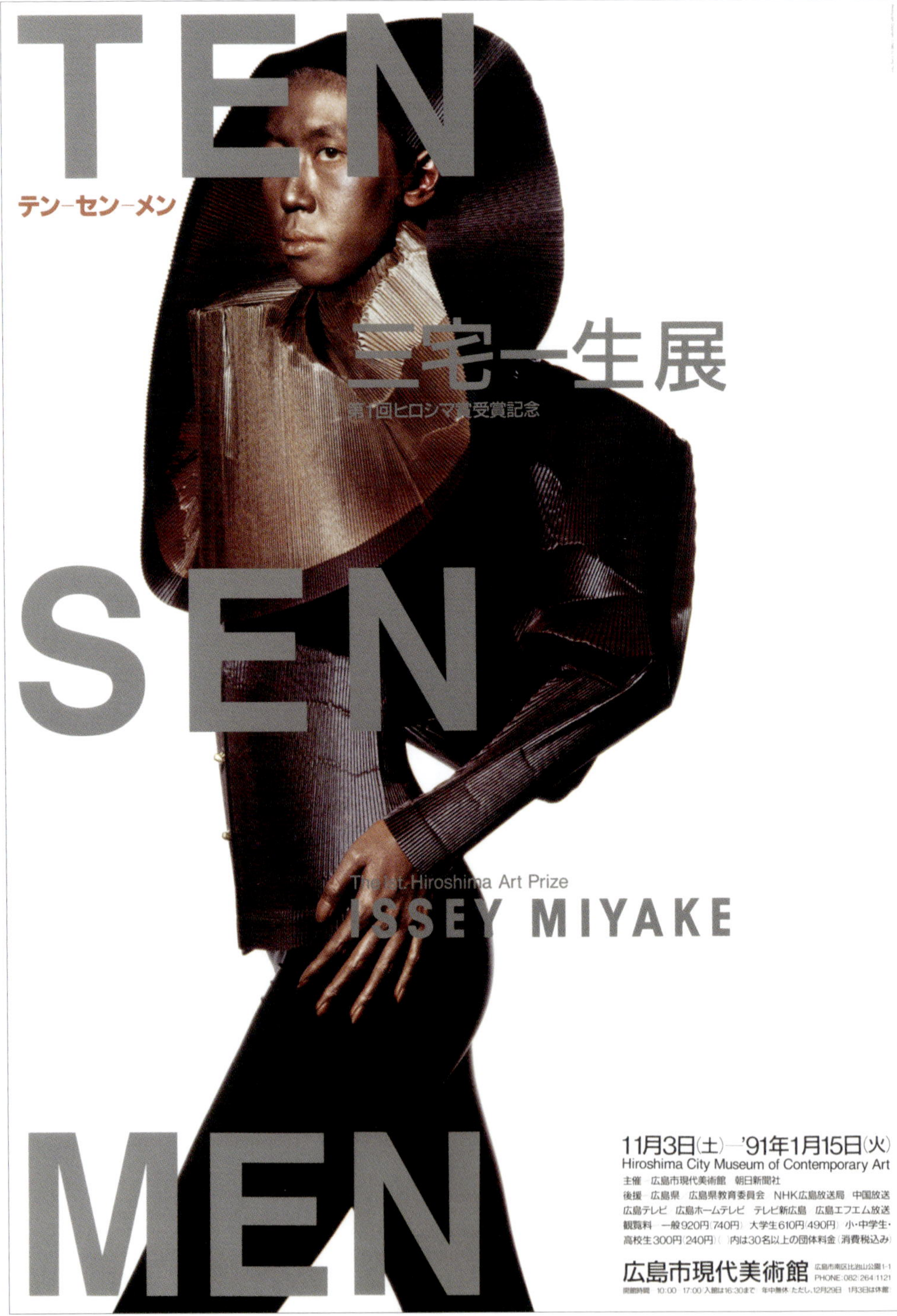
TEN
テン−セン−メン
SEN
MEN
三宅一生展
第1回ヒロシマ賞受賞記念
The 1st Hiroshima Art Prize
ISSEY MIYAKE
11月3日(土)—'91年1月15日(火)
Hiroshima City Museum of Contemporary Art
主催 広島市現代美術館 朝日新聞社
後援 広島県 広島県教育委員会 NHK広島放送局 中国放送
広島テレビ 広島ホームテレビ テレビ新広島 広島エフエム放送
観覧料 一般920円(740円) 大学生610円(490円) 小・中学生・
高校生300円(240円)( )内は30名以上の団体料金(消費税込み)
広島市現代美術館 広島市南区比治山公園1-1
PHONE:082-264-1121
開館時間 10:00−17:00 入館は16:30まで 年中無休 ただし、12月29日−1月3日は休館

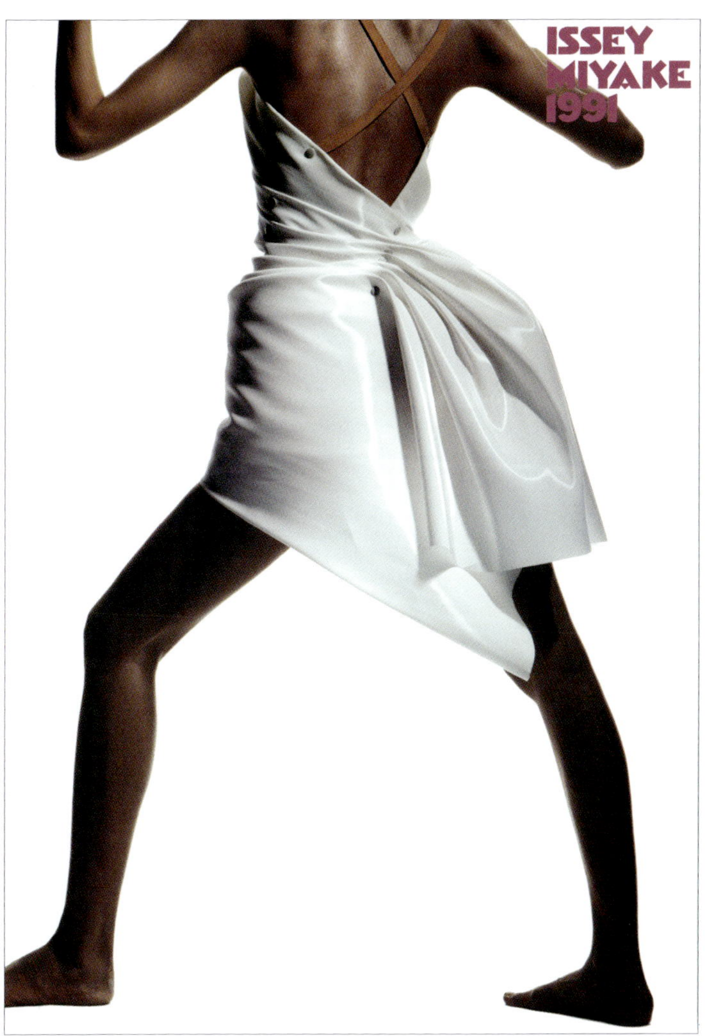

Issey Miyake: Ten Sen Men, a commemorative exhibition in conjunction with the 1st Hiroshima Art Prize. The Hiroshima Art Prize is awarded to an individual or group engaged in a creative field whose work contributes to the promotion of peace. Miyake was the first recipient. To commemorate the award, the *Ten Sen Men* exhibition reviewed work done since 1989. The finale for the opening show, to which the general public was invited, featured white doves, symbols of peace, and white dresses named *Colombe*.
November 3, 1990–January 15, 1991:
Hiroshima City Museum of Contemporary Art

Opposite: ***Issey Miyake: Ten Sen Men*** poster
Lacquer-like Pleats 1989 design/
Spring-Summer 1990 Collection
Photography: Irving Penn; layout and typography:
Ikko Tanaka; model: Yuki Fujii

Above: Spring-Summer 1991 Collection, poster
The *Colombe* is a dress made from monofilament fabric. It was heat-cut instead of using scissors and snaps were used instead of needles and thread to fasten the shapes. 1990 design/Spring-Summer 1991 Collection
Photography: Irving Penn; layout and typography:
Ikko Tanaka; model: Yuki Fujii

1991

> March: Autumn-Winter 1991 Paris Collection at Salle des Arts, Cour Carrée du Louvre
> April: Autumn-Winter 1991 Tokyo Collection at Shibuya On Air
> May: Performance of *The Loss of Small Detail* by William Forsythe and the Ballet Frankfurt
> October: Spring-Summer 1992 Paris Collection at Salle des Arts, Cour Carrée du Louvre
> November: Spring-Summer 1992 Tokyo Collection at EBIS 303

Costumes for William Forsythe and the Ballet Frankfurt

Issey Miyake was developing pleats for more general use when choreographer William Forsythe enlisted his help in designing costumes for a new dance piece. Miyake suspected that light, elastic pleats would be well suited to dance, a suspicion that was confirmed when he saw the dancers darting around playfully during the fittings in Tokyo. The company performed *The Loss of Small Detail* in pleated clothing made from a knit fabric. The dance piece premiered in Frankfurt in May. Miyake and his team did further research and were able to improve the material and the pleating process. All the efforts came to fruition in the launch of an original brand, PLEATS PLEASE ISSEY MIYAKE, in 1993.

1 Autumn-Winter 1991 Paris Collection, March 16, Salle des Arts, Cour Carrée du Louvre
2 Spring-Summer 1992 Paris Collection, October 19, Salle des Arts, Cour Carrée du Louvre

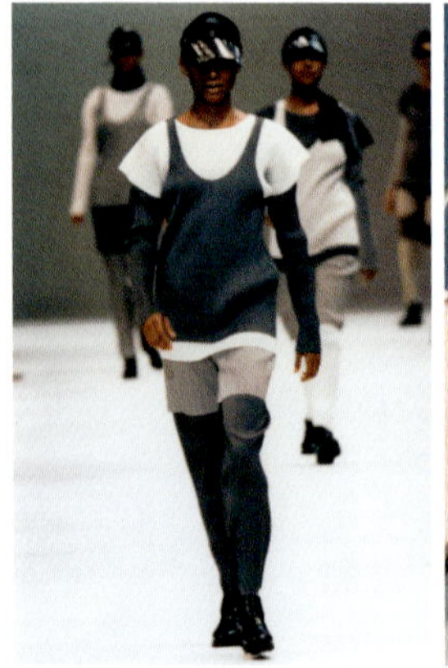

1

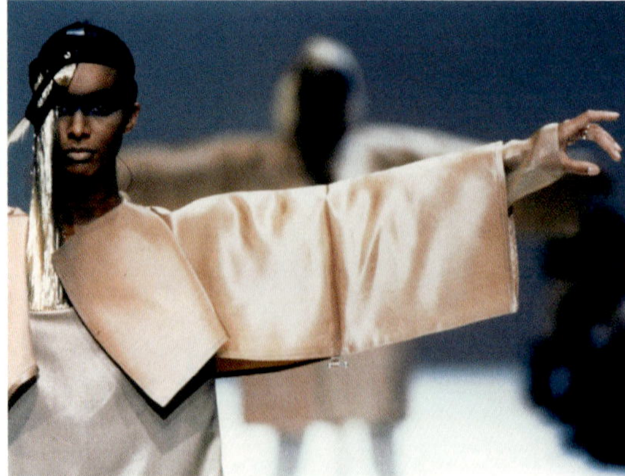

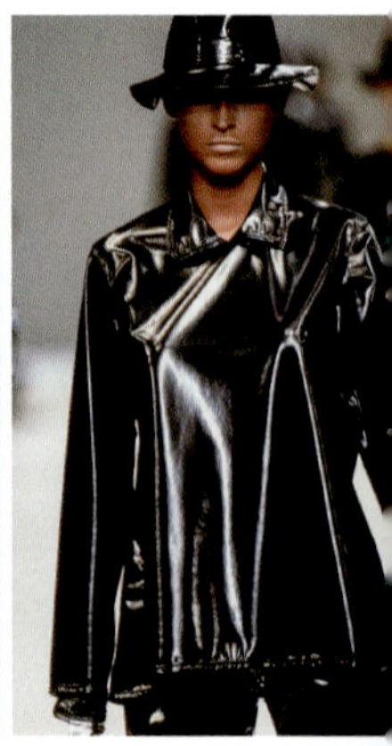

William Forsythe and
Ballet Frankfurt perform
The Loss of Small Detail
Photography:
Dominik Mentzos

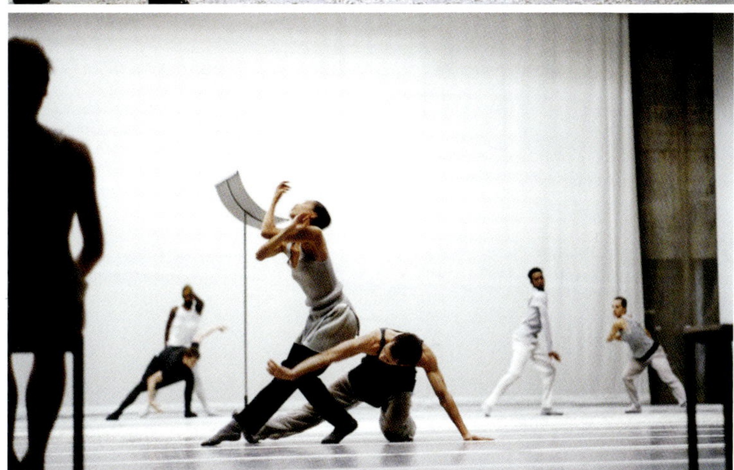

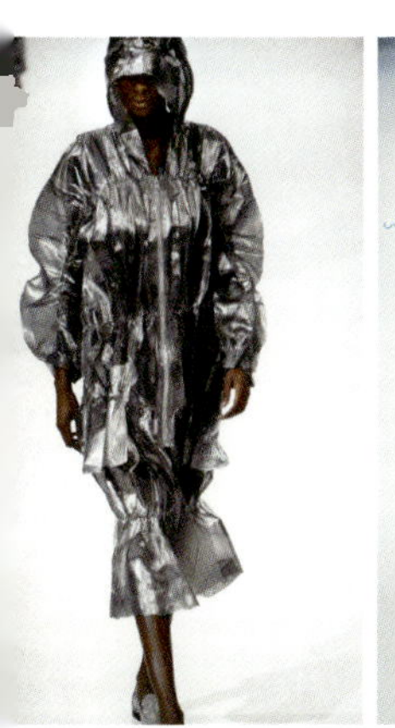
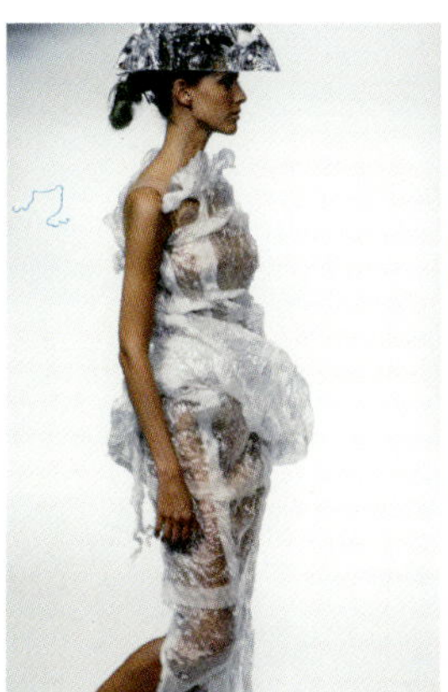
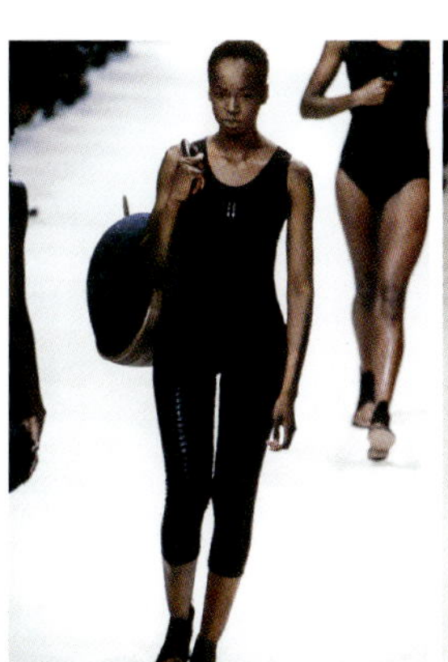
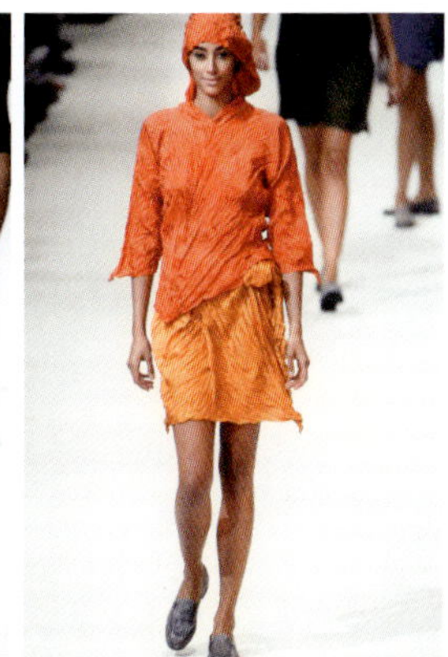

Square on Squares
A jacket made with square elements. It can be easily folded because of the folds made by the heatpress. Metal weights are attached to the hems to give them shape. 1991 design/Autumn-Winter 1991 Collection
Photography: Yuriko Takagi (below), Irving Penn
© The Irving Penn Foundation (opposite)

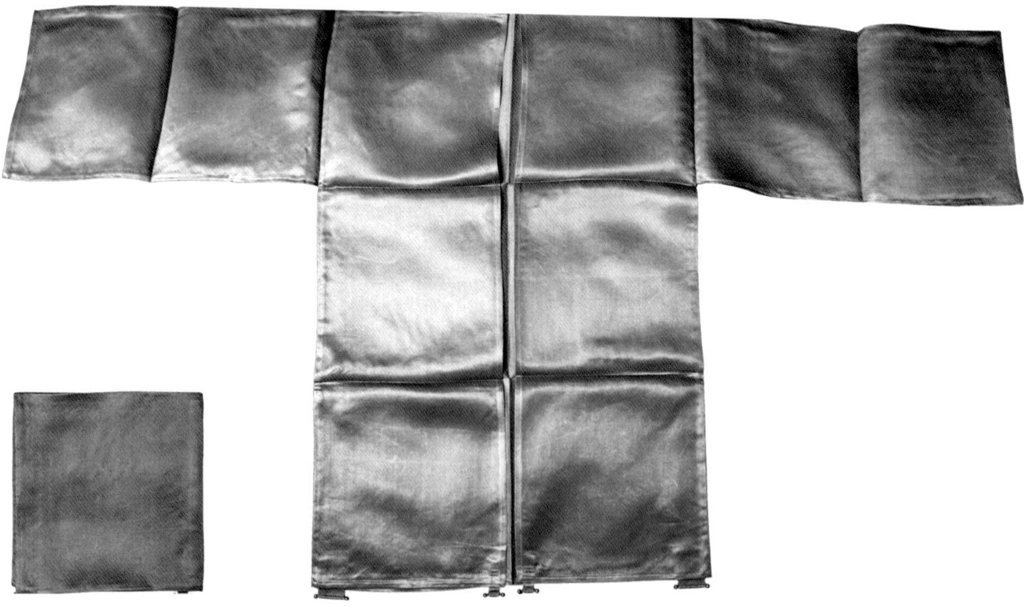

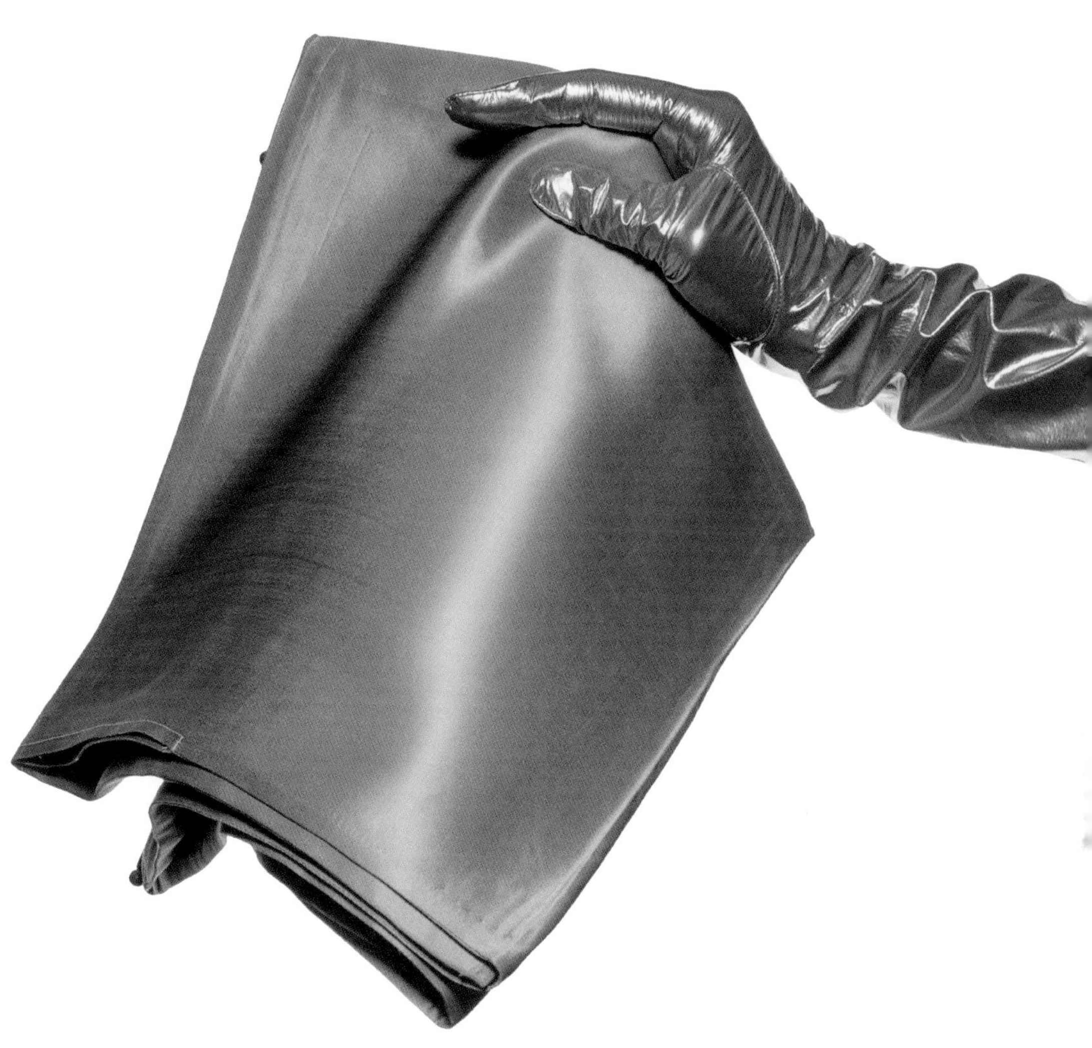

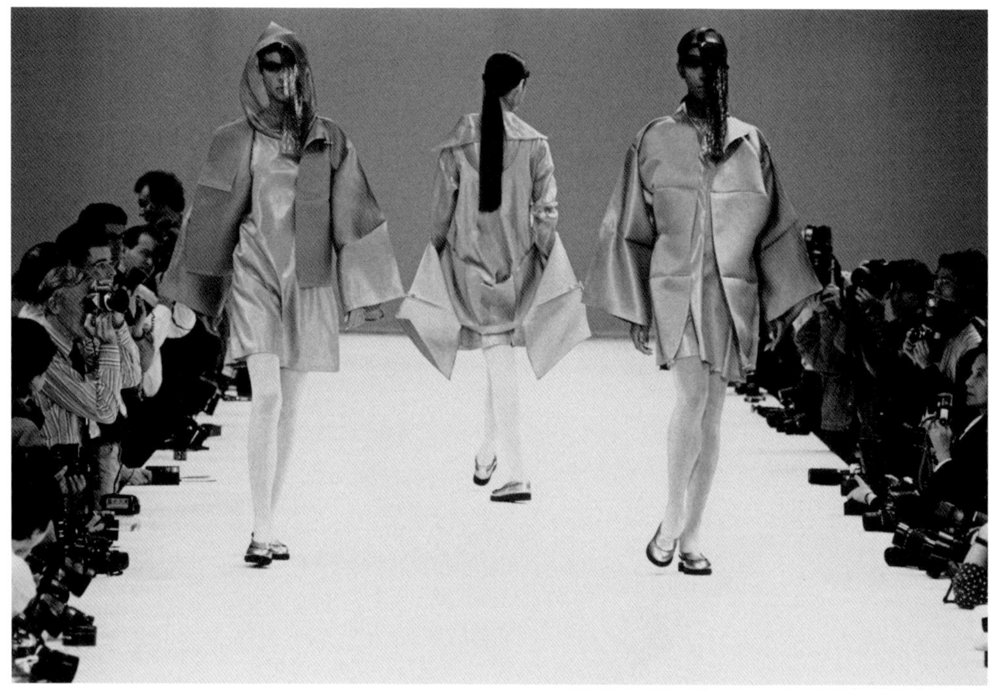

Square on Squares presented at the Autumn-Winter
1991 Paris Collection. Three different lengths,
depending on the layers of squares.
Photography: Michel Quenneville

Opposite: Autumn-Winter 1991 Collection, poster
Photography: Irving Penn; layout and typography:
Ikko Tanaka; model: Yuki Fujii

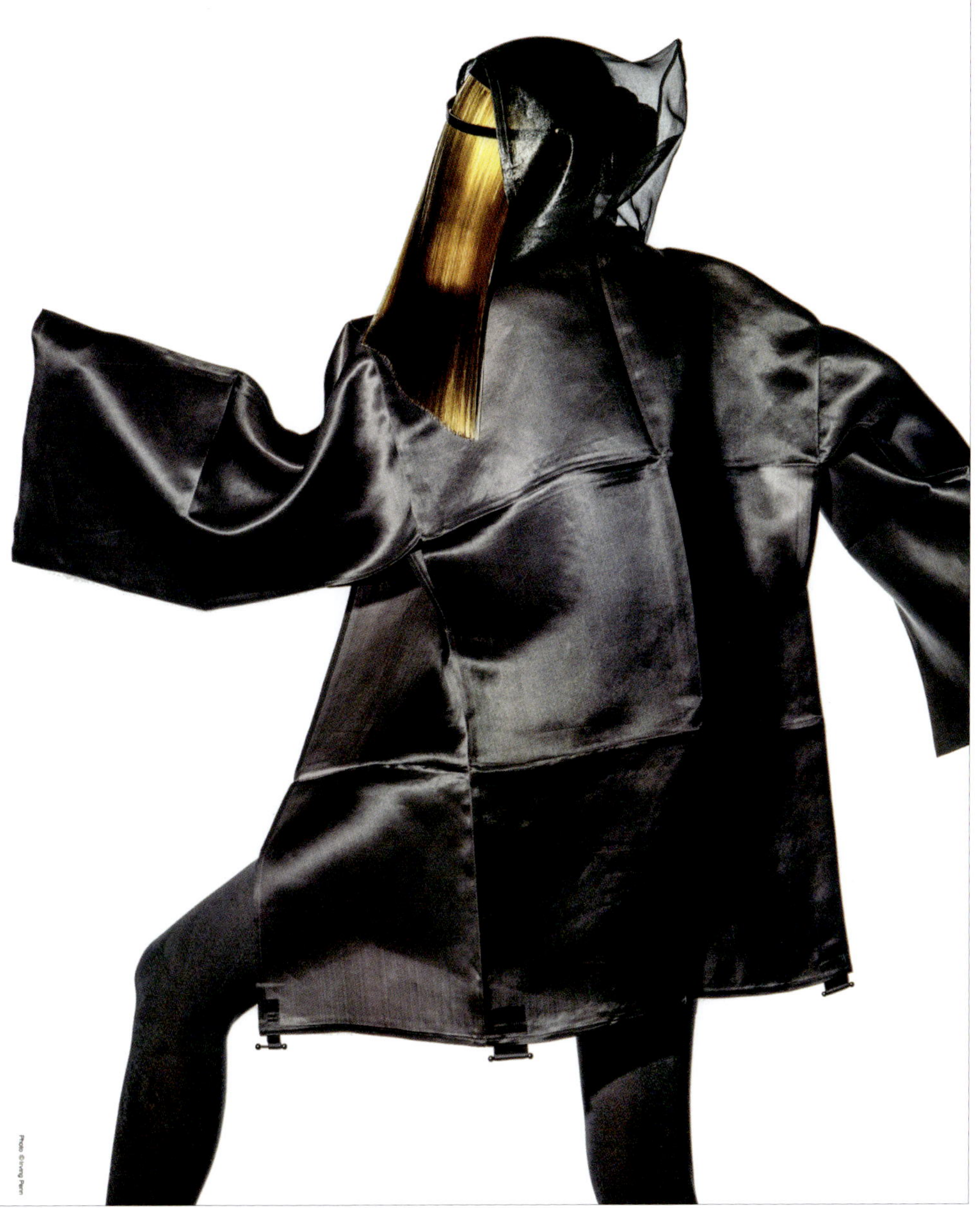

ISSEY MIYAKE 1991

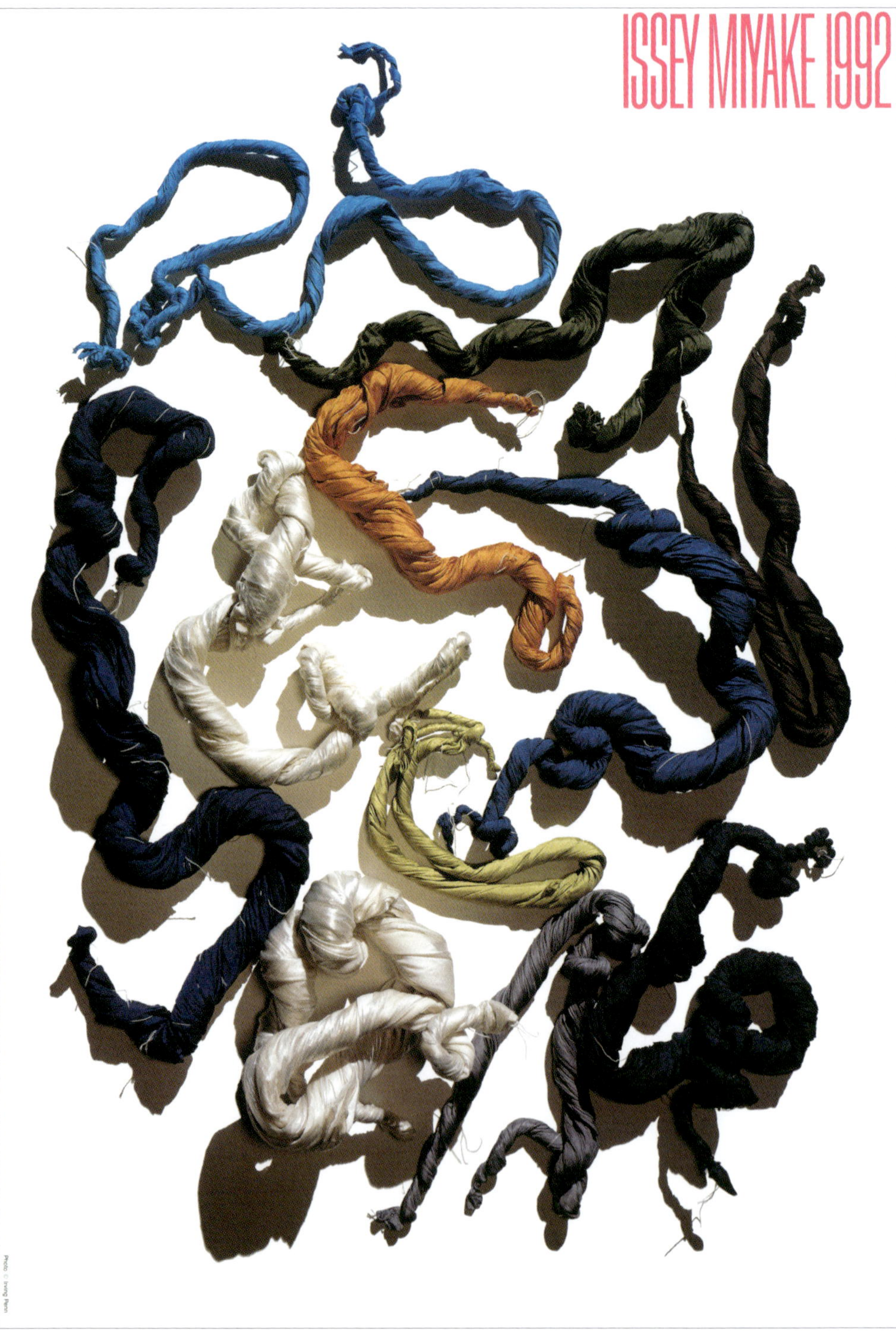
ISSEY MIYAKE 1992

Opposite: Spring-Summer 1992 Collection, poster
Twist. Each of the twisted forms "unfurls" to become
a tank top, shirt, tunic, pants, or dress, each with its
own beautiful, random wrinkles. After being sewn into
clothing, the fabric is folded, twisted by hand at both
ends, fixed in place, and inserted into a kiln for heat
processing. The result is clothing with handmade and
asymmetrical pleats, rather than the regular, orderly
machine pleats.
1991 design/Spring-Summer 1992 Collection
Photography: Irving Penn; layout and typography:
Ikko Tanaka

Spring-Summer 1992 Tokyo Collection
Children appeared on the stage holding a rope with
hanging *Twist* clothes. They also wore *Twist* pieces.
Photography: Masaaki Miyazawa

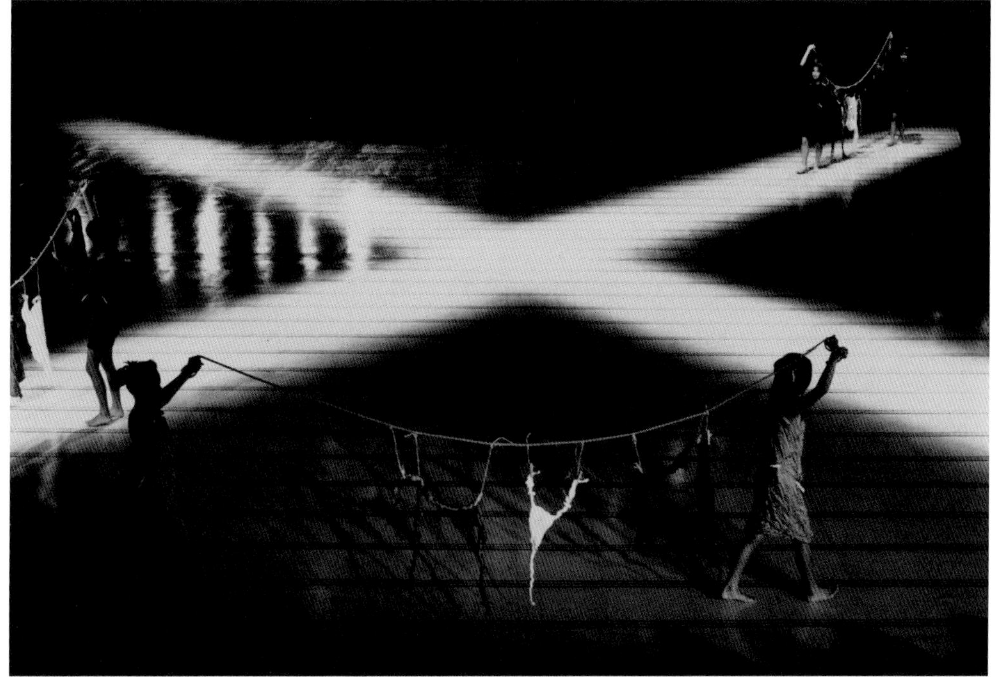

1992

> March: Autumn-Winter 1992 Paris Collection at Salle des Arts, Cour Carrée du Louvre
> March: Launch of L'Eau d'Issey
> April: Autumn-Winter 1992 Tokyo Collection at EBIS 303; joint show with Romeo Gigli
> May: *Issey Miyake Poster* exhibition at Tokyo Designer's Space
> July–November: *Issey Miyake Twist* exhibition at Benesse House, Naoshima Contemporary Art Museum
> October: Spring-Summer 1993 Paris Collection at Salle des Arts, Cour Carrée du Louvre
> November: Spring-Summer 1993 Tokyo Collection at Hamilton Place
> Designed the official uniforms for the Lithuanian team at the Barcelona Olympic Games

Launched L'Eau d'Issey perfume

L'Eau d'Issey (Issey's Water), Miyake's first fragrance, was developed jointly with Beauté Prestige International in France, a company established specifically for the manufacture and sale of perfumes. Miyake considered water to be not only the source of life, but the best source of ideas, a concept that defied conventional wisdom in perfumes and created an international stir. Miyake's concept for the fragrance was: "A message that gives hope, a simple, beautiful, functional bottle, ordinary and universal but still surprising." As he does in his clothing design, he consistently seeks out the essence of the object.

1 Autumn-Winter 1992 Paris Collection, March 21, Salle des Arts, Cour Carrée du Louvre
2 Spring-Summer 1993 Paris Collection, October 17, Salle des Arts, Cour Carrée du Louvre

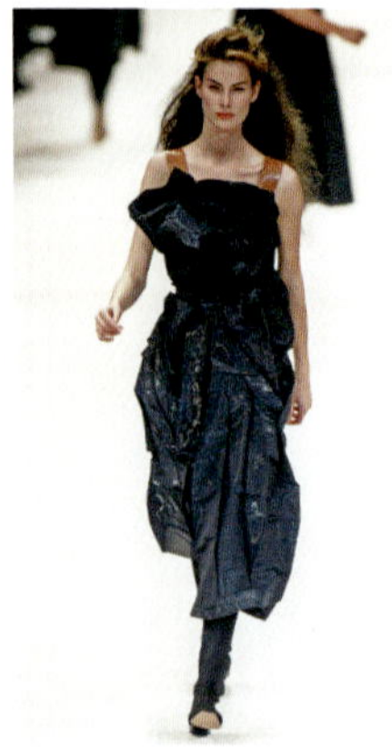
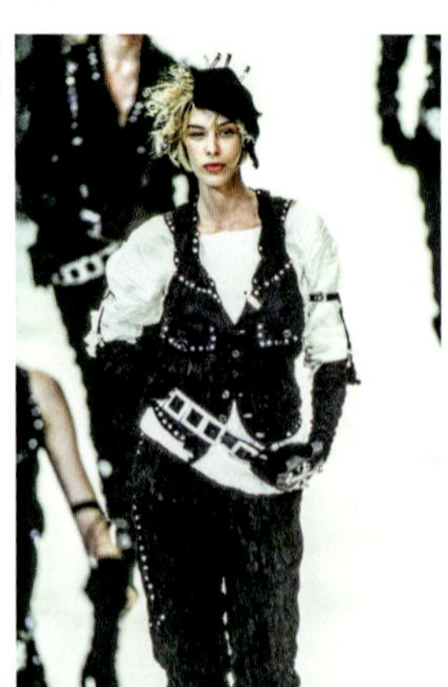
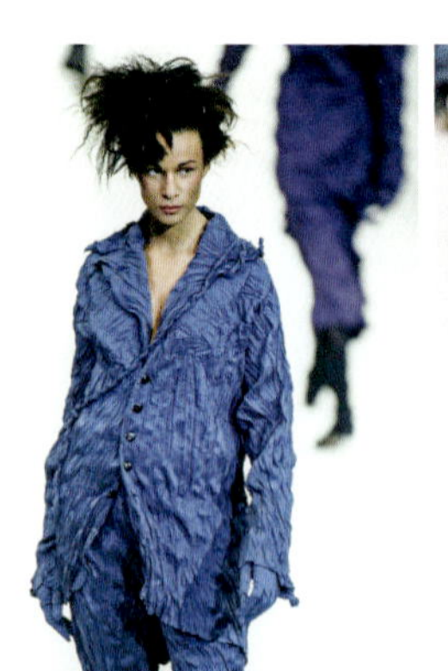
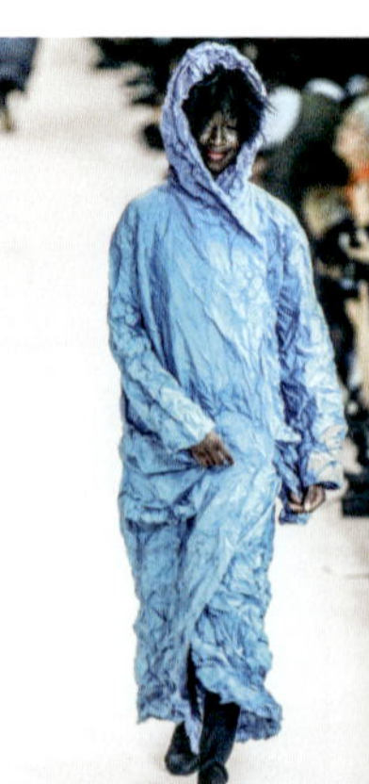

1

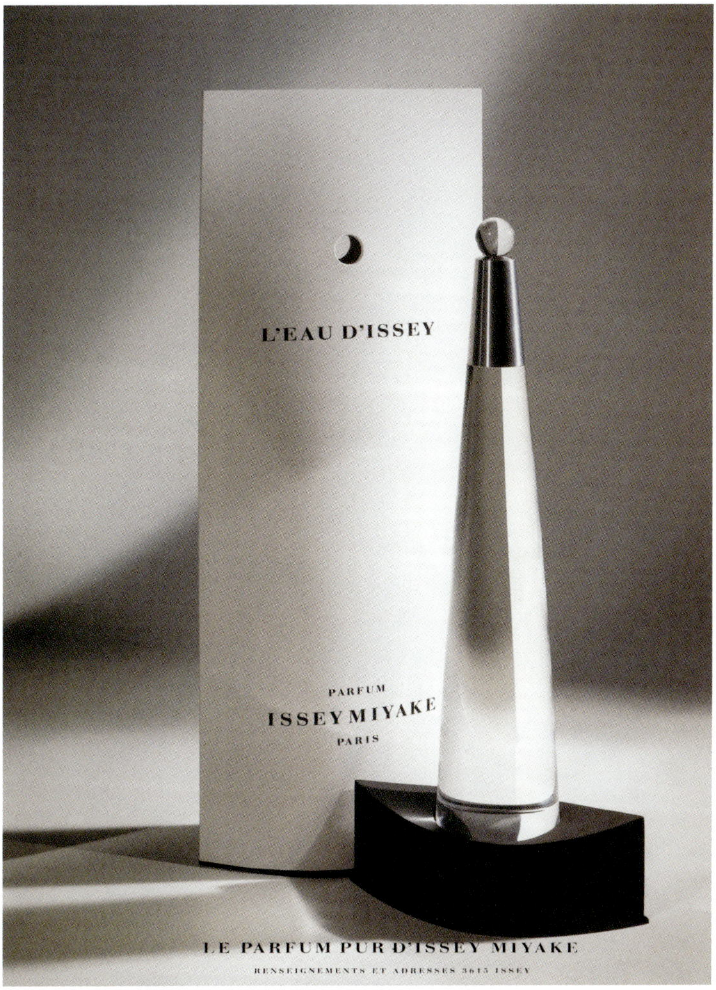

L'Eau d'Issey
advertisement, 1992
Photography: Irving Penn;
bottle design: Issey Miyake,
Fabian Baron, Alain de
Mourgues

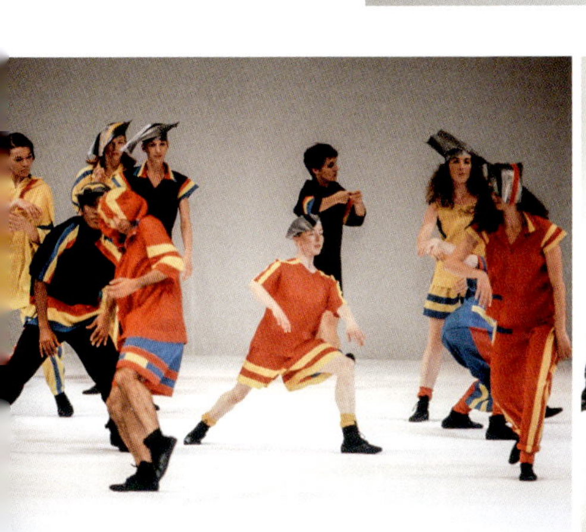

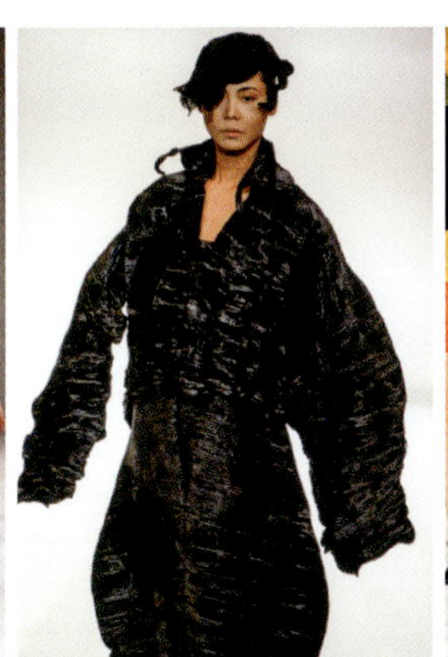

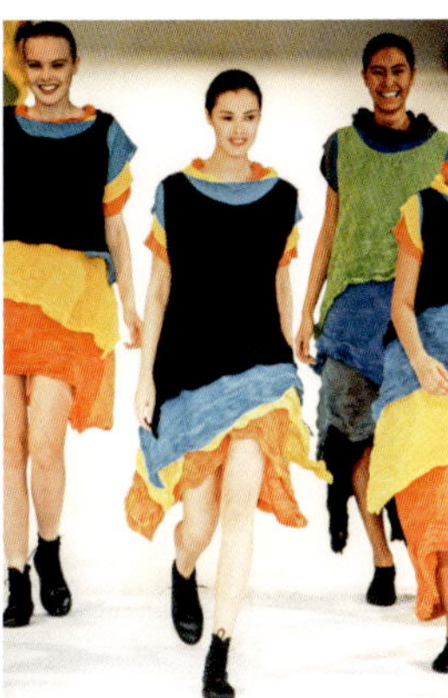

2

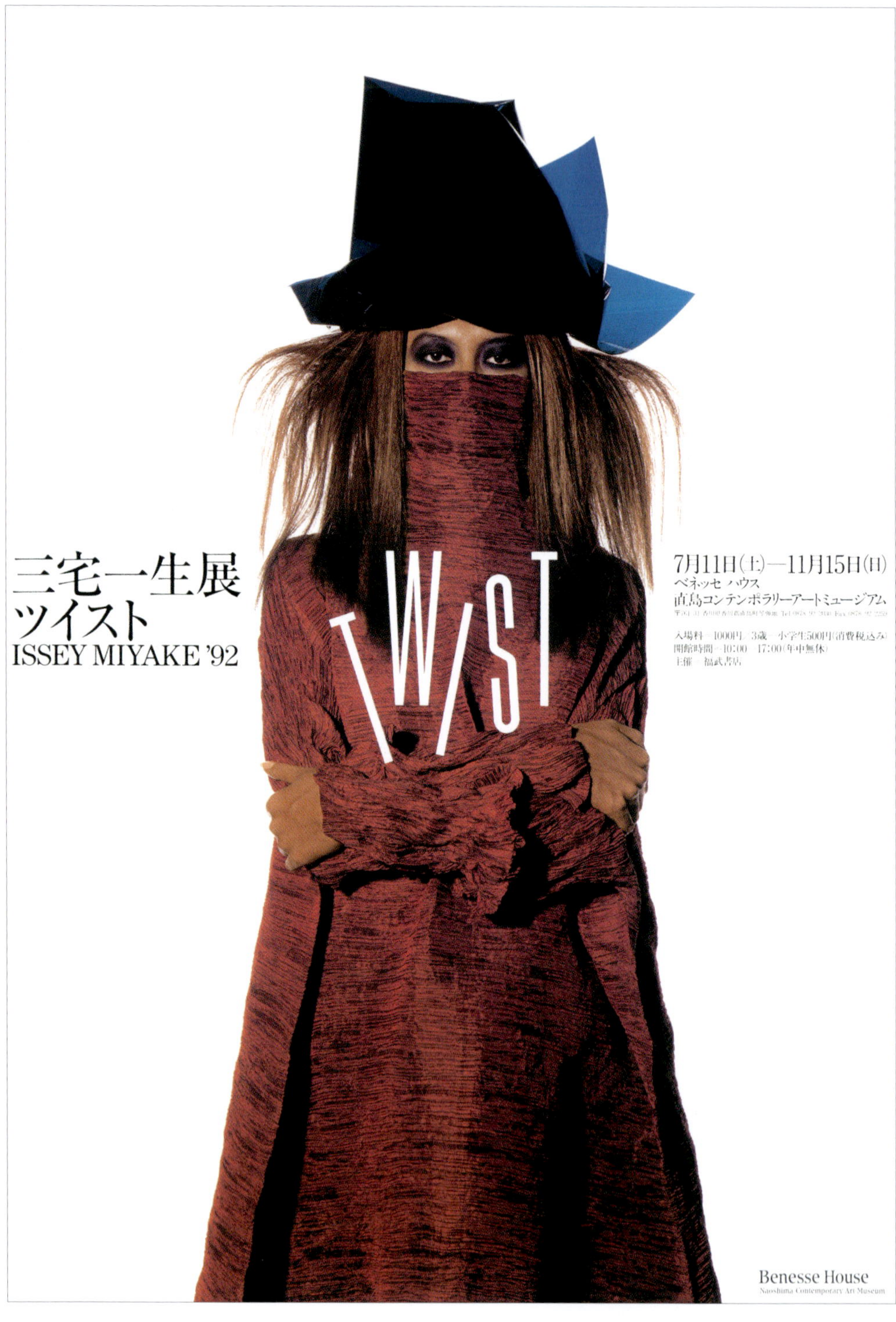
三宅一生展
ツイスト
ISSEY MIYAKE '92
TWIST
7月11日(土)—11月15日(日)
ベネッセ ハウス
直島コンテンポラリーアートミュージアム
入場料―1000円―3歳―小学生500円(消費税込み)
開館時間―10:00―17:00(年中無休)
主催―福武書店
Benesse House
Naoshima Contemporary Art Museum

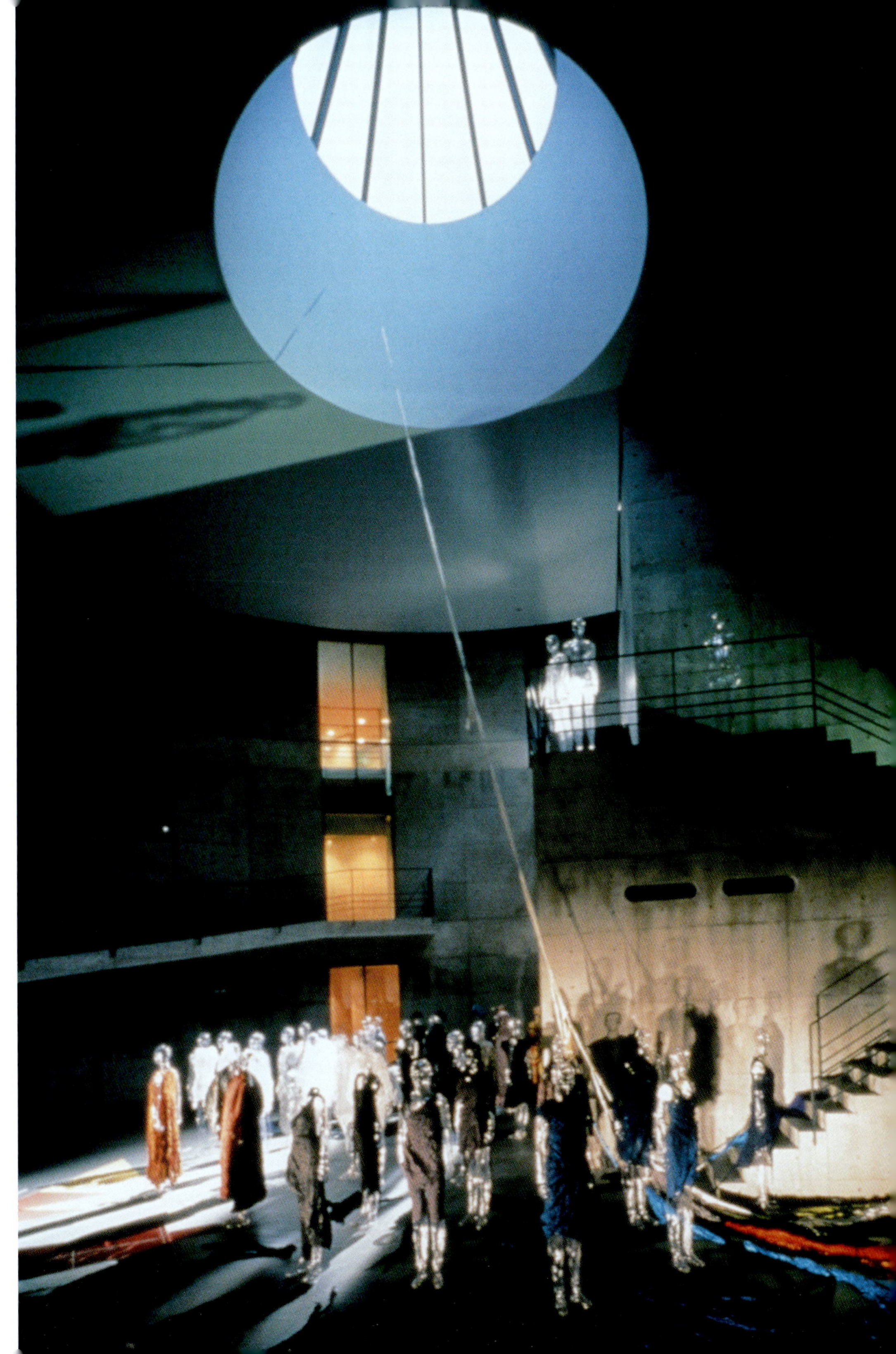

1992

From *Arena* (UK),
September 1992 edition
Photography: Troy Word

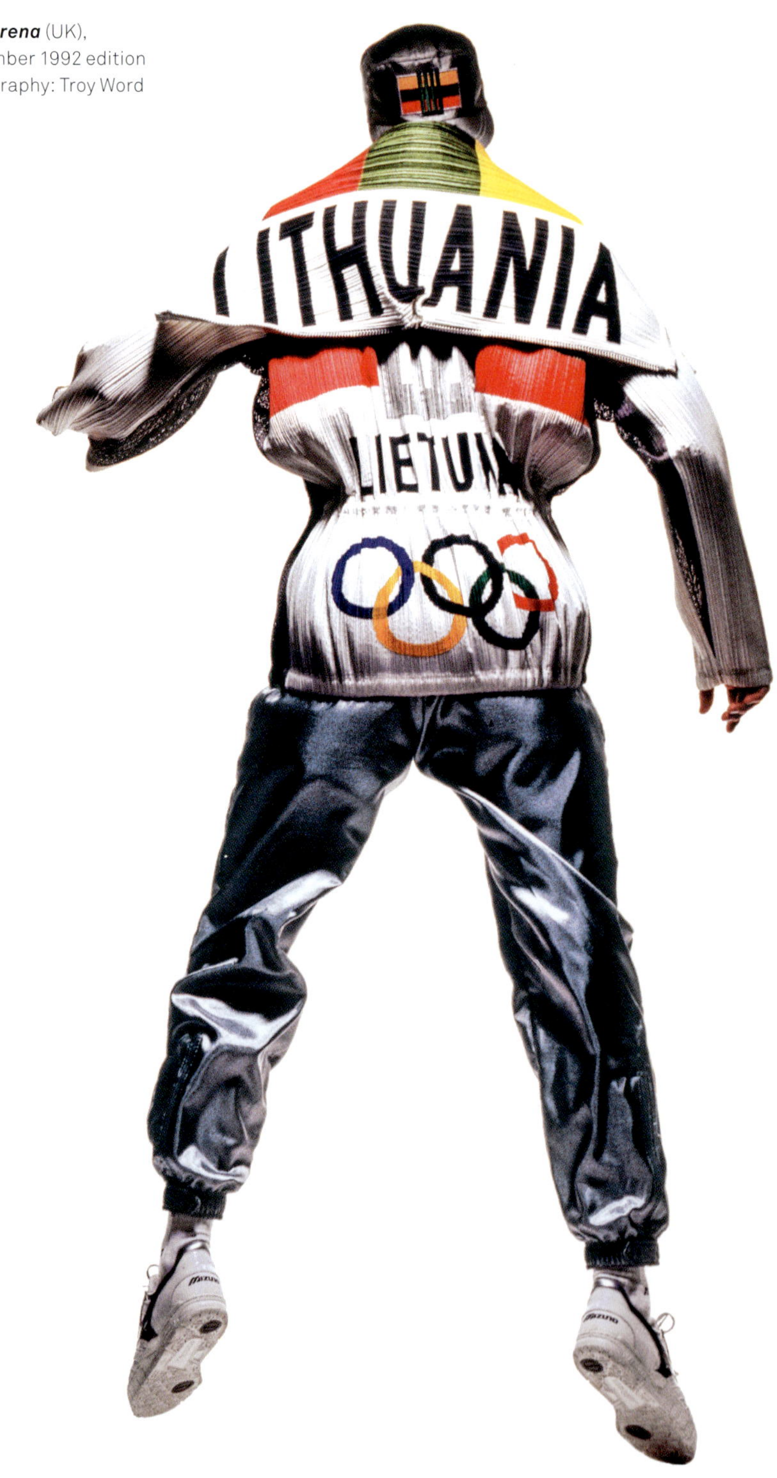

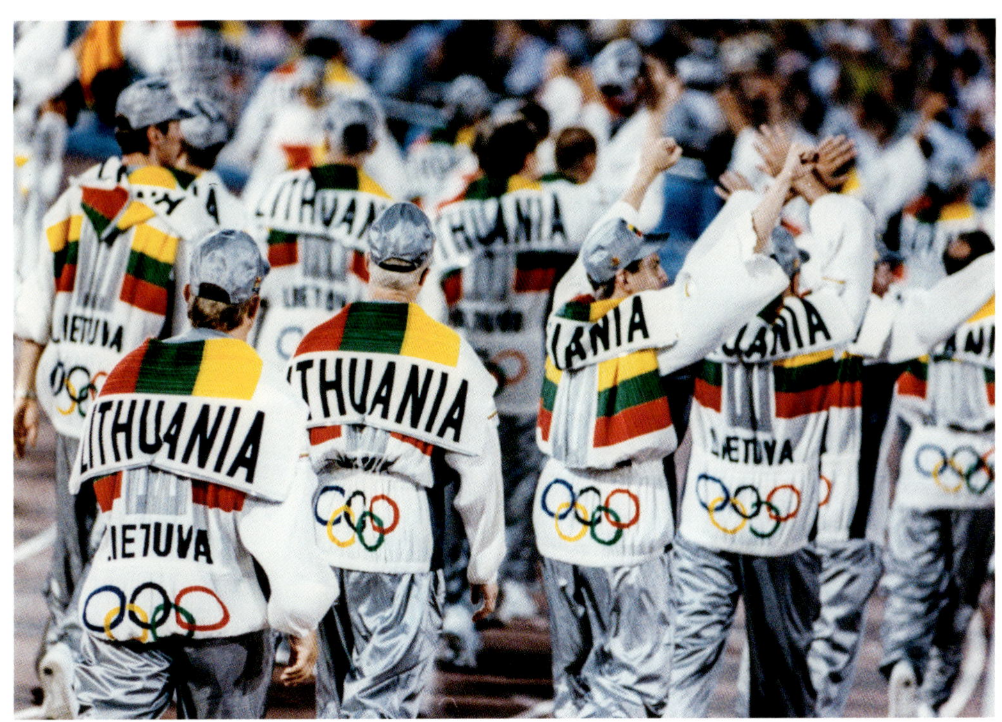
Above: Official uniforms for the Lithuanian team, Barcelona Olympic Games 1992

Page 188: *Issey Miyake Twist* exhibition poster
Tidal Wave. A chambray dress created using the Pleats and Twist method. After sewing, the clothing is given random, horizontal pleats, twisted, and heat processed in a kiln. *Gelatin paper hat*. Both were designed in 1992 for the Autumn-Winter 1992 Collection.
Photography: Irving Penn; layout and typography: Ikko Tanaka; model: Yuki Fujii

Page 189: *Issey Miyake Twist* exhibition
Held as the opening exhibition of the Contemporary Art Museum in Naoshima, in Kagawa prefecture, designed by Tadao Ando. Consisted entirely of Pleats and Twist clothing, showing the original shape and production process.
July 1–November 15: Benesse House, Naoshima Contemporary Art Museum
Exhibition direction: Issey Miyake;
space design: Tokujin Yoshioka
Photography: Shigeo Anzaï

Above: Official uniforms for the Lithuanian team, Barcelona Olympic Games 1992
Having gained its independence from the Soviet Union in 1990, Lithuania was participating in the Olympic Games for the first time in 64 years. They commissioned Miyake to create the design for their official uniform. The result consisted of a hooded jacket made with random pleats, T-shirt, silver pants, cap, and shoes. The fabric was provided by Toray Industries, Inc., the production was done by the Mizuno Corporation, and the pleating by Polytex Industry Co., Ltd. Kensuke Ishizu served as an advisor. The collar featured the national flag and name, and turned into a hood when fastened. A patchwork pattern of the Olympics logo, flag and country name was created in a width several times larger than the desired one prior to pleating to account for the contraction in width during pleating.
Photography: Valdas Malinauskas

1993

> Start of the PLEATS PLEASE ISSEY MIYAKE brand (from Spring-Summer 1994 Collection)
> March: Autumn-Winter 1993 Paris Collection at Salle des Arts, Cour Carrée du Louvre
> April: Autumn-Winter 1993 Tokyo Collection at Issey Miyake Inc. showroom
> October: Spring-Summer 1994 Paris Collection at Salle des Arts, Cour Carrée du Louvre
> November: Spring-Summer 1994 Tokyo Collection at Laforet Roppongi
> November: Documentary *Issey Miyake Moves* shown on Japanese television station WOWOW
> Designed the uniforms for the Japan Pavilion staff at the Daejeon Expo in Korea

PLEATS PLEASE ISSEY MIYAKE

With improvements to the pleating process for knit fabrics and a mass-production system in place, PLEATS PLEASE ISSEY MIYAKE was launched as an independent brand in the Spring-Summer 1994 Collection. The clothing was made with an original "garment pleating" technique that performs pleating after sewing. The result is clothing that fits well with the lives of contemporary women. It offers excellent functionality in terms of easy washing, carrying, and storage, the versatility to be wearable in all aspects of ordinary life, superb comfort, reasonable pricing, and beautiful design. The brand represents the achievement of Issey Miyake's desire to "create universal clothing that everyone can wear" that came out of his encounter with the Paris revolution of 1968.

Opposite: Unveiling of **PLEATS PLEASE ISSEY MIYAKE** during the finale of the Spring-Summer 1994 Paris Collection
During the show's finale, PLEATS PLEASE was worn in layers under the *Flying Saucer* and suddenly revealed. Models in colorful PLEATS PLEASE clothing sang and danced to James Brown's *I Got You (I Feel Good)*.
The felt hats were created by Akio Hirata.
Photography: Philippe Brazil

1 Autumn-Winter 1993 Paris Collection, March 17, Salle des Arts, Cour Carrée du Louvre
2 Spring-Summer 1994 Paris Collection, October 8, Salle des Arts, Cour Carrée du Louvre

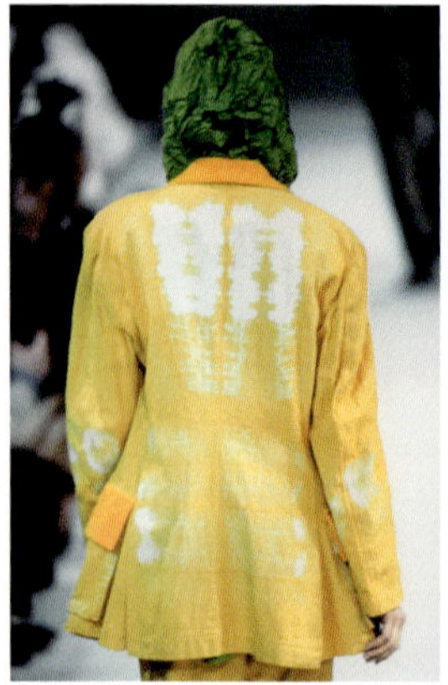
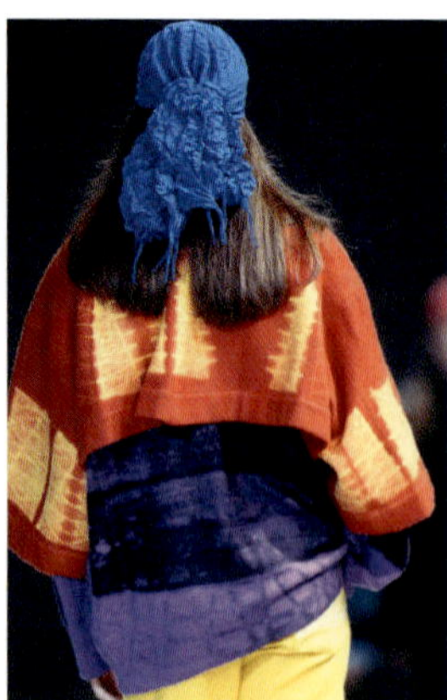
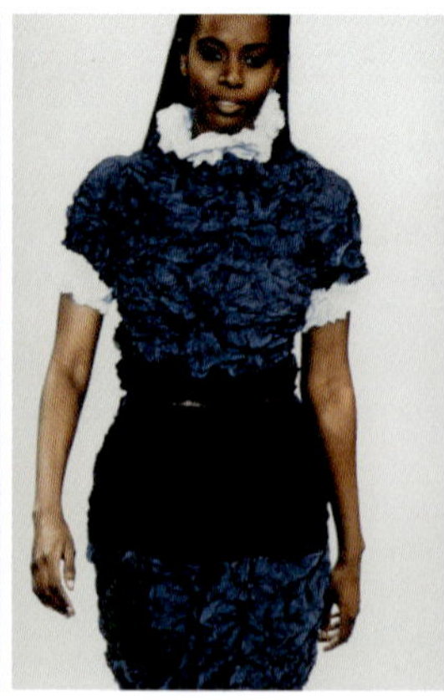
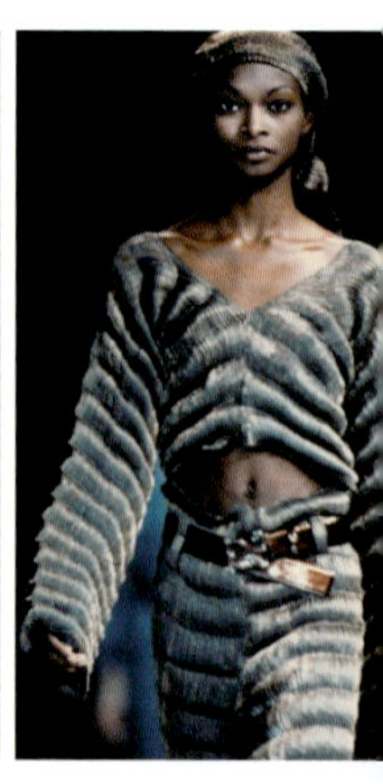

1

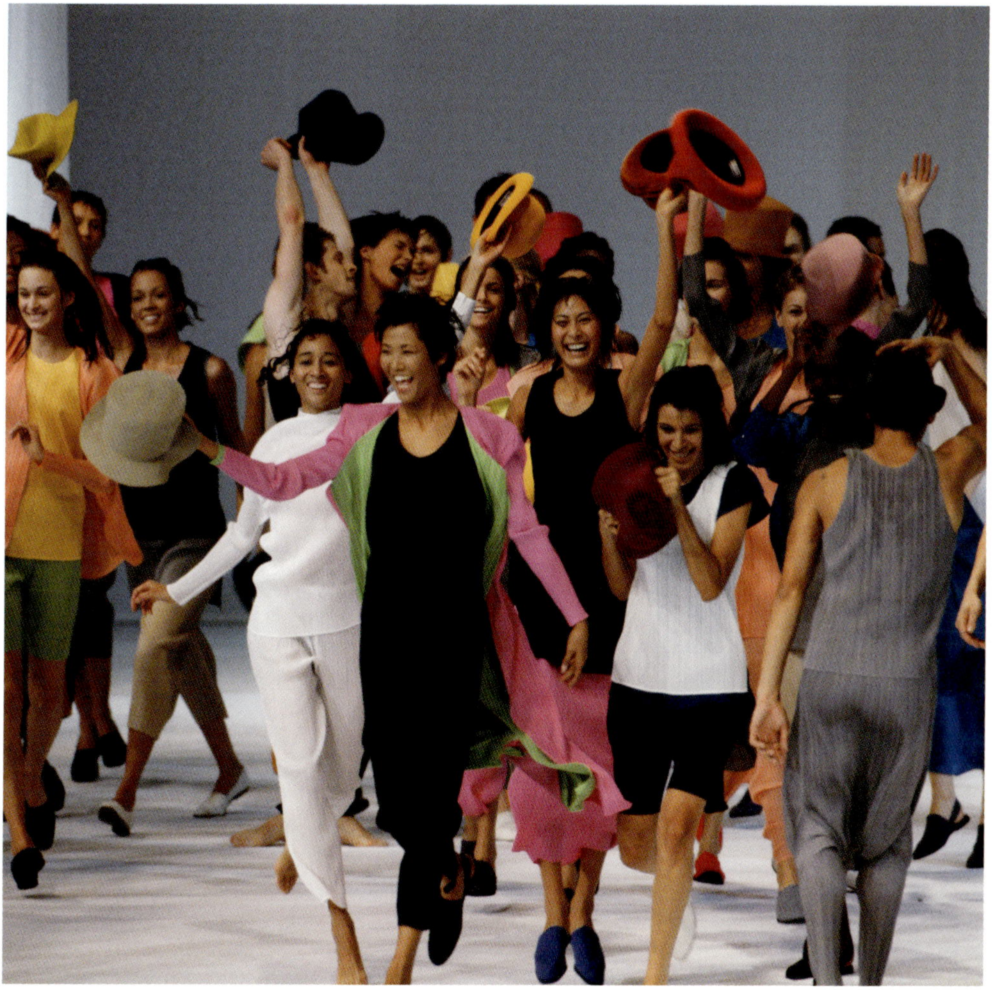

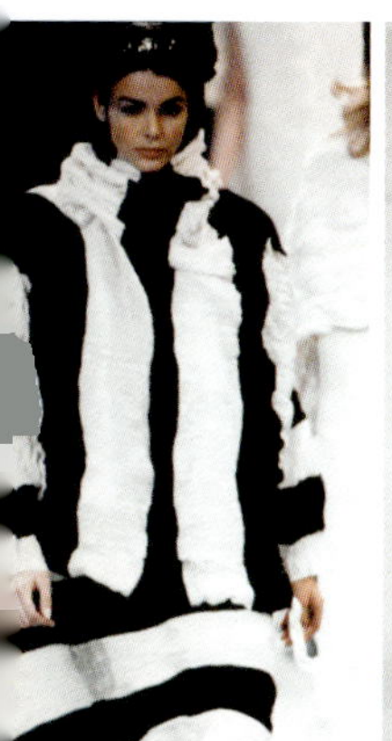
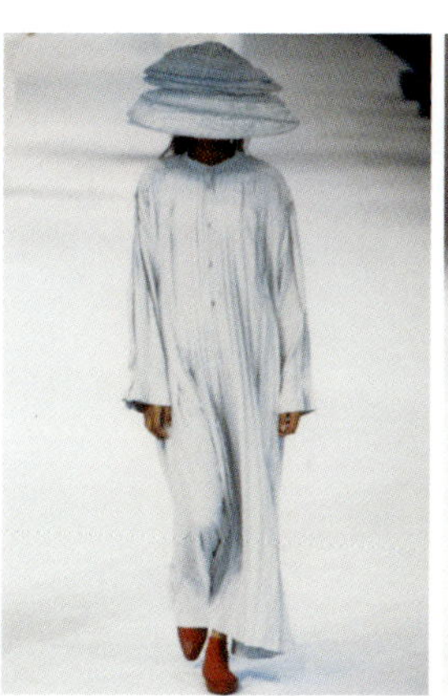
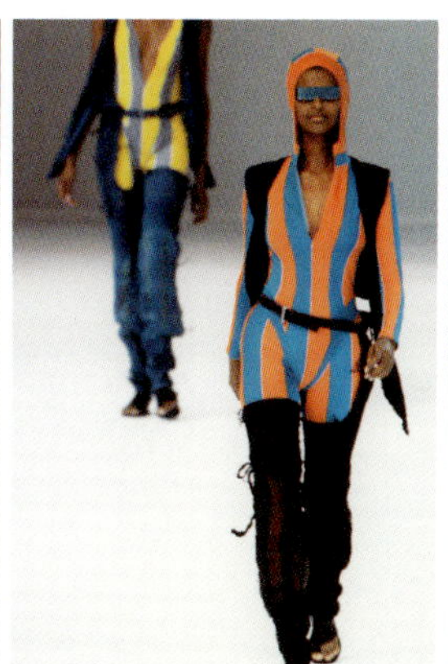
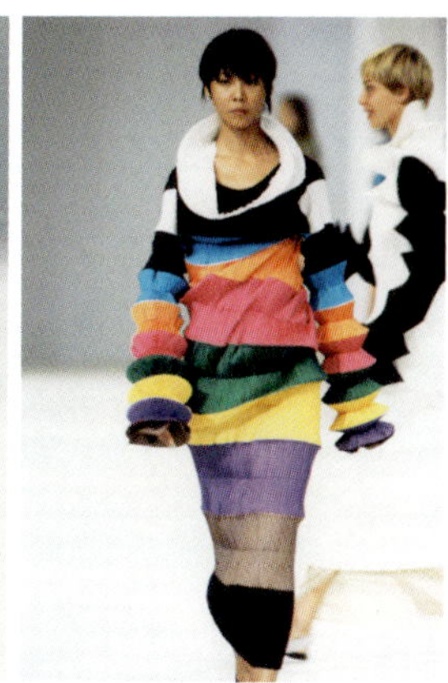

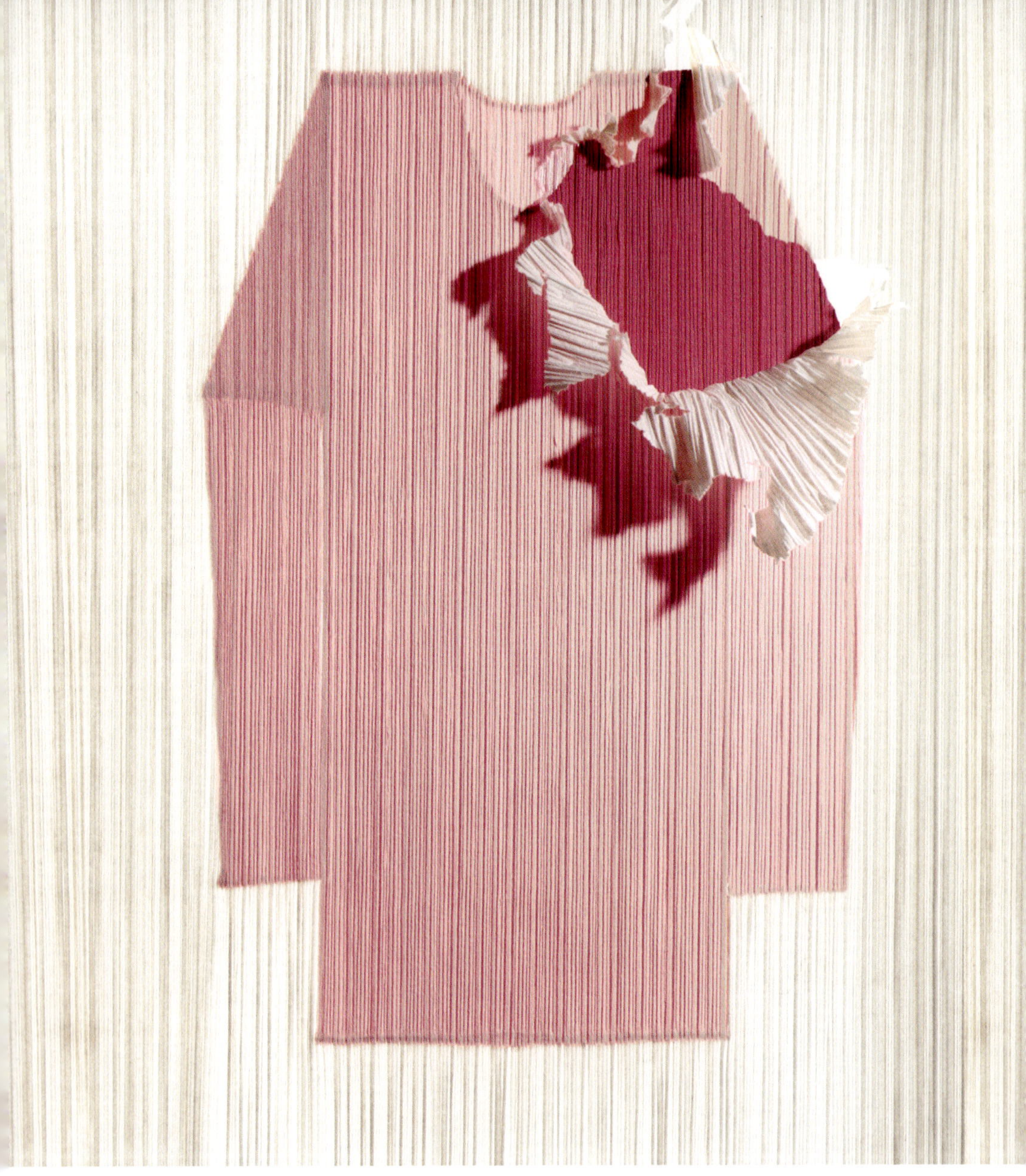

PLEATS PLEASE ISSEY MIYAKE
production process
The clothing is cut and sewn before being placed
between two pieces of paper for pleating. The paper
is then removed to reveal the final product.
Photography: Kazumi Kurigami

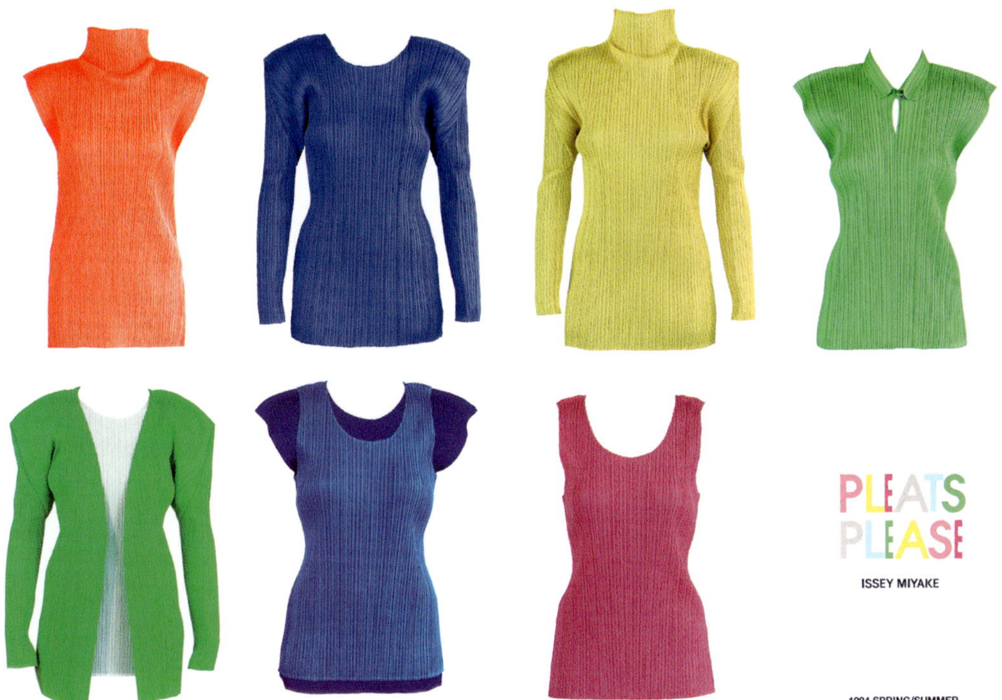

From the **PLEATS PLEASE ISSEY MIYAKE**
Spring-Summer 1994 catalogue
Eight basic tops in the first season catalogue for the
brand. A total of 13 shapes and eight color variations
were offered, including pants, skirts, one-piece
dresses, tunics, and long coats.

Following spread: *Flying Saucer*
1993 design/Spring-Summer 1994 Collection
From the *Issey Miyake Making Things* exhibition
Fondation Cartier pour l'art contemporain, Paris, 1998
Photography: Raymond Meier

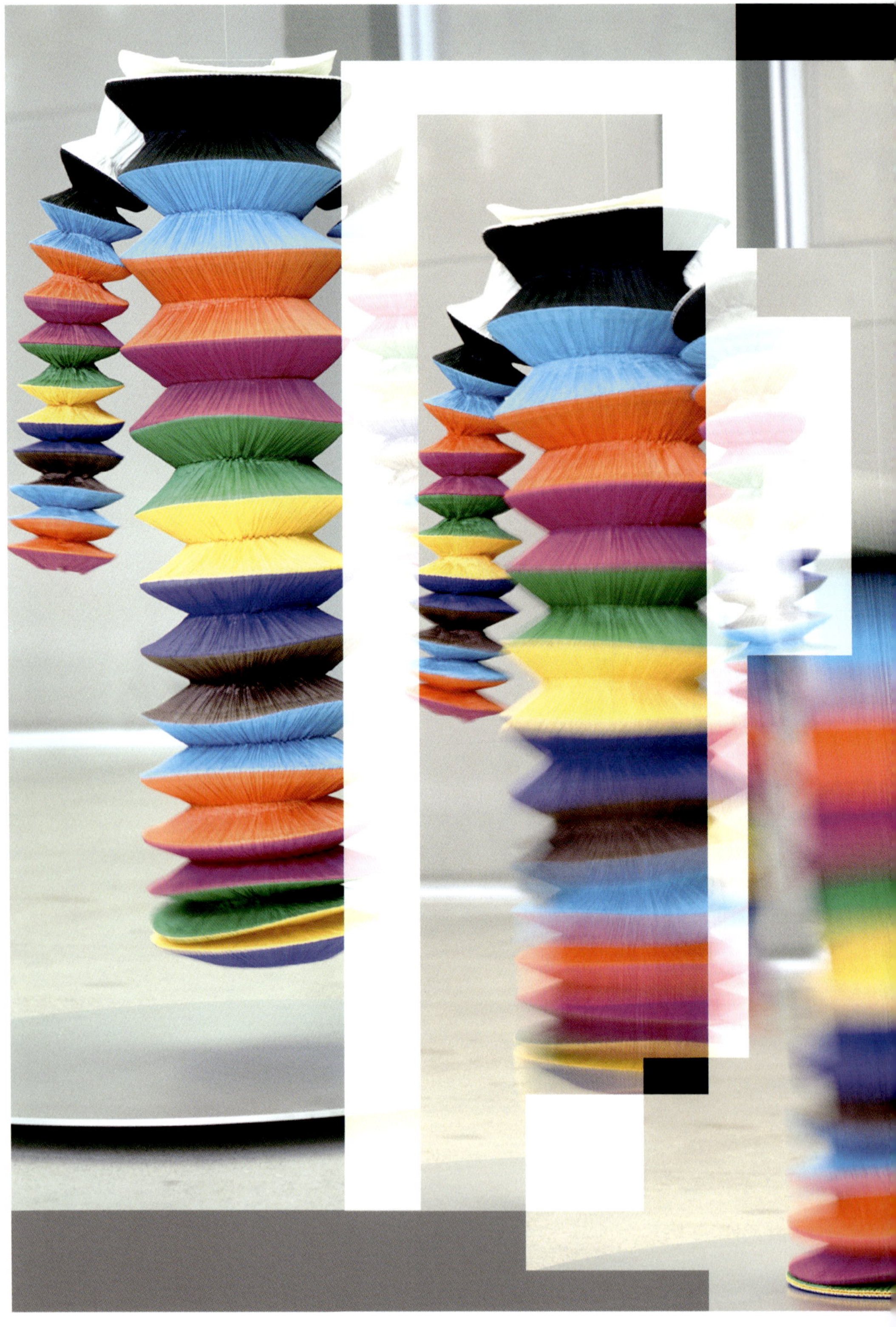

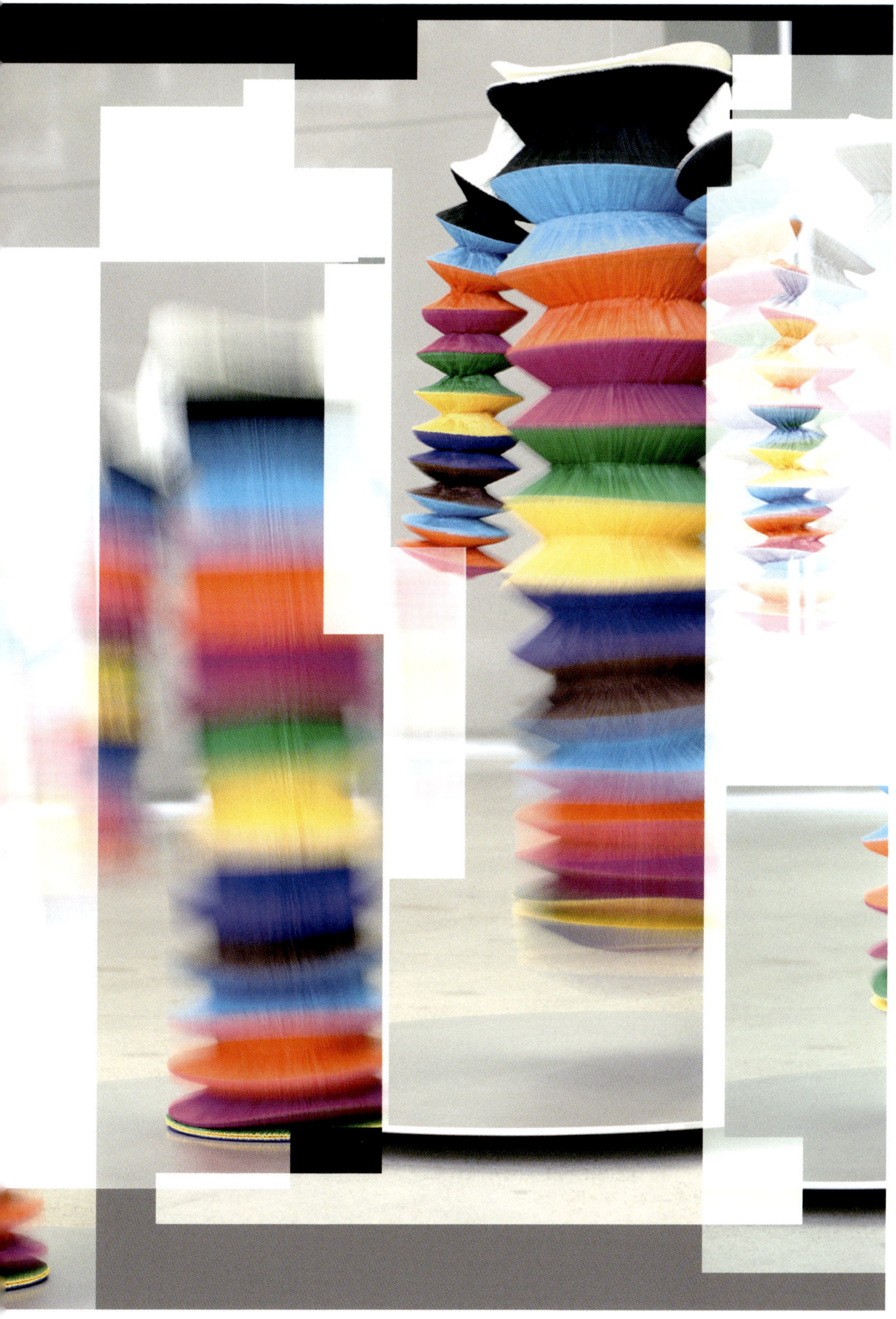

1994

1 Autumn-Winter 1994 Paris Collection, March 7,
Salle Delorme, Carrousel du Louvre
2 Spring-Summer 1995 Paris Collection, October 14,
Salle Le Nôtre, Carrousel du Louvre

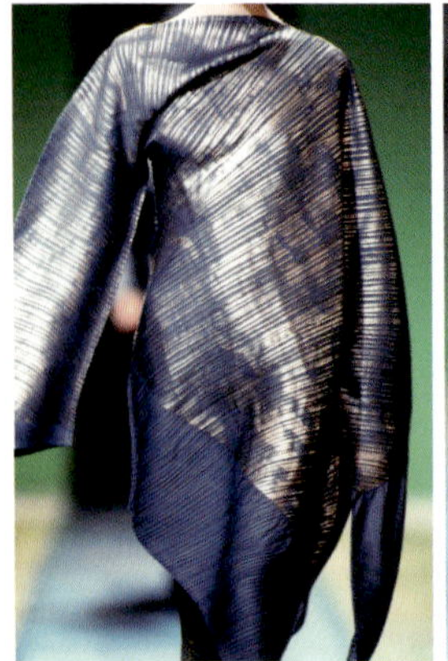
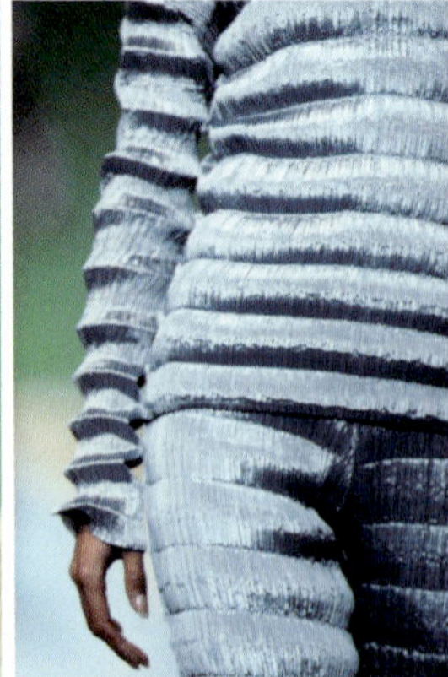
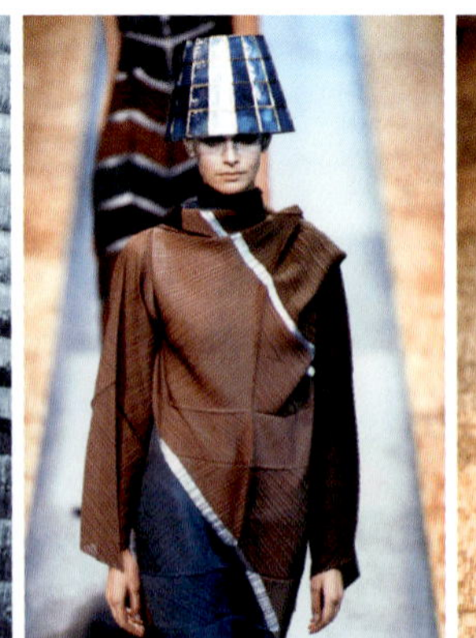
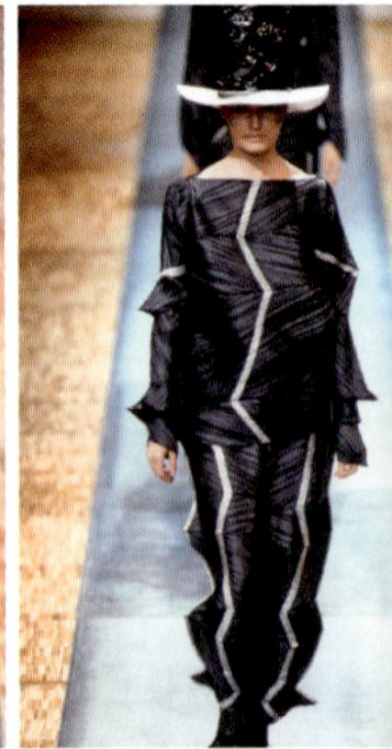

1

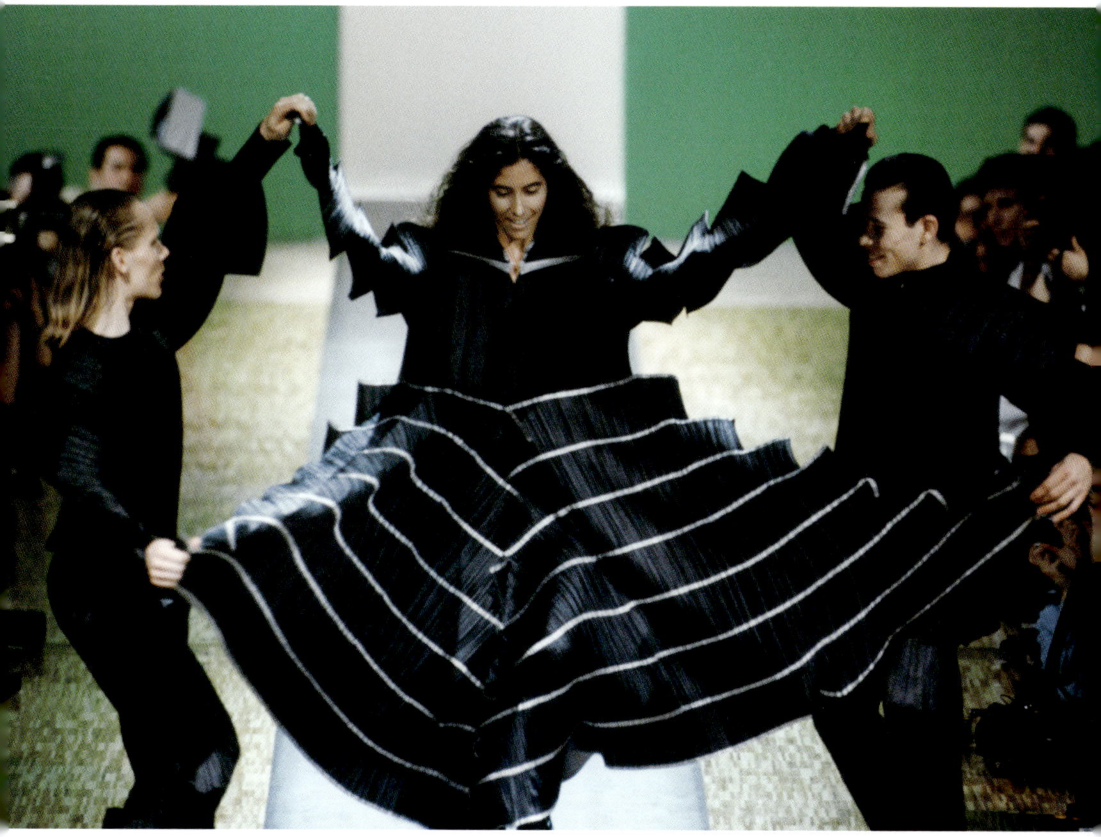

Staircase Dress
From the Paris Collection. Dancers Morleigh Steinberg, Frey Faust, and Tero Saarinen did the modeling.
1994 design/Autumn-Winter 1994 Collection
Photography: Philippe Brazil

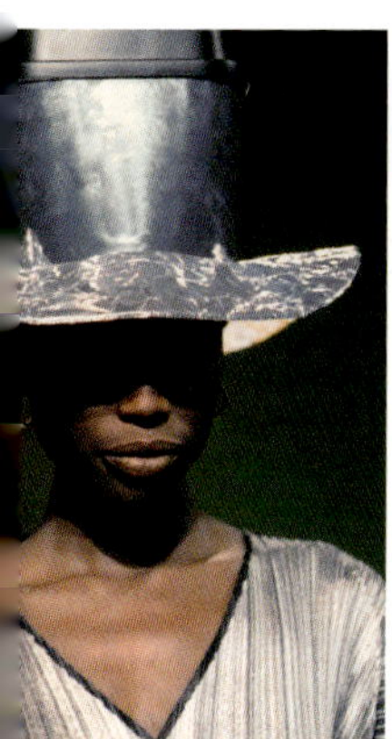
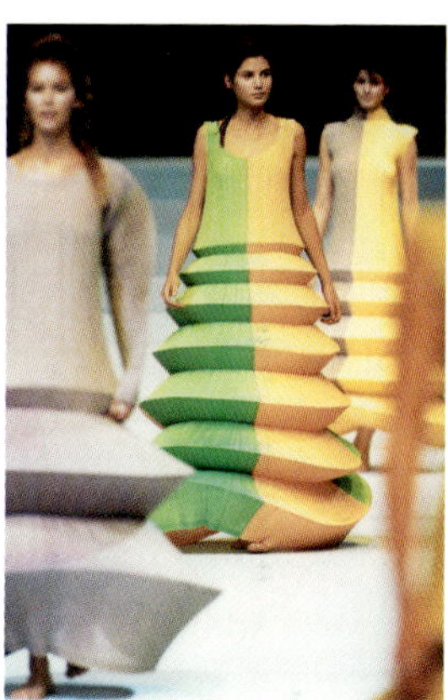
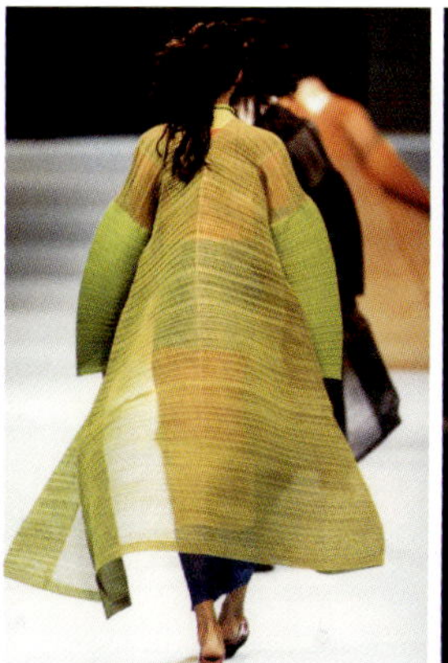
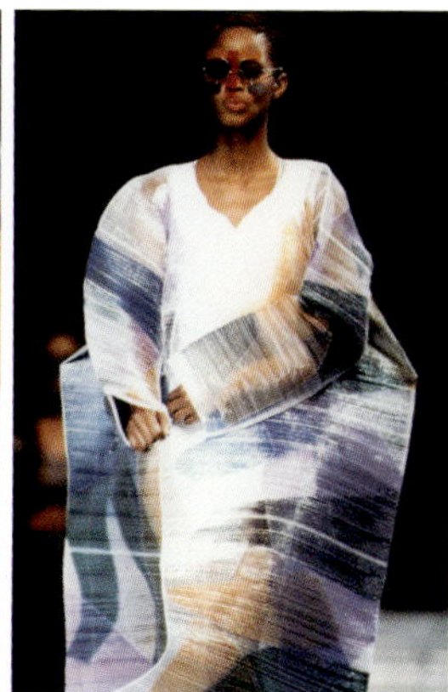

2

1995

Autumn-Winter 1995 Paris Collection
The collection was shown by 23 professional models, special guests Sayoko Yamaguchi and dancer Nora Kimball, and six "Beautiful Ladies" in their 60s to 90s chosen by audition.

Direction: Saburo Teshigawara

Opposite: "Beautiful Ladies" walk on the stage for the Autumn-Winter 1995 Paris Collection
The five are wearing slit-silk shirts and pants sewn with filament thread and silk, polyester-cotton padded jackets and coats.
From left: Claire (doctor and psychiatrist), Jacqueline (ballet instructor), Yvonne (actor, singer, and ballet instructor), Andree (actor) and Elizabeth (actor)
Photography: Philippe Brazil

Autumn-Winter 1995 Paris Collection, March 18, Salle Le Nôtre, Carrousel du Louvre

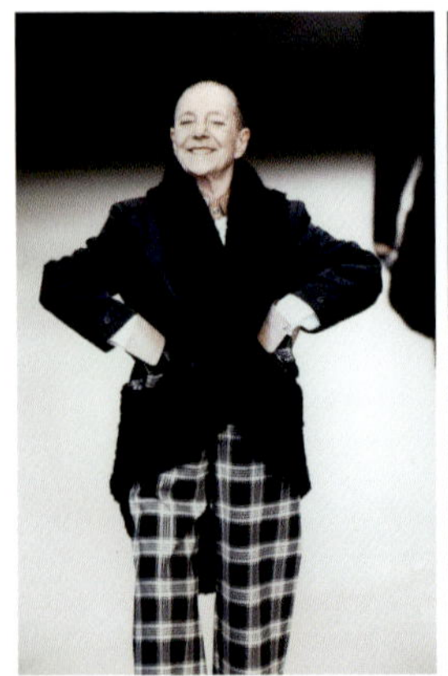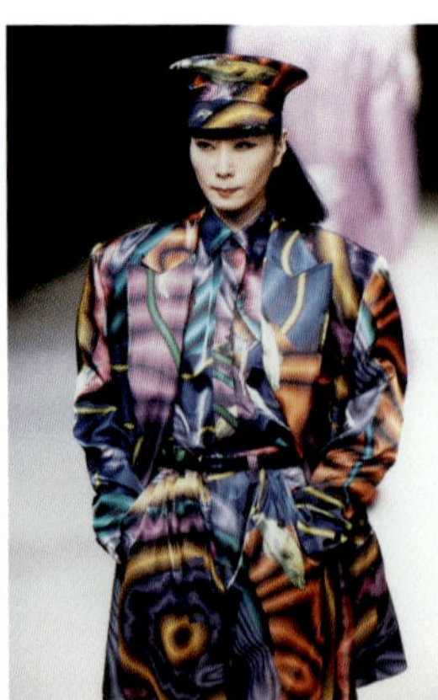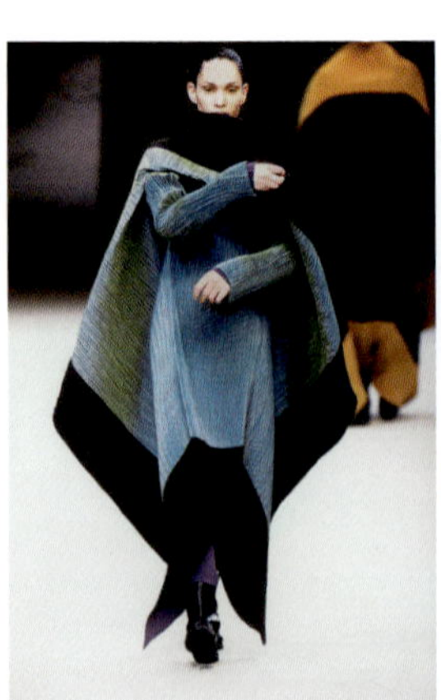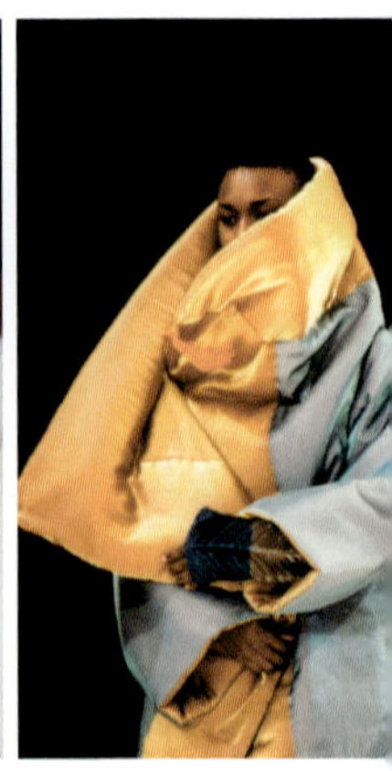

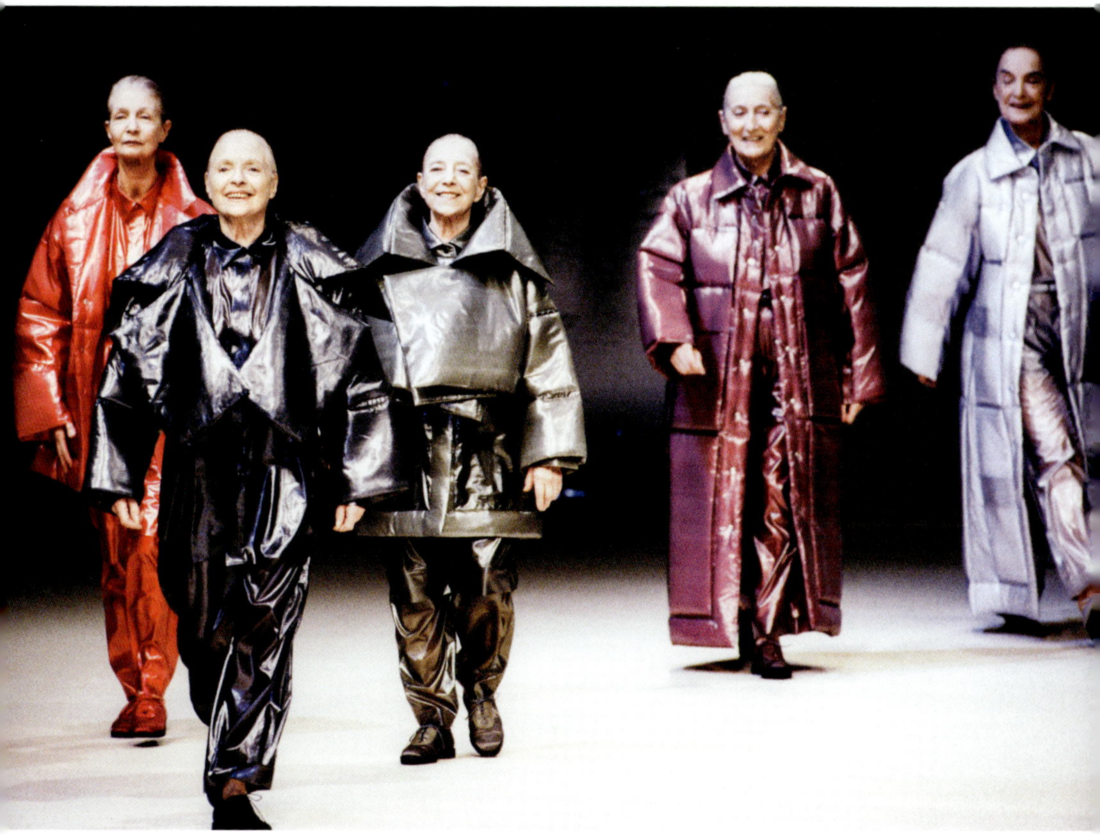

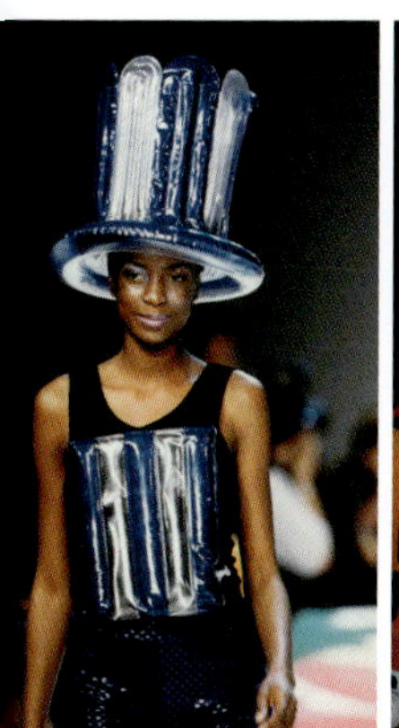

Spring-Summer 1996 Paris Collection, October 16,
Salle Le Nôtre, Carrousel du Louvre

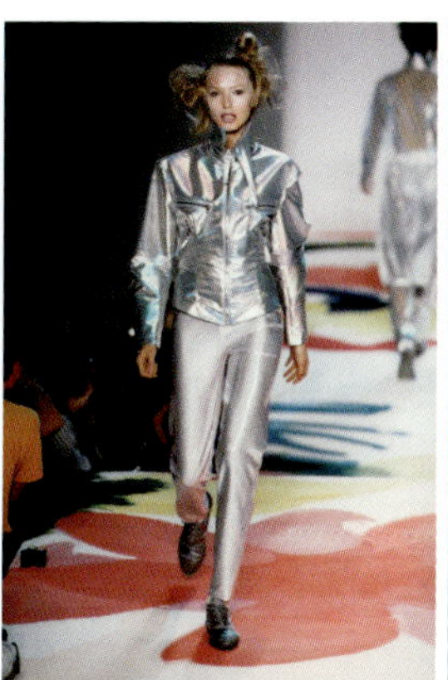
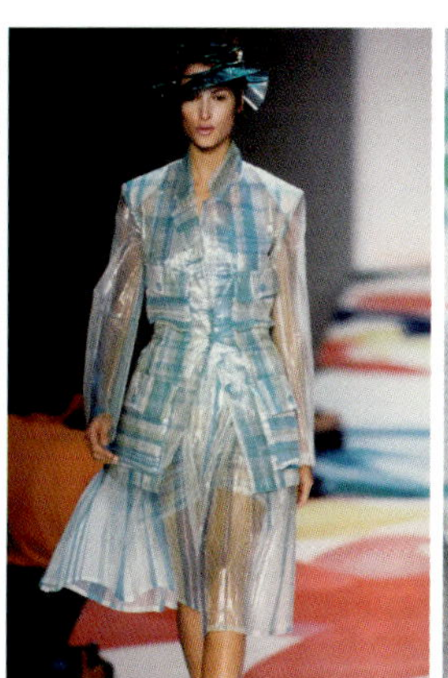
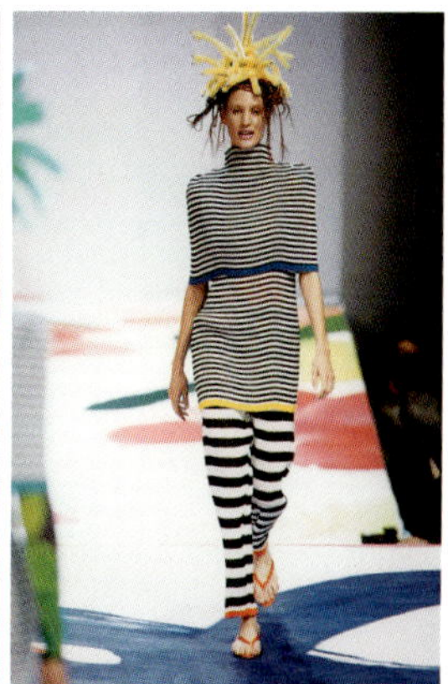

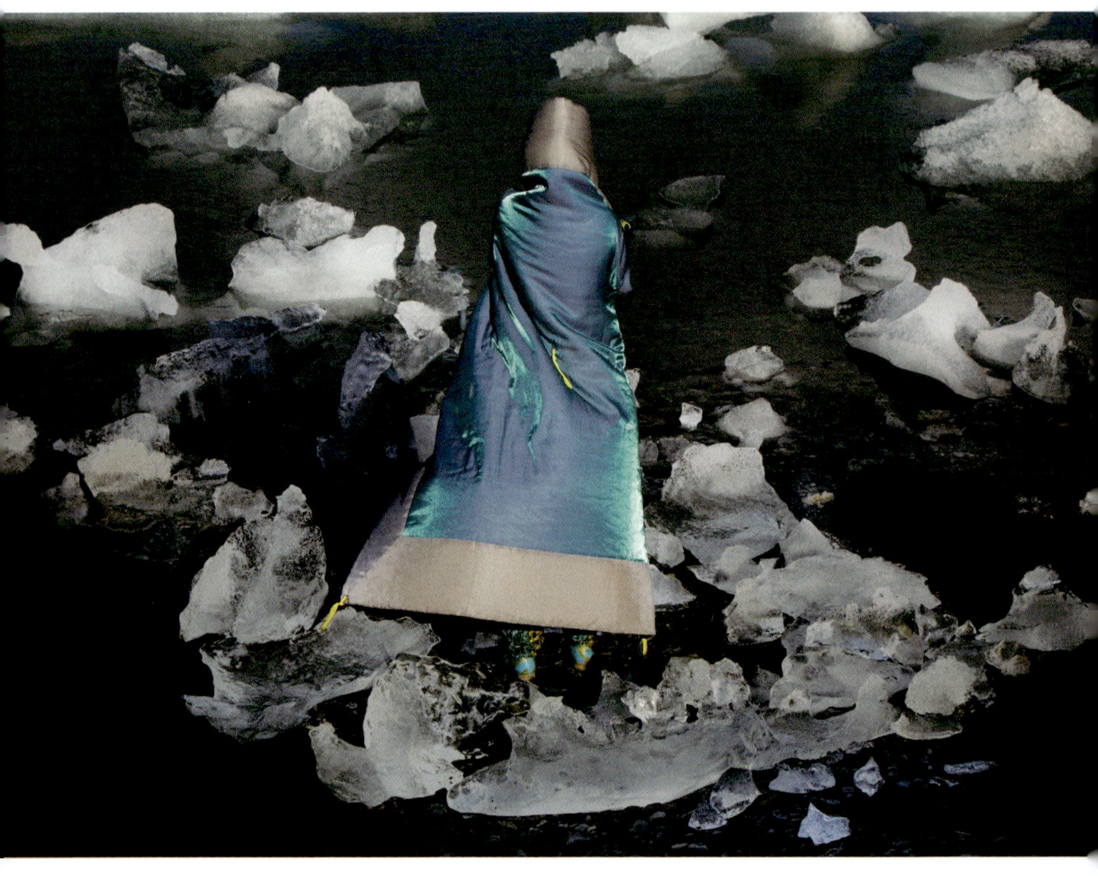

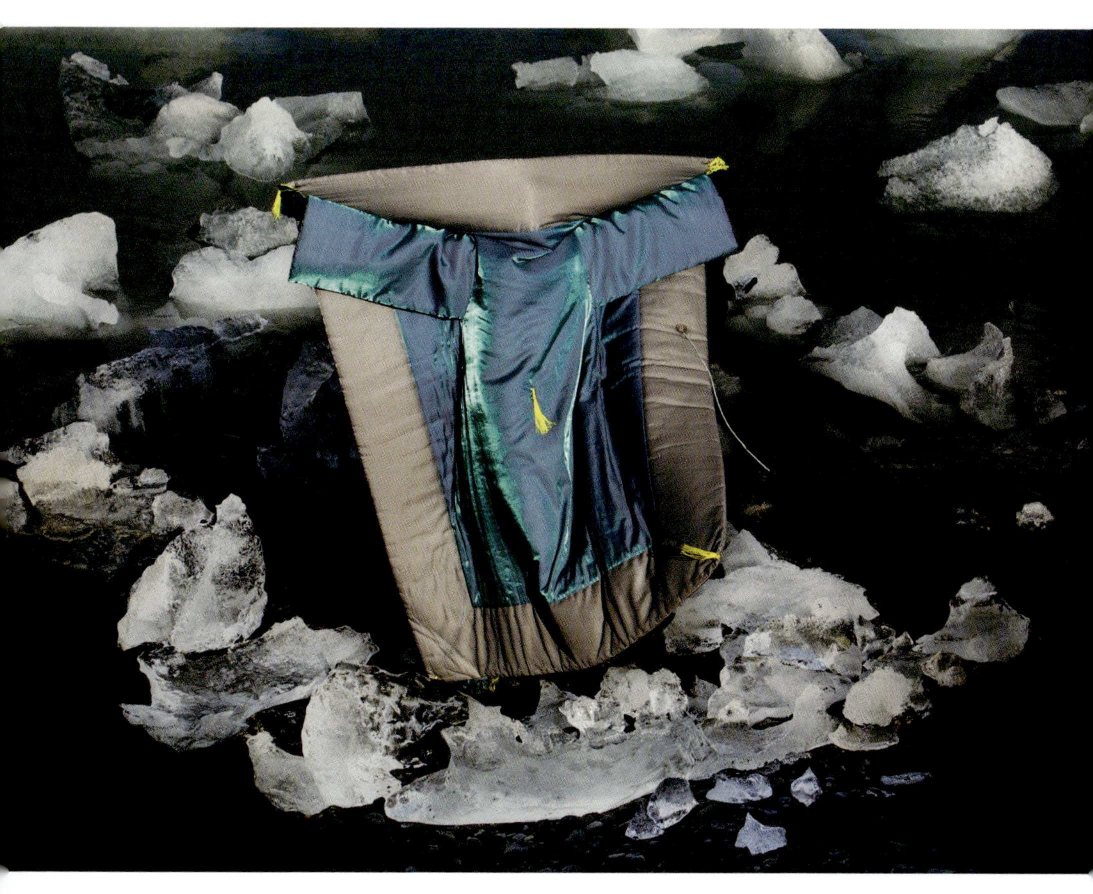

Square Coat
A square coat, inspired by the Japanese futon, in
monofilament fabric stuffed with polyester-cotton.
1995 design/Autumn-Winter 1995 Collection
Photography: Yuriko Takagi

1996

> Announcement of *PLEATS PLEATS ISSEY MIYAKE Guest Artist Series No. 1 Yasumasa Morimura*
> March: Autumn-Winter 1996 Paris Collection at Salle Delorme, Carrousel du Louvre
> September-December: Participated in the First Biennale di Firenze
> October: Spring-Summer 1997 Paris Collection at Salle Delorme, Carrousel du Louvre

PLEATS PLEASE ISSEY MIYAKE Guest Artist Series No. 1 Yasumasa Morimura

Issey Miyake asked artists to collaborate with him by using his PLEATS PLEASE ISSEY MIYAKE as a canvas. Yasumasa Morimura was the first in the series. Morimura's own body is superimposed onto the nude from *La Source*, a Jean-Auguste-Dominique Ingres painting from the collection of the Musée d'Orsay. There were a total of four collaborations in the series: other participants were Nobuyoshi Araki, Tim Hawkinson, and Cai Guo-Qiang.

Autumn-Winter 1996 Paris Collection, March 12, Salle Delorme, Carrousel du Louvre

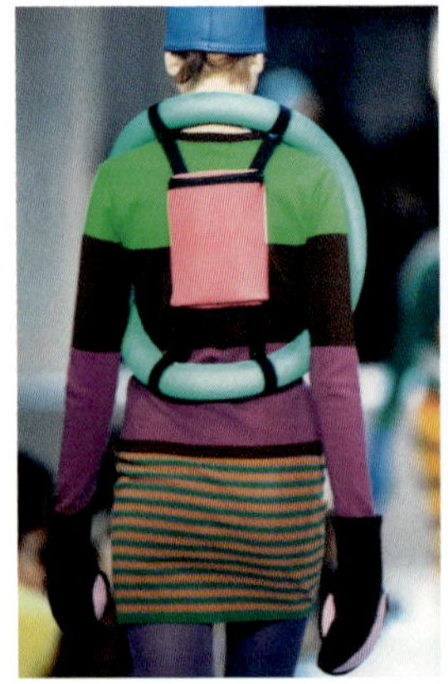
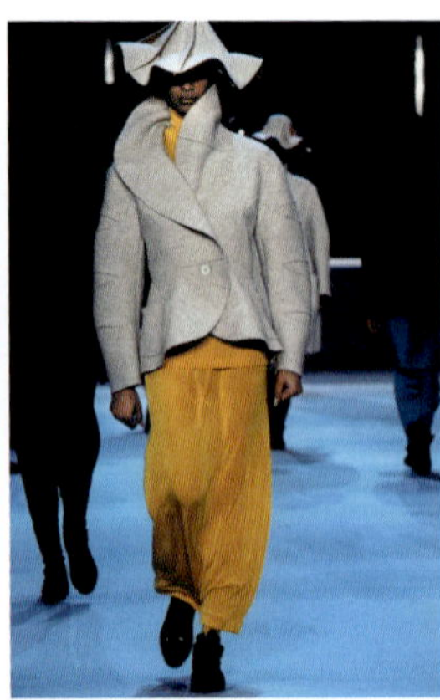
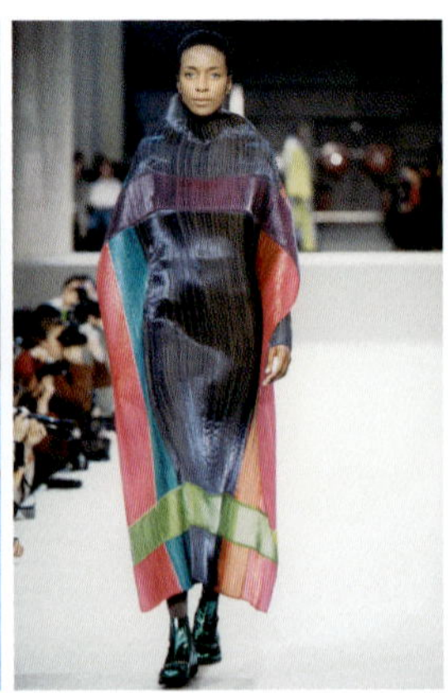
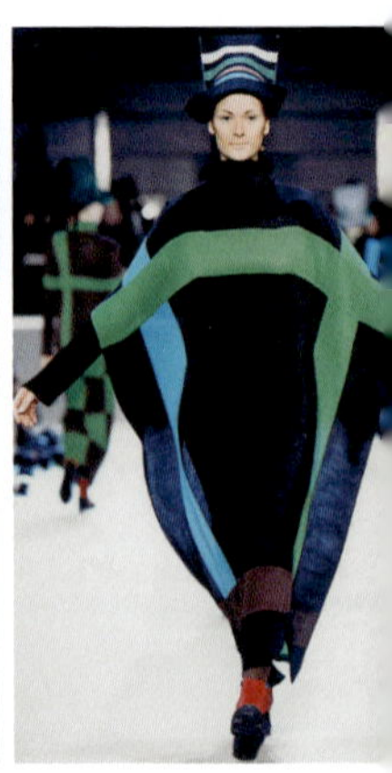

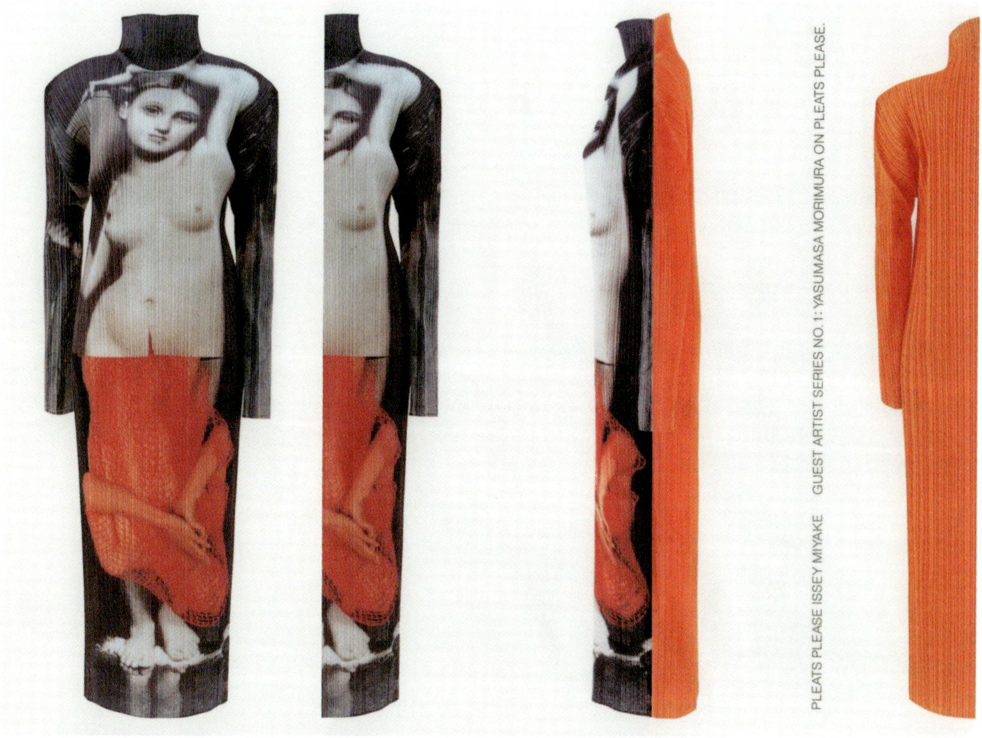

From the **PLEATS PLEASE ISSEY MIYAKE Guest Artist
Series No. 1 Yasumasa Morimura** pamphlet
Photography: Yasuaki Yoshinaga; design:
Gwenael Nicolas

Spring-Summer 1997 Paris Collection, October 8,
Salle Delorme, Carrousel du Louvre

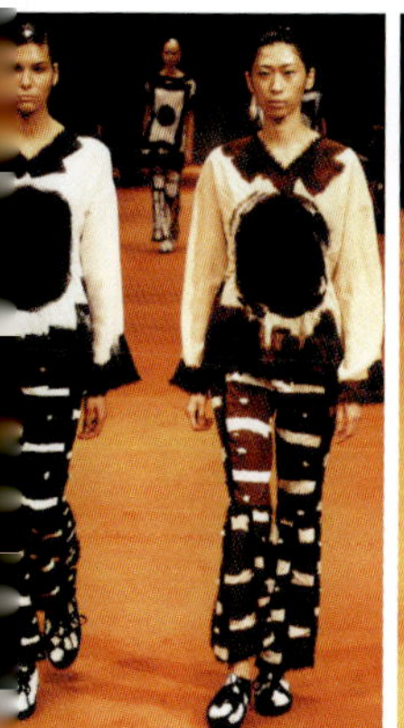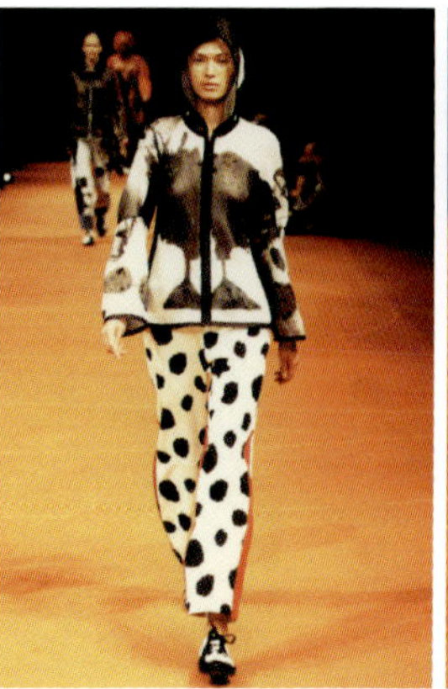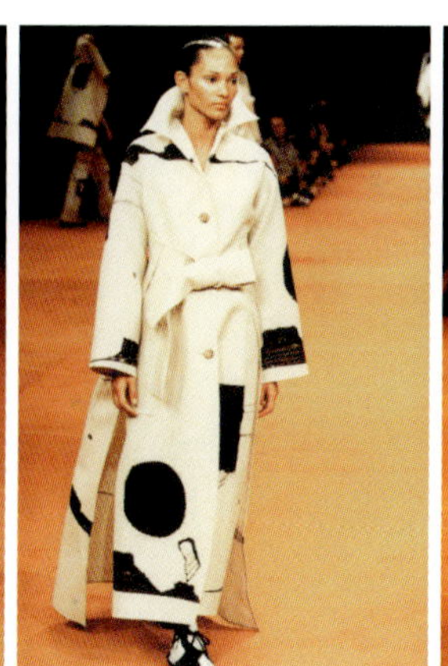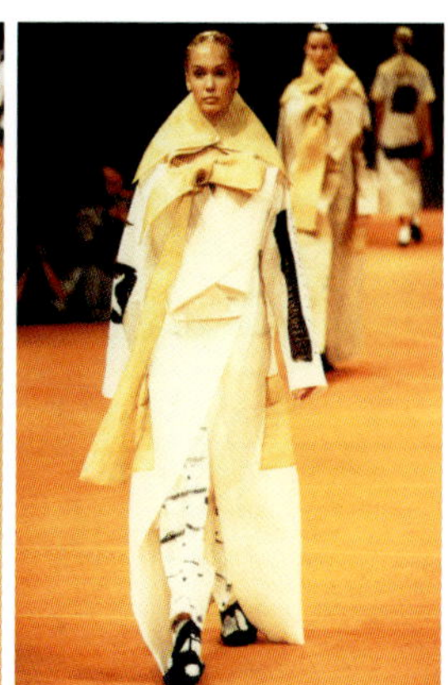

1997

> Announcement of *PLEATS PLEASE ISSEY MIYAKE Guest Artist Series No. 2 Nobuyoshi Araki*
> March: Autumn-Winter 1997 Paris Collection at Salle Delorme, Carrousel du Louvre
> June–August: *Isamu Noguchi and Issey Miyake, Arizona* exhibition at the Marugame Genichiro-Inokuma Museum of Contemporary Art, Kagawa Prefecture
> October: Spring-Summer 1998 Paris Collection at École des Beaux-Arts

PLEATS PLEASE ISSEY MIYAKE Guest Artist Series No. 2 Nobuyoshi Araki

Nobuyoshi Araki, a photographer best known for his female nudes and bondage images, was invited to participate in the Guest Artist Series. He selected photographs shot in the 1970s and self-portraits that harmonized with PLEATS PLEASE to create a new, fresh dialogue with the people wearing the clothing.

Isamu Noguchi and Issey Miyake: Arizona exhibition

Isamu Noguchi's sculptures and lamps, and clothing designed by Issey Miyake were displayed together against a backdrop by Genichiro Inokuma's pen-and-ink canvases inspired by his time in Arizona, USA. Miyake put together an exhibition that utilized the entire museum. While the exhibition ran, workshops were held for children that culminated in a fashion show of "Clothing for the Future."

June 22–August 31: Marugame Genichiro-Inokuma Museum of Contemporary Art, Kagawa Prefecture
Direction: Issey Miyake; space design: Tokujin Yoshioka

1 Autumn-Winter 1997 Paris Collection, March 11, Salle Delorme, Carrousel du Louvre
2 Spring-Summer 1998 Paris Collection, October 15, École des Beaux-Arts

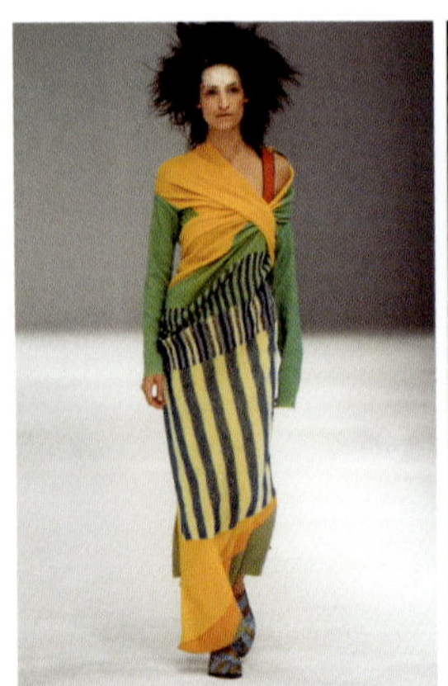
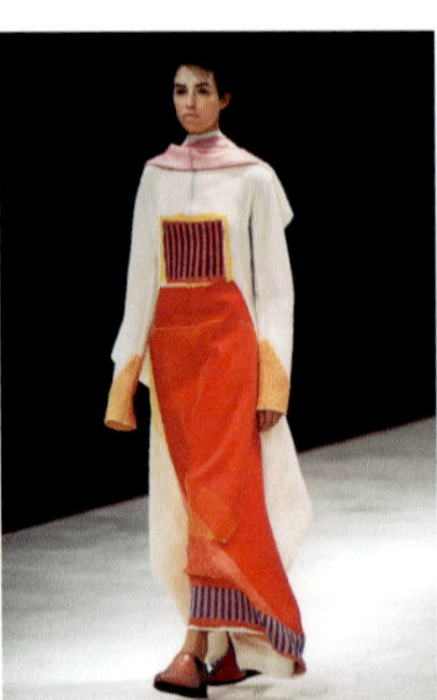
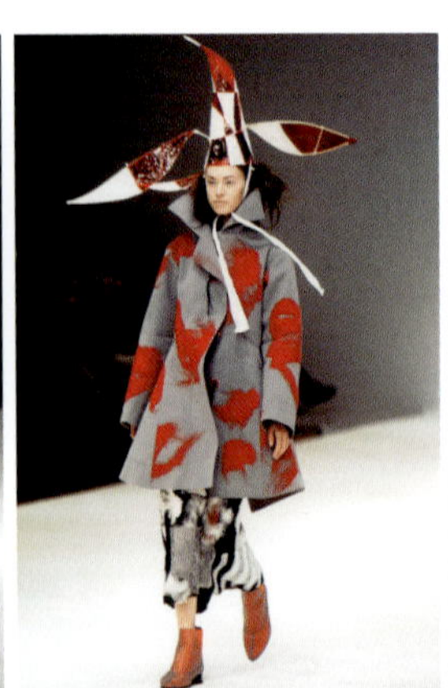
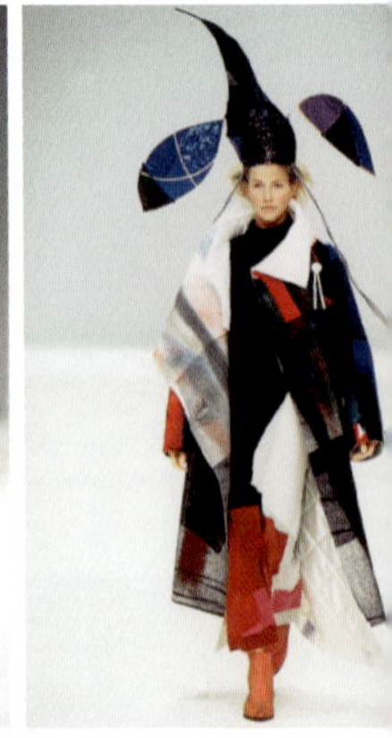

1

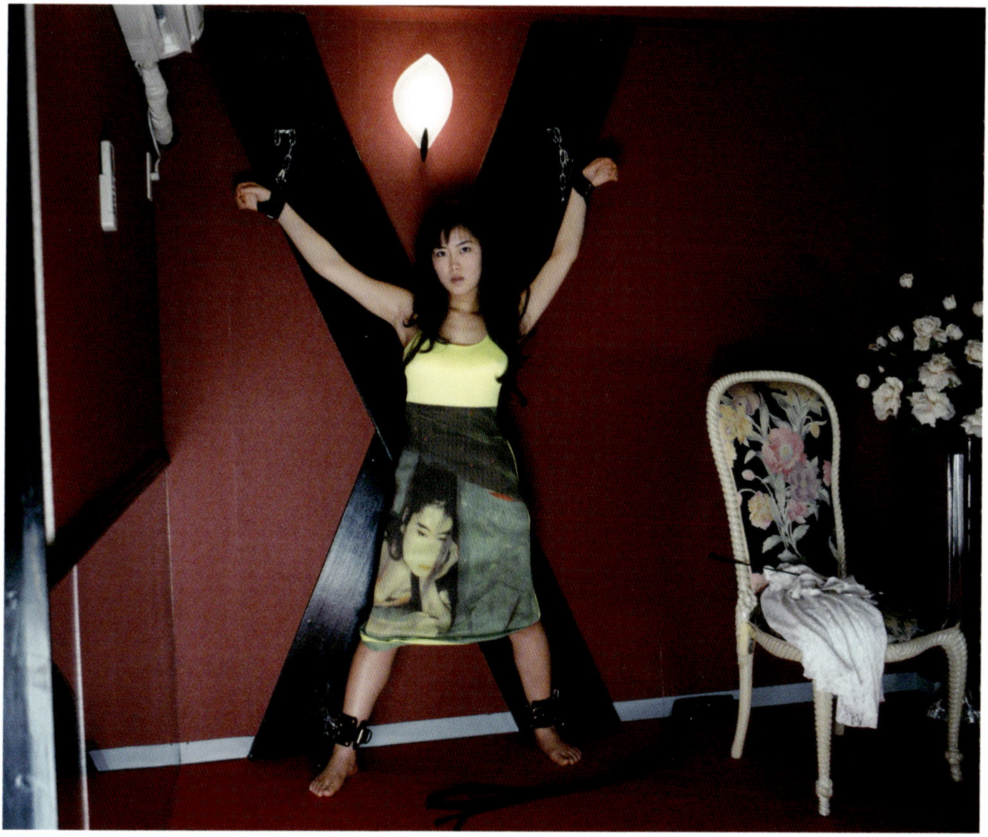

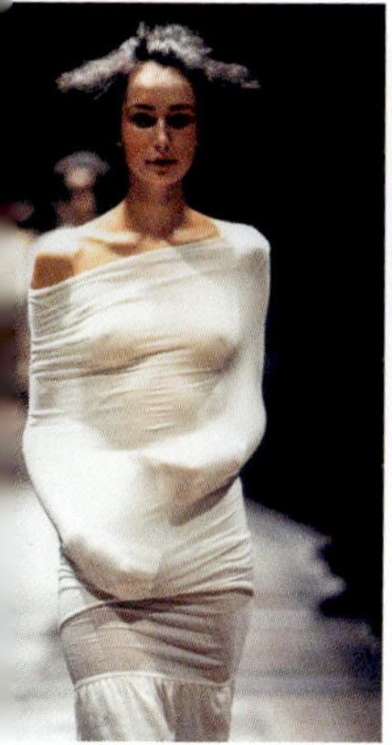

**PLEATS PLEASE ISSEY MIYAKE Guest Artist Series
No. 2 Nobuyoshi Araki**

For *Appear*, the photographs were printed onto the
fabric before pleating; for *Disappear* after pleating.
Photography: Nobuyoshi Araki

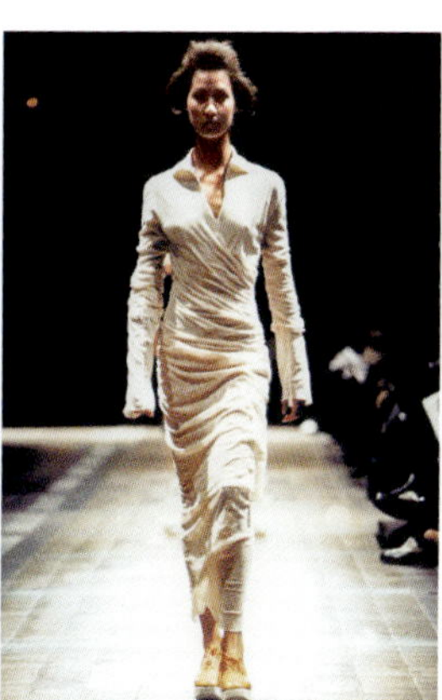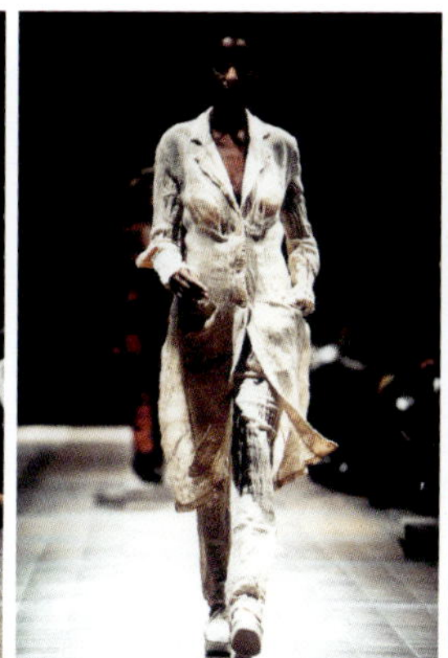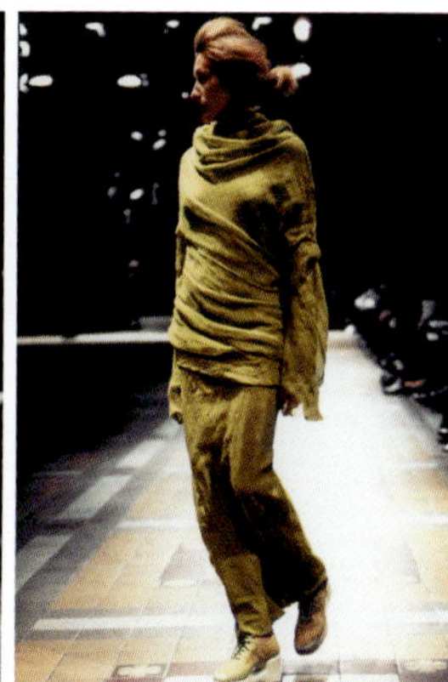

Isamu Noguchi and Issey Miyake:
***Arizona* exhibition**
Below: Isamu Noguchi's sculptures in the front,
and his *Akari* lamps in the back, under which
Origami Pleats are exhibited.
1988 design/Spring-Summer 1989 Collection
Photography: Shigeo Anzaï
Right: Isamu Noguchi's *Akari* and *Origami Pleats*
Photography: Yasuaki Yoshinaga
Opposite: *Arizona* and enlarged drawing
Kachina Doll by Genichiro Inokuma on the high wall.
1996 design/Spring-Summer 1997 Collection
Photography: Shigeo Anzaï

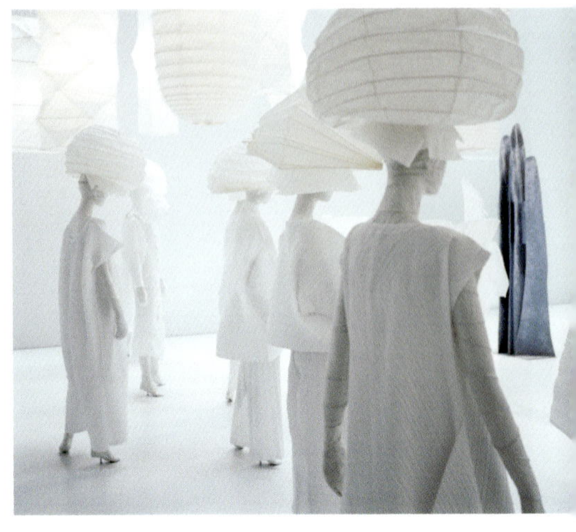

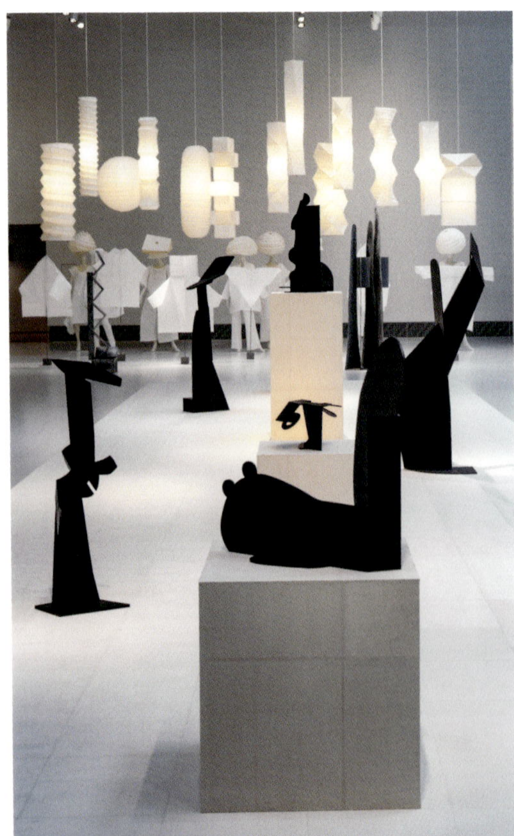

Following spreads: *Prism Collage*
A dress in wool. Floss and chiffon are placed
on the wool and are needle-punched to hold
them and then finally shrink-treated.
1997 design/Autumn-Winter 1997 Collection
Photography: Yasuaki Yoshinaga (pp. 210–211),
Yuriko Takagi (pp. 212–213)

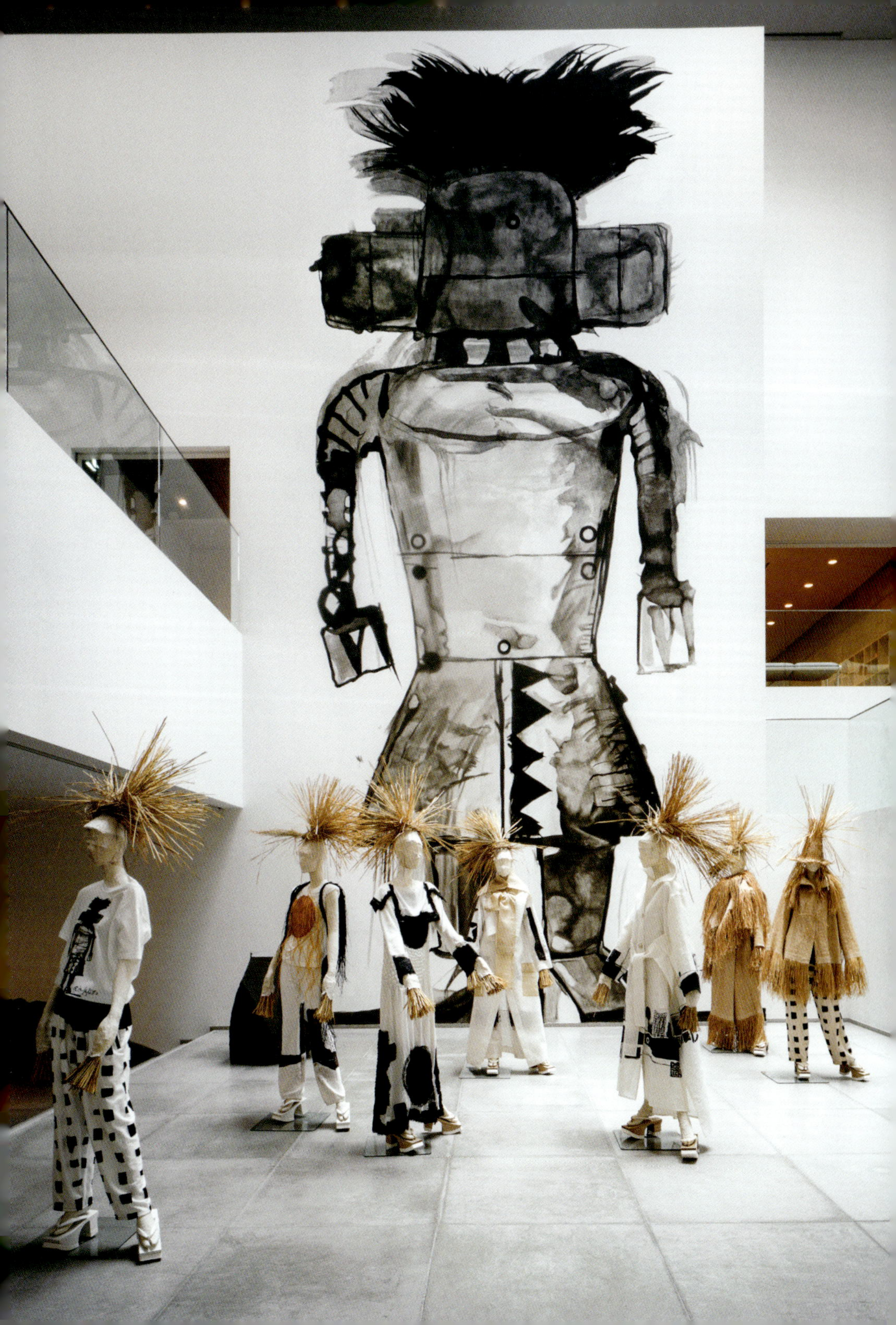

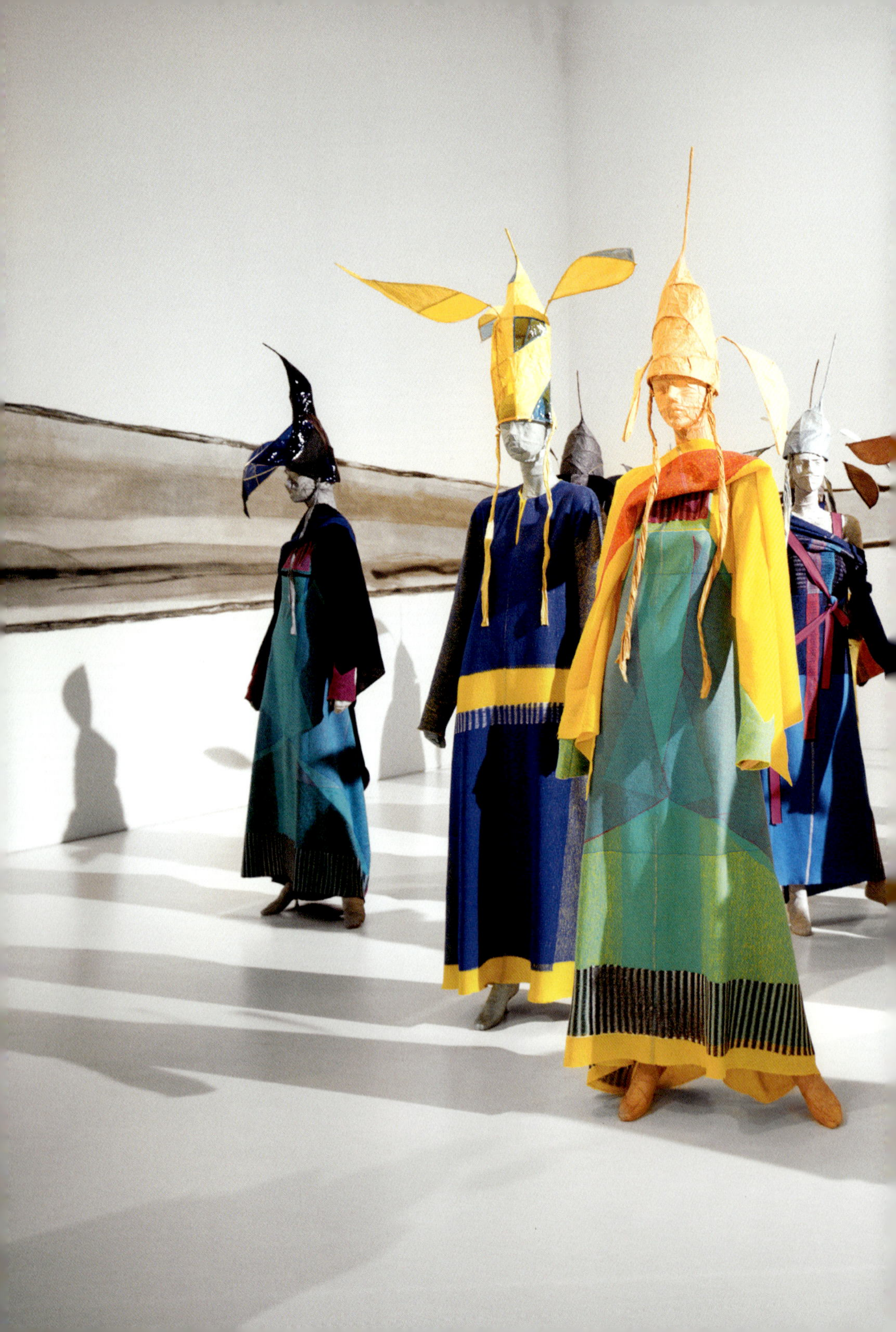

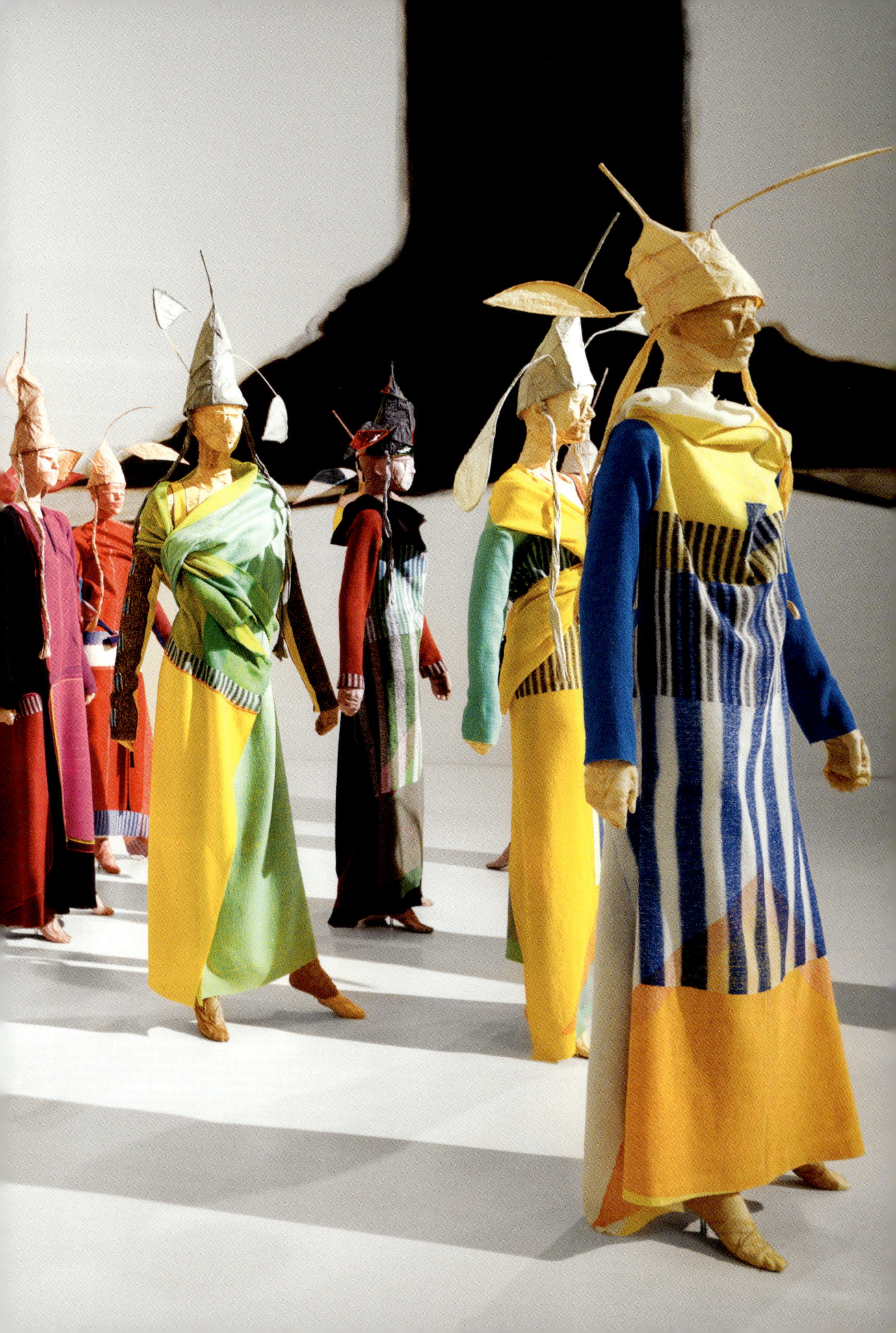

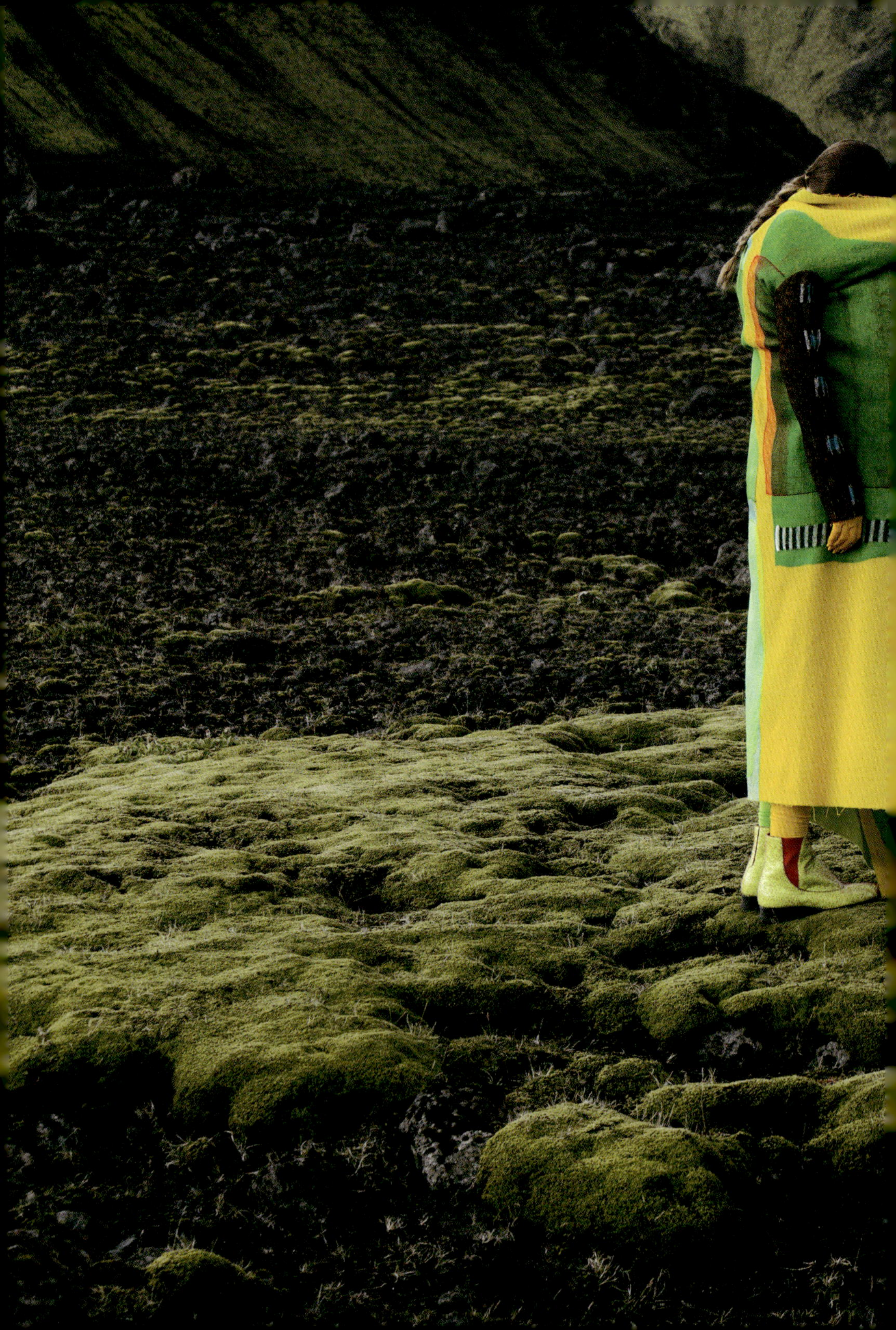

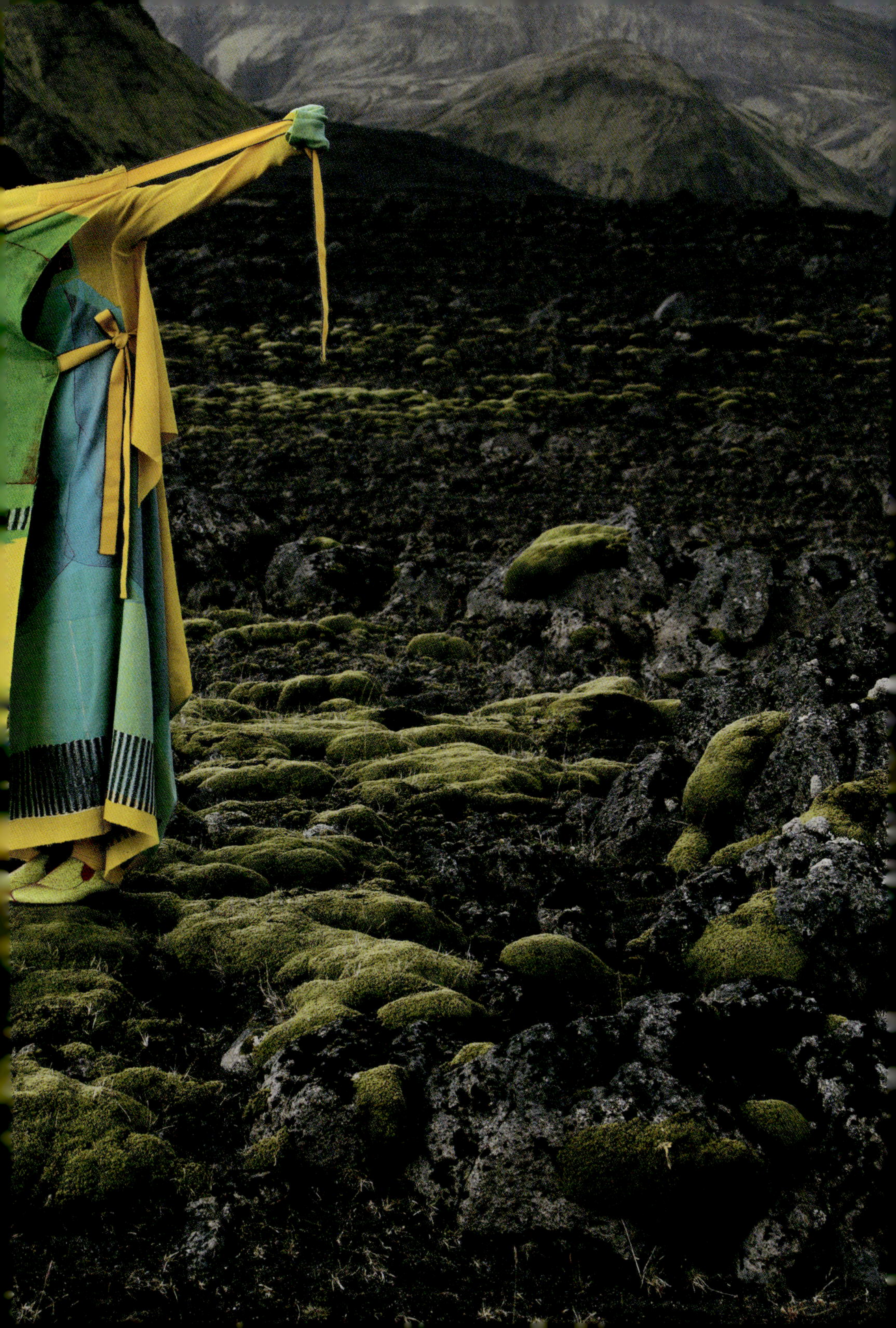

7—IPPON NO ITO, ICHIMAI NO NUNO / ONE THREAD, ONE PIECE OF CLOTH

Essay by
KAZUKO KOIKE

SINGLE-FORM CREATION PROCESS OF CLOTHES

Long before a piece of clothing is ready to be born, there are thread manufacturers, weavers and knitters, dyers and fabric processors, and so on. All are involved in the work, along with the actual clothes designers. In the production process, each of them works separately and with little contact between each other; obviously, in a highly developed capitalist society, such as the one most of us live in, these units, respectively, are incorporated and anonymous.

"We should be able to make clothing that is genuinely original if we trace materials back and become involved in the entire process." This idea occurred to Dai Fujiwara,[1] who joined Miyake Design Studio in 1994. It was inspired by research on jersey, a material important to him and to Miyake. His hunch grew into a methodology where, by using the most advanced technologies available, it became possible to predetermine the design of a given piece of clothing as early as the thread stage.

Thanks to cutting-edge computer programming, the design of the clothes is already inscribed at the stage of making fabrics, making possible the "single-form creation process," the most advanced method of making clothing yet.

But according to Miyake, what is first required for this epoch-making method is imagination. The designer ought to be able to imagine everything about the cloth from the thread stage: how to knit or weave the form, function, and usage of the cloth. Even the total amount of material to be produced must be determined from the beginning. The designer must foresee the finished form, and study how to achieve it. Even if struck by a sudden inspiration, it won't work without imagination and a technical process. "The designer should always search, find, and then grasp it in an instant. No creation without such power."

It is amazing to find that at the basis of Miyake Design Studio's work lies such a vision. This reminds me of how moved I was when I visited the Bauhaus in Dessau and saw a notebook called "Professor Itten's lectures." In it, if I remember correctly, Johannes Itten passionately advocated a vegetarian diet for an institution that was also just a regular school. The quotes just cited come from a conversation on Miyake Design Studio's corporate beliefs, and in this probably lies the key to its success. Their everyday workplace is also one where a certain sort of education occurs, where people can have real lives.

ONE THREAD, ONE PIECE OF CLOTH

A-POC, *A Piece Of Cloth* – Issey Miyake's central philosophy for making clothes – makes us remember that any piece of fabric begins with a single thread, and public awareness of this way of thinking has increased.[2] At the Paris Collection (Spring-Summer 1999) in 1998, studio designers appeared on the runway carrying a tube-shaped knitted fabric in front of the audience. They cut the material and turned it into something wearable. That was the *mise-en-scène*. In the spring of 1999, the same presentation was held in Tokyo. Computerized instructions had been embedded before knitting, and so the knitted material did not even fray at the edges. It was like magic, but no – it was real. The audience had witnessed the approach in action: "Cut material and make a piece of clothing at the same time."

Since the 1970s, Issey Miyake had been interested in the Japanese tradition of tube-weaving, and over time, he tried out a variety of traditional materials in his own creations. PLEATS PLEAwSE appeared on the streets in cities around the world in the 1990s. Many of the clothes are in fact tube-shaped – clothes that are given their forms *a priori*.

To cite a precedent, Coco Chanel's ensemble suit appeared in the 1920s, and this helped jersey fabric be accepted as a material for women's street clothes. A-POC was a result of combining computer technology with industrial knitting machines that were imported to Japan and readjusted here.

Dai Fujiwara says, "As A-POC clothes start from the point of designing, the thread's structural details may be designed to suit the final product's intended use." Research began to look into the possibility that A-POC might develop into an extended project for *mono zukuri,* which would produce not only clothing, but also a wide range of things made from fiber.

An exhibition with the charming title *Nannano? A-POC Miyake Issey + Fujiwara Dai*[3] was held in 2003, and since then hopes and even further questions regarding Fujiwara's ideas have multiplied. If threads possessing a strong structure can be produced, A-POC could possibly even be used, in addition to its application to clothing, for building and other purposes. A-POC might then be akin to a discovery, says the designer Taku Satoh.[4]

He has long been involved in analyzing everyday objects, and once actually performed *The Anatomy of Design = A-POC Baguette*. He examined A-POC's third product, *Baguette*, and, based on his findings, realized an installation work in an exhibition.[5] Briefly, he believes that designing is not an act of covering up and hiding something, but one of discovering and revealing an object's or material's inherent potential. And it is how something is revealed, he says, that differentiates designers, each with his/her own unique and original persona. I had been wondering how to express the essence of A-POC, and found a clue thanks to Satoh. Looking at A-POC within the context of design history, Issey Miyake and Dai Fujiwara discovered new things rather than innovate those which already exist. And it is through this exploration and discovery that we can find the unique characteristics of A-POC.

Here I am reminded of an exhibition of clothing mentioned in chapter two, and which was the first of its kind to be held here. As noted there, the show *Inventive Clothes: 1909–1939* was originally curated by and held at the Costume Institute of New York's Metropolitan Museum of Art; it was then shown at The National Museum of Modern Art, Kyoto, in 1975.[6] The adjective "inventive" had been chosen in view of the context of Western history of clothing, but when it came to Japan the show was renamed *Gendai Ifuku no Genryu Ten* (Sources of Contemporary Clothing). Miyake and all of his collaborators wanted to encourage the public to learn what they could from works representing such varied designers as Poiret,[7] Schiaparelli,[8] Chanel,[9] and Vionnet. Today, 40 years later, A-POC's discovery has encouraged the study of thread and fabric, and shows the possibility of being used for a wide range of products, from clothing to architecture. Issey Miyake understood its potential, and in its history we can also read that of his own work.

A-POC Queen, the knitted tube roll made in 1998, was selected and exhibited in 2006 as a permanent item in the Architecture & Design collection of the Museum of Modern Art, New York.

From 2000 through 2006, A-POC seasonal collections attracted much attention and were appreciated as the fruit of creative research. The form it took at the time of its discovery was knitted fabric; this was followed by further research and development into woven fabric, and followed by thicker versions, such as those bearing patterns like Gobelin tapestries. As well, a very striking jeans-specific A-POC fabric was introduced. Since 2007 the technology has been further enhanced and come to be applied to various brands, to which the label "A-POC-inside" is attached. In 2003, A-POC, by now a much-developed method, lent its technology to PLEATS PLEASE, and this synergized result was named "+A-POC."

EXPANDING STAGES OF EXPRESSION

Issey Miyake excelled in being tuned in to the zeitgeist. He always acted so quickly that I often wonder how his staff were able to keep up with him.

Somebody once proposed that he open a gallery in the neighborhood of the Miyake Design Studio headquarters, and this quickly came into being. A unique, long space of 90 square meters was designed by the architect Shigeru Ban,[10] combining tubes made of industrial-use paper pulp. In its first five years from 2000, the MDS Gallery hosted 20 original exhibitions. What has been noted in the curating of the series is the attitude of openness to creative work from various fields, including design works, craftwork, and art.

Artists shown there have included contemporary artists with distinctive messages such as Tim Hawkinson and Kenji Yanobe,[11] pottery artist Machiko Ogawa,[12] and the German sculptor Ernst Gamperl,[13] known for his wooden containers. But new faces were also featured, such as Ronan & Erwan Bouroullec.[14] This, too, speaks for Miyake's astute eyes and sensibility.

In January 2003, Miyake published an article in the cultural pages of the leading nationwide newspaper, the *Asahi Shimbun*. Its title was "Let's Create a Design Museum," and in it he emphasized that Japan should take advantage of its world-standard resources.[15] Miyake proposed the establishment of a museum that would be based on the idea that creative design is a part of our national intellectual resources. Various cities around the world have design museums where young people have a chance to learn about what has been achieved in the past, and to reflect upon what new directions they might further go in. I interpreted the founding of the MDS Gallery as a part of this message.

If Japan is to find hope, when it has lost full confidence in what it stands for, the key lies in creativity, in particular, design. … What would encourage the Japanese in this context might be to become aware of

the importance of the "legacy of our design work." ... Japan's poverty is not that of any material shortage, but stems from our lack of self-confidence.
The Asahi Shimbun,
January 28, 2003, evening edition

This short excerpt from the article conveys his hope and his message; the essay received a widespread response from a variety of individuals and groups.

As Issey Miyake's determined vision matured, he commenced research into and preparation for establishing an independent, private-sector design foundation.

1   Dai Fujiwara (1967–): Designer. Joined Miyake Design Studio in 1994, worked on the ISSEY MIYAKE design staff. Began the A-POC project with Issey Miyake. ISSEY MIYAKE creative director from 2006 through February of 2012.

2   A-POC: See p. 220.

3   *Nannano? A-POC Miyake Issey + Fujiwara Dai*: See pp. 264, 268–273.

4   Taku Satoh (1955–): Graphic designer. Active in diverse fields such as package design, visual interface, product design, merchandising, art direction for TV programs, etc., while continuing projects to prove that design is also artwork. Director of 21_21 DESIGN SIGHT.

5   *The Anatomy of Design = A-POC Baguette*: See pp. 272–273.

6   *Gendai Ifuku no Genryu Ten – Inventive Clothes: 1909–1939*: See pp. 56–57.

7   Paul Poiret (1879–1944): Fashion designer. Opened a maison in Paris in 1903. In 1906, introduced a corset-less dress. Through his research on linear cutting as well as on clothing from foreign lands, he became a leader in the movement to expand clothing in the 20th century. His work left behind the bodily restrictions of the 19th century.

8   Elsa Schiaparelli (1890–1973): Fashion designer. Opened a maison in Paris in 1927. Was active mainly in the 1930s through the 1940s, and incorporated into fashion elements of the arts by effectively using the texture and gloss of new synthetic materials.

9   Gabrielle "Coco" Chanel (1883–1971), more generally known as Coco Chanel: Fashion designer. Opened a maison in Paris in 1913. In 1916, in an attempt to realize greater simplicity and comfort, came up with a women's suit made of jersey, which until then had been used mainly for women's underwear. In 1954, after having stayed away from fashion design for some time, introduced the "Chanel Suit," which became one of the iconic pieces of attire of the 20th century.

10   Shigeru Ban (1957–): Architect. Established Shigeru Ban Architects in 1985. Representative works include Curtain Wall House, 1995; Japan Pavilion, EXPO 2000 Hanover; Centre Pompidou, Metz, 2010. Well known for using paper tubes and containers, and is actively involved with disaster relief projects around the world.

11   Kenji Yanobe (1965–): Artist. Since his debut in 1990 and his chosen theme of "survival," has produced mechanical sculptures for surviving the future. Shifted his theme to "Revival" at the beginning of the 21st century, and has continued producing large-scale sculptural works.

12   Machiko Ogawa (1946–): Pottery artist. Studied in Paris and West Africa. Her works take advantage of elements that are usually eliminated in pottery, such as cracks, missing pieces, and shrunken baked glazes.

13   Ernst Gamperl (1965–): Wood sculptor. After working as a furniture carpenter, he learned on his own how to use a wood-processing wheel. Opened his studio in 1990 and has continued producing a variety of sculptures.

14   Ronan & Erwan Bouroullec (1971–, 1976–): Furniture and interior designers; formed their two-man team in the 1990s. Designed the A-POC store in Paris in 2000.

15   "Let's Create a Design Museum": See pp. 265–267.

1998

- Embarked upon the A-POC project
- Announcement of *PLEATS PLEASE ISSEY MIYAKE Guest Artist Series No. 3 Tim Hawkinson*, and *No. 4 Cai Guo-Qiang*
- March: Autumn-Winter 1998 Paris Collection at École des Beaux-Arts
- October–February 1999: *Issey Miyake Making Things* exhibition in Paris. Book titled *Issey Miyake Making Things* published in conjunction with the exhibition in France (Actes Sud), UK (Scalo Publishers), and in Japan (AXIS) in 1999
- October: Spring-Summer 1999 Paris Collection at École des Beaux-Arts

***Issey Miyake Making Things* exhibition**

The exhibition focused on Issey Miyake's work during the 1990s and his proposals for future clothing as it explored the approach to design at the heart of his creative activities. It was filled with wit and humor, including a "Laboratory" depicting the production process and "Jumping," a computer-controlled exhibition of the clothing in motion. The exhibition began at the Fondation Cartier pour l'art contemporain in Paris, and then moved to New York and Tokyo.

October 13, 1998–February 28, 1999:
Fondation Cartier pour l'art contemporain, Paris
November 13, 1999–February 29, 2000:
Ace Gallery, New York
April 29–August 20, 2000:
Museum of Contemporary Art, Tokyo
Exhibition direction: Issey Miyake; space design: Tokujin Yoshioka; visual direction: Midori Kitamura; animation: Pascal Roulin; archivist: Masako Omori; poster: Paris/Irving Penn (photography) and Ikko Tanaka (typography and layout); New York/Raymond Meier (photography), Ace Gallery (graphics); Tokyo/Francis Giacobetti (photography), Ikko Tanaka (book design)

1 Autumn-Winter 1998 Paris Collection, March 11, École des Beaux-Arts
2 Spring-Summer 1999 Paris Collection, October 14, École des Beaux-Arts

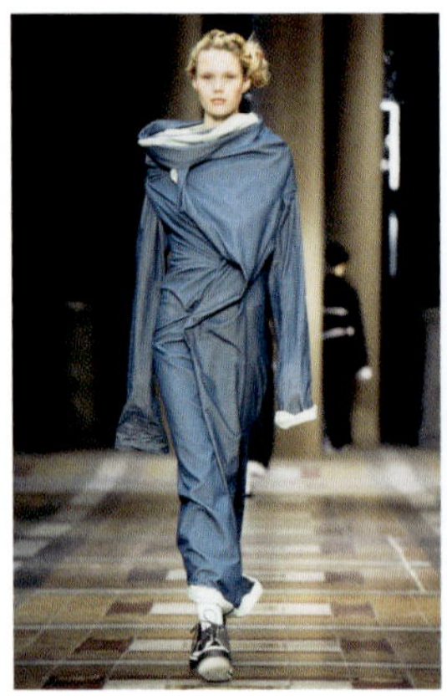
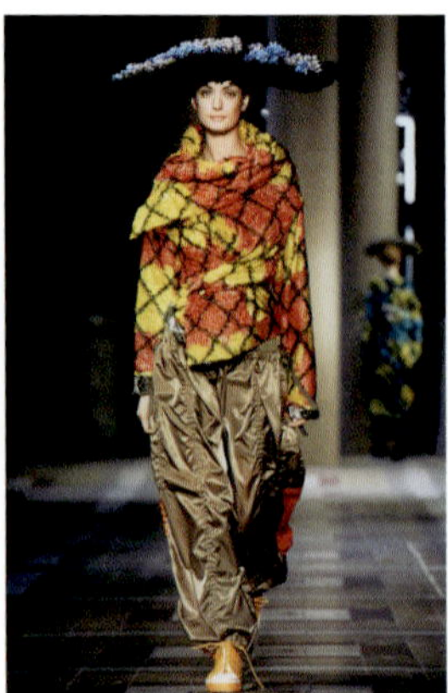
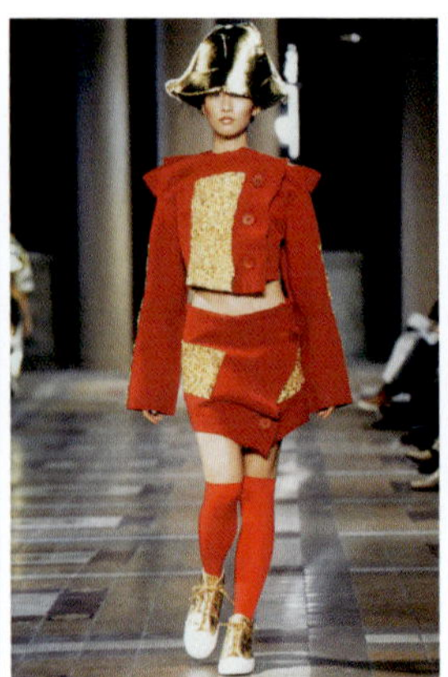
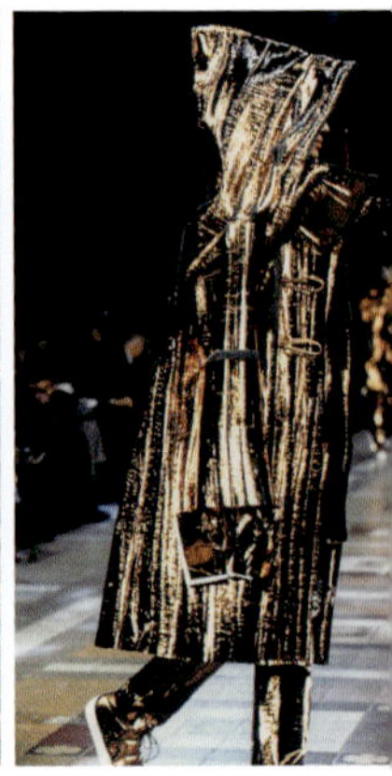

1

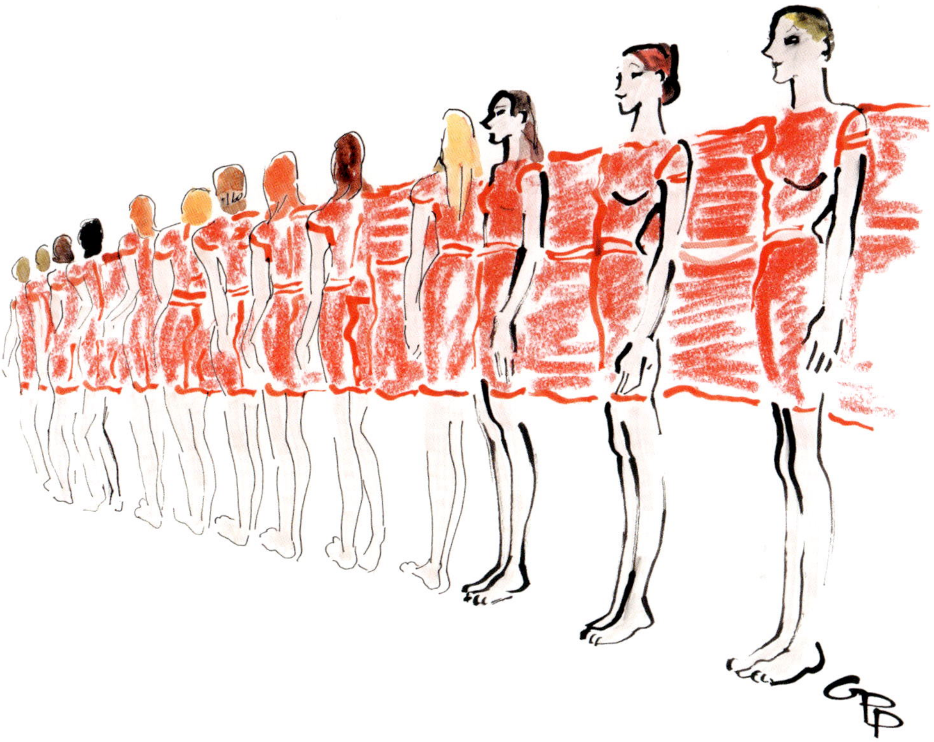

Finale of the Spring-Summer 1999 Paris Collection:
A-POC Le Feu
A-POC borrowed the name from the Le Feu d'Issey
perfume launched in the same year. A repeating
skirt and repeating top are knitted into one tube.
For the finale, the models lined up "inserted" into
the tops and skirts embedded within the two tubes.
Illustrations: Gladys Perint Palmer

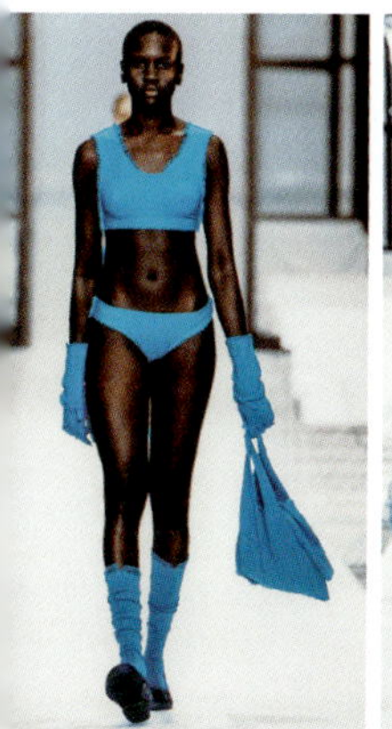
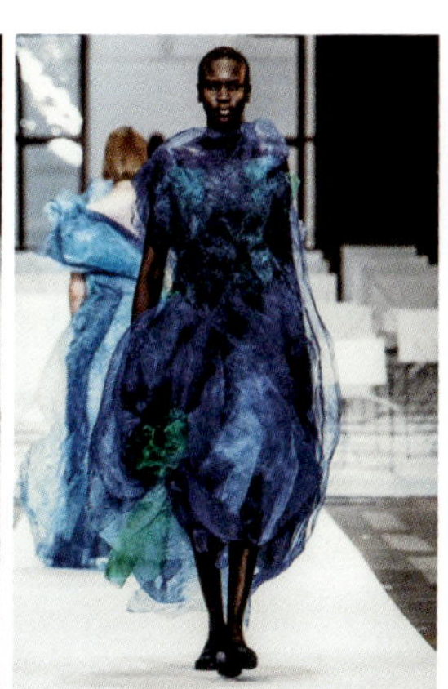
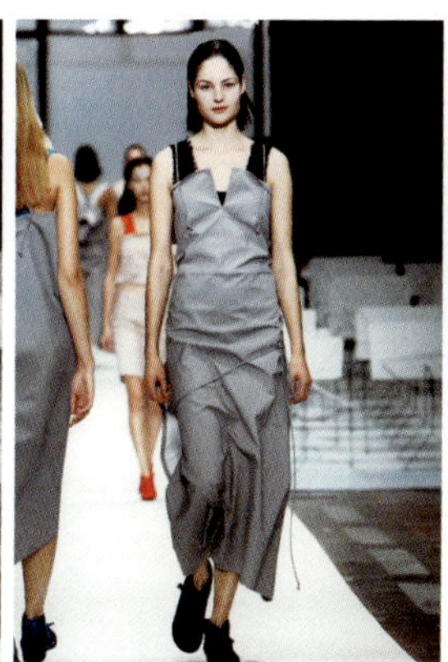
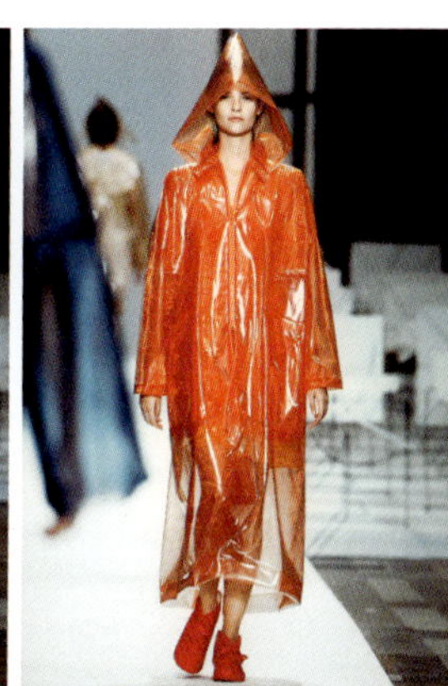

2

A-POC

A-POC is an acronym for Issey Miyake's design touch-stone, *A Piece Of Cloth*. It uses computer technology to create seamless clothing formed in a single process from a single thread. The cloth emerges in tube form, in which the shapes of clothing are embedded. The *Just Before* dress, extruded from lines of demarcation within its tube (shown in 1997), was its immediate predecessor. This innovative production technique provided one of the platforms for Miyake's work in the 21st century.

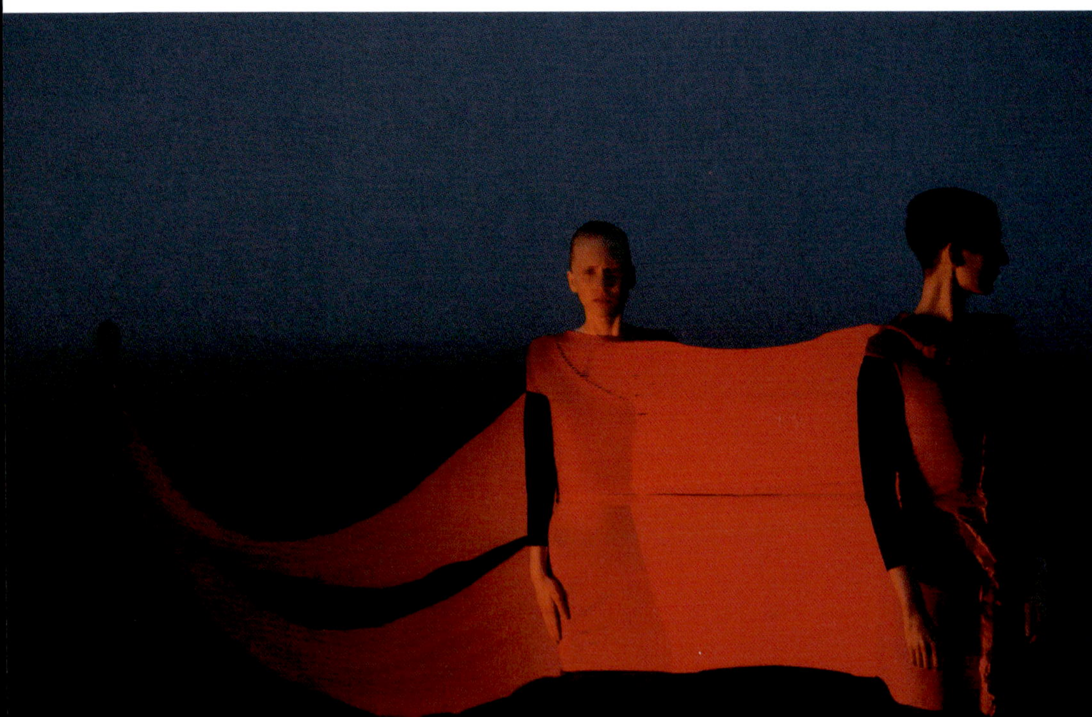

This and following spread: **A-POC Le Feu**
A continuously knitted tube in which either shirts or skirts have been embedded alternately. 1998 design/ Spring-Summer 1999 Collection
Photography: Yuriko Takagi

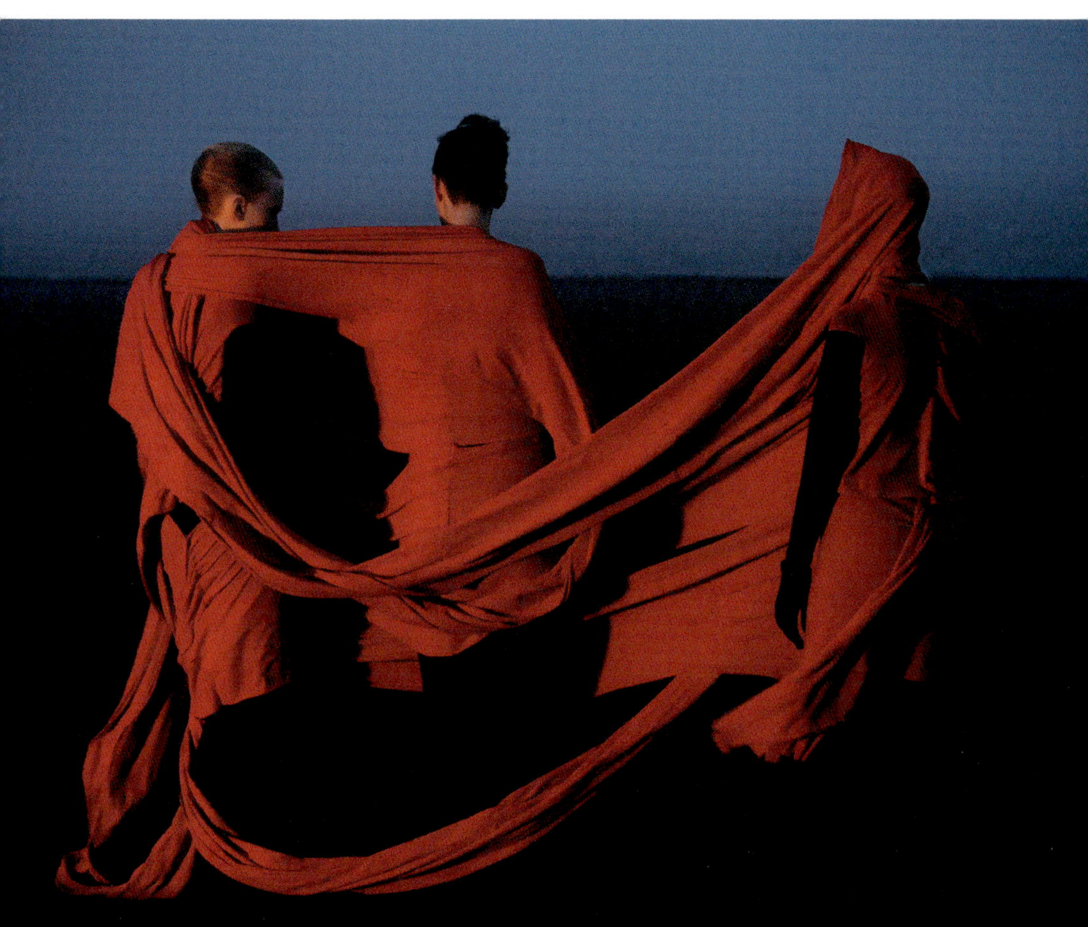

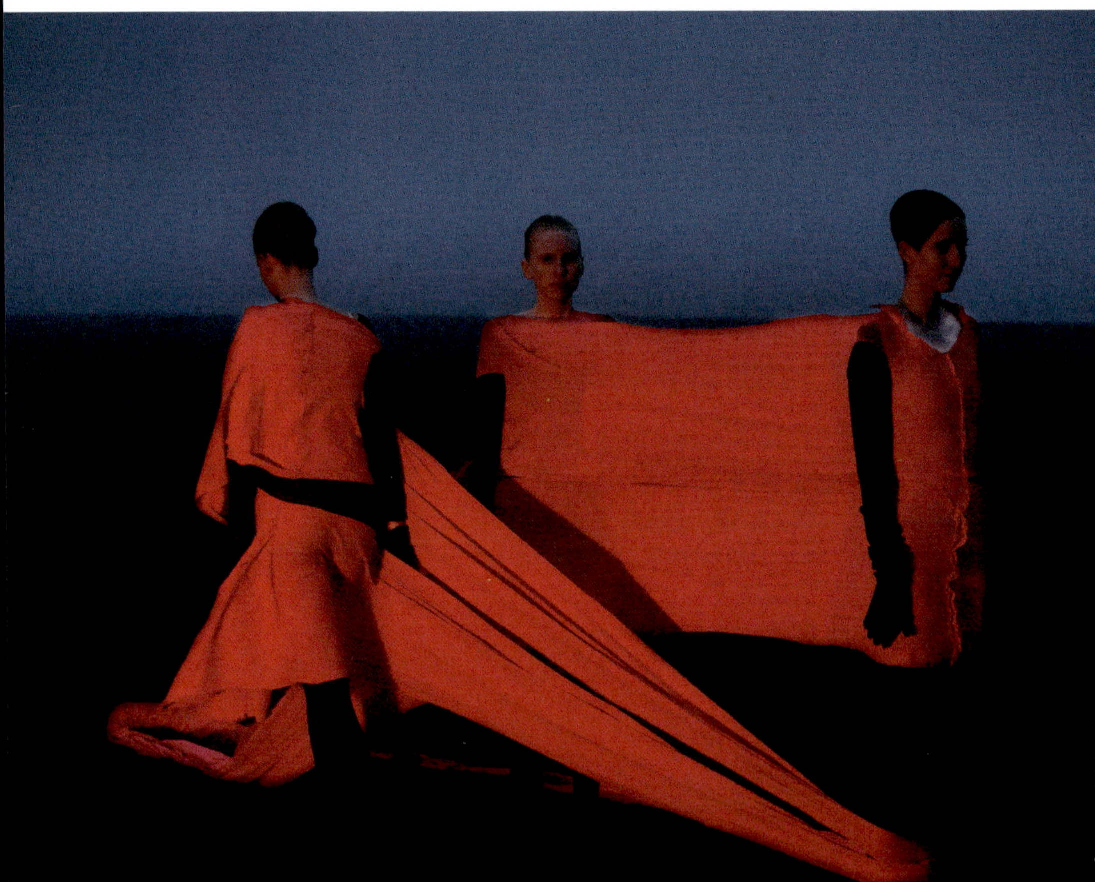

1998

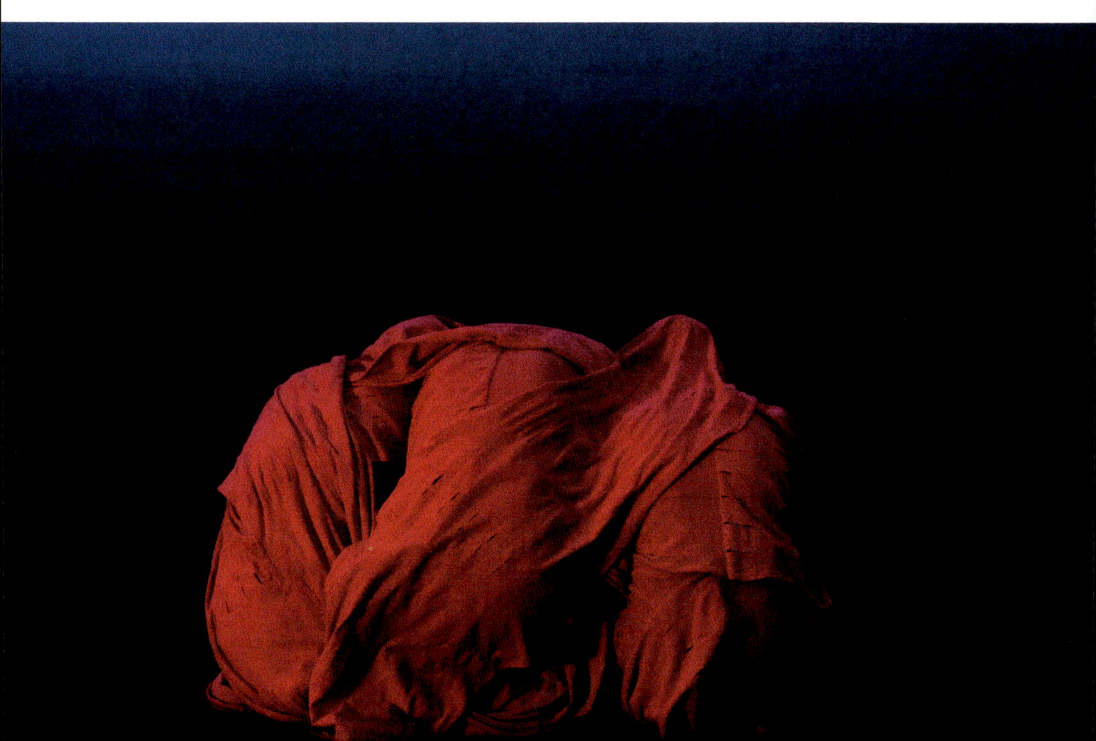

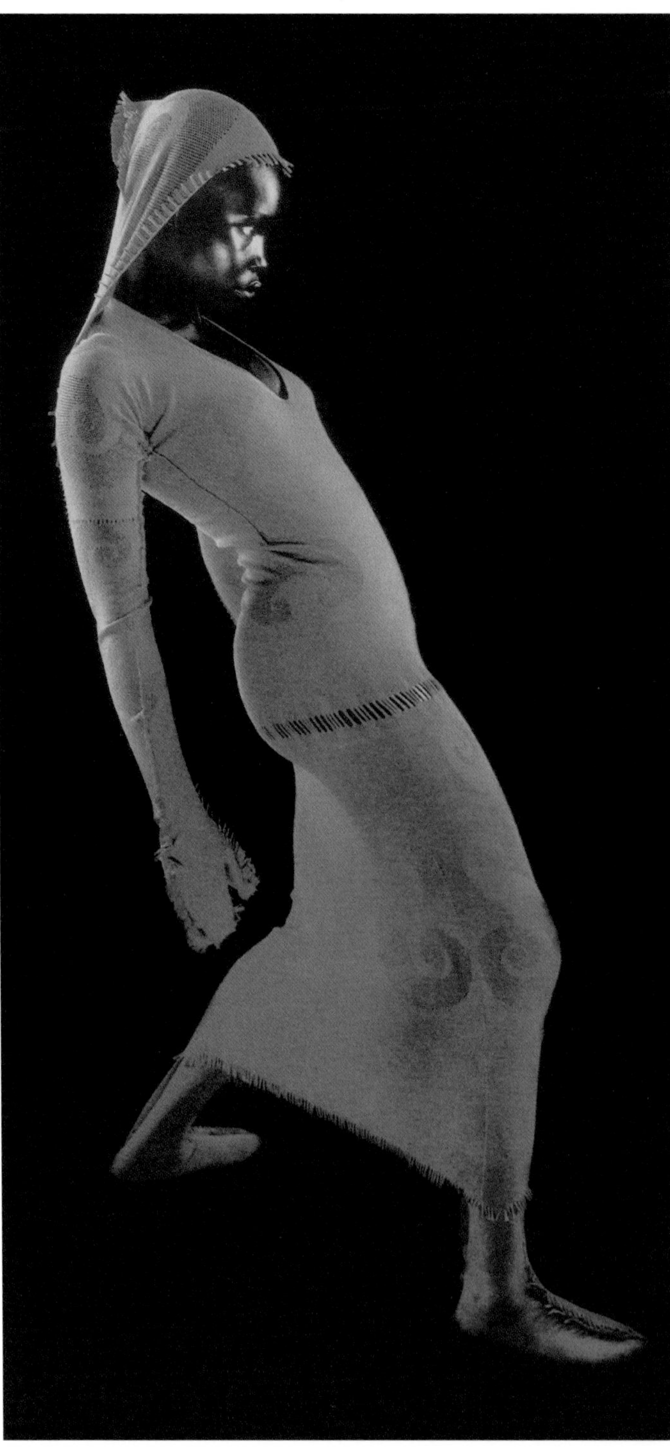

A-POC Queen
From the April 17, 1999 edition of *Independent Magazine* (UK). In addition to the cover, there was a 10-page story titled "Cutting Edge Exclusive: Issey Miyake."
Photography: Sandro Sodano

Following spread: **A-POC Queen**
Arms up is the *Queen*; arms down, the *King*. This was a further evolution of *Just Before* shown the previous year. Multiple components were knit into a single four-meter-long tube: shirt, skirt, underwear, socks, hat, bag, and gloves. The skirt could be shortened by simply cutting across the bottom – the fabric would not unravel. It was hailed as the birth of a new piece of cloth, knit from a single thread and fit for the 21st century, clothing in which the wearer participated in the final step: customization.
1998 design/Spring-Summer 1999 Collection
Animation: Pascal Roulin

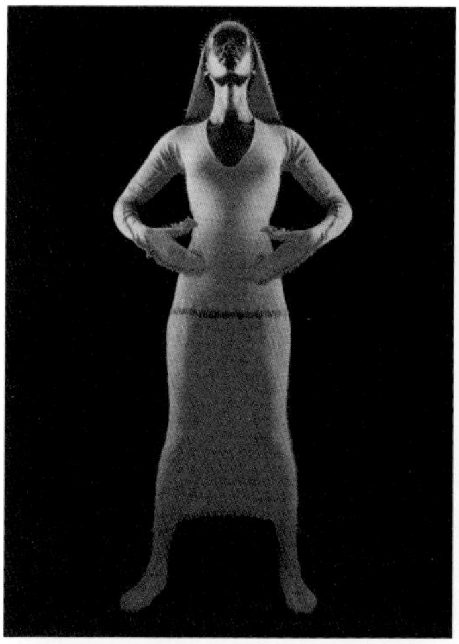

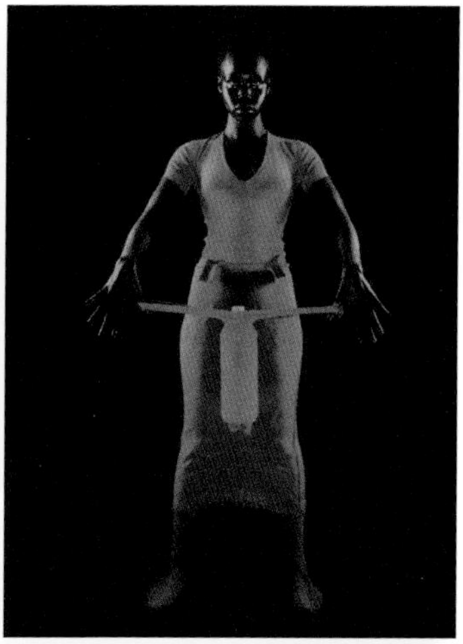

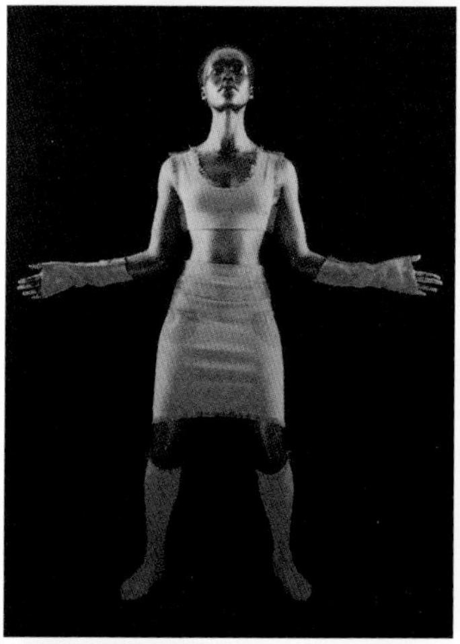

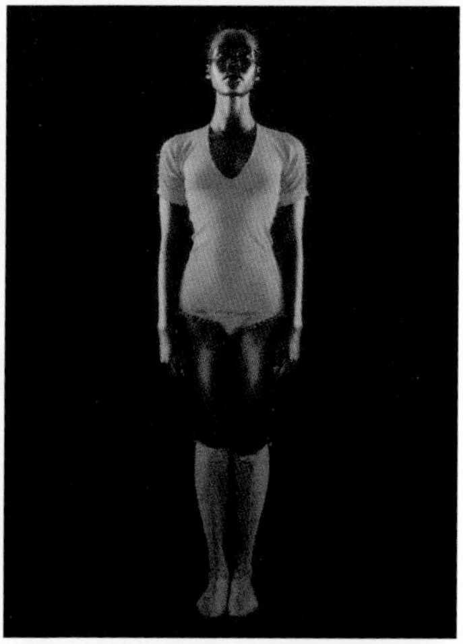

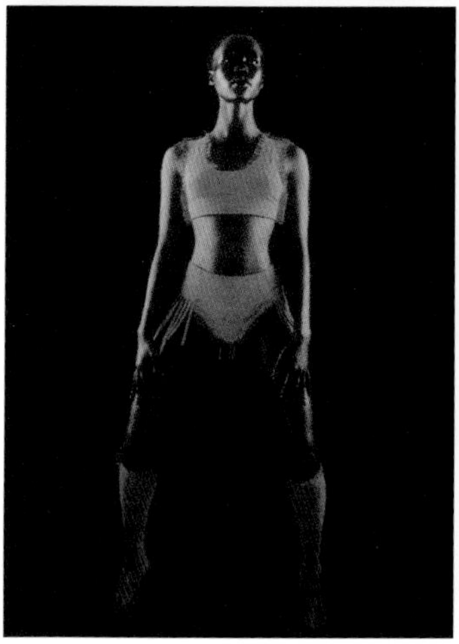

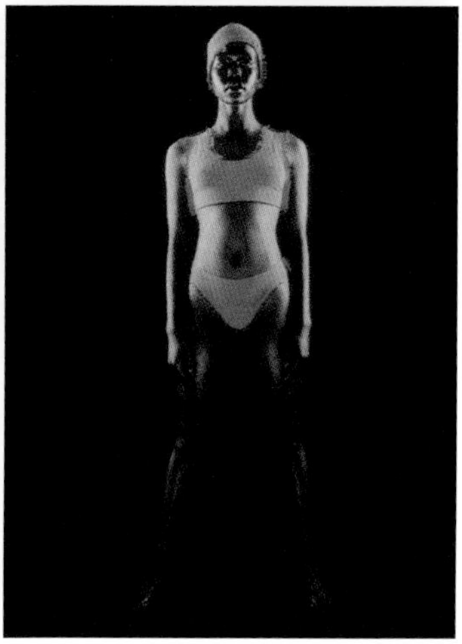

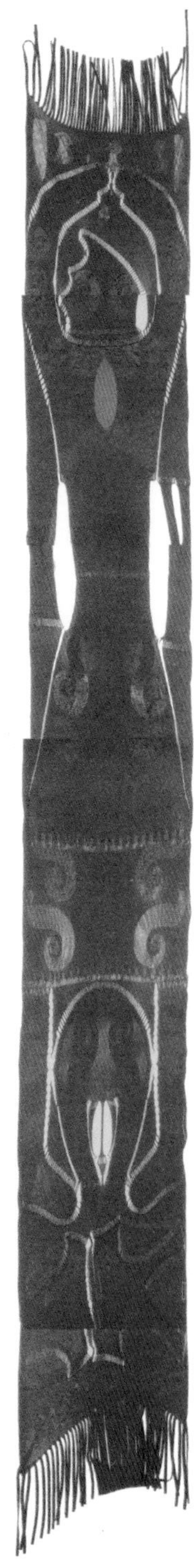

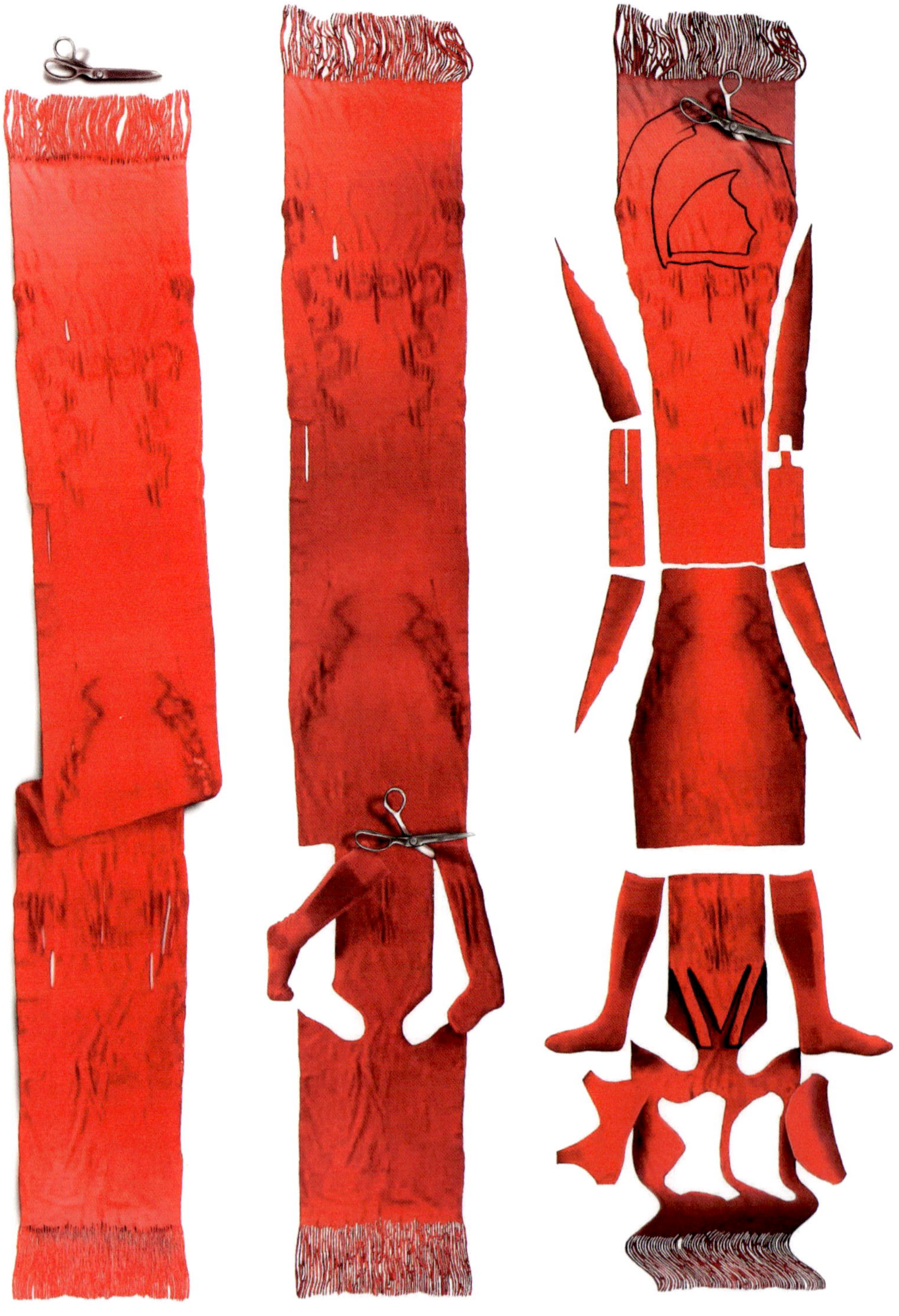

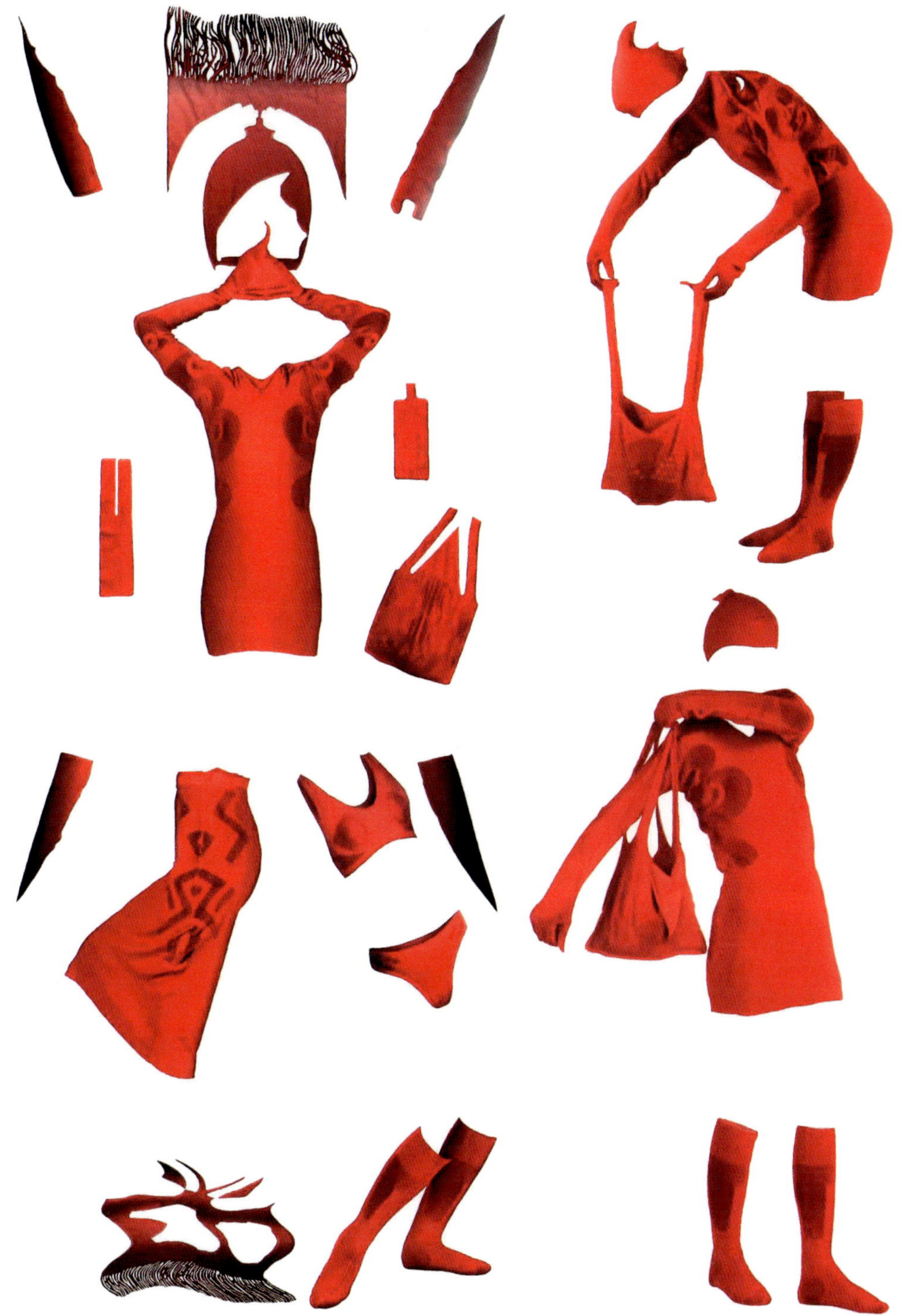

PLEATS PLEASE ISSEY MIYAKE
Guest Artist Series No. 3 Tim Hawkinson

During the 1990s, Tim Hawkinson emerged at the forefront of the American West Coast art scene. His work often makes use of ordinary materials as he explores the contemporary interest in self-expression and the depiction of the human body. Miyake's collaboration with Hawkinson was an attempt to join the two creators' views about the body and mind using clothing as their canvas.

From left: Hawkinson's *Bathtub Generated Contour Lace*, created in 1995, was used as the print for a jumpsuit and dress. *Eye Globe*, created in 1992, had toy eyeballs embedded in a globe, and was used as the print for a jumpsuit.

Pamphlet photography: Yasuaki Yoshinaga; design: Gwenael Nicolas

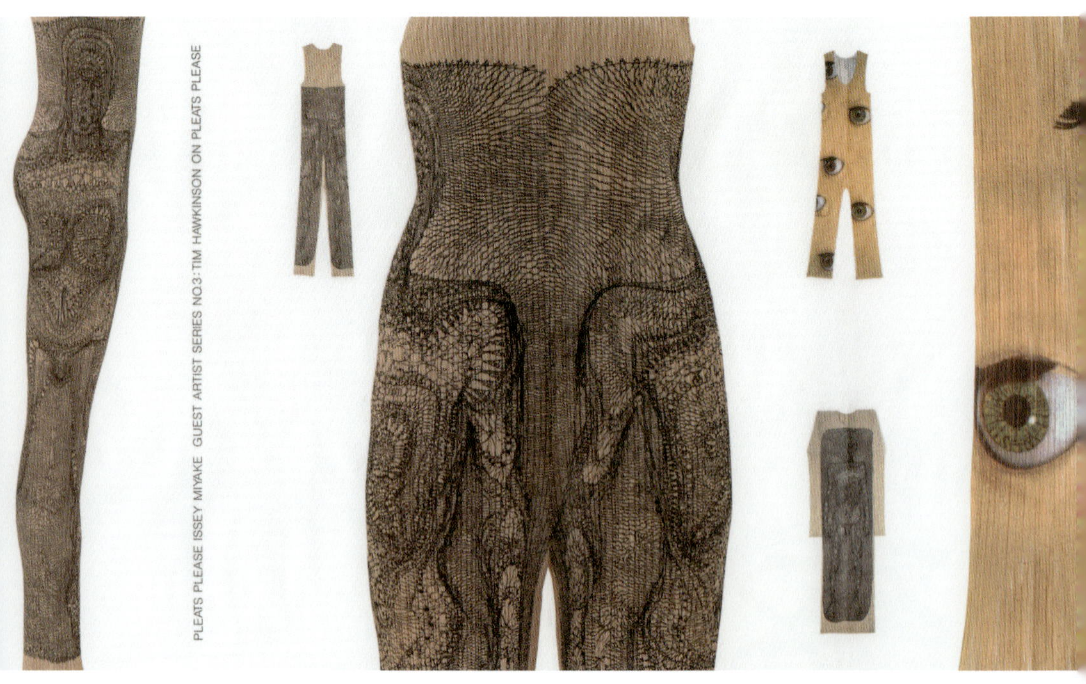

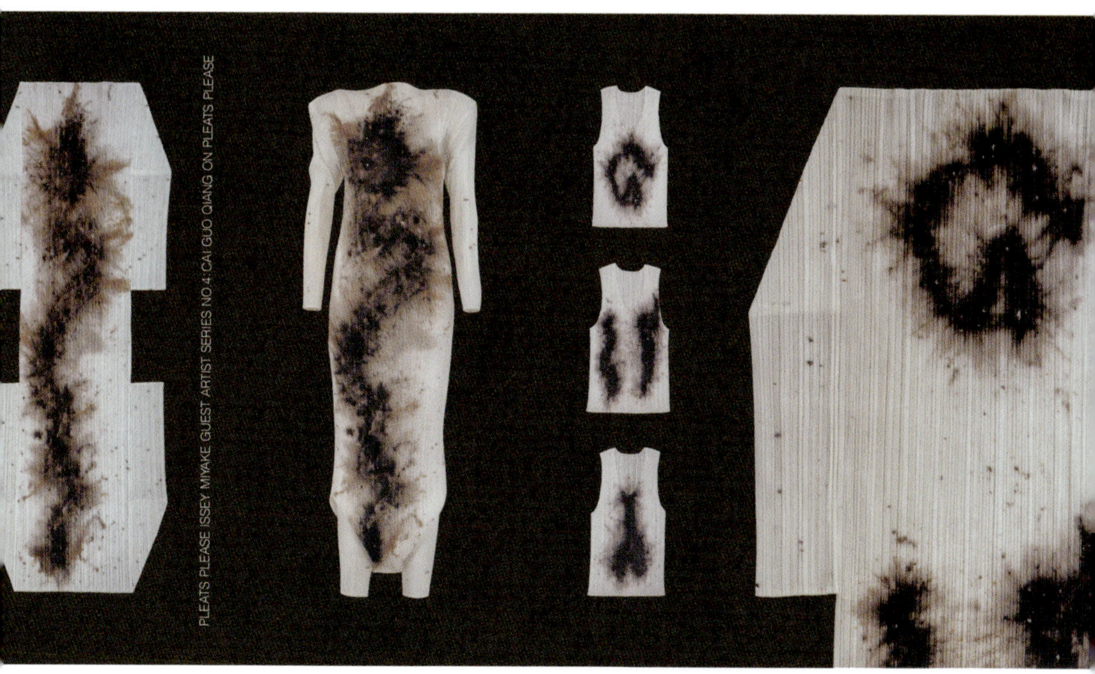

PLEATS PLEASE ISSEY MIYAKE
Guest Artist Series No. 4 Cai Guo-Qiang
Cai Guo-Qiang is an artist born in Fujian, China, who tries to "use my own culture as a starting point to achieve universality." For this work he sprinkled gunpowder, which originated in China, in patterns over the clothing. When ignited, it exploded, creating an abstract image on the fabric of the dragon, a symbol of life.
A jumpsuit, both flat and worn, and tops with three different print patterns: all of them used the burn marks on the clothes as patterns for the final print.
Pamphlet photography: Yasuaki Yoshinaga; design: Gwenael Nicolas

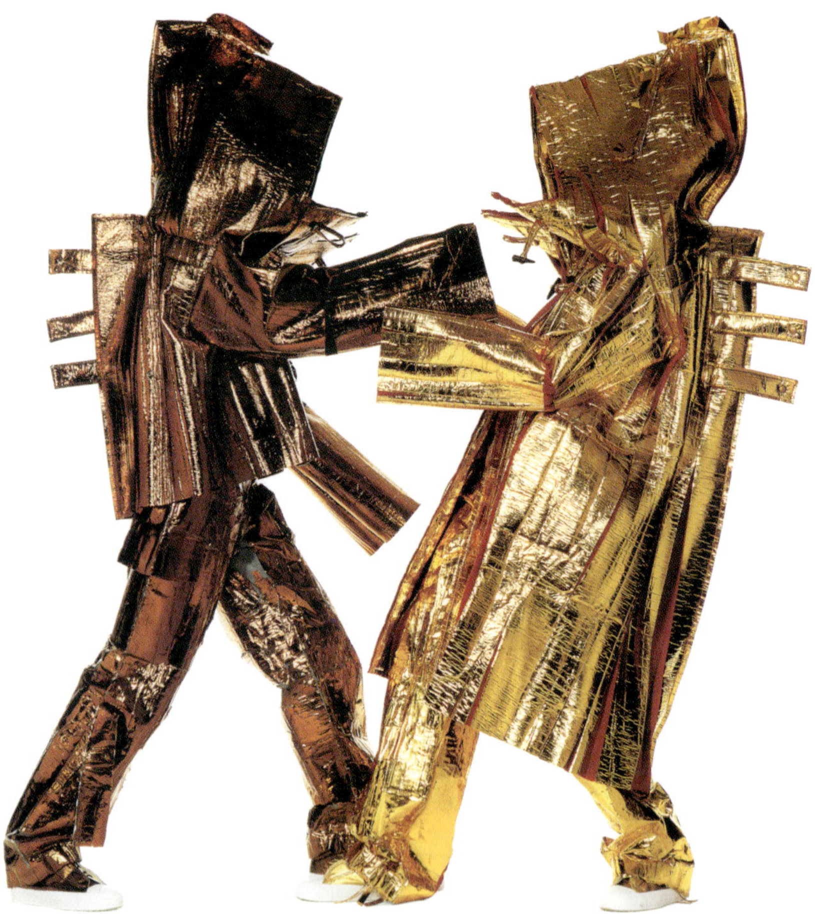
13 octobre 1998 - 17 janvier 1999
ISSEY MIYAKE
Making Things
Fondation Cartier pour l'art contemporain
261 boulevard Raspail 75014 Paris tél 01 42 18 56 50   site Internet : www.fondation.cartier.fr
La Fondation Cartier pour l'art contemporain est ouverte tous les jours, sauf le lundi, de 12h à 20h
Les Soirées Nomades Les jeudis soir à 20h30 (sauf soirées exceptionnelles) Renseignements et réservations (indispensables) : tél 01 42 18 56 72
L'exposition ISSEY MIYAKE Making Things est organisée par la Fondation Cartier pour l'art contemporain, placée sous l'égide de la Fondation de France, et par la Société Cartier.
Photographie © Irving Penn / Conception graphique : Ikko Tanaka

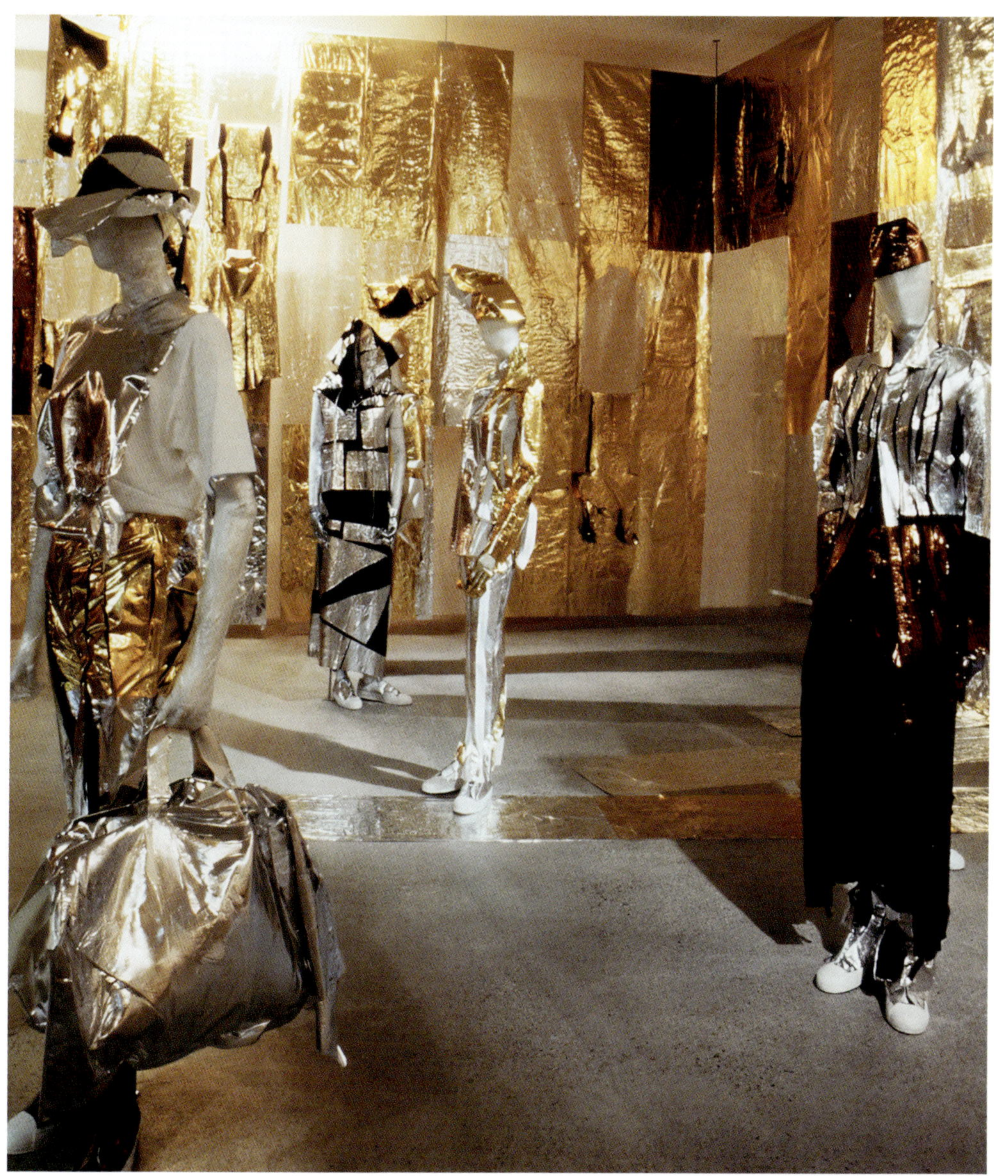

Opposite: ***Issey Miyake Making Things*** poster
Starburst 1998 design/Autumn-Winter 1998 Collection
Photography: Irving Penn; layout and typography:
Ikko Tanaka

Issey Miyake Making Things **exhibition**
Starburst was an idea for reusing old clothing and
accessories. They are given random folds before being
thermobonded with gold, silver, and copper color foil.
When the pressed folds are opened, a new form is
born. For the exhibition, foil sheets were processed to
bring out the silhouettes of shirts, pants, dresses, and
accessories, which were displayed on the wall.
Photography: Yasuaki Yoshinaga

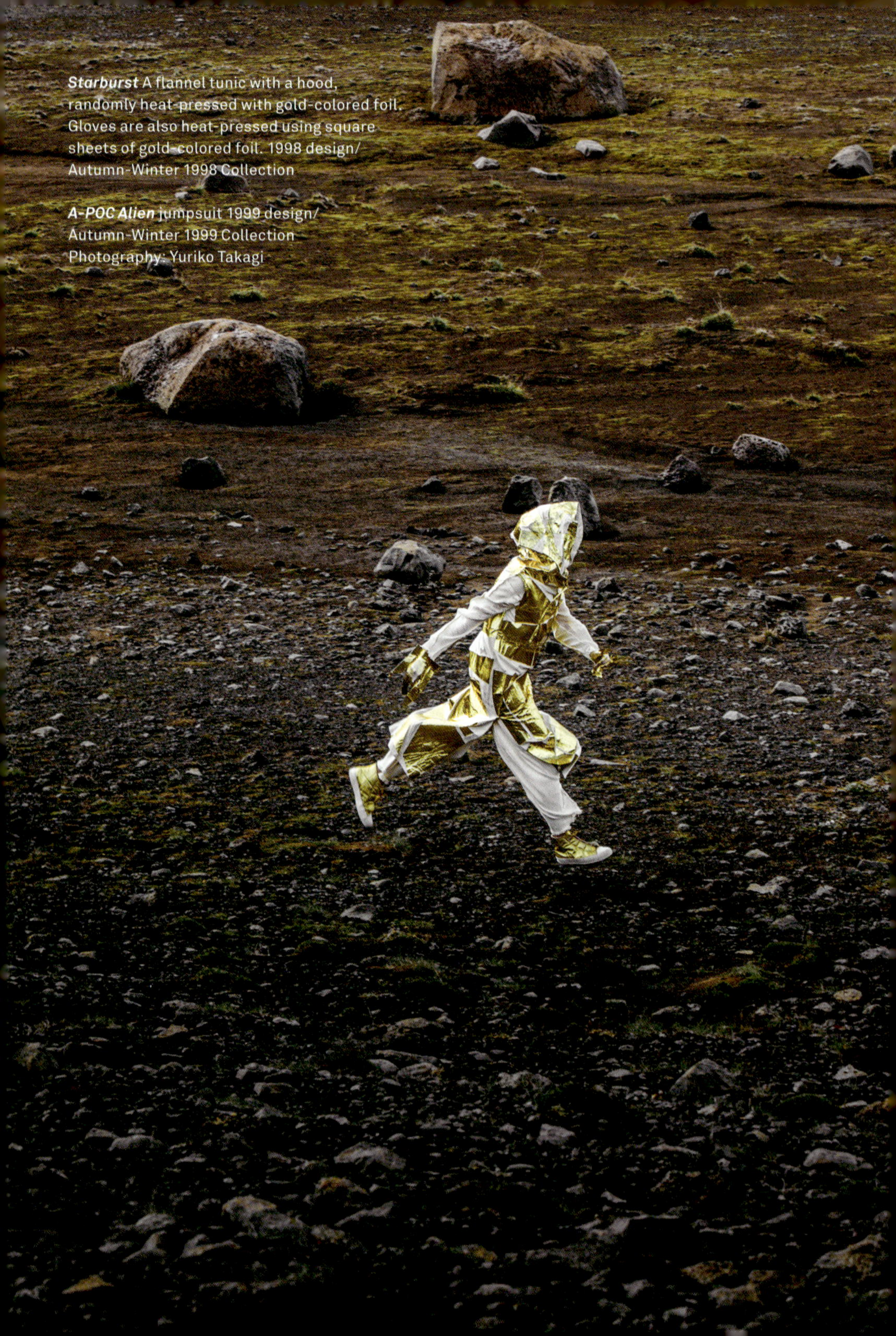

Starburst A flannel tunic with a hood,
randomly heat-pressed with gold-colored foil.
Gloves are also heat-pressed using square
sheets of gold-colored foil. 1998 design/
Autumn-Winter 1998 Collection

A-POC Alien jumpsuit 1999 design/
Autumn-Winter 1999 Collection
Photography: Yuriko Takagi

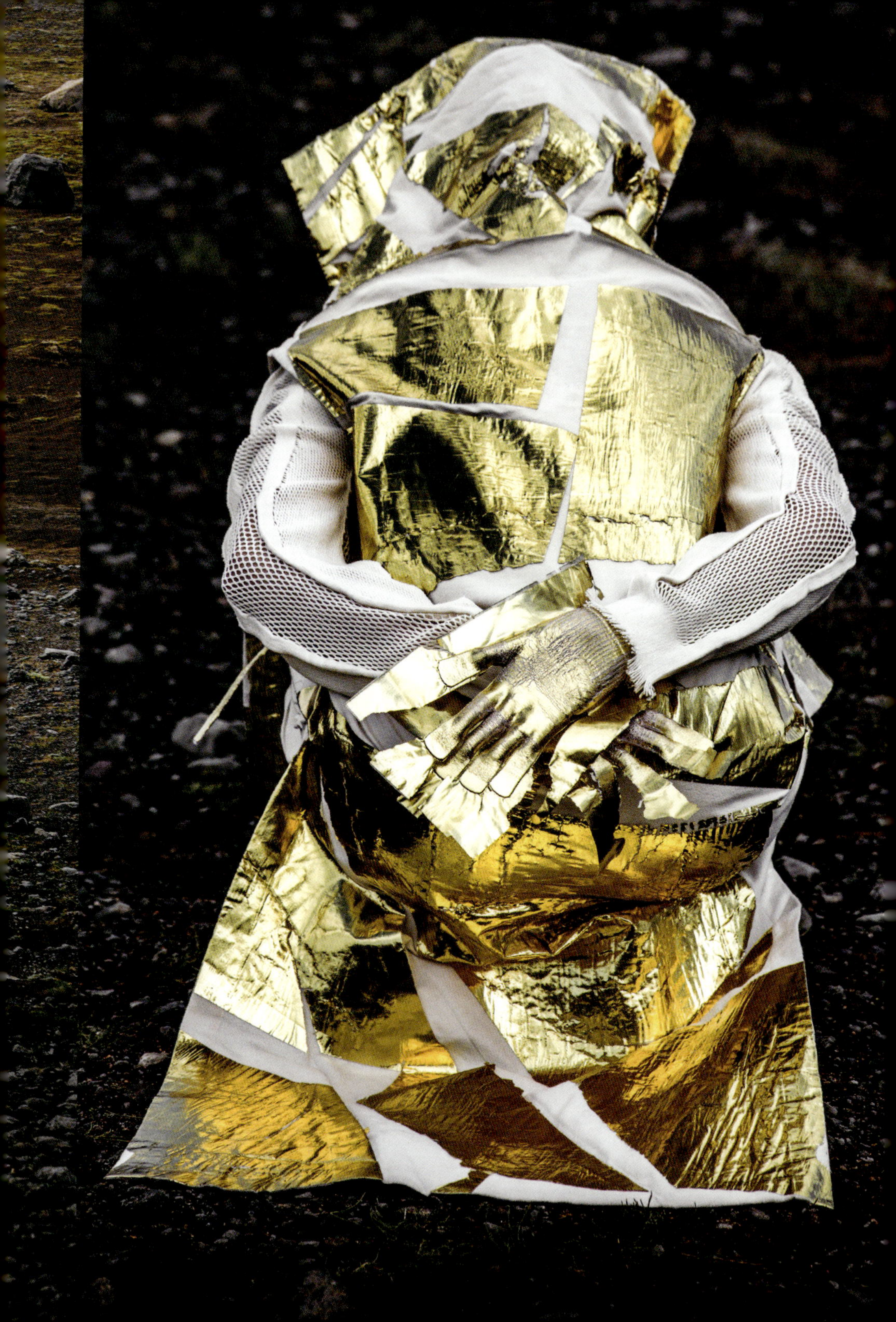

***Issey Miyake Making Things* exhibition**:
installation view of "Laboratory"
A video explained the complete process used to cre-
ate five kinds of clothing, showing the original shape
before the process and the finished design.
Projected onto the floor in front is the process of the
Prism Collage coat (Autumn-Winter 1997 Collection).
Photography: Yasuaki Yoshinaga

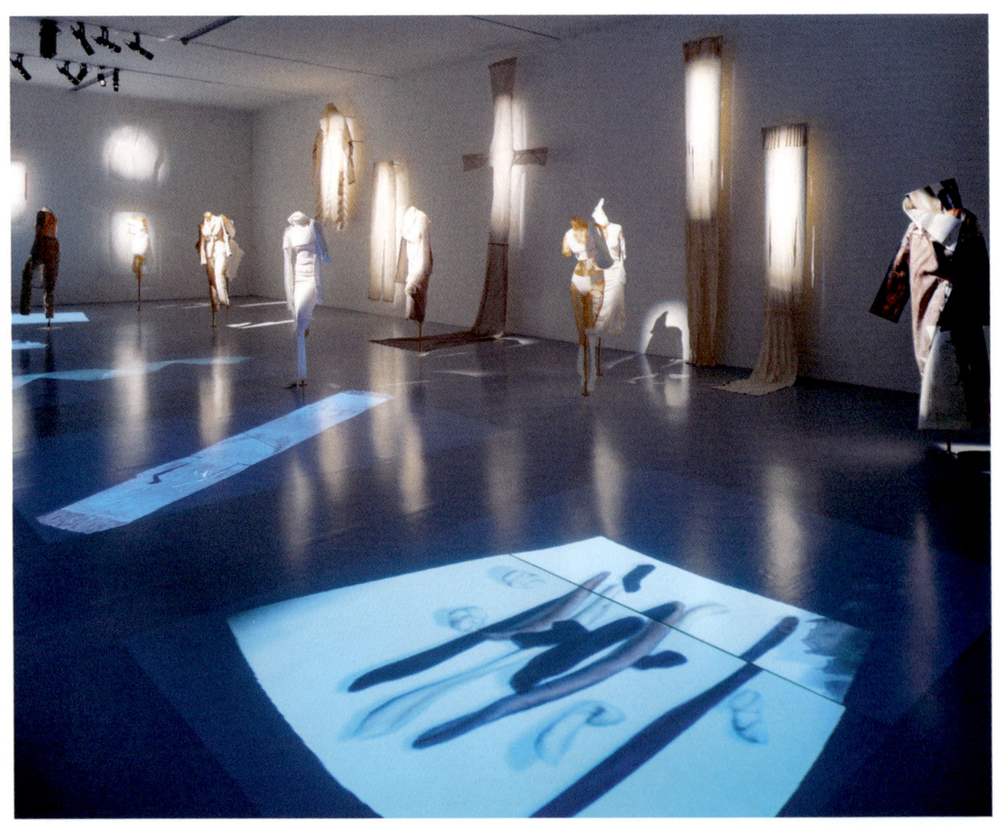

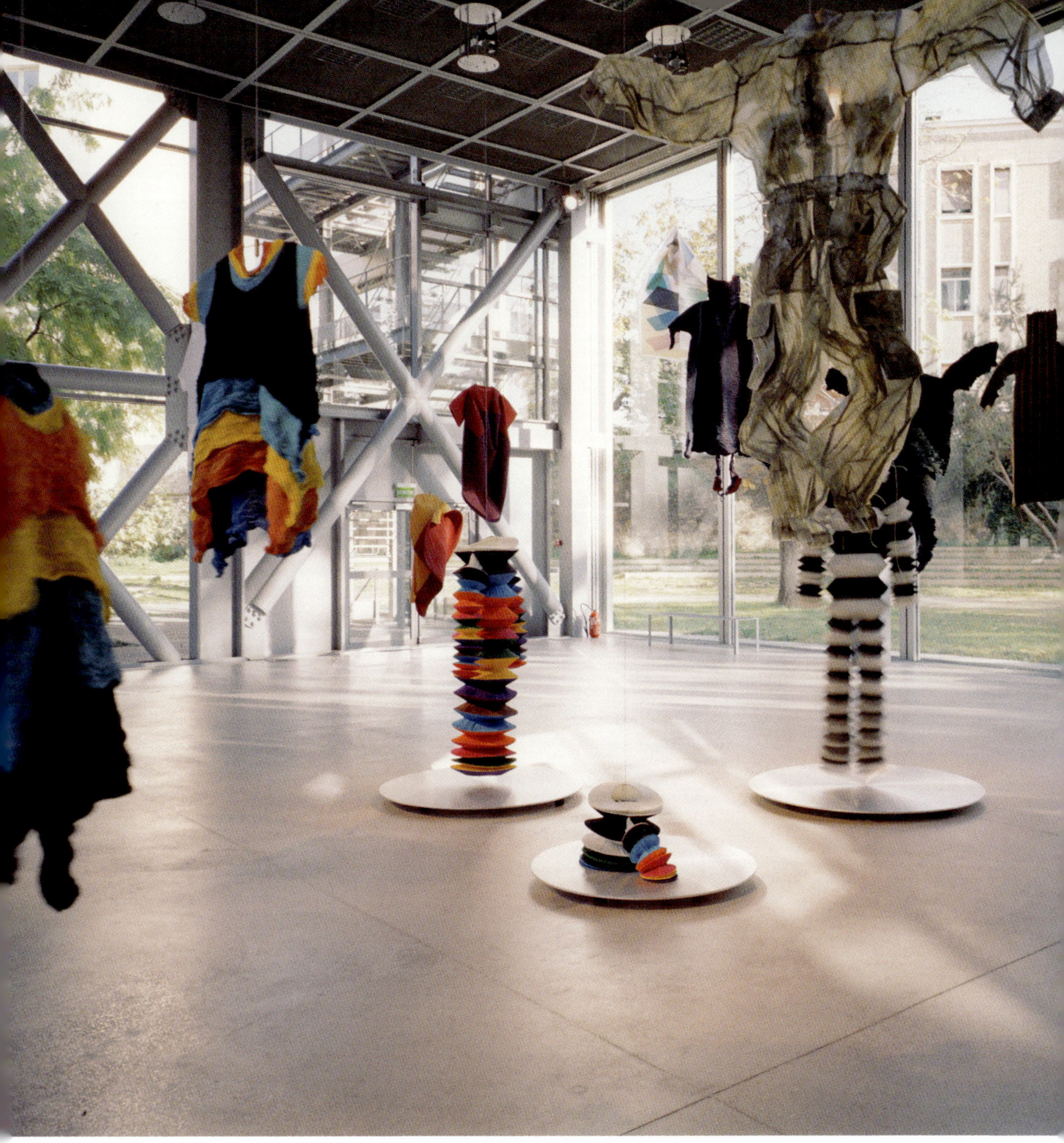

Issey Miyake Making Things exhibition:
installation view of "Jumping"
Exhibited various pleats produced from 1988 to 1998.
The clothing moves up and down by computer control.
The three pieces front right are from *Flying Saucer*,
a saucer-shaped piece of clothing that expands and
contracts up and down (1993 design/Spring-Summer
1994 Collection). The two pieces front left are from
Bouncing Dress (1992 design/Spring-Summer 1993
Collection).
Photography: Yasuaki Yoshinaga

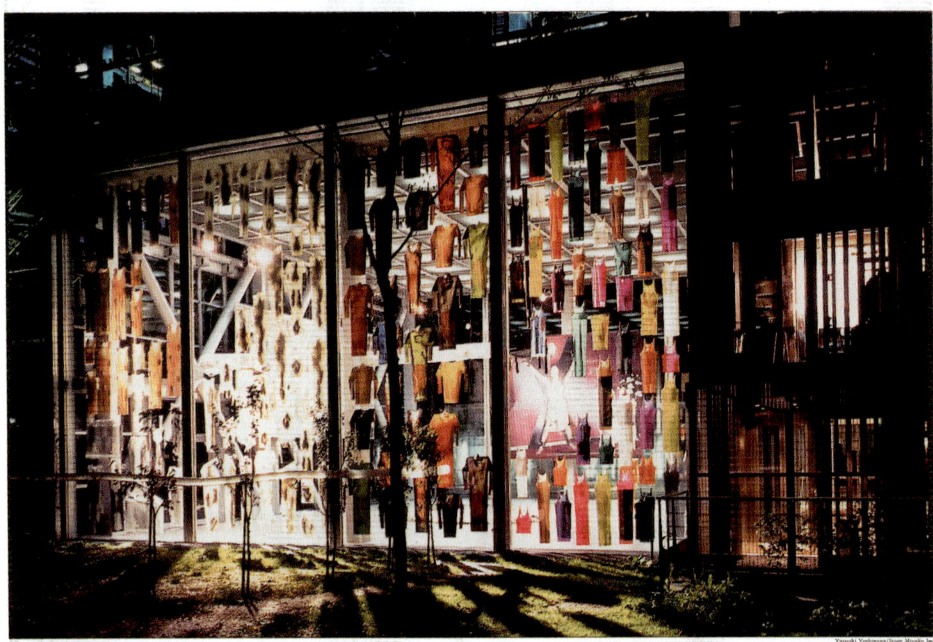

Continued on Page 37

The New York Times, December 27, 1998

"Easy to Pack, Harder to Understand"

Text: Herbert Muschamp

ISSEY MIYAKE is easy to pack. This is often the first thing a smart woman will tell you when you ask her why she wears Miyake's clothes. You can roll his dresses into a ball, they take up practically no room in your luggage, they weigh almost nothing, and when you arrive at your destination you just unroll and wear them. You can brown bag it around the world. In "Issey Miyake: Making Things," a show of the last 10 years of the Japanese designer's work now on view at the Cartier Foundation for Contemporary Art in Paris, Miyake stages a witty play on the ease of traveling with his clothes…"Making Things" extends an invitation to unpack Miyake. Why is Issey Miyake – yet again – the subject of a major show in an art museum? Why are his clothes preferred by so many prominent figures in the arts? Why was he the first fashion designer to be featured on the cover of *Artforum* magazine? Why is Miyake so often singled out as a fashion designer whose work somehow lies above or beyond fashion?

It is often said that Miyake is creating the fashion of the future, or that his work is timeless. These descrip-

Easy to Pack, Harder to Fathom

Continued From Page 1

burst, Miyake's name for this series, is his precious version of environmentally sustainable fashion: the clothes encased within the foil have been recycled.

Other production techniques are demonstrated with slide projections on the floor. Here we see what are, in effect, blueprints for the costumes hanging above: two-dimensional images of cloth cut into bold geometric shapes, awaiting assembly and the application of compression, twisting, folding, shrinking, and other methods that give the completed outfit texture and volume. These diagrammatic pools of cool blue light help explain the appeal Miyake's work holds for architects.

To understand the figure, it helps to appreciate the ground. In an essay called "Fashions in Ballet," published 20 years ago in The New Yorker, the dance critic Arlene Croce noted with disapproval the apparent lack of any rationale behind the Who's In, Who's Out lists published by W and other fashion magazines. "Ins and outs are a good game when the choices are guided by some underlying principle that we can guess at," Croce wrote, "but the lists that W puts together appear to be packs of names selected at random, as if it would be more amusing to have no underlying principle."

To Croce, this abdication of taste was a symptom of exhaustion following the cultural upheavals of the 1960's. But for some thinkers who came of age then, the upheavals of that decade were themselves a symptom of much deeper cultural stresses. To

A 10-year retrospective at the Cartier Foundation in Paris shows off one of the fashion designer's most important tools: the pleat.

the French philosophers Gilles Deleuze and Felix Guattari, for example, the uprisings were a product of advanced capitalism and its discontents.

Their argument might go like this. The market system runs on the excitation of consumer desire. When the system is operating properly, libidinous energies are constantly drawn into the public sphere and channeled into a limitless array of attractions: this laundry detergent or that movie star, this politician or that desktop computer, this TV show or that brand of cat food. The result is a culture of increasing dissociation, a society of personalities that are forever splitting into fractured identities, ideologies and tastes, unbound by any underlying principle that might jeopardize potential market shares.

For Deleuze and Guattari, schizophrenia, with its attendant fugue and dissociative states, is not a simple pathology to be cured by chemical or psychiatric means. It is the natural condition of late capitalist society. Free enterprise induces a free-associational way of life.

I model, therefore I am. It is a sweet coincidence that theory and fashion have converged on Paris. And, to their detractors, at least, philosophers like Deleuze and Guattari are guilty of fashionable thinking: superficial, sensationalistic, without evident rigor, their theory has been attacked as little more than a motley get-up of Nietzsche, Marx, Freud, Lacan and R. D. Laing. But you don't have to buy the theory to see that fashion is a good illustration of it. As Croce observed 20 years ago, no art form has so glorified the random and meaningless. Nor has any consumer product so

lation of desire.

A "fashion week," in Paris, New York or Milan, is a festival of desire overload, a vaudeville of voyeurism and exhibitionism with throbbing musical background. Sex sells. But the splitting evoked in the observer's mind by fashion's fleeting erotic imagery may be more powerful than the imagery itself. Is this what Isaac Mizrahi had in mind when he opened a fashion show a few years back with an excerpt from Bernard Hermann's screeching music for the shower scene in "Psycho"?

There seem to be fashions in multiple-personality disorders as well as colors and silhouettes. Some figures on the national stage, from politicians to movie stars, invite us to regard the self not as an integrated unit, but as a jumble of memories, fantasies, desires, images, that pop up on the national screen like a net surfer's ride through a cybersettlement of chat rooms. With such fractured figures ruling the earth's political life, it's no wonder that fashion has gained inordinate stature in the cultural scheme of things.

NOW for the figure. If Miyake has attained a position above and beyond fashion, that may be largely because he has given differentiation an architectural shape. Unity, duality, multiplicity: Miyake works with the phenomenon of splitting as if it were a basic law of life, not just a contemporary cultural affliction. He has refined the madness of fashion into a contemplative, creative method, almost a form of meditation on the multiple self.

Miyake's wheel of black jersey dresses is a good illustration of this. Viewed from the side, the display begins with the spoke, a point of no dimension. The tube of fabric spirals around the spoke in the form of a line: one dimension. Then the flattened tube is drawn out into a train that reads as a plane: two dimensions. The train rises up into a black dress that conforms to a mannequin's human contours: three dimensions. Then the dress is multiplied in a sequence that evokes the fourth dimension of time.

In the Starburst collection, the splitting of the foil produces a binary tension between the humble (the recycled clothes) and the exalted (silver and gold). Colombe, a serape-like dress of white vinyl, derives its manifold shapes from a series of interplays between point and plane. The garment — a tunic for ancient Greeks from outer space — is made from a white sheet of plastic studded with round metal fasteners. The sheet drapes into different folds depending on what points are snapped together.

For the past decade, Miyake's primary mode of differentiation has been the pleat. Permanent folds that expand a plane of cloth into volumetric space, pleating is the designer's basic binary move, the zig that depends upon the žag. At the Cartier Foundation, the style is represented by examples from Pleats Please a series of chemises, shirts, and jumpsuits that Miyake has issued since 1991, periodically in collaboration with other artists.

For one edition, Miyake printed the cloth with photographs of work by Cai Guo-Quiang, a shamanistic Japanese artist who sets trails of gunpowder ablaze on pieces of fabric. The artist's singed gray and brown images create a dingy, free-form counterpoint to Miyake's crisp, regular pleats. Another edition of dresses features a reproduction of an Ingres nude, "The Source," part of a composite work created by Yasumasa Morimura. The printed image, borrowing Ingres's spatial perspective, supplies the illusion of three dimensions, while the wearer's body dissolves the illusion into three-dimensional space.

Miyake intends the Cartier Foundation show to be seen as a collaboration, too. He has conceived the installation as an exchange between his clothes and Nouvel's building. The mobile dresses echo the elevators that rocket up and down the building's exterior. The clothes hanging inside the ground-floor windows offer both a comple-

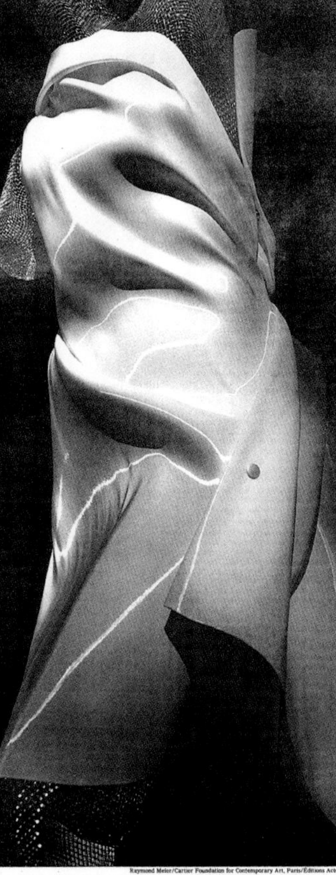

Raymond Meier/Cartier Foundation for Contemporary Art, Paris/Editions Actes

Miyake's Colombe dress is made of a white sheet of plastic with metal fasteners.

Nouvel's exposed steel structure draws out Miyake's architectonic approach. The division between lower and upper galleries spatializes the relationship between creative process and finished work, introspection and presentation, the artist's private and public realms.

What makes this an ideal site for Miyake is not just the formal merits of Nouvel's building, but also the background that both designers share. Both men were living in Paris during the uprisings of 1968, and both

whose traditions had been substantially obliterated by nuclear holocaust and foreign occupation. Artists of Miyake's generation started from ground zero. Their work has been shaped as much by Western as by Japanese influence. It embodies a global perspective unique in the world today.

Miyake moved to Paris in 1960 to study, and later worked for Guy Laroche and Givenchy. After a year in New York, where he was design assistant to Geoffrey Beene, he returned to Tokyo in 1970 and founded the Miyake Design Studio. Today, the studio is based in a building of silky concrete designed by Yoshio Tanaguchi, architect of the new expansion of the Museum of Modern Art in New York. Miyake's outlook has remained global. He regularly shows in Paris, and divides his time between Tokyo and the fashion capital, where he lives in a stunningly spare flat overlooking the Eiffel Tower.

In Japanese Buddhism there is a concept called two but not two. East and West is a good example of it. These are relative terms for two sides of the same planet. Or consider the zig and zag of one pleat. Two but not two represents a holistic way of regarding dualisms that, in the modern West, have been overdefined in terms of the differences between them. We set great store, for instance, on the difference between art and design, but traditionally the distinction has meant little to the Japanese. Miyake has sought to bypass dualism by emphasizing the nature of his craft. He describes himself not as a fashion designer but as a maker of clothes.

Deleuze and Guattari proposed a nomadic philosophy for coping with the schizoid state of advanced capitalist culture. People should rove freely among world views, political perspectives, states of mind, without trying to build any one of them into a rigid hierarchical system. I can't see that this philosophy differs from what writers have practiced for centuries. For that matter, who isn't nomadic in this sense?

But Miyake (easy to pack) does design the fanciest clothes a nomadic philosopher could possibly wear. Even at rest, many of them suggest flux: tents, flying saucers, fisherman jackets, Bedouin burnooses. All of them embrace the body as a metaphor for self-reliance. He is, perhaps, to be regarded as a visual philosopher of modern movement, an architect of traveling light.

MIYAKE'S particular subject is the woman's body, viewed at a historical moment when the social identity of women is a highly mobile abstraction, an entity moving between acting subject and passive object, often occupying both states at once, to excellent and lively confusion. In the service of that entity, his clothes are worn beneath the skin as well as draped over it. Walking through the Cartier show is like drifting through encampments of social possibility: astronaut, insect, idol, hostess, casualty of war. While Miyake's dress forms are female, the roles are transsexual. Anyone could drape a fragment of self within these wrapped, tied, coiled, singed, scrunched-up, levitating pieces of cloth. Two but not two genders per customer.

Does continuity require rupture? Here is a larger issue framed by "Making Things." Miyake and Nouvel are "two children of Marx and Coca-Cola," as Godard once dubbed those who came of age in the 1960's. But both have helped to reinvigorate the modern tradition that this generation was once eager to toss into history's dustbin.

Nouvel has pushed the glass building envelope and structural expression toward a state of transparency far beyond Miesian precedent. Miyake has pursued a wholly modernist exploration of the formal potential of new materials and methods. He has also revived the connection between Japan and the West that was critical to Frank Lloyd Wright, Walter Gropius and other pioneering modernists. Both designers propose a zigzag history to replace the linear unfolding of time.

Is this how it has ended up, then, 30 years after the events of May 1968? Fashionable frocks in a jeweler's showcase? If so, this is no disgrace. One of the achievements of Miyake's generation was to show that art deals with consciousness, and that consciousness can be revolutionized by a song, a film, a photograph, a hemline, the view from a window. Together, Nouvel and

ciate the links between the cultural and the political spheres. Both came to regard art as a form of social action. Both saw themselves as actors in a drama of rupture, a break with the mid-century's High Modern triumphal moment.

But rupture had become a way of life for Miyake long before 1968. Born in 1938, he belonged to the first generation to come of age after the Second World War. Like Arata Isozaki, Shuro Kuramata and other designers and architects who later attained inter-

---

tions are less than useful. His work is grounded in that stretch of history called the present and draws meaning from fashion's immediate context. "Making Things" presents that context with immense glamour and wit…If Miyake has attained a position above and beyond fashion, that may be largely because he has given differentiation an architectural shape. Unity, duality, multiplicity: Miyake works with the phenomenon of splitting as if it were a basic law of life, not just a contemporary cultural affliction. He has refined the madness of fashion into a contemplative, creative method, almost a form of meditation on the multiple self. (Excerpt)

Following spread: ***Issey Miyake Making Things exhibition***: installation view of *PLEATS PLEASE ISSEY MIYAKE Guest Artist Series*
No. 1 through 4 in the series are displayed on the windows. On the floor is the Cai Guo-Qiang work created during the opening performance, *Dragon Explosion on Pleats Please Issey Miyake.*
Photography: Yasuaki Yoshinaga

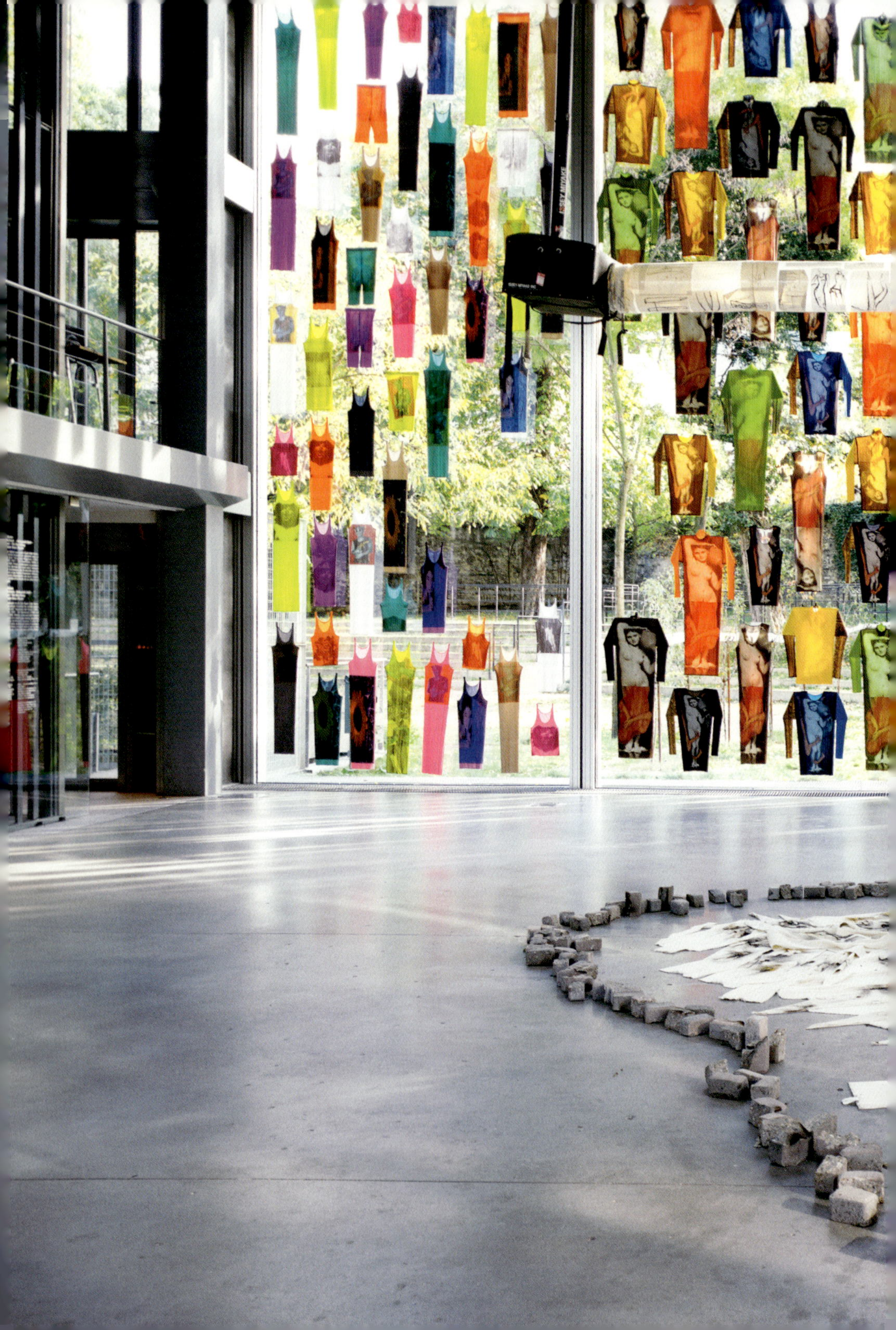

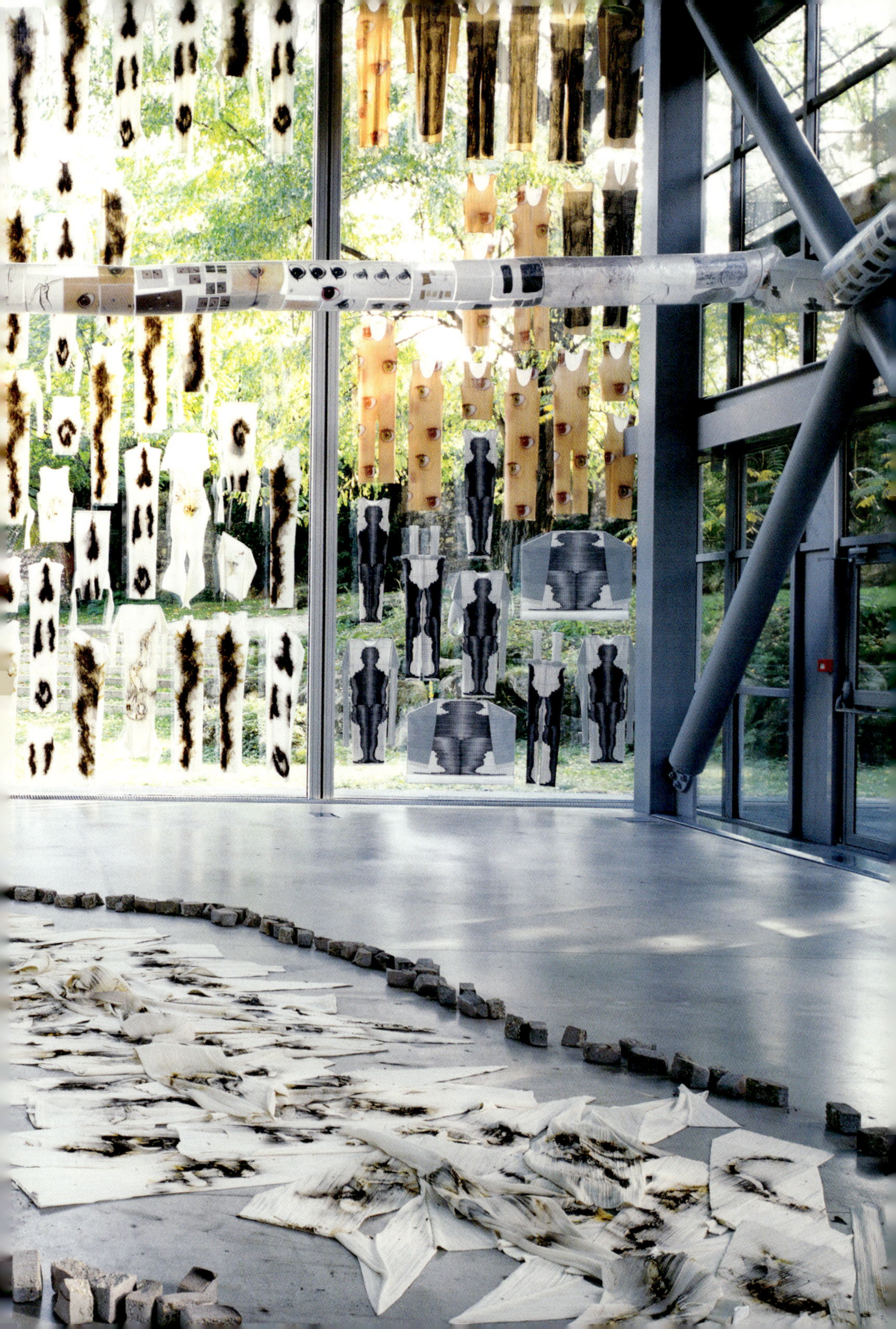

1999

> March: Autumn-Winter 1999 Paris Collection at Salle Charlie Parker. As of 2025, the biannual Paris Collection continues under the direction of Chief Designer Satoshi Kondo
> March: Presented A-POC in a show at Jingumae Studio, Tokyo, together with the Autumn-Winter 1999 Collection
> April: A-POC participated in the Yayoi Kusama performance, *Jeux de Tissu*
> October: First presentation of the A-POC brand in Paris
> October: *Irving Penn Regards the Work of Issey Miyake* (Jonathan Cape, Japanese edition: Kyuryudo Art Publishing)
> November–February 2000: *Issey Miyake Making Things* exhibition in New York
> Selected as one of "the most influential Asians of the 20th century" by the Asia edition of *Time* magazine

Irving Penn Regards the Work of Issey Miyake
Irving Penn photographed the collections twice a year from 1986 to 1998. His collaboration with Issey Miyake, together with photographs previously taken for *Vogue* magazine, were put together in a large-edition photography book. The 112 pieces of clothing were selected by Penn himself and laid out specifically to tell a purely visual story rather than simply listing them in chronological order. The format successfully crystallizes the essence of the collaboration between the two artists, exploring both its tensions and its joys. Mark Holborn, an editor and writer working in New York and London, wrote the essay. To celebrate publication, an exhibition was held at the Ginza Graphic Gallery in Tokyo in December.

Opposite: ***Dots Obsession on A-POC***, 1999
Artist Yayoi Kusama used a white *A-POC King & Queen* as a canvas upon which to paint. Produced at the French embassy to mark the close of the French Year in Japan in 1998.
Photography: Friedemann Hauss;
stylist: Hélène Renault-Kohn

Autumn-Winter 1999 Paris Collection,
March 10, Salle Charlie Parker

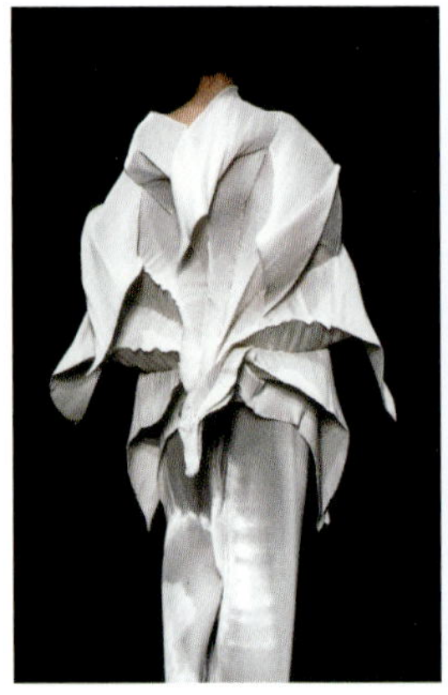
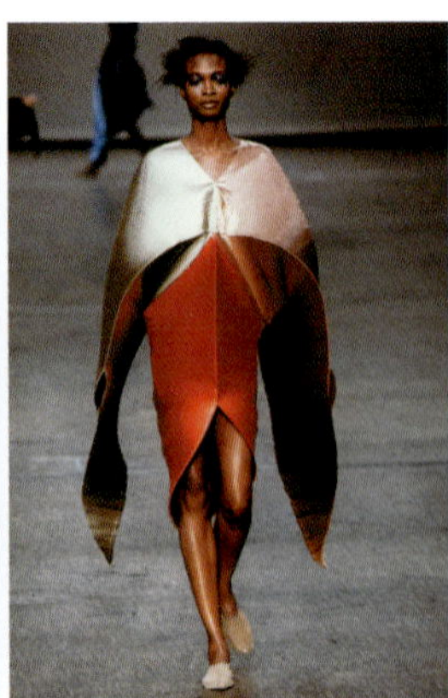
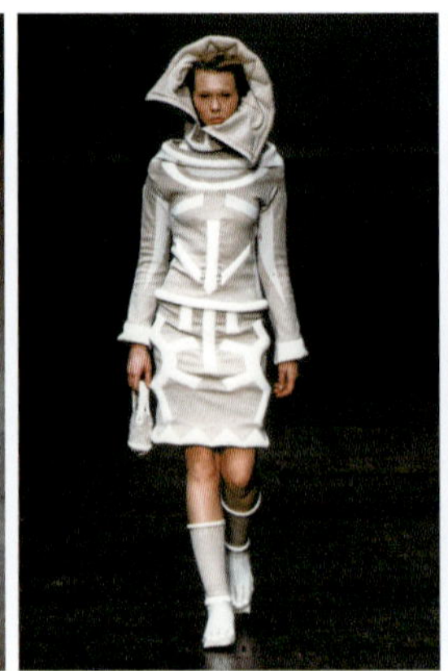
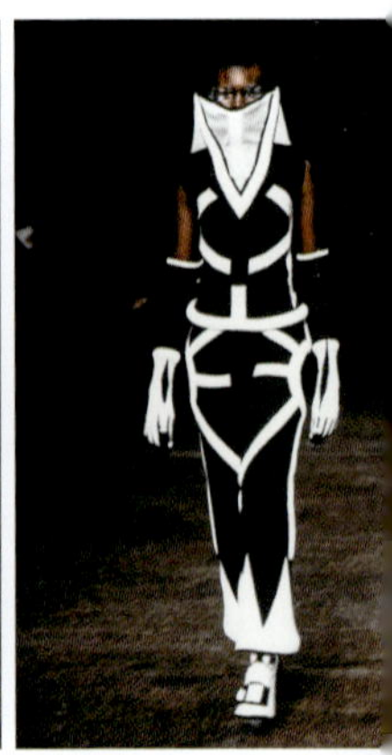

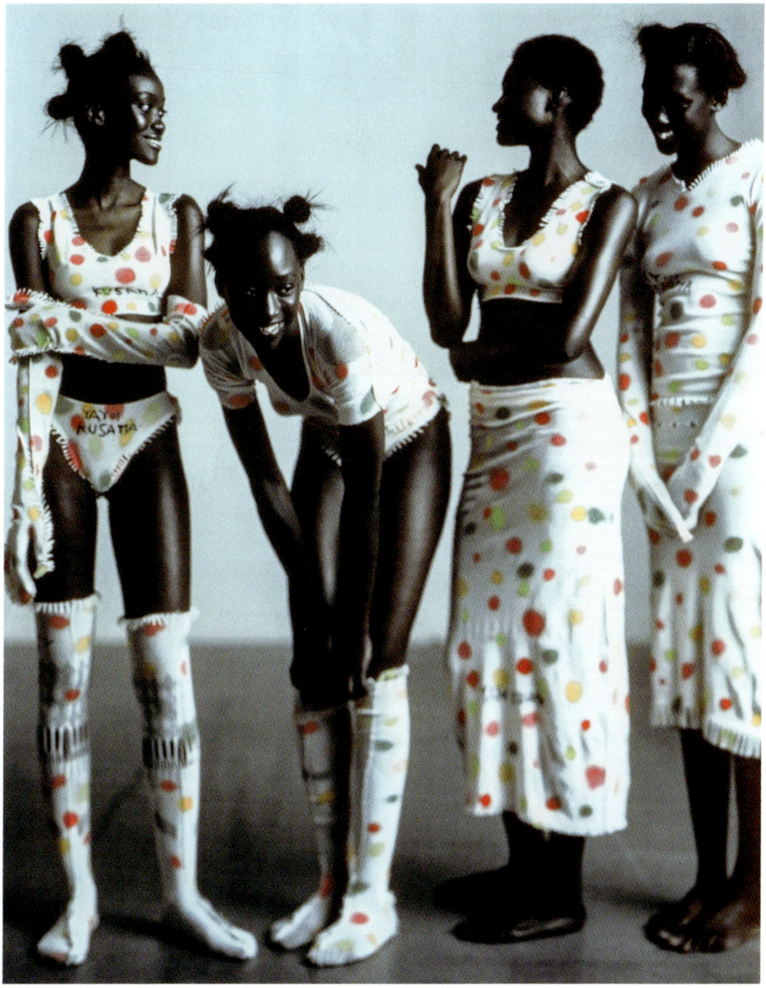

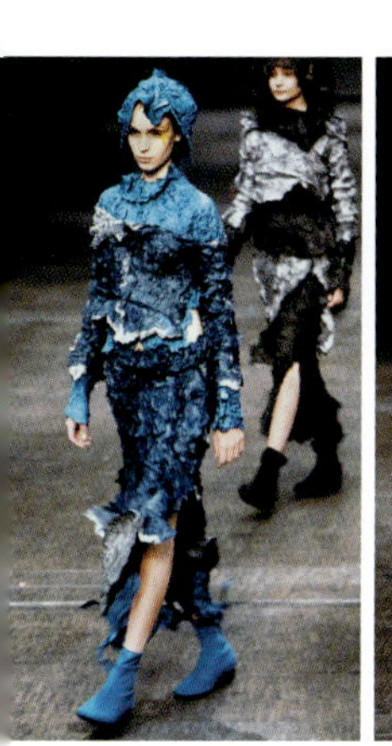
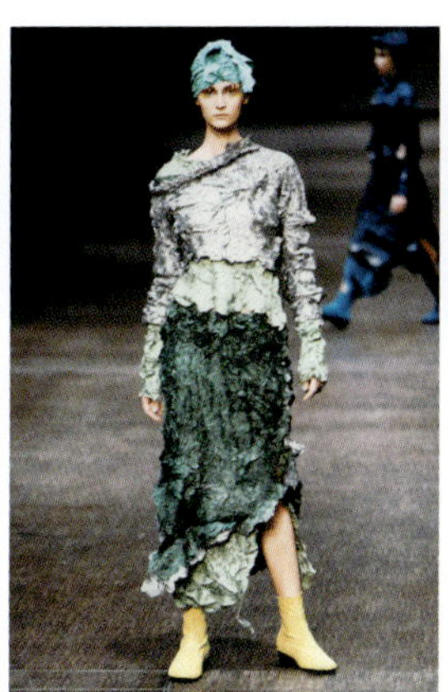
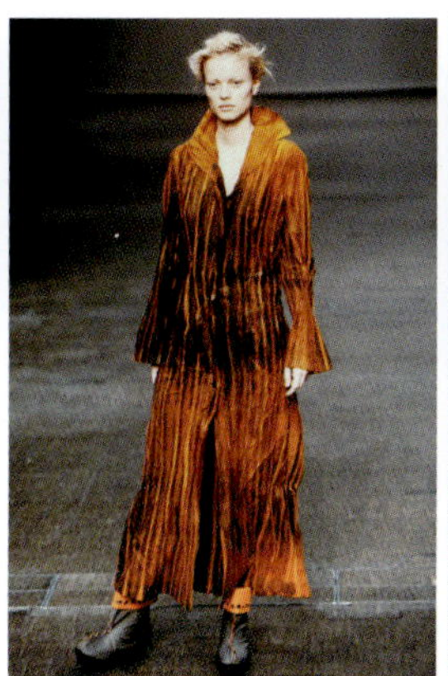
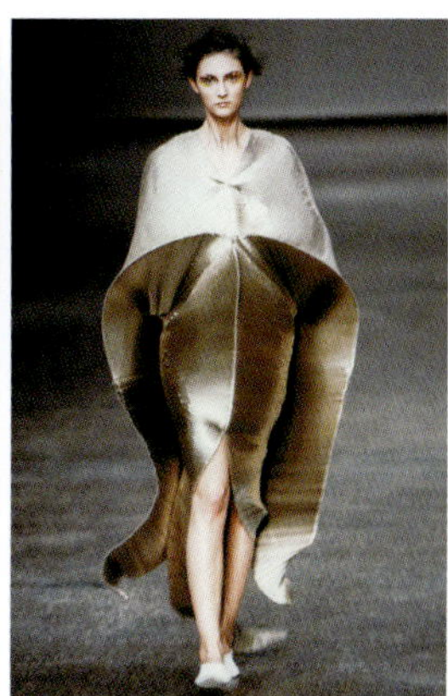

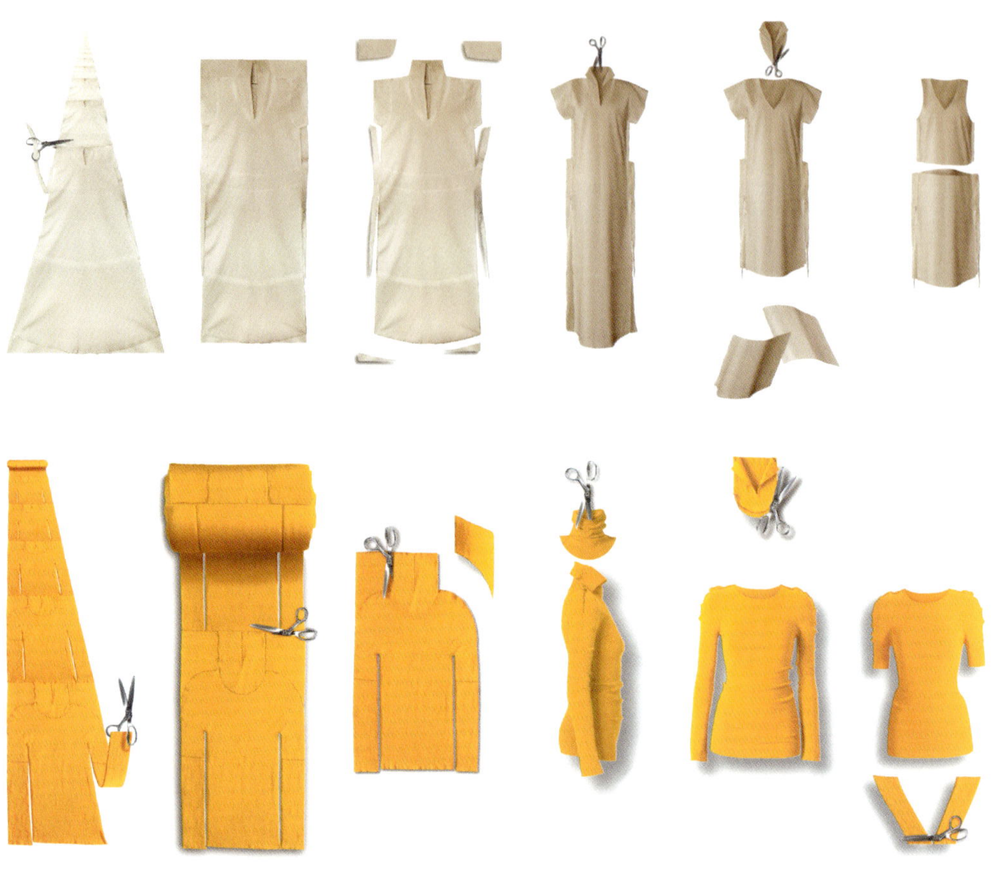

Top: ***A-POC Pain de Mie***
Woven item added at the launch of the A-POC brand.
No sewing is required because the form of the dress
is woven into the tube-shaped fabric. The wearer
simply cuts along the lines with scissors to take out
the finished clothing. Further cutting along lines of
demarcation into the fabric will produce a top and
skirt, and the wearer can cut the length, collar, and
sleeves as desired.
2000 design
Animation: Pascal Roulin

Above: ***A-POC Baguette***
The basic A-POC knit top. By cutting along the lines of
demarcation, also knitted into the fabric, the wearer
can customize both the sleeve length as well as the
shape of the neckline: a turtleneck, jewel neck, or
lapels. As the fabric will not fray, it is possible to cut
the clothes to the desired length.
2000 design
Animation: Pascal Roulin

Opposite: ***A-POC Baguette Flower*** 2000 design
Photography: Friedemann Hauss;
stylist: Hélène Renault-Kohn

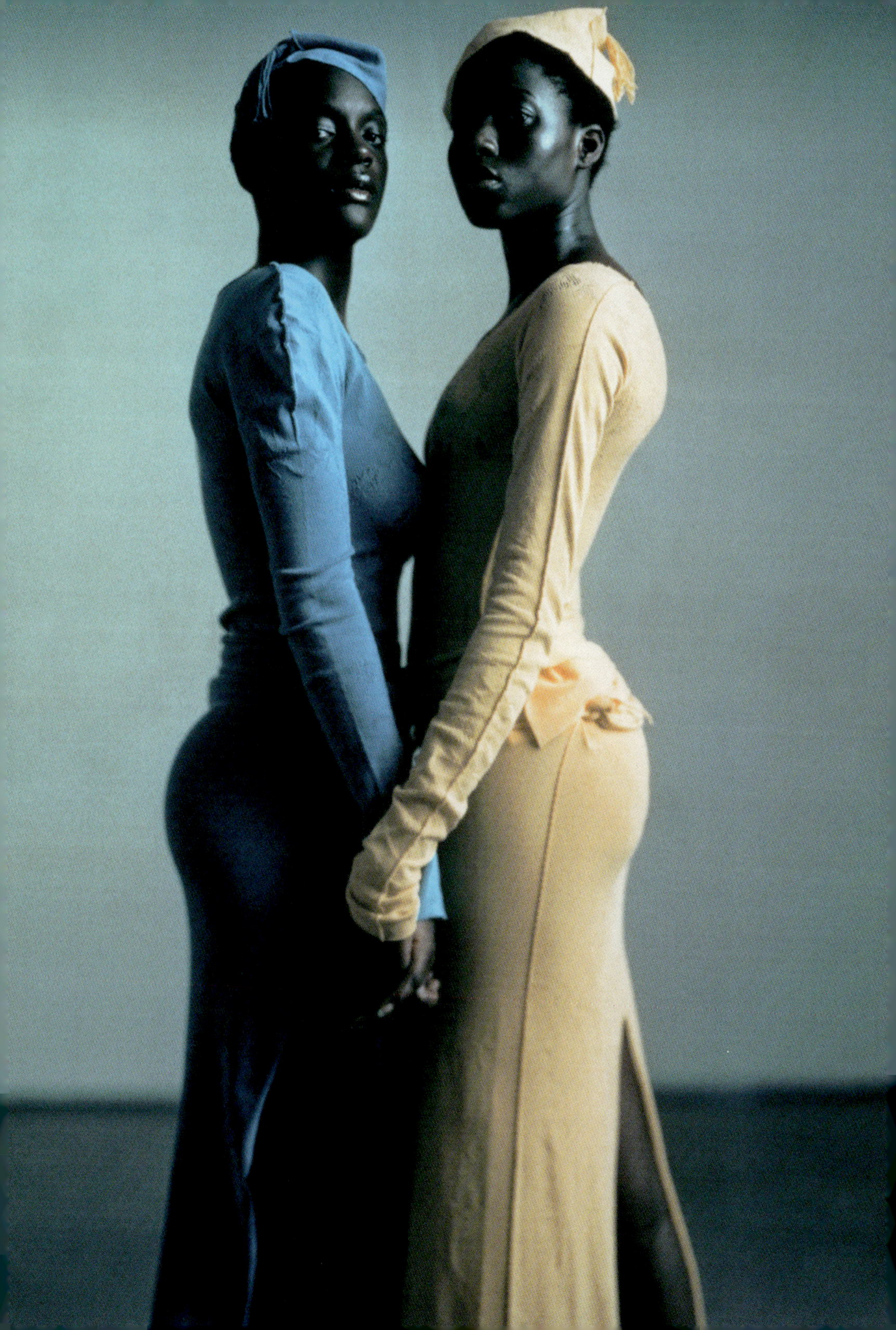

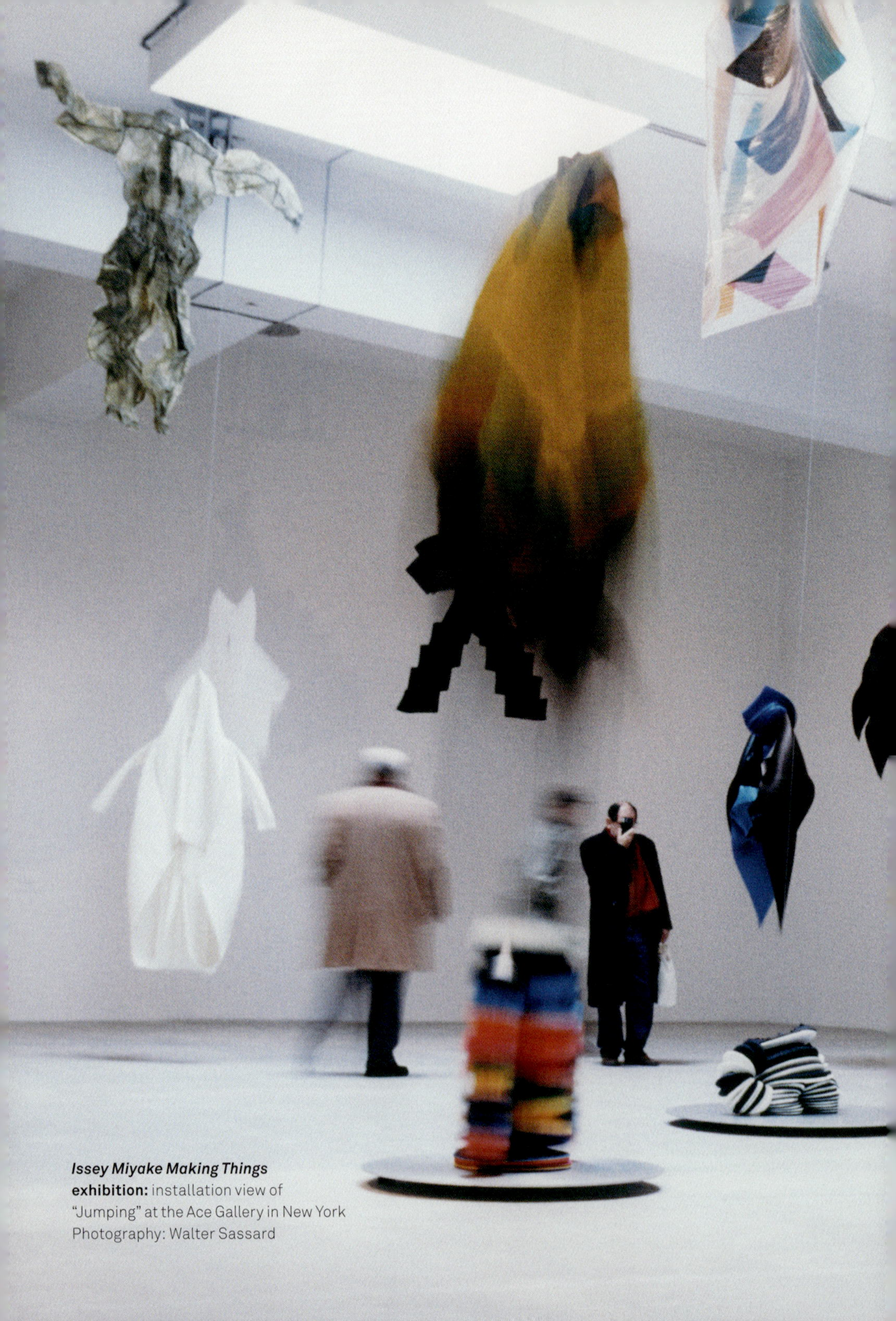

Issey Miyake Making Things
exhibition: installation view of
"Jumping" at the Ace Gallery in New York
Photography: Walter Sassard

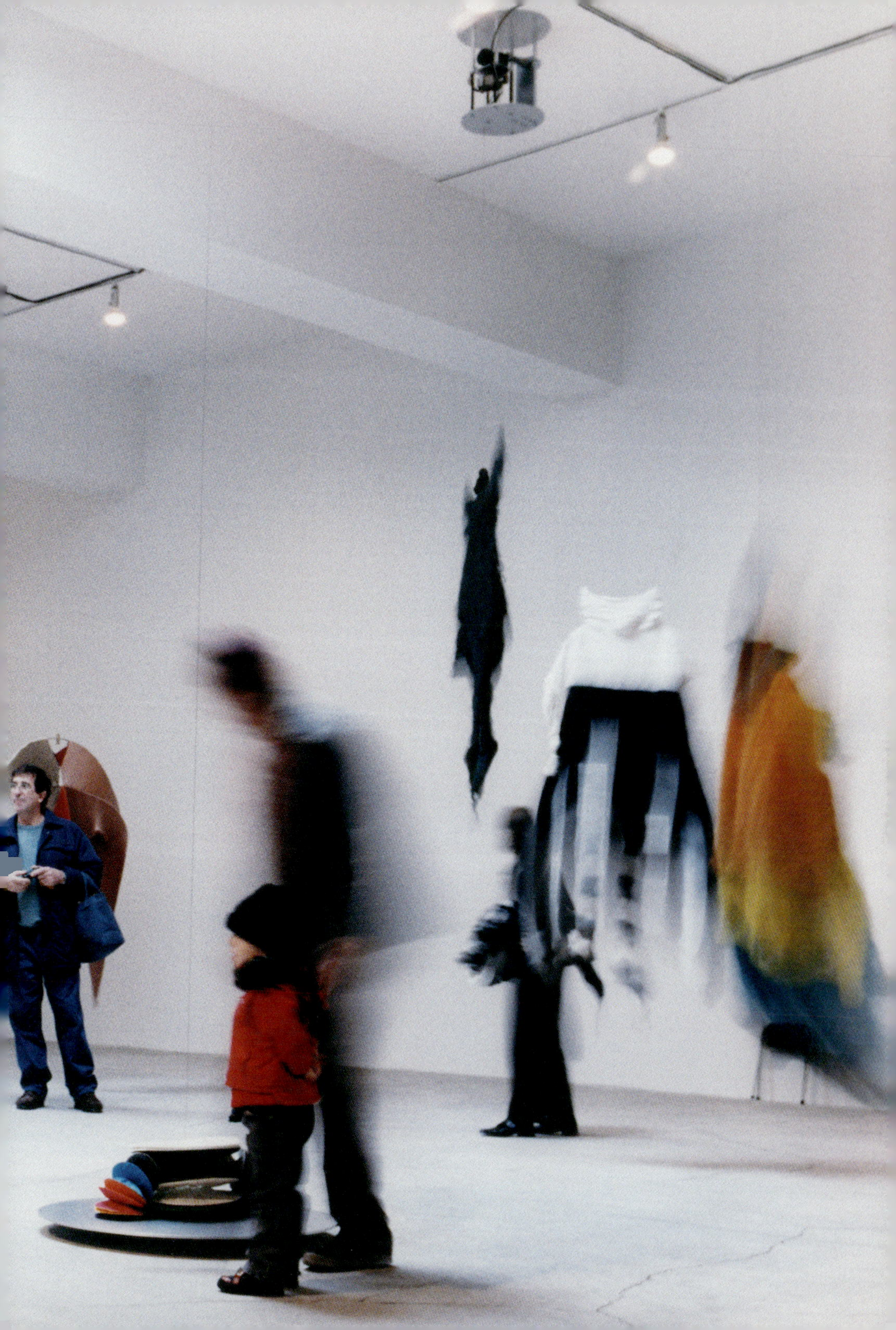

2000

> April–August: *Issey Miyake Making Things* exhibition in Tokyo
> June: A-POC demonstration at the Fondation Cartier pour l'art contemporain. Presentation of A-POC 04, and work in collaboration with Yayoi Kusama
> December: A-POC 05

Issey Miyake Making Things exhibition
Exhibition in Tokyo based upon *Issey Miyake Making Things* in Paris and New York with new additional exhibits.

April 29–August 20: Museum of Contemporary Art, Tokyo Executive direction: Issey Miyake; visual direction: Midori Kitamura; space design: Tokujin Yoshioka; planning support: Fondation Cartier pour l'art contemporain; animation production: Pascal Roulin; poster: Francis Giacobetti (photography) and Ikko Tanaka (graphic design)

Opposite: **Issey Miyake Making Things exhibition**
The black dress is *Just Before*, a shape that is knitted sequentially into a tube. It was presented in 1997, one year before A-POC made its official debut. The installation is a very large roll of the flat, knitted tube, the end of which reveals several of the dresses still embedded within the tube and displayed on mannequins. The red is *A-POC King & Queen* (1998 design/Spring-Summer 1999 Collection), and *A-POC Angel* (2000 design) for small children. Photography: Yasuaki Yoshinaga

A-POC 04

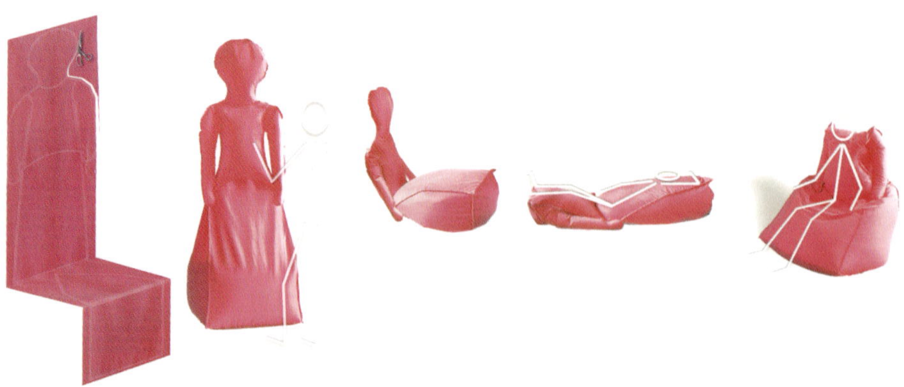

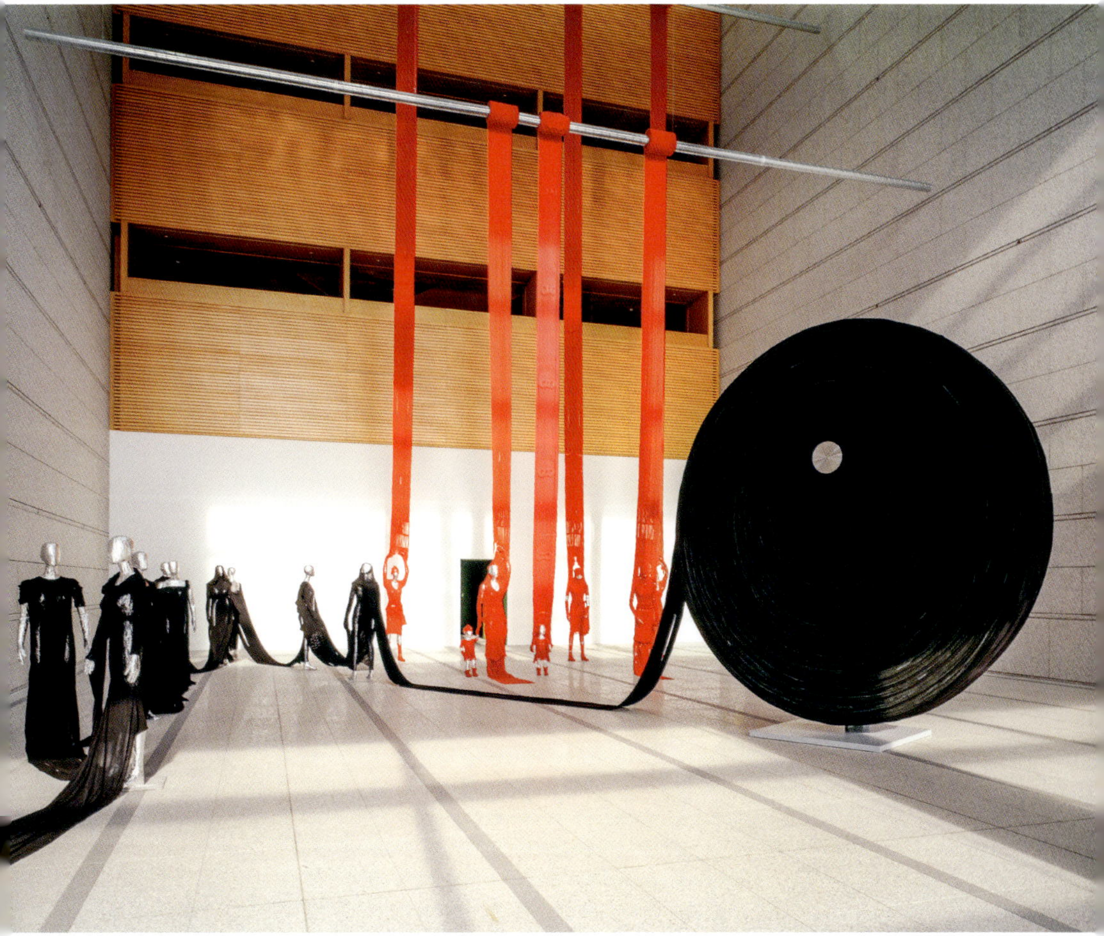

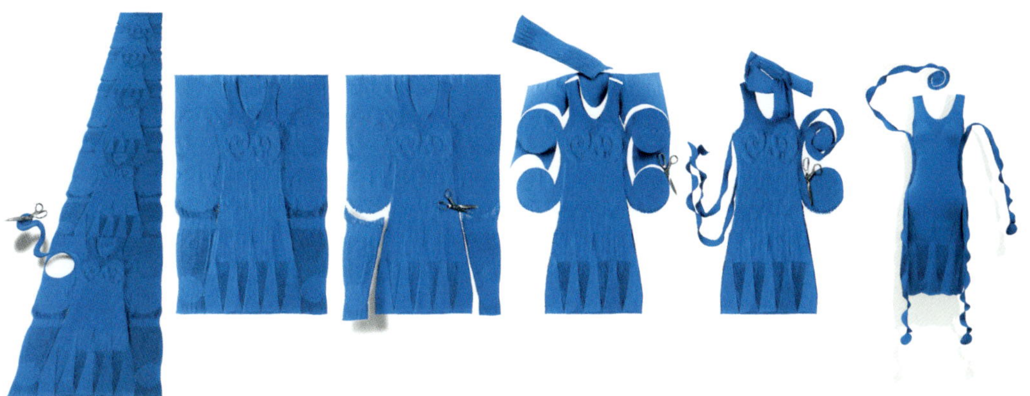

A-POC 05

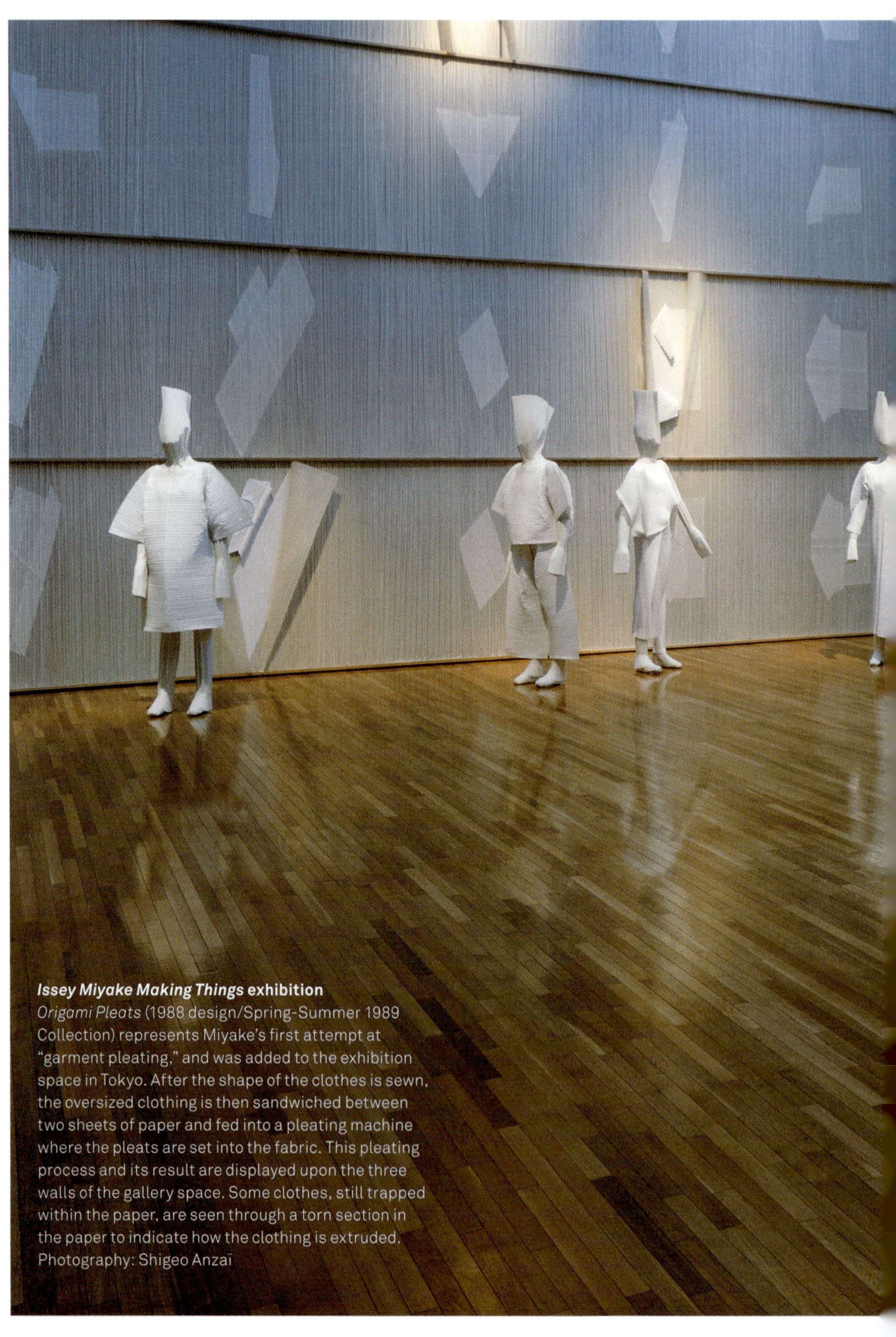

***Issey Miyake Making Things* exhibition**
Origami Pleats (1988 design/Spring-Summer 1989
Collection) represents Miyake's first attempt at
"garment pleating," and was added to the exhibition
space in Tokyo. After the shape of the clothes is sewn,
the oversized clothing is then sandwiched between
two sheets of paper and fed into a pleating machine
where the pleats are set into the fabric. This pleating
process and its result are displayed upon the three
walls of the gallery space. Some clothes, still trapped
within the paper, are seen through a torn section in
the paper to indicate how the clothing is extruded.
Photography: Shigeo Anzaï

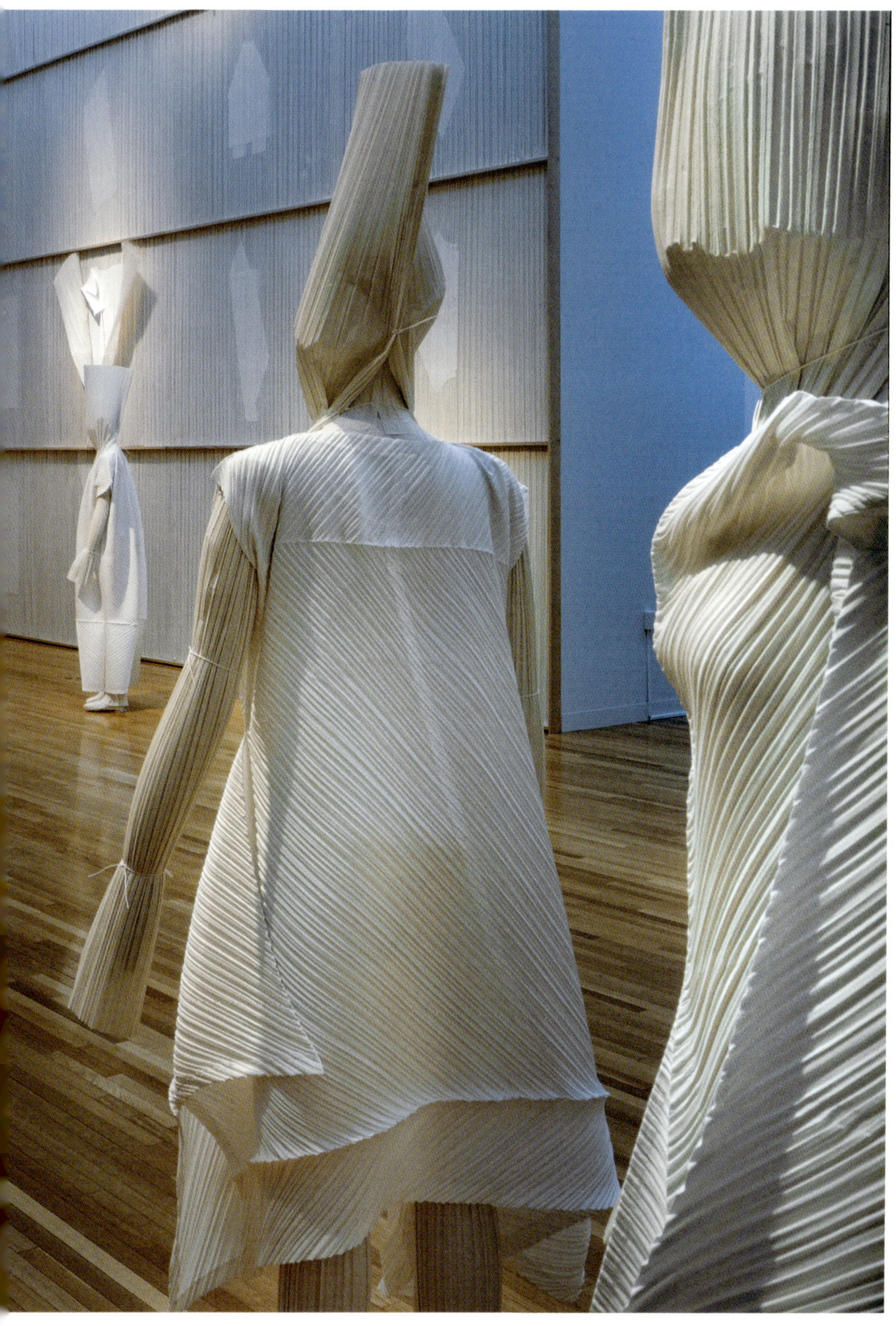

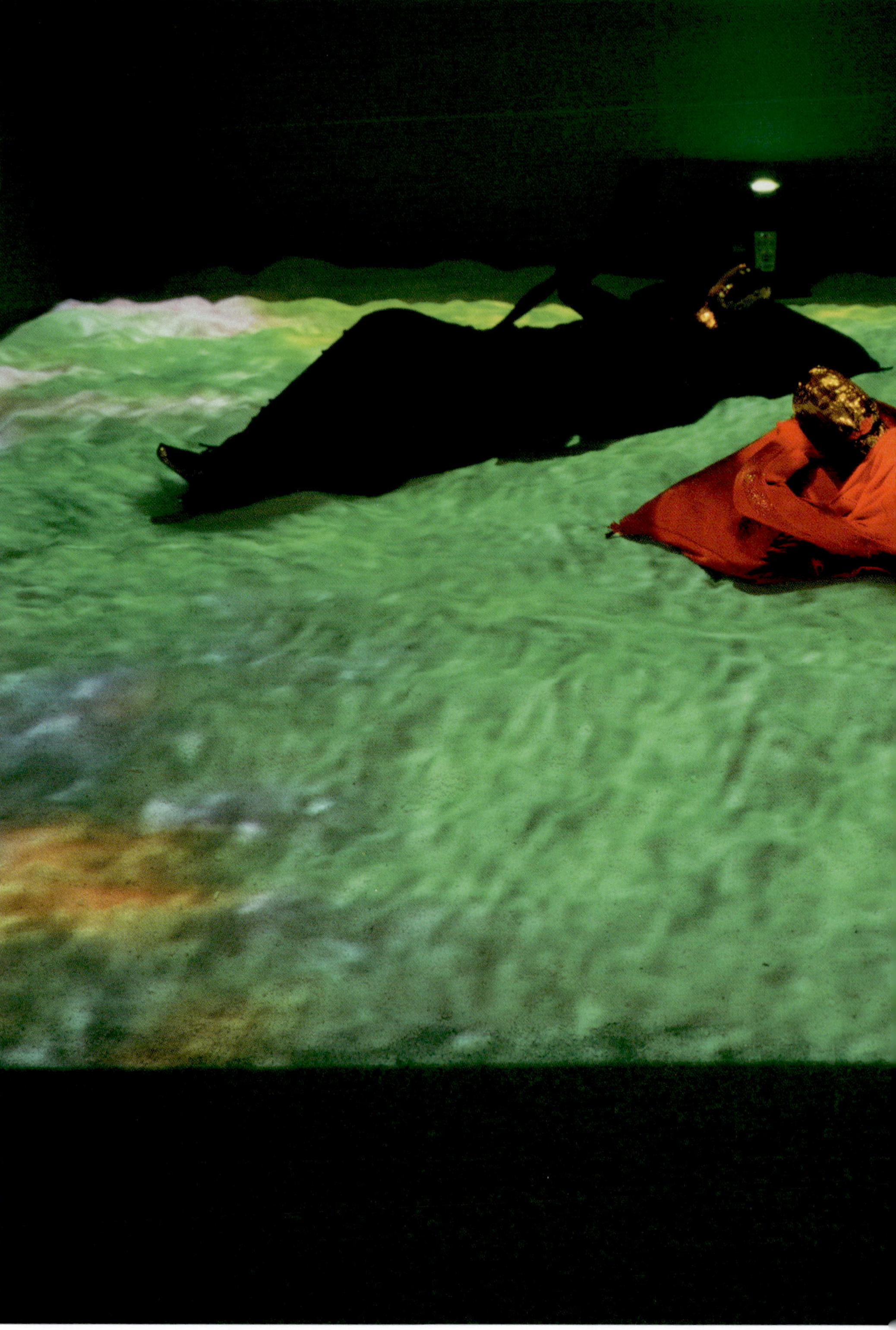

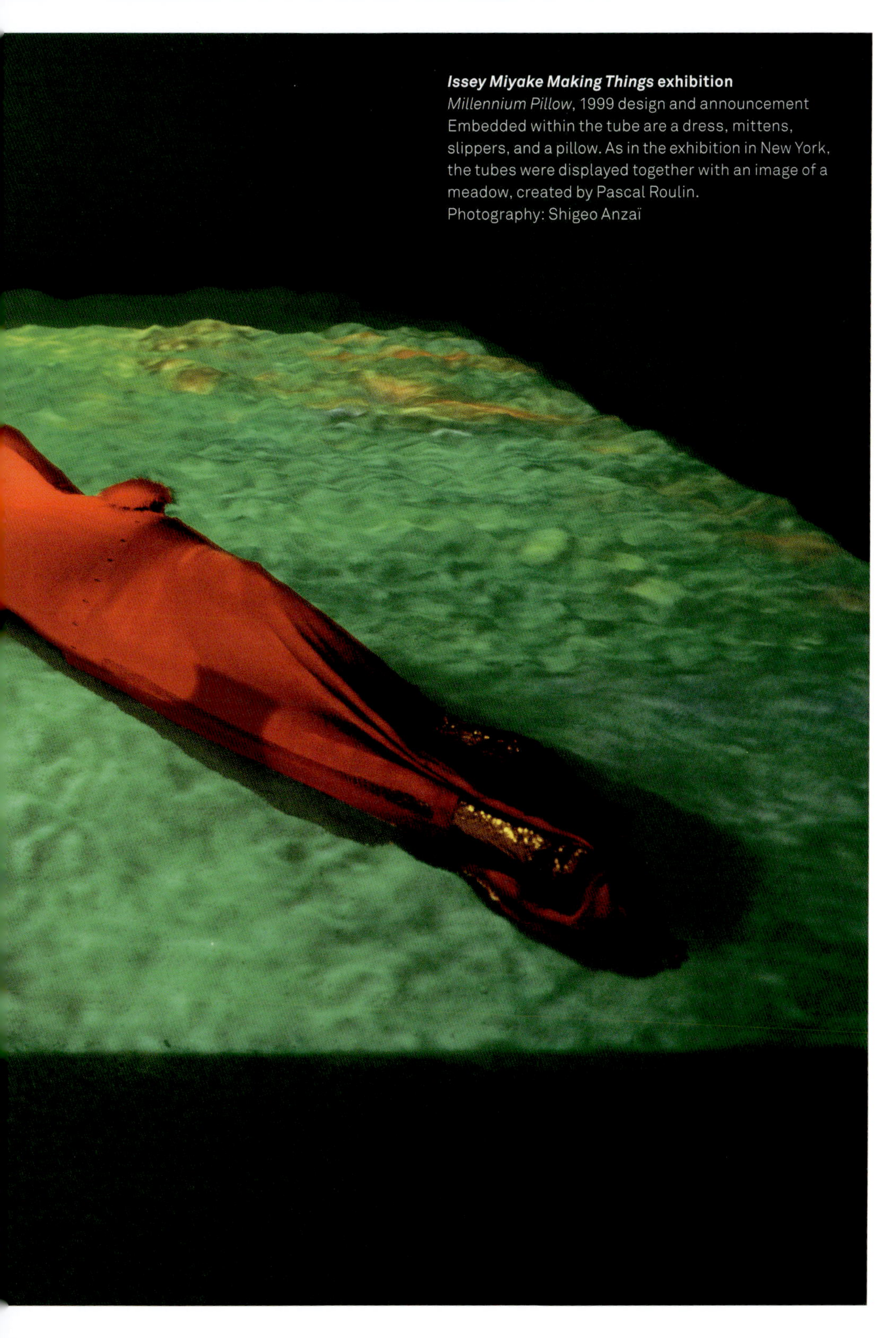

***Issey Miyake Making Things* exhibition**
Millennium Pillow, 1999 design and announcement
Embedded within the tube are a dress, mittens,
slippers, and a pillow. As in the exhibition in New York,
the tubes were displayed together with an image of a
meadow, created by Pascal Roulin.
Photography: Shigeo Anzaï

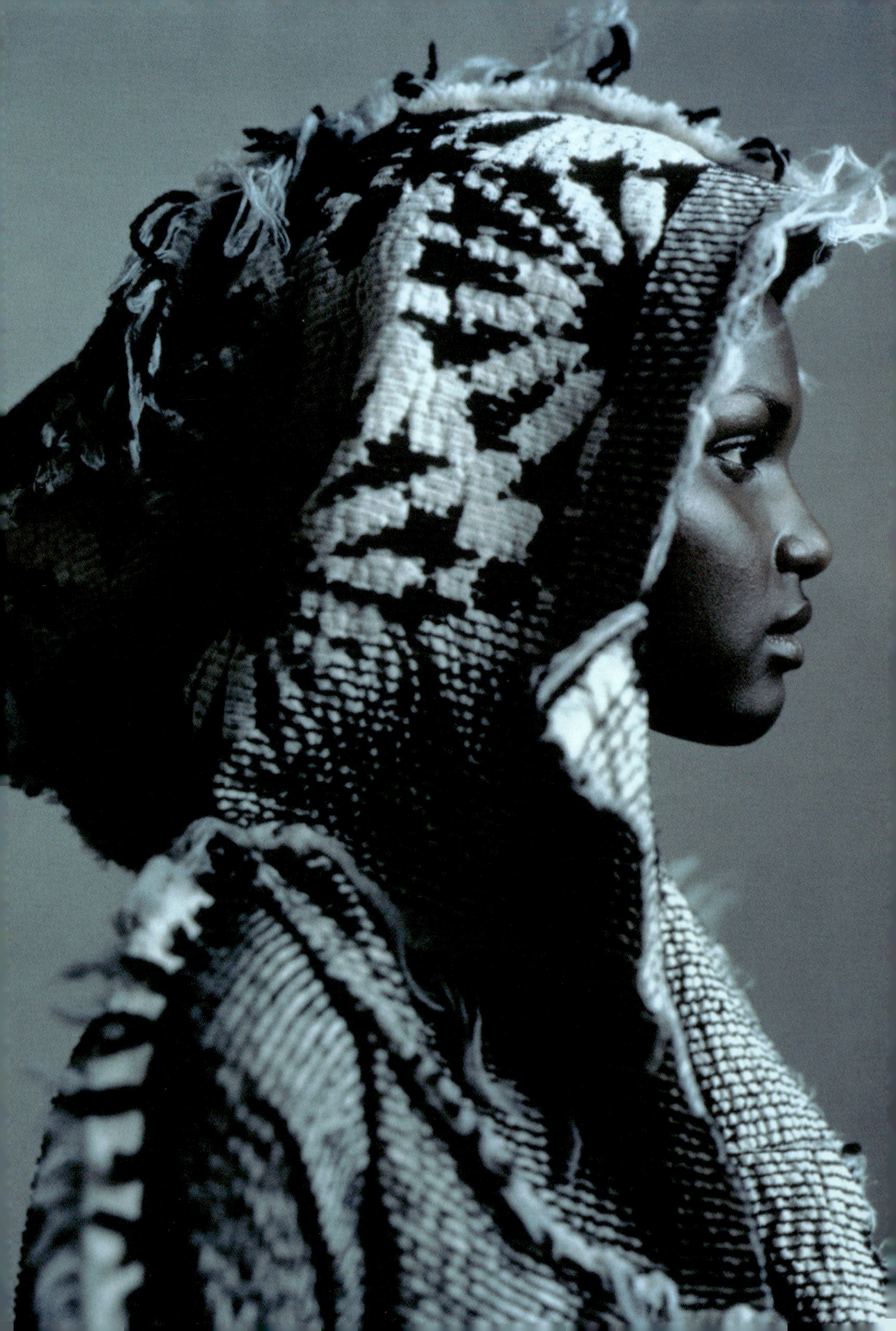

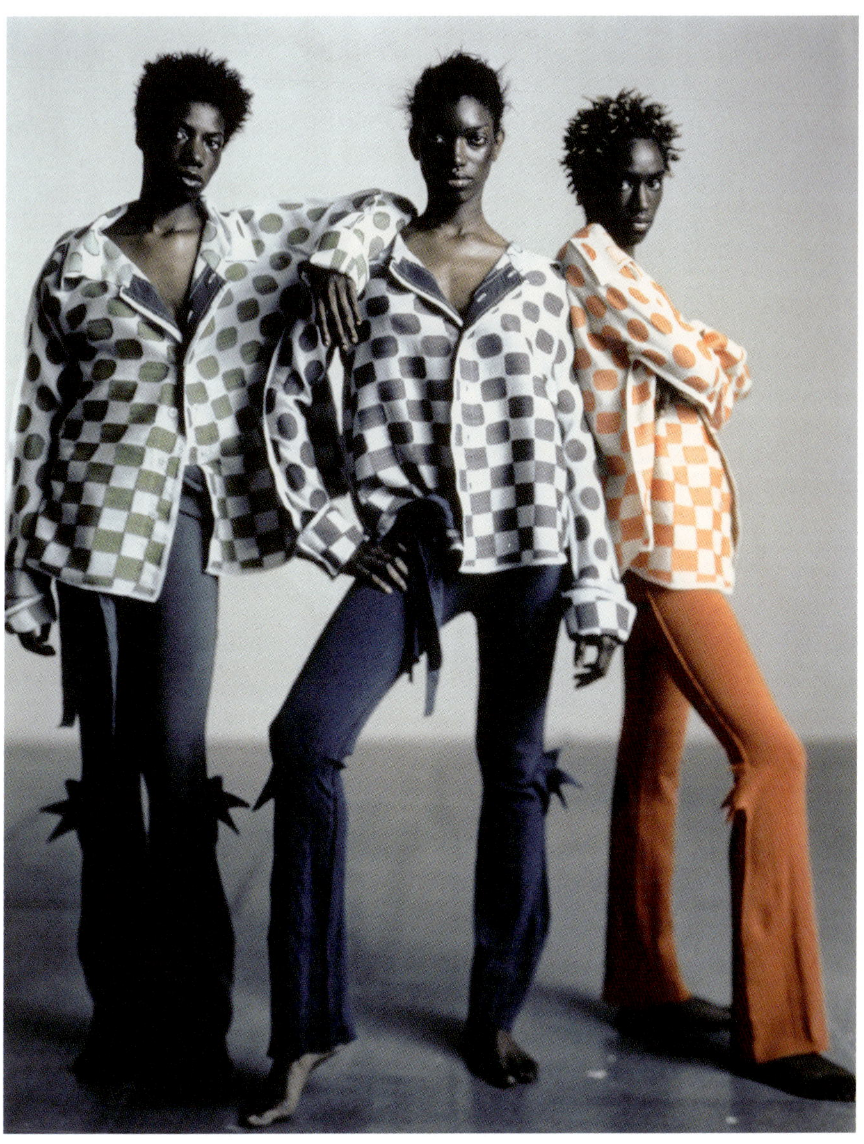

Opposite: *Caravan*
The name is taken from a caravan traveling in the
desert. Hooded coat. Double-woven fabric with cotton
warp and wool weft in which the shape of the clothes'
parts are woven. First A-POC woven clothing that was
sewn after the pieces were made.
2000 design/A-POC 04
Photography: Friedemann Hauss;
styling: Hélène Renault-Kohn

YMC Soda, shirt in silk wool, and pants
in mixed wool knit.
2000 design/A-POC 04
Photography: Friedemann Hauss;
styling: Hélène Renault-Kohn

2001

> April: A-POC 06
> June–July: *A-POC Making: Issey Miyake & Dai Fujiwara* exhibition in Berlin
> October–January 2002: Participated in the *Radical Fashion* exhibition at the Victoria and Albert Museum, London
> November: A-POC 07

A-POC Making: Issey Miyake & Dai Fujiwara exhibition

The A-POC presentation in Berlin was the first to be held outside of Paris or Tokyo. The exhibition featured work from *Just Before* (1997 design / Spring-Summer 1998 Collection) to A-POC 06 (2001 design/Autumn-Winter 2001 Collection). The high ceiling was used to explore the concept of *A Piece of Cloth* and as an opportunity to display its process from textile to clothing.

*June 1–July 1: Vitra Design Museum, Berlin
Exhibition direction: Issey Miyake; concept: Issey Miyake and Dai Fujiwara; visual direction: Midori Kitamura; space design: Tokujin Yoshioka; animation: Pascal Roulin; coordination: Mateo Kries; poster: Irving Penn (photography) and Vitra Design Museum (graphic design)*

Opposite: ***A-POC Making: Issey Miyake & Dai Fujiwara* exhibition** poster
A-POC Face 1999 design/Autumn-Winter 1999 Collection. The bulges are created by stuffing cotton fiber into parts of the fabric after knitting. Photography: Irving Penn; graphic design: Vitra Design Museum

A-POC 06

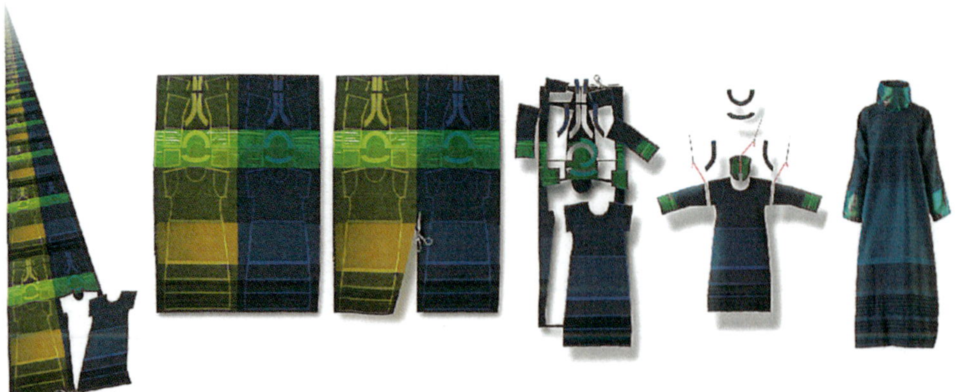

A-POC MAKING: ISSEY MIYAKE & DAI FUJIWARA
1. Juni – 1. Juli 2001, Vitra Design Museum Berlin, Kopenhagener Straße 58, 10437 Berlin/ Prenzlauer Berg, T +49 (0)30 47 37 77 0, Di – Do 11 – 20 Uhr, Fr – So 11 – 22 Uhr

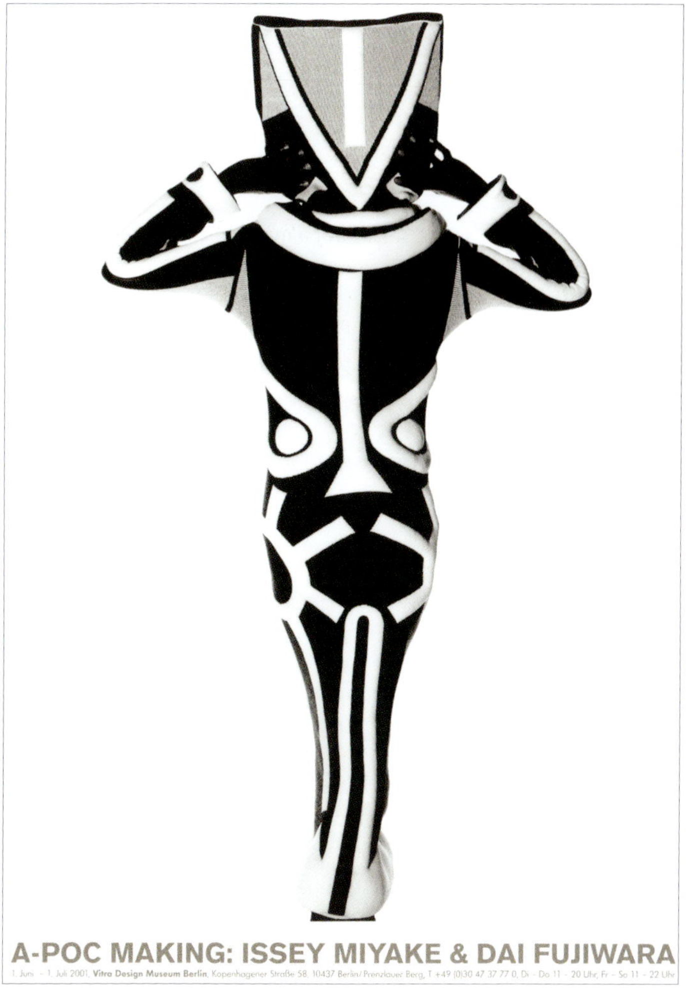

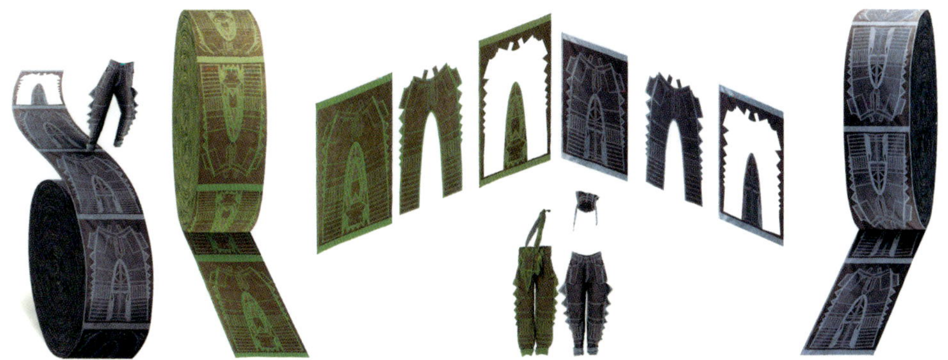

A-POC 07

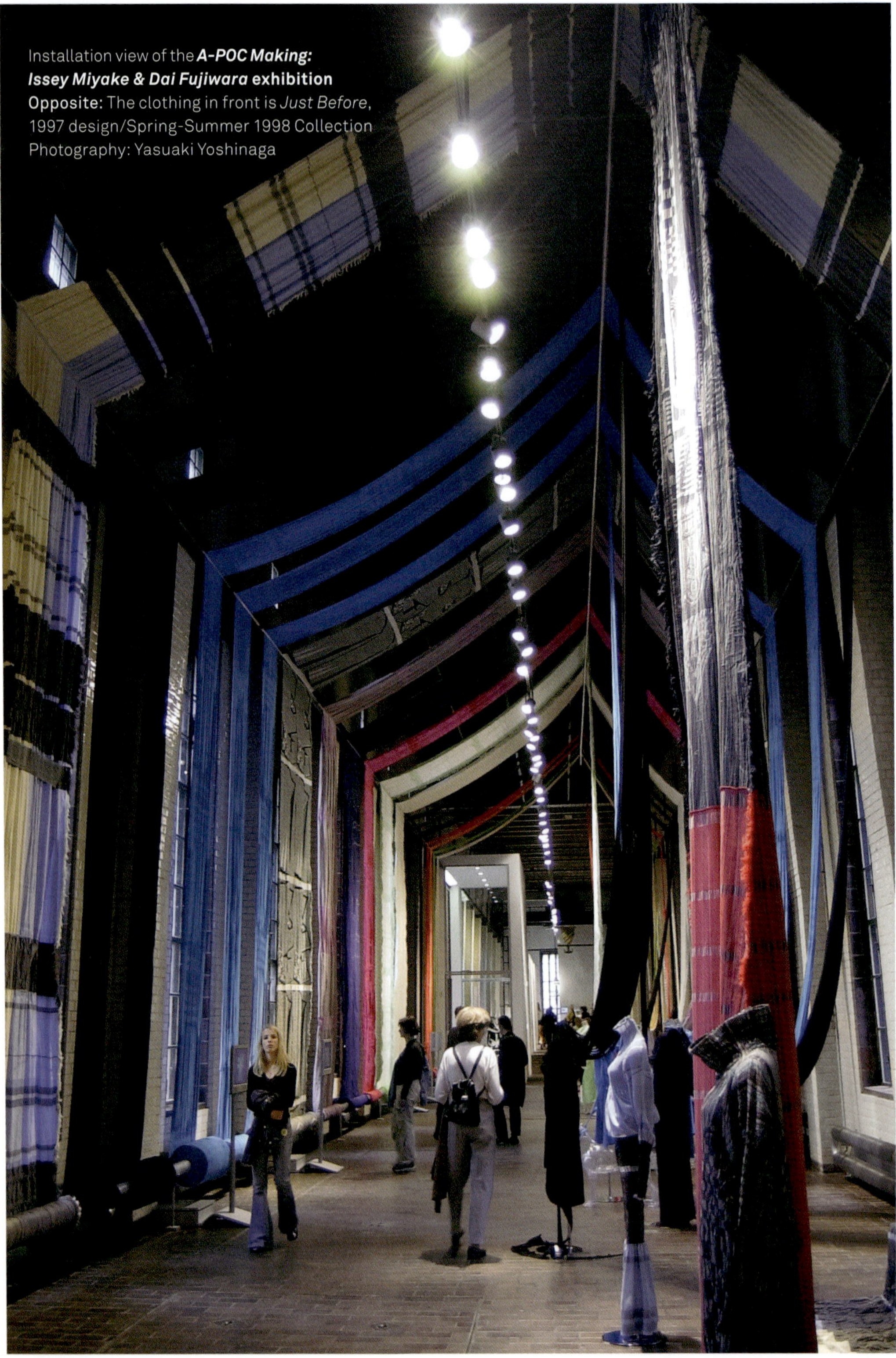

Installation view of the **A-POC Making:
Issey Miyake & Dai Fujiwara exhibition**
Opposite: The clothing in front is *Just Before*,
1997 design/Spring-Summer 1998 Collection
Photography: Yasuaki Yoshinaga

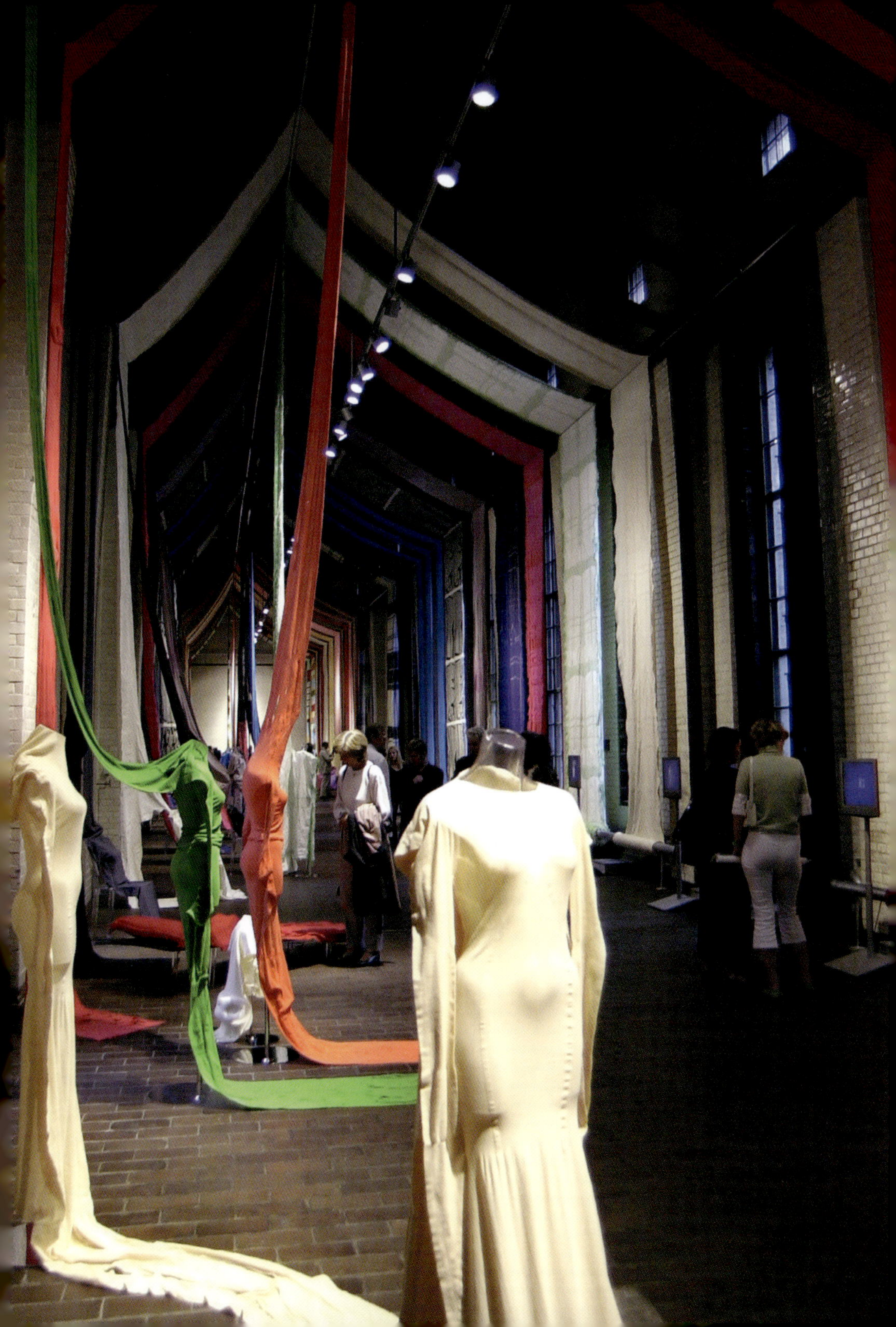

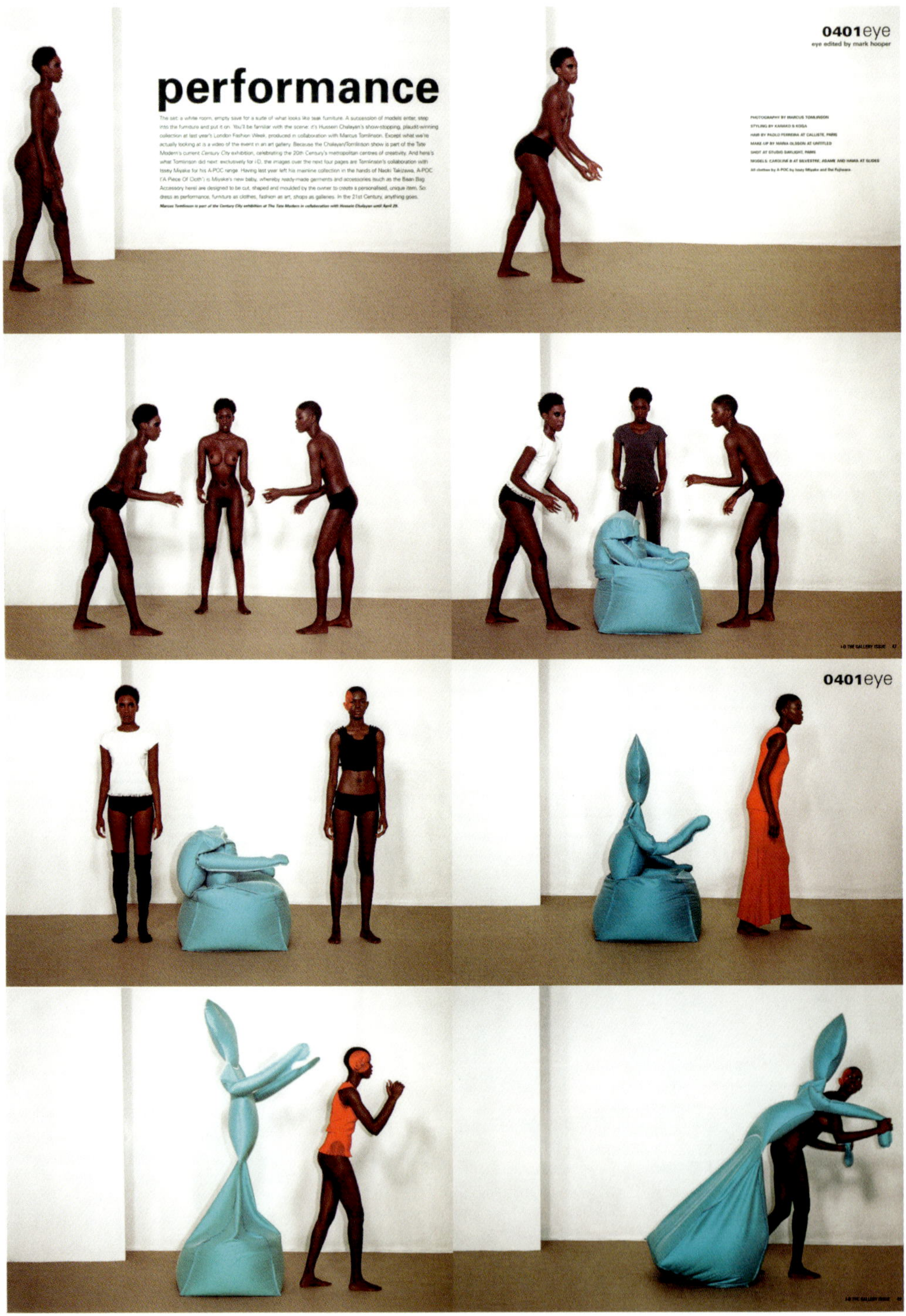

0401eye
eye edited by mark hooper

performance

The set: a white room, empty save for a suite of what looks like teak furniture. A succession of models enter, step into the furniture and put it on. You'll be familiar with the scene: it's Hussein Chalayan's show-stopping, plaudit-winning collection at last year's London Fashion Week, produced in collaboration with Marcus Tomlinson. Except what we're actually looking at is a video of the event in an art gallery. Because the Chalayan/Tomlinson show is part of the Tate Modern's current Century City exhibition, celebrating the 20th Century's metropolitan centres of creativity. And here's what Tomlinson did next: exclusively for i-D, the images over the next four pages are Tomlinson's collaboration with Issey Miyake for his A-POC range. Having last year left his mainline collection in the hands of Naoki Takizawa, A-POC ('A Piece Of Cloth') is Miyake's new baby, whereby ready-made garments and accessories (such as the Bean Bag Accessory here) are designed to be cut, shaped and moulded by the owner to create a personalised, unique item. So: dress as performance, furniture as clothes, fashion as art, shops as galleries. In the 21st Century, anything goes.
Marcus Tomlinson is part of the Century City exhibition at The Tate Modern in collaboration with Hussein Chalayan until April 29.

PHOTOGRAPHY BY MARCUS TOMLINSON
STYLING BY KANAKO B KOGA
HAIR BY PAOLO FERREIRA AT CALLISTE, PARIS
MAKE UP BY MARIA OLSSON AT UNTITLED
SHOT AT STUDIO DAYLIGHT, PARIS
MODELS: CAROLINE B AT SILVESTRE, ADAMI AND HAWA AT SLIDES
All clothes by A-POC by Issey Miyake and Dai Fujiwara.

0401eye

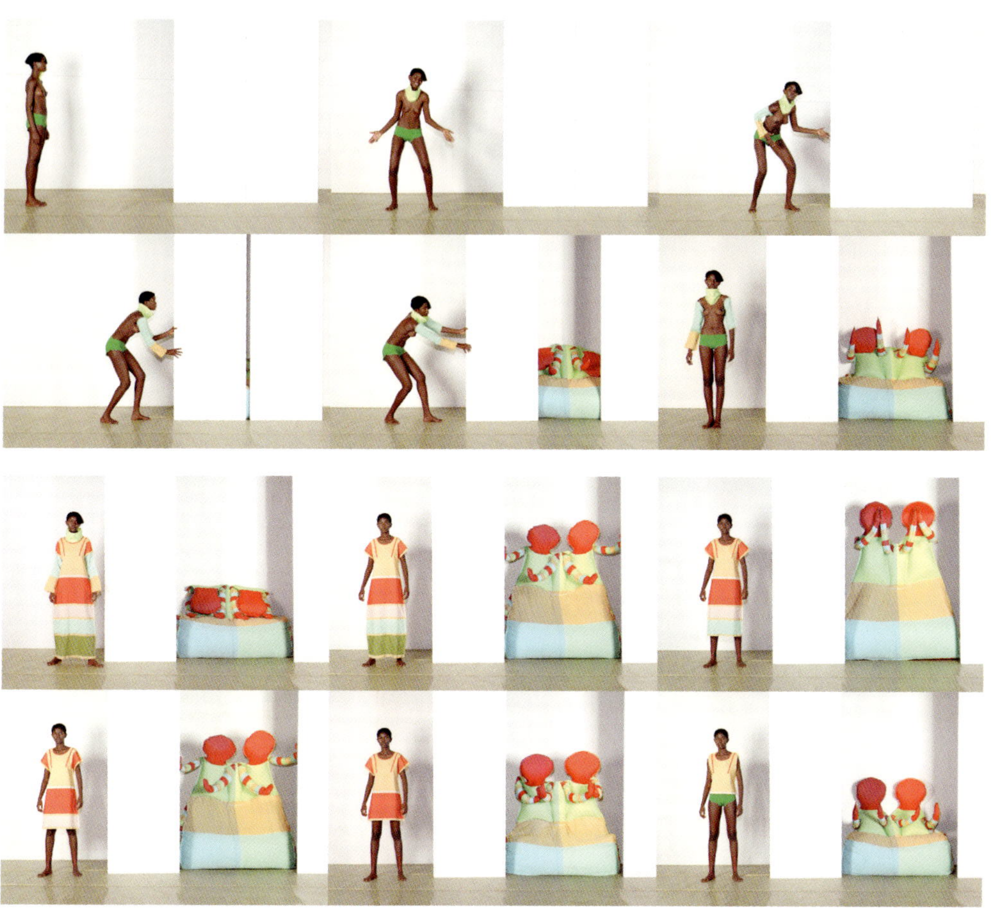

Opposite: "Performance," *i-D,*
The Gallery Issue (UK), No. 208, 2001
A-POC 04 collection and *Midas* chair,
2000 design/A-POC 04
Photography: Marcus Tomlinson

"A-POC Magic," *Vogue Japan*, November 2001
Double Midas sofa and *Framework* dress.
The sofa and clothes are woven using the same threads.
A long-sleeved, turtleneck, and long dress patterns
(frames) are woven into *Framework*'s double cloth.
64 variations of clothing can be made using different
cutting lines and sections. Marcus Tomlinson's photos
show how the various parts can be combined into
different shapes.
2001 design/A-POC 05
Photography: Marcus Tomlinson

2002

Opposite: **A cappella**
Knit with double-width fabric
2002 design/A-POC 08
Photography: Duc Liao

A-POC 08

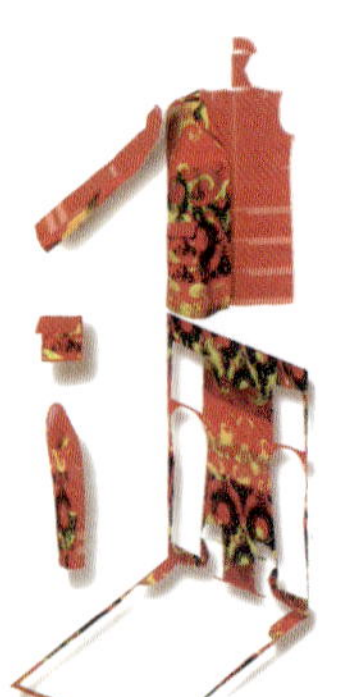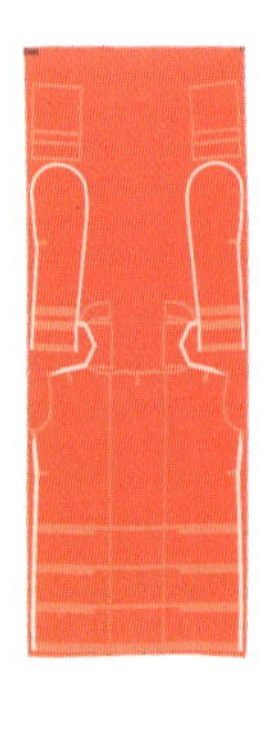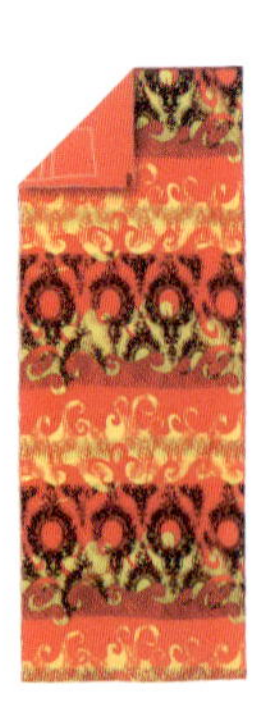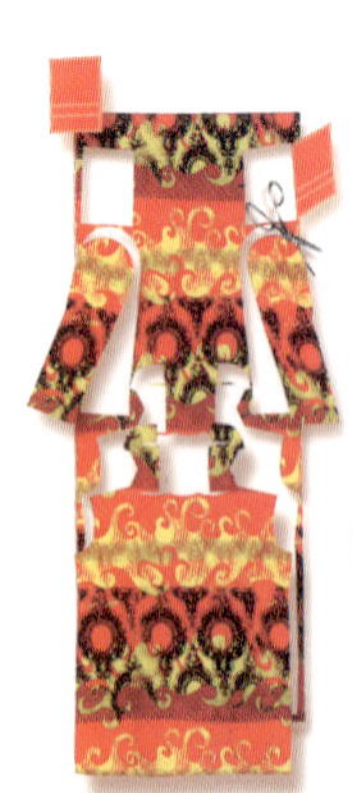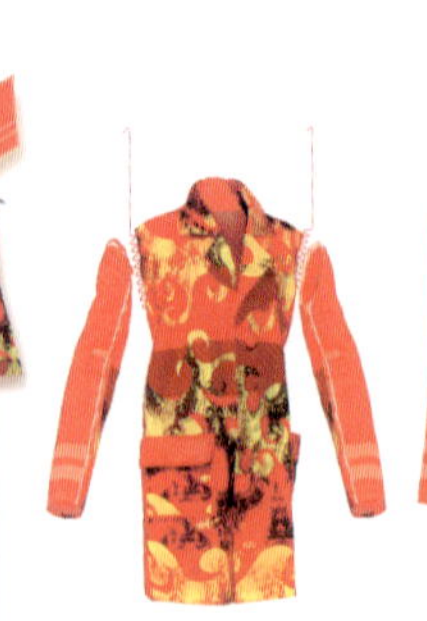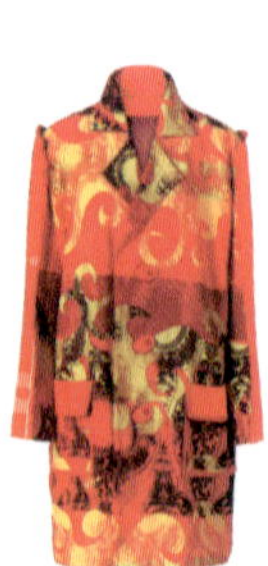

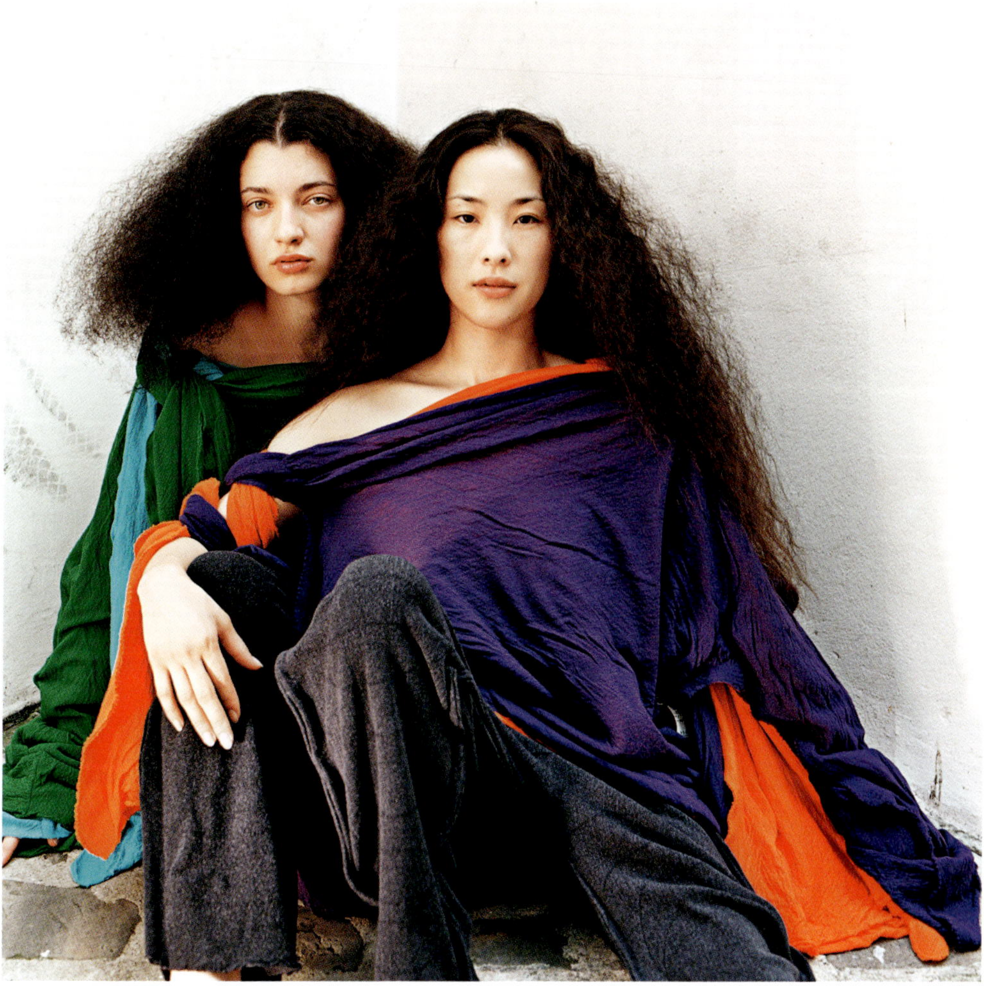

A-POC 09

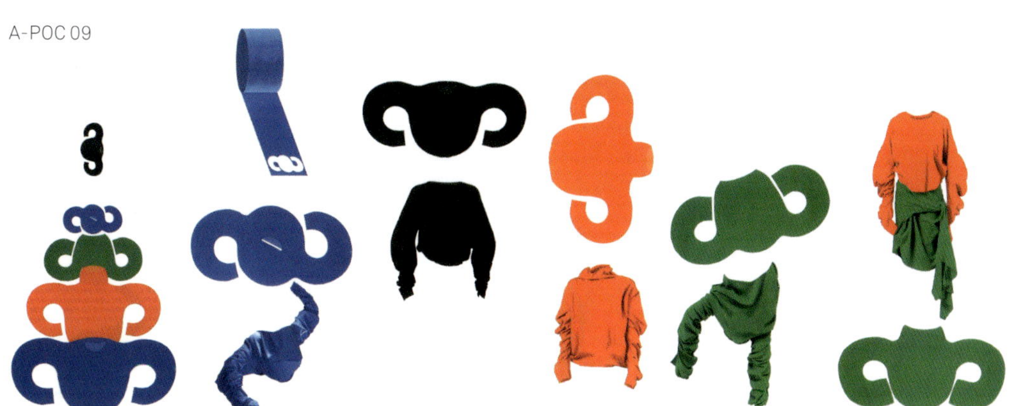

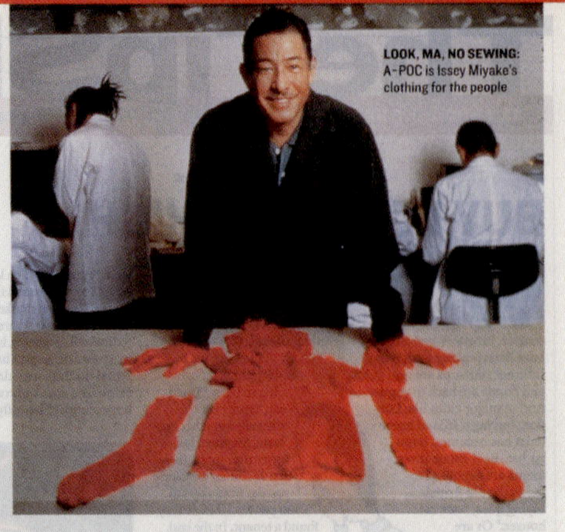

The Epoch Of A-POC

Miyake turns a utopian idea into high fashion

BY DANA THOMAS

A FEW YEARS AGO ISSEY MIYAKE had a crisis of conscience. "I became a fashion designer to make clothes for the people, not to be a top couturier in the French tradition," the 63-year-old Miyake said recently, seated in his spacious, modern headquarters in Tokyo. Yet there he was, "a society designer," as he puts it now, with a hint of disdain. "I questioned everything. I said, 'I am a liar'."

Since then Miyake has gone back to basics. In 2000 he rolled out A-POC—or A Piece of Cloth—clothing that's cut from a single piece of woven or knit tubular fabric. The design is the realization of a utopian idea that Miyake has carried with him since the 1960s: to create "universal clothing," inexpensive items that anyone can wear on any occasion. Last month in London, with the help of his new team of twentysomething assistants—"I love their energy and their ideas!" he says—Miyake presented the latest A-POC line. (In keeping with its revolutionary concept, Miyake does not show A-POC on the runway during fashion week but instead does "demonstrations" periodically during the year. "A-POC," he says, "has no epoch.") The designs, as always with Miyake, are avant-garde, in bold colors like aquamarine, buttercup yellow and strawberry red, and in stark, straight-edged shapes that nevertheless take on the curves of the body.

When the line was introduced, Miyake encouraged wearers to take scissors and fashion each item as they like—change a V neck into a scoop neck, a maxi into a mini, hack off the sleeves or cut out the back. But these days A-POC has grown from a collection of simple snip-and-wear jersey (known as "Baguette") to include more complicated creations, like a cotton-nylon knit flannel suit or a quadruple-weave supershrunk cotton T shirt with mini-smocking.

Miyake created A-POC with help from his chief textile engineer, Dai Fujiwara. One morning Miyake called in Fujiwara, explained his idea and instructed him to focus on knitwear, because, as Miyake says, "the future of fashion is light, durable clothes." As it happened, Fujiwara had been tinkering with an old knitting machine that he had found in an abandoned barn outside Tokyo, trying to figure out how he could meld traditional technology with computers to come up with a new way to produce fabrics. Miyake saw Fujiwara's newfangled contraption as a way to realize his dream, and told the young engineer to keep experimenting.

The resulting method is quite simple: a single thread is fed into a computer-driven knitting or weaving machine that churns out a tube about five feet wide, like a giant tube sock. The seams of the garment—be it a dress, a jacket, pants or mittens—are woven directly into the fabric and are outlined, like paper dolls. Once cut along the seams, the raw edges of this high-tech knit fabric do not unravel—the garment is literally ready to wear straight out of the weaving and cutting machines. No sewing required.

Miyake decided then and there to stop his work as a high-fashion designer, handed over the ready-to-wear duties to one of his protégés, Naoki Takizawa, and focused on A-POC. Fujiwara has since refined the manufacturing process, so A-POC is now produced on two computer-operated machines outside Tokyo—with patents pending. He is already experimenting with other uses for the A-POC principle, like a line of goofy beanbag chairs called Mobile, with arms and hands like a human's. "We can apply A-POC to planes, cars, homes—anything that involves fabric," Fujiwara says. "It's really limitless."

With its easy-to-wear ethic and accessible pricing—from $50 for a handbag to $750 for a coat—A-POC has become the most successful line in the Miyake empire. But most important, it has fulfilled Miyake's lifelong wish to dress the masses well. "A-POC unleashes the freedom of imagination," he says. "It's for people who are curious, who have inner energy—the energy of life and living." And that, for Miyake, is what fashion has always been about. ■

53

Newsweek, July 8, 2002
"The Epoch Of A-POC"
Text: Dana Thomas
In 2000 he rolled out A-POC – or *A Piece of Cloth* – clothing that's cut from a single piece of woven or knitted tubular fabric. The design is the realization of a utopian idea that Miyake has carried with him since the 1960s: to create "universal clothing," inexpensive items that anyone can wear on any occasion…
Miyake created A-POC with help from his chief textile engineer, Dai Fujiwara. As it happened, Fujiwara had been tinkering with an old knitting machine that he had found in an abandoned barn outside Tokyo, trying to figure out how he could meld traditional technology with computers to come up with a new way to produce fabrics. Miyake saw Fujiwara's newfangled contraption as a way to realize his dream, and told the young engineer to keep experimenting.
The resulting method is quite simple: a single thread is fed into a computer-driven knitting or weaving machine that churns out a tube about five feet wide, like a giant tube sock.…
Miyake decided then and there to stop his work as a high-fashion designer, handed over the ready-to-wear duties to one of his proteges, Naoki Takizawa, and focused on A-POC. … "A-POC unleashes the freedom of imagination," he says. "It's for people who are curious, who have inner energy – the energy of life and living." And that, for Miyake, is what fashion has always been about. (Excerpt)

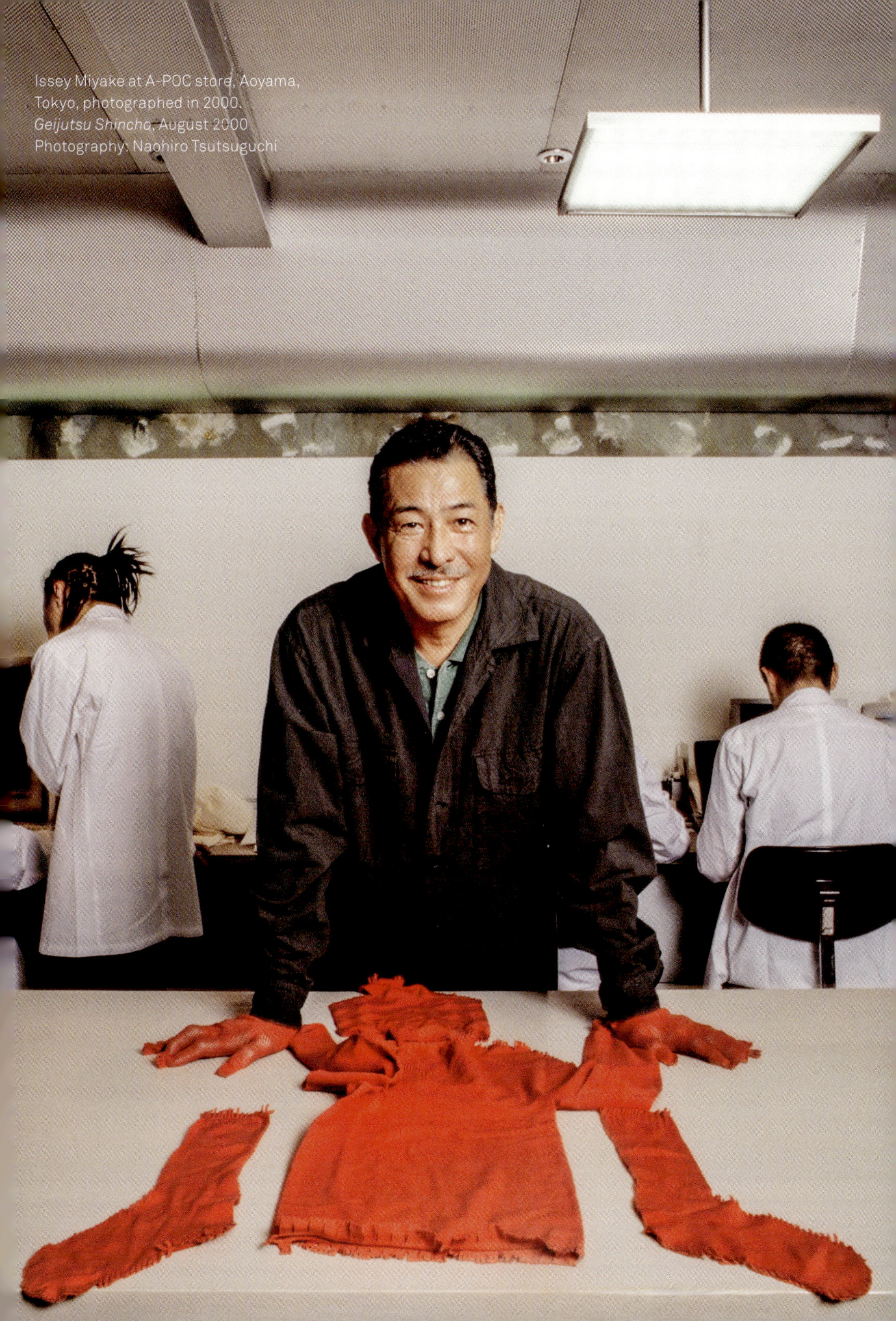

Issey Miyake at A-POC store, Aoyama,
Tokyo, photographed in 2000.
Geijutsu Shincho, August 2000
Photography: Naohiro Tsutsuguchi

2003

> January: Wrote "Let's Create a Design Museum" for the *Asahi Shimbun*
> April: A-POC 10
> September–October: *Nannano? A-POC Miyake Issey + Fujiwara Dai* exhibition in Tokyo
> November: A-POC 11

Opposite: **"Let's Create a Design Museum,"** *The Asahi Shimbun*, January 28, 2003 evening edition
The message described the social relevance of design, and created enough of a stir to eventually lead to the opening of 21_21 DESIGN SIGHT in 2007.

Nannano? A-POC Miyake Issey +
Fujiwara Dai exhibition

The exhibition featured a series of woven fabrics created from its beginning to 2003, illustrating the "single-form creation process" by which the A-POC's clothing design evolved. It also introduced a new methodology for clothing design called "engineering design." In *The Anatomy of Design = A-POC Baguette,* Taku Satoh provided not only graphics, but also texts and three-dimensional exhibits to deconstruct the process by which A-POC is made, including everything from the structure of a single thread to the design of the packaging. This was also the first time *A-POC structure*, which employed braiding techniques to increase strength, was shown.

September 10–October 5: AXIS Gallery, Tokyo
Exhibition concept and direction: Issey Miyake and Dai Fujiwara; space design: Tokujin Yoshioka; posters and graphic design: Kan Akita; produce: Midori Kitamura; "The Anatomy of Design = A-POC Baguette" concept, art direction, and space design: Taku Satoh

A-POC 10

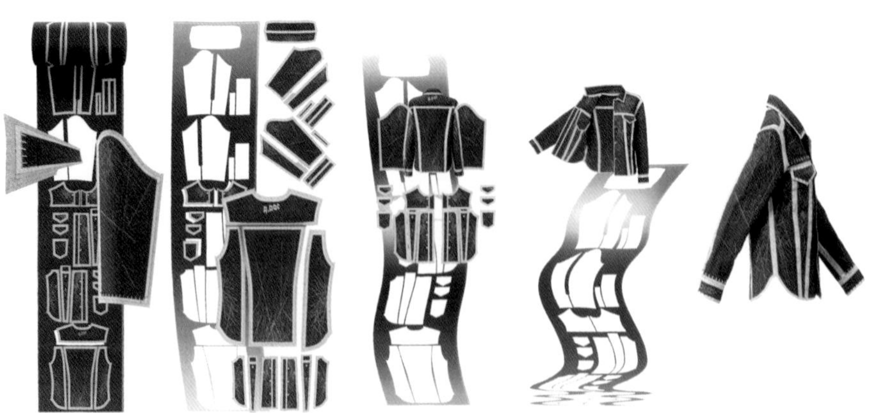

造ろうデザインミュージアム

世界水準の「資源」生かして

三宅　一生

デザイナー

みやけ・いっせい　38年広島県生まれ。63年多摩美大卒。パリとニューヨークで学んだ後、70年に三宅デザイン事務所を設立。パリ・プレタポルテ・コレクションには73年から参加、斬新で創造力豊かなデザインと、素材づくりの独創性で知られる。92年に朝日賞、98年に文化功労者。

バブル経済の崩壊から約10年がたつ。お先真っ暗にも見えるが、どこかに、この状況を打開する道がみつかるかもしれない。自信を失った国に希望があるとすれば、「創造力」さらに言うなら「デザイン」の四文字がその鍵を握っている。私はそんな気がしている。

昨年一月に急逝したデザイナー田中一光さんはあるインタビューにこたえ、次の言葉を遺した。「デザイナーには常に新しい方向を向いていなければ、という強迫観念があるのですが、それだと本当に前を見る時に比較するものがない」

田中さんはいつも、ジャンルを超えた人たちの創造エネルギーの渦の中心にいて、見事なプロデューサーぶりを発揮した。グラフィックと立体の違いなど何もなく、創ることの歓びがあった。いっしょに仕事をするたび、勇気づけられもした。田中さんの遺志を継ぐのは容易ではないが、比較すべ

き「デザインの遺産」の重要性に気づくことが、ひいては日本人の勇気につながるのではないか。

日本の20世紀を振り返れば、戦前の工芸の運動から始まり、戦後は経済成長も手伝ってさまざまな分野のデザインが飛躍的に発展し、人々の生活に深く入り込んできた。プロダクトでは剣持勇氏や柳宗理氏、倉俣史朗氏ら、グラフィックでは亀倉雄策氏や田中一光氏らの巨人たちがすぐれた仕事を

き上げてくれた。彼らの普遍的で汎用性のある仕事は、私たちの生活の一部となっている。

また、日本のすぐれた企業デザインも忘れることはできない。日常品、家電品、建築や環境デザイン等。ファッション・デザインにおいても、世界のクリエーションをエキサイティングなものにしているのは、日本のデザイナーであり、日本の素材であると言える。

だが、独創的なアイデアや技術、それにカタチを与えるデザインに対し、今の日本人はあまりにも無頓着である。オリジナリティのあるデザインによって、生活がうまく機能し、ひいては文化的、精神的な豊かさが育つこと、もっと意識すべきだ。有名ブランドばかりを追い掛けていては、何も始まらない。何か新しいことを始めようとすると「それはちょっとムリですよ」といわれ、さらに「おカネがない」と続く。

そうじゃないでしょう？ わが国の貧しさは、物質的なものではなく、精神的な自信のなさに由来している。それは、美術やデザイン行政の無策ぶりに、企業の文化事業からの後退に、そして明日に希望を持てない若者たちの姿に、端的に表れていると思う。

＊　＊

89年、ロンドンにいち早く「デザインミュージアム」が設立。ニューヨーク、ベルリン、チューリヒ、ヘルシンキ、その他世界の主要都市に「デザインミュージアム」は存在する。世界に誇り得るデザインの宝庫である日本に「デザインミュージアム」ができるのって、世界各地からたくさんの人々を引きつけてくれるはずだ。一つの大きなシンボルとなろう。

「デザインミュージアム」をつくって、術や伝統をカタチにして見せる、面白いアイデアがどんどん出て、街も人も元気が出てくる……。そうした状況をつくり出したいなら、先人たちが遺したすばらしいデザイン遺産を保存・紹介し、未来に向けて同時代の動向も示す「デザインミュージアム」をつくろう。

ロンドンやベルリン、北欧の都市に活気が出てきたのには「デザイン」が作用している。自国の技

デザイン資源を持たない国で、日本人がデザイン・アーカイブをつくることを真剣に考えてほしい。系統だったデザイン・アーカイブをつくるのは生半可な仕事ではない。個人、あるいは一デザイナー事務所の力には限界があり、そして永続性がな

日本の企業にも、自社のデザイン・アーカイブをつくることを真剣に考えてほしい。

＊　＊

これからも胸を張って生きていくには、今以上に知的なエネルギーを発揮するしかない。国際的に通用する「デザイン」立国の道を探る方策もあるのではないか。ただ消費す

るばかりでなく、つくることの大事さをもう一度考えよう。

『明日があるさ』という歌が、リバイバルで少し前にはやった。けれども明日をつくるには、田中一光さんも書いていたとおり、比較するものが欠かせない。

「今、なんだか"日本"が面白いぞ」

世界中でそんな言葉がささやかれるようになり、この国に新しい優れた才能が集まって仕事をし、

すぐれたデザインの伝統を保存・紹介する美術館づくりに、行政、民間、皆で力を合わせてすぐにでも取りかかろう。そこから、次の時代が生まれてくるものと確信している。

最後に、自分自身の感懐を。デザインの仕事は、じつに面白い。私がこの仕事をなんとかめげずにやってこられたのは、「デザインには悲しみはそぐわない、デザインには希望がある、そして、デザインは驚きと喜びを人々に届ける仕事である」ということに

単純素朴な理由からである。

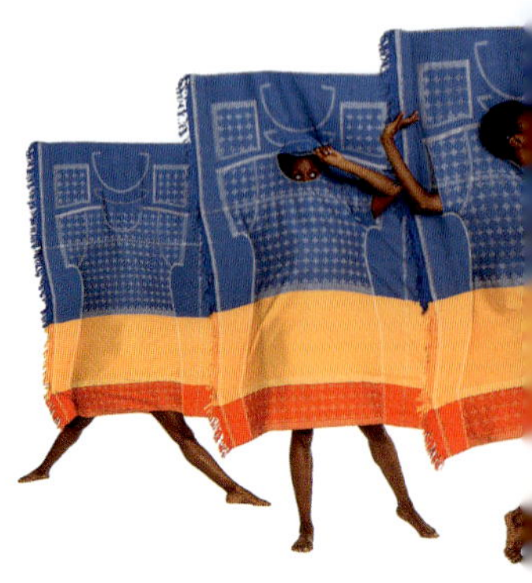

Quadro Cotton, 2001 design/A-POC 07
Photography: Cary Wolinsky and
Barbara Emmel Wolinsky

**Page 265: Let's Create a Design Museum:
Making Use of World-Class "Resources"**
Issey Miyake
It has been roughly a decade since the collapse of the
bubble economy. The path before us may appear dark,
but we can yet find a way through. Our country has lost
its confidence, but I would like to suggest that the key
to our future lies in "creativity," and more particularly,
in "design." At least, that is my opinion. Designer Ikko
Tanaka, who died suddenly in January of last year,
left us the following words in one of his interviews:
"Designers suffer from this obsession that they must
always be heading off in a new direction, but when
you are truly looking forward, you find that you have
nothing to compare to."
Tanaka-san was someone who immersed himself in
the creative energy of people regardless of the genre
in which they worked, and that made him an excellent
producer. It did not matter whether it was graphics or
plastic arts, his was the joy of creation. I came away
encouraged every time I worked with him. It is not easy
to carry on Tanaka-san's legacy, but I think that the
people of Japan may find the courage from the realization of the importance of their "design legacy" and how
it stacks up in the world.
As we look back on design in 20th-century Japan, it
began with the prewar crafts movement and then, with

a boost from postwar economic growth, expanded
into many different fields and directions, and became
deeply embedded in our everyday, ordinary lives.
Japanese design reached world levels in industrial
products with the work of people like Isamu Kenmochi,
Sori Yanagi, and Shiro Kuramata, and in graphics with
giants like Yusaku Kamekura and Ikko Tanaka. Their
works, with their universality and versatility, became
part of our lives.
Nor should we forget Japan's excellent corporate
design. This design extends to household goods,
consumer electronics, architecture, and environmental design. Even in fashion design, it is Japanese
designers and Japanese materials that are bringing
excitement to the world's creations.
For all that, however, we Japanese are still indifferent
to original ideas and technologies, and the designs
that give them form. We need to be more aware of the
originality in designs and how it functions in our lives
and enriches us both culturally and spiritually. Simply
chasing after famous brands is meaningless. Anytime
you try to do something new, you will always be told,
"That's too much of a stretch." This is immediately
followed by, "There's no money for it anyway."
But that's really not the case, is it? The poverty of Japan is not material in nature, but comes from our lack
of spiritual confidence. It is expressed most clearly

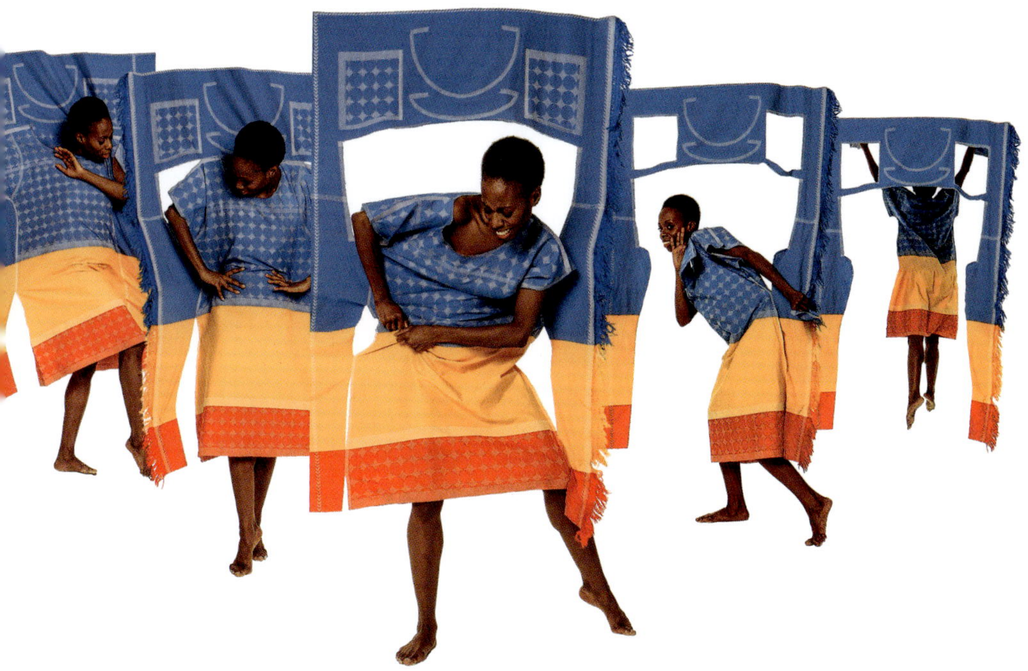

and invisible in our neglect of art and design policy, the waning of our corporate cultural businesses, and in our young people's lack of hope for the future.
London, Berlin, and the cities of Scandinavia have been energized by "design." It brings form to the countries' technologies and traditions, and it is an expression of ambition and motivation.
In 1989, London became one of the first cities to establish a "design museum." Today, you will find design museums in New York, Berlin, Zurich, Helsinki, and most other major cities around the world. How long will it take for Japan to have its own "design museum" to house and display the design treasures of which it can be justifiably proud?
Japan is a country of few resources, and we need even greater intellectual energy than before if we are to continue to take pride in our lives and our work. Can we not find a way to build our country on our international-class "design"? That being said, it is not just enough to consume; we need to consider once again how important it is to create.
There is a song called "There's Always Tomorrow" that enjoyed a bit of a revival recently. But what creates tomorrow is, as Ikko Tanaka wrote, something to compare against.
"Japan is all of a sudden very interesting!"
Could people around the world start to say this? Can

we attract new talent to live and work here? Can we create new and interesting ideas and bring new life and energy to our cities and people? If that is the kind of future we wish to build, then we should start by creating a "design museum" that preserves and displays the wonderful design legacies left to us and shows how our contemporaries are moving us into the future. Such a museum would serve as a symbol and it would attract people from around the world.
I would also like to encourage Japanese companies to think seriously about building their own design archives. It is no easy task to create a systematic design archive. There are limits to what individuals and single designers can do on their own, and they lack the permanence that is required. We need the government, private sector, and public to work together and create a museum that will preserve and display our tradition of excellent design. I'm confident that in doing so we will also give birth to the next generation.
I would like to conclude with some personal impressions.
Design is an extraordinarily interesting job. The reason I have been able to stick with this job throughout everything that's come my way is actually very simple: "Design is not compatible with sadness. Design has hope. Design is the job of surprising and delighting people."

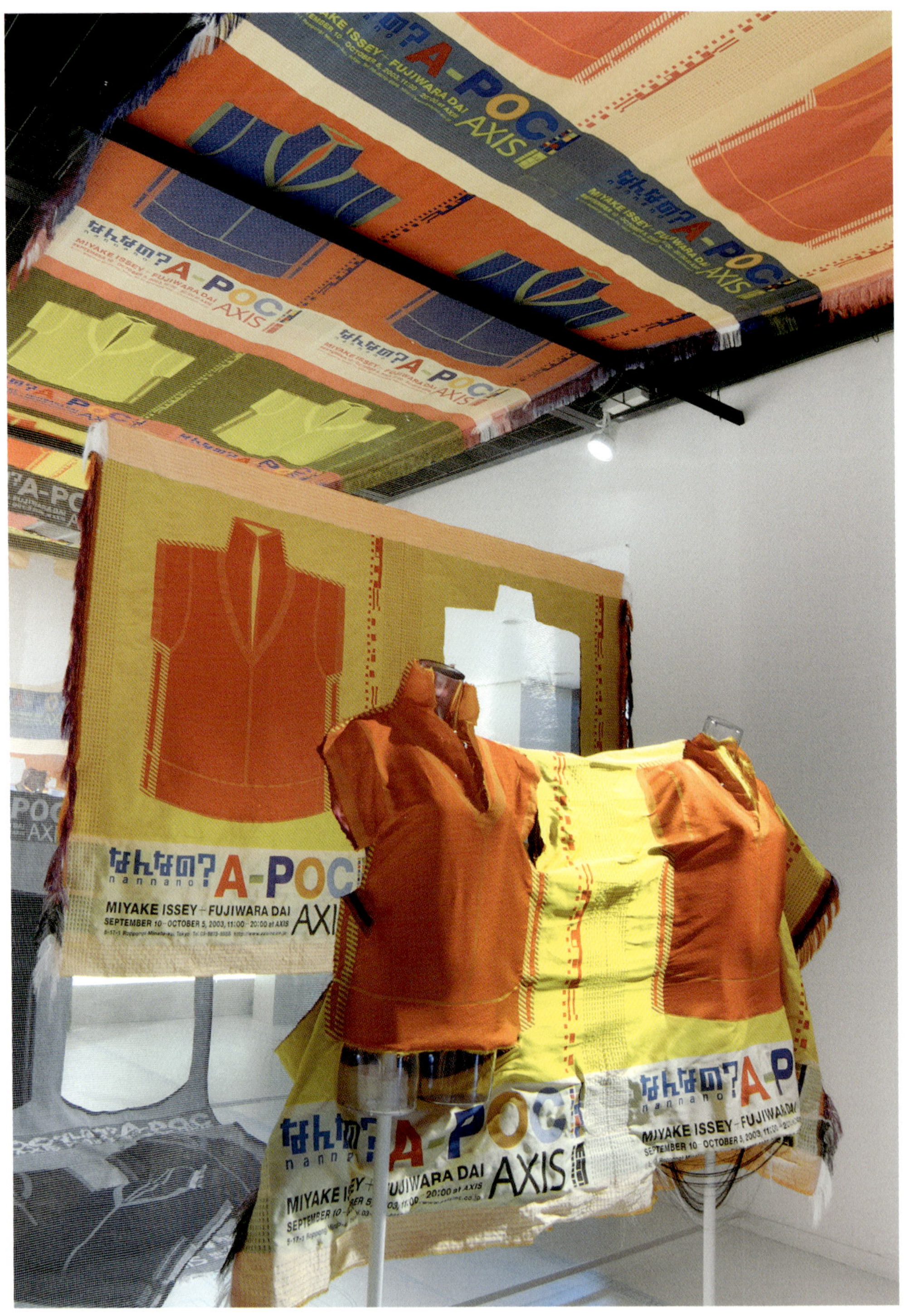
なんなの？A-POC
nannano?
MIYAKE ISSEY + FUJIWARA DAI
SEPTEMBER 10 - OCTOBER 5, 2003, 11:00 - 20:00 at AXIS
AXIS

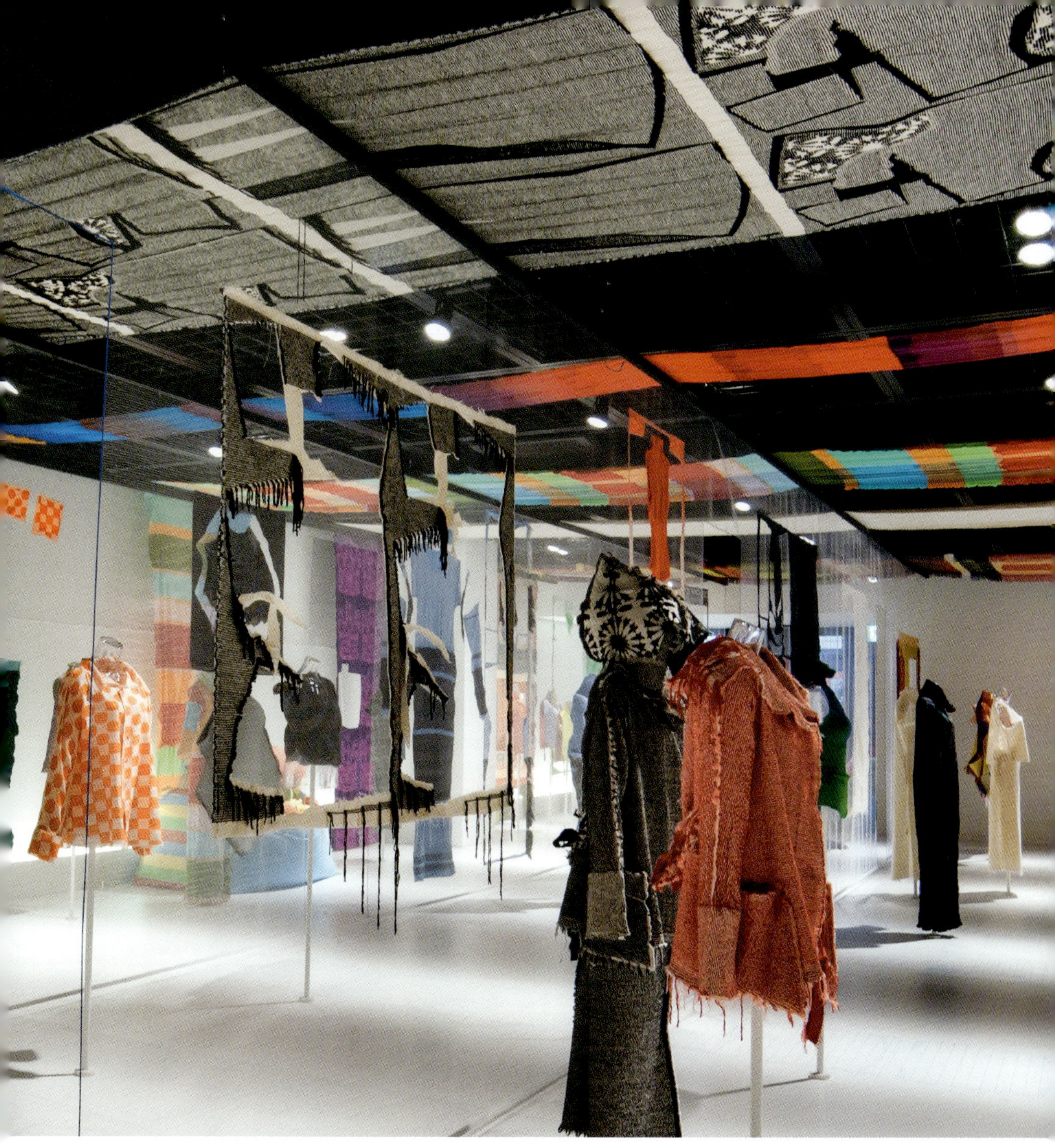

Opposite: *Nannano? A-POC Miyake Issey +*
Fujiwara Dai **exhibition**
A-POC technology was used to create the exhibition
posters. Printing principles were applied to leave
multicolored threads, and when the outlines are cut
out, the poster turns into a wearable shirt.
Photography: Yasuaki Yoshinaga

Nannano? A-POC Miyake Issey +
Fujiwara Dai **exhibition**
Focused on the woven series and the process by
which they were made, clothing patterns were
displayed on the floor.
Photography: Yasuaki Yoshinaga

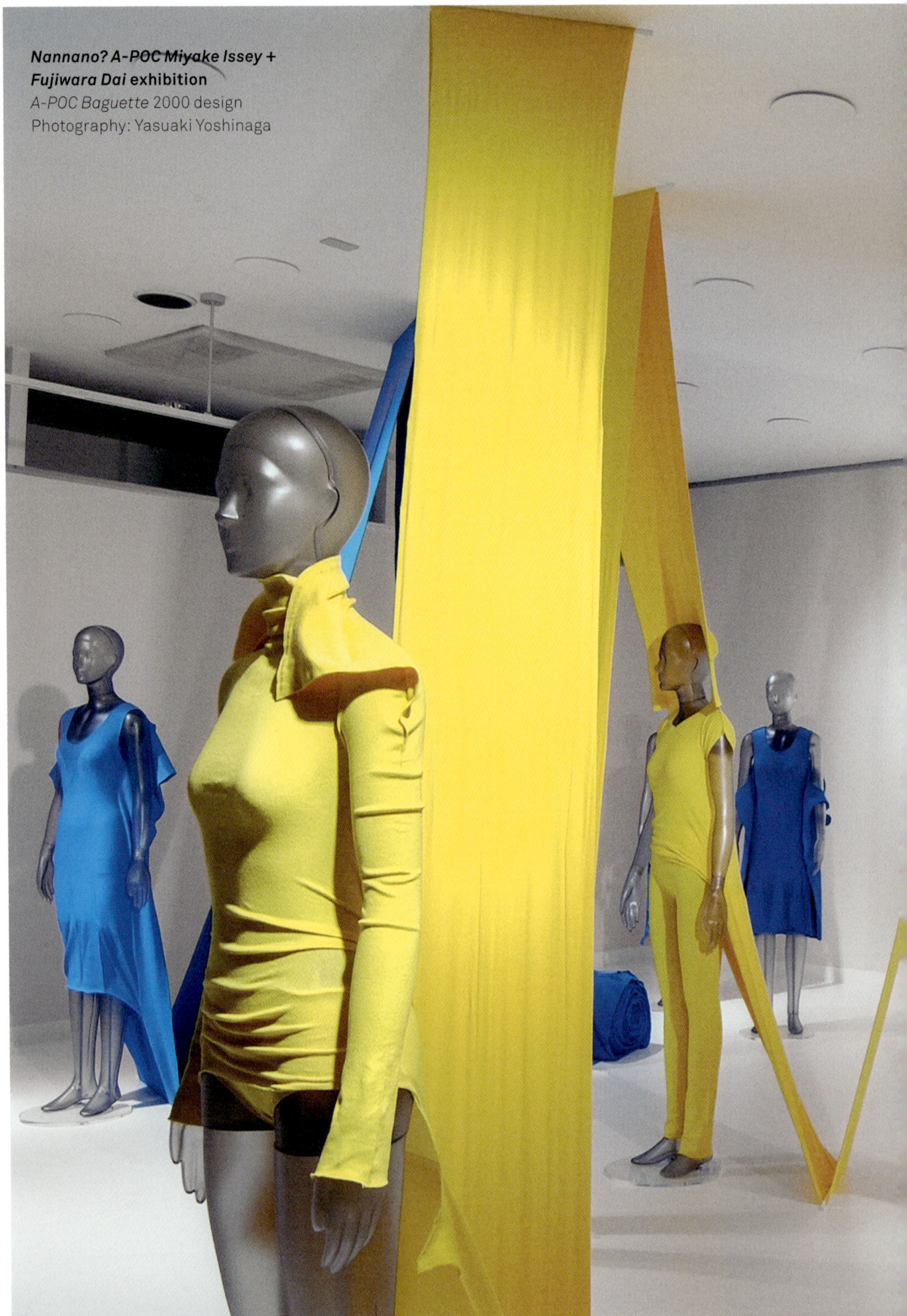

Nannano? A-POC Miyake Issey +
Fujiwara Dai exhibition
A-POC Baguette 2000 design
Photography: Yasuaki Yoshinaga

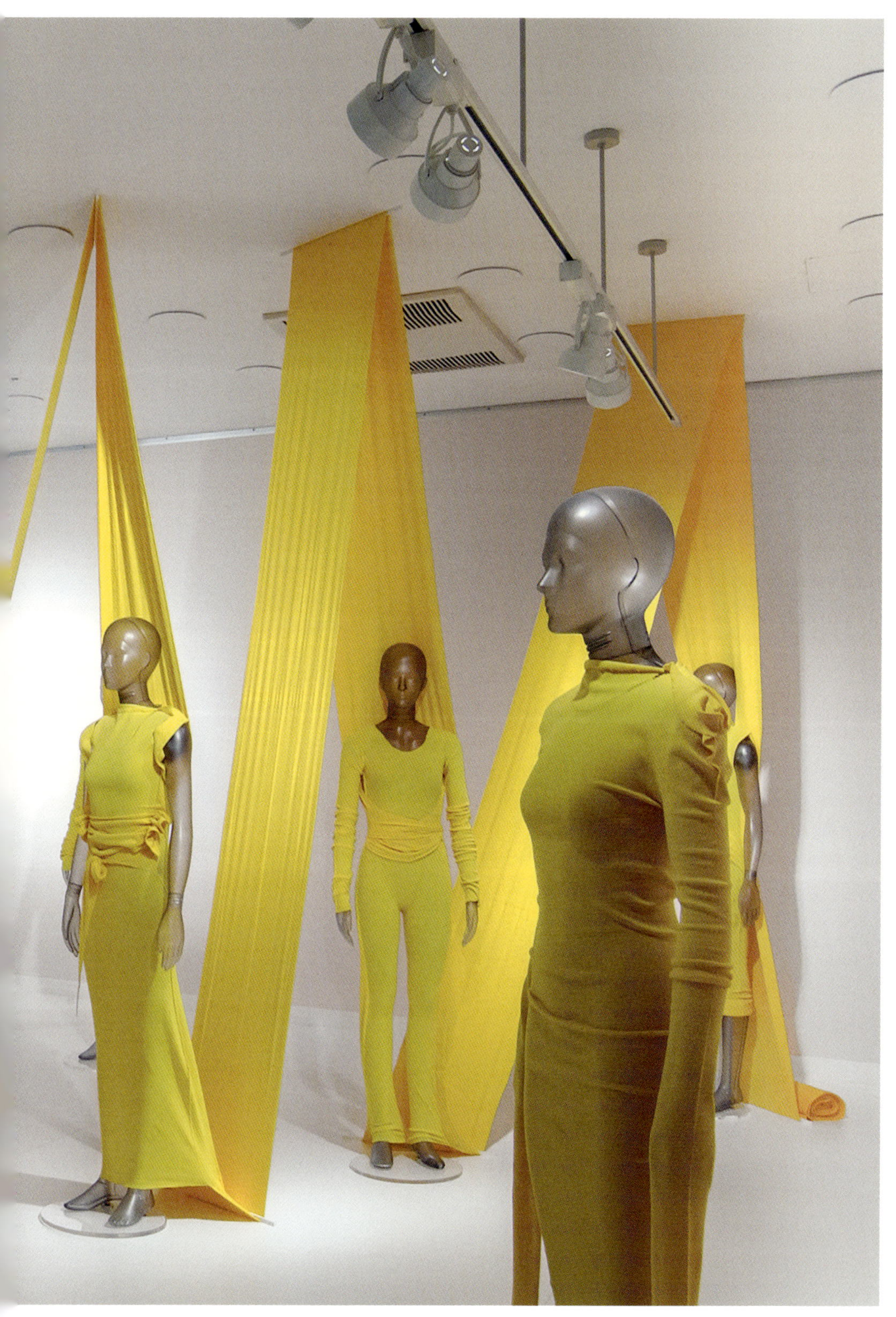

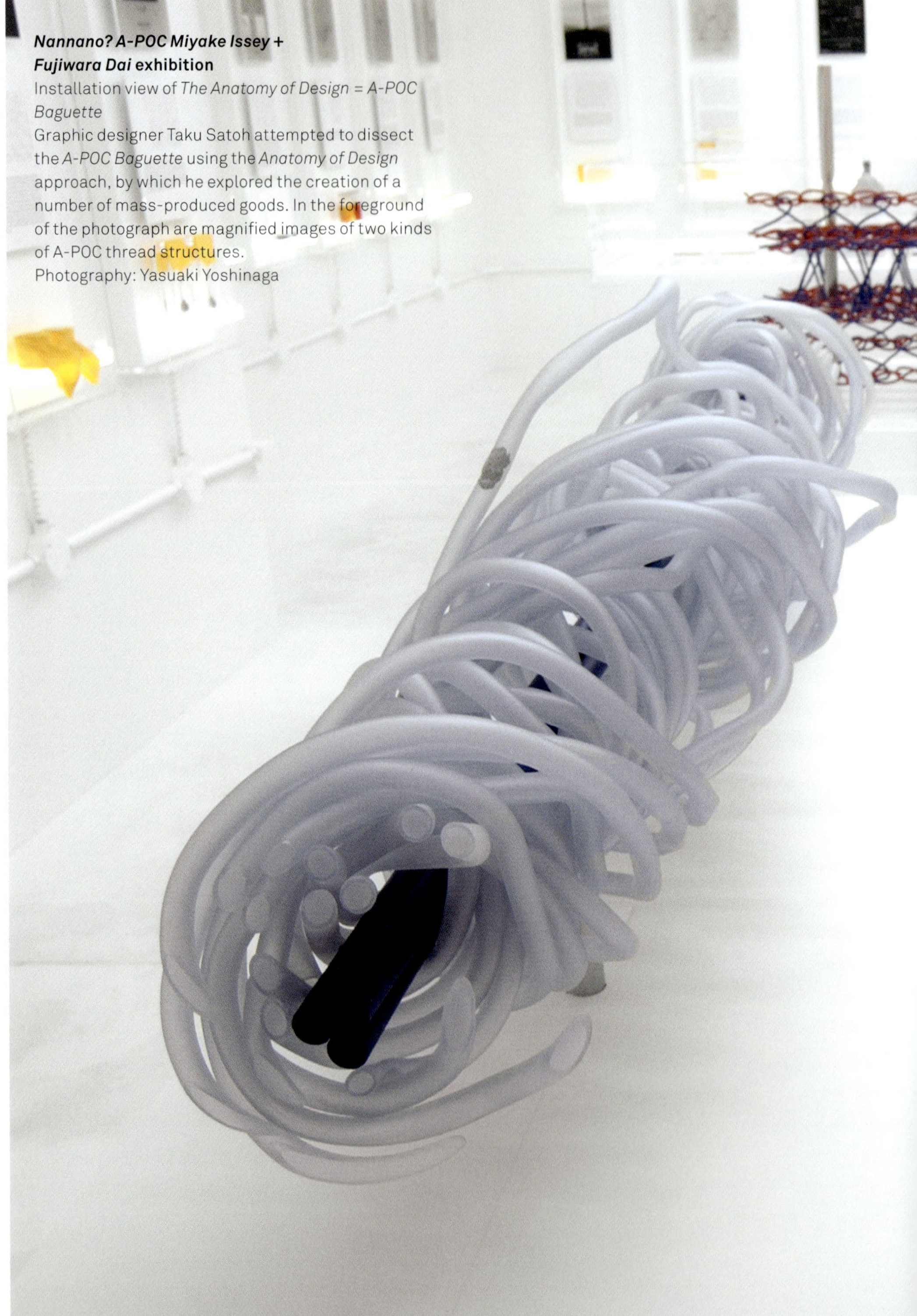

Nannano? A-POC Miyake Issey +
Fujiwara Dai **exhibition**
Installation view of *The Anatomy of Design = A-POC
Baguette*
Graphic designer Taku Satoh attempted to dissect
the *A-POC Baguette* using the *Anatomy of Design*
approach, by which he explored the creation of a
number of mass-produced goods. In the foreground
of the photograph are magnified images of two kinds
of A-POC thread structures.
Photography: Yasuaki Yoshinaga

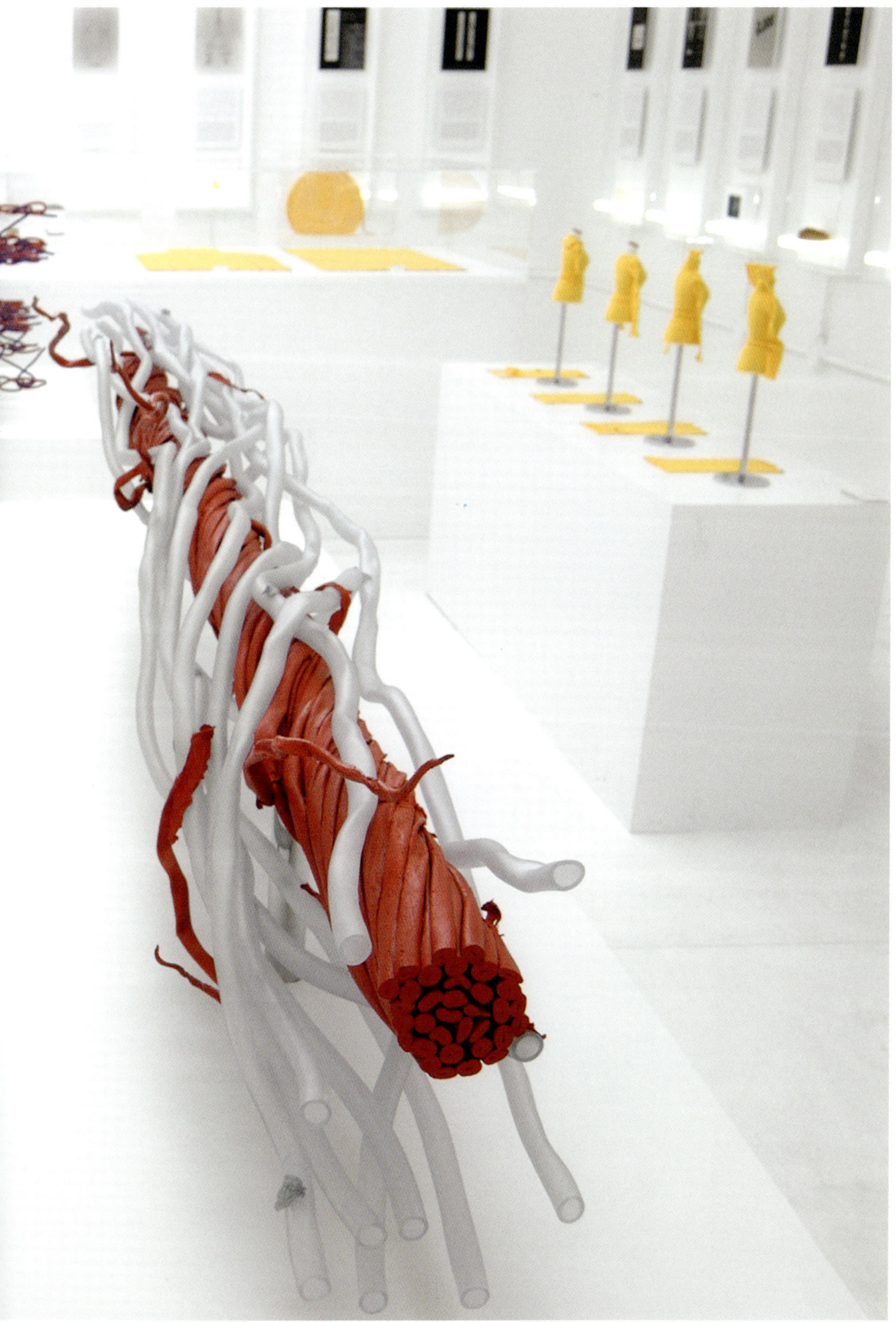

2004

> February: Establishment of the
Miyake Issey Foundation
> April: A-POC 12
> October: A-POC 13
> October–March 2005: Participated in
*The Encounters in the 21st Century:
Polyphony – Emerging Resonances,*
an exhibition to commemorate the
opening of the 21st Century Museum of
Contemporary Art, Kanazawa

*The Encounters in the 21st Century: Polyphony –
Emerging Resonances* **exhibition**

Miyake participated in *The Encounters in the
21st Century: Polyphony – Emerging Resonances,*
an exhibition to commemorate the opening of
the 21st Century Museum of Contemporary
Art, Kanazawa. He exhibited *A-POC Kanazawa,*
a fabric into which the museum's logo (design: Taku
Satoh) was woven as a motif. The museum was designed by SANAA (Kazuyo Sejima, Ryue Nishiza-
wa), and the logo was a floor plan of the building. It
was woven into a knit fabric which, when cut along
the lines of demarcation in the drawing, revealed
eight items: a shirt, cape, skirt, cap, gloves, socks,
bag, and cushion.

*October 9–March 21, 2005: 21st Century Museum of
Contemporary Art, Kanazawa*

Opposite: **A-POC Kanazawa**
2004 design
Photography: Marcus Tomlinson

1 A-POC 12
2 A-POC 13

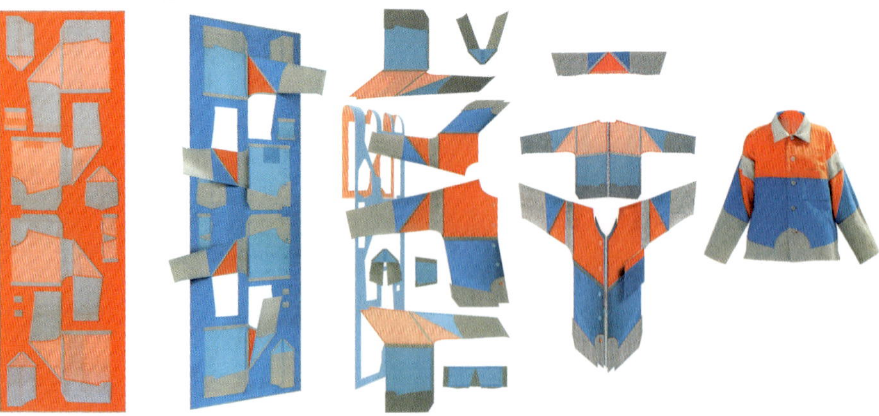

1

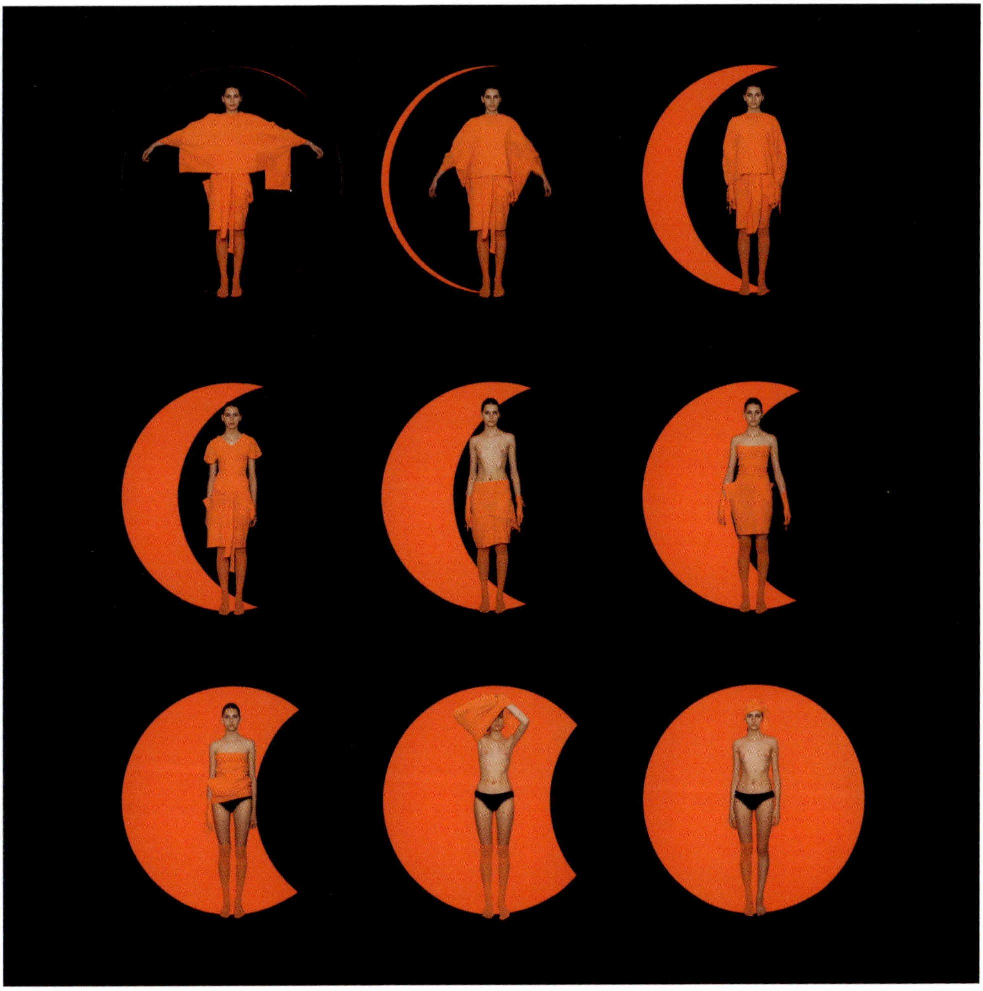

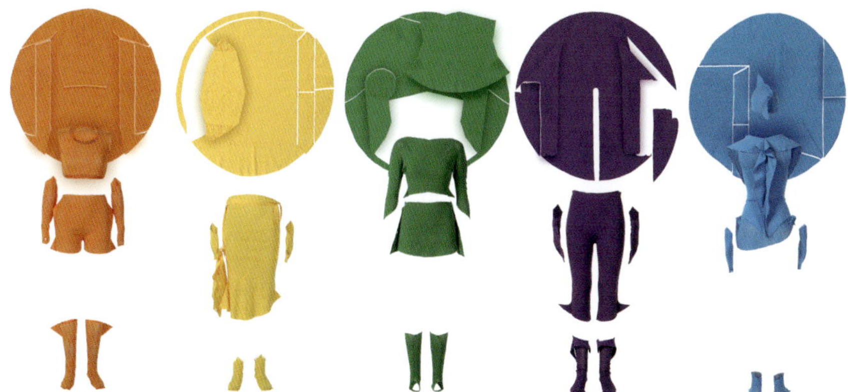

2

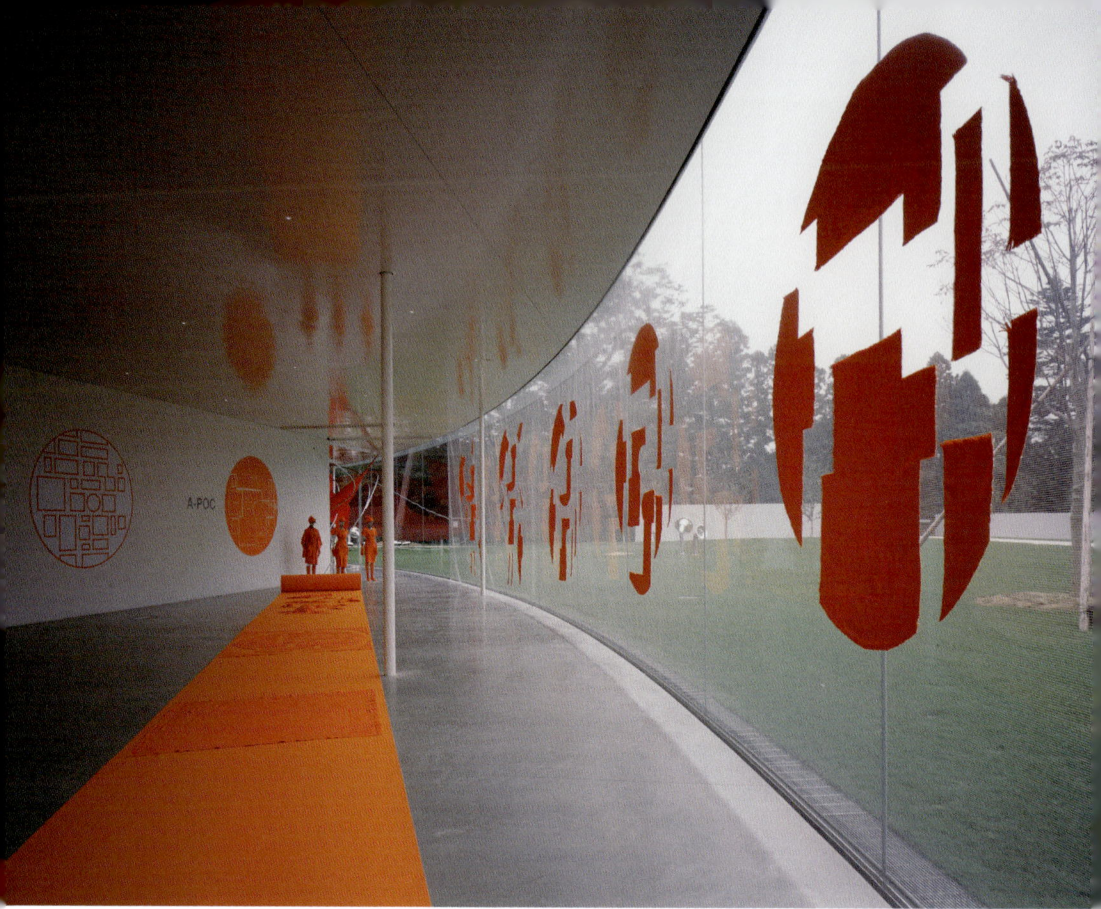

*The Encounters in the 21st Century: Polyphony –
Emerging Resonances* **exhibition** at the 21st Century
Museum of Contemporary Art, Kanazawa
Installation of *A-POC Kanazawa*
Space design: Tokujin Yoshioka
Photography: Shigeo Anzaï

Opposite: *The Encounters in the 21st Century:
Polyphony – Emerging Resonances* **exhibition** at the
21st Century Museum of Contemporary Art, Kanazawa
Installation of *A-POC Kanazawa* as seen from the garden
Photography: Shinkenchiku-sha

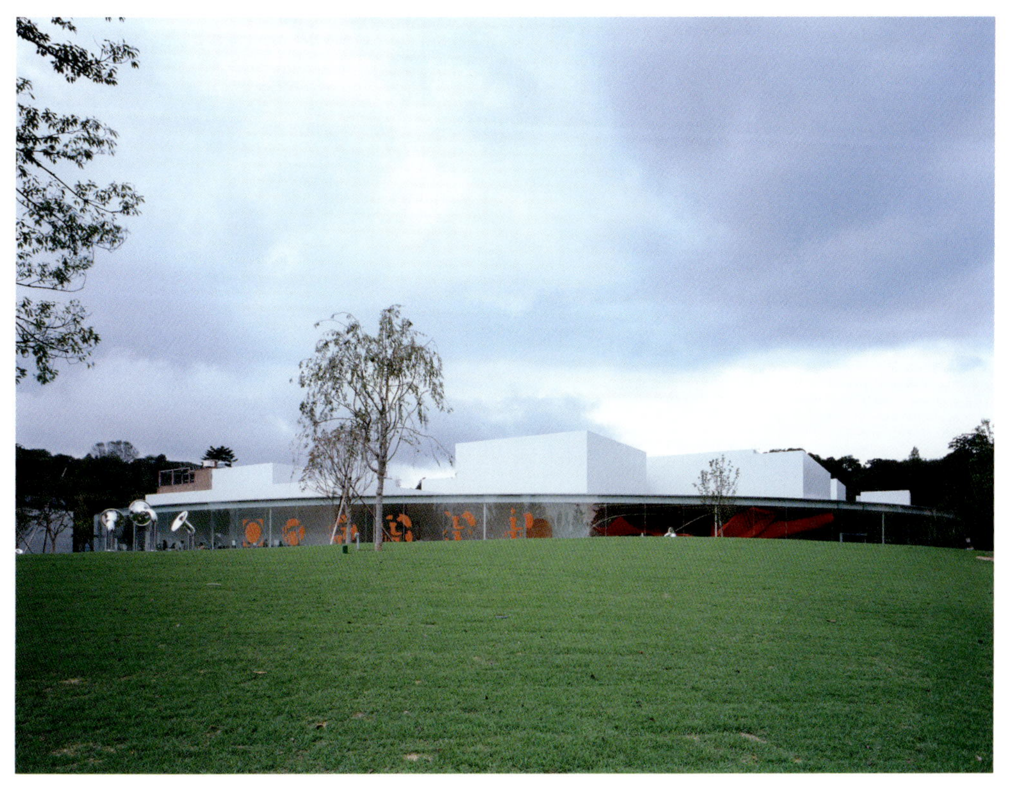

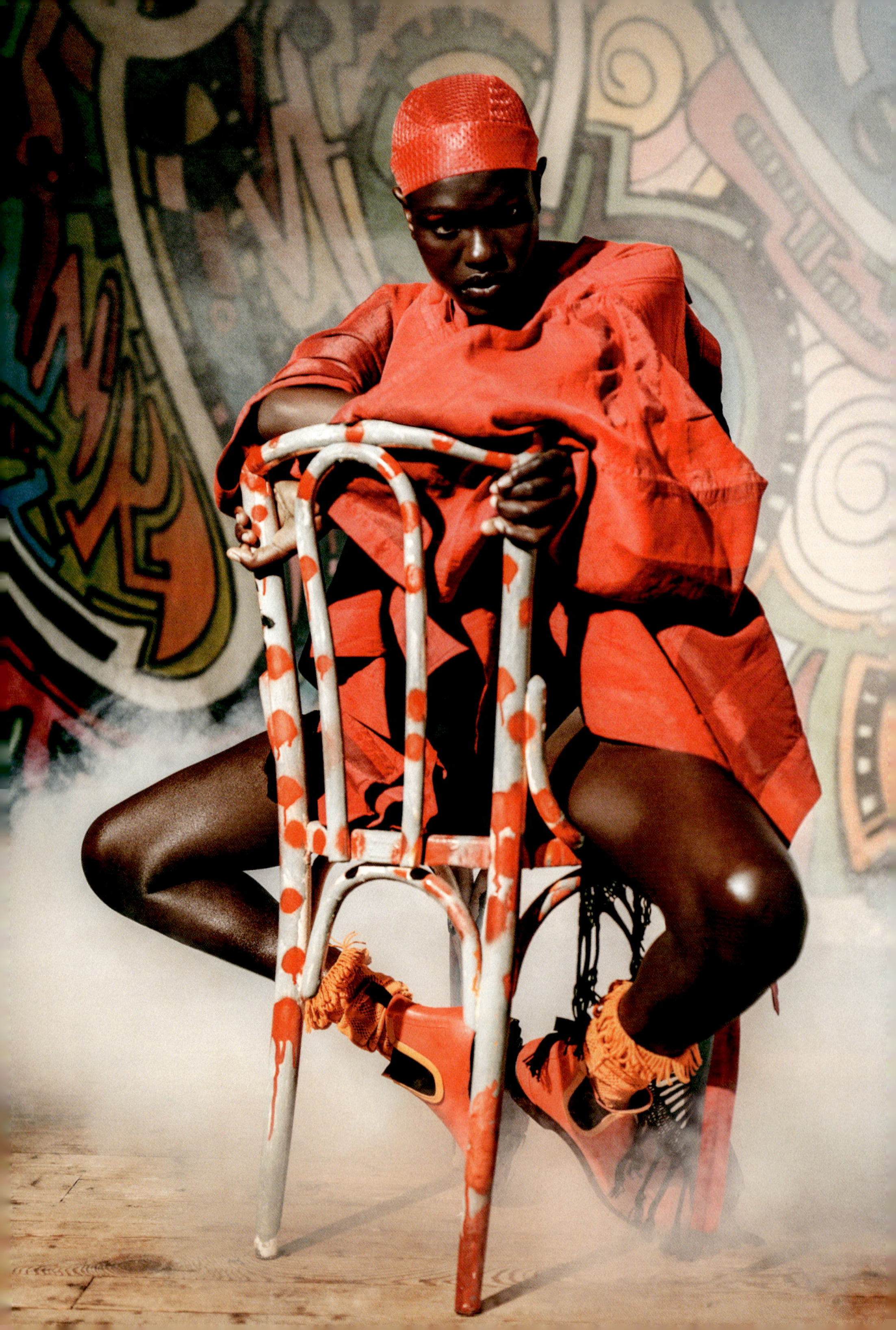

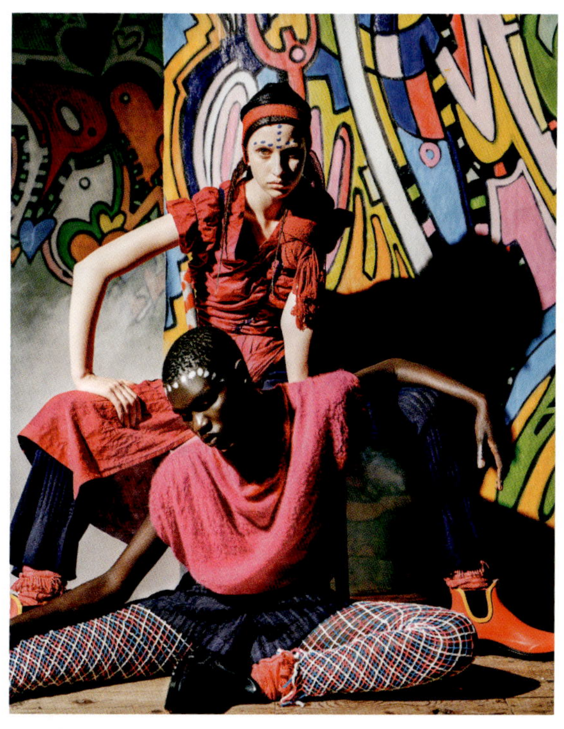

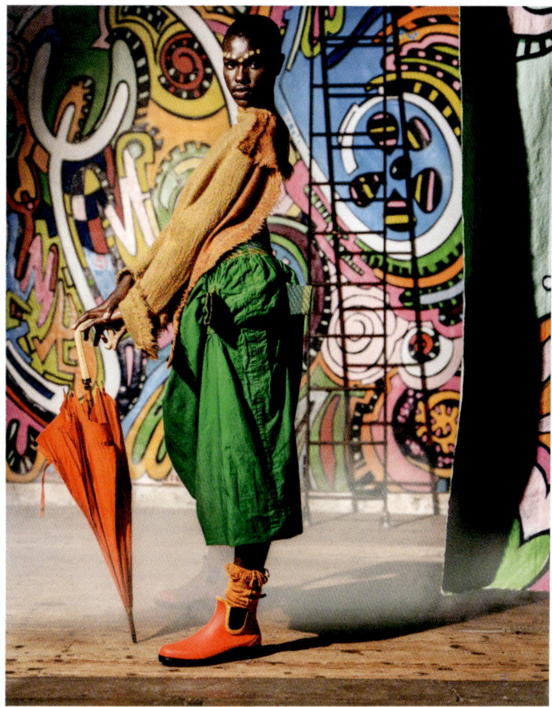

A-POC 12
2004 design
Creative direction and photography:
Hélène Renault-Kohn

2005

> April: A-POC 14
> April–June: Participated in *Big Bang: Destruction et création dans l'art du XXᵉ siècle* at Centre Ponpidou, Paris
> July–September: *Issey Miyake Paris Collections 1977–1999: Invitations by Tadanori Yokoo* exhibition in Toyama Prefecture
> September: A-POC 15
> December: *A-POC Queen* added to permanent collection of the Museum of Modern Art, New York, in the "Architecture & Design" archive

Issey Miyake Paris Collections 1977–1999: Invitations by Tadanori Yokoo exhibition

Tadanori Yokoo has always designed the Issey Miyake Paris Collection invitations; and all have been the same size, with a few exceptions. He continues to design them to this day. This exhibition featured the original drawings and submissions for the Paris Collection invitations from 1977 to 1999, together with large-screen videos of the Issey Miyake Paris Collections and clothes featuring Tadanori Yokoo print designs.

July 16–September 11:
The Museum of Modern Art, Toyama
Exhibition direction: Midori Kitamura; curation: Shoji Katagishi; space design: Tokujin Yoshioka; clothing installation: Naro Tamiya; video editing: Pascal Roulin and Sarah Mallinson; poster: Tadanori Yokoo (source images) and Kazumasa Nagai (graphic design)

A-POC 14

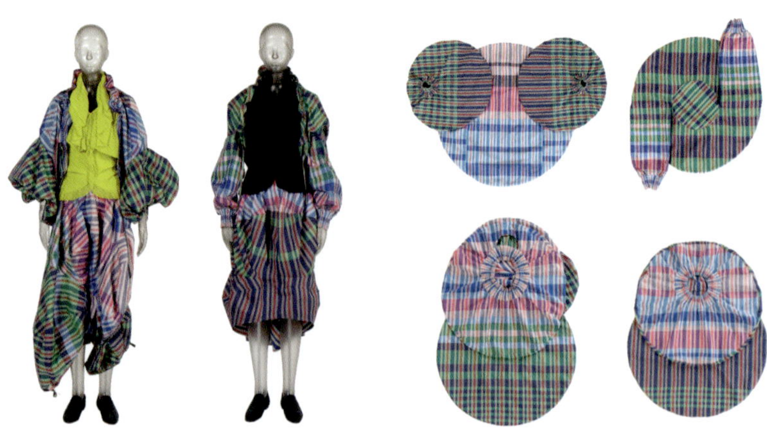

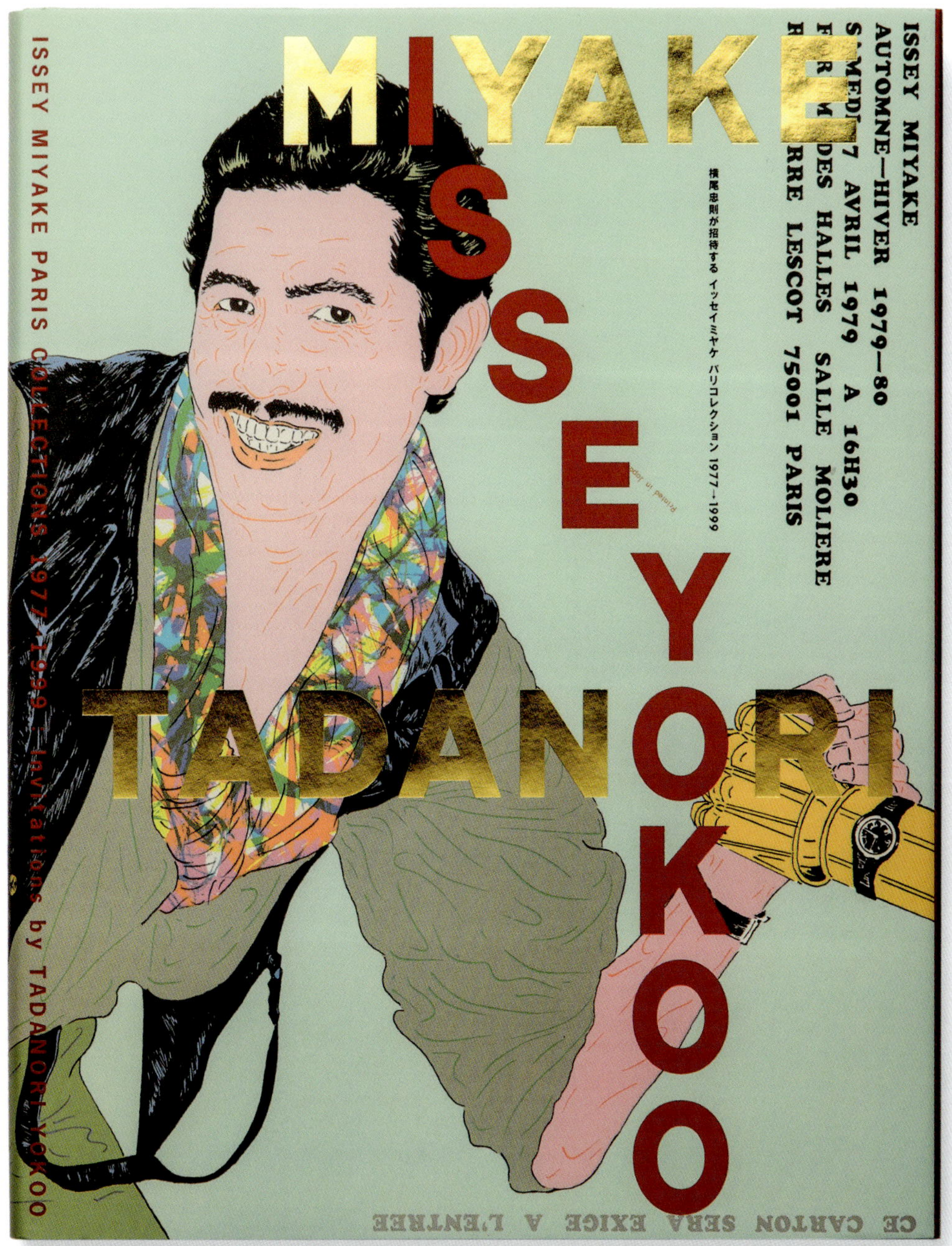

Issey Miyake Paris Collections 1977–1999:
Invitations by Tadanori Yokoo **exhibition** catalogue
published by Bijutsu Shuppan-sha Co., Ltd., 2005
Cover art: Tadanori Yokoo
Art direction: Taku Satoh

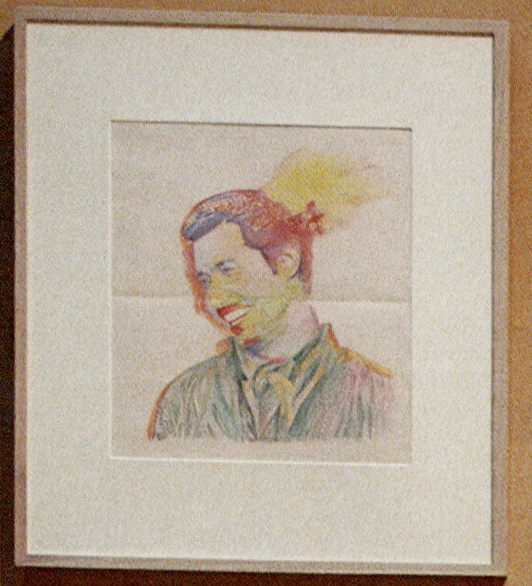

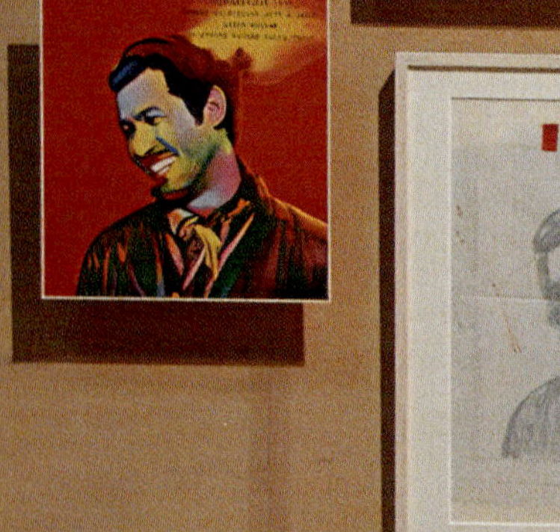

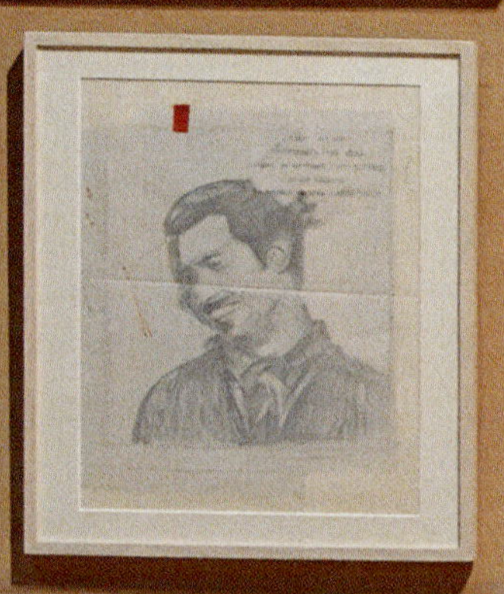

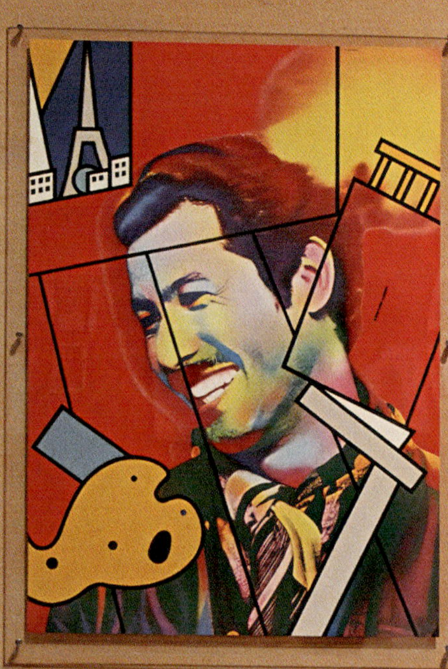

Issey Miyake Paris Collection 1977–1999:
Invitations by Tadanori Yokoo **exhibition**
Design process of the invitation to the
Spring-Summer 1979 Paris Collection.
From left: Invitation, original drawing (above),
mechanical specifications (below).
Poster on the right
Photography: Tadahisa Sakurai

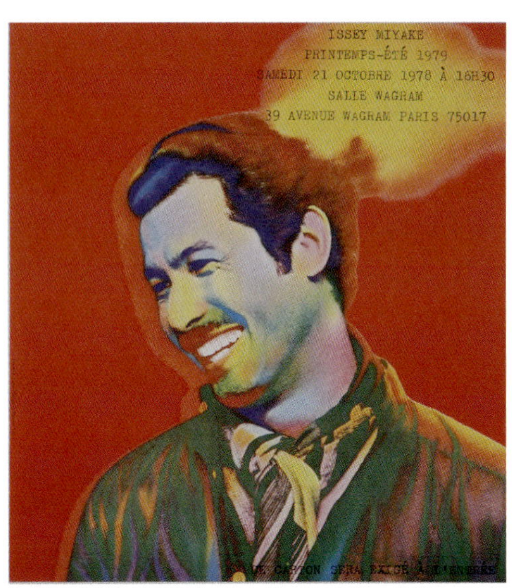

Invitation to the Spring-Summer
1979 Paris Collection
Design: Tadanori Yokoo

Below: Invitation to the Spring-Summer
1989 Paris Collection
Portraits of Issey Miyake were used as
a consistent motif through 1990.
Design: Tadanori Yokoo

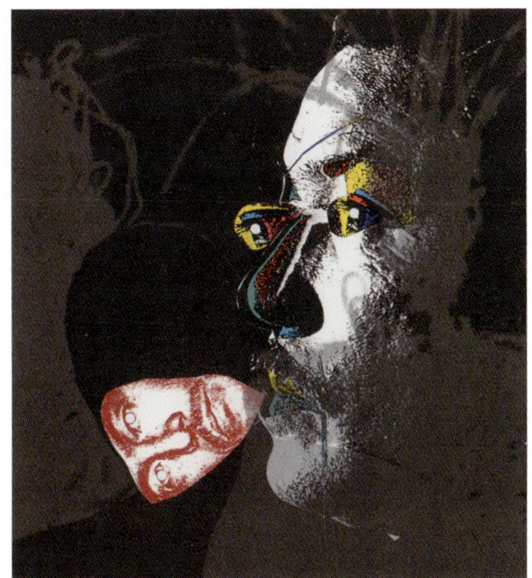

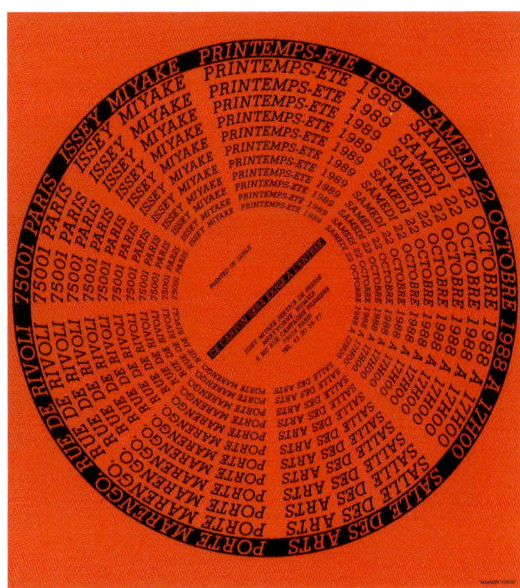

2006

Ron Arad by Moroso + A-POC by MDS
Collaboration between Ron Arad, an architect and product designer, and A-POC. The project began with the idea of putting A-POC clothes on Arad's *Ripple Chair,* designed for Moroso in 2005. The *Trampoline* was both a cover for the chair and a knit that could be worn. The second chair cover was a down vest and stole which became *Gemini.*

Jupiter
The application of A-POC technology to reinvent jeans. Parts for the five pockets on the jeans and the distressed patterns were all woven into the textile before cutting and sewing. This technique was able to reduce the amount of chemicals and water required for the distress-processing.
2006 design/A-POC 16

A-POC 16

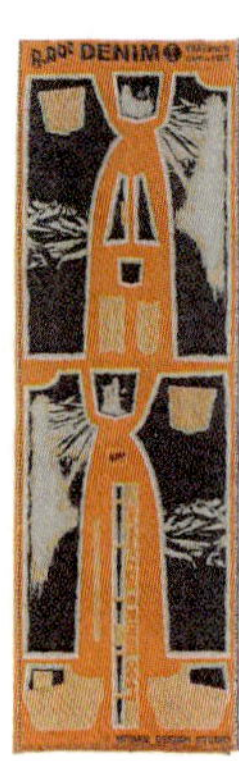
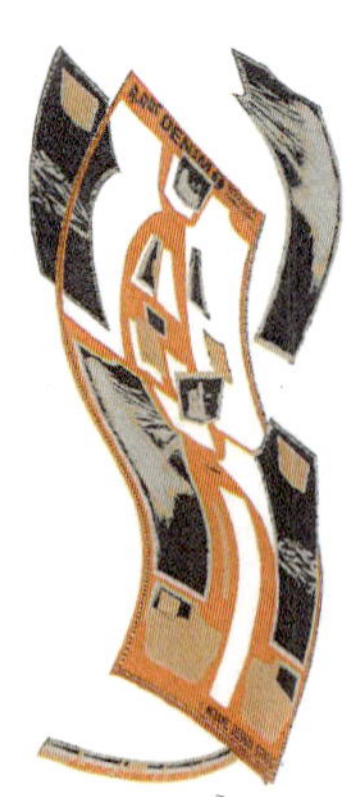
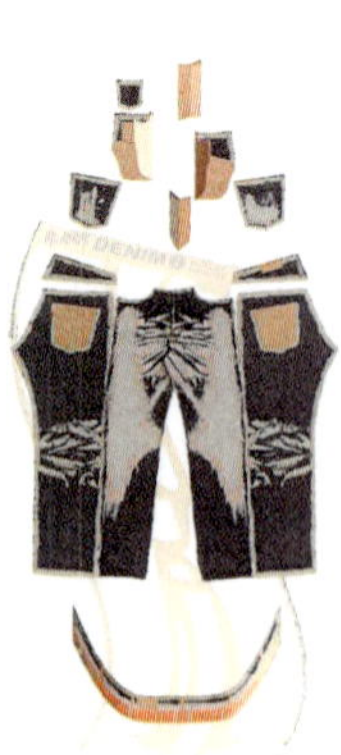
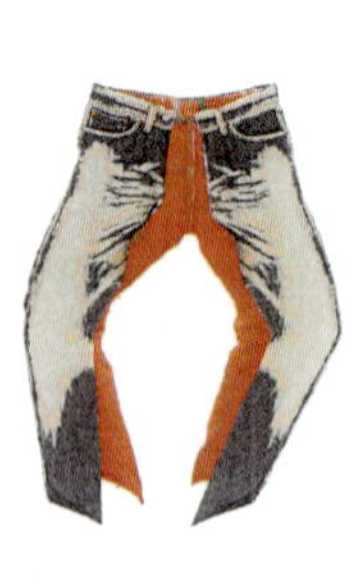
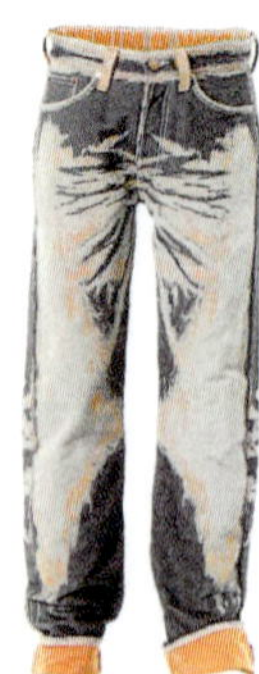

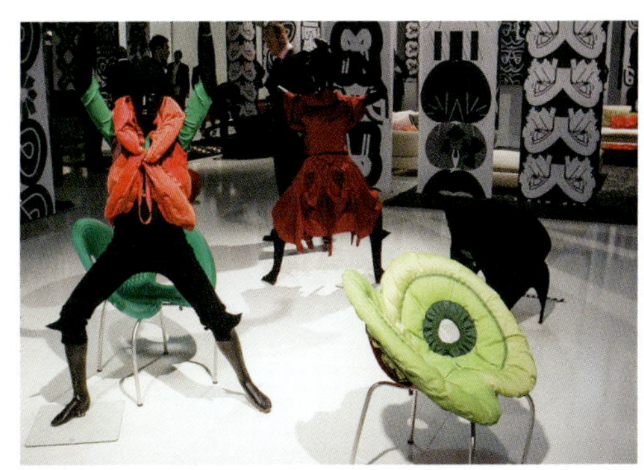

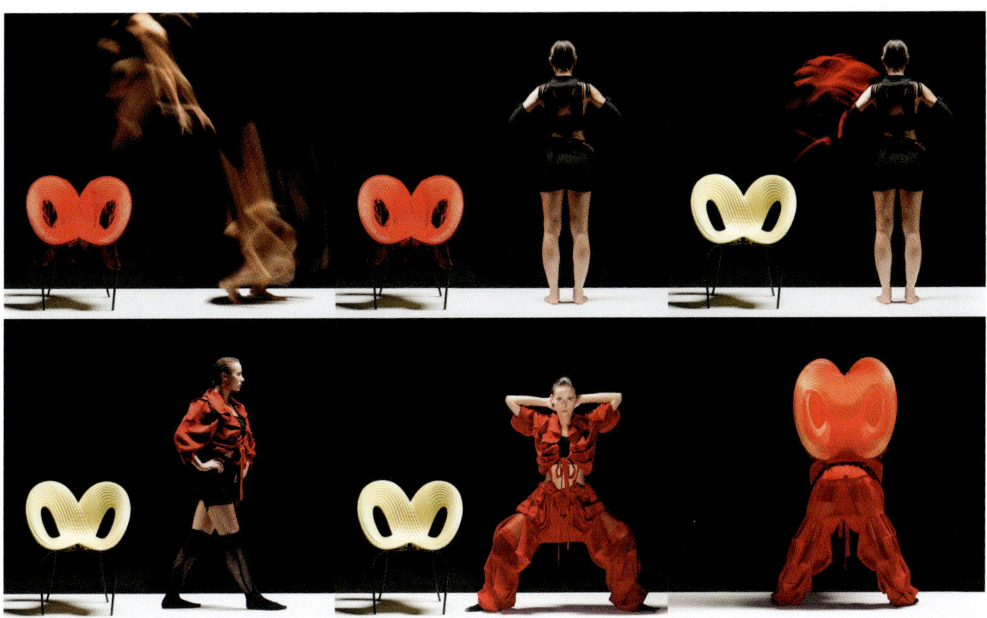

Ron Arad by Moroso + A-POC by MDS
Top: Installation view at the Salone del Mobile,
Milan, April 5–10

Above: ***Trampoline***
Knit jacket, pants, and stole patterned after
the Moroso *Ripple Chair* designed by Ron Arad.
Can also be used as a covering for the chairs.
2005 design/A-POC 15
Photography: Marcus Tomlinson

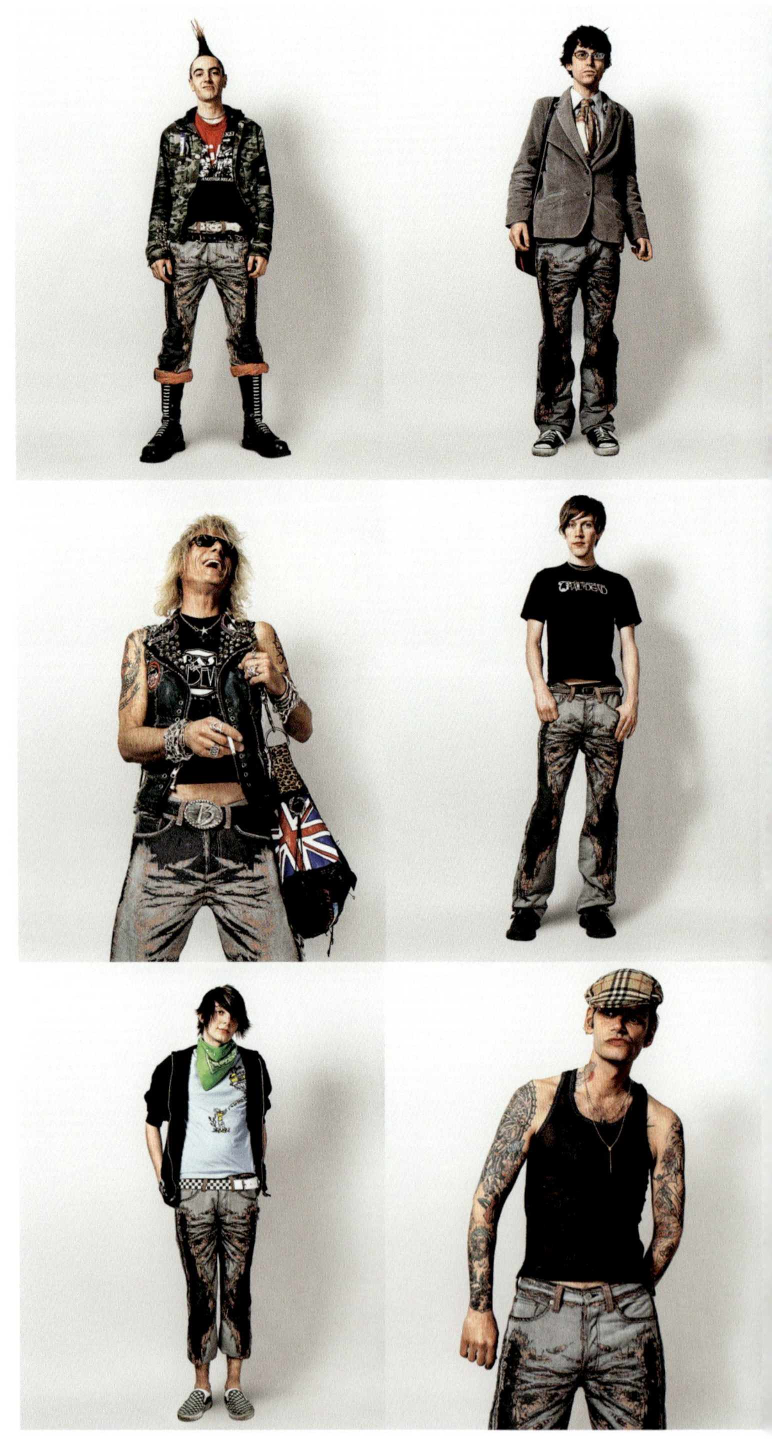

The photographer asked random New Yorkers whom he met on the street to wear the *Jupiter* jeans as they liked, and photographed them in situ.
Photography:
James Mollison

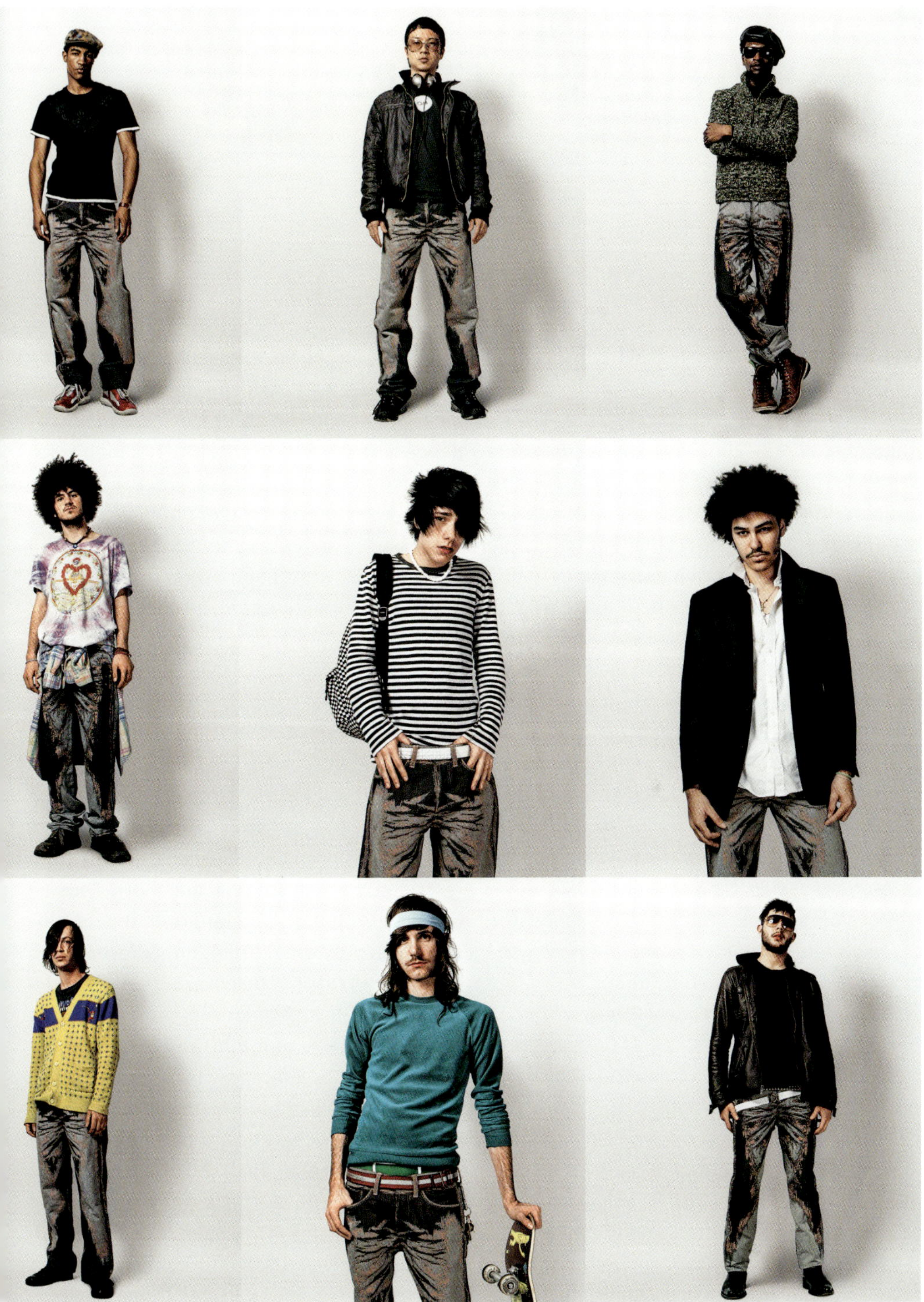

8—A DEVICE FOR TRANSMITTING CULTURE

Essay by
KAZUKO KOIKE

WHAT WAS DISCOVERED AT 21_21 DESIGN SIGHT?

Roppongi, Winter 2007. Exactly as its name suggests, in the center of the immense city, appeared TOKYO MIDTOWN, a multi-feature commercial building. But adjacent to it came another building, this one designed by Tadao Ando,[1] and with a strong presence thanks to its flat rooftop design, 21_21 DESIGN SIGHT.[2] The Miyake Issey Foundation is responsible for planning and realizing the programs presented there.

> *The concept of "a piece of cloth" – "from flatness to volume" – central to Miyake's original inspiration for making clothing – was at the basis too of the building's architectural design. He wondered if it would be possible to deploy that creative concept to an architectural space, and ultimately the one-piece iron roof came about.*
>
> **Tadao Ando, *A Hard-Fought Process: Construction Site 2006 – 21_21 DESIGN SIGHT*, Tadao Ando Exhibition Committee, 2007**

The quotation comes from Ando, and the subtitle of the publication, *Construction Site 2006 – 21_21 DESIGN SIGHT*, echoes the title of the opening exhibition at the new venue. It revealed the architect's twist-and-turn anguish in the process that culminated in the realization of the 54-meter-long, single-piece iron roof, as well as a variety of other technical problems. The show was fully in accordance with 21_21 DESIGN SIGHT's manifesto of its founding mission.

For Issey Miyake, the act of designing always had a verbal quality to it too. Even in those cases where something is made and achieves its creative goal, he considered that each stage in the process itself went through change and growth. He also recognized that design decisions are born out of a deep-rooted relationship with our times and the realities of society. As for the facility's appellation, he adopted the word "sight," suggesting vision, instead of "site," suggesting place, which would have been the choice if one were restricted by conventional concepts. Thus he did away with the signboard term that is generally used by museums and galleries. This was done in favor of discovering yet unknown values. The joy of discovery was a primary source of interest for him, and is at the core of the values he shared with Ando.

To date, 28 exhibitions have been mounted here under the supervision of the three directors, Miyake, Taku Satoh, and Naoto Fukasawa,[3] and by the associate director, Noriko Kawakami.[4] They have attracted much attention for their intriguing content and high quality, and the series of shows were awarded a Special Prize in the 2014 Mainichi Design Awards. Japanese and foreign designers and artists who have participated in the exhibitions have numbered about 300.[5]

The creative and original exhibitions held at 21_21 DESIGN SIGHT have proved important in informing the public of design's great potential, while at the same time enlightening them as to cutting-edge ideas. What the site's promoters hope to see come about is that 21_21 DESIGN SIGHT is regarded as a place where objects and events can be seen and experienced (and not just placed and stored for view), where the public feels that they are looking into something important about their future life and way of thinking. The public evolves together with the artists and designers. Having a design museum is thus crucial in this regard.

HOPE PROPELLED BY CRISIS

Issey Miyake confessed to intense self-questioning as to his capability of grasping the social and global changes to come.[6] Given that clothing is a direct part of quotidian life, he was from early on concerned about and dealt with global warming and pollution. To give one small example, he had long required his design teams to verify at any product's developmental stage if dry-cleaning is a proper choice. He then decided that his theme pertaining to the future should simply read "re-birth, re-creation."

Miyake also knew that petroleum and crude oil are limited resources, and that it must be possible to somehow restore and reuse, and even to upcycle them. This became a mission for him, and he sought to make clothing with enhanced ecological values.

Just as he was moving along this line, he learned that factories and plants in Japan were being closed, one after another.

I found it was not just machines but also people with skills and techniques that were going abroad ... depressing. ... In the past, there were factory teams in each region in the country that by itself could take care of everything required for mono zukuri *(making things). Now, however, we should welcome it if only a single plant per region remains.*
Interview, "Proposition for the Future," *Bijutsu Techo Journal*, December 2012

Despite this situation, Miyake was determined. He found out, "as soon as I started thinking about materials suited for the 21st century, that Teijin Fiber, a major textile manufacturer, was developing a fantastic recycled polyester material," and his wish to "make things from this base, even by developing threads," came true.

Part of Miyake's approach to design was the act of "folding." Folding has been a time-honored practice necessary for storing things, and, especially for kimonos, folding is a traditional and necessary matter of aesthetic beauty. Miyake delegated a young and capable team to pursue restoration and reuse of materials, and also joined with Tsukuba University's researchers specializing in algorithms and started to combine their study of 3D *origami* with his design efforts in using the latest fibers and textiles.

Clothing made of the newly recycled textile was named 132 5. ISSEY MIYAKE[7] and was presented in 2010 in Tokyo in August, and in Paris in September. In November an exhibition was held to announce its launch at 21_21 DESIGN SIGHT under the title *REALITY LAB.*[8] "3D origami structures are made into 2D ones by means of an original method, and from these arise clothes," read the statement. They looked so moving as they embodied what Miyake was now about. He named the production team Reality Lab. They confront reality at all phases and address all of the tasks pertaining to raw materials, threads, fabrics, and the making of clothes, cherishing the work process as a team made up of both textile and patterning experts together with young designers.

INHERITING THE TRADITION OF LIGHT AND SHADOW

Reality Lab was launched in 2007, and their research on the recycled polyester material diverged into the field of lighting devices. "How about applying the material to lamp shades?" When creased, the material demonstrated unique features, and its strength and robustness were also proven. Unwoven fabric was experimented with and tested, and a lighting device that has no structural elements but stands erect by itself came into existence.

I thought it was almost a dream. More than 50 years had passed since Isamu Noguchi was fascinated by the *chochin* paper lanterns of Japan's Gifu prefecture and became intrigued by the beauty of *washi* (Japanese paper) as a material, and these gave birth to AKARI. "Isamu-san! Issey has done a great job using a future-oriented material," I couldn't resist screaming, recalling how I had witnessed their passionate friendship. I also wanted to communicate with overseas friends and designers who have cherished Jun'ichiro Tanizaki's essay "In Praise of Shadows," and thus come to understand the Japanese sensibility, including our sense of space, and to point to how tradition and renovation undergo a ceaseless continuum of creation, as the work of the Reality Lab shows. The night I learned about Issey's new lighting device I slept very little.

Artemide of Italy decided to distribute this IN-EI ISSEY MIYAKE[9] globally. I wonder why Japanese corporations are still so slow in appreciating such heuristic ventures.

ISSEY JUMPS AGAIN

Yoyogi, the district in Tokyo where the forest attached to the Meiji Shrine and the National Olympic Stadium are located, tends to be neglected by Tokyo passersby leading their complicated, busy lives, except for when temporary *Cirque du Soleil* tents are erected, or concerts by foreign opera companies are held at NHK Hall, and very large crowds sweep through the area. Since its inauguration in 1964 for the Olympic Games, the Kenzo Tange–designed National Stadium, with its organic steeple, has been entertaining the eyes of anyone who passes through Yoyogi.

In July 2013, a surprise event happened in the facility's second gym under the steeple, a performance of *Shintaiso* rhythmic gymnastics by the Aomori University Men's Rhythmic Gymnastics Team.[10] The event had been conceived by Miyake. He had created a number of designs and products over the years observing certain aspects of human behavior and movement, and this time he fancied combining clothing with men's physical performance. Men's rhythmic gymnastics had been authorized as a sport in Japan, and Miyake saw the Aomori University Men's Rhythmic Gymnastics Team on a TV program. He was very anxious after an earthquake struck Tohoku, Japan's northeastern region, in 2011 and destroyed grassroots centers of *mono zukuri* in the region, and he made public appeals for help. To name only one example, he organized the exhibition *Tohoku no Sokojikara* (*The Spirit of Tohoku:*

"Clothing" by Issey Miyake)[11] and it was held at 21_21 DESIGN SIGHT in July 2011, immediately after the disaster. The presentation at the Olympic Stadium by the young men of the university, who had entered the school from all over Japan to study, was powerfully beautiful and excited everyone who came to see it.

At the same time, Miyake and the Reality Lab team had by then gone deeper into their research regarding pleated clothes for men. Juxtaposing rhythmic gymnastics into a new kind of men's clothing felt like a chemical reaction, and the idea occurred to him of presenting them in a performance at the Yoyogi National Stadium. It was directed by renowned choreographer Daniel Ezralow, known for directing (in part) the opening ceremony of the 2014 Sochi Winter Olympic Games, and who had also been a part of Miyake's Plantation brand Autumn-Winter 1984 Collection as a dancer and choreographer.

In the students' rhythmic gymnastics performance, the Miyake-designed costumes swung loosely and elegantly in split-second rapport with body movements. The "Issey Miyake and Men's Rhythmic Gymnastics" of that evening ignited the excitement of the audience. Those who had long been in attendance at his shows were reminded of earlier occasions and all their commotion, while younger students and artists, attending such a performance for the first time, were inspired by its empowering force. Later, the gymnasts' costume-like uniforms were made available to the marketplace as the brand HOMME PLISSÉ ISSEY MIYAKE, and it is noteworthy that this clothing line offered the public a new kind of masculine image.[12]

Our dear Issey is to be seen jumping relentlessly across national borders and the would-be boundaries of various creative genres, over many different living creatures' boundaries, and even more.

1 Tadao Ando (1941–): Architect. Self-educated, founded Tadao Ando Architect & Associates in 1969. Representative works include Row House in Sumiyoshi, 1976; Church of the Light, 1989; Modern Art Museum of Fort Worth, 2002; Chichu Art Musuem, 2004, and many others. Serves on the Hanshin-Awaji Earthquake 10th Anniversary Restoration Assistance Committee; in 2000 founded the Setouchi Olive Foundation, promoting olive tree planting.

2 21_21 DESIGN SIGHT: See pp. 292–293.

3 Naoto Fukasawa (1956–): Product designer. In 1989, moved to USA to work at IDEO, design consultants; returned to Japan, and established IDEO Tokyo subsidiary in 1996; started Naoto Fukasawa Design in 2003 and has undertaken numerous projects with Japanese, European, and US corporations. Director of the Japan Folk Crafts Museum since 2012. Director of 21_21 DESIGN SIGHT.

4 Noriko Kawakami: Journalist. After working for *AXIS* design journal, freelance journalist and editor since 1993. Associate director of 21_21 DESIGN SIGHT.

5 Information in this text is based on totals through 2015.

6 From an interview by Yoshiko Ikoma with Issey Miyake, "Proposition for the Future," *Bijutsu Techo* journal, December 2012.

7 132 5. ISSEY MIYAKE: See pp. 298–305.

8 *REALITY LAB* exhibition: See pp. 300–301.

9 IN-EI ISSEY MIYAKE: See pp. 310, 312–313.

10 Aomori University Men's Rhythmic Gymnastics Team: See pp. 314–317.

11 Exhibition *Tohoku no Sokojikara* (*The Spirit of Tohoku: "Clothing" by Issey Miyake*): See pp. 308–309.

12 HOMME PLISSÉ ISSEY MIYAKE: See p. 314.

2007

> March: Opened 21_21 DESIGN SIGHT in Tokyo
> The Reality Lab research and development team was formed to explore new approaches to making things

21_21 DESIGN SIGHT

The Miyake Issey Foundation, established in 2004, opened a design facility in Tokyo Midtown with support from the Mitsui Fudosan Co., Ltd. Issey Miyake's idea of creating a center for design in Japan started in 1988 with a conversation with Isamu Noguchi and Tadao Ando at the time of the *Isamu Noguchi* exhibition in New York and took a step forward with the opening of 21_21 DESIGN SIGHT. Miyake was appointed a director together with Taku Satoh and Naoto Fukasawa. Noriko Kawakami was appointed associate director. The institution offers a changing program of talk events and workshops, focusing on different-themed exhibitions orchestrated by the directors from their individual perspectives.

21_21 DESIGN SIGHT exhibition posters: *Tadao Ando Construction Site 2006 "A Hard-Fought Process," Chocolate, Lucky Luck Show, This Play!,* and *Water*

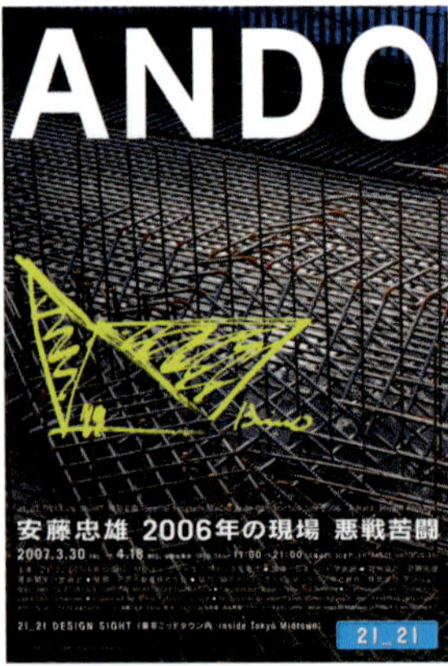

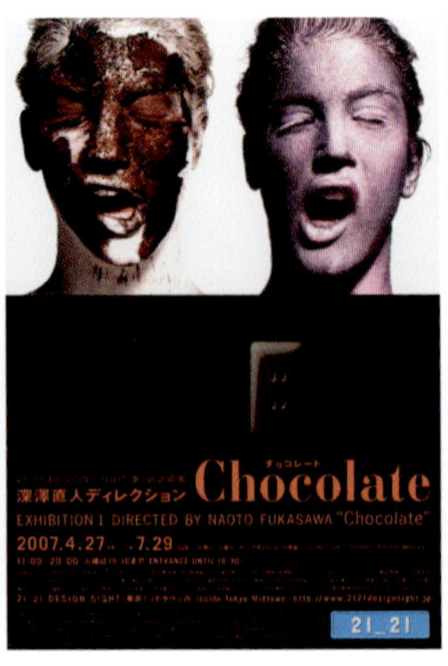

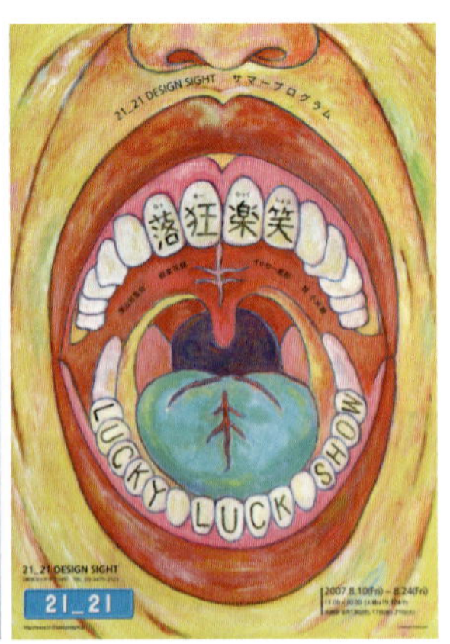

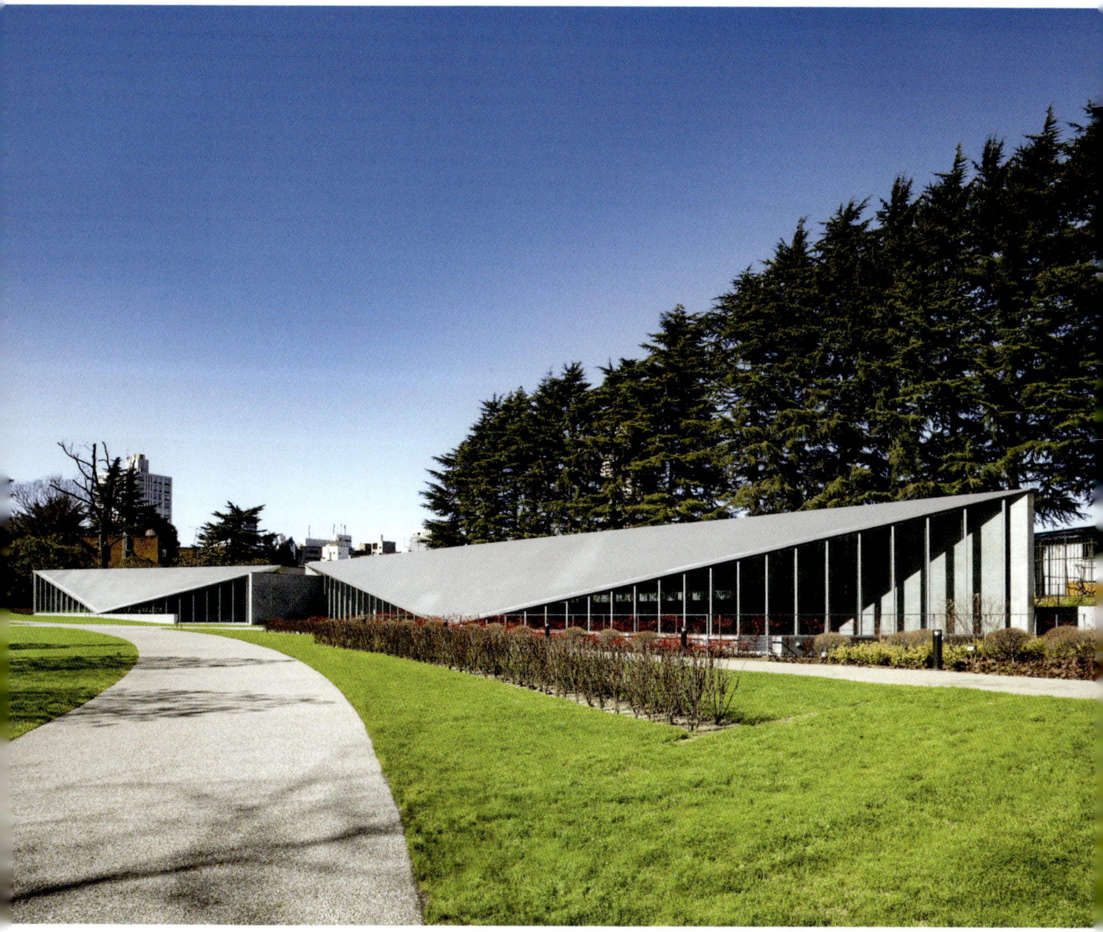

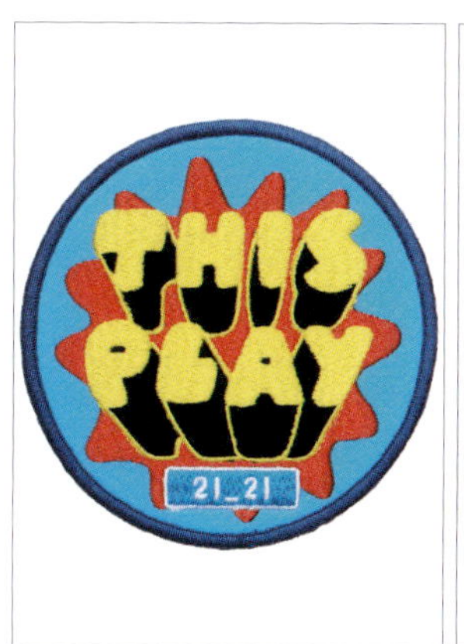

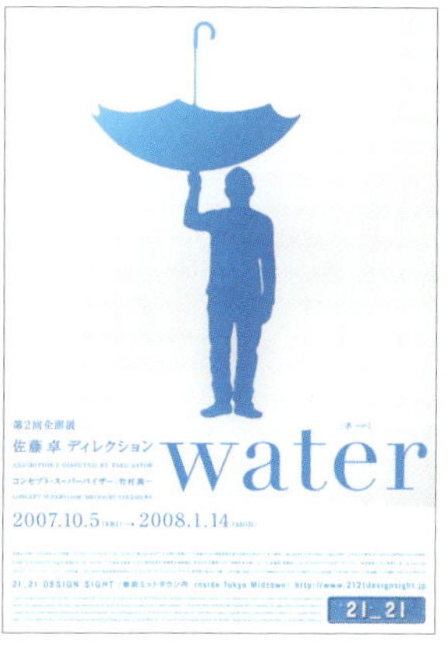

Exterior of 21_21 DESIGN SIGHT
Tadao Ando did the architectural design.
The 54-meter-long roof was built from a
single piece of metal in honor of Miyake's
touchstone concept of creating clothing
from "One Piece of Cloth." More than 70 per-
cent of the building's total volume is underground, and the underground galleries
measure approximately 576 square meters.
Photography: Masaya Yoshimura

2008

> Directed *XXIc. – XXIst Century Man*
exhibition at 21_21 DESIGN SIGHT

XXIc. – XXIst Century Man exhibition

The "XXIc." in the title is a symbol used in archae-ology and museum studies for the 21st century, and the exhibition explored the possibilities of bodies, lives, design, and manufacturing in an age facing serious environmental issues and de-pletion of resources. It featured 11 designers and artists, including an India-ink drawing by Isamu Noguchi. Issey Miyake directed the exhibition and also displayed an installation called *Myth of the 21st Century*. The research and production work done for this installation led to the development of 132 5. ISSEY MIYAKE.

March 30–July 6: 21_21 DESIGN SIGHT
Exhibition direction: Issey Miyake; space design:
Dui Seid; sound design: Masato Hatanaka; poster and
graphic design: Taku Satoh
Participating artists: Isamu Noguchi, Tim Hawkinson,
Ron Arad, Kotaro Sekiguchi, Dui Seid, Dai Fujiwara +
ISSEY MIYAKE Creative Room, Ben Wilson, Yasuhiro
Suzuki, nendo, Yazou Hokama, and Issey Miyake

21_21 DESIGN SIGHT exhibition posters for
Bulls Eye Special 2008, *XXIc.–XXIst Century Man*,
Whispered Prayers, and *Second Nature*

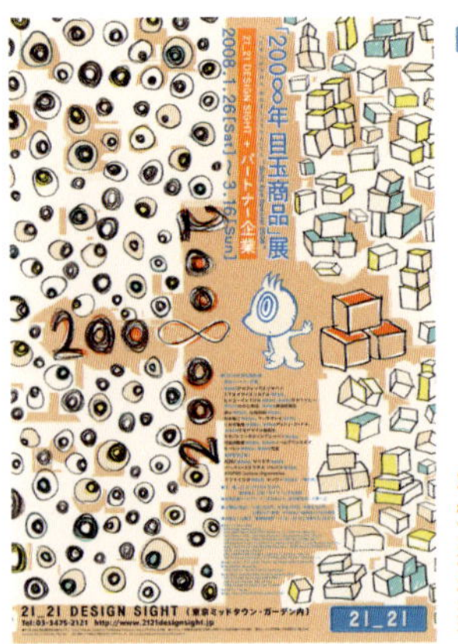
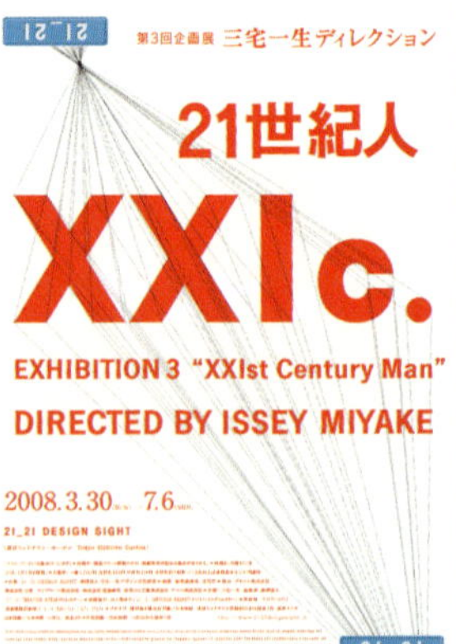

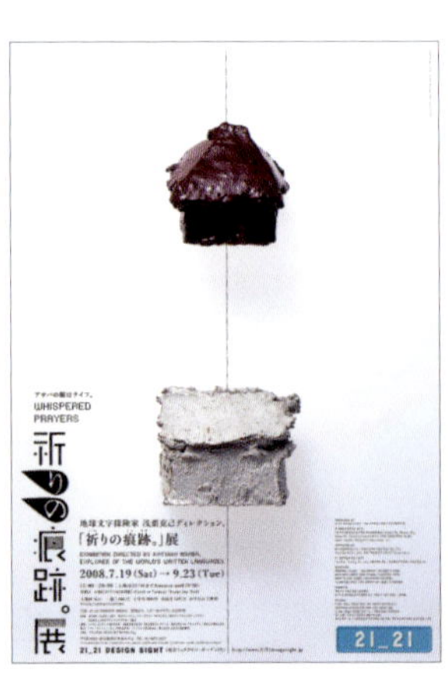

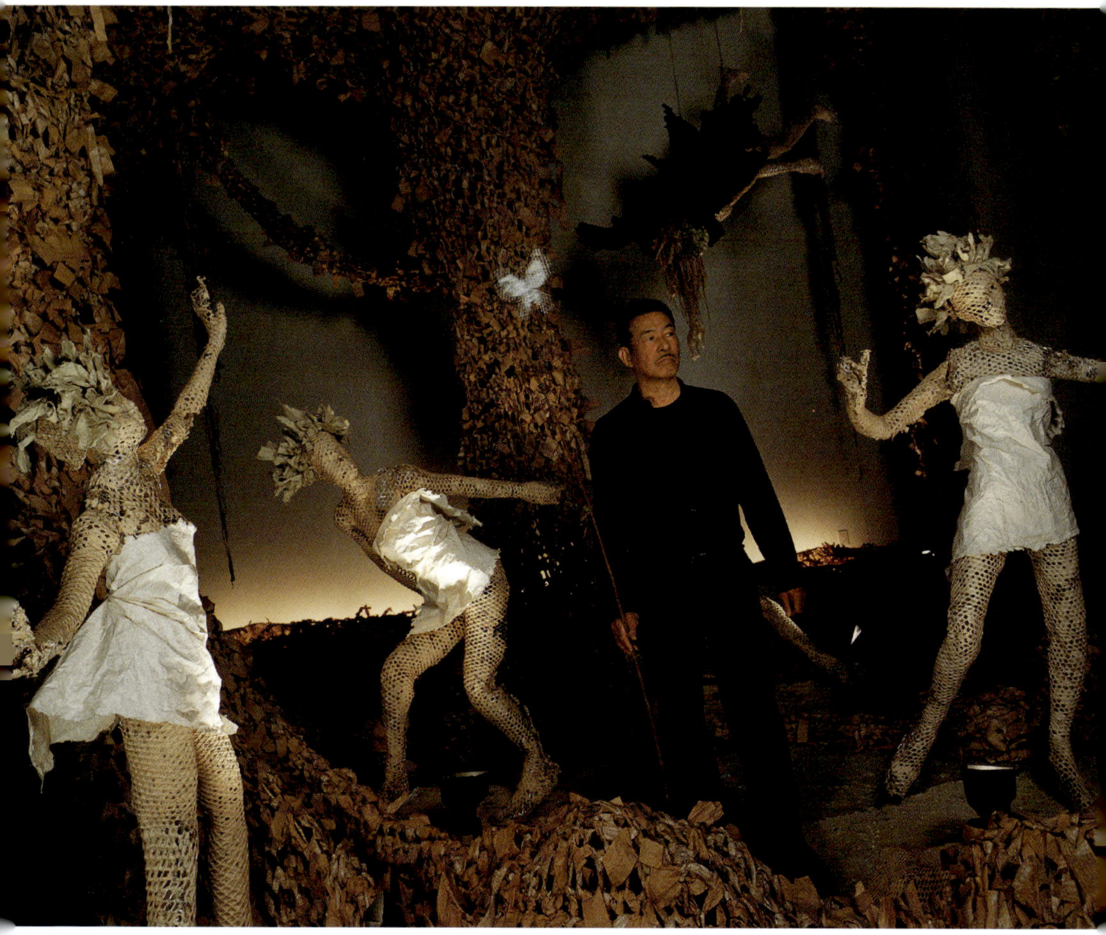

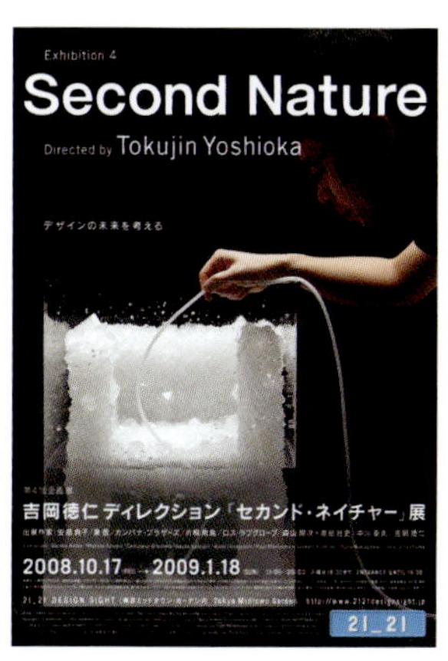

Myth of the 21st Century by Issey Miyake at
the *XXIc. – XXIst Century Man* exhibition
The central motifs for the installation were a giant
paper dragon and eight bodies. It drew upon a variety
of sources, including Japanese mythology and
Stravinsky's ballet *The Rite of Spring*, to express the
21st-century zeitgeist. The materials came from industrial cardboard and paper used in the manufacture
of pleats that was recycled using traditional Japanese
washi papermaking techniques. The construction required 16 members of the Issey Miyake Inc. staff from
design, pattern making, and laboratory departments
to work by hand under Issey Miyake's direction.
Photography: Nobuyoshi Araki

2009

> Directed the *U-Tsu-Wa–Lucie Rie, Jennifer Lee, Ernst Gamperl* exhibition at 21_21 DESIGN SIGHT

U-Tsu-Wa–Lucie Rie, Jennifer Lee, Ernst Gamperl exhibition

Tadao Ando created the design for the space, working from Issey Miyake's concept that started from the Japanese word *utsuwa* (vessel), and transformed it into *uchu no wa* (the rings of space) and *sora no wa* (the rings of the sky). Three artists' creations were displayed along the outlines of their respective constellations on a stage filled with water and strewn with glass powder. Also on display was a collection of Lucie Rie's handmade buttons, the gypsum molds used in their production, and jackets and coats with Rie's buttons from the Autumn-Winter 1989 Collection.

February 13–May 10: 21_21 DESIGN SIGHT
Exhibition direction: Issey Miyake; space design: Tadao Ando; visual direction: Kohei Sugiura; poster: Hiroshi Iwasaki (photography) and Kohei Sugiura (graphic design)

21_21 DESIGN SIGHT exhibition posters for
U-Tsu-Wa–Lucie Rie, Jennifer Lee, Ernst Gamperl,
Bones–Bones and Design. Artificial bones,
bones of future–, and *The Unseen Outline of Things*

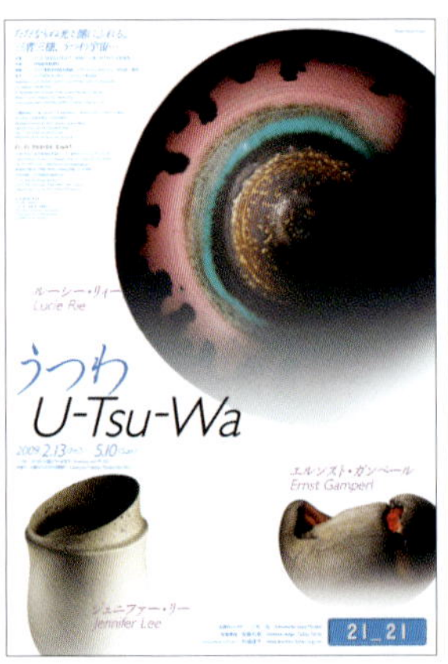
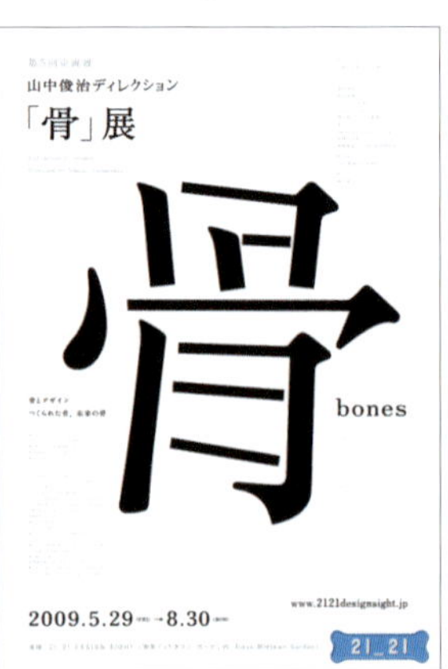
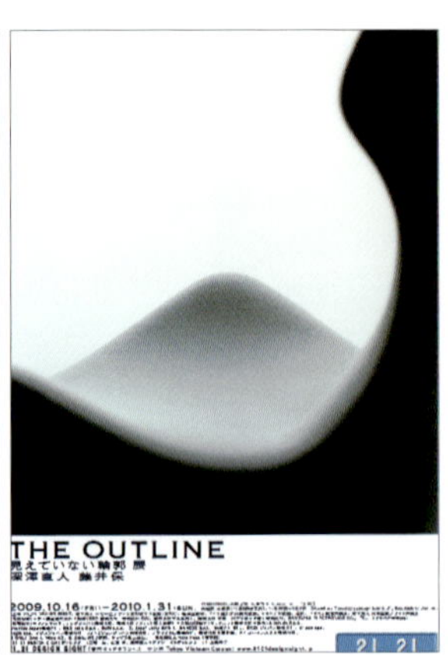

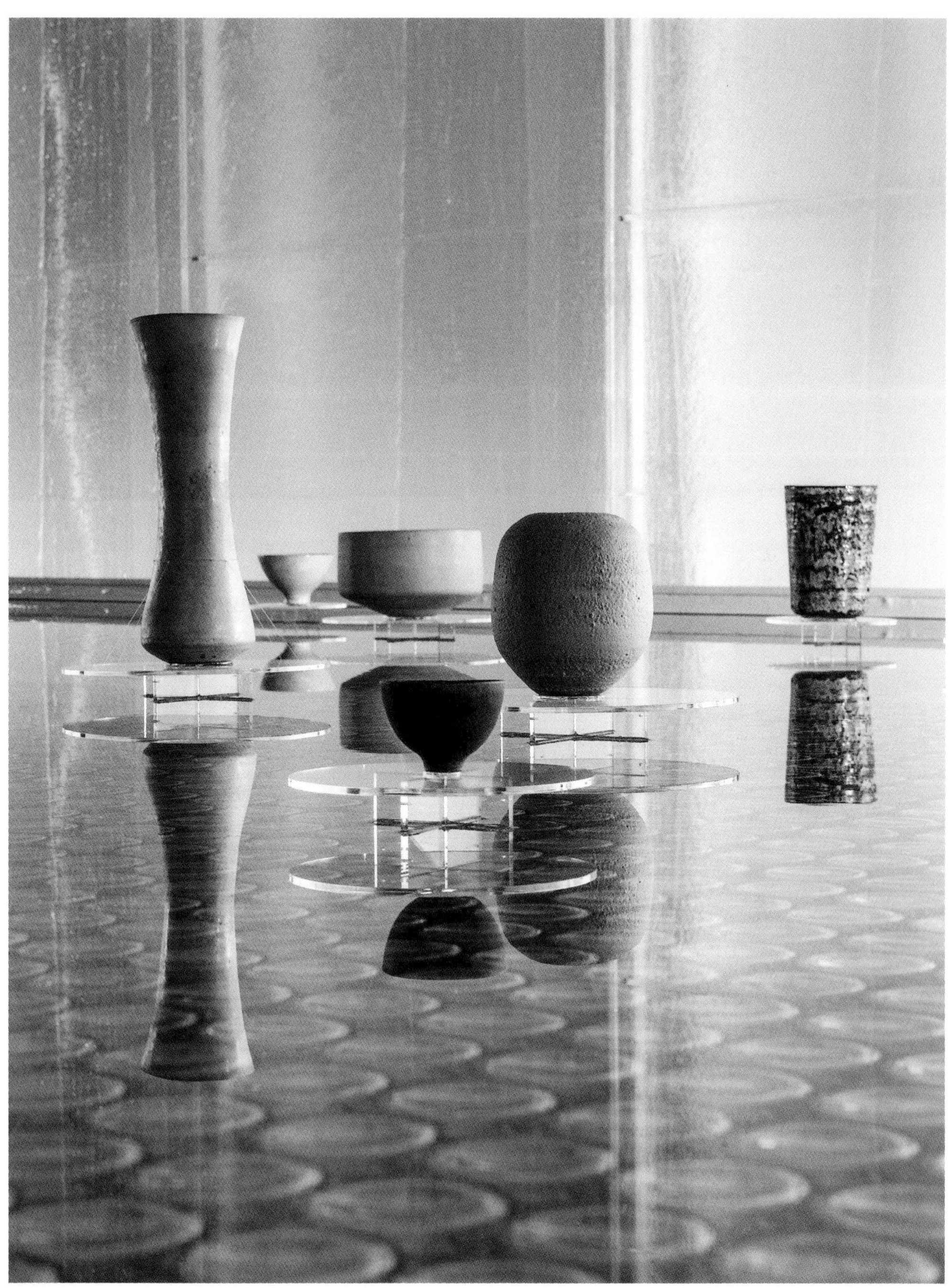

Lucie Rie's works in the *U-Tsu-Wa–Lucie Rie,
Jennifer Lee, Ernst Gamperl* exhibition
Photography: Hiroshi Iwasaki

2010

> April–October: Participated in the *Histoire idéale de la mode contemporaine Vol. I: Les Années 70 & 80* exhibition at the Musée des Arts Décoratifs, Paris

> August: Presentation in Tokyo of 132 5. ISSEY MIYAKE; followed by a similar presentation in Paris in September

> November–December: Directed the *Reality Lab* exhibition at 21_21 DESIGN SIGHT

> November–May 2011: Participated in the *Histoire idéale de la mode contemporaine Vol. II: Les Années 1990–2000* exhibition at the Musée des Arts Décoratifs, Paris

132 5. ISSEY MIYAKE

Issey Miyake began working with the Reality Lab team in 2007 to develop new forms of making things. The brand name expresses his ambitions to move from *A Piece of Cloth* (one dimension) into three-dimensional forms, and then back to objects that become flat when folded (two dimensions); and finally to clothing that transcends time and higher dimensions when worn (five dimensions). He collaborated with computer scientist Jun Mitani to create three-dimensional forms that, when folded and pressed, transform into shirts, skirts, one-piece dresses, and pants according to how the cut-lines are positioned. As materials, he used re-cycled polyester to which he had added numerous improvements, and by doing so challenged the modern notions of making things.

132 5. ISSEY MIYAKE vol. 1–2, 2011

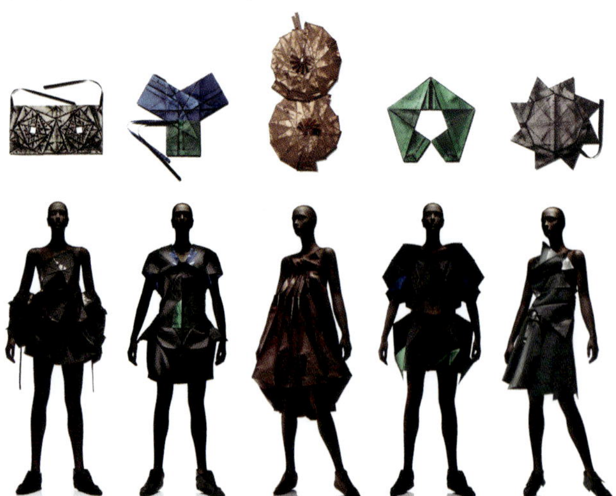

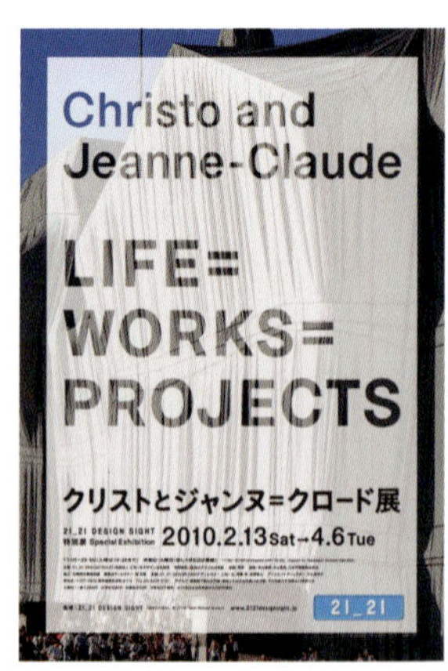

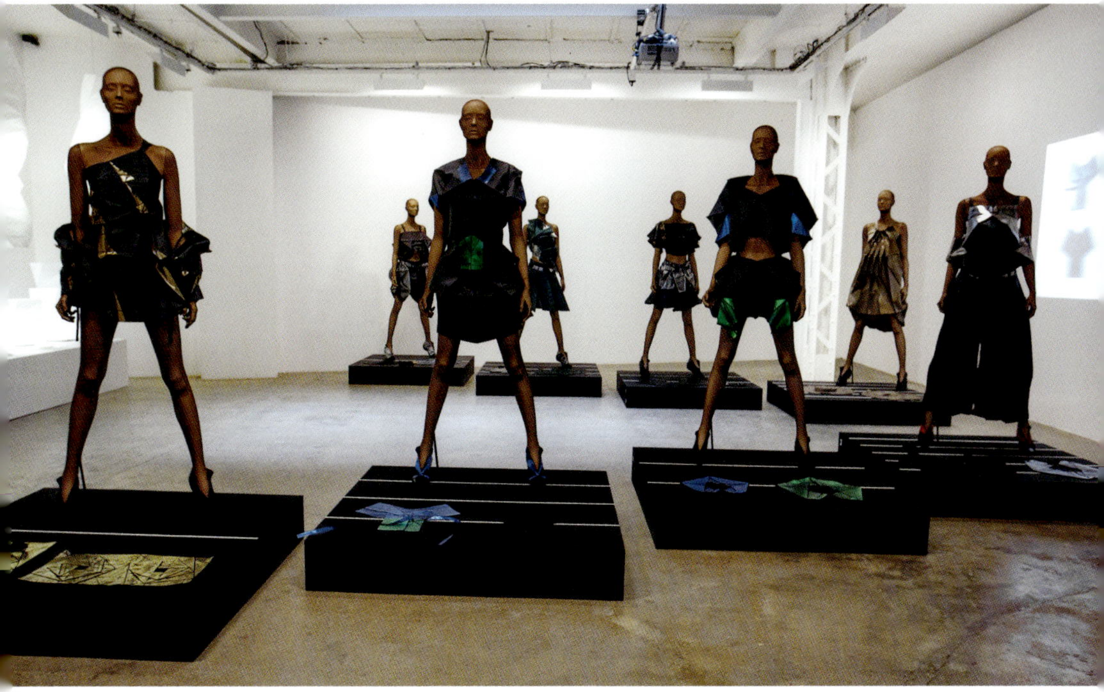

132 5. ISSEY MIYAKE presentation at Galerie Kreo, Paris
Front row from left: *No. 2* shirt and skirt, *No. 4* shirt and skirt, *No. 4* shirt and *No. 3* skirt, all designed in 2010/132 5. ISSEY MIYAKE
Photography: Benjamin Nitôt

Below: 21_21 DESIGN SIGHT exhibition posters for *Christo and Jeanne-Claude Life = Works · Projects*, *Post-Fossil: Excavating 21st Century Creation*, *The Definition of Self*, and *Reality Lab*

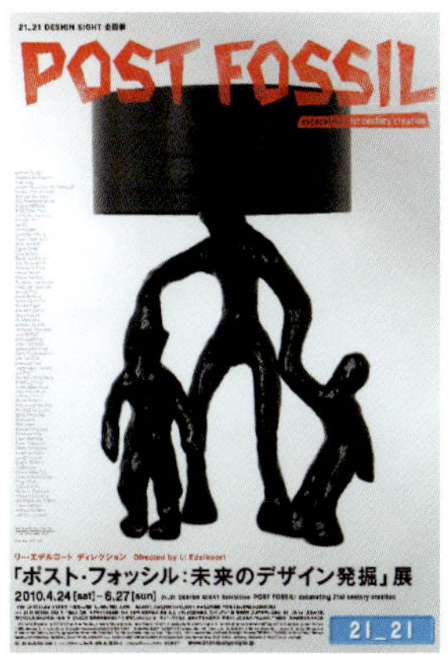

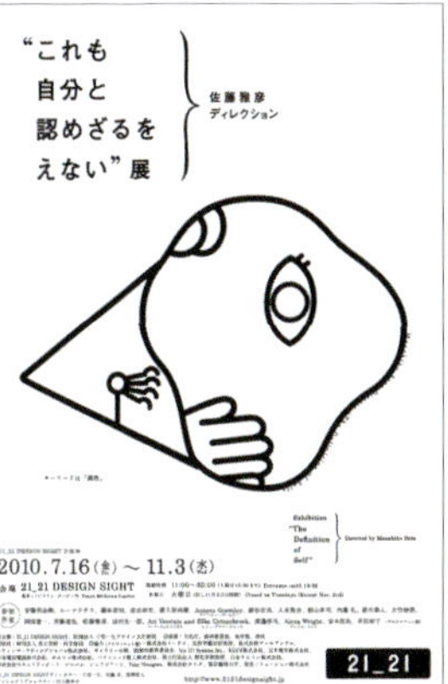

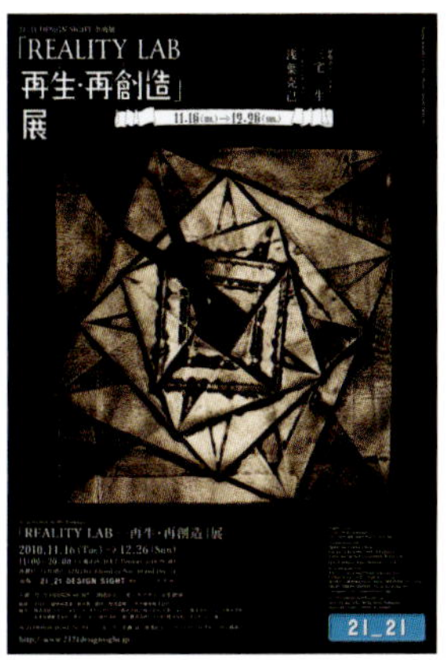

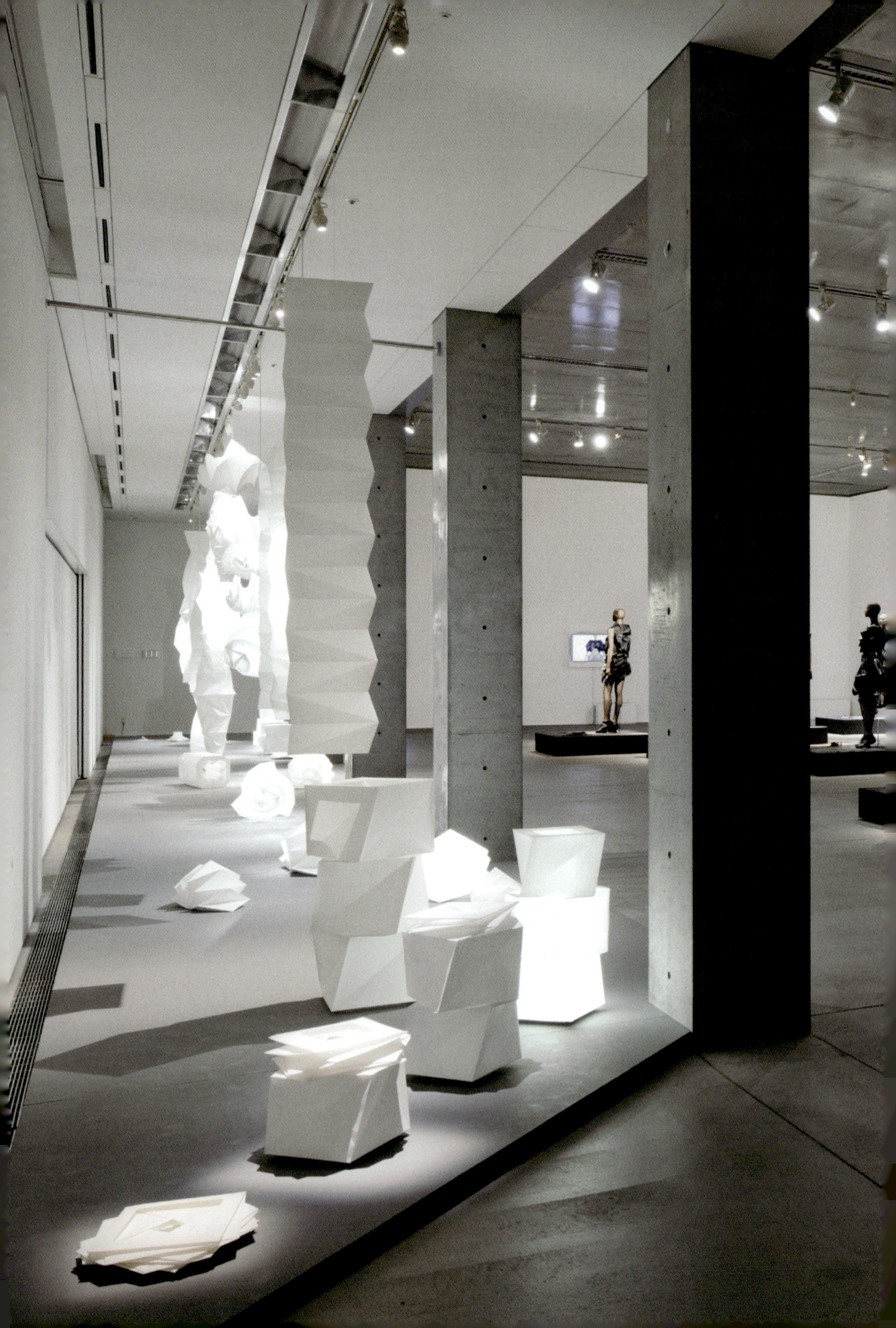

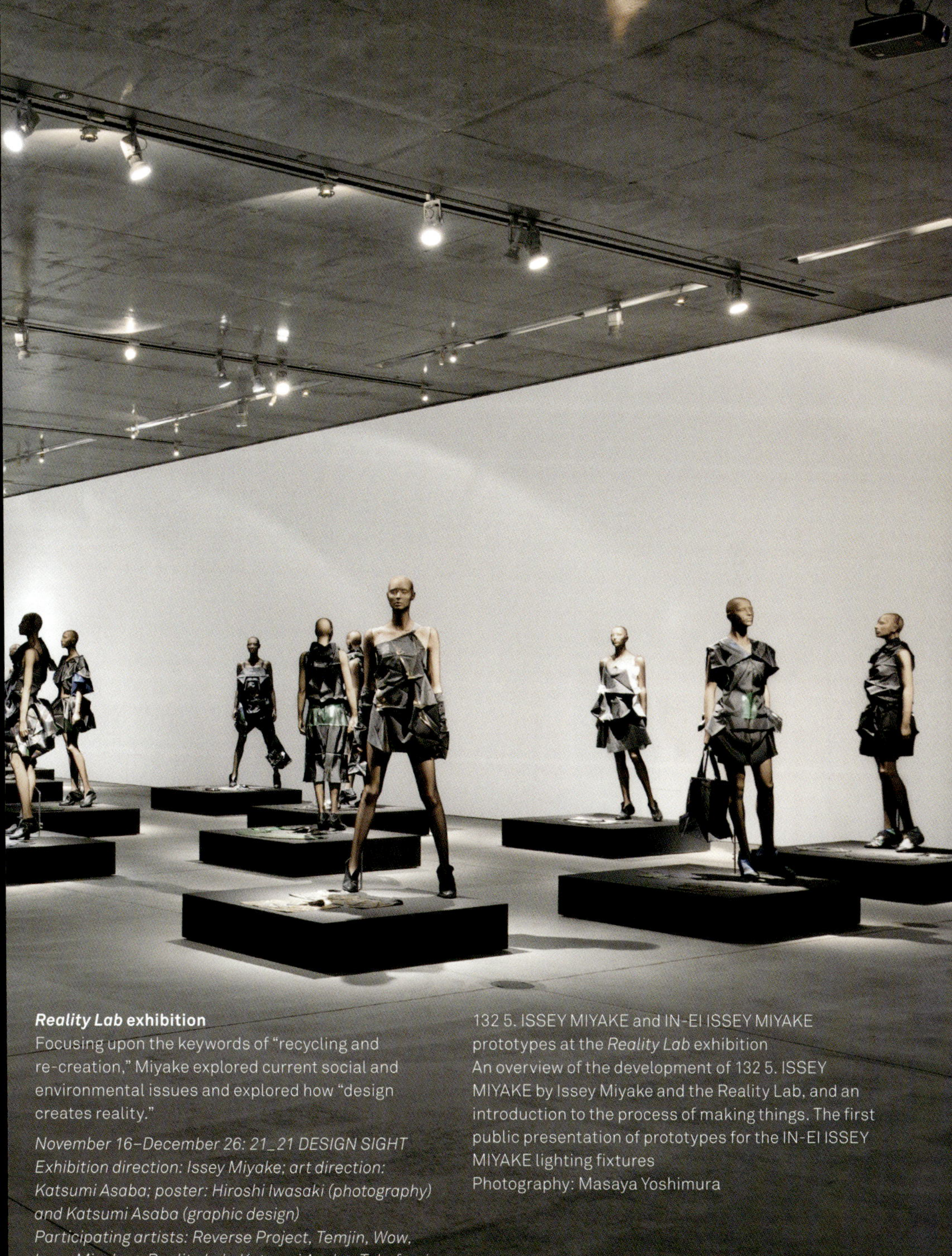

Reality Lab exhibition
Focusing upon the keywords of "recycling and
re-creation," Miyake explored current social and
environmental issues and explored how "design
creates reality."

November 16–December 26: 21_ 21 DESIGN SIGHT
Exhibition direction: Issey Miyake; art direction:
Katsumi Asaba; poster: Hiroshi Iwasaki (photography)
and Katsumi Asaba (graphic design)
Participating artists: Reverse Project, Temjin, Wow,
Issey Miyake + Reality Lab, Katsumi Asaba, Takafumi
Matsui, Pascal Roulin, Arik Levy, Hiroshi Iwasaki,

132 5. ISSEY MIYAKE and IN-EI ISSEY MIYAKE
prototypes at the *Reality Lab* exhibition
An overview of the development of 132 5. ISSEY
MIYAKE by Issey Miyake and the Reality Lab, and an
introduction to the process of making things. The first
public presentation of prototypes for the IN-EI ISSEY
MIYAKE lighting fixtures
Photography: Masaya Yoshimura

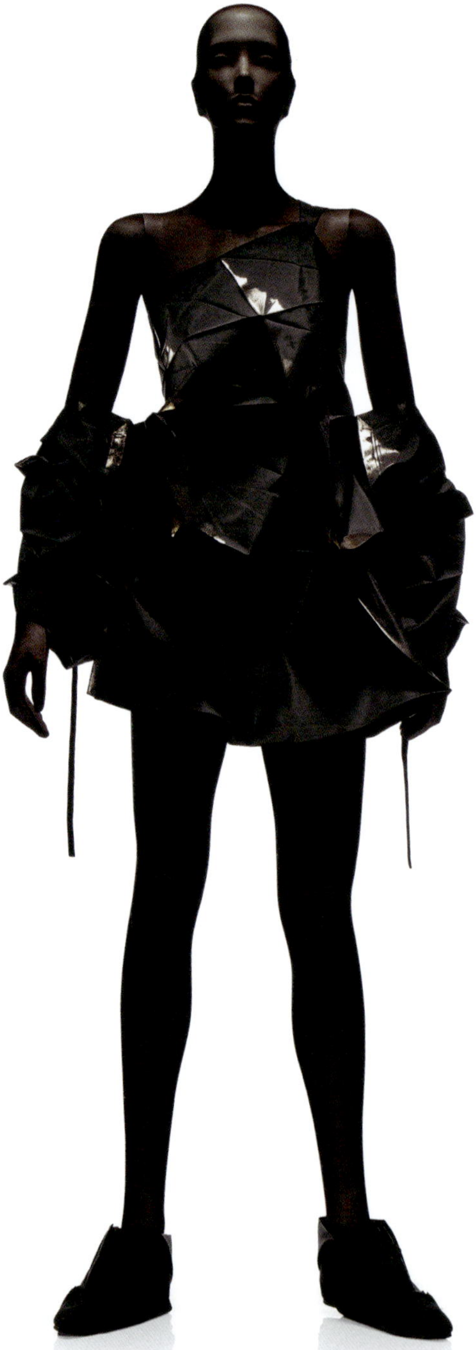

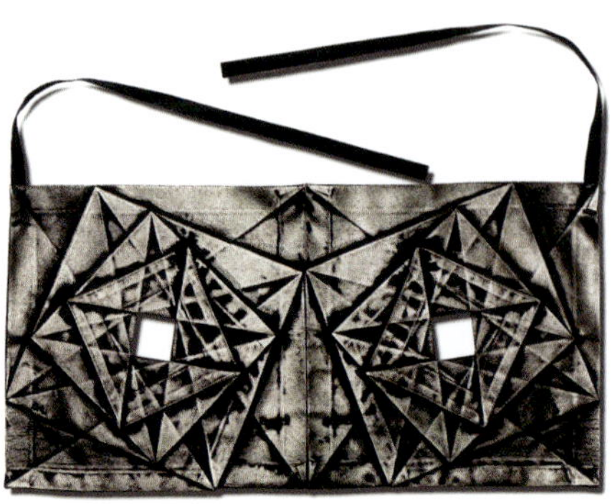

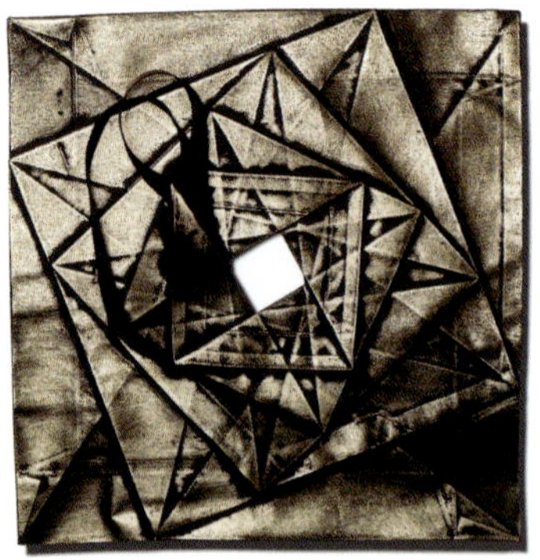

No. 1

No. 1 dress and jacket folded and worn
2010 design/132 5. ISSEY MIYAKE
Photography: Hiroshi Iwasaki

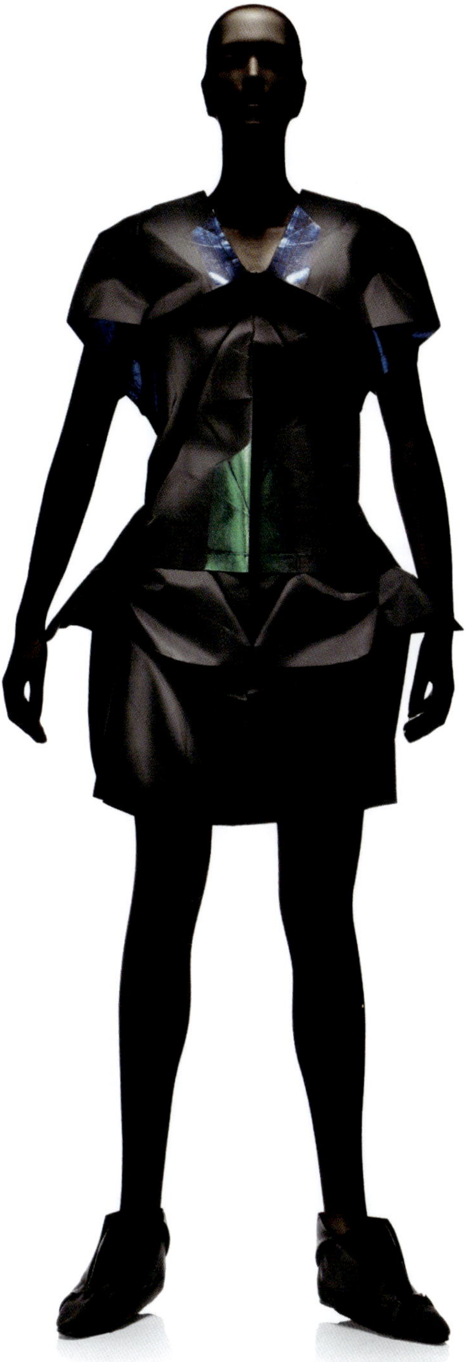

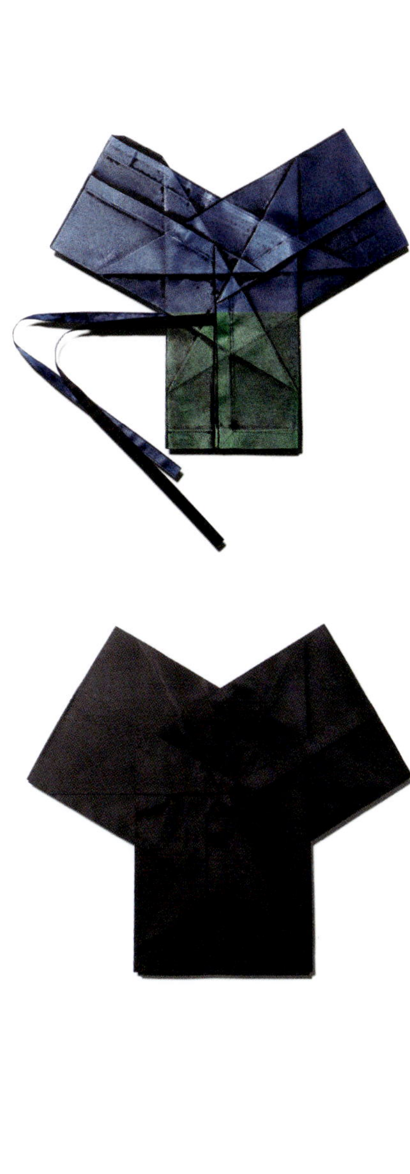

No. 2

No. 2 top and skirt. They are exactly the same when folded, but change into different three-dimensional forms, depending on how the cut-lines are positioned.
2010 design/132 5. ISSEY MIYAKE
Photography: Hiroshi Iwasaki

No. 2 shirt and skirt
Opposite: *No. 7* shirt and *No. 6* skirt
All designed in 2010/132 5. ISSEY MIYAKE
Waraku (Japan), November 2010 edition
Photography: Kazumi Kurigami;
worn by: Shinobu Terajima

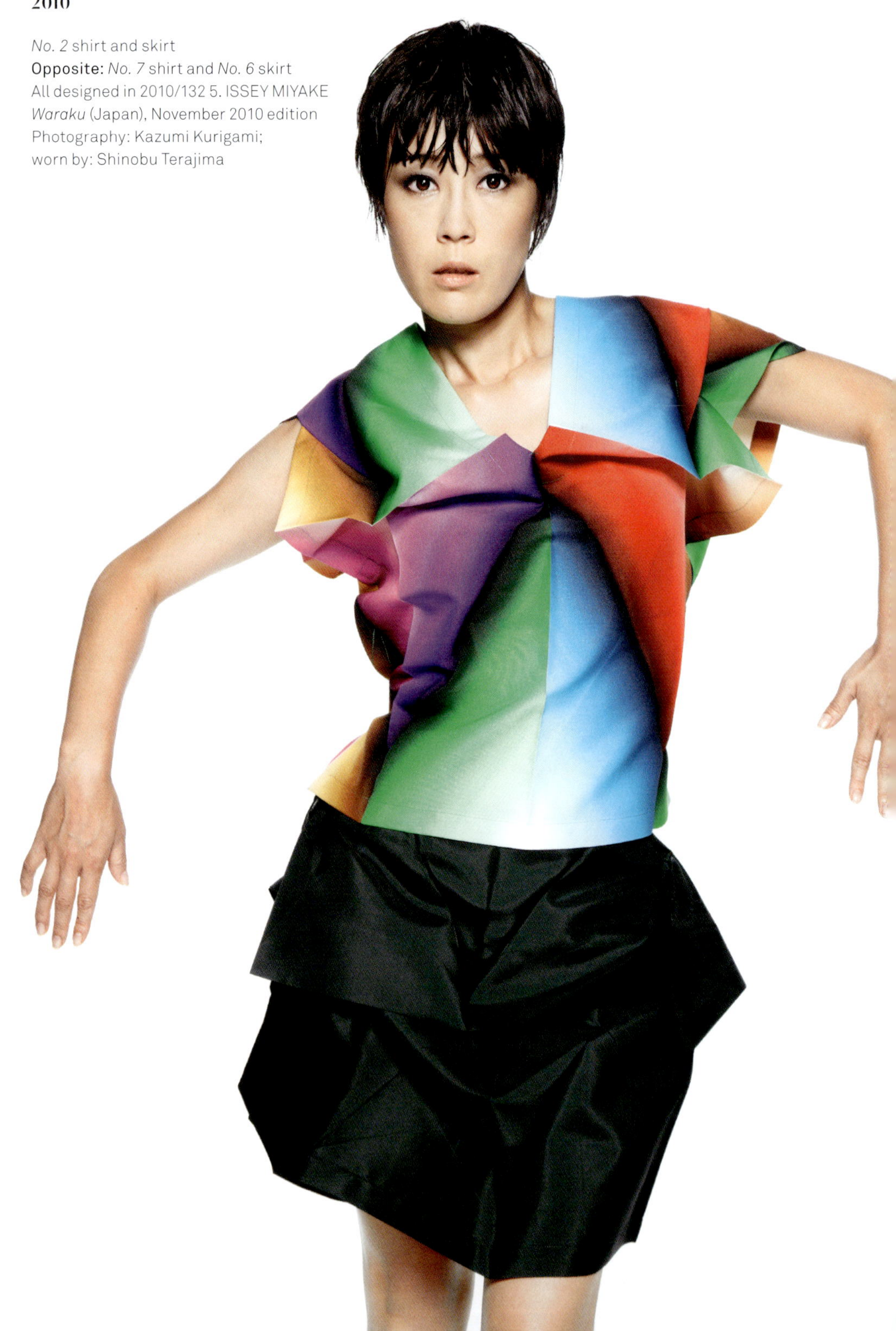

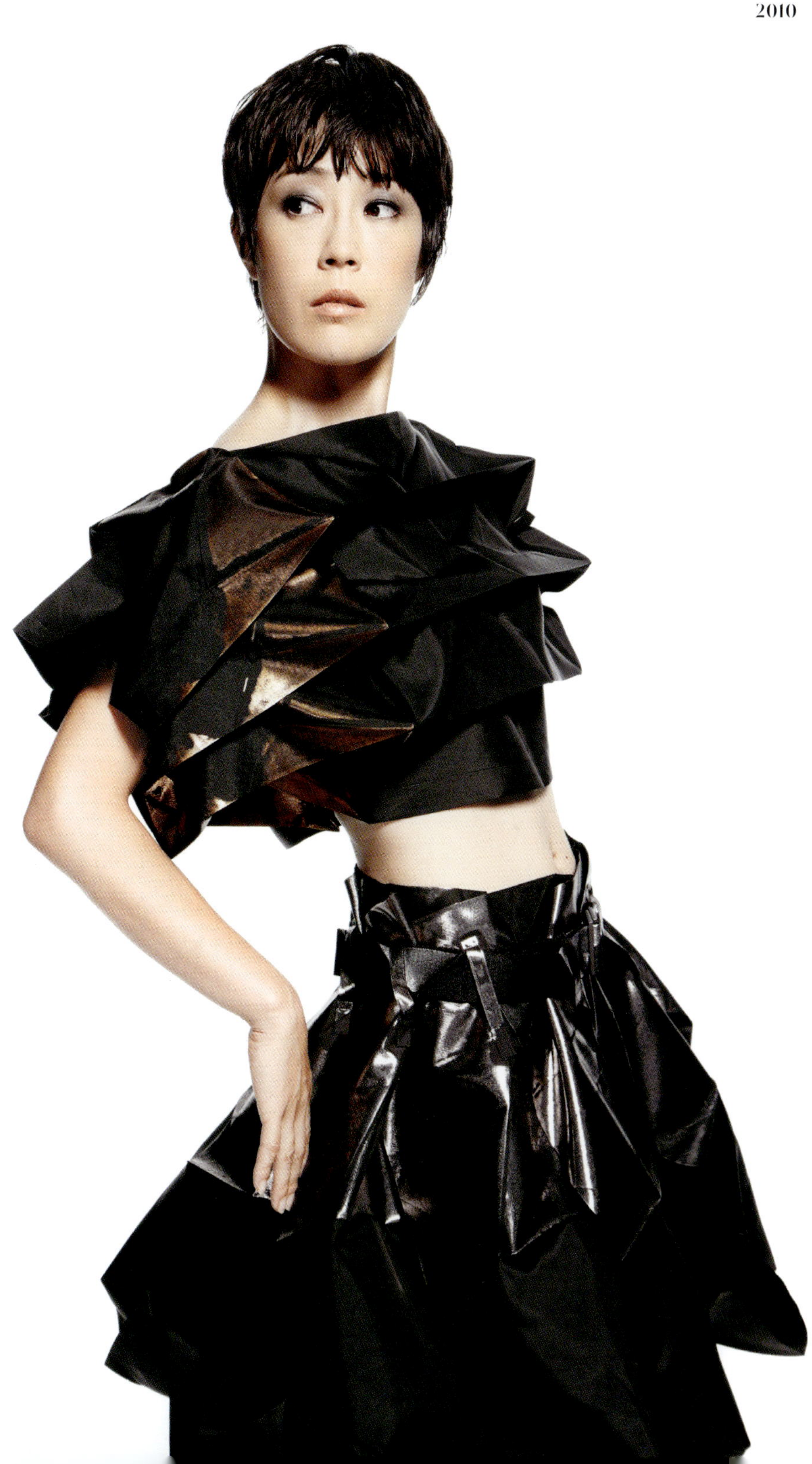

2011

> May: 132 5. ISSEY MIYAKE vol. 3–4, 2011
> July: Directed *The Spirit of Tohoku: "Clothing" by Issey Miyake*: a special exhibition at 21_21 DESIGN SIGHT
> September: 132 5. ISSEY MIYAKE vol. 1–2, 2012
> September-April 2012: *Irving Penn and Issey Miyake: Visual Dialogue* exhibition at 21_21 DESIGN SIGHT

Irving Penn and Issey Miyake: Visual Dialogue exhibition

The exhibition features the results from the 13-year collaboration between the photographer Irving Penn and Issey Miyake. Midori Kitamura served as exhibition director and was present at all the photography sessions to facilitate the two creators' "visual dialogue." The final photographs were selected and arranged by Kitamura herself and shown on a large screen using ultra-high-resolution projectors. Also on display were original pre-photography sketches by Penn, original prints, a Pascal Roulin animation of drawings by Michael Crawford, and 67 posters for which Ikko Tanaka had created the layout and typography.

September 16–April 8, 2012: 21_21 DESIGN SIGHT
Exhibition direction: Midori Kitamura; space design: Shigeru Ban; poster: Irving Penn (photography) and Taku Satoh (graphic design)

132 5. ISSEY MIYAKE vol. 1–2, 2012

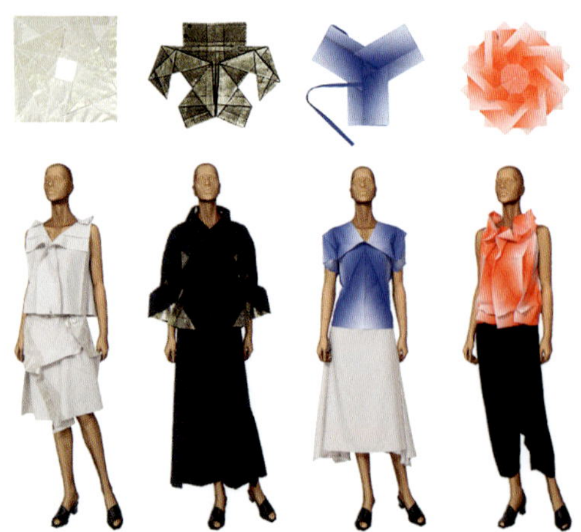

Opposite bottom: 21_21 DESIGN SIGHT exhibition posters for *Shiro Kuramata and Ettore Sottsass*, *The Spirit of Tohoku: "Clothing" by Issey Miyake*, and *Irving Penn and Issey Miyake: Visual Dialogue*

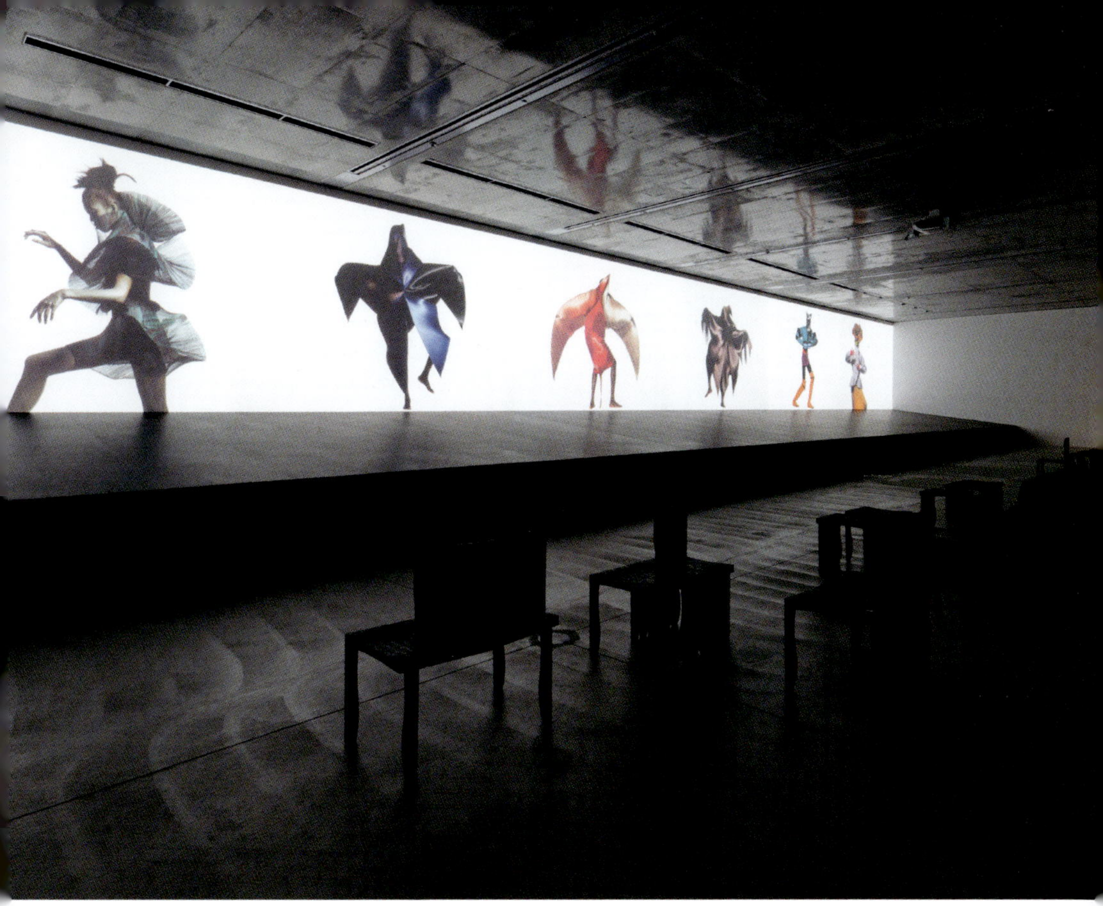

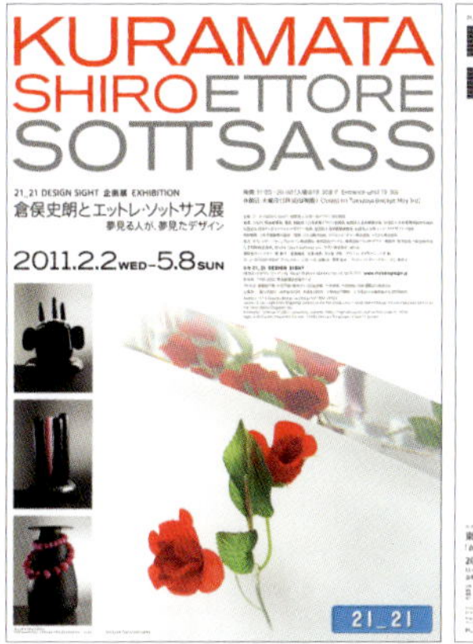

Irving Penn and Issey Miyake:
Visual Dialogue exhibition

Six projectors displayed 148 photographs on a wall, 31 meters long. The chairs, made from recycled materials, were designed by Shigeru Ban.
Photography: Masaya Yoshimura

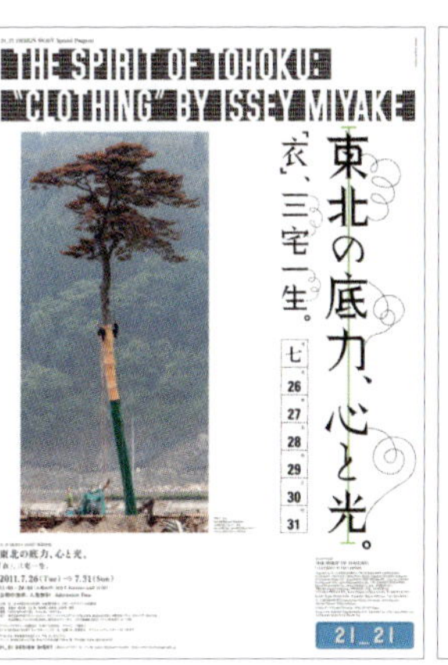

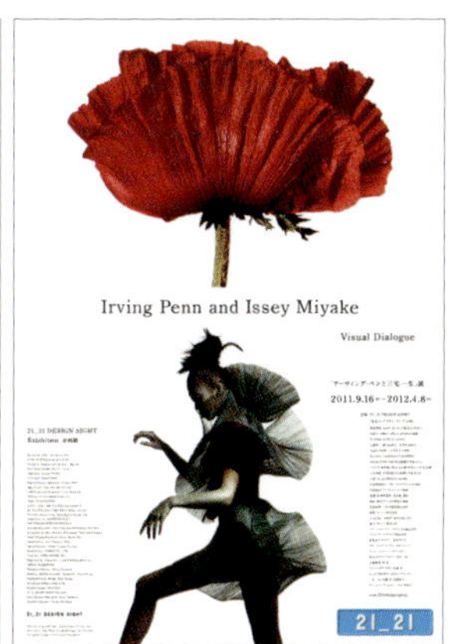

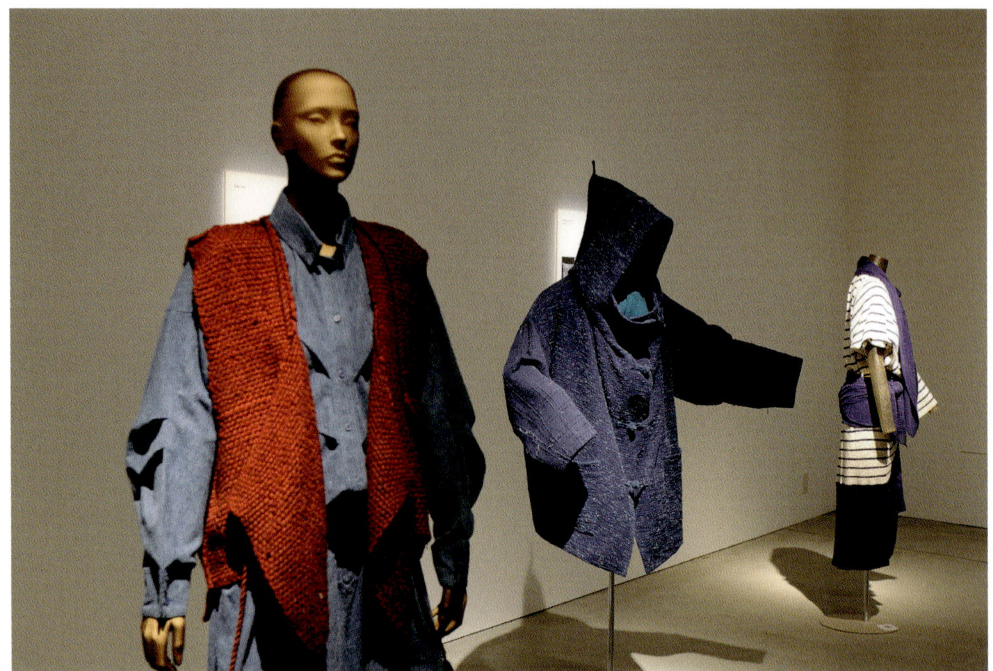

The Spirit of Tohoku: "Clothing" by Issey Miyake
special exhibition at 21_21 DESIGN SIGHT

Issey Miyake quickly put together this exhibition as a
way to help the disaster area after the Great East Japan
Earthquake in March. The focus was upon the "clothing": a component of the essential elements "food,
shelter, and clothing." The exhibition introduced fabric
and clothing from the Tohoku region, the tools used to
produce it, and a view of the lives of the people there.
Also on display was clothing produced in collaboration
with Tohoku creators, from the ISSEY MIYAKE archives.
In addition to the displays, the program featured video
presentations, talks by creators, and production
demonstrations. It ran for six days free of charge.
July 26–31: 21_21 DESIGN SIGHT
Exhibition direction: Issey Miyake; graphic design
and poster: Katsumi Asaba

Above, left: Indigo shirt and *Cotton Vest* created
by Nakamura Kobo in Iwate prefecture. For three
generations, the Nakamura Kobo (studio) in Morioka
has practiced hand-spun wool weaving and vegeta-
ble-dyeing techniques. Issey Miyake first visited the
studio in 1972 with Makiko Minagawa and continued
to collaborate with them. He heard about a son who
had been called to war from the Tohoku region, and
his mother pounded a nail into the work surface, and
wove large cotton threads with her fingers to create

a vest. He commissioned the studio to reproduce it.
1983 design/Autumn-Winter 1983 Collection

Above, center: *Rag Woven Jacket* inspired by the
rag-weaving techniques of the Tohoku region. Tohoku
is a cold place, and cotton is a valuable commodity.
When people were able to get old cotton fabrics, they
did not waste them, no matter how used the clothing
might have been or how small the rags. They developed
a technique of "rag-weaving" in which the threads are
unwound from the fabric and rewoven. The hooded
jacket came from a deep resonance with this spiritual
culture. Indigo cotton was unraveled and woven on a
power loom with two kinds of tape incorporated into
the woof. It symbolizes the warmth of hand weaving.
1983 design/Autumn-Winter 1983 Collection

Above, right: *A Piece of Cloth Knit* woven in Yamagata
prefecture. Yamagata developed as a center for the
knit fabrics industry after World War II. Many of the
farms in the mountainous areas of the prefecture raise
sheep for wool, and all of the associated textile processes, from spinning to dyeing, can be found in the
surrounding cities and towns. The cotton/hemp coat is
worn with an *obi* belt and is symbolic of Issey Miyake's
concept. It was produced by Hokota Meriyasu. 1976
design/Spring-Summer 1977 Collection
Photography: Masaya Yoshimura

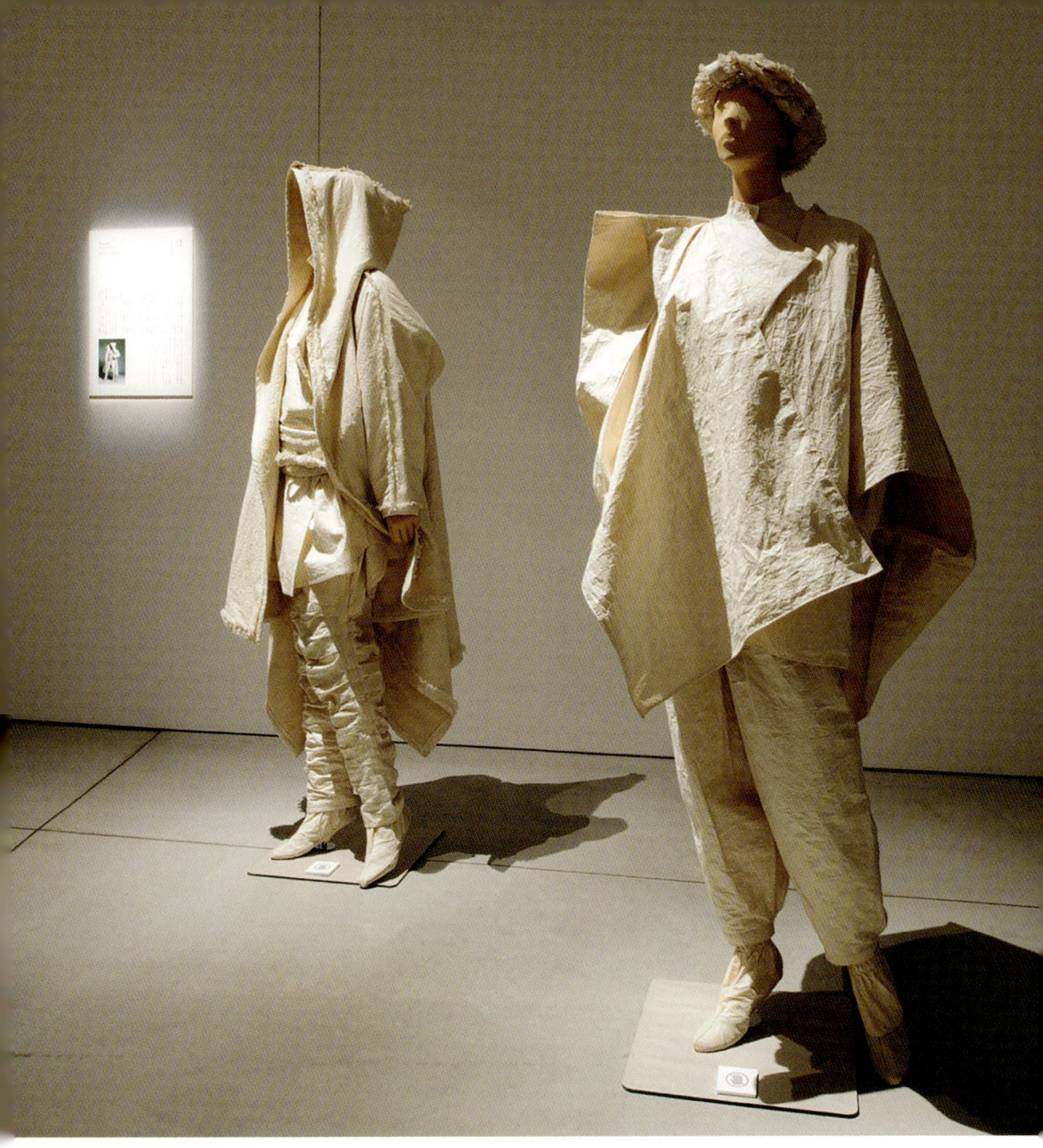

Kamiko using *Shiroishi washi* paper from Miyagi prefecture
Miyake sought out traditional Japanese technologies from modern perspectives, and researched how they could be represented to the public through new forms of creation. In the course of his investigations, he was reintroduced to paper. Paper is widely used in science and medicine, and Issey Miyake had always been interested in its potential as a material for clothing. His *Kamiko* came about because he discovered the

Shiroishi washi paper produced by Tadao Endo and his wife, Mashiko, using the traditional handmade papermaking techniques (*shiroishi washi kobo*). Their paper is used to create the *Kamiko* clothing worn by the monks of Todaiji Temple to collect water at Nigatsu-do. All of the clothing worn by the mannequins is made from *washi* paper. The hooded coat has a wool lining.
1982 design/Autumn-Winter 1982 Collection
Photography: Masaya Yoshimura

2012

> March: 132 5. ISSEY MIYAKE vol. 3–4, 2012
> April: IN-EI ISSEY MIYAKE presented by Artemide at the *Light + Building* in Frankfurt and the Salone del Mobile in Milan
> September: 132 5. ISSEY MIYAKE vol. 1–2, 2013
> November: Established the Society for a Design Museum Japan in cooperation with Masanori Aoyagi and held the first public symposium at the Tokyo Midtown Hall

IN-EI ISSEY MIYAKE

Lighting fixtures that were an evolution of the 132 5. ISSEY MIYAKE development process. Based upon prototypes that had been repeatedly improved by the Reality Lab beginning in 2009, and in 2011, the lamps were then manufactured and launched by Artemide of Italy. Original techniques developed for making clothes such as folding were applied to make the shade. The self-standing shade has no supporting structure and was made from a 100% nonwoven fabric of fibers made out of recycled PET bottles. The wrinkle processing gives the object a unique surface while also improving its strength and robustness.

132 5. ISSEY MIYAKE vol. 3–4, 2012   132 5. ISSEY MIYAKE vol. 1–2, 2013

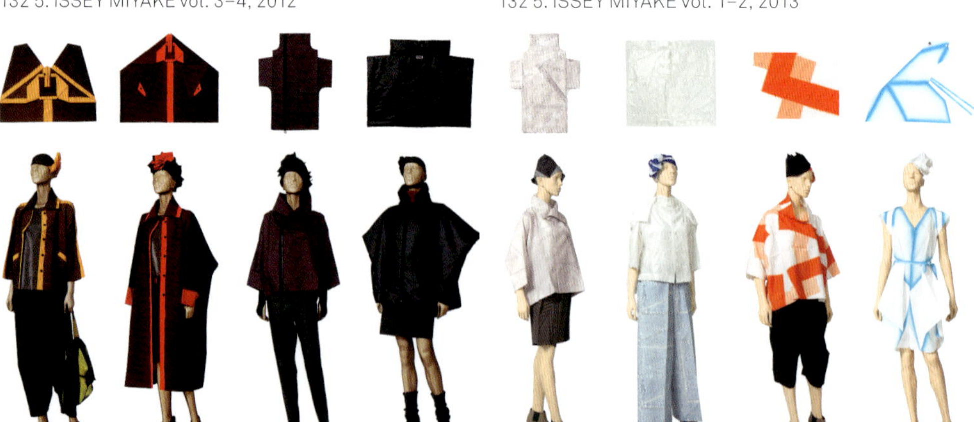

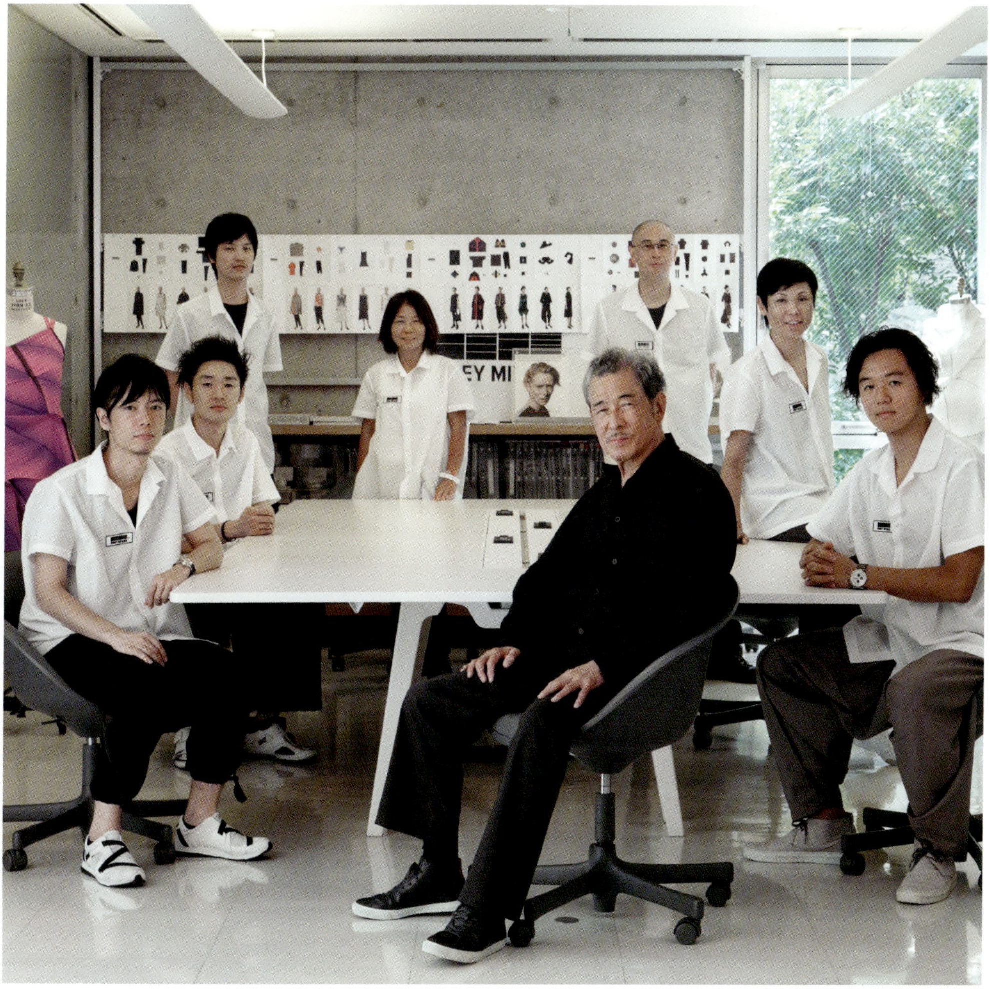

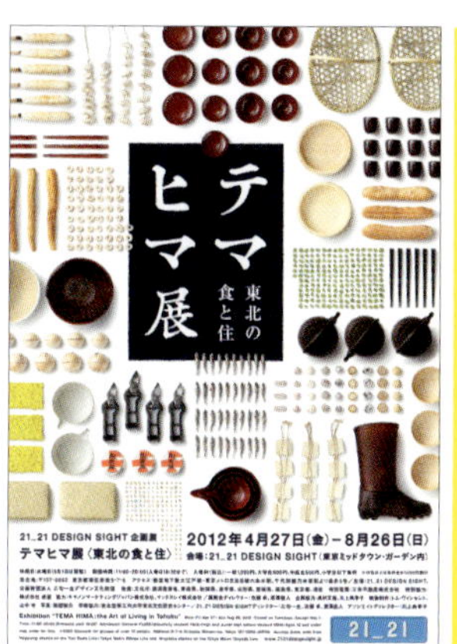

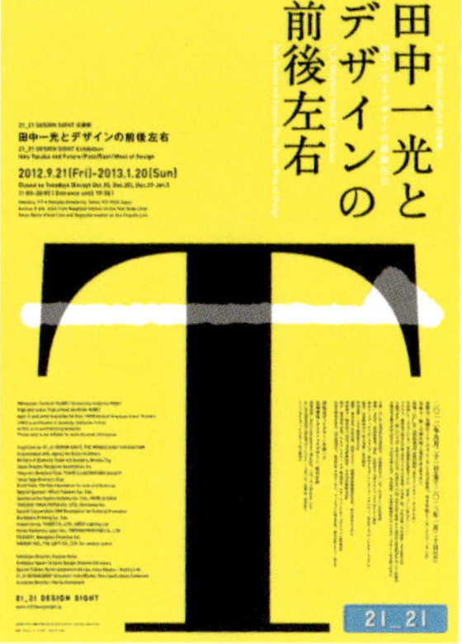

Above: Issey Miyake and the Reality Lab staff
The Wall Street Journal, October 25, 2012
Photography: Tetsuya Miura

Left: 21_21 DESIGN SIGHT posters for *Tema Hima: The Art of Living in Tohoku* and *Ikko Tanaka and Future/Past/East/West of Design*

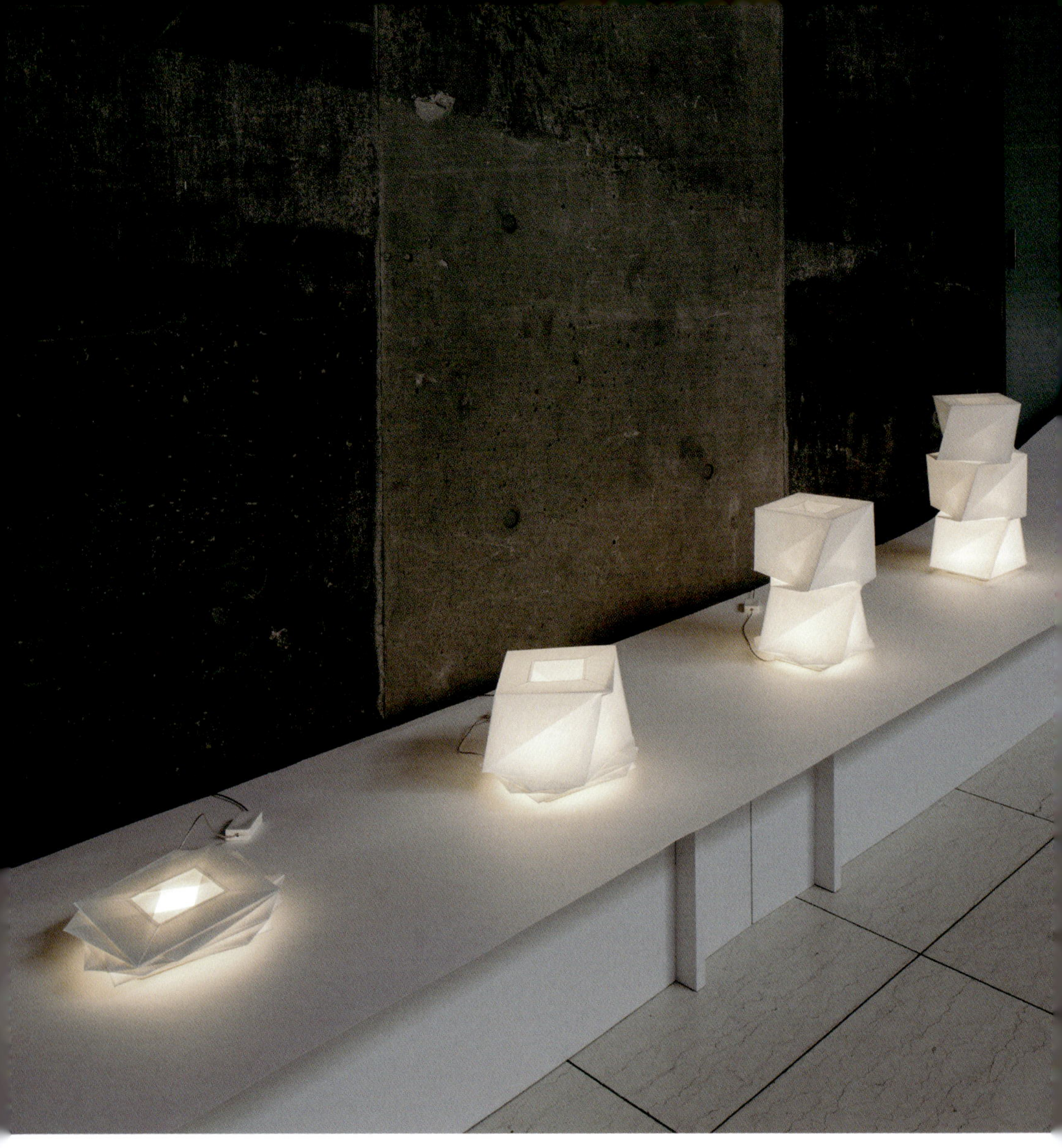

IN-EI ISSEY MIYAKE announced at the GA Gallery,
Tokyo, November 15 and 16
Above: Four stages of folding *MOGURA*
Opopsite: *MINOMUSHI terra* floor type (back left)
FUKUROU pendant (top right)
FUKUROU floor type (bottom right)
Photography: Masaya Yoshimura

312

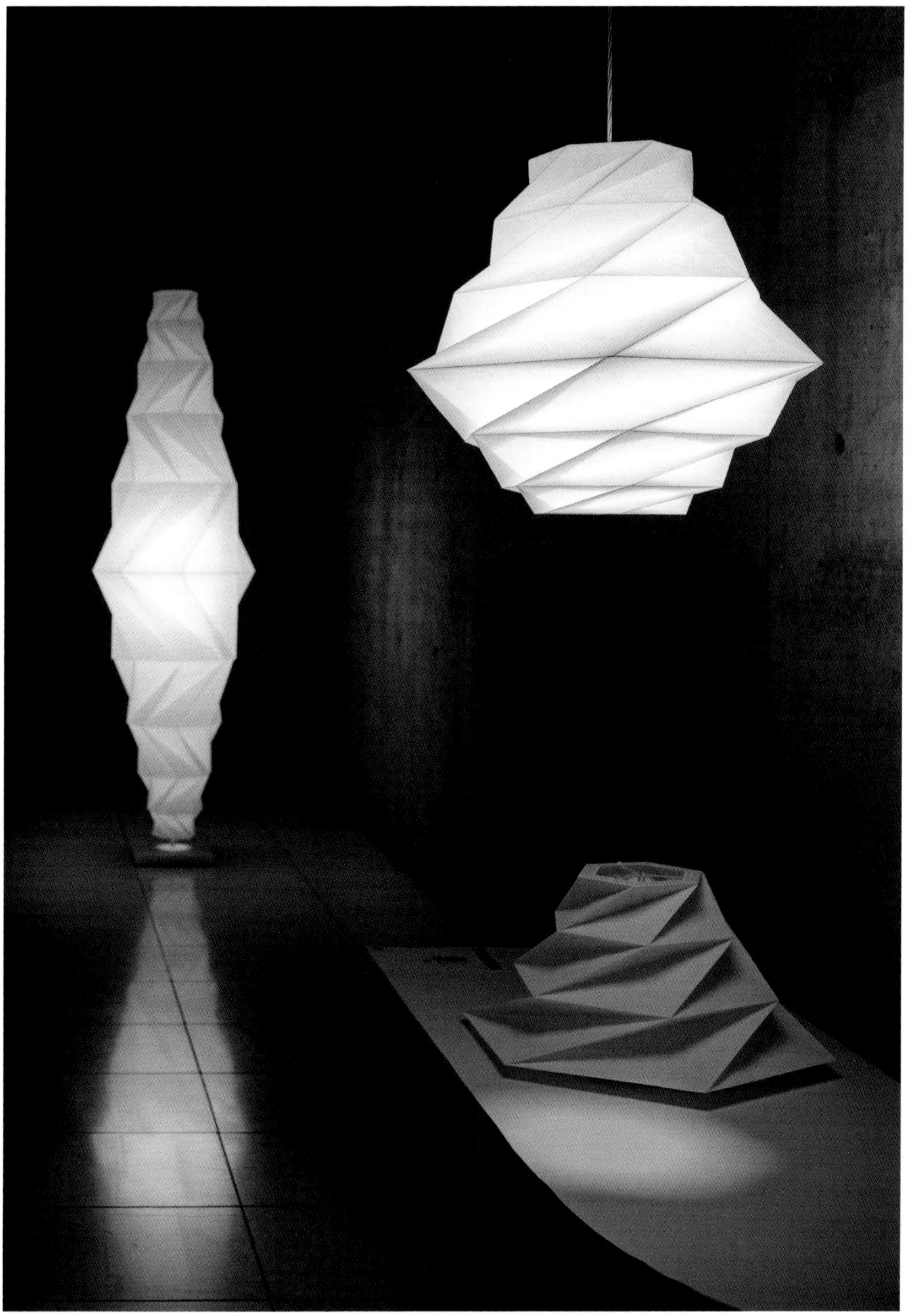

2013

> March: 132 5. ISSEY MIYAKE vol. 3–4, 2013
> April: Second public symposium held
  by the Society for a Design Museum Japan
  at Sendai Mediatheque
> July: 132 5. ISSEY MIYAKE vol. 1–2, 2014
> July: Organized a performance by the
  *Aomori University Men's Rhythmic Gymnastics
  Team* in Tokyo. The planning, production,
  and costume design for the performance was
  by Issey Miyake
> November: Announcement of HOMME PLISSÉ
  ISSEY MIYAKE

Opposite top: *The Aomori University Men's Rhythmic
Gymnastics Team* performance
Daniel Ezralow directed and choreographed based
on their competition performance. Director Hiroyuki
Nakano later turned it into a movie titled *Flying Bodies*.
Issey Miyake's costumes were made from men's pleats
materials. Photography: Takao Fujita

Opposite bottom: 21_21 DESIGN SIGHT exhibition
posters for *Design Ah!*, *Color-Hunting*, and *Toward a
Design Museum Japan*

Aomori University Men's Rhythmic Gymnastics Team performance

Men's rhythmic gymnastics is a sport that was
born in Japan, but the competitive population
is still small. Together with the athletes who had
done much practice and training, Miyake put
together a performance to express the feelings for
the Tohoku region as it began to rebuild from the
earthquake.

*July 18: Yoyogi National Stadium, 2nd Gymnasium
Planning and costume design: Issey Miyake; stage
direction: Daniel Ezralow; lighting: Haruki Kaito; motion
graphics: Yugo Nakamura; music: Open Reel Ensemble;
musical arrangement: Masato Hatanaka; hair and
makeup: Shiseido SABFA*

HOMME PLISSÉ ISSEY MIYAKE

Two decades after the announcement of PLEATS
PLEASE ISSEY MIYAKE, Issey Miyake brought out
a new brand offering pleats as a new form of ordinary clothing for men. Developed with men in mind,
the pleats do not cling to the skin, making it easy to
move about, comfortable to wear, easy to maintain,
and easy to carry.

132 5. ISSEY MIYAKE vol. 3–4, 2013

132 5. ISSEY MIYAKE vol. 1–2, 2014

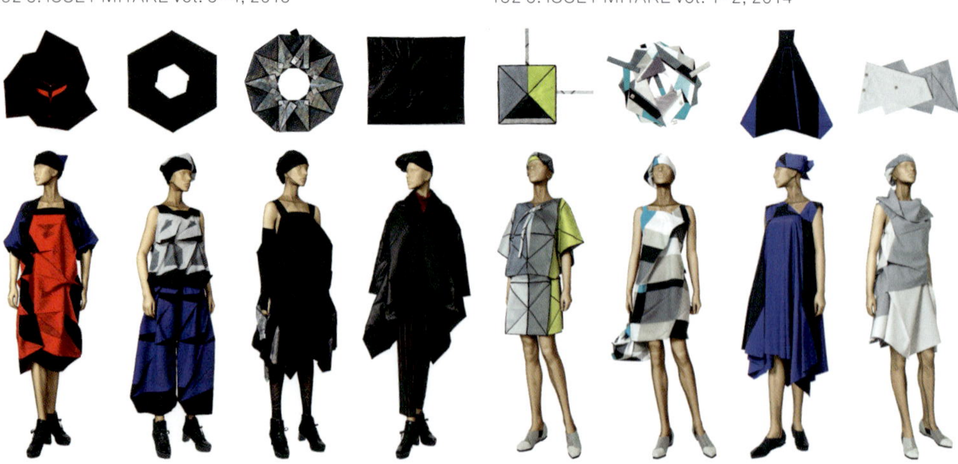

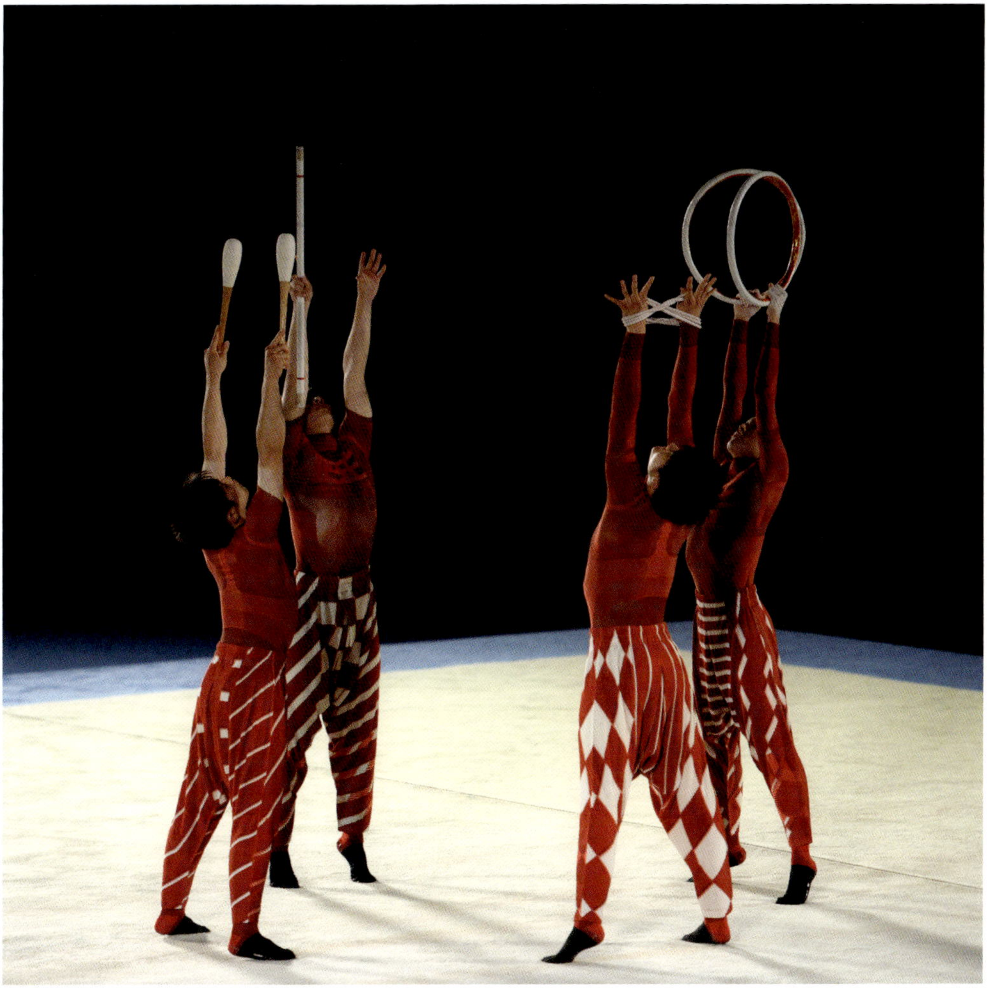

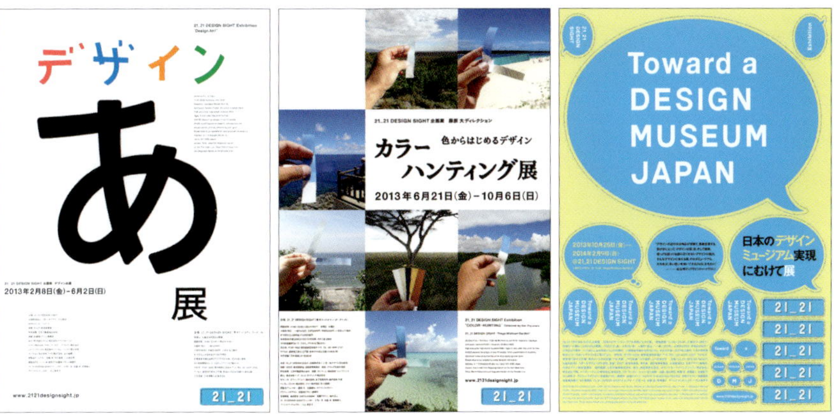

デザイン
あ
展
21_21 DESIGN SIGHT Exhibition
'Design Ah!'
21_21 DESIGN SIGHT 企画展　デザインあ展
2013年2月8日(金)-6月2日(日)
www.2121designsight.jp
21_21

色からはじめるデザイン
21_21 DESIGN SIGHT 企画展　藤原 大ディレクション
カラー
ハンティング展
2013年6月21日(金)-10月6日(日)
21_21 DESIGN SIGHT Exhibition
"COLOR HUNTING" Directed by Dai Fujiwara
www.2121designsight.jp
21_21

Toward a
DESIGN
MUSEUM
JAPAN
2013年10月25日(金)-
2014年2月9日(日)
@21_21 DESIGN SIGHT
日本のデザイン
ミュージアム実現
にむけて展
21_21

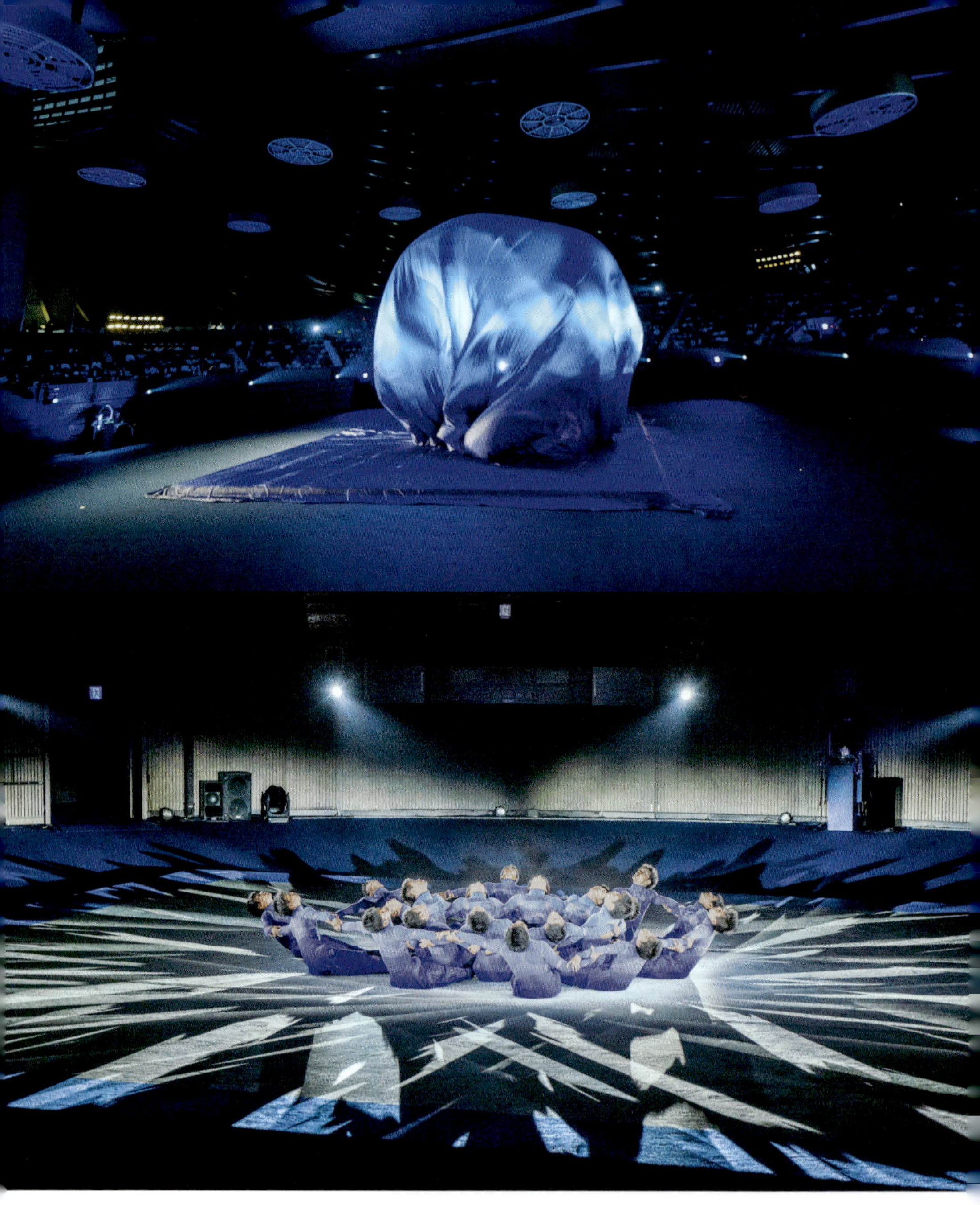

Aomori University Men's Rhythmic Gymnastics
Team performance
Upper left: "Opening"; lower left: "Isoginchaku";
upper right: "Ganba!"; lower right: "Finale"
Photography: Masaya Yoshimura

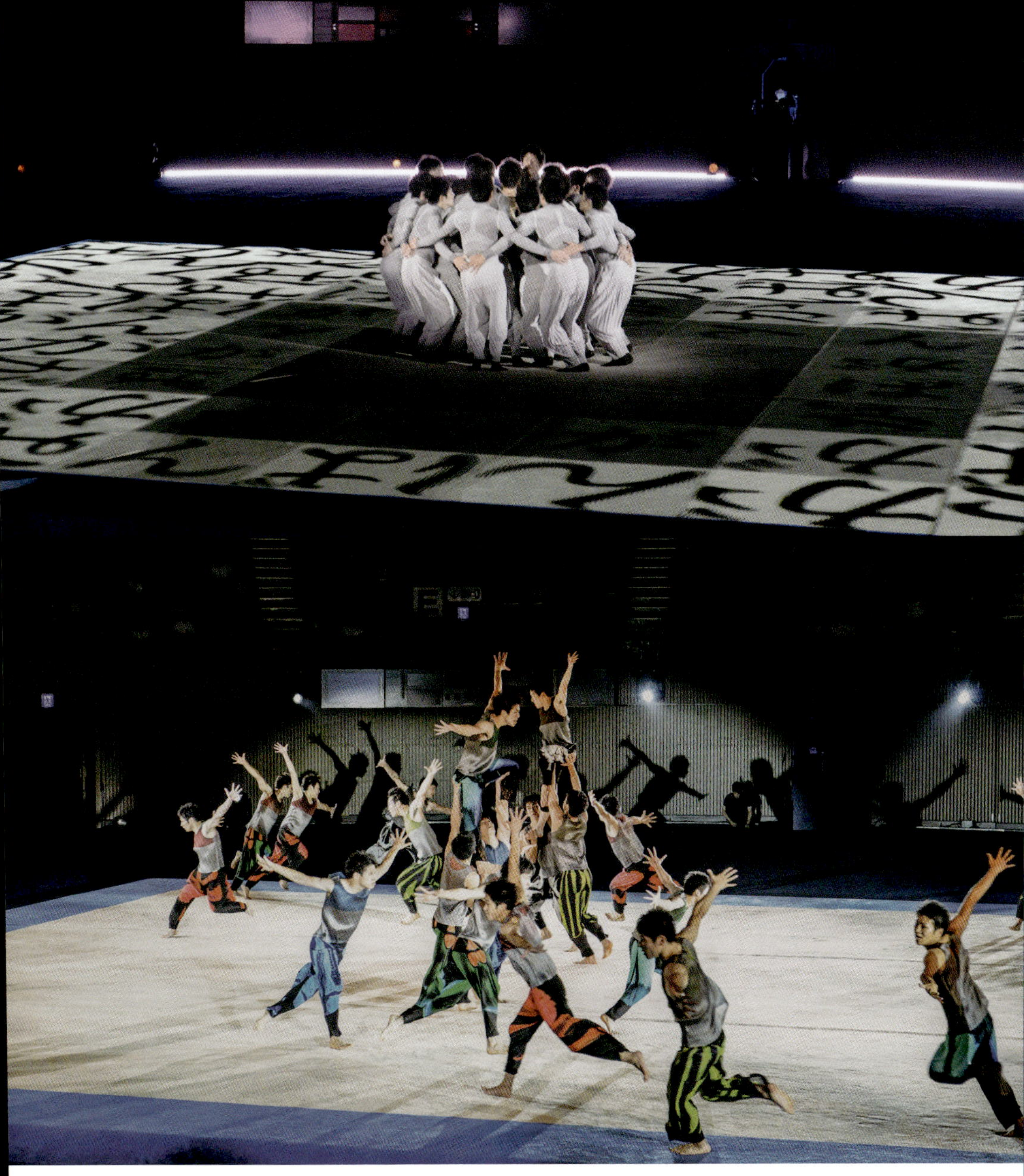

2014

> March: 132 5. ISSEY MIYAKE vol. 3–4, 2014
> May–September: Participated in the
> *Mémoires Vives* exhibition to commemorate
> the 30th anniversary of the Fondation Cartier
> pour l'art contemporain in Paris with IN-EI
> ISSEY MIYAKE
> July: 132 5. ISSEY MIYAKE vol. 1–2, 2015
> July–October: Showed 132 5. ISSEY MIYAKE
> as part of the *Gathering* exhibition at the
> Design Museum Holon in Israel

Opposite top: *Mémoires Vives* exhibition at the
Fondation Cartier pour l'art contemporain, Paris
IN-EI ISSEY MIYAKE displayed amid plantings in the
garden as well as in the gallery.
Photography: Muyard & Foucha, Artemide

Opposite bottom: 21_21 DESIGN SIGHT exhibition
posters for *Kome: The Art of Rice*, *Image-Makers*, and
The Fab Mind: Hints of the Future in a Shifting World

Mémoires Vives **exhibition at the Fondation
Cartier pour l'art contemporain, Paris**
This exhibition commemorated the 30th anniversary of the Fondation Cartier pour l'art contemporain, an institution founded to promote
contemporary art. Issey Miyake was one of the artists who had exhibited at the museum in the past
and had been invited back for the show. He presented IN-EI ISSEY MIYAKE installations both in
the gallery and in the garden. They were designed
specifically for this exhibition.

*May 10–September 21: Fondation Cartier pour l'art
contemporain, Paris*

132 5. ISSEY MIYAKE vol. 3–4, 2014   132 5. ISSEY MIYAKE vol. 1–2, 2015

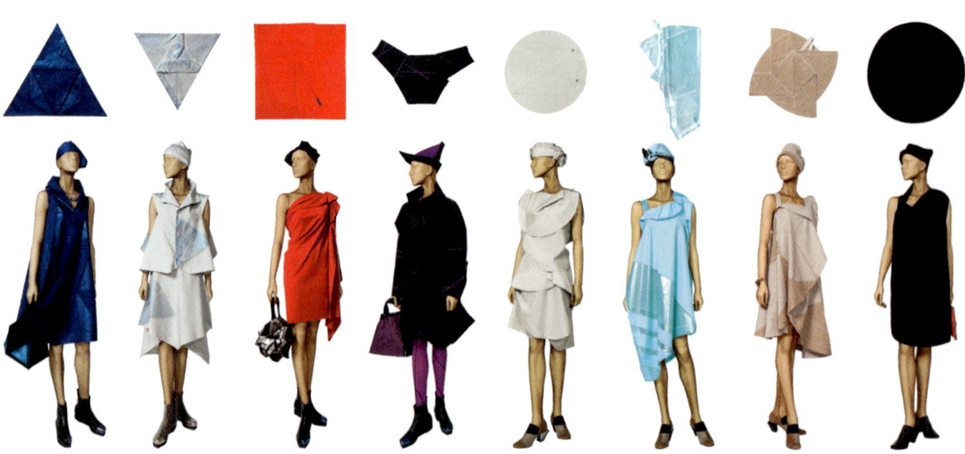

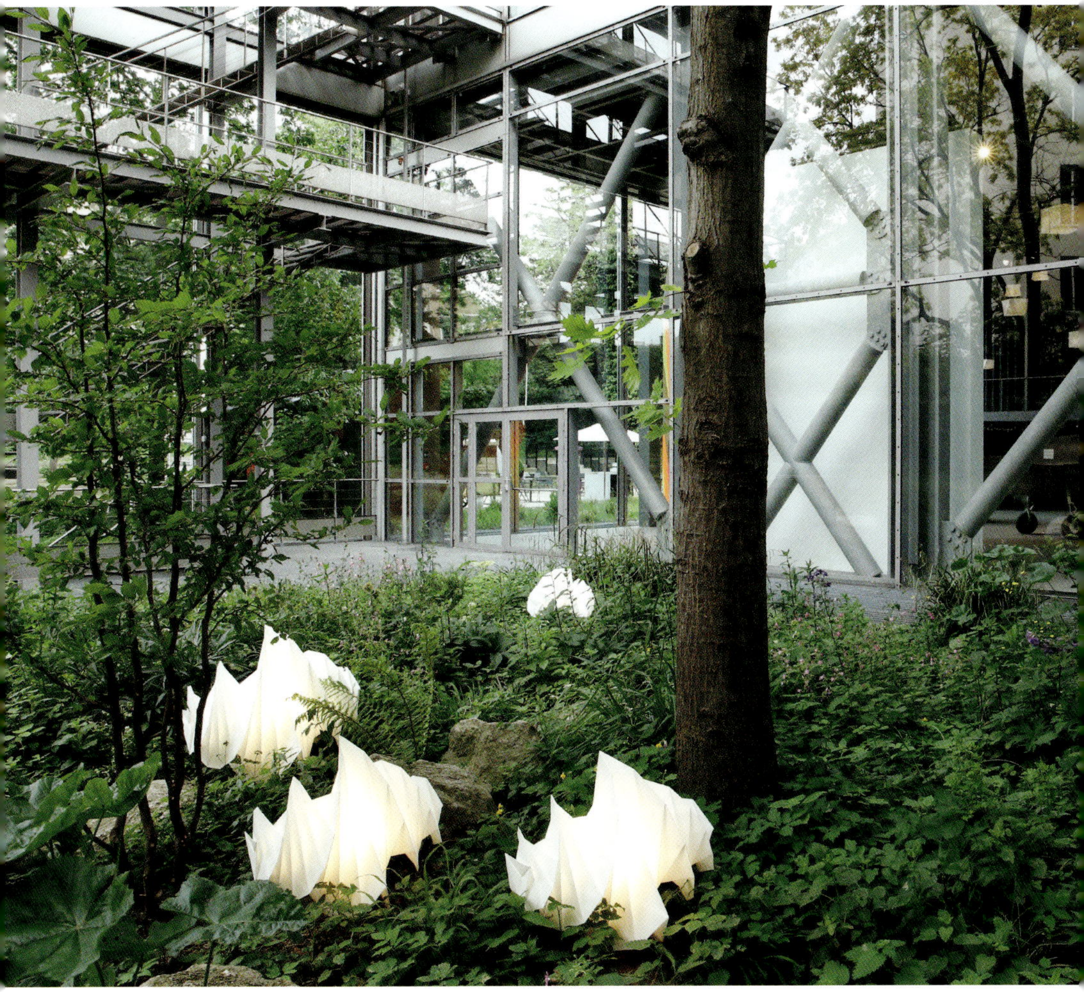

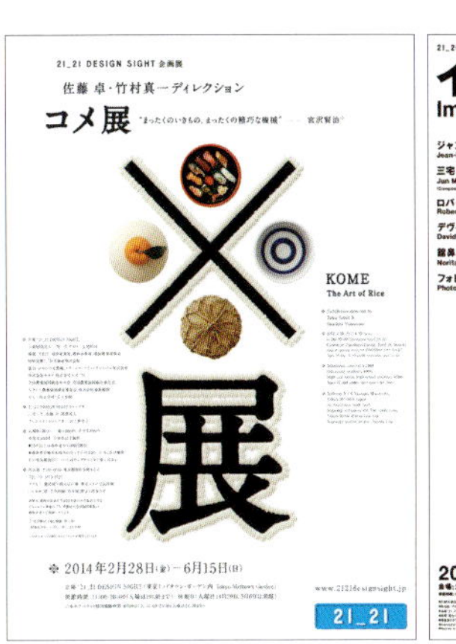

21_21 DESIGN SIGHT 企画展
佐藤 卓・竹村真一ディレクション
コメ展
"まったくのいきもの、まったくの精巧な機械" —— 宮沢賢治
KOME
The Art of Rice
2014年2月28日(金)— 6月15日(日)
www.2121designsight.jp
21_21

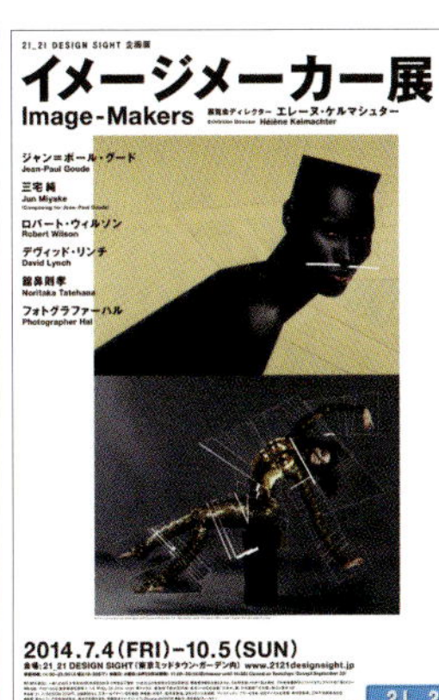

21_21 DESIGN SIGHT 企画展
イメージメーカー展
Image-Makers
展覧会ディレクター エレーヌ・ケルマシュター
Exhibition Director Hélène Kelmachter
ジャン＝ポール・グード
Jean-Paul Goude
三宅純
Jun Miyake
(Composing for Jean-Paul Goude)
ロバート・ウィルソン
Robert Wilson
デヴィッド・リンチ
David Lynch
舘鼻則孝
Noritaka Tatehana
フォトグラファーハル
Photographer Hal
2014.7.4(FRI)—10.5(SUN)
会場：21_21 DESIGN SIGHT（東京ミッドタウン・ガーデン内） www.2121designsight.jp
21_21

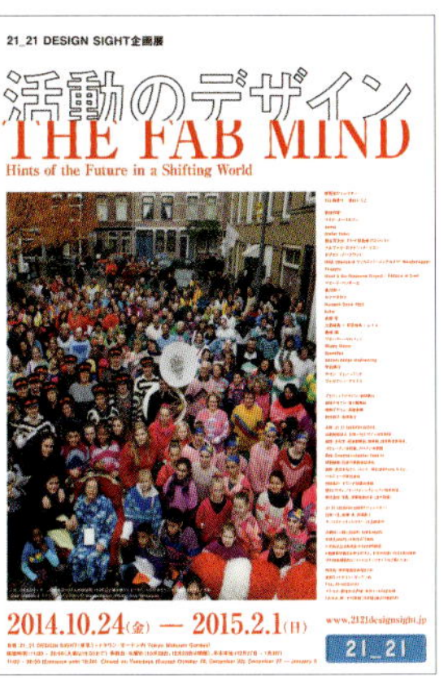

21_21 DESIGN SIGHT企画展
活動のデザイン
THE FAB MIND
Hints of the Future in a Shifting World
2014.10.24(金) — 2015.2.1(日)
www.2121designsight.jp
21_21

HOMME PLISSÉ ISSEY MIYAKE
Autumn-Winter 2014 Collection
For this season, HOMME PLISSÉ ISSEY MIYAKE took its inspiration from capoeira and focused upon clothing able to withstand vigorous movement. Capoeira is a Brazilian form of martial arts in which the competitors are basically not touched. The movements are dance-like and have been linked to the origins of the samba. They are also said to have influenced breakdancing. Photography: Grégoire Alexandre; creative director: Pascal Monfort; production: Sebastien Peretto

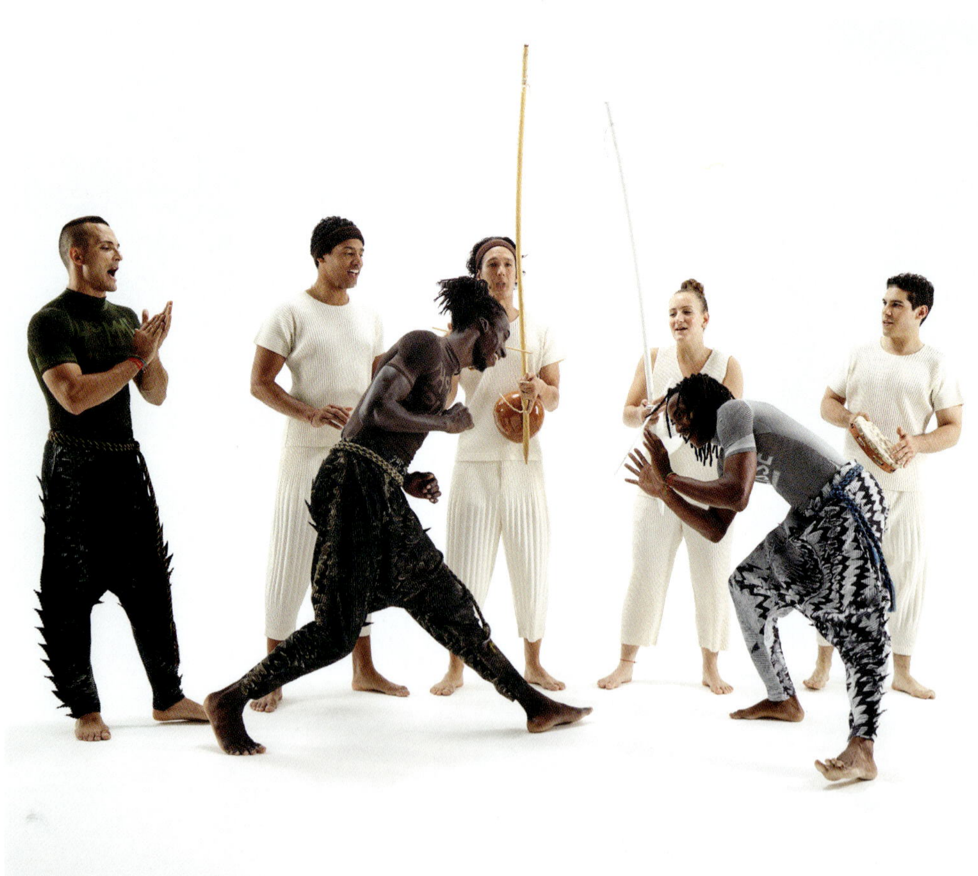

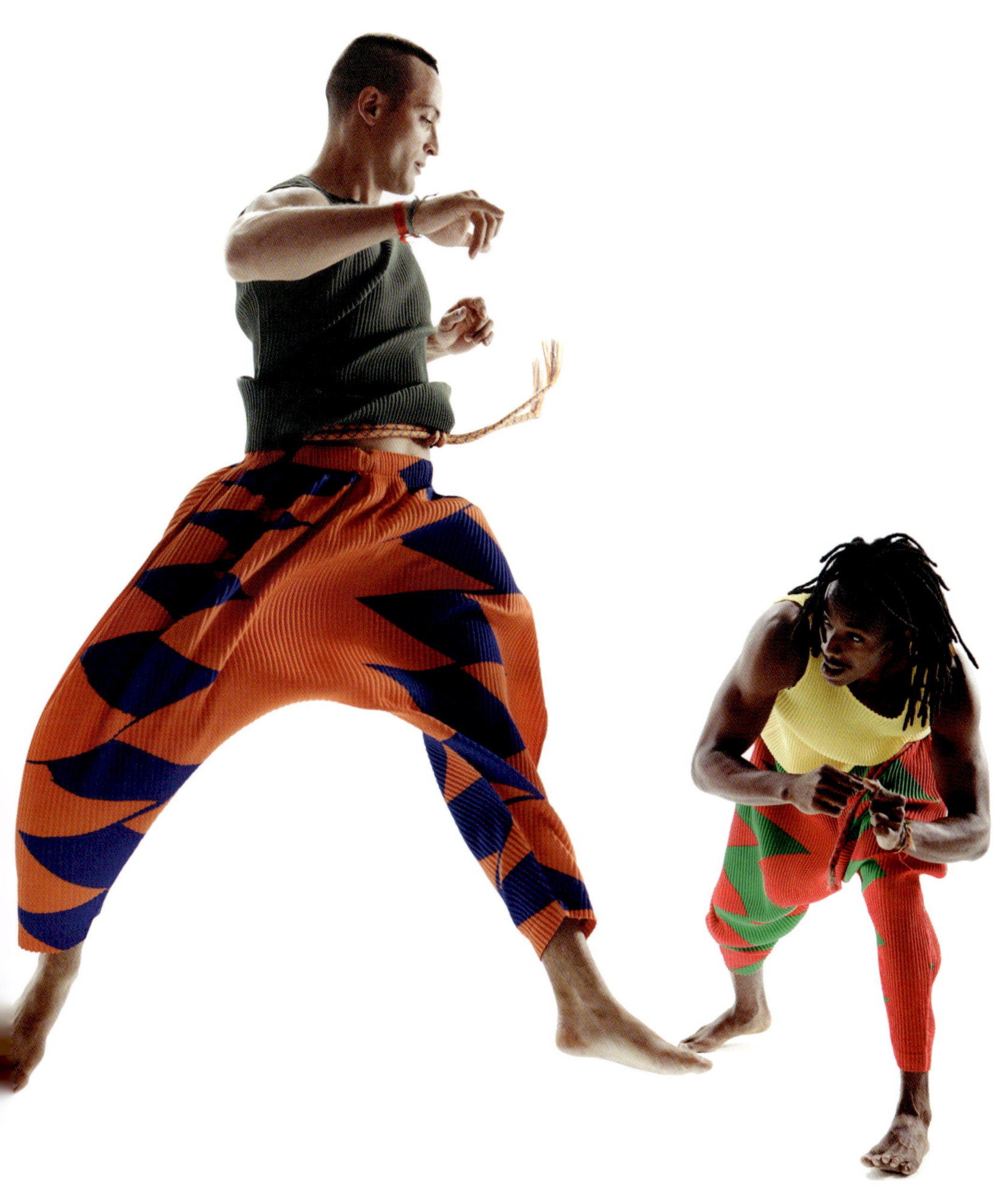

9—I BELIEVE THERE IS HOPE IN DESIGN

Essay by
KAZUKO KOIKE

IKKO TANAKA ISSEY MIYAKE: INVITING IKKO-SAN INTO THE THIRD DIMENSION

A single poster can stand for Japanese aesthetics and what it is to be Japanese. This was the hallmark of the work of the 20th-century graphic designer Ikko Tanaka. He was the designer whom Issey Miyake admired above all, and was closest to. Miyake was still a student when he first met Tanaka, and as he built up his career as a designer in Japan, Tanaka was the one he depended upon for continuous advice and guidance, as his sage and mentor. Tanaka was a true bon vivant, thoroughly expert in details of traditional Japanese wisdom across all aspects of living well – 衣 clothing, 食 eating, and 住 living. He was also alert to the revolutionary transformations that would be brought about by technology from the 20th century onward. Miyake spoke of how their conversations while eating or working together were a constant stream of inspiration. Whenever Tanaka encountered novel work or talent, he tended to immediately incorporate his discoveries in new projects, Miyake being the most remarkable example. Winning the 1976 Mainichi Design Award became the trigger for the monograph *ISSEY MIYAKE East Meets West* (1978),[1] a project that was directly driven by Ikko Tanaka himself, from concept and editing to publication.

Issey Miyake's homage to Ikko Tanaka finally took shape after due thought and reflection in 2015, making it possible to "enjoy Ikko-san's work as wearable designs." The initial collection included wraparound coats, dresses, and bags, based on Tanaka's posters *Nihon Buyo* (1981) for the Asian Performing Arts Institute at UCLA and *the 200th Anniversary of Sharaku* exhibition (1995).[2] Naoto Fukasawa designed the shops to launch this project. This was a clear declaration of Miyake's stance, effectively a manifesto going beyond mere emotional investment, that the graphics were the pillar of these designs. Themes that were truly worthy of inheriting Ikko Tanaka's œuvre and the retail environment for displaying these creations were exhaustively fine-tuned beforehand.

The material for PLEATS PLEASE ISSEY MIYAKE was chosen for its faithful color reproduction qualities, and the pieces were carefully planned to ensure that Ikko Tanaka's design graphics would be seen in their full glory. The production phase was entered via processes that were distinctly and uniquely Miyake Design Studio, the final signing off on color being made in the collection vault of the Ikko Tanaka Archives at the DNP Foundation for Cultural Promotion in Fukushima Prefecture, where his posters are stored.

Tracing Miyake's work in interpreting Ikko Tanaka's œuvre, and its transformation into clothing collections is a significant aspect of Japanese design history in itself. The following phases of this collaboration were launched in quick succession.

Particularly unique was the monochromatic series *Bokugi* (墨 calligraphic ink + 戯 play), a body of work in which Tanaka tackled the ancient Japanese skills of calligraphy.[3] Ink and brush calligraphy is a distinct art form in its own right, one of the important and dedicated arts that are mainstays of traditional Japanese culture, a serious "way" that commands full dedication. Tanaka's forms brim with inventiveness, as if a cherub, in its innocence, had pried open the doors of a conservative world. Playfulness makes the brush and ink dance, and Tanaka discovered how to play with ink, rather in the manner of Action Painting, while installing the fittings for a tea ceremony. Immediately after a white wall had been set up, he requested a bucketful of ink, picked up a piece of rag that happened to be there, and then began to paint. For the *Bokugi*-themed clothes, with this background in mind, Miyake chose to use a natural fiber: thick linen.[4] Ink-black images that were born from play are boldly placed as discrete motifs on brilliantly white heavyweight linen, creating a masterpiece in the IKKO TANAKA ISSEY MIYAKE series.

Gradations, rope, and other motifs from Tanaka's graphics have been worked into collections by Miyake. He conducted careful research into Tanaka's decisions regarding themes, intentionally selecting images that share a sense of optimism and cheer. Whoever wears these items, I dare say, would embrace these choices, and find pleasure in them. The IKKO TANAKA ISSEY MIYAKE series, the inheritor of the gentle and humorous world created by Tanaka, lightheartedly mingles in the street of Tokyo, Osaka, Paris, and Milan.

OPENING OF *MIYAKE ISSEY EXHIBITION: THE WORK OF MIYAKE ISSEY* AT THE NATIONAL ART CENTER, TOKYO

An Issey Miyake exhibition. What shape and form would it take, and how would it be realized? An intriguing question, for design people and those who are simply interested in clothes alike, not just in Japan, but around the world. Miyake was receptive to exhibitions, for he regarded them as spaces of reality, where his vision could be perceived comprehensively. The announcement of a show dedicated to Miyake received a massive response in cities around the world that went far beyond anything that the organizers had imagined.[5]

Any retrospective of his lengthy career, featuring his major achievements from the 1960s to 2016 – the year of the exhibition – was, of course, going to be rich in content. But that was not Miyake's primary interest. The key focus was always on the human being, and how to render visibility to the design thinking that supported the field of clothing and that is born within the context of the surrounding times and society – this was the imperative that drove Miyake and his team.

A "dream team" was organized, with the enthusiastic support of his staff, who had been the constant collaborators in building Issey Miyake's œuvre, in order to give visual expression to his axis, the philosophy that ran through his work from his earliest days, to what was made and sold in 2016. Mannequins being absolute necessities for any display involving clothing, Tokujin Yoshioka created "Grid body," which enabled installations with an unprecedented level of expression of the human form. Midori Kitamura oversaw the exhibition production and creative direction, and Taku Satoh the art direction.

Issey Miyake was well aware that he spearheaded the vanguard of Japan's creative force, but he never tried to restrict privileged access to the research, the studies, the technologies, the people, or any of the factors that enabled this level of achievement. Miyake, in fact, sought to share all of this as much and as widely, as possible. Installing a machine in the National Art Center gallery space, so that the audience could witness the birth of a pleated garment, effectively opening up and sharing the actual sites of making things at Miyake Design Studio, is proof of his stance.

Jack Lang[6] came from Paris for the opening, and there was the added glory of the presentation of the Ordre national de la Légion d'Honneur, Commandeur, granted by President François Hollande of France.

SESSION ONE
LINKING THE SOURCE TO THE LATEST

Something was fermenting, bubbling away inside Issey Miyake, again. The most trusted core members of his design team sensed this, and the initial key word was Jomon. The starting point was to decipher the power that imbued the pottery and statuettes made by the ancient Japanese 5,000 years ago, as a trigger for creativity today. It was, in effect, an act of soaring ambition to aim for creations that transcended our modern consumer market and conventional thinking about clothes.

For Miyake, this philosophical journey in pursuit of the very origin of clothes began with the revelations that he gleaned from the Musée d'Homme while he was studying and working in Paris, and continued throughout his long career. A specific example is his response following the Great East Japan Earthquake (2011 Tohoku Earthquake), when he focused on revisiting and renewing research into the devastated regions where shapes and forms of artifacts continue to be passed down from generation to generation since the Jomon period. His desire to help revitalize the region in the aftermath crystallized in the urgent and speedy planning and realization of the exhibition *The Spirit of Tohoku: "Clothing" by Issey Miyake* at 21_21 DESIGN SIGHT.[7]

What was fermenting inside Miyake was a keen awareness of circularity, how the innate fundamental abilities and forcefulness of humans has developed and flourished throughout our history, and has, in turn, continued to yield new creativity. The ultimate goal was to push the envelope of the limits of technology, and to fully unleash its potential in the outcomes. The project, which could be described as an autodidactic in-house campaign in design capability, was conducted with a select team of the best talent, and was painstakingly planned and organized with a certain degree of tense awareness. This was partly triggered by circumstances such as how the idea of this study in creativity, which was completely free from market trends, resonated with the Italian architect Michele De Lucchi, to the extent that he made a sudden decision to visit Japan expressly in order to write for the design magazine *Domus*.[8]

At the base of what brought forth the Session One pieces lies an imperative to look back at how Miyake Design Studio continued to develop materials to the present day. The starting point was "A Piece of Cloth," leading to techniques such as pleats in the 1980s and A-POC at the end of the 1990s, to which Miyake Design Studio added its latest materials that are processed with a method called

Steam Stretch – which devised optimized fibers, with computer programming drawing the pleat patterns before items are finished with steam compression. Steam Stretch could be why Session One clothing vibrates with "wild raw energy" while simultaneously possessing a distinctive elegance due to their soft texture. By avoiding sewing as far as possible, cloth is shaped using methods such as tying, opening slits, and heat-cutting instead. The prevalence of asymmetrical forms is the result of the designer's natural response, obeying the material.

Issey Miyake removed the separations between planning, technology, and engineering, and formed a team that cut across the different brands in the company in order to tackle the challenge that became known as Session One, which resulted in a powerful visual message sent out across Japan, and around the world.[9]

A-POC ABLE ISSEY MIYAKE
ONE THREAD, ONE PIECE OF CLOTH:
POSSIBILITIES, UNLIMITED

In 1998, Issey Miyake launched A-POC, with the manifesto "to revolutionize the process of clothes-making." A-POC, an acronym for "A Piece Of Cloth," can be understood as a declaration that sums up Miyake Design Studio's commitment to materials research and technological innovation, which, with A-POC ABLE ISSEY MIYAKE,[10] injects, it feels, the wish to see how much fun and pleasure can be had in testing the potential of new technologies. A natural development was the emergence of a rare artistic collaboration with Tadanori Yokoo, a leading contemporary artist and personal friend of Issey Miyake, who had continued to be entrusted with the design of the invitations to the Paris Collection shows since 1977.

Yoshiyuki Miyamae, who has worked with A-POC since the early 2000s, had many in-depth discussions with Yokoo, resulting in blouson jackets that are truly worthy of being described as works of art. The pieces in the first series *TADANORI YOKOO ISSEY MIYAKE 0* used threads in only seven colors to recreate Yokoo's vivid palette on a single piece of cloth. An additional and unexpected synergistic dimension to Yokoo's artwork comes from the focus on the flipped image on the reverse side of the fabric, which emerges from the colors that are not apparent on the surface.[11]

The piece has so much appeal that anyone would obviously choose to wear this artistic collaboration, which effectively doubles the pleasure of dressing up.

A-POC ABLE ISSEY MIYAKE indicates how creative clothes-making will open up after the separation between genres such as crafts, technology, and art that existed until the 20th century has been dismantled.

L'ARC DE TRIOMPHE, WRAPPED
AND THE ARTISTS HEAD FOR
21_21 DESIGN SIGHT

Issey Miyake maintained a close and active relationship with the artists Christo and Jeanne-Claude[12] for more than 30 years. Christo's concepts were significant in inspiring Miyake, of course, and an important part of their relationship was Jeanne-Claude's vibrant personality. The most important element of the factors that linked the three together was cloth. Wrapping requires it, and from their first encounter, as artlessly as a child, Jeanne-Claude would ask their mentor on fabric – Miyake – for answers to their questions, as well as for advice and endorsement. Sometimes they made Miyake smile, such as when they proposed how their product ideas could be applied to a newly developed textile. Miyake enjoyed his trips to Christo and Jeanne-Claude's project sites, such as the fields in Ibaraki in Japan,[13] as well as Central Park in New York,[14] and the Reichstagsgebäude in Berlin,[15] where their reunions were moments of sublime bliss.

Then, L'Arc de Triomphe. To wrap this, the largest monument in Paris, a city where each of them had ties and memories. Miyake's support for the realization of this project was unstinting and tremendous. This was also an event which should be celebrated as the peak experience of the friendship between Christo, Jeanne-Claude, and Miyake. Tragically, however, Jeanne-Claude passed away in 2009, and Christo himself in 2020, before witnessing the project's completion, while the Covid-19 pandemic continued to bar Miyake from traveling.

Miyake then made a decision, one that seemed obvious to him: invite the project to 21_21 DESIGN SIGHT. *L'Arc de Triomphe, Wrapped* was a rejuvenation of the literal heart of Paris by means of an infusion of art – new blood as it were – that concluded with the participation of a total of 60,000 visitors, and finally landed at 21_21 DESIGN SIGHT in Roppongi, Tokyo, a space created by Tadao Ando.[16] Years of painstaking programming and the building of a team of true professionals made the success of this massive project possible in Paris, and a new legend was born when it was transported to Tokyo. This is also how Miyake's stated mission in founding 21_21 DESIGN SIGHT – to design the entirety of how creators' ideas are brought to their audience, their users, including the processes to help to secure acceptance – continues to be sustained.

Issey Miyake injected wisdom from the East into the history of creation in the 20th as well as the 21st century, and created a monumental epoch in world design history. He witnessed the success of this exhibition, was then struck by illness, and quietly slipped away. The response to the sad announcement transcended borders, and a massive wave of condolences were sent to Miyake Design Studio, where, even at this very moment, young designers who were mentored by Miyake continue to strive, in order to achieve the missions that he set.

1   *Issey Miyake East Meets West*: See pp. 82–83.
2   Poster *Nihon Buyo* by Ikko Tanaka and coat *Nihon Buyo* of IKKO TANAKA ISSEY MIYAKE: See pp. 330–331, poster *200th Anniversary of Sharaku* by Ikko Tanaka and coat *Sharaku* of IKKO TANAKA ISSEY MIYAKE: See pp. 332–333.
3   *Bokugi* by Ikko Tanaka: See pp. 352–353.
4   *Bokugi* of IKKO TANAKA ISSEY MIYAKE: See pp. 352–353.
5   Exhibition *Miyake Issey Exhibition: The Work of Miyake Issey*: See pp. 336–349.
6   Jack Lang (1939–): French politician. Established the World Theatre Festival, Nancy, in 1963 and chaired the executive committee. Appointed Minister of Culture by the François Mitterrand government in 1981 and retained that position until 1986. Later responsible for culture and information, and also served as Minister of National Education.
7   Exhibition *The Spirit of Tohoku: "Clothing" by Issey Miyake*: See pp. 308–309.
8   Michele De Lucchi (1951–): Italian architect and designer. Formed the innovative "Memphis" design movement in 1981 together with Ettore Sottsass and others. Involved in product design for Artemide, Olivetti, and other brands, and also active as an architect. "Issey Miyake Session One" in *Domus*: See pp. 368–375.
9   Session One: See pp. 354–367.
10 A-POC ABLE ISSEY MIYAKE: See pp. 402–403.
11 TADANORI YOKOO ISSEY MIYAKE: See pp. 388–397.
12 Christo (1935–2020) and Jeanne-Claude (1935–2009): Artists. Born on the same day (June 13) in the same year, the two met in Paris in 1958 and became lifelong collaborators on monumental environmental art works.
13 *The Umbrellas, Japan – USA, 1984–91*
14 *The Gates, Central Park, New York City, 1979–2005*
15 *Wrapped Reichstag, Berlin, 1971–95*
16 Exhibition *Christo and Jeanne-Claude "L'Arc de Triomphe, Wrapped"*: See pp. 404–415.

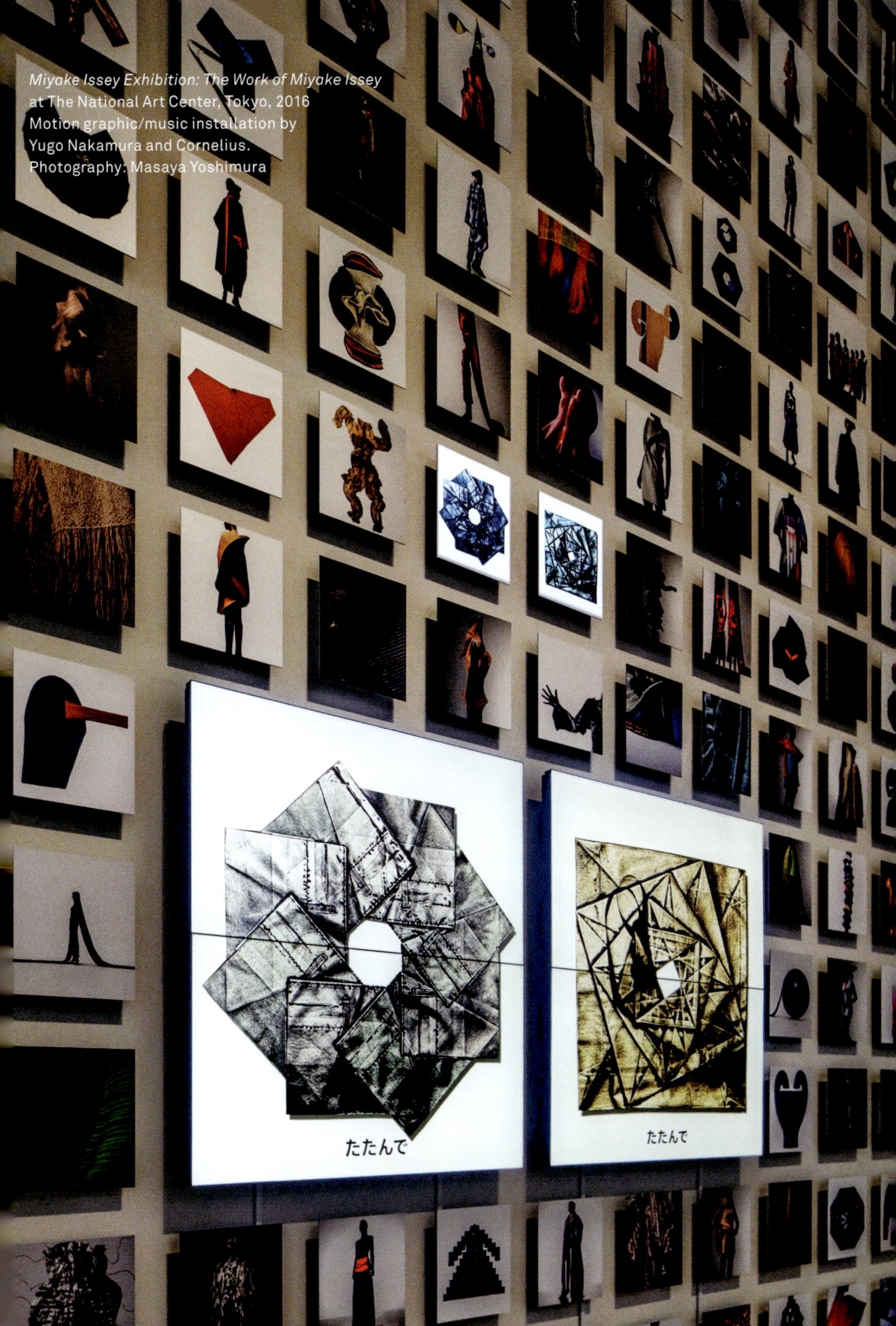

Miyake Issey Exhibition: The Work of Miyake Issey
at The National Art Center, Tokyo, 2016
Motion graphic/music installation by
Yugo Nakamura and Cornelius.
Photography: Masaya Yoshimura

2015

IKKO TANAKA ISSEY MIYAKE

This marked the beginning of a series with motifs based on works by graphic designer Ikko Tanaka. Since becoming acquainted with Tanaka in the 1960s, Issey Miyake respected and was inspired by his work and its ability to bridge Japanese aesthetics like *rinpa* and *ukiyoe* and modern Western design. The garment in this series is an expression of Miyake's gratitude. His goal was to create a new form of appeal for Tanaka's works by having people wear and move around in them. He hoped they would surprise people around the world, and particularly Tanaka. Miyake insisted on the faithful reproduction of the colors of the original works in the manufacturing process.

Opposite bottom: 21_21 DESIGN SIGHT exhibition posters for *Measuring – This much, That much, How much?, Motion Science,* and *Architect Frank Gehry 'I Have an Idea'*

132 5. ISSEY MIYAKE vol. 3–4, 2015

132 5. ISSEY MIYAKE vol. 1–2, 2016

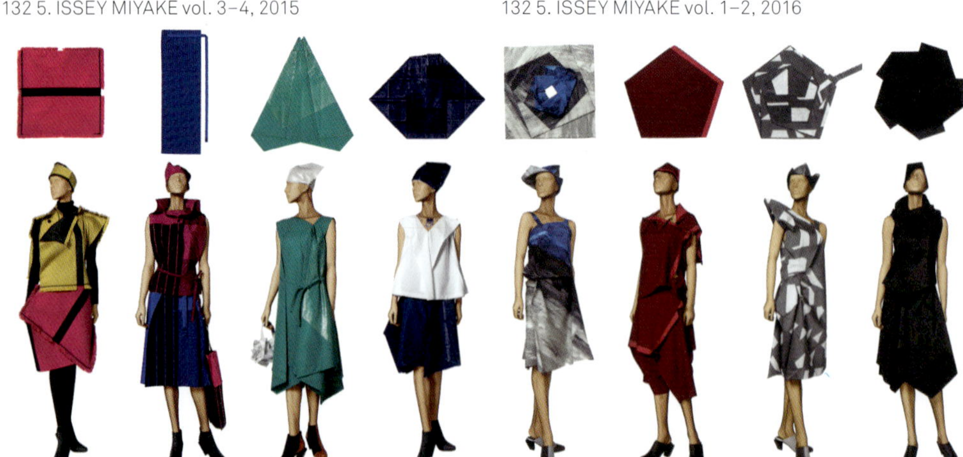

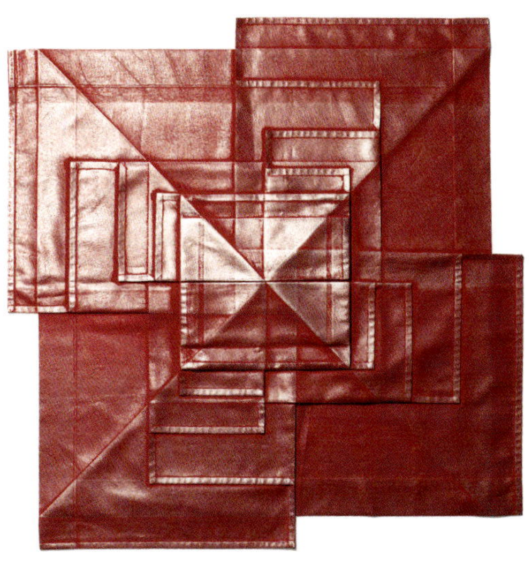

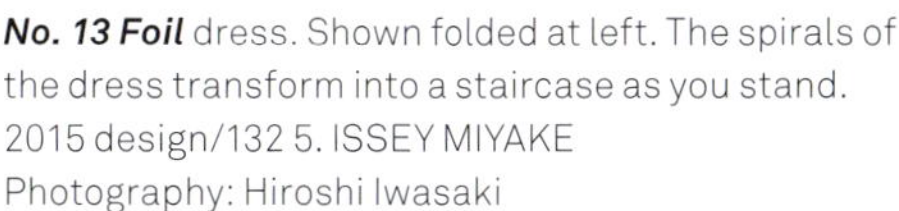

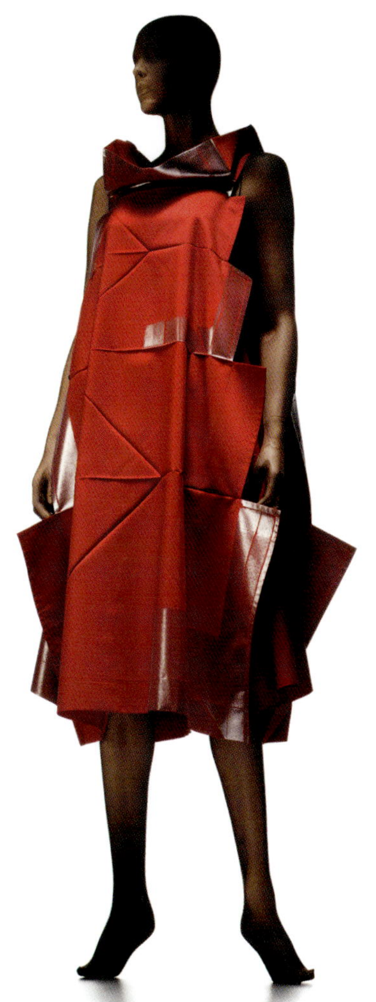

No. 13 Foil dress. Shown folded at left. The spirals of
the dress transform into a staircase as you stand.
2015 design/132 5. ISSEY MIYAKE
Photography: Hiroshi Iwasaki

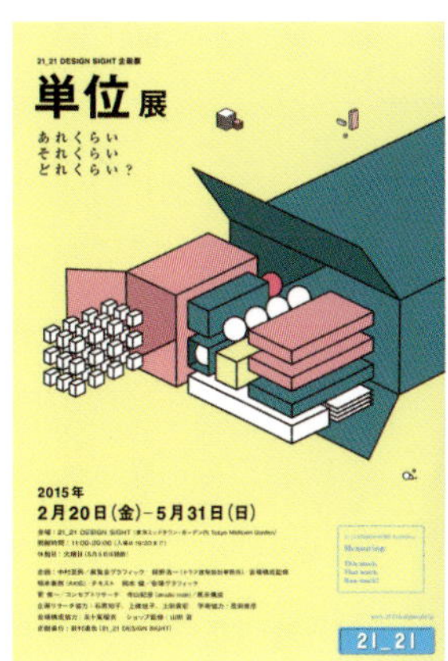

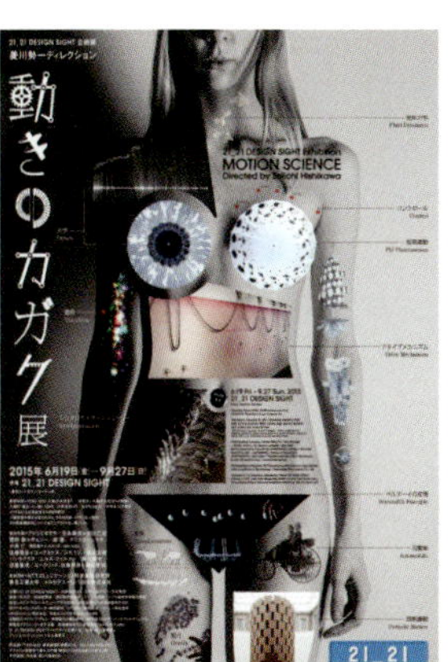

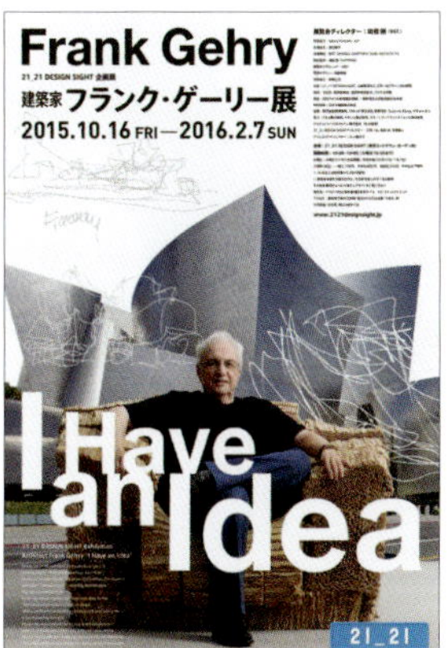

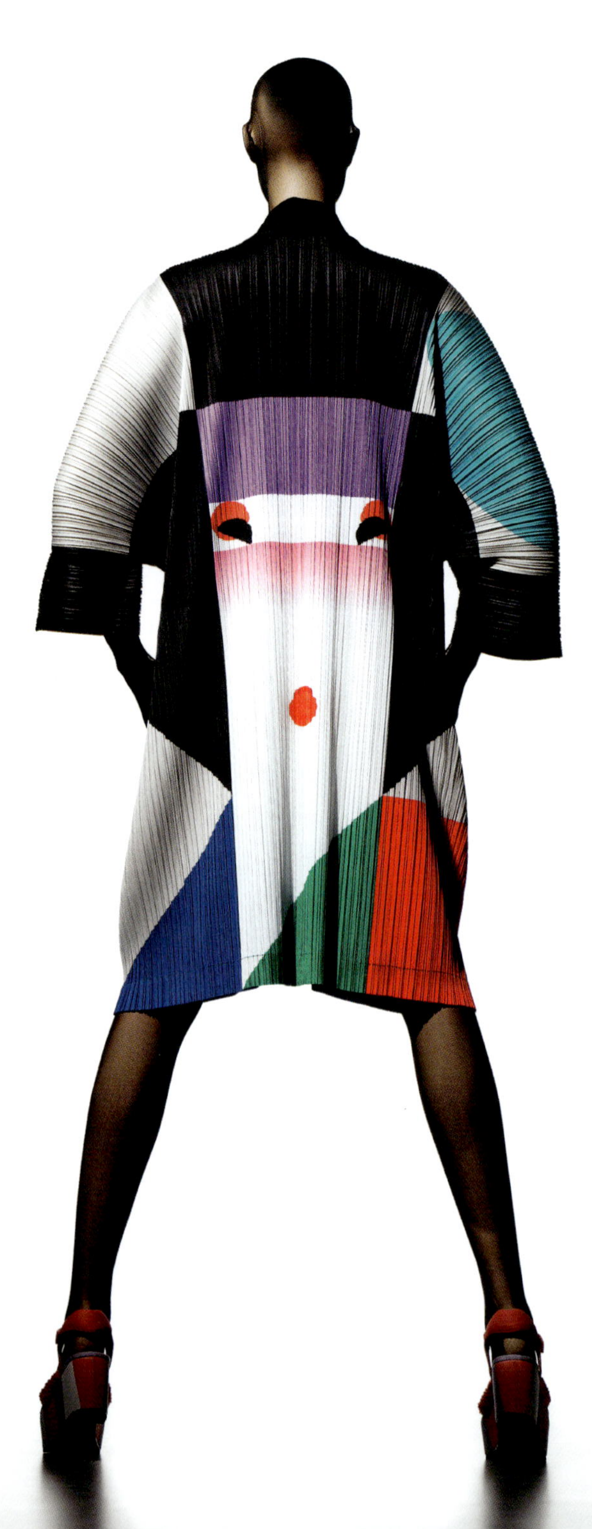

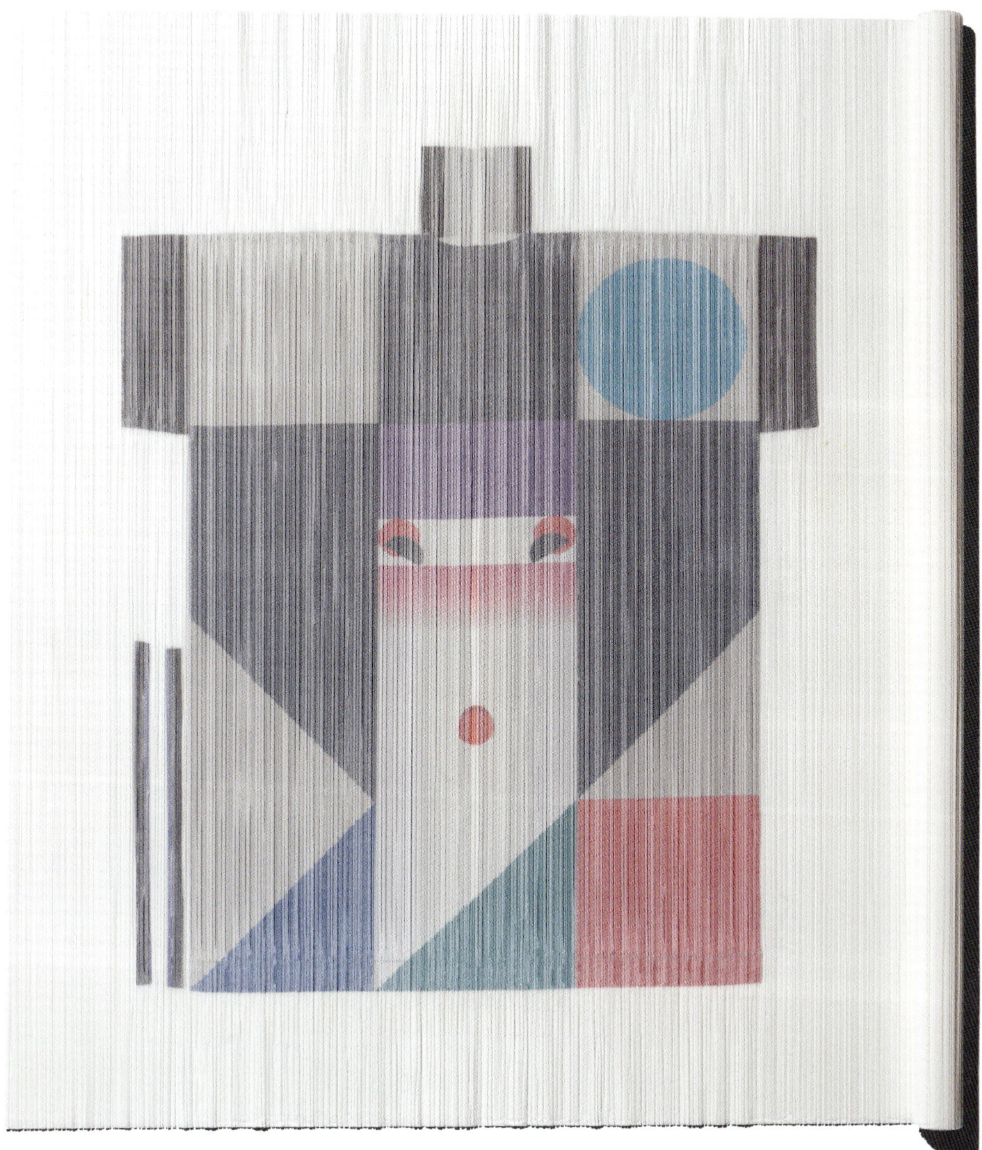

Nihon Buyo coat
The pleats technique was used, and the sizes and colors of the original works were reproduced. Above, the coat with the pleats as it comes out of the machine. The work used as the motif, Tanaka's *Nihon Buyo*, was originally a poster for a Japanese dance performance at UCLA in 1981. It is one of Ikko Tanaka's most famous works and revered for its fusion of Japanese traditional aesthetics and Western rationalism to create a geometrical structure.
2015 design/IKKO TANAKA ISSEY MIYAKE No. 1
Photography: Hiroshi Iwasaki

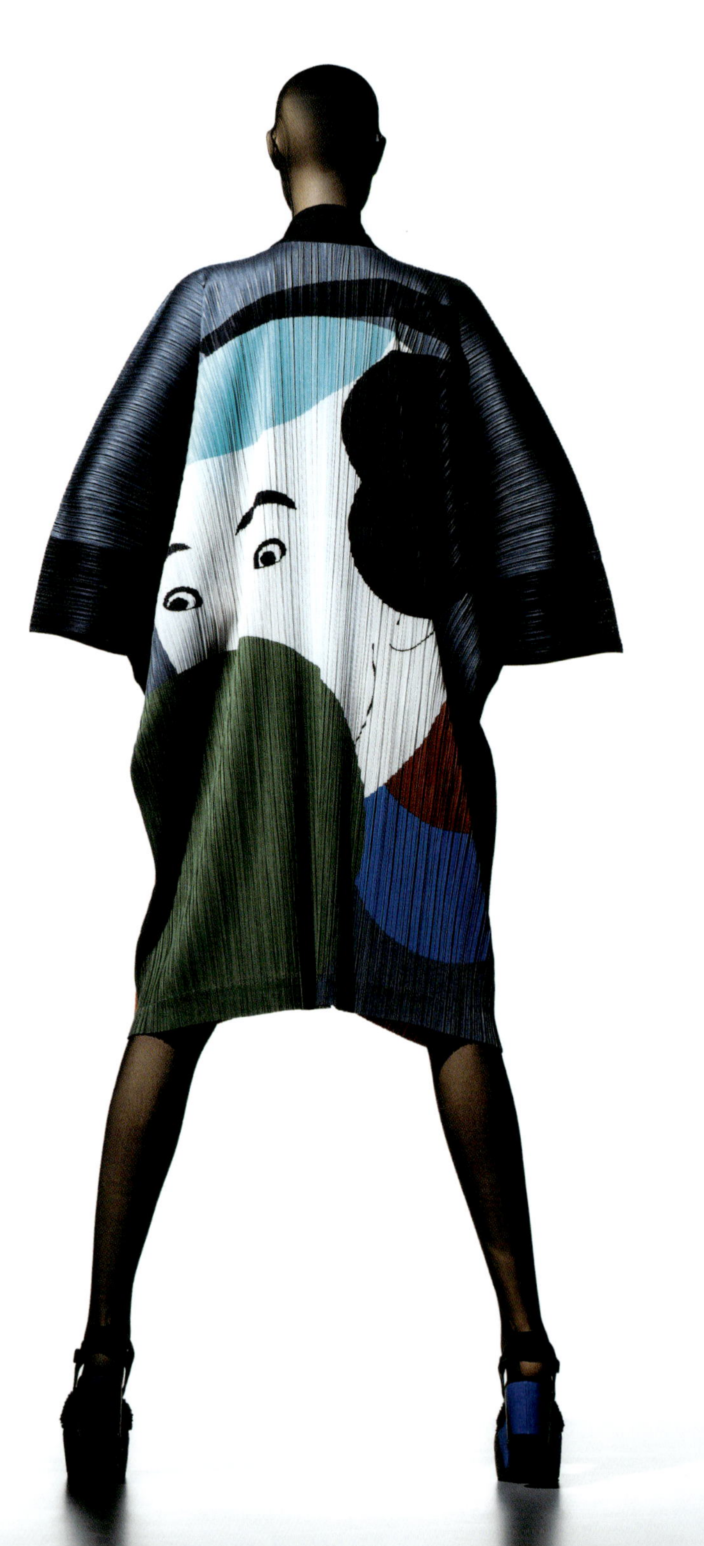

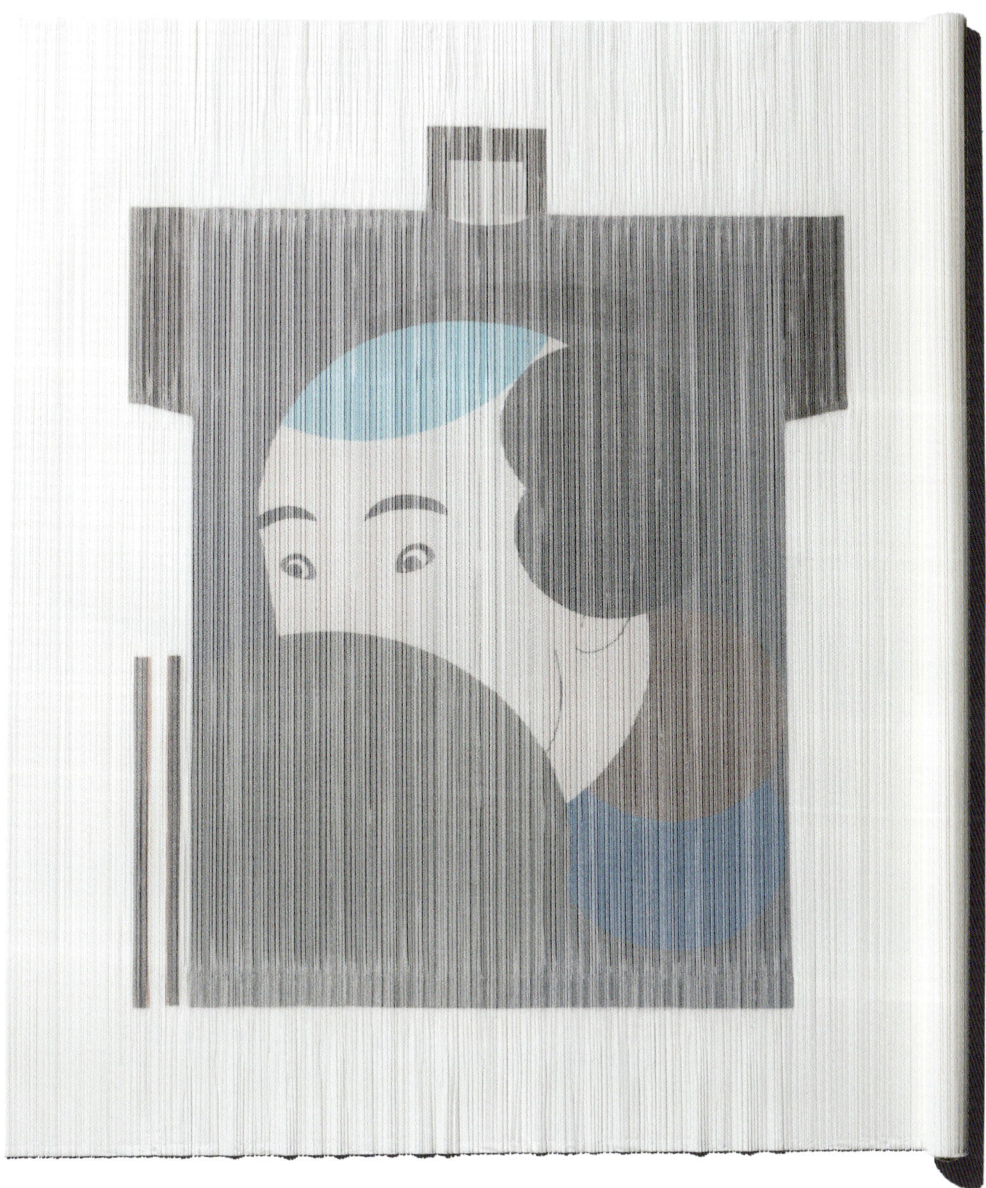

Sharaku coat
The pleats technique was used, and the sizes and colors of the original works were reproduced. Above, the coat with the pleats as it comes out of the machine. The *200th Anniversary of Sharaku* motif uses the simple element of nine circles to create an *okubi-e* by Toshusai Sharaku in this 1995 work to celebrate the 200th anniversary of Sharaku's birth.
2015 design/IKKO TANAKA ISSEY MIYAKE No. 1
Photography: Hiroshi Iwasaki

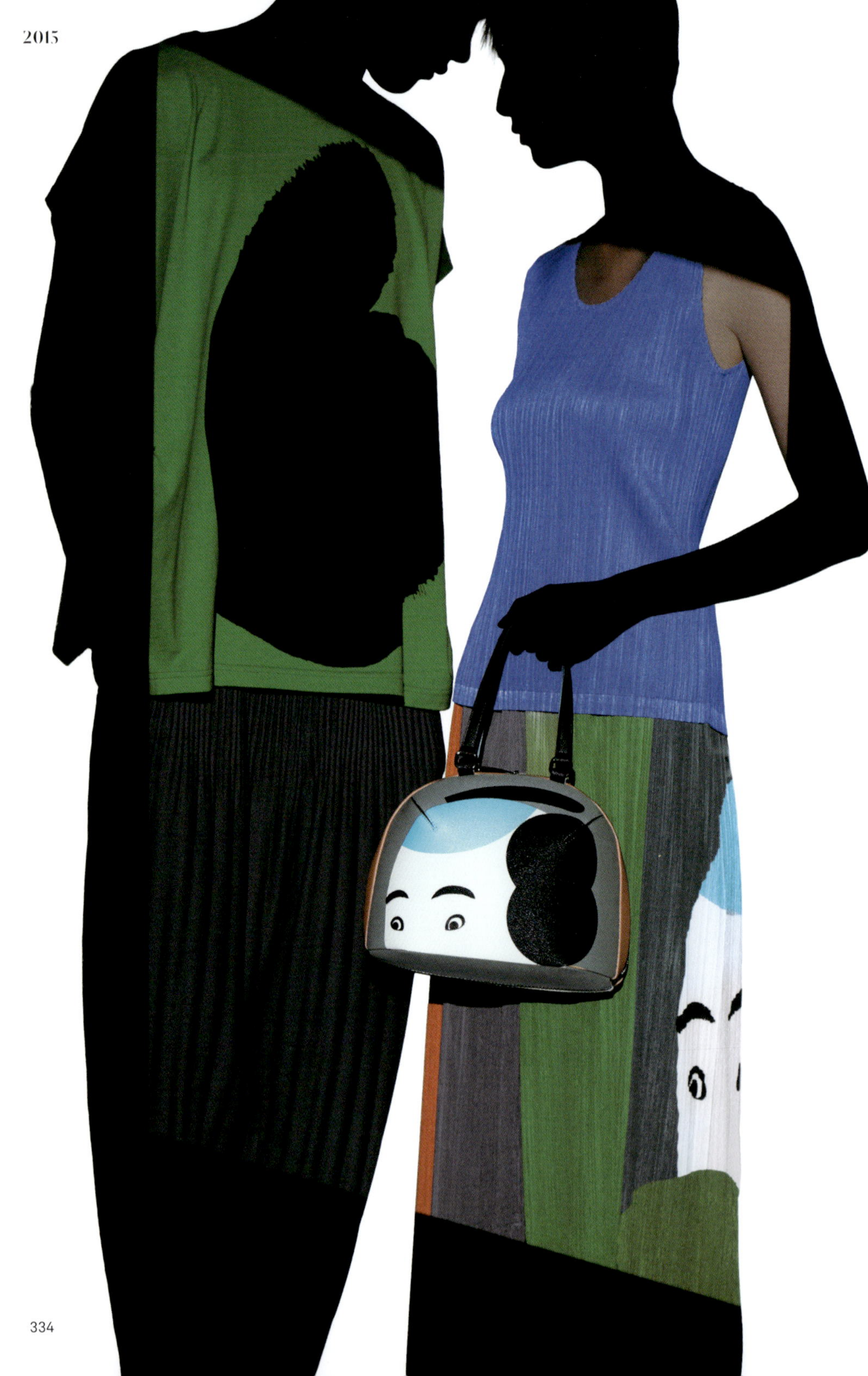

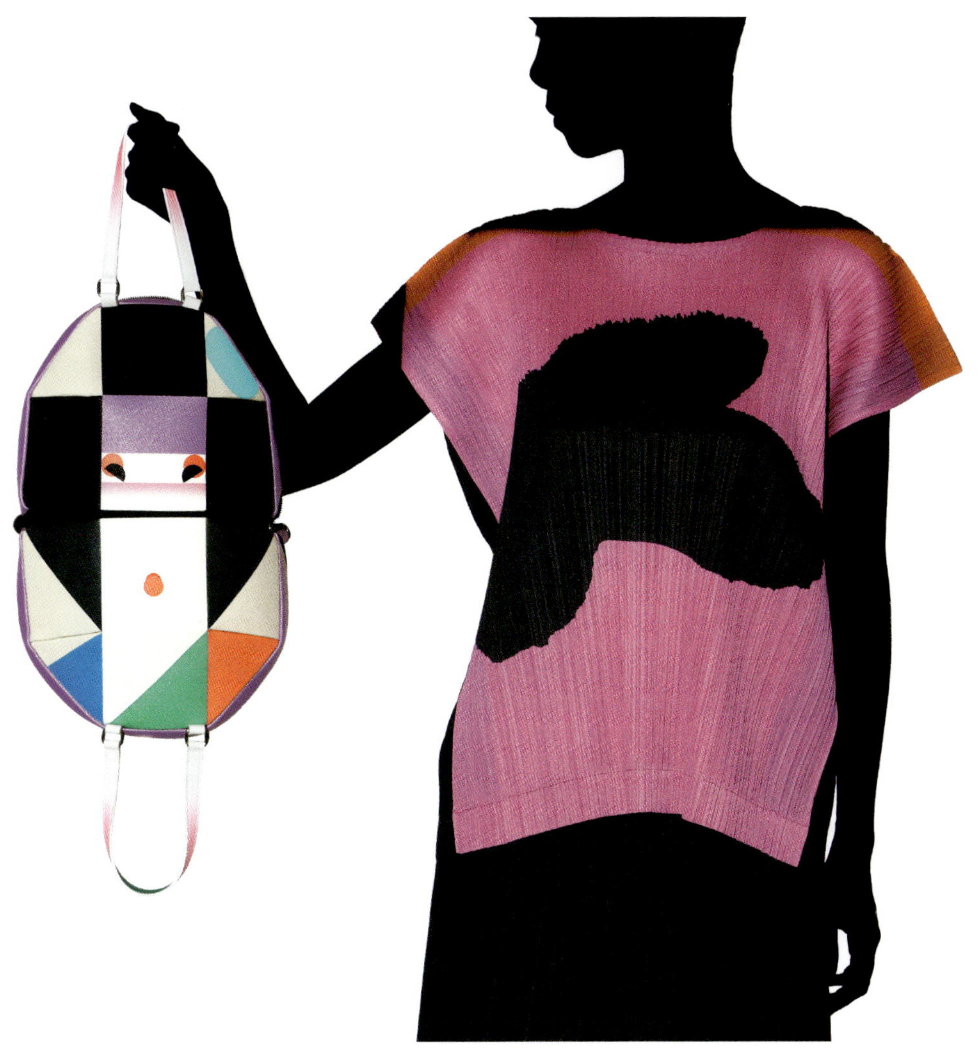

Opposite: *Sharaku* bag, pants, and *Futoi Kigo* top
The motif for the tops, *Variations of Bold Symbols*, was produced as graphic art in 1992. Handwritten symbols are arrayed on a monochrome rectangular base.
2015 design/IKKO TANAKA ISSEY MIYAKE No. 1
Photography: Francis Giacobetti

Nihon Buyo bag and *Futoi Kigo* top
2015 design/IKKO TANAKA ISSEY MIYAKE No. 1
Photography: Francis Giacobetti

2016

- > February: 132 5. ISSEY MIYAKE vol. 3–4, 2016
- > March: *Miyake Issey Exhibition: The Work of Miyake Issey* in Tokyo. A catalogue titled *Miyake Issey Exhibition: The Work of Miyake Issey* was also published by Kyuryudo Art–Publishing Co., Ltd.
- > March: Publication of the book *Issey Miyake* by TASCHEN
- > July: 132 5. ISSEY MIYAKE vol. 1–2, 2017
- > December: IKKO TANAKA ISSEY MIYAKE No. 2

Opposite bottom: 21_21 DESIGN SIGHT exhibition posters for *Zakka – Goods and Things –*, *Doboku: Civil Engineering*, and *Design Anatomy: A Method for Seeing the World through Familiar Objects*

Miyake Issey Exhibition: The Work of Miyake Issey
The exhibition was divided into three parts covering approximately 45 years of work, from early designs to projects still in progress. Issey Miyake wanted to communicate the near future of design culture through his works and his ideas about making things. The exhibition was at the National Art Center in Tokyo and was one of the largest Miyake exhibitions to date.

March 16–June 13: The National Art Center, Tokyo General direction: Issey Miyake, Tamotsu Aoki; production and creative direction: Midori Kitamura; curator: Yayoi Motohashi; art direction: Taku Satoh; grid body installation: Tokujin Yoshioka; video work: Yuriko Takagi, Shinya Nakajima, Yu Yamanaka, Pascal Roulin; collaboration with A-POC: Kotaro Sekiguchi; motion graphic/music installation: Yugo Nakamura, Cornelius; lighting design: Haruki Kaito; graphic design: Shingo Noma

132 5. ISSEY MIYAKE vol. 3–4, 2016   132 5. ISSEY MIYAKE vol. 1–2, 2017

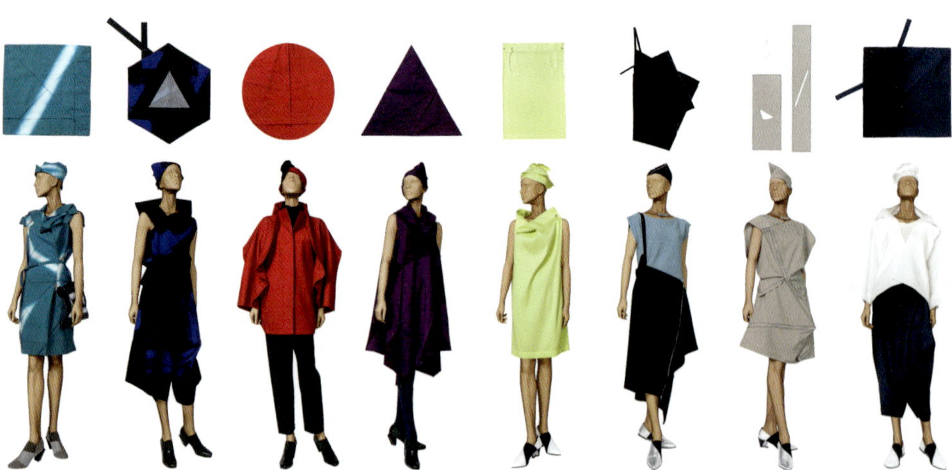

Section A, **_Miyake Issey Exhibition:_**
The Work of Miyake Issey

Exhibition section A was structured around 12 of Miyake's most important works from the 1970s. Tokujin Yoshioka was responsible for the installation here as well as for that in section B. Yoshioka designed the "Grid body" for the exhibit. Here, it can be seen in paper.

Tattoo 1970 design/Spring-Summer 1971 Collection, _Sashiko_ 1972 design/Autumn-Winter 1972 Collection, _Handkerchief dress_ 1970 design/Spring-Summer 1971 Collection, etc. Grid body installation: Tokujin Yoshioka Photography: Masaya Yoshimura

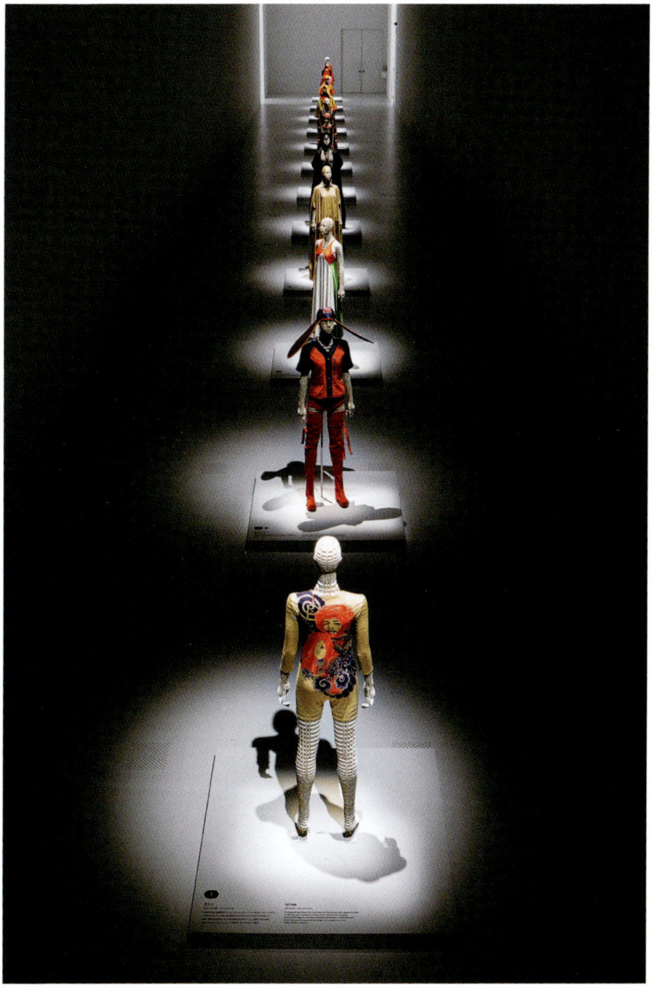

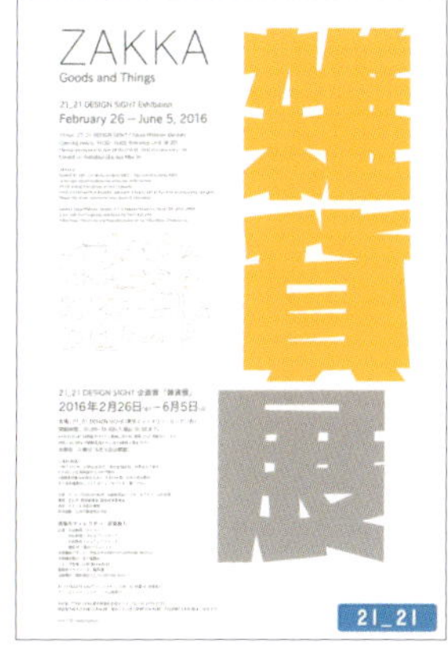

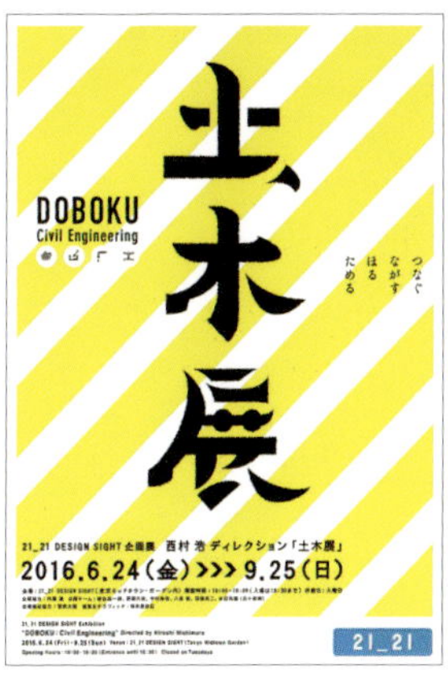

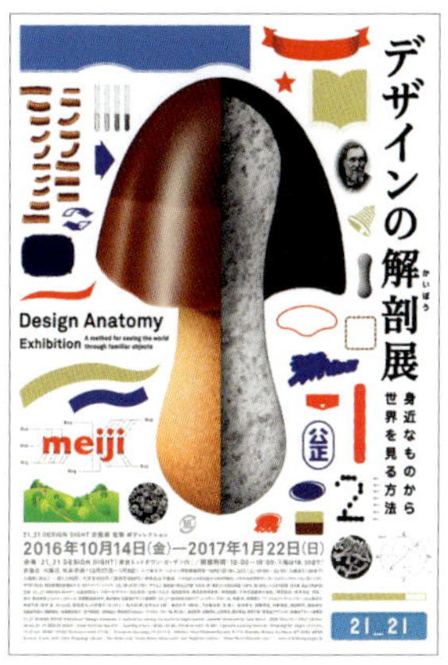

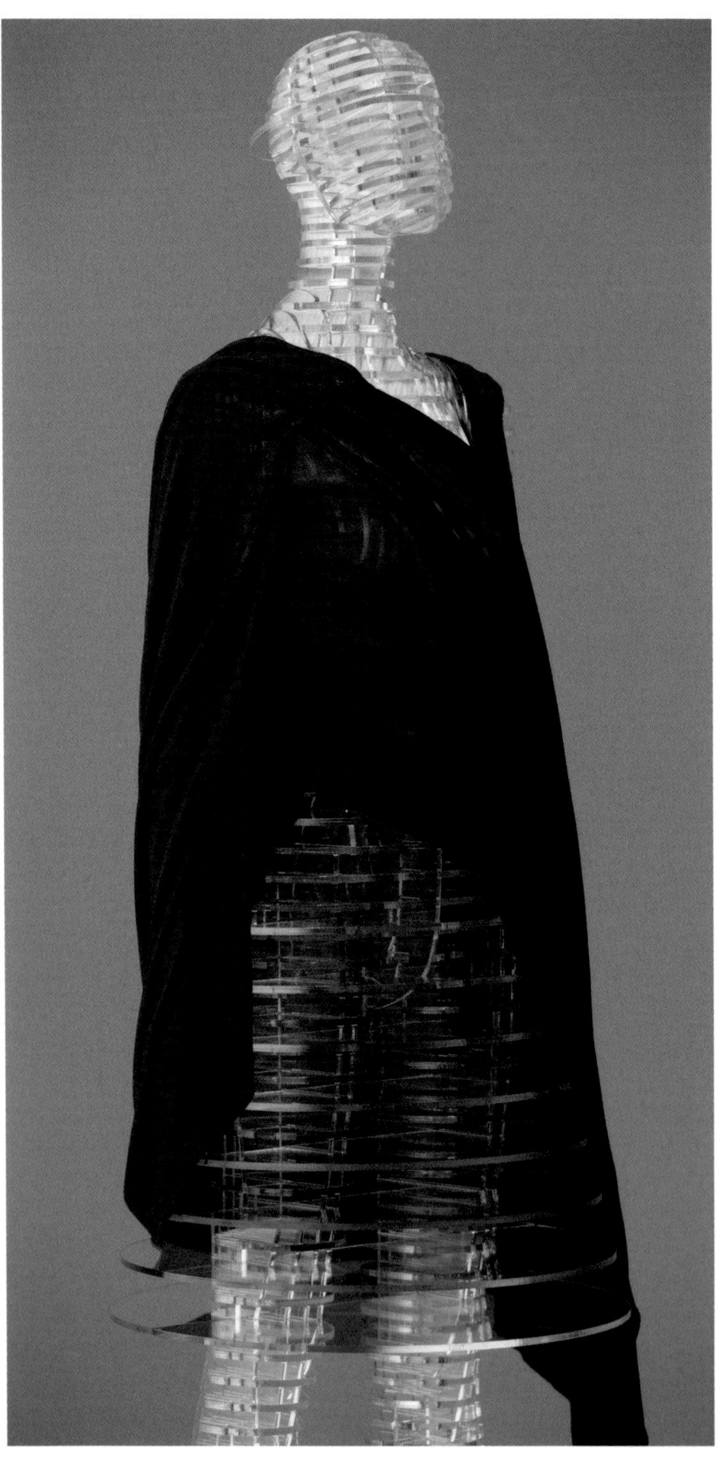

Section B, *Miyake Issey Exhibition: The Work of Miyake Issey*
Exhibition section B contained the Body Series, highlighting Miyake's explorations of the space between clothing and the body during the 1980s. "Grid body" was made from a single sheet of clear plastic laser cut into 365 parts, and it wore a number of Miyake's "Body Works."

Waterfall Body 1984 design/Autumn-Winter 1984 Collection
Grid body installation:
Tokujin Yoshioka
Photography:
Mitsumasa Fujitsuka

Opposite: Section B, *Miyake Issey Exhibition: The Work of Miyake Issey*
Plastic Body 1980 design/ Autumn-Winter 1980 Collection
Grid body installation:
Tokujin Yoshioka
Photography:
Mitsumasa Fujitsuka

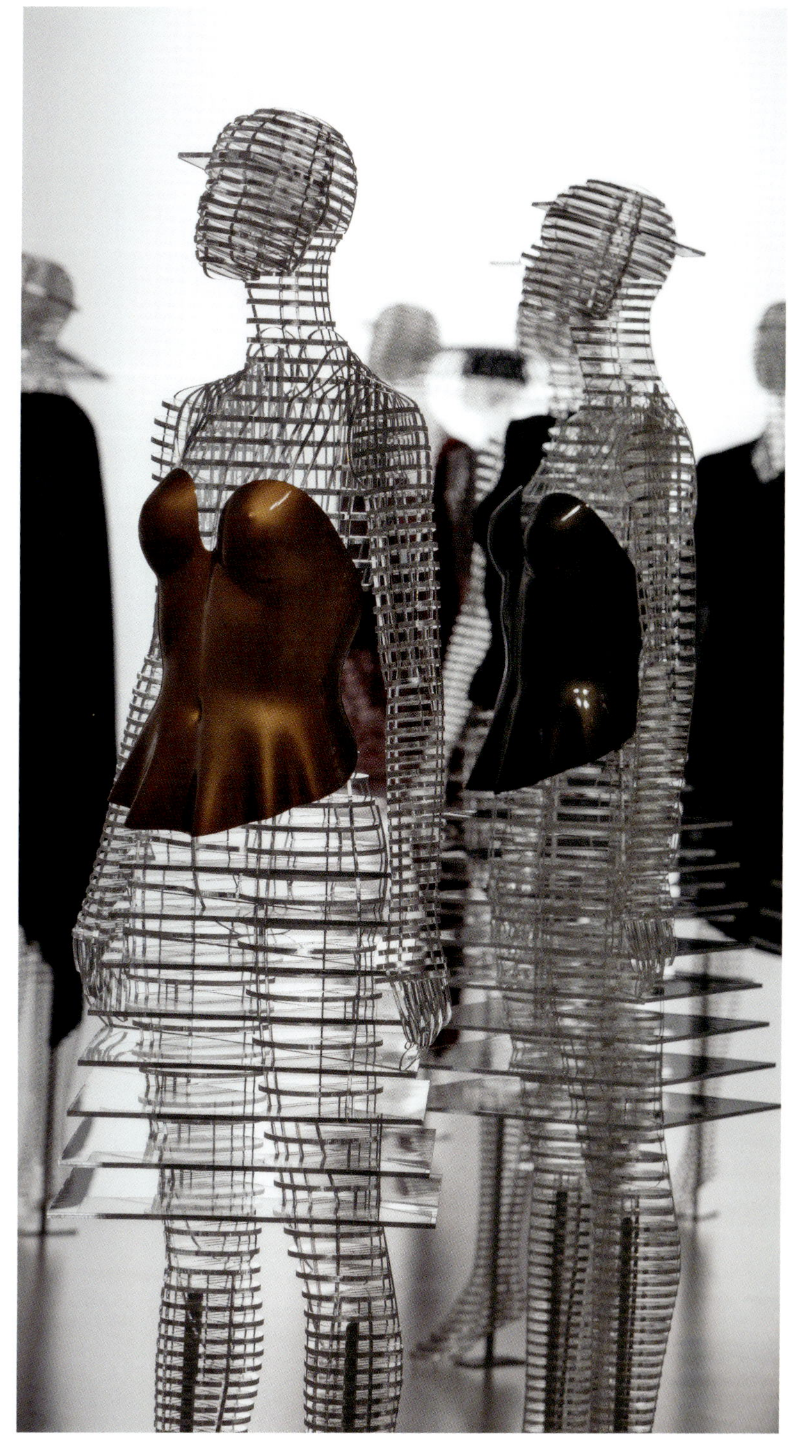

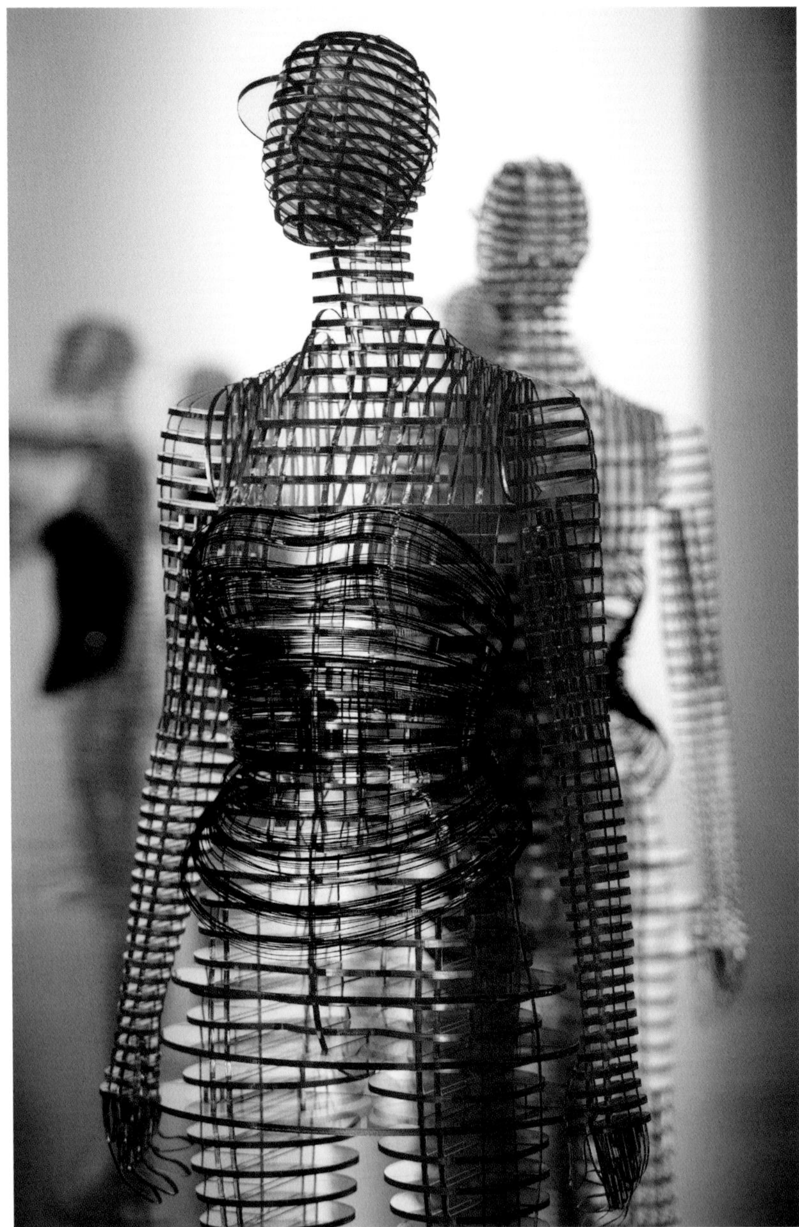

Section B, ***Miyake Issey Exhibition:
The Work of Miyake Issey***
Wire Body 1983 design/Autumn-Winter 1983 Collection
Grid body installation: Tokujin Yoshioka
Photography: Mitsumasa Fujitsuka

Opposite: Section B, ***Miyake Issey Exhibition:
The Work of Miyake Issey***
Rattan Body 1981 design/Spring-Summer 1982
Collection
Grid body installation: Tokujin Yoshioka
Photography: Mitsumasa Fujitsuka

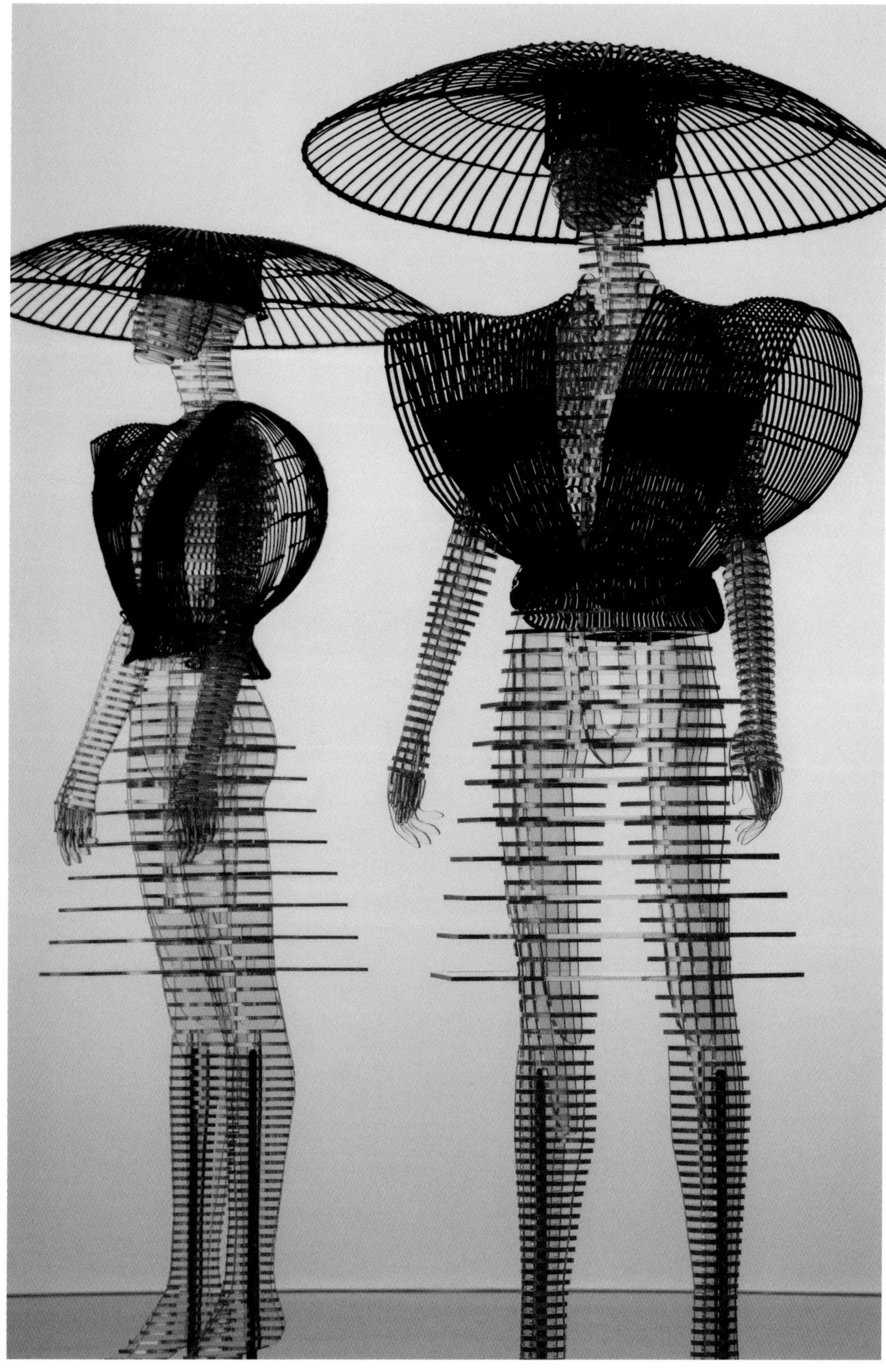

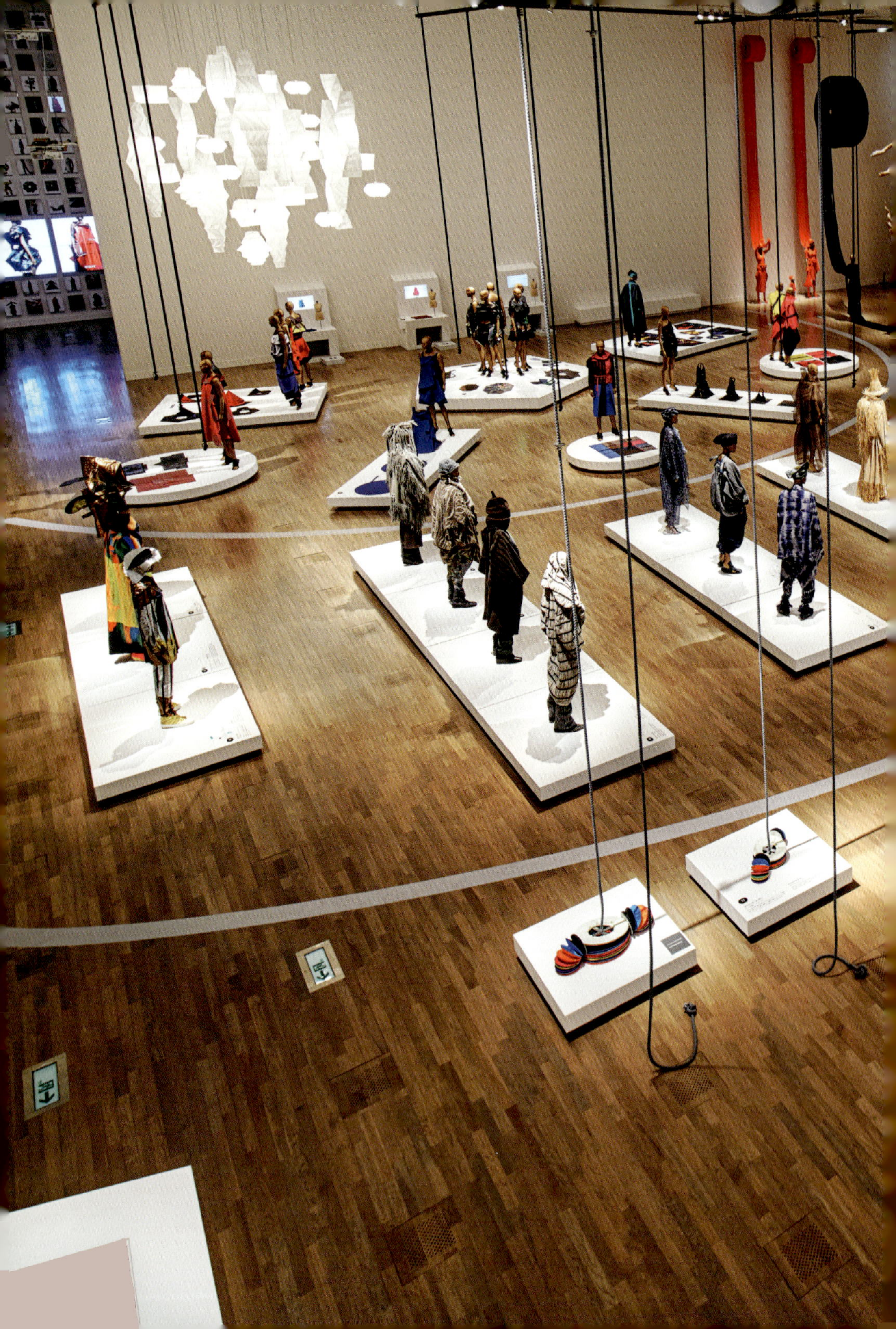

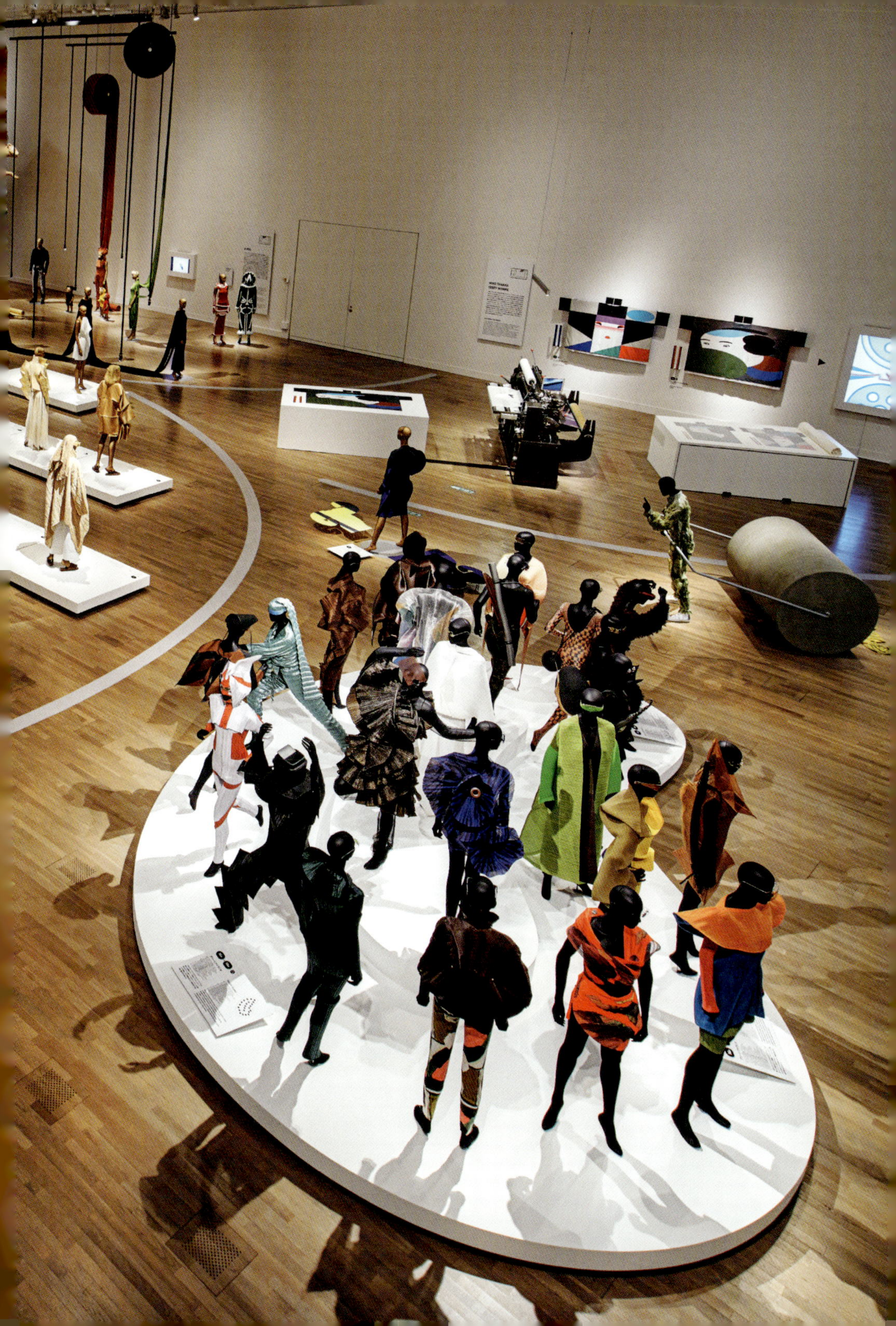

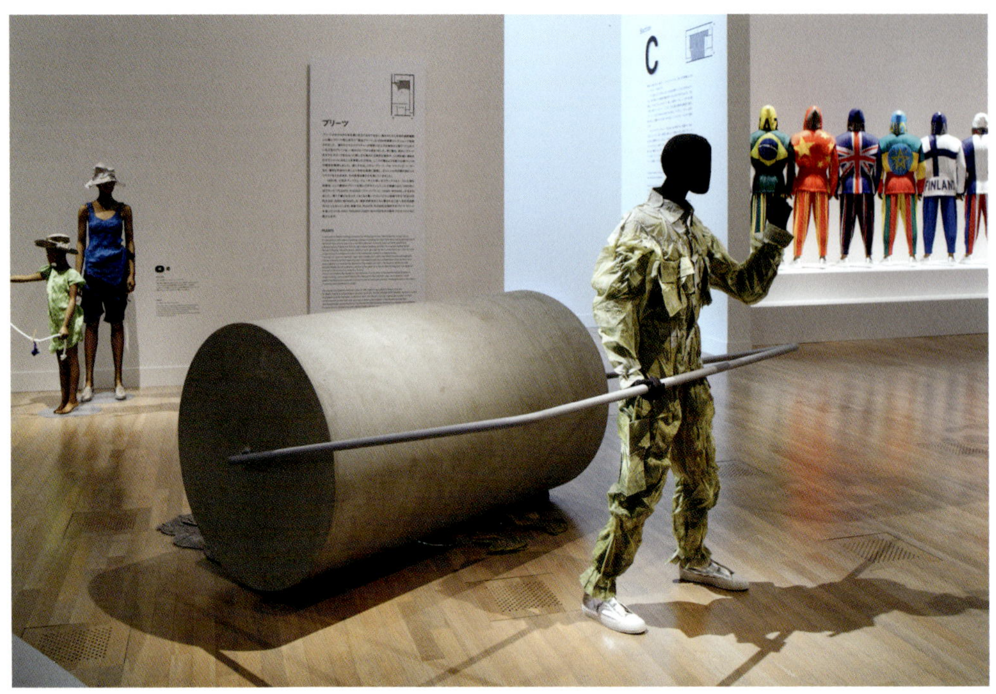

Previous spread: Section C, *Miyake Issey
Exhibition: The Work of Miyake Issey*
Exhibition section C was the largest in the venue and
focused on clothes made from distinctive materials
from the 1980s onward. In addition to the innovative
technologies of pleats, A-POC, and 132 5. ISSEY
MIYAKE, the exhibition highlighted what was then
the newest project, IKKO TANAKA ISSEY MIYAKE, and
installed a pleats machine into the hall (back right)
that was demonstrated by the staff.
Space design: Taku Satoh
Photography: Masaya Yoshimura

Above: Section C, *Miyake Issey Exhibition:
The Work of Miyake Issey*
Gather Press is a technique in which the stitches are
gathered after sewing and then pressed to finish.
Gather Press jumpsuit 1991 design/1996 reproduction
Photography: Masaya Yoshimura

Opposite: *Miyake Issey Exhibition:
The Work of Miyake Issey* poster
Blade of Grass Pleats 1989 design/
Spring-Summer 1990 Collection,
No. 10 2010 design/132 5. ISSEY MIYAKE
Art direction: Taku Satoh; design:
Shingo Noma; photography: Koji Udo

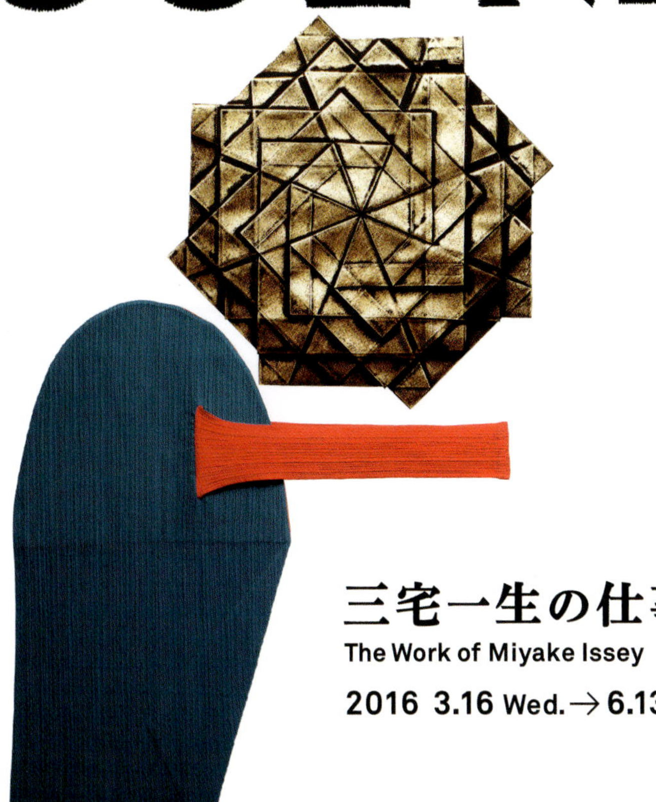

MIYAKE
ISSEY展 EXHIBITION

三宅一生の仕事
The Work of Miyake Issey
2016 3.16 Wed. → 6.13 Mon.

会場｜国立新美術館 企画展示室2E【東京・六本木】
休館日｜毎週火曜日ただし、5月3日（火）㊗は開館
展覧会ホームページ｜http://2016.miyakeissey.org

開館時間｜10:00—18:00 金曜日は20:00まで ※入場は閉館の30分前まで 主催：国立新美術館 共催：公益財団法人 三宅一生デザイン文化財団、株式会社 三宅デザイン事務所 協賛：株式会社 イッセイ ミヤケ 観覧料（税込）：一般 ¥1,300［¥1,100］／大学生 ¥800［¥500］ ※［］内は前売および20名以上の団体料金 ※高校生、18歳未満の方（学生証または年齢のわかるものが必要）および障害者手帳をご持参の方（付添の方1名を含む）は入場無料／5月18日（水）は「国際博物館の日」につき入場無料
お問い合わせ｜03-5777-8600（ハローダイヤル）、国立新美術館 〒106-8558 東京都港区六本木 7-22-2 URL:http://www.nact.jp/

国立新美術館
THE NATIONAL ART CENTER, TOKYO
［Kokuritsu-Shin-Bijutsukan］

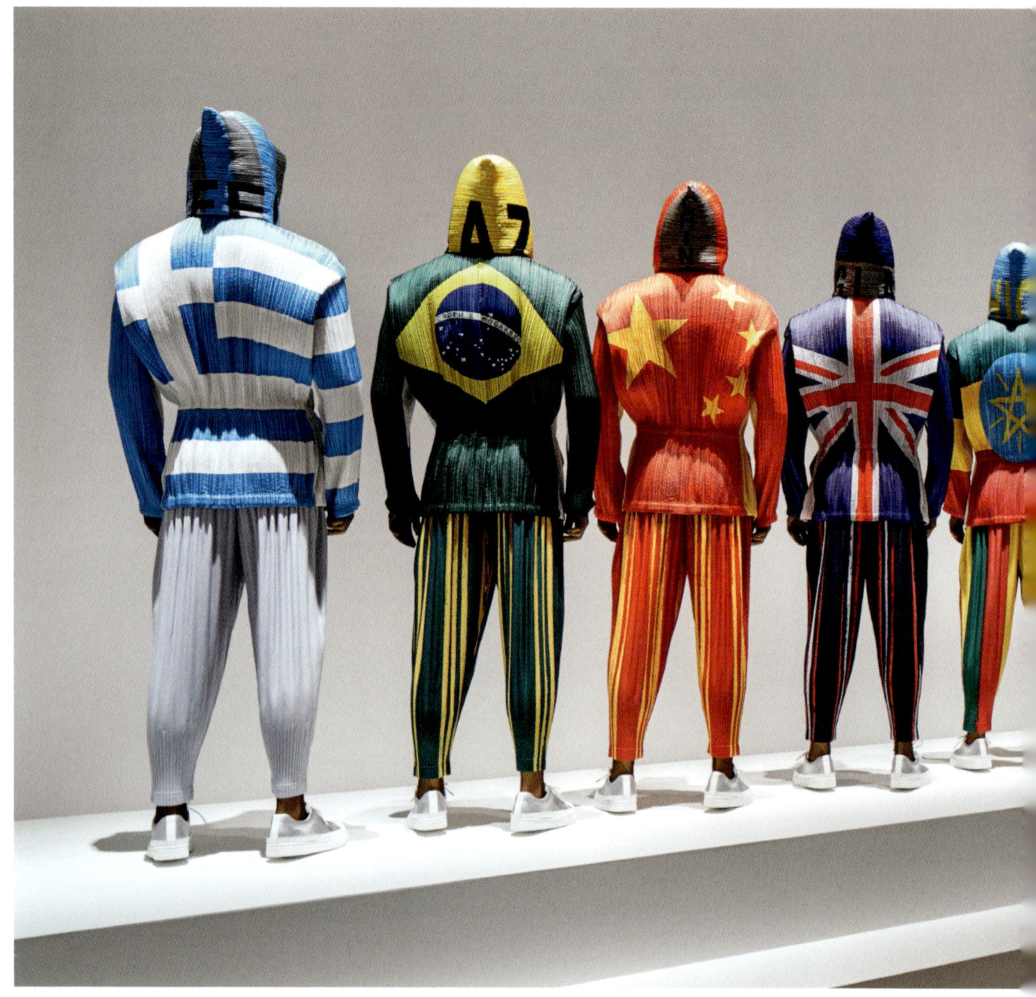

Section C, *Miyake Issey Exhibition:*
The Work of Miyake Issey
Issey Miyake designed the official uniform of the Lithuanian team for the Barcelona Olympics in 1992, and
also presented uniforms for 10 countries in the ISSEY
MIYAKE MEN 1993 Spring-Summer Collection. For the
exhibition, uniforms for an additional 10 countries were
designed, and the Japanese uniform updated.

Virtual Olympic: Lithuania, the United States, the
United Kingdom, Italy, Greece, Switzerland, Spain, China,
Germany, France 1992 design/ISSEY MIYAKE MEN
Spring-Summer 1993 Collection;
India, Ethiopia, the Netherlands, Korea, Kenya, Jamaica,
Japan, Finland, Brazil, South Africa, Russia 2016 design;
the pants 2016 design/HOMME PLISSÉ ISSEY MIYAKE
Photography: Masaya Yoshimura

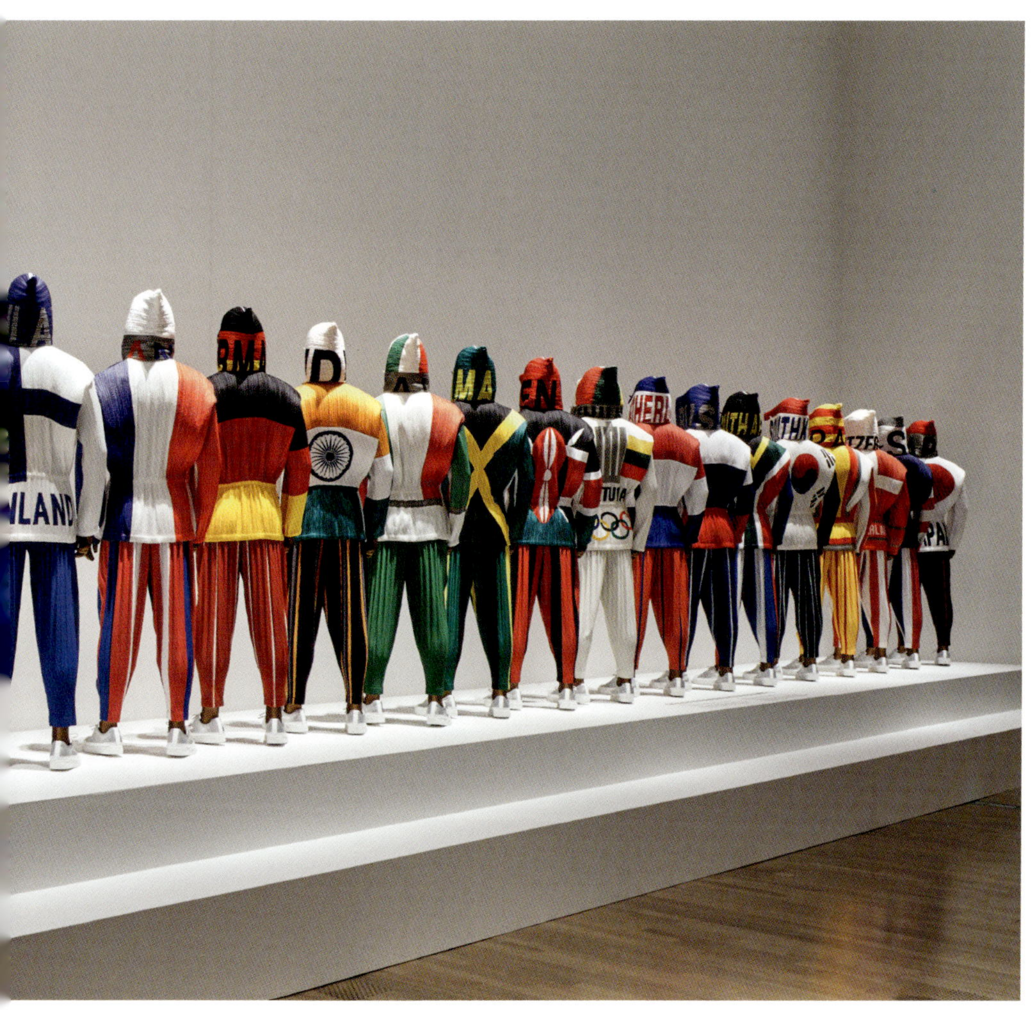

Page 348: Section C, **Miyake Issey Exhibition:**
The Work of Miyake Issey
Artist Kotaro Sekiguchi created masks to go along
with the A-POC *Zoo Series*, which was given animal
names like "Turtle," "Octopus," and "Bear." Sekiguchi's
works were made from newspaper and tape.
Zoo Series 2001 design/A-POC 06
A-POC Collaboration work *Animal Masks*:
Kotaro Sekiguchi
Photography: Masaya Yoshimura

Page 349: Section C, **Miyake Issey Exhibition:**
The Work of Miyake Issey
Jupiter pants used jacquard weaving to create the look
of worn jeans. These were the first A-POC jeans; a single
panel contains all of the parts required to make jeans
woven into the cloth as part of the design. Also, on display was a Kotaro Sekiguchi work depicting adventurers
searching for a bird located on a 5-meter-high box.
Jupiter 2006 design/A-POC 16
A-POC Collaboration work *Adventure*: Kotaro Sekiguchi
Photography: Masaya Yoshimura

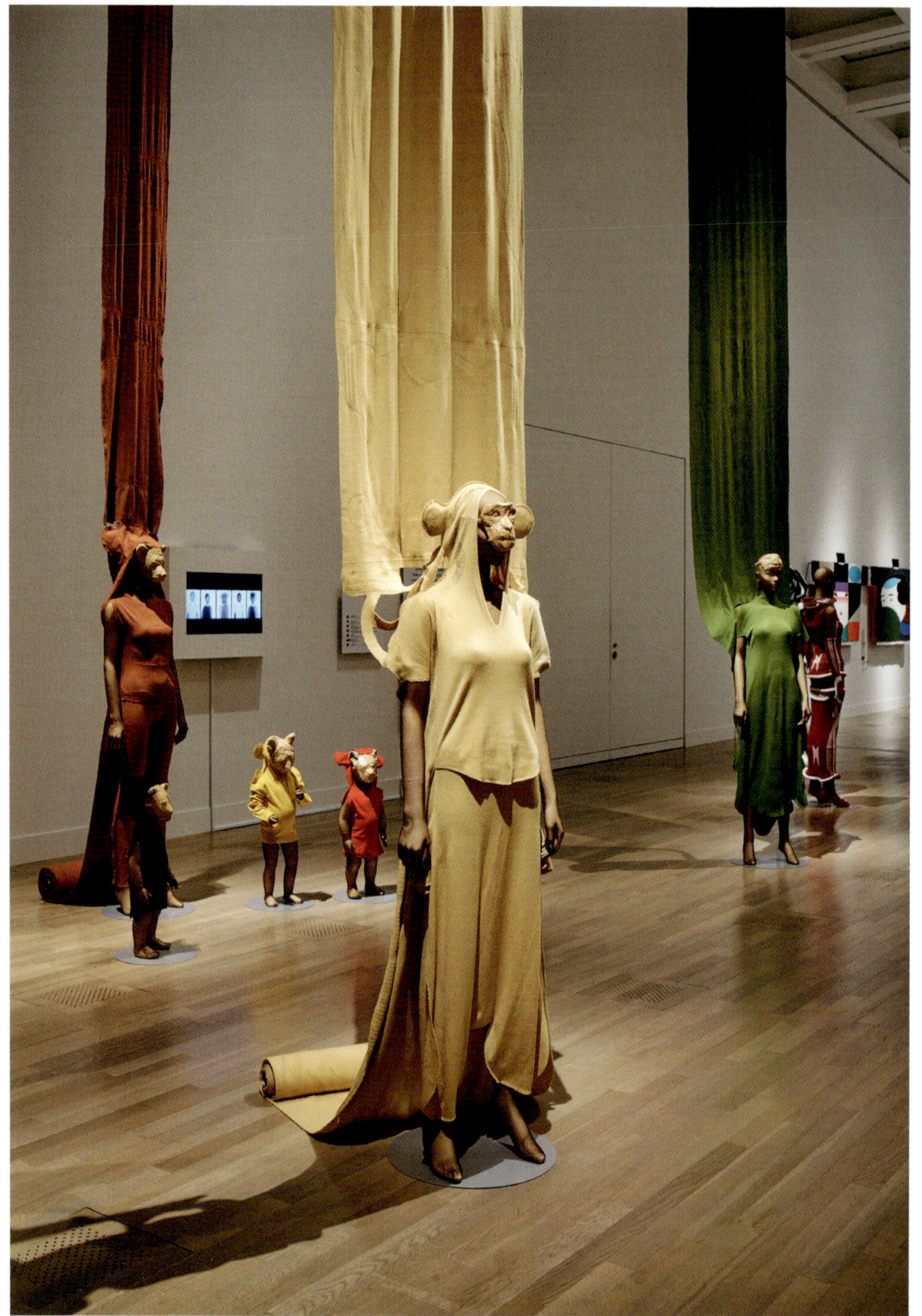

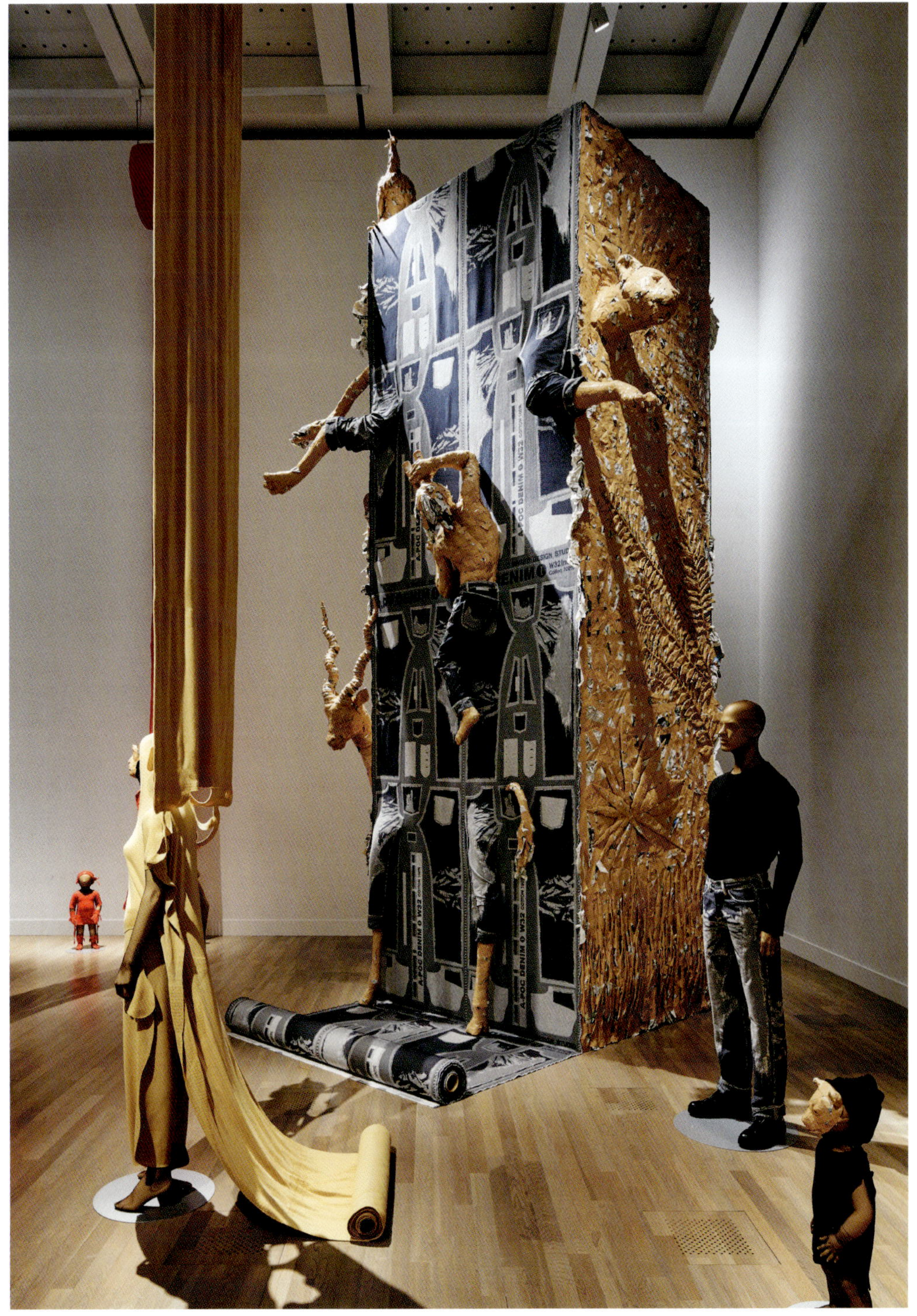

2017

> February: 132 5. ISSEY MIYAKE vol. 3–4, 2017
> March: First shop in Italy, ISSEY MIYAKE/
>   MILAN
> July: 132 5. ISSEY MIYAKE vol. 1–2, 2018
> September: IKKO TANAKA ISSEY MIYAKE No. 3

ISSEY MIYAKE/MILAN

Miyake opened its first flagship store in Italy on Via Bagutta in Milan, next to Via Monte Napoleone. The two-story building with a total of 500 square meters of space was constructed as a home between 1826 and 1831. It was restored, leaving in place the fresco paintings on the ceiling and the pieces of marble embedded in the floor. Tokujin Yoshioka was responsible for the spatial design.

Opposite top: **ISSEY MIYAKE/MILAN**
Space design: Tokujin Yoshioka
Photography: Olivier Baco

Opposite bottom: 21_21 DESIGN SIGHT exhibition posters for *Athlete*, *Grand Projects: How Far Will You Go?*, and *Wild: Untamed Mind*

132 5. ISSEY MIYAKE vol. 3–4, 2017   132 5. ISSEY MIYAKE vol. 1–2, 2018

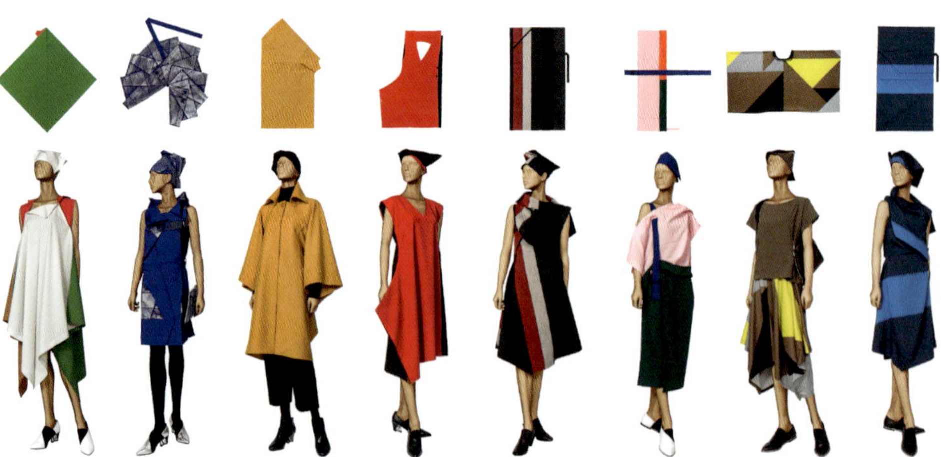

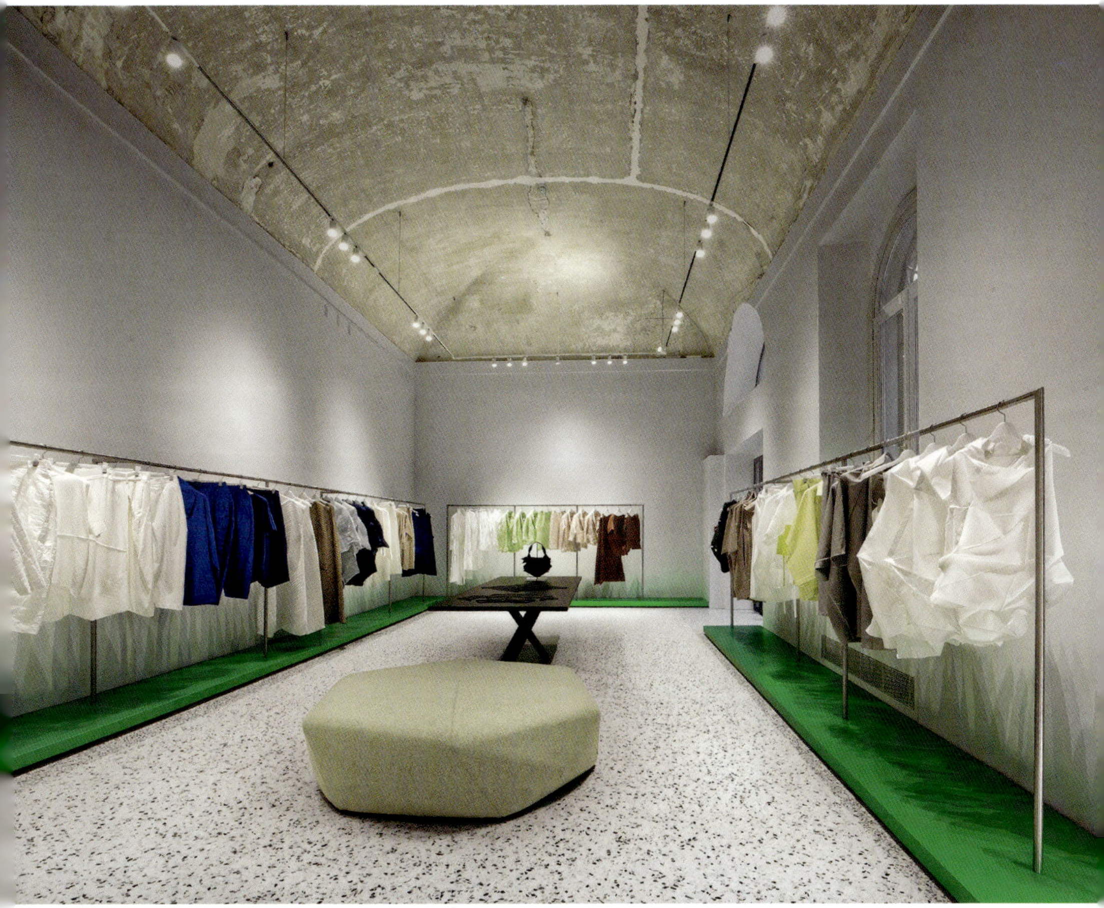

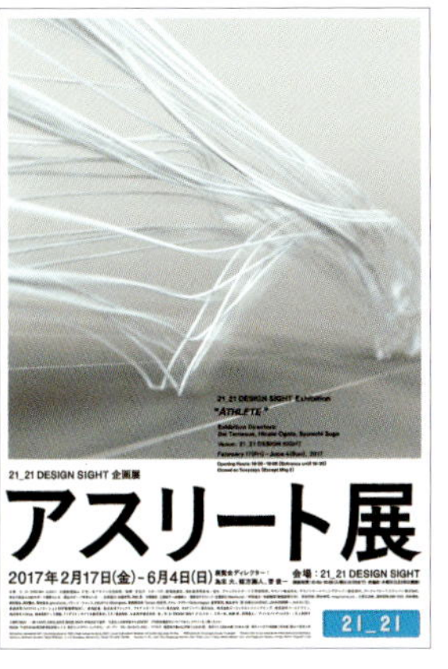

21_21 DESIGN SIGHT Exhibition
"ATHLETE"
21_21 DESIGN SIGHT 企画展
アスリート展
2017年2月17日(金) - 6月4日(日)　会場：21_21 DESIGN SIGHT
21_21

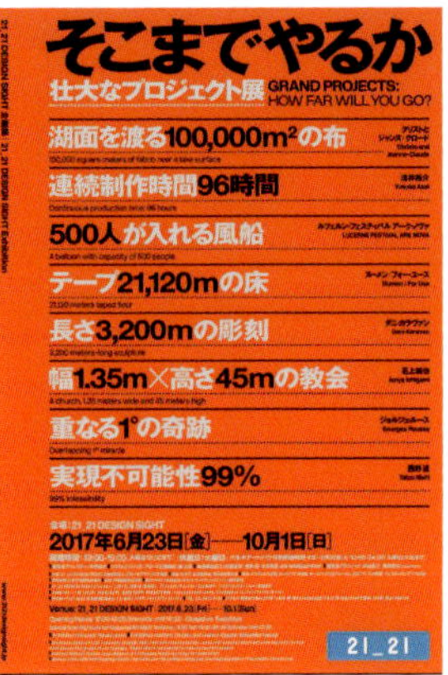

そこまでやるか
壮大なプロジェクト展　GRAND PROJECTS: HOW FAR WILL YOU GO?
湖面を渡る100,000m² の布
連続制作時間96時間
500人 が入れる風船
テープ 21,120m の床
長さ3,200m の彫刻
幅1.35m × 高さ45m の教会
重なる1°の奇跡
実現不可能性99%
2017年6月23日[金] ─── 10月1日[日]
21_21

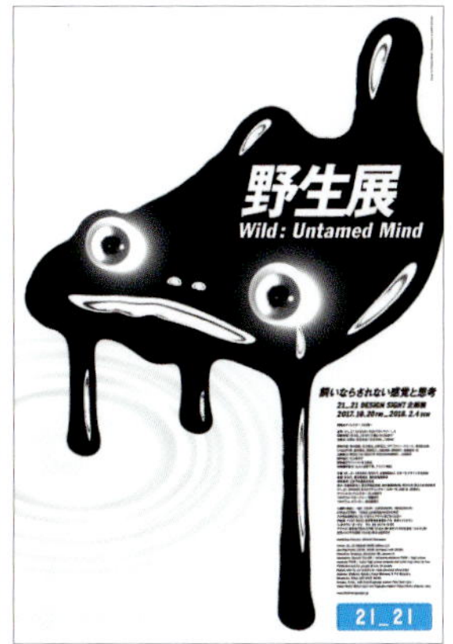

野生展
Wild : Untamed Mind
飼いならされない感覚と思考
21_21 DESIGN SIGHT 企画展
2017.10.20 FRI ─ 2018.2.4 SUN
21_21

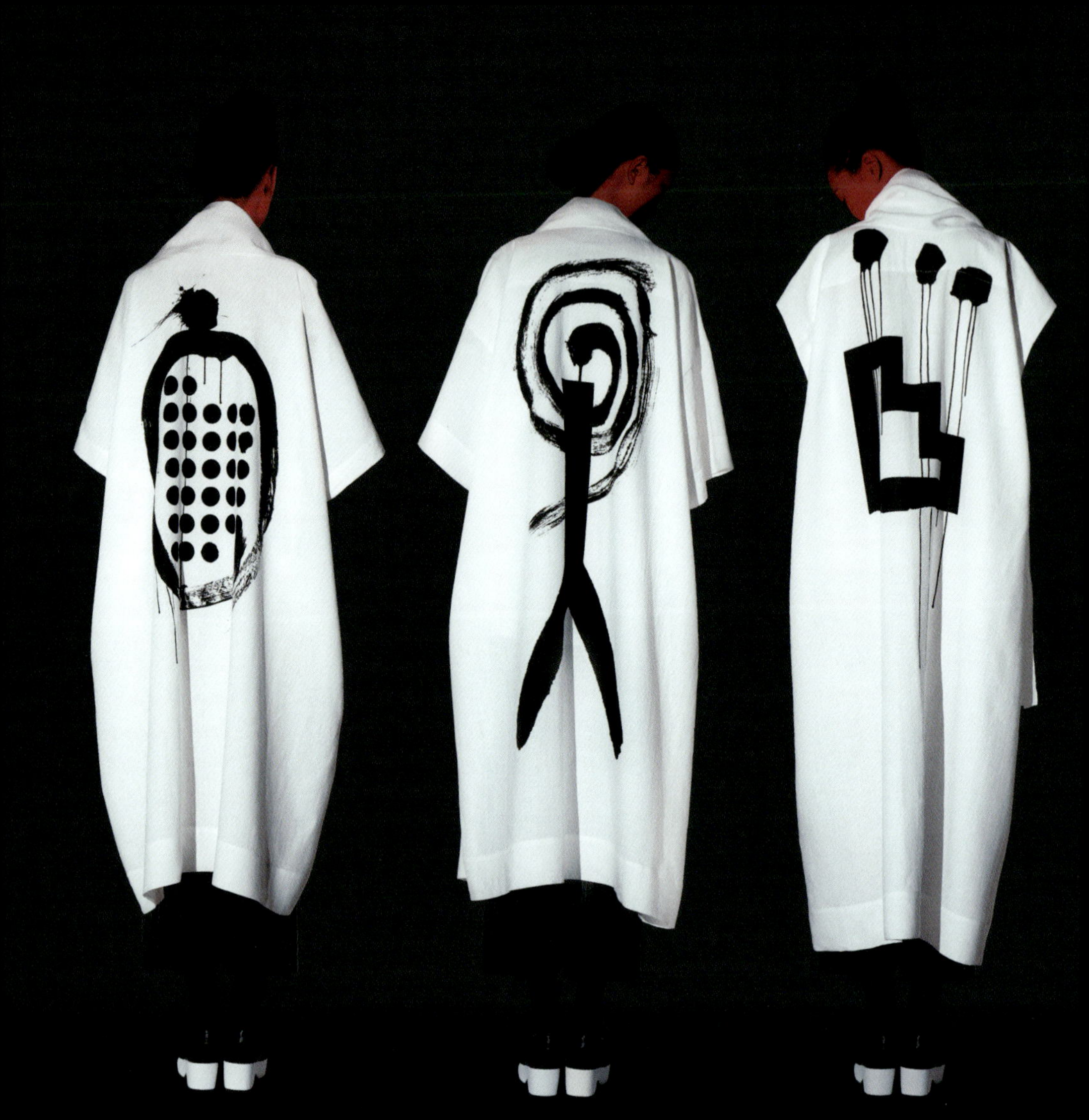

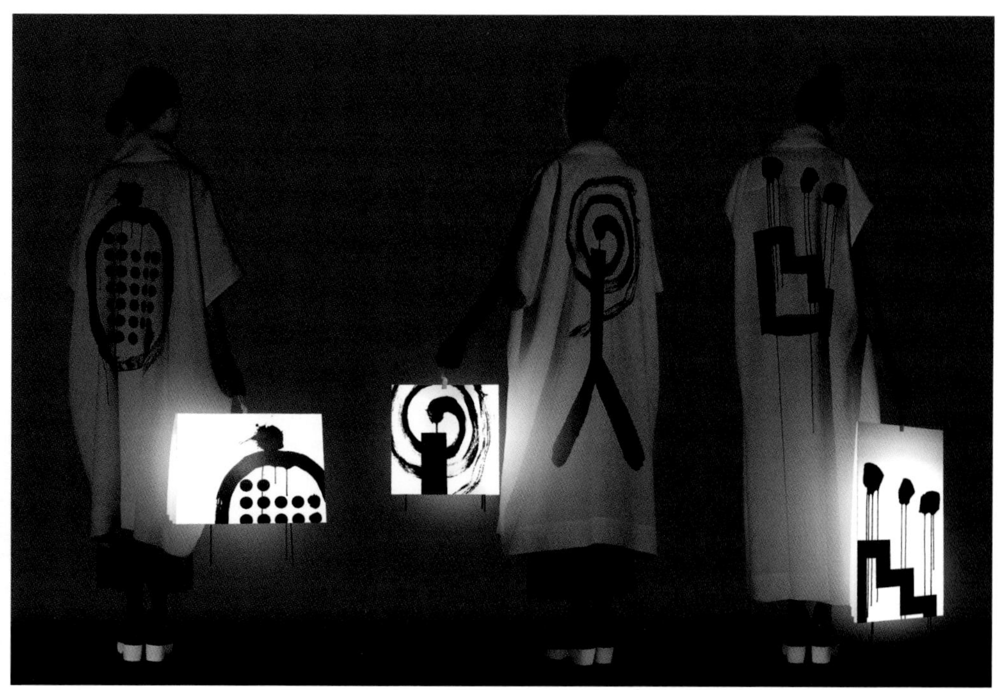

Opposite: *Bokugi*
The material is linen. Tanaka's work providing the motifs is the *Bokugi* series produced in 1996 and expresses the dripping, flowing, and fading of calligraphic ink. It brings together the playfulness of calligraphic ink smears and the tension of graphic design.
Bokugi dress, coat, and long vest, 2016 design/
IKKO TANAKA ISSEY MIYAKE No. 2
Photography: Francis Giacobetti

Bokugi lights
2016 design/IKKO TANAKA ISSEY MIYAKE No. 2
Photography: Francis Giacobetti

2018

> March: 132 5. ISSEY MIYAKE vol. 3–4, 2018
> March: "Issey Miyake Session One," an article by Guest Editor Michele De Lucchi in the April issue of *Domus* (Italy)
> April: *Khadi: The Fabric of India's Tomorrow – Homage to Martand Singh* – at 21_21 DESIGN SIGHT Gallery 3
> June: Session One special presentation
> July: 132 5. ISSEY MIYAKE vol. 1–2, 2019
> September: IKKO TANAKA ISSEY MIYAKE No. 4

Opposite bottom: 21_21 DESIGN SIGHT exhibition posters for *New Planet Photo City – William Klein and Photographers Living in the 22nd Century –*, *Audio Architecture*, and *Mingei – Another Kind of Art*

Session One

The "Session One" project featured in the Italian architectural design magazine *Domus* consisted of research and studies begun by Issey Miyake as part of his intense desire to explore new forms of making things. It was in the fall of 2016 that a team of individuals from different brands of the company was brought together and began its creative work with Miyake. The keyword was "wildness," and numerous prototypes were created around the question of "what kind of clothing would the ancient Jomon people produce if they had modern technology?" This ultimately led to the selection of textiles that combined rough, primitive expression with soft, smooth texture. The materials were produced using the Steam Stretch method of adding steam to a piece of cloth to create a three-dimensional pleat. The textiles are joined together with a minimum of stitching to create clothes with a powerful, asymmetrical form. This project went on to influence the course of future work.

132 5. ISSEY MIYAKE vol. 3–4, 2018

132 5. ISSEY MIYAKE vol. 1–2, 2019

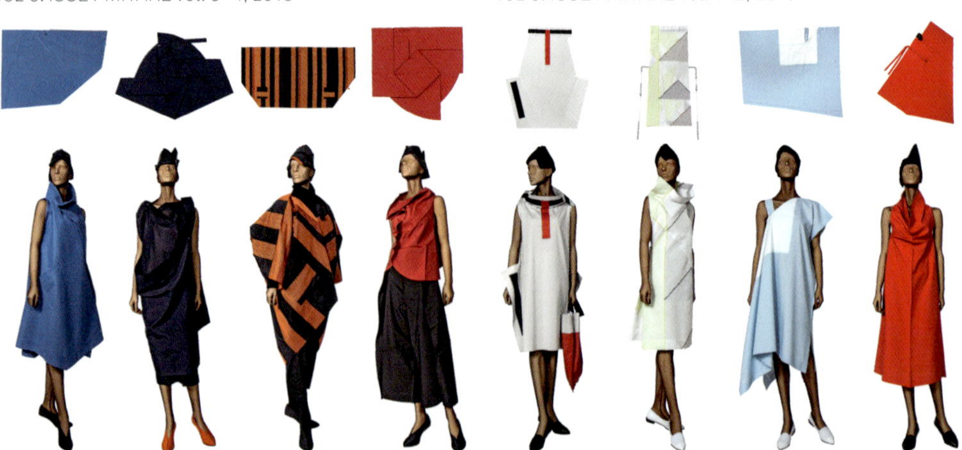

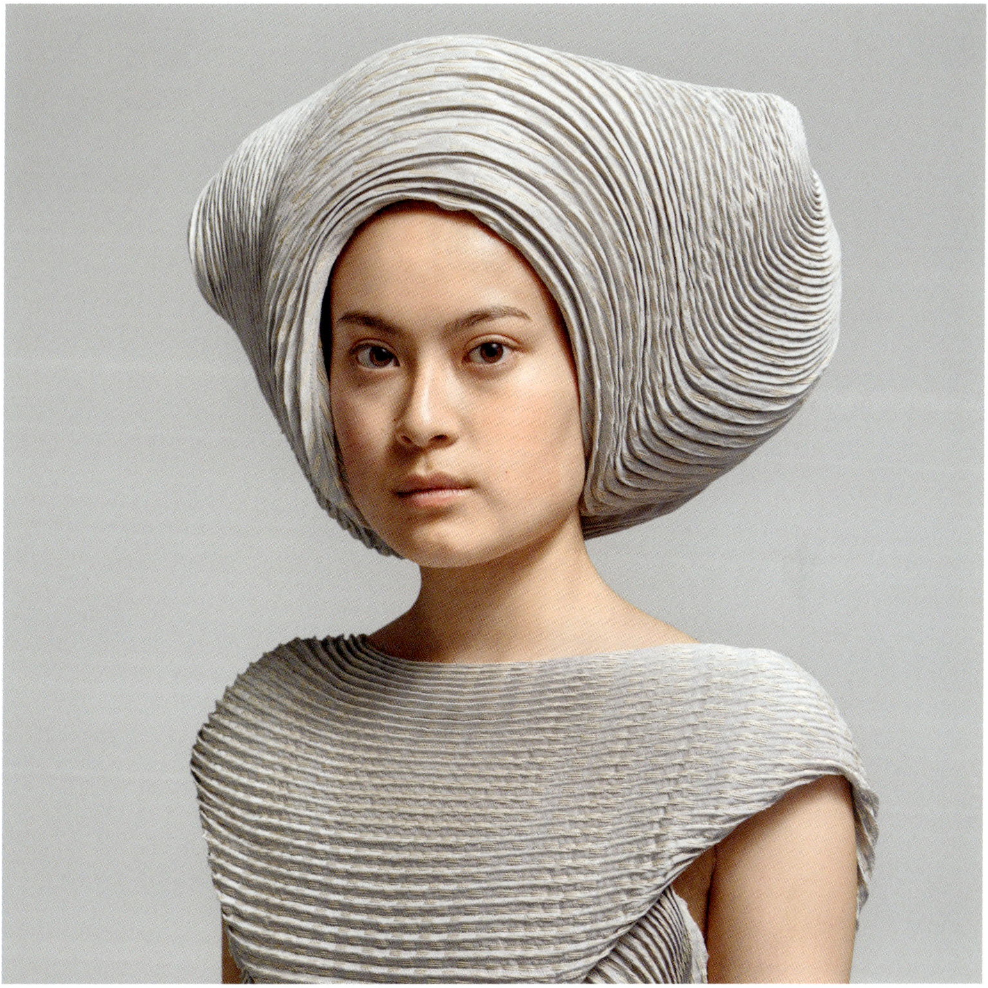

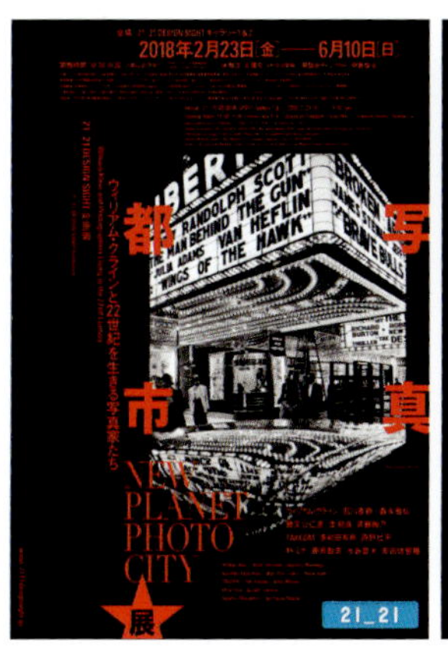

2018年2月23日 金 —— 6月10日 日
都
市
写
真
NEW
PLANET
PHOTO
CITY
展
21_21

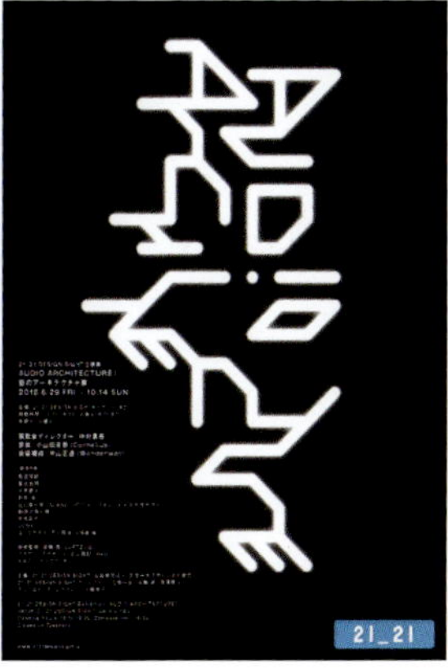

AUDIO ARCHITECTURE
音のカタチ展
2018.6.29 FRI - 10.14 SUN
21_21

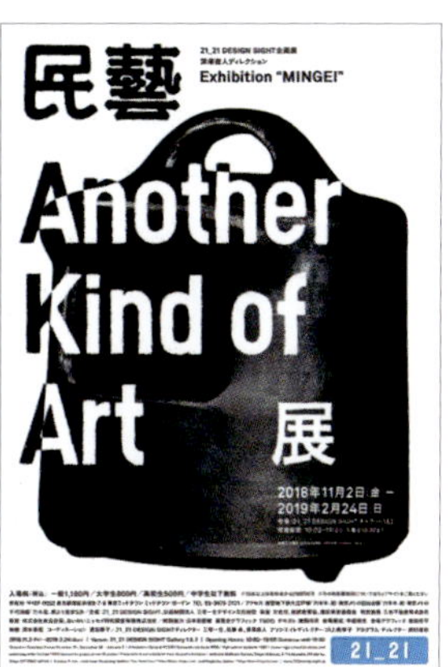

21_21 DESIGN SIGHT企画展
深澤直人ディレクション
Exhibition "MINGEI"
民藝
Another
Kind of
Art
展
2018年11月2日 金 —
2019年2月24日 日

pp. 355–365: *Session One* 2018 design
Photography: James Mollison

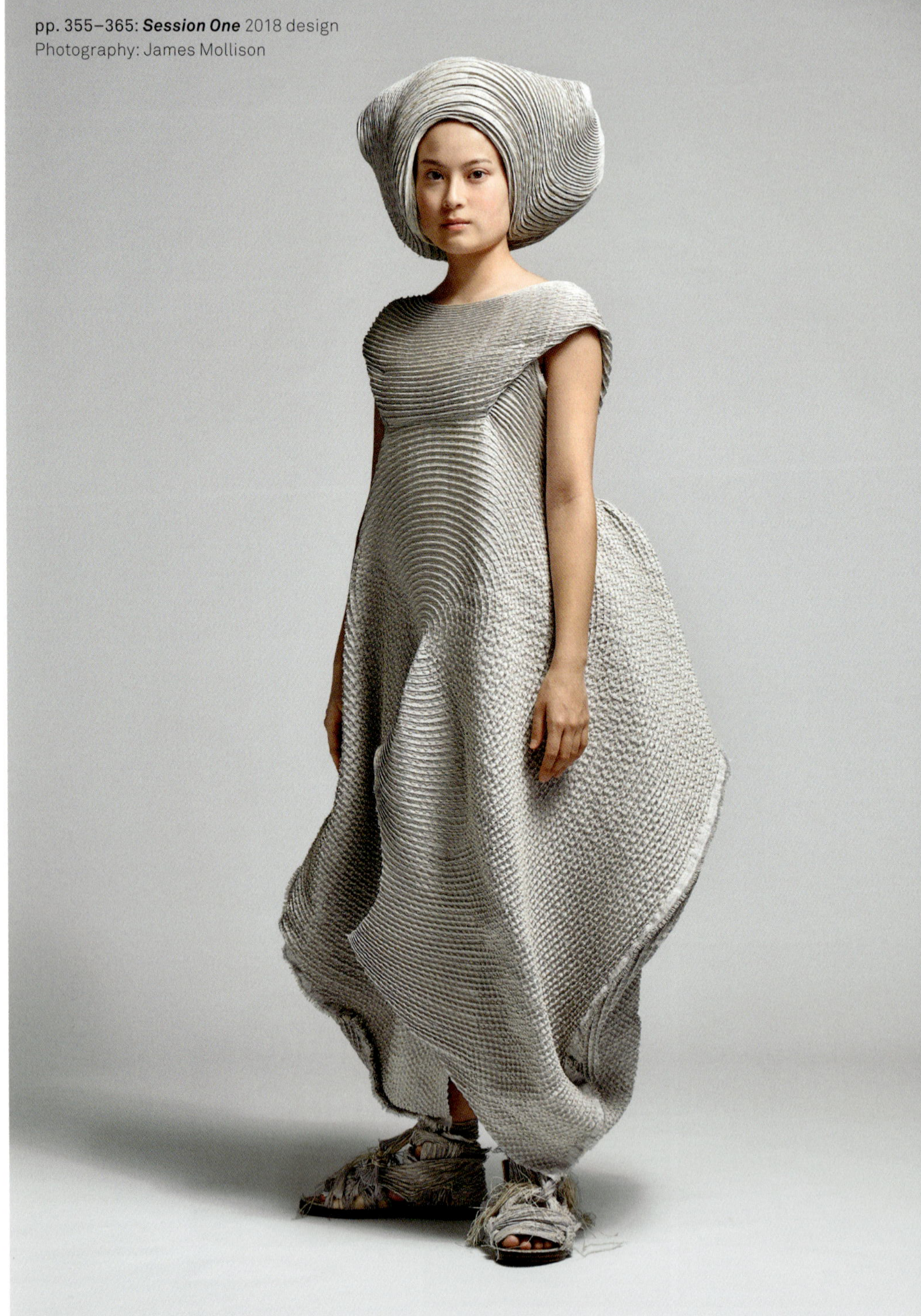

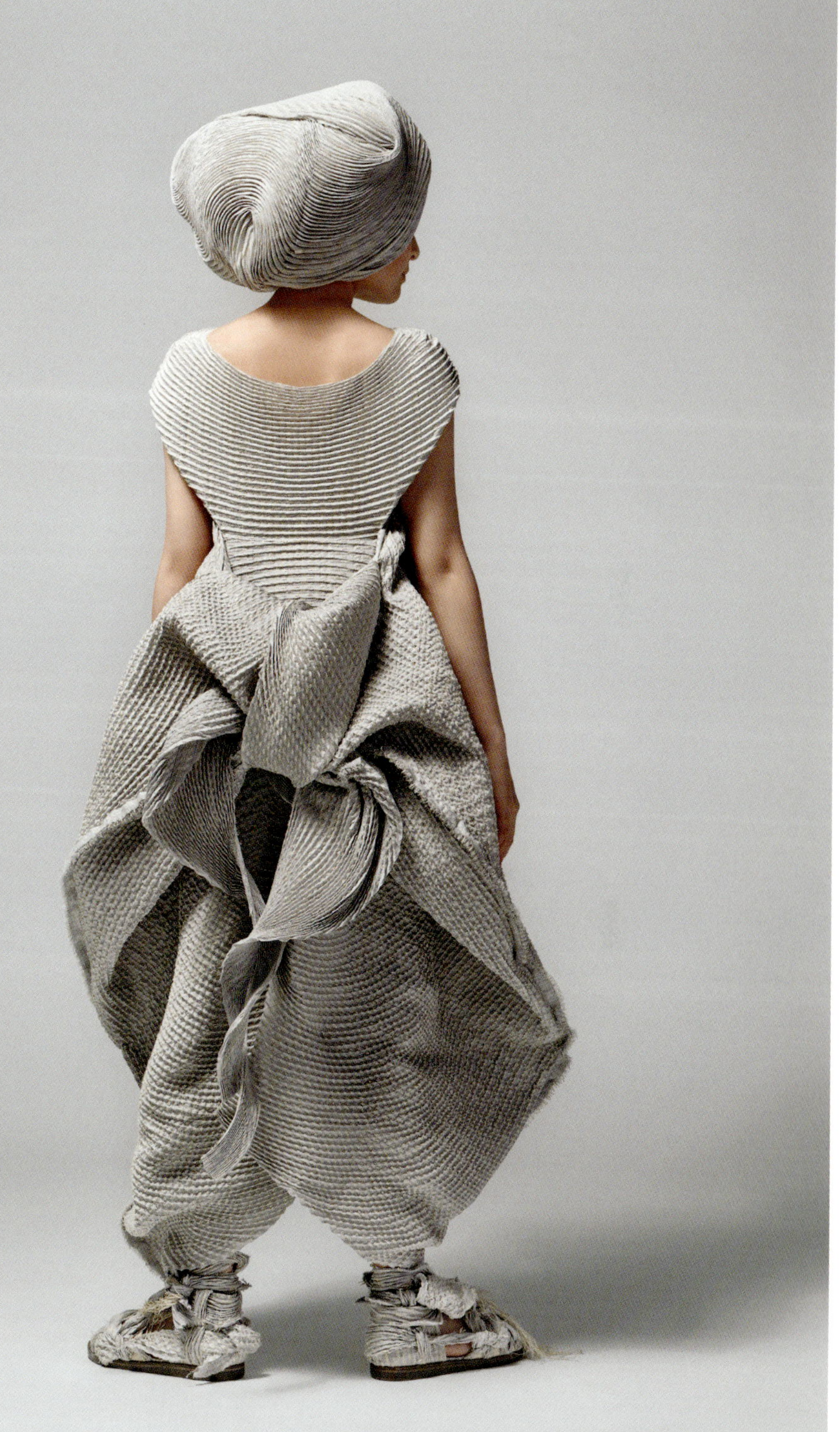

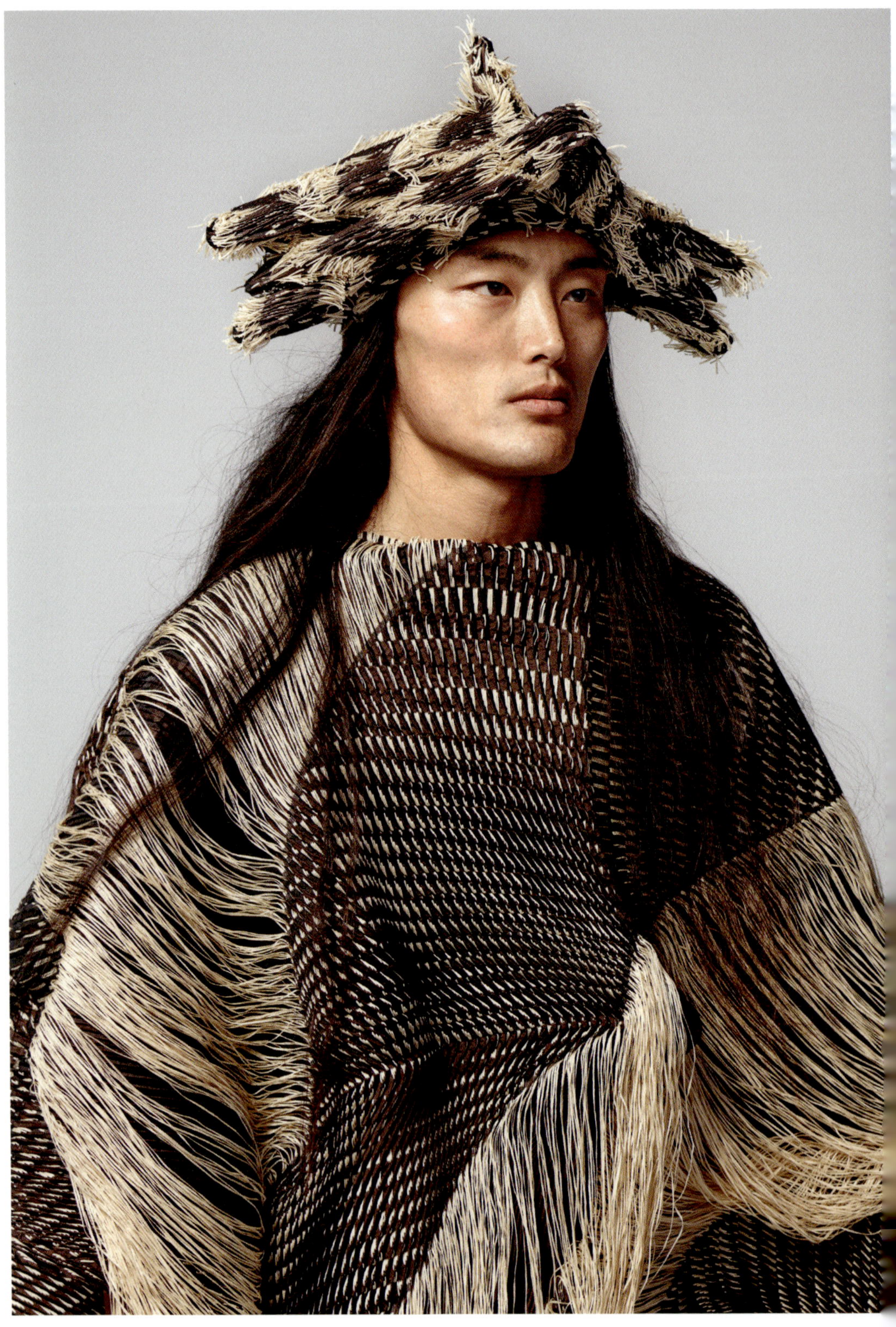

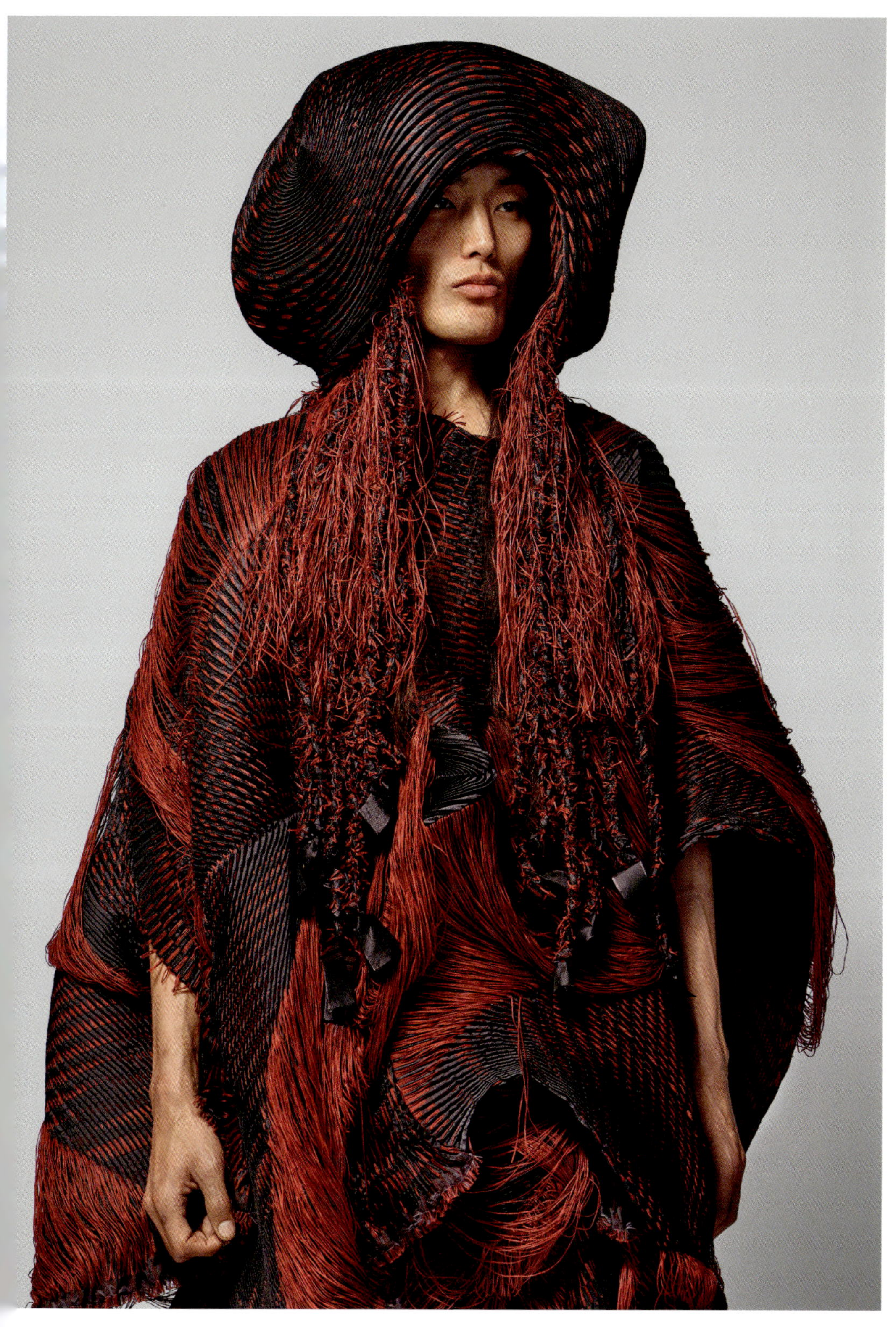

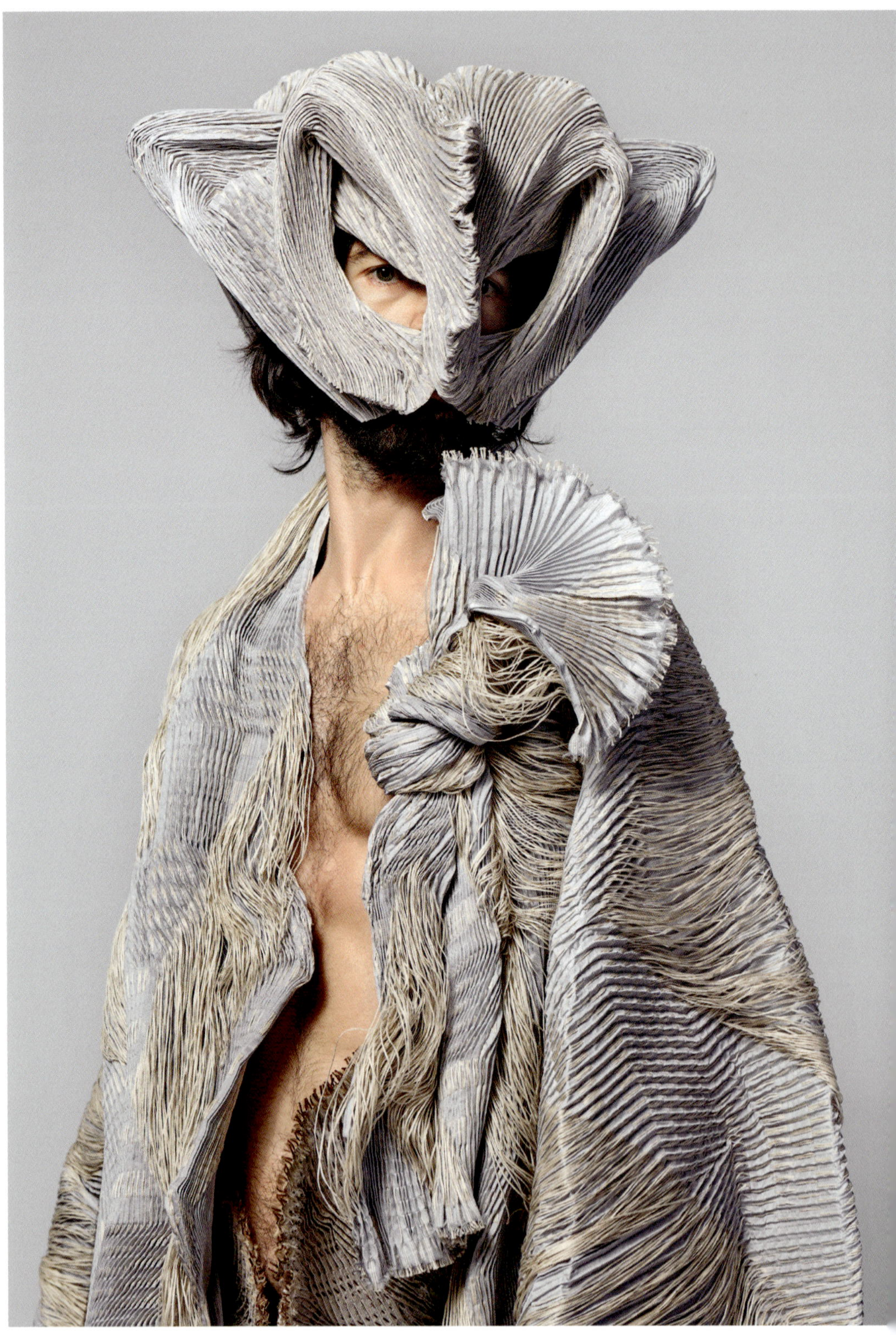

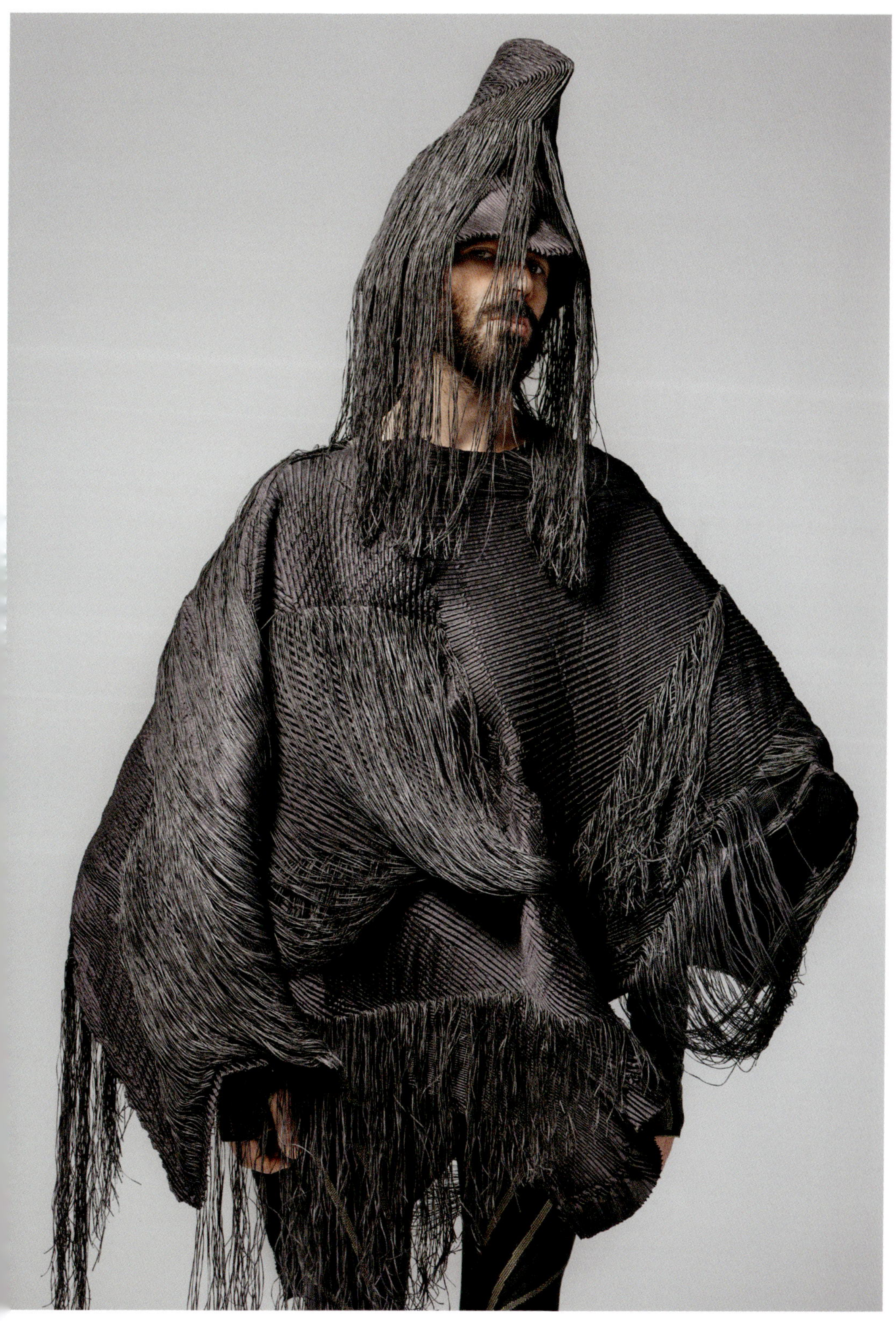

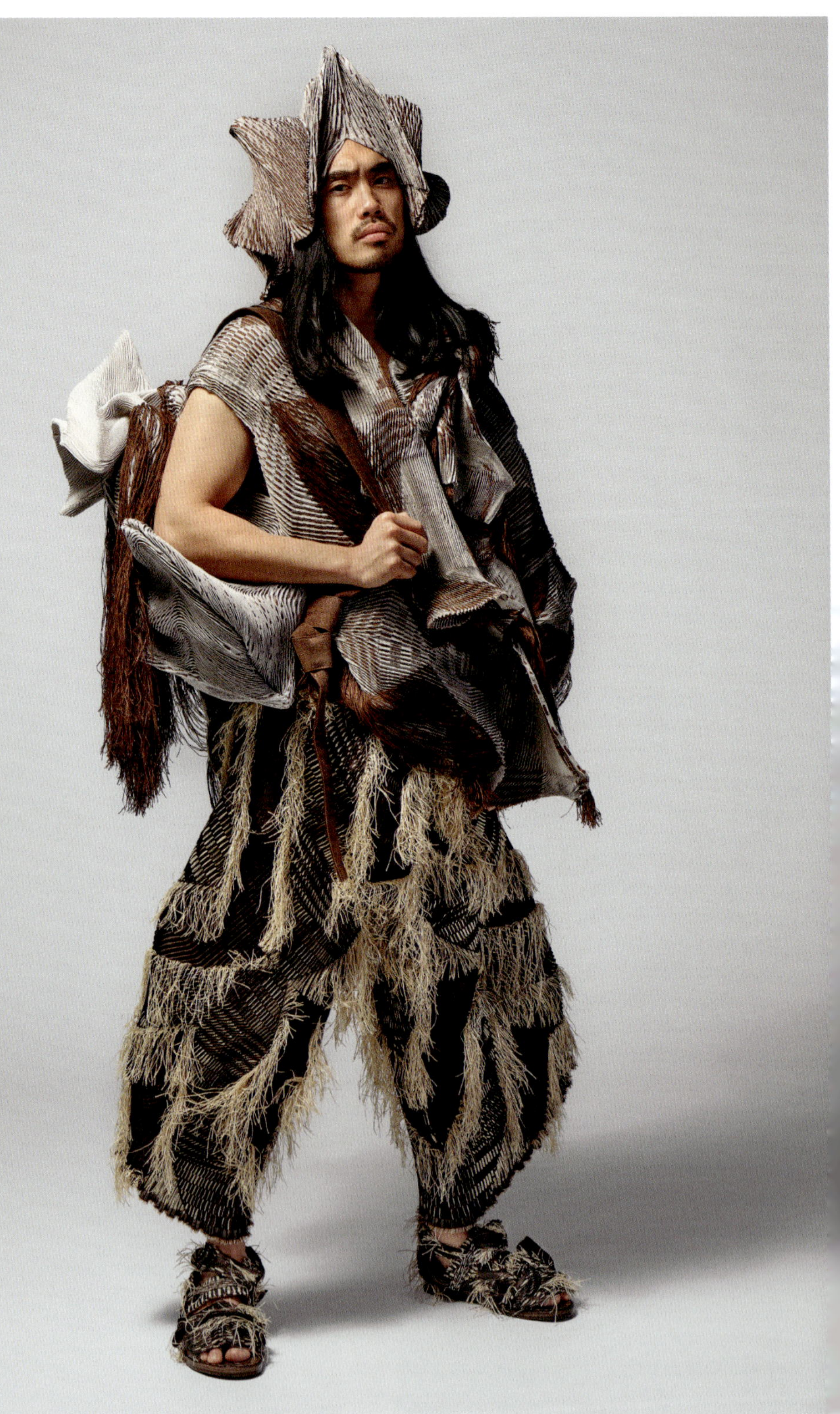

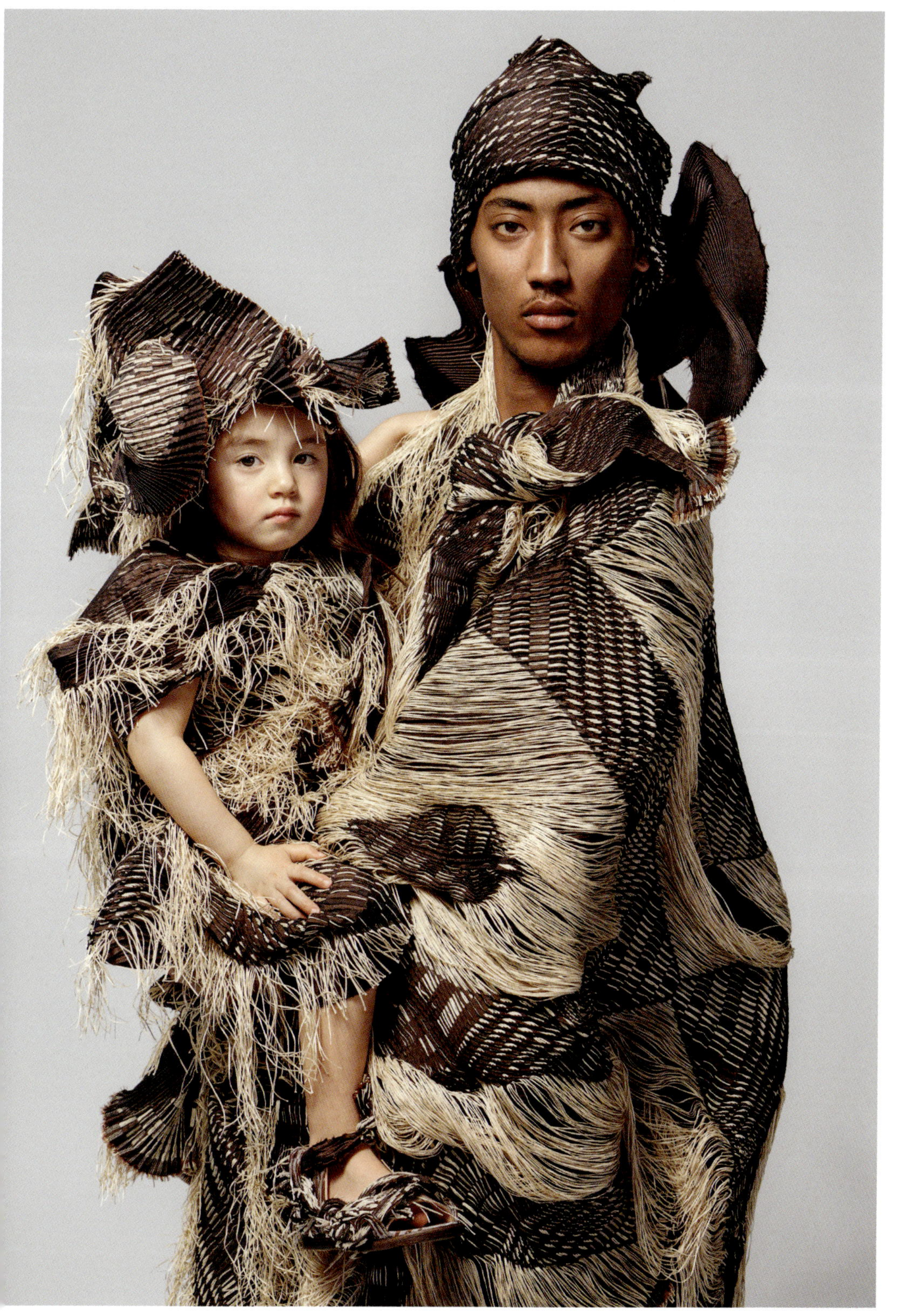

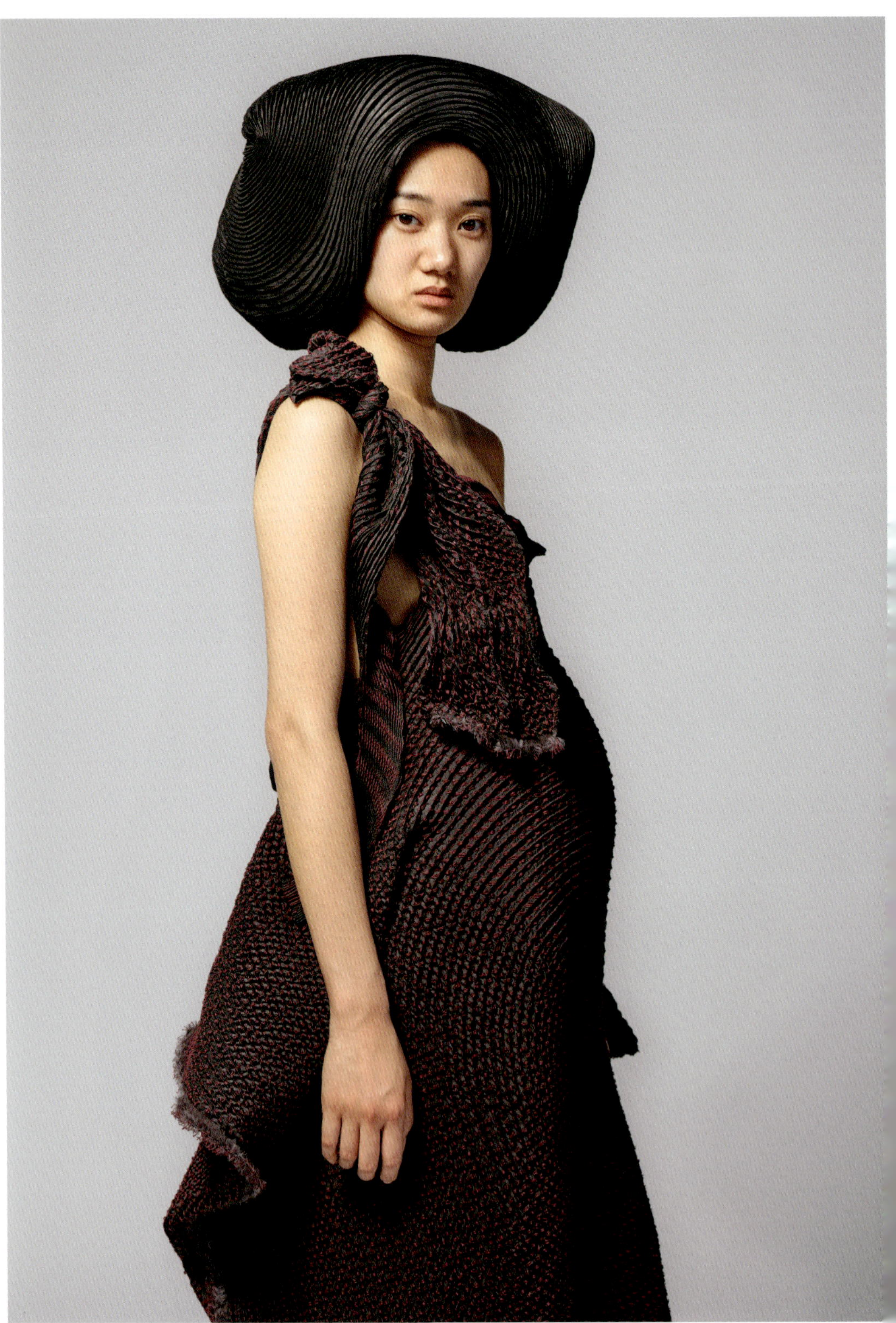

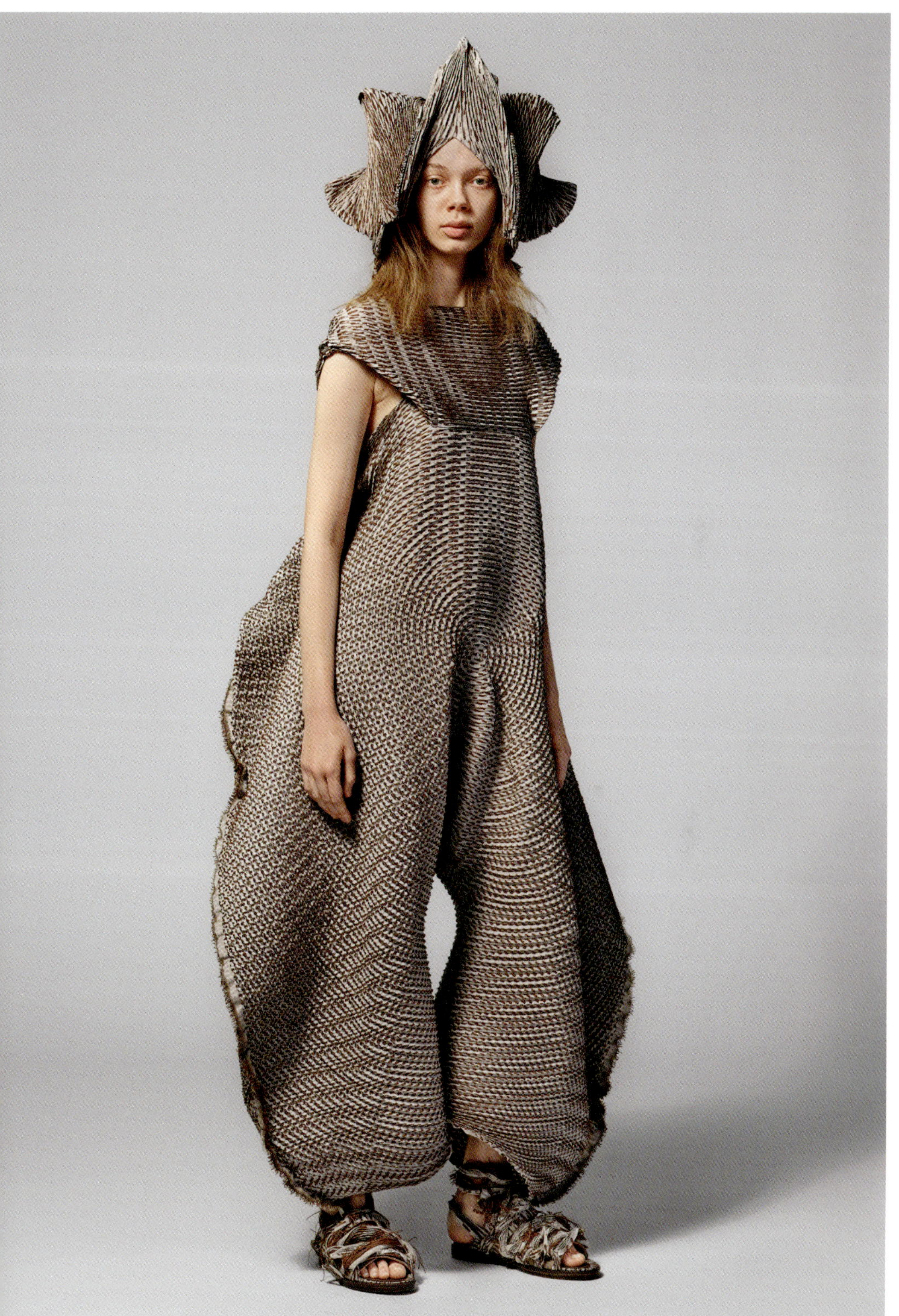

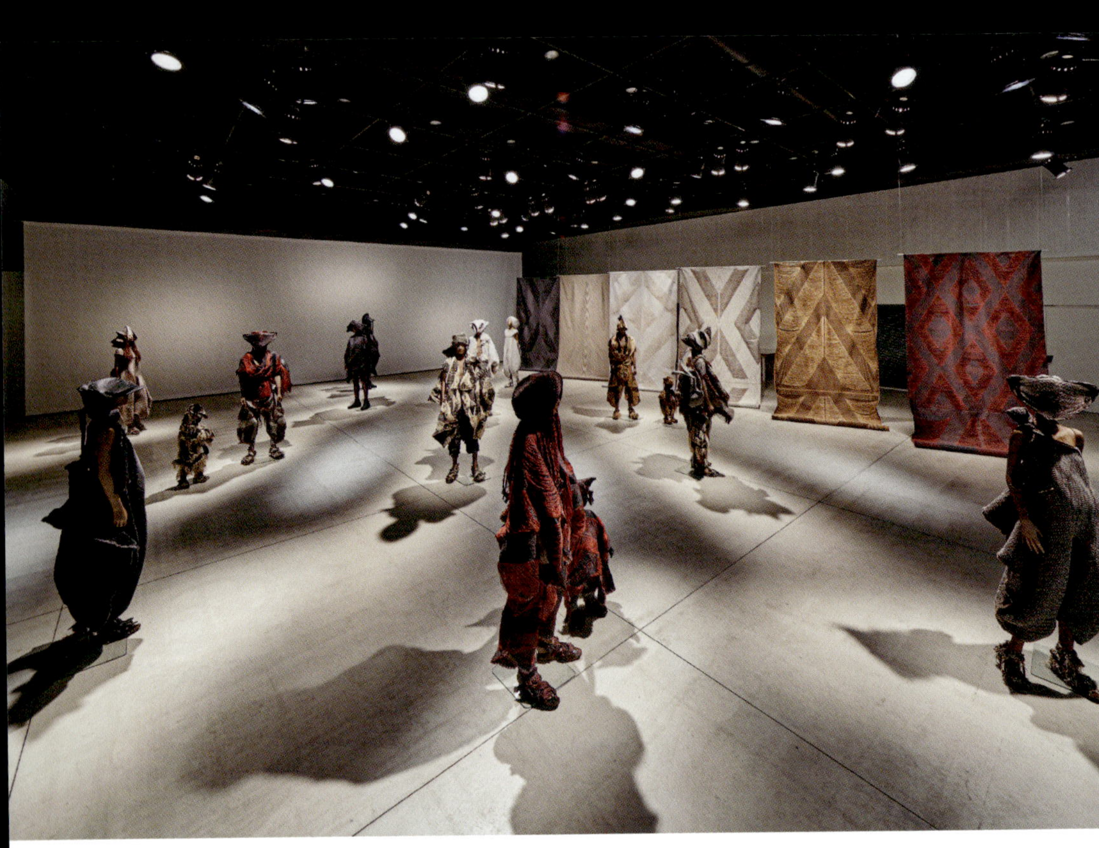

Session One special presentation
June 26–29: Issey Miyake Inc. B1F Hall/Foyer
Project members were present to explain their
process over the course of three days.
Photography: Masaya Yoshimura

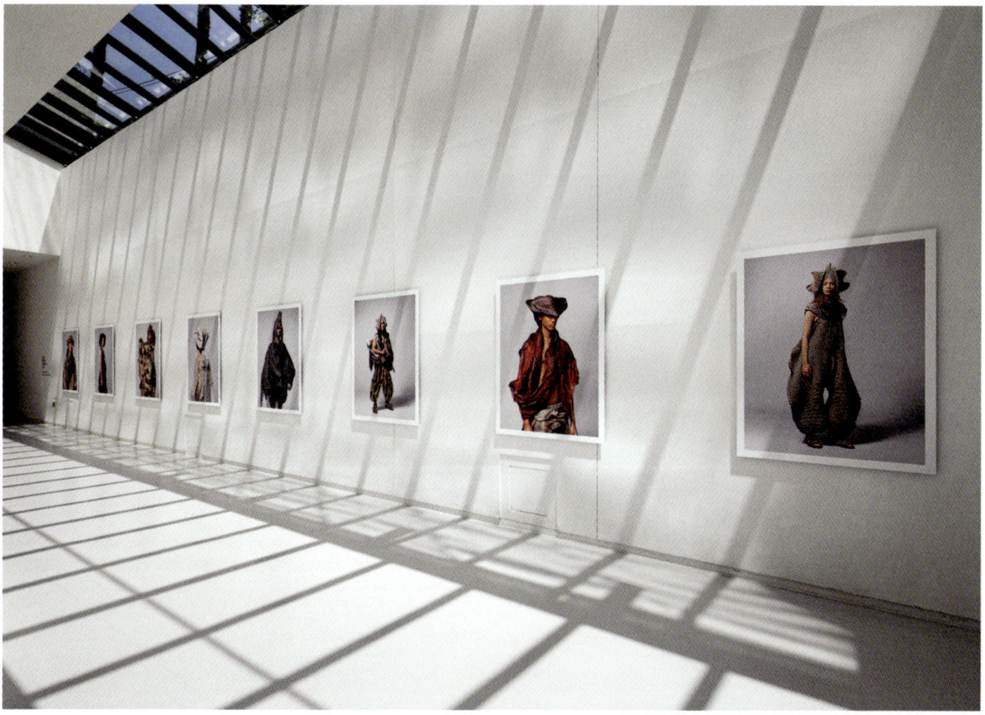

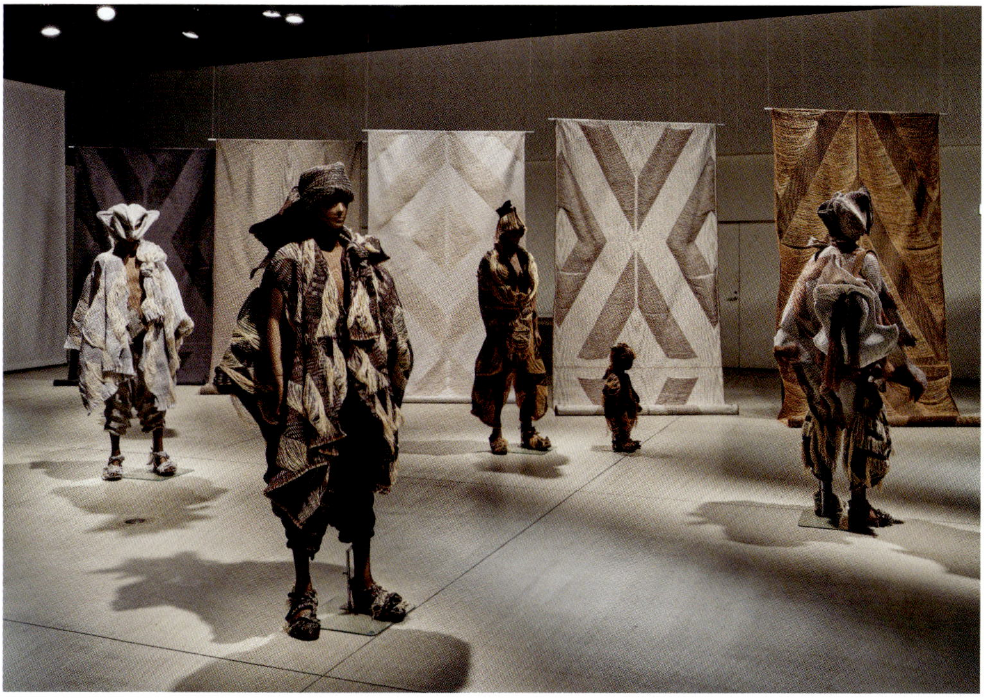

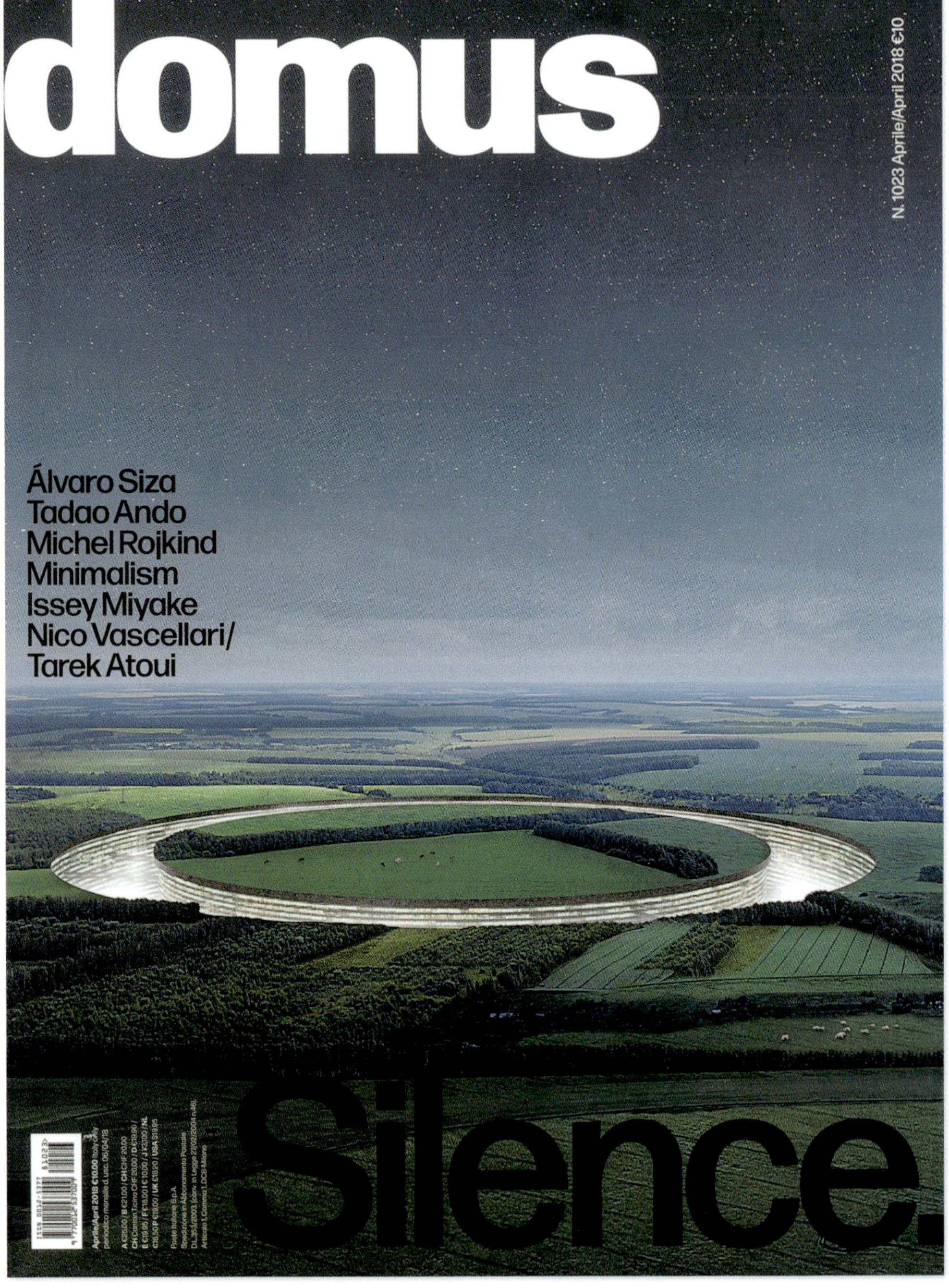

domus

N. 1023 Aprile/April 2018 €10

Álvaro Siza
Tadao Ando
Michel Rojkind
Minimalism
Issey Miyake
Nico Vascellari/
Tarek Atoui

Aprile/April 2018 €10.00 Italy only
periodico mensile d.l rec. 06/04/18
A €20.00 / B €21.00 / CH CHF 20.00
CH Ticino/Ticino CHF 20.00 / D €18.90 /
E €18.90 / F €15.00 / €18.00 / J ¥3300 / NL
€16.50 P €18.00 / UK £15.50 / USA $19.95
Poste Italiane S.p.A.
Spedizione in Abbonamento Postale
D.L.353/2003 (conv. in Legge 27/02/2004 n.46)
Articolo 1 Comma 1 DCB Milano

ISSN 0012-1337

Alla base del lavoro di Miyake c'è la ricerca tecnologica: dall'idea si innesca un processo che può durare molti anni ed è indipendente dalle logiche del mercato

Miyake's work is based on technological research, where the idea gives rise to a process that can last for many years and is independent of market logic

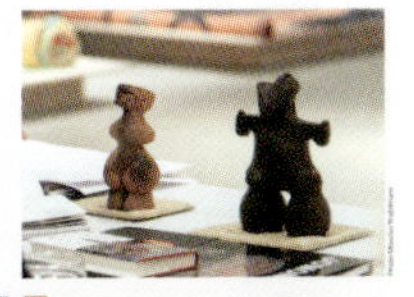

Issey Miyake Session One

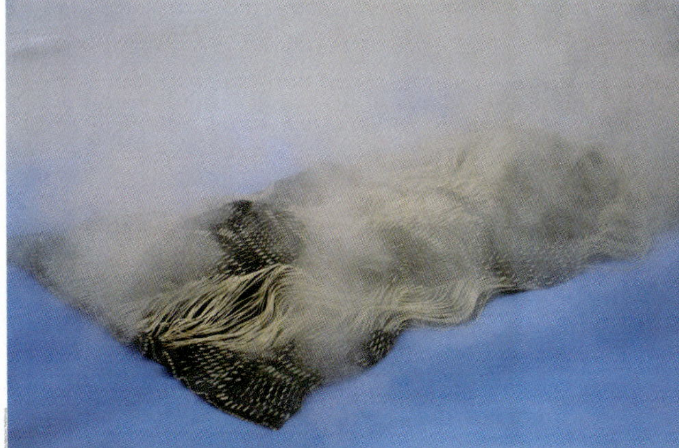

In alto: Session One, il nuovo lavoro di Issey Miyake, è ispirato all'antica civiltà di Jomon (14.000–300 a.C.). Le due statuette in argilla rappresentano la Venere di Jomon (a sinistra) e la Dea mascherata (a destra). A sinistra: le grande macchina per il vapore, programmata attraverso un software ad hoc, trasforma i pannelli di tessuto nella forma tridimensionale del capo finito

Top: Session One, Issey Miyake's new work, is inspired by the ancient civilisation of Jomon (14,500–300 BCE). The two clay figurines represent the Venus of Jomon (left) and the Masked goddess (right). Left: this large steam machine programmed by special software transforms fabric panels into the three-dimensional form of the finished garment

pp. 368–375
Domus, No. 1023, April 2018
Courtesy of Archivio Domus –
© Editoriale Domus S.p.A

Nell'ultimo e inedito lavoro, Issey Miyake progetta tessuti di sofisticata tecnologia con un aspetto primordiale e selvaggio. Oggetti d'arte indossati non per coprire l'uomo, ma per fargli scoprire nuovi linguaggi

Testo di Michele De Lucchi
Foto di James Mollison

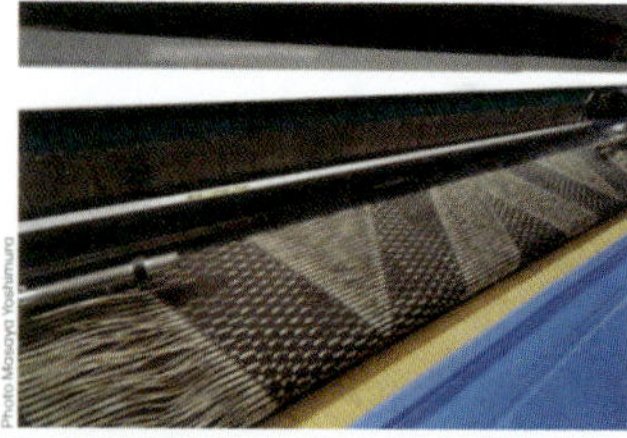

Issey Miyake è calmo, saggio, ti guarda in faccia, ma vede oltre. Impone un lieve senso di soggezione, sufficiente per richiedere rispetto, ma non da tenerti lontano. Anche perché semplicemente lui di rispetto ne porta molto ed è pronto alla sorpresa e all'ammirazione. Lavora molto con altri e coinvolge molto, colleghi, designer, fotografi, grafici, architetti, tutti i creativi di cui si circonda. Possiede una cultura dell'immagine superiore e distingue con immediatezza il nuovo previsto da quello imprevedibile.

Issey Miyake non è certo uno stilista di moda, o un couturier o un sarto né qualcuno che produce vestiti anche se è conosciuto nell'ambiente della moda. Di certo, quello che fa non ha niente a che fare con le stagioni, i colori o i tessuti del momento, i trend e tutte quelle altre cose che i produttori di abbigliamento tengono costantemente sotto controllo per non perdere il contatto con i propri consumatori. Così come è difficile immaginare un saggio agitato e stressato, altrettanto è difficile immaginare questo signore giapponese preoccuparsi per l'evoluzione del gusto e analizzare mese dopo mese l'evoluzione degli stili di vita.

Per una semplice ragione: lui li conosce già ed è lui a indicarli. L'incontro con Issey Miyake, di cui uso i vestiti da tutta la vita, mi fa pensare proprio a questo, a quanto siano poche le persone che sanno determinare l'evoluzione dei comportamenti, dei gusti, delle scelte senza appartenere al mondo della moda. Uomini e donne che con la propria ricerca, l'appassionato lavoro e una costante abnegazione cercano nella propria sensibilità di captare le radici della propria soddisfazione e insoddisfazione, della propria capacità di sorprendersi o annoiarsi. Issey Miyake è un 'progettista' come si dice in italiano, parola difficile da

tradurre in altre lingue, e che si attribuisce a coloro che dedicano la propria vita al progetto, senza utilizzare scorciatoie di comodo, senza beccettare in giro nel lavoro degli altri, senza accontentarsi dei facili risultati. Soddisfatti solo quando il proprio lavoro corrisponde a quanto cercato, desiderato, voluto. Appassionati dalle proprie esigenti pretese, corrisposti dal proprio giudizio e dalla propria approvazione.

Issey Miyake ha una radice di artista grafico, abituato a trattare le due dimensioni, il colore, i segni, i tratti bidimensionali, ma è conquistato dalla terza dimensione e ha fatto diventare questo confronto la matrice del suo lavoro. Il connotato grafico del tessuto è solo l'inizio della ricerca che tende a trasformarlo e renderlo tridimensionale e prende un significato speciale quando ha a che fare con un corpo vivente. Tutto il suo lavoro nasce nel tessuto e nella ricerca del suo potenziale tridimensionale, quasi se nascondesse in sé un'aspirazione alla tridimensionalità. E se c'è, è certo che lui lo trova. Il passaggio tra le due e tre dimensioni è costante, nel progetto dei vestiti, come degli accessori, così come degli allestimenti e delle installazioni spaziali.

Ci si orienta nel mondo Issey Miyake attraverso le parole che identificano i progetti e le collezioni, Pleats Please per i plissé, Bao Bao per le strutture a base triangolo, 132 5. per gli abiti a struttura grafica, IN-EI per le lampade a origami, A-POC (A Piece Of Cloth) per i vestiti ricavati da un unico pezzo di tessuto e così via. L'ultimo progetto, ancora mai presentato e al momento non ancora inserito in alcun programma produttivo, è provvisoriamente chiamato Session One ed è nato proprio da A-POC. Issey Miyake introduce un nuovo connotato non ancora sperimentato, a tutti gli effetti sorprendente, del tutto inaspettato. Il "carattere selvaggio".

Partendo da un tessuto realizzato con particolari accortezze, dopo un controllato passaggio nel vapore, ottiene una materia consistente, di grosso spessore, rude all'aspetto ma estremamente morbida al tatto, con frange e sfilacciamenti.

L'ispirazione viene dal mondo dell'uomo preistorico della cultura jomonese, che ha preso forma in Giappone circa 5.000 anni fa. Il risultato non produce certo vestiti da indossare, ma non era questo l'obiettivo.

Il misterioso anelito alla spazialità delle superfici piane è sempre al centro del suo pensiero e si manifesta in tutto il suo lavoro. C'è un sentore di ricerca scientifica, di fisica quantistica, di analisi di particelle subatomiche.

C'è il **bisogno** di aggiungere una terza dimensione che trasforma un decoro piano in oggetto solido, un segno in una scultura, una traccia in un puro oggetto d'arte.

Issey Miyake (Hiroshima, 1938) fonda il Miyake Design Studio nel 1970 e presenta la prima collezione a Parigi nel 1973. Il suo lavoro si è evoluto partendo sempre da un unico pezzo di stoffa: da Pleats Please del 1993 alla serie A-POC, A Piece of Cloth, del 1998 (dove rotoli continui di tessuto e capi sono realizzati da un singolo pezzo di tessuto). Oggi, collabora con il suo team di progetto Reality Lab per esplorare le caratteristiche dei materiali di recupero.

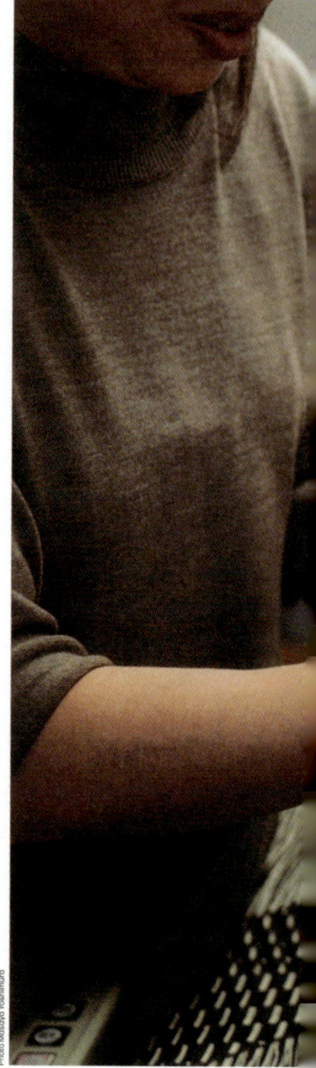

90

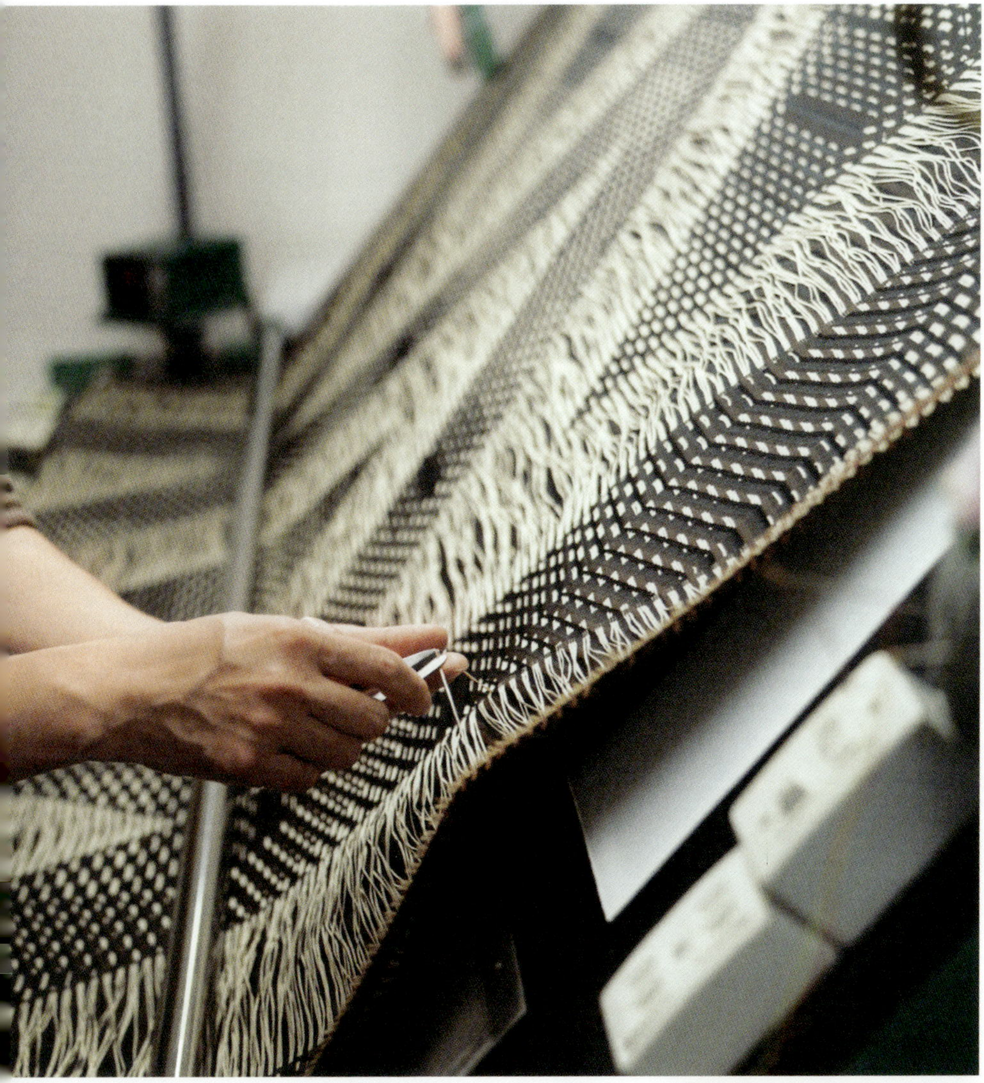

Pagina a fronte: la macchina per la lavorazione jacquard, programmata al computer per la tessitura di Session One. L'azienda, che si trova nella prefettura di Yamanashi (alle pendici del Monte Fuji) e storicamente produceva tessuti in seta, dal 2000 è partner di Miyake ed è stata determinante nello sviluppo del progetto A-POC. In questa pagina. Sopra: fase di controllo del tessuto dopo la tessitura. A destra: Michele De Lucchi e Issey Miyake a Tokyo

Opposite page: the Jacquard loom, computer programmed for weaving Session One. The company, located in Yamanashi Prefecture (on the slopes of Mount Fuji) is a long-established manufacturer of silk fabrics. It has been Miyake's partner since 2000 and was instrumental in developing the A-POC project. This page: inspecting the fabric after weaving. Right: Michele De Lucchi and Issey Miyake in Tokyo

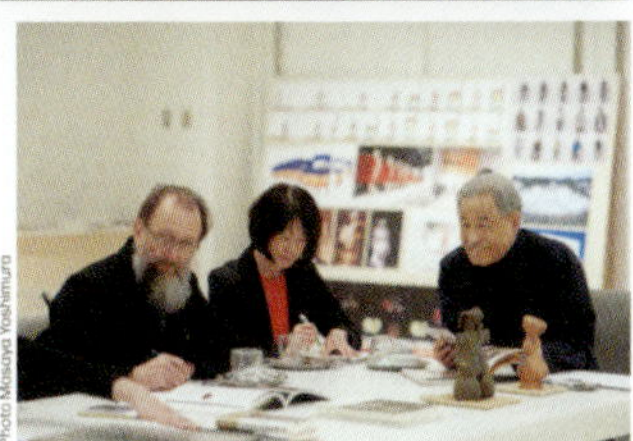

91

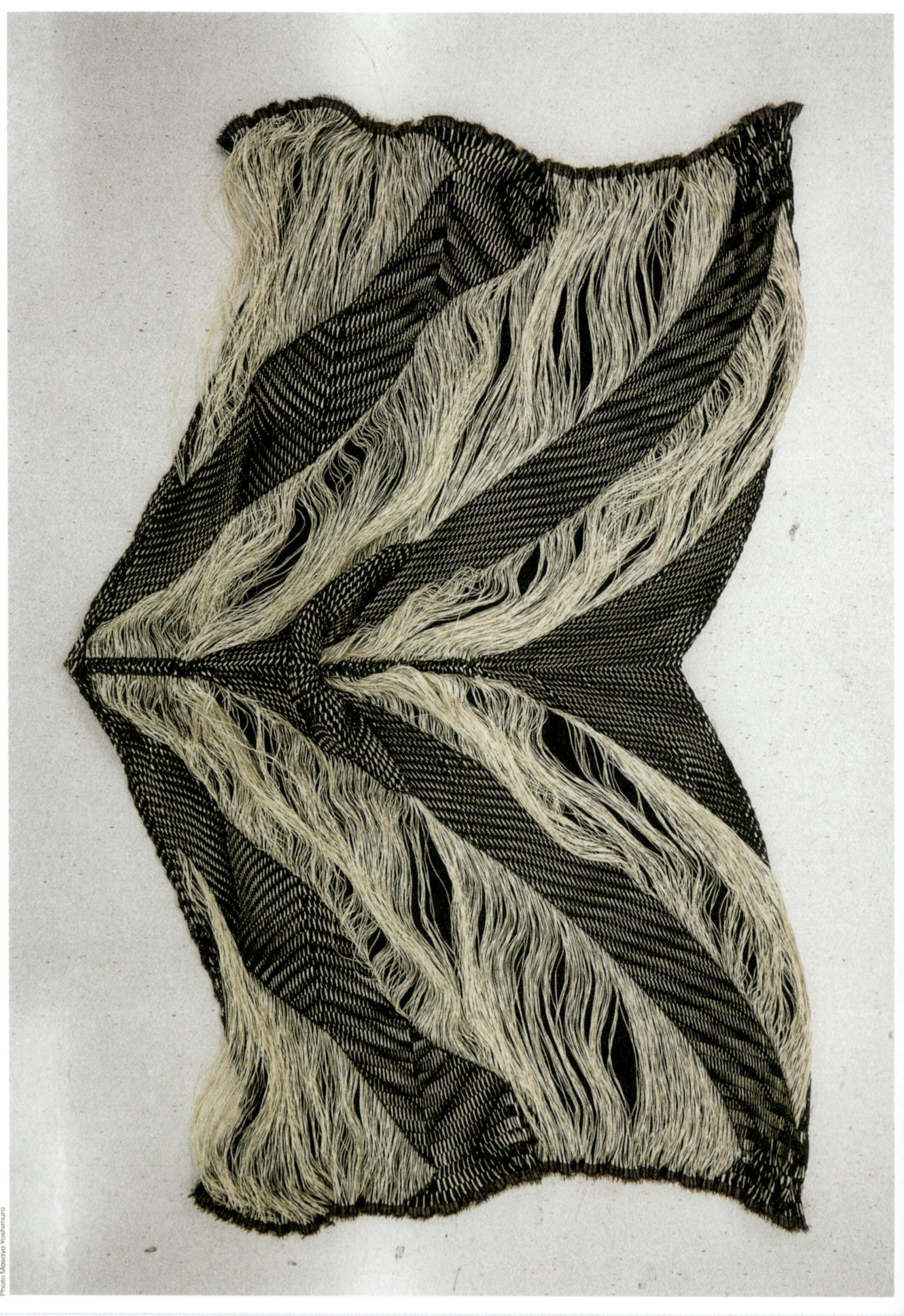
Photo Masayo Yoshimura

In his latest, highly original work, Issey Miyake designs fabrics of sophisticated technology with a wild, primordial appearance. Art objects worn not to clothe the body, but to discover new artistic languages

Text by Michele De Lucchi
Photos by James Mollison

Issey Miyake is calm and wise. He looks you in the face, but sees beyond. He makes you feel slightly in awe of him, sufficiently so to exact respect, but not to keep at a distance. This is simply because he also expresses a great deal of respect and is quick to manifest surprise and admiration. He works extensively with others and involves colleagues, designers, photographers, graphic designers and architects, all the creative people around him, deeply in his work.

He possesses a superior culture of the image and immediately distinguishes the new and foreseen from the unpredictable.

Issey Miyake is certainly not a fashion designer, couturier or tailor, or someone who produces clothes, though he is well known in the fashion world. Of course, what he does has nothing to do with the seasons, the colours or the fabrics of the moment, trends, and all those other things that garment-makers constantly keep under control so as not to lose contact with their consumers.

Just as it is difficult to imagine a sage agitated and stressed, it is equally difficult to imagine this cultivated Japanese man worrying about the evolution of taste and analysing trends in lifestyles month after month. For one simple reason: he already knows them and he is the one who points them out. The meeting with Issey Miyake, whose clothes I have worn all my life, makes me think of this, of how few people are able to determine trends in behaviour, tastes and choices, without belonging to the world of fashion. Men and women who, by their own research, impassioned work and constant self-denial, seek within their own sensibility to capture the roots of their satisfaction and dissatisfaction, their ability to be surprised

or bored. Issey Miyake is a *progettista* as we say in Italian, a designer in the truest sense of the word, which is applied to those who devote their lives to the project, without using convenient shortcuts, without sticking their beaks into others' work, without being content with facile results. They are satisfied only when their work corresponds to what they sought, desired and willed. They are passionate about their exacting wishes, paid for by their own judgment and approval.

Issey Miyake has the root of the graphic artist, accustomed to dealing with two dimensions, colour, signs, two-dimensional features, but he is captivated by the third dimension and has made its exploration the framework of his work. The graphic connotation of a fabric is just the beginning of his research, which tends to transform it and make it three-dimensional, and acquires a special significance when it has to do with a living body. All his work is born in the fabric and the quest for its three-dimensional potential, almost as if it harboured within itself an aspiration to three dimensions. And if it is there, he will certainly find it. He constantly moves between two and three dimensions in the design of clothes as of accessories, in installations as well as spatial set-ups.

We find our bearings in Issey Miyake's world through the words that identify projects and collections: Pleats Please for pleating, Bao Bao for triangle-based structures, 132 5 for garments with a graphic structure, IN-EI for origami lamps, A-POC (A Piece Of Cloth) for garments made from a single fabric, and so forth. The latest project, which has not yet been presented or included in any production programme, is tentatively called Session One and was born out of A-POC. Issey Miyake introduces a new connotation, never before experienced, in all respects surprising, completely unexpected. Its "wild character".

Starting from a fabric made with special care, after a controlled passage through steam, he obtains a thick, dense material, rough in appearance but extremely soft to the touch, with fringes and fraying. The inspiration comes from the world of the prehistoric man of Jomonese culture, which emerged in Japan some 5,000 years ago. The result does not produce clothes for wearing, but that was not the objective.

A mysterious yearning for spatiality in flat surfaces always lies at the centre of his thought and is expressed in all his work. There is a hint of scientific research, of quantum physics, analysis of subatomic particles, a need to add a third dimension that transforms a flat pattern into a solid object, a sign into a sculpture, a trace into a pure art object.

Issey Miyake (Hiroshima, 1938) founded Miyake Design Studio in 1970 and presented his first collection in Paris in 1973. The evolution of his work has always started from a single piece of cloth: from Pleats Please in 1993 to the series titled A-POC, A Piece of Cloth, of 1998 (where continuous rolls of fabric and garments are made from a single piece of yarn). Today, he works with his Reality Lab project team exploring the characteristics of retrieved materials.

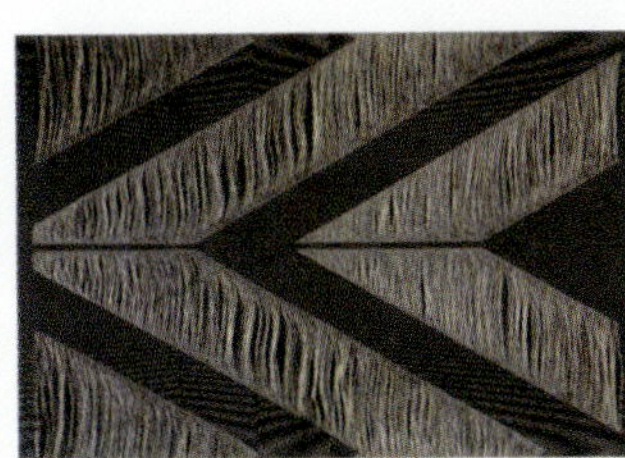

Pagina a fronte: il pannello di tessuto dopo essere stato trattato con il vapore.
In questa pagina. Sopra: lo stesso pannello prima del processo con il vapore. Il tessuto di Session One è realizzato usando tre diversi filati: poliestere (filo base), spandex (da ridurre al vapore) e cotone.
Sotto: una serie di pannelli di tessuto realizzati esclusivamente per Session One. I pannelli hanno una dimensione di circa 2,5 m

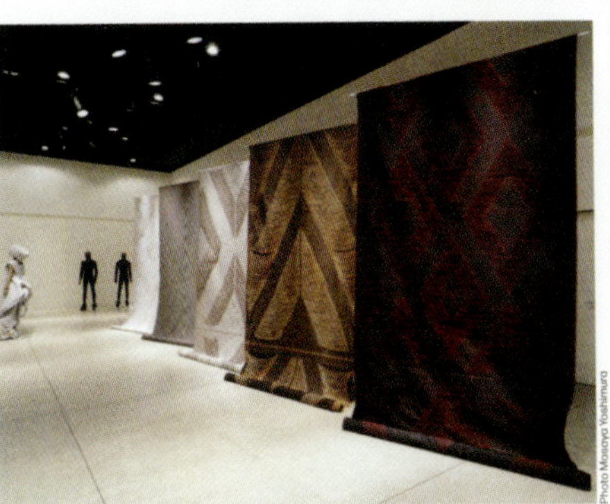

Opposite page: a fabric panel after steam conditioning. This page. Top: the same fabric panel before steam conditioning. The Session One fabric is made using three different yarns: polyester (basic thread), spandex (to be steam-reduced) and cotton. Left: a series of fabric panels made exclusively for Session One. The panels measure about 2.5 m

93

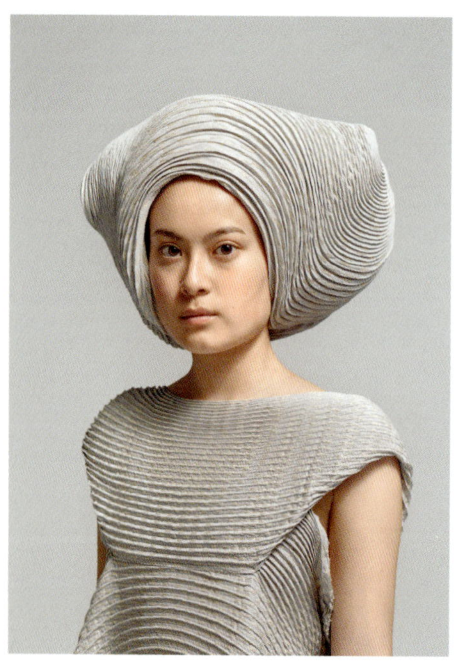

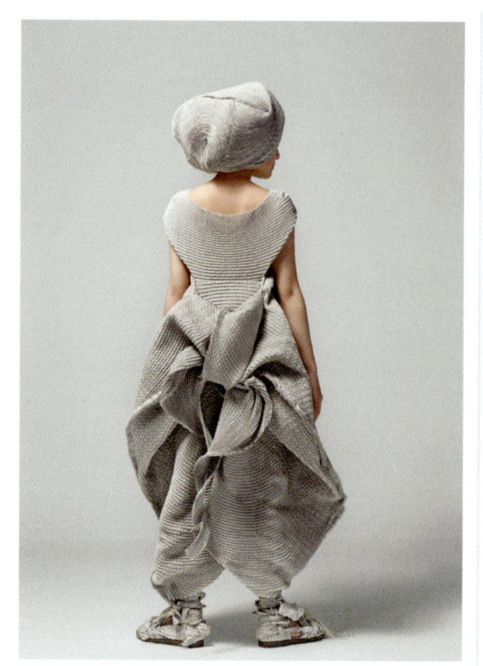

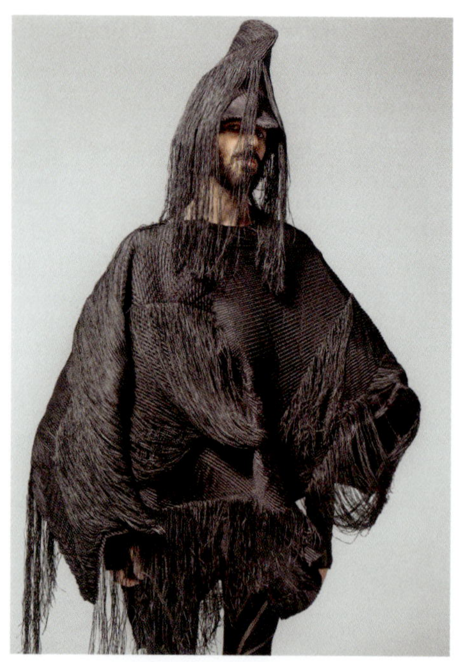

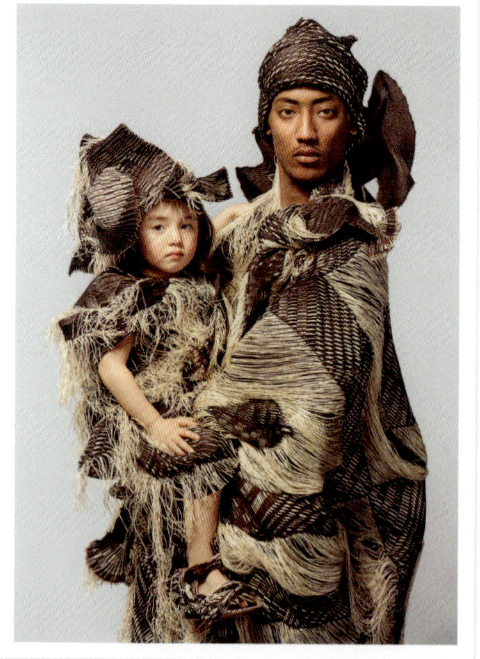

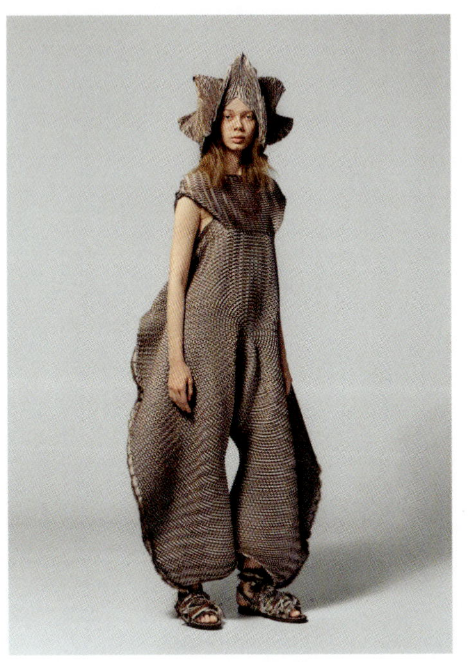

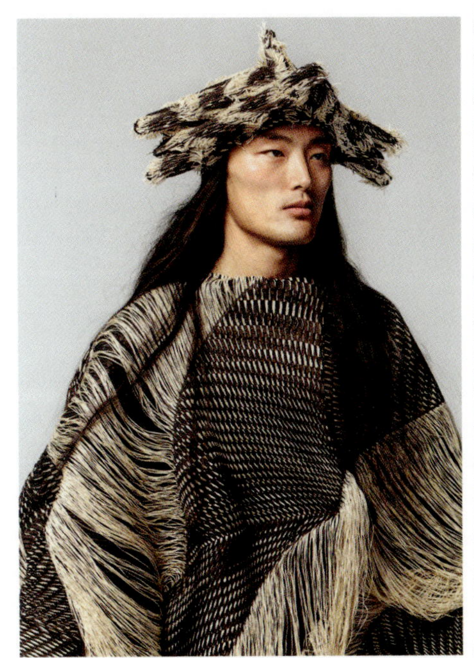

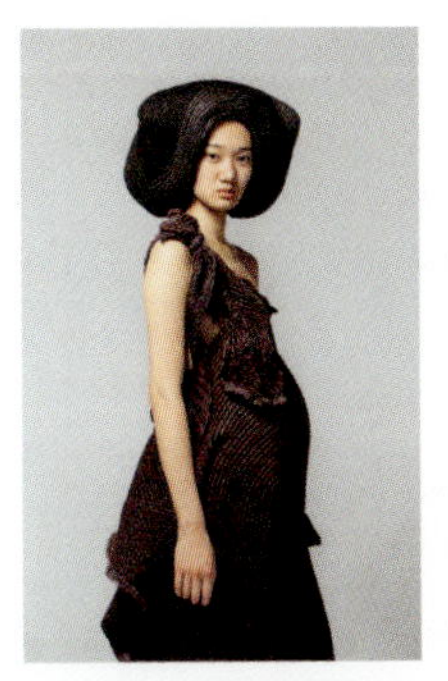

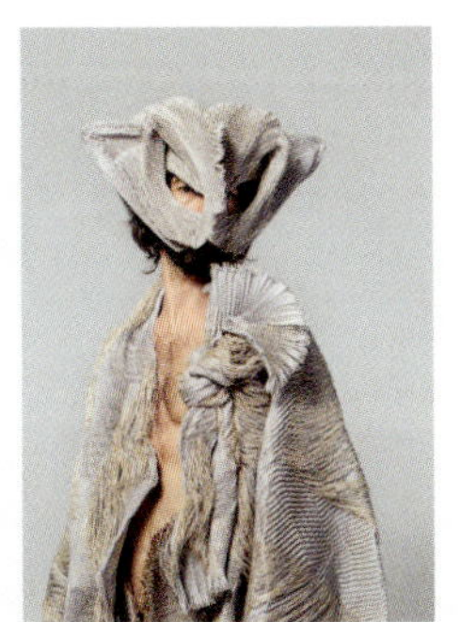

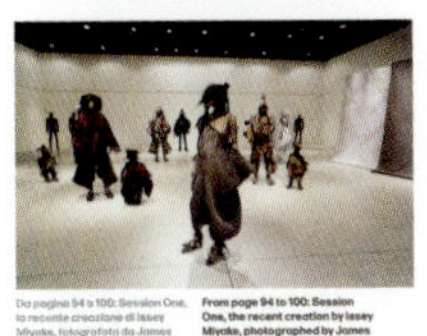

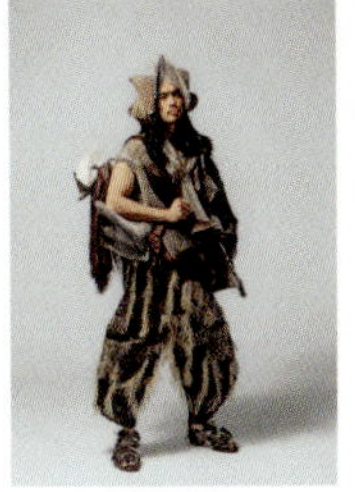

Da pagina 94 a 100: Session One, la recente creazione di Issey Miyake, fotografata da James Mollison. La maggior parte dei look sono realizzati da un unico pannello di tessuto. In rari casi, ne sono stati assemblati due. Session One parte dal metodo di A-POC (A Piece of Cloth), tessuto prodotto da una macchina per la lavorazione jacquard abbinata a una programmazione al computer

From page 94 to 100: Session One, the recent creation by Issey Miyake, photographed by James Mollison. Most of the looks are made from a single panel of fabric. In a few rare cases, two panels were assembled. Session One starts from the A-POC (A Piece of Cloth) method, whereby fabric is produced on a machine for jacquard weaves combined with computer software

100

2019

> January: First presentation of HOMME PLISSÉ ISSEY MIYAKE in Paris (Autumn-Winter 2019 Collection)
> January: Publication of *Pen*, February 1, 2019, Complete Edition: *A Creativity That Ever Flourishes "The Work of Miyake Issey"*
> February: 132 5. ISSEY MIYAKE vol. 3–4, 2019
> July: 132 5. ISSEY MIYAKE vol. 1–2, 2020
> November: IKKO TANAKA ISSEY MIYAKE No. 5

Pen, February 1, 2019

This long, 70-page feature was created by the Editorial Department and inspired by the Session One special presentation. It contains an overview of Miyake's work to that point and related documents.

Opposite top: *Pen*, February 1, 2019, CCC Media House, Complete Edition: *A Creativity That Ever Flourishes "The Work of Issey Miyake"*
Brigitte Lacombe's portraits of Issey Miyake on the cover of *Pen* and the feature pages. Lacombe traveled to Japan for the article and photographed Miyake, his creative team, and the factory.
Photography: Brigitte Lacombe

Opposite bottom: 21_21 DESIGN SIGHT exhibition posters for *Sense of Humor, Insects: Models for Design,* and *Secret Source of Inspiration: Designers' Hidden Sketches and Mockups*

132 5. ISSEY MIYAKE vol. 3–4, 2019

132 5. ISSEY MIYAKE vol. 1–2, 2020

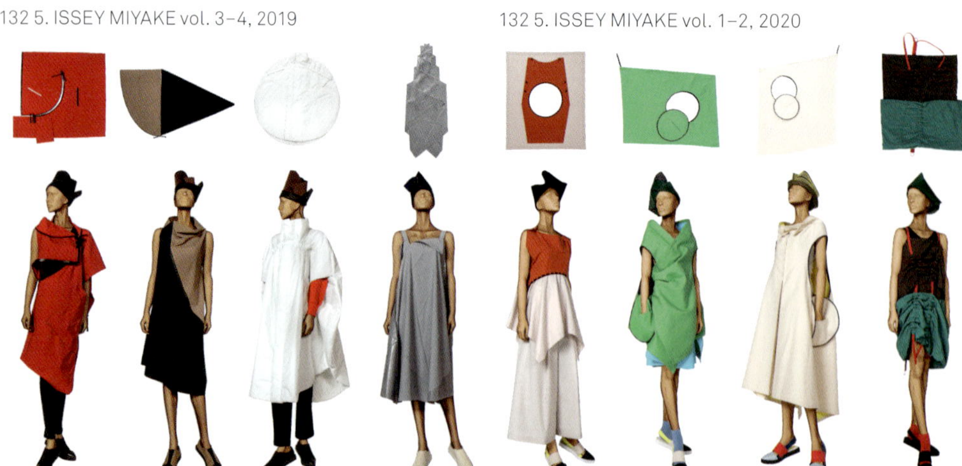

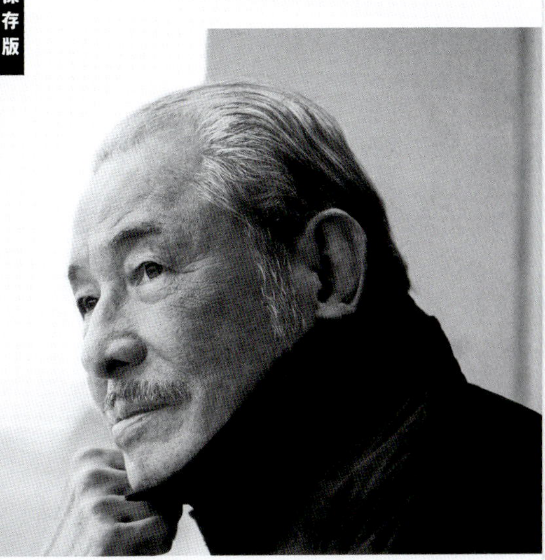
2019年2月1日発行／毎月2日(1日・15日発行)1月15日発売　第23巻2号（通巻467号）
1997年3月10日第三種郵便物認可

pen
with New Attitude

2/1
2019　No.467
特別定価 700 yen

完全保存版
いまも尽きぬ創造のチカラ
三宅一生の仕事。

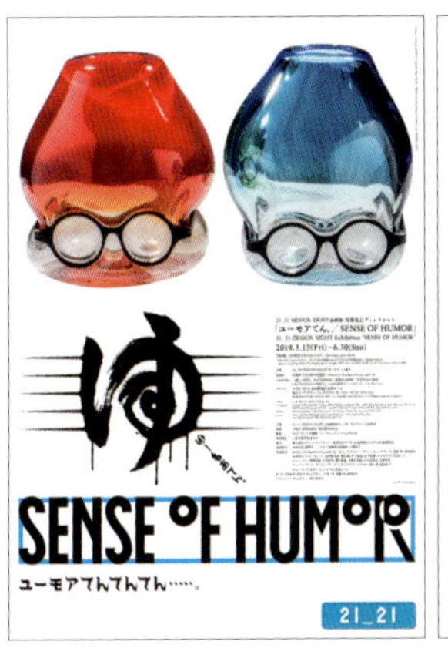
SENSE OF HUMOR
ユーモアてんてんてん……。
21_21

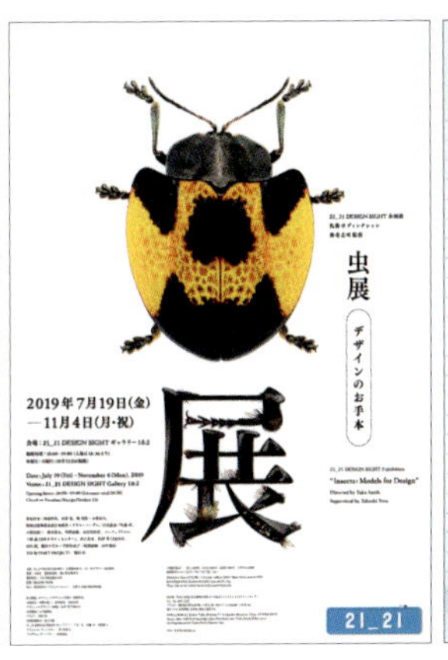
虫展
デザインのお手本
2019年7月19日(金)
—11月4日(月・祝)
展
21_21

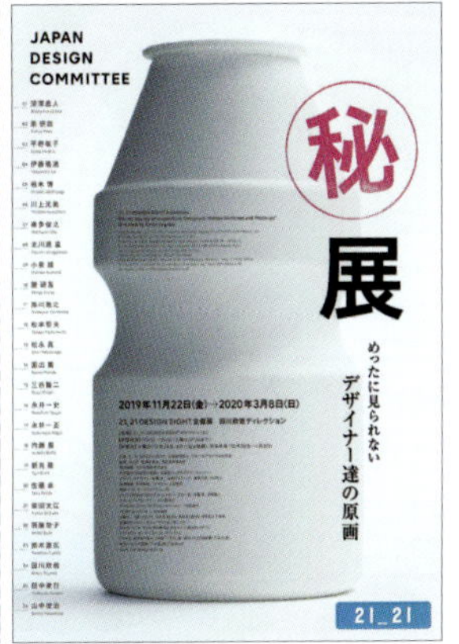
JAPAN
DESIGN
COMMITTEE
秘
展
めったに見られない
デザイナー達の原画
2019年11月22日(金)→2020年3月8日(日)
21_21

Continuous Symbol coats
2018 design/IKKO TANAKA ISSEY MIYAKE No. 4
Photography: Francis Giacobetti

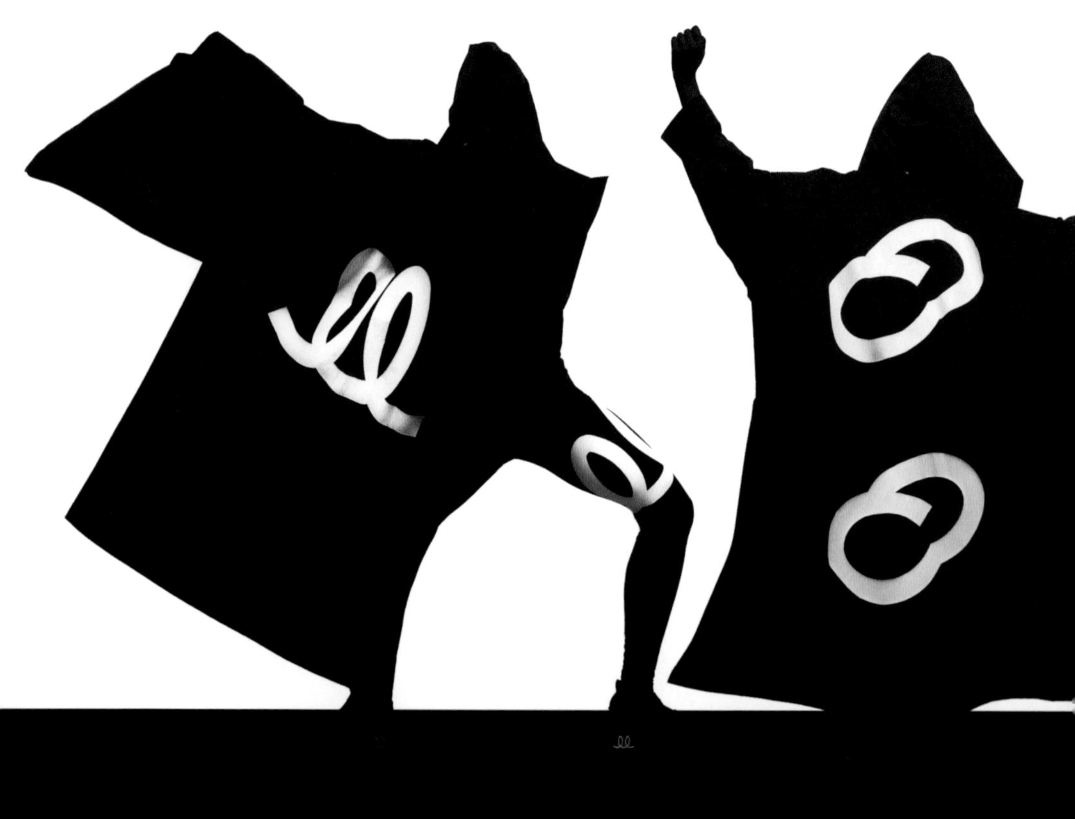

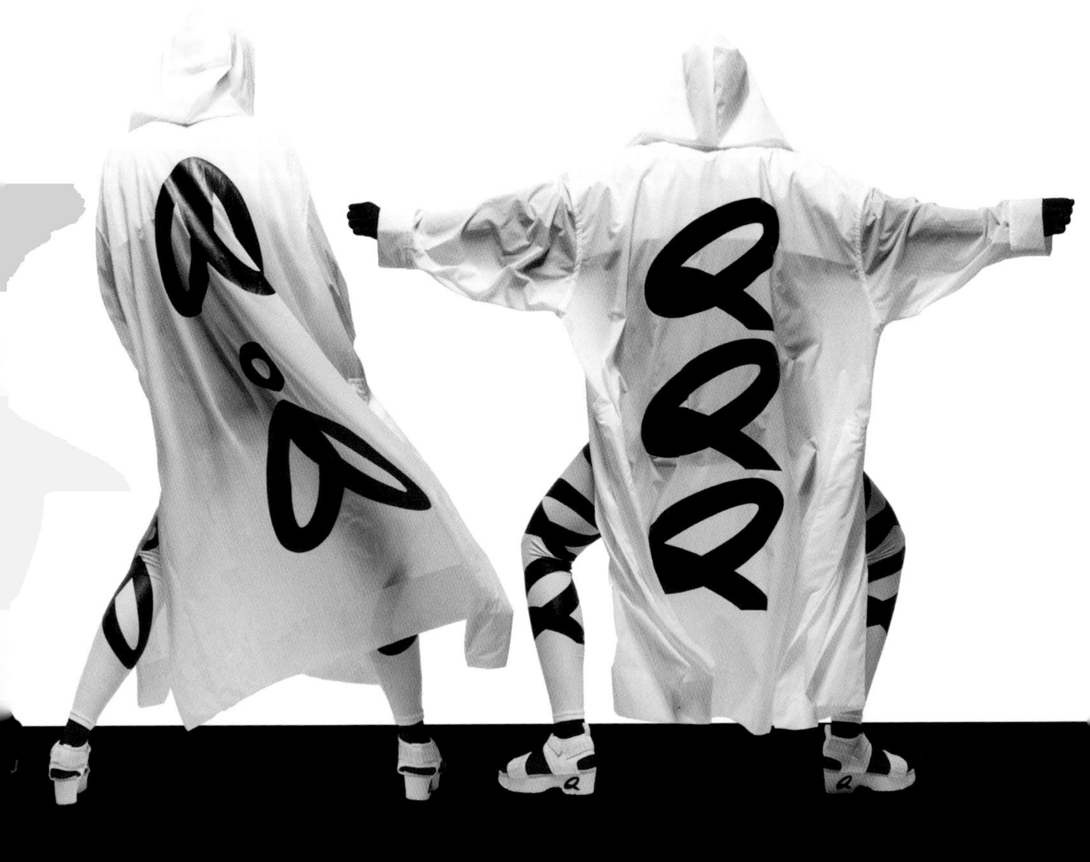

Continuous Symbol dress
A pleated dress. *Continuous Symbol*, Tanaka's work
that served as the motif for the series, was created in
1992 and inspired by the dynamic space of the Ōtemae
Art Center designed by Tadao Ando.
2018 design/IKKO TANAKA ISSEY MIYAKE No. 4
Photography: Francis Giacobetti

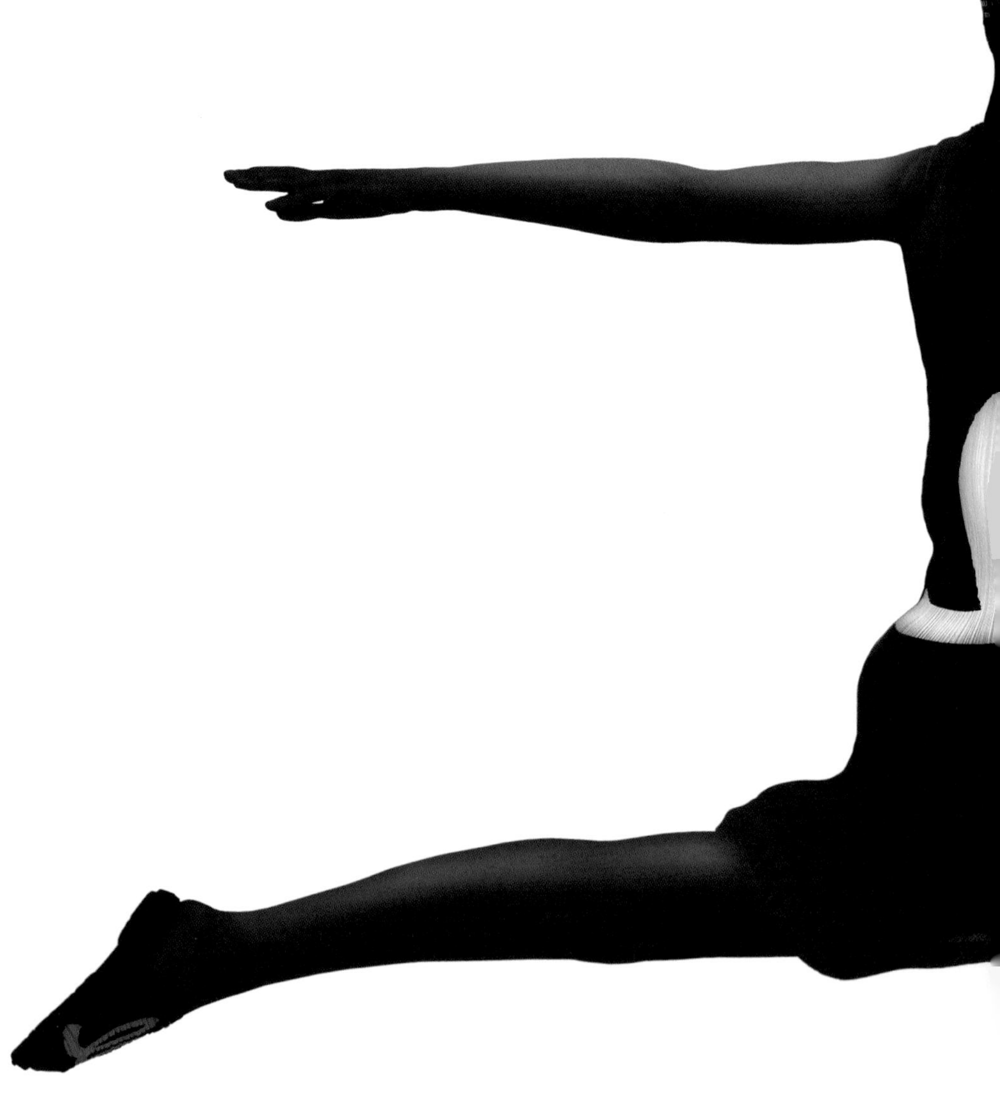

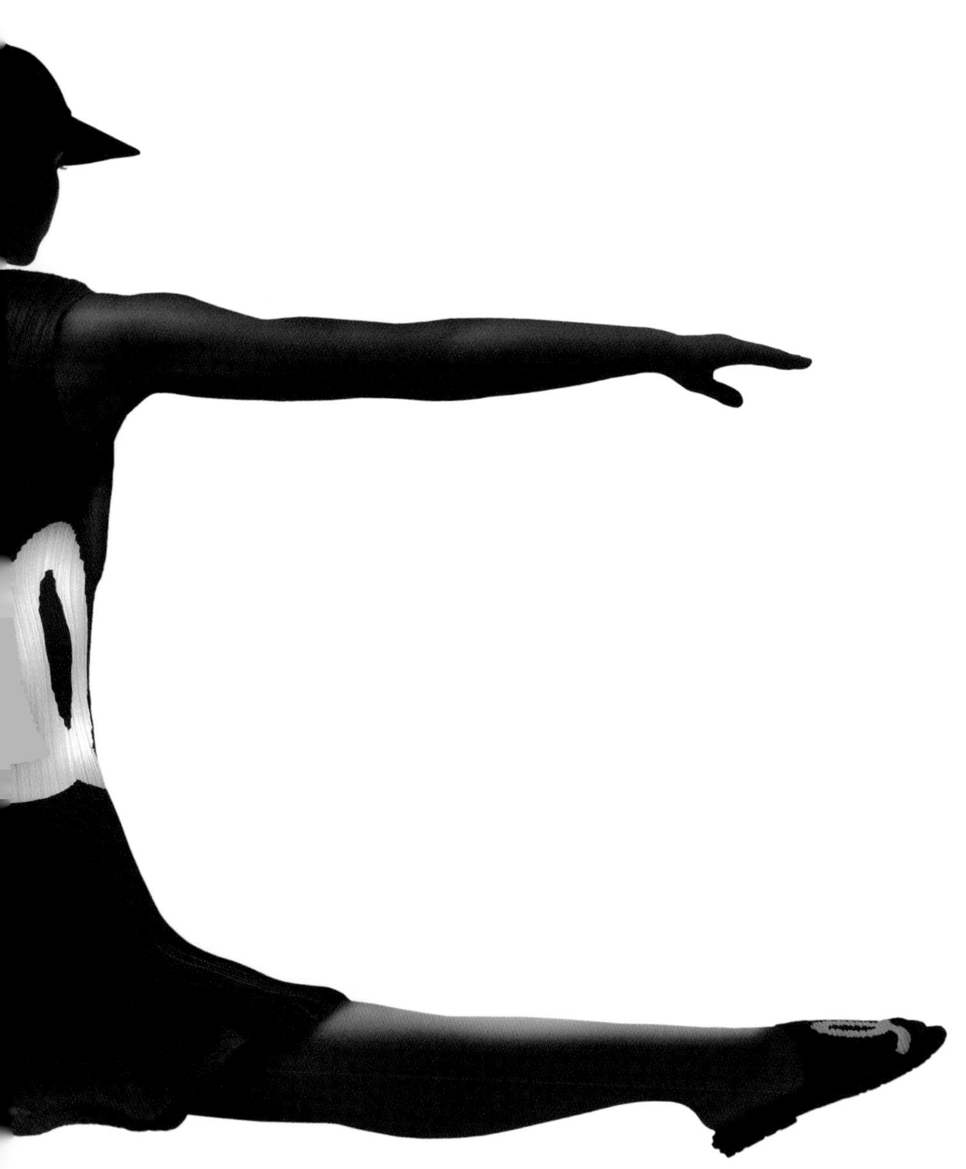

Work coats

Fabric coats. The motifs were *Work: I, Work: Tsu, Work: Q #6*, and *Work: Q #3* created by Ikko Tanaka in 1972. In parallel with his design activities, Tanaka experimented with a number of different planar expressions. He called this "Graphic Art" and presented it in a gallery as "works" of silkscreen and offset printing. 2017 design/IKKO TANAKA ISSEY MIYAKE No.3 Photography: Francis Giacobetti

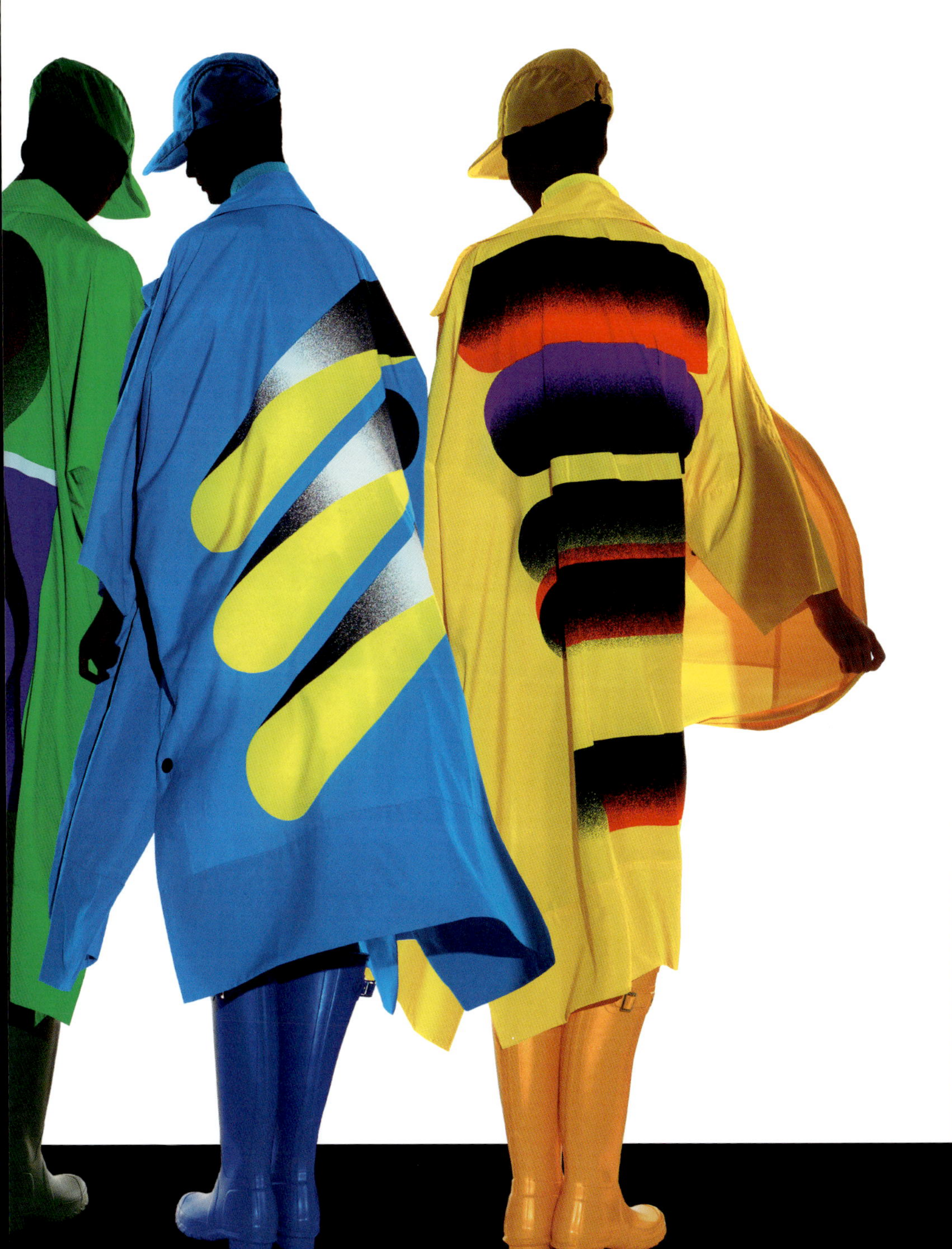

Botanical Garden coat
100% cotton coat.
2019 design/IKKO TANAKA ISSEY MIYAKE No. 5
Photography: Francis Giacobetti

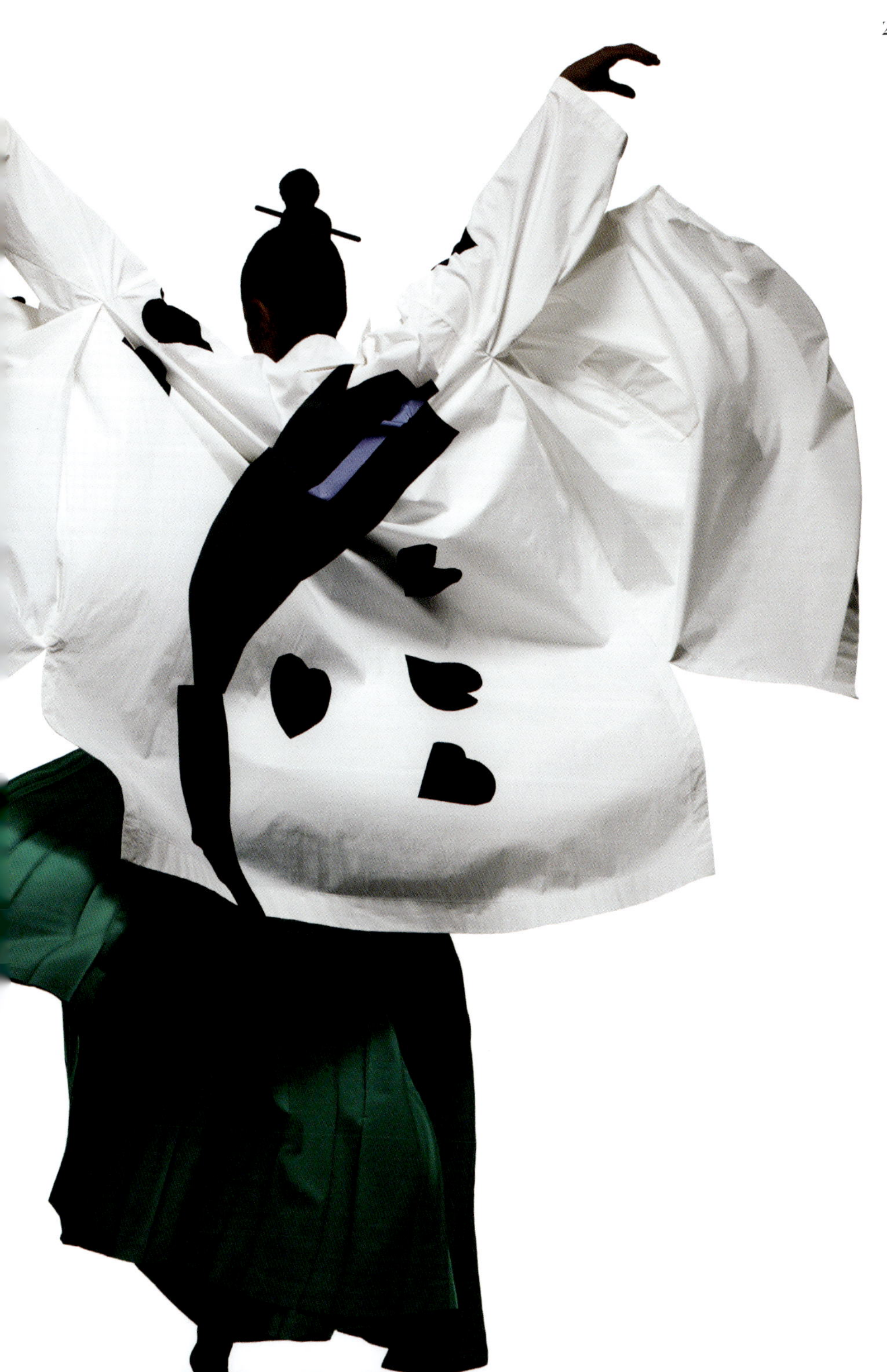

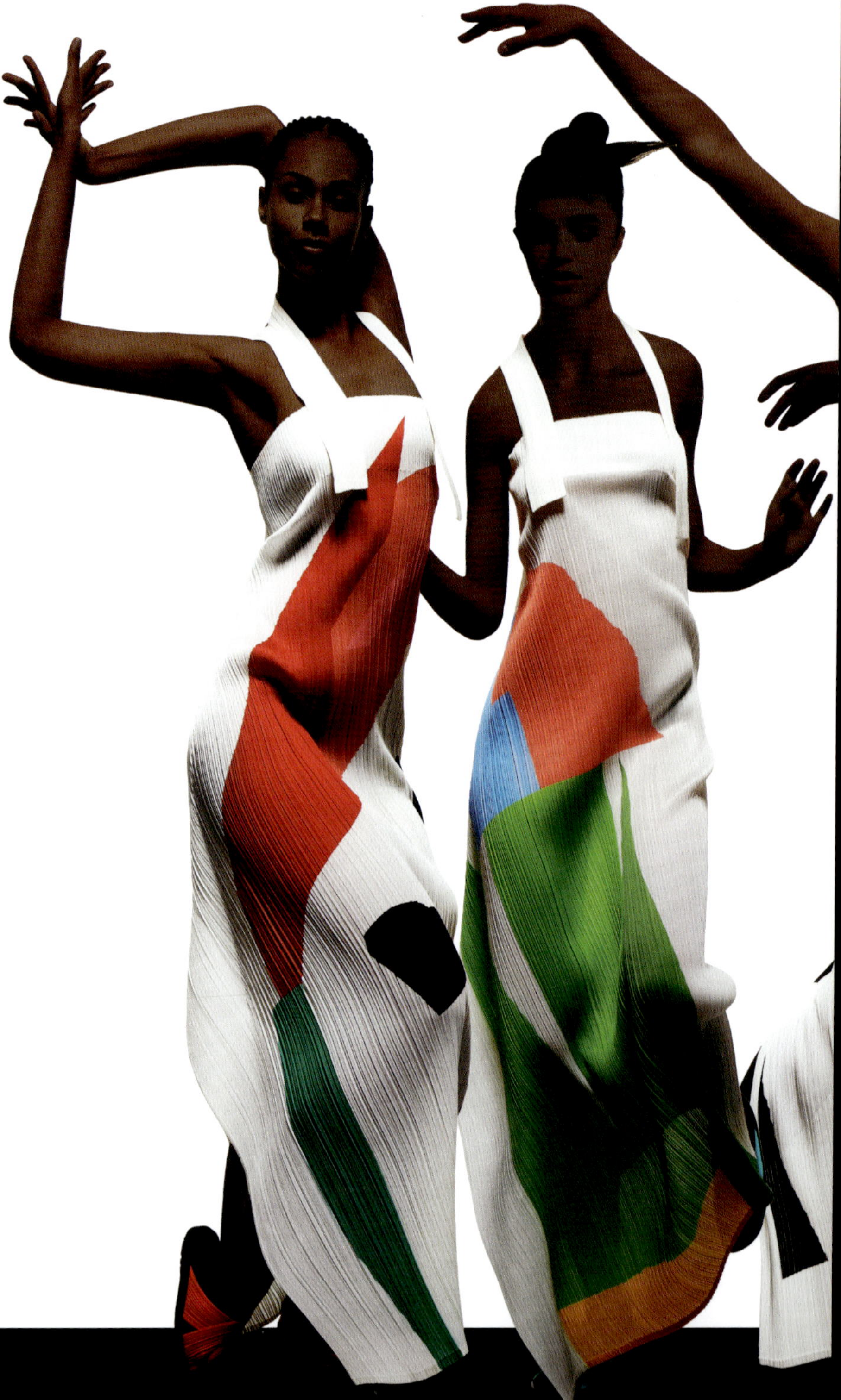

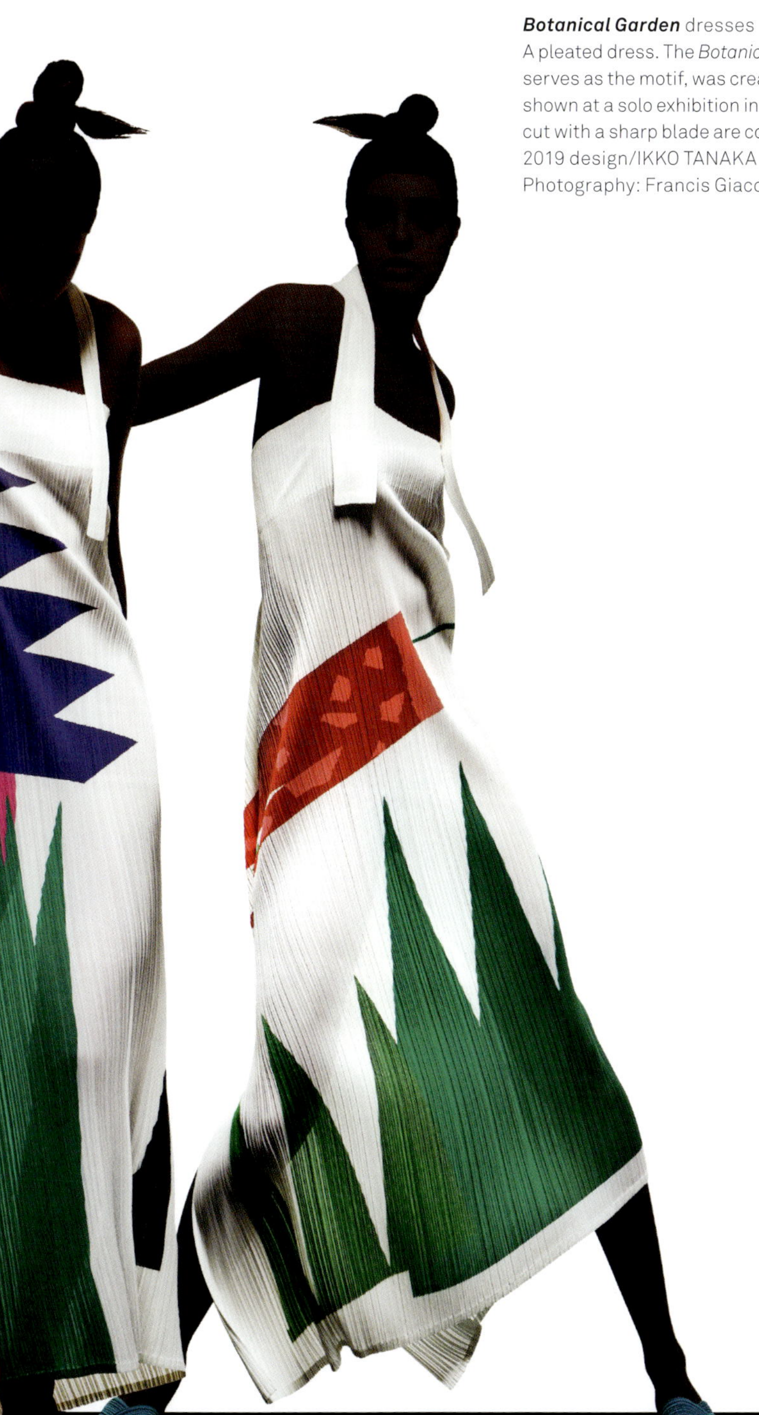

Botanical Garden dresses
A pleated dress. The *Botanical Garden* series which
serves as the motif, was created by Ikko Tanaka and
shown at a solo exhibition in 1990. Pieces of paper
cut with a sharp blade are combined to express plants.
2019 design/IKKO TANAKA ISSEY MIYAKE No. 5
Photography: Francis Giacobetti

2020

- March: 132 5. ISSEY MIYAKE vol. 3–4, 2020
- October: Special presentation of the **TADANORI YOKOO ISSEY MIYAKE project in Tokyo**
- October: 132 5. ISSEY MIYAKE vol. 1–2, 2021

TADANORI YOKOO ISSEY MIYAKE

The TADANORI YOKOO ISSEY MIYAKE project explored new potentials for A-POC by restructuring works of artist and friend Tadanori Yokoo into clothes made from a single piece of cloth. The A-POC technology first developed in the 1990s was combined with progressive concepts to create a series of gender-neutral ageless blousons, everyday clothing suitable for all. A total of eight works were used, mostly from the 1960s, and the clothing was woven from seven colors of recycled polyester thread.

132 5. ISSEY MIYAKE vol. 3–4, 2020   132 5. ISSEY MIYAKE vol. 1–2, 2021

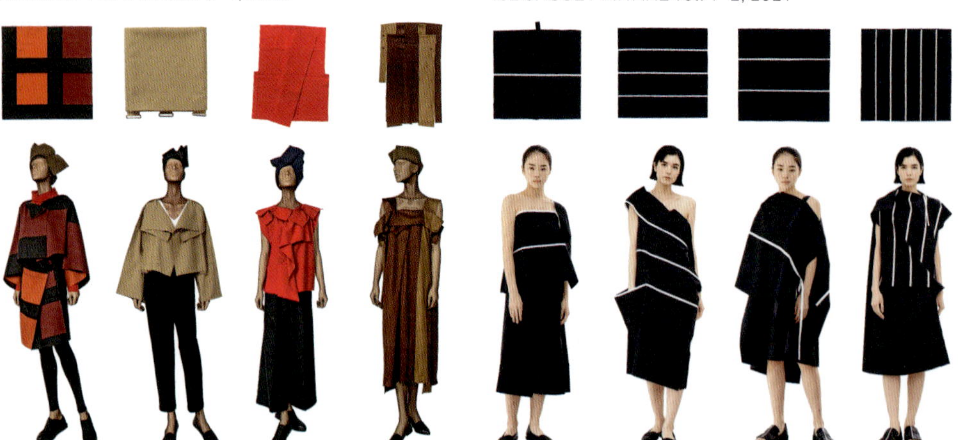

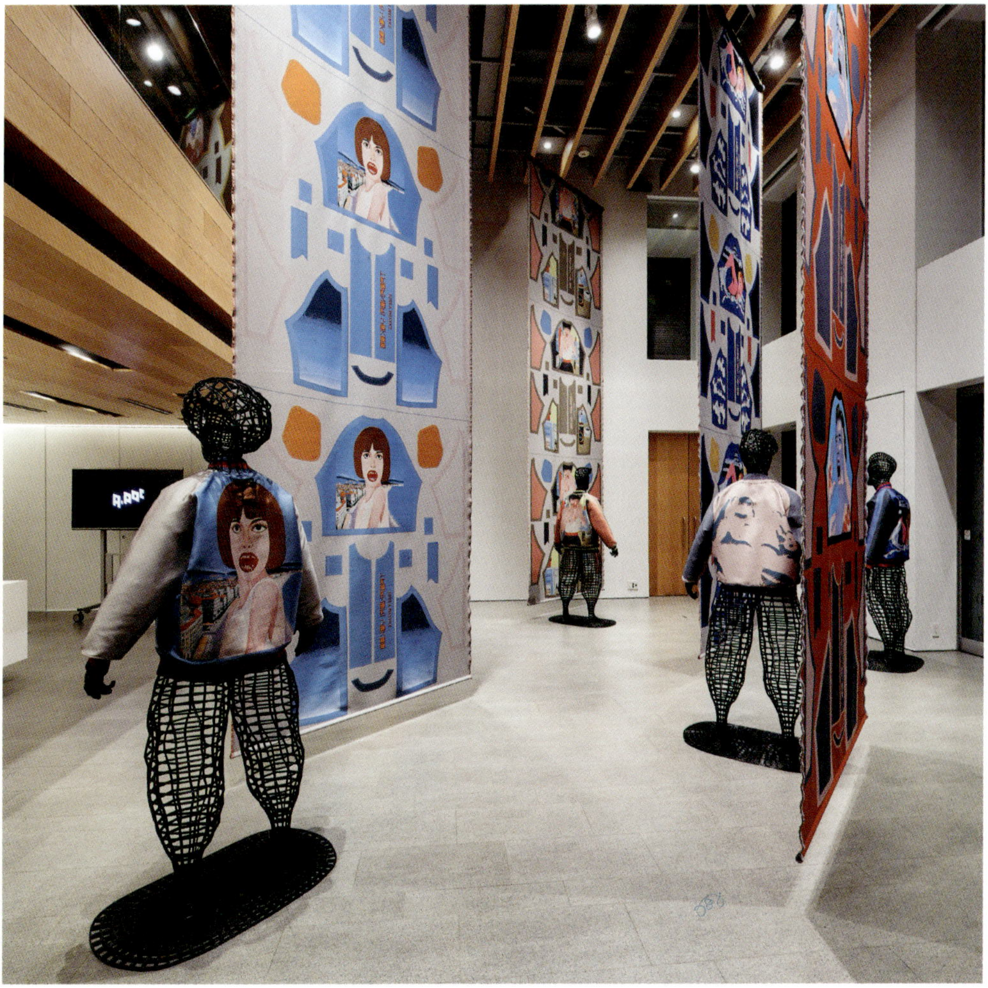

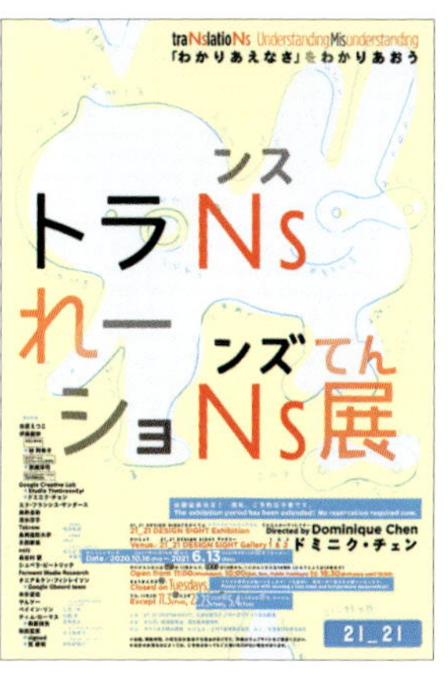

TADANORI YOKOO ISSEY MIYAKE
special presentation

October 23–25: Daikanyama T-SITE Garden Gallery
Along with the blousons, the exhibition included A-POC
textiles containing all of the parts.
Photography: Masaya Yoshimura

Left: 21_21 DESIGN SIGHT exhibition poster for
Translations – Understanding Misunderstanding

TADANORI YOKOO ISSEY MIYAKE 0 blousons
2020 design/ TADANORI YOKOO ISSEY MIYAKE
Photography: Hiroshi Iwasaki

The Tadanori Yokoo works used in the series were,
from left, *Tarzan Is Coming* (1974), *Razor* (1966),
Moat (1966), *Drool* (1966), *Mona Lisa* (1966),
Bride (1966), *KEY BEAUT.Y.* (2017), and *panic Panic
PANIC* (2002–2012).

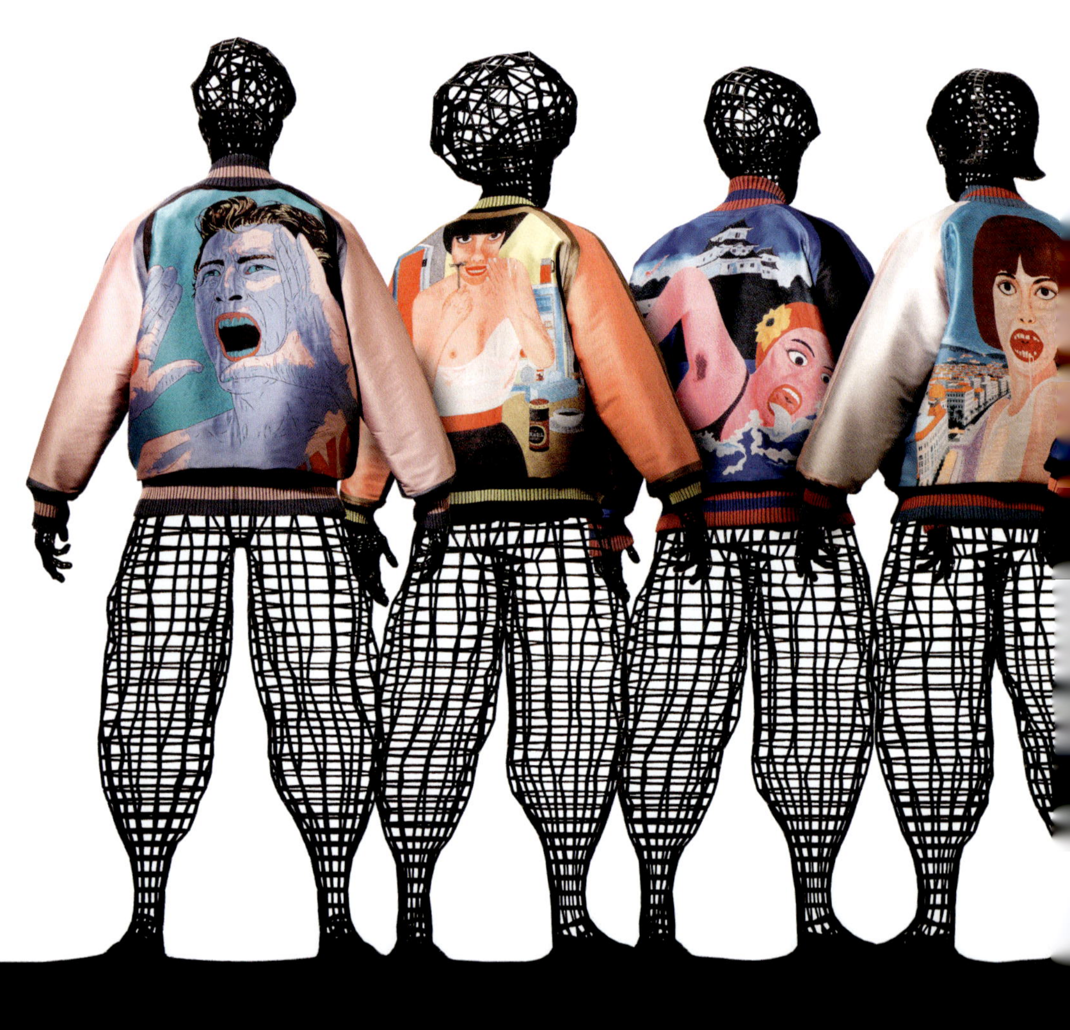

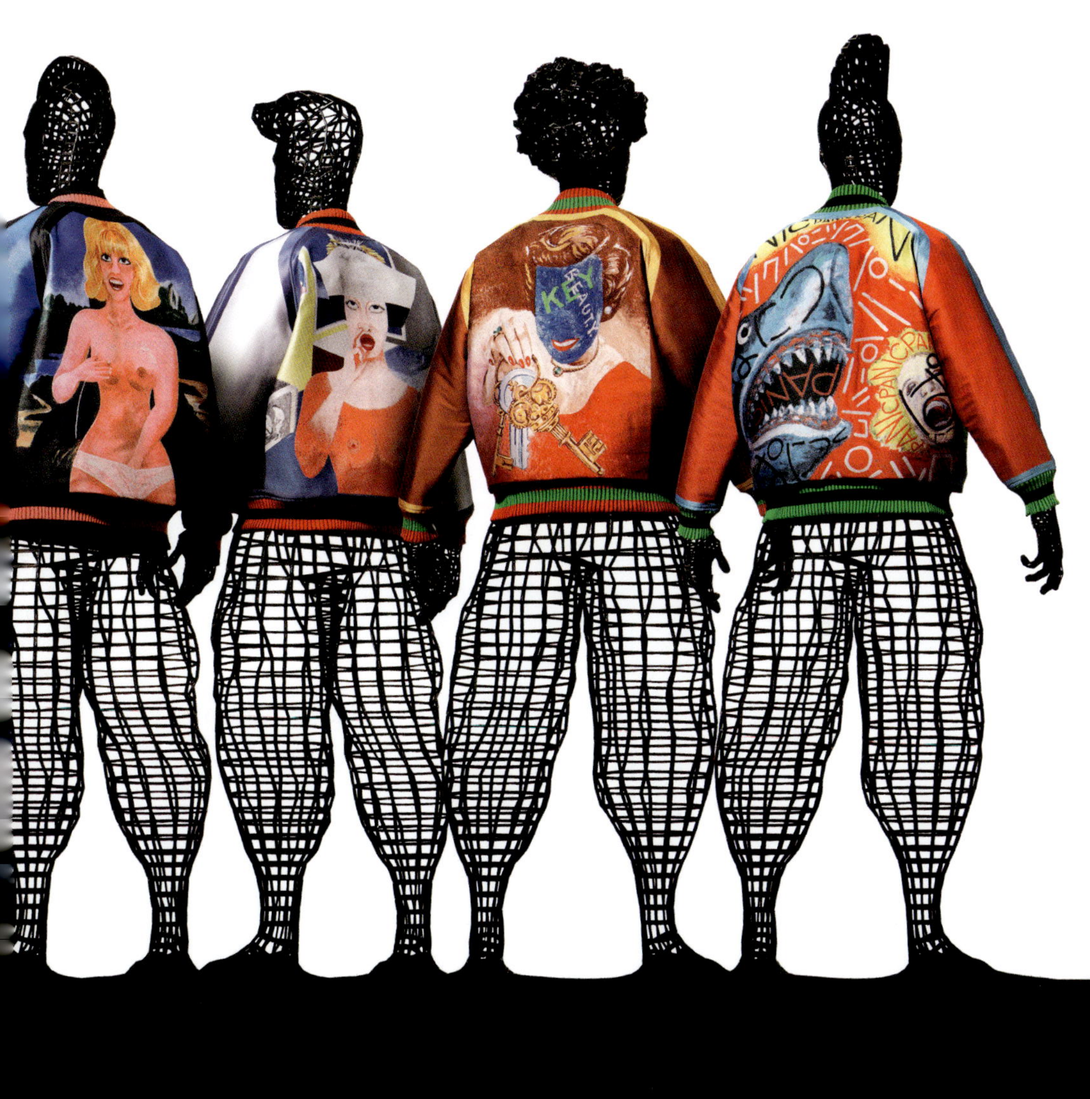

KEY
BEAUTY
PANIC
PANIC

pp. 392–397: *TADANORI YOKOO ISSEY MIYAKE 2*
blousons
The *TADANORI YOKOO ISSEY MIYAKE 2*
series announced in 2022 was based on *the five
constellations*, a recent collaboration between Tadanori Yokoo and a woodblock print artist. The backs
of the blousons use five *okubi-e* of actors created by
Toshusai Sharaku as their motif, emphasizing the
intentional misalignment of the print. The monotone
fronts also express misalignment of the template to
create a humorous and yet refined look.
2022 design/ TADANORI YOKOO
ISSEY MIYAKE
Photography: Hiroshi Iwasaki

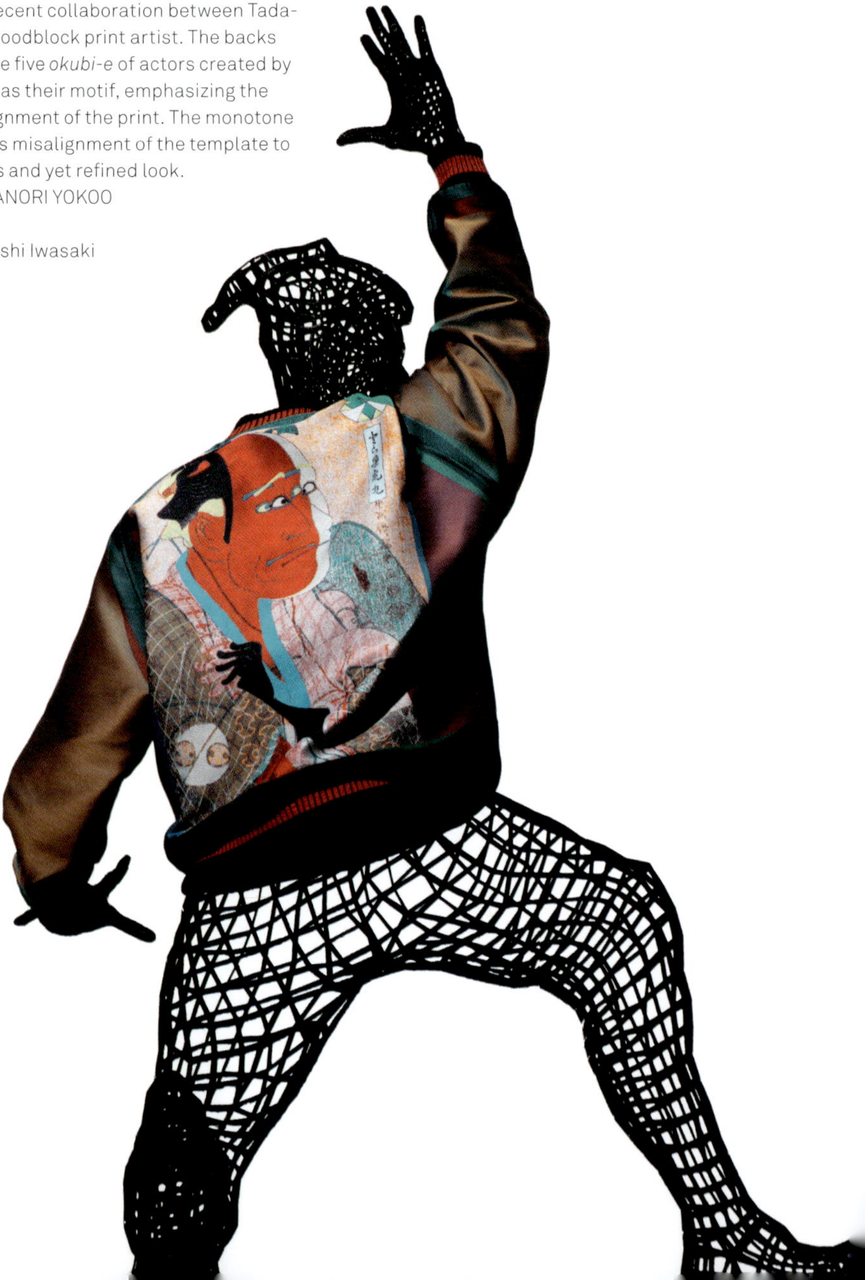

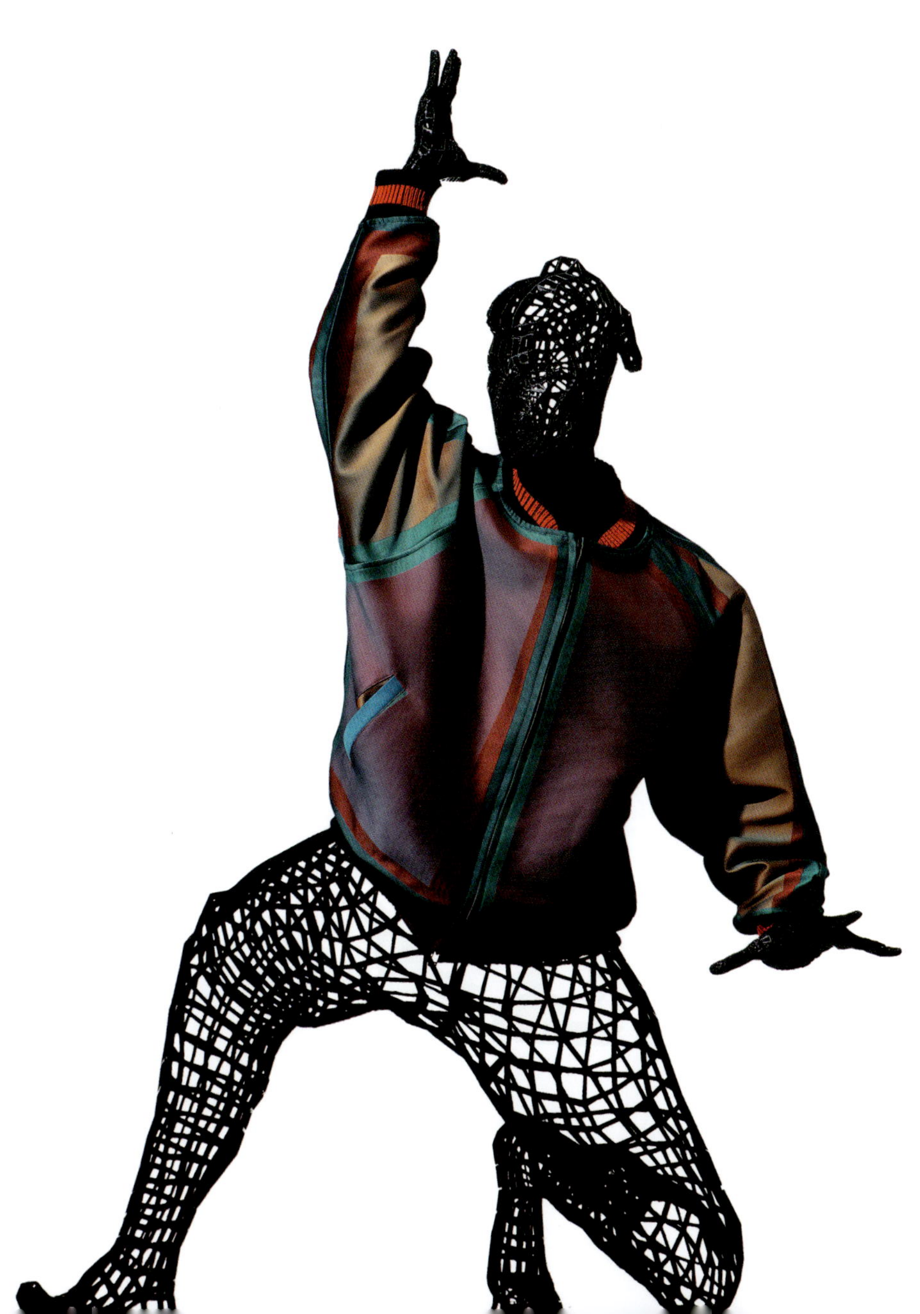

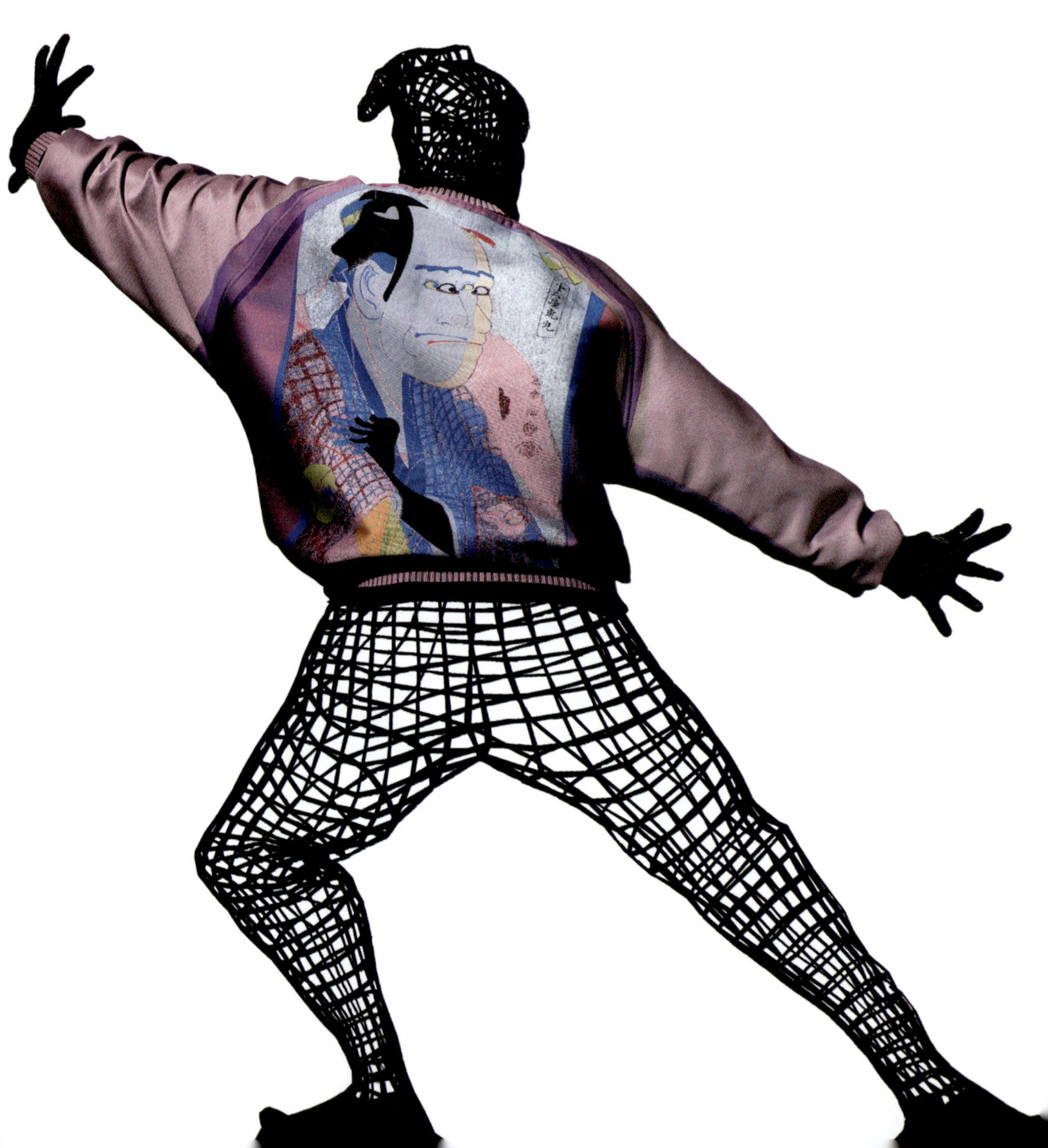

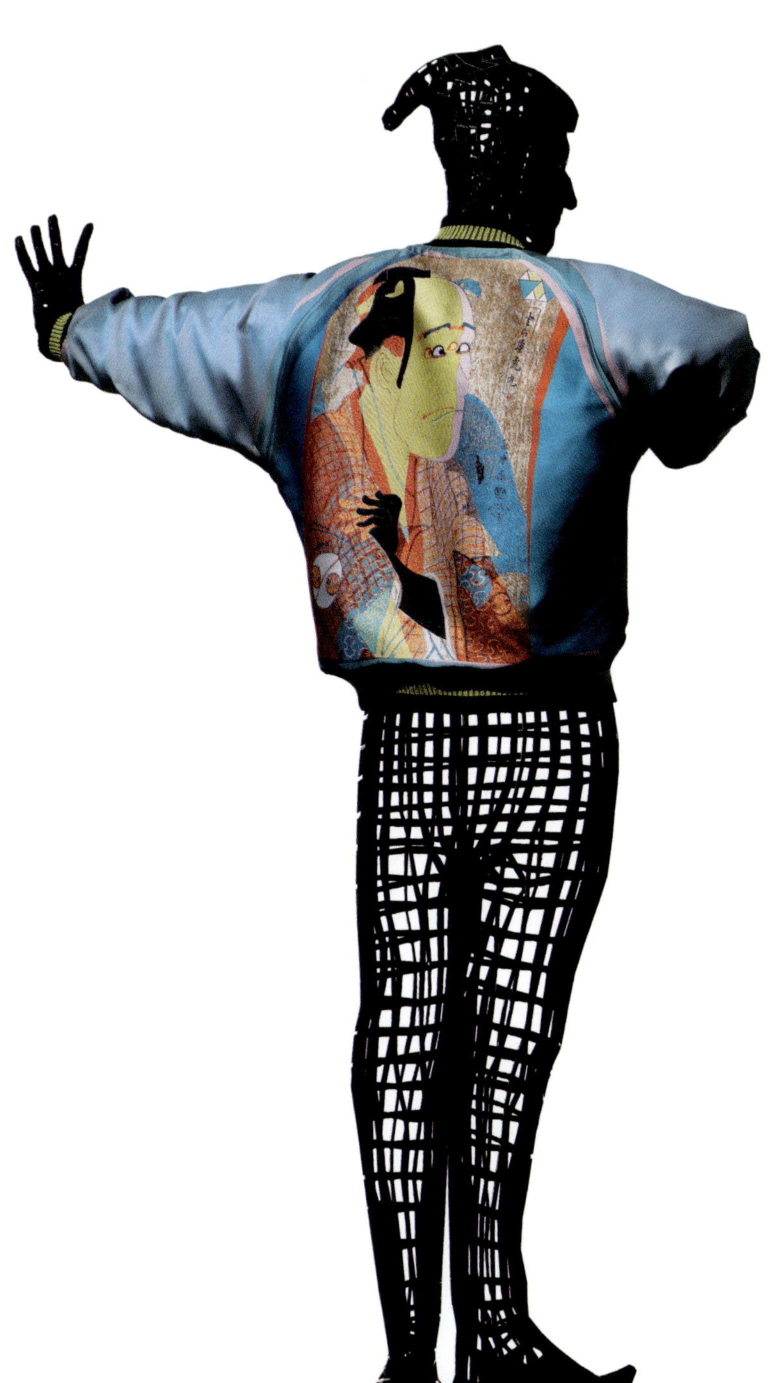

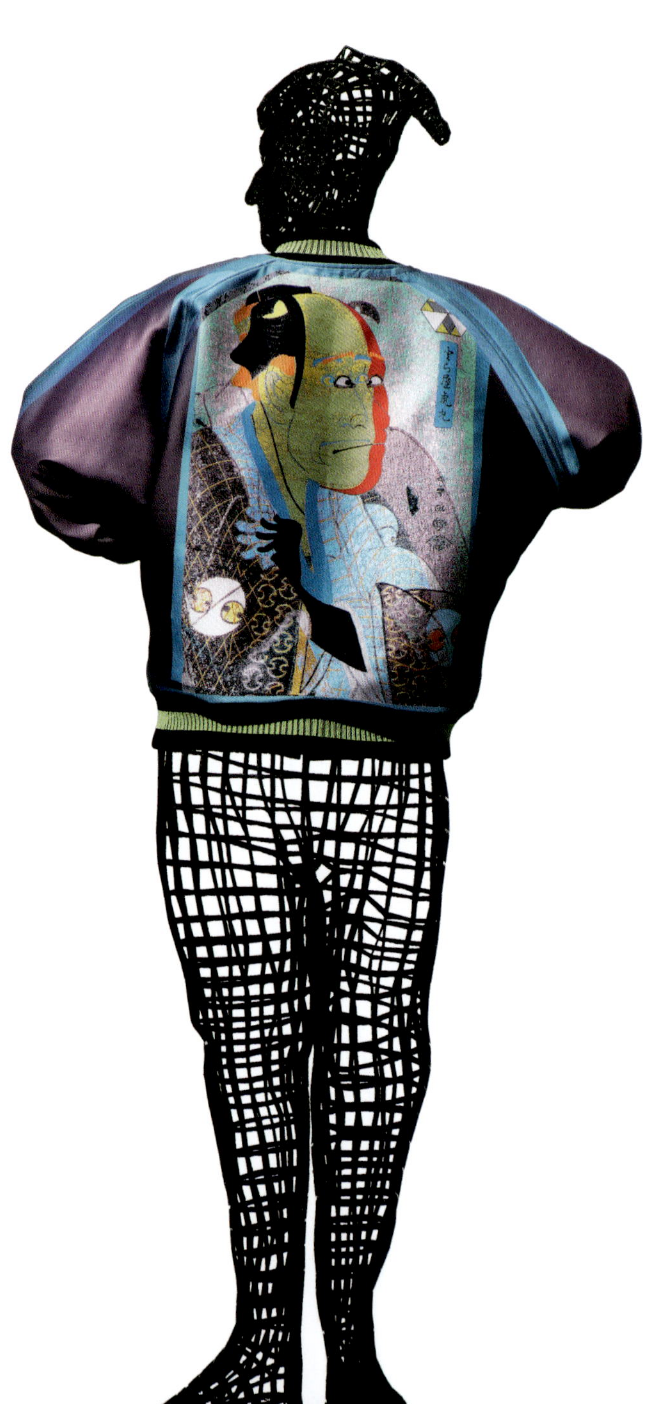

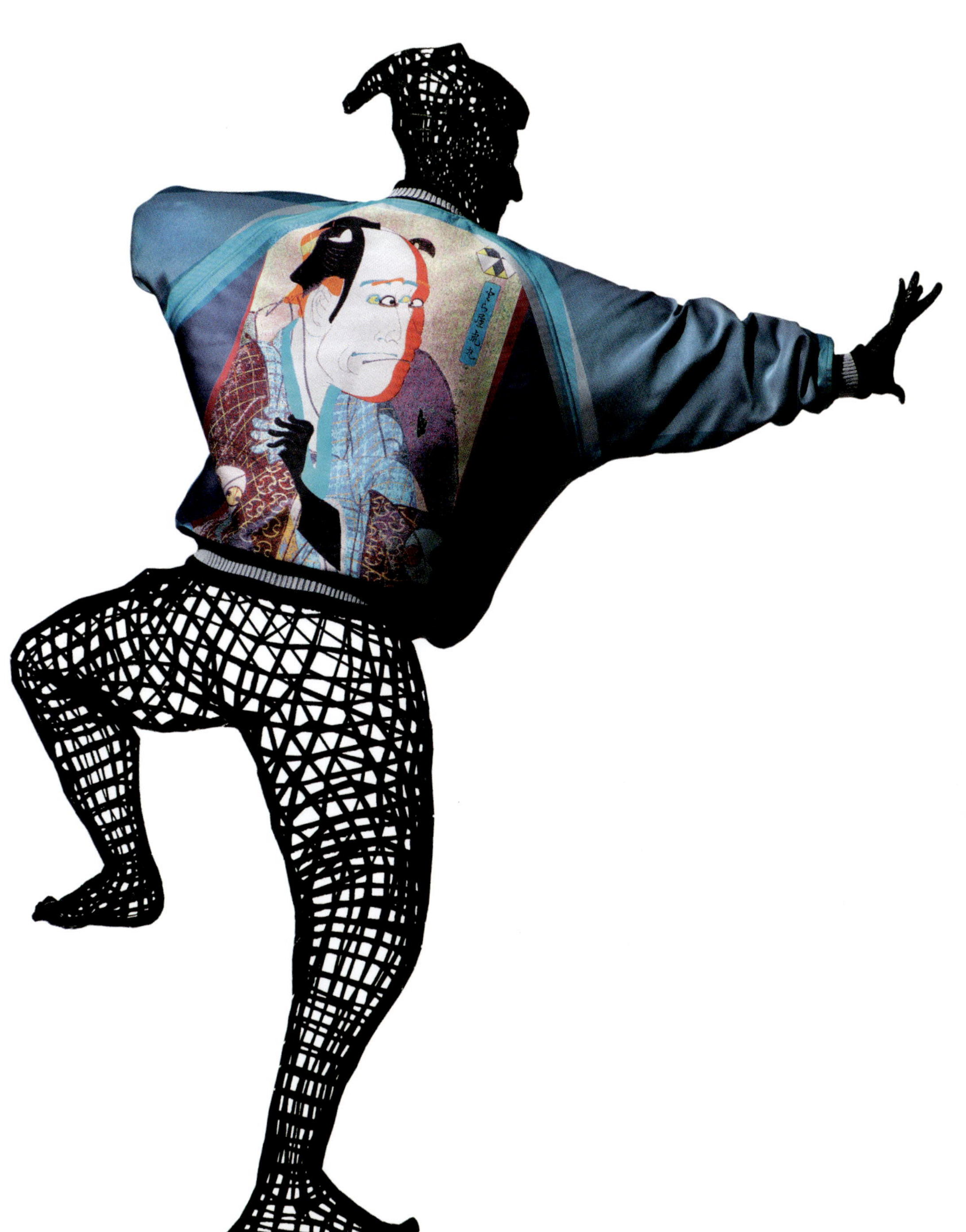

2021

IM MEN

Issey Miyake announced two new brands this year. The first was IM MEN, a collection of everyday clothes for men. It used the recycled materials and the mathematics of folding to investigate the structure clothes developed for 132 5. ISSEY MIYAKE and extend the potential of *A Piece of Cloth* to men's clothing. The items were created by a team of design engineers in the Reality Lab and feature simple shapes, lightweight materials, easy care, and general utility, together with a functional beauty in which even the neatness of the clothes' appearance when folded has been calculated and planned.

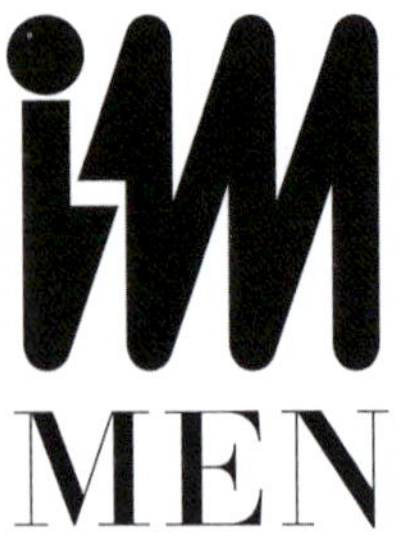

IM MEN brand logo
The brand logo uses the same "im" logo as the original im products. It was designed by Ikko Tanaka and valued by Miyake. Taku Sato created the "MEN" portion.

132 5. ISSEY MIYAKE vol. 3–4, 2021

132 5. ISSEY MIYAKE vol. 1–2, 2022

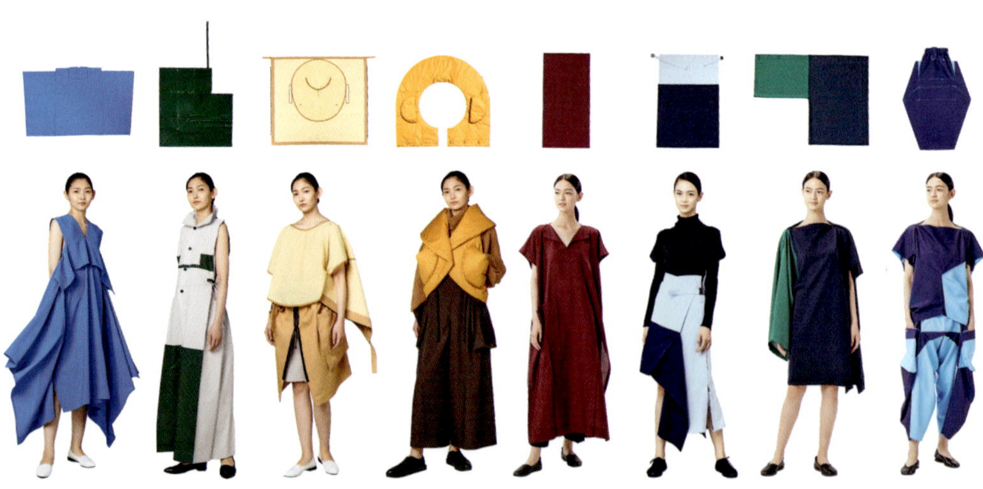

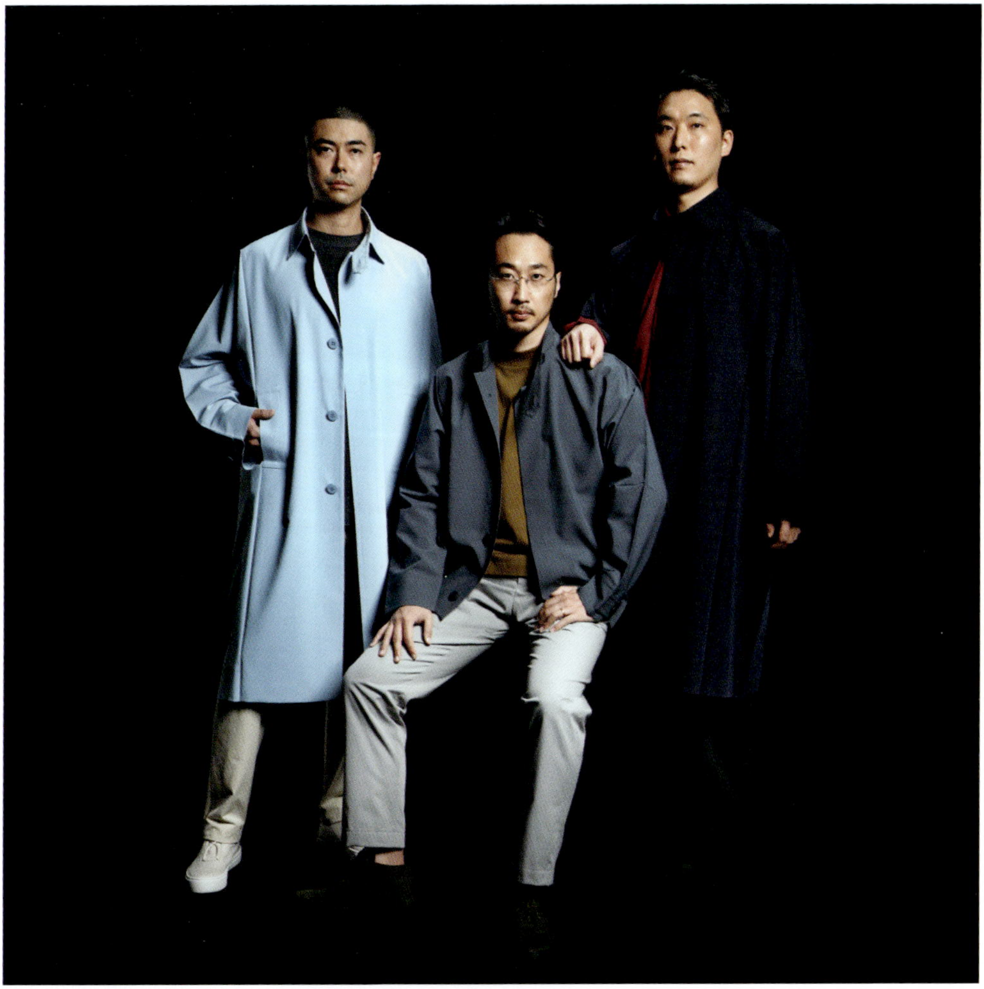

Above: *Flat* series consists of lightweight, wrinkle-resistant clothing created from new materials containing plant-derived polyester. While the designs are simple, it is about more than just simplicity. When folded along the lines, it is compact enough to store in a rain hood.
Flat coats and jacket, 2021 design/IM MEN Spring-Summer 2021 Collection
Photography: Kazumi Kurigami; worn by: Q Asaba, Kent Iitaka and Rei Ishii (Goo Choki Par: Design and art unit)

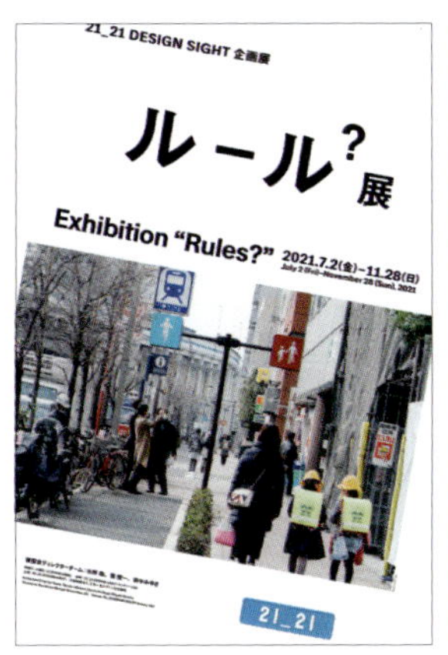

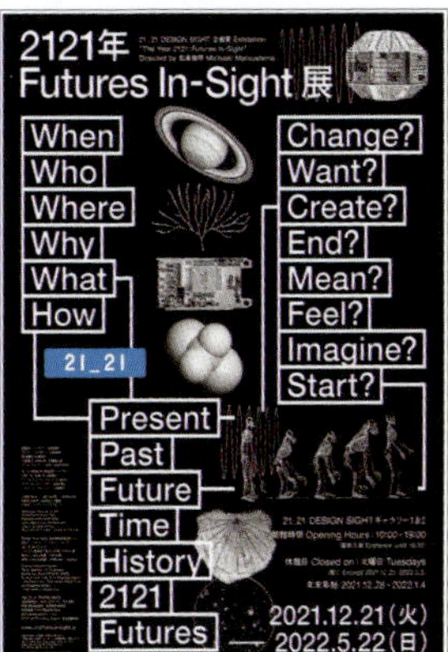

Left: 21_21 DESIGN SIGHT exhibition posters for *Rules?* and *The Year 2121: Futures In-Sight*

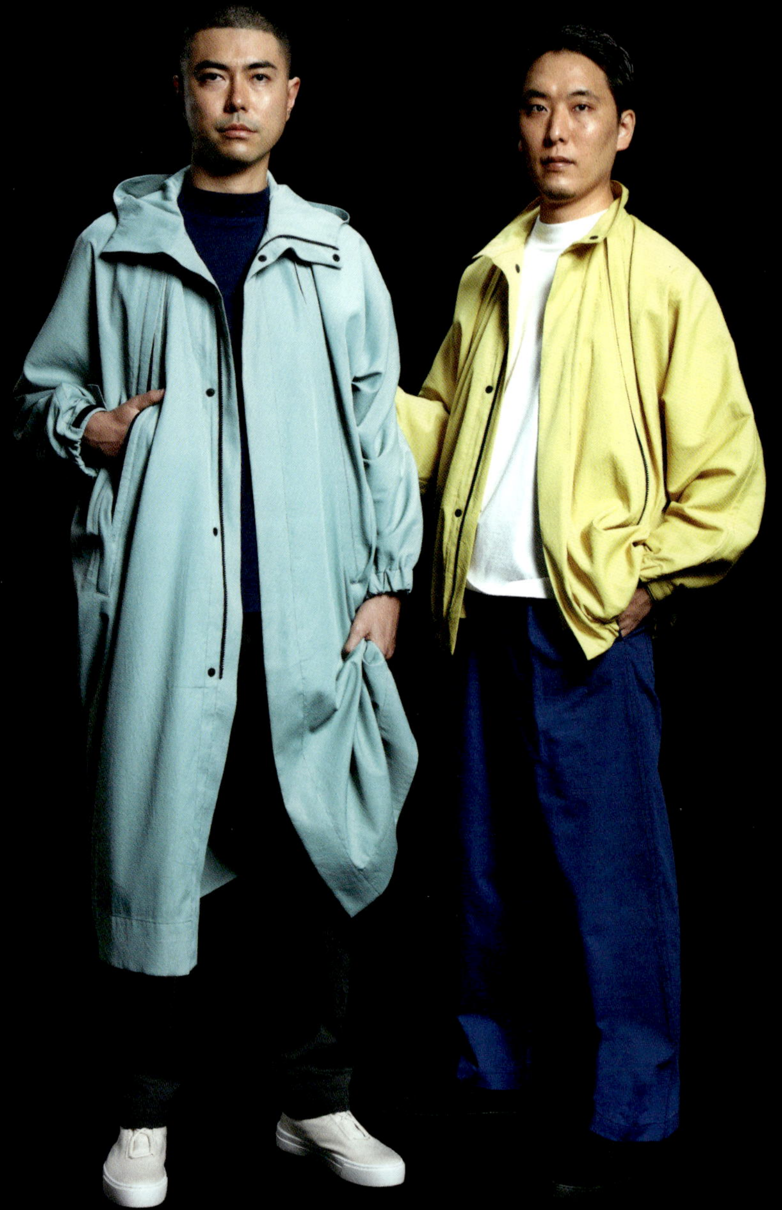

Convertible series exploits the functionality created by new lightweight, wrinkle-resistant materials containing plant-derived polyester. Internal straps in the coats and jackets allow them to hang off the shoulders so that the wearer has their hands free even when the coat or jacket is removed. A pocket in the back provides storage and can be used as a backpack. The pants have a hip pocket for storage, and turn into a sacoche when the strap is extended.
Convertible coat, jacket and pants, 2021 design/IM MEN Spring-Summer 2021 Collection
Photography: Kazumi Kurigami; worn by: Q Asaba and Rei Ishii (Goo Choki Par)

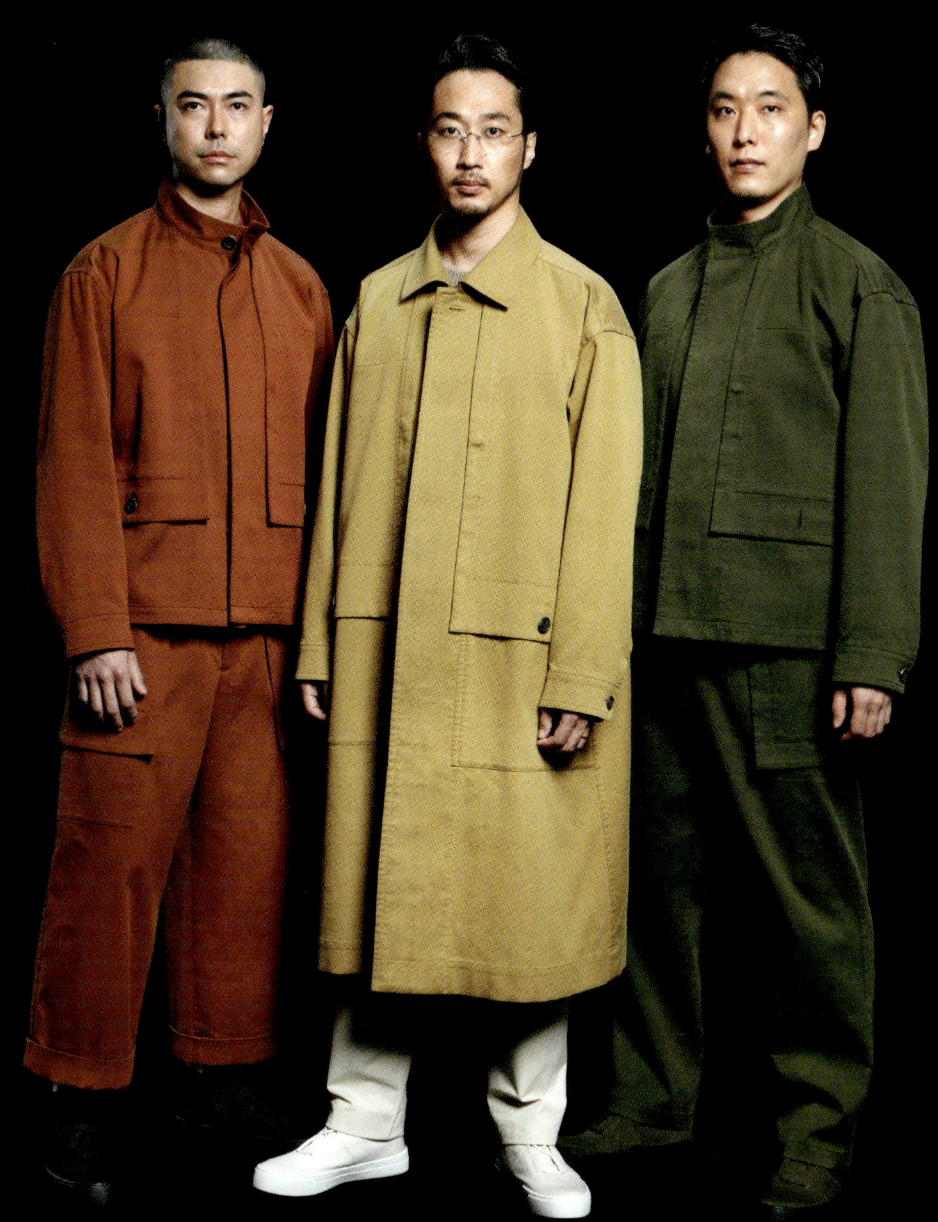

T/C river twill series uses recycled polyester for the
warp and cotton for the woof. Though thick, the textiles are lightweight, and a jacquard machine is used
to create different colors for the inside and outside.

T/C river twill coat and jackets, 2021 design/IM MEN
Spring-Summer 2021 Collection
Photography: Kazumi Kurigami; worn by: Q Asaba,
Kent Iitaka and Rei Ishii (Goo Choki Par)

A-POC ABLE ISSEY MIYAKE

The other brand announced this year was A-POC ABLE ISSEY MIYAKE. It represents an update of the A-POC design thinking, redesigning the basic A-POC manufacturing process to further evolve the communication that takes place between the creator and wearer. The brand combines the two elements of "product" and "project" (collaboration among different fields and industrial sectors) to develop multiple sub-formats, each with their own new approach to making things.

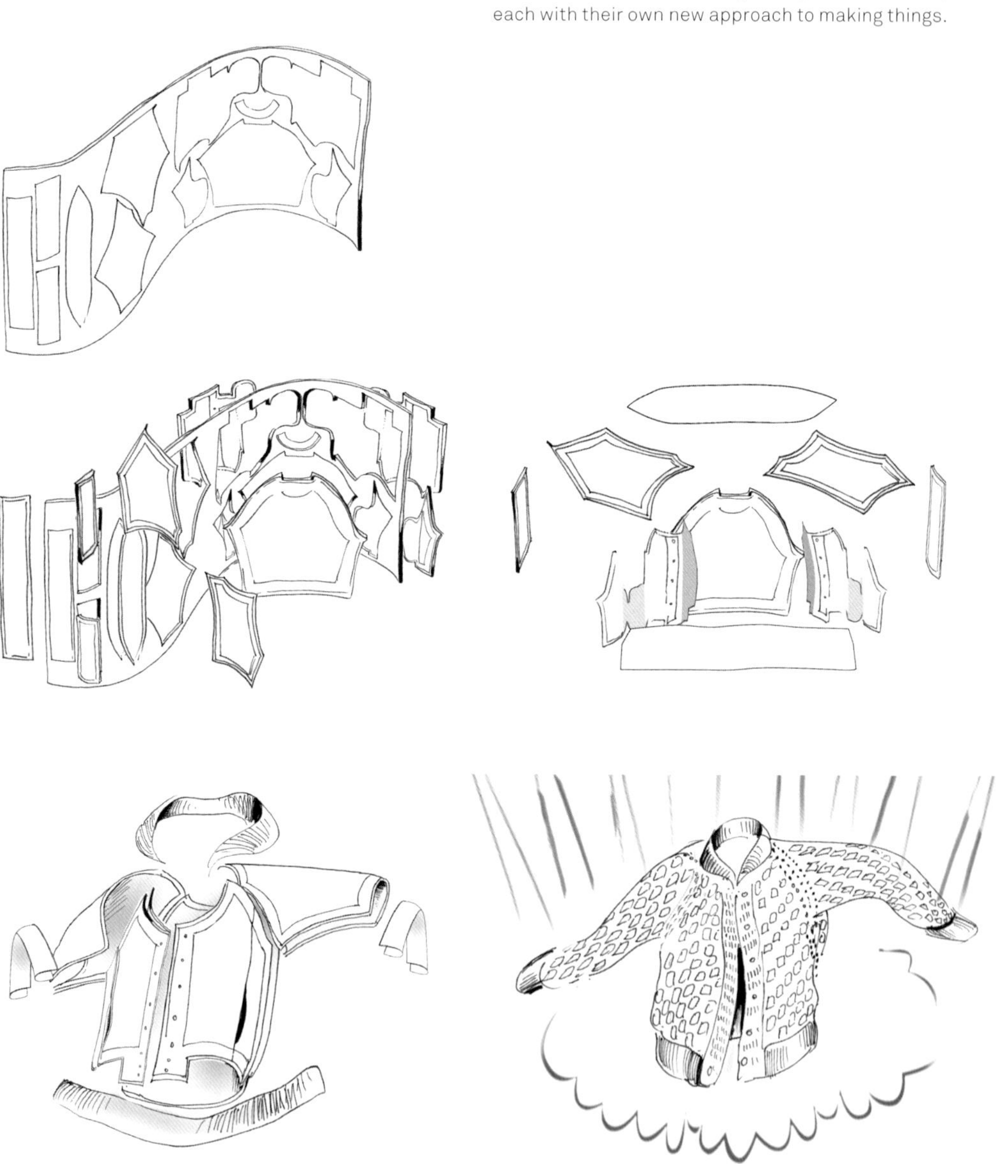

Type-O

Unisex blouson with three-dimensional, geometrical patterns manufactured using the Steam Stretch technique. The *Type O* series uses this technique to investigate a variety of pleat shapes. Threads that shrink under heat are woven with other threads, and then hot steam applied so that only specific threads within the piece of cloth contract. The shrinkage rate is controlled to create commercial products.
2021 design/A-POC ABLE ISSEY MIYAKE
Animation: Pascal Roulin (opposite)
Photography: Hiroshi Iwasaki (below)

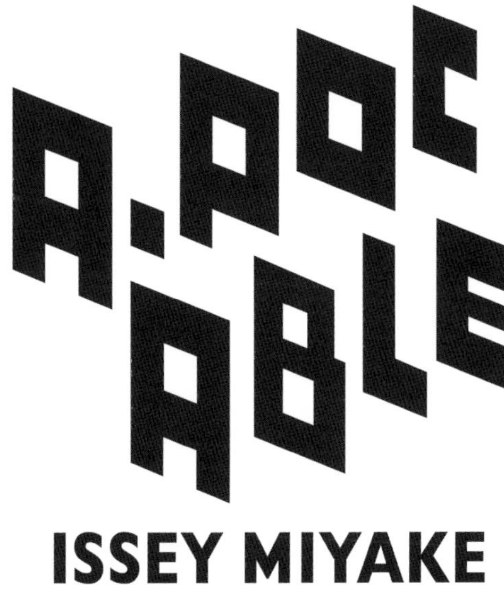

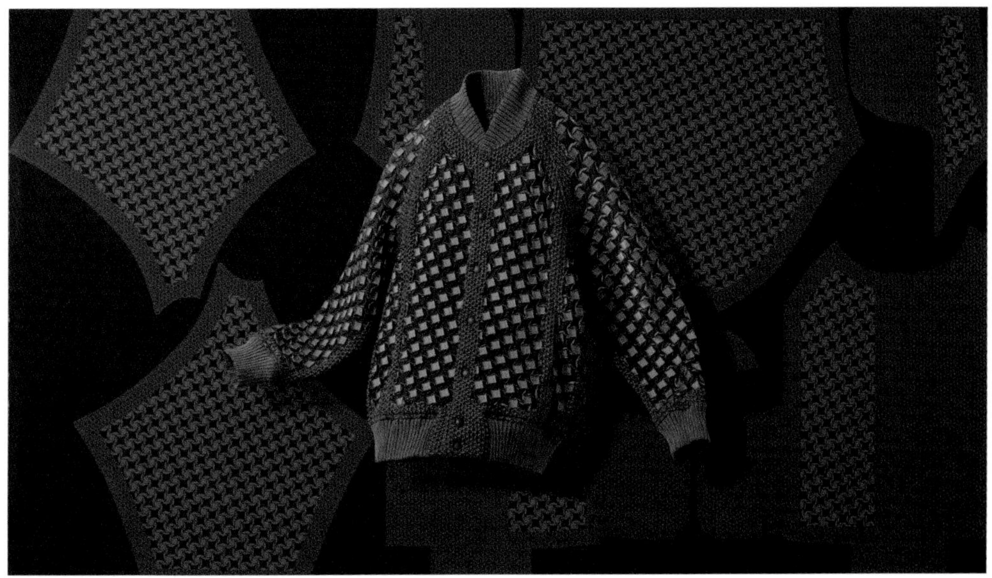

2022

Christo and Jeanne-Claude *"L'Arc de Triomphe, Wrapped"* exhibition

September 2021, this artwork wrapped Paris's Arc de Triomphe de l'Étoile in cloth for 16 days. The project was first conceived by contemporary artists Christo and Jeanne-Claude in 1961, but was only achieved after the deaths of Jeanne-Claude in 2009 and Christo and 2020. Issey Miyake enjoyed a long, close friendship with the two and decided to create an exhibition during the project. Plans began for the exhibition's implementation in the winter of 2021, with direction by Pascal Roulin, the video director. It was a powerful exhibition in which the audience was able to experience, through realistic video and dynamic spatial design, the process from conception to execution of *L'Arc de Triomphe, Wrapped.*

June 13–February 12, 2023: 21_21 DESIGN SIGHT Exhibition direction: Pascal Roulin; graphic design: Shingo Noma; space design: Takashi Nakahara; technical direction: Yutaka Endo (LUFTZUG)

Opposite: *Christo and Jeanne-Claude "L'Arc de Triomphe, Wrapped"* poster
Design: Shingo Noma; photography: Wolfgang Volz, © 2021 Christo and Jeanne-Claude Foundation

132 5. ISSEY MIYAKE vol. 3–4, 2022   132 5. ISSEY MIYAKE vol. 1–2, 2023

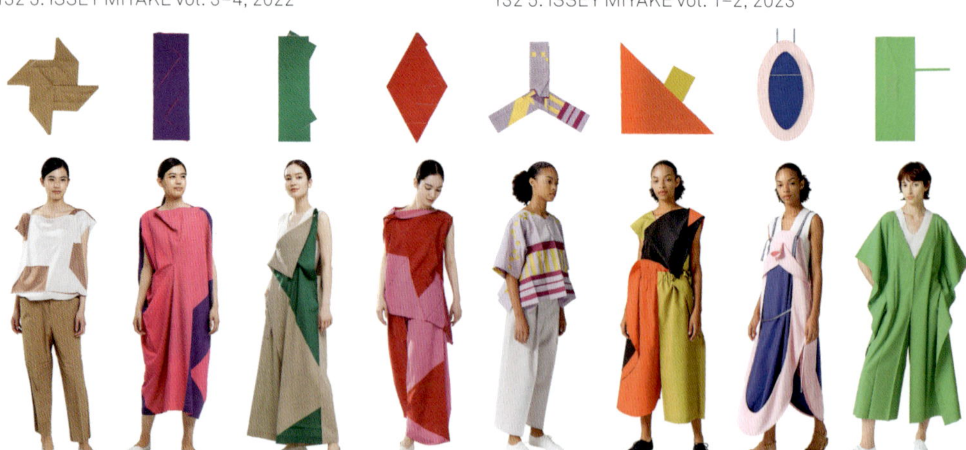

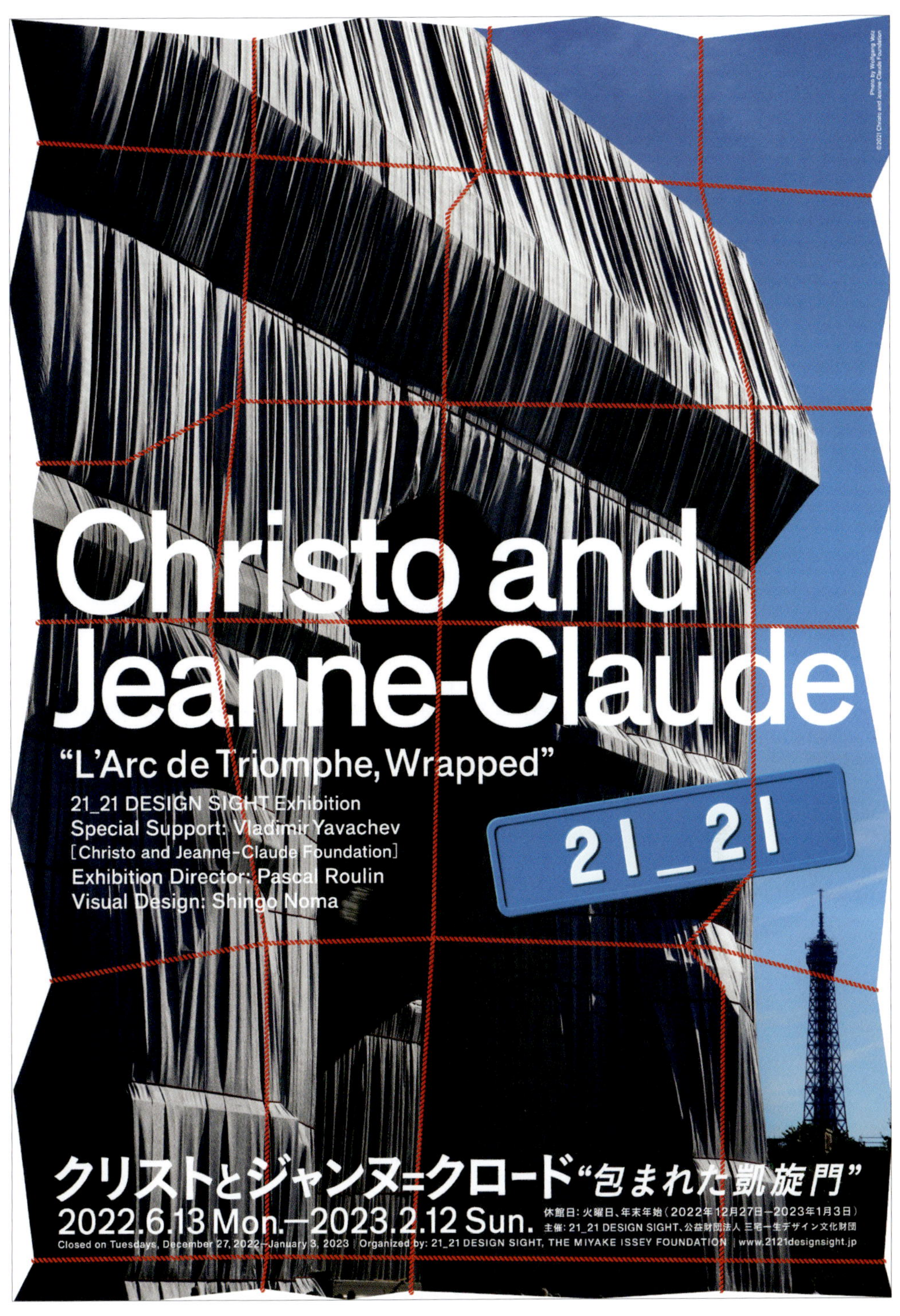
Photo by Wolfgang Volz
©2021 Christo and Jeanne-Claude Foundation

Christo and Jeanne-Claude
"L'Arc de Triomphe, Wrapped"
21_21 DESIGN SIGHT Exhibition
Special Support: Vladimir Yavachev
[Christo and Jeanne-Claude Foundation]
Exhibition Director: Pascal Roulin
Visual Design: Shingo Noma

21_21

クリストとジャンヌ=クロード "包まれた凱旋門"
2022.6.13 Mon.—2023.2.12 Sun.
休館日：火曜日、年末年始（2022年12月27日—2023年1月3日）
主催：21_21 DESIGN SIGHT、公益財団法人 三宅一生デザイン文化財団
Closed on Tuesdays, December 27, 2022—January 3, 2023　Organized by: 21_21 DESIGN SIGHT, THE MIYAKE ISSEY FOUNDATION　www.2121designsight.jp

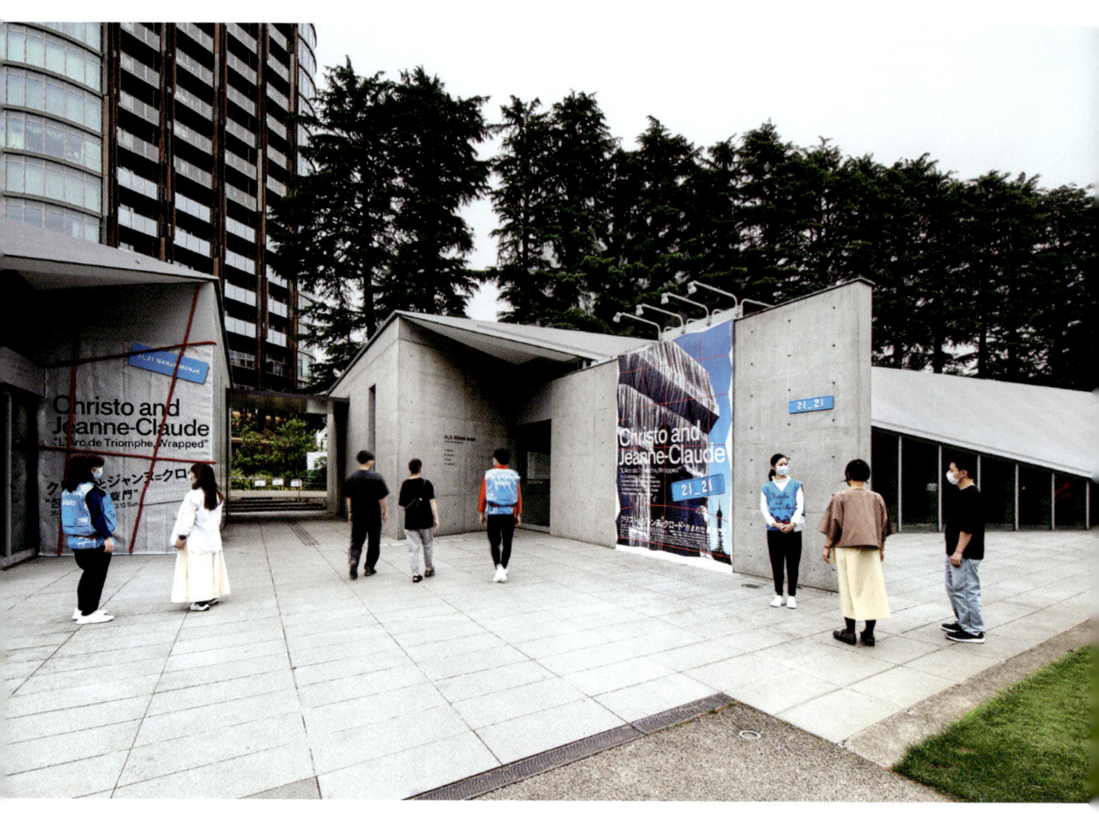

pp. 406–415: Installation view of **Christo and Jeanne-Claude "L'Arc de Triomphe, Wrapped"**
Photography: Masaya Yoshimura

21_21 DESIGN SIGHT staff wearing the same blue vests and uniforms as the guides for *L'Arc de Triomphe, Wrapped*. The design was by Miyake Design Studio.

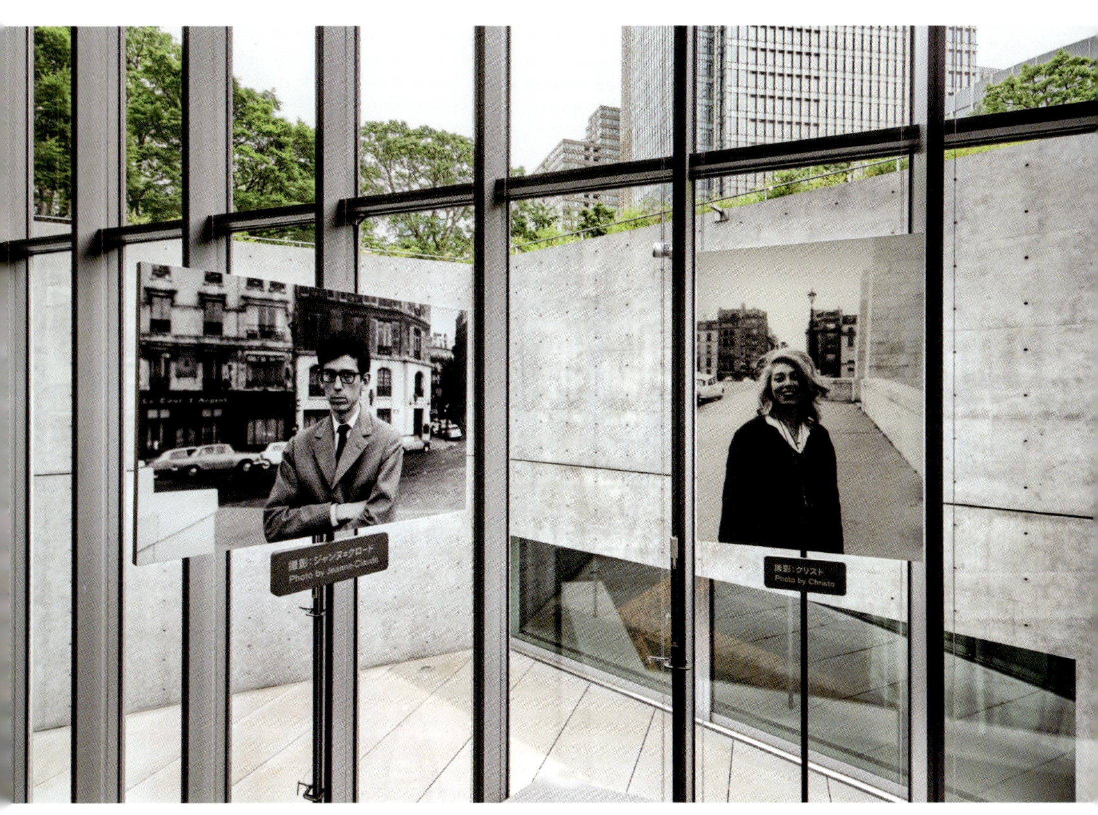

Portraits of young Christo and Jeanne-Claude as
photographed by each other were displayed along
the staircase leading to the hall.

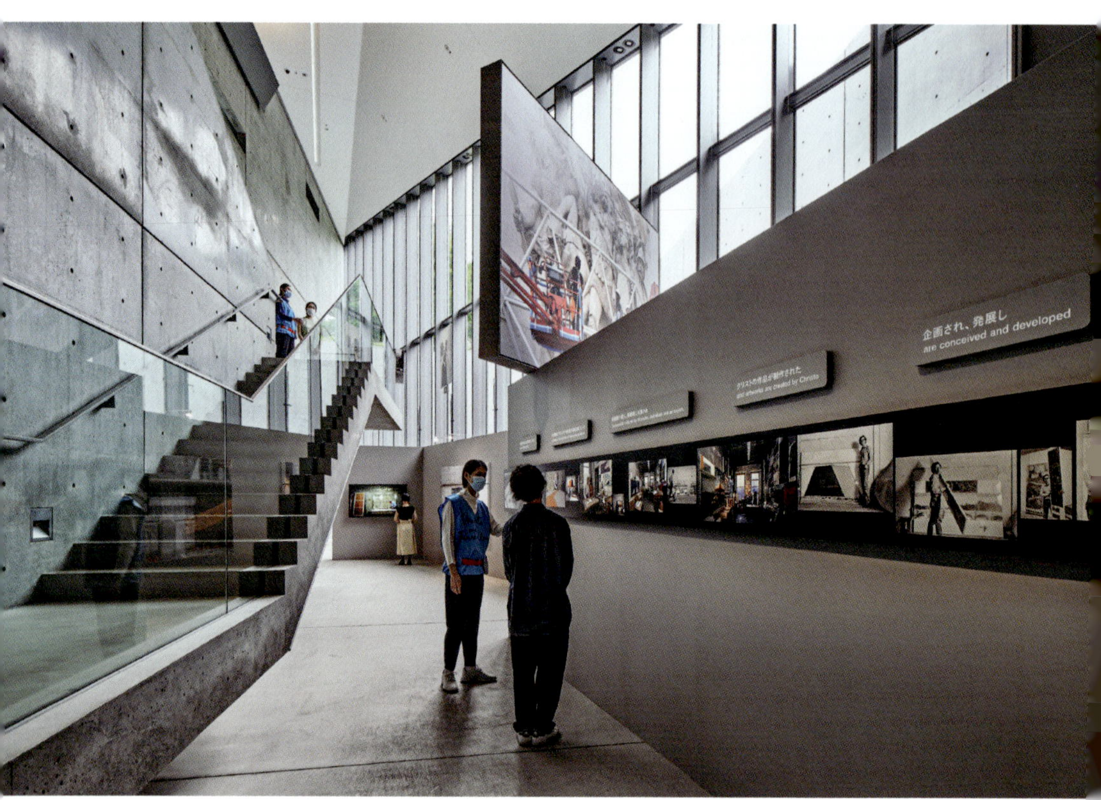

The underground lobby highlighted the activities
and works of Christo and Jeanne-Claude through
photographs, drawings, and videos.

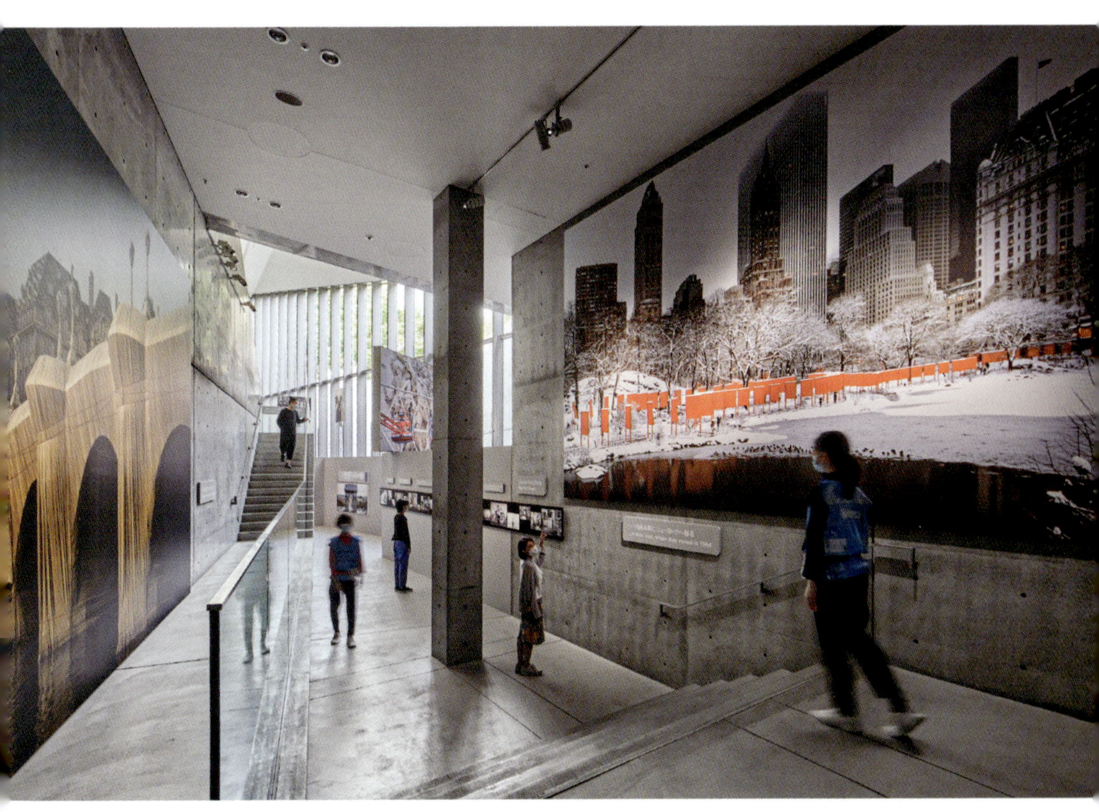

On the right, photographs of *The Gates, Central Park,
New York, 1979–2005*; on the left, *The Pont Neuf
Wrapped, Paris, 1975–85*.

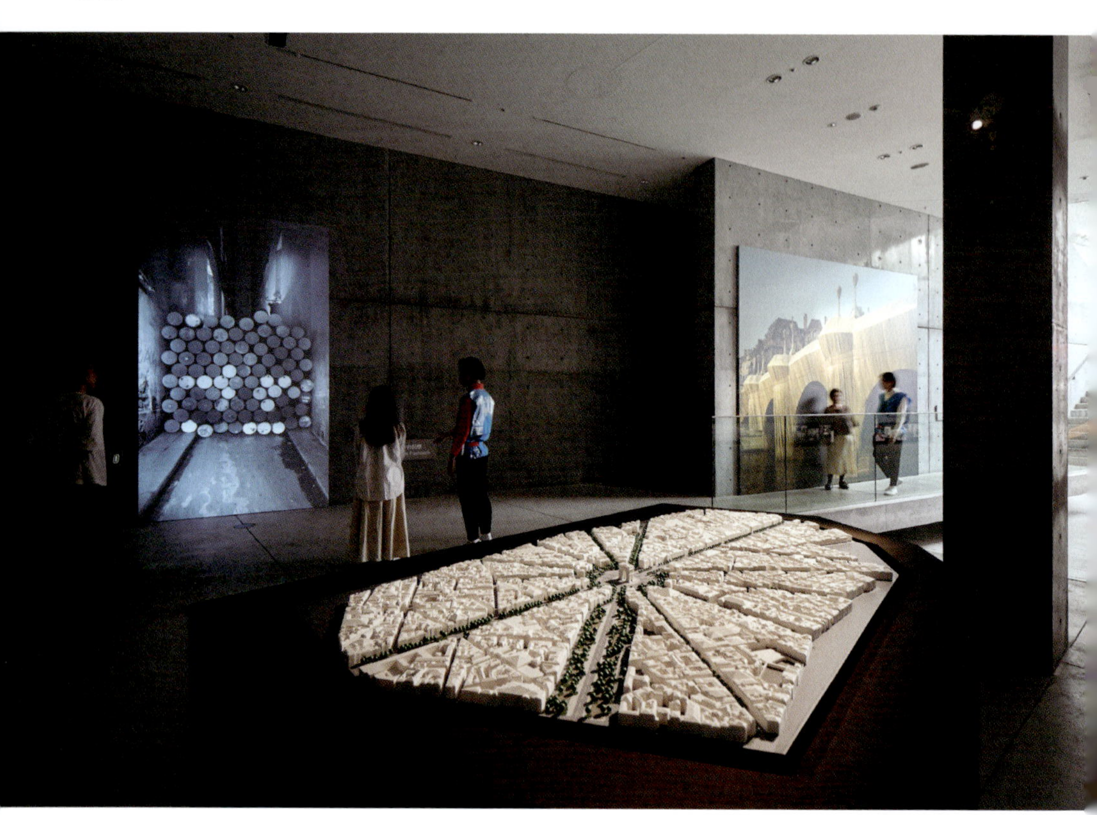

1/1000 scale model of the Arc de Triomphe
and the surrounding area on display in the
underground lobby.

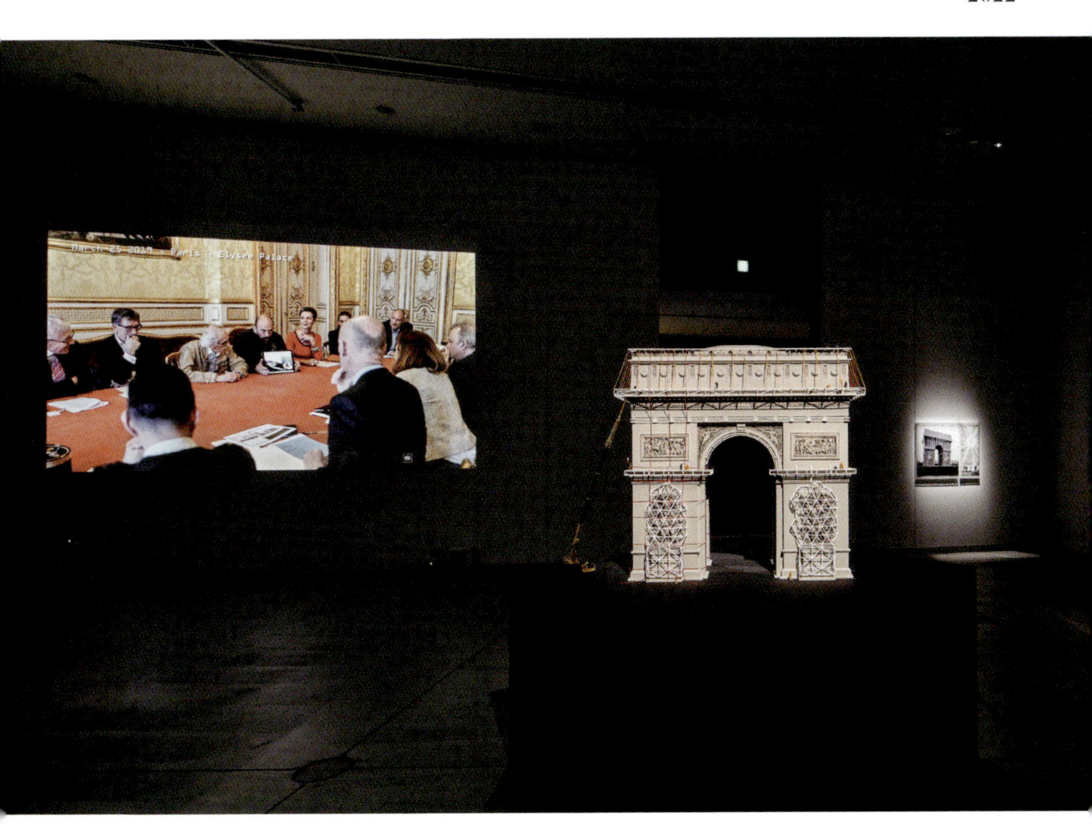

1/50 scale model of the
Arc de Triomphe in Gallery 1.

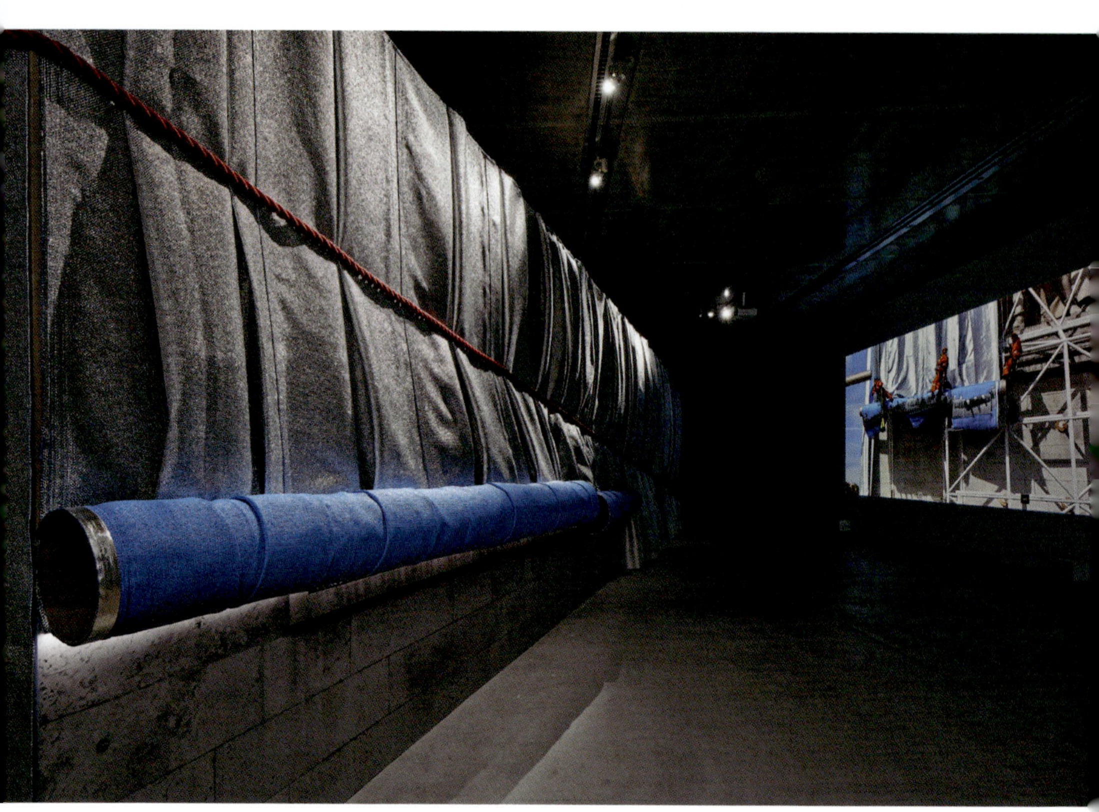

Installation in Gallery 2. Original fabric and ropes
used for *L'Arc de Triomphe, Wrapped.*

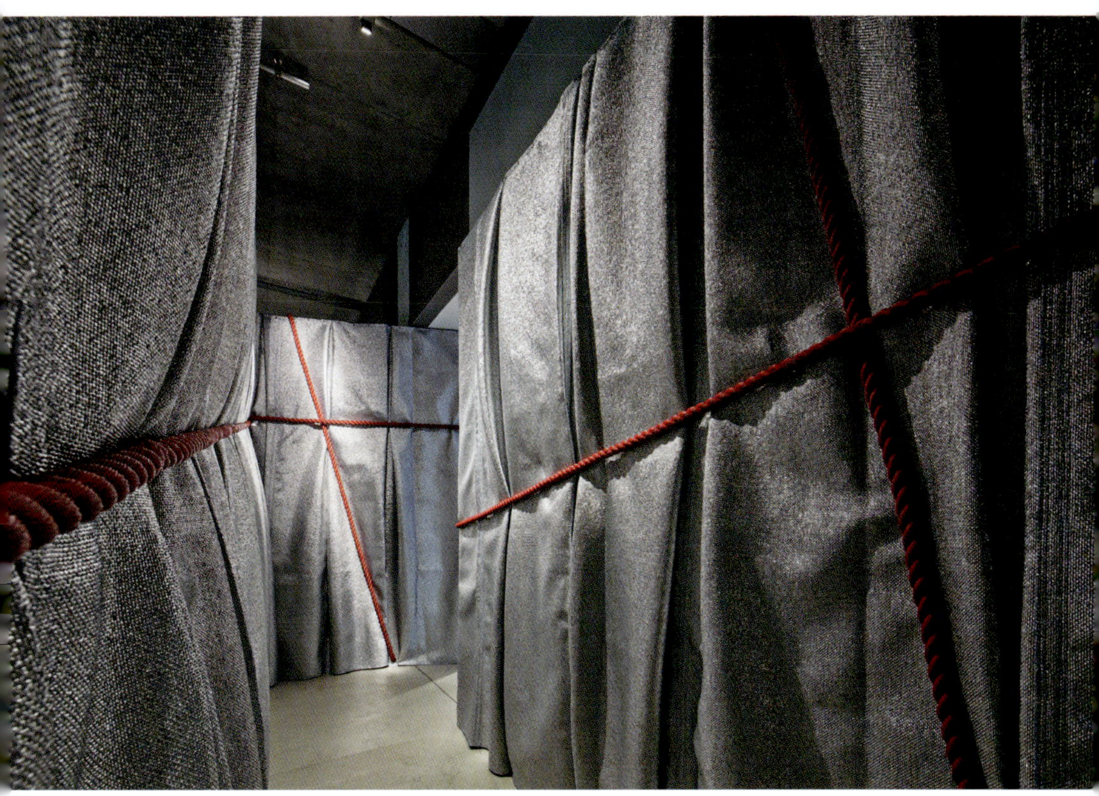

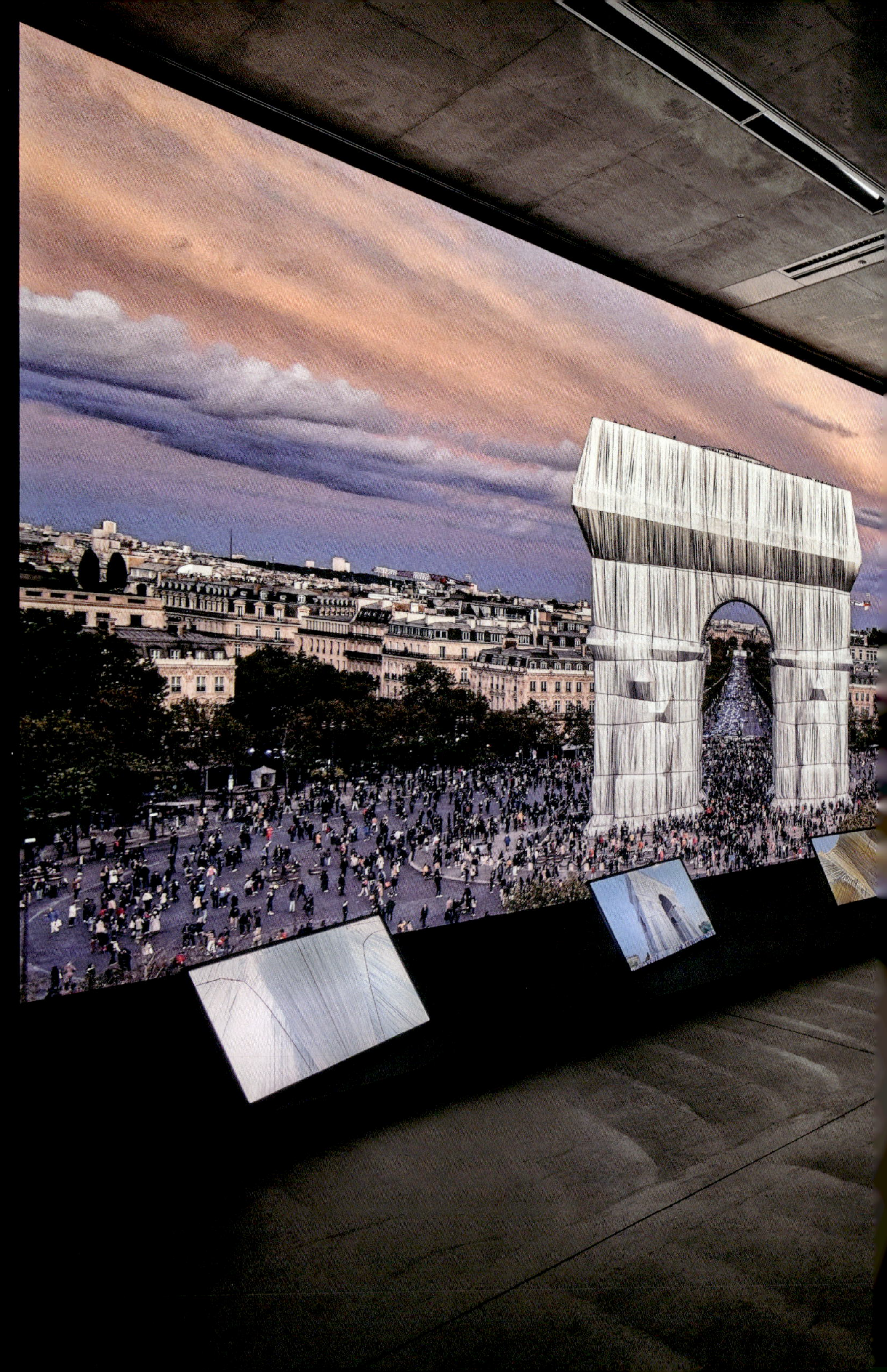

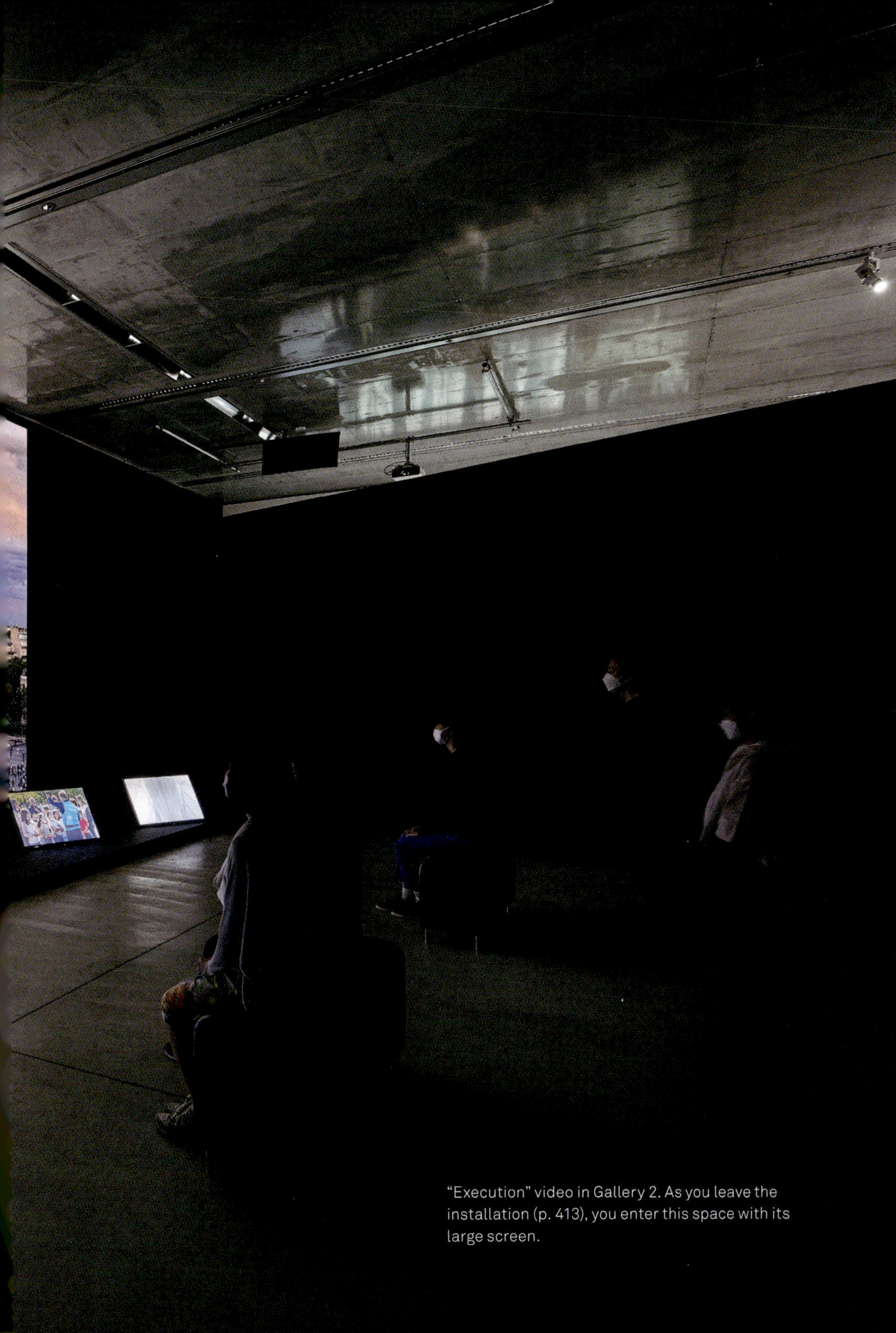

"Execution" video in Gallery 2. As you leave the
installation (p. 413), you enter this space with its
large screen.

**Christo and Jeanne-Claude with Issey Miyake
at The National Art Center, Tokyo, 2007**
Venue for a lecture on *Christo and Jeanne-Claude:
Two Works in Progress* planned and produced by
Issey Miyake.
Photography: Shigeo Anzaï

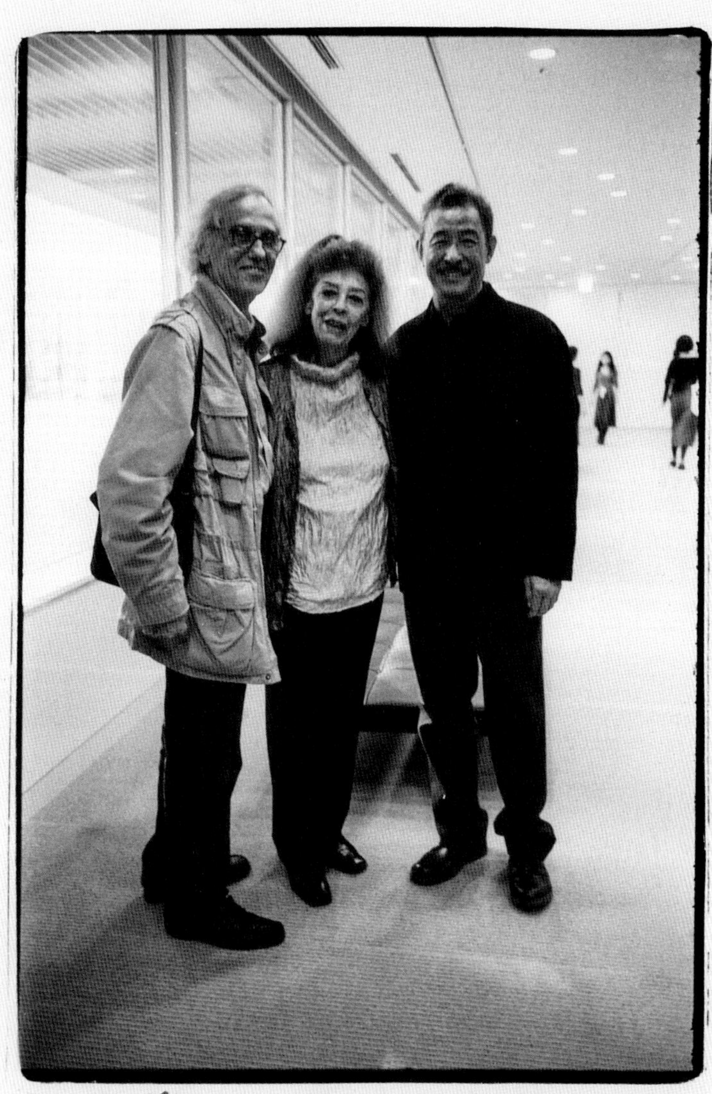
Nov, 8th '07 National Art center
Tokyo

IKKO TANAKA ISSEY MIYAKE No. 6 creation began during the Covid-19 pandemic. Wanting to inspire hope, Miyake turned to rings of flowers as his motif to create a collection of graphic artworks. *Purple Iris* on this page and *Red and White Camellia* on the next are the originals for the ceramic panel murals installed in the Arrivals Lobby at Narita Airport, and the structures of the Tanaka works were incorporated into the clothing.

Purple Iris dress
2023 design/IKKO TANAKA ISSEY MIYAKE No. 6
Photography: Henry Leutwyler

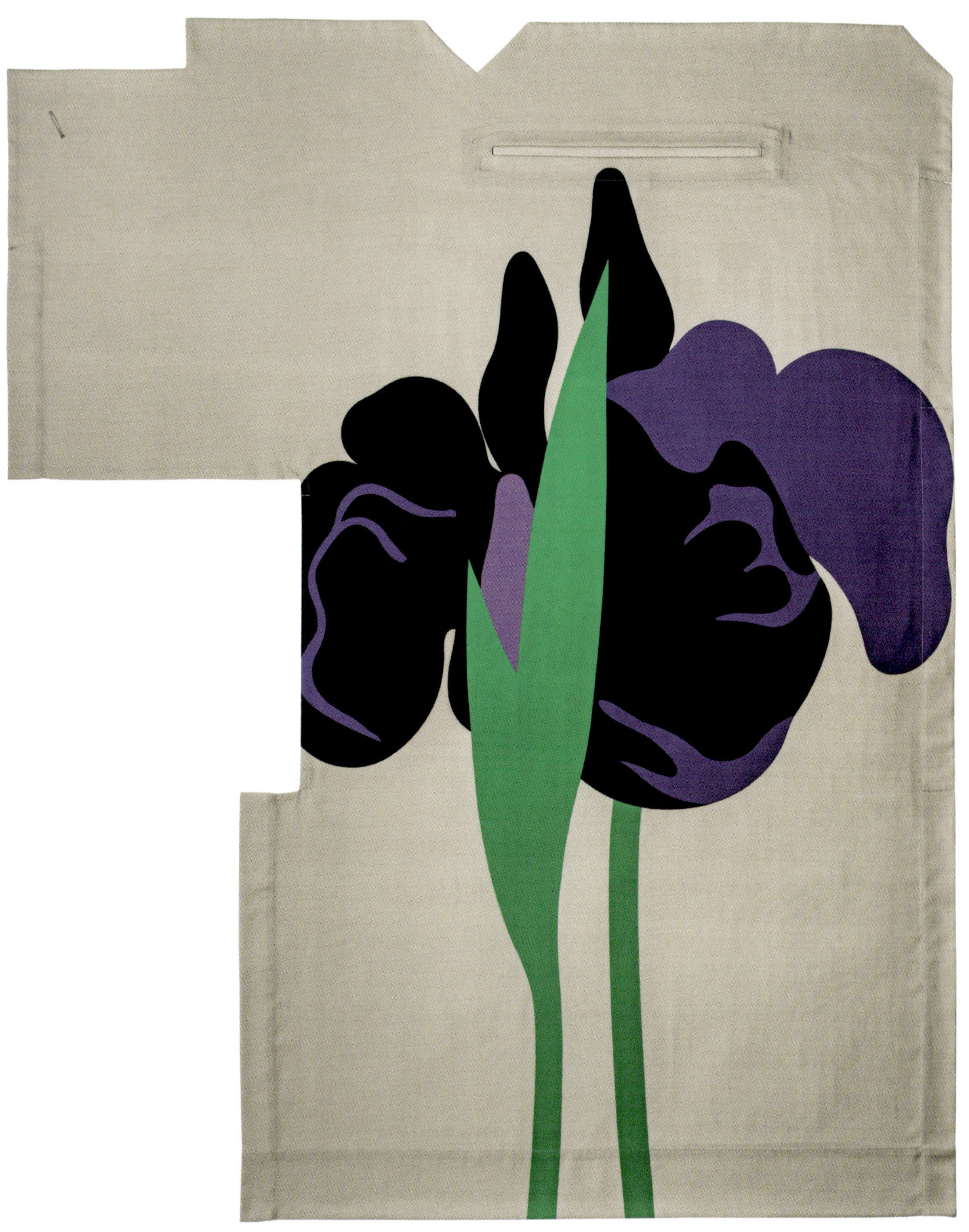

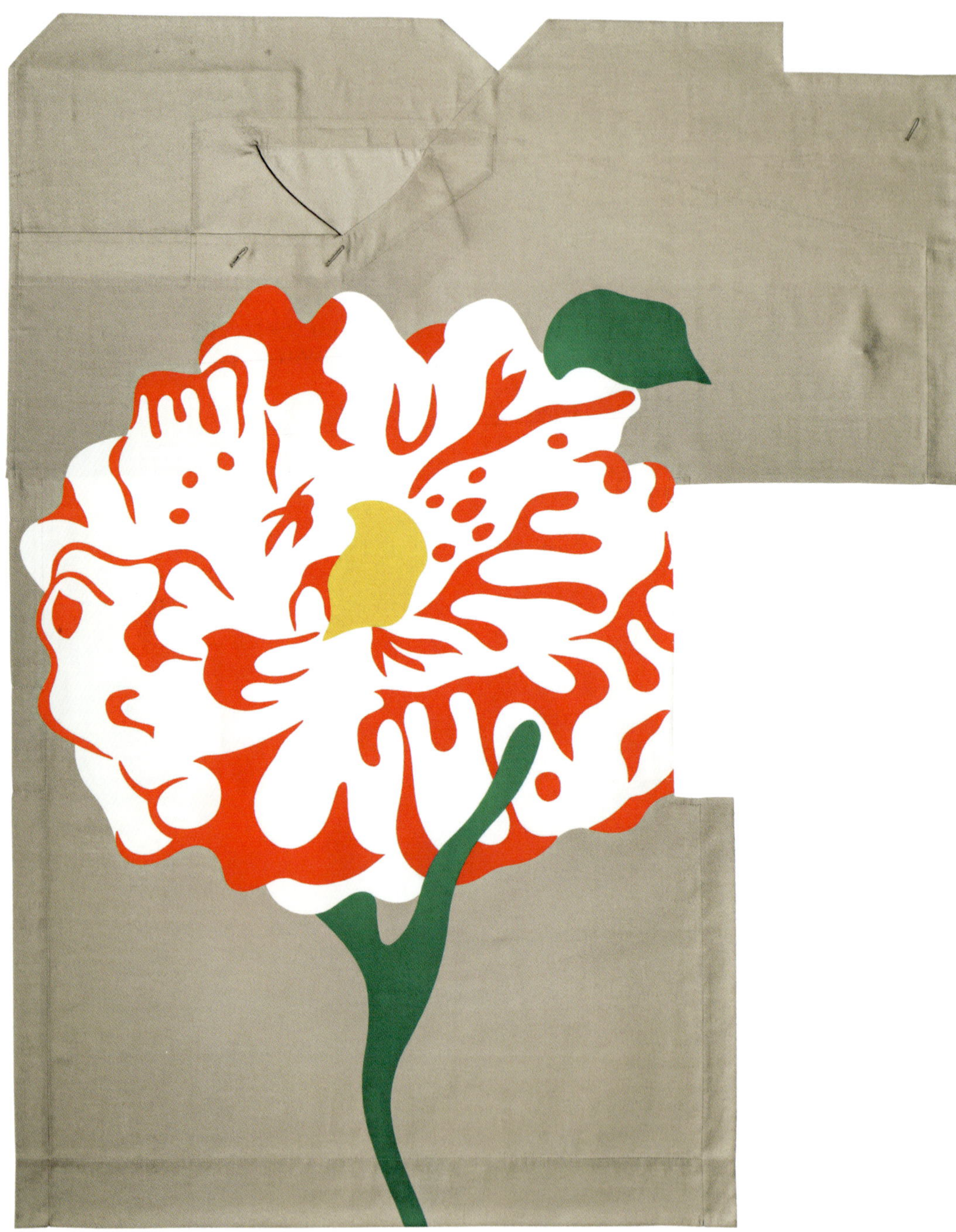

Red and White Camellia long shirt
2023 design / IKKO TANAKA ISSEY MIYAKE No. 6
Photography: Henry Leutwyler

CHRONOLOGY OF EXHIBITIONS AND PUBLICATIONS

SOLO EXHIBITIONS

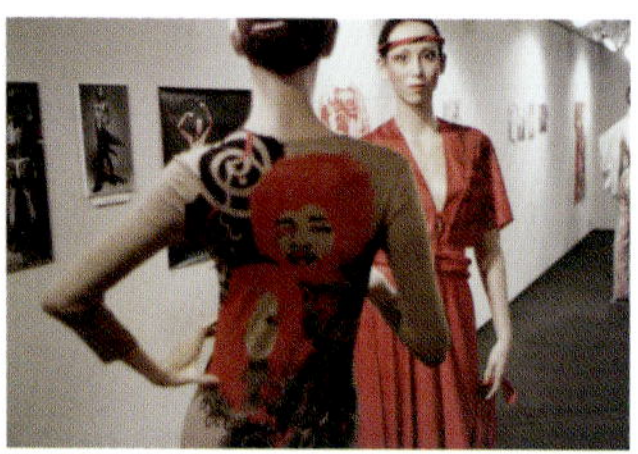

1976
Dec. 2, *One Day One Show – Issey Miyake*,
Tokyo Designer's Space

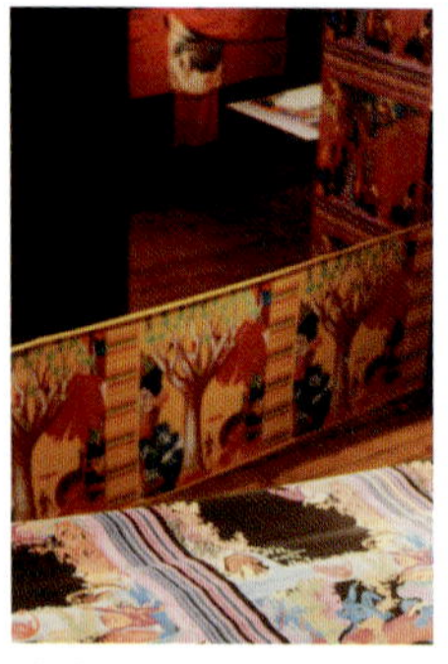

1979
Nov. 29–Feb. 24, 1980, *Les Tissus Imprimés d'Issey Miyake*, Musée de l'Impression sur Étoffes, Mulhouse

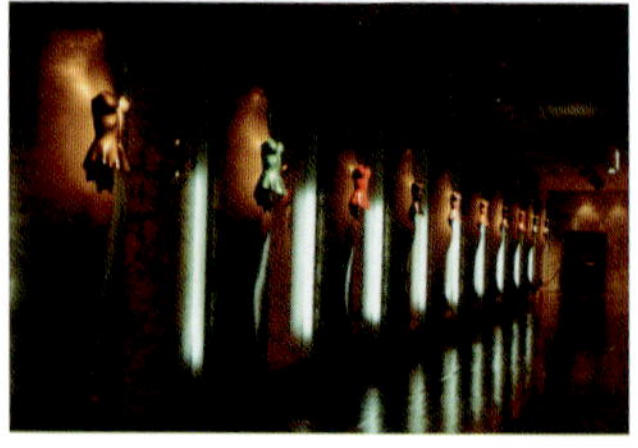

1983
May 1–22, *Issey Miyake Spectacle: Bodyworks*,
Laforet Museum Iigura 800/500, Tokyo

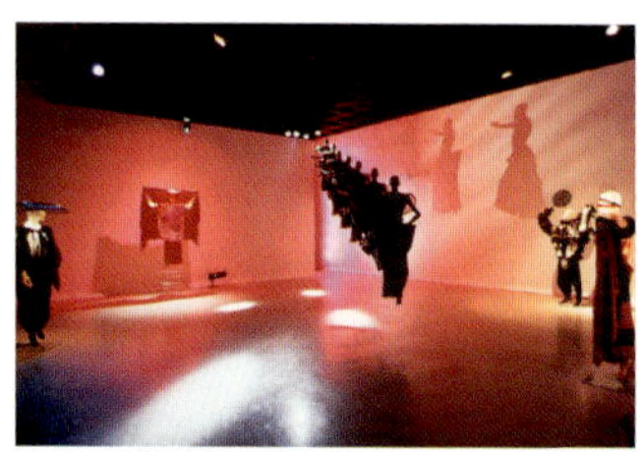

1983
Jun. 15–Jul. 17, *Issey Miyake Spectacle: Bodyworks*, Otis Art Institute of Parsons School of Design, Los Angeles
Photo: Zarko Kalmic

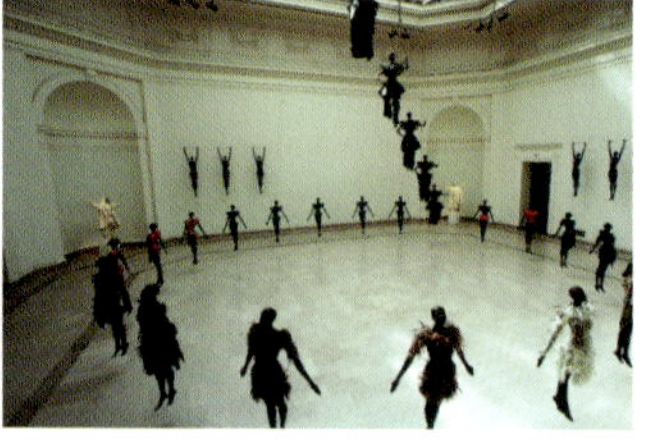

1983
Sep. 20–Nov. 20, *Issey Miyake Spectacle: Bodyworks*, San Francisco Museum of Modern Art
Photo: Mitsumasa Fujitsuka

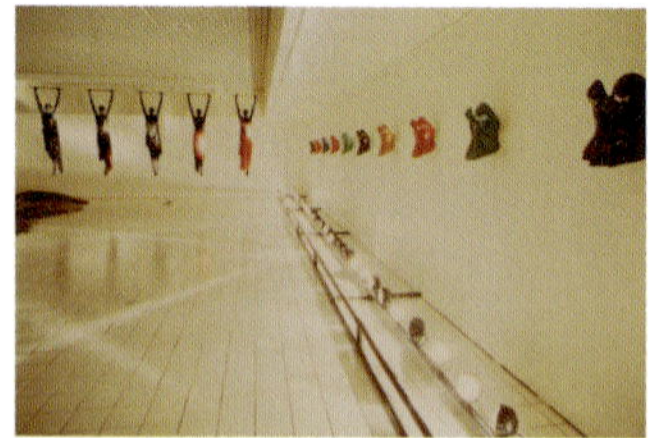

1985
Feb. 27–Apr. 9, *Issey Miyake Bodyworks: Fashion without Taboos*, Boilerhouse Project, Victoria and Albert Museum, London

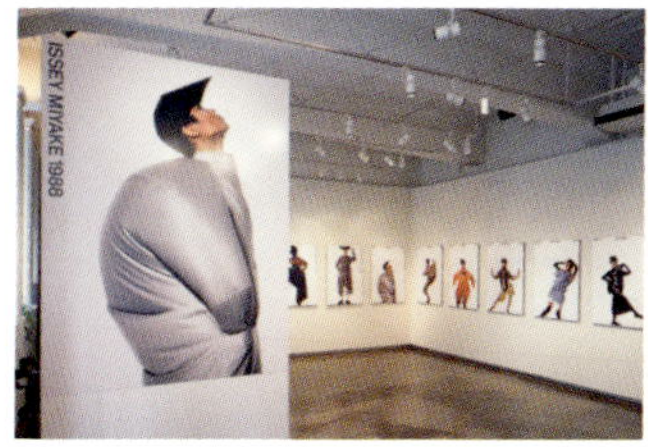

1988

Jun. 6–25, *i.i.i. at ggg Issey Miyake Posters*,
Ginza Graphic Gallery, Tokyo
Photo: Shigeyuki Morishita

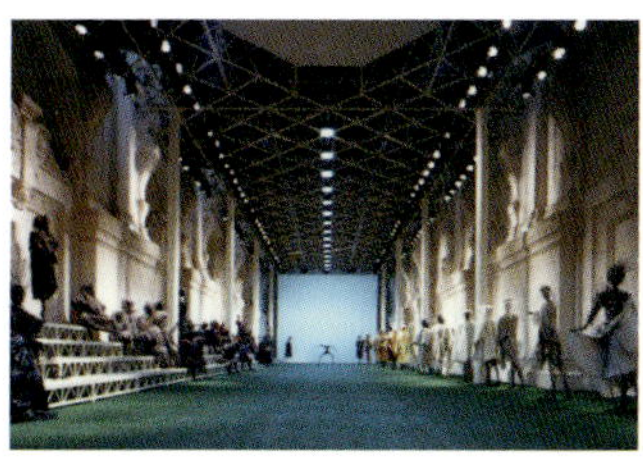

1988

Oct. 5–Dec. 31, *Issey Miyake A–ŪN*,
Musée des Arts Décoratifs, Paris
Photo: Shigeo Anzaï

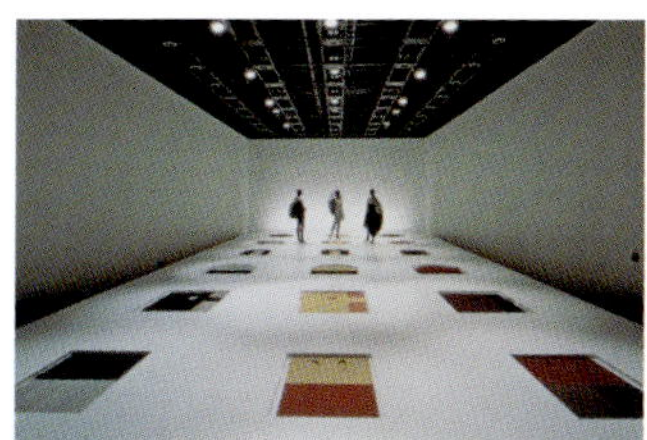

1990

Sep. 1–30, *Issey Miyake Pleats Please*,
Touko Museum of Contemporary Art, Tokyo
Photo: Mitsumasa Fujitsuka

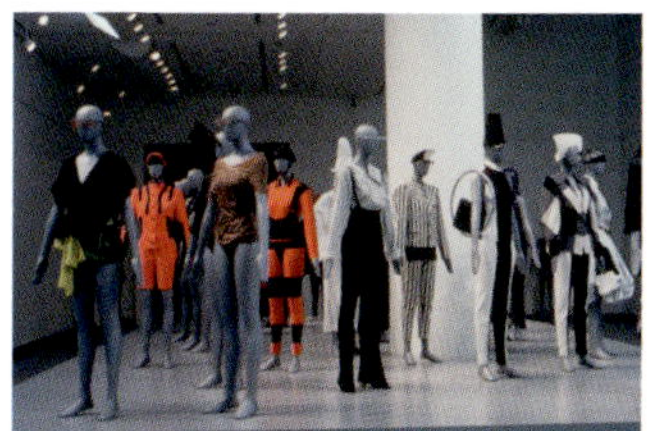

1990

Nov. 3–Jan. 15, 1991, *Issey Miyake: TEN SEN MEN*,
Hiroshima City Museum of Contemporary Art
(on the occasion of the 1st Hiroshima Art Prize)
Photo: Mitsumasa Fujitsuka

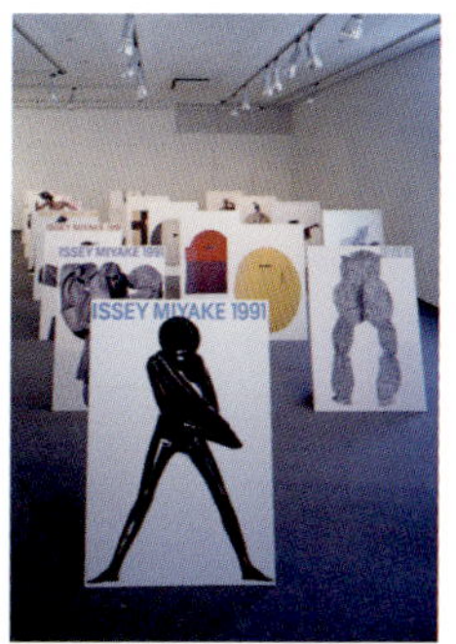

1992

May 19–23, *Issey Miyake Poster Exhibition*,
Tokyo Designer's Space, AXIS, Tokyo

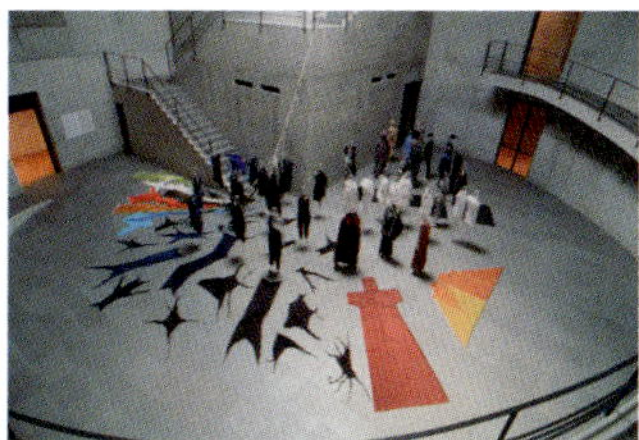

1992

Jul. 11–Nov. 15, *Issey Miyake Twist*, Naoshima
Contemporary Art Museum, Kagawa Prefecture
Photo: Mitsumasa Fujitsuka

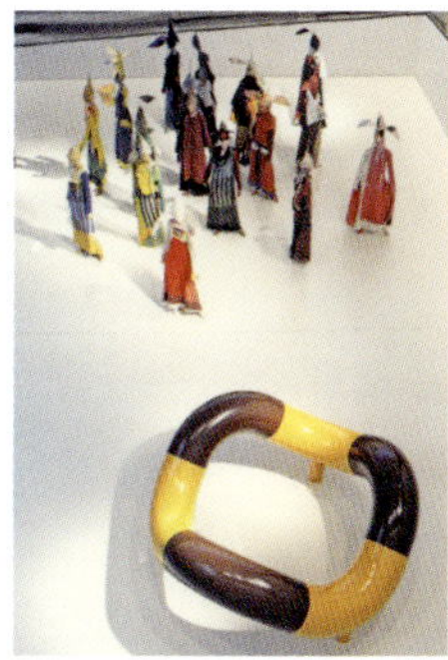

1997

Jun. 22–Aug. 31, *Isamu Noguchi and Issey Miyake:
Arizona*, Marugame Genichiro-Inokuma Museum of
Contemporary Art, Kagawa Prefecture
Photo: Shigeo Anzaï

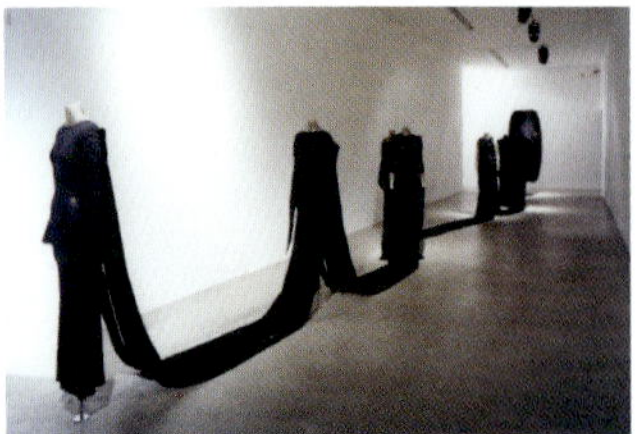

1998

Oct. 13–Feb. 28, 1999, *Issey Miyake Making Things*,
Fondation Cartier pour l'art contemporain, Paris
Photo: Yasuaki Yoshinaga

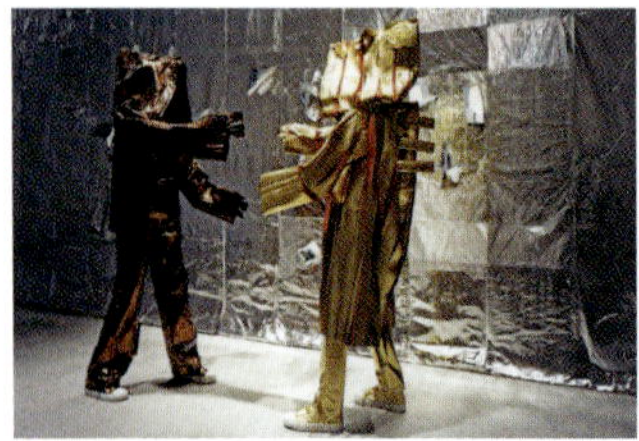

1999

Nov. 13–Feb. 29, 2000, *Issey Miyake Making Things*,
Ace Gallery, New York
Photo: Yasuaki Yoshinaga

1999

Dec. 24–28, *Irving Penn Regards the Work of
Issey Miyake*, Ginza Graphic Gallery, Tokyo

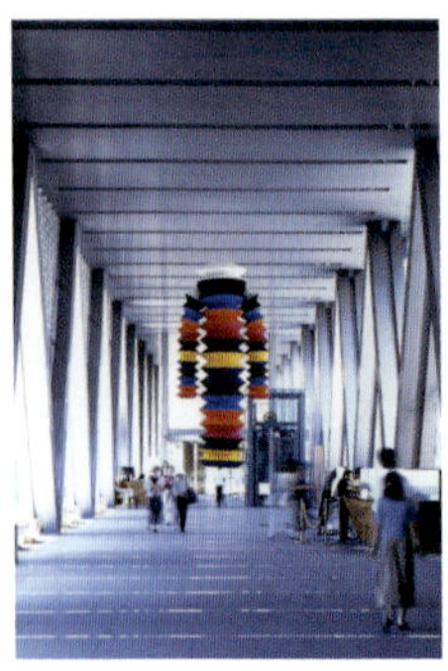

2000

Apr. 29–Aug. 20, *Issey Miyake Making Things*,
Museum of Contemporary Art, Tokyo
Photo: Shigeo Anzaï

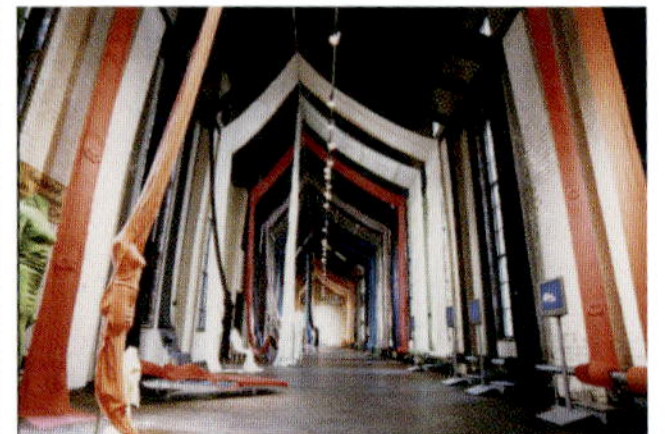

2001

Jun. 1–Jul. 1, *A-POC Making: Issey Miyake & Dai Fujiwara*,
Vitra Design Museum, Berlin
Photo: Yasuaki Yoshinaga

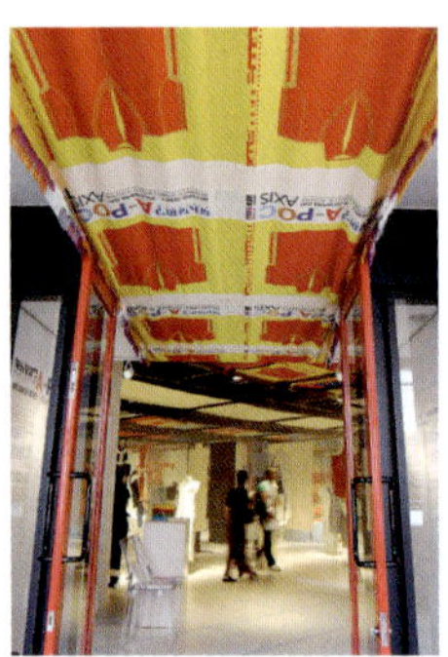

2003

Sep. 10–Oct. 5, *Nannano? A-POC Miyake Issey + Fujiwara
Dai*, AXIS Gallery, Tokyo
Photo: Yasuaki Yoshinaga

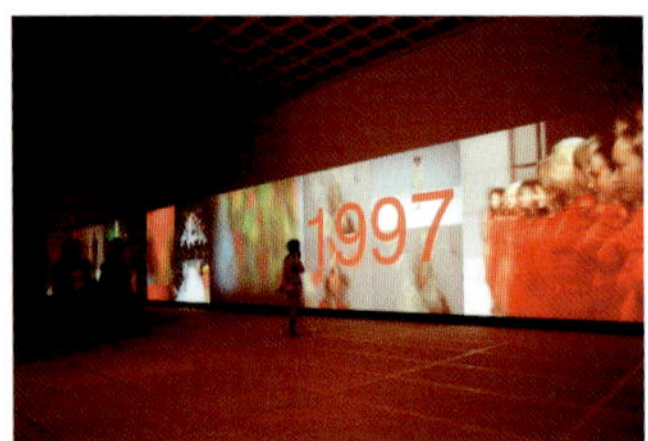

2005

Jul. 16–Sep. 11, *Issey Miyake Paris Collections 1977–1999:
Invitations by Tadanori Yokoo*, The Museum of Modern
Art, Toyama
Photo: Tadahisa Sakurai

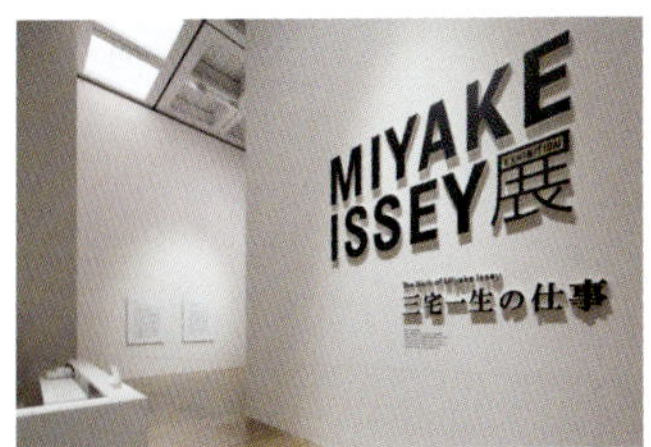

2016
Mar. 16–Jun. 13, *Miyake Issey Exhibition: The Work of Miyake Issey*, The National Art Center, Tokyo
Photo: Masaya Yoshimura

PARTICIPATED IN EXHIBITIONS

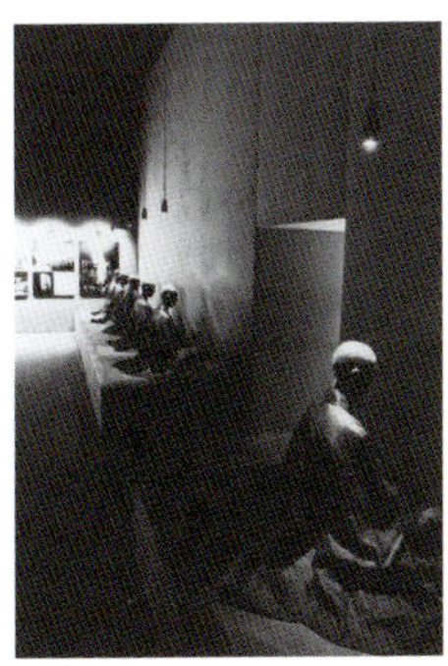

1978
Oct. 11–Dec. 11, *MA Espace-Temps du Japon*, Musée des Arts Décoratifs, Paris
Photo: Syuji Yamada

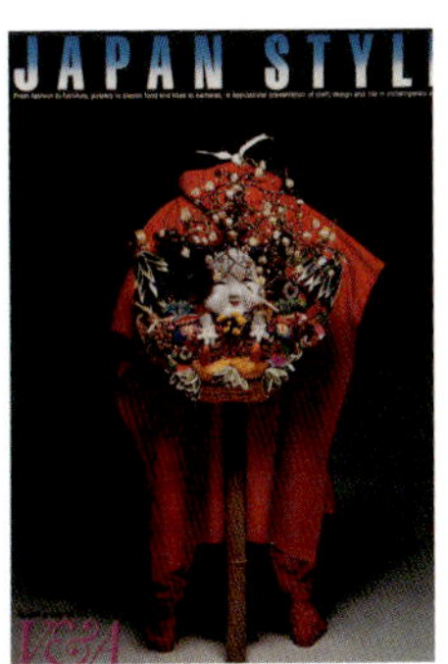

1980
Mar. 12–Jul. 20, *Japan Style*, Victoria and Albert Museum, London
Exhibition poster
Art direction: Ikko Tanaka; photo: Bishin Jumonji; costume: ISSEY MIYAKE

1982
May 15–Jun. 27, *Intimate Architecture: Contemporary Clothing Design*, Massachusetts Institute of Technology

1984
Jul. 10–Aug. 26, *Design in Japan – Tradition and the Present*, The Central House of Artists, Moscow

1985
Apr. 26–May 31, *Giappone avanguardia del futuro*, Palazzo Bianco, Genoa

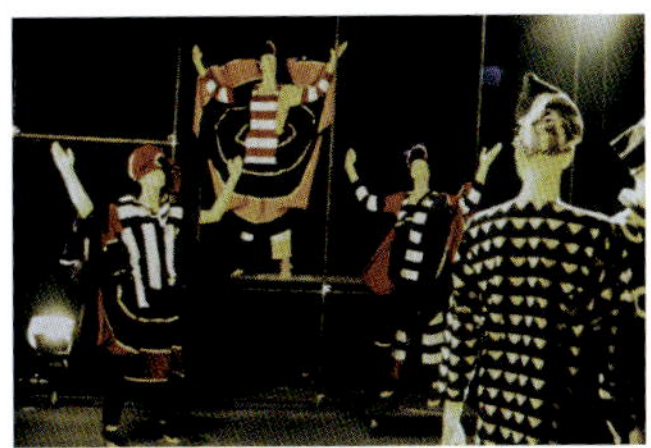

1985
Oct. 16–Dec. 29, *L'Or, la Laine et la Soie, Cotons et Plumes de Paon. Les Textiles de l'Inde et les Modèles Créés par Issey Miyake*, Musée des Arts Décoratifs, Paris
Photo: Yasuhiko Ohgida

1985
Nov. 1–Dec. 15, *A Panorama of Contemporary Art in Japan – Design of Daily Life*, Museum of Modern Art, Toyama

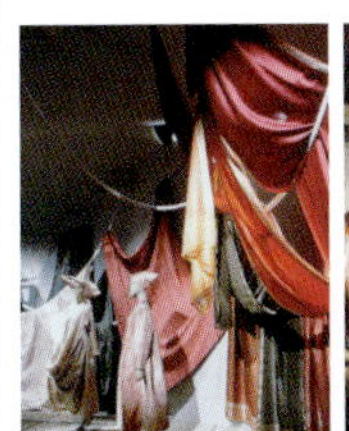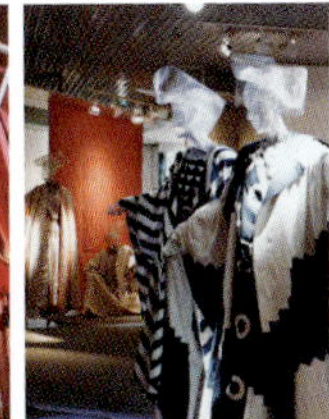

1986
May 2–13, *Haath: Hand Weaving of India and Issey Miyake*, Yurakucho Art Forum, Tokyo

1987
Feb. 2–May 8, *Fashion and Surrealism*, The Fashion Institute of Technology, New York

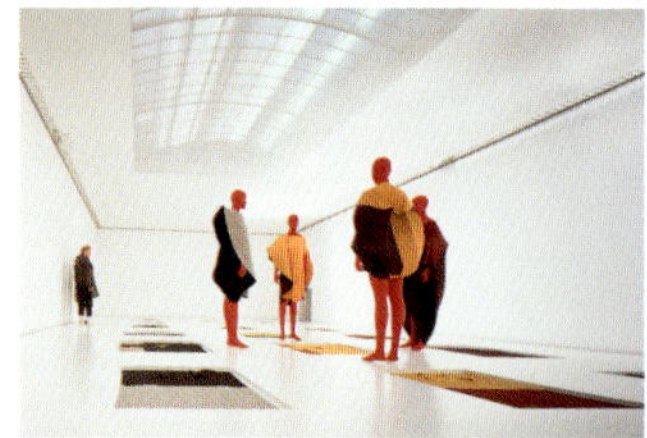

1990

Apr. 8–Jul. 29, *Energieën*, Stedelijk Museum,
Amsterdam
Photo: Shigeo Anzaï

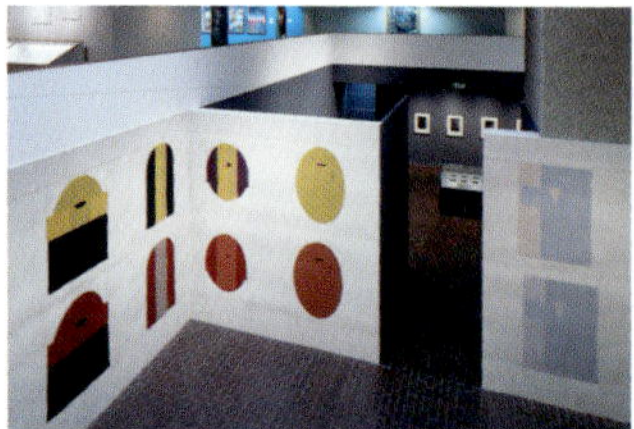

1991

Jul. 11–Sep. 22, *Beyond Japan*,
Barbican Art Gallery, London

1994

Apr. 5–Jun. 19, *Japonism in Fashion*,
The National Museum of Modern Art, Kyoto

1994

Sep. 25–Nov. 20, *Japanese Design:
A Survey Since 1950*, Philadelphia Museum of Art

1994

Nov. 5–Mar. 19, 1995, *Orientalism: Visions
of the East in Western Dress*, The Metropolitan
Museum of Art, New York

1995

Jan. 28–Apr. 30, *In and Out Balance 1975–1995*,
Gemeentemuseum Den Haag

1995

Apr. 19–Jun. 4, *Trace of Post-War Culture 1945–1995*,
Meguro Museum of Art, Tokyo; Jun. 14–Jul. 21,
Hiroshima City Museum of Contemporary Art;
Aug. 15–Sep. 24, Hyogo Prefectural Museum of Art;
Oct. 8–Nov. 5, Fukuoka Prefectural Museum of Art

1995

Sep. 29–Jan. 7, 1996, *Mode & Art 1960–1990*, Palais
des Beaux-Arts, Brussels; Sep. 2, 1996–Jan. 6, 1997,
Musée d'art contemporain de Montréal

1996

Feb. 13–Apr. 29, *Design japonais, 1950–1995*,
Centre Pompidou, Paris

1996

Apr. 17–Aug. 4, *Japonism et mode*, Palais Galliera,
Musée de la Mode de la Ville de Paris;
Sep. 7–Nov. 17, TFT Hall, Tokyo

1996

May 23–Jul. 11, *Made in Japan 1950–1994*,
The Suntory Museum Tempozan, Osaka

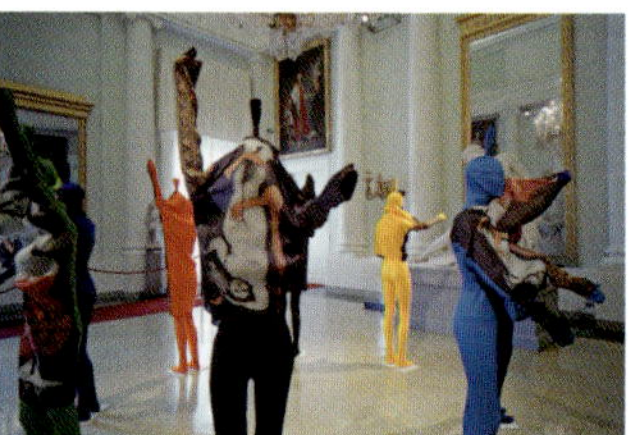

1996

Sep. 21–Dec. 15, *The 1st Biennale di Firenze*,
Galleria d'Arte Moderna in the Palazzo Pitti, Florence
Photo: Yasuaki Yoshinaga

1997

Feb. 8–Mar. 2, *Japanese Textile Design Exhibition*,
Indira Gandhi National Centre for the Arts,
New Delhi

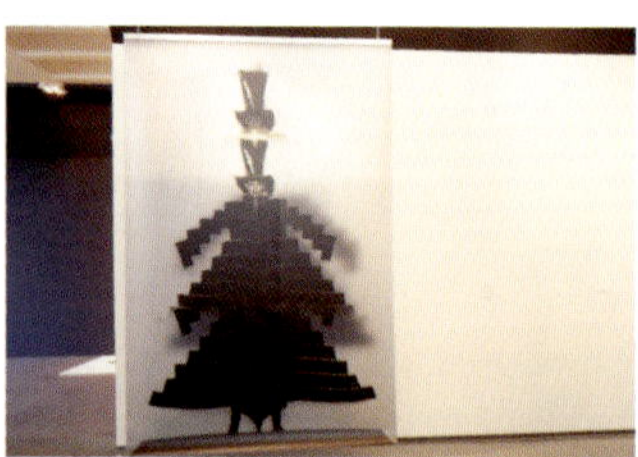

1998

Mar. 4–Apr. 12, *Noir*, Triennale di Milano
Photo: Yasuaki Yoshinaga

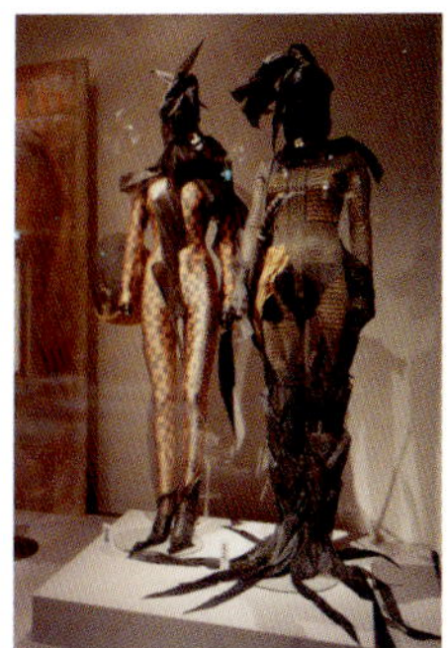

1998
Jan. 24–Mar. 1, 1999, *Touches d'exotisme*
XIVe–XXe siècle, Musée des Arts Décoratifs, Paris
Photo: Yasuaki Yoshinaga

1998
Jul. 21–Sep. 23, *Why Is This Art?,* Toyota Municipal
Museum of Art; Oct. 6–Dec. 6, Kawamura Memorial
DIC Museum of Art, Chiba; Dec. 19–Mar. 22, 1999,
The Contemporary Art Gallery, Art Tower Mito

1998
Oct. 8–Jan. 11, 1999, *Addressing the Century:*
100 Years of Art & Fashion, Hayward Gallery, London

1998
Nov. 12–Jan. 26, 1999, *Structure and Surface:*
Contemporary Japanese Textiles, Museum of
Modern Art, New York

1998
Nov. 22–Jan. 10, 1999, *50 Years of Japanese Life Style,*
Utsunomiya Museum of Art; Jun. 12–Jul. 24, 1999,
Hiroshima City Museum of Contemporary Art

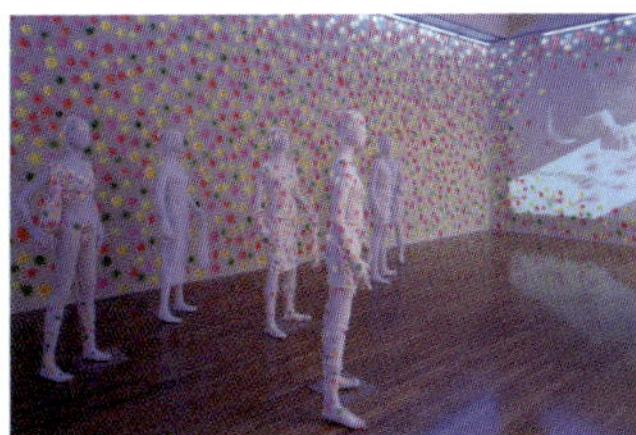

1999
Apr. 6–Jun. 6, *Visions of the Body: Fashion or Invisible*
Corset, The National Museum of Modern Art, Kyoto;
Aug. 7–Nov. 23, Museum of Contemporary Art, Tokyo
Dots Obsessions on A-POC, Yayoi Kusama, 1999
Photo: Naoya Hatakeyama

1999
Apr. 30–Aug. 8, *Design Worlds, Fashion Is,*
Children's Museum, San Diego

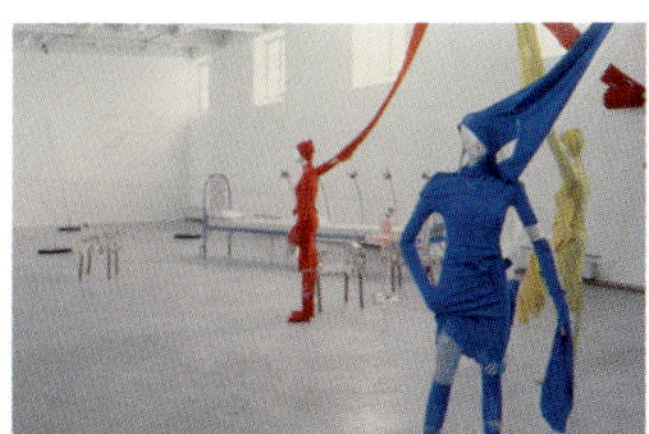

2000
May 29–Aug. 20, *Utsu,* Museum of Far Eastern
Antiquities, Stockholm
Photo: Arata Isozaki & Associates

2000
Oct. 3–Nov. 26, *MA–Twenty Years On,* The University
Art Museum, Tokyo University of the Arts

2000
Oct. 7–Dec. 10, *Plastic Age: Art and Design,*
The Museum of Modern Art, Saitama

2000
Oct. 27–Apr. 25, 2001, *Blow Up – Shaped Air in*
Design, Architecture, Fashion and Art, Vitra Design
Museum, Berlin

2000
Oct. 28–Feb. 11, 2001, *Aluminum by Design, Jewelry*
to Jets, Carnegie Museum of Art, Pittsburgh;
Mar. 20–Jul. 15, 2001, Cooper Hewitt Smithsonian
Design Museum, New York

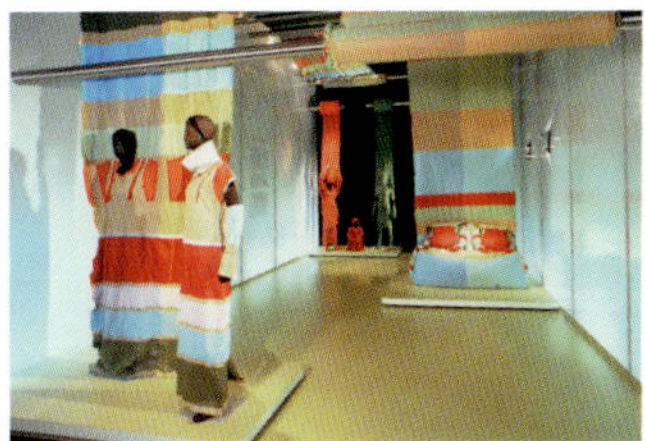

2001
Oct. 18–Jan. 6, 2002, *Radical Fashion,*
Victoria and Albert Museum, London
Photo: Jerry Hardman-Jones
© Victoria and Albert Museum

2003
May 1–Aug. 3, *Goddess: The Classical Mode,*
Metropolitan Museum, New York

2004

Apr. 29–Jun. 20, *Colors in Fashion: Victor & Rolf & KCI,* The National Museum of Modern Art, Kyoto; Aug. 24–Dec. 5, Mori Art Museum, Tokyo

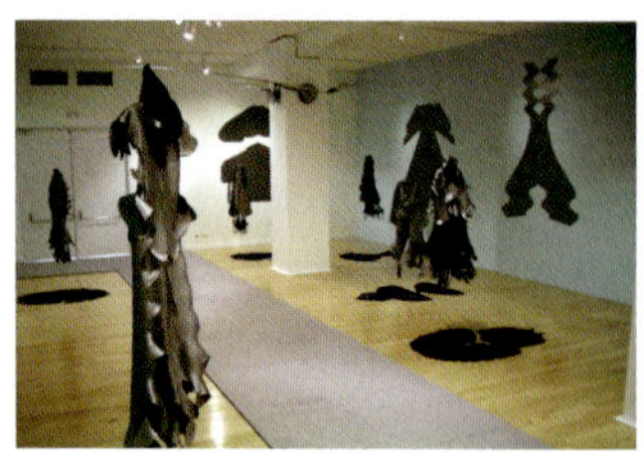

2004

Jun. 22–Oct. 17, *Psychosis = Folds + Pleats: Drapery from Ancient Greek Dress to 21st Century Fashion,* New Benaki Museum, Athens
Photo: The Miyake Issey Foundation

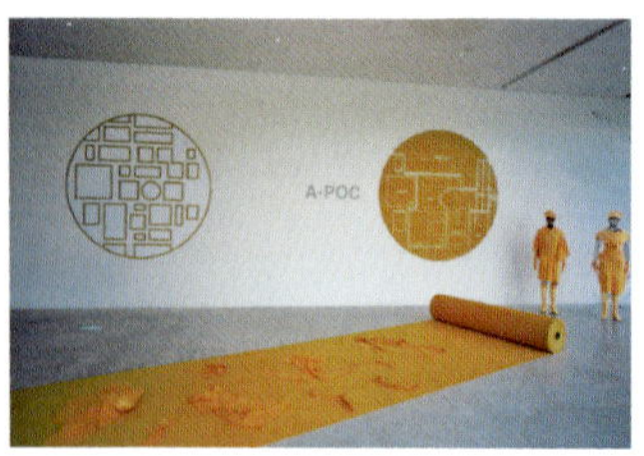

2004

Oct. 9–Mar. 21, 2005, *The Encounters in the 21st Century: Polyphony – Emerging Resonances,* 21st Century Museum of Contemporary Art, Kanazawa
Photo: Shigeo Anzaï

2004

Jul. 10–Aug. 1, The Japan Foundation Traveling Exhibition: *Japanese Design Today 100,* Kawasaki City Museum, Graphic Gallery

2004

Nov. 8–Dec. 13, *On Conceptual Clothing,* Musashino Art University Museum & Library, Tokyo

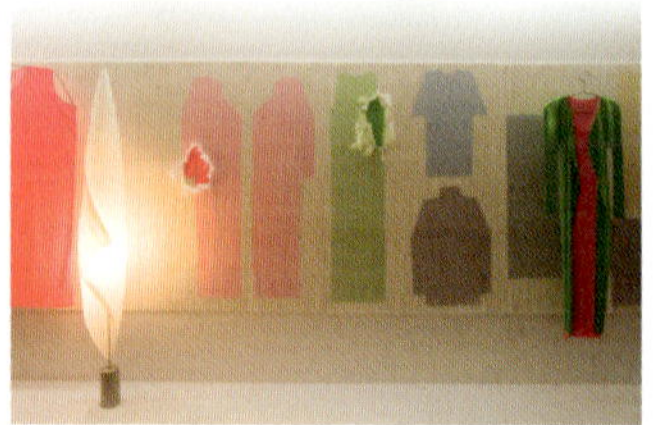

2005

Apr. 3–Jun. 5, *Big Bang: Destruction et création dans l'art du 20ᵉ siècle,* Centre Pompidou, Paris
Photo: Benjamin Nitôt

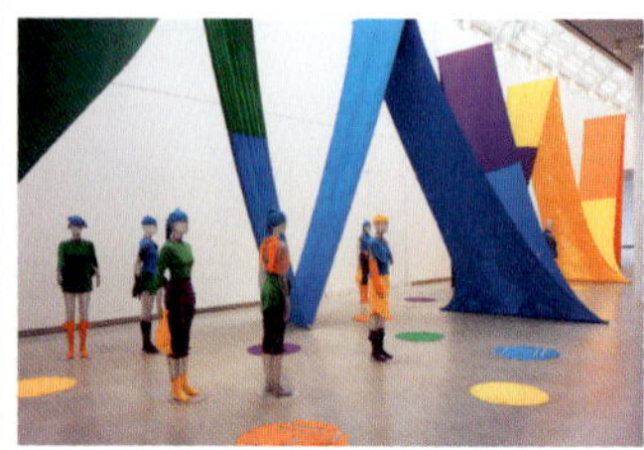

2005

Apr. 16–Jun. 26, *Special Exhibition for the 60th Anniversary of the Hiroshima A-bombing, Toward the Future: Through the Eyes of the Artists Awarded the Hiroshima Art Prize,* Hiroshima City Museum of Contemporary Art
Photo: Oshima Studio

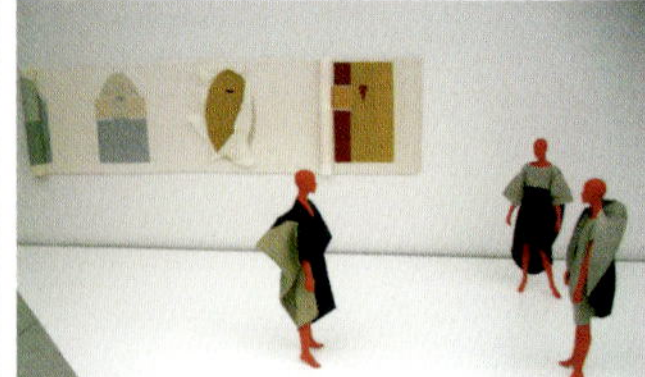

2005

Jul. 21–Sep. 4, *On Conceptual Clothing,* Kirishima Open-Air Museum, Kagoshima
Photo: The Miyake Issey Foundation

2005

Oct. 30–Apr. 30, 2006, *L'Homme Paré,* Musée des Arts Décoratifs, Paris

2005

Dec. 9–Mar. 6, 2006, *Fashion in Colors,* Cooper Hewitt Smithsonian Design Museum, New York

2006

Mar. 4–Jul. 30, *Showtime, le défilé de mode,* Palais Galliera, Musée de la mode de la ville de Paris

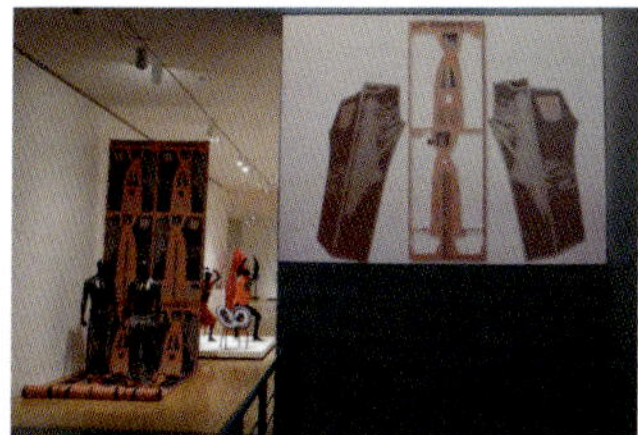

2006

Nov. 19–Mar. 5, 2007, *Skin + Bones: Parallel Practices in Fashion and Architecture*, The Museum of Contemporary Art, Los Angeles
Photo: Brian Forrest. Courtesy of The Museum of Contemporary Art, Los Angeles

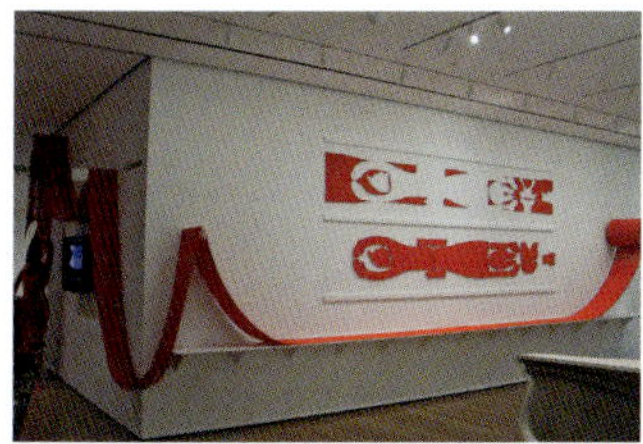

2006

Nov. 22–Nov. 27, 2007, *Digitally Mastered: Recent Acquisitions from the Museum's Collection*, The Museum of Modern Art, New York
Photo: John Peden

2007

Mar. 2–Apr. 7, *Rrripp!! Paper Fashion*, New Benaki Museum, Athens

2007

Mar. 10–May 6, *Second Skin*, Museum of Contemporary Art, Taipei

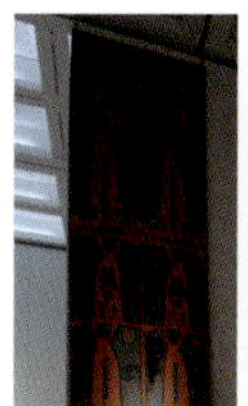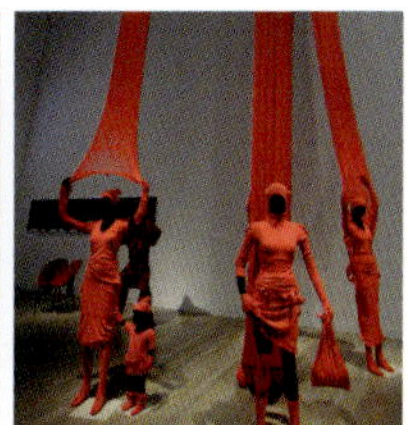

2007

Jun. 6–Aug. 13, *Skin + Bones: Parallel Practices in Fashion and Architecture,* The National Art Center, Tokyo
Photo: Yasuaki Yoshinaga

2007

Jul. 6–Oct. 28, *Fashion Show: Les desfilades de moda,* Museu Tèxtil i d'Indumentària, Barcelona

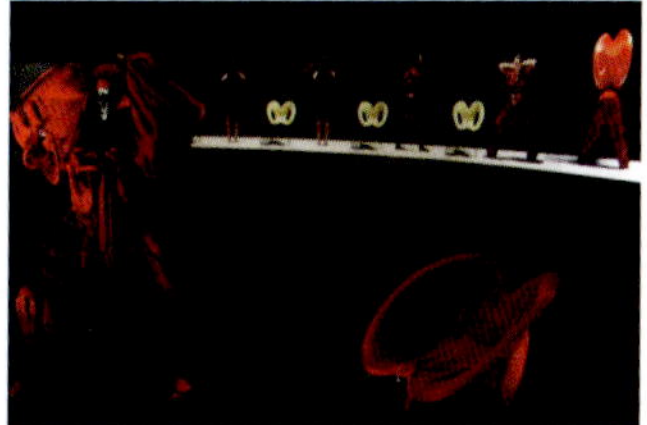

2008

Apr. 24–Aug. 10, *Skin + Bones: Parallel Practice in Fashion and Architecture,* Somerset House, London
Photo: The Miyake Issey Foundation

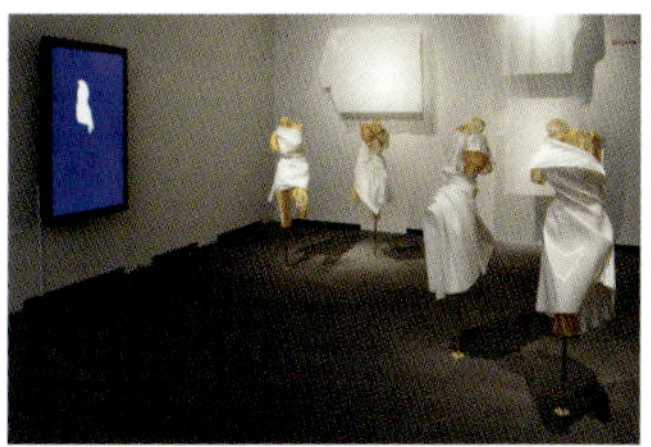

2008

Sep. 27–Nov. 9, *Art of Our Time, Celebrating the 20th Praemium Imperiale in Honor of Prince Takamatsu,* The Ueno Royal Museum, Tokyo
Photo: Yasuaki Yoshinaga

2008

Oct. 22–Jan. 31, 2009, *WA: L'Harmonie au quotidien – design japonais d'aujourd'hui,* Maison de la culture du Japon à Paris

2008

Nov. 20–Mar. 16, 2009, *Ron Arad: No Discipline,* Centre Pompidou, Paris; Aug. 2–Oct. 19, 2009, Museum of Modern Art, New York

2009

Aug. 20–Sep. 20, *WA: The Spirit of Harmony – Japanisches Design heute,* Red Dot Design Museum, Essen; Jan. 14–Mar. 28, The Institute of Industrial Design Warsaw

2009

Nov. 26–Feb. 7, 2010, *Design Real,* Serpentine Gallery, London

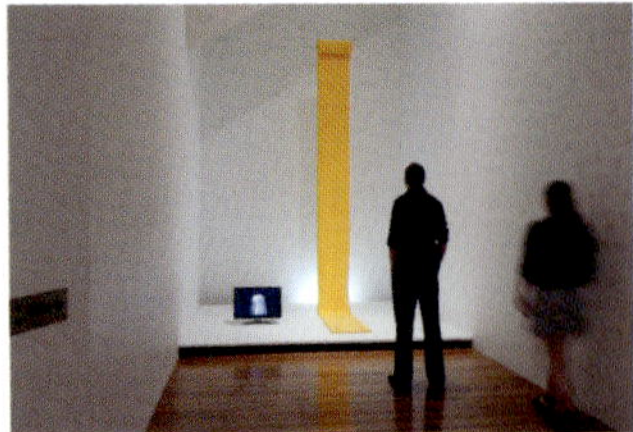

2010

Feb. 12–Mar. 21, *The Endless Garment: The New Craft of Machine Knitting*, RMIT Gallery, Melbourne
Photo: Mark Ashkanasy. Courtesy of RMIT Gallery, Melbourne

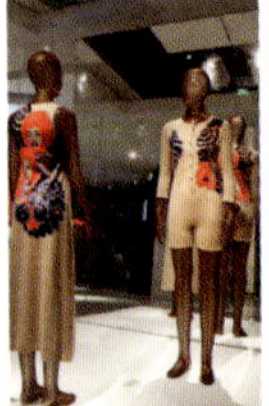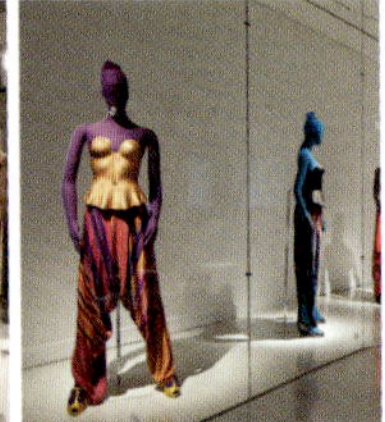

2010

Mar. 31–Oct. 10, *Histoire idéale de la mode contemporaine, Vol. I: Les Années 70 & 80*, Musée des Arts Décoratifs, Paris
Photo: Luc Boegly

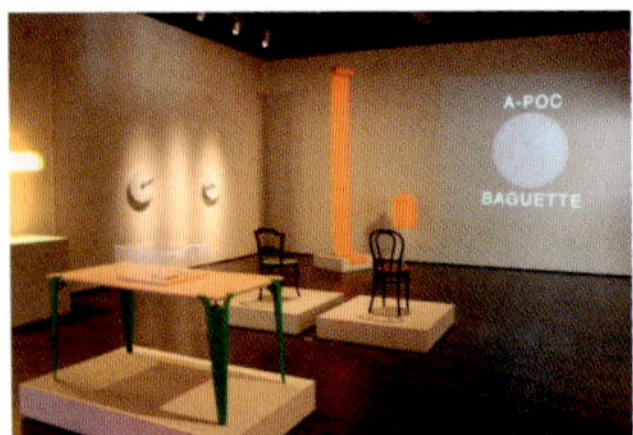

2010

Jul. 10–Oct. 10, *Technocraft: Hackers, Modders, Fabbers, Tweakers and Design in the Age of Individuality*, Yerba Buena Center for the Arts, San Francisco
Photo: Courtesy of Fuseproject

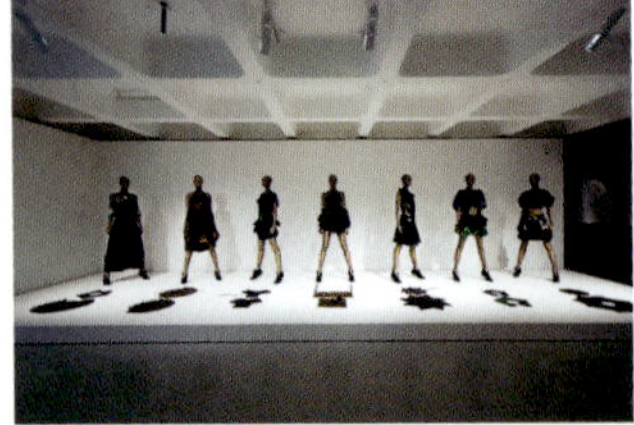

2010

Oct. 15–Feb. 6, 2011, *Future Beauty: 30 Years of Japanese Fashion*, Barbican Art Gallery, London
Photo: Lyndon Douglas, Barbican Art Gallery, London

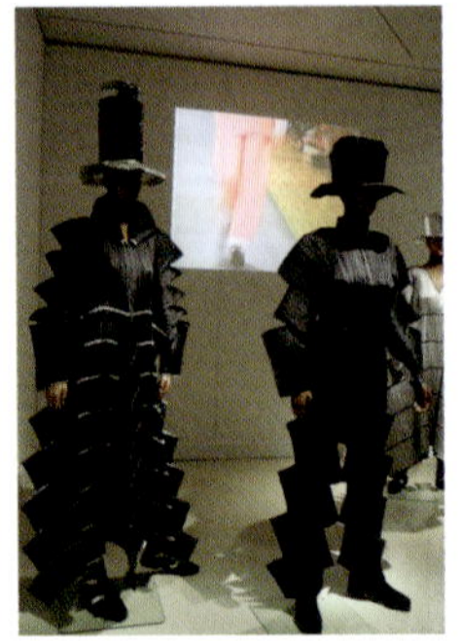

2010

Nov. 25–May 8, 2011, *Histoire idéale de la mode contemporaine Vol. II: Les Années 1990 & 2000*, Musée des Arts Décoratifs, Paris
Photo: The Miyake Issey Foundation

2011

Mar. 4–Jun. 19, *Future Beauty: 30 Years of Japanese Fashion*, Haus der Kunst, Munich

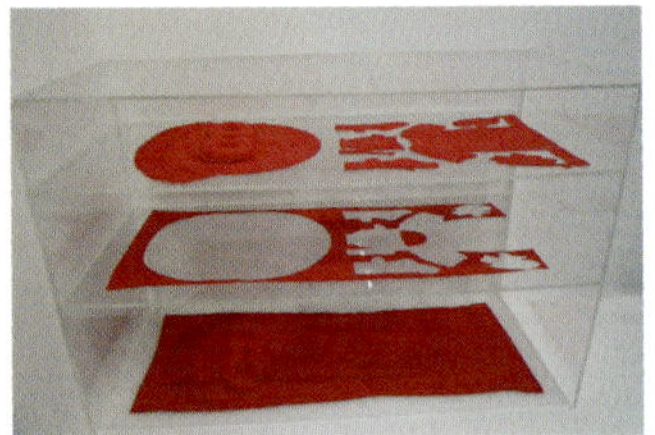

2011

Apr. 6–Feb. 13, 2012, *Collections Contemporaines des Années 1960 à Nos jours*, Centre Pompidou, Paris
Photo: The Miyake Issey Foundation

2011

Jun. 24–Jul. 30, *WA: The Spirit of Harmony and Japanese Design Today*, Musashino Art University Museum & Library, Tokyo

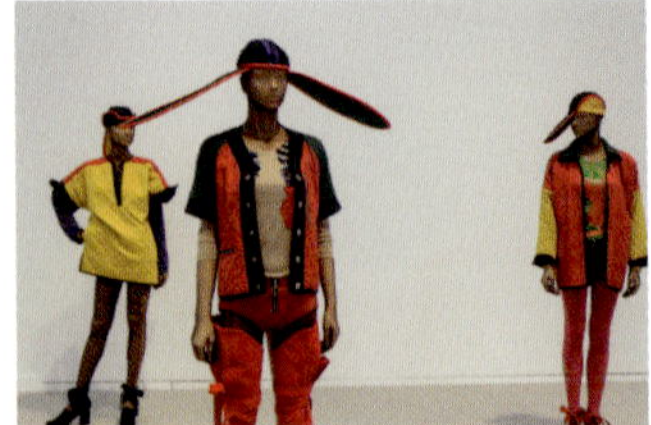

2012

Jul. 28–Oct. 8, *Future Beauty: 30 Years of Japanese Fashion*, Museum of Contemporary Art Tokyo
Photo: Yasuaki Yoshinaga

2013

Mar. 1–May 24, *Papier Glacé*, Palais Galliera,
musée de la Mode de la Ville de Paris

2013

Mar. 2–Jan. 20, 2014, *Applied Design, New Acquisitions
in the Design Collection*, Museum of Modern Art,
New York

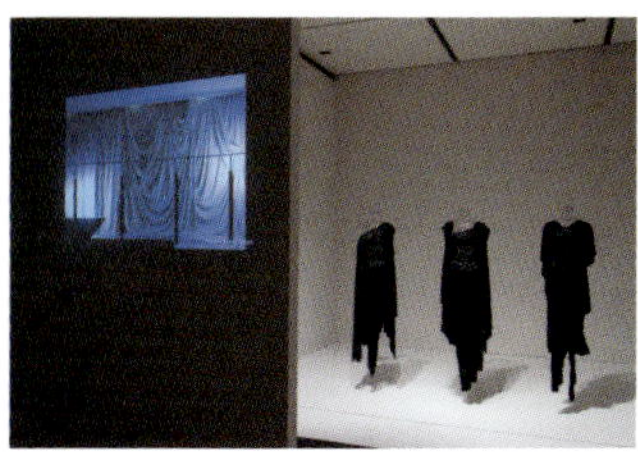

2013

Jul. 6–Sep. 1, *Floating Design: Shiro Kuramata and his
contemporaries*, The Museum of Modern Art, Saitama
Photo: Yasuaki Yoshinaga

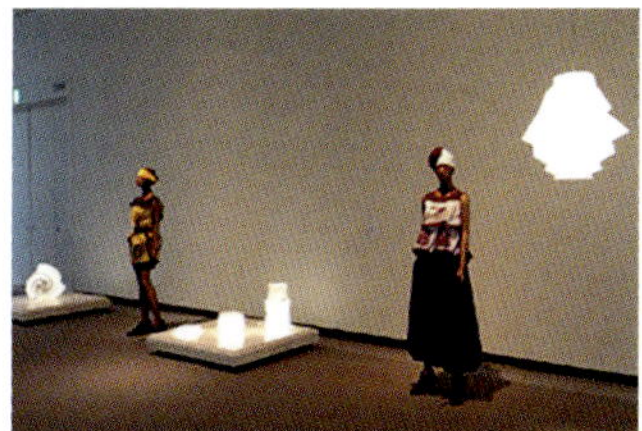

2013

Jul. 20–Oct. 14, *Art Arch Hiroshima 2013, Peace
Meets Art!*, Hiroshima Prefectural Art Museum
Photo: Miyake Design Studio

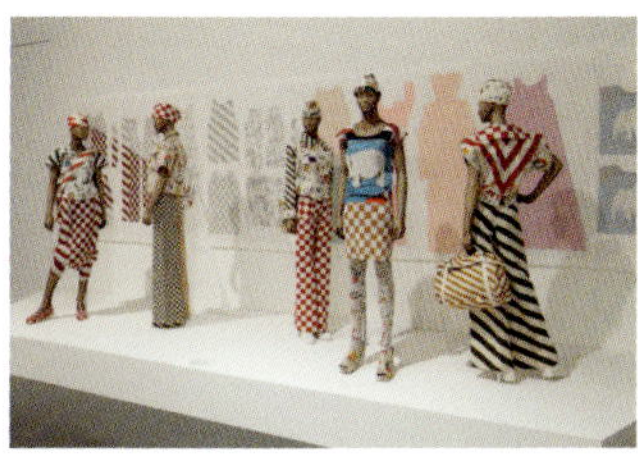

2014

Mar. 21–May 11, *Future Beauty: The Tradition of
Reinvention in Japanese Fashion*, The National
Museum of Modern Art, Kyoto
Photo: Osamu Watanabe, The Kyoto Costume Institute

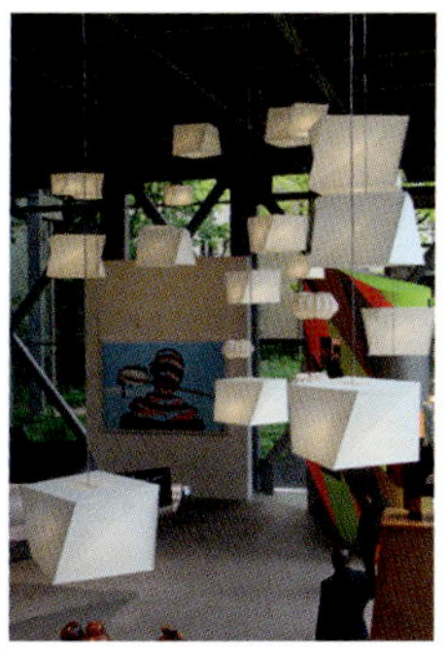

2014

May 10–Sep. 21, *Mémoires Vives, commemorated the
30th anniversary of Fondation Cartier pour l'art contemporain*, Fondation Cartier pour l'art contemporain, Paris
Photo: Miyake Design Studio

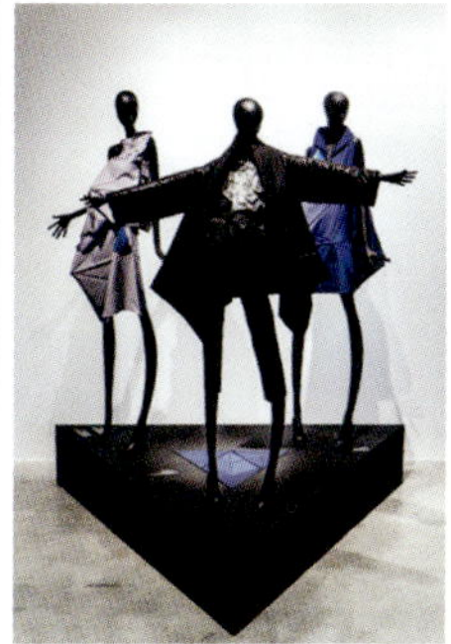

2014

Jul. 3–Nov. 1, *Gathering – From Domestic Craft
to Contemporary Process, Featuring 132 5.
ISSEY MIYAKE*, Design Museum Holon
Photo: Itay Benit. Courtesy of Design Museum Holon

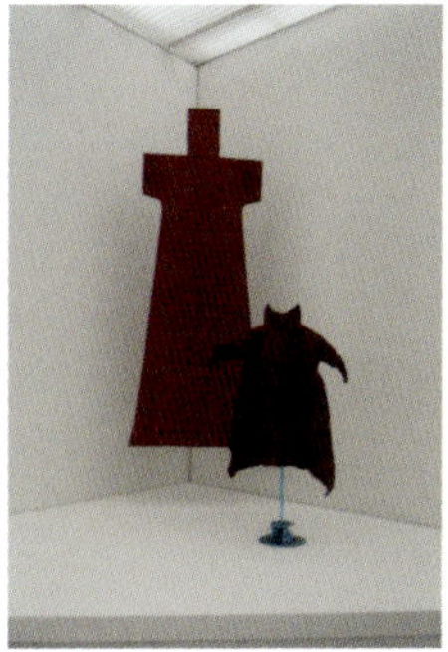

2015

Apr. 24–Jul. 20, *Opening Exhibition vol. 1 Modern:
Blossoming Garden – Oita World Museum*,
Oita Prefectural Art Museum
Photo: The Miyake Issey Foundation

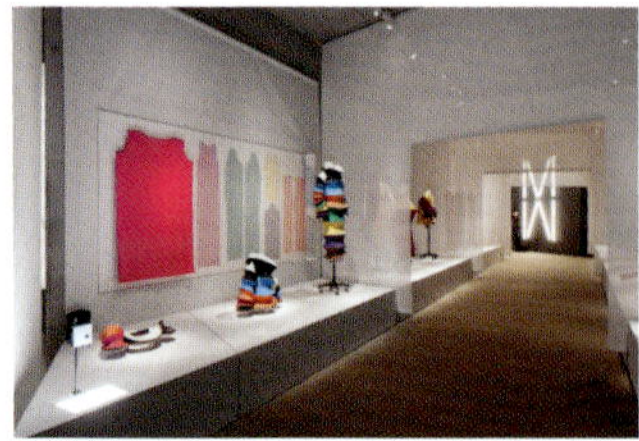

2016

May 5–Sep. 5, *Manus x Machina: Fashion in an Age of Technology*, Metropolitan Museum, New York

Photo: Nicholas Calcott

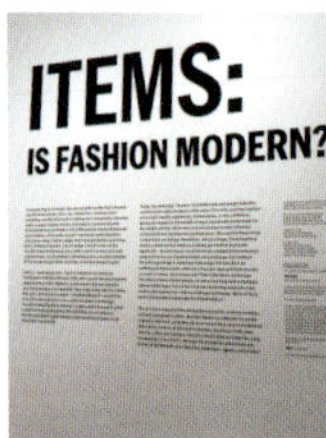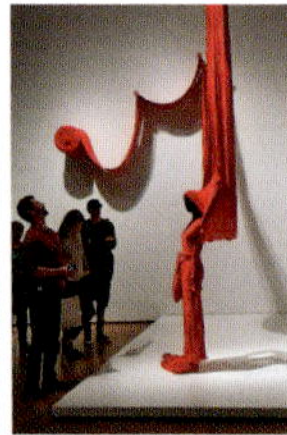

2017

Oct. 1–Jan. 28, 2018, *Items: Is Fashion Modern?*, The Museum of Modern Art, New York

Photo: Miyake Design Studio

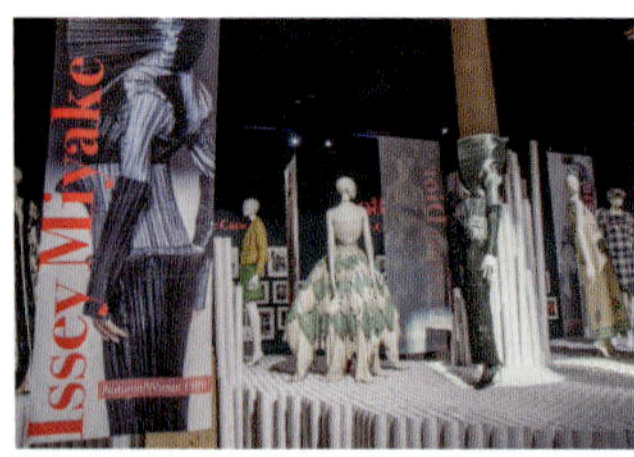

2018

Jul. 7–Jan. 6, 2019, *Catwalking: Fashion Through the Lens of Chris Moore*, The Bowes Museum, Barnard Castle, UK

Photo: The Bowes Museum

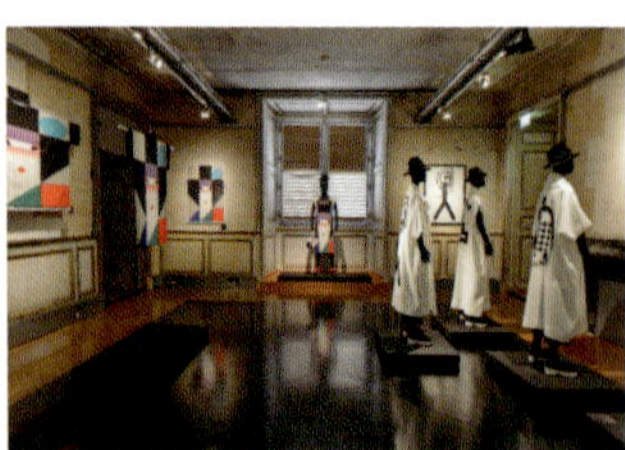

2018

Nov. 15–Mar. 3, 2019, *Japon-Japonismes, Objets Inspirés 1867–2018*, Musée des Arts Décoratifs, Paris

Photo: Manabu Matsunaga

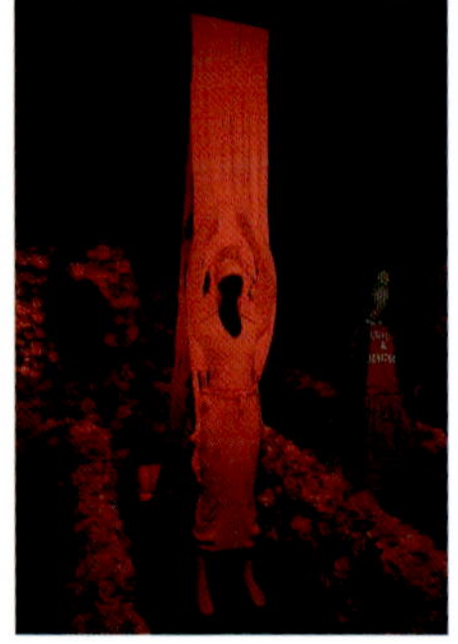

2019

May 11–Sep. 2, 2019, *A Queen Within: Adorned Archetypes*, The Museum of Pop Culture, Seattle

Photo: Mark Woods. Courtesy of Barrett Barrera Projects

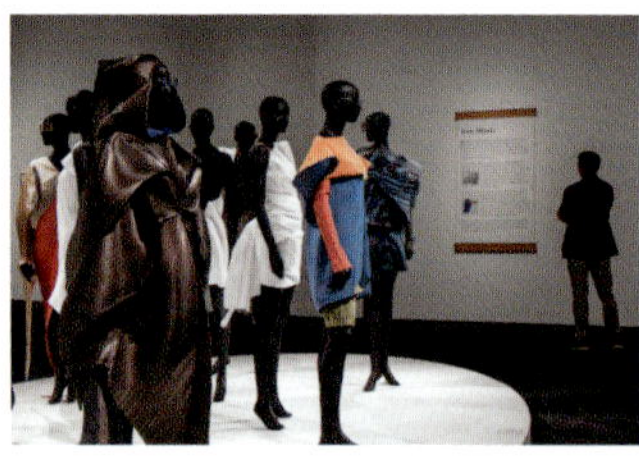

2019

Jun. 2–Aug. 18, *The Life of Animals in Japanese Art*, The National Gallery of Art, Washington, D.C.

Photo: Rob Shelley

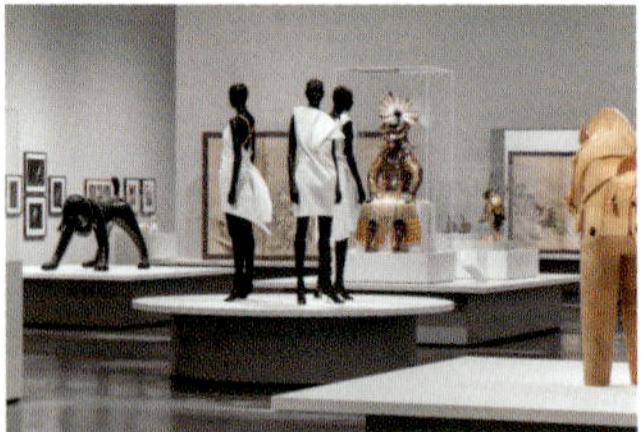

2019

Sep. 22–Dec. 8, *Every Living Thing: Animals in Japanese Art*, Los Angeles County Museum of Art

Photo: Museum Associates/LACMA

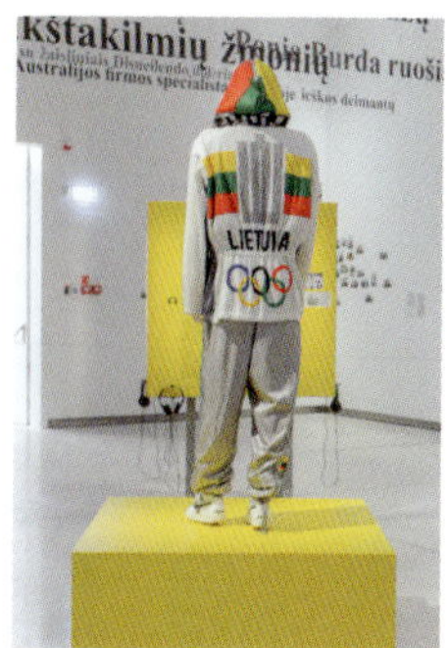

2019

Oct. 5–Feb. 23, 2020, *The Origin of Species: 1990s DNA*, MO Museum, Vilnius, Lithuania

Photo: Norbert Tukaj

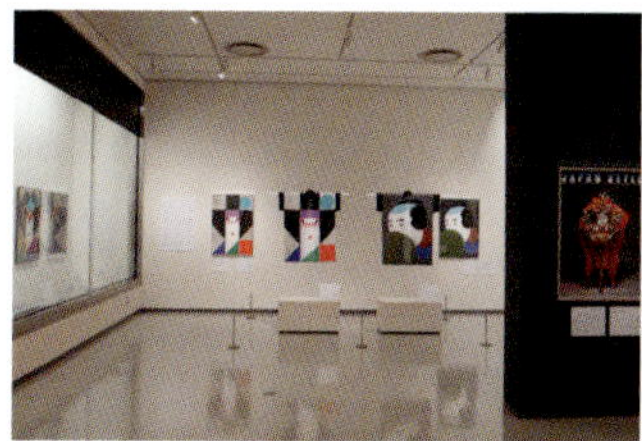

2020

Jan. 25–Mar. 15 (closed between Feb. 28–Mar. 15), *Ikko Tanaka: Design for the Future*, Nara Prefectural Museum of Art

Photo: Nara Prefectural Museum of Art

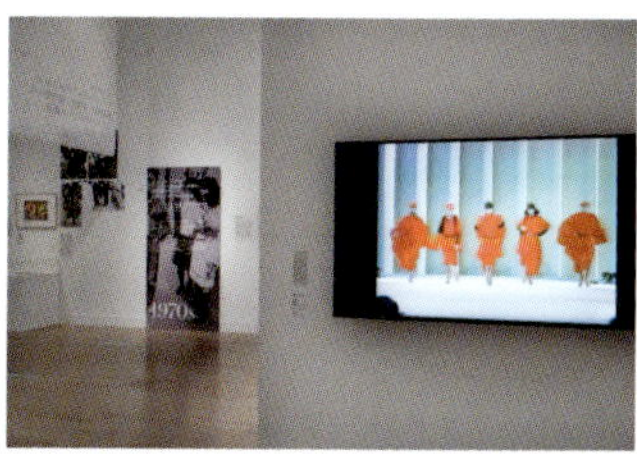

2021

Mar. 20–May 16, *Fashion in Japan 1945–2020*, Iwami Art Museum, Shimane; Jun. 9–Sep. 6, The National Art Center, Tokyo

Photo: Yasuaki Yoshinaga

PARTICIPATED IN THE ORGANIZATION OR CURATION OF EXHIBITIONS OR EVENTS

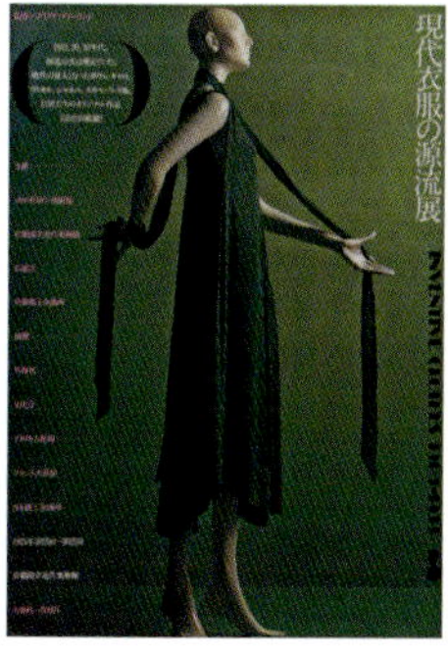

1975

Mar. 25–May 25, *Gendai Ifuku no Genryu Ten – Inventive Clothes: 1909–1939*, The National Museum of Modern Art, Kyoto (participated in the organization of the exhibition)

Exhibition poster

Art direction: Ikko Tanaka

1980

Apr. 5–Jun. 1, *Evolution of Fashion 1835–1895*, The National Museum of Modern Art, Kyoto (participated in the organization of the exhibition)

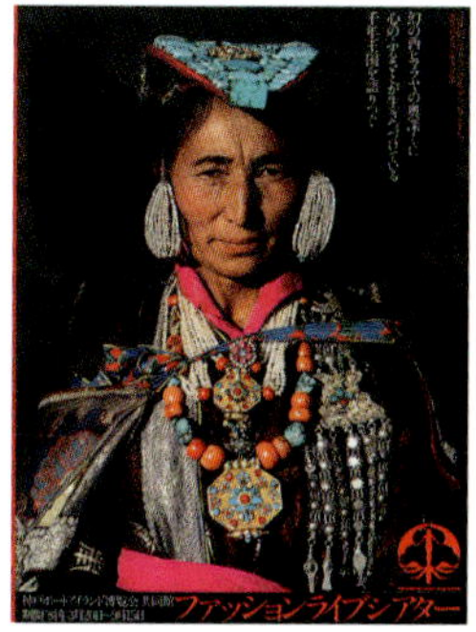

1981

Apr. 28, Fashion Show *Fashion Geograffiti*, The Space, Tokyo, presented by Fashion Live Theater, Kobe Port Island Exposition (participated in the organization as fashion director)

Fashion Live Theater campaign poster

Photo: Tadayuki Naitoh

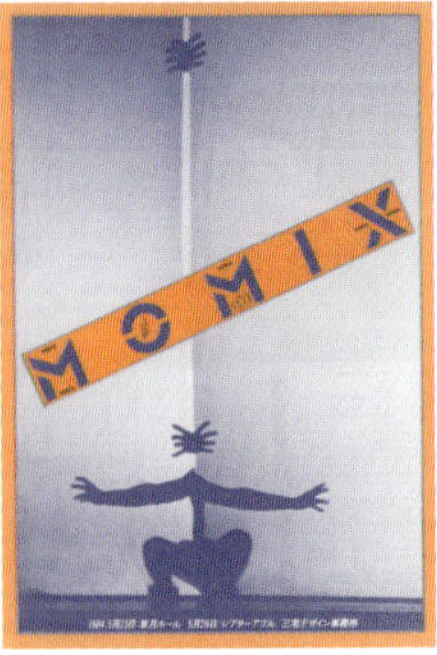

1984

May 25, Invited the American contemporary dance company Momix to perform their work in Tokyo Sogetsu Hall; May 26, Theater Apple

Flyer

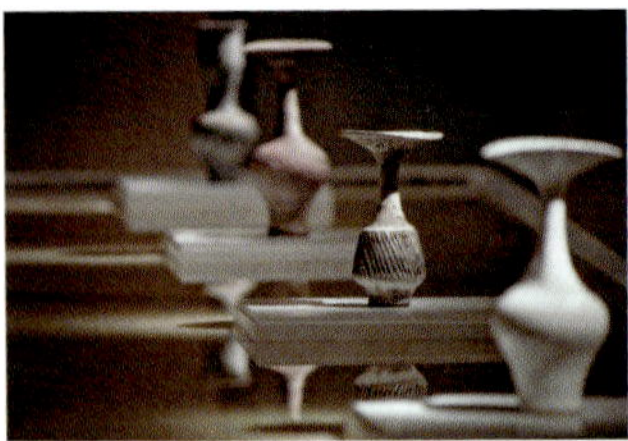

1989

May 10–Jun. 7, *Issey Miyake Meets Lucie Rie*, Sogetsu Gallery, Tokyo; Jun. 27–Jul. 30, Museum of Oriental Ceramics, Osaka

Photo: Mitsumasa Fujitsuka

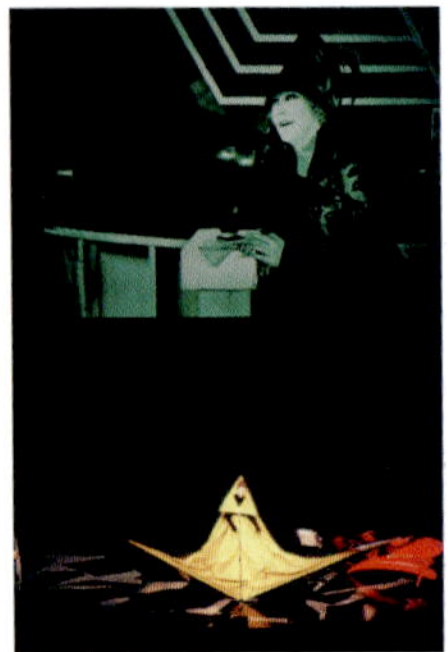

1990

Mar. 2–6, Participated in a multimedia performance based on the film *L'Inhumaine (1924):* costume design, Bunkamura Orchard Hall, Tokyo

Photo: Shigeo Anzaï

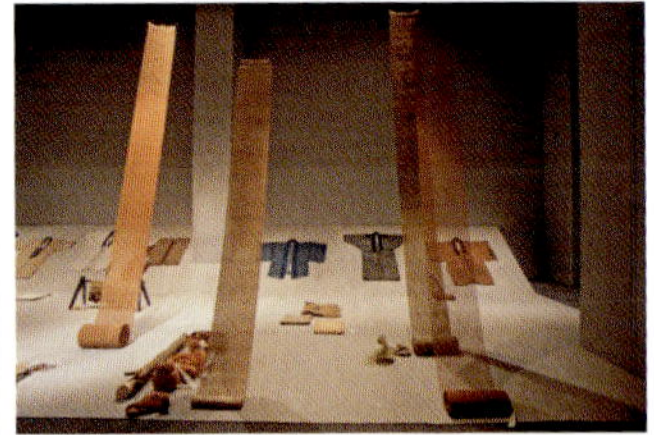

1991

Jun. 7, Series of lectures: *Primitive textiles by Masashi Yamamura, viewing, talking, and thinking about them*, Hamilton Place, Tokyo

Photo: Sasaki Studio

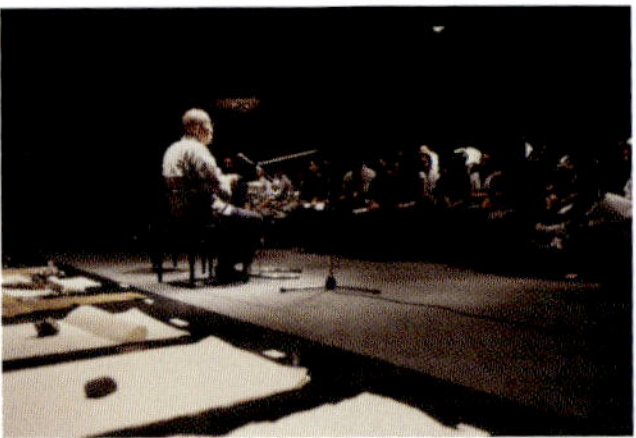

1991

Sep. 5, Series of lectures: *Shiroishi Washi: handscreening paper from Shiroishi by Tadao Endo, viewing, talking, and thinking about them*, Hamilton Place, Tokyo

Photo: Sasaki Studio

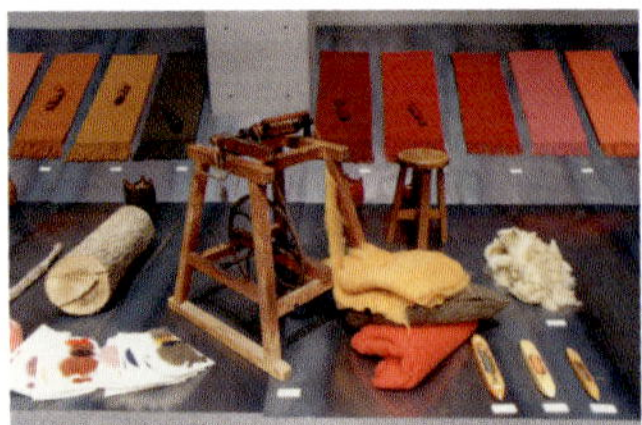

1992

Jan. 24, Series of lectures: *Vegetable dye by Nakamura Kobo, viewing, talking, and thinking about them*, Hamilton Place, Tokyo

Photo: Sasaki Studio

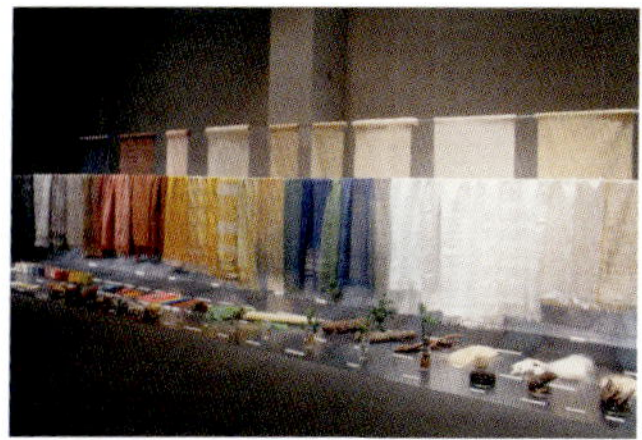

1992

Oct. 2, Series of lectures: *Textile of Akiko Ishigaki from Iriomote Island, viewing, talking, and thinking about them*, Hamilton Place, Tokyo

Photo: Sasaki Studio

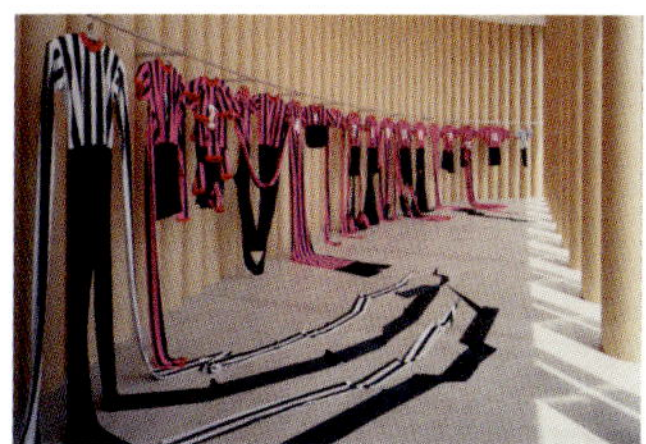

1998

Jun. 4–24, *Matthieu Manche: World Cup*, MDSG (MDS Gallery), Tokyo

Photo: Yasuaki Yoshinaga

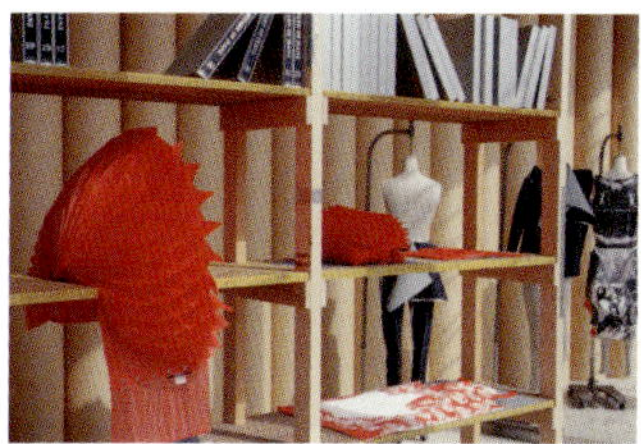

1999

Oct. 16–Nov. 20, *Hiroaki Ohya: Wizard of JeanZ*, MDSG, Tokyo

Photo: Yasuaki Yoshinaga

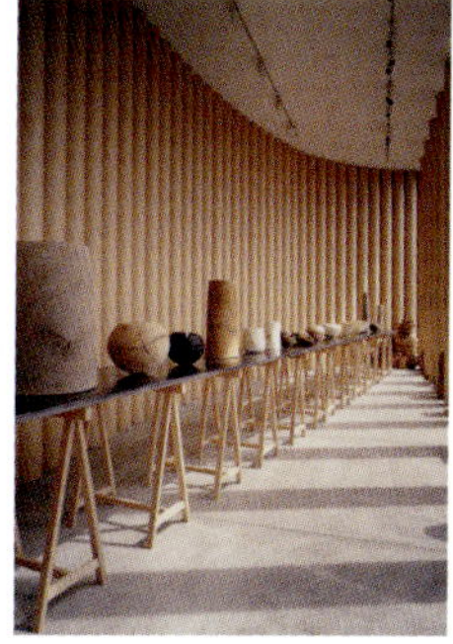

2000

Feb. 16–Mar. 18, *Ernst Gamperl: Volume in Wood*, MDSG, Tokyo

Photo: Yasuaki Yoshinaga

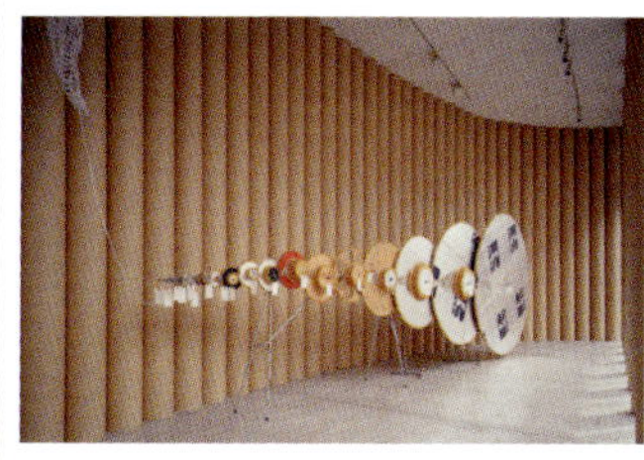

2000

Jul. 13–Aug. 19, *Tim Hawkinson*, MDSG, Tokyo

Photo: Yasuaki Yoshinaga

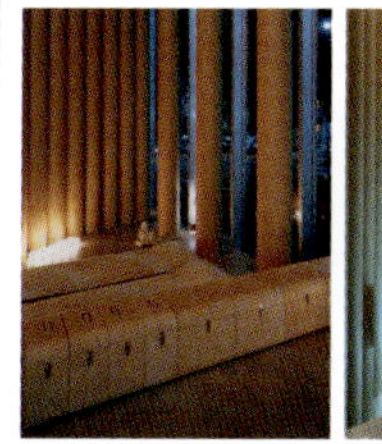

2000

Nov. 17–Dec. 22, *Harri Koskinen: Privacy*, MDSG, Tokyo

Photo: Yasuaki Yoshinaga

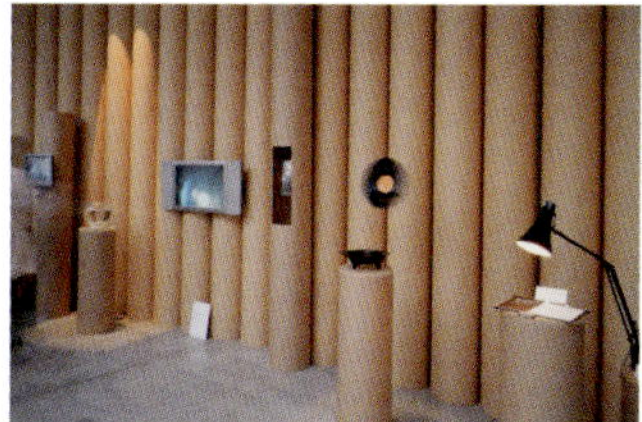

2001

Oct. 10–Nov. 10, *Six Visions – RCA Design Product Students*, Guest Curator Ron Arad, MDSG, Tokyo

Photo: Yasuaki Yoshinaga

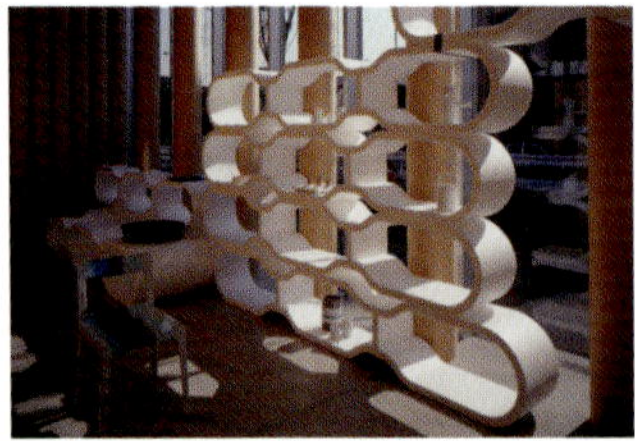

2001
Nov. 24–Dec. 22, *Ronan & Erwan Bouroullec*,
MDSG, Tokyo
Photo: Yasuaki Yoshinaga

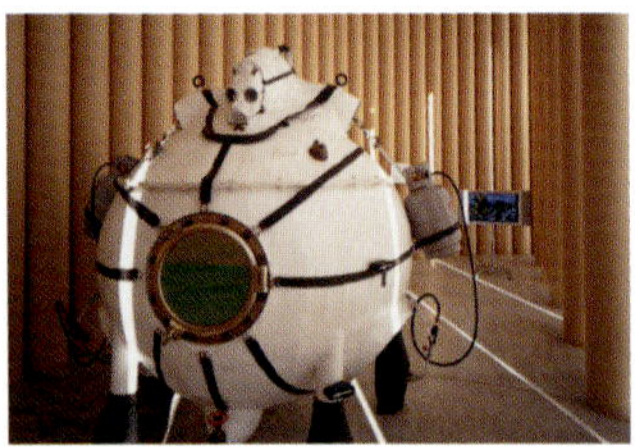

2002
Feb. 23–Apr. 13, *Time Travel Double Cycle Project:
ISSEY MIYAKE FÊTE/Kenji Yanobe Collaboration*,
MDSG, Tokyo
Photo: Yasuaki Yoshinaga

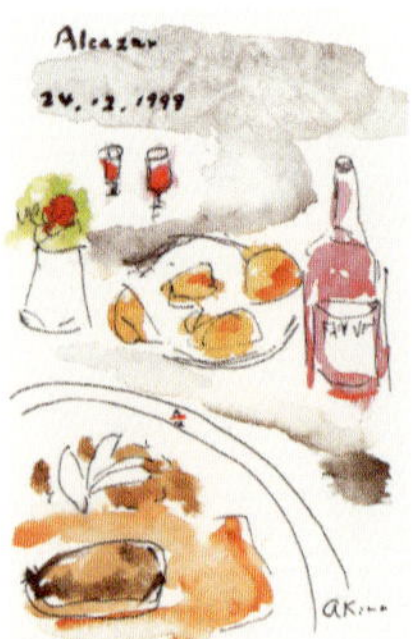

2002
Apr. 23–May 11, *Akira Satoh: World Travel
by Drawing on Postcards*, MDSG, Tokyo
Drawing: Akira Satoh

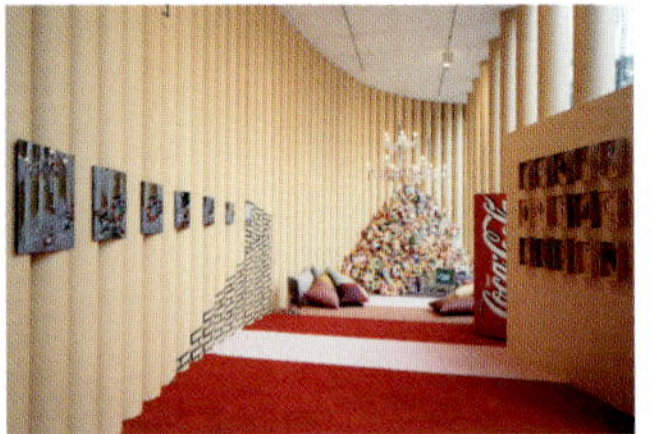

2002
Jun. 8–Jul. 13, *Three Young Artists from Korea*,
curated by Won Kyung-Hwan, MDSG, Tokyo
Photo: Yasuaki Yoshinaga

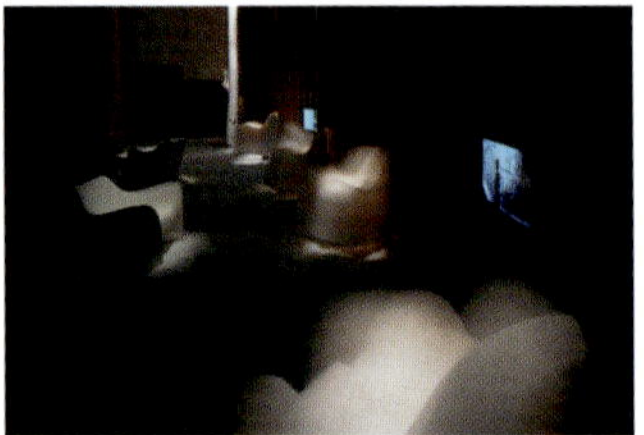

2002
Oct. 8–Nov. 2, *Tokujin Yoshioka: Honey-Pop*,
MDSG, Tokyo
Photo: Yasuaki Yoshinaga

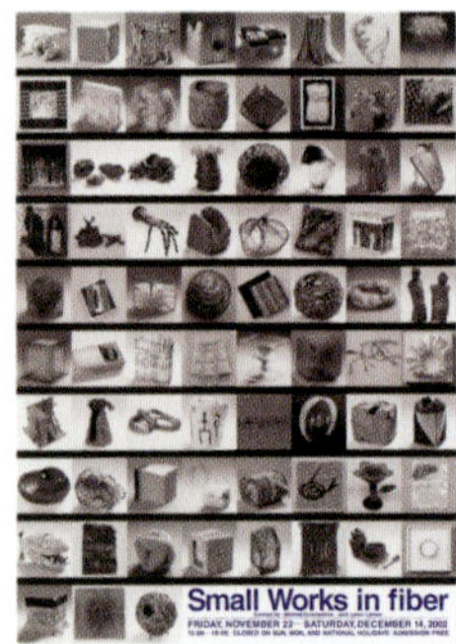

2002
Nov. 22–Dec. 14, *Small Works in Fiber*,
curated by Mildred Constantine,
Jack Lenor Larsen, MDSG, Tokyo

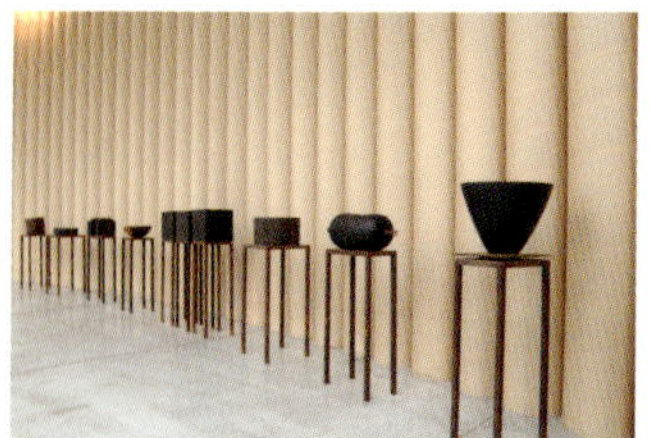

2003

Feb. 22–Mar. 29, *Won Kyung-Hwan:*
Wood Digs Earth, Earth Yields Metal, MDSG, Tokyo
Photo: Yasuaki Yoshinaga

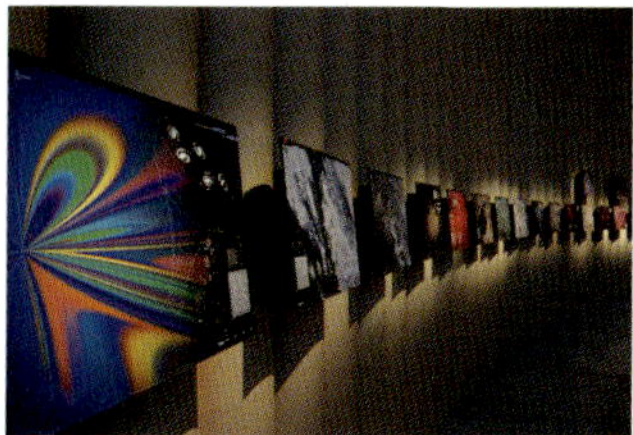

2003

May 9–31, *Mitsuo Katsui: Altered Soil,* MDSG, Tokyo
Photo: Yasuaki Yoshinaga

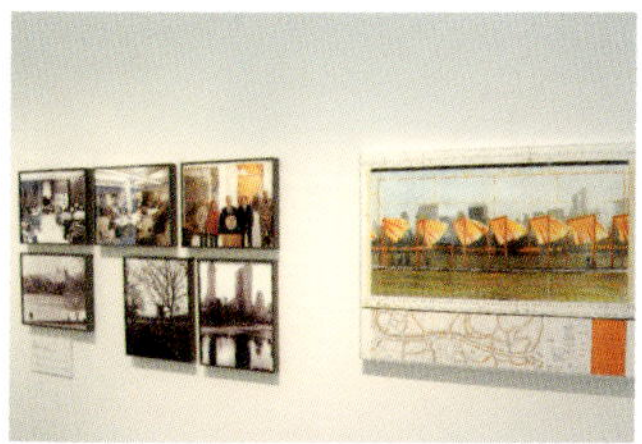

2003

Jun. 7–21, *Christo and Jeanne-Claude: The Gates
(Project for Central Park, New York City)*, MDSG, Tokyo
Photo: Yasuaki Yoshinaga

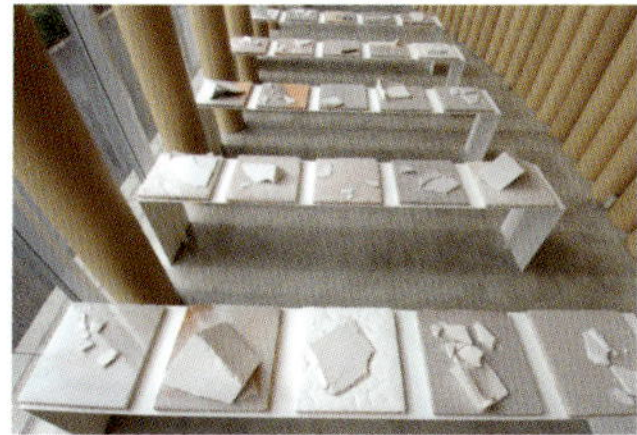

2004

Jan. 22–Feb. 28, *Machiko Ogawa Na2O · ZnO ·
Al2O3 · SiO2 · B2O3*, MDSG, Tokyo
Photo: Yasuaki Yoshinaga

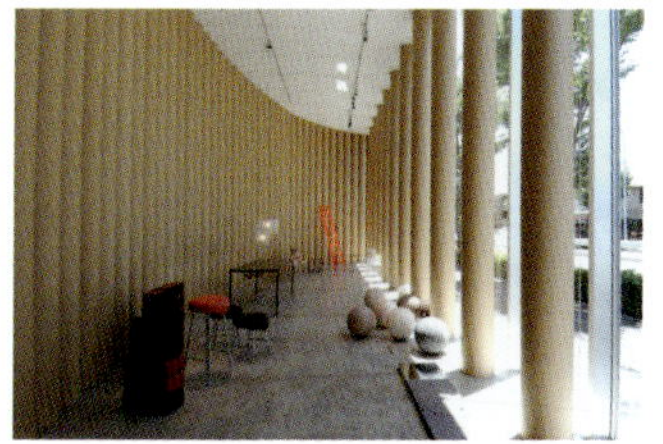

2004

May 27–Jul. 17, *Northern Lights: New Scandinavian
Designers selected by Harri Koskinen*, MDSG, Tokyo
Photo: Yasuaki Yoshinaga

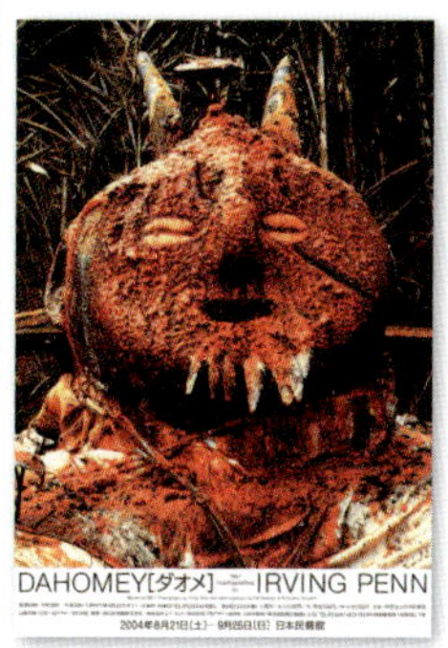

2004

Aug. 21–Sep. 26, *Dahomey 1967: Photographs
by Irving Penn*, Japan Folk Crafts Museum, Tokyo
Exhibition poster
Photo: Irving Penn
Design: Kenichi Samura

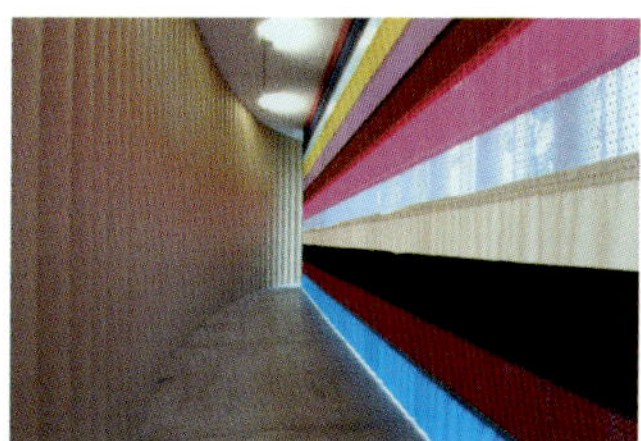

2004

Sep. 30–Nov. 6, *Fransje Killaars:
Installation in Tokyo, 2004*, MDSG, Tokyo
Photo: Yasuaki Yoshinaga

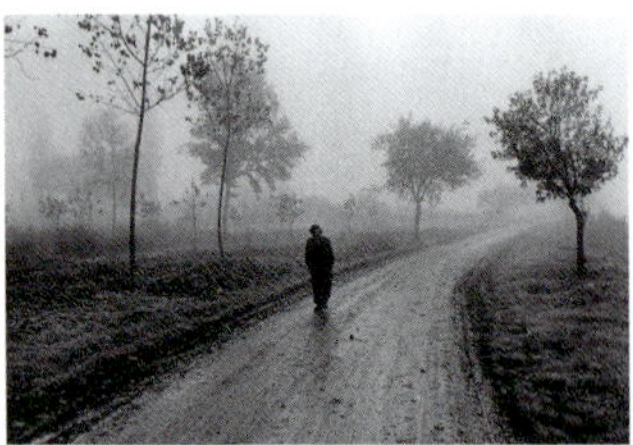

2005

Feb. 17–Mar. 26, *Photographs by Daniel Jouanneau: A Moment in Alsace*; Mar. 29–Apr. 16, *Part II: Aperture – Tokyo 2003*, MDSG, Tokyo

Photo: Daniel Jouanneau

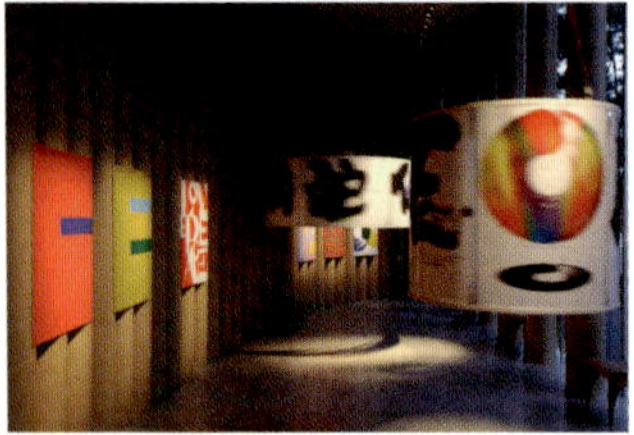

2005

Jul. 28–Aug. 20, *Shu Kataoka: Peace Forever*, MDSG, Tokyo

Photo: Yasuaki Yoshinaga

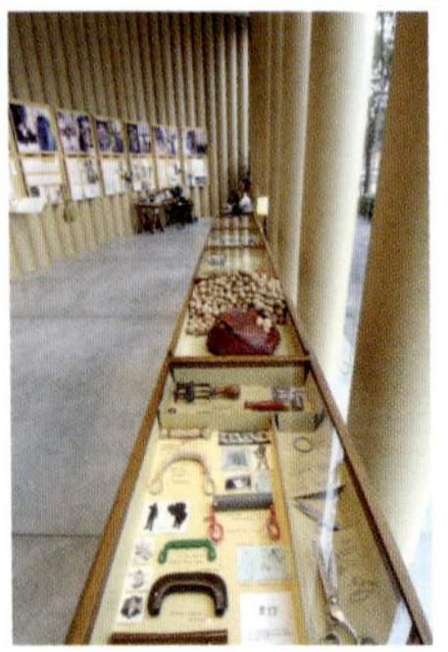

2005

Sep. 30–Nov. 3, *Mike Abelson: Carrying Research*, MDSG, Tokyo

Photo: Yasuaki Yoshinaga

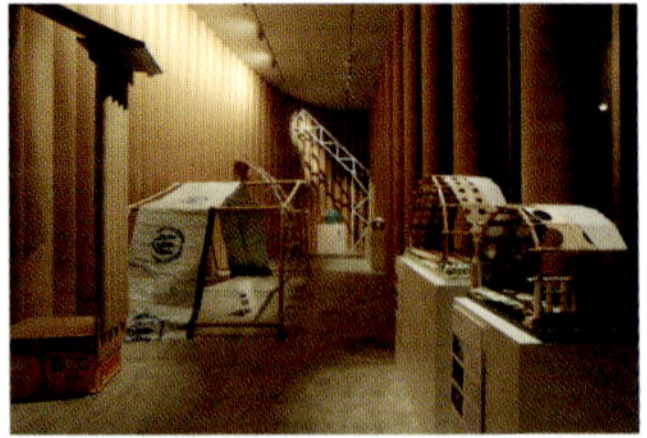

2005

Nov. 11–Dec. 24, *Shigeru Ban: Architecture for Disaster Relief and Student Participation*, MDSG, Tokyo

Photo: Nacása & Partners Inc.

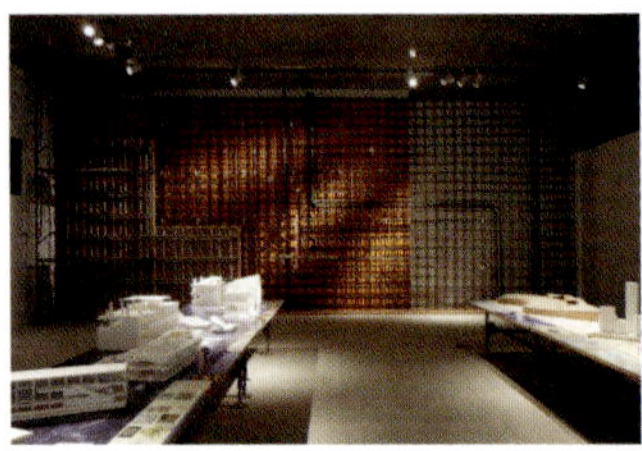

2007

Mar. 30–Apr. 18, Special program *Tadao Ando: Construction Site 2006. "A Hard-Fought Process,"* 21_21 DESIGN SIGHT, Tokyo

Photo: Masaya Yoshimura

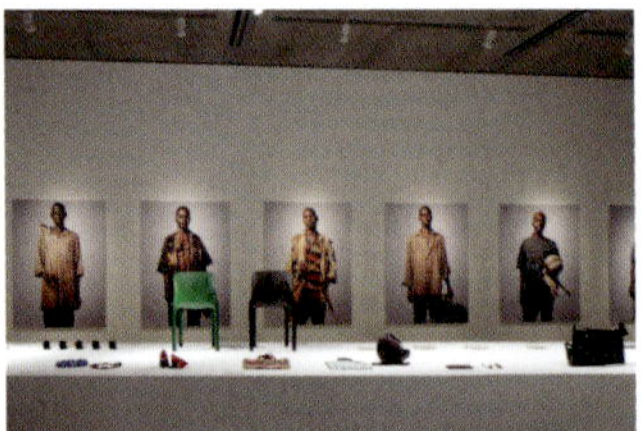

2007

Apr. 27–Jul. 29, Exhibition 1, directed by Naoto Fukasawa, *Chocolate*, 21_21 DESIGN SIGHT, Tokyo

Photo: Masaya Yoshimura

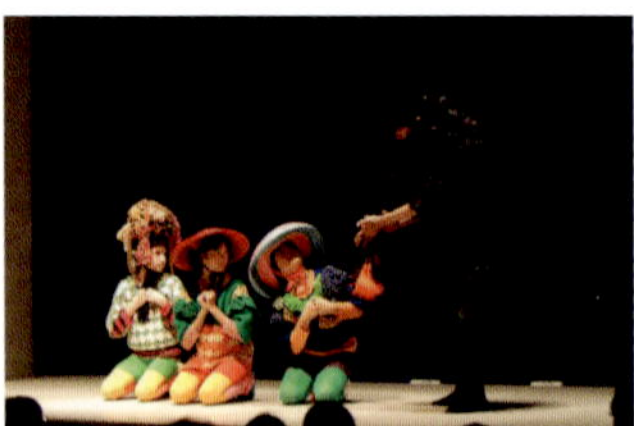

2007

Aug. 10–24, Summer program *Lucky Luck Show*, 21_21 DESIGN SIGHT, Tokyo

Photo: Kazuharu Igarashi

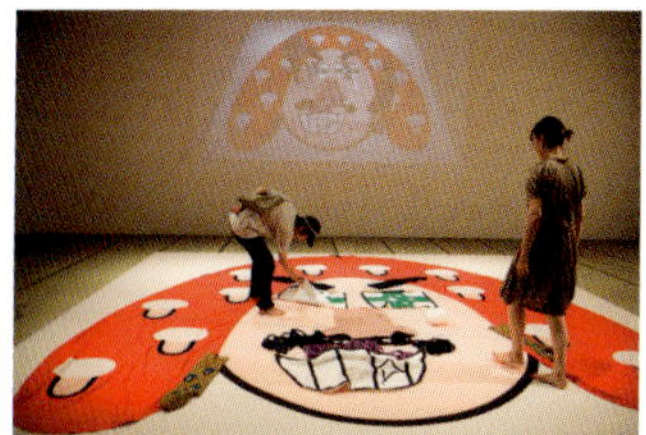

2007

Sep. 11–24, *This Play!*, 21_21 DESIGN SIGHT, Tokyo
Photo: Masaya Yoshimura

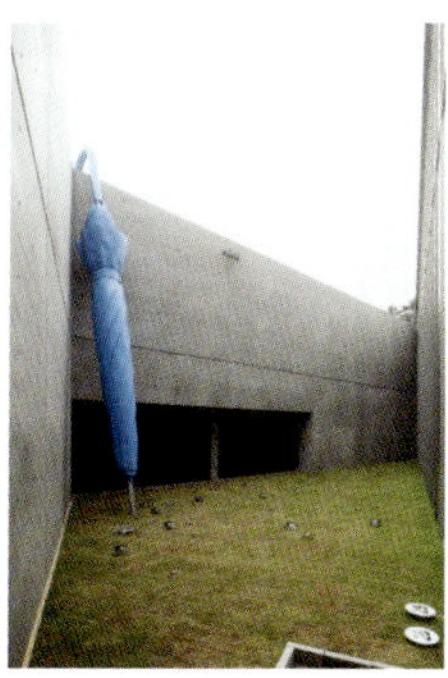

2007

Oct. 5–Jan. 14, 2008, Exhibition 2, directed by
Taku Satoh, *Water*, 21_21 DESIGN SIGHT, Tokyo
Photo: Masaya Yoshimura

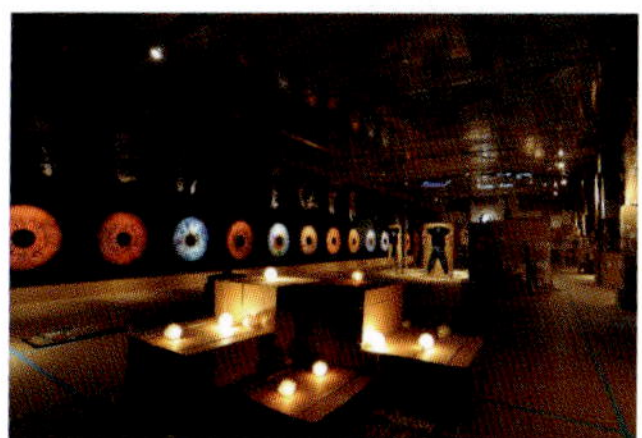

2008

Jan. 26–Mar. 16, 21_21 *DESIGN SIGHT +
Corporate Partners: Bulls Eye Special 2008*,
21_21 DESIGN SIGHT, Tokyo
Photo: Yasuaki Yoshinaga

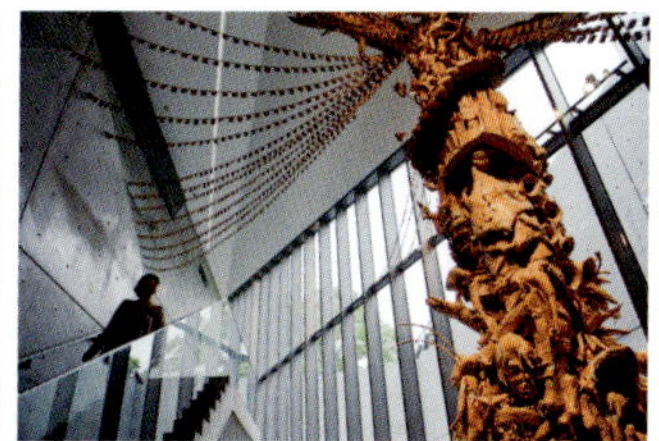

2008

Mar. 30–Jul. 6, Exhibition 3, directed by Issey Miyake,
XXIc.–XXIst Century Man, 21_21 DESIGN SIGHT, Tokyo
Photo: Masaya Yoshimura

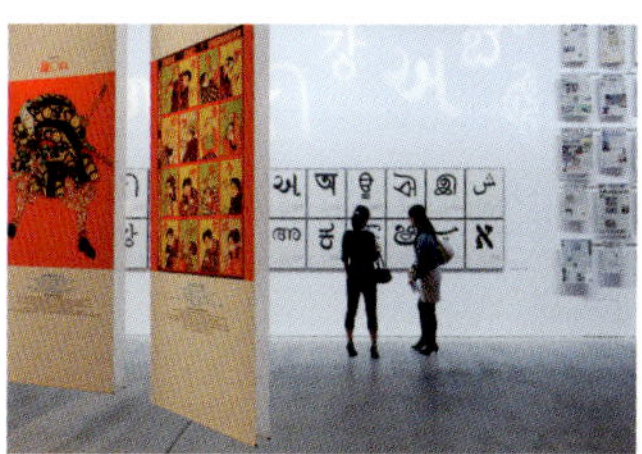

2008

Jul. 19–Sep. 23, *Whispered Prayers*, directed by
Katsumi Asaba, 21_21 DESIGN SIGHT, Tokyo
Photo: Masaya Yoshimura

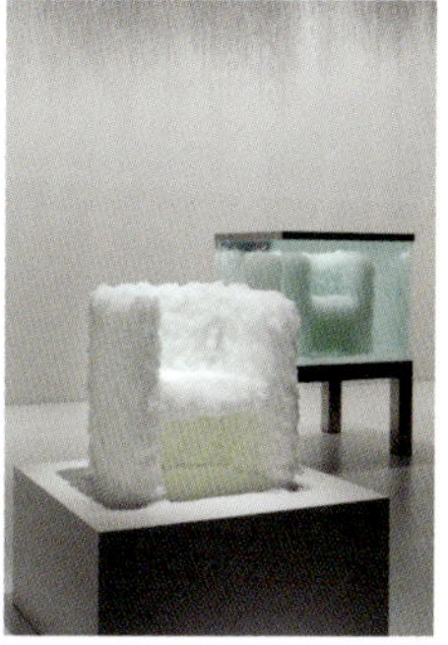

2008

Oct. 17–Jan. 18, 2009, Exhibition 4,
directed by Tokujin Yoshioka, *Second Nature*,
21_21 DESIGN SIGHT, Tokyo
Photo: Masaya Yoshimura

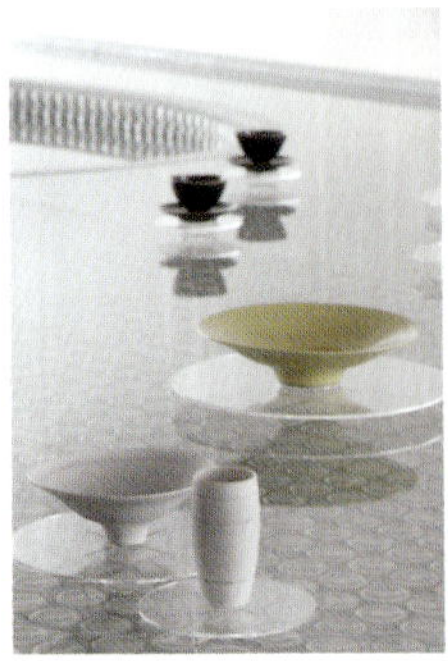

2009

Feb. 13–May 10, *U-tsu-Wa–Lucie Rie, Jennifer Lee, Ernst Gamperl*, 21_21 DESIGN SIGHT, Tokyo

Photo: Hiroshi Iwasaki

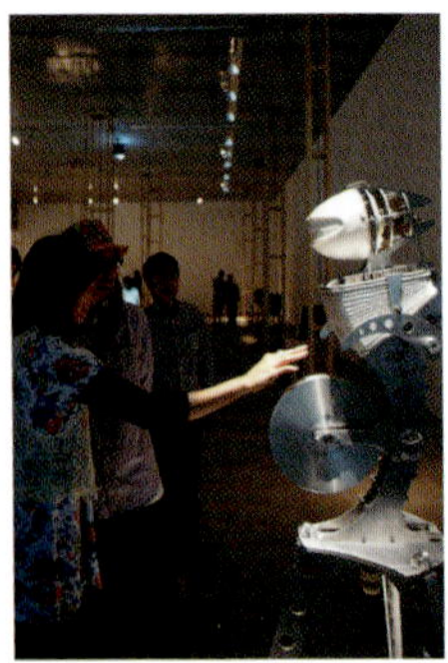

2009

May 29–Aug. 30, Exhibition 5, directed by Shunji Yamanaka, *Bones–Bones and Design. Artificial bones, bones of future–*, 21_21 DESIGN SIGHT, Tokyo

Photo: Masaya Yoshimura

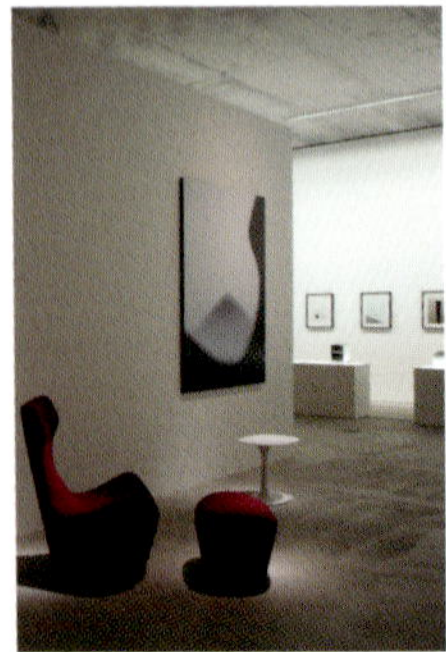

2009

Oct. 16–Jan. 30, 2010, *The Outline: The Unseen Outline of Things*, 21_21 DESIGN SIGHT, Tokyo

Photo: Masaya Yoshimura

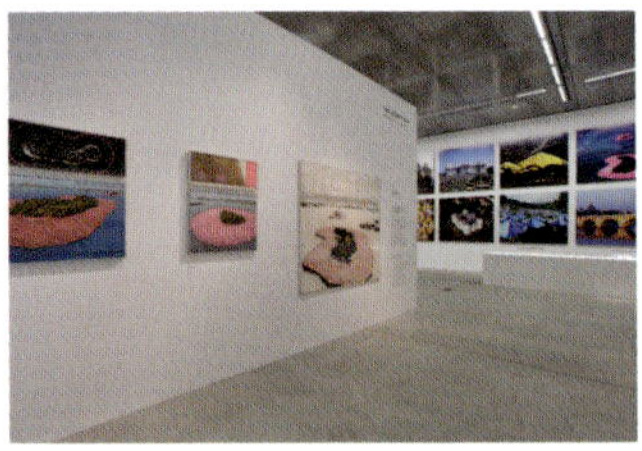

2010

Feb. 13–Apr. 6, Special Exhibition *Christo and Jeanne-Claude Life = Works = Projects*, 21_21 DESIGN SIGHT, Tokyo

Photo: Yasuaki Yoshinaga

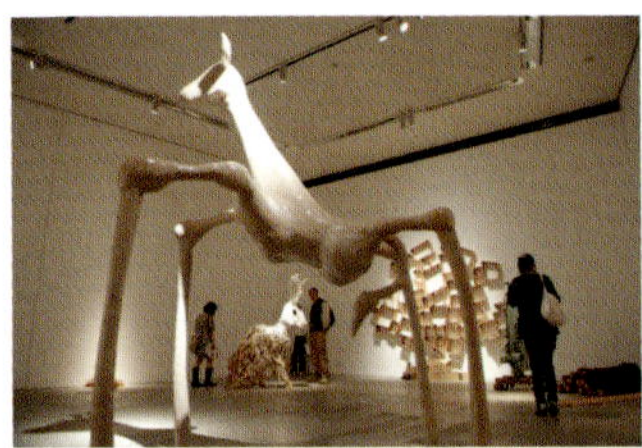

2010

Apr. 24–Jun. 27, *Post Fossil: Excavating 21st Century Creation*, 21_21 DESIGN SIGHT, Tokyo

Photo: Masaya Yoshimura

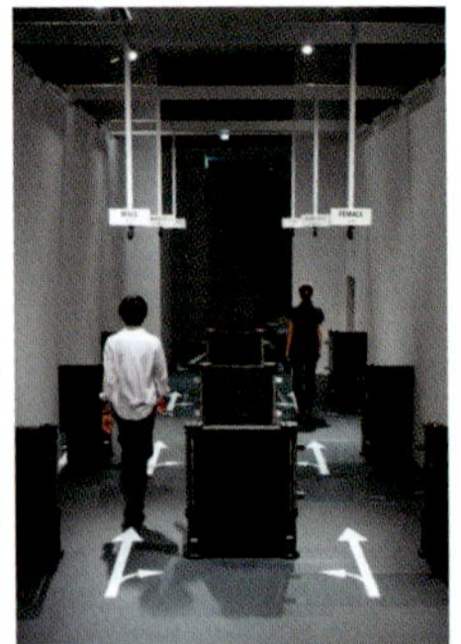

2010

Jul. 16–Nov. 3, *The Definition of Self*, 21_21 DESIGN SIGHT, Tokyo

Photo: Yuichiro Tamura

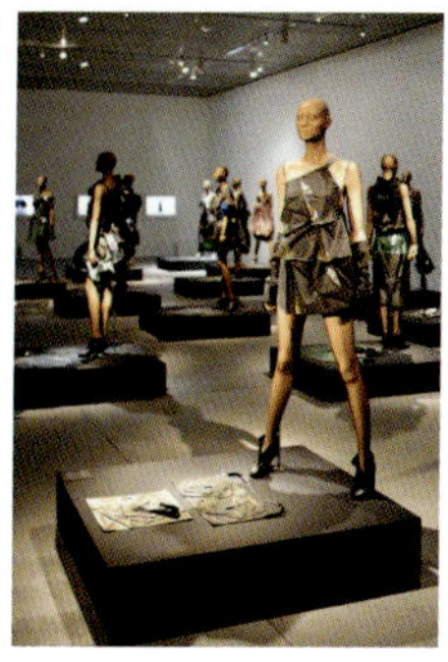

2010

Nov. 16–Dec. 26, *Reality Lab,*
21_21 DESIGN SIGHT, Tokyo

Photo: Masaya Yoshimura

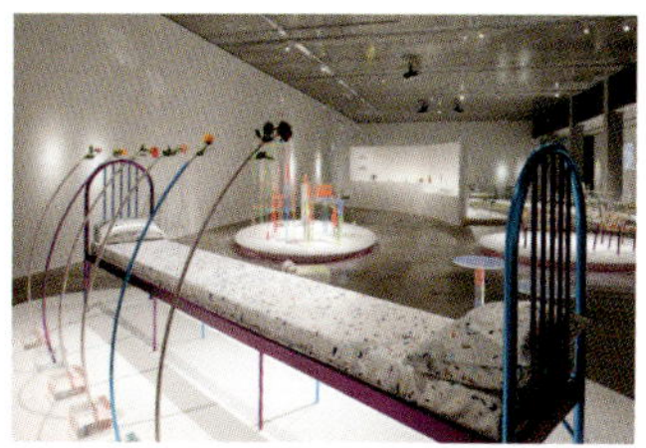

2011

Feb. 2–Jul. 18, *Shiro Kuramata and Ettore Sottsass,*
21_21 DESIGN SIGHT, Tokyo

Photo: Masaya Yoshimura

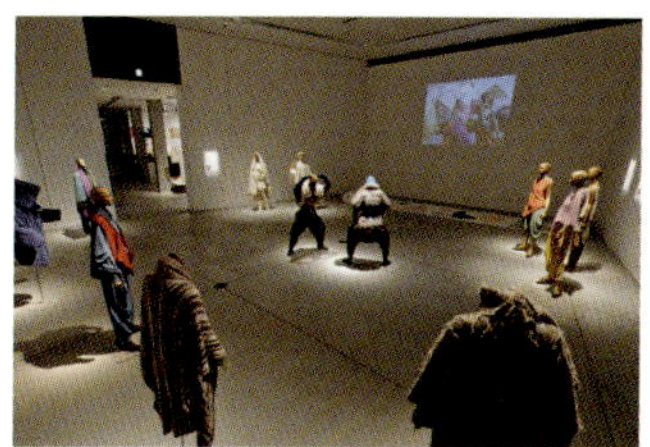

2011

Jul. 26–31, Special program *The Spirit of Tohoku:
"Clothing" by Issey Miyake,* 21_21 DESIGN SIGHT, Tokyo

Photo: Masaya Yoshimura

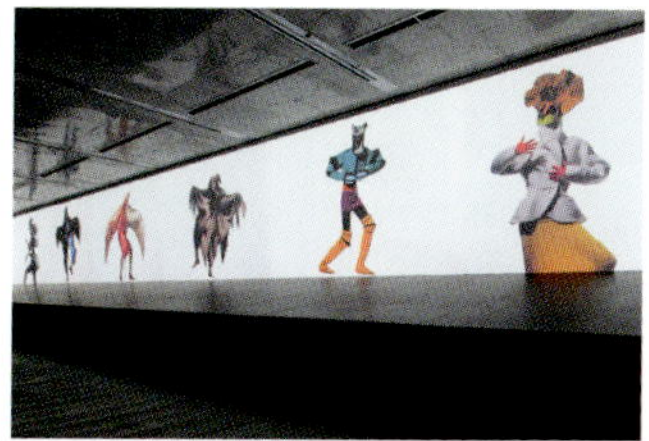

2011

Sep. 16–Apr. 8, 2012, *Irving Penn and Issey Miyake:
Visual Dialogue,* 21_21 DESIGN SIGHT, Tokyo

Photo: Masaya Yoshimura

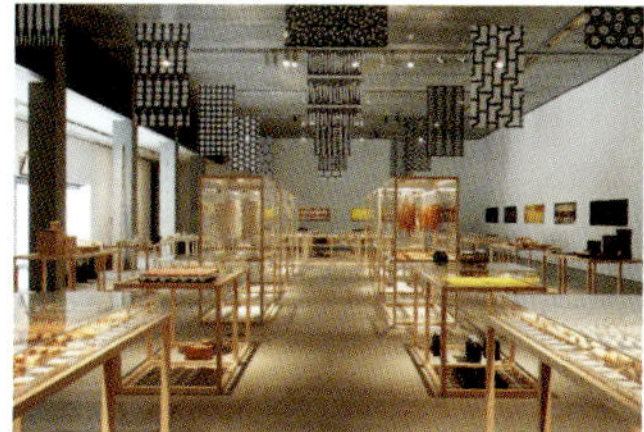

2012

Apr. 27–Aug. 26, *Tema Hima: the Art of Living in Tohoku,*
21_21 DESIGN SIGHT, Tokyo

Photo: Yusuke Nishibe

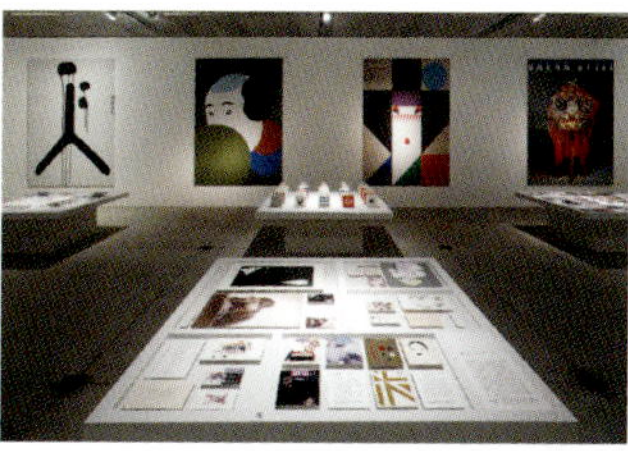

2012

Sep. 21–Jan. 20, 2013, *Ikko Tanaka and Future/Past/
East/West of Design,* 21_21 DESIGN SIGHT, Tokyo

Photo: Masaya Yoshimura

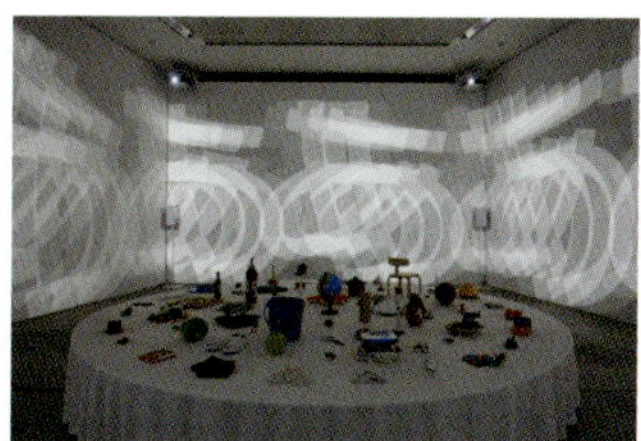

2013

Feb. 8–Jun. 2, *Design Ah!,* 21_21 DESIGN SIGHT, Tokyo

Photo: Masaya Yoshimura

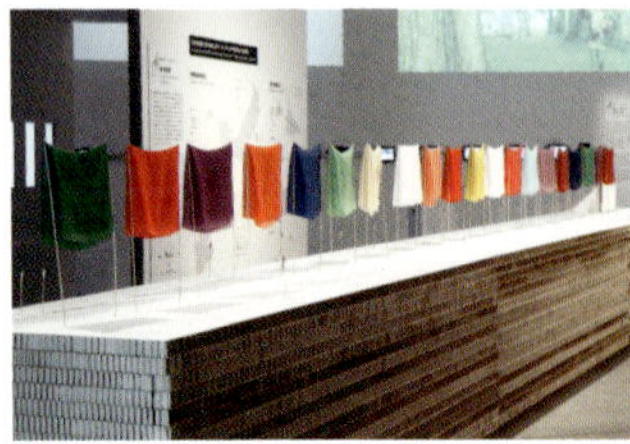

2013

Jun. 21–Oct. 6, *Color-Hunting*,
21_21 DESIGN SIGHT, Tokyo
Photo: Keizo Kioku

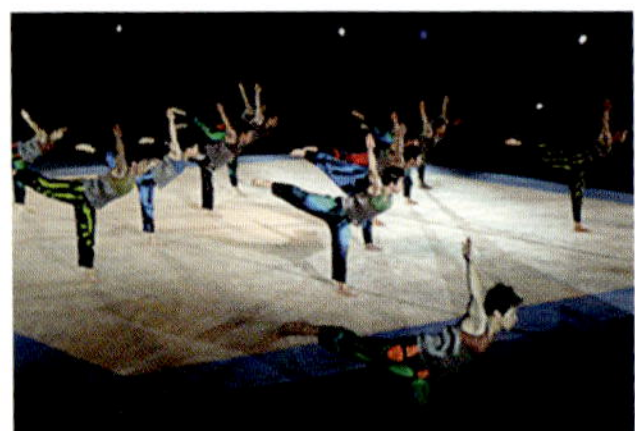

2013

Jul. 18, *Aomori University Men's Rhythmic Gymnastics Team Performance*, Yoyogi National Stadium 2nd Gymnasium, Tokyo
Photo: Masaya Yoshimura

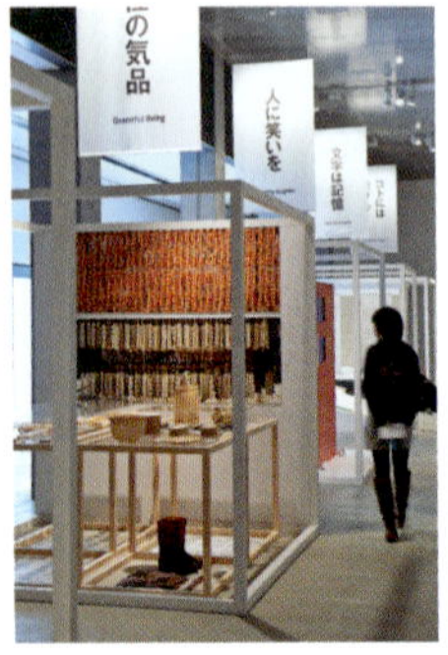

2013

Oct. 25–Feb. 9, 2014, *Toward a Design Museum Japan*, 21_21 DESIGN SIGHT, Tokyo
Photo: Masaya Yoshimura

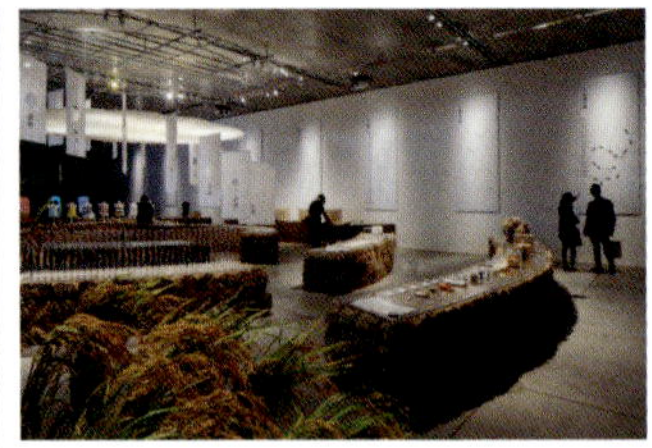

2014

Feb. 28–Jun. 15, *Kome: The Art of Rice*,
21_21 DESIGN SIGHT, Tokyo
Photo: Satoshi Asakawa

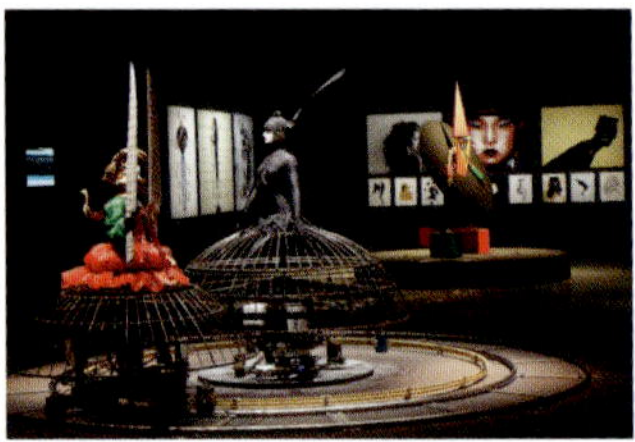

2014

Jul. 4–Oct. 5, *Image-Makers*,
21_21 DESIGN SIGHT, Tokyo
Photo: Keizo Kioku

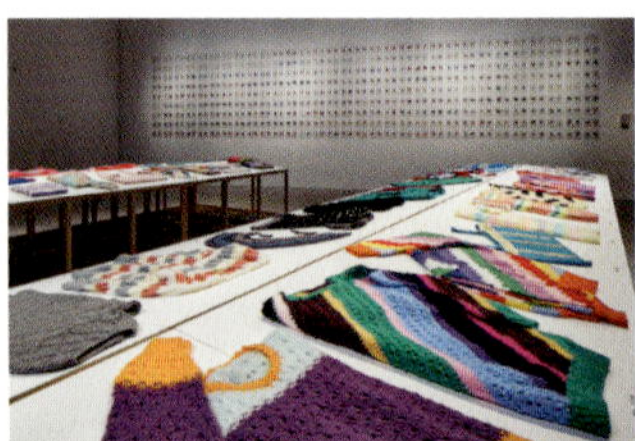

2014

Oct. 24–Feb. 1, 2015, *The Fab Mind: Hints of the Future in a Shifting World*, 21_21 DESIGN SIGHT, Tokyo
Photo: Masaya Yoshimura

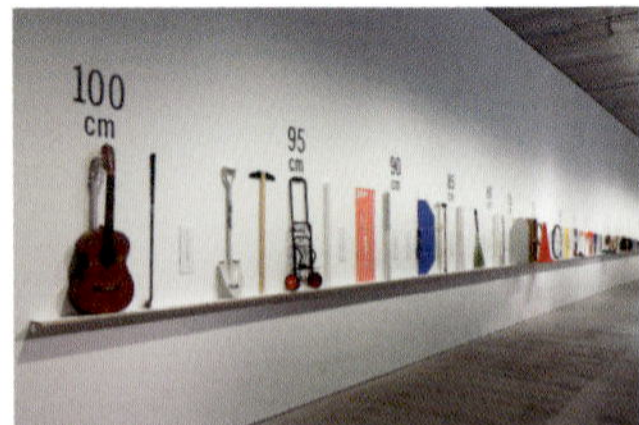

2015

Feb. 20–May 31, *Measuring: This much, That much, How much?*, 21_21 DESIGN SIGHT, Tokyo
Photo: Keizo Kioku

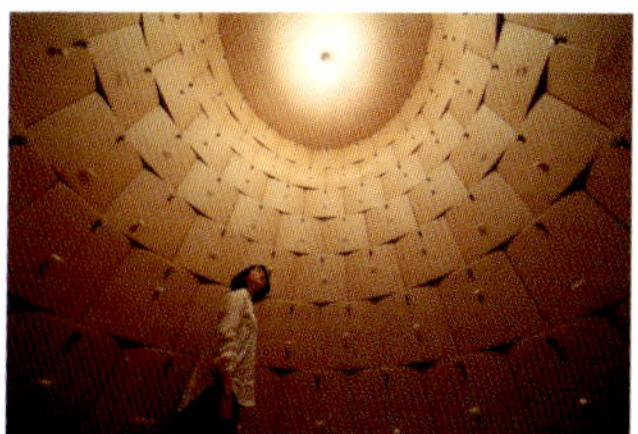

2015
Jun. 19–Sep. 27, *Motion Science*,
21_21 DESIGN SIGHT, Tokyo
Photo: Keizo Kioku

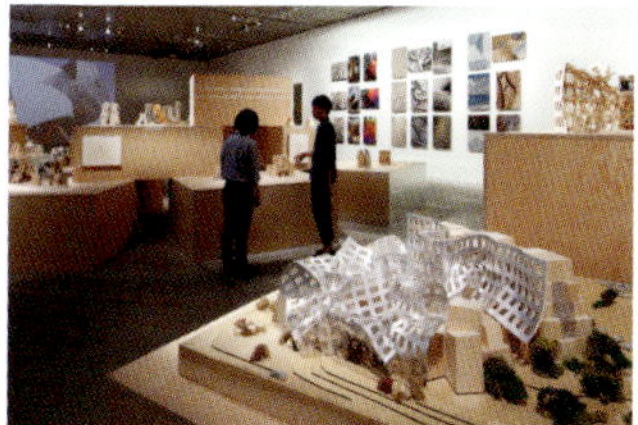

2015
Oct. 16–Feb. 7, 2016, *Architect Frank Gehry
'I Have an Idea'*, 21_21 DESIGN SIGHT, Tokyo
Photo: Keizo Kioku

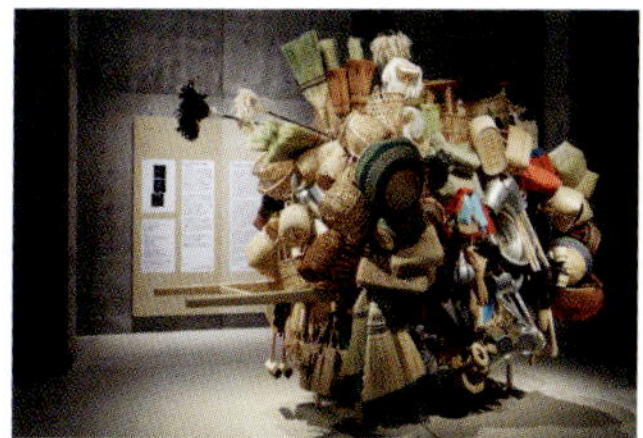

2016
Feb. 26–Jun. 5, *Zakka–Goods and Things–*,
21_21 DESIGN SIGHT, Tokyo
Photo: Sohei Oya (Nacása & Partners Inc.)

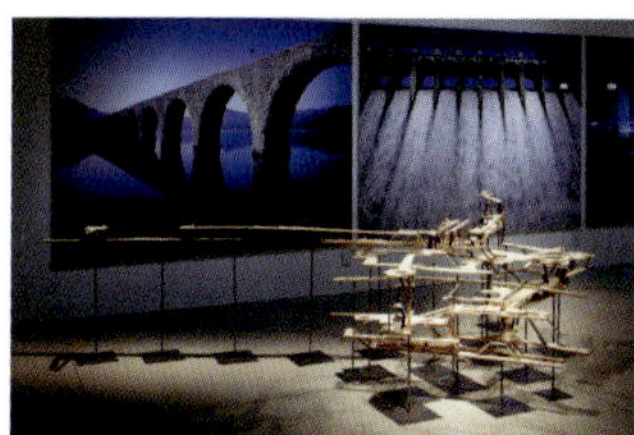

2016
Jun. 24–Sep. 25, *Doboku: Civil Engineering*,
21_21 DESIGN SIGHT, Tokyo
Photo: Keizo Kioku

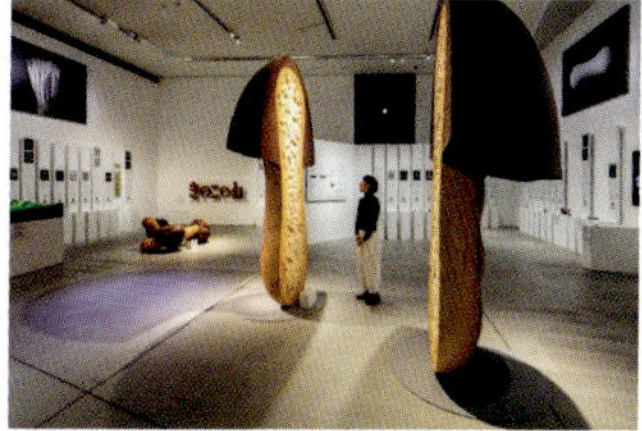

2016
Oct. 14–Jan. 22, 2017, *Design Anatomy: A Method
for Seeing the World through Familiar Objects*,
21_21 DESIGN SIGHT, Tokyo
Photo: Satoshi Asakawa

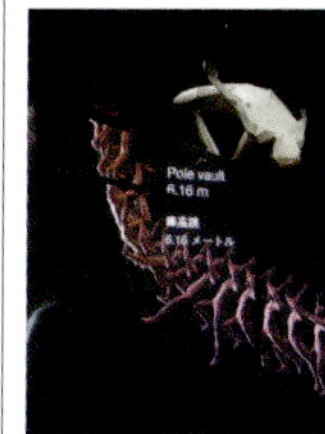
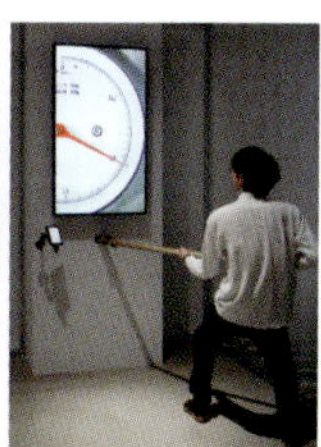

2017
Feb. 17–Jun. 4, *Athlete*, 21_21 DESIGN SIGHT, Tokyo
Photo: Keizo Kioku

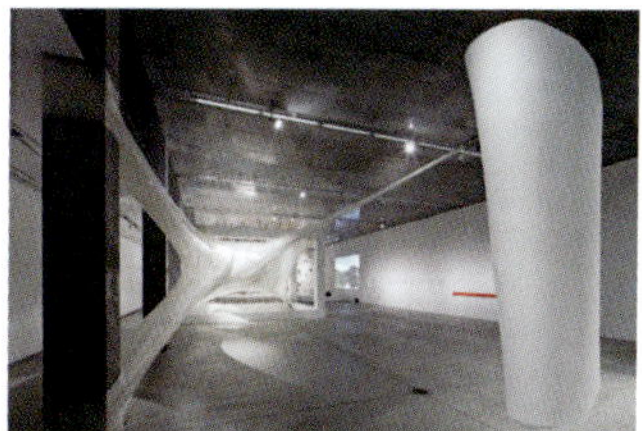

2017
Jun. 23–Oct. 1, *Grand Projects: How Far Will You Go?*,
21_21 DESIGN SIGHT, Tokyo
Photo: Keizo Kioku

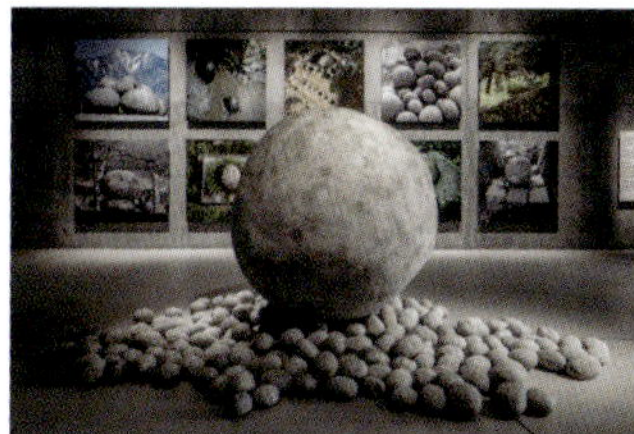

2017
Dec. 20–Feb. 4, 2018, *Wild: Untamed Mind*,
21_21 DESIGN SIGHT, Tokyo
Photo: Satoshi Asakawa

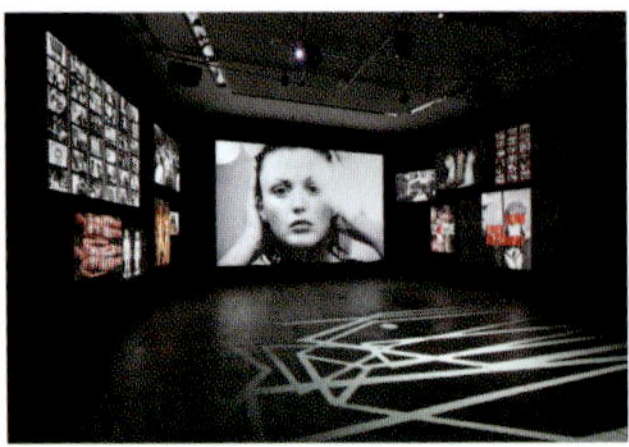

2018

Feb. 23–Jun. 10, *New Planet Photo City–William Klein and Photographers Living in the 22nd Century*, 21_21 DESIGN SIGHT, Tokyo

Photo: Masaya Yoshimura

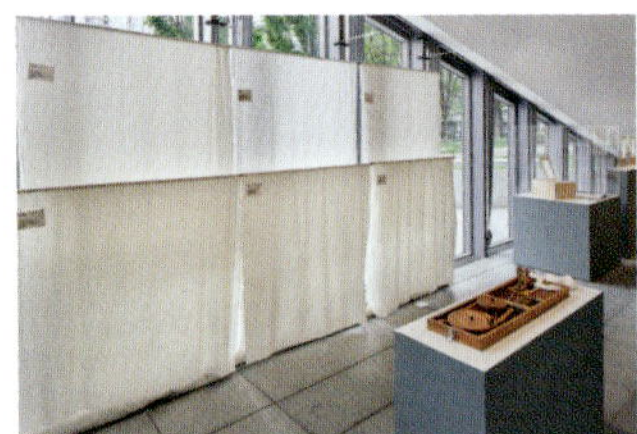

2018

Apr. 18–May 20, *Khadi: The Fabric of India's Tomorrow–Homage to Martand Singh–*, 21_21 DESIGN SIGHT GALLERY 3, Tokyo

Photo: Masaya Yoshimura

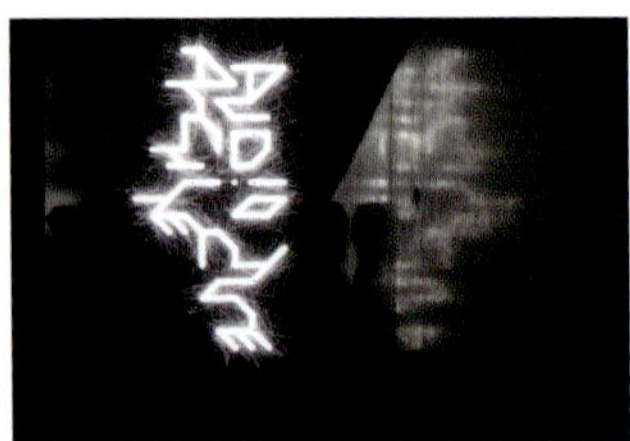

2018

Jun. 29–Oct. 14, *Audio Architecture*, 21_21 DESIGN SIGHT, Tokyo

Photo: Masaya Yoshimura

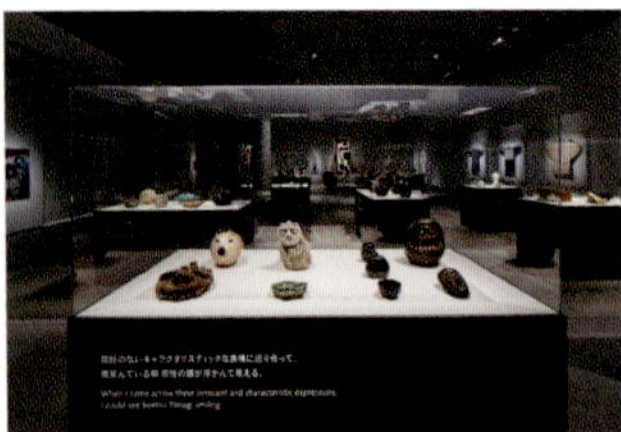

2018

Nov. 2–Feb. 24, 2019, *Mingei–Another Kind of Art*, 21_21 DESIGN SIGHT, Tokyo

Photo: Masaya Yoshimura

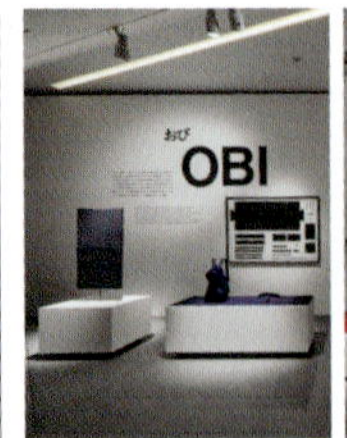
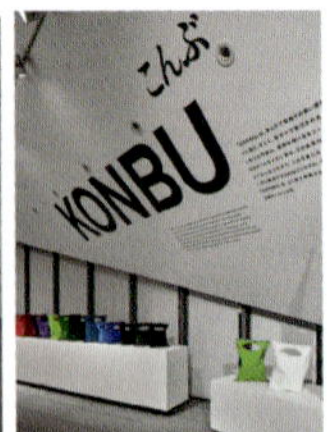

2019

Jun. 19–Feb. 18, *"Obi Konbu" Exhibition: Work by Miyake Design Studio Series* ①, 21_21 DESIGN SIGHT GALLERY 3, Tokyo

Photo: Masaya Yoshimura

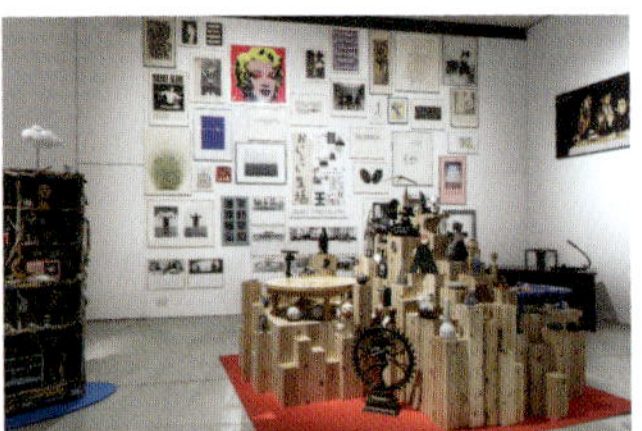

2019

Mar. 15–Jun. 30, *Sense of Humor*, 21_21 DESIGN SIGHT, Tokyo

Photo: Kaoru Suzuki

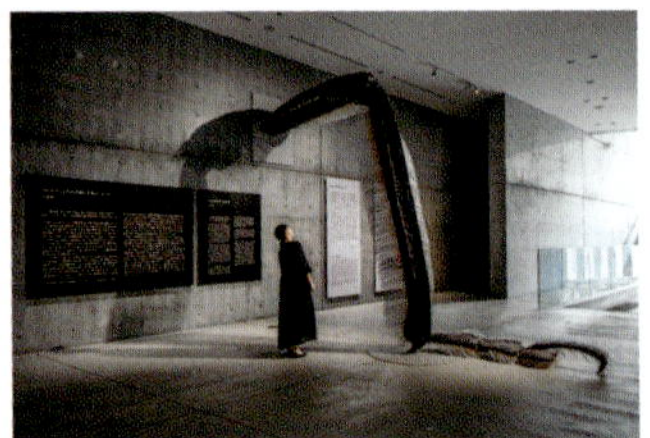

2019

Jul. 14–Nov. 4, *Insects: Models for Design*, 21_21 DESIGN SIGHT, Tokyo

Photo: Satoshi Asakawa

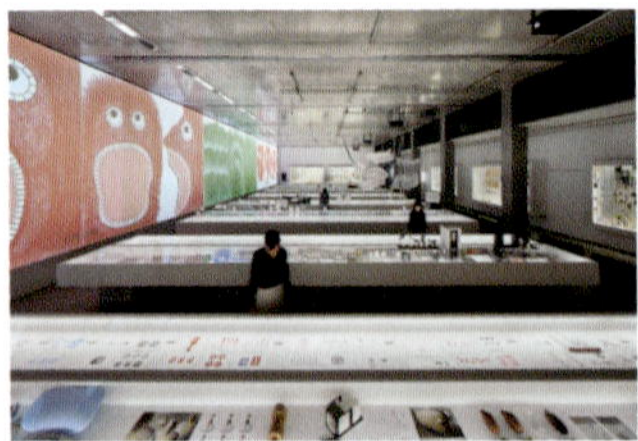

2019

Nov. 22–Sep. 22, 2020 (closed between Feb. 27–May 31, 2020), *Secret Source of Inspiration: Designers' Hidden Sketches and Mockups*, 21_21 DESIGN SIGHT, Tokyo

Photo: Masaya Yoshimura

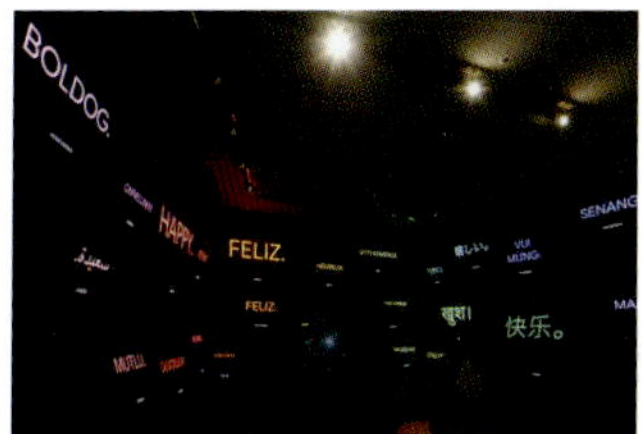

2020

Dec. 16–Jun. 13, 2021 (closed between Apr. 25–
Jun. 1, 2021), *Translations–Understanding
Misunderstanding*, 21_21 DESIGN SIGHT, Tokyo
Photo: Keizo Kioku

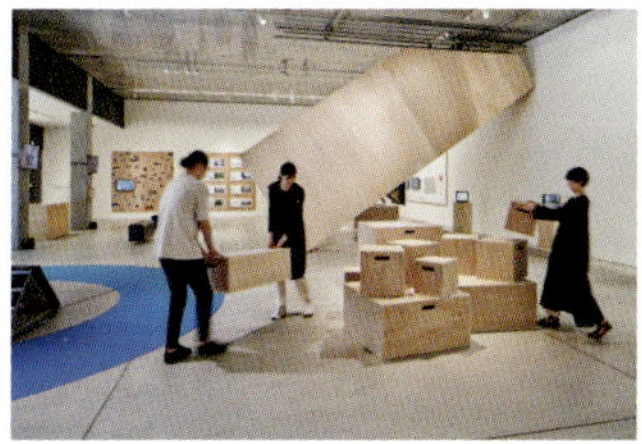

2021

Jul. 2–Nov. 28, *Rules?*, 21_21 DESIGN SIGHT, Tokyo
Photo: Masaya Yoshimura

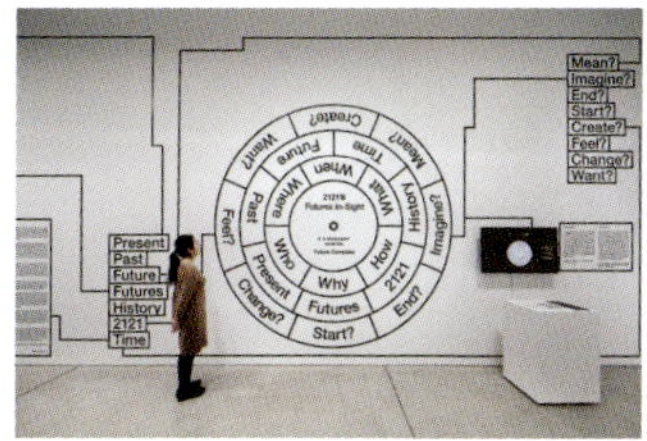

2021

Dec. 21–May 22, 2022, *The Year 2121: Futures
In-Sight*, 21_21 DESIGN SIGHT, Tokyo
Photo: Masaya Yoshimura

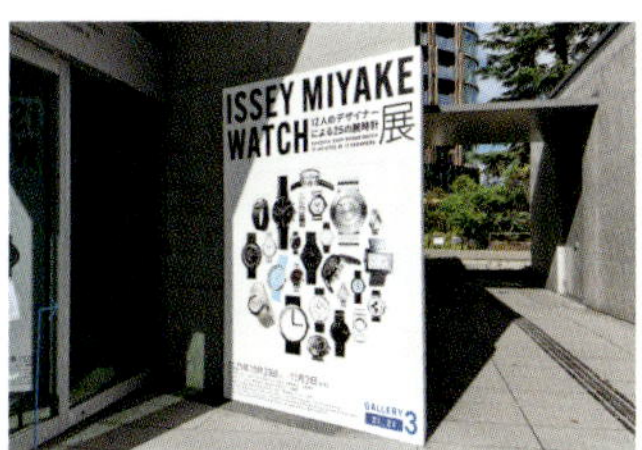

2021

Oct. 23–Nov. 6, *Issey Miyake Watch:
25 Watches by 12 Designers*,
21_21 DESIGN SIGHT GALLERY 3, Tokyo
Photo: Courtesy of Miyake Design Studio

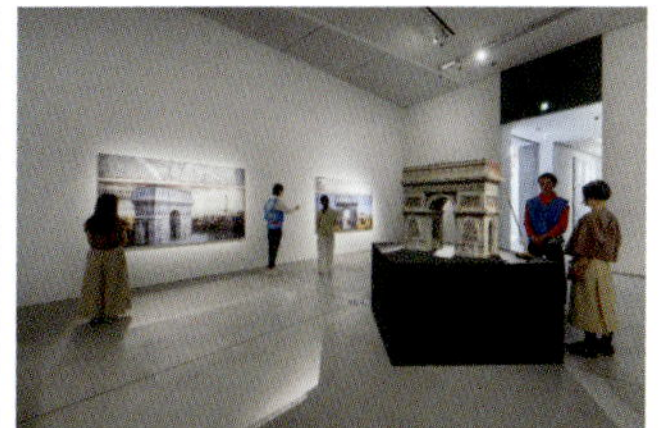

2022

Jun. 13–Feb. 12, 2023, *Christo and Jeanne-Claude
"L'Arc de Triomphe, Wrapped,"* 21_21 DESIGN SIGHT,
Tokyo
Photo: Masaya Yoshimura

PUBLICATIONS
EXHIBITION CATALOGUES

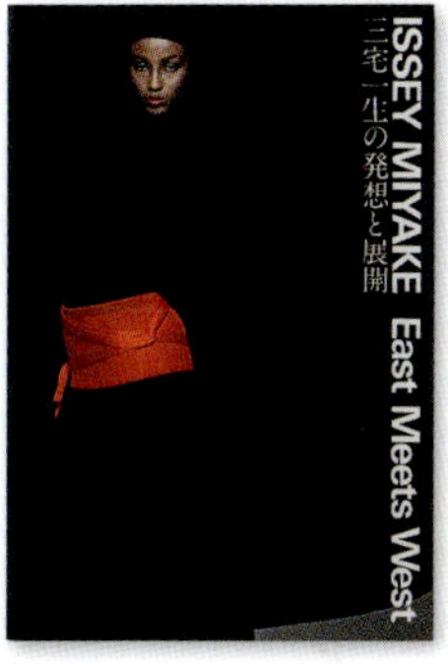

1978

Issey Miyake East Meets West,
Heibonsha Limited

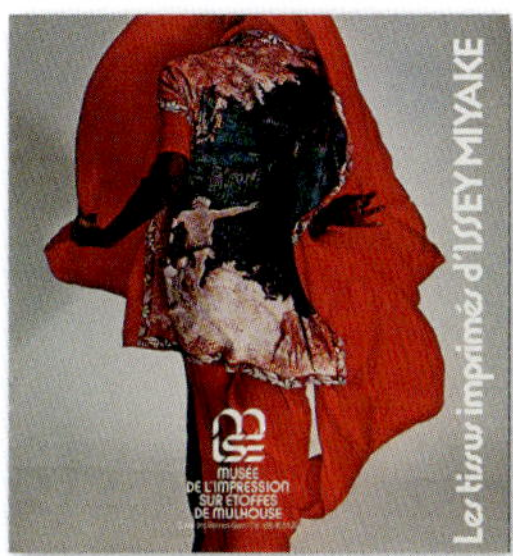

1979

Exhibition catalogue: *Les Tissus Imprimés d'Issey
Miyake*, Musée de l'Impression sur Étoffes, Mulhouse

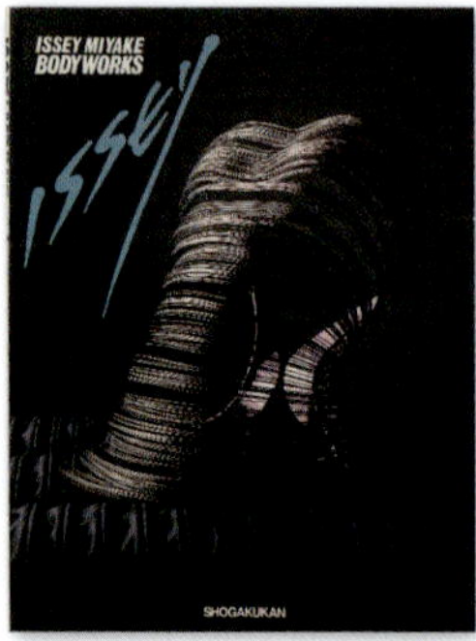

1983

Issey Miyake Bodyworks, Shogakukan, Inc.

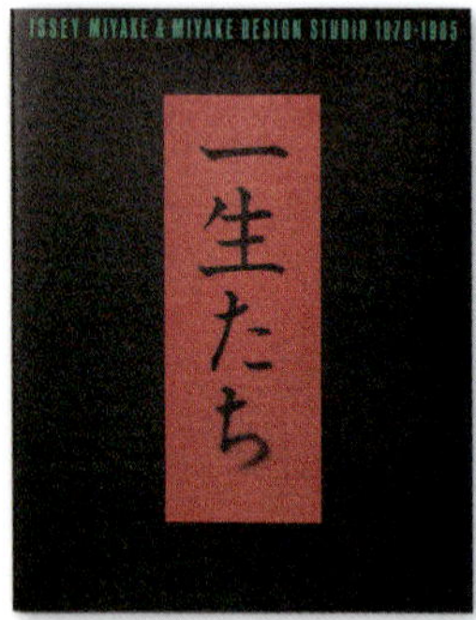

1985

Issey Miyake & Miyake Design Studio 1970–1985, Obunsha Co., Ltd.

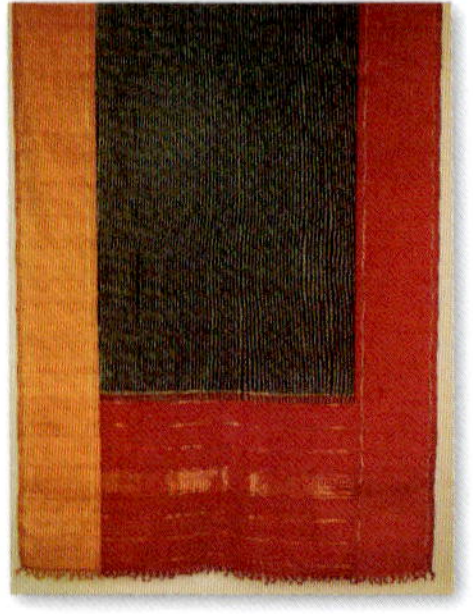

1985

Exhibition catalogue: *L'Or, la Laine et la Soie, Cotons et Plumes de Paon. Les Textiles de l'Inde et les Modèles Créés par Issey Miyake*, Musée des Arts Décoratifs, Paris

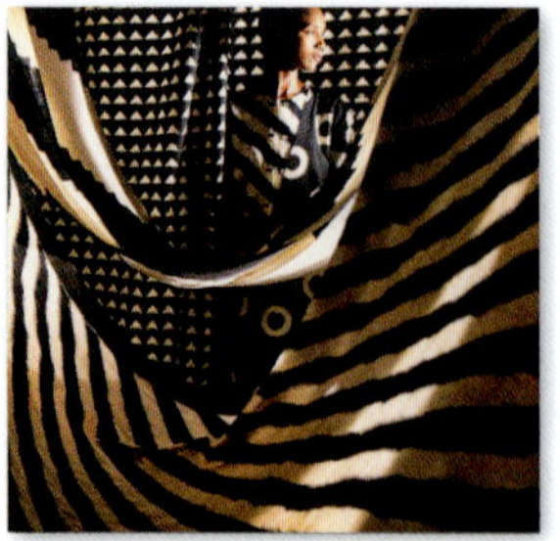

1986

Exhibition catalogue: *Haath: Hand Weaving of India and Issey Miyake*, The Seibu Department Stores, Tokyo

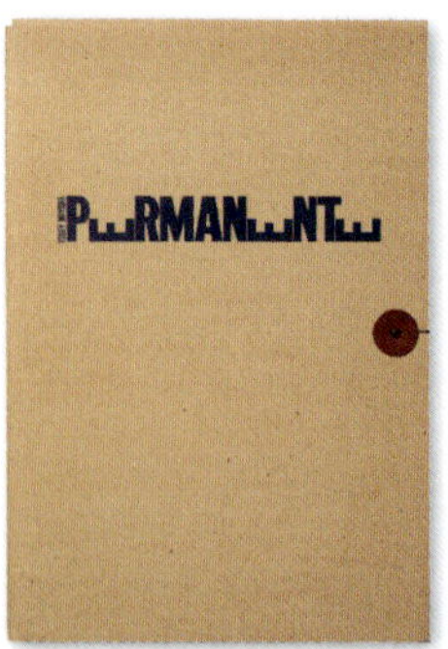

1986

ISSEY MIYAKE PERMANENTE, photographs by Snowdon, Issey Miyake International, Inc. (private publication), issued every collection, 1986–90, 9 issues

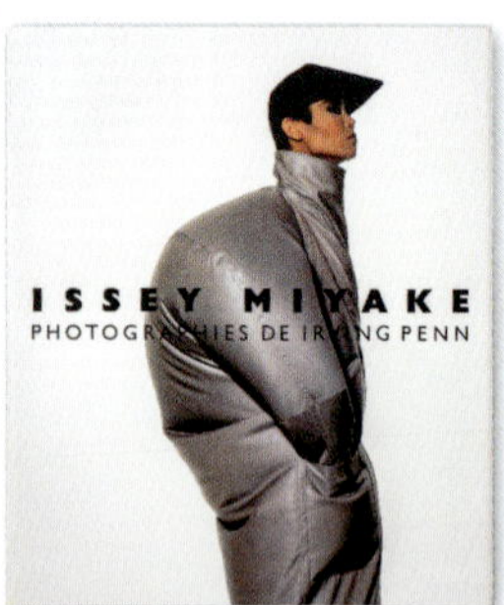

1988

Exhibition catalogue: *Issey Miyake Photographies de Irving Penn*, Pont Royal

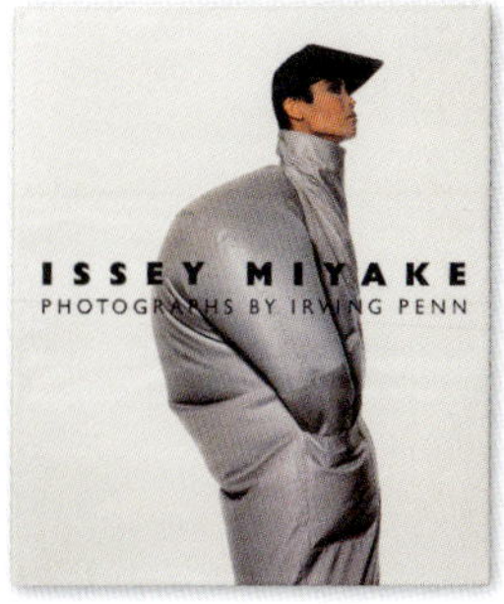

1988

Issey Miyake Photographs by Irving Penn,
Callaway Edition. English edition: New York
Graphic Society Book, Japanese edition:
Libro Port Publishing, French edition:
Edipress Livres, German edition: Edition Stemmle

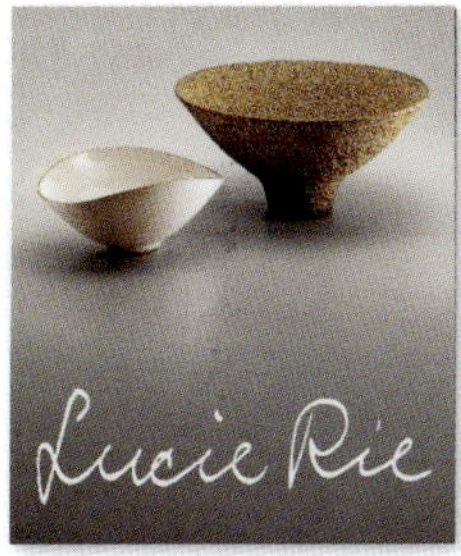

1989

Exhibition catalogue: *Issey Miyake Meets Lucie Rie*,
Miyake Design Studio, Sogetsu-kai foundation,
Museum of Oriental Ceramics, Osaka

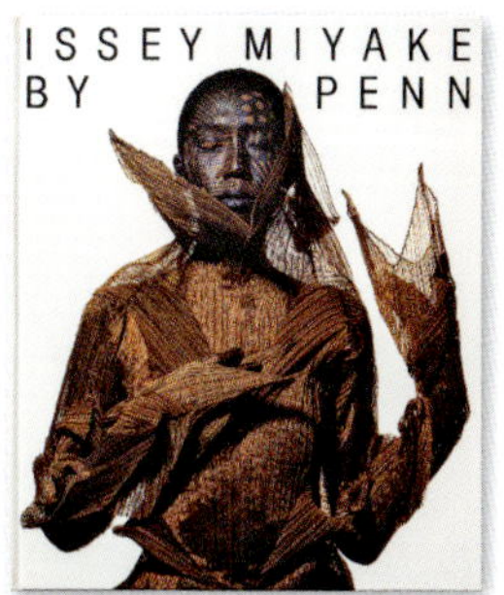

1989

Issey Miyake by Penn,
Miyake Design Studio (private publication)

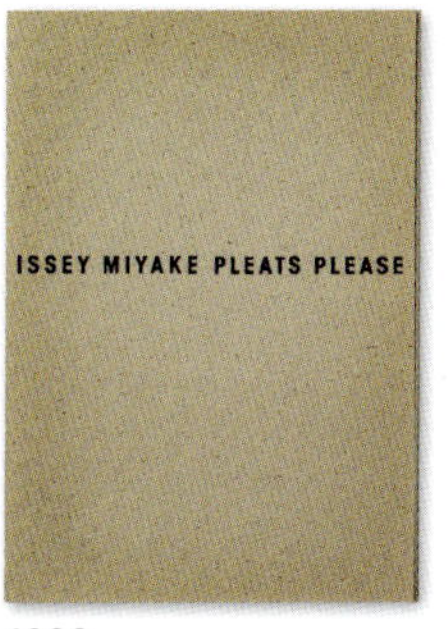

1990

Exhibition catalogue: *Issey Miyake Pleats Please*,
Touko Museum of Contemporary Art

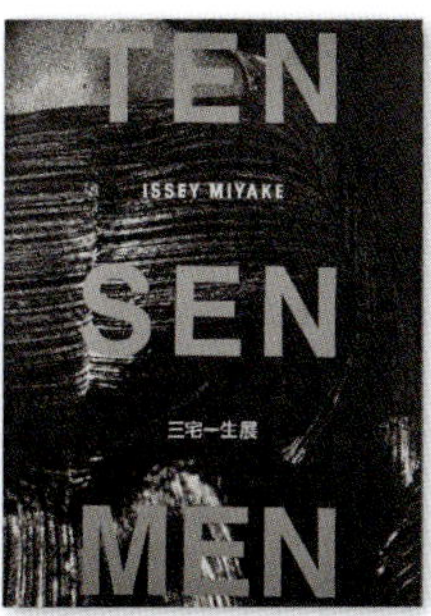

1990

Exhibiton catalogue: *The 1st Hiroshima Art Prize,
Issey Miyake: TEN SEN MEN*, Hiroshima City
Museum of Contemporary Art

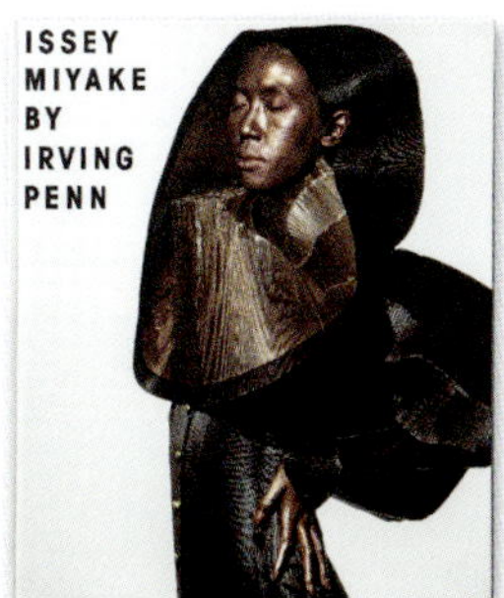

1990

Issey Miyake by Irving Penn 1990,
Miyake Design Studio (private publication)

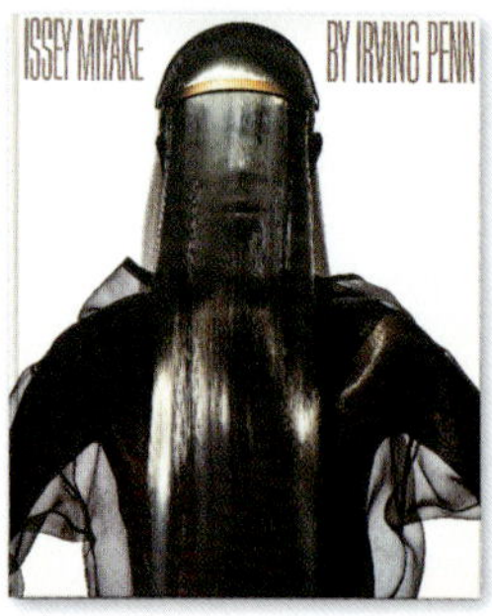

1992

Issey Miyake by Irving Penn 1991–92,
Fukutake Publishing Co., Ltd.

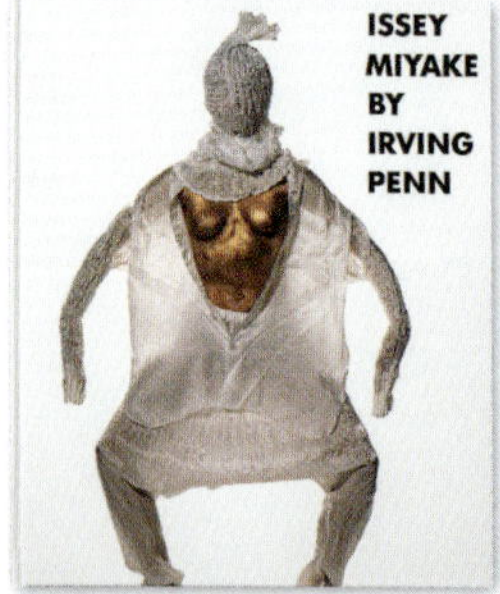

1995

Issey Miyake by Irving Penn 1993–95,
Miyake Design Studio (private publication)

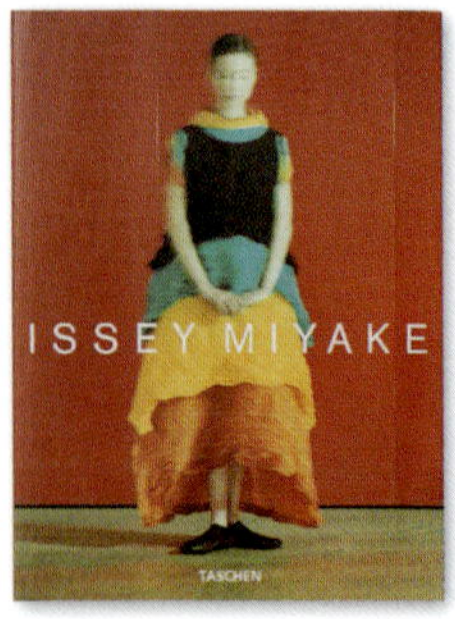

1995

Issey Miyake, TASCHEN, author: Mark Holborn

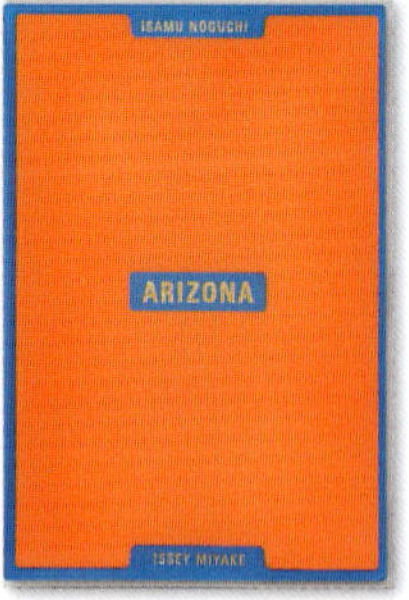

1997

Exhibition catalogue: *Isamu Noguchi and Issey Miyake: Arizona*, Marugame Genichiro-Inokuma Museum of Contemporary Art

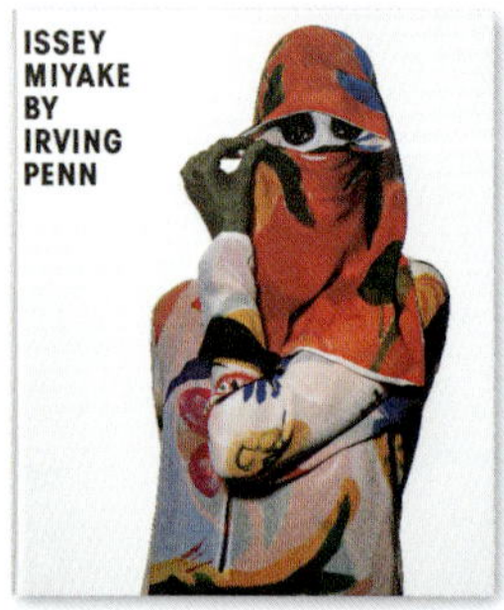

1997

Issey Miyake by Irving Penn 1995–97,
Miyake Design Studio (private publication)

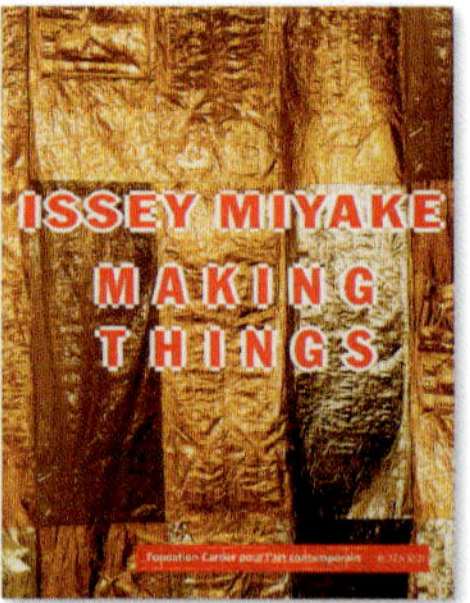

1998

Exhibition catalogue: *Issey Miyake Making Things*,
French edition: Actes Sud, English edition:
Scalo, Japanese edition: AXIS (1999)

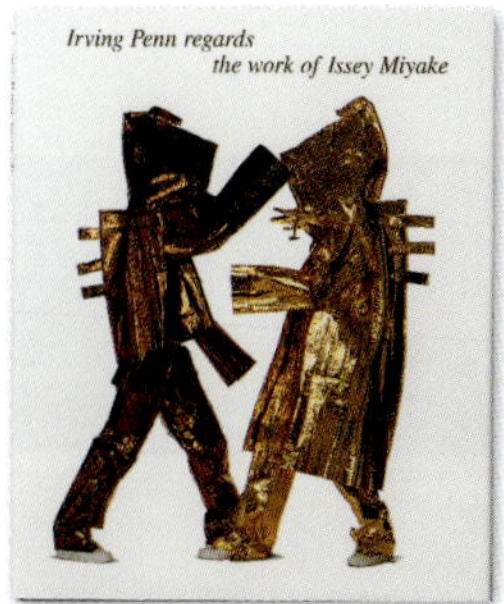

1999

Irving Penn Regards the Work of Issey Miyake,
English edition: Jonathan Cape, American edition:
Bulfinch Press, French edition: Editions Plume,
German edition: Schirmer/Mosel, Japanese edition:
Kyuryudo Art-Publishing Co., Ltd.

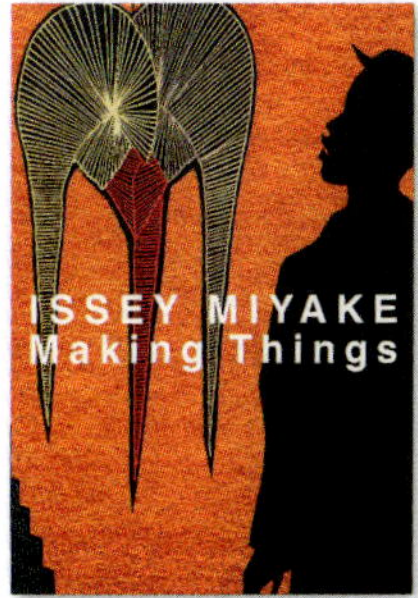

2000

Exhibition catalogue: *Issey Miyake Making Things*,
Museum of Contemporary Art, Tokyo

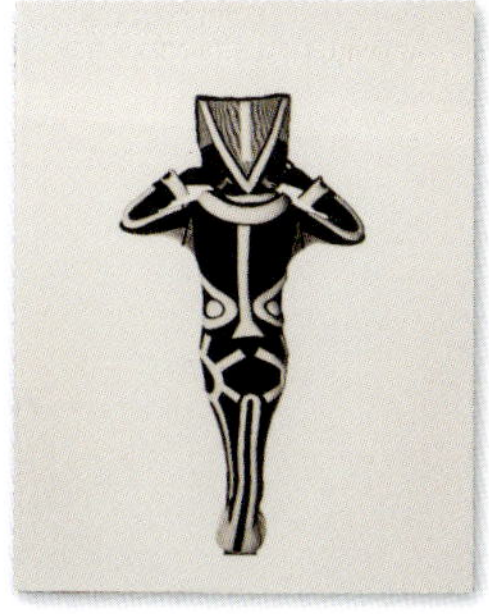

2001

Exhibition catalogue: *A-POC Making: Issey Miyake
& Dai Fujiwara*, Vitra Design Museum, Berlin

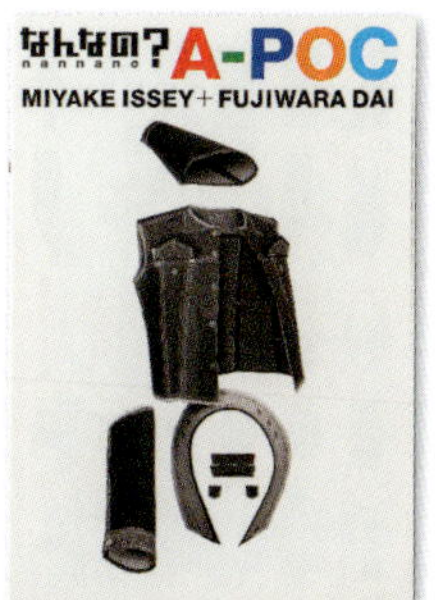

2003

Exhibition catalogue: *Nannano? A-POC Miyake Issey +
Fujiwara Dai*, Axis Inc.

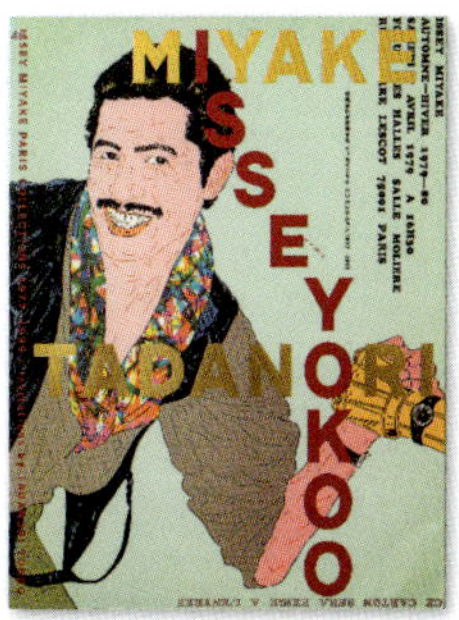

2005

Exhibition catalogue: *Issey Miyake Paris
Collections 1977–1999: Invitations by Tadanori
Yokoo*, The Museum of Modern Art, Toyama

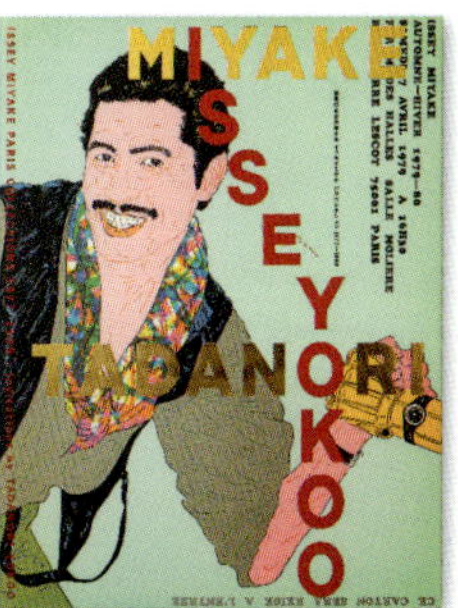

2005

*Issey Miyake Paris Collections 1977–1999:
Invitations by Tadanori Yokoo*, Bijutsu Shuppan-sha

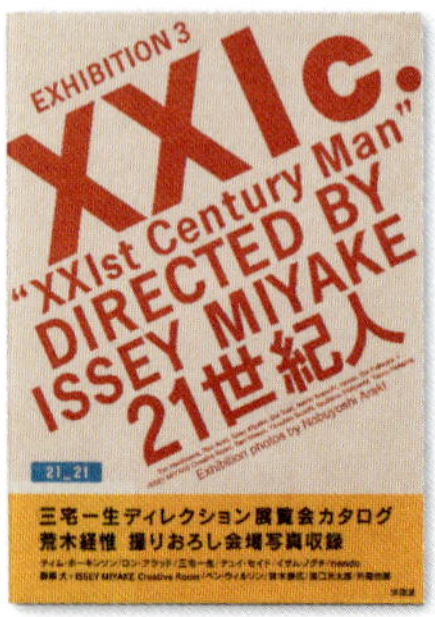

2008

Exhibition catalogue: *XXIc.–XXIst Century Man*,
Kyuryudo Art-Publishing Co., Ltd.

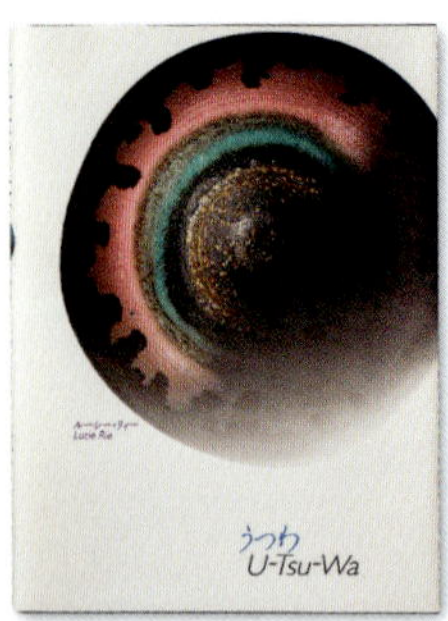

2009

Exhibition catalogue: *U-tsu-Wa–Lucie Rie, Jennifer Lee,
Ernst Gamperl*, Kyuryuko Art-Publishing Co., Ltd

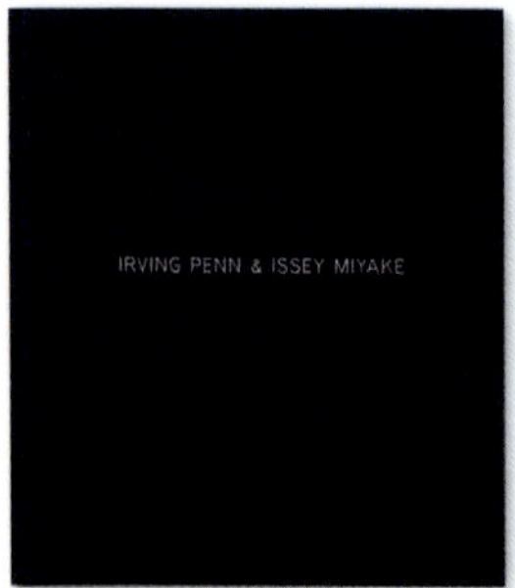

2011

Irving Penn & Issey Miyake, Miyake Design Studio

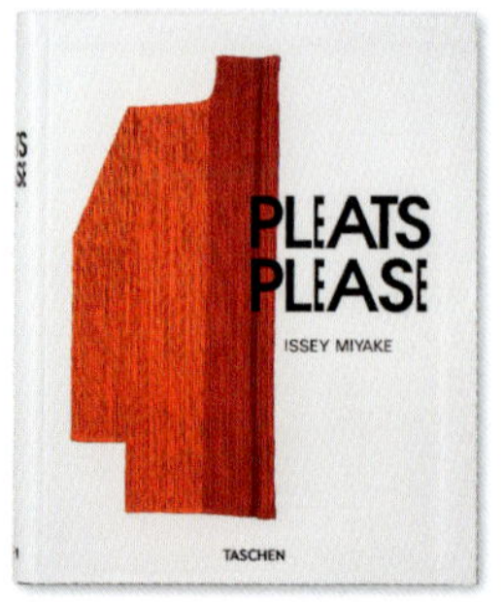

2012

Pleats Please Issey Miyake, TASCHEN

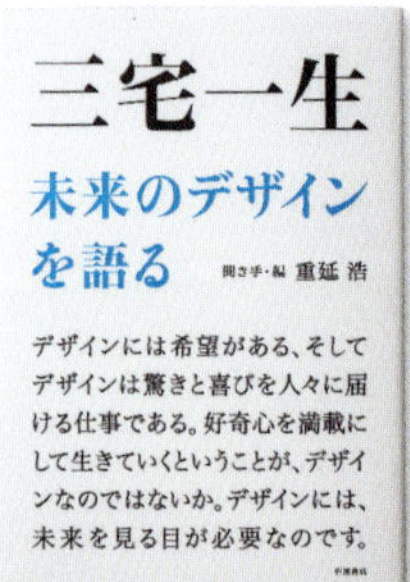

2013

Conversation with Issey Miyake: The Future of Design,
Iwanami Shoten Publishers, interviewer/editor:
Yutaka Shigenobu

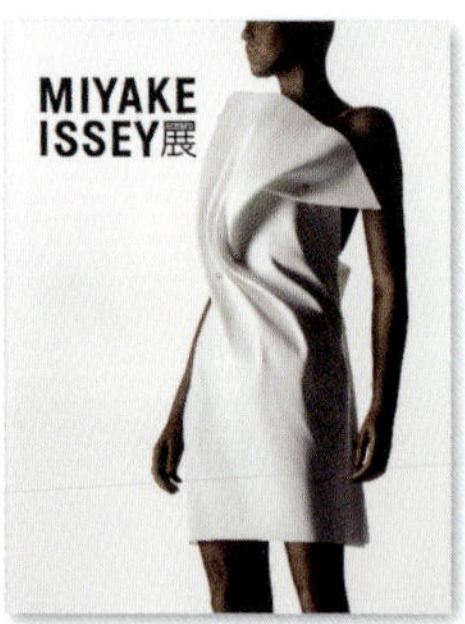

2016

Exhibition catalogue: *Miyake Issey Exhibition: The Work
of Miyake Issey*, Kyuryudo Art-Publishing Co.,Ltd.

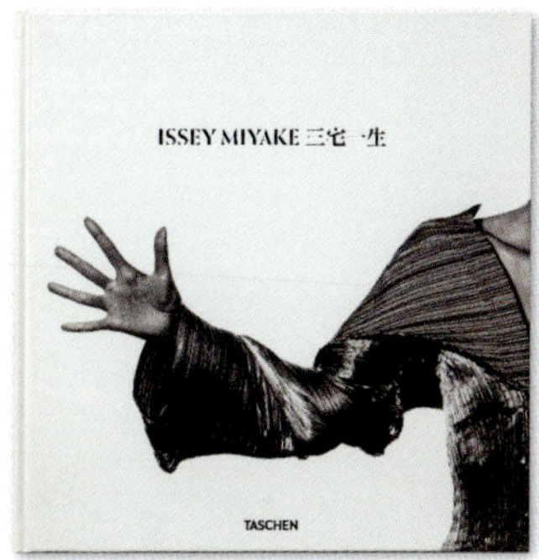

2016

Issey Miyake, TASCHEN

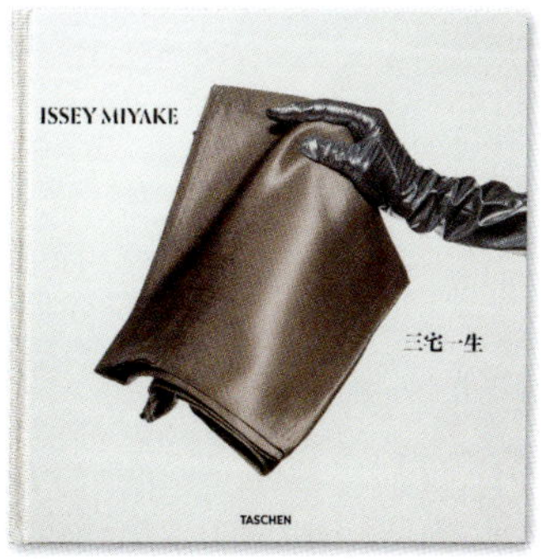

2016

Issey Miyake: Collector's Edition, TASCHEN

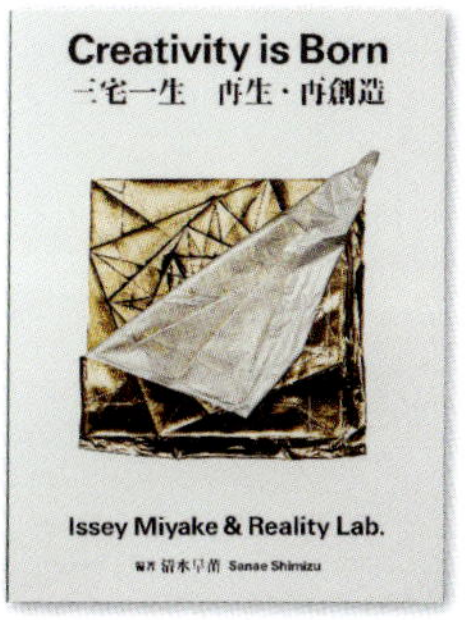

2016

Creativity is Born: Issey Miyake & Reality Lab.,
PIE International Inc., author: Sanae Shimizu

2017

Where Did Issey Come From? The Work of Issey Miyake,
HeHe, author: Kazuko Koike

NOTES

This is a timeline of Issey Miyake's major exhibitions and
publications. For touring exhibitions and shows, the first
exhibition is noted together with the period of the tour
and the places visited. Titles and publishers are noted
for all publications. Names of photographers are noted
when known. All unattributed photographs are in the
collection of The Miyake Issey Foundation.

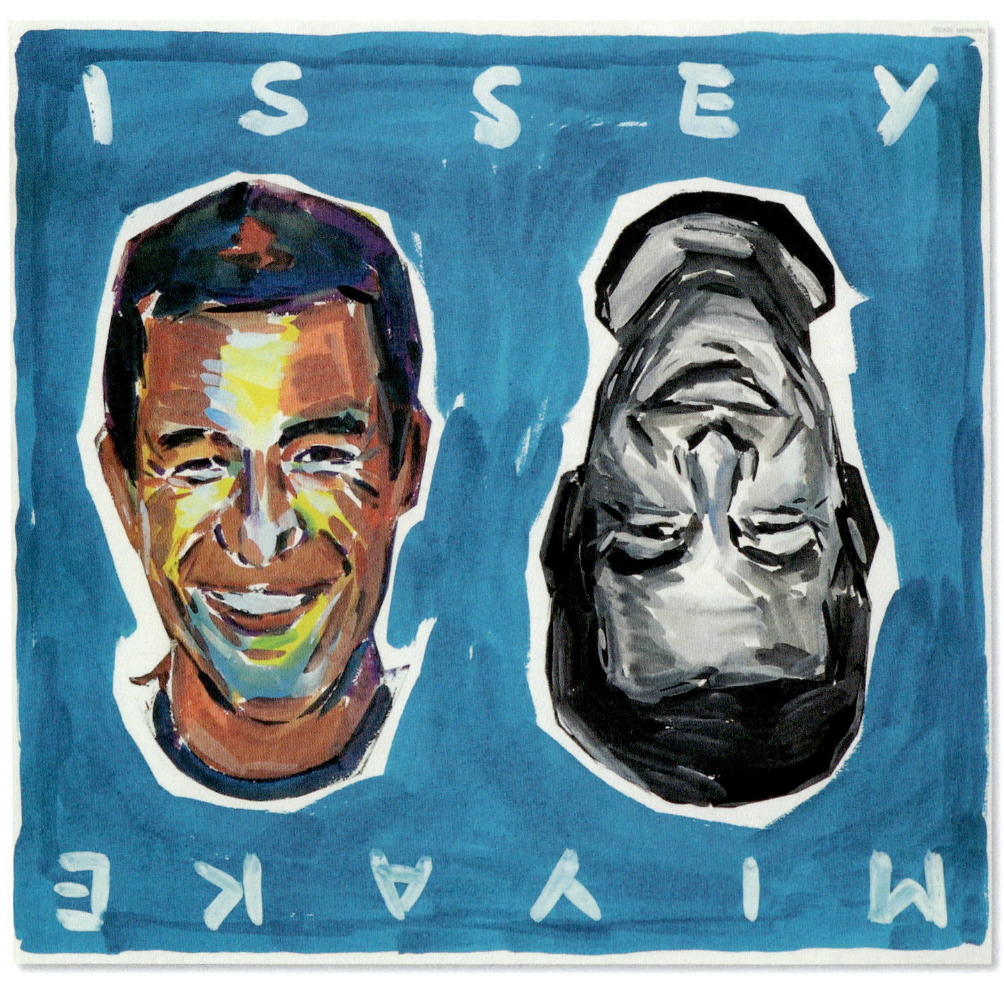

Invitation for the Spring-Summer 1983 Collection
Design: Tadanori Yokoo

APPENDIX

SELECTED BIOGRAPHIES

ISSEY MIYAKE

Designer

Born in Hiroshima in 1938. Graduated from Tama Art University. Established Miyake Design Studio in 1970. Began participating in the Paris Collections in 1973. From the very beginning of his career as a clothing designer, he worked on creative endeavors that examine the relationship between the body and cloth, based upon the concept of "A Piece of Cloth." Throughout his life, he consistently maintained the stance of making things free from preconceived notions, insisting on a process of tenacious research and experimentation.

PRIZES AND AWARDS

1977	1976 Mainichi Design Awards (Japan)
1990	1st Hiroshima Art Prize (Japan)
1991	L'Ordre des Arts et des Lettres (France), rank of Commandeur
1992	1991 Asahi Prize (Japan)
1993	Legion d'Honneur (France), rank of Chevalier Honorary Doctorate, Royal College of Art (UK)
1995	15th Golden Needle Prize (Spain)
1997	Medal with Purple Ribbon (Japan)
1998	Person of Cultural Merit (Japan)
1999	Honorary doctorate, Université de Lyon (France)
2000	1st Georg Jensen Award (Denmark) 18th Mainichi Fashion Grand Prix Millenium Award (Japan) (also won the grand prize in 1984, 1989, and 1993) 2000 Good Design Award Grand Prize (Japan) awarded for A-POC
2001	Chosen as one of the "World's Creative Leaders" by the Toronto Harbourfront Centre (Canada)
2004	11th Wexner Prize, Wexner Center, Ohio State University (USA)
2005	17th Praemium Imperiale Sculpture Prize in Honor of Prince Takamatsu (Japan)
2006	22nd Kyoto Prize (Japan) (Arts and Philosophy)
2010	2010 Order of Culture (Japan) Honorary Citizen, Hiroshima City and Hiroshima Prefecture
2012	"Design of the Year 2012" (fashion) awarded to 132 5. ISSEY MIYAKE by the Design Museum in London 30th anniversary award of Mainichi Fashion Grand Prix (Japan) to Issey Miyake + Reality Lab
2016	Legion d'Honneur (France), rank of Commandeur
2019	Honorary Citizen, Tokyo Honorary Fellow, Royal Academy of Arts (UK)

MIDORI KITAMURA
Chairman of Miyake Design Studio
Chairman of The Miyake Issey Foundation
President of 21_21 DESIGN SIGHT Inc.
Born in Tokyo in 1949. Graduated from Ferris University. Began working with Issey Miyake in 1976 as attaché de presse and involved in all aspects of his professional work, including collections, exhibitions, and publications. Assisted photography of Irving Penn for ISSEY MIYAKE collections over the course of 13 years, from 1986 to 1999. Also provided creative direction and production for perfumes, watches, and other products. Served as exhibition director for the *Irving Penn and Issey Miyake: Visual Dialogue* exhibition (21_21 DESIGN SIGHT) in 2011. Editorial director for the book *Pleats Please Issey Miyake* (TASCHEN, 2012). In 2016, served as exhibition producer and director for the *MIYAKE ISSEY EXHIBITION: The Work of Miyake Issey* (The National Art Center, Tokyo). Editorial director for *Issey Miyake* (TASCHEN, 2016).

KAZUKO KOIKE
Creative director
Born in Tokyo in 1936. Graduated from the School of Humanities and Social Sciences, Waseda University. Involved in the founding of MUJI in 1980 and continues to serve on the advisory board. Planned and directed numerous exhibitions, including *Shojo Toshi* at the Japanese Pavilion in the Biennale di Venezia Architettura (2000) and *Ikko Tanaka and Future/Past/East/West of Design* (21_21 DESIGN SIGHT, 2012). In 1983, developed and led the Sagacho Exhibit Space and was instrumental in introducing many notable contemporary Japanese and international artists (continued to 2000). In 2022, held her first solo exhibit *Alternative! Kazuko Koike Exhibition: Soft-Power Movement of Art & Design* at 3331 Arts Chiyoda. Publications include the book *Art/Mediation: The Work of Kazuko Koike* (Heibonsha, 2020) and the Japanese translation of *Eileen Gray: Architect/Designer* (Misuzu Shobo, 2017). Professor emeritus, Musashino Art University. Awarded the title of "Person of Cultural Merit."

PHOTO CREDITS

The photographs by Yuriko Takagi
on the following pages were taken
for the 2016 edition of *Issey Miyake*.
Shiseido Beauty Creation Center
furnish cooperation for the photography (hair and makeup: Hirofumi
Kera): 50, 51, 144–145, 146–147,
172–173, 202, 203, 212–213, 220,
221, 222, 223, 232, 233

SPECIAL THANKS

Tomoko Komuro

Makiko Minagawa
Tomio Mohri
Akira Onozuka
Naoki Takizawa
Dai Fujiwara

Kaneko Ogasawara
Sachiko Yamamoto
Toshiko Amano
Keiko Neko
Fujiko Hane

NOTES

Issey Miyake's major works are chronicled year by year.
Explanations and records have also been included for
particularly prominent works.
Historical publications and documents have been
followed for records and titles, though clearly erroneous
information has been corrected.
Exhibition data is limited to solo exhibitions by Issey
Miyake or exhibitions for which Issey Miyake provided
planning or direction.

Photographers and graphic designers involved with
poster design have been noted.
Clothes and collections are listed by year of production.
Names of photographers are noted when known.
All unattributed photographs are in the collection of
The Miyake Issey Foundation.

IMPRINT

Revised and updated edition
© 2025 TASCHEN GmbH
Hohenzollernring 53, D–50672 Köln
www.taschen.com

Cover, pp. 2, 6, 460, and back cover
Rhythm Pleats, Spring-Summer 1990 Collection
Photography: Irving Penn
© The Irving Penn Foundation

Concept and editorial direction
Midori Kitamura, Tokyo
Editing
Cawaii Factory | Tamaki Harada and
Mari Nakayama, Tokyo
Editing and project coordination
Sawako Ogitani, Masako Omori,
Ayaka Otake, Masataka Teruya, Tokyo
English translation
Kazue Kobata, Kayoko Yokota, Richard Walker
for bridge corporation, Tokyo
Arturo Silva, Vienna
Editorial cooperation
Akiko Moriyama, Yoshiko Ikoma, Tokyo
Nancy Stanton Talcott, New York
Marie Chalmel, Michi Yamaguchi, Paris
Kerry Francis, London
Giorgiana Ravizza, Milan
Editorial consultant
Jun Kanai, New York
Archive
The Miyake Issey Foundation,
Miyake Design Studio, Tokyo

Printed in Bosnia–Herzegovina
ISBN 978-3-7544-0286-3

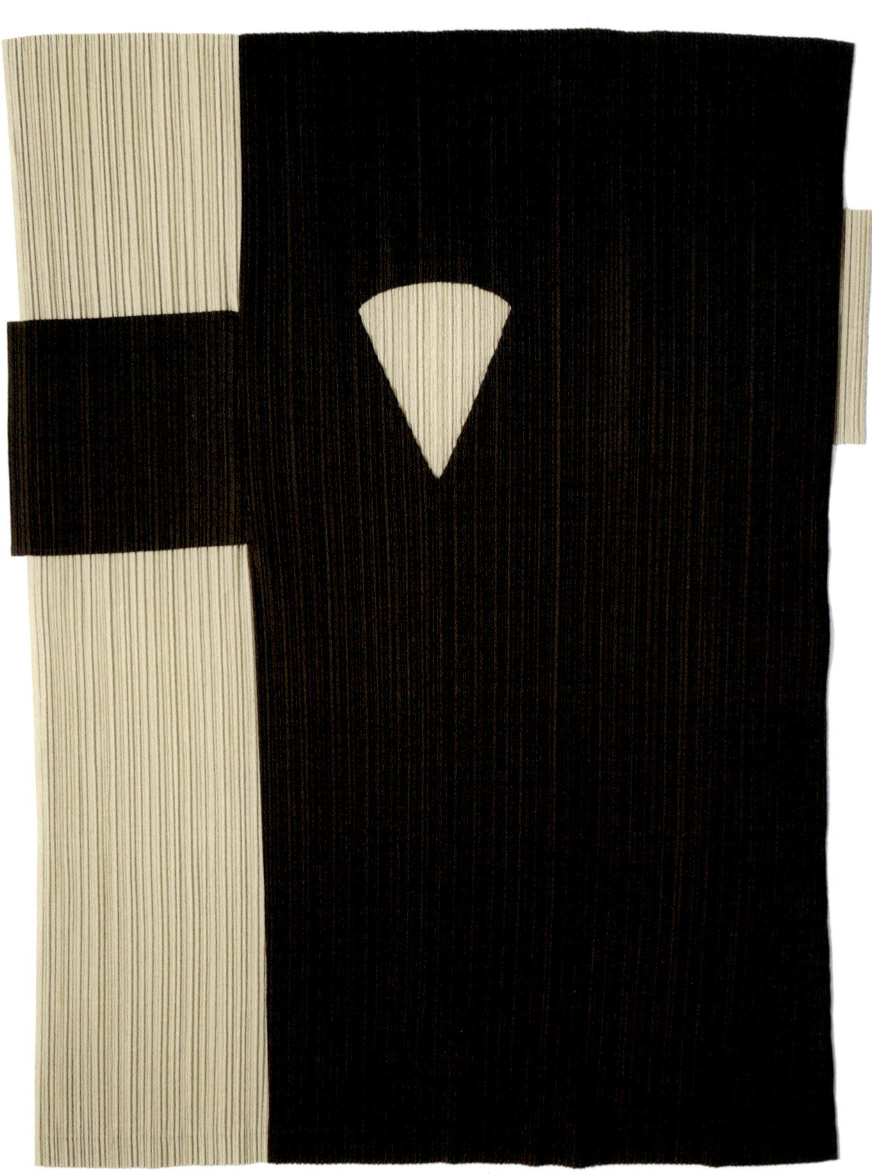

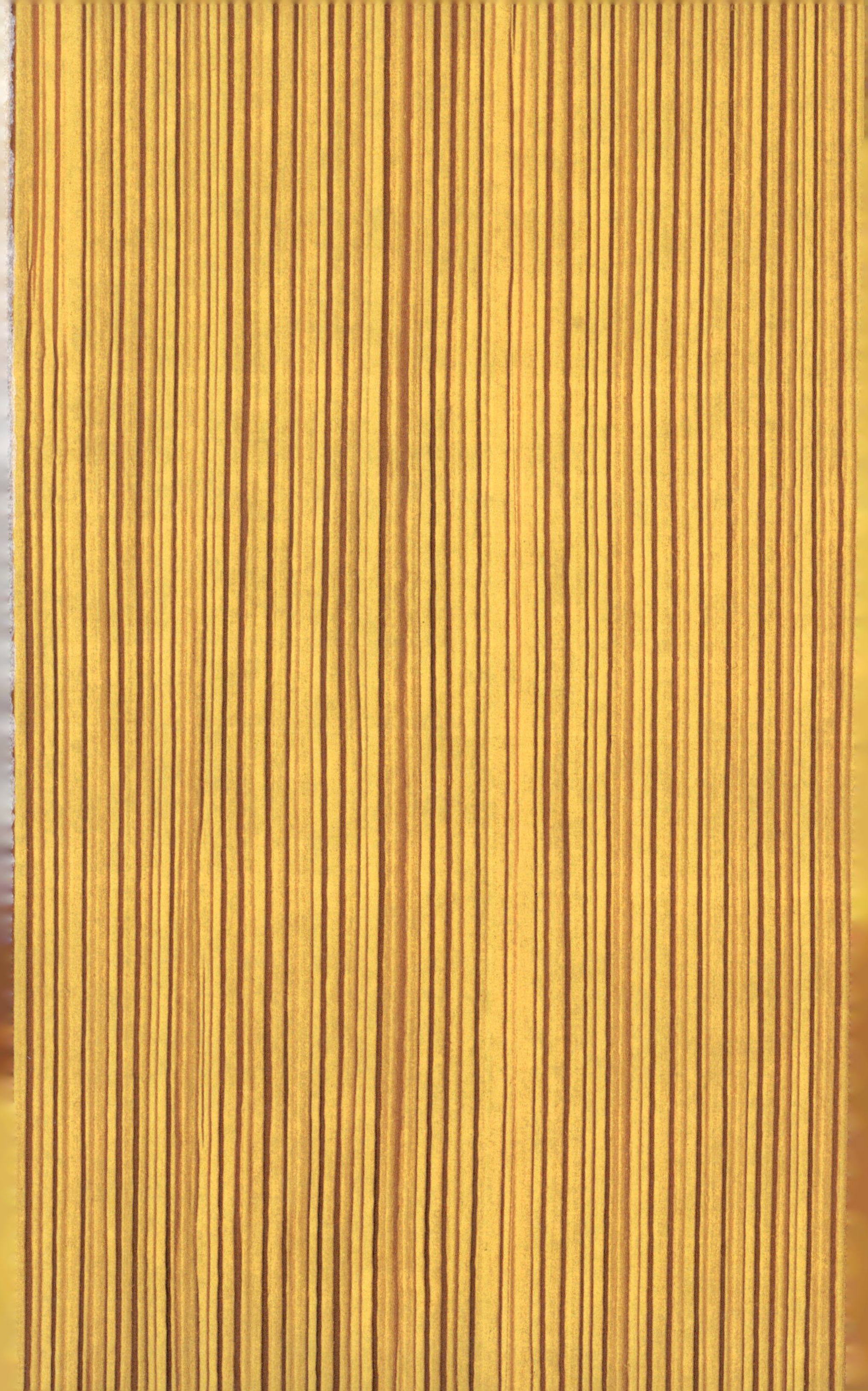

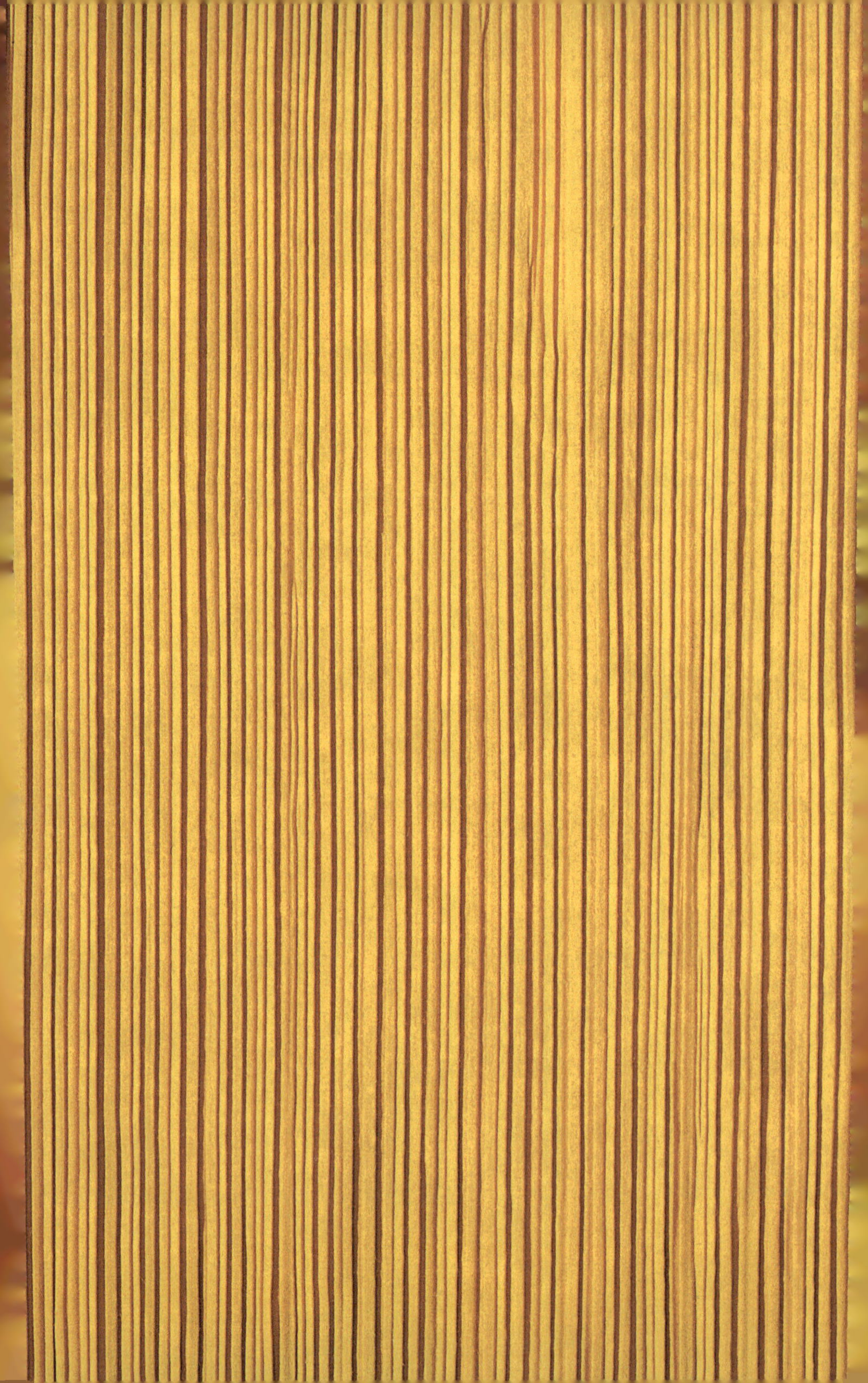